The World Bank

 **World Development Indicators**

If you have questions or comments about this product, please contact:

Development Data Center
The World Bank
1818 H Street NW, Room MC2-812, Washington, DC 20433, USA
Hotline: 800 590 1906 or 202 473 7824; fax 202 522 1498
Email: info@worldbank.org
Web site: www.worldbank.org or www.worldbank.org/data

ISBN 0-8213-5088-9

The World Bank

 2002

World Development Indicators

Eradicating world poverty is the greatest challenge of our age, and the greatest weapon we have to fight poverty is knowledge. Knowledge of policies that work to increase economic growth, of how to protect people from disease and protect the environment from degradation, to train young minds and equip them for productive work, and knowledge of where we stand now and how far we have to go to achieve our goal of a world free from poverty. The *World Development Indicators* gives us access to this last kind of knowledge to helps us assess our past efforts and measure the challenge ahead.

However much the facts and figures tell us about the condition of the world, it is too easy to think that a wall separates the rich world and the poor world. Belief in that separation allowed us to view as normal a world where fewer than 15 percent of us—in rich countries—dominate the world's wealth and take 80 percent of its dollar income. And for too long it has allowed us to view as normal a world where a woman dies in childbirth every minute, and where violence, disenfranchisement, and inequality are seen as problems of poor, weak countries and not our own.

In September 2000, during the Millennium Summit held at the United Nations, more than 140 world leaders agreed to launch a campaign to attack poverty on a number of fronts. Together, we agreed to support the Millennium Declaration—to reduce poverty and hunger, disease and early death, inequality and inequity—and to work together in partnership to make this happen by 2015.

A year later the shattering events of September 11 toppled the imaginary wall that divided the rich world from the poor world and made it clear that there are not two worlds. The process of globalization and growing interdependence has been at work for thousands of years and today we are linked by communication, trade, investment, travel and migration, by environmental degradation, crime, disease, financial crisis, and terror.

It is time to recognize that in this unified world poverty is our collective enemy. We must fight it because it is morally repugnant, and because its existence is like a cancer—weakening the whole of the body not just the parts directly affected.

We have made important progress in the past and we will make progress in the future. Consider these facts:

- Over the past 40 years life expectancy at birth in developing countries has increased by 20 years—about as much as was achieved in all of human history before the middle of the twentieth century.
- Over the past 30 years adult illiteracy in the developing world has been cut nearly in half, from 47 percent to 25 percent.
- Over the past 20 years the number of people living on less than $1 a day has fallen by 200 million, after rising steadily for 200 years.
- Over the past 10 years average incomes in developing countries have risen by 20 percent.

These advances have come not by chance. They have come by action of developing countries themselves in partnership with the richer world and with the international institutions, with civil society, and the private sector. Now, it is more important than ever to continue that partnership, based on shared respect, shared interests, shared experience, and to act on our knowledge to create a better world for all.

James D. Wolfensohn
President
The World Bank Group

Acknowledgements

This book and its companion volumes, the *World Bank Atlas* and *The Little Data Book,* were prepared by a team coordinated by Sulekha Patel. The team consisted of Mehdi Akhlaghi, David Cieslikowski, Mona Fetouh, Richard Fix, Masako Hiraga, M. H. Saeed Ordoubadi, Eric Swanson, K. M. Vijayalakshmi, Vivienne Wang, and Estela Zamora, working closely with other teams in the Development Economics Vice Presidency's Development Data Group. The CD-ROM development team included Azita Amjadi, Elizabeth Crayford, Reza Farivari, and William Prince. The work was carried out under the management of Shaida Badiee.

The choice of indicators and textual content was shaped through close consultation with and substantial contributions from staff in the World Bank's four thematic networks—Environmentally and Socially Sustainable Development; Private Sector Development and Infrastructure; Human Development; and Poverty Reduction and Economic Management—and staff of the International Finance Corporation. Most important, we received substantial help, guidance, and data from our external partners. For individual acknowledgments of contributions to the book's content, please see the *Credits* section. For a listing of our key partners, see the *Partners* section.

We are grateful to Graphic Visions Associates, Mike James, Communication Development Incorporated, and Grundy and Northedge for their contributions to the editing, design and layout of this book. Staff from External Affairs oversaw publication and dissemination of the book.

Preface

This is the 25th edition of the *World Development Indicators*, the 6th in its new format. We offer it now as we did 25 years ago, in the belief that reliable quantitative evidence is essential for understanding economic and social development—evidence to set policies, monitor progress, and evaluate results.

The World Development Indicators begins with a report on the Millennium Development Goals, which set specific, measurable targets for development in the early 21st century. These goals, agreed to by all member states of the United Nations, represent an enormous challenge to the international community to work together to ensure that all the people of the world will share the benefits of social, economic, and technical progress. They focus our efforts on improving people's lives: reducing poverty, educating children, combating illness and disease. To measure progress and ensure that everyone benefits, we must rigorously measure results. And for that we need good statistics.

Most of the statistics in the *World Development Indicators* are the product of national statistical agencies. In poor countries these agencies are often underfunded and their work underused. They need training, equipment, and a clear mandate from their governments to produce better, more reliable, more timely statistics. But the work does not stop there, for the international community also plays a role, by establishing standards, sharing knowledge, and coordinating the collection and dissemination of international statistics.

The World Bank supports national and international efforts to improve statistics. We are working closely with our development partners through the Partnership in Statistics for the 21st Century—PARIS21. The goals are to raise awareness of the need for and value of good statistics and to strengthen international coordination and governance. We have established a trust fund to support statistical capacity-building in countries preparing poverty reduction strategies, drawing on the generous support of several donors. We are working through the International Comparison Programme to improve the measurement of living standards around the world. And we are participating in the International Monetary Fund's General Data Dissemination System initiative to help interested countries document their current statistical practices and develop plans to improve them.

As users of the full array of development statistics we all benefit from the work of national data providers. And we all benefit when the international community is better informed of the challenges and successes of development. That is why we report on the Millennium Development Goals and why we invest in better statistics and disseminate them widely. But in the end, it is the citizens of developing countries who will benefit most when their governments, working in partnership with the World Bank and other development agencies, make better decisions based on good evidence.

Through the *World Development Indicators* we will continue to bring you the latest available information in the most useful and timely ways. We encourage you to send us your comments and suggestions, so that by working together we can improve the quality of the data we publish and our understanding of the world they describe.

Shaida Badiee
Director
Development Data Group

Contents

1   World View

2002 World Development Indicators

2　People

3　Environment

4   Economy

5   States and Markets

6 Global Links

Partners

Defining, gathering, and disseminating international statistics is a collective effort of many people and organizations. The indicators presented in the *World Development Indicators* are the fruit of decades of work at many levels, from the field workers who administer censuses and household surveys to the committees and working parties of the national and international statistical agencies that develop the nomenclature, classifications, and standards fundamental to an international statistical system. Nongovernmental organizations and the private sector have also made important contributions, both in gathering primary data and in organizing and publishing their results. And academic researchers have played a crucial role in developing statistical methods and carrying on a continuing dialogue about the quality and interpretation of statistical indicators. All these contributors have a strong belief that available, accurate data will improve the quality of public and private decision-making.

The organizations listed here have made the *World Development Indicators* possible by sharing their data and their expertise with us. More important, their collaboration contributes to the World Bank's efforts, and to those of many others, to improve the quality of life of the world's people. We acknowledge our debt and gratitude to all who have helped to build a base of comprehensive, quantitative information about the world and its people.

For your easy reference we have included URLs (Web addresses) for organizations that maintain Web sites. The addresses shown were active on 1 March 2002. Information about the World Bank is also provided.

International and government agencies

Bureau of Verification and Compliance, U.S. Department of State

The Bureau of Verification and Compliance, U.S. Department of State, is responsible for international agreements on conventional, chemical, and biological weapons and on strategic forces; treaty verification and compliance; and support to ongoing negotiations, policymaking, and interagency implementation efforts.

For information contact the Public Affairs Officer, Bureau of Verification and Compliance, U.S. Department of State, 2201 C Street NW, Washington, DC 20520, USA; telephone: 202 647 6946; Web site: www.state.gov/www/global/arms/bureauvc.html.

Carbon Dioxide Information Analysis Center

The Carbon Dioxide Information Analysis Center (CDIAC) is the primary global change data and information analysis center of the U.S. Department of Energy. The CDIAC's scope includes potentially anything that would be of value to those concerned with the greenhouse effect and global climate change, including concentrations of carbon dioxide and other radiatively active gases in the atmosphere; the role of the terrestrial biosphere and the oceans in the biogeochemical cycles of greenhouse gases; emissions of carbon dioxide to the atmosphere; long-term climate trends; the effects of elevated carbon dioxide on vegetation; and the vulnerability of coastal areas to rising sea levels.

For information contact the CDIAC, Oak Ridge National Laboratory, PO Box 2008, Oak Ridge, TN 37831-6335, USA; telephone: 865 574 0390; fax: 865 574 2232; email: cdiac@ornl.gov; Web site: cdiac.esd.ornl.gov .

Food and Agriculture Organization

The Food and Agriculture Organization (FAO), a specialized agency of the United Nations, was founded in October 1945 with a mandate to raise nutrition levels and living standards, to increase agricultural productivity, and to better the condition of rural populations. The organization provides direct development assistance; collects, analyzes, and disseminates information; offers policy and planning advice to governments; and serves as an international forum for debate on food and agricultural issues.

Statistical publications of the FAO include the *Production Yearbook, Trade Yearbook,* and *Fertilizer Yearbook.* The FAO makes much of its data available on diskette through its Agrostat PC system.

FAO publications can be ordered from national sales agents or directly from the FAO Sales and Marketing Group, Viale delle Terme di Caracalla, 00100 Rome, Italy; telephone: 39 06 57051; fax: 39 06 5705/3152; email: Publications- sales@fao.org ; Web site: www.fao.org.

International Civil Aviation Organization

The International Civil Aviation Organization (ICAO), a specialized agency of the United Nations, was founded on 7 December 1944. It is responsible for establishing international standards and recommended practices and procedures for the technical, economic, and legal aspects of international civil aviation operations. The ICAO works to achieve the highest practicable degree of uniformity worldwide in civil aviation issues whenever this will facilitate and improve air safety, efficiency, and regularity.

To obtain ICAO publications contact the ICAO, Document Sales Unit, 999 University Street, Montreal, Quebec H3C 5H7, Canada; telephone: 514 954 8022; fax: 514 954 6769; email: sales_unit@icao.int ; Web site: www.icao.int.

International Labour Organization

The International Labour Organization (ILO), a specialized agency of the United Nations, seeks the promotion of social justice and internationally recognized human and labor rights. Founded in 1919, it is the only surviving major creation of the Treaty of Versailles, which brought the League of Nations into being. It became the first specialized agency of the United Nations in 1946. Unique within the United Nations system, the ILO's tripartite structure has workers and employers participating as equal partners with governments in the work of its governing organs.

As part of its mandate, the ILO maintains an extensive statistical publication program. The *Yearbook of Labour Statistics* is its most comprehensive collection of labor force data.

Publications can be ordered from the International Labour Office, 4 route des Morillons, CH-1211 Geneva 22, Switzerland, or from sales agents and major booksellers throughout the world and ILO offices in many countries. Telephone: 41 22 799 78 66; fax: 41 22 799 61 17; email: publns@ilo.org; Web site: www.ilo.org.

International Monetary Fund

The International Monetary Fund (IMF) was established at a conference in Bretton Woods, New Hampshire, United States, on 1–22 July 1944. (The conference also established the World Bank.) The IMF came into official existence on 27 December 1945 and commenced financial operations on 1 March 1947. It currently has 183 member countries.

The statutory purposes of the IMF are to promote international monetary cooperation, facilitate the expansion and balanced growth of international trade, promote exchange rate stability, help to establish a multilateral payments system, make the general resources of the IMF temporarily available to its members under adequate safeguards, and shorten the duration and lessen the degree of disequilibrium in the international balances of payments of members.

The IMF maintains an extensive program for the development and compilation of international statistics and is responsible for collecting and reporting statistics on international financial transactions and the balance of payments. In April 1996 it undertook an important initiative to improve the quality of international statistics, establishing the Special Data Dissemination Standard (SDDS) to guide members that have, or seek, access to international capital markets in providing economic and financial data to the public. In 1997 the IMF established the General Data Dissemination System (GDDS) to guide countries in providing the public with comprehensive, timely, accessible, and reliable economic, financial, and sociodemographic data.

The IMF's major statistical publications include *International Financial Statistics, Balance of Payments Statistics Yearbook, Government Finance Statistics Yearbook,* and *Direction of Trade Statistics Yearbook.*

For more information on IMF statistical publications contact the International Monetary Fund, Publications Services, Catalog Orders, 700 19th Street NW, Washington, DC 20431, USA; telephone: 202 623 7430; fax: 202 623 7201; telex: RCA 248331 IMF UR; email: pubweb@imf.org; Web site: www.imf.org ; SDDS and GDDS bulletin board: dsbb.imf.org.

International Telecommunication Union

Founded in Paris in 1865 as the International Telegraph Union, the International Telecommunication Union (ITU) took its current name in 1934 and became a specialized agency of the United Nations in 1947. The ITU is an intergovernmental organization in which the public and private sectors cooperate for the development of telecommunications. The ITU adopts international regulations and treaties governing all terrestrial and space uses of the frequency spectrum and the use of the geostationary satellite orbit. It also develops standards for the interconnection of telecommunications systems worldwide.

The ITU fosters the development of telecommunications in developing countries by establishing medium-term development policies and strategies in consultation with other partners in the sector and providing specialized technical assistance in management, telecommunications policy, human resource management, research and development, technology choice and transfer, network installation and maintenance, and investment financing and resource mobilization. The ITU's main statistical publication is the *Telecommunications Yearbook.*

Publications can be ordered from ITU Sales and Marketing Service, Place des Nations, CH-1211 Geneva 20, Switzerland; telephone: 41 22 730 6141 (English), 41 22 730 6142 (French), and 41 22 730 6143 (Spanish); fax: 41 22 730 5194; email: sales@itu.int ; telex: 421 000 uit ch; telegram: ITU GENEVE; Web site: www.itu.int .

National Science Foundation

The National Science Foundation (NSF) is an independent U.S. government agency whose mission is to promote the progress of science; to advance the national health, prosperity, and welfare; and to secure the national defense. It is responsible for promoting science and engineering through almost 20,000 research and education projects. In addition, the NSF fosters the exchange of scientific information among scientists and engineers in the United States and other countries, supports programs to strengthen scientific and engineering research potential, and evaluates the impact of research on industrial development and general welfare.

As part of its mandate, the NSF biennially publishes *Science and Engineering Indicators,* which tracks national and international trends in science and engineering research and education.

Electronic copies of NSF documents can be obtained from the NSF's online document system (www.nsf.gov/pubsys/index.htm) or requested by email from its automated mailserver (getpub@nsf.gov). Documents can also be requested from the NSF Publications Clearinghouse by mail, at PO Box 218, Jessup, MD 20794-0218, or by telephone, at 301 947 2722.

For more information contact the National Science Foundation, 4201 Wilson Boulevard, Arlington, VA 22230, USA; telephone: 703 292 5111; Web site: www.nsf.gov .

Organisation for Economic Co-operation and Development

The Organisation for Economic Co-operation and Development (OECD) was set up in 1948 as the Organisation for European Economic Co-operation (OEEC) to administer Marshall Plan funding in Europe. In 1960, when the Marshall Plan had completed its task, the OEEC's member countries agreed to bring in Canada and the United States to form an organization to coordinate policy among industrial countries. The OECD is the international organization of the industrialized, market economy countries.

Representatives of member countries meet at the OECD to exchange information and harmonize policy with a view to maximizing economic growth in member countries and helping nonmember countries develop more rapidly. The OECD has set up a number of specialized committees to further its aims. One of these is the Development Assistance Committee (DAC), whose members have agreed to coordinate their policies on assistance to developing and transition economies.

Also associated with the OECD are several agencies or bodies that have their own governing statutes, including the International Energy Agency and the Centre for Co-operation with Economies in Transition.

The OECD's main statistical publications include *Geographical Distribution of Financial Flows to Aid Recipients, National Accounts of OECD Countries, Labour Force Statistics, Revenue Statistics of OECD Member Countries, International Direct Investment Statistics Yearbook, Basic Science and Technology Statistics, Industrial Structure Statistics,* and *Services: Statistics on International Transactions.*

For information on OECD publications contact the OECD, 2, rue André-Pascal, 75775 Paris Cedex 16, France; telephone: 33 1 45 24 82 00; fax: 33 1 49 10 42 76; email: sales@oecd.org; Web sites: www.oecd.org and www.oecdwash.org.

United Nations

The United Nations and its specialized agencies maintain a number of programs for the collection of international statistics, some of which are described elsewhere in this book. At United Nations headquarters the Statistics Division provides a wide range of statistical outputs and services for producers and users of statistics worldwide.

The Statistics Division publishes statistics on international trade, national accounts, demography and population, gender, industry, energy, environment, human settlements, and disability.

Its major statistical publications include the *International Trade Statistics Yearbook, Yearbook of National Accounts,* and *Monthly Bulletin of Statistics,* along with general statistics compendiums such as the *Statistical Yearbook* and *World Statistics Pocketbook.*

For publications contact United Nations Publications, Room DC2 853, 2 UN Plaza, New York, NY 10017, USA; telephone: 212 963 8302 or 800 253 9646 (toll free); fax: 212 963 3489; email: publications@un.org; Web site: www.un.org.

United Nations Centre for Human Settlements (Habitat), Global Urban Observatory

The Urban Indicators Programme of the United Nations Centre for Human Settlements (Habitat) was established to address the urgent global need to improve the urban knowledge base by helping countries and cities design, collect, and apply policy-oriented indicators related to urban development at the city level. In 1997 the Urban Indicators Programme was integrated into the Global Urban Observatory, the principal United Nations program for monitoring urban conditions and trends and for tracking progress in implementing the goals of the Habitat Agenda. With the Urban Indicators and Best Practices programs, the Global Urban Observatory is establishing a worldwide information, assessment, and capacity building network to help governments, local authorities, the private sector, and nongovernmental and other civil society organizations.

Contact Christine Auclair (guo@unchs.org), Urban Indicators Programme, Global Urban Observatory, UNCHS (Habitat), PO Box 30030, Nairobi, Kenya; telephone: 2542 623694; fax: 2542 624266/7; Web site: www.unchs.org.

United Nations Children's Fund

The United Nations Children's Fund (UNICEF), the only organization of the United Nations dedicated exclusively to children, works with other United Nations bodies and with governments and non-governmental organizations to improve children's lives in more than 140 developing countries through community-based services in primary health care, basic education, and safe water and sanitation.

UNICEF's major publications include *The State of the World's Children* and *The Progress of Nations.*

For information on UNICEF publications contact UNICEF House, 3 United Nations Plaza, New York, NY 10017, USA; telephone: 212 326 7000; fax: 212 888 7465 or 7454; telex: RCA-239521; email: publications@un.org; Web site: www.unicef.org.

United Nations Conference on Trade and Development

UNCTAD

The United Nations Conference on Trade and Development (UNCTAD) is the principal organ of the United Nations General Assembly in the field of trade and development. It was established as a permanent intergovernmental body in 1964 in Geneva with a view to accelerating economic growth and development, particularly in developing countries. UNCTAD discharges its mandate through policy analysis; intergovernmental deliberations, consensus building, and negotiation; monitoring, implementation, and follow-up; and technical cooperation.

UNCTAD produces a number of publications containing trade and economic statistics, including the *Handbook of International Trade and Development Statistic*s.

For information contact UNCTAD, Palais des Nations, CH-1211 Geneva 10, Switzerland; telephone: 41 22 907 12 34 or 917 12 34; fax: 41 22 907 00 43; telex: 42962; email: reference.service@unctad.org; Web site: www.unctad.org.

United Nations Educational, Scientific, and Cultural Organization

The United Nations Educational, Scientific, and Cultural Organization (UNESCO) is a specialized agency of the United Nations established in 1945 to promote "collaboration among nations through education, science, and culture in order to further universal respect for justice, for the rule of law, and for the human rights and fundamental freedoms . . . for the peoples of the world, without distinction of race, sex, language, or religion."

UNESCO's principal statistical publications are the *Statistical Yearbook, World Education Report* (biennial), and *Basic Education and Literacy: World Statistical Indicators*.

For publications contact UNESCO Publishing, Promotion, and Sales Division, 1, rue Miollis F, 75732 Paris Cedex 15, France; fax: 33 1 45 68 57 41; email: publishing.promotion@unesco.org; Web site: www.unesco.org.

United Nations Environment Programme

The mandate of the United Nations Environment Programme (UNEP) is to provide leadership and encourage partnership in caring for the environment by inspiring, informing, and enabling nations and people to improve their quality of life without compromising that of future generations.

UNEP publications include *Global Environment Outlook* and *Our Planet* (a bimonthly magazine).

For information contact the UNEP, PO Box 30552, Nairobi, Kenya; telephone: 254 2 62 1234 or 3292; fax: 254 2 22 6886 or 62 2615; email: oedinfo@unep.org; Web site: www.unep.org.

United Nations Industrial Development Organization

The United Nations Industrial Development Organization (UNIDO) was established in 1966 to act as the central coordinating body for industrial activities and to promote industrial development and cooperation at the global, regional, national, and sectoral levels. In 1985 UNIDO became the 16th specialized agency of the United Nations, with a mandate to help develop scientific and technological plans and programs for industrialization in the public, cooperative, and private sectors.

UNIDO's databases and information services include the Industrial Statistics Database (INDSTAT), Commodity Balance Statistics Database (COMBAL), Industrial Development Abstracts (IDA), and the International Referral System on Sources of Information. Among its publications is the *International Yearbook of Industrial Statistics*.

For information contact UNIDO Public Information Section, Vienna International Centre, PO Box 300, A-1400 Vienna, Austria; telephone: 43 1 260 26 5031; fax: 43 1 213 46 5031 or 260 26 6843; email: publications@unido.org; Web site: www.unido.org.

World Bank Group

The World Bank Group is made up of five organizations: the International Bank for Reconstruction and Development (IBRD), the International Development Association (IDA), the International Finance Corporation (IFC), the Multilateral Investment Guarantee Agency (MIGA), and the International Centre for Settlement of Investment Disputes (ICSID).

Established in 1944 at a conference of world leaders in Bretton Woods, New Hampshire, United States, the World Bank is the world's largest source of development assistance, providing nearly $16 billion in loans annually to its client countries. It uses its financial resources, trained staff, and extensive knowledge base to help each developing country onto a path of stable, sustainable, and equitable growth in the fight against poverty. The World Bank Group has 182 member countries.

For information about the World Bank visit its Web site at www.worldbank.org. For more information about development data contact the Development Data Group, World Bank, 1818 H Street NW, Washington, DC 20433, USA; telephone: 800 590 1906 or 202 473 7824; fax: 202 522 1498; email: data@worldbank.org ; Web site: www.worldbank.org/data .

World Health Organization

The constitution of the World Health Organization (WHO) was adopted on 22 July 1946 by the International Health Conference, convened in New York by the Economic and Social Council. The objective of the WHO, a specialized agency of the United Nations, is the attainment by all people of the highest possible level of health.

The WHO carries out a wide range of functions, including coordinating international health work; helping governments strengthen health services; providing technical assistance and emergency aid; working for the prevention and control of disease; promoting improved nutrition, housing, sanitation, recreation, and economic and working conditions; promoting and coordinating biomedical and health services research; promoting improved standards of teaching and training in health and medical professions; establishing international standards for biological, pharmaceutical, and similar products; and standardizing diagnostic procedures.

The WHO publishes the *World Health Statistics Annual* and many other technical and statistical publications.

For publications contact Distribution and Sales, Division of Publishing, Language, and Library Services, World Health Organization Headquarters, CH-1211 Geneva 27, Switzerland; telephone: 41 22 791 2476 or 2477; fax: 41 22 791 4857; email: publications@who.ch; Web site: www.who.ch.

World Intellectual Property Organization

The World Intellectual Property Organization (WIPO) is a specialized agency of the United Nations based in Geneva, Switzerland. The objectives of WIPO are to promote the protection of intellectual property throughout the world through cooperation among states and, where appropriate, in collaboration with other international organizations and to ensure administrative cooperation among the intellectual property unions—that is, the "unions" created by the Paris and Berne Conventions and several subtreaties concluded by members of the Paris Union. WIPO is responsible for administering various multilateral treaties dealing with the legal and administrative aspects of intellectual property. A substantial part of its activities and resources is devoted to development cooperation with developing countries.

For information contact the World Intellectual Property Organization, 34, chemin des Colombettes, Geneva, Switzerland; mailing address: PO Box 18, CH-1211 Geneva 20, Switzerland; telephone: 41 22 338 9111; fax: 41 22 733 5428; telex: 412912 ompi ch; email: publications.mail@wipo.int; Web site: www.wipo.int.

World Tourism Organization

The World Tourism Organization is an intergovernmental body charged by the United Nations with promoting and developing tourism. It serves as a global forum for tourism policy issues and a source of tourism know-how. The organization began as the International Union of Official Tourist Publicity Organizations, set up in 1925 in The Hague. Renamed the World Tourism Organization, it held its first general assembly in Madrid in May 1975. Its membership includes 132 countries and territories and more than 350 affiliate members representing local governments, tourism associations, and private companies, including airlines, hotel groups, and tour operators.

The World Tourism Organization publishes the *Yearbook of Tourism Statistics, Compendium of Tourism Statistics,* and *Travel and Tourism Barometer* (triannual).

For information contact the World Tourism Organization, Capitán Haya, 42, 28020 Madrid, Spain; telephone: 34 91 567 81 00; fax: 34 91 567 82 18; email: omt@world-tourism.org; Web site: www.world-tourism.org.

World Trade Organization

WORLD
TRADE
ORGANIZATION

The World Trade Organization (WTO), established on 1 January 1995, is the successor to the General Agreement on Tariffs and Trade (GATT). The WTO provides the legal and institutional foundation of the multilateral trading system and embodies the results of the Uruguay Round of trade negotiations, which ended with the Marrakesh Declaration of 15 April 1994. The WTO is mandated with administering and implementing multilateral trade agreements, serving as a forum for multilateral trade negotiations, seeking to resolve trade disputes, overseeing national trade policies, and cooperating with other international institutions involved in global economic policymaking.

The WTO's Statistics and Information Systems Divisions compile statistics on world trade and maintain the Integrated Database, which contains the basic records of the outcome of the Uruguay Round. Its *Annual Report* includes a statistical appendix.

For publications contact the World Trade Organization, Publications Services, Centre William Rappard, 154 rue de Lausanne, CH-1211, Geneva, Switzerland; telephone: 41 22 739 5208 or 5308; fax: 41 22 739 5792; email: publications@wto.org; Web site: www.wto.org.

Private and nongovernmental organizations

EUROMONEY

Euromoney Publications PLC

Euromoney Publications PLC provides a wide range of financial, legal, and general business information. The monthly magazine *Euromoney* carries a semiannual rating of country creditworthiness.

For information contact Euromoney Publications PLC, Nestor House, Playhouse Yard, London EC4V 5EX, UK; telephone: 44 20 7779 8999; fax: 44 20 7779 8602; telex: 2907002; email: hotline@euromoneyplc.com; Web site: www.euromoney.com.

Institutional Investor, Inc.

Institutional Investor, Inc., develops country credit ratings every six months based on information provided by leading international banks. It publishes the magazine *Institutional Investor* monthly.

For information contact Institutional Investor, Inc., 488 Madison Avenue, New York, NY 10022, USA; telephone: 212 224 3300; email: info@iimagazine.com; Web site: www.iimagazine.com.

International Road Federation

The International Road Federation (IRF) is a not-for-profit, nonpolitical service organization. Its purpose is to encourage better road and transport systems worldwide and to help apply technology and management practices that will maximize economic and social returns from national road investments.

The IRF has led global road infrastructure developments and is the international point of affiliation for about 600 member companies, associations, and governments.

The IRF's mission is to promote road development as a key factor in social and economic growth, to provide governments and financial institutions with professional ideas and expertise, to facilitate business exchange among members, to establish links between members and external institutions and agencies, to support national road federations, and to give information to professional groups.

The IRF publishes *World Road Statistics*.

Contact the Geneva office at 2 chemin de Blandonnet, CH-1214 Vernier, Geneva, Switzerland; telephone: 41 22 306 0260; fax: 41 22 306 0270; or the Washington, DC, office at 1010 Massachusetts Avenue NW, Suite 410, Washington, DC 20001, USA; telephone: 202 371 5544; fax: 202 371 5565; email: info@irfnet.com; Web site: www.irfnet.org.

Monetary Research Institute

The Monetary Research Institute (MRI) was founded in 1990 to collect information about the current means of payment in the world. Its flagship publication, the quarterly *MRI Bankers' Guide to Foreign Currency,* is designed for use by banks, foreign exchange bureaus, libraries, universities, coin dealers, travel agents, and those relying on international trade. It features information on and images of all currencies and banknotes in circulation, information on travelers checks, and currency histories, news, and approaching expiration dates. It also lists tourist and parallel exchange rates for every country. The MRI maintains relationships with all currency issuing authorities.

For information contact the Monetary Research Institute, 1014 Wirt Road, Suite 200, Houston, TX 77055, USA; telephone: 713 827 1796; fax: 713 827 8665; email: info@mriguide.com; Web site: www.mriguide.com.

Moody's Investors Service

Moody's Investors Service is a global credit analysis and financial opinion firm. It provides the international investment community with globally consistent credit ratings on debt and other securities issued by North American state and regional government entities, by corporations worldwide, and by some sovereign issuers. It also publishes extensive financial data in both print and electronic form. Its clients include investment banks, brokerage firms, insurance companies, public utilities, research libraries, manufacturers, and government agencies and departments.

Moody's publishes *Sovereign, Subnational and Sovereign-Guaranteed Issuers*. For information contact Moody's Investors Service, 99 Church Street, New York, NY 10007, USA; telephone: 212 553 1658; fax: 212 553 0882; Web site: www.moodys.com.

Netcraft

Netcraft is an Internet consultancy based in Bath, England. Most of its work relates to the development of Internet services for its clients or for itself acting as principal.

For information visit its Web site: www.netcraft.com.

PricewaterhouseCoopers

Drawing on the talents of 150,000 people in more than 150 countries, PricewaterhouseCoopers provides a full range of business advisory services to leading global, national, and local companies and public institutions. Its service offerings have been organized into six lines of service, each staffed with highly qualified, experienced professionals and leaders. These services are audit, assurance, and business advisory services; business process outsourcing; financial advisory services; global human resource solutions; management consulting services; and global tax services.

PricewaterhouseCoopers publishes *Corporate Taxes: Worldwide Summaries* and *Individual Taxes: Worldwide Summaries.*

For information contact PricewaterhouseCoopers, 1301 Avenue of the Americas, New York, NY 10019, USA; telephone: 212 596 8000; fax: 212 259 1301; Web site: www.pwcglobal.com.

The PRS Group

PRS Group is a global leader in political and economic risk forecasting and market analysis and has served international companies large and small for about 20 years. The data it contributed to this year's *World Development Indicators* come from the *International Country Risk Guide* monthly publication that monitors and rates political, financial, and economic risk in 140 countries.

The guide's data series and commitment to independent and unbiased analysis make it the standard for any organization practicing effective risk management.

For information contact the PRS Group, 6320 Fly Road, Suite 102, PO Box 248, East Syracuse, NY 13057-0248, USA; telephone: 315 431 0511; fax: 315 431 0200; email: custserv@PRSgroup.com; Web site: www.prsgroup.com.

Standard & Poor's Equity Indexes and Rating Services

Standard & Poor's, a division of the McGraw-Hill Companies, has provided independent and objective financial information, analysis, and research for nearly 140 years. The S&P 500 index, one of its most popular products, is calculated and maintained by Standard & Poor's Index Services, a leading provider of equity indexes. Standard & Poor's indexes are used by investors around the world for measuring investment performance and as the basis for a wide range of financial instruments.

Standard & Poor's *Sovereign Ratings* provides issuer and local and foreign currency debt ratings for sovereign governments and for sovereign-supported and supranational issuers worldwide. Standard & Poor's Rating Services monitors the credit quality of $1.5 trillion worth of bonds and other financial instruments and offers investors global coverage of debt issuers. Standard & Poor's also has ratings on commercial paper, mutual funds, and the financial condition of insurance companies worldwide.

For information on equity indexes contact Standard & Poor's Index Services, 22 Water Street, New York, NY 10041, USA; telephone: 212 438 2046; fax: 212 438 3523; email: index_services@sandp.com; Web site: www.spglobal.com.

For information on ratings contact the McGraw-Hill Companies, Inc., Executive Offices, 1221 Avenue of the Americas, New York, NY 10020, USA; telephone: 212 512 4105 or 800 352 3566 (toll free); fax: 212 512 4105; email: ratings@mcgraw-hill.com ; Web site http://www.standardandpoor.com/ratingsactions/ratingslists.

World Conservation Monitoring Centre

WORLD CONSERVATION
MONITORING CENTRE

The World Conservation Monitoring Centre (WCMC) provides information on the conservation and sustainable use of the world's living resources and helps others to develop information systems of their own. It works in close collaboration with a wide range of people and organizations to increase access to the information needed for wise management of the world's living resources. Committed to the principle of data exchange with other centers and noncommercial users, the WCMC, whenever possible, places the data it manages in the public domain.

For information contact the World Conservation Monitoring Centre, 219 Huntingdon Road, Cambridge CB3 0DL, UK; telephone: 44 12 2327 7314; fax: 44 12 2327 7136; email: info@wcmc.org.uk; Web site: www.unep-wcmc.org.

World Information Technology and Services Alliance

The World Information Technology and Services Alliance (WITSA) is a consortium of 41 information technology (IT) industry associations from around the world. WITSA members represent more than 97 percent of the world IT market. As the global voice of the IT industry, WITSA is dedicated to advocating policies that advance the industry's growth and development; facilitating international trade and investment in IT products and services; strengthening WITSA's national industry associations by sharing knowledge, experience, and information; providing members with a network of contacts in nearly every region; and hosting the World Congress on Information Technology.

WITSA's publication, *Digital Planet 2000: The Global Information Economy,* uses data provided by the International Data Corporation.

For information contact WITSA, 8300 Boone Boulevard, Suite 450, Vienna, VA 22182, USA; telephone: 703 284 5329; Web site: www.witsa.org.

World Resources Institute

The World Resources Institute is an independent center for policy research and technical assistance on global environmental and development issues. The institute provides—and helps other institutions provide—objective information and practical proposals for policy and institutional change that will foster environmentally sound, socially equitable development. The institute's cur-rent areas of work include trade, forests, energy, economics, technology, biodiversity, human health, climate change, sustainable agriculture, resource and environmental information, and national strategies for environmental and resource management.

For information contact the World Resources Institute, Suite 800, 10 G Street NE, Washington, DC 20002, USA; telephone: 202 729 7600; fax: 202 729 7610; telex 64414 WRIWASH; email: lau-ralee@wri.org; Web site: www.wri.org.

User's guide

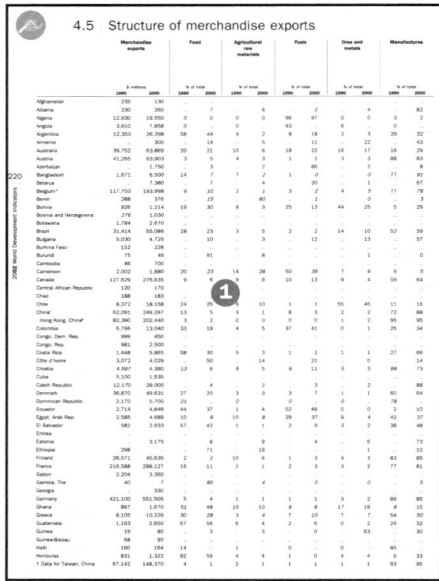

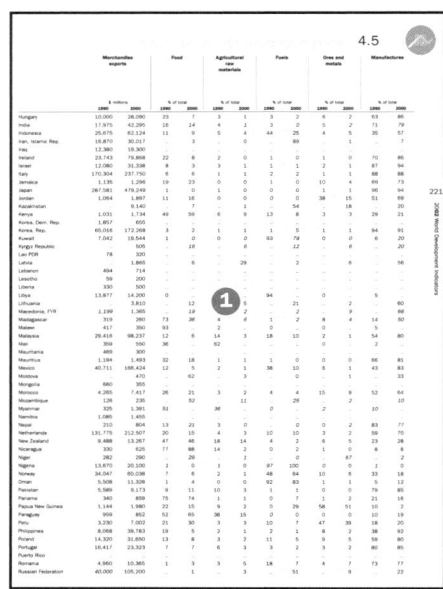

Tables

The tables are numbered by section and display the identifying icon of the section. Countries and economies are listed alphabetically (except for Hong Kong, China, which appears after China). Data are shown for 152 economies with populations of more than 1 million, as well as for Taiwan, China, in selected tables. Selected indicators for 55 other economies—small economies with populations between 30,000 and 1 million, and smaller economies if they are members of the International Bank for Reconstruction and Development (IBRD), or, as it is commonly known, the World Bank—are shown in table 1.6. The term *country*, used interchangeably with *economy*, does not imply political independence, but refers to any territory for which authorities report separate social or economic statistics. When available, aggregate measures for income and regional groups appear at the end of each table.

1 Indicators

Indicators are shown for the most recent year or period for which data are available and, in most tables, for an earlier year or period (usually 1990 in this edition). Time-series data are available on the *World Development Indicators* CD-ROM.

2 Aggregate measures for income groups

The aggregate measures for income groups include 207 economies (the economies listed in the main tables plus those in table 1.6) wherever data are available. Note that in this edition, as in the previous one, table 1.6 does not include France's overseas departments—French Guiana, Guadeloupe, Martinique, and Réunion—which are now included in the national accounts (gross national income and other economic measures) of France. To maintain consistency in the aggregate measures over time and between tables, missing data are imputed where possible. The aggregates are totals (designated by a *t* if the aggregates include gap filled estimates for missing data, and by an *s*, for simple totals, where they do not), median values *(m)*, or weighted averages *(w)*. Gap filling of amounts not allocated to countries may result in discrepancies between subgroup aggregates and overall totals. For further discussion of aggregation methods see *Statistical method*s.

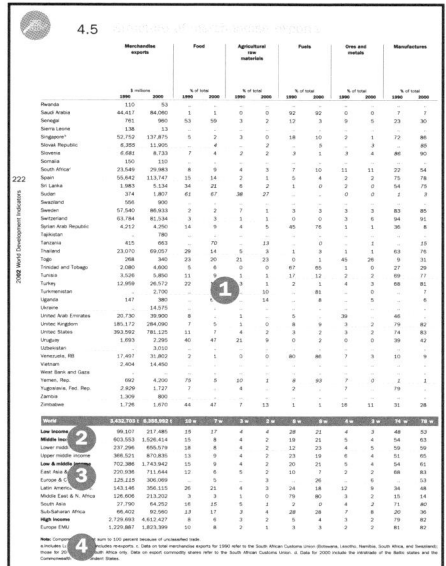 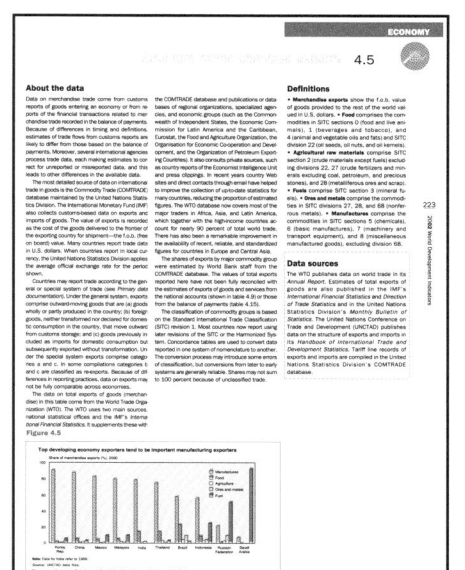

③ Aggregate measures for regions

The aggregate measures for regions include only low- and middle-income economies (note that these measures include developing economies with populations of less than 1 million, including those listed in table 1.6).

The country composition of regions is based on the World Bank's analytical regions and may differ from common geographic usage. For regional classifications see the map on the inside back cover and the list on the back cover flap. For further discussion of aggregation methods see *Statistical method*s.

④ Footnotes

Known deviations from standard definitions or breaks in comparability over time or across countries are either footnoted in the tables or noted in *About the data*. When available data are deemed to be too weak to provide reliable measures of levels and trends or do not adequately adhere to international standards, the data are not shown.

Statistics

Data are shown for economies as they were constituted in 2000, and historical data are revised to reflect current political arrangements. Exceptions are noted throughout the tables.

Additional information about the data is provided in *Primary data documentation*. That section summarizes national and international efforts to improve basic data collection and gives information on primary sources, census years, fiscal years, and other background. *Statistical methods* provides technical information on some of the general calculations and formulas used throughout the book.

Discrepancies in data presented in different editions of the *World Development Indicators* reflect updates by countries as well as revisions to historical series and changes in methodology. Thus readers are advised not to compare data series between editions of the *World Development Indicators* or between different World Bank publications. Consistent time-series data for 1960–2000 are available on the *World Development Indicators* CD-ROM.

Except where noted, growth rates are in real terms. (See *Statistical methods* for information on the methods used to calculate growth rates.) Data for some economic indicators for some economies are presented in fiscal years rather than calendar years; see *Primary data documentation*. All dollar figures are current U.S. dollars unless otherwise stated. The methods used for converting national currencies are described in *Statistical methods*.

China

On 1 July 1997 China resumed its exercise of sovereignty over Hong Kong, and on 20 December 1999 it resumed its exercise of sovereignty over Macao. Unless otherwise noted, data for China do not include data for Hong Kong, China; Taiwan, China; or Macao, China.

Democratic Republic of the Congo

Data for the Democratic Republic of the Congo (Congo, Dem. Rep., in the table listings) refer to the former Zaire. The Republic of Congo is referred to as Congo, Rep., in the table listings.

Czech Republic and Slovak Republic

Data are shown whenever possible for the individual countries formed from the former Czechoslovakia—the Czech Republic and the Slovak Republic.

East Timor

On 25 October 1999 the United Nations Transitional Administration in East Timor (UNTAET) assumed responsibility for the administration of East Timor. Data for Indonesia include East Timor through 1999 unless otherwise noted.

Eritrea

Data are shown for Eritrea whenever possible, but in most cases before 1992 Eritrea is included in the data for Ethiopia.

Jordan

Data for Jordan refer to the East Bank only unless otherwise noted.

Germany

Data for Germany refer to the unified Germany unless otherwise noted.

Union of Soviet Socialist Republics

In 1991 the Union of Soviet Socialist Republics came to an end. Available data are shown for the individual countries now existing on its former territory (Armenia, Azerbaijan, Belarus, Estonia, Georgia, Kazakhstan, Kyrgyz Republic, Latvia, Lithuania, Moldova, the Russian Federation, Tajikistan, Turkmenistan, Ukraine, and Uzbekistan).

República Bolivariana de Venezuela

In December 1999 the official name of Venezuela was changed to República Bolivariana de Venezuela (Venezuela, RB, in the table listings).

Republic of Yemen

Data for the Republic of Yemen refer to that country from 1990 onward; data for previous years refer to aggregated data for the former People's Democratic Republic of Yemen and the former Yemen Arab Republic unless otherwise noted.

Former Socialist Federal Republic of Yugoslavia

Available data are shown for the individual countries formed from the former Socialist Federal Republic of Yugoslavia—Bosnia and Herzegovina, Croatia, the former Yugoslav Republic of Macedonia, Slovenia, and the Federal Republic of Yugoslavia.

Changes in the System of National Accounts

This edition of the *World Development Indicators* uses terminology in line with the 1993 System of National Accounts (SNA). For example, in the 1993 SNA *gross national income* replaces *gross national product*. See *About the data* for tables 1.1 and 4.9.

Most countries continue to compile their national accounts according to the 1968 SNA, but more and more are adopting the 1993 SNA. Countries that use the 1993 SNA are identified in *Primary data documentation*. A few low-income countries still use concepts from older SNA guidelines, including valuations such as factor cost, in describing major economic aggregates.

Classification of economies

For operational and analytical purposes the World Bank's main criterion for classifying economies is gross national income (GNI) per capita. Every economy is classified as low income, middle income (subdivided into lower middle and upper middle), or high income. For income classifications see the map on the inside front cover and the list on the front cover flap. Note that classification by income does not necessarily reflect development status. Because GNI per capita changes over time, the country composition of income groups may change from one edition of the *World Development Indicators* to the next. Once the classification is fixed for
an edition, based on GNI per capita in the most recent year for which data are available (2000 in this edition), all historical data presented are based on the same country grouping.

Low-income economies are those with a GNI per capita of $755 or less in 2000. Middle-income economies are those with a GNI per capita of more than $755 but less than $9,266. Lower-middle-income and upper-middle-income economies are separated at a GNI per capita of $2,995. High-income economies are those with a GNI per capita of $9,266 or more. The 11 participating member countries of the European Monetary Union (EMU) are presented as a subgroup under high-income economies.

Recent revisions of 2000 GNI per capita for Antigua and Barbuda, from $9,190 to $9,440, would place this country in a higher income category; revisions to data for Belize from $2,940 to $3,110, would place this country in a higher income category; revisions to data for Papua New Guinea, from 760 to $700, would place this country in a lower income category; and, revisions to Turkmenistan from $840 to $750, would place this country in a lower income category. However, since the official analytical classifications are fixed during the World Bank's fiscal year (ending on 30 June), these countries remain in the income categories in which they were classified before these revisions: Antigua and Barbuda in the upper-middle-income category, and Belize, Papua New Guinea, and Turkmenistan in the lower-middle-income category.

Symbols

..
means that data are not available or that aggregates cannot be calculated because of missing data in the years shown.

0 or 0.0
means zero or less than half the unit shown.

/
in dates, as in 1990/91, means that the period of time, usually 12 months, straddles two calendar years and refers to a crop year, a survey year, or a fiscal year.

$
means current U.S. dollars unless otherwise noted.

>
means more than.

<
means less than.

Data presentation conventions

- A blank means not applicable or, for an aggregate, not analytically meaningful.
- A billion is 1,000 million.
- A trillion is 1,000 billion.
- Figures in italics refer to years or periods other than those specified.
- Data for years that are more than three years from the range shown are footnoted.

The cutoff date for data is 1 February 2002.

WORLD VIEW

Millennium Development Goals

1	Eradicate extreme poverty and hunger	**5**	Improve maternal health
2	Achieve universal primary education	**6**	Combat HIV/AIDS, malaria, and other diseases
3	Promote gender equality and empower women	**7**	Ensure environmental sustainability
4	Reduce child mortality	**8**	Develop a global partnership for development

"We will spare no effort to free our fellow men, women, and children

At the Millennium Summit in September 2000 the states of the United Nations reaffirmed their commitment to working toward a world in which sustaining development and eliminating poverty would have the highest priority. The Millennium Development Goals grew out of the agreements and resolutions of world conferences organized by the United Nations in the past decade. The goals have been commonly accepted as a framework for measuring development progress.

The goals focus the efforts of the world community on achieving significant, measurable improvements in people's lives. They establish yardsticks for measuring results, not just for developing countries but for rich countries that help to fund development programs and for the multilateral institutions that help countries implement them. The first seven goals are mutually reinforcing and are directed at reducing poverty in all its forms. The last goal—global partnership for development—is about the means to achieve the first seven. Many of the poorest countries will need additional assistance and must look to the rich countries to provide it. Countries that are poor and heavily indebted will need further help in reducing their debt burdens. And all countries will benefit if trade barriers are lowered, allowing a freer exchange of goods and services.

For the poorest countries many of the goals seem far out of reach. Even in better-off countries there may be regions or groups that lag behind. So countries need to set their own goals and work to ensure that poor people are included in the benefits of development.

How many countries are likely to reach the Millennium Development Goals?

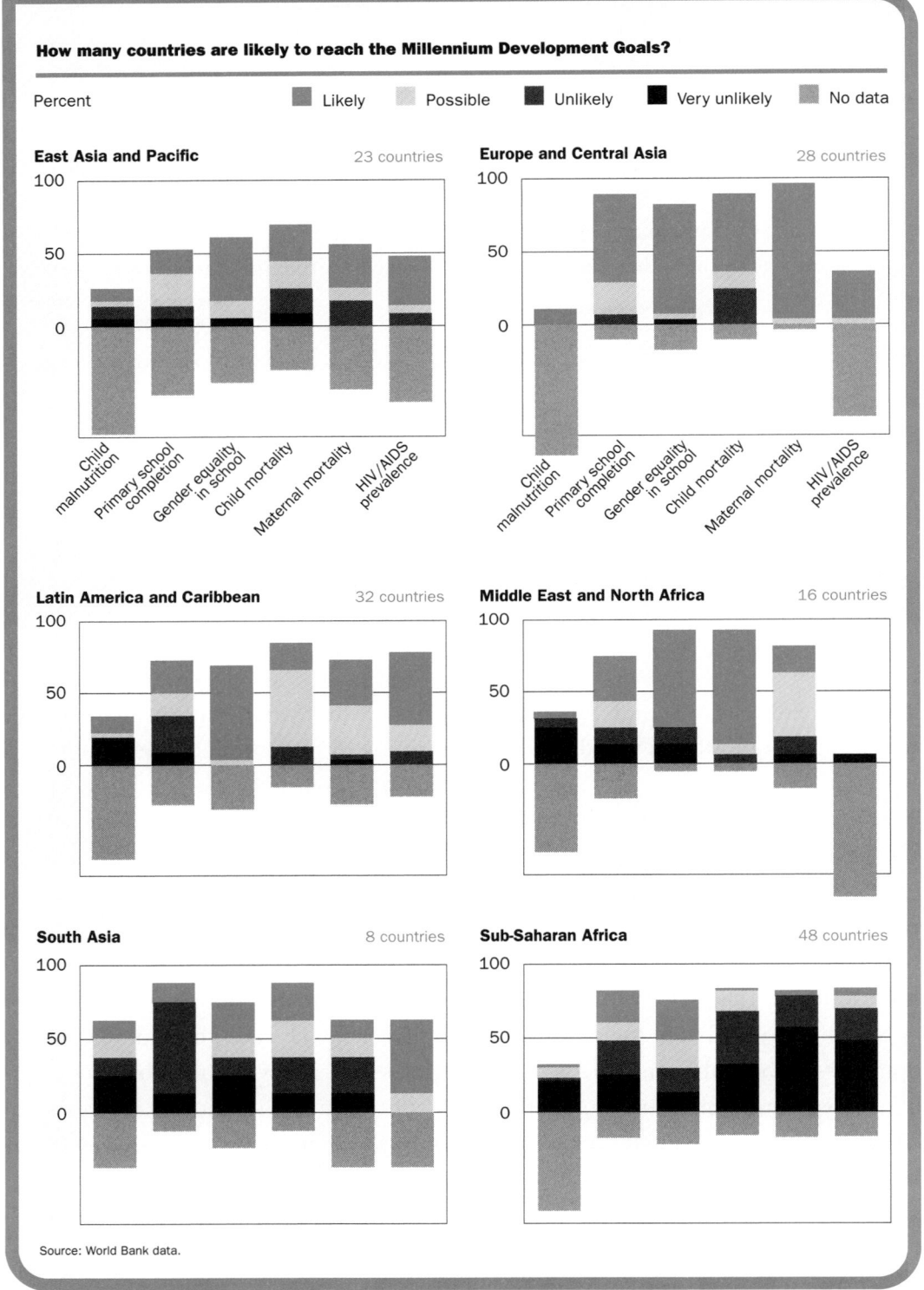

Source: World Bank data.

Are we reaching the goals?

The eight Millennium Development Goals comprise 18 targets and 48 indicators. Where possible, the targets are given as quantified, time-bound values for specific indicators. Data for the indicators come from official statistics and surveys conducted by countries and international agencies. Most of the data are included in this volume, but missing data and the lack of reliable statistics limit the ability to monitor progress.

How many countries are likely to reach the Millennium Development Goals? Much depends on whether the progress in the past decade can be sustained—or accelerated in countries falling behind. The charts show the prospects for low- and middle-income countries of reaching six of the targets of the Millennium Development Goals.

Prospects for each country have been assessed based on their its of progress over the past decade and, in some cases, on its level of attainment. For two indicators lacking time-series data—maternal mortality and HIV prevalence—prospects have been assessed based on level alone. The assessments were made using data available in January 2002 and may be revised in the future.

These assessments are based on past performance and existing data. They are not a final verdict, but they are a warning. Too many countries are falling short of the goals or lack the data to monitor progress. Now is the time to take actions to accelerate progress, not 5 or 10 years from now.

of extreme poverty . . . ."

United Nations Millennium Declaration, September 2000

Regional assessments

- **Countries in dark blue** made progress in the 1990s fast enough to attain the target value in the specified time period (by 2005 for gender equality and by 2015 for all others). They are "likely" to achieve the goals.
- Countries in light blue made progress, but too slowly to reach the goals in the time specified. Continuing at the same rate, they will need as much as twice the time as the "likely" countries to reach the goals. Rated "possible," they need to accelerate progress.

- **Countries in medium gray** made still slower progress. They are "unlikely" to reach the goals. To reach them, they will need to make progress at unprecedented rates.
- For **countries in black,** conditions have worsened since 1990, or they currently have very high maternal mortality and HIV/AIDS prevalence. They are "very unlikely" to reach the goals.
- Countries in light gray lack adequate data to measure progress. Improvements in the statistical systems of many countries are needed to provide a complete and accurate picture of their progress.

The indicators and their targets

- **Child malnutrition Indicator:** Prevalence of malnutrition among children under age five, measured by weight for age (wasting).
Target: Reduce by half between 1990 and 2015.
- **Primary school completion Indicator:** Percentage of children of appropriate age completing last grade of official primary school.
Target: Achieve 100 percent completion by 2015.
- **Gender equality in school Indicator:** Ratio of girls to boys enrolled in primary and secondary school.

Target: Achieve equality in enrollment ratios by 2005.
- **Child mortality Indicator:** Under-five child mortality.
Target: Reduce by two-thirds between 1990 and 2015.
- **Maternal mortality Indicator:** Maternal deaths per 100,000 live births.
Target: Reduce by three-quarters between 1990 and 2015.
- **HIV/AIDS prevalence Indicator:** Prevalence of HIV/AIDS among young women (ages 15–24).
Target: Have halted by 2015 and begun to reverse the spread of HIV/AIDS.

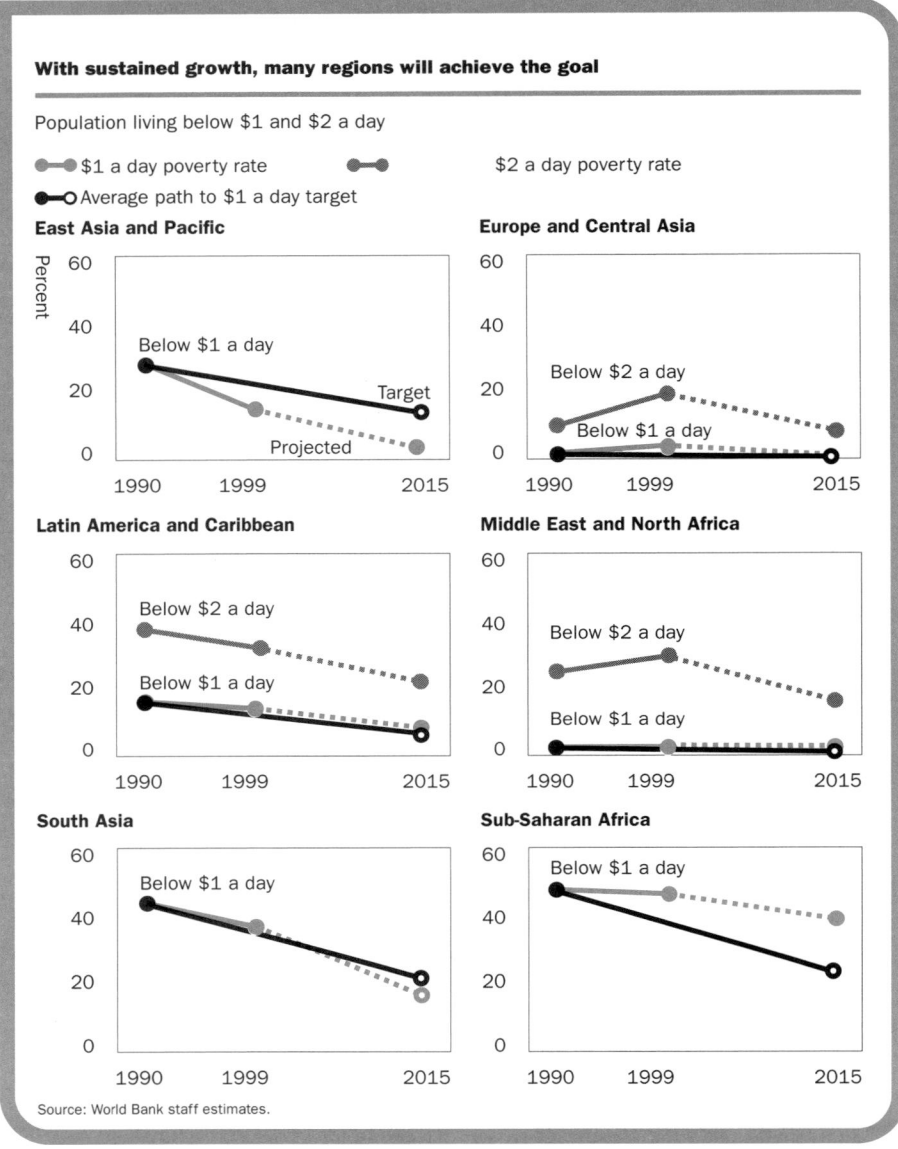

With sustained growth, many regions will achieve the goal

Population living below $1 and $2 a day

●━● $1 a day poverty rate   ●━● $2 a day poverty rate
●━○ Average path to $1 a day target

East Asia and Pacific

Europe and Central Asia

Latin America and Caribbean

Middle East and North Africa

South Asia

Sub-Saharan Africa

Source: World Bank staff estimates.

Eradicate extreme poverty . . .

During the 1990s GDP per capita in developing countries grew by 1.6 percent a year, and the proportion of people living on less than $1 a day fell from 29 percent to 23 percent. By 1999 there were 125 million fewer people living in extreme poverty, continuing a downward trend that began in the early 1980s. But much of the progress has been in Asia, where sustained growth in China lifted nearly 150 million people out of poverty after 1990. Faster growth in parts of South Asia has also led to modest declines in the number of people living in extreme poverty. In other regions the number of poor people has increased, even as the proportion in extreme poverty has fallen.

The Millennium Development Goals call for reducing the proportion of people living on less than $1 a day to half the 1990 level by 2015—from 29 percent of all people in low- and middle-income economies to 14.5 percent. Recent projections by the World Bank show that it is possible to achieve that goal in most regions if growth in per capita income accelerates to an average of 3.6 percent a year. This would be nearly twice the rate achieved over the past decade, but such growth is possible.

. . . and hunger

As average incomes grow, extreme poverty declines and children become better nourished. Very few upper-middle-income countries report significant levels of underweight children. But the data are incomplete, and more systematic monitoring is needed.

Most regions of the world have made dramatic progress in reducing the proportion of underweight children. But progress has been slowing, leaving the prospect of reaching the targets of the Millennium Development Goals in doubt.

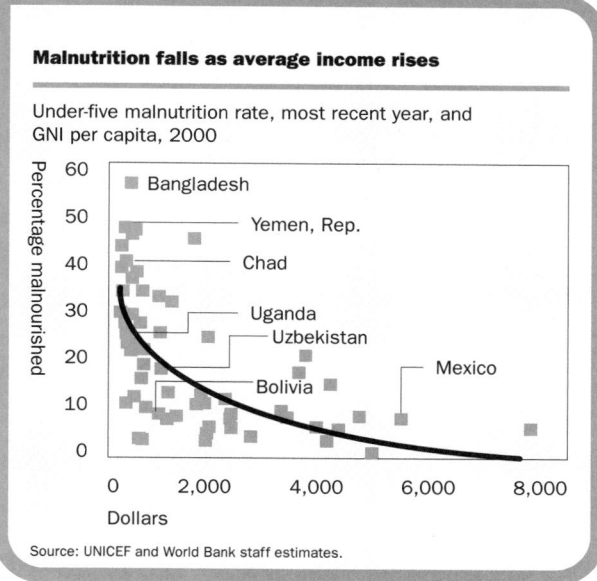

Malnutrition falls as average income rises

Under-five malnutrition rate, most recent year, and GNI per capita, 2000

Percentage malnourished

- Bangladesh
- Yemen, Rep.
- Chad
- Uganda
- Uzbekistan
- Bolivia
- Mexico

Dollars

Source: UNICEF and World Bank staff estimates.

Malnutrition rates among children under five in the developing world fell from 46.5 percent in 1970 to 27 percent in 2000. Even so, 150 million children in low- and middle-income economies are still malnourished, and at current rates of improvement 140 million children will be underweight in 2020.

The number of undernourished people in the developing world fell from 840 million in 1990 to about 777 million in 1997–99 and is expected to decrease by 200 million more by 2015. But greater reductions will be needed to reach the World Food Summit goal of cutting the number of undernourished people in half by 2015.

Malnutrition and hunger

Improving but persistent

Malnutrition in children is caused by consuming too little food energy to meet the body's needs. Adding to the problem are diets that lack essential nutrients, illnesses that deplete those nutrients, and undernourished mothers who give birth to underweight children.

Just as poor countries tend to have high rates of malnutrition, the poorest segment of the population within a country is the most malnourished. Even in countries with relatively low average rates of malnutrition, poor people suffer disproportionately.

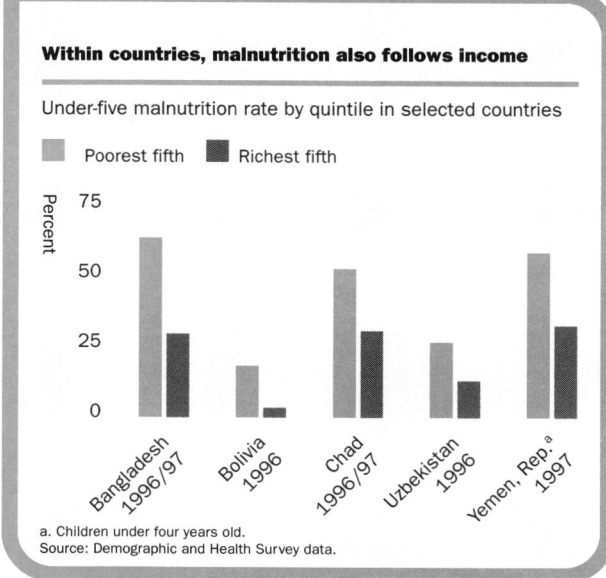

Within countries, malnutrition also follows income

Under-five malnutrition rate by quintile in selected countries

Percent

- Poorest fifth
- Richest fifth

Bangladesh 1996/97
Bolivia 1996
Chad 1996/97
Uzbekistan 1996
Yemen, Rep.ª 1997

a. Children under four years old.
Source: Demographic and Health Survey data.

Raising incomes and reducing poverty is part of the answer. But even poor countries need not suffer high rates of child malnutrition. They can make big improvements through such low-cost measures as nutrition education and food supplementation and fortification. Other things that help include improving the status and education of women, increasing government commitment to health and nutrition, and developing an effective health infrastructure.

Achieve universal primary education

Education is a powerful instrument for reducing poverty and inequality, improving health and social well-being, and laying the basis for sustained economic growth. It is essential for building democratic societies and dynamic, globally competitive economies.

The 1990 Conference on Education for All, held in Jomtien, Thailand, pledged to achieve universal primary education by 2000. But in 1999 there were still 120 million primary-school-age children not in school, 53 percent of them girls

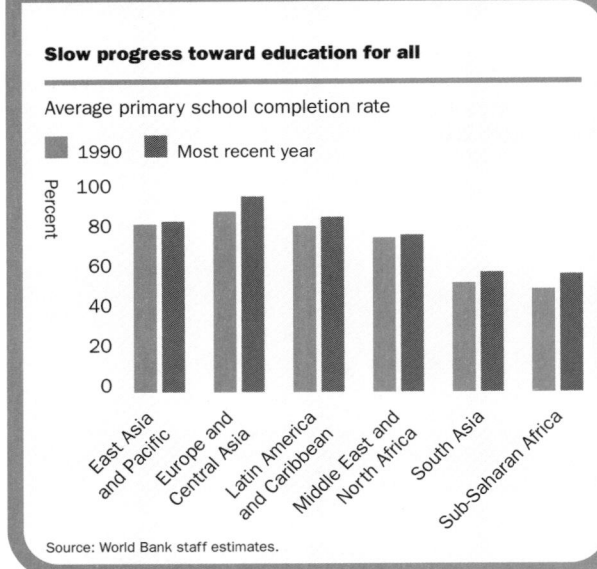

Slow progress toward education for all

Average primary school completion rate

Source: World Bank staff estimates.

and 74 percent living in South Asia and Sub-Saharan Africa. The Millennium Development Goals set a more realistic but still difficult deadline of 2015 when all children everywhere should be able to complete a full course of primary schooling.

Recent work at the World Bank (2002) has produced new estimates of primary completion rates. These show small improvements everywhere, but progress overall has been too slow to reach the goal by 2015.

What can be done? Lower costs to students and their families. Improve the quality of schools. And increase the efficiency of the school system.

Education

Reading, writing, and retention

To reach the goal, schools must first enroll all school-age children and then keep them in school for the full course of the primary stage. In many places schools fail to do both. As a result, there can be large gaps between reported enrollment, attendance, and completion rates. Disparities arise for many reasons. Children may start school late or they may repeat grades, putting them off track. Frequently children drop out of school because of their own or a family member's illness or because their families need their labor. If they return, they re-enroll in the same grade the following year. But many never finish.

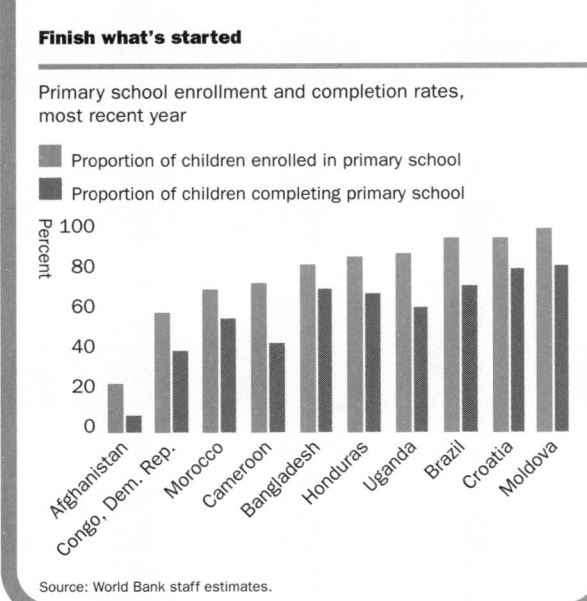

Finish what's started

Primary school enrollment and completion rates, most recent year

Proportion of children enrolled in primary school
Proportion of children completing primary school

Source: World Bank staff estimates.

Some 79 developing countries have already built sufficient schools and places to educate 100 percent of their primary-school-age children. Only 27 of those countries retain 100 percent of children in school through primary graduation.

Since 1990, 17 middle-income and 21 low-income countries have seen completion rates stagnate or decline. Afghanistan fell from an already low 22 percent in 1990 to an estimated 8 percent. A number of middle-income Gulf states, Latin American countries such as Trinidad and Tobago and República Bolivariana de Venezuela, and low-income countries such as Cameroon, Kenya, Madagascar, and Zambia have also lost ground.

Promote gender equality and empower women

In most low-income countries girls are less likely to attend school than boys. And even when girls start school at the same rate as boys, they are more likely to drop out—often because parents think boys' schooling is more important or because girls' work at home seems more valuable than schooling. Concerns about the safety of girls or traditional biases against educating them can mean that they never start school or do not continue beyond the primary stage.

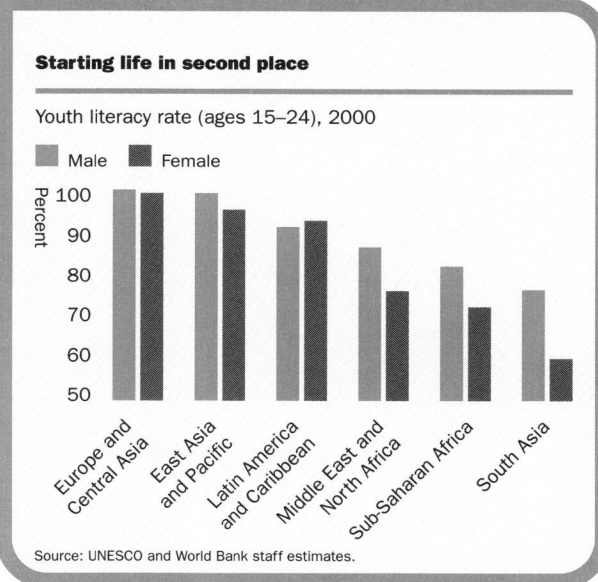

Starting life in second place

Youth literacy rate (ages 15–24), 2000

Source: UNESCO and World Bank staff estimates.

Girls reach adulthood with lower literacy rates than boys (except in Latin America and the Caribbean). Informal training, such as adult literacy classes, can make up some of the difference. But many girls, who begin with fewer opportunities than boys, are at a permanent disadvantage.

Gender equality

Beyond schooling

Educating women and giving them equal rights is important for many reasons:

- It increases their productivity, raising output and reducing poverty.
- It promotes gender equality within households and removes constraints on women's decision-making—thus reducing fertility rates and improving maternal health.
- It increases children's chances of surviving to become healthier and better educated because educated women do a better job caring for children.

Equal access to education is an important step toward greater gender

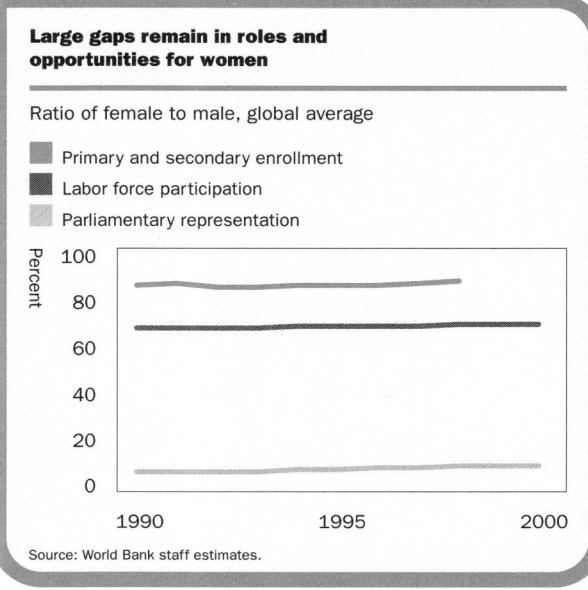

Large gaps remain in roles and opportunities for women

Ratio of female to male, global average

Primary and secondary enrollment
Labor force participation
Parliamentary representation

Source: World Bank staff estimates.

equality, but it is not the only one. Even as gender disparities in education diminish, other differences persist everywhere—in legal rights, labor market opportunities, and the ability to participate in public life and development decision-making.

Recognizing that empowering women extends beyond the classroom and the household, the Millennium Development Goals include three additional indicators of gender equality: illiteracy rates, the proportion of women working outside agriculture, and the proportion of seats women hold in national parliaments. These indicators suggest that even after reaching the goal of full participation in primary and secondary education, the world will still fall short of gender equality.

Reduce child mortality

Deaths of infants and children dropped rapidly over the past 25 years. The number of deaths of children under five fell from 15 million in 1980 to about 11 million in 1990, a period when the number of children being born was still rising. This was success borne on many wings—vaccination programs, the spread of oral rehydration therapy, wider availability of antibiotics to treat pneumonia, and better economic and social conditions all contributed.

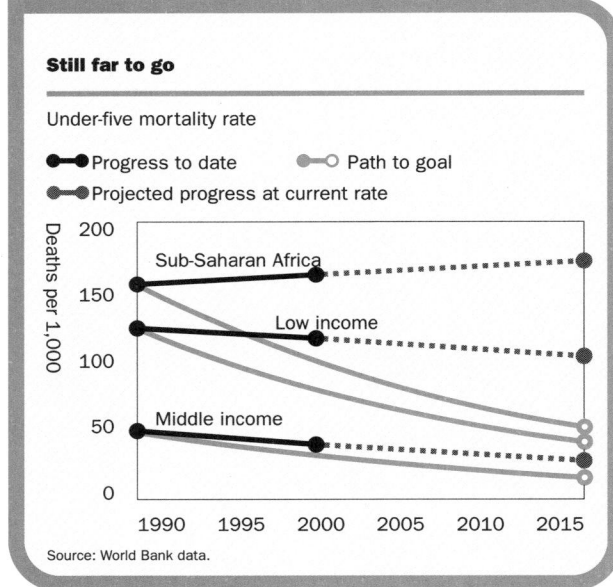

Still far to go

Under-five mortality rate

● Progress to date   ○—○ Path to goal
●—● Projected progress at current rate

Source: World Bank data.

Rapid improvements before 1990 gave hope that mortality rates of children under five could be cut by two-thirds in the following 25 years. But progress slowed almost everywhere in the 1990s, and in parts of Africa infant and child mortality rates increased.

At the end of the 20th century only 36 developing countries were making fast enough progress to reduce under-five child mortality to a third of its 1990 level by 2015. Most of those are middle-income countries, although a few poor countries—notably Bangladesh and Indonesia—and some of the poorest countries of the former Soviet Union are on track to achieve the goal.

Infant and child mortality

Addressing the causes

For 70 percent of children who die before their fifth birthday the cause is a disease or combination of diseases and malnutrition that would be readily preventable in a high-income country: acute respiratory infections, diarrhea, measles, and malaria.

In some parts of the world vaccination coverage has begun to decline. In 1999, 55 countries had not attained 80 percent coverage of measles vaccinations among children under one year; another 48 reported no data.

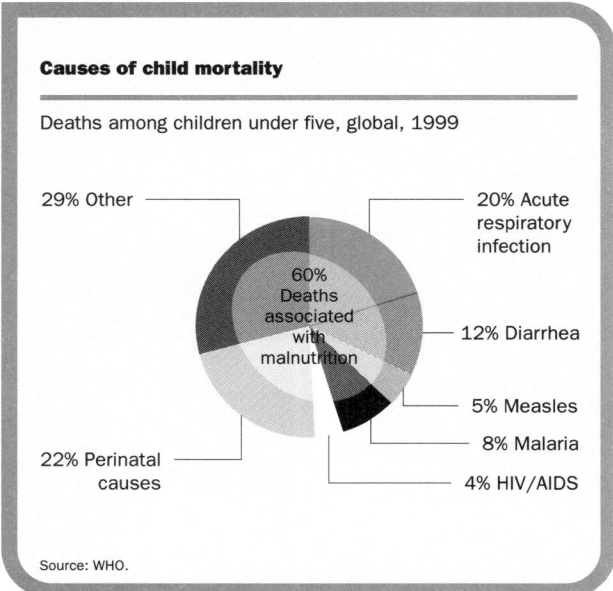

Causes of child mortality

Deaths among children under five, global, 1999

29% Other
20% Acute respiratory infection
60% Deaths associated with malnutrition
12% Diarrhea
5% Measles
8% Malaria
4% HIV/AIDS
22% Perinatal causes

Source: WHO.

One-third of child deaths occur in the neonatal period. They are caused by poor maternal health and lack of care during pregnancy and delivery.

To ensure continuing improvements, disease-specific vaccination and treatment programs must be sustained while new strategies address unmet needs of unserved populations. In all countries the poorest people are least likely to receive health services and so have the highest mortality rates. Addressing the underlying causes of poverty will improve health, and better health will reduce poverty.

Improve maternal health

In 1995 more than 500,000 women died from complications of pregnancy and childbirth, most of them in developing countries, where these complications are the leading cause of death among women of reproductive age. More than half of all maternal deaths occur in Africa. In many African countries one mother dies for every 100 live births. In Rwanda there were more than 2 deaths for every 100 live births. Compare that with Greece, which reported only 2 maternal deaths per 100,000 live births.

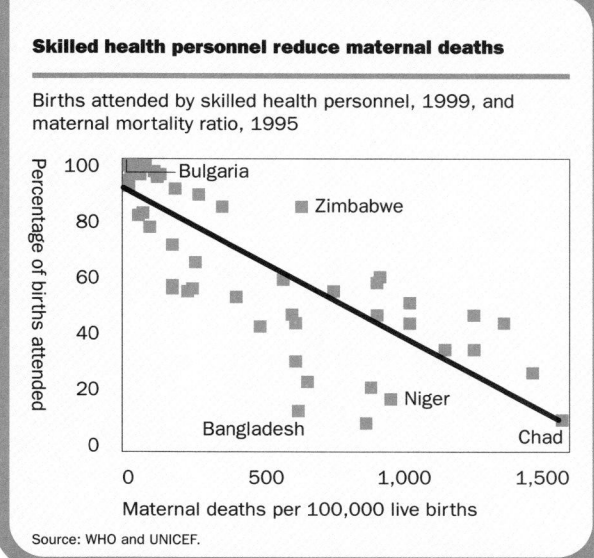

Skilled health personnel reduce maternal deaths

Births attended by skilled health personnel, 1999, and maternal mortality ratio, 1995

Source: WHO and UNICEF.

Many women deliver their children alone or with traditional birth attendants who lack the skills to deal with complications. Skilled birth attendants help to recognize and prevent medical crises. They also provide mothers with basic information about care for themselves and their children before and after giving birth. Lack of current data on maternal deaths limits monitoring of trends over time.

Maternal mortality

Preventing maternal deaths

Women die in childbirth for many reasons, most of them preventable or treatable using cost-effective interventions:

• *Reduce the number of pregnancies.* Early childbearing and closely spaced pregnancies increase the risks for mothers and children. And in some countries unsafe abortions add to the toll. Although many personal and cultural factors affect the desired family size, access to family planning services helps women make decisions about whether and when to have children.

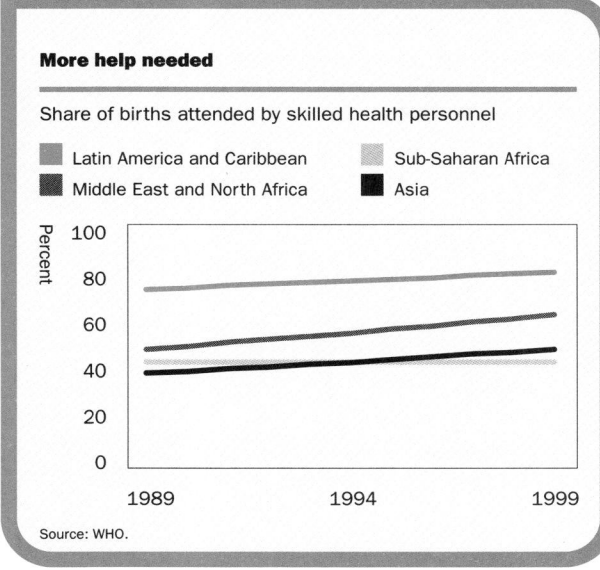

More help needed

Share of births attended by skilled health personnel

■ Latin America and Caribbean ▨ Sub-Saharan Africa
■ Middle East and North Africa ■ Asia

Source: WHO.

• *Prevent complications during pregnancy and childbirth.* Inadequate nutrition, unsafe sex, and poor health care during pregnancy increase the risk of health problems during pregnancy and childbirth. Yet in some countries fewer than 25 percent of pregnant women visit a clinic for care.

• *Prevent deaths when complications arise.* Complications during pregnancy and delivery must be quickly diagnosed and treated in suitable health care facilities. But providing prompt emergency services is beyond the capacity of many countries' health systems.

Combat HIV/AIDS, malaria, and other diseases

With an estimated 40 million people living with HIV/AIDS and 20 million deaths since the disease was first identified, AIDS poses an unprecedented public health, economic, and social challenge. By infecting young people disproportionately—half of all new HIV infections are among 15- to 24-year-olds—and by killing so many adults in their prime, the epidemic seriously undermines development.

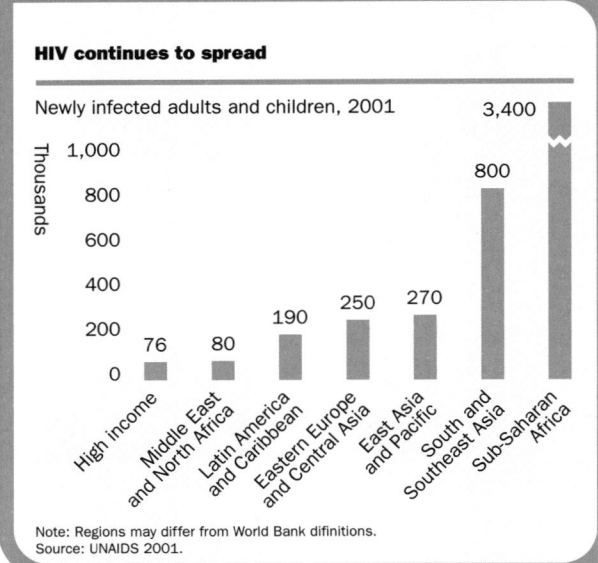

HIV continues to spread

Newly infected adults and children, 2001

Thousands

Note: Regions may differ from World Bank difinitions.
Source: UNAIDS 2001.

HIV/AIDS is the leading cause of death in Sub-Saharan Africa and the fourth largest killer worldwide. Among those lost are teachers, health care workers, and farmers, forcing the closure of schools and clinics and threatening food security. Deaths of parents have left more than 13 million HIV/AIDS orphans—a figure expected to more than double by 2010.

Disease

Epidemic proportions

Malaria is endemic in more than 100 countries and territories and affects an estimated 300 million people each year. Although the mosquitoes that spread the disease have been eradicated in some countries where malaria was not widespread, this has not been possible in wet, tropical climates.

Estimates based on malaria cases reported to the WHO show that almost 90 percent occur in Sub-Saharan Africa, with most of the deaths among young children. Anti-malaria efforts now focus on reducing human exposure and lessening

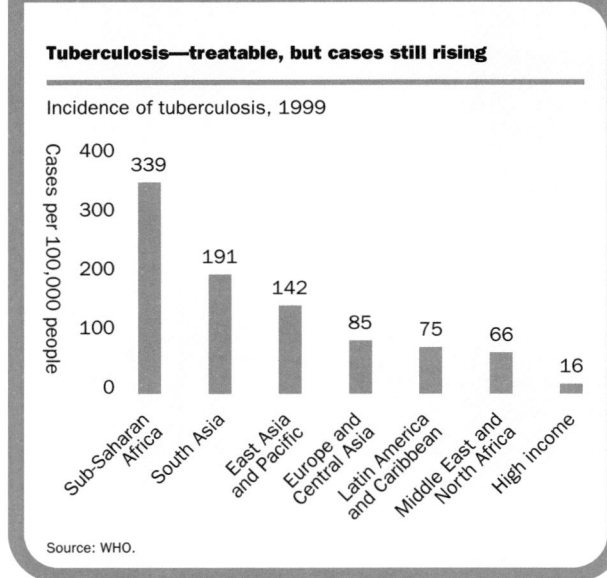

Tuberculosis—treatable, but cases still rising

Incidence of tuberculosis, 1999

Cases per 100,000 people

Source: WHO.

the health effects for those who become infected.

Tuberculosis is the main cause of death from a single infectious agent among adults in developing countries. Over the past decade the incidence of tuberculosis has grown rapidly in Europe and Central Asia, Africa, and parts of South and East Asia. On present trends, there will be 10.2 million new cases in 2005, and Africa will continue to have more cases than other regions. The directly observed treatment, short-course (DOTS) strategy has proven effective, but in 1999 less than half the population in the 23 countries with the largest number of cases had access to DOTS.

Ensure environmental sustainability

The environment provides goods and services that sustain human development—so we must ensure that development sustains the environment. Growing populations are putting greater pressure on land and natural resources. In many places freshwater is already becoming scarce. Forests are disappearing. Soils are being degraded and fisheries overexploited. Poor people are disproportionately affected. Fortunately, good policies and economic growth, which work to improve people's lives, can also work to improve the environment.

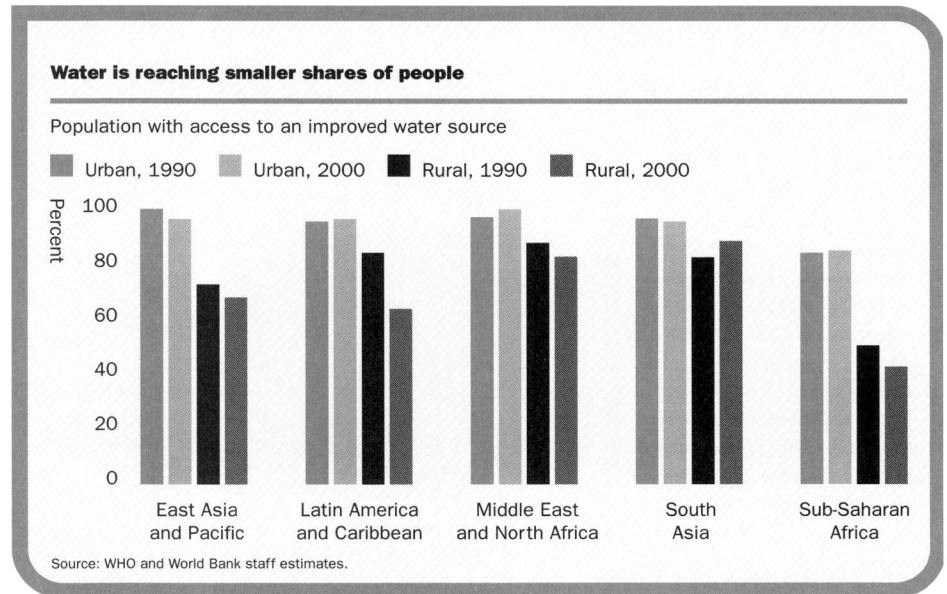

Water is reaching smaller shares of people

Population with access to an improved water source

■ Urban, 1990   ■ Urban, 2000   ■ Rural, 1990   ■ Rural, 2000

Source: WHO and World Bank staff estimates.

Environment

Progress is possible

Greater understanding of how environmental assets and social assets—including markets—work together points the way to truly sustainable development. Poor countries do not need to repeat the mistakes of rich countries. In some high-income countries the abandonment of farmlands has allowed forests to recover. But the world lost more than 900,000 square kilometers of forest in the past decade. And the damage from losing whole species of plants and animals can never be undone.

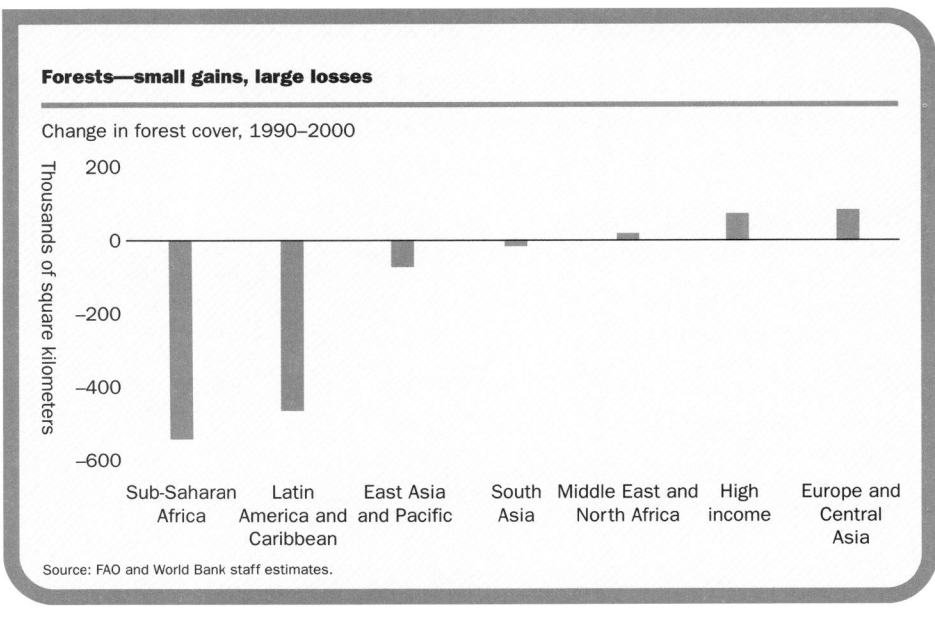

Forests—small gains, large losses

Change in forest cover, 1990–2000

Source: FAO and World Bank staff estimates.

Develop a global partnership for development

What will it take to achieve the Millennium Development Goals? A lot. Economies need to grow to provide jobs and more income for poor people. And growth requires investment in plant and equipment, in energy and transport, in human skills and knowledge. Growth is fastest in a good investment climate—where good economic policies and good governance provide assurance to investors and to workers of receiving the rewards of their efforts.

Great opportunities exist in today's fast changing global economy, but

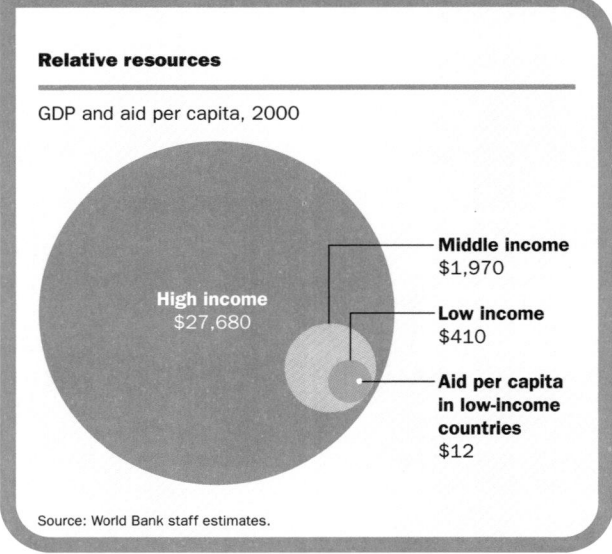

Relative resources

GDP and aid per capita, 2000

High income $27,680

Middle income $1,970

Low income $410

Aid per capita in low-income countries $12

Source: World Bank staff estimates.

many poor countries have been left on the margins, lacking the skills, technologies, and financial resources to participate. To help them eradicate poverty, hunger, and premature death—and to reach the poorest people with the opportunities of growth—will require a new global partnership for development.

The building blocks of that partnership, confirmed at the Monterrey Conference on Financing for Development, are stronger policies and good governance in developing countries, a more open and equitable global trading system, and increased resources through aid and debt reduction for countries working to meet their development goals.

Foundations for

Increasing the effectiveness of development assistance

In the past decade the real value of aid to developing countries has fallen 8 percent. Only half of it goes to low-income economies (average income per capita of less than $755 in 2000) and the rest to middle-income economies (average income per capita ranging upwards to $9,000).

Aid goes for many purposes, but only a small share for such basic social services as basic education, primary health care, nutrition, and safe water and sanitation. In 1999–2000

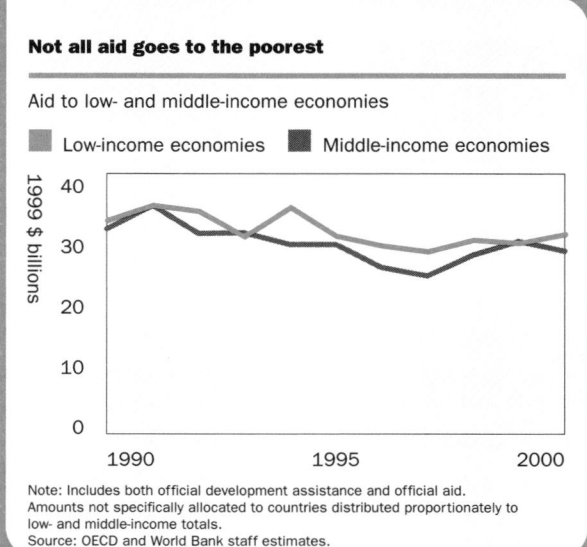

Not all aid goes to the poorest

Aid to low- and middle-income economies

■ Low-income economies   ■ Middle-income economies

1999 $ billions

Note: Includes both official development assistance and official aid.
Amounts not specifically allocated to countries distributed proportionately to low- and middle-income totals.
Source: OECD and World Bank staff estimates.

official development assistance (ODA) for basic social services averaged $4.9 billion, or about 14.5 percent of ODA directed to specific sectors. (Some ODA provided as general budgetary support to country development programs also goes to basic social services.)

Aid is most effective in reducing poverty when it goes to poor countries with good economic policies and sound governance—and advances country-owned poverty reduction programs. But in some cases aid is tied to purchases of goods and services approved by the donor country. Such restrictions reduce the effectiveness of aid and undermine the principle of country ownership. The share of untied aid has been growing.

Easing the burden of debt

The Debt Initiative for Heavily Indebted Poor Countries (HIPCs) provides debt relief to the world's poorest and most heavily indebted countries. Begun in 1996 by the World Bank and the IMF, the initiative was enhanced in 1999 to provide deeper and faster debt relief with a stronger link between debt relief and poverty reduction.

Forty-two countries could qualify for HIPC assistance. At the end of 2001, 24 countries were receiving relief that, in time, will amount to $36 billion. The total debt relief to all countries could reach $50 billion.

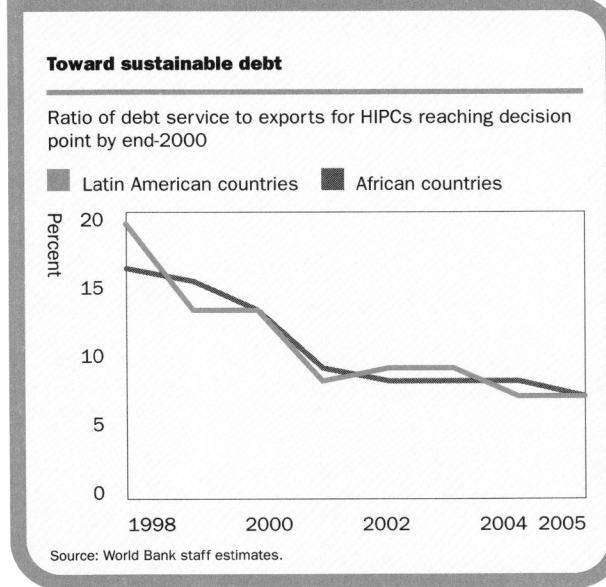

Toward sustainable debt

Ratio of debt service to exports for HIPCs reaching decision point by end-2000

■ Latin American countries   ■ African countries

Source: World Bank staff estimates.

Under the enhanced HIPC initiative, average debt service due in 2001–03 will be about 30 percent less than that paid before relief began in 1998–99.

In 2001–02 social spending in HIPC countries will be about $6.5 billion—45 percent higher than in 1999 and about three times the level of debt service.

The ratio of debt service payments to a country's exports is one of several indicators of whether debt levels are sustainable. For the 24 countries now receiving debt relief, the average annual debt service to export ratio will fall from 17 percent to 8 percent, less than half the average for developing countries.

a new development partnership

Reducing barriers to trade

Tariffs have been falling. After the Uruguay Round of trade negotiations concluded in 1994, average tariffs on agricultural products and textiles and clothing—two important categories of developing country exports—fell in most high-income countries.

But average tariffs don't tell the full story. High tariffs can block access to markets. That is why the European Union's initiative to eliminate tariffs on all exports except arms from least developed countries is so important.

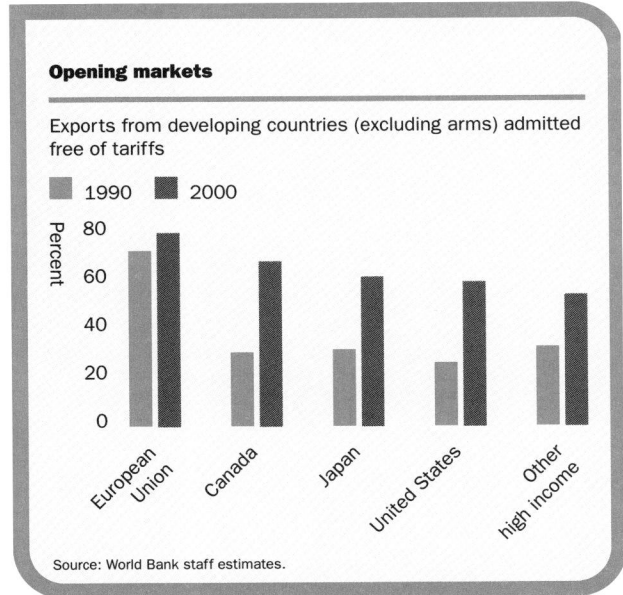

Opening markets

Exports from developing countries (excluding arms) admitted free of tariffs

■ 1990   ■ 2000

European Union   Canada   Japan   United States   Other high income

Source: World Bank staff estimates.

Even if the use of tariffs and quotas is further reduced, many developing countries will still face difficulties realizing the benefits, especially in Africa. One estimate, based on reducing trade protection by half, shows that developing countries would gain about $200 billion by 2015. But only $2.4 billion of this would go to Sub-Saharan Africa, and only another $3.3 billion to South Asia outside of India. To make trade an effective source of growth, developing countries need to increase the efficiency of their trade—their producers, shippers, freight handlers, and customs services. High-income countries can help by providing "aid for trade" and sharing knowledge on establishing competitive export industries.

Millennium Development Goals

Goals and targets	Indicators[a]
Goal 1 Eradicate extreme poverty and hunger	
Halve, between 1990 and 2015, the proportion of people whose income is less than $1 a day	• Proportion of population below $1 a day • Poverty gap ratio [incidence times depth of poverty] • Share of poorest quintile in national consumption
Halve, between 1990 and 2015, the proportion of people who suffer from hunger	• Prevalence of underweight in children (under five years of age) • Proportion of population below minimum level of dietary energy consumption
Goal 2 Achieve universal primary education	
Ensure that, by 2015, children everywhere, boys and girls alike, will be able to complete a full course of primary schooling	• Net enrollment ratio in primary education • Proportion of pupils starting grade 1 who reach grade 5 • Literacy rate of 15- to 24-year-olds
Goal 3 Promote gender equality and empower women	
Eliminate gender disparity in primary and secondary education preferably by 2005 and in all levels of education no later than 2015	• Ratio of girls to boys in primary, secondary, and tertiary education • Ratio of literate females to males among 15- to 24-year-olds • Share of women in wage employment in the nonagricultural sector • Proportion of seats held by women in national parliament
Goal 4 Reduce child mortality	
Reduce by two-thirds, between 1990 and 2015, the under-five mortality rate	• Under-five mortality rate • Infant mortality rate • Proportion of one-year-old children immunized against measles
Goal 5 Improve maternal health	
Reduce by three-quarters, between 1990 and 2015, the maternal mortality ratio	• Maternal mortality ratio • Proportion of births attended by skilled health personnel
Goal 6 Combat HIV/AIDS, malaria, and other diseases	
Have halted by 2015 and begun to reverse the spread of HIV/AIDS	• HIV prevalence among 15- to 24-year-old pregnant women • Contraceptive prevalence rate[b] • Number of children orphaned by HIV/AIDS
Have halted by 2015 and begun to reverse the incidence of malaria and other major diseases	• Prevalence and death rates associated with malaria • Proportion of population in malaria-risk areas using effective malaria prevention and treatment measures • Prevalence and death rates associated with tuberculosis • Proportion of tuberculosis cases detected and cured under directly observed treatment, short-course (DOTS)
Goal 7 Ensure environmental sustainability	
Integrate the principles of sustainable development into country policies and programs and reverse the loss of environmental resources	• Change in land area covered by forest • Land area protected to maintain biological diversity • GDP per unit of energy use • Carbon dioxide emissions (per capita)
Halve, by 2015, the proportion of people without sustainable access to safe drinking water	• Proportion of population with sustainable access to an improved water source
Have achieved, by 2020, a significant improvement in the lives of at least 100 million slum dwellers	• Proportion of population with access to improved sanitation • Proportion of population with access to secure tenure [Urban-rural disaggregation of several of the above indicators may be relevant for monitoring improvement in the lives of slum dwellers]

Goals and targets

Indicators[a]

| Goal 8 | Develop a global partnership for development |

Develop further an open, rule-based, predictable, nondiscriminatory trading and financial system (includes a commitment to good governance, development, and poverty reduction—both nationally and internationally)

Address the special needs of the least developed countries (includes tariff and quota-free access for their exports; enhanced program of debt relief for heavily indebted poor countries and cancellation of official bilateral debt; and more generous ODA for countries committed to poverty reduction)

Address the special needs of landlocked countries and small island developing states (through Barbados Program and 22nd General Assembly provisions)

Deal comprehensively with the debt problems of developing countries through national and international measures in order to make debt sustainable in the long term

Some of the indicators listed below will be monitored separately for the least developed countries (LDCs), Africa, landlocked countries, and small island developing states.

Official development assistance (ODA)
- Net ODA as a percentage of DAC donors' GNI
- Proportion of ODA for basic social services (basic education, primary health care, nutrition, safe water, and sanitation)
- Proportion of ODA that is untied
- Proportion of ODA for the environment in small island developing states
- Proportion of ODA for the transport sector in landlocked countries

Market access
- Proportion of exports (by value, excluding arms) admitted free of duties and quotas
- Average tariffs and quotas on agricultural products and textiles and clothing
- Domestic and export agricultural subsidies in OECD countries
- Proportion of ODA provided to help build trade capacity

Debt sustainability
- Proportion of official bilateral HIPC debt canceled
- Debt service as a percentage of exports of goods and services
- Proportion of ODA provided as debt relief
- Number of countries reaching HIPC decision and completion points

In cooperation with developing countries, develop and implement strategies for decent and productive work for youth

- Unemployment rate of 15- to 24-year-olds

In cooperation with pharmaceutical companies, provide access to affordable, essential drugs in developing countries

- Proportion of population with access to affordable, essential drugs on a sustainable basis

In cooperation with the private sector, make available the benefits of new technologies, especially information and communications

- Telephone lines per 1,000 people
- Personal computers per 1,000 people

a. Some indicators, particularly for goals 7 and 8, remain under discussion. Additions or revisions to the list may be made in the future.

b. Only one form of contraception—condoms—is effective in reducing the spread of HIV.

1.1 | Size of the economy

	Population	Surface area	Population density	Gross national income		Gross national income per capita		PPP gross national income [a]			Gross domestic product	
	millions	thousand sq. km	people per sq. km	$ billions	Rank	$	Rank	$ billions	Per capita $	Rank	% growth	Per capita % growth
	2000	2000	2000	2000[b]	2000	2000[b]	2000	2000	2000	2000	1999-2000	1999-2000
Afghanistan	27 [c]	652	41	..	..	.. [d]	..	..	..	..	..	..
Albania	3	29	124	3.8	126	1,120	130	12	3,600	130	7.8	6.9
Algeria	30	2,382	13	47.9	49	1,580	117	153 [e]	5,040 [e]	107	2.4	0.9
Angola	13	1,247	11	3.8	125	290	178	15 [e]	1,180 [e]	181	2.1	-0.8
Argentina	37	2,780	14	276.2	16	7,460	58	446	12,050	58	-0.5	-1.7
Armenia	4	30	135	2.0	146	520	155	10	2,580	147	6.0	5.9
Australia	19	7,741	2	388.3	15	20,240	27	479 [e]	24,970	19	1.9	0.8
Austria	8	84	98	204.5	21	25,220	14	214	26,330	14	3.0	2.7
Azerbaijan	8	87	93	4.9	115	600	148	22	2,740	142	11.1	10.2
Bangladesh	131	144	1,007	47.9	50	370	167	209	1,590	165	5.9	4.1
Belarus	10	208	48	28.7	60	2,870	94	76	7,550	82	5.8	6.1
Belgium	10	30	331	251.6	18	24,540	20	282	27,470	9	4.0	3.8
Benin	6	113	57	2.3	142	370	167	6	980	186	5.8	3.1
Bolivia	8	1,099	8	8.2	95	990	133	20	2,360	151	2.4	0.0
Bosnia and Herzegovina	4	51	78	4.9	112	1,230	126	..	..	..	5.9	3.1
Botswana	2	582	3	5.3	109	3,300	85	11	7,170	84	3.4	2.5
Brazil	170	8,547	20	610.1	9	3,580	82	1,243	7,300	83	4.5	3.2
Bulgaria	8	111	74	12.4	80	1,520	119	45	5,560	100	5.8	6.3
Burkina Faso	11	274	41	2.4	141	210	193	11 [e]	970 [e]	187	2.2	-0.4
Burundi	7	28	265	0.7	176	110	205	4 [e]	580 [e]	204	0.3	-1.6
Cambodia	12	181	68	3.1	135	260	186	17	1,440	173	5.0	2.7
Cameroon	15	475	32	8.6	90	580	151	24	1,590	165	4.2	2.0
Canada	31	9,971	3	649.8	8	21,130	26	836 [e]	27,170 [e]	11	4.5	3.6
Central African Republic	4	623	6	1.0	166	280	183	4 [e]	1,160 [e]	182	2.5	1.1
Chad	8	1,284	6	1.5	153	200	195	7	870	190	0.6	-2.1
Chile	15	757	20	69.8	43	4,590	73	138	9,100	73	5.4	4.0
China	1,262	9,598 [f]	135	1,062.9	7	840	141	4,951	3,920	124	7.9	7.2
Hong Kong, China	7	..	..	176.2	23	25,920	13	174	25,590	17	10.5	9.2
Colombia	42	1,139	41	85.3	40	2,020	102	256	6,060	94	2.8	1.0
Congo, Dem. Rep.	51	2,345	22	..	..	.. [d]	..	..	..	..	..	..
Congo, Rep.	3	342	9	1.7	151	570	153	2	570	205	7.9	4.9
Costa Rica	4	51	75	14.5	77	3,810	78	30	7,980	80	1.7	-0.5
Côte d'Ivoire	16	322	50	9.6	85	600	148	24	1,500	170	-2.3	-4.9
Croatia	4	57	78	20.2	62	4,620	72	35	7,960	81	3.7	3.6
Cuba	11	111	102	..	..	.. [g]	..	..	..	..	..	..
Czech Republic	10	79	133	53.9	45	5,250	68	142	13,780	55	2.9	3.0
Denmark	5	43	126	172.2	24	32,280	8	145	27,250	10	2.9	2.6
Dominican Republic	8	49	173	17.8	70	2,130	97	48	5,710	97	7.8	6.0
Ecuador	13	284	46	15.3	75	1,210	127	37	2,910	140	2.3	0.4
Egypt, Arab Rep.	64	1,001	64	95.4	38	1,490	120	235	3,670	128	5.1	3.1
El Salvador	6	21	303	12.6	79	2,000	103	28	4,410	117	2.0	0.0
Eritrea	4	118	41	0.7	178	170	200	4	960	188	-8.2	-10.6
Estonia	1	45	32	4.9	113	3,580	82	13	9,340	71	6.4	7.8
Ethiopia	64	1,104	64	6.7	99	100	206	43	660	202	5.4	3.0
Finland	5	338	17	130.1	28	25,130	16	127	24,570	23	5.7	5.5
France	59	552	107	1,438.3 [h]	5	24,090 [h]	23	1,438	24,420	24	3.1	2.6
Gabon	1	268	5	3.9	122	3,190	88	7	5,360	103	2.0	-0.6
Gambia, The	1	11	130	0.4	191	340	173	2 [e]	1,620 [e]	164	5.6	2.3
Georgia	5	70	72	3.2	134	630	146	13	2,680	144	1.9	1.9
Germany	82	357	230	2,063.7	3	25,120	17	2,047	24,920	20	3.0	2.9
Ghana	19	239	85	6.6	102	340	173	37 [e]	1,910 [e]	159	3.7	1.3
Greece	11	132	82	126.3	30	11,960	47	178	16,860	48	4.3	4.1
Guatemala	11	109	105	19.2	67	1,680	111	43	3,770	126	3.3	0.6
Guinea	7	246	30	3.3	132	450	159	14	1,930	158	2.0	-0.3
Guinea-Bissau	1	36	43	0.2	201	180	197	1	710	200	7.5	5.2
Haiti	8	28	289	4.1	121	510	156	12 [e]	1,470 [e]	172	1.1	-0.9
Honduras	6	112	57	5.5	108	860	138	15	2,400	150	4.8	2.2

	Population	Surface area	Population density	Gross national income		Gross national income per capita		PPP gross national income [a]			Gross domestic product	
	millions	thousand sq. km	people per sq. km	$ billions	Rank	$	Rank	$ billions	Per capita $	Rank	% growth	Per capita % growth
	2000	2000	2000	2000[b]	2000	2000[b]	2000	2000	2000	2000	1999-2000	1999-2000
Hungary	10	93	109	47.2	51	4,710	71	120	11,990	59	5.2	5.6
India	1,016	3,287	342	454.8	12	450	159	2,375	2,340	153	3.9	2.0
Indonesia	210	1,905	116	119.9	32	570	153	596	2,830	141	4.8	3.1
Iran, Islamic Rep.	64	1,633	39	106.7	34	1,680	111	376	5,910	95	5.4	3.9
Iraq	23	438	53	..	..	.. [g]	..	..	..	..	..	..
Ireland	4	70	55	86.0	39	22,660	24	97	25,520	18	11.5	10.3
Israel	6	21	302	104.1	35	16,710	36	121	19,330	37	6.0	3.8
Italy	58	301	196	1,163.2	6	20,160	30	1,354	23,470	28	2.9	2.8
Jamaica	3	11	243	6.9	98	2,610	96	9	3,440	135	0.8	-0.9
Japan	127	378	348	4,519.1	2	35,620	5	3,436	27,080	12	2.4	2.2
Jordan	5	89	55	8.4	93	1,710	110	19	3,950	123	3.9	0.8
Kazakhstan	15	2,725	6	18.8	68	1,260	125	82	5,490	101	9.6	10.0
Kenya	30	580	53	10.6	82	350	172	30	1,010	185	-0.2	-2.5
Korea, Dem. Rep.	22	121	185	..	..	.. [d]	..	..	..	..	..	..
Korea, Rep.	47	99	479	421.1	13	8,910	54	818	17,300	46	8.8	7.8
Kuwait	2	18	111	35.8	53	18,030	31	37	18,690	39	1.7	-1.4
Kyrgyz Republic	5	200	26	1.3	158	270	184	13	2,540	149	5.0	3.9
Lao PDR	5	237	23	1.5	154	290	178	8 [e]	1,540 [e]	168	5.7	3.3
Latvia	2	65	38	6.9	97	2,920	93	17	7,070	85	6.6	8.3
Lebanon	4	10	423	17.4	71	4,010	77	20	4,550	113	0.0	-1.3
Lesotho	2	30	67	1.2	163	580	151	5 [e]	2,590 [e]	146	3.8	2.5
Liberia	3	111	32	..	..	.. [d]	..	..	..	..	..	..
Libya	5	1,760	3	..	..	.. [i]	..	..	..	..	..	..
Lithuania	4	65	57	10.8	81	2,930	92	26	6,980	87	3.9	4.0
Macedonia, FYR	2	26	80	3.7	128	1,820	108	10	5,020	108	4.3	3.6
Madagascar	16	587	27	3.9	124	250	188	13	820	191	4.8	1.6
Malawi	10	118	110	1.7	150	170	200	6	600	203	1.7	-0.4
Malaysia	23	330	71	78.7	42	3,380	84	194	8,330	77	8.3	5.7
Mali	11	1,240	9	2.5	138	240	190	8	780	195	4.5	2.1
Mauritania	3	1,026	3	1.0	170	370	167	4	1,630	163	5.2	1.7
Mauritius	1	2	584	4.4	119	3,750	80	12	9,940	70	8.0	6.9
Mexico	98	1,958	51	497.0	11	5,070	69	861	8,790	76	6.9	5.3
Moldova	4	34	130	1.4	157	400	162	10	2,230	154	1.9	2.1
Mongolia	2	1,567	2	0.9	172	390	164	4	1,760	161	1.1	0.3
Morocco	29	447	64	33.9	55	1,180	128	99	3,450	134	0.9	-0.8
Mozambique	18	802	23	3.7	127	210	193	14 [e]	800 [e]	193	1.6	-0.7
Myanmar	48	677	73	..	..	.. [d]	..	..	..	..	..	..
Namibia	2	824	2	3.6	130	2,030	101	11 [e]	6,410 [e]	89	3.9	1.6
Nepal	23	147	161	5.6	107	240	190	32	1,370	176	6.5	3.9
Netherlands	16	42	470	397.5	14	24,970	18	412	25,850	15	3.5	2.8
New Zealand	4	271	14	49.8	48	12,990	45	71	18,530	41	2.5	2.0
Nicaragua	5	130	42	2.1	145	400	162	11 [e]	2,080 [e]	156	4.3	1.6
Niger	11	1,267	9	1.9	148	180	197	8 [e]	740 [e]	199	0.1	-3.2
Nigeria	127	924	139	32.7	56	260	186	102	800	193	3.8	1.3
Norway	4	324	15	155.1	26	34,530	6	133	29,630	6	2.3	1.6
Oman	2	212	11	..	..	.. [i]	..	..	..	..	..	..
Pakistan	138	796	179	61.0	44	440	161	257	1,860	160	4.4	1.9
Panama	3	76	38	9.3	87	3,260	86	16 [e]	5,680 [e]	98	2.7	1.0
Papua New Guinea	5	463	11	3.6	129	700 [j]	144	11 [e]	2,180 [e]	155	0.3	-2.1
Paraguay	5	407	14	7.9	96	1,440	122	24 [e]	4,450 [e]	115	-0.3	-2.8
Peru	26	1,285	20	53.4	46	2,080	100	120	4,660	111	3.1	1.4
Philippines	76	300	253	78.8	41	1,040	131	319	4,220	120	4.0	2.1
Poland	39	323	127	161.8	25	4,190	75	348	9,000	74	4.0	4.0
Portugal	10	92	109	111.3	33	11,120	49	170	16,990	47	3.3	3.1
Puerto Rico	4	9	442	..	..	.. [i]	..	..	..	..	..	..
Romania	22	238	97	37.4	52	1,670	113	143	6,360	90	1.6	1.7
Russian Federation	146	17,075	9	241.0	19	1,660	114	1,165	8,010	79	8.3	8.9

	Population	Surface area	Population density	Gross national income		Gross national income per capita		PPP gross national income [a]			Gross domestic product	
	millions 2000	thousand sq. km 2000	people per sq. km 2000	$ billions 2000[b]	Rank 2000	$ 2000[b]	Rank 2000	$ billions 2000	Per capita $ 2000	Rank 2000	% growth 1999-2000	Per capita % growth 1999-2000
Rwanda	9	26	345	2.0	147	230	192	8	930	189	5.6	3.1
Saudi Arabia	21	2,150	10	149.9	27	7,230	61	236	11,390	60	4.5	1.8
Senegal	10	197	49	4.7	116	490	157	14	1,480	171	5.6	2.9
Sierra Leone	5	72	70	0.6	180	130	204	2	480	207	7.0	4.9
Singapore	4	1	6,587	99.4	37	24,740	19	100	24,910	21	9.9	8.1
Slovak Republic	5	49	112	20.0	66	3,700	81	60	11,040	62	2.2	2.1
Slovenia	2	20	99	20.0	65	10,050	50	34	17,310	45	4.6	4.5
Somalia	9	638	14	..	..	.. [d]	..	..	..	..	..	..
South Africa	43	1,221	35	129.2	29	3,020	91	392 [e]	9,160 [e]	72	3.1	1.4
Spain	39	506	79	595.3	10	15,080	38	760	19,260	38	4.1	3.9
Sri Lanka	19	66	300	16.4	73	850	140	67	3,460	133	6.0	4.3
Sudan	31	2,506	13	9.6	84	310	175	47	1,520	169	8.3	6.4
Swaziland	1	17	61	1.5	156	1,390	123	5	4,600	112	2.6	0.0
Sweden	9	450	22	240.7	20	27,140	11	213	23,970	26	3.6	3.4
Switzerland	7	41	182	273.8	17	38,140	3	219	30,450	5	3.0	2.4
Syrian Arab Republic	16	185	88	15.1	76	940	135	54	3,340	136	2.5	0.0
Tajikistan	6	143	44	1.1	165	180	197	7	1,090	183	8.3	8.1
Tanzania	34	945	38	9.0 [k]	88	270 [k]	184	18	520	206	5.1	2.7
Thailand	61	513	119	121.6	31	2,000	103	384	6,320	92	4.3	3.5
Togo	5	57	83	1.3	159	290	178	6	1,410	175	-0.7	-3.7
Trinidad and Tobago	1	5	254	6.4	104	4,930	70	11	8,220	78	4.8	4.1
Tunisia	10	164	62	20.1	63	2,100	99	58	6,070	93	4.7	3.5
Turkey	65	775	85	202.1	22	3,100	90	459	7,030	86	7.2	5.6
Turkmenistan	5	488	11	3.9	123	750 [j]	143	20	3,800	125	17.6	15.3
Uganda	22	241	113	6.7	100	300	176	27 [e]	1,210 [e]	178	3.5	0.8
Ukraine	50	604	85	34.6	54	700	144	183	3,700	127	5.8	6.7
United Arab Emirates	3	84	35	..	..	.. [i]	..	..	..	..	..	..
United Kingdom	60	243	248	1,459.5	4	24,430	21	1,407	23,550	27	3.1	2.7
United States	282	9,629	31	9,601.5	1	34,100	7	9,601	34,100	3	4.2	3.0
Uruguay	3	176	19	20.0	64	6,000	66	30	8,880	75	-1.3	-2.0
Uzbekistan	25	447	60	8.8	89	360	171	58	2,360	151	4.0	2.5
Venezuela, RB	24	912	27	104.1	36	4,310	74	139	5,740	96	3.2	1.2
Vietnam	79	332	241	30.4	59	390	164	157	2,000	157	5.5	4.1
West Bank and Gaza	3	..	..	4.9	114	1,660	114	..	..	..	-6.4	-10.3
Yemen, Rep.	18	528	33	6.6	103	370	167	14	770	197	5.1	2.4
Yugoslavia, Fed. Rep.	11	102	108	10.0	83	940	135	..	..	..	5.0	4.9
Zambia	10	753	14	3.0	137	300	176	8	750	198	3.5	1.3
Zimbabwe	13	391	33	5.9	106	460	158	32	2,550	148	-4.9	-6.7
World	6,057 s	133,806 s	47 w	31,315 t		5,170 w		44,459 t	7,410 w		3.9 w	2.5 w
Low income	2,460	33,740	76	997		410		4,809	1,980		4.2	2.2
Middle income	2,695	67,751	40	5,319		1,970		15,196	5,680		5.6	4.6
Lower middle income	2,048	44,421	47	2,324		1,130		9,359	4,600		6.3	5.4
Upper middle income	647	23,330	28	3,001		4,640		5,915	9,210		5.1	3.7
Low & middle income	5,154	101,491	52	6,315		1,230		19,980	3,910		5.4	3.9
East Asia & Pacific	1,855	16,385	116	1,962		1,060		7,609	4,130		7.4	6.4
Europe & Central Asia	474	24,217	20	953		2,010		3,140	6,670		6.3	6.2
Latin America & Carib.	516	20,459	26	1,895		3,670		3,624	7,080		3.8	2.3
Middle East & N. Africa	295	11,023	27	618		2,090		1,545	5,270		4.0	2.0
South Asia	1,355	5,140	283	595		440		2,984	2,240		4.2	2.3
Sub-Saharan Africa	659	24,267	28	310		470		1,044	1,600		3.1	0.6
High income	903	32,315	29	24,994		27,680		24,793	27,770		3.5	2.8
Europe EMU	304	2,569	120	6,604		21,730		7,117	23,600		3.4	3.1

a. PPP is purchasing power parity; see *Definitions*. b. Calculated using the World Bank Atlas method. c. Estimate does not account for recent refugee flows. d. Estimated to be low income ($755 or less). e. The estimate is based on regression; others are extrapolated from the latest International Comparison Programme benchmark estimates. f. Includes Taiwan, China; Macao, China; and Hong Kong, China. g. Estimated to be lower middle income ($756-2,995). h. GNI and GNI per capita estimates include the French overseas departments of French Guiana, Guadeloupe, Martinique, and Réunion. i. Estimated to be upper middle income ($2,996-9,265). j. Included under lower-middle income economies in calculating the aggregates based on earlier data. k. Data refer to mainland Tanzania only. l. Estimated to be high income ($9,266 or more).

About the data

Population, land area, income, and output are basic measures of the size of an economy. They also provide a broad indication of actual and potential resources. Therefore, population, land area, income—as measured by gross national income (GNI)—and output—as measured by gross domestic product (GDP)—are used throughout the *World Development Indicators* to normalize other indicators.

Population estimates are generally based on extrapolations from the most recent national census. For further discussion of the measurement of population and population growth see *About the data* for table 2.1 and *Statistical methods*.

The surface area of a country or economy includes inland bodies of water and some coastal waterways. Surface area thus differs from land area, which excludes bodies of water, and from gross area, which may include offshore territorial waters. Land area is particularly important for understanding the agricultural capacity of an economy and the effects of human activity on the environment. (For measures of land area and data on rural population density, land use, and agricultural productivity see tables 3.1–3.3.) Recent innovations in satellite mapping techniques and computer databases have resulted in more precise measurements of land and water areas.

GNI (gross national product, or GNP, in the 1968 SNA terminology) measures the total domestic and foreign value added claimed by residents. GNI comprises GDP plus net receipts of primary income (compensation of employees and property income) from nonresident sources.

The World Bank uses GNI per capita in U.S. dollars to classify countries for analytical purposes and to determine borrowing eligibility. See the *Users guide* for definitions of the income groups used in the *World Development Indicators*. For further discussion of the usefulness of national income as a measure of productivity or welfare see *About the data* for tables 4.1 and 4.2.

When calculating GNI in U.S. dollars from GNI reported in national currencies, the World Bank follows its Atlas conversion method. This involves using a three-year average of exchange rates to smooth the effects of transitory exchange rate fluctuations. (For further discussion of the Atlas method see *Statistical methods*.) Note that growth rates are calculated from data in constant prices and national currency units, not from the Atlas estimates.

Because exchange rates do not always reflect international differences in relative prices, this table also shows GNI and GNI per capita estimates converted into international dollars using purchasing power parity (PPP) rates. PPP rates provide a standard measure allowing comparison of real price levels between countries, just as conventional price indexes allow comparison of real values over time. The PPP conversion factors used here are derived from price surveys covering 118 countries conducted by the International Comparison Programme (ICP). For 62 countries data come from the most recent round of surveys, completed in 1996; the rest are from the 1993 round and have been extrapolated to the 1996 benchmark. Estimates for countries not included in the surveys are derived from statistical models using available data. All economies shown in the *World Development Indicators* are ranked by size, including those that appear in table 1.6. Ranks are shown only in table 1.1. (The *World Bank Atlas* includes a table comparing the GNI per capita rankings based on the Atlas method with those based on the PPP method for all economies with available data.) No rank is shown for economies for which numerical estimates of GNI per capita are not published. Economies with missing data are included in the ranking process at their approximate level, so that the relative order of other economies remains consistent. Where available, rankings for small economies are shown in the *World Bank Atlas*. In 2000 Luxembourg and Liechtenstein were judged to have the highest GNI per capita in the world.

Growth in GDP and growth in GDP per capita are based on GDP measured in constant prices. Growth in GDP is considered a broad measure of the growth of an economy, as GDP in constant prices can be estimated by measuring the total quantity of goods and services produced in a period, valuing them at an agreed set of base year prices, and subtracting the cost of intermediate inputs, also in constant prices. For further discussion of the measurement of economic growth see *About the data* for table 4.1.

Definitions

• **Population** is based on the de facto definition of population, which counts all residents regardless of legal status or citizenship—except for refugees not permanently settled in the country of asylum, who are generally considered part of the population of their country of origin. The values shown are midyear estimates for 2000. See also table 2.1. • **Surface area** is a country's total area, including areas under inland bodies of water and some coastal waterways. • **Population density** is midyear population divided by land area in square kilometers. • **Gross national income** (GNI) is the sum of value added by all resident producers plus any product taxes (less subsidies) not included in the valuation of output plus net receipts of primary income (compensation of employees and property income) from abroad. Data are in current U.S. dollars converted using the World Bank Atlas method (see *Statistical methods*). • **GNI per capita** is gross national income divided by midyear population. GNI per capita in U.S. dollars is converted using the World Bank Atlas method. • **PPP GNI** is gross national income converted to international dollars using purchasing power parity rates. An international dollar has the same purchasing power over GNI as a U.S. dollar has in the United States. • **Gross domestic product** (GDP) is the sum of value added by all resident producers plus any product taxes (less subsidies) not included in the valuation of output. • **GDP per capita** is gross domestic product divided by midyear population. Growth is calculated from constant price GDP data in local currency.

Data sources

Population estimates are prepared by World Bank staff from a variety of sources (see *Data sources* for table 2.1). The data on surface and land area are from the Food and Agriculture Organization (see *Data sources* for table 3.1). GNI, GNI per capita, GDP growth, and GDP per capita growth are estimated by World Bank staff based on national accounts data collected by Bank staff during economic missions or reported by national statistical offices to other international organizations such as the Organisation for Economic Co-operation and Development. Purchasing power parity conversion factors are estimates by World Bank staff based on data collected by the International Comparison Programme.

	Eradicate extreme poverty and hunger			Achieve universal primary education		Promote gender equality		Reduce child mortality		Improve maternal health		
	Share of poorest quintile in national income or consumption %	Child malnutrition weight for age % of children under 5		Net primary enrollment ratio[b, c] %		Ratio of female to male enrollments in primary and secondary school[c] %		Under-five mortality rate per 1,000 live births		Maternal mortality ratio per 100,000 live births modeled estimates	Births attended by skilled health staff % of total	
	1986-2000[a]	1990	2000	1990	1998	1990	1998	1990	2000	1995	1990	1999
Afghanistan	..	..	49	..	..	50	..	257	279	..	9	..
Albania	..	..	8	..	..	90	..	42	..	31	..	..
Algeria	7.0	9	13	93	94	80	91	55	39	150	77	..
Angola	..	20	41	..	57	..	81	..	208	1,300	17	..
Argentina	..	..	5	..	107	..	100	28	22	85	..	..
Armenia	5.5	..	3	..	..	..	..	24	17	29	..	96
Australia	5.9	..	0	99	..	96	..	10	7	6	100	..
Austria	6.9	..	..	90a	88	90	92	9	6	11	..	..
Azerbaijan	6.9	..	17	..	96	94	95	..	21	37	..	99
Bangladesh	8.7	66	61	64	104	72	95	136	83	600	7	14
Belarus	11.4	..	..	..	..	..	96	16	14	33	..	..
Belgium	8.3	..	..	97	..	97	99	9	7	8	..	..
Benin	..	..	29	49	..	..	61	185	143	880	38	60
Bolivia	4.0	11	8	91	97	89	..	120	79	550	43	59
Bosnia and Herzegovina	..	..	..	..	..	..	..	21	18	15	..	..
Botswana	..	..	17	93	81	107	102	62	99	480	79	..
Brazil	2.2	7	6	86	98	..	100	58	39	260	..	88
Bulgaria	10.1	..	..	86	93	94	93	19	16	23	..	99
Burkina Faso	4.6	..	34	27	34	61	66	229	206	1,400	30	27
Burundi	5.1	..	..	52	38	82	81	180	176	1,900	20	..
Cambodia	6.9	..	47	..	104	..	79	119	120	590	47	31
Cameroon	4.6	15	22	..	..	82	81	141	155	720	58	55
Canada	7.5	..	..	97	96	94	95	8	7	6	..	..
Central African Republic	2.0	..	23	53	53	61	..	..	152	1,200	66	..
Chad	..	..	39	..	55	..	53	209	188	1,500	15	11
Chile	3.3	..	1	88	88	98	95	20	12	33	..	100
China	5.9	17	10	97	91	81	89	47	39	60	..	..
Hong Kong, China	..	..	..	..	..	..	..	..	..	..	100	..
Colombia	3.0	10	8	69	87	104	101	40	23	120	94	..
Congo, Dem. Rep.	..	..	34	54	32	69	80	155	163	940	..	..
Congo, Rep.	..	..	..	..	..	88	..	..	106	1,100	..	..
Costa Rica	4.5	3	5	86	..	96	..	16	13	35	97	..
Côte d'Ivoire	7.1	..	24	47	59	..	69	150	180	1,200	50	47
Croatia	8.8	..	1	79	..	97	97	13	9	18	..	..
Cuba	..	..	..	92	97	101	97	13	9	24	..	..
Czech Republic	10.3	1	..	..	90	94	97	12	7	14	..	..
Denmark	9.6	..	..	98	101	96	98	9	6	15	..	..
Dominican Republic	5.1	10	6	..	87	..	103	59	47	110	92	96
Ecuador	5.4	..	..	..	97	97	98	51	34	210	56	..
Egypt, Arab Rep.	9.8	10	4	..	92	78	88	85	52	170	37	56
El Salvador	3.3	15	12	75	81	100	95	54	35	180	90	90
Eritrea	..	..	44	24	34	82	78	140	103	1,100	..	..
Estonia	7.0	..	..	94	96	99	96	17	11	80	..	..
Ethiopia	7.1	48	47	..	35	68	61	211	179	1,800	8	..
Finland	10.0	..	..	99	99	105	100	7	5	6	..	..
France	7.2	..	..	101	100	98	95	10	6	20	..	..
Gabon	..	..	..	..	..	..	95	94	89	620	79	..
Gambia, The	4.0	..	26	51	61	64	80	127	..	1,100	44	..
Georgia	6.1	..	3	..	..	94	95	..	21	22	..	..
Germany	8.2	..	..	84	87	94	..	9	6	12	..	..
Ghana	5.6	30	25	..	..	..	..	119	112	590	55	44
Greece	7.5	..	..	94	95	93	95	11	8	2	..	..
Guatemala	3.8	..	24	..	83	..	..	68	49	270	30	..
Guinea	6.4	..	23	..	46	43	56	215	161	1,200	31	35
Guinea-Bissau	2.1	..	..	..	..	..	..	246	211	910	..	..
Haiti	..	27	28	22	80	..	..	131	111	1,100	78	..
Honduras	2.2	18	25	89	..	103	..	65	44	220	47	55

| | Eradicate extreme poverty and hunger | | | Achieve universal primary education | | Promote gender equality | | Reduce child mortality | | Improve maternal health | | |
| | Share of poorest quintile in national income or consumption % | Child malnutrition weight for age % of children under 5 | | Net primary enrollment ratio[b, c] % | | Ratio of female to male enrollments in primary and secondary school[c] % | | Under-five mortality rate per 1,000 live births | | Maternal mortality ratio per 100,000 live births modeled estimates | Births attended by skilled health staff % of total | |
	1986-2000[a]	1990	2000	1990	1998	1990	1998	1990	2000	1995	1990	1999
Hungary	10.0	2	..	91	82	96	96	17	11	23	..	..
India	8.1	64	47	..	..	68	75	112	88	440	44	..
Indonesia	9.0	..	34	97	..	91	..	83	51	470	47	43
Iran, Islamic Rep.	..	..	11	99	..	80	..	72	41	130	78	..
Iraq	..	12	..	79	80	75	75	50	121	370	50	..
Ireland	6.7	..	..	91	104	99	97	9	7	9	..	..
Israel	6.1	..	..	..	95	99	94	12	7	8	..	..
Italy	8.7	..	..	..	101	95	94	10	7	11	..	..
Jamaica	6.7	5	4	96	92	97	99	32	24	120	92	95
Japan	10.6	..	..	100	102	96	96	6	5	12	100	..
Jordan	7.6	6	5	66	64	93	96	34	30	41	87	97
Kazakhstan	6.7	..	4	..	..	..	97	34	28	80	..	98
Kenya	5.6	..	22	..	..	..	96	97	120	1,300	50	44
Korea, Dem. Rep.	..	..	32	..	..	..	..	35	90	35	..	..
Korea, Rep.	7.5	..	..	104	..	93	..	..	10	20	95	..
Kuwait	..	..	2	45	..	97	97	16	13	25	..	98
Kyrgyz Republic	7.6	..	11	..	85	100	98	41	35	80	..	98
Lao PDR	7.6	..	40	61	76	75	79	170	..	650	..	..
Latvia	7.6	..	..	83	94	96	98	18	17	70	..	..
Lebanon	..	..	3	..	78	..	100	40	30	130	95	95
Lesotho	2.8	16	16	73	60	124	112	148	143	530	50	..
Liberia	..	..	..	..	41	..	71	..	185	..	..	..
Libya	..	..	5	96	..	..	100	42	32	120	76	94
Lithuania	7.8	..	..	..	94	93	96	14	11	27	..	..
Macedonia, FYR	..	..	6	94	96	94	93	33	17	17	88	..
Madagascar	6.4	41	40	..	63	..	96	170	144	580	57	47
Malawi	..	28	30	50	..	79	..	234	193	580	50	..
Malaysia	4.4	25	20	..	98	98	99	21	11	39	..	..
Mali	4.6	..	27	21	42	57	66	268	218	630	..	24
Mauritania	6.4	48	23	..	60	67	90	..	164	870	40	58
Mauritius	..	..	15	95	93	98	98	25	20	45	92	..
Mexico	3.5	17	8	100	102	96	97	46	36	65	..	..
Moldova	5.6	..	..	..	..	103	..	25	22	65	..	..
Mongolia	7.3	12	13	..	85	107	..	102	71	65	100	..
Morocco	6.5	10	..	58	79	67	78	83	60	390	31	..
Mozambique	6.5	..	26	47	41	73	72	238	200	980	..	44
Myanmar	..	32	28	..	..	95	97	130	126	170	94	57
Namibia	..	26	..	89	86	111	103	84	112	370	68	..
Nepal	7.6	..	47	..	..	53	69	138	105	830	8	10
Netherlands	7.3	..	..	95	100	93	92	8	7	10	100	..
New Zealand	..	..	..	101	..	96	..	11	7	15	..	..
Nicaragua	2.3	..	12	72	..	..	..	63	41	250	..	65
Niger	2.6	43	40	25	26	54	64	335	248	920	15	18
Nigeria	4.4	35	27	..	..	76	..	136	153	1,100	31	..
Norway	9.7	..	..	100	102	97	96	9	5	9	..	..
Oman	..	24	23	70	66	86	94	30	22	120	87	..
Pakistan	9.5	40	38	..	..	47	..	138	110	200	40	..
Panama	3.6	6	8	91	..	96	..	..	24	100	..	..
Papua New Guinea	4.5	..	..	..	85	77	79	108	75	390	40	53
Paraguay	1.9	4	..	93	92	95	96	37	28	170	71	71
Peru	4.4	11	8	..	103	93	94	75	41	240	78	56
Philippines	5.4	34	32	97	..	..	..	62	39	240	..	56
Poland	7.8	..	..	97	..	96	..	22	11	12	..	..
Portugal	7.3	..	..	102	108	99	97	15	8	12	98	100
Puerto Rico	..	..	..	..	..	..	..	..	..	30	..	..
Romania	8.0	6	..	77	94	95	96	36	23	60	..	..
Russian Federation	4.4	..	3	..	..	..	74	21	19	75	..	99

	Eradicate extreme poverty and hunger			Achieve universal primary education		Promote gender equality		Reduce child mortality		Improve maternal health		
	Share of poorest quintile in national income or consumption %	Child malnutrition weight for age % of children under 5		Net primary enrollment ratio[b, c] %		Ratio of female to male enrollments in primary and secondary school[c] %		Under-five mortality rate per 1,000 live births		Maternal mortality ratio per 100,000 live births modeled estimates	Births attended by skilled health staff % of total	
	1986-2000[a]	1990	2000	1990	1998	1990	1998	1990	2000	1995	1990	1999
Rwanda	9.7	*29*	27	66	91	98	100	..	203	2,300	*26*	..
Saudi Arabia	..	..	..	59	59	82	89	45	23	23	88	*91*
Senegal	6.4	*22*	13	*48*	59	*69*	78	*148*	129	1,200	*42*	47
Sierra Leone	1.1	29	..	..	..	67	..	323	267	2,100	..	..
Singapore	..	..	..	..	..	89	..	8	6	9	..	*100*
Slovak Republic	11.9	..	..	..	..	*98*	97	14	10	14	..	..
Slovenia	9.1	..	..	..	94	*97*	97	10	7	17	..	..
Somalia	..	..	26	..	..	..	..	215	195	..	..	..
South Africa	2.9	..	9	*103*	..	103	102	73	79	340	..	*84*
Spain	7.5	..	..	103	105	99	98	9	6	8	..	..
Sri Lanka	8.0	..	33	..	102	99	99	23	18	60	85	95
Sudan	..	..	34	..	46	75	86	125	..	1,500	69	..
Swaziland	2.7	..	..	88	77	..	96	115	119	..	*55*	..
Sweden	9.6	..	..	100	103	97	110	7	4	8	11	..
Switzerland	6.9	..	..	84	94	92	91	8	6	8	..	..
Syrian Arab Republic	..	..	13	98	93	82	88	*59*	29	200	64	..
Tajikistan	8.0	..	-18	..	..	..	..	..	30	120	..	..
Tanzania	6.8	29	29	51	48	97	..	*178*	149	1,100	*44*	35
Thailand	6.4	..	..	..	77	94	96	41	33	44	71	..
Togo	..	25	25	75	88	59	67	142	142	980	*32*	*51*
Trinidad and Tobago	5.5	..	..	91	93	98	100	24	19	65	..	*99*
Tunisia	5.7	*10*	4	94	98	82	93	52	30	70	80	82
Turkey	5.8	..	8	89	100	77	..	67	43	55	77	*81*
Turkmenistan	6.1	..	..	..	..	..	..	..	43	65	..	..
Uganda	7.1	*23*	26	..	..	..	88	165	161	1,100	*38*	..
Ukraine	8.8	..	..	..	..	..	106	..	16	45	..	..
United Arab Emirates	..	..	7	94	83	96	96	..	10	30	*96*	..
United Kingdom	6.1	..	..	97	102	97	103	9	7	10	100	..
United States	5.2	..	1	96	95	95	83	*10*	9	12	..	*99*
Uruguay	5.4	6	4	*91*	92	..	108	24	17	50	..	..
Uzbekistan	4.0	..	19	..	..	..	..	..	27	60	..	98
Venezuela, RB	3.0	8	4	88	..	101	..	27	24	43	*97*	..
Vietnam	8.0	45	37	..	97	..	88	54	34	95	95	*77*
West Bank and Gaza	..	..	15	..	..	..	..	*53*	26	..	..	..
Yemen, Rep.	7.4	*30*	46	..	61	..	47	130	95	850	*16*	22
Yugoslavia, Fed. Rep.	..	..	2	69	..	96	96	26	15	15	..	93
Zambia	3.3	25	24	..	73	..	89	*194*	186	870	41	47
Zimbabwe	4.7	*12*	13	..	..	96	..	*77*	116	610	*62*	84
World	.. w	.. w	.. w	.. w	**85 w**	**87 w**	**83 w**	**78 w**			..	..
Low income	..	..	..	..	..	79	123	115			43	..
Middle income	..	13	95	92	84	90	49	39			..	..
Lower middle income	18	11	96	91	82	88	50	41			..	..
Upper middle income	..	..	91	97	93	99	48	35			..	..
Low & middle income	..	..	..	..	82	86	88	84			..	..
East Asia & Pacific	19	13	98	91	84	89	55	45			..	..
Europe & Central Asia	..	..	..	..	90	88	34	25			..	..
Latin America & Carib.	..	9	89	97	..	99	49	37			..	..
Middle East & N. Africa	..	15	..	83	79	84	72	54			..	..
South Asia	64	49	..	..	..	78	121	96			39	..
Sub-Saharan Africa	..	..	..	..	79	80	..	162			..	..
High income	..	..	98	..	96	92	9	7			..	..
Europe EMU	..	..	93	..	97	96	10	6			..	..

a. Data are for the most recent year available. See table 2.8 for survey year and whether share is based on income or consumption expenditure. b. Net enrollment ratios exceeding 100 percent indicate discrepancies between estimates of the school-age population and reported enrollment data. c. Break in series between 1997 and 1998 is due to change from ISCED76 to ISCED97.

Millennium Development Goals:
eradicating poverty and improving lives | 1.2

About the data

This table and the following two provide indicators for 17 of the 18 targets specified by the Millennium Development Goals (MDGs). Each of the eight goals comprises one or more targets and each target has associated with it several indicators by which progress toward the target can be monitored. Most of the targets are set as a value of a specific indicator to be attained by a certain date. In some cases the target value is set relative to a level in 1990. In others it is set at an absolute level. Some of the targets for goals 7 and 8 have not yet been quantified.

The indicators in the table are taken from goals 1-5. Goal 1 has two targets between 1990 and 2015: to reduce by half the proportion of people whose income is less than $1 a day and to reduce by half the proportion of people who suffer from hunger. Estimates of poverty rates can be found in table 2.6. The indicator shown here, the share of the poorest quintile in national income or consumption, is a distributional measure. Countries with less equal income distributions will have a higher rate of poverty for a given average income. There is no single indicator that captures the concept of suffering from hunger. Child malnutrition is a symptom of inadequate food supply, lack of essential nutrients, illnesses that deplete these nutrients, and undernourished mothers who give birth to underweight children.

Progress toward achieving universal primary education has commonly been measured by net enrollment ratios. However, there are sometimes large differences between official enrollments and actual attendance, and even school systems with high average enrollment ratios may have poor completion rates.

Eliminating gender disparities in education would help to increase the status and capabilities of women. The ratio of girls' to boys' enrollment provides an imperfect measure of the relative accessibility of schooling for girls. With a target date of 2005, this is the first of the targets to fall due.

The targets for reducing under-five and maternal mortality are among the most challenging of the Millennium Development Goals. Although estimates of under-five mortality rates are available at regular intervals for most countries, maternal mortality is difficult to measure, in part because it is a relatively rare event.

In addition to the indicators shown in these tables, most of the 48 indicators included in the Millennium Development Goals can be found elsewhere in the *World Development Indicators*. Table 1.2a provides an index for locating the indicators for the first five goals in other tables. More information about data collection methodologies and limitations can be found in *About the data* for those tables.

Table 1.2a

Location of indicators for goals 1- 5
Goal 1. Eradicate extreme poverty and hunger
1. Proportion of population below $1 a day (table 2.6)
2. Poverty gap ratio (table 2.6)
3. Share of poorest quintile in national consumption (table 2.8)
4. Prevalence of underweight in children (under five years of age) (table 2.18)
5. Proportion of population below minimum level of dietary energy consumption (table 2.18)
Goal 2. Achieve universal primary education
6. Net enrollment ratio in primary education (table 2.12)
7. Proportion of pupils starting grade 1 who reach grade 5 (table 2.13)
8. Literacy rate of 15- to 24-year-olds (table 2.14)
Goal 3. Promote gender equality and empower women
9. Ratio of girls to boys in primary, secondary and tertiary education (tables 1.2 and 2.12)
10. Ratio of literate females to males, among 15- to 24-year-olds (tables 1.5 and 2.14)
11. Share of women in wage employment in the nonagricultural sector (table 2.3)
12. Proportion of seats held by women in national parliament (See women in decision-making positions in table 1.5.)
Goal 4. Reduce child mortality
13. Under-five mortality rate (table 2.20)
14. Infant mortality rate (table 2.20)
15. Proportion of one year-old children immunized against measles (table 2.16)
Goal 5. Improve maternal health
16. Maternal mortality ratio (table 2.17)
17. Proportion of births attended by skilled health personnel (table 2.17)

Definitions

- **Share of the poorest quintile in national income or consumption** is the share of consumption or, in some cases, income that accrues to the poorest 20 percent of the population.
- **Child malnutrition** is the percentage of children under five whose weight for age is less than minus two standard deviations from the median for the international reference population ages 0–59 months. The reference population, adopted by the World Health Organization in 1983, is based on children from the United States, who are assumed to be well nourished.
- **Net primary enrollment ratio** is the ratio of the number of children of official school age (as defined by the education system) enrolled in school to the number of children of official school age in the population. • **Ratio of female to male enrollments in primary and secondary school** is the ratio of the number of female students enrolled in primary and secondary school to the number of male students. **Under-five mortality rate** is the probability that a newborn baby will die before reaching age five, if subject to current age-specific mortality rates. The probability is expressed as a rate per 1,000.
- **Maternal mortality ratio** is the number of women who die during pregnancy and childbirth, per 100,000 live births. The data shown here have been collected in various years and adjusted to a common 1995 base year. • **Births attended by skilled health staff** are the percentage of deliveries attended by personnel trained to give the necessary supervision, care, and advice to women during pregnancy, labor, and the postpartum period, to conduct deliveries on their own, and to care for newborns.

Data sources

The indicators here, and where they appear throughout the rest of the book, have been compiled by World Bank staff from primary and secondary sources. More information can be found in *About the data*, *Definitions*, and *Data sources* entries that accompany each table in subsequent sections. More information about the Millennium Development Goals and related indicators can be found at www.developmentgoals.org.

Millennium Development Goals:
1.3 | protecting our common environment

	Combat HIV/AIDS and other diseases			Ensure environmental sustainability						Develop a global partnership for development	
	HIV prevalence male % ages 15-24 1999[b]	HIV prevalence female % ages 15-24 1999[b]	Incidence of tuberculosis per 100,000 people 1999	CO_2 emissions per capita metric tons 1990	CO_2 emissions per capita metric tons 1998	Access to an improved water source % of population 1990	Access to an improved water source % of population 2000	Access to improved sanitation facilities % of population 1990	Access to improved sanitation facilities % of population 2000	Unemployment % ages 15-24 1999	Telephone[a] lines per 1,000 people 2000
Afghanistan	..	..	325	0.1	0.0	..	13	..	12	..	1
Albania	..	..	29	2.2	0.5	..	..	..	..	..	39
Algeria	..	..	45	3.2	3.6	..	94	..	73	..	57
Angola	1.3	2.7	271	0.5	0.5	..	38	..	44	..	5
Argentina	0.9	0.3	55	3.4	3.8	..	79	..	85	..	213
Armenia	..	..	58	1.0	0.9	..	..	..	..	..	152
Australia	0.1	0.0 [c]	8	15.6	17.7	100	100	100	100	14	525
Austria	0.2	0.1	16	7.4	7.9	100	100	100	100	6	467
Azerbaijan	..	..	62	6.4	4.9	..	..	..	..	..	104
Bangladesh	0.0 [c]	0.0 [c]	241	0.1	0.2	91	97	97	53	..	4
Belarus	0.4	0.2	80	9.3	6.0	..	100	..	..	..	269
Belgium	0.1	0.1	15	10.1	9.9	..	..	..	..	23	498
Benin	0.9	2.2	266	0.1	0.1	..	63	20	23	..	8
Bolivia	0.1	0.0 [c]	238	0.8	1.5	74	79	55	66	..	61
Bosnia and Herzegovina	..	..	87	..	1.2	..	..	..	..	..	103
Botswana	15.8	34.3	702	1.7	2.4	95	..	61	..	..	93
Brazil	0.7	0.3	70	1.4	1.8	82	87	72	77	18	182
Bulgaria	..	..	46	8.6	5.7	..	..	..	..	33	350
Burkina Faso	2.3	5.8	319	0.1	0.1	53	..	24	29	..	4
Burundi	5.7	11.6	382	0.0	0.0	65	..	89	..	..	3
Cambodia	2.4	3.5	560	0.0	0.1	..	30	..	18	..	2
Cameroon	3.8	7.8	335	0.1	0.1	52	62	87	92	..	6
Canada	0.3	0.1	7	15.4	15.4	100	100	100	100	14	677
Central African Republic	6.9	14.1	415	0.1	0.1	59	60	30	31	..	3
Chad	1.9	3.0	270	0.0	0.0	..	27	18	29	..	1
Chile	0.3	0.1	26	2.7	4.1	90	94	97	97	21	221
China	0.1	0.0 [c]	103	2.1	2.5	71	75	29	38	3	112
Hong Kong, China	0.1	0.0 [c]	91	4.6	5.4	..	..	..	..	10	583
Colombia	0.4	0.1	51	1.6	1.7	87	91	82	85	24	169
Congo, Dem. Rep.	2.5	5.1	301	0.1	0.1	..	45	..	20	..	0
Congo, Rep.	3.2	6.5	318	0.9	0.6	..	51	..	..	..	7
Costa Rica	0.6	0.3	17	1.0	1.4	..	98	..	96	12	249
Côte d'Ivoire	3.8	9.5	375	1.0	0.9	65	77	49	..	..	18
Croatia	0.0 [c]	0.0 [c]	61	3.5	4.5	..	95	..	100	30	365
Cuba	0.1	0.0 [c]	15	3.0	2.2	..	95	..	95	..	44
Czech Republic	0.1	0.0 [c]	19	13.1	11.5	..	..	..	..	17	378
Denmark	0.2	0.1	12	9.9	10.1	..	100	..	..	10	720
Dominican Republic	2.6	2.8	135	1.3	2.5	78	79	60	71	..	105
Ecuador	0.4	0.1	172	1.6	2.2	..	71	..	59	24	100
Egypt, Arab Rep.	..	..	39	1.4	1.7	94	95	87	94	..	86
El Salvador	0.7	0.3	67	0.5	1.0	..	74	..	83	13	100
Eritrea	..	..	272	..	..	..	46	..	13	..	8
Estonia	..	..	61	15.9	12.1	..	..	..	..	16	363
Ethiopia	7.5	11.9	373	0.1	0.0	22	24	13	15	..	4
Finland	0.0 [c]	0.0 [c]	12	10.6	10.3	100	100	100	100	22	550
France	0.3	0.2	16	6.3	6.3	..	..	..	..	27	579
Gabon	2.3	4.7	289	7.1	2.4	..	70	..	21	..	32
Gambia, The	0.9	2.2	260	0.2	0.2	..	62	..	37	..	26
Georgia	..	..	72	2.8	1.0	..	76	..	99	..	139
Germany	0.1	0.0 [c]	13	11.1	10.1	..	..	..	..	9	611
Ghana	1.4	3.4	281	0.2	0.2	56	64	60	63	..	12
Greece	0.1	0.1	22	7.1	8.1	..	..	..	..	30	532
Guatemala	1.2	0.9	85	0.6	0.9	78	92	77	85	..	57
Guinea	0.6	1.4	255	0.2	0.2	45	48	55	58	..	8
Guinea-Bissau	1.0	2.5	267	0.8	0.8	..	49	..	47	..	9
Haiti	4.9	2.9	361	0.2	0.2	46	46	25	28	..	9
Honduras	1.4	1.7	92	0.5	0.8	84	90	..	77	6	46

	Combat HIV/AIDS and other diseases			Ensure environmental sustainability						Develop a global partnership for development	
	HIV prevalence male % ages 15-24 1999[b]	HIV prevalence female % ages 15-24 1999[b]	Incidence of tuberculosis per 100,000 people 1999	CO_2 emissions per capita metric tons 1990	CO_2 emissions per capita metric tons 1998	Access to an improved water source % of population 1990	Access to an improved water source % of population 2000	Access to improved sanitation facilities % of population 1990	Access to improved sanitation facilities % of population 2000	Unemployment % ages 15-24 1999	Telephone[a] lines per 1,000 people 2000
Hungary	0.1	0.0 [c]	40	5.6	5.8	99	99	99	99	12	372
India	0.4	0.6	185	0.8	1.1	78	88	21	31	..	32
Indonesia	0.0 [c]	0.0 [c]	282	0.9	1.1	69	76	54	66	..	31
Iran, Islamic Rep.	..	..	54	3.9	4.7	86	95	81	81	..	149
Iraq	..	..	156	2.7	3.7	..	85	..	79	..	29
Ireland	0.1	0.0 [c]	15	8.5	10.3	..	..	..	..	9	420
Israel	0.1	0.1	8	7.4	10.1	..	..	..	..	17	482
Italy	0.3	0.2	9	7.0	7.2	..	..	..	..	33	474
Jamaica	0.6	0.4	8	3.3	4.3	..	71	..	84	34	199
Japan	0.0 [c]	0.0 [c]	29	8.7	9.0	..	..	..	..	9	586
Jordan	..	..	11	3.2	3.0	97	96	98	99	..	93
Kazakhstan	0.1	..	130	15.6	8.2	..	91	..	99	..	113
Kenya	6.4	13.0	417	0.2	0.3	40	49	84	86	..	10
Korea, Dem. Rep.	..	..	176	12.3	10.3	..	..	..	..	..	46
Korea, Rep.	0.0 [c]	0.0 [c]	69	5.6	7.8	..	92	..	63	14	464
Kuwait	..	..	31	19.9	26.3	..	..	..	..	..	244
Kyrgyz Republic	..	..	130	2.5	1.3	..	77	..	100	..	77
Lao PDR	0.0 [c]	0.1	171	0.1	0.1	..	90	..	46	..	8
Latvia	0.2	0.1	105	4.8	3.2	..	..	..	..	23	303
Lebanon	..	..	24	2.5	3.9	..	100	..	99	..	195
Lesotho	12.1	26.4	542	..	..	..	91	..	92	..	10
Liberia	..	..	271	0.2	0.1	..	..	..	..	..	2
Libya	..	..	24	8.8	7.2	71	72	97	97	..	108
Lithuania	..	..	99	5.7	4.2	..	..	..	..	25	321
Macedonia, FYR	..	..	50	5.5	6.1	..	99	..	99	..	255
Madagascar	0.0 [c]	0.1	236	0.1	0.1	44	47	36	42	..	3
Malawi	7.0	15.3	443	0.1	0.1	49	57	73	77	..	4
Malaysia	0.6	0.1	111	3.0	5.4	..	..	..	..	..	199
Mali	1.3	2.1	261	0.0	0.0	55	65	70	69	..	3
Mauritania	0.4	0.6	241	1.3	1.2	37	37	30	33	..	7
Mauritius	0.0 [c]	0.0 [c]	68	1.1	1.5	100	100	100	99	..	235
Mexico	0.4	0.1	39	3.7	3.9	83	86	69	73	3	125
Moldova	0.3	0.1	130	4.8	2.2	..	100	..	..	..	133
Mongolia	..	..	205	4.7	3.3	..	60	..	30	..	56
Morocco	..	..	119	1.0	1.2	75	82	62	75	35	50
Mozambique	6.7	14.7	407	0.1	0.1	..	60	..	43	..	4
Myanmar	1.0	1.7	169	0.1	0.2	64	68	45	46	..	6
Namibia	9.1	19.8	490	..	0.0	72	77	33	41	..	63
Nepal	0.1	0.2	209	0.0	0.1	66	81	21	27	..	12
Netherlands	0.2	0.1	10	10.0	10.4	100	100	100	100	7	618
New Zealand	0.1	0.0 [c]	6	6.9	7.9	..	..	..	..	14	500
Nicaragua	0.2	0.1	88	0.7	0.7	70	79	76	84	..	31
Niger	0.9	1.5	252	0.1	0.1	53	59	15	20	..	2
Nigeria	2.5	5.1	301	0.9	0.6	49	57	60	63	..	4
Norway	0.1	0.0 [c]	5	7.5	7.6	100	100	..	..	10	532
Oman	..	..	10	7.1	8.8	37	39	84	92	..	89
Pakistan	0.1	0.0 [c]	177	0.6	0.7	84	88	34	61	10	22
Panama	1.6	1.4	54	1.3	2.1	..	87	..	94	29	151
Papua New Guinea	0.1	0.2	250	0.6	0.5	42	42	82	82	..	13
Paraguay	0.1	0.0 [c]	68	0.5	0.9	63	79	89	95	..	50
Peru	0.4	0.2	228	1.0	1.1	72	77	64	76	..	64
Philippines	0.0 [c]	0.1	314	0.7	1.0	87	87	74	83	19	40
Poland	..	..	39	9.1	8.3	..	..	..	..	30	282
Portugal	0.6	0.2	53	4.3	5.5	..	..	..	..	9	430
Puerto Rico	..	..	9	3.3	4.6	..	..	..	..	23	332
Romania	0.0 [c]	0.0 [c]	130	6.7	4.1	..	58	..	53	20	175
Russian Federation	0.3	0.1	123	13.3	9.8	..	99	..	..	27	218

	Combat HIV/AIDS and other diseases			Ensure environmental sustainability						Develop a global partnership for development	
	HIV prevalence male % ages 15-24 1999^b	HIV prevalence female % ages 15-24 1999^b	Incidence of tuberculosis per 100,000 people 1999	CO$_2$ emissions per capita metric tons 1990	CO$_2$ emissions per capita metric tons 1998	Access to an improved water source % of population 1990	Access to an improved water source % of population 2000	Access to improved sanitation facilities % of population 1990	Access to improved sanitation facilities % of population 2000	Unemployment % ages 15-24 1999	Telephone[a] lines per 1,000 people 2000
Rwanda	5.2	10.6	381	0.1	0.1	..	41	..	8	..	2
Saudi Arabia	..	..	45	11.3	14.4	..	95	..	100	..	137
Senegal	0.7	1.6	258	0.4	0.4	72	78	57	70	..	22
Sierra Leone	1.2	2.9	274	0.1	0.1	..	28	..	28	..	4
Singapore	0.2	0.2	48	13.8	21.0	100	100	100	100	7	484
Slovak Republic	0.0^c	0.0^c	28	8.1	7.1	..	100	..	100	32	314
Slovenia	0.0^c	0.0^c	27	6.1	7.4	100	100	..	..	18	386
Somalia	..	..	365	0.0	0.0	..	..	..	..	..	2
South Africa	11.3	24.8	495	8.3	8.3	..	86	..	86	58	114
Spain	0.5	0.2	59	5.5	6.3	..	..	..	..	29	421
Sri Lanka	0.0^c	0.1	59	0.2	0.4	66	83	82	83	28	41
Sudan	..	..	195	0.1	0.1	67	75	58	62	..	12
Swaziland	..	..	564	0.6	0.4	..	..	..	..	..	32
Sweden	0.1	0.0^c	4	5.7	5.5	100	100	100	100	14	682
Switzerland	0.4	0.3	9	6.4	5.9	100	100	100	100	6	727
Syrian Arab Republic	..	..	85	3.0	3.3	..	80	..	90	..	103
Tajikistan	..	..	105	3.7	0.8	..	..	..	..	..	36
Tanzania	4.0	8.1	340	0.1	0.1	50	54	88	90	..	5
Thailand	1.2	2.3	141	1.7	3.2	71	80	86	96	7	92
Togo	2.2	5.5	313	0.2	0.2	51	54	37	34	..	9
Trinidad and Tobago	0.8	0.6	12	13.9	17.4	..	86	..	88	25	231
Tunisia	..	..	37	1.6	2.4	80	..	76	..	..	90
Turkey	..	..	38	2.6	3.2	80	83	87	91	15	280
Turkmenistan	..	..	90	6.9	5.7	..	58	..	100	..	82
Uganda	3.8	7.8	343	0.0	0.1	44	50	84	75	..	3
Ukraine	1.3	0.8	73	11.5	7.0	..	..	..	..	23	199
United Arab Emirates	..	..	21	33.0	32.4	..	..	..	..	..	391
United Kingdom	0.1	0.0^c	12	9.9	9.2	100	100	100	100	12	589
United States	0.5	0.2	6	19.3	19.8	100	100	100	100	10	700
Uruguay	0.4	0.2	29	1.3	1.8	..	98	..	95	24	278
Uzbekistan	..	..	97	5.3	4.5	..	85	..	100	..	67
Venezuela, RB	0.7	0.1	42	5.8	6.7	..	84	..	74	26	108
Vietnam	0.3	0.1	189	0.3	0.6	48	56	73	73	..	32
West Bank and Gaza	..	..	28	..	..	..	..	..	..	..	..
Yemen, Rep.	..	..	108	0.7	0.9	66	69	39	45	..	19
Yugoslavia, Fed. Rep.	..	..	47	12.4	..	..	..	..	..	..	226
Zambia	8.2	17.8	495	0.3	0.2	52	64	63	78	..	8
Zimbabwe	11.3	24.5	562	1.6	1.2	77	85	64	68	..	18
World	0.7 w	1.1 w	142 w	3.4 w	3.9 w	76 w	80 w	49 w	56 w		163 w
Low income	1.1	2.0	229	0.7	1.0	70	76	40	45		23
Middle income	0.5	0.6	104	2.7	3.5	75	81	47	59		139
Lower middle income	0.2	0.2	110	2.2	3.1	74	80	41	52		116
Upper middle income	1.5	2.2	84	4.1	4.9	..	87	..	81		213
Low & middle income	0.8	1.3	163	1.8	2.3	73	79	44	52		84
East Asia & Pacific	0.2	0.2	142	2.0	2.4	70	75	38	47		101
Europe & Central Asia	0.4	..	85	9.2	6.8	..	90	..	..		222
Latin America & Carib.	0.7	0.3	75	2.2	2.6	81	85	72	78		148
Middle East & N. Africa	..	..	66	3.3	3.9	84	89	78	83		92
South Asia	0.3	0.5	191	0.7	0.9	80	87	31	37		27
Sub-Saharan Africa	4.5	9.2	339	0.9	0.8	49	55	55	55		14
High income	0.3	0.1	16	12.1	12.6	..	..	..	..		604
Europe EMU	0.3	0.2	20	6.9	8.0	..	..	..	..		534

a. Data are from International Telecommunications Union's (ITU) *World Telecommunication Development Report 2001*. Please cite the ITU for third party use of these data. b. Average of high and low estimates. c. Less than 0.05.

About the data

The Millennium Development Goals address issues of common concern to people of all nations. Diseases and environmental degradation do not respect national boundaries. Wherever epidemic diseases persist, they pose a threat to people everywhere. And damage done to the environment in one location may affect the wellbeing of plants, animals, and human beings in distant locations.

The indicators in the table are taken from goals 6 and 7 and the targets of goal 8 that address youth employment and access to new technologies. For the other targets of goal 8 see table 1.4.

Measuring the prevalence or incidence of a disease can be difficult. Much of the developing world lacks reporting systems needed for monitoring the course of a disease. Estimates are often derived from surveys and reports from sentinel sites that must be extrapolated to the general population. Tracking diseases such as HIV/AIDS, which has a long latency between contracting the disease and the appearance of outward symptoms, or malaria, which has periods of dormancy, can be particularly difficult. For some of the most serious illnesses international organizations have formed coalitions such as UNAIDS and the Roll Back Malaria campaign to gather information and coordinate global efforts to treat victims and prevent the diseases from spreading.

Antenatal care clinics are a key site for monitoring sexually transmitted diseases such as HIV and syphilis. The prevalence of HIV in young people provides an indicator of the spread of the epidemic. Prevalence rates in the older population can be affected by life-prolonging treatment. The indicator shown here is the estimated prevalence among women, ages 15-24.

The incidence of tuberculosis is based on data on case notifications and estimates of the proportion of cases detected in the population.

Carbon dioxide emissions are the primary source of greenhouse gases, which are believed to contribute to global warming.

Access to reliable supplies of safe drinking water and sanitary disposal of excrement are two of the most important means of improving human health and protecting the environment. There is no widespread program for testing the quality of water. The indicator shown here measures the proportion of households with access to an improved source, such as piped water or protected wells. Improved sanitation services prevent human, animal, and insect contact with excreta, but do not include treatment to render sewage outflows innocuous.

The eighth goal—to develop a global partnership for development—takes note of the need for decent and productive work for youth. Labor market information, such as unemployment rates, is still not generally available for most low- and middle-income economies. Telephone lines are one element of the new telecommunications technologies that are changing the way the global economy works.

Definitions

• **HIV Prevalence** refers to the percentage of people ages 15-24 who are infected with HIV.
• **Incidence of tuberculosis** is the estimated number of new tuberculosis cases (pulmonary, smear positive, extrapulmonary). • **Carbon dioxide emissions** are those stemming from the burning of fossil fuels and the manufacture of cement. They include carbon dioxide produced during consumption of solid, liquid, and gas fuels and gas flaring. • **Access to an improved water source** refers to the share of the population with reasonable access to an adequate amount of water from an improved source, such as a household connection, public standpipe, borehole, protected well or spring, or rainwater collection. Unimproved sources include vendors, tanker trucks, and unprotected wells and springs. Reasonable access is defined as the availability of at least 20 liters a person a day from a source within one kilometer of the dwelling. • **Access to improved sanitation facilities** refers to the percentage of the population with at least adequate excreta disposal facilities (private or shared, but not public) that can effectively prevent human, animal, and insect contact with excreta. Improved facilities range from simple but protected pit latrines to flush toilets with a sewerage connection. To be effective, facilities must be correctly constructed and properly maintained. • **Unemployment** refers to the share of the labor force without work but available for and seeking employment. Definitions of labor force and unemployment differ by country. • **Telephone lines** are telephone mainlines connecting a customer's equipment to the public switched telephone network.

Table 1.3a

Location of indicators for goals 6 and 7
Goal 6. Combat HIV/AIDS, malaria, and other diseases
18. HIV prevalence among 15-to-24-year-old pregnant women (tables 1.3 and 2.19)
19. Contraceptive prevalence rate (table 2.17)
20. Number of children orphaned by HIV/AIDS (no data currently available)
21. Prevalence and death rates associated with malaria (no data currently available)
22. Proportion of population in malaria-risk areas using effective malaria prevention and treatment measures (no data currently available)
23. Incidence of tuberculosis (per 100,000 people) (table 2.19)
24. Proportion of tuberculosis cases detected and cured under directly observed treatment, short course (table 2.16)
Goal 7. Ensure environmental sustainability
25. Change in land area covered by forest (table 3.4)
26. Land area protected to maintain biological diversity (table 3.4)
27. GDP per unit of energy use (table 3.8)
28. Carbon dioxide emissions per capita (table 3.8)
29. Proportion of population with sustainable access to an improved water source (tables 2.16 and 3.5)
30. Proportion of population with access to improved sanitation (table 2.16)
31. Proportion of population with access to secure tenure (table 3.11)

Data sources

Data on HIV/AIDS and the incidence of tuberculosis come from UNAIDS and the WHO's *AIDS Epidemic Update* (2000), and the WHO's *World Health Report 2000* and *Global Tuberculosis Control Report 1999*. The data on CO$_2$ emissions are from the Carbon Dioxide Information Analysis Center, Environmental Sciences Division, Oak Ridge National Laboratory, in the U.S. state of Tennessee. Data on access to water and sanitation come from the WHO and UNICEF's *Global Water Supply and Sanitation Assessment 2000 Report*. Unemployment data are from the International Labour Organization, database Key Indicators of the Labour Market (2001-02 issue). Data on telephone lines are from the International Telecommunication Union's (ITU) *World Telecommunication Development Report 2001*.

Millennium Development Goals:
1.4 | overcoming obstacles

Development Assistance Committee members	Official aid by donor		Market access to high-income countries						Support to agriculture	Debt sustainability
	Net official development assistance (ODA)	ODA provided for basic social services[a]	Goods (excluding arms) admitted free of tariffs		Tariffs on exports of low- and middle-income economies					Proportion of ODA provided by donors as debt relief
					Agricultural products		Textiles and clothing			
	% of donor GNI	% of total ODA commitments	%	%	Simple mean tariff %	Simple mean tariff %	Simple mean tariff %	Simple mean tariff %	Total support as share of GDP %	%
	2000	2000	1990	2000	1990	2000	1990	2000	2000	2000
Australia	0.27	14	*38.8*	42.7	*1.9*	1.6	*29.3*	14.6	0.3	1.3
Canada	0.25	6	*27.8*	65.2	*3.6*	2.7	*20.0*	11.5	0.5	5.0
European Union			48.2	72.9	11.1	4.9	6.3	4.3	1.52	
Austria	0.23	8	..	..	..	..	..	..	..	13.2
Belgium	0.36	12	..	..	..	..	..	..	..	5.0
Denmark	1.06	6	..	..	..	..	..	..	..	1.6
Finland	0.31	7	..	..	..	..	..	..	..	..
France	0.32	..	..	..	..	..	..	..	..	12.1
Germany	0.27	14	..	..	..	..	..	..	..	4.7
Greece	0.20	..	..	..	..	..	..	..	..	..
Ireland	0.30	35	..	..	..	..	..	..	..	1.5
Italy	0.13	7	..	..	..	..	..	..	..	17.3
Luxembourg	0.71	27	..	..	..	..	..	..	..	..
Netherlands	0.84	17	..	..	..	..	..	..	..	5.3
Portugal	0.26	5	..	..	..	..	..	..	..	9.6
Spain	0.22	12	..	..	..	..	..	..	..	1.4
Sweden	0.80	15	..	..	..	..	..	..	..	2.1
United Kingdom	0.32	24	..	..	..	..	..	..	..	3.4
Japan	0.28	3	42.2	57.2	9.4	9.1	5.0	4.1	1.4	3.4
New Zealand	0.25	9	*54.4*	52.4	*5.7*	1.7	*18.4*	8.2	0.3	1.4
Norway	0.80	10	*87.1*	71.7	*0.5*	15.2	*14.0*	11.6	1.4	2.2
Switzerland	0.34	13	*2.6*	61.8	..	..	..	..	2.0	2.3
United States	0.10	20	20.3	56.2	3.7	4.4	11.8	10.2	0.9	1.3

Highly indebted poor countries (HIPC)

	HIPC decision point[b]	HIPC completion point[c]	Estimated total nominal debt service relief		HIPC decision point[b]	HIPC completion point[c]	Estimated total nominal debt service relief
	date	date	$ millions		date	date	$ millions
Benin	Jul 00	floating	460	Malawi	Dec 00	floating	1,000
Bolivia	Feb 00	Jun 01	2,060	Mali	Sep 00	floating	870
Burkina Faso	Jul 00	floating	700	Mauritania	Feb 00	floating	1,100
Cameroon	Oct 00	floating	2,000	Mozambique	Apr 00	Sep 01	4,300
Chad	May 01	floating	260	Nicaragua	Dec 00	floating	4,500
Côte d'Ivoire	Mar 98	..	800	Niger	Dec 00	floating	900
Ethiopia	Nov 01	floating	1,930	Rwanda	Dec 00	floating	800
Gambia	Dec 00	floating	90	São Tomé & Principe	Dec 00	floating	200
Ghana[d]	Feb 02	floating	3,700	Senegal	Jun 00	floating	850
Guinea	Dec 00	floating	800	Sierra Leone[d]	..	..	900
Guinea-Bissau	Dec 00	floating	790	Tanzania	Apr 00	Nov 01	3,000
Guyana	Nov 00	floating	1,030	Uganda	Feb 00	May 00	1,950
Honduras	Jul 00	floating	900	Zambia	Dec 00	floating	3,820
Madagascar	Dec 00	floating	1,500				

a. Includes basic health, education, nutrition, and water and sanitation services. b. Except for Côte d'Ivoire, Ghana and Sierra Leone, data refer to the enhanced framework date; the following countries also reached decision points under the original framework on these dates: Bolivia, Sept. 1997; Burkina Faso, Sept. 1997; Guyana, Dec. 1997; Mali, Sept. 1998; Mozambique, April 1998; Uganda, April 1997. c. Except for Côte d'Ivoire, Ghana and Sierra Leone, data refer to the enhanced framework date; the following countries also reached completion points under the original framework on these dates: Bolivia, Sept. 1998; Burkina Faso, July 2000; Guyana, May 1999; Mali, Sept. 2000; Mozambique, July 1999; Uganda, April 1998. d. Figures are based on preliminary assessments at the time of the issuance of the preliminary HIPC document and are subject to change.

Millennium Development Goals:
overcoming obstacles | 1.4

About the data

Achieving the Millennium Development Goals (MDGs) will require an open, rule-based, global economy in which all countries, rich and poor, participate. Many poor countries, lacking the resources needed to finance their own development, burdened by unsustainable levels of debt, and unable to compete in the global marketplace, need assistance from rich countries. Therefore, many of the indicators for goal 8 monitor the actions of members of the Development Assistance Committee (DAC) of the Organisation for Economic Co-operation and Development (OECD).

Official development assistance (ODA) has been decreasing in recent years, both in real value and as a share of the gross national income of donor countries. The poorest countries will need additional assistance to achieve the Millennium Development Goals. Recent estimates suggest that $40-60 billion more a year, if provided to countries with good policies, would allow most of them to achieve the goals.

One of the most important things that high-income economies can do to help is to reduce barriers to the exports of low- and middle-income economies. The European Union has announced a program to eliminate tariffs on developing country exports of "everything but arms." The data in the table reflect the tariff schedules applied by high-income OECD members to low- and middle-income economies. Agricultural commodities and clothing and textiles are two of the most

important categories of goods exported by developing economies. Although average tariffs have been falling, averages may disguise high tariffs targeted at specific goods. (See table 6.6 for an estimate of the number of "international peaks" in each country's tariff schedule.) Only ad valorem duties are included in the averages. No data are shown for Switzerland, which applies specific duties almost exclusively. Comparable data on nontariff barriers are not currently available.

Subsidies to agricultural producers and exporters in OECD countries are another form of barrier to developing economies' exports. The table shows the value of total support to the agricultural sector as a share of the economy's GDP. In 2000 the total value of all subsidies in high-income OECD economies was $277 billion.

The heavily indebted poor country (HIPC) debt initiative is the first comprehensive approach to reducing the external debt of the world's poorest, most heavily indebted countries. It represents an important step forward in placing debt relief within an overall framework of poverty reduction. While the HIPC initiative yielded significant early progress, multilateral organizations, bilateral creditors, HIPC governments, and civil society have engaged in an intensive dialogue about the strengths and weaknesses of the program. A major review in 1999 resulted in an enhancement of the original framework.

Definitions

• **Net Official development assistance** comprises grants and loans that meet the DAC definition of ODA and are made to developing countries and territories in Part 1 of the DAC list of recipient countries. • **ODA provided for basic social services** is aid reported by DAC donors for basic health, education, nutrition, and water and sanitation services. • **Goods admitted free of tariffs** is the value of exports of goods (excluding arms) received from developing countries and admitted without tariff as a share of total exports from developing countries. • **Agricultural products** comprise plant and animal products, including tree crops but excluding timber and fish products. • **Textiles and clothing** include natural and man-made fibers and fabrics and articles of clothing made from them. • **Simple mean tariff** is the unweighted average of the effectively applied rates for all products subject to tariffs. • **Support to agriculture** is the value of subsidies to the agricultural sector. • **Proportion of ODA provided as debt relief** is the share of aid from DAC donors going to debt relief. • **HIPC decision point** is the date at which a heavily indebted poor country with an established track record of good performance under adjustment programs supported by the International Monetary Fund and the World Bank, commits to undertake additional reforms and to develop and implement a poverty reduction strategy. • **HIPC completion point** is the date at which the country successfully completes the key structural reforms agreed at the decision point, including the development and implementation of its poverty reduction strategy. The country then receives the bulk of debt relief under the HIPC initiative without any further policy conditions.

Data sources

Data on official development assistance are compiled by the DAC and published in the DAC chairman's annual report, *Development Co-operation*. Data on tariffs and trade flows are calculated by World Bank staff using the World Integrated Trade Solution system. Data on supports to agriculture were provided by the OECD. Information on the HIPC program is available from the World Bank's HIPC Web site www.worldbank.org/hipc.

Table 1.4a

Location of indicators for goal 8
Goal 8. Develop a global partnership for development
32. Net ODA as a percentage of DAC donors' gross national income (table 6.9)
33. Proportion of ODA for basic social services (table 1.4)
34. Proportion of ODA that is untied (table 6.9)
35. Proportion of ODA for the environment in small island developing states (no data currently available)
36. Proportion of ODA for the transport sector in landlocked countries (no data currently available)
37. Proportion of exports (by value, excluding arms) admitted free of duties and quotas (table 1.4)
38. Average tariffs and quotas on agricultural products and textiles and clothing (See related indicators in table 6.6)
39. Domestic and export agricultural subsidies in OECD countries (table 1.4)
40. Proportion of ODA provided to help build trade capacity (no data currently available)
41. Proportion of official bilateral HIPC debt canceled (no data currently available)
42. Debt service as a percentage of exports of goods and services (table 4.17)
43. Proportion of ODA provided as debt relief (table 1.4)
44. Number of countries reaching HIPC decision and completion points (table 1.4)
45. Unemployment rate of 15-to-24-year-olds (See table 2.4 for related indicators)
46. Proportion of population with access to affordable, essential drugs on a sustainable basis (no data currently available)
47. Telephone lines per 1,000 people (tables 1.3 and 5.9)
48. Personal computers per 1,000 people (table 5.10)

1.5 | Women in development

	Female population	Life expectancy at birth		Pregnant women receiving prenatal care	Literacy gender parity index	Labor force gender parity index		Maternity leave benefits	Women in decision-making positions	
	% of total	Male years	Female years	%	ages 15-24			% of wages paid in covered period	% at ministerial level	
	2000	2000	2000	1996	2000	1990	2000	1998	1994	1998
Afghanistan	48.4	43	43	..	..	0.5	0.6	..	..	..
Albania	48.9	72	76	..	1.0	0.7	0.7	..	0	11
Algeria	49.3	69	73	58	0.9	0.3	0.4	100	4	0
Angola	50.5	45	48	25	..	0.9	0.9	100	7	14
Argentina	51.0	70	77	..	1.0	0.4	0.5	100	0	8
Armenia	51.6	71	77	95	1.0	0.9	0.9	..	3	0
Australia	50.2	76	82	..	..	0.7	0.8	0	13	14
Austria	51.2	75	81	..	..	0.7	0.7	100	16	20
Azerbaijan	50.8	68	75	95	..	0.8	0.8	..	5	10
Bangladesh	48.4	61	62	23	0.7	0.7	0.7	100	8	5
Belarus	53.4	62	74	..	1.0	1.0	1.0	100	3	3
Belgium	51.0	75	81	..	..	0.7	0.7	82 [a]	11	3
Benin	50.7	51	55	60	0.5	0.9	0.9	100	10	13
Bolivia	50.2	61	64	52	1.0	0.6	0.6	70 [b]	0	6
Bosnia and Herzegovina	50.5	71	76	..	..	0.6	0.6	..	0	6
Botswana	51.0	39	39	92	1.1	0.9	0.8	25	6	14
Brazil	50.6	64	72	74	1.0	0.5	0.6	100	5	4
Bulgaria	51.4	68	75	..	1.0	0.9	0.9	100	0	..
Burkina Faso	51.7	44	45	59	0.5	0.9	0.9	100	7	10
Burundi	51.4	41	43	88	0.9	1.0	0.9	50	7	8
Cambodia	51.2	52	55	52	0.9	1.2	1.1	50	0	..
Cameroon	50.2	49	51	73	1.0	0.6	0.6	100	3	6
Canada	50.5	76	82	..	..	0.8	0.8	55 [c]	14	..
Central African Republic	51.3	43	44	67	0.8	..	..	50	5	4
Chad	50.5	47	50	30	0.8	0.8	0.8	50	5	0
Chile	50.5	73	79	91	1.0	0.4	0.5	100	13	13
China	48.6	69	72	79	1.0	0.8	0.8	100	6	..
Hong Kong, China	49.1	77	82	100	1.0	0.6	0.6	..	..	..
Colombia	50.6	68	75	83	1.0	0.6	0.6	100	11	18
Congo, Dem. Rep.	50.4	45	46	66	0.8	0.8	0.8	67	6	..
Congo, Rep.	51.0	49	53	55	1.0	0.8	0.8	100	6	6
Costa Rica	49.3	75	80	95	1.0	0.4	0.5	100	10	15
Côte d'Ivoire	48.8	45	46	83	0.8	0.5	0.5	100	8	3
Croatia	51.6	69	78	..	1.0	0.7	0.8	..	4	12
Cuba	49.9	75	78	100	1.0	0.6	0.7	100	0	5
Czech Republic	51.4	72	78	..	..	0.9	0.9	..	0	17
Denmark	50.5	74	79	..	..	0.9	0.9	100 [e]	29	41
Dominican Republic	49.2	65	70	97	1.0	0.4	0.4	100	4	10
Ecuador	49.8	68	71	75	1.0	0.3	0.4	100	6	20
Egypt, Arab Rep.	49.4	66	69	53	0.8	0.4	0.4	100	4	6
El Salvador	50.9	67	73	69	1.0	0.5	0.6	75	10	6
Eritrea	50.3	51	53	19	0.8	0.9	0.9	..	7	5
Estonia	53.4	65	76	..	..	1.0	1.0	..	15	12
Ethiopia	50.3	41	43	20	0.8	0.7	0.7	100	10	5
Finland	51.2	74	81	..	..	0.9	0.9	80	39	29
France	51.3	75	83	..	..	0.8	0.8	100	7	12
Gabon	50.5	51	54	86	..	0.8	0.8	100	7	3
Gambia, The	50.5	52	55	91	0.7	0.8	0.8	100	0	29
Georgia	52.3	69	77	95	..	0.9	0.9	..	0	4
Germany	51.0	74	81	..	..	0.7	0.7	100	16	8
Ghana	50.2	56	58	86	0.9	1.0	1.0	50	11	9
Greece	50.7	75	81	..	1.0	0.5	0.6	75	4	5
Guatemala	49.6	62	68	53	0.9	0.3	0.4	100	19	0
Guinea	49.7	46	47	59	..	0.9	0.9	100	9	8
Guinea-Bissau	50.7	43	46	50	0.6	0.7	0.7	100	4	18
Haiti	51.0	51	56	68	1.0	0.8	0.8	100 [e]	13	0
Honduras	49.7	63	69	73	1.0	0.4	0.5	100 [f]	11	11

	Female population	Life expectancy at birth		Pregnant women receiving prenatal care	Literacy gender parity index	Labor force gender parity index		Maternity leave benefits	Women in decision-making positions	
	% of total 2000	Male years 2000	Female years 2000	% 1996	ages 15-24 2000	1990	2000	% of wages paid in covered period 1998	% at ministerial level 1994	1998
Hungary	52.3	67	76	..	1.0	0.8	0.8	100	0	5
India	48.4	62	63	62	0.8	0.5	0.5	100	3	..
Indonesia	49.8	64	68	82	1.0	0.6	0.7	100	6	3
Iran, Islamic Rep.	48.8	68	70	62	1.0	0.3	0.4	67	0	0
Iraq	49.2	60	62	59	0.9	0.2	0.2	100	0	0
Ireland	50.3	74	79	..	..	0.5	0.5	70 d	16	21
Israel	50.7	76	80	90	1.0	0.6	0.7	75	4	0
Italy	51.5	76	82	..	1.0	0.6	0.6	80	12	13
Jamaica	50.7	73	77	98	1.1	0.9	0.9	100 g	5	12
Japan	51.1	78	84	..	..	0.7	0.7	60	6	0
Jordan	48.0	70	73	80	1.0	0.2	0.3	100	3	2
Kazakhstan	51.5	60	71	92	..	0.9	0.9	..	6	5
Kenya	50.2	47	47	95	1.0	0.8	0.9	100	0	0
Korea, Dem. Rep.	49.8	59	62	100	..	0.8	0.8	..	0	..
Korea, Rep.	49.7	70	77	96	1.0	0.6	0.7	100	4	..
Kuwait	41.8	75	79	99	1.0	0.3	0.5	100	0	0
Kyrgyz Republic	51.0	63	72	90	..	0.9	0.9	..	0	4
Lao PDR	50.1	53	55	25	0.7	..	..	100	0	0
Latvia	53.9	65	76	..	1.0	1.0	1.0	..	0	7
Lebanon	51.1	69	72	85	1.0	0.4	0.4	100	0	0
Lesotho	50.4	44	44	91	1.2	0.6	0.6	0	6	6
Liberia	49.7	46	48	0	0.6	0.6	0.7	0	0	0
Libya	48.2	69	73	100	0.9	0.2	0.3	50	0	7
Lithuania	52.8	68	78	..	1.0	0.9	0.9	..	0	6
Macedonia, FYR	50.0	71	75	..	..	0.7	0.7	..	8	9
Madagascar	50.3	53	56	78	0.9	0.8	0.8	100 d	0	19
Malawi	50.3	39	39	90	0.8	1.0	0.9	..	9	4
Malaysia	49.3	70	75	90	1.0	0.6	0.6	100	7	16
Mali	50.5	41	44	25	0.8	0.9	0.9	100	10	21
Mauritania	50.4	50	53	49	0.7	0.8	0.8	100	0	4
Mauritius	50.2	68	76	99	1.0	0.4	0.5	100	3	..
Mexico	50.5	70	76	71	1.0	0.4	0.5	100	5	5
Moldova	52.2	64	72	..	1.0	0.9	0.9	..	0	0
Mongolia	49.9	65	69	90	..	0.9	0.9	..	0	0
Morocco	49.9	66	69	45	0.8	0.5	0.5	100	0	0
Mozambique	50.6	41	44	54	0.6	0.9	0.9	100	4	0
Myanmar	50.3	54	59	80	1.0	0.8	0.8	67	0	0
Namibia	50.6	47	47	88	1.0	0.7	0.7	..	10	8
Nepal	48.7	59	59	15	0.6	0.7	0.7	100	0	3
Netherlands	50.4	75	81	..	..	0.6	0.7	100	31	28
New Zealand	50.7	76	81	..	..	0.8	0.8	0	8	8
Nicaragua	50.2	67	71	71	1.0	0.5	0.6	60	10	5
Niger	49.6	44	48	30	0.4	0.8	0.8	50	5	10
Nigeria	49.6	46	48	60	0.9	0.5	0.6	50	3	6
Norway	50.5	76	81	..	..	0.8	0.9	100	35	20
Oman	46.9	72	75	98	1.0	0.1	0.2	..	0	0
Pakistan	48.6	62	64	27	0.6	0.3	0.4	100	4	7
Panama	49.5	72	77	72	1.0	0.5	0.5	100	13	6
Papua New Guinea	47.9	58	59	70	0.9	0.7	0.7	0	0	0
Paraguay	49.6	68	73	83	1.0	0.4	0.4	50 h	0	7
Peru	50.4	67	72	64	1.0	0.4	0.5	100	6	10
Philippines	49.6	67	71	83	1.0	0.6	0.6	100	8	10
Poland	51.4	69	78	..	1.0	0.8	0.9	100	17	12
Portugal	51.9	72	79	..	1.0	0.7	0.8	100	10	10
Puerto Rico	51.9	72	81	99	1.0	0.5	0.6	..	..	..
Romania	51.1	66	74	..	1.0	0.8	0.8	50-94	0	8
Russian Federation	53.2	59	72	..	1.0	0.9	1.0	100	0	8

	Female population	Life expectancy at birth		Pregnant women receiving prenatal care	Literacy gender parity index	Labor force gender parity index		Maternity leave benefits	Women in decision-making positions	
		Male years	Female years		ages 15-24			% of wages paid in covered period	% at ministerial level	
	% of total 2000	2000	2000	% 1996	2000	1990	2000	1998	1994	1998
Rwanda	50.5	39	40	94	1.0	1.0	1.0	67	9	5
Saudi Arabia	46.6	71	74	87	1.0	0.1	0.2	50-100	0	0
Senegal	50.1	51	54	74	0.7	0.7	0.7	100	7	7
Sierra Leone	50.8	38	41	30	..	0.6	0.6	..	0	10
Singapore	49.6	76	80	100	1.0	0.6	0.6	100	0	0
Slovak Republic	51.4	69	77	..	..	0.9	0.9	..	5	19
Slovenia	51.4	72	79	..	1.0	0.9	0.9	..	5	0
Somalia	50.4	47	50	0	..	0.8	0.8	0	0	0
South Africa	50.8	47	49	89	1.0	0.6	0.6	45	6	..
Spain	51.1	75	82	..	1.0	0.5	0.6	100	14	18
Sri Lanka	48.6	71	76	100	1.0	0.5	0.6	100	3	13
Sudan	49.7	55	58	54	0.9	0.4	0.4	100	0	0
Swaziland	50.7	45	46	0	1.0	0.6	0.6	0	0	0
Sweden	50.5	77	82	..	..	0.9	0.9	75	30	43
Switzerland	50.5	77	83	..	..	0.6	0.7	100	17	17
Syrian Arab Republic	49.3	67	72	33	0.8	0.3	0.4	100	7	8
Tajikistan	50.2	66	72	90	1.0	0.7	0.8	..	3	6
Tanzania	50.4	44	45	92	0.9	1.0	1.0	100	13	13
Thailand	50.5	67	71	77	1.0	0.9	0.9	100 i	0	4
Togo	50.3	48	50	43	0.7	0.7	0.7	100	5	9
Trinidad and Tobago	50.3	70	75	98	1.0	0.5	0.5	60-100	19	14
Tunisia	49.5	70	74	71	0.9	0.4	0.5	67	4	3
Turkey	49.5	67	72	62	1.0	0.5	0.6	67	5	5
Turkmenistan	50.5	63	70	90	..	0.8	0.8	..	3	4
Uganda	50.1	42	42	87	0.8	0.9	0.9	100 j	10	13
Ukraine	53.6	63	74	..	1.0	1.0	1.0	100	0	5
United Arab Emirates	33.9	74	77	95	1.1	0.1	0.2	100	0	0
United Kingdom	50.8	75	80	..	..	0.7	0.8	90 k	9	24
United States	50.7	74	80	..	..	0.8	0.9	0	14	26
Uruguay	51.5	71	78	80	1.0	0.6	0.7	100	0	7
Uzbekistan	50.3	67	73	90	1.0	0.8	0.9	..	3	3
Venezuela, RB	49.7	71	76	74	1.0	0.5	0.5	100	11	3
Vietnam	50.2	67	72	78	1.0	1.0	1.0	100	5	0
West Bank and Gaza	49.3	70	74	..	..	..	..	..	..	..
Yemen, Rep.	50.2	56	57	26	0.6	0.4	0.4	100	0	0
Yugoslavia, Fed. Rep.	50.3	70	75	..	..	0.7	0.8	..	..	5
Zambia	49.8	38	38	92	0.9	0.8	0.8	100	5	3
Zimbabwe	50.0	40	40	93	1.0	0.8	0.8	60-75	3	12
World	**49.4 w**	**65 w**	**69 w**	**70 w**	**.. w**	**0.7 w**	**0.7 w**		**6 w**	**.. w**
Low income	49.3	58	60	62	0.8	0.6	0.6		4	..
Middle income	49.5	67	72	77	1.0	0.7	0.7		5	..
Lower middle income	49.2	67	72	76	1.0	0.8	0.8		5	..
Upper middle income	50.2	67	73	80	1.0	0.5	0.6		6	6
Low & middle income	49.4	63	66	70	0.9	0.7	0.7		5	..
East Asia & Pacific	49.0	67	71	80	1.0	0.8	0.8		5	..
Europe & Central Asia	51.8	64	74	..	1.0	0.8	0.9		3	7
Latin America & Carib.	50.4	67	74	75	1.0	0.5	0.5		6	7
Middle East & N. Africa	48.6	66	69	58	0.9	0.3	0.4		2	2
South Asia	48.5	62	63	55	0.8	0.5	0.5		4	..
Sub-Saharan Africa	50.1	46	47	65	0.9	0.7	0.7		6	7
High income	49.5	75	81	..	..	0.7	0.8		12	16
Europe EMU	51.2	75	81	..	..	0.7	0.7		14	13

a. For 30 days, 75 percent thereafter. b. Benefit is 70 percent of wages above the minimum wage, 100 percent of national minimum wage. c. For 15 weeks. d. Up to a ceiling. e. For 6 weeks. f. For 84 days. g. For 8 weeks. h. For 9 weeks. i. Benefit is 100 percent for the first 45 days, then 50 percent for 15 days. j. For 1 month. k. For 6 weeks; flat rate thereafter.

About the data

Despite considerable progress in recent decades, gender inequalities remain pervasive in many dimensions of life—worldwide. But while disparities exist throughout the world, they are most prevalent in poor developing countries. The differences in outcomes between men and women—and between boys and girls—are a consequence of differences in the opportunities and resources available to them. Inequalities in the allocation of resources such as education, health care, and nutrition matter because of the strong association of these resources with well-being, productivity, and growth. This pattern of inequality begins at an early age, with boys routinely receiving a larger share of education and health spending than girls do, for example.

Life expectancy has increased for both men and women in all regions, but female morbidity and mortality rates sometimes exceed male rates, particularly during early childhood and the reproductive years. In high-income countries women tend to outlive men by four to eight years on average, while in low-income countries the difference is narrower—about two to three years. The female disadvantage is best reflected in differences in child mortality rates (see table 2.20). Child mortality captures the effect of preferences for boys because adequate nutrition and medical interventions are particularly important for the age group 1–5. Because of the natural female biological advantage, when female child mortality is as high as or higher than male child mortality, there is good reason to believe that girls are discriminated against.

Female disadvantage in mortality is carried into adolescence and the reproductive years. Serious health risks for adolescents arise when they become sexually active. And while in high-income countries women have universal access to health care during pregnancy, in developing countries it is estimated that 35 percent of pregnant women—some 45 million each year—receive no care at all (United Nations 2000b). Prenatal care is essential for recognizing, diagnosing, and promptly treating complications that arise during pregnancy.

Girls in many developing countries are allowed less education by their families than boys are—a disparity reflected in lower female primary enrollment (see table 1.2) and higher female illiteracy. As a result, women have fewer employment opportunities, especially in the formal sector. A labor force gender parity index of less than 1.0 shows that women's labor force participation in the formal sector is lower than men's. (A ratio of 1.0 indicates gender equality).

Women who work outside the home continue to bear a disproportionate share of the responsibility for housework and child rearing. They also face discriminatory practices in the workplace, especially relating to equal pay and maternity benefits. The maternity benefits data in the table relate only to legislated benefits and do not include contractual benefits negotiated through labor union contracts. The benefits generally apply only in the formal sector, leaving out the vast majority of working women in developing countries. As a result, while the situation in the United States is much better than the data indicate, the situation in Thailand is likely to be much worse.

Women are vastly underrepresented in decision-making positions in government, although there is some evidence of recent improvement. While 6 percent of the world's cabinet ministers were women in 1994, 8 percent were in 1998. Without representation at this level, it is difficult for women to influence policy.

For information on other aspects of gender, see tables 1.2 (Millennium Development Goals: eradicating poverty and improving lives), 2.3 (employment by economic activity), 2.4 (unemployment), 2.13 (education efficiency), 2.14 (education outcomes), 2.17 (reproductive health), 2.19 (health: risk factors and future challenges), and 2.20 (mortality).

Figure 1.5

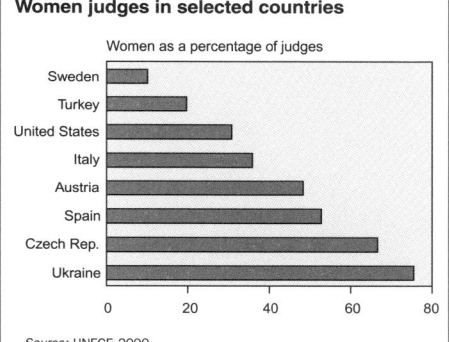

Women judges in selected countries

Women as a percentage of judges

Source: UNECE 2000.

Women have begun to make inroads in various political, governmental, and civic aspects of life that give them decision-making power and influence and place them on a more equal footing with men. However, they still have a long way to go to achieve their share of positions where they can make a difference. Judgeships are the only positions of power and influence in which women have reached parity in a number of countries.

Definitions

• **Female population** is the percentage of the population that is female. • **Life expectancy at birth** is the number of years a newborn infant would live if prevailing patterns of mortality at the time of its birth were to stay the same throughout its life. • **Pregnant women receiving prenatal care** are the percentage of women attended at least once during pregnancy by skilled health personnel for reasons related to pregnancy. • **Literacy gender parity index** is the ratio of the female literacy rate to the male rate, for the age group 15–24. • **Labor force gender parity index** is the ratio of the percentage of women who are economically active to the percentage of men who are. According to the International Labour Organization (ILO) definition, the economically active population is all those who supply labor for the production of goods and services during a specified period. It includes both the employed and the unemployed. While national practices vary in the treatment of such groups as the armed forces and seasonal or part-time workers, in general the labor force includes the armed forces, the unemployed, and first-time job seekers, but excludes homemakers and other unpaid caregivers and workers in the informal sector. • **Maternity leave benefits** refer to the compensation provided to women during maternity leave, as a share of their full wages. • **Women in decision-making positions** are those in ministerial or equivalent positions in the government.

Data sources

The data are from the World Bank's population database; electronic databases of the United Nations Educational, Scientific, and Cultural Organization (UNESCO); the ILO database Estimates and Projections of the Economically Active Population, 1950–2010; and the United Nations' *World's Women: Trends and Statistics 2000.*

1.6 | Key indicators for other economies

	Population	Surface area	Population density	Gross national income		PPP[a]		Gross domestic product		Life expectancy at birth	Adult illiteracy rate	Carbon dioxide emissions
					Per capita		Per capita		Per capita		% of people 15 and above	
	thousands 2000	thousand sq. km 2000	people per sq. km 2000	$ millions 2000[b]	$ 2000[b]	$ millions 2000	$ 2000	% growth 1999-2000	% growth 1999-2000	years 2000	2000	thousand metric tons 1998
American Samoa	65	0.2	327	..	.. [c]	..	..	..	..	..	..	282
Andorra	67	0.5	149	..	.. [d]	..	..	..	..	80	..	..
Antigua and Barbuda	68	0.4	155	642	9,440 [e]	680	10,000	3.7	2.8	75	..	337
Aruba	101	0.2	532	..	.. [d]	..	..	..	..	..	..	1,883
Bahamas, The	303	13.9	30	4,533	14,960	4,969	16,400	4.5	2.9	69	5	1,792
Bahrain	691	0.7	1,001	..	.. [c]	..	..	..	..	73	12	18,688
Barbados	267	0.4	621	2,469	9,250 [f]	4,010	15,020	4.1	3.8	75	..	1,569
Belize	240	23.0	11	746	3,110 [g]	1,258	5,240	10.2	6.6	74	7	399
Bermuda	63	0.1	1,260	..	.. [d]	..	..	..	..	..	..	462
Bhutan	805	47.0	17	479	590	1,161	1,440	7.0	3.9	62	..	386
Brunei	338	5.8	64	..	.. [d]	..	..	..	..	76	8	5,488
Cape Verde	441	4.0	109	588	1,330	2,100 [h]	4,760 [h]	6.8	3.6	69	26	121
Cayman Islands	35	0.3	135	..	.. [d]	..	..	..	..	..	..	289
Channel Islands	149	0.2	768	..	.. [d]	..	..	..	..	79	..	..
Comoros	558	2.2	250	212	380	887 [h]	1,590 [h]	-1.1	-3.6	61	44	70
Cyprus	757	9.3	82	9,361	12,370	15,734 [h]	20,780 [h]	4.8	4.4	78	3	5,918
Djibouti	632	23.2	27	553	880	..	..	0.7	-1.3	46	35	366
Dominica	73	0.8	97	..	.. [c]	..	..	0.5	..	76	..	84
Equatorial Guinea	457	28.1	16	363	800	2,560	5,600	16.9	13.8	51	17	253
Faeroe Islands	45	1.4	32	..	.. [d]	..	..	..	..	..	..	641
Fiji	812	18.3	44	1,480	1,820	3,636	4,480	-8.0	-9.2	69	7	721
French Polynesia	235	4.0	64	4,064	17,290	5,486	23,340	4.0	2.4	73	..	561
Greenland	56	341.7	0	..	.. [d]	..	..	..	..	..	..	528
Grenada	98	0.3	288	370	3,770	682	6,960	6.5	5.4	72	..	183
Guam	155	0.6	281	..	.. [d]	..	..	..	..	78	..	4,111
Guyana	761	215.0	4	652	860	2,795	3,670	-0.7	-1.3	63	2	1,649
Iceland	281	103.0	3	8,540	30,390	8,069	28,710	5.0	3.7	80	..	2,083
Isle of Man	75	0.6	131	..	.. [c]	..	..	..	..	..	..	..
Kiribati	91	0.7	124	86	950	..	..	-1.8	-4.2	62	..	22
Liechtenstein	32	0.2	200	..	.. [d]	..	..	..	..	..	..	..
Luxembourg	438	2.6	169	18,439	42,060	19,934	45,470	8.5	6.9	77	..	7,678
Macao, China	438	..	..	6,385 [i]	14,580 [i]	7,967	18,190	4.6	3.7	79	6	1,630
Maldives	276	0.3	920	541	1,960	1,171	4,240	4.8	2.3	68	3	330
Malta	390	0.3	1,219	3,559	9,120 [f]	6,448	16,530	4.7	4.2	78	8	1,803
Marshall Islands	52	0.2	286	102	1,970	..	..	0.5	..	65	..	..
Mayotte	145	0.4	388	..	.. [c]	..	..	..	..	..	..	..
Micronesia, Fed. Sts.	118	0.7	168	250	2,110	..	..	3.0	1.2	68	..	..
Monaco	32	0.0	16,410	..	.. [d]	..	..	..	..	..	..	..
Netherlands Antilles	215	0.8	269	..	.. [d]	..	..	..	..	76	3	7,753
New Caledonia	213	18.6	12	3,203	15,060	4,641	21,820	2.1	0.3	73	..	1,746
Northern Mariana Islands	72	0.5	151	..	.. [d]	..	..	..	..	..	..	..
Palau	19	0.5	41	..	.. [c]	..	..	5.4	..	70	..	242
Qatar	585	11.0	53	..	.. [d]	..	..	..	..	75	19	46,772
Samoa	170	2.8	60	246	1,450	859	5,050	7.0	6.4	69	20	132
São Tomé and Principe	148	1.0	154	43	290	..	..	2.9	0.7	65	..	77
Seychelles	81	0.5	181	573	7,050	..	..	1.2	-0.3	72	..	198
Solomon Islands	447	28.9	16	278	620	766 [h]	1,710 [h]	-14.0	-16.9	69	..	161
San Marino	27	0.1	450	..	.. [d]	..	..	..	..	80	..	..
St. Kitts and Nevis	41	0.4	114	269	6,570	449	10,960	2.6	2.3	71	..	103
St. Lucia	156	0.6	256	642	4,120	842	5,400	2.0	0.5	71	..	198
St. Vincent and the Grenadines	115	0.4	295	313	2,720	599	5,210	2.3	1.4	73	..	161
Suriname	417	163.3	3	788	1,890	1,450	3,480	-7.3	-7.9	70	..	2,139
Tonga	100	0.8	139	166	1,660	..	..	6.2	5.5	71	..	117
Vanuatu	197	12.2	16	226	1,150	583 [h]	2,960 [h]	2.2	0.1	68	..	62
Virgin Islands (U.S.)	121	0.3	356	..	.. [d]	..	..	..	..	78	..	11,706

a. PPP is purchasing power parity; see *Definitions*. b. Calculated using the World Bank Atlas method. c. Estimated to be upper middle income ($2,996-9,265). d. Estimated to be high income ($9,266 or more). e. Included under upper middle income economies in calculating the aggregates based on earlier data. f. Included under high income economies in calculating the aggregates based on earlier data. g. Included under lower middle income economies in calculating the aggregates based on earlier data. h. The estimate is based on regression; others are extrapolated from the latest International Comparison Programme benchmark estimates. i. Refers to GDP and GDP per capita.

About the data

This table shows data for 55 economies—small economies with populations between 30,000 and 1 million and smaller economies if they are members of the World Bank. Where data on gross national income (GNI) per capita are not available, the estimated range is given. For more information on the calculation of GNI (gross national product, or GNP, in the 1968 System of National Accounts), see *About the data* for table 1.1. As in last year's edition, this table excludes France's overseas departments—French Guiana, Guadeloupe, Martinique, and Réunion—for which GNI and other economic measures are now included in the French national accounts.

Definitions

• **Population** is based on the de facto definition of population, which counts all residents regardless of legal status or citizenship—except for refugees not permanently settled in the country of asylum, who are generally considered part of the population of their country of origin. The values shown are midyear estimates for 2000. See also table 2.1. • **Surface area** is a country's total area, including areas under inland bodies of water and some coastal waterways. • **Population density** is midyear population divided by land area in square kilometers. • **Gross national income** (GNI) is the sum of value added by all resident producers plus any product taxes (less subsidies) not included in the valuation of output plus net receipts of primary income (compensation of employees and property income) from abroad. Data are in current U.S. dollars converted using the World Bank Atlas method (see *Statistical methods*). • **GNI per capita** is gross national income divided by midyear population. GNI per capita in U.S. dollars is converted using the World Bank Atlas method. • **PPP GNI** is gross national income converted to international dollars using purchasing power parity rates. An international dollar has the same purchasing power over GNI as a U.S. dollar has in the United States. • **Gross domestic product** (GDP) is the sum of value added by all resident producers plus any product taxes (less subsidies) not included in the valuation of output. Growth is calculated from constant price GDP data in local currency. • **Life expectancy at birth** is the number of years a newborn infant would live if prevailing patterns of mortality at the time of its birth were to stay the same throughout its life. • **Adult illiteracy rate** is the percentage of adults ages 15 and above who cannot, with understanding, read and write a short, simple statement about their everyday life. • **Carbon dioxide emissions** are those stemming from the burning of fossil fuels and the manufacture of cement. They include carbon dioxide produced during consumption of solid, liquid, and gas fuels and gas flaring.

Data sources

The indicators here and throughout the rest of the book have been compiled by World Bank staff from primary and secondary sources. More information about the indicators and their sources can be found in the *About the data, Definitions,* and *Data sources* entries that accompany each table in subsequent sections.

PEOPLE

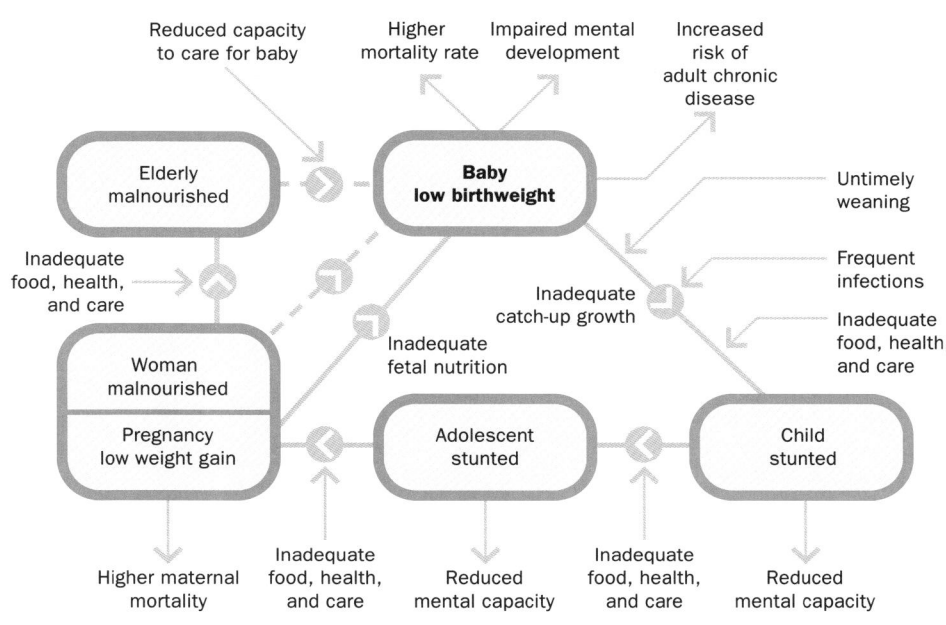

Higher maternal mortality

Inadequate food, health, and care

Reduced mental capacity

Inadequate food, health, and care

Reduced mental capacity

Source: UN ACC/SCN 2000.

Hunger and malnutrition

Hunger and malnutrition still pose a major challenge to many developing countries. In countries already saddled with poverty, malnutrition starts a vicious cycle of ill health, lower learning capacity, and poor physical growth. Because that undermines a country's social and economic development, investing in better nutrition is essential.

Reflecting this development priority, the Millennium Development Goals adopted a target to halve, between 1990 and 2015, the proportion of people in developing countries who suffer from hunger. Two indicators were identified to track progress: the prevalence of underweight in children under age five and the proportion of undernourished people.

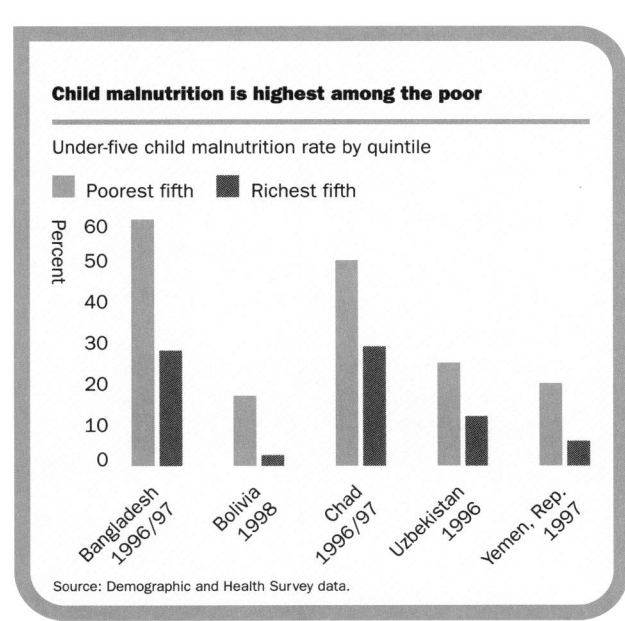

Child malnutrition is highest among the poor

Under-five child malnutrition rate by quintile

Source: Demographic and Health Survey data.

Malnutrition is pervasive

The prevalence of child malnutrition in the developing world fell from 46.5 percent in 1970 to 27 percent in 2000. Even so, 150 million children under five are still malnourished. The situation is bleakest in Africa, where both the number and the proportion of malnourished children have been rising. At current rates of improvement, now slowing, halving child malnutrition by 2015 is unlikely. In 2020, 140 million children under five in developing countries will still be underweight, or about 50 million short of the goal (Smith and Haddad 2000).

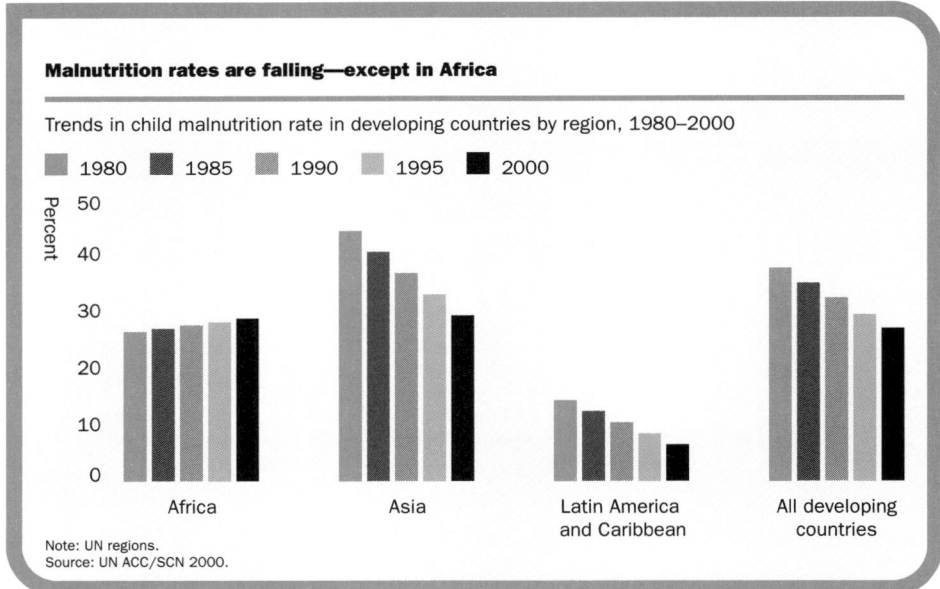

Malnutrition rates are falling—except in Africa

Trends in child malnutrition rate in developing countries by region, 1980–2000

■ 1980　■ 1985　■ 1990　■ 1995　■ 2000

Note: UN regions.
Source: UN ACC/SCN 2000.

Why focus on malnutrition?

Overweight and underweight

Some wealthier developing countries are also starting to have worrisome rates of overweight children. These countries are undergoing a rapid nutrition transition, often to diets high in saturated fats, sugar, and refined foods (UN ACC/SCN 2000). In these countries obesity coexists with undernutrition (de Onis and Blossner 2000).

Data on nutritional status during the life cycle are slowly becoming available, mainly for women. The limited data suggest that women in developing countries fall on average

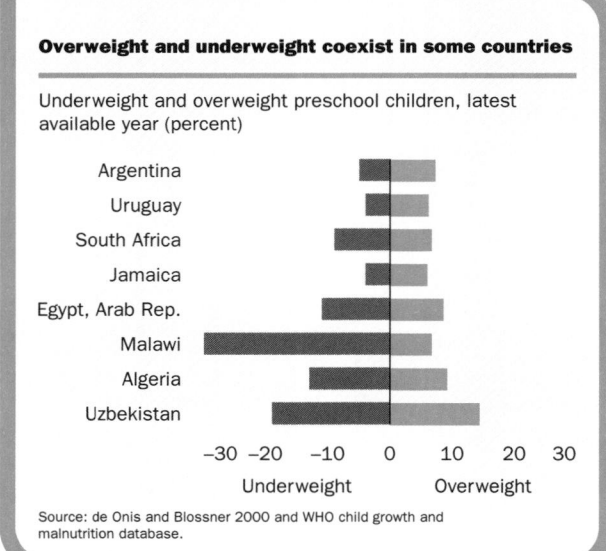

Overweight and underweight coexist in some countries

Underweight and overweight preschool children, latest available year (percent)

Source: de Onis and Blossner 2000 and WHO child growth and malnutrition database.

in the bottom quarter of weight-for-height standards and the bottom fifth of height. In addition, weight gains during pregnancy are usually half or less of those recommended (McGuire 1996).

The number of undernourished people in the developing world is expected to decline, from 777 million in 1997–99 to 576 million in 2015, halving the proportion of the population that was undernourished in 1990–92 and thus meeting the Millennium Development Goal. But the number of people undernourished in 2015 will still be around 70 percent of the 840 million people undernourished in 1990–92, far short of the World Food Summit goal of a reduction by half in the number of undernourished people.

Undernourishment and food insecurity

The chronic undernourishment measure, based on average caloric consumption (also called food inadequacy or food insecurity), developed by the Food and Agriculture Organization (FAO 2000), has the value of focusing world attention on food insecurity and food-insecure people. It also focuses the attention of national governments and international development agencies on a numerical goal and the political will to attain it, as part of the Millennium Development Goals.

However, the measure, derived largely from food supply data and an estimate of the distribution of food consumption across households, has its limitations:

• Food insecurity is an individual, household, or national phenomenon. And the average amount of food available to each person in the population, even if corrected for the possible effects of low income, is not a good predictor of food insecurity in the population. Furthermore, food insecurity can be a seasonal phenomenon even when there is aggregate food security.
• In addition to being influenced by access to food, nutrition security is also determined by the quality of care for mothers and children and the quality of the household's health environment.
• Food-insecure households often have well-nourished children, which shows that some households have adaptive behaviors that contribute to better nutrition.
• The estimation method has problems because distribution of consumption among households is often not directly measured, and food availability at the national level is subject to many unmeasured errors.

These limitations become harder to ignore with the increasing numbers of nationally representative household food consumption and expenditure surveys that are now available.

Source: Adapted from Smith 1998.

Because it is a powerful indicator of extreme poverty.

Stunting—a strong indicator of poverty

Malnutrition affects the poor more than the rich because factors associated with income poverty—such as female illiteracy, food insecurity, and a poor health environment—also cause malnutrition. Malnutrition is thus a cause and a consequence of poverty. Tracking trends in nutritional status is therefore useful in tracking the overall effectiveness of poverty reduction strategies. Stunting in children under five is the most appropriate indicator for populationwide monitoring. Stunting is an inexpensive and robust indicator when measured in a representative sample.

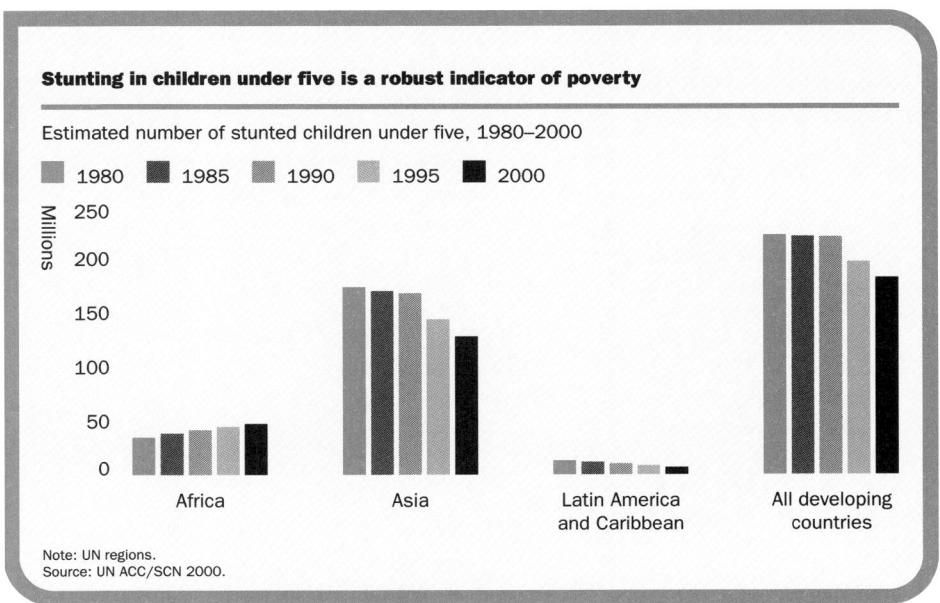

Stunting in children under five is a robust indicator of poverty

Estimated number of stunted children under five, 1980–2000

Note: UN regions.
Source: UN ACC/SCN 2000.

Higher mortality

Nearly a third of poor health outcomes are associated with malnutrition. More than half of child deaths—mostly from diarrheal diseases and respiratory infections—are associated with low weight for age. In India underweight children had two to four times the mortality rate of normal weight children (McGuire 1996). Mortality is also associated with essential micronutrient deficiencies. Severely anemic women are at considerably greater risk of death during childbirth, since anemia lowers the tolerance to blood loss and the resistance to infection. Anemia may account for almost 20 percent of maternal

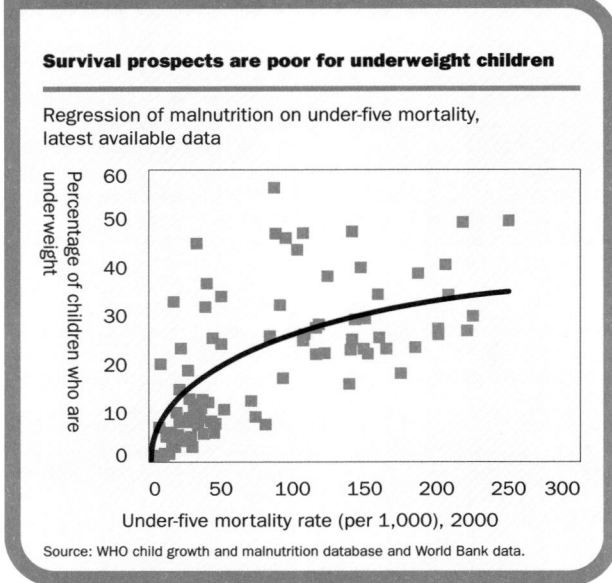

Survival prospects are poor for underweight children

Regression of malnutrition on under-five mortality, latest available data

Percentage of children who are underweight

Under-five mortality rate (per 1,000), 2000

Source: WHO child growth and malnutrition database and World Bank data.

deaths. And addressing vitamin A deficiency in areas where it is common can result in a 23 percent reduction in mortality among children between ages two and six.

The costs of malnutrition are high

Poorer health

Morbidity indicators are also linked with malnutrition. Chronic noncommunicable diseases, such as diabetes and cardiovascular disease, are associated with inadequate diets for mothers and low birthweights for infants. Malnourished children have less resistance to infection. Malnutrition has been associated with a 10–45 percent increase in the incidence of diarrhea and a 30–55 percent increase in its duration. Similarly, vitamin A–deficient children are two to four times as susceptible to respiratory disease and twice as susceptible to diarrhea.

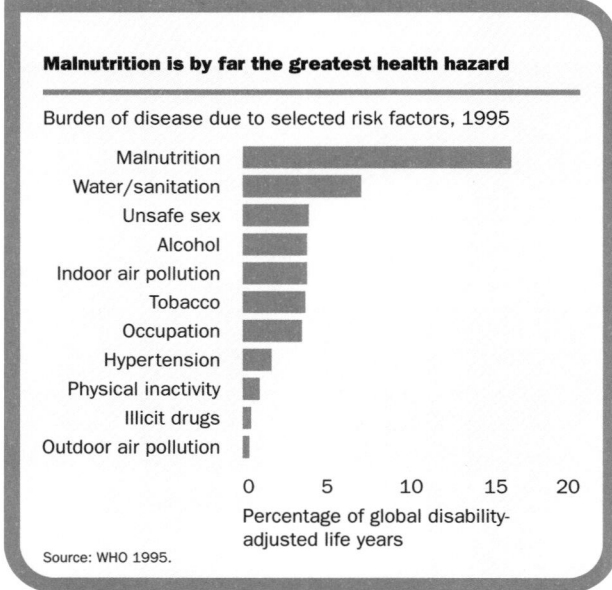

Malnutrition is by far the greatest health hazard

Burden of disease due to selected risk factors, 1995

Malnutrition
Water/sanitation
Unsafe sex
Alcohol
Indoor air pollution
Tobacco
Occupation
Hypertension
Physical inactivity
Illicit drugs
Outdoor air pollution

Percentage of global disability-adjusted life years

Source: WHO 1995.

Costs to the national health system are substantial. Poor nutritional status is by far the largest single risk factor for disease in the WHO's calculations of the total burden of disease, leading to 1.1 billion days of illness a year worldwide.

Women in poor developing countries are disproportionately affected by malnutrition and health risks, causing an intergenerational vicious circle. The incidence of low-birthweight infants is higher among women who are short and undernourished. Low-birthweight infants are more likely to be stunted. And stunted girls grow up to be short women.

Less education and learning

Childhood malnutrition is often caused by improper feeding and caring practices, making the knowledge and values of caregivers very important. Women with at least a secondary education tend to have fewer children. They also have the knowledge and skills to provide them with better nutritional care. Women's education levels therefore influence nutritional status, and nutritional status affects children's educational attainment.

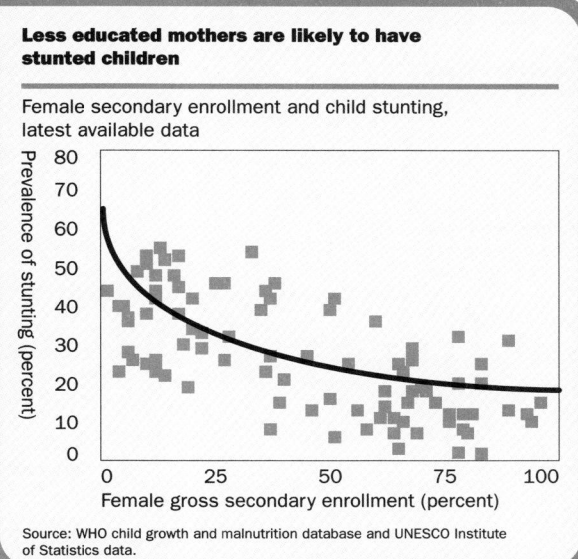

Less educated mothers are likely to have stunted children

Female secondary enrollment and child stunting, latest available data

Prevalence of stunting (percent)

Female gross secondary enrollment (percent)

Source: WHO child growth and malnutrition database and UNESCO Institute of Statistics data.

Chronic malnutrition and bouts of hunger in children affect school enrollment, attendance, and cognitive development. In Brazil a 12 percent reduction in malnutrition resulted in a 4 percent improvement in passing rates for first and second grades (McGuire 1996). A study of 9- to 11-year-olds in Indonesia found that the achievement scores of anemic children improved by more than 10 percent after 12 weeks of iron supplementation (Soemantri, Pollitt, and Kim 1985). Nutrition affects school performance indirectly as well. Stunted children tend to enroll later in school than better-nourished children. In Ghana a 10 percent increase in stunting caused a 3.5 percent increase in the age of first enrollment in school (UN ACC/SCN 2000).

throughout childhood and adult life.

Lower productivity

The economic livelihood of populations depends on the health and nutrition of adults. This reflects the legacy of malnutrition in childhood as well as whether adults have sufficient food intake to sustain both normal body weight and the physical activity needed for the tasks of daily life. Child malnutrition manifests itself in reduced schooling and shorter stature, both linked to lower wages in rural and urban settings (Thomas and Strauss 1997).

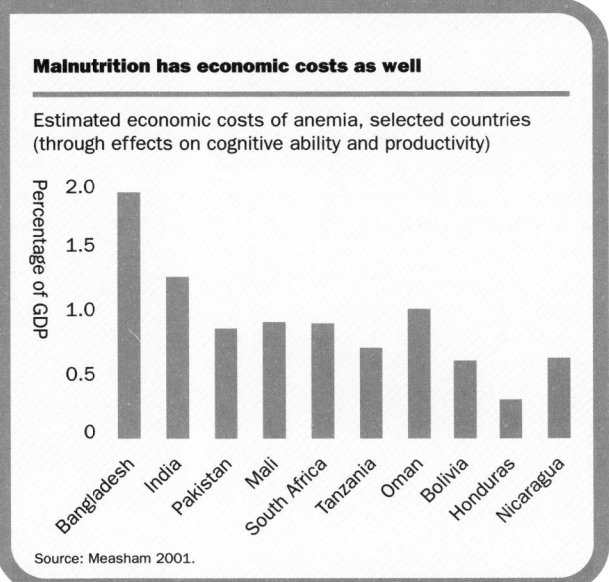

Malnutrition has economic costs as well

Estimated economic costs of anemia, selected countries (through effects on cognitive ability and productivity)

Percentage of GDP

Bangladesh, India, Pakistan, Mali, South Africa, Tanzania, Oman, Bolivia, Honduras, Nicaragua

Source: Measham 2001.

Adult nutrition affects body mass. In India a 30 percent reduction in lean body mass was associated with 20 percent lower wages (McGuire 1996). Deficiencies in vitamin A, iron, and iodine can also cause prolonged impairment, reducing productivity and gross domestic product.

Causes of poor nutrition

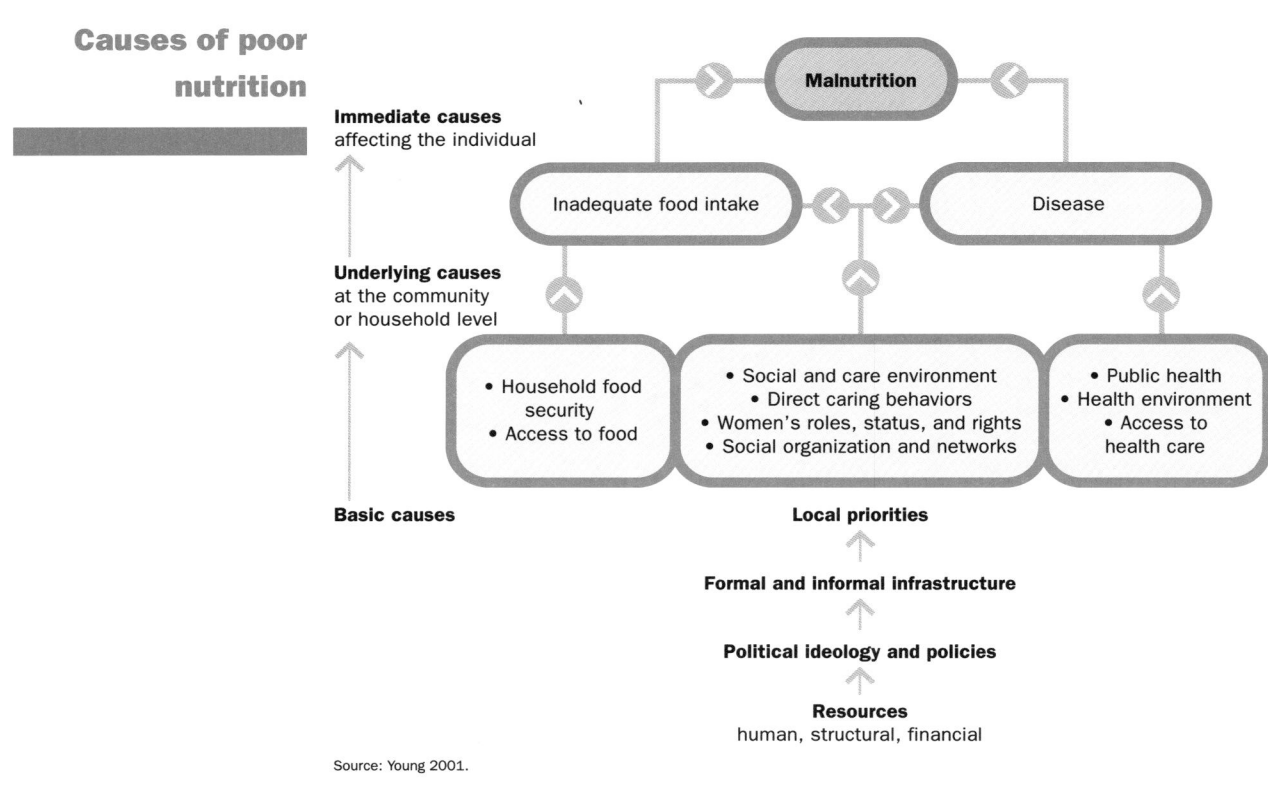

Immediate causes
affecting the individual

Underlying causes
at the community
or household level

Basic causes

Malnutrition

Inadequate food intake

Disease

- Household food
  security
- Access to food

- Social and care environment
- Direct caring behaviors
- Women's roles, status, and rights
- Social organization and networks

- Public health
- Health environment
- Access to
  health care

Local priorities

Formal and informal infrastructure

Political ideology and policies

Resources
human, structural, financial

Source: Young 2001.

Slow progress against malnutrition

There are three main reasons for the generally slow progress in tackling malnutrition (Measham 2001). First, malnutrition is a complex intersectoral problem. It encompasses biological and socioeconomic causes at both micro and macro levels. It therefore rarely has an institutional home, such as a single ministry.

Second, because malnutrition is not highly visible, its severity and effects may be ignored. Even countries with national nutrition plans may not have a clearly articulated strategy for addressing malnutrition because politicians and decision-makers fail to see the urgency and significance of the problem. And unlike education or health, malnutrition does not have a constituency to demand policies and programs to address it. Poor people often say that food is their first priority, but they lack the political power to get government to respond. If govern-

ment does respond, it usually tries to increase agricultural output or undertake expensive, ineffective food giveaways. This does not necessarily mean additional food consumption or increased income for the malnourished. Seldom is there a well-defined strategy for translating the demand for food into ways of increasing the nutritional well-being of those in need.

Third, even when confronting malnutrition is a priority, lack of government capacity results in inappropriate policies and programs, such as untargeted and unaffordable food subsidies, with implementation depending on institutions that are already overburdened. Good nutrition programs need not be expensive, but they require skilled administrators and appropriate design. As nongovernmental organizations conduct more nutrition programs, government resources become less of a constraint.

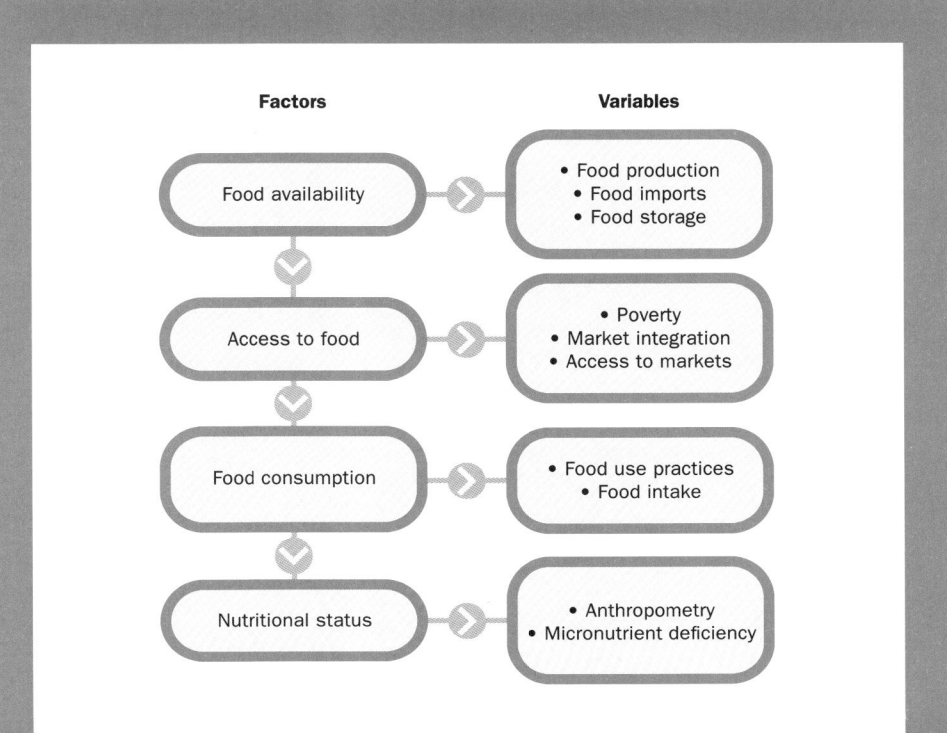

Factors		Variables
Food availability	→	• Food production • Food imports • Food storage
↓		
Access to food	→	• Poverty • Market integration • Access to markets
↓		
Food consumption	→	• Food use practices • Food intake
↓		
Nutritional status	→	• Anthropometry • Micronutrient deficiency

Food security and food policy

Food security and food policy are important in dealing with the underlying and basic causes of malnutrition. The need for adequate information on food security at global, national, and subnational levels received attention when international targets for the eradication of hunger and malnutrition were adopted. The World Food Conference in 1974 called for eradicating

hunger and malnutrition, and the World Food Summit in 1996 set the less ambitious goal of reducing the number of undernourished people by half no later than 2015.

Food security is determined by four sets of factors:
- Food availability.
- Access to food.
- Food consumption.
- Nutritional status.

Policymakers often assume that interventions at any point in the chain will have a direct effect in reducing undernutrition or food insecurity. But links are more complex than they appear. For example, a school feeding scheme may have little impact on nutritional status if parents reallocate household resources away from providing food to the child.

To monitor food security, most countries collect information from a variety of sources, including national population censuses, agricultural surveys, agroecological zoning, market monitoring, health center records, livelihood monitoring, vulnerability mapping, and income, consumption, and expenditure surveys. Often not all these data sources are fully exploited because data collection and reporting tend to be divided among ministries, and as a result databases and information are not always coordinated.

Source: Adapted from Devereux 2001.

46

The way forward

Sustained income growth can do much to reduce malnutrition in the next two decades. But economic growth by itself is unlikely to achieve the Millennium Development Goal for malnutrition (Alderman and others 2001). Although economic growth can foster improvements in nutrition, many other factors influence the process. The most important appears to be women's education, followed by food availability (or income), the government's commitment to health at local and national levels, and women's status (Smith and Haddad 2000).

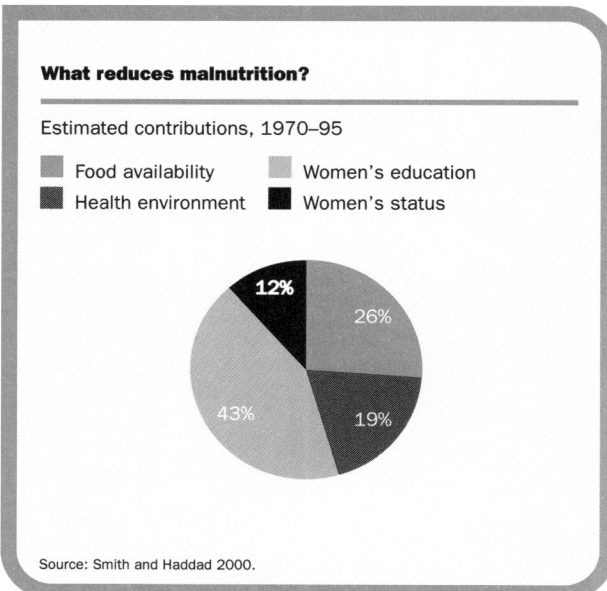

What reduces malnutrition?

Estimated contributions, 1970–95

Food availability   Women's education
Health environment   Women's status

Source: Smith and Haddad 2000.

Income growth should therefore be part of a balanced strategy for addressing nutritional problems. As income rises, so does investment in other factors that influence nutrition, notably education and health.

Monitoring and measuring malnutrition tells a vivid story.

Some impressive returns

But given the difficulty many countries face in achieving sustained economic growth, especially those in Sub-Saharan Africa, nutrition education, supplementation, fortification, and supply and price mechanisms should be considered at both national and community levels.

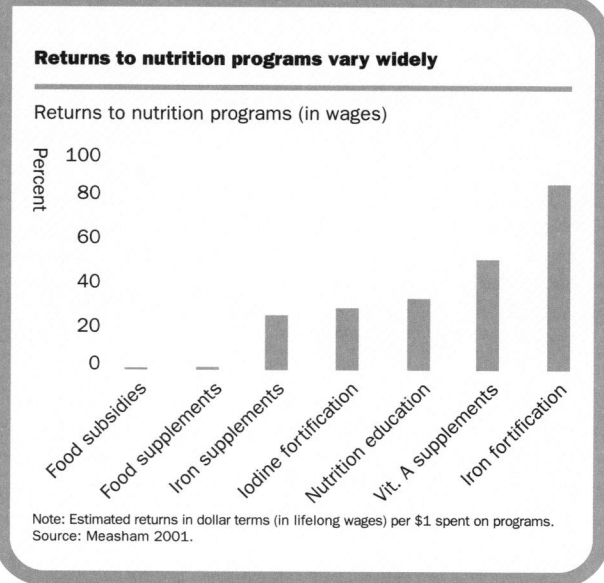

Returns to nutrition programs vary widely

Returns to nutrition programs (in wages)

Note: Estimated returns in dollar terms (in lifelong wages) per $1 spent on programs.
Source: Measham 2001.

The World Bank estimates that sustained elimination of micronutrient deficiencies could alone contribute as much as 5 percent of GDP annually to an affected country—for an investment of less than 0.3 percent of GDP (McGuire 1996). The returns per dollar invested in higher lifelong wages and lower disability are impressive.

Nutrition needs are still great

Over the past two decades progress has been dramatic in some areas of nutrition, especially in reducing micronutrient deficiencies. The proportion of stunted and underweight preschool children has declined in all regions except parts of Sub-Saharan Africa.

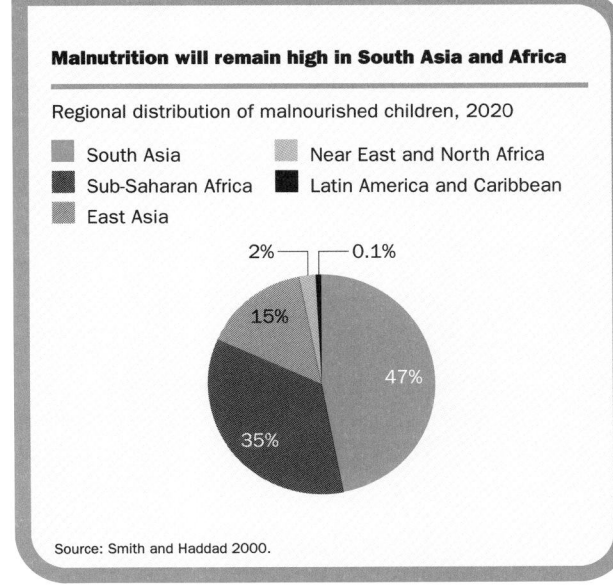

Malnutrition will remain high in South Asia and Africa

Regional distribution of malnourished children, 2020

- South Asia
- Sub-Saharan Africa
- East Asia
- Near East and North Africa
- Latin America and Caribbean

2% 0.1%
15%
47%
35%

Source: Smith and Haddad 2000.

But high proportions of Asian and African mothers are malnourished, and the numbers are expected to grow. In developing countries some 30 million children are born each year with their growth already retarded. More than 150 million preschool children are still underweight, many with anemia and vitamin A deficiency. And more children and adults are becoming overweight or obese.

Making malnutrition visible

Because malnutrition is not very visible, it is often overlooked until it becomes severe. Making it visible is central to an effective strategy. Countries need to identify appropriate indicators of nutritional status and trends—and strengthen their statistical systems for collecting, analyzing, publishing, and using data.

Tracking malnutrition

Indicators that focus attention on nutritional status and behavior can be identified at household, community, and national levels.

Household
- Growth promotion
- Breastfeeding practices
- Access to health care
- Household food security

Community
- Well-functioning food markets
- Access to clean water and sanitation
- Availability of health care
- Nutrition education

National
- Trends in child growth
- Women's health
- Girls' education
- Trends in childhood infections
- Immunization trends
- Food prices and price variability across time and regions
- Wage and employment rates, especially among the rural poor
- Income of the poor

2.1 | Population dynamics

	Total population (millions)			Average annual population growth rate (%)		Population age composition			Dependency ratios (dependents as proportion of working age population)		Crude death rate (per 1,000 people)	Crude birth rate (per 1,000 people)
						Ages 0-14 %	Ages 15-64 %	Ages 65+ %	young	old		
	1980	2000	2015	1980-2000	2000-2015	2000	2000	2000	2000	2000	2000	2000
Afghanistan	16.0	26.6 ª	37.8	2.5	2.4	43.5	53.7	2.8	0.8	0.1	22	48
Albania	2.7	3.4	4.0	1.2	1.0	30.0	64.2	5.9	0.5	0.1	6	17
Algeria	18.7	30.4	39.1	2.4	1.7	34.8	61.0	4.1	0.6	0.1	5	25
Angola	7.1	13.1	19.6	3.1	2.7	48.2	49.0	2.8	1.0	0.1	19	48
Argentina	28.1	37.0	42.8	1.4	1.0	27.7	62.6	9.7	0.4	0.2	8	19
Armenia	3.1	3.8	4.0	1.0	0.4	23.7	67.6	8.6	0.4	0.1	6	11
Australia	14.7	19.2	21.5	1.3	0.8	20.5	67.2	12.3	0.3	0.2	7	13
Austria	7.6	8.1	8.0	0.4	-0.1	16.6	67.8	15.6	0.3	0.2	10	10
Azerbaijan	6.2	8.0	9.2	1.3	0.9	29.0	64.2	6.8	0.5	0.1	6	15
Bangladesh	85.4	131.1	167.7	2.1	1.6	38.7	58.2	3.1	0.7	0.1	9	28
Belarus	9.6	10.0	9.4	0.2	-0.4	18.7	68.0	13.3	0.3	0.2	14	9
Belgium	9.8	10.3	10.3	0.2	0.0	17.3	65.7	17.0	0.3	0.3	10	11
Benin	3.5	6.3	9.0	3.0	2.4	46.4	50.9	2.7	1.0	0.1	13	39
Bolivia	5.4	8.3	10.9	2.2	1.8	39.6	56.4	4.0	0.7	0.1	9	31
Bosnia and Herzegovina	4.1	4.0	4.4	-0.1	0.6	18.9	71.2	9.9	0.3	0.1	8	12
Botswana	0.9	1.6	1.7	2.8	0.6	42.1	55.1	2.8	0.8	0.1	20	32
Brazil	121.6	170.4	201.3	1.7	1.1	28.8	66.1	5.1	0.4	0.1	7	20
Bulgaria	8.9	8.2	7.4	-0.4	-0.6	15.7	68.1	16.1	0.2	0.2	14	9
Burkina Faso	7.0	11.3	15.6	2.4	2.2	48.7	48.1	3.2	1.0	0.1	19	44
Burundi	4.1	6.8	8.8	2.5	1.7	47.6	49.6	2.9	1.0	0.1	20	40
Cambodia	6.8	12.0	15.2	2.8	1.6	43.9	53.3	2.8	0.8	0.1	12	30
Cameroon	8.7	14.9	19.4	2.7	1.8	43.1	53.2	3.7	0.8	0.1	14	37
Canada	24.6	30.8	33.6	1.1	0.6	19.1	68.3	12.6	0.3	0.2	8	11
Central African Republic	2.3	3.7	4.6	2.4	1.5	43.0	53.0	4.0	0.8	0.1	20	36
Chad	4.5	7.7	11.8	2.7	2.9	46.5	50.4	3.1	0.9	0.1	16	45
Chile	11.1	15.2	17.7	1.6	1.0	28.5	64.4	7.2	0.4	0.1	6	17
China	981.2	1,262.5	1,392.6	1.3	0.7	24.8	68.3	6.9	0.4	0.1	7	15
Hong Kong, China	5.0	6.8	7.5	1.5	0.6	16.3	73.1	10.6	0.2	0.2	5	8
Colombia	28.4	42.3	51.6	2.0	1.3	32.8	62.5	4.7	0.5	0.1	6	23
Congo, Dem. Rep.	26.9	50.9	75.6	3.2	2.6	48.8	48.4	2.9	1.0	0.1	17	46
Congo, Rep.	1.7	3.0	4.6	3.0	2.8	46.3	50.4	3.3	0.9	0.1	14	43
Costa Rica	2.3	3.8	4.7	2.6	1.5	32.4	62.5	5.1	0.5	0.1	4	20
Côte d'Ivoire	8.2	16.0	20.5	3.3	1.7	42.1	54.8	3.1	0.8	0.1	17	37
Croatia	4.6	4.4	4.2	-0.2	-0.3	18.0	67.8	14.1	0.3	0.2	12	10
Cuba	9.7	11.2	11.7	0.7	0.3	21.2	69.2	9.6	0.3	0.1	7	13
Czech Republic	10.2	10.3	9.9	0.0	-0.2	16.4	69.7	13.8	0.2	0.2	11	9
Denmark	5.1	5.3	5.4	0.2	0.1	18.3	66.7	15.0	0.3	0.2	11	12
Dominican Republic	5.7	8.4	10.1	1.9	1.3	33.5	62.2	4.3	0.5	0.1	6	23
Ecuador	8.0	12.6	15.8	2.3	1.5	33.8	61.5	4.7	0.6	0.1	6	24
Egypt, Arab Rep.	40.9	64.0	80.7	2.2	1.6	35.4	60.5	4.1	0.6	0.1	6	25
El Salvador	4.6	6.3	8.0	1.6	1.6	35.6	59.4	5.0	0.6	0.1	6	26
Eritrea	2.4	4.1	5.9	2.7	2.4	43.9	53.2	2.9	0.8	0.1	13	39
Estonia	1.5	1.4	1.3	-0.4	-0.5	17.7	67.9	14.4	0.3	0.2	13	9
Ethiopia	37.7	64.3	88.1	2.7	2.1	45.2	51.9	3.0	0.9	0.1	20	44
Finland	4.8	5.2	5.3	0.4	0.1	18.0	67.0	14.9	0.3	0.2	10	11
France	53.9	58.9	61.6	0.4	0.3	18.7	65.3	16.0	0.3	0.2	9	13
Gabon	0.7	1.2	1.7	2.9	2.2	40.2	54.0	5.8	0.7	0.1	16	36
Gambia, The	0.6	1.3	1.8	3.5	2.1	40.3	56.6	3.1	0.7	0.1	13	39
Georgia	5.1	5.0	4.8	0.0	-0.3	20.5	66.6	12.9	0.3	0.2	9	9
Germany	78.3	82.2	80.0	0.2	-0.2	15.5	68.1	16.4	0.2	0.2	11	9
Ghana	10.7	19.3	24.7	2.9	1.6	40.9	55.8	3.2	0.7	0.1	11	30
Greece	9.6	10.6	10.3	0.5	-0.2	15.1	67.4	17.6	0.2	0.3	11	12
Guatemala	6.8	11.4	16.3	2.6	2.4	43.6	52.8	3.5	0.8	0.1	7	33
Guinea	4.5	7.4	9.8	2.5	1.9	44.1	53.2	2.8	0.8	0.1	17	39
Guinea-Bissau	0.8	1.2	1.7	2.3	2.2	43.5	52.9	3.6	0.8	0.1	20	42
Haiti	5.4	8.0	10.3	2.0	1.7	40.6	55.7	3.7	0.7	0.1	13	32
Honduras	3.6	6.4	8.5	2.9	1.9	41.8	54.8	3.4	0.8	0.1	6	31

	Total population			Average annual population growth rate		Population age composition			Dependency ratios		Crude death rate	Crude birth rate
									dependents as proportion of working age population			
						Ages 0-14 %	Ages 15-64 %	Ages 65+ %	young	old	per 1,000 people	per 1,000 people
	millions 1980	2000	2015	% 1980-2000	2000-2015	2000	2000	2000	2000	2000	2000	2000
Hungary	10.7	10.0	9.4	-0.3	-0.4	16.9	68.4	14.6	0.3	0.2	14	10
India	687.3	1,015.9	1,227.9	2.0	1.3	33.5	61.5	5.0	0.5	0.1	9	25
Indonesia	148.3	210.4	250.5	1.7	1.2	30.8	64.4	4.8	0.5	0.1	7	22
Iran, Islamic Rep.	39.1	63.7	80.4	2.4	1.6	37.4	59.2	3.4	0.6	0.1	6	22
Iraq	13.0	23.3	31.2	2.9	2.0	41.6	55.5	2.9	0.8	0.1	9	31
Ireland	3.4	3.8	4.3	0.5	0.8	21.6	67.1	11.3	0.3	0.2	8	14
Israel	3.9	6.2	7.9	2.4	1.6	28.3	61.9	9.9	0.5	0.2	6	21
Italy	56.4	57.7	54.8	0.1	-0.3	14.3	67.6	18.1	0.2	0.3	10	9
Jamaica	2.1	2.6	3.1	1.1	1.0	31.5	61.3	7.2	0.5	0.1	6	21
Japan	116.8	126.9	124.6	0.4	-0.1	14.7	68.1	17.2	0.2	0.3	8	9
Jordan	2.2	4.9	6.8	4.0	2.2	40.0	57.2	2.8	0.7	0.1	4	29
Kazakhstan	14.9	14.9	15.3	0.0	0.2	27.0	66.2	6.9	0.4	0.1	10	15
Kenya	16.6	30.1	37.5	3.0	1.5	43.5	53.7	2.8	0.8	0.1	14	35
Korea, Dem. Rep.	17.2	22.3	24.2	1.3	0.6	26.5	67.6	5.9	0.4	0.1	11	18
Korea, Rep.	38.1	47.3	50.3	1.1	0.4	20.8	72.1	7.1	0.3	0.1	6	13
Kuwait	1.4	2.0	2.7	1.8	2.1	31.3	66.5	2.2	0.5	0.0	2	20
Kyrgyz Republic	3.6	4.9	5.8	1.5	1.1	33.9	60.0	6.0	0.6	0.1	7	21
Lao PDR	3.2	5.3	7.3	2.5	2.2	42.7	53.8	3.5	0.8	0.1	13	37
Latvia	2.5	2.4	2.1	-0.4	-0.7	17.4	67.8	14.8	0.3	0.2	14	9
Lebanon	3.0	4.3	5.2	1.8	1.2	31.1	62.8	6.1	0.5	0.1	6	20
Lesotho	1.4	2.0	2.3	2.0	0.8	39.3	56.6	4.2	0.7	0.1	17	33
Liberia	1.9	3.1	4.5	2.6	2.5	42.7	54.5	2.9	0.8	0.1	17	44
Libya	3.0	5.3	7.0	2.8	1.9	33.9	62.7	3.4	0.5	0.1	5	27
Lithuania	3.4	3.7	3.6	0.4	-0.2	19.5	67.2	13.4	0.3	0.2	11	9
Macedonia, FYR	1.9	2.0	2.2	0.4	0.4	22.6	67.4	10.0	0.3	0.2	8	13
Madagascar	8.9	15.5	22.5	2.8	2.5	44.7	52.3	3.0	0.9	0.1	12	40
Malawi	6.2	10.3	13.6	2.6	1.8	46.3	50.7	2.9	0.9	0.1	24	46
Malaysia	13.8	23.3	29.3	2.6	1.5	34.1	61.8	4.1	0.6	0.1	4	25
Mali	6.6	10.8	15.0	2.5	2.2	46.1	49.9	4.0	0.9	0.1	20	46
Mauritania	1.6	2.7	3.9	2.7	2.5	44.1	52.7	3.2	0.8	0.1	15	42
Mauritius	1.0	1.2	1.4	1.0	0.9	25.6	68.2	6.2	0.4	0.1	7	17
Mexico	67.6	98.0	121.1	1.9	1.4	33.1	62.1	4.7	0.5	0.1	5	25
Moldova	4.0	4.3	4.2	0.3	-0.1	23.1	67.6	9.3	0.3	0.1	11	10
Mongolia	1.7	2.4	2.9	1.8	1.3	35.2	61.0	3.8	0.6	0.1	6	22
Morocco	19.4	28.7	35.4	2.0	1.4	34.7	61.2	4.1	0.6	0.1	6	24
Mozambique	12.1	17.7	22.7	1.9	1.7	43.9	52.8	3.2	0.8	0.1	20	40
Myanmar	33.7	47.7	55.8	1.7	1.0	33.1	62.3	4.6	0.5	0.1	12	25
Namibia	1.0	1.8	2.1	2.9	1.2	43.7	52.5	3.8	0.8	0.1	17	36
Nepal	14.6	23.0	31.1	2.3	2.0	41.0	55.2	3.7	0.7	0.1	10	33
Netherlands	14.2	15.9	16.9	0.6	0.4	18.3	68.1	13.6	0.3	0.2	9	13
New Zealand	3.1	3.8	4.1	1.0	0.5	23.0	65.4	11.7	0.4	0.2	7	15
Nicaragua	2.9	5.1	7.0	2.8	2.1	42.6	54.3	3.0	0.8	0.1	5	30
Niger	5.6	10.8	16.8	3.3	2.9	49.9	48.1	2.0	1.0	0.0	19	51
Nigeria	71.1	126.9	169.4	2.9	1.9	45.1	51.9	3.0	0.9	0.1	16	40
Norway	4.1	4.5	4.8	0.5	0.4	19.8	64.9	15.4	0.3	0.2	10	13
Oman	1.1	2.4	3.3	3.9	2.2	44.1	53.4	2.5	0.8	0.1	3	28
Pakistan	82.7	138.1	192.8	2.6	2.2	41.8	54.5	3.7	0.8	0.1	8	34
Panama	2.0	2.9	3.5	1.9	1.3	31.3	63.2	5.5	0.5	0.1	5	21
Papua New Guinea	3.1	5.1	6.9	2.5	2.0	40.1	57.5	2.4	0.7	0.0	9	32
Paraguay	3.1	5.5	7.5	2.8	2.1	39.5	57.0	3.5	0.7	0.1	5	30
Peru	17.3	25.7	31.4	2.0	1.3	33.4	61.8	4.8	0.5	0.1	7	23
Philippines	48.0	75.6	97.3	2.3	1.7	37.5	58.9	3.5	0.6	0.1	5	27
Poland	35.6	38.7	38.8	0.4	0.0	19.2	68.7	12.1	0.3	0.2	10	10
Portugal	9.8	10.0	9.9	0.1	-0.1	16.7	67.7	15.6	0.3	0.2	11	12
Puerto Rico	3.2	3.9	4.4	1.0	0.7	23.8	65.7	10.5	0.4	0.2	8	15
Romania	22.2	22.4	21.4	0.1	-0.3	18.3	68.4	13.3	0.3	0.2	11	10
Russian Federation	139.0	145.6	134.5	0.2	-0.5	18.0	69.6	12.5	0.3	0.2	15	9

2.1 | Population dynamics

	Total population			Average annual population growth rate		Population age composition			Dependency ratios		Crude death rate	Crude birth rate
						Ages 0-14 %	Ages 15-64 %	Ages 65+ %	dependents as proportion of working age population		per 1,000 people	per 1,000 people
	millions			%					young	old		
	1980	2000	2015	1980-2000	2000-2015	2000	2000	2000	2000	2000	2000	2000
Rwanda	5.2	8.5	11.1	2.5	1.8	44.3	53.1	2.6	0.9	0.1	22	44
Saudi Arabia	9.4	20.7	32.1	4.0	2.9	42.9	54.1	3.0	0.8	0.1	4	33
Senegal	5.5	9.5	13.0	2.7	2.1	44.3	53.2	2.5	0.8	0.1	13	37
Sierra Leone	3.2	5.0	6.9	2.2	2.1	44.2	52.8	2.9	0.8	0.1	23	44
Singapore	2.4	4.0	4.9	2.5	1.3	21.9	70.9	7.2	0.3	0.1	4	12
Slovak Republic	5.0	5.4	5.4	0.4	0.0	19.5	69.1	11.4	0.3	0.2	10	10
Slovenia	1.9	2.0	1.9	0.2	-0.2	15.9	70.2	13.9	0.2	0.2	10	9
Somalia	6.5	8.8	14.2	1.5	3.2	48.0	49.6	2.4	1.0	0.1	17	51
South Africa	27.6	42.8	45.8	2.2	0.5	34.0	62.4	3.6	0.6	0.1	16	26
Spain	37.4	39.5	38.8	0.3	-0.1	14.7	68.3	17.0	0.2	0.3	9	10
Sri Lanka	14.7	19.4	23.0	1.4	1.1	26.3	67.4	6.3	0.4	0.1	6	18
Sudan	19.3	31.1	41.8	2.4	2.0	40.1	56.4	3.4	0.7	0.1	11	34
Swaziland	0.6	1.0	1.3	3.1	1.3	41.6	55.0	3.5	0.8	0.1	15	36
Sweden	8.3	8.9	8.8	0.3	-0.1	18.2	64.4	17.4	0.3	0.3	11	10
Switzerland	6.3	7.2	7.1	0.6	0.0	16.7	67.3	16.0	0.3	0.2	9	10
Syrian Arab Republic	8.7	16.2	22.1	3.1	2.1	40.8	56.0	3.1	0.7	0.1	5	29
Tajikistan	4.0	6.2	7.7	2.2	1.5	39.4	56.0	4.6	0.7	0.1	5	19
Tanzania	18.6	33.7	43.9	3.0	1.8	45.0	52.6	2.4	0.9	0.1	17	39
Thailand	46.7	60.7	68.7	1.3	0.8	26.7	68.1	5.2	0.4	0.1	7	17
Togo	2.5	4.5	6.0	2.9	1.9	44.3	52.6	3.1	0.8	0.1	15	37
Trinidad and Tobago	1.1	1.3	1.5	0.9	0.8	25.0	68.4	6.7	0.4	0.1	7	15
Tunisia	6.4	9.6	11.6	2.0	1.3	29.7	64.4	5.9	0.5	0.1	6	17
Turkey	44.5	65.3	77.8	1.9	1.2	30.0	64.2	5.8	0.5	0.1	6	20
Turkmenistan	2.9	5.2	6.4	3.0	1.3	37.6	58.1	4.3	0.7	0.1	7	21
Uganda	12.8	22.2	31.6	2.8	2.4	49.2	48.3	2.5	1.0	0.1	19	45
Ukraine	50.0	49.5	44.9	-0.1	-0.6	17.8	68.3	13.8	0.3	0.2	15	9
United Arab Emirates	1.0	2.9	3.8	5.1	1.8	26.0	71.3	2.7	0.4	0.0	3	17
United Kingdom	56.3	59.7	59.7	0.3	0.0	19.0	65.3	15.8	0.3	0.2	11	11
United States	227.2	281.6	317.8	1.1	0.8	21.7	66.0	12.3	0.3	0.2	9	15
Uruguay	2.9	3.3	3.7	0.7	0.6	24.8	62.3	12.9	0.4	0.2	10	16
Uzbekistan	16.0	24.8	30.1	2.2	1.3	36.3	59.1	4.7	0.6	0.1	6	22
Venezuela, RB	15.1	24.2	30.3	2.4	1.5	34.0	61.5	4.4	0.6	0.1	4	22
Vietnam	53.7	78.5	94.4	1.9	1.2	33.4	61.3	5.3	0.5	0.1	6	19
West Bank and Gaza	..	3.0	5.0	..	3.5	..	..	..	..	..	4	40
Yemen, Rep.	8.5	17.5	27.0	3.6	2.9	50.1	47.6	2.3	1.1	0.1	11	40
Yugoslavia, Fed. Rep.	9.8	10.6	10.7	0.4	0.1	20.0	66.9	13.1	0.3	0.2	11	12
Zambia	5.7	10.1	12.2	2.8	1.3	46.5	50.5	2.9	0.9	0.1	21	40
Zimbabwe	7.1	12.6	14.0	2.9	0.7	45.2	51.6	3.2	0.9	0.1	18	30

World	4,429.3 s	6,057.3 s	7,101.2 s	1.6 w	1.1 w	30.0 w	63.1 w	6.9 w	0.47 w	0.11 w	9 w	22 w
Low income	1,609.5	2,459.8	3,090.3	2.1	1.5	36.9	58.7	4.4	0.6	0.1	11	29
Middle income	2,030.0	2,694.6	3,063.4	1.4	0.9	27.4	66.0	6.6	0.4	0.1	8	18
Lower middle income	1,563.7	2,047.6	2,306.4	1.3	0.8	26.9	66.4	6.8	0.4	0.1	8	17
Upper middle income	466.3	647.0	757.1	1.6	1.0	29.1	64.6	6.2	0.5	0.1	7	20
Low & middle income	3,639.5	5,154.4	6,153.7	1.7	1.2	31.9	62.5	5.6	0.5	0.1	9	23
East Asia & Pacific	1,396.9	1,855.2	2,097.8	1.4	0.8	26.9	66.8	6.2	0.4	0.1	7	17
Europe & Central Asia	425.8	474.3	478.8	0.5	0.1	22.0	67.1	10.8	0.3	0.2	11	12
Latin America & Carib.	359.6	515.7	625.4	1.8	1.3	31.5	63.0	5.4	0.5	0.1	6	22
Middle East & N. Africa	174.0	295.2	388.7	2.6	1.8	37.8	58.6	3.6	0.6	0.1	6	26
South Asia	901.4	1,355.1	1,681.9	2.0	1.4	35.1	60.3	4.6	0.6	0.1	9	27
Sub-Saharan Africa	381.7	658.9	881.1	2.7	1.9	44.4	52.6	3.0	0.8	0.1	17	39
High income	789.8	902.9	947.5	0.7	0.3	18.5	66.9	14.7	0.3	0.2	9	12
Europe EMU	286.7	304.0	302.3	0.3	0.0	16.2	67.3	16.4	0.2	0.2	10	11

a. Estimate does not account for recent refugee flows.

About the data

Population estimates are usually based on national population censuses, but the frequency and quality of these vary by country. Most countries conduct a complete enumeration no more than once a decade. Pre- and postcensus estimates are interpolations or extrapolations based on demographic models. Errors and undercounting occur even in high-income countries; in developing countries such errors may be substantial because of limits in the transport, communications, and other resources required to conduct a full census. The quality and reliability of official demographic data are also affected by the public trust in the government, the government's commitment to full and accurate enumeration, the confidentiality and protection against misuse accorded to census data, and the independence of census agencies from undue political influence. Moreover, the international comparability of population indicators is limited by differences in the concepts, definitions, data collection procedures, and estimation methods used by national statistical agencies and other organizations that collect population data.

Of the 152 economies listed in the table, 118 (about 78 percent) conducted a census between 1990 and 2001. The currentness of a census, along with the availability of complementary data from surveys or registration systems, is one of many objective ways to judge the quality of demographic data. In some European countries registration systems offer complete information on population in the absence of a census. See *Primary data documentation* for the most recent census or survey year and for registration completeness.

Current population estimates for developing countries that lack recent census-based data, and pre- and postcensus estimates for countries with census data, are provided by national statistical offices, the United Nations Population Division, and other agencies. The standard estimation method requires fertility, mortality, and net migration data, which are often collected from sample surveys, some of which may be small or limited in coverage. The population estimates are the product of demographic modeling and so are susceptible to biases and errors because of shortcomings in the model as well as in the data. Population projections are made using the cohort component method.

The growth rate of the total population conceals the fact that different age groups may grow at very different rates. In many developing countries the population under 15 was earlier growing rapidly, but is now starting to shrink. Previously high fertility rates and declining mortality rates are now reflected in the larger share of the working-age population.

The variations in the proportions of children, aged persons, and persons of working age are taken into account in the dependency ratio.

Separate calculations of young-age dependency and old-age dependency reflect the burden of dependency that the working-age population must bear in relation to the proportion of children and the aged in the population. Age dependency ratios are a measure of the age composition, not of economic dependency. It should be noted that some people in the dependent age range are part of the labor force, and many persons in the working age range are not in the labor force.

The vital rates shown in the table are based on data derived from birth and death registration systems, censuses, and sample surveys conducted by national statistical offices, United Nations agencies, and other organizations. The estimates for 2000 for many countries are based on extrapolations of levels and trends measured in earlier years.

Vital registers are the preferred source of these data, but in many developing countries systems for registering births and deaths do not exist or are incomplete because of deficiencies in geographic coverage or coverage of events. Many developing countries carry out specialized household surveys that estimate vital rates by asking respondents about births and deaths in the recent past. Estimates derived in this way are subject to sampling errors as well as errors due to inaccurate recall by the respondents.

The United Nations Statistics Division monitors the completeness of vital registration systems. The share of countries with at least 90 percent complete vital registration increased from 45 percent in 1988 to 53 percent in 1999. Still, some of the most populous developing countries—China, India, Indonesia, Brazil, Pakistan, Bangladesh, Nigeria—do not have complete vital registration systems. Fewer than 30 percent of births and fewer than 40 percent of deaths worldwide are thought to be registered and reported.

International migration is the only other factor besides birth and death rates that directly determines a country's population growth. In the high-income countries about 40 percent of annual population growth in 1990–95 was due to migration, while in the developing countries migration reduced population growth by about 3 percent. Estimating international migration is difficult. At any time many people are located outside their home country as tourists, workers, or refugees or for other reasons. Standards relating to the duration and purpose of international moves that qualify as migration vary, and accurate estimates require information on flows into and out of countries that is difficult to collect.

Definitions

- **Total population** of an economy includes all residents who are present regardless of legal status or citizenship— except for refugees not permanently settled in the country of asylum, who are generally considered part of the population of their country of origin. The indicators shown are midyear estimates for 1980 and 2000 and projections for 2015.
- **Average annual population growth rate** is the exponential change for the period indicated. See *Statistical methods* for more information.
- **Population age composition** represents the percentage of the total population that is in specific age groups. • **Dependency ratios** are the ratios of dependents—people younger than 15 and older than 64—to the working-age population—those between ages 15–64.
- **Crude death rate** and **crude birth rate** are the number of deaths and the number of live births occurring during the year, per 1,000 population estimated at midyear. Subtracting the crude death rate from the crude birth rate provides the rate of natural increase, which is equal to the population growth rate in the absence of migration.

Data sources

The World Bank's population estimates are produced by its Human Development Network and Development Data Group in consultation with its operational staff and country offices. Important inputs to the World Bank's demographic work come from the following sources: census reports and other statistical publications from national statistical offices; Demographic and Health Surveys conducted by national agencies, Macro International, and the U.S. Centers for Disease Control and Prevention; United Nations Statistics Division, *Population and Vital Statistics Report* (quarterly); United Nations Population Division, *World Population Prospects: The 2000 Revision;* Eurostat, *Demographic Statistics* (various years); Centro Latinoamericano de Demografía, *Boletín Demográfico* (various years); and U.S. Bureau of the Census, International Database.

2.2 | Labor force structure

	Population ages 15-64		Labor force						
	millions			Total millions		Average annual growth rate %		Female % of labor force	
	1980	2000	1980	2000	2010	1980-2000	2000-2010	1980	2000
Afghanistan	8.5	14.2	6.8	11.2	13.8	2.5	2.1	34.8	35.5
Albania	1.6	2.2	1.2	1.7	2.0	1.7	1.5	38.8	41.3
Algeria	9.3	18.6	4.8	10.2	14.6	3.7	3.5	21.4	27.6
Angola	3.7	6.4	3.5	6.0	8.1	2.7	3.0	47.0	46.3
Argentina	17.2	23.2	10.7	15.0	18.5	1.7	2.1	27.6	33.2
Armenia	2.0	2.6	1.4	1.9	2.2	1.4	1.3	47.9	48.6
Australia	9.6	12.9	6.7	9.8	10.6	1.9	0.8	36.8	43.7
Austria	4.8	5.5	3.4	3.8	3.8	0.6	0.0	40.5	40.3
Azerbaijan	3.7	5.2	2.7	3.6	4.3	1.4	1.9	47.5	44.6
Bangladesh	44.8	76.2	40.3	69.2	86.7	2.7	2.3	42.3	42.4
Belarus	6.4	6.8	5.1	5.3	5.3	0.2	0.1	49.9	49.0
Belgium	6.5	6.7	3.9	4.3	4.2	0.4	-0.2	33.9	40.9
Benin	1.8	3.2	1.7	2.8	3.7	2.7	2.8	47.0	48.3
Bolivia	2.9	4.7	2.0	3.4	4.4	2.6	2.5	33.3	37.8
Bosnia and Herzegovina	2.7	2.8	1.6	1.9	2.0	0.7	0.9	32.8	38.1
Botswana	0.4	0.9	0.4	0.7	0.8	2.9	0.9	50.1	45.3
Brazil	70.3	112.6	47.7	79.7	90.0	2.6	1.2	28.4	35.5
Bulgaria	5.8	5.6	4.6	4.2	3.9	-0.5	-0.7	45.3	48.2
Burkina Faso	3.4	5.4	3.8	5.6	6.7	1.9	1.9	47.6	46.5
Burundi	2.1	3.4	2.3	3.7	4.6	2.5	2.2	50.2	48.7
Cambodia	3.9	6.4	3.7	6.3	7.9	2.7	2.3	55.4	51.7
Cameroon	4.5	7.9	3.6	6.1	7.5	2.5	2.1	36.8	38.0
Canada	16.7	21.0	12.2	16.5	17.5	1.5	0.6	39.5	45.8
Central African Republic	1.3	2.0	1.2	1.8	2.1	1.9	1.5	..	..
Chad	2.3	3.9	2.2	3.7	5.0	2.6	3.0	43.4	44.7
Chile	6.8	9.8	3.8	6.2	7.5	2.4	1.9	26.3	33.6
China	586.3	862.2	538.7	756.8	818.3	1.7	0.8	43.2	45.2
Hong Kong, China	3.4	5.0	2.5	3.6	3.9	1.9	0.8	34.3	37.1
Colombia	15.8	26.4	9.4	18.5	23.0	3.4	2.2	26.2	38.7
Congo, Dem. Rep.	13.8	24.6	12.0	21.0	28.2	2.8	3.0	44.5	43.4
Congo, Rep.	0.9	1.5	0.7	1.2	1.7	2.9	3.0	42.4	43.5
Costa Rica	1.3	2.4	0.8	1.5	1.9	3.3	2.1	20.8	31.1
Côte d'Ivoire	4.2	8.8	3.3	6.4	8.0	3.3	2.3	32.2	33.4
Croatia	3.1	3.0	2.2	2.1	2.0	-0.2	-0.2	40.2	44.2
Cuba	5.9	7.7	3.7	5.5	5.9	2.0	0.7	31.4	39.5
Czech Republic	6.5	7.2	5.3	5.8	5.5	0.4	-0.4	47.1	47.3
Denmark	3.3	3.6	2.7	2.9	2.8	0.4	-0.5	44.0	46.4
Dominican Republic	3.1	5.2	2.1	3.7	4.6	2.8	2.2	24.7	30.8
Ecuador	4.2	7.8	2.5	4.9	6.5	3.3	2.7	20.1	28.0
Egypt, Arab Rep.	23.1	38.7	14.3	24.4	32.2	2.7	2.8	26.5	30.4
El Salvador	2.4	3.7	1.6	2.7	3.6	2.8	2.9	26.5	36.5
Eritrea	1.3	2.2	1.2	2.1	2.7	2.6	2.7	47.4	47.4
Estonia	1.0	0.9	0.8	0.8	0.7	-0.4	-0.2	50.6	49.0
Ethiopia	19.9	33.4	16.9	27.6	34.6	2.4	2.3	42.3	40.9
Finland	3.2	3.5	2.4	2.6	2.5	0.4	-0.5	46.5	48.1
France	34.4	38.5	23.8	26.7	27.6	0.6	0.3	40.1	45.1
Gabon	0.4	0.7	0.4	0.6	0.7	2.2	2.0	45.0	44.7
Gambia, The	0.3	0.7	0.3	0.7	0.8	3.5	2.4	44.8	45.1
Georgia	3.3	3.3	2.6	2.5	2.5	-0.2	0.1	49.3	46.8
Germany	51.6	55.9	37.5	40.9	40.8	0.4	0.0	40.1	42.3
Ghana	5.5	10.8	5.1	9.2	11.2	2.9	2.0	51.0	50.5
Greece	6.2	7.1	3.8	4.6	4.6	1.0	0.1	27.9	37.8
Guatemala	3.5	6.0	2.3	4.2	6.0	2.9	3.5	22.4	28.9
Guinea	2.3	3.9	2.3	3.5	4.3	2.1	2.0	47.1	47.2
Guinea-Bissau	0.4	0.6	0.4	0.6	0.7	1.9	2.3	39.9	40.5
Haiti	2.9	4.4	2.5	3.5	4.2	1.6	1.8	44.6	42.9
Honduras	1.8	3.5	1.2	2.4	3.4	3.5	3.3	25.2	31.8

	Population ages 15-64		Labor force						
	millions		Total millions			Average annual growth rate %		Female % of labor force	
	1980	2000	1980	2000	2010	1980-2000	2000-2010	1980	2000
Hungary	6.9	6.9	5.1	4.8	4.6	-0.3	-0.5	43.3	44.7
India	394.5	625.2	299.5	450.8	543.6	2.0	1.9	33.7	32.3
Indonesia	83.2	135.6	58.6	101.8	124.5	2.8	2.0	35.2	40.8
Iran, Islamic Rep.	20.5	37.7	11.7	19.7	27.7	2.6	3.4	20.4	27.1
Iraq	6.7	12.9	3.5	6.5	8.6	3.0	2.8	17.3	19.7
Ireland	2.0	2.5	1.3	1.6	1.8	1.2	1.3	28.1	34.5
Israel	2.3	3.9	1.5	2.7	3.5	3.1	2.5	33.7	41.2
Italy	36.4	39.0	22.6	25.7	24.7	0.7	-0.4	32.9	38.5
Jamaica	1.1	1.6	1.0	1.4	1.6	1.8	1.5	46.3	46.2
Japan	78.7	86.4	57.2	68.3	66.1	0.9	-0.3	37.9	41.4
Jordan	1.0	2.8	0.5	1.5	2.0	5.2	3.4	14.7	24.6
Kazakhstan	9.1	9.8	7.0	7.3	7.7	0.2	0.6	47.6	47.1
Kenya	7.8	16.2	7.8	15.5	19.0	3.4	2.0	46.0	46.1
Korea, Dem. Rep.	10.5	15.1	7.5	11.7	12.3	2.2	0.5	44.8	43.3
Korea, Rep.	23.7	34.1	15.5	24.2	26.6	2.2	0.9	38.7	41.4
Kuwait	0.8	1.3	0.5	0.8	1.2	2.4	4.0	13.1	31.3
Kyrgyz Republic	2.1	2.9	1.5	2.1	2.6	1.6	2.1	47.5	47.3
Lao PDR	1.8	2.8	1.7	2.5	3.3	2.1	2.6	..	..
Latvia	1.7	1.6	1.4	1.3	1.3	-0.5	-0.4	50.8	50.5
Lebanon	1.6	2.7	0.8	1.5	2.0	2.9	2.6	22.6	29.6
Lesotho	0.7	1.2	0.6	0.8	0.9	1.9	1.2	37.9	36.9
Liberia	1.0	1.7	0.8	1.3	1.6	2.3	2.1	38.4	39.6
Libya	1.6	3.3	0.9	1.5	1.9	2.4	2.4	18.6	23.1
Lithuania	2.2	2.5	1.8	1.9	2.0	0.3	0.2	49.7	48.0
Macedonia, FYR	1.2	1.4	0.8	1.0	1.0	0.8	0.6	36.1	41.7
Madagascar	4.6	8.1	4.3	7.3	9.7	2.6	2.9	45.2	44.7
Malawi	3.1	5.2	3.1	5.0	6.0	2.3	1.9	50.6	48.6
Malaysia	7.8	14.4	5.3	9.6	12.7	3.0	2.8	33.7	37.9
Mali	3.3	5.4	3.4	5.3	6.6	2.2	2.3	46.7	46.2
Mauritania	0.8	1.4	0.7	1.2	1.6	2.5	2.7	45.0	43.6
Mauritius	0.6	0.8	0.3	0.5	0.6	2.0	1.1	25.7	32.6
Mexico	34.5	60.9	22.0	40.4	50.9	3.0	2.3	26.9	33.2
Moldova	2.6	2.9	2.1	2.2	2.2	0.1	0.2	50.3	48.6
Mongolia	0.9	1.5	0.8	1.2	1.5	2.2	2.1	45.7	47.0
Morocco	10.2	17.6	7.0	11.5	14.7	2.5	2.5	33.5	34.7
Mozambique	6.4	9.3	6.7	9.2	11.1	1.6	1.9	49.0	48.4
Myanmar	18.6	29.7	17.1	25.4	29.3	2.0	1.5	43.7	43.4
Namibia	0.5	0.9	0.4	0.7	0.8	2.6	1.4	40.1	40.9
Nepal	8.1	12.7	7.1	10.7	13.6	2.1	2.4	38.8	40.5
Netherlands	9.4	10.8	5.6	7.4	7.6	1.4	0.2	31.5	40.6
New Zealand	2.0	2.5	1.3	1.9	2.0	1.9	0.6	34.3	45.0
Nicaragua	1.5	2.8	1.0	2.1	2.9	3.6	3.4	27.6	35.9
Niger	2.7	5.2	2.8	5.1	7.0	3.0	3.2	44.6	44.3
Nigeria	37.0	65.9	29.5	50.3	63.2	2.7	2.3	36.2	36.5
Norway	2.6	2.9	1.9	2.3	2.4	0.9	0.3	40.5	46.4
Oman	0.6	1.3	0.3	0.6	0.8	3.3	2.7	6.2	17.1
Pakistan	45.4	75.3	29.3	51.7	71.4	2.8	3.2	22.7	28.6
Panama	1.1	1.8	0.7	1.2	1.5	2.8	2.0	29.9	35.3
Papua New Guinea	1.7	2.9	1.5	2.5	3.2	2.5	2.3	41.7	42.2
Paraguay	1.7	3.1	1.1	2.1	2.8	3.0	3.0	26.7	30.0
Peru	9.4	15.9	5.4	9.7	12.6	2.9	2.6	23.9	31.3
Philippines	25.8	44.5	18.7	31.9	41.0	2.7	2.5	35.0	37.8
Poland	23.3	26.6	18.5	19.9	20.3	0.4	0.2	45.3	46.4
Portugal	6.2	6.8	4.6	5.1	5.0	0.5	-0.1	38.7	44.0
Puerto Rico	1.9	2.6	1.0	1.5	1.7	1.9	1.2	31.8	37.2
Romania	14.0	15.4	10.9	10.7	10.6	-0.1	-0.1	45.8	44.5
Russian Federation	94.7	101.2	76.0	77.7	77.0	0.1	-0.1	49.4	49.2

2.2 | Labor force structure

	Population ages 15-64		Labor force						
	millions			Total millions		Average annual growth rate %		Female % of labor force	
	1980	2000	1980	2000	2010	1980-2000	2000-2010	1980	2000
Rwanda	2.5	4.5	2.6	4.6	5.8	2.8	2.2	49.1	48.8
Saudi Arabia	5.0	11.2	2.8	6.8	9.6	4.5	3.4	7.6	16.1
Senegal	2.9	5.1	2.5	4.3	5.4	2.6	2.3	42.2	42.6
Sierra Leone	1.7	2.7	1.2	1.9	2.4	2.0	2.4	35.5	36.8
Singapore	1.6	2.8	1.1	2.0	2.2	2.9	1.1	34.6	39.1
Slovak Republic	3.2	3.7	2.5	3.0	3.0	0.9	0.2	45.3	47.8
Slovenia	1.2	1.4	1.0	1.0	1.0	0.3	-0.3	45.8	46.5
Somalia	3.3	4.4	3.0	3.8	5.2	1.2	3.3	43.4	43.4
South Africa	15.2	26.7	10.3	17.0	18.4	2.5	0.8	35.1	37.8
Spain	23.5	27.0	14.0	17.4	17.6	1.1	0.1	28.3	37.2
Sri Lanka	8.9	13.1	5.4	8.5	10.1	2.2	1.7	26.9	36.6
Sudan	10.2	17.6	7.1	12.4	16.2	2.8	2.6	26.9	29.5
Swaziland	0.3	0.6	0.2	0.4	0.5	3.2	2.0	33.5	37.7
Sweden	5.3	5.7	4.2	4.8	4.6	0.7	-0.3	43.8	48.0
Switzerland	4.2	4.8	3.1	3.9	3.9	1.2	0.0	36.7	40.5
Syrian Arab Republic	4.2	9.1	2.5	5.2	7.5	3.7	3.8	23.5	27.0
Tajikistan	2.1	3.5	1.5	2.4	3.3	2.3	3.0	46.9	44.9
Tanzania	9.3	17.7	9.5	17.3	21.1	3.0	2.0	49.8	49.1
Thailand	26.9	41.4	24.4	36.8	40.8	2.1	1.0	47.4	46.3
Togo	1.3	2.4	1.1	1.9	2.3	2.7	2.3	39.3	40.0
Trinidad and Tobago	0.7	0.9	0.4	0.6	0.7	1.6	1.6	31.4	34.3
Tunisia	3.5	6.2	2.2	3.8	4.8	2.7	2.4	28.9	31.7
Turkey	24.9	41.9	18.7	31.3	37.1	2.6	1.7	35.5	37.6
Turkmenistan	1.6	3.0	1.2	2.3	2.9	3.2	2.4	47.0	45.9
Uganda	6.4	10.7	6.6	10.9	14.0	2.5	2.5	47.9	47.6
Ukraine	33.4	33.8	26.4	25.1	24.4	-0.3	-0.3	50.2	48.9
United Arab Emirates	0.7	2.1	0.6	1.4	1.7	4.7	1.9	5.1	14.8
United Kingdom	36.1	39.0	26.9	29.9	29.7	0.5	-0.1	38.9	44.1
United States	150.6	185.8	110.1	144.7	158.0	1.4	0.9	41.0	46.0
Uruguay	1.8	2.1	1.2	1.5	1.7	1.4	0.9	30.8	41.8
Uzbekistan	8.6	14.6	6.5	10.5	13.3	2.4	2.4	48.0	46.9
Venezuela, RB	8.5	14.9	5.2	9.9	12.8	3.3	2.6	26.7	34.8
Vietnam	28.6	48.1	25.6	40.4	48.0	2.3	1.7	48.1	48.9
West Bank and Gaza	..	..	..	..	..	..	..	..	..
Yemen, Rep.	4.0	8.3	2.5	5.5	7.7	4.0	3.3	32.5	28.1
Yugoslavia, Fed. Rep.	6.5	7.1	4.5	5.1	5.2	0.6	0.3	38.7	42.9
Zambia	2.9	5.1	2.4	4.3	5.1	2.9	1.8	45.4	44.8
Zimbabwe	3.5	6.5	3.2	5.8	6.6	3.0	1.2	44.4	44.5

World	**2,600.9 s**	**3,806.4 s**	**2,036.1 s**	**2,943.2 s**	**3,380.2 s**	**1.8 w**	**1.4 w**	**39.1 w**	**40.6 w**
Low income	894.7	1,443.2	708.7	1,115.1	1,367.6	2.3	2.0	37.8	37.8
Middle income	1,200.1	1,774.6	969.3	1,388.8	1,558.3	1.8	1.2	40.2	42.1
Lower middle income	929.9	1,356.8	785.4	1,100.4	1,223.6	1.7	1.1	41.9	43.4
Upper middle income	270.2	417.8	183.9	288.4	334.7	2.2	1.5	33.0	36.7
Low & middle income	2,094.8	3,217.8	1,678.0	2,503.9	2,926.0	2.0	1.6	39.2	40.2
East Asia & Pacific	820.4	1,239.7	719.3	1,051.7	1,170.0	1.9	1.1	42.5	44.4
Europe & Central Asia	274.2	318.4	214.1	238.1	249.0	0.5	0.4	46.7	46.3
Latin America & Carib.	201.0	324.9	129.8	222.1	269.1	2.7	1.9	27.8	34.8
Middle East & N. Africa	91.6	171.2	54.1	99.0	134.5	3.0	3.1	23.8	27.7
South Asia	510.7	817.4	388.7	602.6	739.9	2.2	2.1	33.8	33.4
Sub-Saharan Africa	197.0	346.3	172.0	290.5	363.5	2.6	2.2	42.0	42.0
High income	506.2	588.6	358.1	439.4	454.3	1.0	0.3	38.4	43.2
Europe EMU	185.1	204.6	123.4	141.0	141.2	0.7	0.0	36.4	41.3

2002 World Development Indicators

About the data

The labor force is the supply of labor available for the production of goods and services in an economy. It includes people who are currently employed and people who are unemployed but seeking work as well as first-time job-seekers. Not everyone who works is included, however. Unpaid workers, family workers, and students are among those usually omitted, and in some countries members of the military are not counted. The size of the labor force tends to vary during the year as seasonal workers enter and leave it.

Data on the labor force are compiled by the International Labour Organization (ILO) from censuses or labor force surveys. For international comparisons the most comprehensive source is labor force surveys. Despite the ILO's efforts to encourage the use of international standards, labor force data are not fully comparable because of differences among countries, and sometimes within countries, in their scope and coverage. In some countries data on the labor force refer to people above a specific age, while in others there is no specific age provision. The reference period of the census or survey is another important source of differences: in some countries data refer to people's status on the day of the census or survey or during a specific period before the inquiry date, while in others the data are recorded without reference to any period. In developing countries, where the household is often the basic unit of production and all members contribute to output, but some at low intensity or irregular intervals, the estimated labor force may be significantly smaller than the numbers actually working (ILO, *Yearbook of Labour Statistics 1997*).

The labor force estimates in the table were calculated by World Bank staff by applying economic activity rates from the ILO database to World Bank population estimates to create a series consistent with these population estimates. This procedure sometimes results in estimates of labor force size that differ slightly from those in the ILO's *Yearbook of Labour Statistics*. The population ages 15–64 is often used to provide a rough estimate of the potential labor force. But in many developing countries children under 15 work full or part time. And in some high-income countries many workers postpone retirement past age 65. As a result, labor force participation rates calculated in this way may systematically over- or underestimate actual rates.

In general, estimates of women in the labor force are lower than those of men and are not comparable internationally, reflecting the fact that for women, demographic, social, legal, and cultural trends and norms determine whether their activities are regarded as economic. In many countries large numbers of women work on farms or in other family enterprises without pay, while others work in or near their homes, mixing work and family activities during the day. Countries differ in the criteria used to determine the extent to which such workers are to be counted as part of the labor force.

Figure 2.2

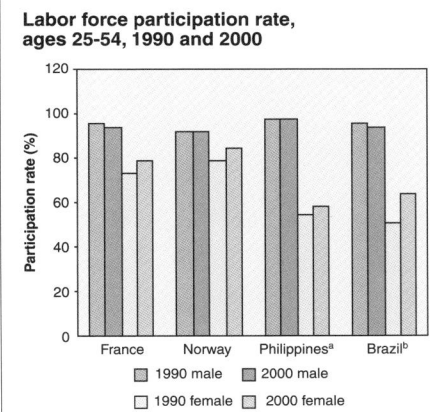

Labor force participation rate, ages 25-54, 1990 and 2000

Participation rate (%) — France, Norway, Philippines[a], Brazil[b]

☐ 1990 male   ■ 2000 male
☐ 1990 female   ☐ 2000 female

a. Data refer to 1999 rather than 2000. b. Data refer to 1998 rather than 2000.

Source: ILO. *Key Indicators of the Labour Market* database (2001-02).

The analysis of labor force participation by sex shows that for economies for which information is available, women are less likely than men to participate in the labor force. This reflects whether their work is regarded as economic as it does the competing demands of household work and childbearing and childcare.

For the majority of economies, the gap between male and female labor force participation has been falling. This results from both the reduced rates for men and the rising rates for women.

Definitions

• **Population ages 15–64** is the number of people who could potentially be economically active. • **Total labor force** comprises people who meet the ILO definition of the economically active population: all people who supply labor for the production of goods and services during a specified period. It includes both the employed and the unemployed. While national practices vary in the treatment of such groups as the armed forces and seasonal or part-time workers, the labor force generally includes the armed forces, the unemployed, and first-time job-seekers, but excludes homemakers and other unpaid caregivers and workers in the informal sector. • **Average annual growth rate of the labor force** is calculated using the exponential endpoint method (see *Statistical methods* for more information). • **Females as a percentage of the labor force** show the extent to which women are active in the labor force.

Data sources

The population estimates are from the World Bank's population database. The economic activity rates are from the ILO database Estimates and Projections of the Economically Active Population, 1950–2010. The ILO publishes estimates of the economically active population in its *Yearbook of Labour Statistics*.

2.3 | Employment by economic activity

2002 World Development Indicators

	Agriculture				Industry				Services			
	Male % of male labor force		Female % of female labor force		Male % of male labor force		Female % of female labor force		Male % of male labor force		Female % of female labor force	
	1980-82ᵃ	1998-2000ᵃ	1980-82ᵃ	1998-2000ᵃ	1980-82ᵃ	1998-2000ᵃ	1980-82ᵃ	1998-2000ᵃ	1980-82ᵃ	1998-2000ᵃ	1980-82ᵃ	1998-2000ᵃ
Afghanistan	66	..	86	..	9	..	12	..	26	..	2	..
Albania	..	..	..	..	..	..	..	..	..	..	..	..
Algeria	27	..	69	..	33	..	6	..	40	..	25	..
Angola	67	..	87	..	13	..	1	..	20	..	11	..
Argentina	..	1	..	0 ᵇ	..	34	..	10	..	65	..	89
Armenia	..	..	..	..	..	..	..	..	..	..	..	..
Australia	8	6	4	4	39	30	16	10	53	64	79	86
Austria	..	6	..	7	..	43	..	14	..	52	..	79
Azerbaijan	..	..	..	..	..	..	..	..	..	..	..	..
Bangladesh	..	..	..	..	..	..	..	..	..	..	..	..
Belarus	..	..	..	..	..	..	..	..	..	..	..	..
Belgium	..	3	..	2	..	37	..	13	..	60	..	86
Benin	66	..	69	..	10	..	4	..	24	..	27	..
Bolivia	52	58 ᶜ	28	2 ᶜ	21	40 ᶜ	19	16 ᶜ	27	58 ᶜ	53	82 ᶜ
Bosnia and Herzegovina	26	..	38	..	45	..	24	..	30	..	39	..
Botswana	6	..	3	..	41	..	8	..	53	..	89	..
Brazil	34	26	20	19	30	27	13	10	36	47	67	71
Bulgaria	..	..	..	..	..	..	..	..	..	..	..	..
Burkina Faso	92	..	93	..	3	..	2	..	5	..	5	..
Burundi	..	..	..	..	..	..	..	..	..	..	..	..
Cambodia	..	..	..	..	..	..	..	..	..	..	..	..
Cameroon	65	..	87	..	11	..	2	..	24	..	11	..
Canada	7	5	3	2	37	32	16	11	56	63	81	87
Central African Republic	79	..	90	..	5	..	1	..	15	..	9	..
Chad	82	..	95	..	6	..	0 ᵇ	..	..	..	4	..
Chile	22	19	3	5	27	31	16	14	51	49	81	82
China	..	..	..	..	..	..	..	..	..	..	..	..
Hong Kong, China	2	0 ᵇ	1	0 ᵇ	47	28	56	12	52	71	43	88
Colombia	2	2	1	1	39	27	26	20	59	71	74	79
Congo, Dem. Rep.	62	..	84	..	18	..	4	..	20	..	12	..
Congo, Rep.	42	..	81	..	20	..	2	..	38	..	17	..
Costa Rica	34	27	6	5	25	26	20	17	40	46	74	77
Côte d'Ivoire	60	..	75	..	10	..	5	..	30	..	20	..
Croatia	..	15	..	13	..	34	..	21	..	51	..	66
Cuba	30	..	10	..	32	..	22	..	39	..	68	..
Czech Republic	13	6	11	4	57	49	39	28	30	48	50	69
Denmark	11	5	4	2	41	37	16	15	48	58	80	83
Dominican Republic	..	..	..	..	..	..	..	..	..	..	..	..
Ecuador	..	11	..	2	..	26	..	14	..	63	..	84
Egypt, Arab Rep.	45	29	10	35	21	25	13	9	33	46	69	56
El Salvador	51	37	10	6	21	24	21	25	28	38	69	69
Eritrea	79	..	88	..	7	..	2	..	14	..	11	..
Estonia	..	11	..	7	..	40	..	23	..	49	..	70
Ethiopia	..	..	..	..	..	..	..	..	..	..	..	..
Finland	15	8	12	4	44	40	23	14	41	52	65	82
France	3	2	1	1	50	35	25	13	48	63	75	86
Gabon	59	..	74	..	18	..	6	..	24	..	21	..
Gambia, The	78	..	93	..	10	..	3	..	13	..	5	..
Georgia	..	..	..	..	..	..	..	..	..	..	..	..
Germany	..	3	..	2	..	46	..	19	..	50	..	79
Ghana	..	..	..	..	..	..	..	..	..	..	..	..
Greece	26	16	42	20	34	29	18	12	40	54	40	67
Guatemala	..	..	..	..	..	..	..	..	..	..	..	..
Guinea	86	..	97	..	2	..	1	..	12	..	3	..
Guinea-Bissau	81	..	98	..	3	..	..	..	17	..	3	..
Haiti	81	..	53	..	8	..	8	..	11	..	39	..
Honduras	..	50	..	9	..	21	..	25	..	30	..	67

	Agriculture				Industry				Services			
	Male % of male labor force		Female % of female labor force		Male % of male labor force		Female % of female labor force		Male % of male labor force		Female % of female labor force	
	1980-82[a]	1998-2000[a]	1980-82[a]	1998-2000[a]	1980-82[a]	1998-2000[a]	1980-82[a]	1998-2000[a]	1980-82[a]	1998-2000[a]	1980-82[a]	1998-2000[a]
Hungary	24	9	19	4	45	42	36	25	31	48	45	71
India	..	..	..	..	..	..	..	..	..	..	..	..
Indonesia	57	..	54	..	13	..	13	..	29	..	33	..
Iran, Islamic Rep.	..	..	..	..	..	..	..	..	..	..	..	..
Iraq	21	..	62	..	24	..	11	..	55	..	28	..
Ireland	..	12	..	2	..	38	..	15	..	50	..	83
Israel	8	3	4	1	39	35	16	13	52	61	79	86
Italy	13	6	16	5	43	39	28	21	44	55	56	74
Jamaica	47	30	23	10	20	26	8	9	33	45	69	81
Japan	9	5	13	6	40	38	28	22	51	57	58	73
Jordan	..	..	..	..	..	..	..	..	..	..	..	..
Kazakhstan	..	..	..	..	..	..	..	..	..	..	..	..
Kenya	23	20	25	16	24	23	9	10	53	57	65	75
Korea, Dem. Rep.	39	..	52	..	37	..	20	..	24	..	28	..
Korea, Rep.	31	10	39	13	32	34	24	19	37	56	37	68
Kuwait	2	..	..	..	36	..	3	..	62	..	97	..
Kyrgyz Republic	..	52	..	53	..	14	..	8	..	34	..	38
Lao PDR	77	..	82	..	7	..	4	..	16	..	13	..
Latvia	..	17	..	14	..	35	..	18	..	49	..	69
Lebanon	13	..	20	..	29	..	21	..	58	..	59	..
Lesotho	26	..	64	..	52	..	5	..	22	..	31	..
Liberia	69	..	89	..	9	..	1	..	22	..	10	..
Libya	16	..	63	..	29	..	3	..	55	..	34	..
Lithuania	..	24	..	..	..	33	..	..	..	43	..	..
Macedonia, FYR	..	..	..	..	..	..	..	..	..	..	..	..
Madagascar	73	77	93	76	9	6	2	4	19	16	5	20
Malawi	..	..	..	..	..	..	..	..	..	..	..	..
Malaysia	34	21	44	13	26	33	20	29	40	46	36	58
Mali	86	..	92	..	2	..	1	..	12	..	7	..
Mauritania	65	..	79	..	11	..	2	..	25	..	19	..
Mauritius	29	..	30	..	19	..	40	..	47	..	31	..
Mexico	..	27	..	9	..	27	..	21	..	45	..	69
Moldova	..	..	..	..	..	..	..	..	..	..	..	..
Mongolia	..	..	..	..	..	..	..	..	..	..	..	..
Morocco	..	6	..	6	..	32	..	40	..	63	..	54
Mozambique	72	..	97	..	14	..	1	..	14	..	2	..
Myanmar	..	..	..	..	..	..	..	..	..	..	..	..
Namibia	52	..	42	..	22	..	10	..	27	..	47	..
Nepal	..	..	..	..	..	..	..	..	..	..	..	..
Netherlands	7	4	3	2	39	31	13	9	54	63	84	84
New Zealand	..	11	..	6	..	32	..	12	..	56	..	81
Nicaragua	..	..	..	..	..	..	..	..	..	..	..	..
Niger	7	..	6	..	69	..	29	..	25	..	66	..
Nigeria	..	..	..	..	..	..	..	..	..	..	..	..
Norway	10	6	6	2	41	33	13	9	49	61	81	88
Oman	52	..	24	..	21	..	33	..	27	..	43	..
Pakistan	..	..	..	..	..	..	..	..	..	..	..	..
Panama	37	25	6	2	21	22	12	10	39	52	81	88
Papua New Guinea	76	..	92	..	8	..	2	..	16	..	6	..
Paraguay	2	..	0 [b]	..	35	..	13	..	63	..	86	..
Peru	..	8	..	3	..	25	..	11	..	67	..	86
Philippines	60	47	37	27	16	18	15	13	25	36	48	61
Poland	..	19	..	19	..	41	..	21	..	39	..	60
Portugal	22	11	35	14	44	44	25	24	34	45	40	62
Puerto Rico	8	3	0 [b]	0 [b]	27	28	24	14	65	69	75	85
Romania	22	39	39	45	52	33	34	22	26	29	27	33
Russian Federation	19	15	13	8	50	36	37	23	31	49	50	69

	Agriculture				Industry				Services			
	Male % of male labor force		Female % of female labor force		Male % of male labor force		Female % of female labor force		Male % of male labor force		Female % of female labor force	
	1980-82[a]	1998-2000[a]	1980-82[a]	1998-2000[a]	1980-82[a]	1998-2000[a]	1980-82[a]	1998-2000[a]	1980-82[a]	1998-2000[a]	1980-82[a]	1998-2000[a]
Rwanda	88	..	98	..	5	..	1	..	7	..	1	..
Saudi Arabia	45	..	25	..	17	..	5	..	39	..	70	..
Senegal	74	..	90	..	9	..	2	..	17	..	8	..
Sierra Leone	63	..	82	..	20	..	4	..	17	..	14	..
Singapore	2	0 [b]	1	0 [b]	33	33	40	23	65	67	59	77
Slovak Republic	..	10	..	5	..	49	..	26	..	42	..	69
Slovenia	..	11	..	11	..	46	..	28	..	42	..	61
Somalia	69	..	90	..	12	..	2	..	19	..	8	..
South Africa	..	..	..	..	..	..	..	..	..	..	..	..
Spain	20	9	18	5	42	40	21	14	39	51	60	81
Sri Lanka	44	38	51	49	19	23	18	22	30	37	28	27
Sudan	66	..	88	..	9	..	4	..	24	..	8	..
Swaziland	40	..	38	..	29	..	14	..	30	..	48	..
Sweden	8	4	3	1	45	38	16	12	47	59	81	87
Switzerland	8	5	5	4	47	36	23	13	46	59	72	83
Syrian Arab Republic	..	..	..	..	..	..	..	..	..	..	..	..
Tajikistan	..	..	..	..	..	..	..	..	..	..	..	..
Tanzania	..	..	..	..	..	..	..	..	..	..	..	..
Thailand	68	50	74	47	13	20	8	17	20	31	18	36
Togo	70	..	67	..	12	..	7	..	19	..	26	..
Trinidad and Tobago	11	11	9	3	44	37	21	13	45	52	70	83
Tunisia	33	..	53	..	30	..	32	..	37	..	16	..
Turkey	4	34	9	72	36	25	31	10	60	41	60	18
Turkmenistan	..	..	..	..	..	..	..	..	..	..	..	..
Uganda	..	..	..	..	..	..	..	..	..	..	..	..
Ukraine	..	..	..	..	..	..	..	..	..	..	..	..
United Arab Emirates	5	..	..	..	40	..	7	..	55	..	93	..
United Kingdom	4	2	1	1	48	36	23	12	49	61	76	87
United States	5	4	2	1	39	32	19	12	56	64	80	86
Uruguay	..	6	..	1	..	34	..	14	..	61	..	85
Uzbekistan	..	..	..	..	..	..	..	..	..	..	..	..
Venezuela, RB	20	..	2	..	31	..	18	..	49	..	79	..
Vietnam	..	..	..	..	..	..	..	..	..	..	..	..
West Bank and Gaza	22	..	25	..	43	..	25	..	36	..	50	..
Yemen, Rep.	60	..	98	..	19	..	1	..	21	..	1	..
Yugoslavia, Fed. Rep.	..	..	..	..	..	..	..	..	..	..	..	..
Zambia	69	..	85	..	13	..	3	..	19	..	13	..
Zimbabwe	29	..	50	..	31	..	8	..	40	..	42	..
World	.. w	.. w	.. w	.. w	.. w	.. w	.. w	.. w	.. w	.. w	.. w	.. w
Low income	..	..	..	..	..	..	..	..	..	..	..	..
Middle income	..	..	..	..	..	..	..	..	..	..	..	..
Lower middle income	..	..	..	..	..	..	..	..	..	..	..	..
Upper middle income	..	22	..	21	..	31	..	16	..	48	..	64
Low & middle income	..	..	..	..	..	..	..	..	..	..	..	..
East Asia & Pacific	..	..	..	..	..	..	..	..	..	..	..	..
Europe & Central Asia	..	21	..	21	..	35	..	21	..	44	..	58
Latin America & Carib.	..	20	..	11	..	28	..	14	..	52	..	75
Middle East & N. Africa	..	..	..	..	..	..	..	..	..	..	..	..
South Asia	..	..	..	..	..	..	..	..	..	..	..	..
Sub-Saharan Africa	..	..	..	..	..	..	..	..	..	..	..	..
High income	7	4	6	2	42	36	22	15	51	60	72	82
Europe EMU	..	4	..	2	..	41	..	17	..	55	..	80

a. Data are for the most recent year available. b. Less than 0.5. c. Break in series between 1980 and 1990.

About the data

The International Labour Organization (ILO) classifies economic activity on the basis of the International Standard Industrial Classification (ISIC) of All Economic Activities. Because this classification is based on where work is performed (industry) rather than on what type of work is performed (occupation), all of an enterprise's employees are classified under the same industry, regardless of their trade or occupation. The categories should add up to 100 percent. Where they do not, the differences arise because of people who are not classifiable by economic activity.

Data on employment are drawn from labor force surveys, establishment censuses and surveys, administrative records of social insurance schemes, and official national estimates. The concept of employment generally refers to people above a certain age who worked, or who held a job, during a reference period. Employment data include both full-time and part-time workers. There are, however, many differences in how countries define and measure employment status, particularly for part-time workers, students, members of the armed forces, and household or contributing family workers. When the armed forces are included, they are allocated to the service sector, causing that sector to be somewhat overstated in comparison with economies where they are excluded. Where data are obtained from establishment surveys, they cover only employees; thus self-employed and contributing family workers are excluded. In such cases the employment share of the agricultural sector is severely underreported. Countries also take very different approaches to the treatment of unemployed people. In most countries unemployed people with previous job experience are classified according to their last job. But in some countries the unemployed and people seeking their first job are not classifiable by economic activity. Because of these differences, the size and distribution of employment by economic activity may not be fully comparable across countries (ILO, *Yearbook of Labour Statistics 1996*, p. 64).

The ILO's *Yearbook of Labour Statistics* and *Key Indicators of the Labour Market* database report data by major divisions of the ISIC revision 2 or ISIC revision 3. In this table the reported divisions or categories are aggregated into three broad groups: agriculture, industry, and services. An increasing number of countries report economic activity according to the ISIC. Where data are supplied according to national classifications, however, industry definitions and descriptions may differ. In addition, classification into broad groups may obscure fundamental differences in countries' industrial patterns.

The distribution of economic activity by gender reveals some interesting patterns. Agriculture accounts for the largest share of female employment in much of Africa and Asia. Services

account for much of the increase in women's labor force participation in North Africa, Latin America and the Caribbean, and high-income economies. Worldwide, women are underrepresented in industry.

Segregating one sex in a narrow range of occupations significantly reduces economic efficiency by reducing labor market flexibility and thus the economy's ability to adapt to change. This segregation is particularly harmful for women, who have a much narrower range of labor market choices and lower levels of pay than men. But it is also detrimental to men when job losses are concentrated in industries dominated by men and job growth is centered in service occupations, where women often dominate, as has been the recent experience in many countries.

There are several explanations for the rising importance of service jobs for women. Many service jobs— such as nursing and social and clerical work—are considered "feminine" because of a perceived similarity to women's traditional roles. Women often do not receive the training needed to take advantage of changing employment opportunities. And the greater availability of part-time work in service industries may lure more women, although it is not clear whether this is a cause or an effect.

Definitions

- **Agriculture** includes hunting, forestry, and fishing, corresponding to division 1 (ISIC revision 2) or tabulation categories A and B (ISIC revision 3). • **Industry** includes mining and quarrying (including oil production), manufacturing, construction, electricity, gas, and water, corresponding to divisions 2–5 (ISIC revision 2) or tabulation categories C–F (ISIC revision 3). • **Services** include wholesale and retail trade and restaurants and hotels; transport, storage, and communications; financing, insurance, real estate, and business services; and community, social, and personal services—corresponding to divisions 6–9 (ISIC revision 2) or tabulation categories G–P (ISIC revision 3).

Data sources

The employment data are from the ILO database Key Indicators of the Labour Market (2001-02 issue).

Figure 2.3

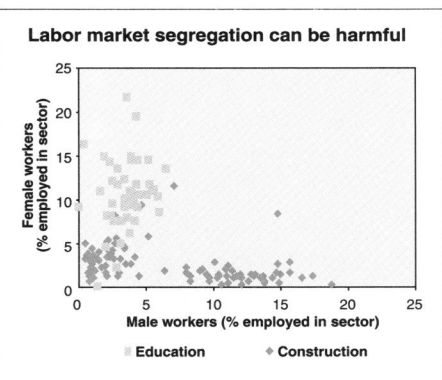

Labor market segregation can be harmful

Source: ILO. *Key Indicators of the Labour Market* database (2001-02).

Labor market segregation is a consequence of men's and women's tendency to be employed in different occupations. The interest in studying occupational segregation ranges from concerns to identify whether market forces or policies produced the existing occupational structure, to the practical issues of advancing the equality of women and men in employment.

2.4 | Unemployment

	Unemployment						Long term unemployment			Unemployment by level of educational attainment		
	Male % of male labor force		Female % of female labor force		Total % of total labor force		% of total unemployment			% of total unemployment		
							Male	Female	Total	Primary	Secondary	Tertiary
	1980-82[a]	1998-2000[a]	1980-82[a]	1998-2000[a]	1980-82[a]	1998-2000[a]	1998-2000[a]	1998-2000[a]	1998-2000[a]	1997-99[a]	1997-99[a]	1997-99[a]
Afghanistan	..	..	..	..	..	..	..	..	..	..	..	..
Albania	..	15.8	..	20.9	5.6	18.0	..	..	..	..	..	..
Algeria	..	..	..	..	..	..	..	..	..	..	..	..
Angola	..	..	..	..	..	..	..	..	..	..	..	..
Argentina	..	11.9	..	14.3	2.3	12.8	..	..	..	..	..	..
Armenia	..	4.9	..	15.0	..	9.3	..	..	..	..	..	..
Australia	5.0	7.2	7.4	6.7	5.9	6.4	30.6	24.0	27.9	53.3	32.1	11.8
Austria	1.6	4.7	2.3	4.8	1.9	4.7	28.1	36.1	31.7	35.2	60.3	4.6
Azerbaijan	..	1.0	..	1.4	..	1.2	..	..	..	6.7	30.8	62.5
Bangladesh	..	..	..	..	..	..	..	..	..	..	..	..
Belarus	..	..	..	..	..	2.0	..	..	..	7.8	15.5	76.7
Belgium	5.5	5.8	15.0	8.7	9.1	7.0	60.1	60.9	60.5	53.1	33.4	13.6
Benin	..	..	..	..	..	..	..	..	..	..	..	..
Bolivia	..	..	..	..	..	..	..	..	..	..	..	..
Bosnia and Herzegovina	..	..	..	..	..	..	..	..	..	..	..	..
Botswana	..	..	..	..	..	..	..	..	..	..	..	..
Brazil	2.8	7.2	2.8	11.6	2.8	9.6	..	..	..	..	..	..
Bulgaria	..	16.7	..	15.9	..	16.3	58.6	58.7	58.7	7.4	85.3	7.3
Burkina Faso	..	..	..	..	..	..	..	..	..	..	..	..
Burundi	..	..	..	..	..	..	..	..	..	..	..	..
Cambodia	..	..	..	..	..	..	..	..	..	..	..	..
Cameroon	..	..	..	..	..	..	..	..	..	..	..	..
Canada	7.0	6.9	8.2	6.7	7.5	6.8	11.7	9.5	10.7	25.9	31.2	35.6
Central African Republic	..	..	..	..	..	..	..	..	..	..	..	..
Chad	..	..	..	..	..	..	..	..	..	..	..	..
Chile	10.6	7.0	10.0	7.6	10.4	9.9	..	..	..	28.5	56.2	14.6
China	..	..	..	..	4.9	3.1	..	..	..	..	..	..
Hong Kong, China	3.9	5.1	3.4	4.0	3.8	5.0	..	..	..	..	..	..
Colombia	7.5	17.2	11.5	23.3	9.1	20.1	..	..	..	21.3	57.8	19.1
Congo, Dem. Rep.	..	..	..	..	..	..	..	..	..	..	..	..
Congo, Rep.	..	..	..	..	..	..	..	..	..	..	..	..
Costa Rica	5.3	4.9	7.8	8.2	5.9	6.0	..	..	..	75.1	12.7	8.1
Côte d'Ivoire	..	..	..	..	..	..	..	..	..	..	..	..
Croatia	3.4	12.8	8.2	14.5	5.3	16.1	56.3	53.6	60.7	19.5	69.1	11.4
Cuba	..	..	..	..	..	..	..	..	..	..	..	..
Czech Republic	..	7.3	..	10.6	..	8.8	47.5	49.8	48.8	24.2	72.1	3.7
Denmark	6.5	4.5	7.6	5.9	7.0	5.4	20.9	20.1	20.5	34.6	47.7	16.7
Dominican Republic	..	..	..	..	..	..	..	..	..	50.4	31.1	9.6
Ecuador	..	8.4	..	16.0	..	11.5	..	..	..	..	..	..
Egypt, Arab Rep.	3.9	5.1	19.2	19.9	5.2	8.2	..	..	..	..	..	..
El Salvador	..	8.2	..	6.0	12.9	7.3	..	..	..	57.1	23.4	7.5
Eritrea	..	..	..	..	..	..	..	..	..	..	..	..
Estonia	..	13.0	..	10.2	..	14.8	45.4	49.1	47.0	22.5	54.4	23.1
Ethiopia	3.6	..	9.5	..	5.2	..	..	..	..	26.9	61.3	8.1
Finland	4.6	9.7	4.7	10.7	4.7	9.8	30.1	25.2	27.6	41.1	49.8	9.1
France	4.1	8.5	9.1	11.9	6.1	10.0	41.1	43.6	42.5	..	..	..
Gabon	..	..	..	..	..	..	..	..	..	..	..	..
Gambia, The	..	..	..	..	..	..	..	..	..	..	..	..
Georgia	..	15.3	..	12.2	..	13.8	..	..	..	3.9	32.4	60.8
Germany	..	7.6	..	8.6	..	8.1	49.9	54.0	51.7	28.9	57.5	13.6
Ghana	..	..	..	..	..	..	..	..	..	..	..	..
Greece	3.3	7.0	5.7	16.5	2.4	10.8	44.7	61.5	54.9	36.9	40.5	21.9
Guatemala	..	..	..	..	..	..	..	..	..	..	..	..
Guinea	..	..	..	..	..	..	..	..	..	..	..	..
Guinea-Bissau	..	..	..	..	..	..	..	..	..	..	..	..
Haiti	..	..	..	..	..	..	..	..	..	..	..	..
Honduras	8.6	3.7	6.0	3.8	7.3	3.7	..	..	..	63.2	22.4	5.8

2002 World Development Indicators

	Unemployment						Long term unemployment			Unemployment by level of educational attainment		
	Male % of male labor force		Female % of female labor force		Total % of total labor force		% of total unemployment			% of total unemployment		
							Male	Female	Total	Primary	Secondary	Tertiary
	1980-82ᵃ	1998-2000ᵃ	1980-82ᵃ	1998-2000ᵃ	1980-82ᵃ	1998-2000ᵃ	1998-2000ᵃ	1998-2000ᵃ	1998-2000ᵃ	1997-99ᵃ	1997-99ᵃ	1997-99ᵃ
Hungary	..	7.5	..	6.3	..	6.5	45.0	43.2	44.3	35.2	61.6	3.2
India	..	..	..	..	..	..	..	..	..	..	..	..
Indonesia	..	..	..	..	..	6.1	..	..	..	38.3	47.9	9.2
Iran, Islamic Rep.	..	..	..	..	..	..	..	..	..	..	..	..
Iraq	..	..	..	..	..	..	..	..	..	..	..	..
Ireland	11.4	4.8	8.2	4.6	10.5	4.7	44.9	23.4	36.5	60.7	20.8	16.1
Israel	4.1	8.5	6.0	8.1	4.8	8.3	..	..	..	23.9	42.2	33.1
Italy	4.8	8.7	13.2	15.7	7.6	10.8	62.1	60.7	61.4	52.3	39.0	6.9
Jamaica	16.3	10.0	39.6	22.5	27.3	15.7	18.0	29.6	25.6	..	..	..
Japan	2.0	5.0	2.0	4.5	2.0	4.8	30.7	17.1	25.5	23.3	51.2	25.6
Jordan	..	11.8	..	20.7	..	13.2	..	..	..	..	..	..
Kazakhstan	..	..	..	..	..	13.7	..	..	..	7.2	52.5	40.3
Kenya	..	..	..	..	..	..	..	..	..	..	..	..
Korea, Dem. Rep.	..	..	..	..	..	..	..	..	..	..	..	..
Korea, Rep.	6.2	7.1	3.5	5.1	5.2	4.1	3.1	0.7	2.3	16.4	52.7	20.0
Kuwait	..	..	..	..	..	..	..	..	..	..	..	..
Kyrgyz Republic	..	..	..	..	..	..	..	..	..	33.4	55.7	10.9
Lao PDR	..	..	..	..	..	..	..	..	..	..	..	..
Latvia	..	15.5	..	13.3	..	8.4	50.5	52.8	51.5	20.8	68.1	8.5
Lebanon	..	..	..	..	..	..	..	..	..	..	..	..
Lesotho	..	..	..	..	..	..	..	..	..	..	..	..
Liberia	..	..	..	..	..	..	..	..	..	..	..	..
Libya	..	..	..	..	..	..	..	..	..	..	..	..
Lithuania	..	17.3	..	13.3	..	11.1	23.4	19.2	21.6	15.4	56.2	28.5
Macedonia, FYR	15.6	32.5	32.8	37.5	22.0	34.5	..	..	..	..	..	..
Madagascar	..	..	..	..	..	..	..	..	..	..	..	..
Malawi	..	..	..	..	..	..	..	..	..	..	..	..
Malaysia	..	..	..	..	..	3.0	..	..	..	..	..	..
Mali	..	..	..	..	..	..	..	..	..	..	..	..
Mauritania	..	..	..	..	..	..	..	..	..	..	..	..
Mauritius	..	..	..	..	..	..	..	..	..	33.2	66.1	..
Mexico	..	1.8	..	2.6	..	2.0	0.4	1.5	0.8	15.5	36.0	37.7
Moldova	..	..	..	..	..	11.1	..	..	..	..	..	..
Mongolia	..	5.2	..	6.3	..	5.7	..	..	..	47.9	24.1	17.3
Morocco	..	20.3	..	27.6	..	22.0	..	..	..	..	..	..
Mozambique	..	..	..	..	..	..	..	..	..	..	..	..
Myanmar	..	..	..	..	..	..	..	..	..	..	..	..
Namibia	..	..	..	..	..	..	..	..	..	..	..	..
Nepal	..	1.5	..	0.7	..	1.1	..	..	..	..	..	..
Netherlands	4.3	2.7	5.2	4.9	4.6	3.6	47.7	40.4	43.5	30.4	33.0	14.3
New Zealand	..	6.1	..	5.8	..	6.0	20.7	12.6	17.1	0.5	38.5	22.6
Nicaragua	..	8.8	..	14.5	..	13.3	..	..	..	54.9	24.7	14.9
Niger	..	..	..	..	..	..	..	..	..	..	..	..
Nigeria	..	..	..	..	..	..	..	..	..	..	..	..
Norway	1.2	3.7	2.1	3.2	1.7	3.4	6.7	2.9	5.0	25.3	54.7	17.3
Oman	..	..	..	..	..	..	..	..	..	..	..	..
Pakistan	3.0	4.2	7.5	14.9	3.6	5.9	..	..	..	..	..	..
Panama	6.3	8.9	13.3	16.9	8.4	11.8	..	..	..	..	..	..
Papua New Guinea	..	..	..	..	..	..	..	..	..	..	..	..
Paraguay	3.8	..	4.8	..	4.1	..	..	..	..	..	..	..
Peru	..	7.5	..	8.6	..	8.0	..	..	..	13.1	52.6	33.3
Philippines	3.2	10.3	7.5	9.9	4.8	10.1	..	..	..	..	..	..
Poland	..	15.2	..	18.5	..	16.7	34.2	41.4	37.9	33.1	64.8	2.0
Portugal	3.3	2.9	12.2	4.8	6.7	3.8	39.5	42.9	41.2	73.9	14.9	5.8
Puerto Rico	19.5	11.9	12.3	7.8	17.1	10.1	..	..	..	..	..	..
Romania	..	7.4	..	6.2	..	10.8	41.0	48.4	44.0	21.7	70.6	6.4
Russian Federation	..	13.6	..	13.1	..	11.4	..	..	11.9	16.8	41.6	41.6

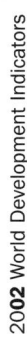

	Unemployment						Long term unemployment			Unemployment by level of educational attainment		
	Male % of male labor force		Female % of female labor force		Total % of total labor force		% of total unemployment			% of total unemployment		
							Male	Female	Total	Primary	Secondary	Tertiary
	1980-82[a]	1998-2000[a]	1980-82[a]	1998-2000[a]	1980-82[a]	1998-2000[a]	1998-2000[a]	1998-2000[a]	1998-2000[a]	1997-99[a]	1997-99[a]	1997-99[a]
Rwanda	..	..	..	..	..	..	..	..	..	..	..	..
Saudi Arabia	..	..	..	..	..	..	..	..	..	..	..	..
Senegal	..	..	..	..	..	..	..	..	..	..	..	..
Sierra Leone	..	..	..	..	..	..	..	..	..	..	..	..
Singapore	2.9	4.5	3.4	4.6	3.0	4.4	..	..	..	26.8	27.4	28.6
Slovak Republic	..	15.9	..	16.4	..	18.9	43.2	49.7	46.1	..	75.6	3.0
Slovenia	..	7.5	..	7.4	..	7.5	44.3	36.8	40.7	28.2	64.8	7.0
Somalia	..	..	..	..	..	..	..	..	..	..	..	..
South Africa	..	19.8	..	27.8	..	23.3	..	..	..	..	..	..
Spain	10.4	9.7	12.8	20.5	11.1	14.1	39.5	52.4	46.8	52.3	19.1	21.5
Sri Lanka	..	5.9	..	11.0	..	7.7	..	..	..	49.8	..	50.2
Sudan	..	..	..	..	..	..	..	..	..	..	..	..
Swaziland	..	..	..	..	..	..	..	..	..	..	..	..
Sweden	1.9	7.4	2.6	6.7	2.2	5.1	33.3	26.1	30.1	32.0	50.6	15.8
Switzerland	0.2	2.3	0.3	3.1	0.2	2.7	27.5	29.1	28.3	..	..	..
Syrian Arab Republic	3.8	..	3.8	..	3.9	..	..	..	..	..	..	..
Tajikistan	..	..	..	..	..	..	..	..	..	10.6	83.2	6.3
Tanzania	..	..	..	..	..	..	..	..	..	..	..	..
Thailand	1.0	3.0	0.7	3.0	0.8	2.4	..	..	..	71.7	12.3	12.9
Togo	..	..	..	..	..	..	..	..	..	..	..	..
Trinidad and Tobago	8.0	10.9	14.0	16.8	10.0	13.1	19.9	42.3	31.0	38.2	60.7	0.8
Tunisia	..	..	..	..	..	..	..	..	..	..	33.7	4.1
Turkey	9.0	7.6	23.0	6.6	10.9	8.3	29.8	44.1	33.7	..	..	..
Turkmenistan	..	..	..	..	..	..	..	..	..	..	..	..
Uganda	..	..	..	..	..	..	..	..	..	..	..	..
Ukraine	..	12.2	..	11.5	..	11.9	..	..	..	9.4	27.2	63.4
United Arab Emirates	..	..	..	..	..	..	..	..	..	..	..	..
United Kingdom	8.3	6.7	4.8	5.1	6.8	5.3	34.8	21.6	29.8	9.3	43.4	12.1
United States	6.9	3.7	7.4	4.6	7.1	4.1	6.7	5.3	6.0	22.2	35.6	42.1
Uruguay	..	8.7	..	14.6	..	11.3	..	..	..	..	..	..
Uzbekistan	..	..	..	..	..	..	..	..	..	..	..	..
Venezuela, RB	..	..	..	..	5.9	14.9	..	..	..	..	..	..
Vietnam	..	..	..	..	..	..	..	..	..	..	..	..
West Bank and Gaza	..	..	..	..	..	14.1	..	..	..	..	..	..
Yemen, Rep.	..	..	..	..	..	..	..	..	..	..	..	..
Yugoslavia, Fed. Rep.	..	..	..	..	..	..	..	..	..	..	..	..
Zambia	32.7	..	59.0	..	42.2	..	..	..	..	..	..	..
Zimbabwe	..	7.3	..	4.6	..	6.0	..	..	..	..	..	..
World	.. w	.. w	.. w	.. w	.. w	.. w	.. w	.. w	.. w	.. w	.. w	.. w
Low income	..	..	..	..	..	..	..	..	..	..	..	..
Middle income	..	..	..	..	4.8	4.9	..	..	..	..	..	..
Lower middle income	..	..	..	..	4.9	4.3	..	..	..	..	..	..
Upper middle income	..	7.0	..	8.9	..	9.0	..	..	..	..	..	..
Low & middle income	..	..	..	..	..	..	..	..	..	..	..	..
East Asia & Pacific	..	..	..	..	4.7	3.7	..	..	..	..	..	..
Europe & Central Asia	..	11.3	..	11.1	..	11.1	..	..	27.1	17.6	47.3	34.8
Latin America & Carib.	..	7.2	..	10.5	..	9.2	..	..	..	..	..	..
Middle East & N. Africa	..	..	..	..	..	..	..	..	..	..	..	..
South Asia	..	..	..	..	..	..	..	..	..	..	..	..
Sub-Saharan Africa	..	..	..	..	..	..	..	..	..	..	..	..
High income	5.5	5.4	7.0	6.7	6.0	6.2	28.4	25.6	27.3	27.3	41.2	27.4
Europe EMU	5.5	7.9	10.8	11.6	7.1	9.8	48.5	50.9	49.8	42.3	42.9	12.9

a. Data are for the most recent year available.

About the data

Unemployment and total employment in a country are the broadest indicators of economic activity as reflected by the labor market. The International Labour Organization (ILO) defines the unemployed as members of the economically active population who are without work but available for and seeking work, including people who have lost their jobs and those who have voluntarily left work. Some unemployment is unavoidable in all economies. At any time some workers are temporarily unemployed—between jobs as employers look for the right workers and workers search for better jobs. Such unemployment, often called frictional unemployment, results from the normal operation of labor markets.

Changes in unemployment over time may reflect changes in the demand for and supply of labor, but they may also reflect changes in reporting practices. Ironically, low unemployment rates can often disguise substantial poverty in a country, while high unemployment rates can occur in countries with a high level of economic development and low incidence of poverty. In countries without unemployment or welfare benefits, people eke out a living in the informal sector. In countries with well-developed safety nets, workers can afford to wait for suitable or desirable jobs. But high and sustained unemployment indicates serious inefficiencies in the allocation of resources.

The ILO definition of unemployment notwithstanding, reference periods, the criteria for those considered to be seeking work, and the treatment of people temporarily laid off and those seeking work for the first time vary across countries. In many developing countries it is especially difficult to measure employment and unemployment in agriculture. The timing of a survey, for example, can maximize the effects of seasonal unemployment in agriculture. And informal sector employment is difficult to quantify where informal activities are not registered and tracked.

Data on unemployment are drawn from labor force sample surveys and general household sample surveys, social insurance statistics, employment office statistics, and official estimates, which are usually based on information drawn from one or more of the above sources. Labor force surveys generally yield the most comprehensive data because they include groups—particularly people seeking work for the first time—not covered in other unemployment statistics. These surveys generally use a definition of unemployment that follows the international recommendations more closely than that used by other sources and therefore generate statistics that are more comparable internationally.

In contrast, the quality and completeness of data obtained from employment offices and social insurance programs vary widely. Where employment offices work closely with social insurance schemes, and registration with such of-

fices is a prerequisite for receipt of unemployment benefits, the two sets of unemployment estimates tend to be comparable. Where registration is voluntary, and where employment offices function only in more populous areas, employment office statistics do not give a reliable indication of unemployment. Most commonly excluded from both these sources are discouraged workers who have given up their job search because they believe that no employment opportunities exist or do not register as unemployed after their benefits have been exhausted. Thus measured unemployment may be higher in economies that offer more or longer unemployment benefits.

Long-term unemployment is measured in terms of duration, that is, the length of time that an unemployed person has been without work and looking for a job. The underlying assumption is that shorter periods of joblessness are of less concern, especially when the unemployed are covered by unemployment benefits or similar forms of welfare support. The length of time a person has been unemployed is difficult to measure, because the ability to recall the length of that time diminishes as the period of joblessness extends. Women's long-term unemployment is likely to be lower in countries where women constitute a large share of the unpaid family workforce. Such women have more access than men to nonmarket work and are more likely to drop out of the labor force and not be counted as unemployed.

No data are given in the table for economies for which unemployment data are not consistently available or are deemed unreliable.

Definitions

• **Unemployment** refers to the share of the labor force without work but available for and seeking employment. Definitions of labor force and unemployment differ by country (see *About the data*). • **Long-term unemployment** refers to the number of people with continuous periods of unemployment extending for a year or longer, expressed as a percentage of the total unemployed. • **Unemployment by level of educational attainment** shows the unemployed by level of educational attainment, as a percentage of the total unemployed. The levels of educational attainment accord with the United Nations Educational, Cultural, and Scientific Organization's (UNESCO) International Standard Classification of Education.

Data sources

The unemployment data are from the ILO database Key Indicators of the Labour Market (2001-02 issue).

Figure 2.4

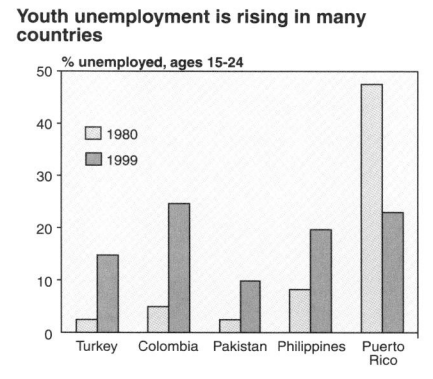

Youth unemployment is rising in many countries

% unemployed, ages 15-24

Legend: 1980, 1999

(Countries: Turkey, Colombia, Pakistan, Philippines, Puerto Rico)

Source: ILO. *Key Indicators of the Labour Market* database (2001-02).

The youth unemployment rate refers to the share of the labor force ages 15-24 who are unemployed. Youth unemployment is generally viewed as an important policy issue for many economies. Low unemployment among youth does not necessarily imply a high level of school enrollment, it could indicate the difficulties young people have in finding a job.

2.5 | Wages and productivity

	Average hours worked per week		Minimum wage $ per year		Agricultural wage $ per year		Labor cost per worker in manufacturing $ per year		Value added per worker in manufacturing $ per year	
	1980-84	1995-99ª	1980-84	1995-99ª	1980-84	1995-99ª	1980-84	1995-99ª	1980-84	1995-99ª
Afghanistan	..	..	..	..	..	..	..	..	..	..
Albania	..	..	..	..	..	..	..	..	..	..
Algeria	..	..	..	1,340	..	..	6,242	2,638	11,306	..
Angola	..	..	..	..	..	..	..	..	..	..
Argentina	41	40	..	2,400	..	..	6,768	7,338	33,694	37,480
Armenia	..	..	..	..	..	..	..	..	..	..
Australia	37	39	..	12,712	11,212	15,124	14,749	26,087	27,801	57,857
Austria	33	32	..	b	..	..	11,949	28,342	20,956	53,061
Azerbaijan	..	..	..	..	..	..	..	..	..	..
Bangladesh	..	52	..	492	192	360	556	671	1,820	1,711
Belarus	..	..	..	..	1,641	410	2,233	754	..	..
Belgium	..	38	7,661	15,882	6,399	..	12,805	24,132	25,579	58,678
Benin	..	..	..	..	..	..	..	..	..	..
Bolivia	..	46	..	529	..	..	4,432	2,343	21,519	26,282
Bosnia and Herzegovina	..	..	..	..	..	..	..	..	..	..
Botswana	45	..	894	961	650	1,223	3,250	2,884	7,791	..
Brazil	..	..	1,690	1,308	..	..	10,080	14,134	43,232	61,595
Bulgaria	..	..	..	573	..	1,372	2,485	1,179	..	..
Burkina Faso	..	..	695	585	..	..	3,282	..	15,886	..
Burundi	..	..	..	..	..	..	..	..	..	..
Cambodia	..	..	..	..	..	..	..	..	..	..
Cameroon	..	..	..	..	..	..	..	..	..	..
Canada	38	38	4,974	7,897	20,429	30,625	17,710	28,424	36,903	60,712
Central African Republic	..	..	..	..	..	..	..	..	..	..
Chad	..	..	..	..	..	..	..	..	..	..
Chile	43	45	663	1,781	..	..	6,234	5,822	32,805	32,977
China	..	..	..	..	349	325	472	729	3,061	2,885
Hong Kong, China	48	46	..	..	..	..	4,127	10,353	7,886	32,611
Colombia	..	..	..	1,128	..	..	2,988	2,507	15,096	17,061
Congo, Dem. Rep.	..	..	..	..	..	..	..	..	..	..
Congo, Rep.	..	..	..	..	..	..	..	..	..	..
Costa Rica	..	47	1,042	1,638	982	1,697	2,433	2,829	7,185	7,184
Côte d'Ivoire	..	..	1,246	871	..	..	5,132	9,995	16,158	..
Croatia	..	..	..	..	..	..	..	..	..	..
Cuba	..	..	..	..	..	..	..	..	..	..
Czech Republic	43	43	..	942	2,277	3,090	2,306	3,815	5,782	5,094
Denmark	..	37	9,170	19,933	..	..	16,169	29,235	27,919	49,273
Dominican Republic	44	44	..	1,439	..	..	2,191	1,806	8,603	..
Ecuador	..	..	1,637	492	..	..	5,065	3,738	12,197	9,747
Egypt, Arab Rep.	58	..	343	415	..	..	2,210	1,863	3,691	5,976
El Salvador	..	..	..	790	..	..	3,654	..	14,423	..
Eritrea	..	..	..	..	..	..	..	..	..	..
Estonia	..	..	..	..	..	..	..	..	..	..
Ethiopia	..	..	..	..	..	..	..	1,596	..	7,094
Finland	..	38	..	b	..	..	11,522	26,615	25,945	55,037
France	40	39	6,053	12,072	..	..	18,488	..	26,751	61,019
Gabon	..	..	..	..	..	..	..	..	..	..
Gambia, The	..	..	..	..	..	..	..	..	..	..
Georgia	..	..	..	..	..	..	..	..	..	..
Germany	41	40	..	b	..	..	15,708	33,226	34,945	79,616
Ghana	..	..	..	..	1,470	..	2,306	..	12,130	..
Greece	..	41	..	6,057	..	..	6,461	12,296	14,561	30,429
Guatemala	..	..	..	459	..	..	2,605	1,802	11,144	9,235
Guinea	40	..	..	..	..	..	..	..	..	..
Guinea-Bissau	48	..	..	..	..	..	..	..	..	..
Haiti	..	..	..	..	..	..	..	..	..	..
Honduras	..	44	..	..	1,623	..	2,949	2,658	7,458	7,427

	Average hours worked per week		Minimum wage $ per year		Agricultural wage $ per year		Labor cost per worker in manufacturing $ per year		Value added per worker in manufacturing $ per year	
	1980-84	**1995-99ᵃ**	**1980-84**	**1995-99ᵃ**	**1980-84**	**1995-99ᵃ**	**1980-84**	**1995-99ᵃ**	**1980-84**	**1995-99ᵃ**
Hungary	35	*33*	1,186	1,132	1,186	2,676	1,410	3,755	4,307	10,918
India	46	..	..	*408*	205	*245*	1,035	*1,192*	2,108	*3,118*
Indonesia	40	43	..	*241*	..	..	898	3,054	3,807	*5,139*
Iran, Islamic Rep.	..	..	..	..	..	..	9,737	*30,562*	17,679	*89,787*
Iraq	..	..	..	..	..	..	4,624	*13,288*	13,599	*34,316*
Ireland	41	*41*	5,556	12,087	..	..	10,190	*22,681*	26,510	*86,036*
Israel	36	*36*	..	*5,861*	4,582	*7,906*	13,541	*21,150*	23,459	*35,526*
Italy	..	*32*	..	ᵇ	..	..	9,955	*34,859*	24,580	*50,760*
Jamaica	..	*39*	782	*692*	..	..	5,218	*3,655*	12,056	*11,091*
Japan	47	47	3,920	12,265	..	..	12,306	*31,687*	34,456	*92,582*
Jordan	..	*50*	ᵇ	ᵇ	..	..	4,643	2,082	16,337	*11,906*
Kazakhstan	..	..	..	..	..	..	..	..	..	..
Kenya	41	*39*	..	551	508	*568*	1,043	810	2,345	1,489
Korea, Dem. Rep.	..	..	..	..	..	..	..	..	..	..
Korea, Rep.	52	*48*	..	3,903	..	..	3,153	*10,743*	11,617	*40,916*
Kuwait	..	..	..	*8,244*	..	..	10,281	..	30,341	..
Kyrgyz Republic	..	..	..	65	1,695	168	2,287	687	..	..
Lao PDR	..	..	..	..	..	..	..	..	..	..
Latvia	..	..	..	..	..	..	..	*366*	..	..
Lebanon	..	..	..	..	..	..	..	..	..	..
Lesotho	..	*45*	..	..	..	..	1,442	..	6,047	..
Liberia	..	..	..	..	..	..	..	..	..	..
Libya	..	..	..	..	..	..	8,648	..	21,119	..
Lithuania	..	..	..	..	..	..	..	..	..	..
Macedonia, FYR	..	..	..	..	..	..	..	..	..	..
Madagascar	..	*40*	..	..	..	..	1,575	..	3,542	..
Malawi	..	..	..	..	..	..	..	..	..	..
Malaysia	..	..	..	ᵇ	1,435	..	2,519	*3,429*	8,454	*12,661*
Mali	..	..	321	*459*	..	..	2,983	..	10,477	..
Mauritania	..	..	..	..	..	..	..	..	..	..
Mauritius	..	..	..	..	..	..	1,465	*1,973*	2,969	*4,217*
Mexico	43	*45*	1,343	768	1,031	*908*	3,772	7,607	17,448	*25,931*
Moldova	..	..	..	..	..	..	..	..	..	..
Mongolia	..	..	..	..	..	..	..	..	..	..
Morocco	..	..	..	*1,672*	..	..	2,583	*3,391*	6,328	9,089
Mozambique	..	..	..	..	..	..	..	..	..	..
Myanmar	..	..	..	..	..	..	..	..	..	..
Namibia	..	..	..	..	..	..	..	..	..	..
Nepal	..	..	..	..	..	..	371	..	1,523	..
Netherlands	40	*40*	9,074	15,170	..	..	18,891	*34,326*	27,491	*56,801*
New Zealand	39	*39*	3,309	9,091	..	..	10,605	*18,419*ᵃ	16,835	*32,723*
Nicaragua	..	*44*	..	..	..	..	..	..	..	..
Niger	40	..	..	..	..	..	4,074	..	22,477	..
Nigeria	..	..	..	*300*	..	..	4,812	..	20,000	..
Norway	35	*35*	..	ᵇ	..	..	14,935	38,415	24,905	*51,510*
Oman	..	..	..	..	..	..	..	3,099	..	*61,422*
Pakistan	48	..	..	*600*	427	*416*	1,264	..	6,214	..
Panama	..	..	..	..	..	..	4,768	*6,351*	15,327	*17,320*
Papua New Guinea	44	..	..	..	..	..	4,825	..	13,563	..
Paraguay	36	*39*	..	..	1,606	*1,210*	2,509	*3,241*	..	*14,873*
Peru	48	..	..	..	..	*944*	2,988	..	15,962	..
Philippines	47	*43*	915	1,472	382	..	1,240	*2,450*	5,266	*10,781*
Poland	36	*33*	320	1,584	1,726	*1,301*	1,682	*1,714*	6,242	*7,637*
Portugal	39	*40*	1,606	4,086	..	..	3,115	*6,237*	7,161	*17,273*
Puerto Rico	..	..	..	..	..	..	..	..	..	..
Romania	34	*34*	..	531	1,669	*1,864*	1,757	*1,190*	..	*3,482*
Russian Federation	..	..	863	297	2,417	659	2,524	1,528	..	..

	Average hours worked per week		Minimum wage		Agricultural wage		Labor cost per worker in manufacturing		Value added per worker in manufacturing	
			$ per year		$ per year		$ per year		$ per year	
	1980-84	1995-99ᵃ	1980-84	1995-99ᵃ	1980-84	1995-99ᵃ	1980-84	1995-99ᵃ	1980-84	1995-99ᵃ
Rwanda	..	..	..	..	..	..	1,871	..	9,835	..
Saudi Arabia	..	..	..	..	..	..	9,814	..	..	..
Senegal	..	..	993	848	..	..	2,828	7,754	6,415	..
Sierra Leone	44	..	..	..	..	..	1,624	..	7,807	..
Singapore	46	47	..	..	..	4,856	5,576	21,317	16,442	40,674
Slovak Republic	43	40	..	..	2,277	1,885	2,306	1,876	5,782	5,094
Slovenia	..	..	..	..	..	..	..	9,632	..	12,536
Somalia	..	..	..	..	..	..	..	..	..	..
South Africa	42	41	..ᵇ	888	..	6,261	8,475	12,705	16,612	
Spain	38	37	3,058	5,778	..	..	8,276	19,329	18,936	47,016
Sri Lanka	50	53	..	..	198	264	447	604	2,057	3,405
Sudan	..	..	..	..	..	..	..	..	..	..
Swaziland	..	..	..	..	..	..	..	..	..	..
Sweden	36	37	..	..	9,576	27,098	13,038	26,601	32,308	56,675
Switzerland	44	42	..	..ᵇ	..	..	..	..	..	61,848
Syrian Arab Republic	..	..	..	..	..	..	2,844	4,338	9,607	9,918
Tajikistan	..	..	..	..	..	..	..	..	..	..
Tanzania	..	..	..	..	..	..	1,123	..	3,339	..
Thailand	50	47	749	1,159	..	..	2,305	3,868	11,072	19,946
Togo	..	..	..	..	..	..	..	..	..	..
Trinidad and Tobago	..	40	..	2,974	..	..	..	..	14,008	..
Tunisia	..	..	1,381	1,525	668	968	3,344	3,599	7,111	..
Turkey	..	48	594	1,254	1,015	2,896	3,582	7,958	13,994	32,961
Turkmenistan	..	..	..	..	..	..	..	..	..	..
Uganda	43	..	..	..	..	..	253	..	..	..
Ukraine	..	..	..	..	..	..	..	..	..	..
United Arab Emirates	..	..	..	..	..	..	6,968	..	20,344	..
United Kingdom	42	40	..	ᵇ	..	..	11,406	23,843	24,716	55,060
United States	40	41	6,006	8,056	..	..	19,103	28,907	47,276	81,353
Uruguay	48	42	1,262	1,027	1,289	..	4,128	3,738	13,722	16,028
Uzbekistan	..	..	..	..	..	..	..	..	..	..
Venezuela	41	..	1,869	1,463	..	..	11,188	4,667	37,063	24,867
Vietnam	..	47	..	134	..	442	..	711	..	..
West Bank and Gaza	..	..	..	..	..	..	..	..	..	..
Yemen, Rep.	..	..	..	..	..	..	4,492	1,291	17,935	5,782
Yugoslavia, FR (Serb./Mont.)	..	..	..	..	..	..	..	..	..	..
Zambia	..	45	..	..	..	..	3,183	4,292	11,753	16,615
Zimbabwe	..	..	..	..	1,065	..	4,097	3,422	9,625	11,944

a. Figures in italics refer to 1990-94. b. Country has sectoral minimum wage but no minimum wage policy.

About the data

Much of the available data on labor markets are collected through national reporting systems that depend on plant-level surveys. Even when these data are compiled and reported by international agencies such as the International Labour Organization or the United Nations Industrial Development Organization, differences in definitions, coverage, and units of account limit their comparability across countries. The indicators in this table are the result of a research project at the World Bank that has compiled results from more than 300 national and international sources in an effort to provide a set of uniform and representative labor market indicators. Nevertheless, many differences in reporting practices persist, some of which are described below.

Analyses of labor force participation, employment, and underemployment often rely on the number of hours of work per week. The indicator reported in the table is the time spent at the workplace working, preparing for work, or waiting for work to be supplied or for a machine to be fixed. It also includes the time spent at the workplace when no work is being performed but for which payment is made under a guaranteed work contract, or time spent on short periods of rest. Hours paid for but not spent at the place of work—such as paid annual and sick leave, paid holidays, paid meal breaks, and time spent in commuting between home and workplace—are not included. When this information is not available, the table reports the number of hours paid for, comprising the hours actually worked plus the hours paid for but not spent in the workplace. Data on hours worked are influenced by differences in methods of compilation and coverage as well as by national practices relating to the number of days worked and overtime, making comparisons across countries difficult.

Wages refer to remuneration in cash and in kind paid to employees at regular intervals. They exclude employers' contributions to social security and pension schemes as well as other benefits received by employees under these schemes. In some countries the national minimum wage represents a "floor," with higher minimum wages for particular occupations and skills set through collective bargaining. In those countries the agreements reached by employers associations and trade unions are extended by the government to all firms in the sector, or at least to large firms. Changes in the national minimum wage are generally associated with parallel changes in the minimum wages set through collective bargaining.

In many developing countries agricultural workers are hired on a casual or daily basis and lack any social security benefits. International comparisons of agricultural wages are subject to greater reservations than those of wages in other activities. The nature of the work carried out by different categories of agricultural workers and the length of the workday and workweek vary considerably from one country to another. Seasonal fluctuations in agricultural wages are more important in some countries than in others. And the methods followed in different countries for estimating the monetary value of payments in kind are not uniform.

Labor cost per worker in manufacturing is sometimes used as a measure of international competitiveness. The indicator reported in the table is the ratio of total compensation to the number of workers in the manufacturing sector. Compensation includes direct wages, salaries, and other remuneration paid directly by employers plus all contributions by employers to social security programs on behalf of their employees. But there are unavoidable differences in concepts and reference periods and in reporting practices. Remuneration for time not worked, bonuses and gratuities, and housing and family allowances should be considered part of the compensation costs, along with severance and termination pay. These indirect labor costs can vary substantially from country to country, depending on the labor laws and collective bargaining agreements in force.

International competitiveness also depends on productivity, which is often measured by value added per worker in manufacturing. The indicator reported in the table is the ratio of total value added in manufacturing to the number of employees engaged in that sector. Total value added is estimated as the difference between the value of industrial output and the value of materials and supplies for production (including fuel and purchased electricity) and cost of industrial services received.

Observations on labor costs and value added per worker are from plant-level surveys covering relatively large establishments, usually employing 10 or more workers and mostly in the formal sector. In high-income countries the coverage of these surveys tends to be quite good. In developing countries there is often a substantial bias toward very large establishments in the formal sector. As a result, the data may not be strictly comparable across countries. The data are converted into U.S. dollars using the average exchange rate for each year.

The data in the table are period averages and refer to workers of both sexes.

Definitions

• **Average hours worked per week** refer to all workers (male and female) in nonagricultural activities or, if unavailable, in manufacturing. The data correspond to hours actually worked, to hours paid for, or to statutory hours of work in a normal workweek. • **Minimum wage** corresponds to the most general regime for nonagricultural activities. When rates vary across sectors, only that for manufacturing (or commerce, if the manufacturing wage is unavailable) is reported. • **Agricultural wage** is based on daily wages in agriculture. • **Labor cost per worker in manufacturing** is obtained by dividing the total payroll by the number of employees, or the number of people engaged, in manufacturing establishments. • **Value added per worker in manufacturing** is obtained by dividing the value added of manufacturing establishments by the number of employees, or the number of people engaged, in those establishments.

Data sources

The data in the table are drawn from Martin Rama and Raquel Artecona's *"Database of Labor Market Indicators across Countries,"* (2001).

2.6 | Poverty

	National poverty line								International poverty line				
		Population below the poverty line				Population below the poverty line				Population below $1 a day %	Poverty gap at $1 a day %	Population below $2 a day %	Poverty gap at $2 a day %
	Survey year	Rural %	Urban %	National %	Survey year	Rural %	Urban %	National %	Survey year				
Afghanistan	..	..	..	..		..	..	..		..	..	..	..
Albania	1994	28.9	..	..	1996	..	15.0	..		..	..	..	..
Algeria	1988	16.6	7.3	12.2	1995	30.3	14.7	22.6	1995	<2	<0.5	15.1	3.6
Angola		..	..	..		..	..	..		..	..	..	..
Argentina	1991	..	..	25.5	1993	..	..	17.6		..	..	..	..
Armenia		..	..	..		..	..	..	1996	7.8	1.7	34.0	11.3
Australia		..	..	..		..	..	..		..	..	..	..
Austria		..	..	..		..	..	..		..	..	..	..
Azerbaijan	1995	..	..	68.1		..	..	..	1995	<2	<0.5	9.6	2.3
Bangladesh	1991-92	46.0	23.3	42.7	1995-96	39.8	14.3	35.6	1996	29.1	5.9	77.8	31.8
Belarus	2000	..	..	41.9		..	..	..	1998	<2	<0.5	<2	<0.5
Belgium		..	..	..		..	..	..		..	..	..	..
Benin	1995	..	..	33.0		..	..	..		..	..	..	..
Bolivia	1993	..	29.3	..	1995	79.1	..	..	1999	14.4	5.4	34.3	14.9
Bosnia and Herzegovina		..	..	..		..	..	..		..	..	..	..
Botswana		..	..	..		..	..	..	1985-86	33.3	12.5	61.4	30.7
Brazil	1990	32.6	13.1	17.4		..	..	..	1998	11.6	3.9	26.5	11.6
Bulgaria		..	..	..		..	..	..	1997	<2	<0.5	21.9	4.2
Burkina Faso		..	..	..		..	..	..	1994	61.2	25.5	85.8	50.9
Burundi	1990	..	..	36.2		..	..	..		..	..	..	..
Cambodia	1993-94	43.1	24.8	39.0	1997	40.1	21.1	36.1		..	..	..	..
Cameroon	1984	32.4	44.4	40.0		..	..	..	1996	33.4	11.8	64.4	31.2
Canada		..	..	..		..	..	..		..	..	..	..
Central African Republic		..	..	..		..	..	..	1993	66.6	38.1	84.0	58.4
Chad	1995-96	67.0	63.0	64.0		..	..	..		..	..	..	..
Chile	1996	..	..	24.6	1998	..	..	21.2	1998	<2	<0.5	8.7	2.3
China	1996	7.9	<2	6.0	1998	4.6	<2	4.6	1999	18.8	4.4	52.6	20.9
Hong Kong, China		..	..	..		..	..	..		..	..	..	..
Colombia	1991	29.0	7.8	16.9	1992	31.2	8.0	17.7	1998	19.7	10.8	36.0	19.4
Congo, Dem. Rep.		..	..	..		..	..	..		..	..	..	..
Congo, Rep.		..	..	..		..	..	..		..	..	..	..
Costa Rica	1992	25.5	19.2	22.0		..	..	..	1998	12.6	6.2	26.0	12.8
Côte d'Ivoire	1993	..	..	32.3	1995	..	..	36.8	1995	12.3	2.4	49.4	16.8
Croatia		..	..	..		..	..	..	1998	<2	<0.5	<2	<0.5
Cuba		..	..	..		..	..	..		..	..	..	..
Czech Republic		..	..	..		..	..	..	1996	<2	<0.5	<2	<0.5
Denmark		..	..	..		..	..	..		..	..	..	..
Dominican Republic	1989	27.4	23.3	24.5	1992	29.8	10.9	20.6	1996	3.2	0.7	16.0	5.0
Ecuador	1994	47.0	25.0	35.0		..	..	..	1995	20.2	5.8	52.3	21.2
Egypt, Arab Rep.	1995-96	23.3	22.5	22.9		..	..	..	1995	3.1	<0.5	52.7	13.9
El Salvador	1992	55.7	43.1	48.3		..	..	..	1998	21.0	7.8	44.5	20.6
Eritrea	1993-94	..	..	53.0		..	..	..		..	..	..	..
Estonia	1995	14.7	6.8	8.9		..	..	..	1998	<2	<0.5	5.2	0.8
Ethiopia		..	..	..		..	..	..	1995	31.3	8.0	76.4	32.9
Finland		..	..	..		..	..	..		..	..	..	..
France		..	..	..		..	..	..		..	..	..	..
Gabon		..	..	..		..	..	..		..	..	..	..
Gambia, The	1992	..	..	64.0		..	..	..	1998	59.3	28.8	82.9	51.1
Georgia	1997	9.9	12.1	11.1		..	..	..	1996	<2	<0.5	<2	<0.5
Germany		..	..	..		..	..	..		..	..	..	..
Ghana	1992	34.3	26.7	31.4		..	..	..	1999	44.8	17.3	78.5	40.8
Greece		..	..	..		..	..	..		..	..	..	..
Guatemala	1989	71.9	33.7	57.9		..	..	..	1998	10.0	2.2	33.8	11.8
Guinea	1994	..	..	40.0		..	..	..		..	..	..	..
Guinea-Bissau	1991	..	..	48.7		..	..	..		..	..	..	..
Haiti	1987	..	..	65.0	1995	66.0	..	..		..	..	..	..
Honduras	1992	46.0	56.0	50.0	1993	51.0	57.0	53.0	1998	24.3	11.9	45.1	23.5

2002 World Development Indicators

	National poverty line								International poverty line				
		Population below the poverty line				Population below the poverty line				Population below $1 a day %	Poverty gap at $1 a day %	Population below $2 a day %	Poverty gap at $2 a day %
	Survey year	Rural %	Urban %	National %	Survey year	Rural %	Urban %	National %	Survey year				
Hungary	1989	..	..	1.6	1993	..	..	8.6	1998	<2	<0.5	7.3	1.7
India	1992	43.5	33.7	40.9	1994	36.7	30.5	35.0	1997	44.2	12.0	86.2	41.4
Indonesia	1996	..	..	15.7	1999	..	..	27.1	1999	7.7	1.0	55.3	16.5
Iran, Islamic Rep.		..	..	..		..	..	..		..	..	..	..
Iraq		..	..	..		..	..	..		..	..	..	..
Ireland		..	..	..		..	..	..		..	..	..	..
Israel		..	..	..		..	..	..		..	..	..	..
Italy		..	..	..		..	..	..		..	..	..	..
Jamaica	1992	..	..	33.9	2000	..	..	18.7	1996	3.2	0.7	25.2	6.9
Japan		..	..	..		..	..	..		..	..	..	..
Jordan	1991	..	..	15.0	1997	..	..	11.7	1997	<2	<0.5	7.4	1.4
Kazakhstan	1996	39.0	30.0	34.6		..	..	..	1996	<2	<0.5	15.3	3.9
Kenya	1992	46.4	29.3	42.0		..	..	..	1994	26.5	9.0	62.3	27.5
Korea, Dem. Rep.		..	..	..		..	..	..		..	..	..	..
Korea, Rep.		..	..	..		..	..	..	1993	<2	<0.5	<2	<0.5
Kuwait		..	..	..		..	..	..		..	..	..	..
Kyrgyz Republic	1993	48.1	28.7	40.0	1997	64.5	28.5	51.0		..	..	..	..
Lao PDR	1993	53.0	24.0	46.1		..	..	..	1997	26.3	6.3	73.2	29.6
Latvia		..	..	..		..	..	..	1998	<2	<0.5	8.3	2.0
Lebanon		..	..	..		..	..	..		..	..	..	..
Lesotho	1993	53.9	27.8	49.2		..	..	..	1993	43.1	20.3	65.7	38.1
Liberia		..	..	..		..	..	..		..	..	..	..
Libya		..	..	..		..	..	..		..	..	..	..
Lithuania		..	..	..		..	..	..	1996	<2	<0.5	7.8	2.0
Macedonia, FYR		..	..	..		..	..	..		..	..	..	..
Madagascar	1993-94	77.0	47.0	70.0		..	..	..	1999	49.1	18.3	83.3	44.0
Malawi	1990-91	..	..	54.0		..	..	..		..	..	..	..
Malaysia	1989	..	..	15.5		..	..	..		..	..	..	..
Mali		..	..	..		..	..	..	1994	72.8	37.4	90.6	60.5
Mauritania	1989-90	..	..	57.0		..	..	..	1995	28.6	9.1	68.7	29.6
Mauritius	1992	..	..	10.6		..	..	..		..	..	..	..
Mexico	1988	..	..	10.1		..	..	..	1998	15.9	5.2	37.7	16.0
Moldova	1997	26.7	..	23.3		..	..	..	1997	11.3	3.0	38.4	14.0
Mongolia	1995	33.1	38.5	36.3		..	..	..	1995	13.9	3.1	50.0	17.5
Morocco	1990-91	18.0	7.6	13.1	1998-99	27.2	12.0	19.0	1990-91	<2	<0.5	7.5	1.3
Mozambique		..	..	..		..	..	..	1996	37.9	12.0	78.4	36.8
Myanmar		..	..	..		..	..	..		..	..	..	..
Namibia		..	..	..		..	..	..	1993	34.9	14.0	55.8	30.4
Nepal	1995-96	44.0	23.0	42.0		..	..	..	1995	37.7	9.7	82.5	37.5
Netherlands		..	..	..		..	..	..		..	..	..	..
New Zealand		..	..	..		..	..	..		..	..	..	..
Nicaragua	1993	76.1	31.9	50.3		..	..	..		..	..	..	..
Niger	1989-93	66.0	52.0	63.0		..	..	..	1995	61.4	33.9	85.3	54.8
Nigeria	1985	49.5	31.7	43.0	1992-93	36.4	30.4	34.1	1997	70.2	34.9	90.8	59.0
Norway		..	..	..		..	..	..		..	..	..	..
Oman		..	..	..		..	..	..		..	..	..	..
Pakistan	1991	36.9	28.0	34.0		..	..	..	1996	31.0	6.2	84.7	35.0
Panama	1997	64.9	15.3	37.3		..	..	..	1998	14.0	5.9	29.0	13.8
Papua New Guinea		..	..	..		..	..	..	..	..	..	..	..
Paraguay	1991	28.5	19.7	21.8		..	..	..	1998	19.5	9.8	49.3	26.3
Peru	1994	67.0	46.1	53.5	1997	64.7	40.4	49.0	1996	15.5	5.4	41.4	17.1
Philippines	1994	53.1	28.0	40.6	1997	50.7	21.5	36.8	..	..	..	..	..
Poland	1993	..	..	23.8		..	..	..	1998	<2	<0.5	<2	<0.5
Portugal		..	..	..		..	..	..	1994	<2	<0.5	<2	<0.5
Puerto Rico		..	..	..		..	..	..		..	..	..	..
Romania	1994	27.9	20.4	21.5		..	..	..	1994	2.8	0.8	27.5	6.9
Russian Federation	1994	..	..	30.9		..	..	..	1998	7.1	1.4	25.1	8.7

2.6 | Poverty

	National poverty line								International poverty line				
		Population below the poverty line				Population below the poverty line				Population below $1 a day %	Poverty gap at $1 a day %	Population below $2 a day %	Poverty gap at $2 a day %
	Survey year	Rural %	Urban %	National %	Survey year	Rural %	Urban %	National %	Survey year				
Rwanda	1993	..	..	51.2		..	..	..	1983-85	35.7	7.7	84.6	36.7
Saudi Arabia		..	..	..		..	..	..		..	..	..	..
Senegal	1992	40.4	..	33.4		..	..	..	1995	26.3	7.0	67.8	28.2
Sierra Leone	1989	76.0	53.0	68.0		..	..	..	1989	57.0	39.5	74.5	51.8
Singapore		..	..	..		..	..	..		..	..	..	..
Slovak Republic		..	..	..		..	..	..	1992	<2	<0.5	<2	<0.5
Slovenia		..	..	..		..	..	..	1998	<2	<0.5	<2	<0.5
Somalia		..	..	..		..	..	..		..	..	..	..
South Africa		..	..	..		..	..	..	1993	11.5	1.8	35.8	13.4
Spain		..	..	..		..	..	..		..	..	..	..
Sri Lanka	1990-91	..	..	20.0	1995-96	..	..	25.0	1995	6.6	1.0	45.4	13.5
Sudan		..	..	..		..	..	..		..	..	..	..
Swaziland	1995	..	..	40.0		..	..	..		..	..	..	..
Sweden		..	..	..		..	..	..		..	..	..	..
Switzerland		..	..	..		..	..	..		..	..	..	..
Syrian Arab Republic		..	..	..		..	..	..		..	..	..	..
Tajikistan		..	..	..		..	..	..		..	..	..	..
Tanzania	1991	..	..	51.1	1993	49.7	24.4	41.6	1993	19.9	4.8	59.7	23.0
Thailand	1990	..	..	18.0	1992	15.5	10.2	13.1	1998	<2	<0.5	28.2	7.1
Togo	1987-89	..	..	32.3		..	..	..		..	..	..	..
Trinidad and Tobago	1992	20.0	24.0	21.0		..	..	..	1992	12.4	3.5	39.0	14.6
Tunisia	1985	29.2	12.0	19.9	1990	21.6	8.9	14.1	1995	<2	<0.5	10.0	2.3
Turkey		..	..	..		..	..	..	1994	2.4	0.5	18.0	5.0
Turkmenistan		..	..	..		..	..	..	1998	12.1	2.6	44.0	15.4
Uganda	1993	..	..	55.0		..	..	..		..	..	..	..
Ukraine	1995	..	..	31.7		..	..	..	1999	2.9	0.6	31.0	8.0
United Arab Emirates		..	..	..		..	..	..		..	..	..	..
United Kingdom		..	..	..		..	..	..		..	..	..	..
United States		..	..	..		..	..	..		..	..	..	..
Uruguay		..	..	..		..	..	..	1989	<2	<0.5	6.6	1.9
Uzbekistan		..	..	..		..	..	..	1993	3.3	0.5	26.5	7.3
Venezuela, RB	1989	..	..	31.3		..	..	..	1998	23.0	10.8	47.0	23.0
Vietnam	1993	57.2	25.9	50.9		..	..	..		..	..	..	..
West Bank and Gaza		..	..	..		..	..	..		..	..	..	..
Yemen, Rep.	1992	19.2	18.6	19.1		..	..	..	1998	15.7	4.5	45.2	15.0
Yugoslavia, FR (Serb./Mont.)		..	..	..		..	..	..		..	..	..	..
Zambia	1991	88.0	46.0	68.0	1993	..	..	86.0	1998	63.7	32.7	87.4	55.4
Zimbabwe	1990-91	31.0	10.0	25.5		..	..	..	1990-91	36.0	9.6	64.2	29.4

Poverty 2.6

About the data

International comparisons of poverty data entail both conceptual and practical problems. Different countries have different definitions of poverty, and consistent comparisons between countries can be difficult. Local poverty lines tend to have higher purchasing power in rich countries, where more generous standards are used than in poor countries. Is it reasonable to treat two people with the same standard of living—in terms of their command over commodities—differently because one happens to live in a better-off country? Can we hold the real value of the poverty line constant across countries, just as we do when making comparisons over time?

Poverty measures based on an international poverty line attempt to do this. The commonly used $1 a day standard, measured in 1985 international prices and adjusted to local currency using purchasing power parities (PPPs), was chosen for the World Bank's *World Development Report 1990: Poverty* because it is typical of the poverty lines in low-income countries. PPP exchange rates, such as those from the Penn World Tables or the World Bank, are used because they take into account the local prices of goods and services not traded internationally. But PPP rates were designed not for making international poverty comparisons but for comparing aggregates from national accounts. As a result, there is no certainty that an international poverty line measures the same degree of need or deprivation across countries.

Past editions of the *World Development Indicators* used PPPs from the Penn World Tables. Because the Penn World Tables updated to 1993 are not yet available, this year's edition (like last year's) uses 1993 consumption PPP estimates produced by the World Bank. The international poverty line, set at $1 a day in 1985 PPP terms, has been recalculated in 1993 PPP terms at about $1.08 a day. Any revisions in the PPP of a country to incorporate better price indexes can produce dramatically different poverty lines in local currency.

Problems also exist in comparing poverty measures within countries. For example, the cost of living is typically higher in urban than in rural areas. (Food staples, for example, tend to be more expensive in urban areas.) So the urban monetary poverty line should be higher than the rural poverty line. But it is not always clear that the difference between urban and rural poverty lines found in practice properly reflects the difference in the cost of living. In some countries the urban poverty line in common use has a higher real value—meaning that it allows the purchase of more commodities for consumption—than does the rural poverty line. Sometimes the difference has been so large as to imply that the incidence of poverty is greater in urban than in rural areas, even though the reverse is found when adjustments are made only

for differences in the cost of living. As with international comparisons, when the real value of the poverty line varies, it is not clear how meaningful such urban-rural comparisons are.

The problems of making poverty comparisons do not end there. More issues arise in measuring household living standards. The choice between income and consumption as a welfare indicator is one issue. Income is generally more difficult to measure accurately, and consumption accords better with the idea of the standard of living than does income, which can vary over time even if the standard of living does not. But consumption data are not always available, and when they are not there is little choice but to use income. There are still other problems. Household survey questionnaires can differ widely, for example, in the number of distinct categories of consumer goods they identify. Survey quality varies, and even similar surveys may not be strictly comparable.

Comparisons across countries at different levels of development also pose a potential problem, because of differences in the relative importance of consumption of nonmarket goods. The local market value of all consumption in kind (including consumption from own production, particularly important in underdeveloped rural economies) should be included in the measure of total consumption expenditure. Similarly, the imputed profit from production of nonmarket goods should be included in income. This is not always done, though such omissions were a far bigger problem in surveys before the 1980s. Most survey data now include valuations for consumption or income from own production. Nonetheless, valuation methods vary. For example, some surveys use the price in the nearest market, while others use the average farm gate selling price.

Whenever possible, consumption has been used as the welfare indicator for deciding who is poor. When only household income was available, average income has been adjusted to accord with either a survey-based estimate of mean consumption (when available) or an estimate based on consumption data from national accounts. This procedure adjusts only the mean, however; nothing can be done to correct for the difference in Lorenz (income distribution) curves between consumption and income.

Empirical Lorenz curves were weighted by household size, so they are based on percentiles of population, not households. In all cases the measures of poverty have been calculated from primary data sources (tabulations or household data) rather than existing estimates. Estimation from tabulations requires an interpolation method; the method chosen was Lorenz curves with flexible functional forms, which have proved reliable in past work.

Definitions

• **Survey year** is the year in which the underlying data were collected. • **Rural poverty rate** is the percentage of the rural population living below the national rural poverty line. • **Urban poverty rate** is the percentage of the urban population living below the national urban poverty line. • **National poverty rate** is the percentage of the population living below the national poverty line. National estimates are based on population-weighted subgroup estimates from household surveys. • **Population below $1 a day** and **population below $2 a day** are the percentages of the population living on less than $1.08 a day and $2.15 a day at 1993 international prices (equivalent to $1 and $2 in 1985 prices, adjusted for purchasing power parity). Poverty rates are comparable across countries, but as a result of revisions in PPP exchange rates, they cannot be compared with poverty rates reported in previous editions for individual countries. • **Poverty gap** is the mean shortfall from the poverty line (counting the nonpoor as having zero shortfall), expressed as a percentage of the poverty line. This measure reflects the depth of poverty as well as its incidence.

Data sources

The poverty measures are prepared by the World Bank's Development Research Group. The national poverty lines are based on the Bank's country poverty assessments. The international poverty lines are based on nationally representative primary household surveys conducted by national statistical offices or by private agencies under the supervision of government or international agencies and obtained from government statistical offices and World Bank country departments. The World Bank has prepared an annual review of poverty work in the Bank since 1993. *Poverty Reduction and the World Bank: Operationalizing the World Develoment Report 2000/01* is forthcoming.

2.7 | Social indicators of poverty

	Survey year	Infant mortality rate		Delivery attendance by a medically trained person		Prevalence of child malnutrition		Low mother's body-mass index		Total fertility rate	
		per 1,000 live births		% of births in the five years prior to the survey		% of children under five		% of women		births per woman	
		Poorest quintile	**Richest quintile**	**Poorest quintile**	**Richest quintile**	**Poorest quintile**	**Richest quintile**	**Poorest quintile**	**Richest quintile**	**Poorest quintile**	**Richest quintile**
Bangladesh	1996-97	96	57	2	30	60	28	64.4	32.6	3.8	2.2
Benin	1996	119	63	34	98	37	19	21.0	7.0	7.3	3.8
Bolivia	1998	107	26	20	98	17	3	0.5	2.2	7.4	2.1
Brazil	1996	83	29	72	99	12	3	8.8	5.4	4.8	1.7
Burkina Faso	1992-93	114	80	26	86	36	22	15.7	10.2	7.5	4.6
Cameroon	1991	104	51	32	95	25	6	..	..	6.2	4.8
Central African Republic	1994-95	132	54	14	82	37	20	16.3	11.2	5.1	4.9
Chad	1996-97	80	89	3	47	50	29	27.5	21.0	7.1	6.2
Colombia	1995	41	16	61	98	15	3	5.9	1.2	5.2	1.7
Comoros	1996	87	65	26	85	36	18	7.4	8.6	6.4	3.0
Côte d'Ivoire	1994	117	63	17	84	31	13	11.0	5.7	6.4	3.7
Dominican Republic	1996	67	23	89	98	13	1	8.9	3.0	5.1	2.1
Egypt, Arab Rep.	1995-96	110	32	21	86	17	8	2.9	0.4	4.4	2.7
Ghana	1993	78	46	25	85	33	13	11.3	7.2	6.7	3.4
Guatemala	1995	57	35	9	92	35	7	4.2	2.0	8.0	2.4
Haiti	1994-95	94	74	24	78	39	10	24.9	9.3	7.0	2.3
India	1992-93	109	44	12	79	60	34	..	..	4.1	2.1
Indonesia	1997	78	23	21	89	..	..	..	..	3.3	2.0
Kazakhstan	1995	35	29	99	100	11	3	7.9	3.8	3.2	1.3
Kenya	1998	103	50	23	80	32	10	17.6	6.0	6.6	3.0
Kyrgyz Republic	1997	83	46	96	100	13	8	5.6	3.7	4.6	2.0
Madagascar	1997	119	58	30	89	45	32	24.3	15.1	8.1	3.4
Malawi	1992	141	106	45	78	34	17	14.1	6.0	7.2	6.1
Mali	1995-96	151	93	11	81	47	28	15.9	12.2	6.9	5.1
Morocco	1993	80	35	5	78	17	2	6.2	1.8	6.7	2.3
Mozambique	1997	188	95	18	82	37	14	17.2	4.2	5.2	4.4
Namibia	1992	64	57	51	91	36	13	19.3	5.3	6.9	3.6
Nepal	1996	96	64	3	34	53	28	25.7	21.4	6.2	2.9
Nicaragua	1997-98	51	26	33	92	18	4	4.0	4.1	6.6	1.9
Niger	1998	131	86	4	63	52	37	26.7	12.8	8.4	5.7
Nigeria	1990	102	69	12	70	40	22	..	..	6.6	4.7
Pakistan	1990-91	89	63	5	55	54	26	..	..	5.1	4.0
Paraguay	1990-91	43	16	41	98	6	1	..	..	7.9	2.7
Peru	1996	78	20	14	97	17	1	1.3	1.1	6.6	1.7
Philippines	1998	49	21	21	92	..	..	..	..	6.5	2.1
Senegal	1997	85	45	20	86	..	..	..	..	7.4	3.6
Tanzania	1996	87	65	27	81	40	18	12.2	7.1	7.8	3.9
Togo	1998	84	66	25	91	32	12	13.3	7.9	7.3	2.9
Turkey	1993	100	25	43	99	22	3	2.7	3.2	3.7	1.5
Uganda	1995	109	63	23	70	31	16	12.7	5.8	7.5	5.4
Uzbekistan	1996	50	47	92	100	25	12	11.4	5.7	4.4	2.1
Vietnam	1997	43	17	49	99	..	..	..	..	3.1	1.6
Yemen, Rep.	1997	109	60	7	50	20	6	39.0	13.1	7.3	4.7
Zambia	1996	124	70	19	91	32	13	10.2	7.9	7.4	4.4
Zimbabwe	1994	52	42	55	93	19	9	5.7	1.2	6.2	2.8

About the data

The data in the table describe the health status of individuals in different socioeconomic groups within countries. The data are from Demographic and Health Surveys conducted by Macro International with the support of the U.S. Agency for International Development. These large-scale household sample surveys, conducted periodically in about 50 developing countries, collect information on a large number of health, nutrition, and population measures as well as on respondents' social, demographic, and economic characteristics using a standard set of questionnaires.

In the table socioeconomic status is defined in terms of household assets, including ownership of consumer items, characteristics of the household's dwelling, and other characteristics related to wealth. Each household asset for which information was collected was assigned a weight generated through principal component analysis. The resulting scores were standardized and then used to create break points defining wealth quintiles, expressed as quintiles of individuals.

The choice of the asset index for defining socioeconomic status was based on pragmatic rather than conceptual considerations: Demographic and Health Surveys do not provide income or consumption data but do have detailed information on household ownership of consumer goods and access to a variety of goods and services. Like income or consumption, the asset index defines disparities in primarily economic terms. It therefore excludes other possibilities of disparities among groups, such as those based on gender, education, ethnic background, or other facets of social exclusion. To that extent the index provides only a partial view of the multidimensional concepts of poverty, inequality, and inequity.

The analysis has been carried out for 45 countries, with the results issued in country reports. The table shows the estimates for the poorest and richest quintiles only; the full set of estimates for more than 20 indicators is available in the country reports (see *Data sources*).

Figure 2.7

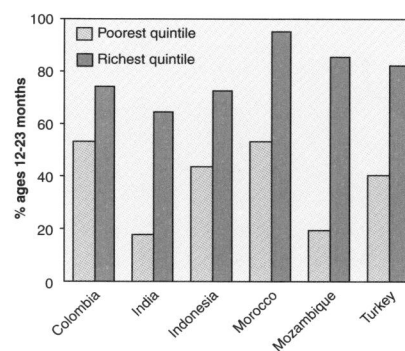

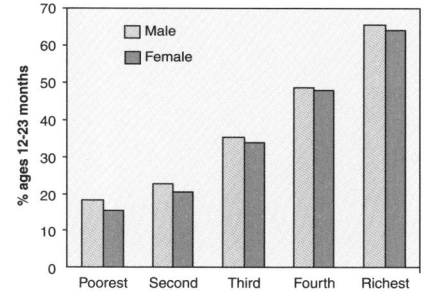

Source: Demographic and Health Survey data.

Governments in developing countries usually finance immunization against childhood diseases as part of the basic health package. The large discrepancies between poor and rich quintiles indicate the lack of access to basic health care among the poor. And while the differences in immunization rates for boys and girls across quintiles in India points to female disadvantage, the data underscore that poverty has a larger impact on access to health care than does gender.

Definitions

• **Survey year** is the year in which the underlying data were collected. • **Infant mortality rate** is the number of infants dying before reaching one year of age, per 1,000 live births. The estimates are based on births in the 10 years preceding the survey and may therefore differ from the estimates in table 2.20. • **Delivery attendance by a medically trained person** refers to births attended by a doctor, nurse, or nurse-midwife. • **Prevalence of child malnutrition** is the percentage of children whose weight is more than two standard deviations below the median reference standard for their age as established by the U.S. National Center for Health Statistics, the U.S. Centers for Disease Control and Prevention, and the World Health Organization. The data are based on a sample of children who survived to age three, four, or five years, depending on the country. • **Low mother's body mass index** refers to the percentage of women whose body mass index (BMI) is less than 18.5, a cutoff point indicating acute malnutrition. The BMI is the weight in kilograms divided by the square of the height in meters. • **Total fertility rate** is the number of children that would be born to a woman if she were to live to the end of her childbearing years and bear children in accordance with current age-specific fertility rates. The estimates are based on births during the three years preceding the survey and may therefore differ from those in table 2.17.

Data sources

Data are from an analysis of Demographic and Health Surveys by the World Bank and Macro International. Country reports are available at www.worldbank.org/poverty/health/data/index.htm.

2.8 | Distribution of income or consumption

	Survey year	Gini Index	Percentage share of income or consumption						
			Lowest 10%	Lowest 20%	Second 20%	Third 20%	Fourth 20%	Highest 20%	Highest 10%
Afghanistan		..	..	..	..	..	..	..	..
Albania		..	..	..	..	..	..	..	..
Algeria	1995 [a,b]	35.3	2.8	7.0	11.6	16.1	22.7	42.6	26.8
Angola		..	..	..	..	..	..	..	..
Argentina		..	..	..	..	..	..	..	..
Armenia	1996 [a,b]	44.4	2.3	5.5	9.4	13.9	20.6	50.6	35.2
Australia	1994 [c,d]	35.2	2.0	5.9	12.0	17.2	23.6	41.3	25.4
Austria	1995 [c,d]	31.0	2.5	6.9	13.2	18.1	23.9	38.0	22.5
Azerbaijan	1995 [c,d]	36.0	2.8	6.9	11.5	16.1	22.3	43.3	27.8
Bangladesh	1995-96 [a,b]	33.6	3.9	8.7	12.0	15.7	20.8	42.8	28.6
Belarus	1998 [a,b]	21.7	5.1	11.4	15.2	18.2	21.9	33.3	20.0
Belgium	1996 [c,d]	28.7	3.2	8.3	13.9	18.0	22.6	37.3	23.0
Benin		..	..	..	..	..	..	..	..
Bolivia	1999 [a,b]	44.7	1.3	4.0	9.2	14.8	22.9	49.1	32.0
Bosnia and Herzegovina		..	..	..	..	..	..	..	..
Botswana		..	..	..	..	..	..	..	..
Brazil	1998 [c,d]	60.7	0.7	2.2	5.4	10.1	18.3	64.1	48.0
Bulgaria	1997 [c,d]	26.4	4.5	10.1	13.9	17.4	21.9	36.8	22.8
Burkina Faso	1998 [a,b]	55.1	2.0	4.6	7.2	10.8	17.1	60.4	46.8
Burundi	1998 [a,b]	42.5	1.8	5.1	10.3	15.1	21.5	48.0	32.9
Cambodia	1997 [a,b]	40.4	2.9	6.9	10.7	14.7	20.1	47.6	33.8
Cameroon	1996 [a,b]	47.7	1.9	4.6	8.3	13.1	20.9	53.1	36.6
Canada	1994 [c,d]	31.5	2.8	7.5	12.9	17.2	23.0	39.3	23.8
Central African Republic	1993 [a,b]	61.3	0.7	2.0	4.9	9.6	18.5	65.0	47.7
Chad		..	..	..	..	..	..	..	..
Chile	1998 [c,d]	56.7	1.3	3.3	6.5	10.9	18.4	61.0	45.6
China	1998 [c,d]	40.3	2.4	5.9	10.2	15.1	22.2	46.6	30.4
Hong Kong, China	1996 [c,d]	52.2	1.8	4.4	8.0	12.2	18.3	57.1	43.5
Colombia	1996 [c,d]	57.1	1.1	3.0	6.6	11.1	18.4	60.9	46.1
Congo, Dem. Rep.		..	..	..	..	..	..	..	..
Congo, Rep.		..	..	..	..	..	..	..	..
Costa Rica	1997 [c,d]	45.9	1.7	4.5	8.9	14.1	21.6	51.0	34.6
Côte d'Ivoire	1995 [a,b]	36.7	3.1	7.1	11.2	15.6	21.9	44.3	28.8
Croatia	1998 [c,d]	29.0	3.7	8.8	13.3	17.4	22.6	38.0	23.3
Cuba		..	..	..	..	..	..	..	..
Czech Republic	1996 [c,d]	25.4	4.3	10.3	14.5	17.7	21.7	35.9	22.4
Denmark	1992 [c,d]	24.7	3.6	9.6	14.9	18.3	22.7	34.5	20.5
Dominican Republic	1998 [c,d]	47.4	2.1	5.1	8.6	13.0	20.0	53.3	37.9
Ecuador	1995 [a,b]	43.7	2.2	5.4	9.4	14.2	21.3	49.7	33.8
Egypt, Arab Rep.	1995 [a,b]	28.9	4.4	9.8	13.2	16.6	21.4	39.0	25.0
El Salvador	1998 [c,d]	52.2	1.2	3.3	7.3	12.4	20.7	56.4	39.5
Eritrea		..	..	..	..	..	..	..	..
Estonia	1998 [c,d]	37.6	3.0	7.0	11.0	15.3	21.6	45.1	29.8
Ethiopia	1995 [a,b]	40.0	3.0	7.1	10.9	14.5	19.8	47.7	33.7
Finland	1991 [c,d]	25.6	4.2	10.0	14.2	17.6	22.3	35.8	21.6
France	1995 [c,d]	32.7	2.8	7.2	12.6	17.2	22.8	40.2	25.1
Gabon		..	..	..	..	..	..	..	..
Gambia, The	1998 [a, b]	50.2	1.6	4.0	7.6	12.4	20.8	55.3	38.2
Georgia	1996 [c,d]	37.1	2.3	6.1	11.4	16.3	22.7	43.6	27.9
Germany	1994 [c,d]	30.0	3.3	8.2	13.2	17.5	22.7	38.5	23.7
Ghana	1999 [a,b]	40.7	2.2	5.6	10.0	15.1	22.6	46.7	30.1
Greece	1993 [c,d]	32.7	3.0	7.5	12.4	16.9	22.8	40.3	25.3
Guatemala	1998 [c,d]	55.8	1.6	3.8	6.8	10.9	17.9	60.6	46.0
Guinea	1994 [a,b]	40.3	2.6	6.4	10.4	14.8	21.2	47.2	32.0
Guinea-Bissau	1991 [a,b]	56.2	0.5	2.1	6.5	12.0	20.6	58.9	42.4
Guyana	1993 [a,b]	40.2	2.4	6.3	10.7	15.0	21.2	46.9	32.0
Haiti		..	..	..	..	..	..	..	..
Honduras	1998 [c,d]	56.3	0.6	2.2	6.4	11.8	20.3	59.4	42.7

	Survey year	Gini Index	Percentage share of income or consumption						
			Lowest 10%	Lowest 20%	Second 20%	Third 20%	Fourth 20%	Highest 20%	Highest 10%
Hungary	1998 a,b	24.4	4.1	10.0	14.7	18.3	22.7	34.4	20.5
India	1997 a,b	37.8	3.5	8.1	11.6	15.0	19.3	46.1	33.5
Indonesia	1999 a,b	31.7	4.0	9.0	12.5	16.1	21.3	41.1	26.7
Iran, Islamic Rep.		..	..	..	..	..	..	..	..
Iraq		..	..	..	..	..	..	..	..
Ireland	1987 c,d	35.9	2.5	6.7	11.6	16.4	22.4	42.9	27.4
Israel	1997 c,d	38.1	2.4	6.1	10.7	15.9	23.0	44.2	28.3
Italy	1995 c,d	27.3	3.5	8.7	14.0	18.1	22.9	36.3	21.8
Jamaica	2000 a,b	37.9	2.7	6.7	10.7	15.0	21.8	46.0	30.3
Japan	1993 c,d	24.9	4.8	10.6	14.2	17.6	22.0	35.7	21.7
Jordan	1997 a,b	36.4	3.3	7.6	11.4	15.5	21.1	44.4	29.8
Kazakhstan	1996 a,b	35.4	2.7	6.7	11.5	16.4	23.1	42.3	26.3
Kenya	1997 a,b	44.9	2.4	5.6	9.3	13.6	20.3	51.2	36.1
Korea, Dem. Rep.		..	..	..	..	..	..	..	..
Korea, Rep.	1993 a,b	31.6	2.9	7.5	12.9	17.4	22.9	39.3	24.3
Kuwait		..	..	..	..	..	..	..	..
Kyrgyz Republic	1999 a,b	34.6	3.2	7.6	11.7	16.1	22.1	42.5	27.2
Lao PDR	1997 a,b	37.0	3.2	7.6	11.4	15.3	20.8	45.0	30.6
Latvia	1998 c,d	32.4	2.9	7.6	12.9	17.1	22.1	40.3	25.9
Lebanon		..	..	..	..	..	..	..	..
Lesotho	1986-87 a,b	56.0	0.9	2.8	6.5	11.2	19.4	60.1	43.4
Liberia		..	..	..	..	..	..	..	..
Libya		..	..	..	..	..	..	..	..
Lithuania	1996 a,b	32.4	3.1	7.8	12.6	16.8	22.4	40.3	25.6
Luxembourg	1994 c,d	26.9	4.0	9.4	13.8	17.7	22.6	36.5	22.0
Macedonia, FYR		..	..	..	..	..	..	..	..
Madagascar	1999 a,b	38.1	2.6	6.4	10.7	15.6	22.5	44.9	28.6
Malawi		..	..	..	..	..	..	..	..
Malaysia	1997 c,d	49.2	1.7	4.4	8.1	12.9	20.3	54.3	38.4
Mali	1994 a,b	50.5	1.8	4.6	8.0	11.9	19.3	56.2	40.4
Mauritania	1995 a,b	37.3	2.5	6.4	11.2	16.0	22.4	44.1	28.4
Mauritius		..	..	..	..	..	..	..	..
Mexico	1998 c,d	53.1	1.3	3.5	7.3	12.1	19.7	57.4	41.7
Moldova	1997 c,d	40.6	2.2	5.6	10.2	15.2	22.2	46.8	30.7
Mongolia	1995 a,b	33.2	2.9	7.3	12.2	16.6	23.0	40.9	24.5
Morocco	1998-99 a,b	39.5	2.6	6.5	10.6	14.8	21.3	46.6	30.9
Mozambique	1996-97 a,b	39.6	2.5	6.5	10.8	15.1	21.1	46.5	31.7
Myanmar		..	..	..	..	..	..	..	..
Namibia		..	..	..	..	..	..	..	..
Nepal	1995-96 a,b	36.7	3.2	7.6	11.5	15.1	21.0	44.8	29.8
Netherlands	1994 c,d	32.6	2.8	7.3	12.7	17.2	22.8	40.1	25.1
New Zealand		..	..	..	..	..	..	..	..
Nicaragua	1998 a,b	60.3	0.7	2.3	5.9	10.4	17.9	63.6	48.8
Niger	1995 a,b	50.5	0.8	2.6	7.1	13.9	23.1	53.3	35.4
Nigeria	1996-97 a,b	50.6	1.6	4.4	8.2	12.5	19.3	55.7	40.8
Norway	1995 c,d	25.8	4.1	9.7	14.3	17.9	22.2	35.8	21.8
Oman		..	..	..	..	..	..	..	..
Pakistan	1996-97 a,b	31.2	4.1	9.5	12.9	16.0	20.5	41.1	27.6
Panama	1997 a,b	48.5	1.2	3.6	8.1	13.6	21.9	52.8	35.7
Papua New Guinea	1996 a,b	50.9	1.7	4.5	7.9	11.9	19.2	56.5	40.5
Paraguay	1998 c,d	57.7	0.5	1.9	6.0	11.4	20.1	60.7	43.8
Peru	1996 c,d	46.2	1.6	4.4	9.1	14.1	21.3	51.2	35.4
Philippines	1997 a,b	46.2	2.3	5.4	8.8	13.2	20.3	52.3	36.6
Poland	1998 a,b	31.6	3.2	7.8	12.8	17.1	22.6	39.7	24.7
Portugal	1994-95 c,d	35.6	3.1	7.3	11.6	15.9	21.8	43.4	28.4
Puerto Rico		..	..	..	..	..	..	..	..
Romania	1998 a,b	31.1	3.2	8.0	13.1	17.2	22.3	39.5	25.0
Russian Federation	1998 a,b	48.7	1.7	4.4	8.6	13.3	20.1	53.7	38.7

	Survey year	Gini Index	Percentage share of income or consumption						
			Lowest 10%	Lowest 20%	Second 20%	Third 20%	Fourth 20%	Highest 20%	Highest 10%
Rwanda	1983-85 a,b	28.9	4.2	9.7	13.2	16.5	21.6	39.1	24.2
Saudi Arabia		..	..	..	..	..	..	..	..
Senegal	1995 a,b	41.3	2.6	6.4	10.3	14.5	20.6	48.2	33.5
Sierra Leone	1989 a,b	62.9	0.5	1.1	2.0	9.8	23.7	63.4	43.6
Singapore		..	..	..	..	..	..	..	..
Slovak Republic	1992 c,d	19.5	5.1	11.9	15.8	18.8	22.2	31.4	18.2
Slovenia	1998 c,d	28.4	3.9	9.1	13.4	17.3	22.5	37.7	23.0
Somalia		..	..	..	..	..	..	..	..
South Africa	1993-94 a,b	59.3	1.1	2.9	5.5	9.2	17.7	64.8	45.9
Spain	1990 c,d	32.5	2.8	7.5	12.6	17.0	22.6	40.3	25.2
Sri Lanka	1995 a,b	34.4	3.5	8.0	11.8	15.8	21.5	42.8	28.0
St. Lucia	1995 c,d	42.6	2.0	5.2	9.9	14.8	21.8	48.3	32.5
Sudan		..	..	..	..	..	..	..	..
Swaziland	1994 c,d	60.9	1.0	2.7	5.8	10.0	17.1	64.4	50.2
Sweden	1992 c,d	25.0	3.7	9.6	14.5	18.1	23.2	34.5	20.1
Switzerland	1992 c,d	33.1	2.6	6.9	12.7	17.3	22.9	40.3	25.2
Syrian Arab Republic		..	..	..	..	..	..	..	..
Tajikistan	1998 a,b	34.7	3.2	8.0	12.9	17.0	22.1	40.0	25.2
Tanzania	1993 a,b	38.2	2.8	6.8	11.0	15.1	21.6	45.5	30.1
Thailand	1998 a,b	41.4	2.8	6.4	9.8	14.2	21.2	48.4	32.4
Togo		..	..	..	..	..	..	..	..
Trinidad and Tobago	1992 c,d	40.3	2.1	5.5	10.3	15.5	22.7	45.9	29.9
Tunisia	1995 a,b	41.7	2.3	5.7	9.9	14.7	21.8	47.9	31.8
Turkey	1994 a,b	41.5	2.3	5.8	10.2	14.8	21.6	47.7	32.3
Turkmenistan	1998 a,b	40.8	2.6	6.1	10.2	14.7	21.5	47.5	31.7
Uganda	1996 a,b	37.4	3.0	7.1	11.1	15.4	21.5	44.9	29.8
Ukraine	1999 a,b	29.0	3.7	8.8	13.3	17.4	22.7	37.8	23.2
United Arab Emirates		..	..	..	..	..	..	..	..
United Kingdom	1995 c,d	36.8	2.3	6.1	11.6	16.4	22.7	43.2	27.7
United States	1997 c,d	40.8	1.8	5.2	10.5	15.6	22.4	46.4	30.5
Uruguay	1989 c,d	42.3	2.1	5.4	10.0	14.8	21.5	48.3	32.7
Uzbekistan	1998 a,b	44.7	1.2	4.0	9.5	15.0	22.4	49.1	32.8
Venezuela, RB	1998 c,d	49.5	0.8	3.0	8.2	13.8	21.8	53.2	36.5
Vietnam	1998 a,b	36.1	3.6	8.0	11.4	15.2	20.9	44.5	29.9
West Bank and Gaza		..	..	..	..	..	..	..	..
Yemen, Rep.	1998 a,b	33.4	3.0	7.4	12.2	16.7	22.5	41.2	25.9
Yugoslavia, FR (Serb./Mont.)		..	..	..	..	..	..	..	.. ..
Zambia	1998 a,b	52.6	1.1	3.3	7.6	12.5	20.0	56.6	41.0
Zimbabwe	1995 a,b	50.1	2.0	4.7	8.0	12.3	19.4	55.7	40.4

a. Refers to expenditure shares by percentiles of population.   b. Ranked by per capita expenditure.   c. Refers to income shares by percentiles of population.   d. Ranked by per capita income.

About the data

Inequality in the distribution of income is reflected in the percentage shares of either income or consumption accruing to segments of the population ranked by income or consumption levels. The segments ranked lowest by personal income receive the smallest share of total income. The Gini index provides a convenient summary measure of the degree of inequality.

Data on personal or household income or consumption come from nationally representative household surveys. The data in the table refer to different years between 1985 and 2000. Footnotes to the survey year indicate whether the rankings are based on per capita income or consumption. Each distribution is based on percentiles of population—rather than of households—with households ranked by income or expenditure per person.

Where the original data from the household survey were available, they have been used to directly calculate the income (or consumption) shares by quintile. Otherwise, shares have been estimated from the best available grouped data.

The distribution indicators have been adjusted for household size, providing a more consistent measure of per capita income or consumption. No adjustment has been made for spatial differences in cost of living within countries, because the data needed for such calculations are generally unavailable. For further details on the estimation method for low- and middle-income economies see Ravallion and Chen (1996).

Because the underlying household surveys differ in method and in the type of data collected, the distribution indicators are not strictly comparable across countries. These problems are diminishing as survey methods improve and become more standardized, but achieving strict comparability is still impossible (see *About the data* for table 2.6).

Two sources of noncomparability should be noted. First, the surveys can differ in many respects, including whether they use income or consumption expenditure as the living standard indicator. The distribution of income is typically more unequal than the distribution of consumption. In addition, the definitions of income used usually differ among surveys. Consumption is usually a much better welfare indicator, particularly in developing countries. Second, households differ in size (number of members) and in the extent of income sharing among members. And individuals differ in age and consumption needs. Differences among countries in these respects may bias comparisons of distribution.

World Bank staff have made an effort to ensure that the data are as comparable as possible. Whenever possible, consumption has been used rather than income. The income distribution and Gini indexes for high-income countries are calculated directly from the Luxembourg Income Study database, using an estimation method consistent with that applied for developing countries.

Definitions

• **Survey year** is the year in which the underlying data were collected. • **Gini index** measures the extent to which the distribution of income (or, in some cases, consumption expenditure) among individuals or households within an economy deviates from a perfectly equal distribution. A Lorenz curve plots the cumulative percentages of total income received against the cumulative number of recipients, starting with the poorest individual or household. The Gini index measures the area between the Lorenz curve and a hypothetical line of absolute equality, expressed as a percentage of the maximum area under the line. Thus a Gini index of zero represents perfect equality, while an index of 100 implies perfect inequality. • **Percentage share of income or consumption** is the share that accrues to subgroups of population indicated by deciles or quintiles. Percentage shares by quintile may not sum to 100 because of rounding.

Data sources

The data on distribution are compiled by the World Bank's Development Research Group using primary household survey data obtained from government statistical agencies and World Bank country departments. The data for high-income economies are from the Luxembourg Income Study database.

2.9 | Assessing vulnerability

	Urban informal sector employment			Children 10-14 in the labor force		Pension contributors			Private health expenditure	
	% of urban employment			% of age group				% of working age population		% of total
	Male 1995-99[a]	Female 1995-99[a]	Total 1995-99[a]	1980	2000	Year	% of labor force		Year	
Afghanistan	..	..	..	28	24		..	..		..
Albania	..	..	..	4	0	1995	32.0	31.0	1999	25.9
Algeria	..	..	..	7	0	1997	31.0	23.0	1998	27.8
Angola	..	..	..	30	26					
Argentina	48	36	43	8	2	1995	53.0	39.0	1999	71.9
Armenia	..	..	..	0	0	1995	66.6	49.4	1995	60.3
Australia	..	..	..	0	0				1998	30.0
Austria	..	..	..	0	0	1993	95.8	76.6	1999	27.9
Azerbaijan	..	..	..	0	0	1996	52.0	46.0	1997	32.5
Bangladesh	..	..	..	35	28	1993	3.5	2.6	1998	52.5
Belarus	..	..	..	0	0	1992	97.0	94.0	1998	18.1
Belgium	..	..	..	0	0	1995	86.2	65.9	1999	28.7
Benin	..	..	..	30	26	1996	4.8	..	1998	50.6
Bolivia	..	..	53	19	11	1999	14.8	13.3	1998	36.6
Bosnia and Herzegovina	..	..	..	1	0					..
Botswana	12	28	19	26	14		..	..	1998	38.3
Brazil	43	31	38	19	14	1996	36.0	31.0	1998	55.9
Bulgaria	..	..	..	0	0	1994	64.0	63.0	1999	5.7
Burkina Faso	..	..	..	71	43	1993	3.1	3.0	1998	68.1
Burundi	..	..	..	50	49	1993	3.3	3.0	1999	5.7
Cambodia	..	..	..	27	24		..	..	1998	91.6
Cameroon	..	..	..	34	23	1993	13.7	11.5	1997	79.9
Canada	..	..	..	0	0	1992	91.9	80.2	1998	29.9
Central African Republic	..	..	..	..	..		..	..	1998	33.0
Chad	..	..	..	42	37	1990	1.1	1.0	1998	21.4
Chile	33	32	32	0	0	1995	70.0	43.0	1998	53.5
China	..	..	..	30	8	1994	17.6	17.4	1999	59.2
Hong Kong, China	..	..	..	6	0		..	..	1995	55.0
Colombia	49	44	47	12	6	1999	35.0	29.3	1998	44.8
Congo, Dem. Rep.	..	..	..	33	29		..	..		..
Congo, Rep.	..	..	..	27	25	1992	5.8	5.6	1998	65.8
Costa Rica	43	36	40	10	4	1998	50.6	38.5	1998	22.6
Côte d'Ivoire	37	73	53	28	19	1997	9.3	9.1	1998	67.6
Croatia	6	7	6	0	0	1997	66.0	57.0	1997	16.4
Cuba	..	..	..	0	0		..	..	1994	9.4
Czech Republic	..	..	..	0	0	1995	85.0	67.2	1999	8.5
Denmark	..	..	..	0	0	1993	89.6	88.0	1999	17.8
Dominican Republic	..	..	..	25	13	1999	14.4	12.4	1998	61.3
Ecuador	54	55	53	9	4	1999	43.1	33.8	1998	54.1
Egypt, Arab Rep.	..	..	..	18	9	1994	50.0	34.2	1997	52.6
El Salvador	..	..	..	17	14	1996	26.2	25.0	1998	64.2
Eritrea	..	..	..	44	38		..	..	1994	45.1
Estonia	..	..	..	0	0	1995	76.0	67.0	1999	16.6
Ethiopia	19	53	33	46	41		..	..	1998	58.4
Finland	..	..	..	0	0	1993	90.3	83.6	1999	24.3
France	..	..	..	0	0	1993	88.4	74.6	1999	21.9
Gabon	..	..	..	29	14	1991	7.3	7.0	1998	33.3
Gambia, The	..	..	..	44	34		..	..	1998	50.1
Georgia	..	..	..	0	0	1996	77.0	72.0	1999	73.0
Germany	..	..	..	0	0	1995	94.2	82.3	1999	24.7
Ghana	..	..	79	16	12	1993	7.2	9.0	1998	61.4
Greece	..	..	..	5	0	1996	88.0	73.0	1998	43.7
Guatemala	..	..	..	19	14	1999	22.8	19.3	1998	52.5
Guinea	..	..	..	41	31	1993	1.5	1.8	1998	39.6
Guinea-Bissau	..	..	..	43	37		..	..		..
Haiti	..	..	..	33	23		..	..	1998	66.0
Honduras	53	58	55	14	7	1999	20.6	17.7	1998	54.4

	Urban informal sector employment			Children 10-14 in the labor force		Pension contributors			Private health expenditure	
	% of urban employment							% of		
	Male	Female	Total	% of age group			% of	working age		% of
	1995-99[a]	1995-99[a]	1995-99[a]	1980	2000	Year	labor force	population	Year	total
Hungary	..	..	..	0	0	1996	77.0	65.0	1998	23.5
India	..	..	..	21	12	1992	10.6	7.9	1997	85.0
Indonesia	19	23	21	13	8	1995	8.0	7.0	1998	53.7
Iran, Islamic Rep.	3	90	18	14	3	1994	29.8	..	1998	59.3
Iraq	..	..	..	11	2		..	..	1998	32.1
Ireland	..	..	..	1	0	1992	79.3	64.7	1998	23.2
Israel	..	..	..	0	0	1992	82.0	63.0	1998	37.4
Italy	..	..	..	2	0	1997	87.0	68.0	1999	32.0
Jamaica	26	21	24	0	0	1999	44.4	45.8	1998	44.6
Japan	..	..	..	0	0	1994	97.5	92.3	1998	21.5
Jordan	..	..	..	4	0	1995	40.0	25.0	1998	47.0
Kazakhstan	..	..	..	0	0	1997	51.0	44.0	1999	51.9
Kenya	..	..	58	45	39	1995	18.0	24.0	1998	69.8
Korea, Dem. Rep.	..	..	..	3	0		..	..		..
Korea, Rep.	..	..	..	0	0	1996	58.0	43.0	1999	56.1
Kuwait	..	..	..	0	0		..	..	1998	12.1
Kyrgyz Republic	..	..	..	0	0	1997	44.0	42.0	1999	50.5
Lao PDR	..	..	..	31	25		..	..	1998	51.6
Latvia	..	..	17	0	0	1995	60.5	52.3	1998	38.3
Lebanon	..	..	..	5	0		..	..	1998	80.1
Lesotho	..	..	..	28	21		..	..		..
Liberia	..	..	..	26	15		..	..		..
Libya	..	..	..	9	0		..	..		..
Lithuania	12	5	9	0	0		..	..	1998	24.2
Macedonia, FYR	..	..	..	1	0	1995	49.0	47.0	1998	15.4
Madagascar	..	..	58	40	34	1993	5.4	4.8	1998	46.7
Malawi	..	..	..	45	31		..	..	1998	56.0
Malaysia	..	..	..	8	2	1993	48.7	37.8	1998	42.3
Mali	..	..	71	61	51	1990	2.5	2.0	1998	51.4
Mauritania	..	..	..	30	22		..	..	1998	71.1
Mauritius	..	..	..	5	2		..	..	1998	46.4
Mexico	38	30	35	9	5	1997	30.0	31.0	1998	52.0
Moldova	..	..	..	3	0		..	..	1998	32.7
Mongolia	..	..	..	4	1		..	..	1992	8.0
Morocco	..	..	..	21	1	1994	20.9	17.8	1998	72.7
Mozambique	..	..	..	39	32		..	..	1998	19.0
Myanmar	53	57	54	28	23		..	..	1998	87.0
Namibia	..	..	..	34	17		..	..	1998	47.8
Nepal	..	..	..	56	42		..	..	1998	76.5
Netherlands	..	..	..	0	0	1993	91.7	75.4	1999	31.5
New Zealand	..	..	..	0	0		..	..	1999	22.5
Nicaragua	..	..	..	19	12	1999	14.3	13.3	1998	32.1
Niger	..	..	..	48	44	1992	1.3	1.5	1998	53.1
Nigeria	..	..	..	29	24	1993	1.3	1.3	1998	70.1
Norway	..	..	..	0	0	1993	94.0	85.8	1999	24.2
Oman	..	..	..	6	0		..	..	1998	17.1
Pakistan	..	..	..	23	15	1993	3.5	2.1	1998	76.4
Panama	36	28	32	6	3	1998	51.6	40.7	1998	32.3
Papua New Guinea	..	..	..	28	17		..	..	1998	21.6
Paraguay	..	..	58	15	6	1997	31.0	29.0	1998	68.0
Peru	45	53	48	4	2	1997	20.0	16.0	1998	61.0
Philippines	16	19	17	14	5	1996	28.3	13.6	1999	57.1
Poland	14	11	13	0	0	1996	68.0	64.0	1999	24.9
Portugal	..	..	..	8	1	1996	84.3	80.0	1998	33.1
Puerto Rico	..	..	..	0	0		..	..		..
Romania	..	..	..	0	0	1994	55.0	48.0	1998	32.6
Russian Federation	..	..	..	0	0		..	..	1997	27.8

	Urban informal sector employment			Children 10-14 in the labor force		Pension contributors			Private health expenditure	
	% of urban employment			% of age group				% of working age population		% of total
	Male 1995-99[a]	Female 1995-99[a]	Total 1995-99[a]	1980	2000	Year	% of labor force		Year	
Rwanda	..	..	..	43	41	1993	9.3	13.3	1998	51.8
Saudi Arabia	..	..	..	5	0		..	..	1997	20.0
Senegal	..	..	..	43	27	1998	4.3	4.7	1998	41.6
Sierra Leone	..	..	..	19	14		..	..	1998	83.4
Singapore	..	..	..	2	0	1995	73.0	56.0	1998	64.0
Slovak Republic	25	11	19	0	0	1996	73.0	72.0	1998	21.2
Slovenia	..	..	..	0	0	1995	86.0	68.7	1998	12.0
Somalia	..	..	..	38	31		..	..		..
South Africa	11	26	17	1	0		..	..	1998	53.4
Spain	..	..	..	0	0	1994	85.3	61.4	1998	23.1
Sri Lanka	..	..	..	4	2	1992	28.8	20.8	1999	51.0
Sudan	..	..	..	33	27	1996	3.9	..	1997	79.1
Swaziland	..	..	..	17	12		..	..	1998	28.0
Sweden	..	..	..	0	0	1994	91.1	88.9	1998	16.2
Switzerland	..	..	..	0	0	1994	98.1	96.8	1998	26.4
Syrian Arab Republic	..	..	..	14	2		..	..	1998	65.0
Tajikistan	..	..	..	0	0		..	..	1998	14.5
Tanzania	60	85	67	43	37	1996	2.0	2.0	1998	58.0
Thailand	75	79	77	25	12	1999	18.0	17.0	1998	68.7
Togo	..	..	..	36	27	1997	6.0	3.0	1998	50.0
Trinidad and Tobago	..	..	..	1	0		..	..	1998	42.4
Tunisia	..	..	..	6	0	1991	39.4	27.2	1998	56.5
Turkey	..	..	..	21	8	1990	34.6	..	1998	28.1
Turkmenistan	..	..	..	0	0		..	..	1998	20.8
Uganda	..	..	..	49	44	1994	8.2	..	1998	68.8
Ukraine	5	5	5	0	0	1995	69.8	66.1	1999	33.3
United Arab Emirates	..	..	..	0	0		..	..	1998	90.3
United Kingdom	..	..	..	0	0	1994	89.7	84.5	1999	16.7
United States	..	..	..	0	0	1993	94.0	91.9	1999	55.5
Uruguay	39	41	36	4	1	1995	82.0	78.0	1998	79.4
Uzbekistan	..	..	..	0	0		..	..	1998	15.6
Venezuela, RB	47	46	47	4	0	1999	23.6	18.2	1998	38.1
Vietnam	..	..	..	22	5	1998	8.4	10.0	1998	83.5
West Bank and Gaza	..	..	..	..	..		..	..		..
Yemen, Rep.	..	..	..	26	19		..	..	1997	57.1
Yugoslavia, FR (Serb./Mont.)	..	..	..	0	0		..	..		..
Zambia	..	..	..	19	16	1994	10.2	7.9	1998	48.3
Zimbabwe	..	..	..	37	27		..	..	1999	50.1
World				**20 w**	**11 w**					**57.3 w**
Low income				25	18					71.4
Middle income				21	6					52.7
Lower middle income				24	6					54.6
Upper middle income				10	6					46.8
Low & middle income				23	12					61.3
East Asia & Pacific				26	8					60.3
Europe & Central Asia				3	1					28.1
Latin America & Carib.				13	8					54.2
Middle East & N. Africa				14	4					50.6
South Asia				23	15					80.2
Sub-Saharan Africa				35	29					60.6
High income				0	0					35.1
Europe EMU				1	0					26.3

a. Data are for the most recent year available.

About the data

As traditionally defined and measured, poverty is a static concept, and vulnerability a dynamic one. Vulnerability reflects a household's resilience in the face of shocks and the likelihood that a shock will lead to a decline in well-being. It is therefore primarily a function of a household's asset endowment and insurance mechanisms. Because poor people have fewer assets and less diversified sources of income than the better-off, fluctuations in income affect them more.

Poor households face many risks, and vulnerability is thus multidimensional. The indicators in the table focus on individual risks—informal sector employment, child labor, income insecurity in old age—and the extent to which publicly provided services may be capable of mitigating some of these risks. Poor people face labor market risks, often having to take up precarious, low-quality jobs in the informal sector and to increase their household's labor market participation through their children. Income security is a prime concern for the elderly. And affordable access to health care is a primary concern for all poor people, for whom illness and injury have both direct and opportunity costs.

For informal sector employment the most common sources of data are labor force and special informal sector surveys, based on a mixed household and enterprise survey approach or an economic or establishment census approach. Other sources include multipurpose household surveys, household income and expenditure surveys, surveys of household industries or economic activities, small and micro enterprise surveys, and official estimates. The international comparability of the data is affected by differences among countries in definitions and coverage and in the treatment of domestic workers and those who have a secondary job in the informal sector. The data in the table are based on national definitions of urban areas established by countries. For details on country definitions see the notes in the data source.

Reliable estimates of child labor are hard to obtain. In many countries child labor is officially presumed not to exist and so is not included in surveys or in official data. Underreporting also occurs because data exclude children engaged in agricultural or household activities with their families. Most child workers are in Asia. But the share of children working is highest in Africa, where, on average, one in three children ages 10–14 is engaged in some form of economic activity, mostly in agriculture (Fallon and Tzannatos 1998). Available statistics suggest that more boys than girls work. But the number of girls working is often underestimated because surveys exclude those working as unregistered domestic help or doing full-time household work to enable their parents to work outside the home.

Data on pension contributors come from national sources, the International Labour Organization, and International Monetary Fund country reports. Coverage by pension schemes may be broad or even universal where eligibility is determined by citizenship, residency, or income status. In contribution-related schemes, however, eligibility is usually restricted to individuals who have made contributions for a minimum number of years. Definitional issues—relating to the labor force, for example—may arise in comparing coverage by contribution-related schemes over time and across countries (for country-specific information see Palacios and Pallares-Miralles 2000). Coverage may be overstated in countries that do not attempt to count informal sector workers as part of the labor force.

Total expenditure on health in a country can be divided into two main categories by source of funding: public and private. Public health expenditure consists of spending by central and local governments, including social health insurance funds. Private health expenditure includes private insurance, direct out-of-pocket payments by households, and spending by non-profit institutions serving households, and private corporations. In countries where the proportion of out-of-pocket private expenditure is large, lower-income households may be particularly vulnerable to the impoverishing effects of necessary health care.

Definitions

• **Urban informal sector employment** is broadly characterized as employment in units in urban areas that produce goods or services on a small scale with the primary objective of generating employment and income for those concerned. These units typically operate at a low level of organization, with little or no division between labor and capital as factors of production. Labor relations are based on casual employment, kinship, or social relationships rather than contractual arrangements. • **Children 10–14 in the labor force** refer to the share of that age group active in the labor force. • **Pension contributors** refer to the share of the labor force or working-age population (here defined as ages 20–59) covered by a pension scheme. • **Private health expenditure** includes direct household (out-of-pocket) spending, private insurance, spending by non-profit institutions serving households (other than social insurance), and direct service payments by private corporations.

Data sources

The data on urban informal sector employment are from the International Labour Organization (ILO) database Key Indicators of the Labour Market (2001-02 issue). The child labor force participation rates are from the ILO database Estimates and Projections of the Economically Active Population, 1950–2010. The data on pension contributors are drawn from Robert Palacios and Montserrat Pallares-Miralles's "International Patterns of Pension Provision" (2000). For updates and further notes and sources go to the World Bank's Web site on pensions (www.worldbank.org/pensions). The data on private health expenditure for developing countries are largely from the World Health Organization's *World Health Report 2000* and *World Health Report 2001,* from household surveys and from World Bank poverty assessments and sector studies. The data on private health expenditure for member countries of the Organisation for Economic Co-operation and Development (OECD) are from the OECD.

2.10 | Enhancing security

	Public expenditure on pensions				Public expenditure on health		Public expenditure on education[a]	
	Year	% of GDP	Year	Average pension % of per capita income	Year	% of GDP	% of GDP 1998	Per student % of GDP per capita 1998
Afghanistan	..			..		..	..	..
Albania	1995	5.1		..	1999	2.0	..	..
Algeria	1997	2.1	1991	75.0	1998	2.6	6.0	22.2
Angola	..	..		..		..	2.6	19.1
Argentina	1994	6.2		..	1999	2.4	..	14.7
Armenia	1996	3.1	1996	18.7	1999	4.0	2.0	..
Australia	1997	5.9	1989	37.3	1998	6.0	4.8	..
Austria	1997	14.4	1993	69.3	1999	5.9	6.3	36.5
Azerbaijan	1996	2.5	1996	51.4	1999	1.0	3.4	15.1
Bangladesh	1992	0.0		..	1998	1.7	..	..
Belarus	1997	7.7	1995	31.2	1998	4.6	5.6	..
Belgium	1997	12.9		..	1999	6.3	..	..
Benin	1993	0.4	1993	189.7	1998	1.6	2.6	13.8
Bolivia	1995	2.5		..	1998	4.1	..	..
Bosnia and Herzegovina		..		..	1999	8.0	..	..
Botswana		..		..	1998	2.5	9.1	30.1
Brazil	1996	4.9		..	1999	2.9	4.6	16.1
Bulgaria	1996	7.3	1995	39.3	1999	3.9	3.4	..
Burkina Faso	1992	0.3	1992	207.3	1999	1.5	3.0	..
Burundi	1991	0.2	1991	57.4	1998	0.6	3.9	39.9
Cambodia		..		..	1998	0.6	5.5	26.0
Cameroon	1993	0.4		..	1998	1.0	2.6	13.7
Canada	1997	5.4	1994	54.3	1999	6.6	5.6	27.6
Central African Republic	1990	0.3		..	1998	2.0	1.9	..
Chad	1997	0.1		..	1998	2.3	1.7	..
Chile	1993	5.8	1993	56.1	1998	2.7	3.7	15.5
China	1996	2.7		..	1999	2.1	..	..
Hong Kong, China		..		..	1996	2.1	..	..
Colombia	1994	1.1	1989	72.2	1998	5.2	..	..
Congo, Dem. Rep.		..		..		..	..	..
Congo, Rep.	1992	0.9		..	1998	2.0	4.7	..
Costa Rica	1996	3.8	1993	76.1	1998	5.2	6.0	..
Côte d'Ivoire	1997	0.3		..	1998	1.2	4.2	24.3
Croatia	1997	11.6		..	1999	9.5	..	..
Cuba	1992	12.6		..	1994	8.3	..	..
Czech Republic	1999	9.8	1996	37.0	1999	6.6	4.2	23.8
Denmark	1997	8.8	1994	46.7	1999	6.9	8.2	44.3
Dominican Republic		..		..	1998	1.9	..	..
Ecuador	1997	1.0		..	1998	1.7	..	..
Egypt, Arab Rep.	1994	2.5	1994	45.0	1997	1.8	..	..
El Salvador	1996	1.3		..	1998	2.6	..	..
Eritrea		..		..	1997	2.9	5.0	51.3
Estonia	1995	7.0	1995	56.7	1999	5.1	6.8	32.8
Ethiopia	1993	0.9		..	1999	1.3	4.3	41.6
Finland	1997	12.1	1994	57.4	1999	5.2	..	..
France	1997	13.4		..	1999	7.3	5.9	28.9
Gabon		..		..	1998	2.1	3.3	10.8
Gambia, The		..		..	1999	2.3	4.8	..
Georgia	2000	2.7	1996	12.6	1999	0.8	..	..
Germany	1997	12.1	1995	62.8	1999	7.9	4.6	27.2
Ghana	1993	0.1		..	1999	1.7	4.0	..
Greece	1993	11.9	1990	85.6	1998	4.7	..	..
Guatemala	1995	0.7	1995	27.6	1998	2.1	2.0 [b]	..
Guinea		..		..	1998	2.3	1.8	..
Guinea-Bissau		..		..	1994	1.1	..	..
Haiti		..		..	1998	1.4	..	..
Honduras	1994	0.6		..	1998	3.9	4.0	..

	Year	Public expenditure on pensions % of GDP	Year	Average pension % of per capita income	Public expenditure on health Year	% of GDP	Public expenditure on education[a] % of GDP 1998	Per student % of GDP per capita 1998
Hungary	1996	9.7	1996	33.6	1998	5.2	4.6	25.8
India		..		..	1997	0.8	..	..
Indonesia		..		..	1999	0.8	1.4	..
Iran, Islamic Rep.	1994	1.5		..	1998	1.7	4.6	..
Iraq		..		..	1998	3.8	..	..
Ireland	1997	4.6	1993	77.9	1998	5.2	4.5	17.4
Israel	1996	5.9	1992	48.1	1998	6.0	7.7	29.7
Italy	1997	17.6		..	1999	5.6	4.7	29.8
Jamaica	1996	0.3	1989	25.9	1998	3.1	6.3	28.7
Japan	1997	6.9	1989	33.9	1998	5.7	3.5	21.3
Jordan	1995	4.2	1995	144.0	1998	3.6	..	..
Kazakhstan	1997	5.0	1996	18.8	1999	2.7	..	..
Kenya	1993	0.5		..	1998	2.4	6.6	28.2
Korea, Dem. Rep.		..				..	..	..
Korea, Rep.	1997	1.3		..	1999	2.4	4.1	..
Kuwait	1990	3.5		..	1997	2.9	6.5	29.9
Kyrgyz Republic	1997	6.4	1994	35.0	1999	2.2	5.4	21.1
Lao PDR		..		..	1998	1.2	2.4	11.2
Latvia	1995	10.2	1994	47.6	1999	4.0	6.8	35.0
Lebanon		..		..	1998	2.2	2.1	9.8
Lesotho		..		..	1995	3.4	13.0	57.9
Liberya		..		..		..	..	..
Libya		..		..		..	..	..
Lithuania	1998	7.3	1995	21.3	1998	4.8	6.4	32.2
Macedonia, FYR	1998	8.7	1996	91.6	1998	5.3	..	..
Madagascar	1990	0.2		..	1998	1.1	1.9	11.4
Malawi		..		..	1998	2.8	4.6	..
Malaysia	1999	6.5		..	1998	1.4	..	..
Mali	1991	0.4		..	1998	2.1	3.0	25.8
Mauritania	1992	0.2		..	1998	1.4	4.3	25.6
Mauritius	1999	4.4		..	1998	1.8	4.0	19.5
Mexico	1997	4.6		..	1998	2.6	..	15.9
Moldova	1996	7.5		..	1999	2.9	..	..
Mongolia		..		..	1995	4.7	..	..
Morocco	1994	1.8	1994	118.0	1998	1.2	..	..
Mozambique	1996	0.0		..	1998	2.8	2.9	22.6
Myanmar		..		..	1998	0.2	..	..
Namibia		..		..	1999	3.3	8.1	26.8
Nepal		..		..	1998	1.3	2.5	11.0
Netherlands	1997	11.1	1989	48.5	1999	6.0	4.9	24.8
New Zealand	1997	6.5		..	1999	6.3	7.2	..
Nicaragua	1996	4.3		..	1998	8.5	4.2	..
Niger	1992	0.1		..	1998	1.2	2.7	..
Nigeria	1991	0.1	1991	40.5	1998	0.8	..	..
Norway	1997	8.2	1994	49.9	1999	7.0	7.7	34.8
Oman		..		..	1998	2.9	3.9	..
Pakistan	1993	0.9		..	1999	0.7	..	..
Panama	1996	4.3		..	1998	4.9	..	..
Papua New Guinea		..		..	1998	2.5	..	..
Paraguay		..		..	1998	1.7	4.5	..
Peru	1996	1.2		..	1998	2.4	3.2	11.0
Philippines	1993	1.0		..	1999	1.6	3.2	..
Poland	1997	15.5	1995	61.2	1999	4.7	5.4	..
Portugal	1997	10.0	1989	44.6	1998	5.1	5.7	27.9
Puerto Rico		..		..		..	..	..
Romania	1996	5.1	1994	34.1	1999	3.8	4.4	..
Russian Federation	1996	5.7	1995	18.3	1997	4.6	..	..

		Public expenditure on pensions			Public expenditure on health		Public expenditure on education[a]	
	Year	% of GDP	Year	Average pension % of per capita income	Year	% of GDP	% of GDP 1998	Per student % of GDP per capita 1998
Rwanda		..		..	1998	2.0	..	..
Saudi Arabia		..		..	1997	6.4	..	..
Senegal	1998	1.5		..	1998	2.6	3.5	24.1
Sierra Leone		..		..	1998	0.9	1.0	..
Singapore	1996	1.4		..	1998	1.2	..	..
Slovak Republic	1994	9.1	1994	44.5	1998	5.7	4.3	20.7
Slovenia	1996	13.6	1996	49.3	1998	6.7	5.8	29.3
Somalia		..		..		..	..	..
South Africa		..		..	1998	3.3	6.1	19.6
Spain	1997	10.9	1995	54.1	1998	5.4	4.5	23.3
Sri Lanka	1996	2.4		..	1999	1.7	..	..
Sudan		..		..	1997	0.7	3.7	30.1
Swaziland		..		..	1998	2.5	6.1	21.9
Sweden	1997	11.1	1994	78.0	1998	6.6	8.0	34.2
Switzerland	1997	13.4	1993	44.4	1998	7.6	5.5	31.7
Syrian Arab Republic	1991	0.5		..	1998	0.9	..	..
Tajikistan	1996	3.0		..	1998	5.2	..	..
Tanzania		..		..	1998	1.3	2.1	..
Thailand		..		..	1998	1.9	4.7	20.0
Togo	1997	0.6	1993	178.8	1998	1.3	4.5	15.8
Trinidad and Tobago	1996	0.6		..	1998	2.5	..	..
Tunisia	1991	2.6	1991	89.5	1998	2.2	7.6	26.5
Turkey	1997	4.5	1993	112.7	1999	3.3	..	..
Turkmenistan	1996	2.3		..	1998	4.1	..	..
Uganda	1997	0.8		..	1998	1.9	1.6	4.6
Ukraine	1996	8.6	1995	30.9	1999	2.9	4.4	25.6
United Arab Emirates		..		..	1998	0.8	1.9	10.7
United Kingdom	1997	10.3		..	1999	5.8	4.7	18.8
United States	1997	7.5	1989	33.0	1999	5.7	5.0	22.5
Uruguay	1996	15.0	1996	64.1	1998	1.9	2.5	11.4
Uzbekistan	1995	5.3	1995	45.8	1998	3.4	..	..
Venezuela, RB	1990	0.5		..	1998	2.6	..	..
Vietnam	1998	1.6		..	1998	0.8	..	..
West Bank and Gaza		..		..	1996	4.9	..	..
Yemen, Rep.	1994	0.1		..	1997	2.4	6.7	31.5
Yugoslavia, FR (Serb./Mont.)		..		..		..	4.2	31.5
Zambia	1993	0.1		..	1998	3.6	2.3	12.0
Zimbabwe		..		..	1999	3.0	10.8	..
World						5.3 w	4.5 m	24.3 m
Low income						0.9	3.4	24.1
Middle income						2.9	4.5	..
Lower middle income						2.7	..	..
Upper middle income						3.2	4.2	17.8
Low & middle income						2.5	4.1	22.2
East Asia & Pacific						1.8	..	..
Europe & Central Asia						4.4	4.4	25.7
Latin America & Carib.						2.8	..	..
Middle East & N. Africa						2.9	..	..
South Asia						0.9	..	..
Sub-Saharan Africa						2.0	3.6	23.4
High income						6.0	5.6	28.4
Europe EMU						6.7	4.8	27.6

a. Break in series between 1997 and 1998 due to change from ISCED76 to ISCED97. b. Data refer to 1999.

About the data

Enhancing security for poor people means reducing their vulnerability to such risks as ill health, providing them the means to manage risk themselves, and strengthening market or public institutions for managing risk. The tools include microfinance programs, old age assistance and pensions, and public provision of basic health care and education.

Public interventions and institutions can provide services directly to poor people, although whether these work well for the poor is debated. State action is often ineffective, in part because governments can influence only a few of the many sources of well-being and in part because of difficulties in delivering goods and services. The effectiveness of public provision is further constrained by the fiscal resources at governments' disposal and the fact that state institutions may not be responsive to the needs of poor people.

Data on public pension spending are from national sources and cover all government expenditures, including the administrative costs of pension programs. They cover noncontributory pensions or social assistance targeted to the elderly and disabled and spending by social insurance schemes for which contributions had previously been made. The pattern of spending in a country is correlated with its demographic structure—spending increases as the population ages.

The lack of consistent national health accounting systems in most developing countries makes cross-country comparisons of health spending

difficult. Compiling estimates of public health expenditures is complicated in countries where state or provincial and local governments are involved in health care financing and delivery because the data on public spending often are not aggregated. The data in the table are the product of an effort to collect all available information on health expenditures from national and local government budgets, national accounts, household surveys, insurance publications, international donors, and existing tabulations.

The data on education spending in the table refer solely to public spending—government spending on public education plus subsidies for private education. The data generally exclude foreign aid for education. They may also exclude spending by religious schools, which play a significant role in many developing countries. Data for some countries and for some years refer to spending by the ministry of education only (excluding education expenditures by other ministries and departments, local authorities, and so on). The share of gross domestic product (GDP) devoted to education can be interpreted as reflecting a country's effort in education. It often bears a weak relationship to measures of output of the education system, as reflected in educational attainment. The pattern in this relationship suggests wide variations across countries in the efficiency with which the government's resources are translated into education outcomes.

Definitions

- **Public expenditure on pensions** includes all government expenditures on cash transfers to the elderly, the disabled, and survivors and the administrative costs of these programs.
- **Average pension** is estimated by dividing total pension expenditure by the number of pensioners. • **Public expenditure on health** consists of recurrent and capital spending from government (central and local) budgets and social (or compulsory) health insurance funds.
- **Public expenditure on education** consists of public spending on public education plus subsidies to private education at the primary, secondary, and tertiary levels.

Data sources

The data on pension spending are drawn from Robert Palacios and Montserrat Pallares-Miralles's "International Patterns of Pension Provision" (2000). For updates and further notes and sources go to the World Bank's Web site on pensions (www.worldbank.org/pensions). The estimates of health expenditure come from the World Health Organization's *World Health Report 2000* and *World Health Report 2001,* from the Organisation for Economic Co-operation and Development for its member countries, from National Health Accounts of a country, from the web site *The European Observatory on Health Care Systems* (www.observatory.dk), supplemented by World Bank country and sector studies, including the Human Development Network's *Sector Strategy: Health, Nutrition, and Population* (World Bank 1997a). Data are also drawn from World Bank public expenditure reviews, the International Monetary Fund's Government Finance Statistics database, and other studies. The data on education expenditure are from the UNESCO Institute for Statistics.

Figure 2.10

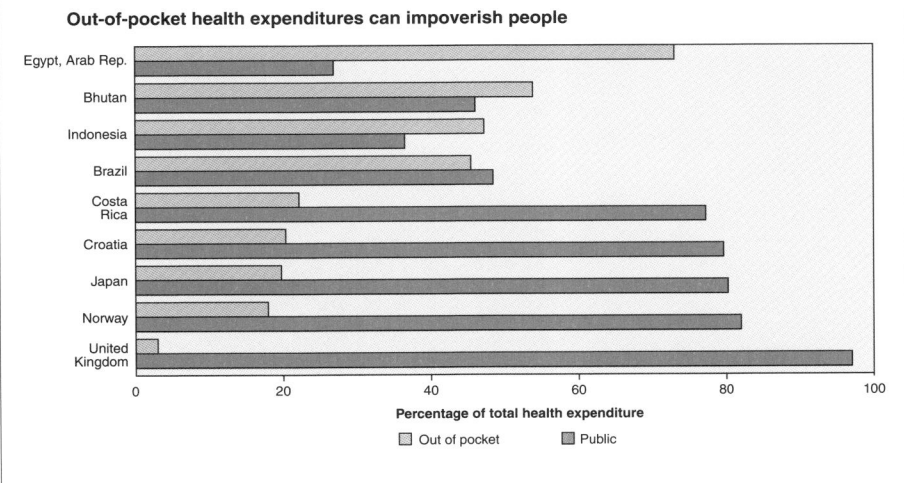

Out-of-pocket health expenditures can impoverish people

Percentage of total health expenditure

☐ Out of pocket   ▨ Public

Source: WHO, *World Health Report 2000.*

Out-of-pocket payments are generally regressive because they have the potential not only to impoverish people but also to deter the poor from obtaining care. Exempting the poor from user fees at public facilities, or imposing a sliding scale, based on socioeconomic characteristics, are attempts to reduce the risks associated with out-of-pocket payments. However, such schemes require relatively high administrative costs to distinguish users, and may end up affecting only a small amount of total risk-related payments.

2.11 | Education inputs

| | Expenditure per student | | | | | | Expenditure on teachers' compensation | | Primary teachers with required academic qualifications | Primary pupil-teacher ratio[b] |
| | Primary % of GDP per capita | | Secondary % of GDP per capita | | Tertiary % of GDP per capita | | % of total current education expenditure | | % of total | pupils per teacher |
	1980	1997	1980	1997	1980	1997	1980	1997	1992-98[a]	1998
Afghanistan	10.8	..	46.7	..	..	..	46.8	..	18	..
Albania	..	..	..	..	..	..	..	..	..	..
Algeria	8.7	..	23.2	..	..	..	63.6	74.3 [c]	93	28
Angola	..	..	..	..	..	..	..	..	..	..
Argentina	..	9.0	11.0	16.2	29.8	..	..	84.1	..	21
Armenia	..	..	..	..	..	26.3	..	..	89	..
Australia	..	14.0	42.5	15.8	48.8	27.9	..	54.1 [d]	..	..
Austria	15.4	21.4	19.6	24.4	36.7	34.8	53.1	61.7	..	13
Azerbaijan	..	21.6	..	..	..	17.3	..	..	100	19
Bangladesh	..	..	9.3	..	33.9	..	33.5	..	68	59
Belarus	..	45.8	..	28.6	..	17.7	..	..	100	..
Belgium	..	8.5	32.4	13.5	50.3	17.6	73.0	73.6 [e]	..	..
Benin	..	11.6	..	..	..	244.2	..	..	100	53
Bolivia	..	10.9	..	..	..	53.3	..	..	64	..
Bosnia and Herzegovina	..	..	..	..	..	..	..	..	84	..
Botswana	..	..	..	..	..	..	54.9	..	..	28
Brazil	..	11.0	..	..	..	..	..	..	83	33
Bulgaria	17.2	29.6	..	..	50.5	16.7	..	..	99	18
Burkina Faso	..	..	102.9	..	2,938.5	..	61.0	67.8	100	49
Burundi	..	..	..	..	..	..	74.3	..	..	46
Cambodia	..	..	..	..	..	..	..	..	91	48
Cameroon	..	..	..	..	..	..	65.4	..	90	52
Canada	..	..	..	..	37.7	..	52.2	..	..	18
Central African Republic	..	..	23.9	..	938.8	..	..	..	..	99
Chad	..	6.3	..	24.0	..	234.5	..	64.4	..	68
Chile	9.2	10.5	15.7	11.4	107.8	19.9	76.8	..	96	27
China	3.8	6.5	12.4	11.5	246.2	65.3	..	..	95	21
Hong Kong, China	..	7.8	8.2	12.6	..	..	72.9	..	..	..
Colombia	5.2	..	7.7	10.3	43.6	30.1	93.4	82.0 [f]	90	23
Congo, Dem. Rep.	..	..	..	..	..	..	..	..	..	26
Congo, Rep.	..	10.7	15.4	5.7	334.4	..	70.8	..	100	61
Costa Rica	..	..	24.5	17.9	72.4	..	50.2	..	86	..
Côte d'Ivoire	..	..	..	..	357.4	..	..	..	..	43
Croatia	..	..	..	..	..	..	..	..	94	..
Cuba	..	16.3	..	34.0	..	98.2	38.8	..	100	13
Czech Republic	..	13.0	..	20.8	..	33.7	..	44.4	..	18
Denmark	..	24.1	11.0	34.2	48.7	49.2	49.3	43.1	..	10
Dominican Republic	..	..	5.8	4.7	..	9.3	62.2	..	..	37
Ecuador	..	..	12.5	15.0	23.0	34.4	77.4	..	83	27
Egypt, Arab Rep.	..	..	..	..	54.1	..	..	..	100	23
El Salvador	..	7.0	13.9	5.5	138.4	7.7	..	..	..	..
Eritrea	..	11.1	..	11.9	..	..	..	..	..	47
Estonia	..	..	..	45.2	..	37.9	..	..	..	16
Ethiopia	..	26.5	..	71.2	..	862.6	68.4	..	..	..
Finland	..	21.9	21.2	26.2	35.9	43.5	50.5	47.7	..	17
France	11.7	15.8	19.7	26.4	28.6	27.6	68.1	..	..	19
Gabon	..	..	..	..	..	..	..	..	56	44
Gambia, The	18.4	13.5	43.2	29.0	..	..	..	..	100	33
Georgia	..	..	..	..	..	..	..	..	94	17
Germany	..	..	..	..	..	37.0	..	..	..	17
Ghana	..	..	10.3	..	..	..	60.0	..	..	..
Greece	..	..	..	15.0	..	22.1	84.8	..	..	14
Guatemala	..	6.1	..	5.1	..	30.7	..	62.8	..	38
Guinea	..	..	..	27.9	..	421.9	..	..	89	47
Guinea-Bissau	19.0	..	63.5	..	..	..	73.5	..	..	..
Haiti	..	..	12.8	..	128.6	..	66.9	..	86	31
Honduras	..	..	13.8	..	73.2	59.4	71.1	67.8	100	..

	Expenditure per student						Expenditure on teachers' compensation		Primary teachers with required academic qualifications	Primary pupil-teacher ratio[b]
	Primary % of GDP per capita		Secondary % of GDP per capita		Tertiary % of GDP per capita		% of total current education expenditure		% of total	pupils per teacher
	1980	1997	1980	1997	1980	1997	1980	1997	1992-98[a]	1998
Hungary	13.7	17.9	25.5	17.6	83.8	30.4	45.2	..	..	11
India	..	8.4	15.1	16.4	83.3	92.5	..	..	88	72
Indonesia	..	..	..	..	..	12.3	..	..	94	..
Iran, Islamic Rep.	22.6	8.0	36.4	10.8	..	7.4	..	47.4 [g]	38	..
Iraq	..	..	6.5	..	87.5	..	..	..	..	22
Ireland	10.7	11.6	22.5	18.2	55.6	30.1	67.6	73.6 [h]	100	22
Israel	15.6	..	41.7	..	71.6	..	51.2	..	..	13
Italy	..	21.7	..	27.7	..	20.6	..	67.3 [h]	..	11
Jamaica	12.7	11.8	..	..	185.5	..	65.6	64.1	100	31
Japan	14.6	..	16.4	..	20.7	..	49.8	..	..	21
Jordan	..	..	..	..	61.7	75.8	70.5	70.4	47	..
Kazakhstan	..	..	..	..	..	21.3	..	..	98	..
Kenya	..	..	35.2	..	899.2	..	..	..	..	28
Korea, Dem. Rep.	..	..	..	..	..	..	..	..	100	..
Korea, Rep.	..	17.4	9.1	11.9	15.7	5.5	69.2	..	100	..
Kuwait	..	23.6	..	6.6	43.8	102.6	46.5	..	100	..
Kyrgyz Republic	..	..	..	39.7	..	48.2	..	..	95	24
Lao PDR	..	6.5	..	13.9	..	61.0	..	67.1	87	31
Latvia	..	..	16.1	51.3	13.6	33.1	..	40.5	80	15
Lebanon	..	..	..	..	..	23.1	..	..	..	14
Lesotho	12.7	18.1	107.3	70.4	1,500.8	1,022.3	60.9	57.6	79	25
Liberia	..	..	..	..	..	..	..	..	90	39
Libya	..	..	..	..	..	..	..	..	..	8
Lithuania	..	..	..	27.8	..	41.9	..	..	..	17
Macedonia, FYR	..	..	..	24.2	..	61.5	..	..	100	22
Madagascar	..	..	..	..	397.9	..	81.8	..	..	47
Malawi	7.0	8.2	89.2	25.4	1,685.7	1,492.0	43.4	..	..	..
Malaysia	..	10.7	20.5	17.2	140.9	53.6	57.5	58.6	..	22
Mali	29.6	13.3	87.3	28.5	..	369.4	51.0	..	..	62
Mauritania	28.8	10.1	167.6	56.1	..	191.2	..	..	..	47
Mauritius	..	9.7	20.2	15.3	337.1	140.6	31.4	..	100	26
Mexico	4.2	..	10.0	..	25.5	..	..	..	84	27
Moldova	..	..	..	..	..	60.6	..	..	..	..
Mongolia	..	..	..	..	95.5	45.9	..	..	97	32
Morocco	..	..	53.6	43.1	150.3	67.5	..	78.0	..	28
Mozambique	..	..	..	..	..	..	..	..	..	61
Myanmar	..	..	..	..	..	..	..	..	..	31
Namibia	..	..	..	34.7	..	103.4	..	..	25	32
Nepal	..	9.3	..	12.1	274.9	110.7	59.2	..	96	39
Netherlands	13.2	14.1	22.3	20.6	70.1	45.8	73.5	..	..	..
New Zealand	14.7	16.6	13.4	22.1	58.5	42.4	82.7	..	..	..
Nicaragua	..	12.6	..	6.4	..	..	66.7	..	63	..
Niger	..	..	..	81.0	..	..	..	..	..	41
Nigeria	..	..	..	..	..	..	..	..	90	..
Norway	..	27.6	14.5	18.7	37.1	45.1	..	..	..	..
Oman	..	8.9	..	16.4	..	30.1	..	..	..	25
Pakistan	..	..	17.1	..	..	..	..	..	99	32
Panama	..	..	10.2	11.2	26.5	39.2	65.3	..	100	..
Papua New Guinea	..	..	..	..	..	..	..	..	100	36
Paraguay	..	10.9	..	12.0	..	90.6	..	..	59	20
Peru	6.9	4.8	8.0	7.3	4.7	16.4	59.4	40.1	74	25
Philippines	..	9.3	4.2	9.8	13.7	14.8	..	..	100	..
Poland	..	16.7	..	15.9	..	25.4	..	..	..	..
Portugal	..	18.7	19.2	20.8	34.4	23.7	..	..	98	..
Puerto Rico	..	..	..	..	..	..	..	..	..	..
Romania	..	19.9	..	8.7	..	31.3	..	..	23	19
Russian Federation	..	..	..	..	..	..	..	..	..	..

2.11 | Education inputs

| | Expenditure per student | | | | | | Expenditure on teachers' compensation | | Primary teachers with required academic qualifications | Primary pupil-teacher ratio[b] |
| | Primary % of GDP per capita | | Secondary % of GDP per capita | | Tertiary % of GDP per capita | | % of total current education expenditure | | % of total | pupils per teacher |
	1980	1997	1980	1997	1980	1997	1980	1997	1992-98[a]	1998
Rwanda	11.1	..	112.4	..	902.7	..	74.8	..	47	54
Saudi Arabia	..	..	..	..	109.5	58.1	..	..	100	12
Senegal	..	..	68.5	63.8	432.5	..	..	..	99	49
Sierra Leone	..	..	..	..	..	..	..	..	..	..
Singapore	..	..	12.4	..	41.5	34.1	47.5	..	..	25
Slovak Republic	..	21.8	..	9.7	..	29.3	..	37.9	79	19
Slovenia	..	20.6	..	24.6	..	37.9	..	62.2	..	14
Somalia	..	..	..	..	..	..	..	..	..	..
South Africa	..	..	..	..	..	..	..	64.5 ᶜ	..	37
Spain	..	16.4	..	21.1	..	16.8	..	..	..	15
Sri Lanka	..	..	..	..	..	84.2	..	..	100	..
Sudan	..	45.6	601.0	38.0	..	..	..	..	..	26
Swaziland	..	8.6	35.3	23.0	139.5	229.8	86.3	..	100	33
Sweden	41.7	26.2	14.0	31.4	33.9	66.6	46.4	..	..	12
Switzerland	..	20.1	31.0	30.3	60.8	47.4	61.0	59.9	..	13
Syrian Arab Republic	..	..	15.1	14.6	74.7	..	57.8	..	..	23
Tajikistan	..	..	..	..	..	..	..	..	..	..
Tanzania	..	..	..	..	..	..	..	..	..	38
Thailand	8.8	11.9	9.8	10.5	59.7	25.4	80.3	56.8 ᵍ	84	21
Togo	7.7	8.8	..	24.8	828.7	455.1	68.3	74.2	..	41
Trinidad and Tobago	..	4.8	12.4	..	56.4	..	73.2	..	100	21
Tunisia	..	..	36.4	20.8	188.1	75.0	81.3	77.0	..	24
Turkey	..	..	8.7	..	96.3	..	..	..	100	..
Turkmenistan	..	..	..	..	..	..	..	..	..	..
Uganda	..	..	..	..	..	..	..	..	..	60
Ukraine	2.1	..	1.2	..	2.0	22.4	..	..	..	..
United Arab Emirates	..	..	..	..	..	..	..	30.2	..	16
United Kingdom	..	17.2	22.2	20.1	80.1	39.9	52.1	41.0 ⁱ	..	19
United States	..	..	17.3	..	47.8	..	..	..	..	15
Uruguay	8.9	..	13.6	9.3	27.0	21.3	56.9	41.5	100	21
Uzbekistan	..	..	..	..	..	..	..	..	..	..
Venezuela, RB	5.8	2.1	..	4.7	71.4	..	68.8	..	..	..
Vietnam	..	7.3	..	..	..	86.1	..	66.0	77	30
West Bank and Gaza	..	..	..	..	..	..	..	..	..	..
Yemen, Rep.	..	..	..	..	..	..	..	..	74	30
Yugoslavia, Fed. Rep.	..	..	..	..	..	71.1	..	..	..	17
Zambia	9.8	4.7	56.4	..	..	..	52.6	..	71	45
Zimbabwe	19.5	19.3	103.8	34.6	326.8	..	75.2	91.1	100	..

World	.. m	.. m	.. m	.. m	.. m	.. m	64.5 m	62.0 m	89 m	25 w
Low income	..	..	..	..	..	..	66.7	67.5	88	42
Middle income	..	..	..	..	66.5	40.8	65.3	58.6	91	22
Lower middle income	..	..	..	..	..	38.1	65.6	64.1	91	22
Upper middle income	..	..	..	..	71.4	..	61.4	47.8	87	28
Low & middle income	..	..	..	..	..	..	65.5	64.4	89	38
East Asia & Pacific	..	8.3	..	..	..	42.4	69.2	62.3	94	23
Europe & Central Asia	..	..	..	..	..	31.3	45.2	40.5	..	..
Latin America & Carib.	..	..	12.4	8.4	56.4	..	66.7	57.0	84	28
Middle East & N. Africa	..	..	..	..	87.5	..	67.1	74.3	76	24
South Asia	..	..	16.1	..	83.3	84.2	46.4	..	87	66
Sub-Saharan Africa	..	..	..	..	..	..	65.4	67.8	..	..
High income	..	18.7	19.6	20.4	45.8	36.9	52.6	57.3	..	17
Europe EMU	..	..	..	..	..	..	67.9	67.4	..	16

a. Data are for the most recent year available. b. Break in series between 1997 and 1998 due to change from ISCED76 to ISCED97. c. Not including tertiary education. d. Not including preprimary education. e. Flemish Community only. f. Ministry of Education only. g. Not including expenditure on universities. h. Data refer to expenditure on public institutions only. i. Not including expenditure on independent private institutions.

About the data

Data on education are compiled by the United Nations Educational, Scientific, and Cultural Organization (UNESCO) from official responses to surveys and from reports provided by education authorities in each country. Such data are used for monitoring, policymaking, and resource allocation. For a variety of reasons, however, education statistics generally fail to provide a complete and accurate picture of a country's education system. Statistics often have two to three years' time lag, but an effort is being made to shorten the delay. Coverage and data collection methods vary across countries and over time within countries and should be interpreted with caution. (For further discussion of the reliability of education data see Behrman and Rosenzweig 1994.)

The data on education spending in the table refer solely to public spending—government spending on public education plus subsidies for private education. The data generally exclude foreign aid for education. They may also exclude spending by religious schools, which play a significant role in many developing countries. Data for some countries and for some years refer to spending by the ministry of education only (excluding education expenditures by other ministries and departments and local authorities).

Many developing countries have sought to supplement public funds for education. Some countries have adopted tuition fees to recover part of the cost of providing education services or to encourage development of private schools. Charging fees raises difficult questions relating to equity, efficiency, access, and taxation, however, and some governments have used scholarships, vouchers, and other methods of public finance to counter this criticism. Data for a few countries include private spending, although national practices vary with respect to whether parents or schools pay for books, uniforms, and other supplies. For greater detail see the country- and indicator-specific notes in the source.

Well-trained and motivated teachers are a critical input to education, but they come at a cost: teachers' compensation (gross salaries and other benefits) typically accounts for two-thirds of education spending. Teachers are defined here as including both full- and part-time teaching staff. Teachers assigned to nonteaching duties are excluded, but country reporting varies. Comparisons should thus be made with caution.

The share of teachers with required academic qualifications measures the quality of the teaching staff available in primary schools. It does not take account of competencies acquired by teachers through their professional experience or self-instruction, or of such factors as work experience, teaching methods and materials, or classroom conditions, all of which may affect the quality of teaching. The qualifications are specified by the national authorities of each country and may not relate specifically to teaching. Since the indicator is based on minimum national qualifications, which may vary greatly, care should be taken in comparing across countries.

The comparability of pupil-teacher ratios across countries is affected by the definition of teachers and by differences in class size by grade and in the number of hours taught. Moreover, the underlying enrollment levels are subject to a variety of reporting errors (for further discussion of enrollment data see *About the data* for table 2.12). While the pupil-teacher ratio is often used to compare the quality of schooling across countries, it is often weakly related to the value added of schooling systems (Behrman and Rosenzweig 1994).

The International Standard Classification of Education 1976 (ISCED76) was used for two decades as an instrument to assemble, compile and present education statistics. In 1998 ISCED97 was introduced and UNESCO's data collection program and country reporting of education statistics were adjusted to this new classification. The adjustments were made to facilitate the international compilation and comparison of educational statistics as well as to take into account new types of learning opportunities and activities available for both children and adults. Thus the time series data up to 1997 are not consistent with data for 1998 and after. Any time series analysis should therefore be made with extreme caution.

ISCED97 introduced a new level 4, "postsecondary nontertiary education". The students who fall into this category are not counted as either secondary or tertiary even though they are in the education system.

Definitions

• **Expenditure per student** is the public current spending on education divided by the total number of students by level, as a percentage of gross domestic product (GDP) per capita.
• **Expenditure on teachers' compensation** is the public expenditure on teachers' gross salaries and other benefits as a percentage of the total public current spending on education.
• **Primary teachers with required academic qualifications** refer to the percentage of primary school teachers with at least the minimum academic qualifications required by national public authorities for teaching in primary education. • **Primary pupil-teacher ratio** is the number of pupils enrolled in primary school divided by the number of primary school teachers (regardless of their teaching assignment).

Data sources

International data on education are compiled by the UNESCO Institute for Statistics in cooperation with national commissions and national statistical services. Data on qualified teachers come from UNESCO's special data collection for the Education for All initiative.

Table 2.11a

Why the break in data? Comparing ISCED76 with ISCED97.

ISCED76

0 Education preceding the first level
1 Education at the first level
2 Education at the second level, first stage
3 Education at the second level, second stage
5 Education at the third level, first stage, of the type that leads to an award not equivalent to a first university degree
6 Education at the third level, first stage, of the type that leads to a first university degree or equivalent
7 Education at the third level, second stage of the type that leads to a post-graduate university degree or equivalent
9 Education not definable by level

ISCED97

0 Pre-primary education
1 Primary education or first stage of basic education
2 Lower secondary or second stage of basic education (2A, 2B and 2C)
3 Upper secondary education (3A, 3B, 3C)
4 Postsecondary non-tertiary education (4A, 4B)
5 First stage of tertiary education not leading directly to an advanced research qualification (5A, 5B)
6 Second stage of tertiary education leading to an advanced research qualification

ISCED97 provides an improved set of definitions and criteria aiming to ensure international comparability in the classification of educational programs by level and field of education. It includes seven levels of education while the earlier version had eight levels. Other differences are that a new level 4 'post-secondary non-tertiary education' has been introduced while level 9 has been deleted.

| | Gross enrollment ratio[a] | | | | | | | | Net enrollment ratio[a, b] | | | |
| | Preprimary % of relevant age group | Primary % of relevant age group | | Secondary % of relevant age group | | Tertiary % of relevant age group | | Primary % of relevant age group | | Secondary % of relevant age group | |
	1998	1980	1998	1980	1998	1980	1998	1980	1998	1980	1998
Afghanistan	..	34	..	10	..	..	..	29	..	..	..
Albania	..	113	..	67	..	5	..	..	..	..	..
Algeria	2	94	109	33	66	6	15	81	94	31	58
Angola	..	175	91	21	16	0 [c]	1	..	57	..	..
Argentina	57	106	120	56	89	22	47	..	107	..	74
Armenia	..	..	..	..	..	..	..	..	..	..	..
Australia	..	112	..	71	..	25	..	102	..	70	..
Austria	80	99	100	93	96	22	50	87	88	..	..
Azerbaijan	19	115	103	95	84	24	22	..	96	..	82
Bangladesh	31	61	122	18	47	3	5	..	104	..	..
Belarus	..	104	..	98	..	39	..	..	..	..	..
Belgium	..	104	..	91	..	26	..	97	..	..	..
Benin	5	67	84	16	21	1	3	..	..	..	16
Bolivia	..	87	..	37	..	15	..	79	97	16	..
Bosnia and Herzegovina	..	..	..	..	..	..	..	..	..	..	..
Botswana	..	91	105	19	77	1	4	76	81	14	57
Brazil	55	98	154	33	83	11	14	80	98	14	..
Bulgaria	63	98	101	84	87	16	43	96	93	73	81
Burkina Faso	2	17	42	3	10	0 [c]	..	15	34	..	9
Burundi	1	26	51	3	7	0 [c]	1	20	38	..	..
Cambodia	6	139	119	..	22	0 [c]	1	..	104	..	20
Cameroon	12	98	90	18	20	2	5	..	..	15	..
Canada	66	99	97	88	105	57	58	..	96	..	94
Central African Republic	..	71	57	14	..	1	2	56	53	..	..
Chad	..	..	67	..	11	..	..	..	55	..	7
Chile	74	109	106	53	85	12	34	..	88	..	70
China	39	113	107	46	62	2	6	..	91	..	50
Hong Kong, China	..	107	..	64	..	10	..	95	..	61	..
Colombia	35	112	112	39	53	9	..	..	87	..	..
Congo, Dem. Rep.	..	92	46	24	18	1	1	..	32	..	12
Congo, Rep.	2	141	57	74	..	5	..	96	..	..	..
Costa Rica	..	105	..	47	..	21	..	89	..	39	..
Côte d'Ivoire	3	75	78	19	23	3	7	..	59	..	..
Croatia	..	..	..	77	..	19	..	..	..	..	..
Cuba	96	106	100	81	79	17	19	95	97	..	75
Czech Republic	90	95	104	99	82	17	26	..	90	..	79
Denmark	93	95	103	105	126	28	55	95	101	88	89
Dominican Republic	34	118	133	42	66	..	..	..	87	..	53
Ecuador	63	117	113	53	56	35	..	..	97	..	46
Egypt, Arab Rep.	10	73	100	50	81	16	39	..	92	..	..
El Salvador	40	75	111	24	50	9	18	..	81	..	37
Eritrea	5	..	53	..	24	..	1	..	34	..	19
Estonia	90	103	101	127	104	25	47	..	96	..	77
Ethiopia	2	37	63	9	17	0 [c]	1	..	35	..	16
Finland	48	96	99	100	121	32	83	..	99	..	95
France	83	111	105	85	111	25	51	100	100	79	94
Gabon	..	..	154	..	55	..	8	..	..	..	..
Gambia, The	26	53	81	11	31	..	..	50	61	..	23
Georgia	28	93	95	109	79	30	34	..	..	..	78
Germany	94	..	105	..	98	..	46	..	87	..	88
Ghana	..	79	..	41	..	2	..	..	..	..	..
Greece	70	103	97	81	96	17	50	96	95	..	86
Guatemala	47	71	102	19	33	8	..	59	83	13	..
Guinea	..	36	59	17	15	5	..	..	46	..	13
Guinea-Bissau	..	68	..	6	..	..	..	47	..	3	..
Haiti	63	77	152	14	..	1	..	38	80	..	..
Honduras	..	98	..	30	..	7	13	78	..	..	..

	Gross enrollment ratio[a]								Net enrollment ratio[a, b]			
	Preprimary % of relevant age group	Primary % of relevant age group		Secondary % of relevant age group		Tertiary % of relevant age group		Primary % of relevant age group		Secondary % of relevant age group	
	1998	1980	1998	1980	1998	1980	1998	1980	1998	1980	1998
Hungary	106	96	103	70	98	14	34	95	82	..	85
India	29	83	100	30	49	5	..	..	..	..	39
Indonesia	..	107	..	29	..	4	..	88	..	..	..
Iran, Islamic Rep.	..	87	..	42	..	..	..	..	..	..	..
Iraq	11	113	88	57	20	9	13	99	80	47	31
Ireland	3	100	141	90	109	18	45	90	104	78	77
Israel	77	95	107	73	89	29	49	..	95	..	85
Italy	95	100	102	72	95	27	47	..	101	..	88
Jamaica	83	103	98	67	90	7	9	96	92	64	79
Japan	83	101	102	93	102	31	44	101	102	93	..
Jordan	20	82	69	59	66	13	..	73	64	53	60
Kazakhstan	14	84	97	93	87	34	23	..	..	..	74
Kenya	39	115	92	20	31	1	1	91	..	..	..
Korea, Dem. Rep.	..	..	..	..	..	..	..	..	..	..	..
Korea, Rep.	..	110	..	78	..	15	..	104	..	70	..
Kuwait	..	102	..	80	..	11	..	85	..	..	..
Kyrgyz Republic	14	116	104	110	86	16	30	..	85	..	..
Lao PDR	7	113	111	21	33	0 [c]	3	..	76	..	27
Latvia	54	102	103	99	87	24	51	..	94	..	83
Lebanon	64	111	110	59	89	30	38	..	78	..	76
Lesotho	20	103	102	18	32	1	2	67	60	13	14
Liberia	48	48	83	22	24	..	7	..	41	..	..
Libya	4	125	153	76	77	8	57	..	..	62	71
Lithuania	50	79	101	114	90	35	41	..	94	..	85
Macedonia, FYR	27	100	103	61	83	28	22	..	96	..	79
Madagascar	..	130	93	..	16	3	2	..	63	..	13
Malawi	..	60	..	5	..	0 [c]	0	43	..	..	7
Malaysia	55	93	99	48	98	4	..	..	98	..	93
Mali	2	26	53	8	14	1	2	20	42	..	..
Mauritania	..	37	83	11	18	..	6	..	60	..	..
Mauritius	100	93	108	50	71	1	7	79	93	..	63
Mexico	76	120	114	49	71	14	18	..	102	..	56
Moldova	..	83	..	78	..	30	..	..	..	..	..
Mongolia	24	107	94	92	..	22	25	..	85	..	53
Morocco	69	83	97	26	40	6	9	62	79	20	..
Mozambique	..	99	71	5	9	0 [c]	1	36	41	..	7
Myanmar	3	91	114	22	36	5	..	..	..	..	..
Namibia	..	..	126	..	59	..	7	..	86	..	31
Nepal	..	86	114	22	48	3	3	..	..	..	..
Netherlands	98	100	108	93	125 [d]	29	49	93	100	81	93
New Zealand	..	111	..	83	..	27	..	..	..	81	..
Nicaragua	..	94	..	41	..	12	..	70	..	22	..
Niger	1	25	31	5	7	0 [c]	..	21	26	4	6
Nigeria	..	109	..	18	..	3	..	..	..	..	..
Norway	77	99	102	94	121	25	65	98	102	84	96
Oman	10	51	75	12	67	0 [c]	..	43	66	10	58
Pakistan	8	40	86	14	37	..	..	..	..	..	..
Panama	..	106	..	61	..	21	..	89	..	46	..
Papua New Guinea	20	59	85	12	22	2	2	..	85	..	22
Paraguay	77	106	115	27	51	9	..	89	92	..	42
Peru	60	114	126	59	81	17	29	86	103	..	61
Philippines	..	112	..	64	..	24	28	94	..	45	..
Poland	..	100	..	77	..	18	..	98	..	70	..
Portugal	67	123	124	37	113 [d]	11	45	98	108	..	88
Puerto Rico	..	..	..	..	..	42	..	..	..	..	..
Romania	132	104	103	94	80	12	..	..	94	..	76
Russian Federation	..	102	..	96	..	46	..	..	..	..	..

2.12 | Participation in education

	Gross enrollment ratio[a]							Net enrollment ratio[a, b]			
	Preprimary % of relevant age group	Primary % of relevant age group		Secondary % of relevant age group		Tertiary % of relevant age group		Primary % of relevant age group		Secondary % of relevant age group	
	1998	1980	1998	1980	1998	1980	1998	1980	1998	1980	1998
Rwanda	..	63	114	3	9	0 [c]	1	59	91	..	..
Saudi Arabia	5	61	71	29	66	7	19	49	59	21	..
Senegal	3	46	70	11	20	3	4	37	59	..	..
Sierra Leone	..	52	..	14	..	1	..	..	..	..	..
Singapore	..	108	92	60	67	8	..	99	..	..	..
Slovak Republic	80	..	101	..	86	..	27	..	..	..	..
Slovenia	72	98	98	..	99	20	53	..	94	..	89
Somalia	..	21	..	9	..	..	..	16	..	5	..
South Africa	26	90	127	..	104	..	17	..	..	..	..
Spain	75	109	108	87	113	23	56	102	105	74	92
Sri Lanka	..	103	111	55	71	3	..	..	102	..	..
Sudan	24	50	56	16	29	2	7	..	46	..	..
Swaziland	..	103	117	38	56	4	5	80	77	..	35
Sweden	77	97	111	88	161 [d]	31	63	..	103	..	100
Switzerland	89	84	102	94	94	18	35	79	94	78	83
Syrian Arab Republic	9	100	104	46	42	17	6	89	93	39	38
Tajikistan	..	..	..	..	..	24	..	..	..	..	..
Tanzania	..	93	65	3	..	0 [c]	1	68	48	..	4
Thailand	92	99	94	29	88	15	30	..	77	..	55
Togo	3	118	124	33	33	2	4	..	88	..	23
Trinidad and Tobago	12	99	102	69	80	4	6	90	93	..	72
Tunisia	14	102	119	27	73	5	17	82	98	23	55
Turkey	7	96	..	35	70	5	14	..	100	..	..
Turkmenistan	..	..	..	..	..	22	..	..	..	..	..
Uganda	..	50	154	5	16	1	2	..	..	..	9
Ukraine	..	102	..	94	..	42	..	..	..	..	..
United Arab Emirates	73	89	94	52	78	3	13	74	83	..	70
United Kingdom	78	103	102	83	156 [d]	19	58	97	102	79	94
United States	59	99	102	91	97	56	77	..	95	..	90
Uruguay	56	107	113	62	88	17	35	..	92	..	66
Uzbekistan	..	81	..	105	..	28	..	..	..	..	..
Venezuela, RB	..	93	..	21	..	21	..	82	..	14	..
Vietnam	39	109	110	42	61	2	11	95	97	..	49
West Bank and Gaza	..	..	..	..	..	..	..	..	..	..	..
Yemen, Rep.	1	..	78	..	45	..	10	..	61	..	35
Yugoslavia, Fed. Rep.	..	..	..	..	..	..	..	..	..	..	..
Zambia	3	90	86	16	27	1	3	77	73	..	22
Zimbabwe	..	85	..	8	..	1	..	..	..	..	..
World	37 w	97 w	104 w	49 w	60 w	13 w	.. w	.. w	.. w	.. w	.. w
Low income	25	83	96	29	42	6	..	..	..	..	..
Middle income	41	106	111	52	67	10	12	..	92	..	..
Lower middle income	39	107	106	52	63	9	10	..	91	..	51
Upper middle income	48	102	129	50	81	13	19	..	97	..	..
Low & middle income	34	96	104	41	56	8	..	..	..	..	..
East Asia & Pacific	40	111	107	44	62	4	8	..	91	..	51
Europe & Central Asia	..	99	..	86	..	31	..	..	..	..	..
Latin America & Carib.	60	105	130	42	75	14	20	..	97	..	..
Middle East & N. Africa	17	87	97	42	60	11	22	..	83	..	..
South Asia	27	77	101	27	48	5	..	..	..	..	39
Sub-Saharan Africa	..	80	78	15	..	1	4	..	..	..	..
High income	..	102	..	87	..	36	..	..	..	..	..
Europe EMU	..	106	..	81	..	24	..	..	..	..	..

a. Break in series between 1997 and 1998 due to change from ISCED76 to ISCED97. b. Net enrollment ratios exceeding 100 percent indicate discrepancies between estimates of the school-age population and reported enrollment data. c. Less than 0.5. d. Includes training for the unemployed.

About the data

School enrollment data are reported to the United Nations Educational, Scientific, and Cultural Organization (UNESCO) by national education authorities. Enrollment ratios help to monitor two important issues for universal primary education: an international development goal that implies achieving a net primary enrollment ratio of 100 percent; and gross enrollment ratios that help to assess whether an education system has sufficient capacity to meet the needs of universal primary education. Net enrollment ratios also show the proportion of children of primary school age who are enrolled in school and consequently also the proportion who are not in formal education.

Enrollment ratios, while a useful measure of participation in education, also have significant limitations. They are based on data collected during annual school surveys, which are typically conducted at the beginning of the school year. They do not reflect actual rates of attendance or dropouts during the school year. And school administrators may report exaggerated enrollments, especially if there is a financial incentive to do so. Often the number of teachers paid by the government is related to the number of pupils enrolled. Behrman and Rosenzweig (1994), comparing official school enrollment data for Malaysia in 1988 with gross school attendance rates from a household survey, found that the official statistics systematically overstated enrollment.

Overage or underage enrollments frequently occur, particularly when parents prefer, for cultural or economic reasons, to have children start school at other than the official age. Children's age at enrollment may be inaccurately estimated or misstated, especially in communities where registration of births is not strictly enforced. Parents who want to enroll their underage children in primary school may do so by overstating the age of the children. And in some education systems ages for children repeating a grade may be deliberately or inadvertently underreported.

As an international indicator, the gross primary enrollment ratio has been used to indicate broad levels of participation as well as school capacity. It has an inherent weakness: the length of primary education differs significantly across countries. A short duration tends to increase the ratio and a long duration to decrease it (in part because there are more dropouts among older children).

Other problems affecting cross-country comparisons of enrollment data stem from errors in estimates of school-age populations. Age-gender structures from censuses or vital registration systems, the primary sources of data on school-age populations, are commonly subject to underenumeration (especially of young children) aimed at circumventing laws or regulations; errors are also introduced when parents round up children's ages. While census data are often adjusted for age bias, adjustments are rarely made for inadequate vital registration systems. Compounding these problems, pre-and post-census estimates of school-age children are interpolations or projections based on models that may miss important demographic events (see the discussion of demographic data in *About the data* for table 2.1).

In using enrollment data, it is also important to consider repetition rates, which are quite high in some developing countries, leading to a substantial number of overage children enrolled in each grade and raising the gross enrollment ratio. A common error that may also distort enrollment ratios is the lack of distinction between new entrants and repeaters, which, other things equal, leads to underreporting of repeaters and overestimation of dropouts. Thus gross enrollment ratios provide an indication of the capacity of each level of the education system, but a high ratio does not necessarily indicate a successful education system. The net enrollment ratio excludes overage students in an attempt to capture more accurately the system's coverage and internal efficiency. It does not solve the problem completely, however, because some children fall outside the official school age because of late or early entry rather than because of grade repetition. The difference between gross and net enrollment ratios shows the incidence of overage and underage enrollments.

In 1998, ISCED97 was introduced and UNESCO's data collection program and country reporting of education statistics were adjusted to this new classification. This was to facilitate the international compilation and comparison of educational statistics, as well as to take into account new types of learning opportunities and activities available for both children and adults. Thus the time series data up to 1997 are not consistent with data for 1998 and after. Any time series analysis should therefore be made with extreme caution.

ISCED97 introduced a new level 4 labeled "post-secondary non-tertiary education". The students who fall into this category are not counted as either secondary or tertiary although they are in the education system.

The year shown in the table usually indicates the beginning of the school year but in most of the countries school year ends the following year.

Definitions

• **Gross enrollment ratio** is the ratio of total enrollment, regardless of age, to the population of the age group that officially corresponds to the level of education shown. • **Net enrollment ratio** is the ratio of the number of children of official school age (as defined by the national education system) who are enrolled in school to the population of the corresponding official school age. Based on the International Standard Classification of Education 1976 (ISCED76) and 1997 (ISCED97), • **Preprimary** education refers to the initial stage of organized instruction, designed primarily to introduce very young children to a school-type environment. • **Primary** education provides children with basic reading, writing, and mathematics skills along with an elementary understanding of such subjects as history, geography, natural science, social science, art, and music. • **Secondary** education completes the provision of basic education that began at the primary level, and aims at laying the foundations for lifelong learning and human development, by offering more subject- or skill-oriented instruction using more specialized teachers. • **Tertiary** education, whether or not leading to an advanced research qualification, normally requires, as a minimum condition of admission, the successful completion of education at the secondary level.

Data sources

The data are from the UNESCO Institute for Statistics.

	Net intake rate in grade 1		Percentage of cohort reaching grade 5				Primary completion rate			Avearge years of schooling		
	% of school-age population		% of grade one students who reach grade 5				% of all children who complete primary school					
	Male	Female	Male		Female		Total	Male	Female	Total	Male	Female
	1998	1998	1980	1997	1980	1997	1992-2000[a]	1992-2000[a]	1992-2000[a]	2000	2000	2000
Afghanistan	..	..	62	..	61	..	8	15	0	1.7	2.6	0.8
Albania	97	103	..	81	..	83	89	84	95	..	..	..
Algeria	78	75	90	93	85	95	91	93	88	5.4	6.2	4.5
Angola	27	22	..	..	..	..	..	..	..	..	..	..
Argentina	107	105	..	70	..	70	96	97	98	8.8	8.8	8.9
Armenia	..	..	..	..	..	..	82	..	..	..	..	..
Australia	..	..	..	..	..	..	..	..	..	10.9	11.2	10.7
Austria	..	..	..	..	..	..	..	..	..	8.4	9.2	7.6
Azerbaijan	12	13	..	..	..	..	101	103	100	..	..	..
Bangladesh	95	91	18	..	26	..	70	68	72	2.6	3.3	1.8
Belarus	..	..	..	..	..	..	93	95	92	..	..	..
Belgium	..	..	75	..	77	..	..	..	..	9.3	9.6	9.1
Benin	..	..	59	64	62	57	39	52	25	2.3	3.3	1.4
Bolivia	..	..	..	..	..	..	77	80	75	5.6	6.1	5.1
Bosnia and Herzegovina	..	..	..	..	..	..	88	..	..	..	..	..
Botswana	20	23	80	87	84	93	102	96	107	6.3	6.2	6.3
Brazil	73	65	..	..	..	..	71	..	..	4.9	5.4	4.4
Bulgaria	..	..	..	..	..	..	92	92	92	..	..	..
Burkina Faso	22	15	76	74	74	77	25	29	20	..	..	..
Burundi	27	23	100	..	96	..	43	45	41	..	..	..
Cambodia	80	77	..	51	..	46	60	68	51	..	..	..
Cameroon	..	..	70	..	69	..	43	..	..	3.5	4.2	2.9
Canada	..	..	..	..	..	..	..	..	..	11.6	11.7	11.6
Central African Republic	..	..	63	..	50	..	19	..	..	2.5	3.4	1.7
Chad	27	19	..	62	..	53	19	26	10	..	..	..
Chile	37	38	..	100	..	100	92	92	92	7.5	7.6	7.5
China	..	..	..	93	..	94	108	111	106	6.4	7.6	5.1
Hong Kong, China	..	..	98	..	99	..	..	..	..	9.4	9.9	8.9
Colombia	56	55	..	70	..	76	85	84	87	5.3	4.9	5.7
Congo, Dem. Rep.	20	22	56	..	59	..	40	..	..	3.0	4.1	2.0
Congo, Rep.	11	10	81	40	83	78	44	45	43	5.1	5.8	4.6
Costa Rica	58	60	77	86	82	89	89	91	87	6.0	6.1	6.0
Côte d'Ivoire	34	27	..	77	..	71	40	50	31	..	..	..
Croatia	..	..	..	..	..	..	79	80	79	..	..	..
Cuba	90	90	..	..	..	..	..	..	..	..	..	..
Czech Republic	..	..	..	..	..	..	109	110	107	..	..	..
Denmark	..	..	99	100	99	99	..	..	..	9.7	9.8	9.5
Dominican Republic	59	60	..	..	..	..	82	78	86	4.9	4.9	5.0
Ecuador	82	83	..	84	..	86	96	96	96	6.4	6.4	6.4
Egypt, Arab Rep.	..	..	92	..	88	..	99	104	92	5.5	6.5	4.5
El Salvador	54	55	17	76	16	77	76	77	75	5.2	5.2	5.1
Eritrea	18	16	..	73	..	67	35	43	28	..	..	..
Estonia	..	..	..	96	..	97	88	89	86	..	..	..
Ethiopia	25	20	50	51	51	50	24	31	18	..	..	..
Finland	..	..	..	100	..	100	..	..	..	10.0	10.2	9.8
France	..	..	..	..	..	..	..	..	..	7.9	8.1	7.6
Gabon	62	63	57	58	56	61	80	79	80	..	..	..
Gambia, The	10	10	74	78	71	83	70	80	60	2.3	3.0	1.6
Georgia	..	..	..	..	..	..	90	..	..	..	..	..
Germany	..	..	..	..	..	..	..	..	..	10.2	10.5	9.9
Ghana	..	..	..	..	..	..	64	..	..	3.9	5.7	2.2
Greece	..	..	99	..	98	..	..	..	..	8.7	9.8	7.6
Guatemala	59	56	..	52	..	47	56	63	50	3.5	3.8	3.1
Guinea	23	20	..	..	..	..	34	49	19	..	..	..
Guinea-Bissau	..	..	25	..	17	..	31	..	..	0.8	0.9	0.7
Haiti	37	48	20	..	21	..	..	..	..	2.8	3.5	2.1
Honduras	46	47	..	..	..	..	67	64	71	4.8	5.6	4.0

	Net intake rate in grade 1		Percentage of cohort reaching grade 5				Primary completion rate			Avearge years of schooling		
	% of school-age population		% of grade one students who reach grade 5					% of all children who complete primary school				
	Male	Female	Male		Female		Total	Male	Female	Total	Male	Female
	1998	1998	1980	1997	1980	1997	1992-2000[a]	1992-2000[a]	1992-2000[a]	2000	2000	2000
Hungary	..	..	96	..	97	..	102	..	..	9.1	9.6	8.7
India	..	..	..	..	..	..	76	88	63	5.1	6.3	3.7
Indonesia	..	..	..	88	..	89	91	90	92	5.0	5.5	4.5
Iran, Islamic Rep.	..	..	..	..	..	..	92	95	89	5.3	6.1	4.5
Iraq	76	71	..	..	..	..	55	59	51	4.0	4.6	3.3
Ireland	..	..	..	..	..	..	..	..	..	9.4	9.3	9.4
Israel	..	..	..	..	..	..	..	..	..	9.6	9.8	9.4
Italy	..	..	99	98	99	99	..	..	..	7.2	7.6	6.8
Jamaica	..	..	..	..	..	..	89	85	93	5.3	4.9	5.6
Japan	..	..	100	..	100	..	..	..	..	9.5	9.9	9.1
Jordan	46	47	100	..	98	..	..	..	..	6.9	7.7	6.0
Kazakhstan	..	..	..	..	..	..	100	99	101	..	..	..
Kenya	..	..	60	..	62	..	58	58	57	4.2	4.7	3.7
Korea, Dem. Rep.	..	..	..	..	..	..	..	..	..	..	..	..
Korea, Rep.	..	..	94	98	94	99	96	95	98	10.8	11.7	10.0
Kuwait	..	..	..	..	..	..	70	69	71	7.1	7.2	6.9
Kyrgyz Republic	..	..	..	..	..	..	100			..	..	..
Lao PDR	52	50	..	57	..	54	64	70	59	..	..	..
Latvia	..	..	..	..	..	..	86			..	..	..
Lebanon	14	14	..	..	..	..	70	..	..	..	..	..
Lesotho	16	15	50	55	68	71	69	55	83	4.2	3.6	4.8
Liberia	48	31	..	..	..	..	..	..	..	2.5	3.3	1.5
Libya	..	..	..	..	..	..	..	..	..	..	..	..
Lithuania	..	..	..	..	..	..	95	97	94	..	..	..
Macedonia, FYR	..	..	..	95	..	95	91	94	87	..	..	..
Madagascar	56	46	..	49	..	33	26	26	27	..	..	..
Malawi	..	..	48	36	40	32	50	61	40	3.2	3.6	2.8
Malaysia	95	94	97	..	97	..	90	89	90	6.8	7.4	6.2
Mali	..	..	..	92	..	70	23	33	14	0.9	1.2	0.6
Mauritania	..	..	..	61	..	68	46	52	39	..	..	..
Mauritius	27	27	..	98	..	99	111	..	..	6.0	6.5	5.6
Mexico	92	93	..	85	..	86	89	87	86	7.2	7.6	6.9
Moldova	..	..	..	..	..	..	81	82	81	..	..	..
Mongolia	..	..	..	..	..	..	82	77	88	..	..	..
Morocco	59	55	79	76	78	74	55	63	47	..	..	..
Mozambique	13	12	..	52	..	39	36	43	29	1.1	1.4	0.8
Myanmar	..	..	..	..	..	..	..	..	..	2.8	3.0	2.5
Namibia	63	67	..	76	..	82	90	86	94	..	..	..
Nepal	..	..	..	..	..	..	57	70	42	2.4	3.4	1.5
Netherlands	..	..	94	..	98	..	..	..	..	9.4	9.6	9.1
New Zealand	..	..	93	97	94	97	..	..	..	11.7	12.0	11.5
Nicaragua	..	..	..	43	..	52	65	61	70	4.6	4.5	4.6
Niger	32	21	74	72	72	73	20	25	15	1.0	1.4	0.7
Nigeria	..	..	..	..	..	..	67	75	59	..	..	..
Norway	..	..	100	100	100	100	..	..	..	11.8	12.2	11.6
Oman	57	56	..	96	..	96	76	76	76	..	..	..
Pakistan	1	4	..	..	..	..	..	..	..	3.9	5.1	2.5
Panama	83	69	74	..	79	..	..	..	..	8.6	8.6	8.5
Papua New Guinea	108	97	..	59	..	60	59	64	53	2.9	3.3	2.4
Paraguay	70	72	58	77	58	80	86	85	87	6.2	6.3	6.1
Peru	97	96	78	..	74	..	90	90	89	7.6	8.0	7.1
Philippines	..	..	..	..	..	..	92	..	..	8.2	8.2	8.2
Poland	..	..	..	..	..	..	96	..	..	9.8	10.0	9.7
Portugal	..	..	..	..	..	..	..	..	..	5.9	6.1	5.7
Puerto Rico	..	..	..	..	..	..	..	..	..	..	..	..
Romania	..	..	..	..	..	..	98	..	..	..	..	..
Russian Federation	..	..	..	..	..	..	90	91	90	..	..	..

2.13 | Education efficiency

	Net intake rate in grade 1		Percentage of cohort reaching grade 5				Primary completion rate			Avearge years of schooling		
	% of school-age population		% of grade one students who reach grade 5				Total	% of all children who complete primary school Male	Female	Total	Male	Female
	Male 1998	Female 1998	Male 1980	1997	Female 1980	1997	1992-2000[a]	1992-2000[a]	1992-2000[a]	2000	2000	2000
Rwanda	..	..	69	..	74	..	..	..	..	2.6	3.0	2.2
Saudi Arabia	49	33	82	87	86	92	69	68	69	..	..	..
Senegal	78	..	89	89	82	85	41	48	34	2.6	3.1	2.0
Sierra Leone	..	..	..	..	..	..	..	..	..	2.4	3.1	1.7
Singapore	..	..	..	..	..	..	..	..	..	7.0	7.5	6.6
Slovak Republic	..	..	..	..	..	..	97	96	97	9.3	..	..
Slovenia	..	..	..	..	..	..	92	90	94	7.1	..	..
Somalia	..	..	..	..	..	..	..	..	..	..	..	..
South Africa	36	34	..	..	..	..	98	95	100	6.1	5.7	6.6
Spain	..	..	95	..	94	..	..	..	..	7.3	7.4	7.1
Sri Lanka	..	..	..	83	..	84	100	98	102	6.9	7.2	6.6
Sudan	..	..	68	75	71	73	35	38	33	2.1	2.7	1.6
Swaziland	41	43	77	73	81	79	81	78	85	6.0	5.8	6.2
Sweden	..	..	98	97	98	97	..	..	..	11.4	11.4	11.4
Switzerland	..	..	75	..	74	..	..	..	..	10.5	11.1	9.9
Syrian Arab Republic	62	60	93	93	88	94	90	95	86	5.8	6.8	4.8
Tajikistan	..	..	..	..	..	..	95	..	..	..	..	..
Tanzania	11	13	89	78	90	84	59	58	60	2.7	3.1	2.3
Thailand	..	..	..	..	..	..	84	..	..	6.5	7.0	6.0
Togo	43	38	59	79	44	60	63	86	41	3.3	4.6	2.1
Trinidad and Tobago	86	94	85	98	87	97	81	79	84	7.8	7.5	8.0
Tunisia	79	80	89	90	84	92	91	93	90	5.0	5.8	4.2
Turkey	..	..	..	..	..	..	92	95	89	5.3	6.2	4.3
Turkmenistan	..	..	..	..	..	..	..	..	..	..	..	..
Uganda	..	..	..	..	..	..	61	74	49	3.5	4.3	2.7
Ukraine	..	..	..	..	..	..	55	55	55	..	..	..
United Arab Emirates	53	53	100	83	100	84	80	76	86	..	..	..
United Kingdom	..	..	..	..	..	..	..	..	..	9.4	9.5	9.4
United States	..	..	..	..	..	..	..	..	..	12.0	12.1	12.0
Uruguay	49	49	..	96	..	99	98	95	101	7.6	7.2	7.9
Uzbekistan	..	..	..	..	..	..	100	..	..	..	..	..
Venezuela, RB	..	..	..	86	..	92	78	77	79	6.6	6.5	6.8
Vietnam	78	83	..	..	..	..	..	..	..	..	..	..
West Bank and Gaza	..	..	..	..	..	..	..	..	..	..	..	..
Yemen, Rep.	32	21	..	..	..	..	..	..	..	..	..	..
Yugoslavia, Fed. Rep.	..	..	..	..	..	..	96	..	..	..	..	..
Zambia	40	42	88	..	82	..	80	..	..	5.5	6.0	5.0
Zimbabwe	..	..	..	78	..	79	113	116	111	5.4	6.0	4.7
World	.. w	.. w	.. w	.. w	.. w	.. w	84 w	90 w	80 w	6.4 w	7.2 w	5.7 w
Low income	..	..	..	..	..	..	69	77	61	4.4	5.4	3.3
Middle income	..	..	..	..	..	..	..	..	..	6.4	7.3	5.5
Lower middle income	..	..	..	91	..	92	101	104	99	6.3	7.3	5.2
Upper middle income	74	70	..	..	..	..	..	..	..	6.9	7.3	6.5
Low & middle income	..	..	..	..	..	..	84	90	80	5.6	6.5	4.6
East Asia & Pacific	..	..	..	92	..	93	103	107	102	6.3	7.3	5.2
Europe & Central Asia	..	..	..	..	..	..	..	..	..	..	..	..
Latin America & Carib.	77	74	..	..	..	..	..	..	..	6.0	6.3	5.8
Middle East & N. Africa	..	..	..	..	..	..	84	88	80	5.3	6.1	4.4
South Asia	..	..	..	..	..	..	74	84	63	4.7	5.8	3.4
Sub-Saharan Africa	..	..	..	..	..	..	53	59	48	..	..	..
High income	..	..	..	..	..	..	..	..	..	10.0	10.2	9.8
Europe EMU	..	..	..	..	..	..	..	..	..	8.4	8.8	8.1

a. Data are for the most recent year available.

About the data

Indicators of students' progress through school, estimated by the United Nations Educational, Scientific, and Cultural Organization (UNESCO) and the World Bank, measure an education system's success in extending coverage to all students, maintaining the flow of students from one grade to the next, and, ultimately, imparting a particular level of education.

Low net intake rates in grade 1 reflect the fact that many children do not enter primary school at the official age, even though school attendance, at least through the primary level, is mandatory in all countries. Once enrolled, students drop out for a variety of reasons, including the low quality of schooling, discouragement over poor performance, and the direct and indirect costs of schooling. Students' progress to higher grades may also be limited by the availability of teachers, classrooms, and educational materials.

The cohort survival rate is estimated as the proportion of an entering cohort of grade 1 students that eventually reaches grade 5. It measures the holding power and internal efficiency of an education system. Cohort survival rates approaching 100 percent indicate a high level of retention and a low level of dropout.

Cohort survival rates are typically estimated from data on enrollment and repetition by grade for two consecutive years, in a procedure called the reconstructed cohort method. This method makes three simplifying assumptions: dropouts never return to school; promotion, repetition, and dropout rates remain constant over the entire period in which the cohort is enrolled in school; and the same rates apply to all pupils enrolled in a given grade, regardless of whether they previously repeated a grade (Fredricksen 1993). Given these assumptions, cross-country comparisons should be made with caution, because other flows—caused by new entrants, reentrants, grade skipping, migration, or school transfers during the school year—are not considered.

UNESCO measures cohort survival to grade 5 because research suggests that five to six years of schooling is a critical threshold for the achievement of sustainable basic literacy and numeracy skills. However, it should be noted that the cohort survival rate does not guarantee these learning outcomes, and only indirectly reflects the quality of schooling. Measuring actual learning outcomes requires setting curriculum standards and measuring students' learning progress against those standards through standardized assessments, or tests.

The primary completion rate is being used increasingly by the World Bank as a core indicator of education system performance. Because it measures both education system coverage and student attainment, the primary completion rate is a more accurate indicator of human capital formation and school system quality and efficiency than are either gross or net enrollment ratios. It is also the most direct measure of national progress toward the Millennium Development Goal of universal primary education.

The primary completion rate reflects the primary cycle as nationally defined, ranging from a very small number of countries with 3 or 4 years of primary education, to a majority of countries with 5 or 6 years, and a relatively small number of countries with 7 or 8 years. For any given country it is therefore consistent with the gross and net enrollment ratios. The numerator may include overage children who have repeated one or more grades of primary school but are now graduating successfully. For countries where the number of primary graduates is not reported, a proxy primary completion rate is calculated: the total number of students in the final year of primary school, minus the number of students who repeat the grade in a typical year, divided by the total number of children of official graduation age in the population.

Average years of schooling measure the educational attainment of the population ages 15 and over, which provides another indication of the human capital stock of the country. However, the data do not directly measure the human skills obtained in schools and, specifically, do not take account of differences in the quality of schooling across countries. Average years of schooling are computed using a perpetual inventory method. For further details, see Barro and Lee (2000).

Definitions

• **Net intake rate in grade 1** is the number of new entrants in the first grade of primary education who are of official primary school entrance age, expressed as a percentage of the population of the corresponding age.
• **Percentage of cohort reaching grade 5** is the share of children enrolled in the first grade of primary school who eventually reach grade 5. The estimate is based on the reconstructed cohort method (see *About the data*). • **Primary completion rate** is the total number of students successfully completing (or graduating from) the last year of primary school in a given year, divided by the total number of children of official graduation age in the population.
• **Average years of schooling** are the years of formal schooling received, on average, by adults ages 15 and over. Because of data limitations it is not possible to adjust this number for students who drop out during the final year of school. Thus, proxy rates should be taken as an upper-bound estimate of the likely actual primary completion rate.

Data sources

Data on the net intake rate come from UNESCO's special data collection for the Education for All initiative. The data on the cohort reaching grade 5 are from the UNESCO Institute for Statistics. The data on the primary completion rate are compiled by staff in the education group of the World Bank's Human Development Network. Data on average years of schooling are from Robert Barro and Jong-Wha Lee's *International Data on Educational Attainment Updates and Implications,* (2000).

2.14 | Education outcomes

	Adult illiteracy rate				Youth illiteracy rate				Expected years of schooling			
	Male % ages 15 and over		Female % ages 15 and over		Male % ages 15-24		Female % ages 15-24		Males		Females	
	1990	2000	1990	2000	1990	2000	1990	2000	1990	1998	1990	1998
Afghanistan	..	..	..	..	..	..	..	..	..	..	..	..
Albania	13	8	33	23	3	1	8	4	..	..	..	..
Algeria	36	24	59	43	14	6	32	16	11	11	9	11
Angola	..	..	..	..	..	..	..	..	..	6	..	5
Argentina	4	3	4	3	2	2	2	1	..	14	..	15
Armenia	1	1	4	2	0 a	0 a	1	0 a	..	..	..	..
Australia	..	..	..	..	..	..	..	..	13	..	13	..
Austria	..	..	..	..	..	..	..	..	15	..	14	..
Azerbaijan	..	..	..	..	..	..	..	..	..	11	..	11
Bangladesh	54	48	77	70	45	39	68	60	6	8	4	8
Belarus	0 a	0 a	1	1	0 a	0 a	0 a	0 a	..	..	..	..
Belgium	..	..	..	..	..	..	..	..	14	..	14	..
Benin	62	48	85	76	43	29	75	64	..	8	..	5
Bolivia	13	8	30	21	4	2	11	6	..	13	..	12
Bosnia and Herzegovina	..	..	..	..	..	..	..	..	..	..	..	..
Botswana	34	25	30	20	21	15	13	8	10	12	11	12
Brazil	18	15	20	15	12	9	9	6	..	13	..	13
Bulgaria	2	1	4	2	0 a	0 a	1	0 a	12	..	12	..
Burkina Faso	75	66	92	86	64	54	86	77	3	4	2	3
Burundi	51	44	73	60	42	34	55	38	6	4	4	3
Cambodia	22	20	52	43	19	17	34	25	..	9	..	7
Cameroon	28	18	47	31	10	6	16	7	..	13	..	11
Canada	..	..	..	..	..	..	..	..	17	15	17	15
Central African Republic	53	40	79	65	34	24	61	41	..	6	..	3
Chad	63	48	81	66	42	27	62	40	..	7	..	3
Chile	5	4	6	4	2	1	2	1	..	13	..	13
China	14	8	33	24	3	1	8	4	..	9	..	9
Hong Kong, China	5	3	16	10	2	1	1	0 a	..	..	..	..
Colombia	11	8	12	8	6	4	4	2	..	11	..	11
Congo, Dem. Rep.	39	27	66	50	20	12	42	25	..	5	..	4
Congo, Rep.	23	13	42	26	5	2	10	3	..	7	..	5
Costa Rica	6	4	6	4	3	2	2	1	..	11	..	11
Côte d'Ivoire	57	46	77	61	40	30	59	40	..	8	..	5
Croatia	1	1	5	3	0 a	0 a	0 a	0 a	..	..	..	..
Cuba	5	3	5	3	1	0 a	1	0 a	12	11	13	12
Czech Republic	..	..	..	..	..	..	..	..	..	..	..	..
Denmark	..	..	..	..	..	..	..	..	14	..	14	..
Dominican Republic	20	16	21	16	13	10	12	8	..	11	..	12
Ecuador	10	7	15	10	4	2	5	3	..	11	..	11
Egypt, Arab Rep.	40	33	66	56	29	24	49	37	..	12	..	11
El Salvador	24	18	31	24	15	11	17	13	..	11	..	10
Eritrea	42	33	65	55	27	20	51	40	..	5	..	4
Estonia	..	..	..	..	..	..	..	..	12	..	12	..
Ethiopia	62	53	80	69	48	39	66	52	..	5	..	3
Finland	..	..	..	..	..	..	..	..	15	..	16	..
France	..	..	..	..	..	..	..	..	14	..	15	..
Gabon	..	..	..	..	..	..	..	..	..	12	..	11
Gambia, The	68	56	80	71	49	34	66	51	..	8	..	6
Georgia	..	..	..	..	..	..	..	..	..	5	..	5
Germany	..	..	..	..	..	..	..	..	15	..	14	..
Ghana	30	20	53	37	12	6	25	12	..	3	..	2
Greece	2	1	8	4	1	0 a	0 a	0 a	13	..	13	..
Guatemala	31	24	47	39	20	14	34	27	..	10	..	8
Guinea	..	..	..	..	..	..	..	..	..	6	..	3
Guinea-Bissau	57	46	87	77	37	27	74	57	..	8	..	5
Haiti	57	48	63	52	44	36	46	35	..	12	..	12
Honduras	31	25	32	25	22	18	21	15	..	8	..	9

	Adult illiteracy rate				Youth illiteracy rate				Expected years of schooling			
	Male % ages 15 and over		Female % ages 15 and over		Male % ages 15-24		Female % ages 15-24		Males		Females	
	1990	2000	1990	2000	1990	2000	1990	2000	1990	1998	1990	1998
Hungary	1	1	1	1	0 [a]	0 [a]	0 [a]	0 [a]	11	..	11	..
India	38	32	64	55	27	20	46	35	..	9	..	8
Indonesia	13	8	27	18	3	2	7	3	10	..	9	..
Iran, Islamic Rep.	28	17	46	31	8	4	19	8	..	..	..	..
Iraq	43	34	67	54	29	22	48	33	..	9	..	7
Ireland	..	..	..	..	..	..	..	..	12	..	13	..
Israel	5	3	13	8	1	0 [a]	2	1 [a]	..	14	..	15
Italy	2	1	3	2	0 [a]	0 [a]	0 [a]	0 [a]	..	..	..	..
Jamaica	22	17	14	9	13	9	5	3	11	11	11	11
Japan	..	..	..	..	..	..	..	..	..	14	..	14
Jordan	10	5	29	16	2	1	4	1 [a]	9	9	9	9
Kazakhstan	..	..	..	..	..	..	..	..	..	10	..	10
Kenya	19	11	39	24	7	4	13	6	..	8	..	8
Korea, Dem. Rep.	..	..	..	..	..	..	..	..	..	..	..	..
Korea, Rep.	2	1	7	4	0 [a]	0 [a]	0 [a]	0 [a]	14	..	13	..
Kuwait	21	16	27	20	12	8	13	7	7	9	7	10
Kyrgyz Republic	..	..	..	..	..	..	..	..	..	11	..	10
Lao PDR	47	36	80	67	28	17	62	42	9	9	6	7
Latvia	0 [a]	0 [a]	0 [a]	0 [a]	0 [a]	0 [a]	0 [a]	0 [a]	..	..	..	..
Lebanon	12	8	27	20	5	3	11	7	..	13	..	14
Lesotho	35	28	11	6	23	17	3	1	9	9	11	10
Liberia	45	30	77	62	25	15	60	46	..	6	..	4
Libya	17	9	49	32	1	0 [a]	17	7	..	13	..	13
Lithuania	0 [a]	0 [a]	1	1	0 [a]	0 [a]	0 [a]	0 [a]	..	..	..	..
Macedonia, FYR	..	..	..	..	..	..	..	..	..	..	..	..
Madagascar	34	26	50	40	22	16	33	23	..	6	..	6
Malawi	31	26	64	53	24	19	49	39	..	10	..	10
Malaysia	13	9	26	17	5	3	6	2	..	10	..	11
Mali	67	51	81	66	46	28	63	40	3	5	1	3
Mauritania	54	49	76	70	44	43	64	59	..	7	..	6
Mauritius	15	12	25	19	9	7	9	6	..	12	..	12
Mexico	9	7	15	10	4	3	6	3	..	12	..	11
Moldova	1	0 [a]	4	2	0 [a]	0 [a]	0 [a]	0 [a]	..	..	..	..
Mongolia	1	1	2	1	1	1	1	0 [a]	..	7	..	9
Morocco	47	38	75	64	32	24	58	42	..	10	..	8
Mozambique	51	40	82	71	34	25	68	54	4	5	3	4
Myanmar	13	11	26	19	10	9	14	9	..	7	..	8
Namibia	23	17	28	19	14	10	11	7	..	13	..	13
Nepal	52	40	86	76	33	23	73	57	..	10	..	7
Netherlands	..	..	..	..	..	..	..	..	15	..	15	..
New Zealand	..	..	..	..	..	..	..	..	14	10	15	11
Nicaragua	37	34	37	33	32	29	31	28	..	10	..	10
Niger	82	76	95	92	75	68	91	86	..	3	..	2
Nigeria	40	28	62	44	19	10	34	16	..	7	..	5
Norway	..	..	..	..	..	..	..	..	14	..	14	..
Oman	33	20	62	38	5	0 [a]	25	4	10	9	9	8
Pakistan	51	43	80	72	37	29	69	58	..	5	..	3
Panama	10	7	12	9	4	3	5	4	..	12	..	12
Papua New Guinea	36	29	52	43	26	20	38	29	..	9	..	8
Paraguay	8	6	12	8	4	3	5	3	9	10	8	11
Peru	8	5	21	15	3	2	8	5	..	13	..	11
Philippines	7	5	8	5	3	2	3	1	..	1	..	2
Poland	0 [a]	0 [a]	0 [a]	0 [a]	0 [a]	0 [a]	0 [a]	0 [a]	12	..	12	..
Portugal	9	5	16	10	1	0 [a]	0 [a]	0 [a]	13	..	14	..
Puerto Rico	8	6	9	6	5	3	3	2	..	..	..	..
Romania	1	1	4	3	1	0 [a]	1	0 [a]	11	..	11	..
Russian Federation	0 [a]	0 [a]	1	1	0 [a]	0 [a]	0 [a]	0 [a]	..	..	..	..

	Adult illiteracy rate				Youth illiteracy rate				Expected years of schooling			
	Male % ages 15 and over		Female % ages 15 and over		Male % ages 15-24		Female % ages 15-24		Males		Females	
	1990	2000	1990	2000	1990	2000	1990	2000	1990	1998	1990	1998
Rwanda	37	26	56	40	22	15	33	19	..	8	..	8
Saudi Arabia	24	17	50	33	9	5	21	10	9	9	7	9
Senegal	62	53	81	72	50	40	70	58	..	6	..	5
Sierra Leone	..	..	..	..	..	..	..	..	..	..	..	..
Singapore	6	4	17	12	1	0 ᵃ	1	0 ᵃ	..	..	..	..
Slovak Republic	..	..	..	..	..	..	..	..	..	..	..	..
Slovenia	0 ᵃ	0 ᵃ	0 ᵃ	0 ᵃ	0 ᵃ	0 ᵃ	0 ᵃ	0 ᵃ	..	..	..	..
Somalia	..	..	..	..	..	..	..	..	..	..	..	..
South Africa	18	14	20	15	11	9	12	9	13	14	13	14
Spain	2	1	5	3	0 ᵃ	0 ᵃ	0 ᵃ	0 ᵃ	..	..	..	..
Sri Lanka	7	6	15	11	4	3	6	3	..	11	..	11
Sudan	40	31	68	54	24	17	46	29	..	5	..	5
Swaziland	26	19	30	21	15	10	15	9	11	11	10	10
Sweden	..	..	..	..	..	..	..	..	13	..	13	..
Switzerland	..	..	..	..	..	..	..	..	14	..	13	..
Syrian Arab Republic	18	12	52	40	8	5	33	21	11	9	9	9
Tajikistan	1	0 ᵃ	3	1	0 ᵃ	0 ᵃ	0 ᵃ	0 ᵃ	..	..	..	..
Tanzania	24	16	49	33	11	7	23	12	..	5	..	5
Thailand	5	3	11	6	1	1	2	2	..	10	..	11
Togo	39	28	71	58	21	13	52	36	11	12	6	8
Trinidad and Tobago	6	4	11	8	3	2	4	3	11	12	11	12
Tunisia	28	19	53	39	7	3	25	11	11	13	10	12
Turkey	11	7	33	23	3	1	12	6	..	10	..	9
Turkmenistan	..	..	..	..	..	..	..	..	..	..	..	..
Uganda	31	22	57	43	20	14	40	28	..	11	..	10
Ukraine	0 ᵃ	0 ᵃ	1	1	0 ᵃ	0 ᵃ	0 ᵃ	0 ᵃ	..	..	..	..
United Arab Emirates	29	25	29	21	18	13	11	6	10	11	11	11
United Kingdom	..	..	..	..	..	..	..	..	14	..	14	..
United States	..	..	..	..	..	..	..	..	15	16	16	15
Uruguay	4	3	3	2	1	1	1	0 ᵃ	..	11	..	14
Uzbekistan	1	0 ᵃ	2	1	0 ᵃ	0 ᵃ	0 ᵃ	0 ᵃ	..	..	..	..
Venezuela, RB	10	7	12	8	5	3	3	1	..	10	..	11
Vietnam	6	4	13	9	5	3	5	3	..	10	..	10
West Bank and Gaza	..	..	..	..	..	..	..	..	..	..	..	..
Yemen, Rep.	45	32	87	75	26	17	75	54	..	11	..	5
Yugoslavia, Fed. Rep.	..	..	..	..	..	..	..	..	..	..	..	..
Zambia	21	15	41	29	14	9	24	15	..	8	..	7
Zimbabwe	13	7	25	15	3	1	9	4	..	..	..	..
World	.. w	.. w	.. w	.. w	.. w	.. w	.. w	.. w	.. w	.. w	.. w	.. w
Low income	35	28	56	47	24	18	40	31	..	..	..	..
Middle income	13	9	26	19	5	4	10	6	..	..	..	..
Lower middle income	14	9	29	21	5	3	10	7	..	..	..	..
Upper middle income	11	8	16	12	6	4	7	4	..	..	..	..
Low & middle income	22	18	39	31	13	11	23	19	..	..	..	..
East Asia & Pacific	13	8	29	21	3	2	8	4	..	..	..	..
Europe & Central Asia	2	2	6	5	1	1	3	2	..	..	..	..
Latin America & Carib.	14	11	17	13	8	6	8	6	..	..	..	..
Middle East & N. Africa	34	25	59	46	18	12	37	24	..	..	..	..
South Asia	40	34	66	57	29	23	50	40	..	..	..	..
Sub-Saharan Africa	40	30	60	47	25	17	40	27	..	..	..	..
High income	..	..	..	..	..	..	..	..	15	..	16	..
Europe EMU	..	..	..	..	..	..	..	..	15	..	15	..

a. Less than 0.5.

About the data

Many governments collect and publish statistics that indicate how their education systems are working and developing—statistics on enrollment and on such efficiency indicators as pupil-teacher ratios, repetition rates, and cohort progression through school. But until recently, despite an obvious interest in what education achieves, few systems in high-income or developing countries had systematically collected information on outcomes of education.

Basic student outcomes include achievements in reading and mathematics judged against established standards. In many countries national learning assessments are enabling ministries of education to monitor progress in these outcomes. Internationally, the United Nations Educational, Scientific, and Cultural Organization (UNESCO) has established literacy as an outcome indicator based on an internationally agreed definition. The rate of illiteracy is defined as the percentage of people who cannot, with understanding, read and write a short, simple statement about their everyday life. In practice, illiteracy is difficult to measure. To estimate illiteracy using such a definition requires census or survey measurements under controlled conditions. Many countries estimate the number of illiterate people from self-reported data, or by taking people with no schooling as illiterate.

Literacy statistics for most countries cover the population ages 15 and above, by five-year age groups, but some include younger ages or are confined to age ranges that tend to inflate literacy rates. As an alternative, UNESCO has proposed the narrower age range of 15–24, which better captures the ability of participants in the formal education system. The youth illiteracy rate reported in the table measures the accumulated outcomes of primary education over the previous 10 years or so by indicating the proportion of people who have passed through the primary education system (or never entered it) without acquiring basic literacy and numeracy skills. Reasons for this may include difficulties in attending school or dropping out before reaching grade 5 (see *About the data* for table 2.13) and thereby failing to achieve basic learning competencies.

The indicator expected years of schooling is an estimate of the total years of schooling that an average child at the age of school entry will receive, including years spent on repetition, given the current patterns of enrollment across cycles of education. It may also be interpreted as an indicator of the total education resources, measured in school years, that a child will acquire over his or her "lifetime" in school—or as an indicator of an education system's overall level of development.

Because the calculation of this indicator assumes that the probability of a child's being enrolled in school at any future age is equal to the current enrollment ratio for that age, it does not account for changes and trends in future enrollment ratios. The expected number of years and the expected number of grades completed are not necessarily consistent, because the first includes years spent in repetition. Comparability across countries and over time may be affected by differences in the length of the school year or changes in policies on automatic promotions and grade repetition.

Figure 2.14

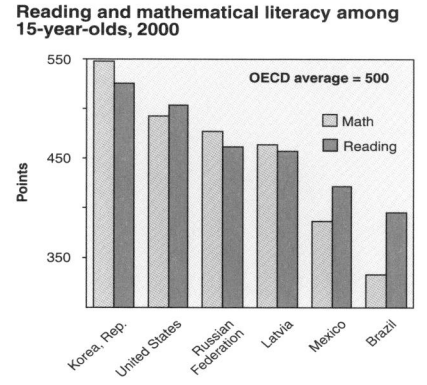

Reading and mathematical literacy among 15-year-olds, 2000

Source: Programme for International Student Assessment survey.

The absence of regular and reliable measures of education outcomes across countries, especially measures of skills, remains the most signifiant gap in education indicators. The Programme for International Student Assessment (PISA) was carried out by OECD and participating countries to measure skills for life— reading literacy, mathematical literacy, and scientific literacy—among 15-year-old students. Thirty two countries, including eight developing countries, conducted the first PISA survey in 2000. The PISA scale for each literacy area was devised so that across OECD countries the average score is 500 points.

Definitions

• **Adult illiteracy rate** is the percentage of people ages 15 and over who cannot, with understanding, read and write a short, simple statement about their everyday life. • **Youth illiteracy rate** is the illiteracy rate among people ages 15–24. • **Expected years of schooling** are the average number of years of formal schooling that children are expected to receive, including university education and years spent in repetition. They are the sum of the underlying age-specific enrollment ratios for primary, secondary, and tertiary education.

Data sources

The data on illiteracy are based on the UNESCO Institute for Statistics estimates and projections assessed in 2000 and 2002. The data on expected years of schooling are from the UNESCO Institute for Statistics.

2.15 | Health expenditure, services, and use

	Health expenditure			Health expenditure per capita	Physicians		Hospital beds		Inpatient admission rate	Average length of stay	Outpatient visits per capita
	Public % of GDP 1995-99[a]	Private % of GDP 1995-99[a]	Total % of GDP 1995-99[a,b]	$ 1995-99[a]	per 1,000 people		per 1,000 people		% of population 1990-99[a]	days 1990-99[a]	1990-99[a]
					1980	1990-99[a]	1980	1990-99[a]			
Afghanistan	..	..	..	..	..	0.1	..	0.2	..	..	..
Albania	2.0	0.9	3.3 [c]	36	..	1.3	..	3.2	..	13	2
Algeria	2.6	1.0	3.6	68	..	1.0	..	2.1	..	..	..
Angola	..	..	..	..	..	0.1	..	1.3	..	..	..
Argentina	2.4	6.1	8.4	654	..	2.7	..	3.3	..	..	..
Armenia	4.0	4.2	7.8	27	3.5	3.2	8.4	0.7	8	15	2
Australia	6.0	2.6	8.6	1,714	1.8	2.5	..	8.5	16	16	6
Austria	5.9	2.3	8.2	2,121	..	3.0	11.2	8.7	29	9	7
Azerbaijan	1.0	0.6	1.8	9	3.4	3.6	9.7	9.7	6	18	1
Bangladesh	1.7	1.9	3.6	12	0.1	0.2	0.2	0.3	..	..	..
Belarus	4.6	1.0	5.6	85	3.4	4.4	12.5	12.2	26	18	11
Belgium	6.3	2.5	8.8	2,137	2.5	3.8	..	7.3	20	11	8
Benin	1.6	1.6	3.3	12	0.1	0.1	1.5	0.2	..	..	..
Bolivia	4.1	2.4	6.5	69	..	1.3	..	1.7	..	..	..
Bosnia and Herzegovina	8.0	..	..	..	..	1.4	..	1.8	..	15	..
Botswana	2.5	1.5	4.0	127	0.1	0.2	2.4	1.6	..	..	..
Brazil	2.9	3.6	6.5	308	..	1.3	..	3.1	0 [e]	..	2
Bulgaria	3.9	0.2	4.1	62	2.5	3.5	11.1	8.6	18	12	5
Burkina Faso	1.5	2.8	4.1	9	0.0 [d]	0.0 [d]	..	1.4	2	3	0 [e]
Burundi	0.6	3.0	3.7	5	..	0.1	..	0.7	..	..	..
Cambodia	0.6	6.3	6.9	17	..	0.3	..	2.1	..	..	..
Cameroon	1.0	4.0	5.0	31	..	0.1	..	2.6	..	..	..
Canada	6.6	2.7	9.3	1,939	..	2.1	..	4.1	10	8	7
Central African Republic	2.0	1.0	3.0	9	0.0 [d]	0.0 [d]	1.6	0.9	..	..	..
Chad	2.3	0.6	2.9	7	..	0.0 [d]	..	0.7	..	..	..
Chile	2.7	3.1	5.9	289	..	1.1	3.4	2.7	..	..	..
China	2.1	3.0	5.1	40	0.9	1.7	2.0	2.4	4	12	..
Hong Kong, China	2.1	2.8	5.0	1,134	0.8	1.3	4.0	..	2	..	1
Colombia	5.2	4.2	9.4	227	..	1.2	1.6	1.5	..	..	..
Congo, Dem. Rep.	..	..	..	..	..	0.1	..	1.4	..	..	.. ..
Congo, Rep.	2.0	3.8	5.8	40	..	0.3	..	3.4	..	..	..
Costa Rica	5.2	1.5	6.7	257	..	0.9	3.3	1.7	9	6	1
Côte d'Ivoire	1.2	2.5	3.7	28	..	0.1	..	0.8	..	..	..
Croatia	9.5	2.0	9.6	440	..	2.3	..	5.9	12	..	..
Cuba	..	..	..	..	..	5.3	..	5.1	..	..	..
Czech Republic	6.6	0.6	7.2	380	..	3.0	..	8.7	20	11	12
Denmark	6.9	1.5	8.4	2,785	..	3.4	..	4.5	20	7	6
Dominican Republic	1.9	3.0	4.8	95	..	2.2	..	1.5	..	..	..
Ecuador	1.7	2.0	3.6	59	..	1.7	1.9	1.6	..	..	..
Egypt, Arab Rep.	1.8	2.0	3.8	48	1.1	1.6	2.0	2.1	3	6	4
El Salvador	2.6	4.6	7.2	143	0.3	1.1	..	1.6	..	..	..
Eritrea	2.9	..	..	..	..	0.0 [d]	..	..	..	..	..
Estonia	5.1	1.3	6.6 [c]	243	4.2	3.0	12.4	7.4	18	9	5
Ethiopia	1.3	2.4	4.1	4	0.0 [d]	0.0 [d]	0.3	0.2	..	..	..
Finland	5.2	1.7	6.8	1,704	1.9	3.1	15.5	7.5	27	11	4
France	7.3	2.0	9.3	2,288	..	3.0	..	8.5	23	11	7
Gabon	2.1	1.0	3.1	122	..	0.2	..	3.2	..	..	..
Gambia, The	2.3	1.9	3.7	13	..	0.0 [d]	..	0.6	..	..	..
Georgia	0.8	2.0	2.8	16	4.8	4.4	10.7	4.8	5	11	1
Germany	7.9	2.6	10.5	2,697	2.2	3.5	..	9.3	21	12	7
Ghana	1.7	2.9	4.7	19	..	0.1	..	1.5	..	..	..
Greece	4.7	3.6	8.4	965	2.4	4.1	6.2	5.0	15	8	..
Guatemala	2.1	2.3	4.3	78	..	0.9	..	1.0	..	..	..
Guinea	2.3	1.5	3.8	19	..	0.1	..	0.6	..	..	..
Guinea-Bissau	..	..	..	..	0.1	0.2	1.9	1.5	..	..	..
Haiti	1.4	2.8	4.2	21	..	0.2	0.7	0.7	..	..	..
Honduras	3.9	4.7	8.6	74	..	0.8	1.3	1.1	..	..	..

	Health expenditure			Health expenditure per capita	Physicians		Hospital beds		Inpatient admission rate	Average length of stay	Outpatient visits per capita
	Public % of GDP 1995-99[a]	Private % of GDP 1995-99[a]	Total % of GDP 1995-99[a,b]	$ 1995-99[a]	per 1,000 people 1980	1990-99[a]	per 1,000 people 1980	1990-99[a]	% of population 1990-99[a]	days 1990-99[a]	1990-99[a]
Hungary	5.2	1.6	6.8	318	2.5	3.2	9.1	8.3	24	10	15
India	0.8	4.2	5.4	20	0.4	0.4	0.8	0.8	..	..	..
Indonesia	0.8	0.9	1.6	8	..	0.2	..	0.7	..	..	..
Iran, Islamic Rep.	1.7	2.5	4.2	128	..	0.9	1.5	1.6	..	..	..
Iraq	3.8	1.8	5.6	..	0.6	0.5	1.9	1.4	..	..	..
Ireland	5.2	1.6	6.8	1,569	1.3	2.3	9.7	3.7	14	8	..
Israel	6.0	3.6	9.5	1,607	..	3.9	5.1	6.0	..	..	..
Italy	5.6	2.6	8.2	1,676	..	5.9	..	5.5	18	8	5
Jamaica	3.0	2.5	5.5	157	..	1.4	..	2.1	..	..	..
Japan	5.7	1.6	7.2	2,243	..	1.9	11.3	16.4	10	40	16
Jordan	3.6	3.8	8.0 [c]	139	0.8	1.7	1.3	1.8	11	4	3
Kazakhstan	2.7	2.9	5.5	62	3.2	3.5	13.2	8.5	15	16	0 [e]
Kenya	2.4	5.5	7.8	31	..	0.1	..	1.6	..	..	..
Korea, Dem. Rep.	..	..	..	..	..	3.0	..	..	..	..	..
Korea, Rep.	2.4	3.0	5.4	470	0.6	1.3	1.7	5.5	6	12	10
Kuwait	2.9	0.4	3.3	551	1.7	1.9	4.1	2.8	..	..	..
Kyrgyz Republic	2.2	2.2	4.4	11	2.9	3.0	12.0	9.5	21	15	1
Lao PDR	1.2	1.3	2.5	6	..	0.2	..	2.6	..	..	..
Latvia	4.0	2.6	6.7	166	4.1	2.8	13.7	10.3	21	14	4
Lebanon	2.2	9.7	12.1 [c]	469	..	2.1	..	2.7	17	4	..
Lesotho	3.4	2.2	..	..	..	0.1	..	..	..	..	..
Liberia	..	..	..	..	..	0.0 [d]	..	..	..	..	..
Libya	..	..	..	..	1.3	1.3	..	4.3	..	..	..
Lithuania	4.7	1.5	6.3	183	3.9	4.0	12.1	9.2	24	11	7
Macedonia, FYR	5.3	1.0	4.9	90	..	2.2	..	4.7	9	13	3
Madagascar	1.1	1.0	2.1	5	..	0.1	..	0.9	..	..	..
Malawi	2.8	3.5	6.3	11	..	0.0 [d]	..	1.3	..	..	2
Malaysia	1.4	1.0	2.5	81	0.3	0.7	..	2.0	..	..	..
Mali	2.1	2.2	4.3	11	0.0 [d]	0.1	..	0.2	1	7	0 [e]
Mauritania	1.4	3.4	4.8	19	..	0.1	..	0.7	..	..	..
Mauritius	1.8	1.6	3.4	120	0.5	0.9	3.1	3.1	0 [e]	..	4
Mexico	2.6	2.8	5.3	236	..	1.7	..	1.1	6	4	2
Moldova	2.9	2.1	6.4	25	3.1	3.5	12.0	12.1	19	18	8
Mongolia	4.7	..	..	..	..	2.4	11.2	11.5	..	..	..
Morocco	1.2	3.2	4.4	49	..	0.5	..	1.0	3	7	..
Mozambique	2.8	0.7	3.5	8	0.0 [d]	..	1.1	0.9	..	..	..
Myanmar	0.2	1.6	1.8	97	..	0.3	0.9	0.6	..	..	..
Namibia	3.3	3.3	7.0	142	..	0.3	..	..	..	..	..
Nepal	1.3	4.2	5.4	11	0.0 [d]	0.0 [d]	0.2	0.2	..	..	.. ..
Netherlands	6.0	2.8	8.7	2,173	..	3.1	12.5	11.3	11	34	6
New Zealand	6.3	1.8	8.1	1,163	1.6	2.3	..	6.2	13	9	..
Nicaragua	8.5	4.0	12.5	54	0.4	0.9	..	1.5	..	..	..
Niger	1.2	1.4	2.6	5	..	0.0 [d]	..	0.1	28	5	0 [e]
Nigeria	0.8	2.0	2.8	30	0.1	0.2	0.9	1.7	..	..	..
Norway	7.0	2.2	9.2	3,182	1.9	2.8	15.0	14.4	16	9	4
Oman	2.9	0.6	3.5	..	0.5	1.3	1.6	2.2	9	4	4
Pakistan	0.7	3.1	4.0	18	0.3	0.6	0.6	0.7	..	..	3
Panama	4.9	2.3	7.3	246	..	1.7	..	2.2	..	..	..
Papua New Guinea	2.5	0.7	3.2	25	0.1	0.1	5.5	4.0	..	..	..
Paraguay	1.7	3.6	5.2	86	..	1.1	..	1.3	..	..	..
Peru	2.4	3.8	6.2	141	0.7	0.9	..	1.5	1	6	2
Philippines	1.6	2.1	3.6	37	0.1	1.2	1.7	1.1	..	..	..
Poland	4.7	1.5	6.2	248	1.8	2.3	5.6	5.1	15	9	5
Portugal	5.1	2.5	7.7	859	..	3.2	..	4.0	12	9	3
Puerto Rico	..	..	..	..	..	1.7	..	3.3	..	..	..
Romania	3.8	1.5	4.6	86	1.5	1.8	8.8	7.6	18	10	4
Russian Federation	4.6	1.2	4.6	133	4.0	4.2	13.0	12.1	22	17	8

	Health expenditure			Health expenditure per capita	Physicians		Hospital beds		Inpatient admission rate	Average length of stay	Outpatient visits per capita
	Public % of GDP 1995-99[a]	Private % of GDP 1995-99[a]	Total % of GDP 1995-99[a,b]	$ 1995-99[a]	per 1,000 people 1980	1990-99[a]	per 1,000 people 1980	1990-99[a]	% of population 1990-99[a]	days 1990-99[a]	1990-99[a]
Rwanda	2.0	2.1	4.1	10	0.0 [d]	0.0 [d]	1.5	1.7	..	..	..
Saudi Arabia	6.4	1.6	8.0	611	..	1.7	..	2.3	11	4	1
Senegal	2.6	1.9	4.5	23	..	0.1	..	0.4	22	10	1
Sierra Leone	0.9	4.4	5.3	8	0.1	0.1	1.2	..	..	..	..
Singapore	1.1	2.1	3.2	678	0.9	1.6	4.0	3.6	12	..	..
Slovak Republic	5.7	1.5	6.5	285	..	3.5	..	7.1	20	9	4
Slovenia	6.7	0.9	7.6	746	..	2.3	7.0	5.7	16	11	..
Somalia	..	..	..	..	0.0 [d]	0.0 [d]	..	0.8	..	..	..
South Africa	3.3	3.8	7.2	230	..	0.6	..	..	..	..	..
Spain	5.4	1.6	7.0	1,043	..	3.1	..	3.9	11	10	..
Sri Lanka	1.7	1.8	3.5	29	0.1	0.4	2.9	2.7	..	..	..
Sudan	0.7	2.6	3.3	119	0.1	0.1	0.9	1.1	..	..	..
Swaziland	2.5	1.0	3.5	46	..	0.2	..	..	..	..	..
Sweden	6.6	1.3	7.9	2,145	2.2	3.1	14.8	3.7	17	7	3
Switzerland	7.6	2.8	10.4	3,857	..	3.4	..	18.1	17	14	11
Syrian Arab Republic	0.9	1.6	2.5	116	0.4	1.3	1.1	1.4	..	..	..
Tajikistan	5.2	0.9	6.1	13	2.4	2.0	10.0	8.8	16	15	..
Tanzania	1.3	1.8	3.0	8	..	0.0 [d]	1.4	0.9	..	..	..
Thailand	1.9	4.1	6.0	112	0.1	0.4	1.5	2.0	..	..	1
Togo	1.3	1.3	2.6	9	0.1	0.1	..	1.5	..	..	..
Trinidad and Tobago	2.5	1.8	4.3	204	0.7	0.8	..	5.1	..	..	..
Tunisia	2.2	2.9	5.1	108	0.3	0.7	2.1	1.7	8	..	..
Turkey	3.3	1.4	4.8	153	0.6	1.2	2.2	2.6	7	6	2
Turkmenistan	4.1	1.1	5.2	30	2.9	3.0	10.6	11.5	17	15	..
Uganda	1.9	4.1	5.9	18	..	0.0 [d]	..	0.9	..	..	..
Ukraine	2.9	1.5	4.4	28	3.7	3.0	12.5	11.8	20	17	10
United Arab Emirates	0.8	7.6	8.4	1,428	1.1	1.8	2.8	2.6	11	5	..
United Kingdom	5.8	1.2	6.9	1,675	..	1.8	9.3	4.1	15	10	6
United States	5.7	7.1	12.9	4,271	1.8	2.7	5.9	3.6	13	7	6
Uruguay	1.9	7.3	9.1	621	..	3.7	..	4.4	..	..	..
Uzbekistan	3.4	0.6	4.1	25	2.9	3.1	11.5	8.3	19	14	..
Venezuela, RB	2.6	1.6	4.2	171	0.8	2.4	0.3	1.5	..	..	..
Vietnam	0.8	4.0	4.8	17	0.2	0.5	3.5	1.7	8	7	3
West Bank and Gaza	4.9	3.7	8.6	82	..	0.5	..	1.2	9	3	4
Yemen, Rep.	2.4	3.2	5.6	18	..	0.2	..	0.6	..	..	..
Yugoslavia, Fed. Rep.	..	..	..	..	..	2.0	..	5.3	8	12	2
Zambia	3.6	3.4	6.9	23	0.1	0.1	..	..	..	..	..
Zimbabwe	3.0	4.0	8.1 [c]	36	0.2	0.1	3.0	0.5	..	..	..
World	**5.3 w**	**3.8 w**	**9.0 w**	**483 w**	**1.0 w**	**1.4 w**	**3.4 w**	**3.2 w**	**9 w**	**13 w**	**6 w**
Low income	0.9	2.7	3.8	21	0.5	0.5	1.7	1.3	13	11	4
Middle income	2.9	2.9	5.7	119	1.2	1.7	3.4	3.4	6	12	4
Lower middle income	2.7	2.6	5.0	62	1.2	1.7	3.4	3.5	6	13	5
Upper middle income	3.2	3.1	6.2	303	..	1.6	..	3.2	6	7	4
Low & middle income	2.5	2.9	5.3	74	0.9	1.1	2.7	2.5	7	12	4
East Asia & Pacific	1.8	2.7	4.5	51	0.8	1.3	2.0	2.5	4	13	4
Europe & Central Asia	4.4	1.4	5.2	126	3.0	3.1	10.4	8.8	17	14	6
Latin America & Carib.	2.8	3.7	6.5	264	..	1.6	..	2.2	2	5	2
Middle East & N. Africa	2.9	2.2	5.1	125	..	1.0	..	1.7	5	6	3
South Asia	0.9	3.8	5.1	19	0.3	0.4	0.7	0.7	..	..	3
Sub-Saharan Africa	2.0	2.8	4.9	41	..	0.1	..	1.1	12	6	1
High income	6.0	4.0	10.1	2,733	..	2.9	..	7.2	15	14	8
Europe EMU	6.7	2.4	9.1	2,029	..	3.8	..	7.4	19	12	6

a. Data are for the most recent year available. b. Data may not sum to total because of rounding and because of differences in the year for which the most recent data are available. c. A country has one more category, external resources, in addition to public and private. d. Less than 0.05.

About the data

National health accounts track financial flows in the health sector, including both public and private expenditures by sources of funding. In contrast with high-income countries, few developing countries have health accounts that are methodologically consistent with national accounting approaches. The difficulties in creating national health accounts go beyond data collection. To establish a national health accounting system, a country needs to define the boundaries of the health care system and a taxonomy of health care delivery institutions. The accounting system should be comprehensive and standardized, providing not only accurate measurements of financial flows, but also information on the equity and efficiency of health financing to inform health policy.

The absence of consistent national health accounting systems in most developing countries makes cross-country comparisons of health spending difficult. Records of private out-of-pocket expenditures are often lacking. And compiling estimates of public health expenditures is complicated in countries where state or provincial and local governments are involved in health care financing and delivery because the data on public spending often are not aggregated. The data in the table are the product of an effort by the World Health Organization (WHO), the Organisation for Economic Co-operation and Development (OECD), and the World Bank to collect all available information on health expenditures from national and local government budgets, national accounts, household surveys, insurance publications, international donors, and existing tabulations.

Health service indicators (physicians and hospital beds per 1,000 people) and health care utilization indicators (inpatient admission rates, average length of stay, and outpatient visits) come from a variety of sources (see *Data sources*). Data are lacking for many countries, and for others comparability is limited by differences in definitions. In estimates of health personnel, for example, some countries incorrectly include retired physicians (because deletions are made only periodically) or those working outside the health sector. There is no universally accepted definition of hospital beds. Moreover, figures on physicians and hospital beds are indicators of availability, not of quality or use. They do not show how well trained the physicians are or how well equipped the hospitals or medical centers are. And physicians and hospital beds tend to be concentrated in urban areas, so these indicators give only a partial view of health services available to the entire population.

The average length of stay in hospitals is an indicator of the efficiency of resource use. Longer stays may reflect a waste of resources if patients are kept in hospitals beyond the time medically required, inflating demand for hospital beds and increasing hospital costs. Aside from differences in cases and financing methods, cross-country variations in average length of stay may result from differences in the role of hospitals. Many developing countries do not have separate extended care facilities, so hospitals become the source of both long-term and acute care. Other factors may also explain the variations. Data for some countries may not include all public and private hospitals. Admission rates may be overstated in some countries if outpatient surgeries are counted as hospital admissions. And in many countries outpatient visits, especially emergency visits, may result in double counting if a patient receives treatment in more than one department.

Definitions

• **Public health expenditure** consists of recurrent and capital spending from government (central and local) budgets and social (or compulsory) health insurance funds. • **Private health expenditure** includes direct household (out-of-pocket) spending, private insurance, spending by non-profit institutions serving households (other than social insurance) and direct service payments by private corporations. • **Total health expenditure** is the sum of public and private health expenditure, plus, for some countries, external sources (mainly foreign assistance). It covers the provision of health services (preventive and curative), family planning activities, nutrition activities, and emergency aid designated for health but does not include provision of water and sanitation. • **Physicians** are defined as graduates of any faculty or school of medicine who are working in the country in any medical field (practice, teaching, research). • **Hospital beds** include inpatient beds available in public, private, general, and specialized hospitals and rehabilitation centers. In most cases beds for both acute and chronic care are included. • **Inpatient admission rate** is the percentage of the population admitted to hospitals during a year. • **Average length of stay** is the average duration of inpatient hospital admissions. • **Outpatient visits per capita** are the number of visits to health care facilities per capita, including repeat visits.

Data sources

The estimates of health expenditure come from the WHO's *World Health Report 2000* and *World Health Report 2001*, from the OECD for its member countries, from national health accounts of a country, from the Web site *The European Observatory on Health Care Systems* (www.observatory.dk), supplemented by World Bank country and sector studies, and poverty assessments, including the Human Development Network's *Sector Strategy: Health, Nutrition, and Population* (World Bank 1997). Data are also drawn from World Bank public expenditure reviews, the International Monetary Fund's *Government Finance Statistics* database, and other studies. The data on private expenditure in developing countries are largely drawn from household surveys conducted by a government, or statistical or international organizations. The data on physicians, hospital beds, and utilization of health services are from the WHO and OECD, supplemented by country data.

Table 2.15a

How important are the different elements of client responsiveness?

Respect for persons	Client orientation
Respect for dignity	Prompt attention
Confidentiality	Quality of amenities
Autonomy	Access to social support networks
	Choice of providers

Source: WHO, *World Health Report 2000.*

Use of health services depends not only on easy access, but on responsiveness to clients by health providers. In a survey of 35 countries the poor were identified as the main disadvantaged group. They were considered to be treated with less respect for their dignity, to have less choice of providers, and to be offered poorer quality amenities than the nonpoor. Rural populations were regarded as being treated worse than urban dwellers, suffering especially from less prompt attention. In several countries women, children or adolescents, and indigenous or tribal groups received worse treatment than the rest of the population.

	Access to an improved water source % of population		Access to improved sanitation facilities % of population		Tetanus vaccinations % of pregnant women	Child immunization rate % of children under 12 months measles	DPT	Tuberculosis treatment success rate % of cases	DOTS detection rate % of cases
	1990	2000	1990	2000	1996-2000[a]	1995-99[a]	1995-99[a]	1995-99[a]	1995-99[a]
Afghanistan	..	13	..	12	..	40	35	33	5
Albania	..	..	..	..	65	85	97	..	..
Algeria	..	94	..	73	52	83	83	..	..
Angola	..	38	..	44	24	46	22	68	62
Argentina	..	79	..	85	..	99	88	55	18
Armenia	..	..	..	..	..	91	91	81	42
Australia	100	100	100	100	..	89	88	75	23
Austria	100	100	100	100	..	90	90	..	..
Azerbaijan	..	..	..	..	..	99	99	86	9
Bangladesh	91	97	37	53	64	71	72	80	25
Belarus	..	100	..	..	..	98	99	..	..
Belgium	..	..	..	..	..	83	96	..	..
Benin	..	63	20	23	50	79	79	77	31
Bolivia	74	79	55	66	27	79	78	62	77
Bosnia and Herzegovina	..	..	..	..	..	83	90	88	52
Botswana	95	..	61	..	54	86	90	47	65
Brazil	82	87	72	77	45	99	90	91	4
Bulgaria	..	..	..	..	..	96	96	..	..
Burkina Faso	53	..	24	29	33	53	42	59	9
Burundi	65	..	89	..	9	75	74	74	28
Cambodia	..	30	..	18	31	55	49	95	57
Cameroon	52	62	87	92	49	62	48	75	10
Canada	100	100	100	100	..	96	97	..	..
Central African Republic	59	60	30	31	6	39	33	..	..
Chad	..	27	18	29	24	30	21	64	33
Chile	90	94	97	97	..	96	94	83	85
China	71	75	29	38	13	90	90	97	32
Hong Kong, China	..	..	..	..	..	..	..	85	56
Colombia	87	91	82	85	..	75	74	74	30
Congo, Dem. Rep.	..	45	..	20	10	..	..	70	53
Congo, Rep.	..	51	..	..	30	23	29	..	..
Costa Rica	..	98	..	96	..	88	86	..	30
Côte d'Ivoire	65	77	49	..	49	62	62	62	44
Croatia	..	95	..	100	..	92	93	..	..
Cuba	..	95	..	95	..	96	94	94	95
Czech Republic	..	..	..	..	..	95	98	65	51
Denmark	..	100	..	..	..	92	99	..	..
Dominican Republic	78	79	60	71	86	96	73	..	7
Ecuador	..	71	..	59	..	99	80	..	26
Egypt, Arab Rep.	94	95	87	94	36	95	94	87	25
El Salvador	..	74	..	83	..	86	86	77	55
Eritrea	..	46	..	13	34	88	93	73	12
Estonia	..	..	..	..	..	92	95	..	..
Ethiopia	22	24	13	15	17	27	21	74	22
Finland	100	100	100	100	..	96	99	..	..
France	..	..	..	..	..	84	98	..	..
Gabon	..	70	..	21	54	55	37	..	..
Gambia, The	..	62	..	37	96	..	..	..	..
Georgia	..	76	..	99	..	80	90	78	46
Germany	..	..	..	..	..	75	85	..	..
Ghana	56	64	60	63	51	73	72	59	23
Greece	..	..	..	..	..	88	88	..	..
Guatemala	78	92	77	85	39	83	78	79	54
Guinea	45	48	55	58	61	52	46	73	43
Guinea-Bissau	..	49	..	47	46	70	38	..	..
Haiti	46	46	25	28	52	85	43	79	24
Honduras	84	90	..	77	..	98	95	93	15

	Access to an improved water source		Access to an improved sanitation facilities		Tetanus vaccinations	Child immunization rate		Tuberculosis treatment success rate	DOTS detection rate
	% of population		% of population		% of pregnant women	% of children under 12 months		% of cases	% of cases
	1990	2000	1990	2000	1996-2000[a]	measles 1995-99[a]	DPT 1995-99[a]	1995-99[a]	1995-99[a]
Hungary	99	99	99	99	..	99	99	80	36
India	78	88	21	31	67	50	55	84	6
Indonesia	69	76	54	66	54	71	72	58	19
Iran, Islamic Rep.	86	95	81	81	75	..	..	83	31
Iraq	..	85	..	79	56	63	76	83	5
Ireland	..	..	..	..	..	77	86	..	..
Israel	..	..	..	..	..	94	96	..	83
Italy	..	..	..	..	..	70	95	72	54
Jamaica	..	71	..	84	..	96	84	89	105
Japan	..	..	..	..	..	94	71	..	..
Jordan	97	96	98	99	15	94	97	92	33
Kazakhstan	..	91	..	99	..	99	98	79	73
Kenya	40	49	84	86	51	79	79	77	53
Korea, Dem. Rep.	..	..	..	..	5	34	37	91	2
Korea, Rep.	..	92	..	63	..	85	74	..	..
Kuwait	..	..	..	..	8	96	94	..	..
Kyrgyz Republic	..	77	..	100	..	97	98	82	60
Lao PDR	..	90	..	46	32	71	56	..	..
Latvia	..	..	..	..	..	97	95	71	52
Lebanon	..	100	..	99	..	88	94	73	72
Lesotho	..	91	..	92	17	77	85	..	..
Liberia	..	..	..	..	..	..	..	..	..
Libya	71	72	97	97	..	..	..	68	134
Lithuania	..	..	..	..	..	97	93	79	2
Macedonia, FYR	..	99	..	99	..	..	..	..	..
Madagascar	44	47	36	42	35	55	55	..	..
Malawi	49	57	73	77	81	83	84	69	42
Malaysia	..	..	..	..	71	88	93	..	..
Mali	55	65	70	69	32	57	52	70	19
Mauritania	37	37	30	33	63	62	40	..	50
Mauritius	100	100	100	99	78	79	85	91	34
Mexico	83	86	69	73	..	95	96	78	38
Moldova	..	100	..	..	..	..	..	..	..
Mongolia	..	60	..	30	..	93	94	84	63
Morocco	75	82	62	75	33	90	91	82	90
Mozambique	..	60	..	43	29	57	61	..	..
Myanmar	64	68	45	46	78	85	83	82	33
Namibia	72	77	33	41	70	66	72	60	105
Nepal	66	81	21	27	33	73	76	89	44
Netherlands	100	100	100	100	..	96	97	65	40
New Zealand	..	..	..	..	..	83	88	..	..
Nicaragua	70	79	76	84	42	99	83	82	80
Niger	53	59	15	20	41	36	28	..	..
Nigeria	49	57	60	63	44	41	26	73	11
Norway	100	100	..	..	..	93	95	69	20
Oman	37	39	84	92	96	99	99	86	106
Pakistan	84	88	34	61	58	54	56	66	2
Panama	..	87	..	94	..	90	92	51	9
Papua New Guinea	42	42	82	82	11	58	56	72	5
Paraguay	63	79	89	95	..	92	66	..	..
Peru	72	77	64	76	59	93	93	92	95
Philippines	87	87	74	83	35	79	79	84	20
Poland	..	..	..	..	..	97	98	75	3
Portugal	..	..	..	..	..	96	97	74	77
Puerto Rico	..	..	..	..	..	..	..	..	..
Romania	..	58	..	53	..	98	97	85	4
Russian Federation	..	99	..	..	..	97	95	68	2

	Access to an improved water source		Access to improved sanitation facilities		Tetanus vaccinations	Child immunization rate		Tuberculosis treatment success rate	DOTS detection rate
	% of population		% of population		% of pregnant women	% of children under 12 months		% of cases	% of cases
						measles	DPT		
	1990	2000	1990	2000	1996-2000[a]	1995-99[a]	1995-99[a]	1995-99[a]	1995-99[a]
Rwanda	..	41	..	8	43	87	85	72	37
Saudi Arabia	..	95	..	100	66	94	96	57	22
Senegal	72	78	57	70	64	60	60	48	48
Sierra Leone	..	28	..	28	42	62	46	..	..
Singapore	100	100	100	100	..	93	94	..	..
Slovak Republic	..	100	..	100	..	99	99	85	36
Slovenia	100	100	..	..	..	98	92	78	68
Somalia	..	..	..	..	..	26	18	88	22
South Africa	..	86	..	86	26	82	76	74	68
Spain	..	..	..	..	..	93	94	..	..
Sri Lanka	66	83	82	83	78	95	99	76	76
Sudan	67	75	58	62	55	53	50	65	32
Swaziland	..	..	..	..	..	82	99	..	..
Sweden	100	100	100	100	..	96	99	..	..
Switzerland	100	100	100	100	79	81	94	..	..
Syrian Arab Republic	..	80	..	90	53	97	94	88	17
Tajikistan	..	..	..	..	..	79	81	..	..
Tanzania	50	54	88	90	61	..	..	76	51
Thailand	71	80	86	96	81	96	97	68	40
Togo	51	54	37	34	41	43	41	..	..
Trinidad and Tobago	..	86	..	88	..	91	90	65	123
Tunisia	80	..	76	..	50	84	96	91	79
Turkey	80	83	87	91	30	80	79	..	..
Turkmenistan	..	58	..	100	..	97	98	..	..
Uganda	44	50	84	75	38	53	55	62	59
Ukraine	..	..	..	..	87	99	99	..	..
United Arab Emirates	..	..	..	..	..	95	94	..	..
United Kingdom	100	100	100	100	..	91	93	..	..
United States	100	100	100	100	..	92	96	72	90
Uruguay	..	98	..	95	..	93	93	84	91
Uzbekistan	..	85	..	100	..	96	99	78	2
Venezuela, RB	..	84	..	74	..	82	77	81	82
Vietnam	48	56	73	73	55	93	93	93	80
West Bank and Gaza	..	..	..	..	31	..	..	..	..
Yemen, Rep.	66	69	39	45	9	74	72	..	..
Yugoslavia, Fed. Rep.	..	..	..	..	..	..	..	..	..
Zambia	52	64	63	78	35	90	84	..	..
Zimbabwe	77	85	64	68	58	79	81	70	55
World	**76 w**	**80 w**	**48 w**	**56 w**		**73 w**	**72 w**		
Low income	70	76	36	45		57	57		
Middle income	75	81	47	59		90	89		
Lower middle income	74	80	41	52		89	89		
Upper middle income	..	87	..	81		92	88		
Low & middle income	73	79	42	52		71	70		
East Asia & Pacific	70	75	38	47		85	85		
Europe & Central Asia	..	90	..	..		93	93		
Latin America & Carib.	81	85	72	78		93	87		
Middle East & N. Africa	84	89	78	83		86	88		
South Asia	80	87	25	37		53	57		
Sub-Saharan Africa	49	55	55	55		53	46		
High income	..	..	..	..		89	92		
Europe EMU	..	..	..	..		82	93		

a. Data are for the most recent year available.

About the data

The indicators in the table are based on data provided to the World Health Organization (WHO) by member states as part of their efforts to monitor and evaluate progress in implementing national health strategies. Because reliable, observation-based statistical data for these indicators do not exist in some developing countries, the data are at times estimated.

People's health is influenced by the environment in which they live. Lack of clean water and basic sanitation is the main reason diseases transmitted by feces are so common in developing countries. Drinking water contaminated by feces deposited near homes and an inadequate water supply cause diseases accounting for 10 percent of the disease burden in developing countries (World Bank 1993c). The data on access to an improved water source measure the share of the population with ready access to water for domestic purposes. The data are based on surveys and estimates provided by governments to the WHO-UNICEF Joint Monitoring Programme. The coverage rates for water and sanitation are based on information from service users on the facilities their households actually use, rather than on information from service providers, who may include nonfunctioning systems. Access to drinking water from an improved source does not ensure that the water is adequate or safe, as these characteristics are not tested at the time of the surveys.

Neonatal tetanus is an important cause of infant mortality in some developing countries. It can be prevented through immunization of the mother during pregnancy. Recommended doses for full protection are generally two tetanus shots during the first pregnancy and one booster shot during each subsequent pregnancy, with five doses considered adequate for lifetime protection. Information on tetanus shots during pregnancy is collected through surveys in which pregnant respondents are asked to show antenatal cards on which tetanus shots have been recorded. Because not all women have antenatal cards, respondents are also asked about their receipt of these injections. Poor recall may result in a downward bias in estimates of the share of births protected. But in settings where receiving injections is common, respondents may erroneously report having received tetanus toxoid.

Governments in developing countries usually finance immunization against measles and diphtheria, pertussis (whooping cough), and tetanus (DPT) as part of the basic public health package. According to the World Bank's *World Development Report 1993: Investing in Health,* these diseases accounted for about 10 percent of the disease burden among children under five in 1990, compared with an expected 23 percent at 1970 levels of vaccination. In many developing countries, however, lack of precise in-

formation on the size of the cohort of children under one year of age makes immunization coverage difficult to estimate. The data shown here are based on an assessment of national immunization coverage rates carried out in 2000-01 by the WHO and UNICEF. The assessment considered both administrative data from service providers and household survey data on children's immunization histories. Based on the data available, consideration of potential biases, and contributions of local experts, the most likely true level of immunization coverage was determined for each year.

Data on the success rate of tuberculosis treatment are provided for countries that have implemented the recommended control strategy: directly observed treatment, short course (DOTS). Countries that have not adopted DOTS or have only recently done so are omitted because of lack of data or poor comparability or reliability of reported results. The treatment success rate for tuberculosis provides a useful indicator of the quality of health services. A low rate or no success suggests that infectious patients may not be receiving adequate treatment. An essential complement to the tuberculosis treatment success rate is the DOTS detection rate, which indicates whether there is adequate coverage by the recommended case detection and treatment strategy. A country with a high treatment success rate may still face big challenges if its DOTS detection rate remains low.

Definitions

• **Access to an improved water source** refers to the percentage of the population with reasonable access to an adequate amount of water from an improved source, such as a household connection, public standpipe, borehole, protected well or spring, and rainwater collection. Unimproved sources include vendors, tanker trucks, and unprotected wells and springs. Reasonable access is defined as the availability of at least 20 liters a person a day from a source within one kilometer of the dwelling. • **Access to improved sanitation facilities** refers to the percentage of the population with at least adequate excreta disposal facilities (private or shared, but not public) that can effectively prevent human, animal, and insect contact with excreta. Improved facilities range from simple but protected pit latrines to flush toilets with a sewerage connection. To be effective, facilities must be correctly constructed and properly maintained. • **Tetanus vaccinations** refer to the percentage of pregnant women who receive two tetanus toxoid injections during their first pregnancy and one booster shot during each subsequent pregnancy. • **Child immunization rate** is the percentage of children under one year of age receiving vaccination coverage for four diseases—measles and diphtheria, pertussis (whooping cough), and tetanus (DPT). A child is considered adequately immunized against measles after receiving one dose of vaccine, and against DPT after receiving three doses. • **Tuberculosis treatment success rate** refers to the percentage of new, registered smear-positive (infectious) cases that were cured or in which a full course of treatment was completed. • **DOTS detection rate** is the percentage of estimated new infectious tuberculosis cases detected under the directly observed treatment, short-course (DOTS) case detection and treatment strategy.

Data sources

The table was produced using information provided to the WHO by countries, the WHO's EPI Information System, and its *Global Tuberculosis Control Report 2001;* the United Nations Children's Fund's (UNICEF) *State of the World's Children 2001;* and the WHO and UNICEF's *Global Water Supply and Sanitation Assessment 2000 Report.*

2.17 | Reproductive health

	Total fertility rate		Adolescent fertility rate	Women at risk of unintended pregnancy	Contraceptive prevalence rate	Births attended by skilled health staff		Maternal mortality ratio	
	births per woman		births per 1,000 women ages 15-19	% of married women ages 15-49	% of women ages 15-49	% of total		per 100,000 live births National estimates	Modelled estimates
	1980	2000	2000	1990-2000[a]	1990-2000[a]	1982	1996-99[a]	1990-98[a]	1995
Afghanistan	7.0	6.7	153	..	..	..	..	..	..
Albania	3.6	2.1	16	..	..	99	..	..	31
Algeria	6.7	3.2	24	..	51	15	..	220	150
Angola	6.9	6.6	219	..	..	34	..	..	1,300
Argentina	3.3	2.5	61	..	..	..	..	38	85
Armenia	2.3	1.3	44	..	..	..	96	35	29
Australia	1.9	1.8	18	..	..	99	..	..	6
Austria	1.6	1.3	21	..	..	..	..	..	11
Azerbaijan	3.2	2.0	32	..	..	..	99	43	37
Bangladesh	6.1	3.1	142	15	54	2	14	440	600
Belarus	2.0	1.3	28	..	..	..	..	28	33
Belgium	1.7	1.6	11	..	..	..	..	..	8
Benin	7.0	5.5	123	21	16	..	60	500	880
Bolivia	5.5	3.9	80	26	49	..	59	390	550
Bosnia and Herzegovina	2.1	1.6	23	..	..	..	..	10	15
Botswana	6.1	4.0	78	..	..	61	..	330	480
Brazil	3.9	2.2	70	7	77	98	88	160	260
Bulgaria	2.0	1.3	49	..	..	..	99	15	23
Burkina Faso	7.5	6.5	144	26	12	12	27	..	1,400
Burundi	6.8	6.0	55	..	..	12	..	..	1,900
Cambodia	5.7	4.0	60	..	24	..	31	470	590
Cameroon	6.4	4.8	142	13	19	10	55	430	720
Canada	1.7	1.5	20	..	..	..	..	..	6
Central African Republic	5.8	4.7	140	16	15	..	..	1,100	1,200
Chad	6.9	6.4	194	9	4	24	11	830	1,500
Chile	2.8	2.2	49	..	..	95	100	20	33
China	2.5	1.9	17	..	83	..	..	55	60
Hong Kong, China	2.0	1.0	7	..	..	100	..	..	..
Colombia	3.9	2.6	80	8	77	..	..	80	120
Congo, Dem. Rep.	6.6	6.1	215	..	..	..	..	..	940
Congo, Rep.	6.3	6.0	141	..	..	..	..	..	1,100
Costa Rica	3.6	2.5	85	..	..	..	..	29	35
Côte d'Ivoire	7.4	4.8	130	43	15	13	47	600	1,200
Croatia	1.9	1.4	19	..	69	..	..	6	18
Cuba	2.0	1.6	65	..	..	..	..	27	24
Czech Republic	2.1	1.2	23	..	69	..	..	9	14
Denmark	1.5	1.7	9	..	..	..	..	10	15
Dominican Republic	4.2	2.7	90	13	64	..	96	230	110
Ecuador	5.0	3.0	72	..	66	62	..	160	210
Egypt, Arab Rep.	5.1	3.3	53	11	56	..	56	170	170
El Salvador	4.9	3.1	10	8	60	35	90	120	180
Eritrea	7.5	5.4	119	28	8	..	..	1,000	1,100
Estonia	2.0	1.2	25	..	..	..	..	50	80
Ethiopia	6.6	5.6	152	36	8	58	..	870	1,800
Finland	1.6	1.7	11	..	..	..	..	6	6
France	1.9	1.9	9	..	71	..	..	10	20
Gabon	4.5	4.2	172	28	33	..	..	520	620
Gambia, The	6.5	5.0	139	..	..	41	..	..	1,100
Georgia	2.3	1.1	47	21	41	..	..	70	22
Germany	1.4	1.4	13	..	..	..	..	8	12
Ghana	6.5	4.2	90	23	22	47	44	210	590
Greece	2.2	1.3	18	..	..	99	..	1	2
Guatemala	6.3	4.6	117	23	38	40	..	190	270
Guinea	6.1	5.2	168	24	6	..	35	670	1,200
Guinea-Bissau	6.0	5.8	190	..	..	..	..	910	910
Haiti	5.9	4.3	80	40	28	34	..	525	1,100
Honduras	6.5	3.9	102	11	50	50	55	110	220

	Total fertility rate		Adolescent fertility rate	Women at risk of unintended pregnancy	Contraceptive prevalence rate	Births attended by skilled health staff		Maternal mortality ratio	
	births per woman		births per 1,000 women ages 15-19	% of married women ages 15-49	% of women ages 15-49	% of total		per 100,000 live births National estimates	Modelled estimates
	1980	2000	2000	1990-2000[a]	1990-2000[a]	1982	1996-99[a]	1990-98[a]	1995
Hungary	1.9	1.3	28	..	73	..	..	15	23
India	5.0	3.1	104	16	52	23	..	410	440
Indonesia	4.3	2.5	60	11	57	31	43	450	470
Iran, Islamic Rep.	6.7	2.6	45	..	73	..	..	37	130
Iraq	6.4	4.3	38	..	..	..	..	..	370
Ireland	3.2	1.9	14	..	60	..	..	6	9
Israel	3.2	2.8	19	..	..	99	..	5	8
Italy	1.6	1.2	8	..	..	100	..	7	11
Jamaica	3.7	2.5	84	15	65	89	95	120	120
Japan	1.8	1.4	4	..	..	100	..	8	12
Jordan	6.8	3.7	33	14	50	75	97	41	41
Kazakhstan	2.9	2.0	40	11	66	..	98	70	80
Kenya	7.8	4.4	111	24	39	..	44	590	1,300
Korea, Dem. Rep.	2.8	2.1	2	..	..	100	..	110	35
Korea, Rep.	2.6	1.4	4	..	..	70	..	20	20
Kuwait	5.3	2.7	34	..	..	..	98	5	25
Kyrgyz Republic	4.1	2.6	40	12	60	..	98	65	80
Lao PDR	6.7	5.0	91	..	25	..	..	650	650
Latvia	1.9	1.2	32	..	..	..	..	45	70
Lebanon	4.0	2.3	30	..	61	..	95	100	130
Lesotho	5.5	4.4	86	..	23	28	..	..	530
Liberia	6.8	6.0	230	..	..	89	..	..	..
Libya	7.3	3.5	35	..	45	76	94	75	120
Lithuania	2.0	1.3	36	..	..	..	..	18	27
Macedonia, FYR	2.5	1.8	26	..	..	..	..	3	17
Madagascar	6.6	5.4	180	26	19	62	47	490	580
Malawi	7.6	6.3	136	30	31	59	..	1,120	580
Malaysia	4.2	3.0	25	..	..	82	..	39	39
Mali	7.1	6.3	180	26	7	14	24	580	630
Mauritania	6.4	5.7	147	..	..	23	58	550	870
Mauritius	2.7	2.0	37	..	75	84	..	50	45
Mexico	4.7	2.6	64	..	65	..	..	55	65
Moldova	2.4	1.4	57	..	74	..	..	42	65
Mongolia	5.3	2.6	58	10	60	100	..	150	65
Morocco	5.4	2.9	50	16	59	24	..	230	390
Mozambique	6.5	5.1	172	7	6	28	44	1,100	980
Myanmar	4.9	3.0	29	..	..	97	57	230	170
Namibia	5.9	5.0	105	22	29	..	..	230	370
Nepal	6.1	4.3	120	28	29	10	10	..	830
Netherlands	1.6	1.7	4	..	75	100	..	7	10
New Zealand	2.0	2.0	30	..	..	99	..	15	15
Nicaragua	6.3	3.5	135	15	60	..	65	150	250
Niger	8.0	7.2	215	17	8	20	18	590	920
Nigeria	6.9	5.3	128	22	15	..	..	700	1,100
Norway	1.7	1.9	12	..	..	100	..	6	9
Oman	9.9	4.3	80	..	24	60	..	19	120
Pakistan	7.0	4.7	64	32	28	..	..	..	200
Panama	3.7	2.5	75	..	..	83	..	70	100
Papua New Guinea	5.8	4.4	77	29	26	34	53	370	390
Paraguay	5.2	4.0	75	17	57	22	71	190	170
Peru	4.5	2.8	66	10	69	44	56	265	240
Philippines	4.8	3.4	33	26	47	57	56	170	240
Poland	2.3	1.4	21	..	..	..	..	8	12
Portugal	2.2	1.5	22	..	..	..	100	8	12
Puerto Rico	2.6	1.9	73	..	78	..	..	..	30
Romania	2.4	1.3	36	..	48	99	..	41	60
Russian Federation	1.9	1.2	46	..	34	..	99	50	75

	Total fertility rate		Adolescent fertility rate	Women at risk of unintended pregnancy	Contraceptive prevalence rate	Births attended by skilled health staff		Maternal mortality ratio	
	births per woman		births per 1,000 women ages 15-19	% of married women ages 15-49	% of women ages 15-49	% of total		per 100,000 live births National estimates	Modelled estimates
	1980	2000	2000	1990-2000[a]	1990-2000[a]	1982	1996-99[a]	1990-98[a]	1995
Rwanda	8.3	5.9	56	37	21	20	..	..	2,300
Saudi Arabia	7.3	5.5	105	..	21	74	91	..	23
Senegal	6.8	5.1	103	33	11	..	47	560	1,200
Sierra Leone	6.5	5.8	212	..	..	25	..	..	2,100
Singapore	1.7	1.5	9	..	..	100	100	6	9
Slovak Republic	2.3	1.3	26	..	..	..	..	9	14
Slovenia	2.1	1.2	10	..	..	..	..	11	17
Somalia	7.3	7.1	210	..	..	2	..	..	..
South Africa	4.6	2.9	70	..	62	..	84	..	340
Spain	2.2	1.2	9	..	..	96	..	6	8
Sri Lanka	3.5	2.1	20	..	..	87	95	60	60
Sudan	6.1	4.6	62	25	10	20	..	500	1,500
Swaziland	6.2	4.4	121	..	..	50	..	..	..
Sweden	1.7	1.6	11	..	..	..	..	5	8
Switzerland	1.5	1.5	5	..	..	..	..	5	8
Syrian Arab Republic	7.4	3.6	44	..	45	43	..	110	200
Tajikistan	5.6	3.1	35	..	..	..	..	65	120
Tanzania	6.7	5.3	125	13	25	74	35	530	1,100
Thailand	3.5	1.9	65	..	72	52	..	44	44
Togo	6.8	5.0	89	..	24	..	51	480	980
Trinidad and Tobago	3.3	1.8	40	..	..	90	99	..	65
Tunisia	5.2	2.1	13	..	60	50	82	70	70
Turkey	4.3	2.4	60	11	64	76	81	130	55
Turkmenistan	4.9	2.3	20	..	..	..	..	65	65
Uganda	7.2	6.2	204	29	15	..	..	510	1,100
Ukraine	2.0	1.2	43	..	68	..	..	27	45
United Arab Emirates	5.4	3.2	73	..	..	96	..	3	30
United Kingdom	1.9	1.7	28	..	..	98	..	7	10
United States	1.8	2.1	48	..	64	99	99	8	12
Uruguay	2.7	2.2	70	..	..	..	..	26	50
Uzbekistan	4.8	2.6	56	14	56	..	98	21	60
Venezuela, RB	4.2	2.8	98	..	..	82	..	60	43
Vietnam	5.0	2.2	31	..	75	100	77	160	95
West Bank and Gaza	..	5.7	90	..	42	..	..	..	..
Yemen, Rep.	7.9	6.2	105	39	21	..	22	350	850
Yugoslavia, Fed. Rep.	2.3	1.7	32	..	..	..	93	10	15
Zambia	7.0	5.3	156	27	26	..	47	650	870
Zimbabwe	6.4	3.8	112	15	54	69	84	695	610

World	**3.7 w**	**2.7 w**	**69 w**	**.. w**
Low income	5.3	3.6	104	..
Middle income	3.2	2.2	39	..
Lower middle income	3.0	2.1	32	80
Upper middle income	3.7	2.3	59	..
Low & middle income	4.1	2.8	74	..
East Asia & Pacific	3.0	2.1	28	83
Europe & Central Asia	2.5	1.6	43	..
Latin America & Carib.	4.1	2.6	72	..
Middle East & N. Africa	6.2	3.4	51	..
South Asia	5.3	3.3	105	52
Sub-Saharan Africa	6.6	5.2	138	..
High income	1.8	1.7	25	..
Europe EMU	1.8	1.5	11	..

a. Data are for most recent year available.

About the data

Reproductive health is a state of physical and mental well-being in relation to the reproductive system and its functions and processes. Means of achieving reproductive health include education and services during pregnancy and childbirth, provision of safe and effective contraception, and prevention and treatment of sexually transmitted diseases. Health conditions related to sex and reproduction have been estimated to account for 25 percent of the global disease burden in women (Murray and Lopez 1998). Reproductive health services will need to expand rapidly over the next two decades, when the number of women and men of reproductive age is projected to increase by more than 300 million.

Total and adolescent fertility rates are based on data on registered live births from vital registration systems or, in the absence of such systems, from censuses or sample surveys. As long as the surveys are fairly recent, the estimated rates are generally considered reliable measures of fertility in the recent past. In cases where no empirical information on age-specific fertility rates is available, a model is used to estimate the share of births to adolescents. For countries without vital registration systems, fertility rates for 2000 are generally based on extrapolations from trends observed in censuses or surveys from earlier years.

An increasing number of couples in the developing world want to limit or postpone childbearing but are not using effective contraceptive methods. These couples face the risk of unintended pregnancy, shown in the table as the percentage of married women of reproductive age who do not want to become pregnant but are not using contraception (Bulatao 1998). Information on this indicator is collected through surveys and excludes women not exposed to the risk of pregnancy because of postpartum anovulation, menopause, or infertility. Common reasons for not using contraception are lack of knowledge about contraceptive methods and concerns about their possible health side-effects.

Contraceptive prevalence reflects all methods—ineffective traditional methods as well as highly effective modern methods. Contraceptive prevalence rates are obtained mainly from Demographic and Health Surveys and contraceptive prevalence surveys (see *Primary data documentation* for the most recent survey year). Unmarried women are often excluded from such surveys, which may bias the estimates.

The share of births attended by skilled health staff is an indicator of a health system's ability to provide adequate care for pregnant women. Good antenatal and postnatal care improves maternal health and reduces maternal and infant mortality. But data may not reflect such improvements because health information systems are often weak, maternal deaths are underreported, and rates of maternal mortality are difficult to measure.

Maternal mortality ratios are generally of unknown reliability, as are many other cause-specific mortality indicators. Household surveys such as the Demographic and Health Surveys attempt to measure maternal mortality by asking respondents about survivorship of sisters. The main disadvantage of this method is that the estimates of maternal mortality that it produces pertain to 12 years or so before the survey, making them unsuitable for monitoring recent changes or observing the impact of interventions. In addition, measurement of maternal mortality is subject to many types of errors. Even in high-income countries with vital registration systems, misclassification of maternal deaths has been found to lead to serious underestimation.

The maternal mortality ratios shown in the table as reported are estimates based on national surveys, vital registration, or surveillance or are derived from community and hospital records. Those shown as modeled are based on an exercise carried out by the World Health Organization (WHO) and United Nations Children's Fund (UNICEF). In this exercise maternal mortality was estimated with a regression model using information on fertility, birth attendants, and HIV prevalence. Neither set of ratios can be assumed to provide an accurate estimate of maternal mortality in any of the countries in the table.

Definitions

• **Total fertility rate** is the number of children that would be born to a woman if she were to live to the end of her childbearing years and bear children in accordance with current age-specific fertility rates. • **Adolescent fertility rate** is the number of births per 1,000 women ages 15–19. • **Women at risk of unintended pregnancy** are fertile, married women of reproductive age who do not want to become pregnant and are not using contraception. • **Contraceptive prevalence rate** is the percentage of women who are practicing, or whose sexual partners are practicing, any form of contraception. It is usually measured for married women ages 15–49 only. • **Births attended by skilled health staff** are the percentage of deliveries attended by personnel trained to give the necessary supervision, care, and advice to women during pregnancy, labor, and the postpartum period, to conduct deliveries on their own, and to care for newborns. • **Maternal mortality ratio** is the number of women who die during pregnancy and childbirth, per 100,000 live births.

Data sources

The data on reproductive health come from Demographic and Health Surveys, the WHO's *Coverage of Maternity Care* (1997) and other WHO sources, UNICEF, and national statistical offices. Modelled estimates for maternal mortality ratios are from Kenneth Hill, Carla AbouZhar and Tessa Wordlaw's "Estimates of Maternal Mortality for 1995," (2001).

	Prevalence of undernourishment % of population		Prevalence of child malnutrition Weight for age		Prevalence of overweight Height for age		Prevalence of anemia % of pregnant women	Low-birthweight babies % of births	Breast feeding exclusive breastfeeding less then 4 months		Consumption of iodized salt % of households	Vitamin A supplemen-tation % of children 6-59 months
			% of children under 5	% of children under 5	% of children under 5							
	1990-92	1996-98	1993-2000[a]	1993-2000[a]	Year	%	1985-99[a]	1993-99[a]	Year	%	1992-98[a]	1998-2000
Afghanistan	63	70	49	48	1997	4	..	..	..	..	..	78
Afghanistan	63	70	49	48	1997	4	..	..	..	..	..	78
Albania	14	3	8	15	..	..	..	8	..	..	..	..
Algeria	5	5	13	18	1995	9	42	..	..	..	92	..
Angola	51	43	41	53	..	..	29	..	..	..	10	94
Argentina	..	..	5	12	1994	7	26	7	..	..	90	..
Armenia	..	21	3	12	1998	6	..	..	..	..	70	..
Australia	..	..	0	0	1995-96	5	..	7	..	..	..	..
Austria	..	..	..	..	..	..	..	6	..	..	..	..
Azerbaijan	..	32	17	20	1996	4	..	6	..	..	..	..
Bangladesh	35	38	61	55	1996-97	1	53	50	1996-97	26	55	79
Belarus	..	..	..	..	..	..	..	6	..	..	37	..
Belgium	..	..	..	..	..	..	..	..	..	..	..	..
Benin	21	14	29	25	1996	1	41	9	1996	2	79	100
Bolivia	25	23	8	27	1998	7	54	9	1998	32	91	85
Bosnia and Herzegovina	..	10	..	..	..	..	..	..	..	..	..	..
Botswana	20	27	17	29	..	..	..	..	1988	8	27	..
Brazil	13	10	6	11	1996	5	33	8	1996	20	95	20
Bulgaria	..	13	..	..	..	..	..	7	..	..	..	..
Burkina Faso	32	32	34	37	1992-93	2	24	..	1998-99	6	23	99
Burundi	44	68	..	..	1987	1	68	16	1987	47	80	92
Cambodia	41	33	47	53	..	..	..	18	..	..	7	79
Cameroon	29	19	22	29	1991	3	44	..	1998	5	83	100
Canada	..	..	..	..	1970-72	5	..	6	..	..	..	..
Central African Republic	46	41	23	28	1995	1	67	..	1994-95	0	87	100
Chad	58	38	39	40	..	..	37	..	1996-97	1	55	92
Chile	8	4	1	2	1996	7	13	5	..	..	100	..
China	17	11	10	14	1992	4	52	..	..	..	91	..
Hong Kong, China	..	..	..	..	..	..	..	5	..	..	..	..
Colombia	17	13	8	15	1995	3	24	17	1995	4	92	..
Congo, Dem. Rep.	37	61	34	45	..	..	..	20	..	..	90	78
Congo, Rep.	34	32	..	..	..	..	..	..	..	..	..	74
Costa Rica	6	6	5	6	1996	6	27	6	..	..	97	..
Côte d'Ivoire	15	14	24	24	1994	2	34	..	1994	2	..	..
Croatia	..	12	1	1	1995-96	6	..	..	..	..	90	..
Cuba	4	19	..	..	..	..	47	8	..	..	45	..
Czech Republic	..	..	..	..	1991	4	23	6	..	..	..	..
Denmark	..	..	..	..	..	..	..	..	..	..	..	..
Dominican Republic	29	28	6	11	1996	3	..	14	1996	8	13	53
Ecuador	8	5	..	..	..	..	17	17	1987	20	99	42
Egypt, Arab Rep.	5	4	4	19	1995-96	9	24	..	1995	25	84	..
El Salvador	12	11	12	23	1993	2	14	11	..	..	91	..
Eritrea	..	65	44	38	..	..	..	..	1995	41	80	94
Estonia	..	6	..	..	..	..	..	..	..	..	..	..
Ethiopia	..	49	47	51	..	..	42	9	..	..	0	86
Finland	..	..	..	..	..	..	..	..	..	..	..	..
France	..	..	..	..	..	..	..	6	..	..	..	..
Gabon	11	8	..	..	..	..	..	..	..	..	..	..
Gambia, The	18	16	26	30	..	..	80	..	..	..	9	..
Georgia	..	23	3	12	..	..	..	..	..	..	..	..
Germany	..	..	..	..	..	..	..	..	..	..	..	..
Ghana	29	10	25	26	1993-94	2	64	8	1998	18	28	91
Greece	..	..	..	..	1995	4	..	..	..	..	..	..
Guatemala	14	24	24	46	..	..	45	8	1998-99	27	49	..
Guinea	37	29	23	26	..	..	..	13	1999	10	37	100
Guinea-Bissau	..	..	..	..	..	..	74	..	..	..	..	77
Haiti	64	62	28	32	1994-95	3	64	15	1994-95	1	10	..
Honduras	23	22	25	39	1996	1	14	9	..	..	80	53

	Prevalence of undernourishment		Prevalence of child malnutrition		Prevalence of overweight		Prevalence of anemia	Low-birthweight babies	Breast feeding		Consumption of iodized salt	Vitamin A supplementation
	% of population		Weight for age % of children under 5	% of children under 5	Height for age % of children under 5		% of pregnant women	% of births	exclusive breastfeeding less then 4 months		% of households	% of children 6-59 months
	1990-92	1996-98	1993-2000ª	1993-2000ª	Year	%	1985-99ª	1993-99ª	Year	%	1992-98ª	1998-2000
Hungary	..	..	..	..	1980-88	2	..	8	..	..	..	..
India	26	21	47	46	1992-93	2	88	34	1999	28	70	15
Indonesia	10	6	34	42	1995	4	64	15	1997	20	64	64
Iran, Islamic Rep.	6	6	11	15	1995	3	17	10	..	..	94	..
Iraq	9	17	..	..	..	..	18	24	..	..	10	..
Ireland	..	..	..	..	..	..	..	..	..	..	..	..
Israel	..	..	..	..	..	..	..	8	..	..	..	..
Italy	..	..	..	..	1975-77	4	..	..	..	..	..	..
Jamaica	12	10	4	7	2000	5	40	11	..	..	100	..
Japan	..	..	..	..	1978-81	2	..	8	..	..	..	..
Jordan	4	5	5	8	1990	6	50	2	1997	4	95	..
Kazakhstan	..	5	4	10	1995	4	27	9	1995	4	53	..
Kenya	47	43	22	33	1993	4	35	..	1998	3	100	80
Korea, Dem. Rep.	19	57	32	15	..	..	71	..	..	..	5	100
Korea, Rep.	..	..	..	..	..	..	..	..	..	..	..	..
Kuwait	22	4	2	3	1996-97	6	40	7	..	..	..	..
Kyrgyz Republic	..	17	11	25	..	..	..	6	1997	8	27	..
Lao PDR	31	29	40	47	..	..	62	60	..	..	95	80
Latvia	..	4	..	..	..	..	..	4	..	..	..	..
Lebanon	..	..	3	12	..	..	49	19	..	..	92	..
Lesotho	31	29	16	44	..	..	7	..	..	..	73	..
Liberia	49	46	..	..	..	..	78	..	1986	7	..	93
Libya	..	..	5	15	..	..	..	..	..	..	90	..
Lithuania	..	..	..	..	..	..	..	4	..	..	..	..
Macedonia, FYR	..	7	6	7	..	..	..	8	..	..	..	..
Madagascar	33	40	40	48	1992	1	..	15	1997	17	73	94
Malawi	47	32	30	48	1992	7	55	..	1992	5	58	..
Malaysia	3	..	20	..	..	..	56	8	..	..	..	..
Mali	24	32	27	49	1995-96	1	58	..	1996	3	9	100
Mauritania	15	13	23	44	..	..	24	9	..	..	3	83
Mauritius	6	6	15	10	1995	4	29	..	..	..	0	..
Mexico	5	5	8	18	1988	4	41	9	1987	22	97	..
Moldova	..	11	..	..	..	..	20	5	..	..	..	..
Mongolia	34	45	13	25	1997	4	45	11	..	..	68	87
Morocco	5	5	..	..	1992	7	45	4	1992	30	..	0
Mozambique	67	58	26	36	..	..	58	..	1997	13	62	100
Myanmar	10	7	28	42	..	..	58	..	..	..	65	42
Namibia	27	31	..	..	1992	3	16	..	1992	4	59	83
Nepal	21	28	47	54	1996	1	65	23	1996	52	55	85
Netherlands	..	..	..	..	..	..	..	..	..	..	..	..
New Zealand	..	..	..	..	..	..	..	6	..	..	..	..
Nicaragua	29	31	12	25	1993	3	36	8	1997-98	8	86	63
Niger	42	46	40	40	1992	1	41	..	1998	0	64	100
Nigeria	16	8	27	46	1993	3	55	..	1990	2	98	23
Norway	..	..	..	..	..	..	..	5	..	..	..	..
Oman	..	..	23	23	1994-95	1	54	8	..	..	61	..
Pakistan	26	20	38	36	1990-91	3	37	25	1990-91	20	19	88
Panama	19	16	8	18	1980	4	..	8	..	..	95	..
Papua New Guinea	26	29	..	..	1982-83	2	16	16	..	..	..	..
Paraguay	18	13	..	..	1990	4	44	9	1990	4	83	..
Peru	40	18	8	26	1996	7	53	6	1996	34	93	5
Philippines	24	21	32	32	1993	1	48	11	1998	22	15	78
Poland	..	..	..	..	..	..	..	8	..	..	..	..
Portugal	..	..	..	..	..	..	..	7	..	..	..	..
Puerto Rico	..	..	..	..	1991	2	..	14	..	..	..	..
Romania	3	..	..	..	..	..	31	10	..	..	..	..
Russian Federation	..	6	3	13	..	..	30	..	..	..	30	..

	Prevalence of undernourishment		Prevalence of child malnutrition		Prevalence of overweight		Prevalence of anemia	Low-birthweight babies	Breast feeding		Consumption of iodized salt	Vitamin A supplementation
	% of population		Weight for age		Height for age		% of pregnant women	% of births	exclusive breastfeeding less then 4 months		% of households	% of children 6-59 months
			% of children under 5	% of children under 5	% of children under 5							
	1990-92	**1996-98**	**1993-2000ᵃ**	**1993-2000ᵃ**	**Year**	**%**	**1985-99ᵃ**	**1993-99ᵃ**	**Year**	**%**	**1992-98ᵃ**	**1998-2000**
Rwanda	37	39	27	42	1992	2	..	..	1992	76	95	93
Saudi Arabia	3	3	..	..	..	..	..	5	..	..	..	..
Senegal	21	23	13	23	1992-93	3	26	..	1997	3	9	87
Sierra Leone	45	43	..	..	..	..	31	..	..	..	75	80
Singapore	..	..	..	..	1970-77	1	..	7	..	..	..	..
Slovak Republic	..	4	..	..	..	..	..	..	..	..	..	..
Slovenia	..	3	..	..	..	..	..	5	..	..	..	..
Somalia	67	75	26	23	..	..	78	..	..	..	..	63
South Africa	..	..	9	23	1994-95	7	37	..	..	..	62	..
Spain	..	..	..	..	..	..	..	..	..	..	..	..
Sri Lanka	28	25	33	20	1987	0	39	18	1987	4	47	..
Sudan	30	18	34	34	..	..	36	15	1990	10	0	79
Swaziland	9	14	..	..	..	..	..	..	..	..	..	..
Sweden	..	..	..	..	..	..	..	..	..	..	..	..
Switzerland	..	..	..	..	..	..	..	5	..	..	..	..
Syrian Arab Republic	..	..	13	21	..	..	..	7	..	..	40	..
Tajikistan	..	32	..	..	..	..	50	..	..	..	20	..
Tanzania	31	41	29	44	1996	3	59	..	1996	7	74	21
Thailand	31	21	18	13	1987	1	57	7	1987	4	50	..
Togo	29	18	25	22	1988	3	48	..	1998	2	73	100
Trinidad and Tobago	12	13	..	..	1987	3	53	14	1987	7	..	..
Tunisia	..	..	4	8	1988	4	38	16	1988	13	98	..
Turkey	..	..	8	16	1993	3	74	..	1998	2	18	..
Turkmenistan	..	10	..	..	..	..	..	..	..	..	0	..
Uganda	23	30	26	38	1995	3	30	..	1995	35	69	79
Ukraine	..	5	..	..	..	..	..	8	..	..	4	..
United Arab Emirates	..	..	7	..	..	..	..	..	..	..	..	..
United Kingdom	..	..	..	..	1973-79	3	..	6	..	..	..	..
United States	..	..	1	2	1988-94	5	..	7	..	..	..	..
Uruguay	7	4	4	10	1992-93	6	20	8	..	..	..	..
Uzbekistan	..	11	19	31	1996	14	..	..	1996	0	17	..
Venezuela, RB	11	16	4	13	1997	3	29	12	..	..	90	..
Vietnam	28	22	37	39	1998	1	..	11	1997	1	89	55
West Bank and Gaza	..	..	15	..	..	..	..	6	..	..	..	..
Yemen, Rep.	37	35	46	52	1996	4	..	26	1997	7	39	100
Yugoslavia, Fed. Rep.	..	3	2	7	1996	5	..	..	..	..	63	..
Zambia	40	45	24	42	1996-97	3	34	10	1996	4	90	75
Zimbabwe	41	37	13	27	1994	4	..	11	1994	1	80	..

World	**21w**	**18w**	**..w**	**..w**			**55w**	**..w**			**67w**	**..w**
Low income	27	24	..	..			69	..			61	50
Middle income	15	11	13	..			44	..			69	..
Lower middle income	17	11	11	17			46	..			87	..
Upper middle income	9	8	..	..			40	..			67	..
Low & middle income	21	18	..	..			55	..			74	..
East Asia & Pacific	17	12	13	18			54	..			25	..
Europe & Central Asia	..	8	..	..			40	..			89	..
Latin America & Carib.	14	12	9	19			34	10			53	..
Middle East & N. Africa	7	8	15	..			28	..			66	..
South Asia	27	24	49	47			78	34			60	34
Sub-Saharan Africa	32	33	..	..			46	..			..	69
High income	..	..	..	..			..	..			..	..
Europe EMU	..	..	..	..			..	..			..	..

a. Data are for the most recent year available.

About the data

Data on undernourishment are produced by the Food and Agriculture Organization (FAO) based on the calories available from local food production, trade, and stocks; the number of calories needed by different age and gender groups; the proportion of the population represented by each age group; and a coefficient of distribution to take account of inequality in access to food (FAO, 2000). From a policy and program standpoint, however, this measure has its limits. First, food insecurity exists even where food availability is not a problem because of inadequate access of poor households to food. Second, food insecurity is an individual or household phenomenon, and the average food available to each person, even corrected for possible effects of low income, is not a good predictor of food insecurity among the population. And third, nutrition security is determined not only by food security, but also by the quality of care of mothers and children and the quality of the household's health environment (Smith and Haddad 2000).

Estimates of child malnutrition, based on both weight for age (underweight) and height for age (stunting), are from national survey data. The proportion of children underweight is the most common indicator of malnutrition. Being underweight, even mildly, increases the risk of death and inhibits cognitive development in children. Moreover, it perpetuates the problem from one generation to the next, as malnourished women are more likely to have low-birthweight babies. Height for age reflects linear growth achieved pre- and postnatally, and a deficit indicates long-term, cumulative effects of inadequacies of health, diet, or care. It is often argued that stunting is a proxy for multifaceted deprivation.

Estimates of children overweight are also from national survey data. Overweight in children has become a matter of growing concern in developing countries. Researchers show an association between obesity in childhood and high prevalences of high blood pressure, diabetes, respiratory disease and psychosocial and orthopedic disorders (de Onis and Blossner, 2000). The survey data were analyzed in a standardized way by the World Health Organization (WHO) to allow comparisons across countries.

Adequate quantities of micronutrients (vitamins and minerals) are essential for healthy growth and development. Studies indicate that more people are deficient in iron (anemic) than any other micronutrient, and most are women of reproductive age. Anemia during pregnancy can harm both the mother and the fetus, causing loss of the baby, premature birth, or low birthweight. Estimates of the prevalence of anemia among pregnant women are generally drawn from clinical data, which suffer from two weaknesses: the sample is based on those who seek care and is therefore not random, and private clinics or hospitals may not be part of the reporting network.

Low birthweight, which is associated with maternal malnutrition, raises the risk of infant mortality and stunts growth in infancy and childhood. Estimates of low-birthweight infants are drawn mostly from hospital records. But many births in developing countries take place at home, and these births are seldom recorded. A hospital birth may indicate higher income and therefore better nutrition, or it could indicate a higher-risk birth, possibly skewing the data on birthweights downward. The data should therefore be treated with caution.

It is estimated that breastfeeding can save some 1.5 million children a year. Breast milk alone contains all the nutrients, antibodies, hormones, and antioxidants an infant needs to thrive. It protects babies from diarrhea and acute respiratory infections, stimulates their immune systems and response to vaccination, and, according to some studies, confers cognitive benefits as well. The data are derived from national surveys.

Iodine deficiency is the single most important cause of preventable mental retardation, and it contributes significantly to the risk of stillbirth and miscarriage. Iodized salt is the best source of iodine, and a global campaign to iodize edible salt is significantly reducing the risks (UNICEF, *The State of the World's Children 1999*).

Vitamin A is essential for the functioning of the immune system. A child deficient in vitamin A faces a 25 percent greater risk of dying from a range of childhood ailments such as measles, malaria, or diarrhea. Improving the vitamin A status of pregnant women may reduce their risk of dying during pregnancy and childbirth, improves their resistance to infection, and helps reduce anemia. Giving vitamin A to new mothers who are breastfeeding helps to protect their children during the first months of life. Food fortification with vitamin A is also being introduced in many developing countries.

Definitions

• **Prevalence of undernourishment** refers to the percentage of the population that is undernourished. • **Prevalence of child malnutrition** is the percentage of children under five whose weight for age and height for age are less than minus two standard deviations from the median for the international reference population ages 0–59 months. For children up to two years of age, height is measured by recumbent length. For older children, height is measured by stature while standing. The reference population, adopted by the WHO in 1983, is based on children from the United States, who are assumed to be well nourished. • **Prevalence of overweight** is the percentage of children under five whose weight for height is greater than two standard deviations from the National Center for Health Statistics and WHO international reference median value, as recommended by a WHO Expert Committee. • **Prevalence of anemia**, or iron deficiency, refers to the percentage of pregnant women with hemoglobin levels less than 11 grams per deciliter. • **Low-birthweight babies** are newborns weighing less than 2,500 grams, with the measurement taken within the first hours of life, before significant postnatal weight loss has occurred. • **Exclusive breastfeeding** is the proportion of children less than 4-6 months old who are fed breast milk alone (no other liquids). • **Consumption of iodized salt** refers to the percentage of households that use edible salt fortified with iodine. • **Vitamin A supplementation** is the percentage of children ages 6-59 months who received at least one high dose vitamin A capsule in the previous six months.

Data sources

Data are drawn from a variety of sources, including FAO's *The State of Food Insecurity in the World 2000*; the United Nations Administrative Committee on Coordination, Subcommittee on Nutrition's *Update on the Nutrition Situation;* the WHO's *World Health Report 2000*; and UNICEF's *State of the World's Children 2001.*

| | | Prevalence of smoking | | Incidence of tuberculosis | Prevalence of HIV | | |
| | | | % of adults | | per 100,000 | % of | male % age 15-24 | female % age 15-24 |
	Year	Males	Females	people **1999**	adults **1999**	**1999**[a]	**1999**[a]
Afghanistan		..	..	325	<0.01	..	..
Albania	1996	44	6	29	<0.01	..	..
Algeria	1998	44	7	45	0.07	..	..
Angola		..	..	271	2.78	1.25	2.72
Argentina	2000	47	34	55	0.69	0.86	0.29
Armenia		..	..	58	0.01	..	..
Australia	1995	27	23	8	0.15	0.14	0.02
Austria	1997	30	19	16	0.23	0.19	0.10
Azerbaijan	1999	30	1	62	<0.01	..	..
Bangladesh	1998	40	10	241	0.02	0.01	0.01
Belarus	1999	55	5	80	0.28	0.40	0.19
Belgium	1999	31	26	15	0.15	0.11	0.11
Benin		..	..	266	2.45	0.89	2.24
Bolivia	1998	43	18	238	0.10	0.13	0.03
Bosnia and Herzegovina		..	..	87	0.04	..	..
Botswana		..	..	702	35.80	15.84	34.31
Brazil	1995	38	29	70	0.57	0.70	0.28
Bulgaria	1996	49	24	46	0.01	..	..
Burkina Faso		..	..	319	6.44	2.31	5.79
Burundi		..	..	382	11.32	5.69	11.60
Cambodia	1994	65	..	560	4.04	2.36	3.51
Cameroon		..	..	335	7.73	3.82	7.78
Canada	1999	27	23	7	0.30	0.29	0.07
Central African Republic		..	..	415	13.84	6.91	14.07
Chad		..	..	270	2.69	1.92	3.03
Chile	1997	26	18	26	0.19	0.29	0.08
China	1996	63	4	103	0.07	0.12	0.02
Hong Kong, China		..	..	91	0.06	0.10	0.05
Colombia	1997	24	21	51	0.31	0.44	0.10
Congo, Dem. Rep.		..	..	301	5.07	2.49	5.07
Congo, Rep.		..	..	318	6.43	3.17	6.46
Costa Rica	1995	29	7	17	0.54	0.65	0.28
Côte d'Ivoire		..	..	375	10.76	3.78	9.51
Croatia		..	..	61	0.02	0.02	0.01
Cuba	1995	48	26	15	0.03	0.06	0.02
Czech Republic	1998	28	12	19	0.04	0.06	0.03
Denmark	1998	32	30	12	0.17	0.16	0.08
Dominican Republic	1993	24	17	135	2.80	2.58	2.78
Ecuador	1991	46	17	172	0.29	0.37	0.08
Egypt, Arab Rep.	1997	43	5	39	0.02	..	..
El Salvador	1989	38	12	67	0.60	0.68	0.27
Eritrea		..	..	272	2.87	..	..
Estonia	1996	48	22	61	0.04	..	..
Ethiopia		..	..	373	10.63	7.50	11.86
Finland	1999	27	20	12	0.05	0.03	0.02
France	1997	39	27	16	0.44	0.33	0.23
Gabon		..	..	289	4.16	2.32	4.72
Gambia, The		..	..	260	1.95	0.86	2.17
Georgia	1999	60	15	72	<0.01	..	..
Germany	1997	43	30	13	0.10	0.09	0.04
Ghana		..	..	281	3.60	1.36	3.42
Greece	1994	46	28	22	0.16	0.12	0.05
Guatemala	1989	38	18	85	1.38	1.16	0.92
Guinea	1998	60	44	255	1.54	0.57	1.43
Guinea-Bissau		..	..	267	2.50	0.99	2.48
Haiti	1990	11	9	361	5.17	4.88	2.91
Honduras	1988	36	11	92	1.92	1.40	1.66

		Prevalence of smoking		Incidence of tuberculosis	Prevalence of HIV		
						Young people	
						male	female
		% of adults		per 100,000	% of	% age 15-24	% age 15-24
	Year	Males	Females	people **1999**	adults **1999**	**1999**[a]	**1999**[a]
Hungary	1999	44	27	40	0.05	0.08	0.02
India		..	..	185	0.70	0.36	0.61
Indonesia	1995	69	3	282	0.05	0.03	0.03
Iran, Islamic Rep.	1998	25	5	54	<0.01	..	..
Iraq	1990	40	5	156	<0.01	..	..
Ireland	1998	32	31	15	0.10	0.06	0.05
Israel	1999	33	25	8	0.08	0.06	0.06
Italy	1998	32	17	9	0.35	0.29	0.24
Jamaica		..	..	8	0.71	0.59	0.40
Japan	1998	53	13	29	0.02	0.03	0.01
Jordan	1996	44	5	11	0.02	..	..
Kazakhstan		..	..	130	0.04	0.07	..
Kenya	1995	67	32	417	13.95	6.39	13.02
Korea, Dem. Rep.		..	..	176	<0.01	..	..
Korea, Rep.		..	..	69	0.01	0.02	0.00
Kuwait	1996	34	2	31	0.12	..	..
Kyrgyz Republic	1998	60	16	130	<0.01	..	..
Lao PDR		..	..	171	0.05	0.04	0.05
Latvia	1998	53	18	105	0.11	0.18	0.06
Lebanon		..	..	24	0.09	..	..
Lesotho	1992	39	1	542	23.57	12.05	26.40
Liberia		..	..	271	2.80		
Libya		..	..	24	0.05	..	..
Lithuania	1997	41	9	99	0.02	..	..
Macedonia, FYR		..	..	50	<0.01	..	..
Madagascar		..	..	236	0.14	0.04	0.13
Malawi	1996	20	9	443	15.96	7.04	15.26
Malaysia	1996	49	4	111	0.42	0.57	0.09
Mali		..	..	261	2.03	1.31	2.07
Mauritania		..	..	241	0.52	0.37	0.59
Mauritius	1998	42	3	68	0.08	0.04	0.04
Mexico	1998	51	18	39	0.29	0.40	0.06
Moldova	1998	44	3	130	0.20	0.28	0.11
Mongolia	1999	55	19	205	<0.01	..	..
Morocco	1999	30	10	119	0.03	..	..
Mozambique		..	..	407	13.22	6.73	14.74
Myanmar	1993	74	46	169	1.99	1.04	1.72
Namibia	1994	65	35	490	19.54	9.14	19.80
Nepal	1998	20	15	209	0.29	0.14	0.20
Netherlands	1998	37	30	10	0.19	0.18	0.08
New Zealand	1998	26	24	6	0.06	0.05	0.02
Nicaragua		..	..	88	0.20	0.22	0.06
Niger		..	..	252	1.35	0.95	1.50
Nigeria		..	..	301	5.06	2.52	5.12
Norway	1998	34	32	5	0.07	0.06	0.03
Oman	1995	13	0	10	0.11	..	..
Pakistan	1994	36	9	177	0.10	0.06	0.04
Panama	1993	56	20	54	1.54	1.65	1.36
Papua New Guinea		..	..	250	0.22	0.08	0.25
Paraguay	1990	24	6	68	0.11	0.13	0.04
Peru	1998	42	16	228	0.35	0.39	0.17
Philippines	1999	75	18	314	0.07	0.03	0.06
Poland	1998	39	19	39	0.06	..	..
Portugal	1996	30	7	53	0.74	0.57	0.25
Puerto Rico		..	..	9	..	..	..
Romania	1994	43	15	130	0.02	0.02	0.02
Russian Federation	1996	63	14	123	0.18	0.25	0.12

	Year	Prevalence of smoking % of adults Males	Prevalence of smoking % of adults Females	Incidence of tuberculosis per 100,000 people 1999	Prevalence of HIV % of adults 1999	Prevalence of HIV Young people male % age 15-24 1999[a]	Prevalence of HIV Young people female % age 15-24 1999[a]
Rwanda	1994	7	4	381	11.21	5.22	10.63
Saudi Arabia	1994	40	8	45	0.01	..	..
Senegal		..	..	258	1.77	0.71	1.60
Sierra Leone		..	..	274	2.99	1.16	2.92
Singapore	1998	27	3	48	0.19	0.22	0.16
Slovak Republic	1996	55	30	28	<0.01	0.02	0.01
Slovenia	1999	30	20	27	0.02	0.03	0.01
Somalia		..	..	365	..		
South Africa	1998	42	11	495	19.94	11.34	24.82
Spain	1997	42	25	59	0.58	0.48	0.22
Sri Lanka	1998	41	..	59	0.07	0.04	0.05
Sudan	1999	24	2	195	0.99	..	..
Swaziland	1994	25	2	564	25.25		
Sweden	1998	17	22	4	0.08	0.06	0.04
Switzerland	1997	38	27	9	0.46	0.37	0.33
Syrian Arab Republic	2000	53	9	85	0.01	..	..
Tajikistan		..	..	105	<0.01	..	..
Tanzania	1995	50	12	340	8.10	3.96	8.06
Thailand	1999	39	2	141	2.15	1.18	2.32
Togo		..	..	313	5.98	2.20	5.53
Trinidad and Tobago		..	..	12	1.05	0.84	0.59
Tunisia	1996	61	4	37	0.04	..	..
Turkey	1997	51	49	38	0.01	..	..
Turkmenistan	1990	27	1	90	<0.01	..	..
Uganda	1995	52	17	343	8.30	3.84	7.82
Ukraine	2000	58	14	73	0.96	1.29	0.79
United Arab Emirates	1995	24	1	21	0.18	..	..
United Kingdom	1997	29	28	12	0.11	0.09	0.05
United States	1997	28	22	6	0.61	0.50	0.23
Uruguay	1995	32	14	29	0.33	0.41	0.21
Uzbekistan	1991	40	1	97	<0.01	..	..
Venezuela, RB	1992	42	39	42	0.49	0.65	0.15
Vietnam	1995	73	4	189	0.24	0.27	0.09
West Bank and Gaza		..	..	28	..	..	..
Yemen, Rep.	1997	60	29	108	0.01	..	..
Yugoslavia, FR (Serb./Mont.)		..	..	47	0.10	..	..
Zambia	1996	35	10	495	19.95	8.20	17.77
Zimbabwe	1993	34	1	562	25.06	11.31	24.50
World		**47 w**	**12 w**	**142 w**	**1.05 w**	**0.70 w**	**1.07 w**
Low income		43	9	229	2.01	1.13	2.00
Middle income		55	11	104	0.53	0.49	0.59
Lower middle income		58	7	110	0.18	0.21	0.16
Upper middle income		44	26	84	1.84	1.47	2.23
Low & middle income		50	10	163	1.19	0.79	1.25
East Asia & Pacific		64	6	142	0.22	0.19	0.16
Europe & Central Asia		51	20	85	0.18	0.39	..
Latin America & Carib.		37	25	75	0.58	0.67	0.30
Middle East & N. Africa		40	7	66	0.03	..	..
South Asia		40	8	191	0.56	0.29	0.48
Sub-Saharan Africa		..	..	339	8.38	4.54	9.20
High income		35	22	16	0.33	0.28	0.14
Europe EMU		38	25	20	0.31	0.25	0.15

a. Average of high and low estimates.

About the data

The limited availability of data on health status is a major constraint in assessing the health situation in developing countries. Surveillance data are lacking for a number of major public health concerns. Estimates of prevalence and incidence are available for some diseases but are often unreliable and incomplete. National health authorities differ widely in their capacity and willingness to collect or report information. To compensate for the paucity of data and ensure reasonable reliability and international comparability, the World Health Organization (WHO) prepares estimates in accordance with epidemiological models and statistical standards.

Smoking is the most common form of tobacco use in many countries, and the prevalence of smoking is therefore a good measure of the extent of the tobacco epidemic (Corrao and others 2000). While the prevalence of smoking has been declining in some high-income countries, it has been increasing in many low- and middle-income countries. Tobacco use causes heart and other vascular diseases, and cancers of the lung and other organs. Given the long delay between starting to smoke and the onset of disease, the health impact of smoking in developing countries will increase rapidly in the next few decades. Because the data present a one-time estimate, with no information on intensity of smoking or duration, they should be interpreted with caution. The data in the table are based on surveys and other studies compiled in *Tobacco Control Country Profiles* (Corrao and others 2000), issued for the 2000 World Conference on Tobacco or Health.

Tuberculosis is the main cause of death from a single infectious agent among adults in developing countries. In high-income countries tuberculosis has reemerged largely as a result of cases among immigrants. The estimates of tuberculosis incidence in the table are based on a new approach in which reported cases are adjusted using the ratio of case notifications to the estimated share of cases detected by panels of 80 epidemiologists convened by the WHO.

Adult HIV prevalence rates reflect the rate of HIV infection in each country's population. Low national prevalence rates, however, can be very misleading. They often disguise serious epidemics that are initially concentrated in certain localities or among specific population groups and that threaten to spill over into the wider population. In many parts of the developing world the majority of new infections occur in young adults, with young women especially vulnerable. About one-third of those currently living with HIV/AIDS are in the age group 15-24. The estimates of HIV prevalence are based on extrapolations from data collected through surveys and surveillance of small, nonrepresentative groups.

Table 2.19a

Bednets save lives

Percentage of children under five who sleep under a treated bednet

São Tomé and Principe	53
Malawi	38
Niger	35
Gambia, The	35
Vietnam	32
Tajikistan	32
Cameroon	12
Senegal	11
Guyana	11
Azerbaijan	11
Sierra Leone	10
Tanzania	10
Chad	2
Madagascar	1
Lao, PDR	0

Source: UNICEF Multiple Indicator Cluster Surveys, (www.childinfo.org).

Malaria is endemic in the poorest countries in the world, causing 300-500 million clinical cases and more than one million deaths per year. More than 90 percent of malaria deaths occur in Sub-Saharan Africa, and almost all deaths are in children under five. Over the last two decades, morbidity and mortality from malaria have been increasing as a result of growing drug and insecticide resistance, deteriorating health systems, changes in weather patterns, and population displacement.

Roll Back Malaria is a partnership, founded by the WHO, UNICEF, the United Nations Development Programme, and the World Bank in 1998 with the objective of halving the malaria burden world-wide by the year 2010. This goal can be achieved only if a number of strategies that have proven effective, sustainable, and cost-effective are implemented. Among the core strategies is the widespread use of insecticide-treated bednets to limit human-mosquito contact. In areas of Sub-Saharan Africa with high levels of malaria transmission, regular use of an insecticide-treated bednet can reduce mortality in children under five by as much as 30 percent.

Definitions

- **Prevalence of smoking** is the percentage of men and women who smoke cigarettes. The age range varies among countries, but in most is 18 and above or 15 and above.
- **Incidence of tuberculosis** is the estimated number of new tuberculosis cases (pulmonary, smear positive, extrapulmonary). • **Prevalence of HIV** refers to the percentage of people who are infected with HIV.

Data sources

The data are drawn from a variety of sources, including the WHO's *World Health Report 2000* and *Global Tuberculosis Control Report 1999;* the NATIONS database (http://apps.nccd.cdc.gov/nations/) and UNAIDS and the WHO's *AIDS Epidemic Update* (2000).

2.20 | Mortality

	Life expectancy at birth		Infant mortality rate		Under-five mortality rate		Child mortality rate		Adult mortality rate		Survival to age 65	
	years		per 1,000 live births		per 1,000		Male per 1,000 1988-2000[a]	Female per 1,000 1988-2000[a]	Male per 1,000	Female per 1,000	% of cohort	
											Male	Female
	1980	2000	1980	2000	1980	2000			2000	2000	2000	2000
Afghanistan	40	43	177	163	280	279	..	..	394	353	31	31
Albania	69	74	47	20	57	..	15	15	171	86	76	84
Algeria	59	71	98	33	139	39	..	..	149	127	73	79
Angola	41	47	154	128	261	208	..	..	442	391	34	38
Argentina	70	74	35	17	38	22	..	..	178	89	74	86
Armenia	73	74	26	15	..	17	..	..	171	76	74	86
Australia	74	79	11	5	13	7	..	..	102	54	83	91
Austria	73	78	14	5	17	6	..	..	126	60	81	90
Azerbaijan	69	72	30	13	..	21	..	..	207	103	68	83
Bangladesh	49	61	132	60	211	83	28	38	278	272	57	59
Belarus	71	68	16	11	..	14	..	..	361	128	53	80
Belgium	73	78	12	5	15	7	..	..	129	66	81	90
Benin	48	53	116	87	214	143	89	90	373	322	42	48
Bolivia	52	63	118	57	170	79	26	26	258	214	58	66
Bosnia and Herzegovina	70	73	31	13	..	18	..	..	165	90	73	84
Botswana	58	39	71	58	94	99	18	16	792	747	13	17
Brazil	63	68	71	32	..	39	8	9	252	137	61	78
Bulgaria	71	72	20	13	25	16	..	..	227	106	67	82
Burkina Faso	44	44	134	104	..	206	131	128	557	524	27	31
Burundi	47	42	122	102	193	176	101	114	620	582	25	28
Cambodia	39	54	183	88	330	120	34	30	381	322	41	47
Cameroon	50	50	103	76	173	155	69	75	490	433	34	39
Canada	75	79	10	5	13	7	..	..	105	60	83	91
Central African Republic	46	43	117	96	..	152	63	64	612	561	24	28
Chad	42	48	123	101	235	188	106	99	433	383	37	42
Chile	69	76	32	10	35	12	3	2	153	83	77	87
China	67	70	42	32	65	39	10	11	161	115	71	77
Hong Kong, China	74	80	11	3	..	..	..	..	102	52	84	91
Colombia	66	72	41	20	58	23	4	3	203	114	70	82
Congo, Dem. Rep.	49	46	112	85	210	163	..	..	514	481	30	33
Congo, Rep.	50	51	88	68	125	106	..	..	476	403	35	42
Costa Rica	73	77	19	10	29	13	..	..	120	72	81	89
Côte d'Ivoire	49	46	108	111	170	180	71	58	535	506	30	33
Croatia	70	73	21	8	23	9	..	..	154	117	69	86
Cuba	74	76	20	6	22	9	..	..	121	76	80	87
Czech Republic	70	75	16	4	19	7	..	..	168	78	74	86
Denmark	74	76	8	4	10	6	..	..	132	83	79	87
Dominican Republic	63	67	76	39	92	47	13	13	233	148	61	73
Ecuador	63	70	74	28	101	34	12	9	185	123	70	75
Egypt, Arab Rep.	56	67	121	42	175	52	15	16	189	153	67	73
El Salvador	57	70	84	29	120	35	17	20	243	141	67	80
Eritrea	44	52	..	60	..	103	89	78	466	417	37	41
Estonia	69	71	17	8	25	11	..	..	294	104	58	83
Ethiopia	42	42	155	98	213	179	83	86	575	530	25	29
Finland	73	77	8	4	9	5	..	..	137	60	79	90
France	74	79	10	4	14	6	..	..	138	59	81	91
Gabon	48	53	104	58	..	89	32	33	391	348	44	49
Gambia, The	40	53	159	73	216	..	83	79	436	388	40	46
Georgia	71	73	25	17	..	21	..	..	211	82	70	85
Germany	73	77	12	4	16	6	..	..	127	61	79	89
Ghana	53	57	94	58	157	112	53	51	334	294	46	49
Greece	74	78	18	5	23	8	..	..	114	51	81	89
Guatemala	57	65	84	39	..	49	15	18	288	185	58	70
Guinea	40	46	151	95	..	161	101	98	448	443	31	32
Guinea-Bissau	39	45	169	126	290	211	..	..	473	420	33	37
Haiti	51	53	124	73	200	111	52	54	459	355	38	46
Honduras	60	66	70	35	103	44	..	..	245	152	58	70

	Life expectancy at birth		Infant mortality rate		Under-five mortality rate		Child mortality rate		Adult mortality rate		Survival to age 65	
	years		per 1,000 live births		per 1,000		Male per 1,000 1988-2000[a]	Female per 1,000 1988-2000[a]	Male per 1,000	Female per 1,000	% of cohort Male	Female
	1980	2000	1980	2000	1980	2000	1988-2000[a]	1988-2000[a]	2000	2000	2000	2000
Hungary	70	71	23	9	26	11	..	..	272	116	65	83
India	54	63	115	69	177	88	25	37	222	209	60	63
Indonesia	55	66	90	41	125	51	19	20	232	180	62	70
Iran, Islamic Rep.	58	69	98	33	126	41	..	..	166	148	71	74
Iraq	62	61	80	93	95	121	..	..	225	185	62	66
Ireland	73	76	11	6	14	7	..	..	112	67	78	87
Israel	73	78	16	6	19	7	..	..	104	62	83	89
Italy	74	79	15	5	17	7	..	..	113	52	80	91
Jamaica	71	75	33	20	39	24	..	..	127	85	79	86
Japan	76	81	8	4	10	5	..	..	96	44	85	93
Jordan	..	72	41	25	..	30	7	5	153	116	73	79
Kazakhstan	67	65	33	21	..	28	11	6	378	166	49	73
Kenya	55	47	75	78	115	120	36	38	600	558	28	32
Korea, Dem. Rep.	67	61	32	54	43	90	..	..	315	233	53	60
Korea, Rep.	67	73	26	8	27	10	..	..	186	81	71	85
Kuwait	71	77	27	9	35	13	..	..	117	70	81	87
Kyrgyz Republic	65	67	43	23	..	35	10	11	297	136	57	77
Lao PDR	45	54	127	92	200	..	..	..	374	313	43	48
Latvia	69	70	20	10	26	17	..	..	296	121	59	83
Lebanon	65	70	48	26	..	30	..	..	171	127	70	77
Lesotho	53	44	119	91	168	143	..	..	557	523	25	28
Liberia	51	47	153	111	235	185	..	..	431	395	34	38
Libya	60	71	53	26	80	32	6	5	181	135	71	80
Lithuania	71	73	20	9	24	11	..	..	248	86	65	86
Macedonia, FYR	..	73	54	14	69	17	..	..	159	100	74	83
Madagascar	51	55	119	88	216	144	75	68	324	283	48	53
Malawi	44	39	169	103	265	193	101	102	593	574	19	22
Malaysia	67	73	30	8	42	11	4	4	186	110	71	81
Mali	42	42	184	120	..	218	136	138	496	441	25	28
Mauritania	47	52	120	101	188	164	..	..	360	307	44	49
Mauritius	66	72	32	16	40	20	..	..	199	102	69	83
Mexico	67	73	51	29	74	36	15	17	155	94	74	84
Moldova	66	68	35	18	..	22	..	..	306	172	58	74
Mongolia	58	67	82	56	..	71	27	22	196	168	68	73
Morocco	58	67	99	47	152	60	21	19	195	142	66	74
Mozambique	44	42	145	129	..	200	84	82	591	527	24	29
Myanmar	51	56	113	89	134	126	..	..	357	262	44	55
Namibia	53	47	90	62	114	112	30	34	588	542	21	24
Nepal	48	59	132	74	180	105	..	..	260	265	57	54
Netherlands	76	78	9	5	11	7	..	..	100	65	81	89
New Zealand	73	78	13	6	16	7	..	..	119	69	82	89
Nicaragua	59	69	84	33	143	41	12	11	200	136	67	76
Niger	42	46	135	114	317	248	184	202	476	389	30	36
Nigeria	46	47	99	84	196	153	66	69	468	418	32	35
Norway	76	79	8	4	11	5	..	..	107	61	82	90
Oman	60	74	41	17	95	22	..	..	136	101	77	82
Pakistan	55	63	127	83	157	110	22	37	194	164	63	68
Panama	70	75	32	20	36	24	..	..	133	81	77	85
Papua New Guinea	51	59	78	56	..	75	28	21	360	329	49	52
Paraguay	67	70	50	23	61	28	10	12	184	119	68	79
Peru	60	69	81	32	126	41	19	20	193	132	68	77
Philippines	61	69	65	31	81	39	21	19	190	142	68	76
Poland	70	73	26	9	..	11	..	..	221	86	70	86
Portugal	71	76	24	6	31	8	..	..	153	69	76	88
Puerto Rico	74	76	19	10	..	..	..	..	151	57	75	90
Romania	69	70	29	19	36	23	7	5	250	117	63	79
Russian Federation	67	65	22	16	..	19	3	2	416	148	47	75

	Life expectancy at birth		Infant mortality rate		Under-five mortality rate		Child mortality rate		Adult mortality rate		Survival to age 65	
	years		per 1,000 live births		per 1,000		Male per 1,000	Female per 1,000	Male per 1,000	Female per 1,000	% of cohort	
											Male	Female
	1980	2000	1980	2000	1980	2000	1988-2000[a]	1988-2000[a]	2000	2000	2000	2000
Rwanda	46	40	128	123	..	203	87	73	614	581	22	24
Saudi Arabia	61	73	65	18	85	23	..	..	155	120	75	81
Senegal	45	52	117	60	..	129	76	74	401	303	32	40
Sierra Leone	35	39	190	154	336	267	..	..	527	477	26	30
Singapore	71	78	12	3	13	6	..	..	122	68	82	88
Slovak Republic	70	73	21	8	23	10	..	..	212	85	69	85
Slovenia	70	75	15	5	18	7	..	..	165	73	75	88
Somalia	43	48	145	117	246	195	..	..	397	340	38	44
South Africa	57	48	67	63	91	79	..	..	549	487	26	32
Spain	76	78	12	4	16	6	..	..	125	52	80	91
Sri Lanka	68	73	34	15	48	18	10	9	161	92	76	83
Sudan	48	56	117	81	145	..	62	63	330	289	51	55
Swaziland	52	46	100	89	151	119	..	..	567	526	25	29
Sweden	76	80	7	3	8	4	..	..	91	56	84	91
Switzerland	76	80	9	4	11	6	..	..	105	58	84	92
Syrian Arab Republic	62	70	56	24	73	29	..	..	180	134	68	77
Tajikistan	66	69	58	21	..	30	..	..	236	142	63	75
Tanzania	50	44	108	93	176	149	61	58	562	521	26	30
Thailand	64	69	49	28	58	33	11	11	229	144	66	75
Togo	49	49	100	75	188	142	75	90	473	431	37	41
Trinidad and Tobago	68	73	35	16	40	19	4	3	181	133	72	80
Tunisia	62	72	69	26	100	30	19	19	166	121	74	81
Turkey	61	70	109	34	133	43	12	14	188	125	68	78
Turkmenistan	64	66	54	27	..	43	..	..	282	157	58	73
Uganda	48	42	116	83	180	161	82	72	604	590	24	27
Ukraine	69	68	17	13	..	16	..	..	335	132	55	79
United Arab Emirates	68	75	55	7	..	10	..	..	127	91	79	84
United Kingdom	74	77	12	6	14	7	..	..	113	66	80	88
United States	74	77	13	7	15	9	..	..	138	81	80	90
Uruguay	70	74	37	14	42	17	..	..	166	74	73	87
Uzbekistan	67	70	47	22	..	27	15	9	226	127	65	78
Venezuela, RB	68	73	36	19	42	24	..	..	176	100	74	84
Vietnam	60	69	57	27	105	34	..	..	206	141	66	76
West Bank and Gaza	..	72	..	22	..	26	10	7	160	103	73	82
Yemen, Rep.	49	56	141	76	198	95	33	36	311	288	49	51
Yugoslavia, Fed. Rep.	70	72	33	13	..	15	..	..	174	105	72	81
Zambia	50	38	90	115	149	186	96	93	655	634	16	20
Zimbabwe	55	40	80	69	108	116	35	31	630	594	18	19
World	**63 w**	**66 w**	**80 w**	**54 w**	**124 w**	**78 w**	**.. w**	**.. w**	**224 w**	**168 w**	**69 w**	**78 w**
Low income	53	59	112	76	176	115	..	..	294	261	64	69
Middle income	66	70	55	31	79	39	..	..	199	127	63	80
Lower middle income	66	69	54	33	81	41	10	11	192	125	61	78
Upper middle income	65	70	57	28	..	35	..	..	224	136	68	82
Low & middle income	60	64	87	58	136	84	..	..	242	187	64	73
East Asia & Pacific	64	69	56	35	82	45	10	11	183	132	69	76
Europe & Central Asia	68	69	41	20	..	25	..	..	298	127	59	80
Latin America & Carib.	65	70	61	29	..	37	..	..	208	121	67	81
Middle East & N. Africa	58	68	98	43	136	54	..	..	183	151	68	73
South Asia	54	62	119	73	179	96	25	37	227	212	62	65
Sub-Saharan Africa	48	47	116	91	187	162	..	..	504	459	40	46
High income	74	78	12	6	15	7	..	..	122	64	81	90
Europe EMU	74	78	13	5	16	6	..	..	125	58	80	90

a. Data are for the most recent year available.

About the data

Mortality rates for different age groups—infants, children, or adults—and overall indicators of mortality—life expectancy at birth or survival to a given age—are important indicators of health status in a country. Because data on the incidence and prevalence of diseases (morbidity data) frequently are unavailable, mortality rates are often used to identify vulnerable populations. And they are among the indicators most frequently used to compare levels of socioeconomic development across countries.

The main sources of mortality data are vital registration systems and direct or indirect estimates based on sample surveys or censuses. A "complete" vital registration system—one covering at least 90 percent of vital events in the population—is the best source of age-specific mortality data. But such systems are fairly uncommon in developing countries. Thus estimates must be obtained from sample surveys or derived by applying indirect estimation techniques to registration, census, or survey data. Survey data are subject to recall error, and surveys estimating infant deaths require large samples because households in which a birth or an infant death has occurred during a given year cannot ordinarily be preselected for sampling. Indirect estimates rely on estimated actuarial ("life") tables that may be inappropriate for the population concerned. Because life expectancy at birth is constructed using infant mortality data and model life tables, similar reliability issues arise for this indicator.

Life expectancy at birth and age-specific mortality rates for 2000 are generally estimates based on vital registration or the most recent census or survey available (see *Primary data documentation*). Extrapolations based on outdated surveys may not be reliable for monitoring changes in health status or for comparative analytical work.

Specific problems arise in calculating infant mortality rates in developing countries, where routine data collection in the health system often omits many infant deaths. In countries where civil registration of deaths is incomplete, many infants dying during the first weeks of life may not even have been registered as having been born. Rates based on civil registration in these countries, or on hospital data covering mainly urban areas, are therefore biased because they reflect the more privileged population. Infant and child mortality rates are higher for boys than for girls in countries in which parental gender preferences are absent. Child mortality captures the effect of gender discrimination better than does infant mortality, as malnutrition and medical interventions are more important in this age group. Where female child mortality is higher, as in some countries in South Asia, it is likely that girls have unequal access to resources.

Adult mortality rates have increased in many countries in Sub-Saharan Africa and Europe and

Central Asia. In Sub-Saharan Africa the increase stems from AIDS-related mortality and affects both men and women. In Europe and Central Asia the causes are more diverse and affect men more. They include a high prevalence of smoking, a high-fat diet, excessive alcohol use, and stressful conditions related to the economic transition.

The percentage of a cohort surviving to age 65 reflects both child and adult mortality rates. Like life expectancy, it is a synthetic measure based on current age-specific mortality rates and used in the construction of life tables. It shows that even in countries where mortality is high, a certain share of the current birth cohort will live well beyond the life expectancy at birth, while in low-mortality countries close to 90 percent will reach at least age 65.

Table 2.20a

Differences in life expectancy shrink at older ages

Additional years of life expectancy at age 60, selected countries

	2000 (estimate)	2020 (projection)
Brazil	17.1	18.6
China	17.9	19.5
India	15.6	16.8
Nigeria	15.1	15.8
Russian Federation	15.7	17
Turkey	17.8	19.4

Source: World Bank staff estimates

Changes in life expectancy at birth are strongly influenced by trends in infant and child mortality. The rapid improvements in life expectancy in the second half of the 20th century were the result of declining childhood mortality. Improvements in mortality at the oldest ages add fewer years of life to overall life expectancy, and differences among countries in life expectancy at older ages are therefore considerably smaller than at birth. Nevertheless, mortality at older ages has also declined, and is expected to continue to do so in the next decades. This trend, together with the increasing number of people who are entering the older ages, will result in a rapidly growing elderly population.

Definitions

• **Life expectancy at birth** is the number of years a newborn infant would live if prevailing patterns of mortality at the time of its birth were to stay the same throughout its life. • **Infant mortality rate** is the number of infants dying before reaching the age of one year, per 1,000 live births in a given year. • **Under-five mortality rate** is the probability that a newborn baby will die before reaching age five, if subject to current age-specific mortality rates. • **Child mortality rate** is the probability of dying between the ages of one and five, if subject to current age-specific mortality rates. • **Adult mortality rate** is the probability of dying between the ages of 15 and 60—that is, the probability of a 15-year-old dying before reaching age 60, if subject to current age-specific mortality rates between ages 15 and 60. • **Survival to age 65** refers to the percentage of a cohort of newborn infants that would survive to age 65, if subject to current age-specific mortality rates.

Data sources

The data are from the United Nations Statistics Division's *Population and Vital Statistics Report;* publications and other releases from country statistical offices; Demographic and Health Surveys from national sources and Macro International; and the United Nations Children's Fund's (UNICEF) *State of the World's Children 2000.*

ENVIRONMENT

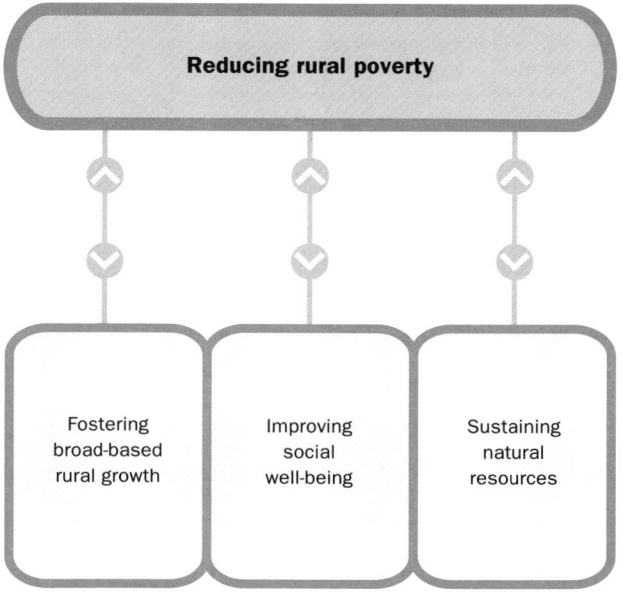

To reduce rural poverty . . .

Poverty is overwhelmingly rural, with some 70 percent of the poorest people in developing countries living in rural areas. Although the number and proportion of poor people in cities are expected to grow rapidly in the next decades, the majority of the poor will continue to live in the countryside. So reducing poverty and ending hunger require more attention to the rural economy and to rural development.

But there's a problem: most countries—in their development strategies and in their allocations of resources—favor cities. Rural people, especially women and ethnic minorities, have little political clout, so they cannot influence public policy to attract more public investment to rural areas. Reducing rural poverty requires dealing with the entire rural space—with all of rural society and with both farm and nonfarm aspects of the economy.

What will contribute most to faster growth in rural economies and to more poverty reduction? Three things: fostering broad-based rural growth, improving social well-being (in part by managing risk and reducing vulnerability), and sustaining natural resources. Each country's priorities will depend on its level of development—and its success on a policy and institutional environment conducive to rural development.

Agricultural yields growing, but low-income countries lagging

It took more than 1,000 years for the United Kingdom to increase wheat yields from 0.5 to 2 tons a hectare (in the 1950s) but only 40 years to triple yields to 6 tons a hectare. What made such a dramatic breakthrough possible? Massive public investment in agricultural research—research that has allowed most industrial and many developing countries to sustain food surpluses.

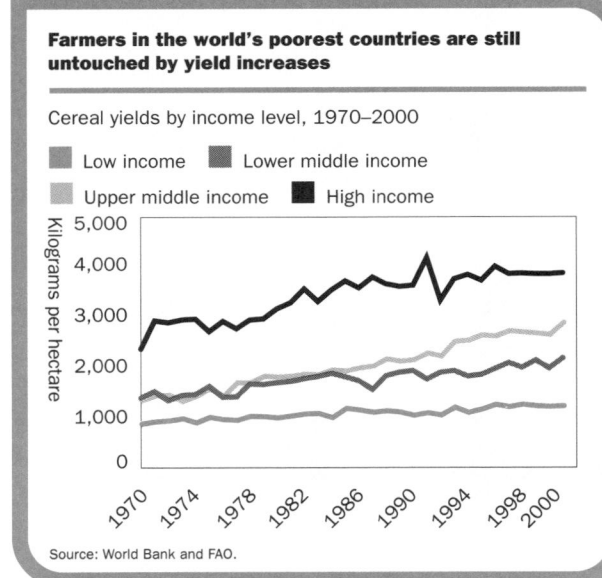

Farmers in the world's poorest countries are still untouched by yield increases

Cereal yields by income level, 1970–2000

■ Low income ■ Lower middle income
■ Upper middle income ■ High income

Source: World Bank and FAO.

About 900 million of the world's poor people live in rural areas, most of them farmers, many of them untouched by the yield advances in industrial countries. Yet for many poorer developing countries agriculture is the main source of economic growth, and agricultural growth is the cornerstone of poverty reduction.

Increasing the productivity of agriculture is thus essential for these countries. A 10 percent increase in crop yields can reduce the proportion of people living on less than $1 a day by between 6 and 12 percent (Thirtle and others 2000). Imagine what a tripling of yields might do.

Increase agricultural productivity.

Food production outpaces population, but malnourishment persists

The rise in food production has outpaced population growth in all regions except Africa. And this has been achieved with only small increases in cropland. For example, Asia doubled cereal production after 1970 with only 4 percent more cropland (Hazell 2001).

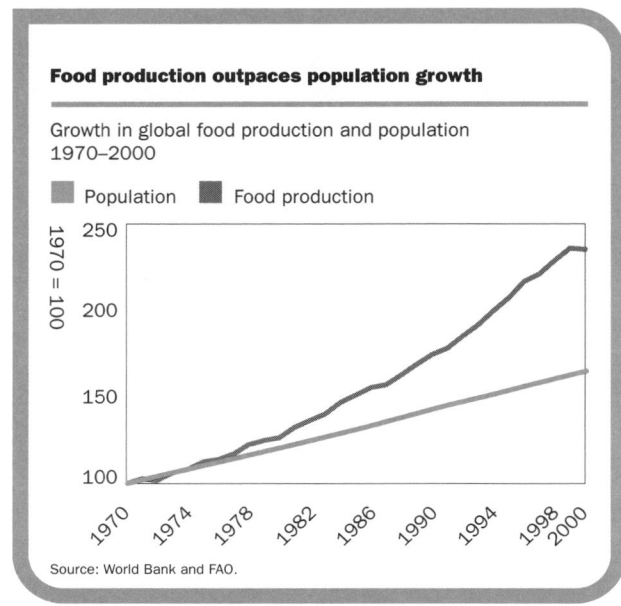

Food production outpaces population growth

Growth in global food production and population 1970–2000

■ Population ■ Food production

Source: World Bank and FAO.

Because of such productivity gains (and the food aid from industrial countries that subsidize agriculture), food prices have been falling. Even so, more than 150 million children under five are malnourished—because of low incomes and poor food distribution.

Agriculture is not enough

As economies develop, activities off the farm become much more important, providing jobs and reducing poverty. Workers follow a diverse array of opportunities, often sending much of their income back home. The new activities, generally linked to agriculture and infrastructure, contribute 30–50 percent of total income in rural areas.

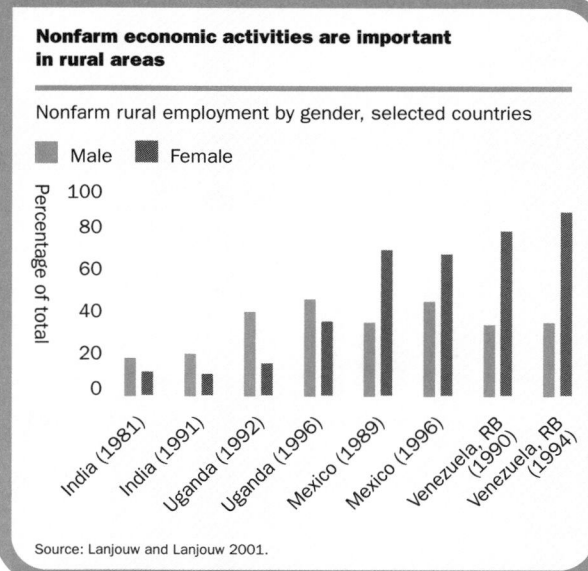

Nonfarm economic activities are important in rural areas

Nonfarm rural employment by gender, selected countries

■ Male ■ Female

Percentage of total

Source: Lanjouw and Lanjouw 2001.

The new activities off the farm provide work in the slack periods of the agricultural cycle. Studies of African farm households suggest that 15–65 percent of farmers also work off the farm and that 15–40 percent of family labor hours go to such income-generating activities. And these are underestimates. Much nonfarm activity in developing countries, especially that of women, is not taken into account. Activities such as clothing production, food processing, and education for the household are not included in figures on income generation.

Boost the nonfarm economy.

Rapid urban growth affects the rural space

In the next 30 years almost all population growth will be concentrated in urban areas. The pace will be fastest in developing countries, where the urban population is forecast to increase from 1.94 billion to 3.88 billion. The number of people in African cities will jump from 297 million to 766 million, or more than the total population today. In Asia the urban population will almost double from 1.35 billion to 2.61 billion.

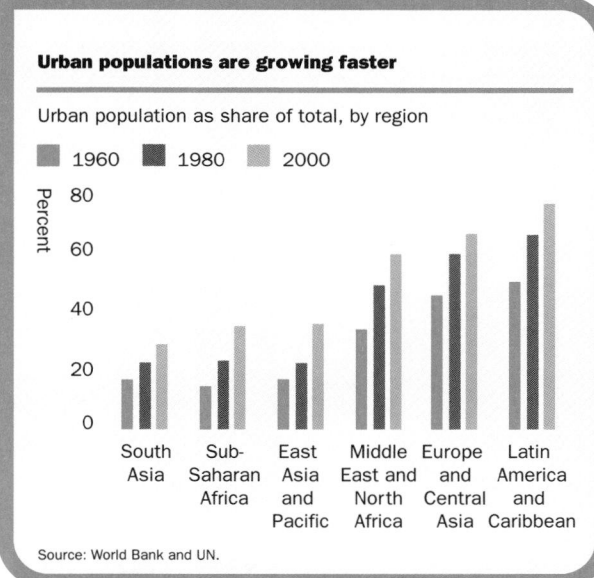

Urban populations are growing faster

Urban population as share of total, by region

■ 1960 ■ 1980 ■ 2000

Percent

South Asia | Sub-Saharan Africa | East Asia and Pacific | Middle East and North Africa | Europe and Central Asia | Latin America and Caribbean

Source: World Bank and UN.

Rapid urbanization has strengthened the links between rural and urban economies, blurring the distinction between them, in part because rural workers now take advantage of the new opportunities in small towns and cities.

But it has also increased air and water pollution and traffic congestion. Such environmental problems stretch beyond urban boundaries, affecting rural people as well. Industrial effluents in rivers can poison agriculture downstream. And in some parts of the world urban sprawl is encroaching on prime agricultural land.

Rural infrastructure is lagging

Rural residents are often more deprived of health and education than they are of income, since their access to those services is often limited and the services available are lower in quality than those in urban areas. They are also deprived of physical infrastructure, again of low quality if it is available. This "urban bias" imposes substantial costs on almost all rural economic activity.

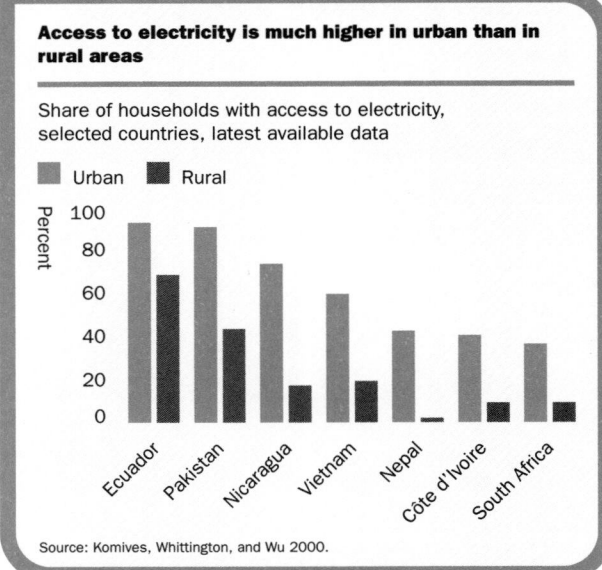

Access to electricity is much higher in urban than in rural areas

Share of households with access to electricity, selected countries, latest available data

Urban ■ Rural

Source: Komives, Whittington, and Wu 2000.

Dependence on the weather makes the rural poor more vulnerable to economic shocks. Nor are they spared a country's financial shocks, which often hurt them as much as urban dwellers, sometimes even more. Better social and physical infrastructure can do much to help reduce their vulnerability, to manage their risks, and to improve their well-being.

Improve physical and social infrastructure.

Limited infrastructure hurts rural well-being

The availability of transport, energy, water supply, sanitation, and communication services in rural areas remains limited. Access to electricity, in-house water supply, and telephones is on average two to five times higher in urban areas than in rural (Komives, Whittington, and Wu 2000). That is bad for markets, which thrive on good transport and information. It is also bad for households. The lack of safe water is a major contributor to diarrhea,

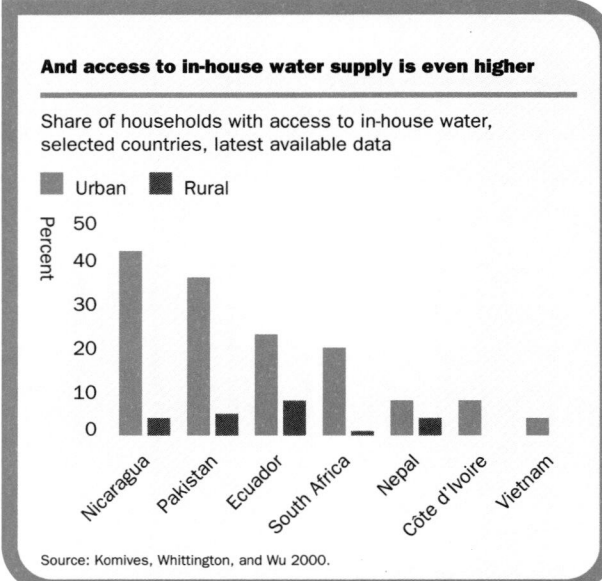

And access to in-house water supply is even higher

Share of households with access to in-house water, selected countries, latest available data

Urban ■ Rural

Source: Komives, Whittington, and Wu 2000.

a frequent cause of death among children in rural areas. Also contributing to illness for the rural poor is their lack of access to appropriate sanitation. Globally, the number of people with access to improved sanitation increased from 2.9 billion in 1990 to 3.7 billion in 2000. But 2.4 billion people still lack access. Most—2 billion of them—live in rural areas.

Schooling helps

Education—by enabling individuals and households to harness knowledge, increase and diversify incomes, manage risks, and increase social mobility—offers the prospect of breaking out of the cycle of poverty. In the rural space it also improves agricultural productivity and efficiency. And it is good for taking advantage of opportunities off the farm. But investments in education can bring even more benefits for development, as improved women's education is associated with lower fertility and slower population growth.

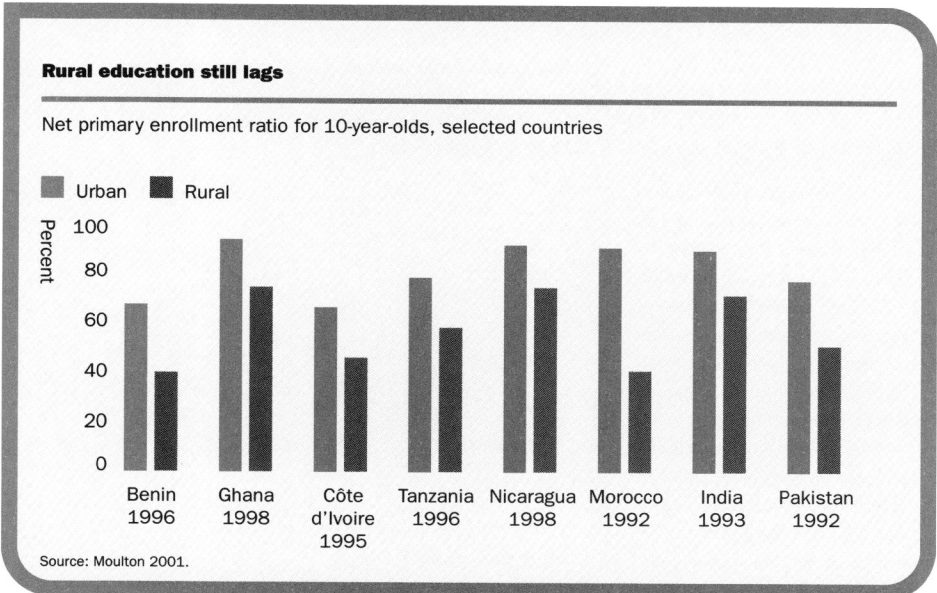

Rural education still lags

Net primary enrollment ratio for 10-year-olds, selected countries

Source: Moulton 2001.

Narrow the urban and rural access gap,

So do better health and nutrition

Poverty exposes people to illness and disease. And illness and disease push families into poverty—a vicious cycle. Rural communities routinely report that poor health afflicts their poorest members. Disease and illness also reduce labor productivity and economic growth, by keeping adults out of the labor force and reducing the intensity of their work effort. And child malnutrition even affects future work, since it increases the risks of illness and death in adulthood. Another vicious cycle.

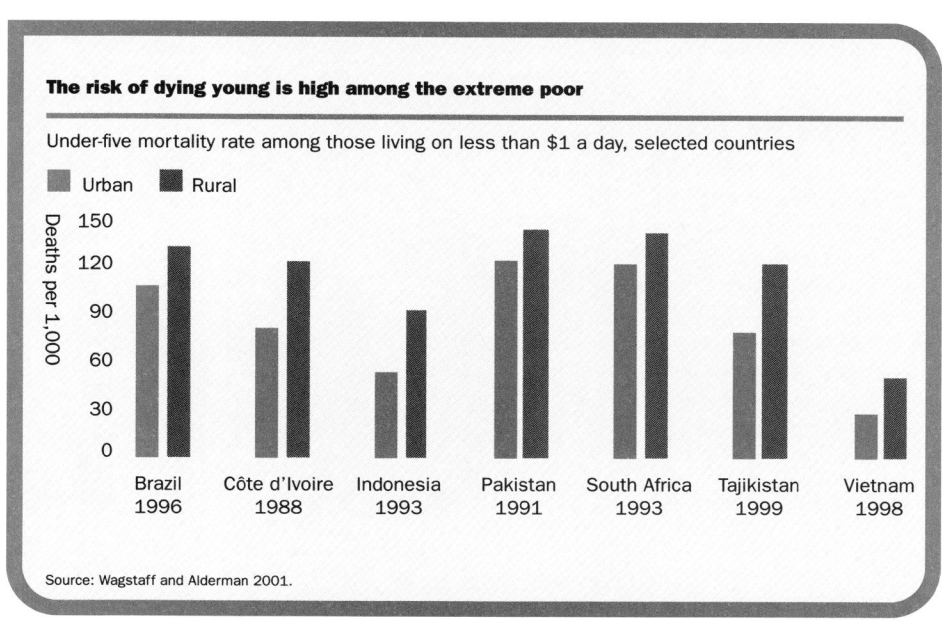

The risk of dying young is high among the extreme poor

Under-five mortality rate among those living on less than $1 a day, selected countries

Source: Wagstaff and Alderman 2001.

Degrading natural resources affects the poor most

Whether the world will continue to feed itself depends in large part on the future of the world's natural resource base. That depends, in turn, on whether poverty is reduced, for poverty and environmental degradation are often closely linked. Natural resources provide fundamental support to life and economic processes in the rural space. Soils are the food of agriculture. Forests protect water sources and provide income for more than 1.6 billion people. Biodiversity, the basis for protecting and

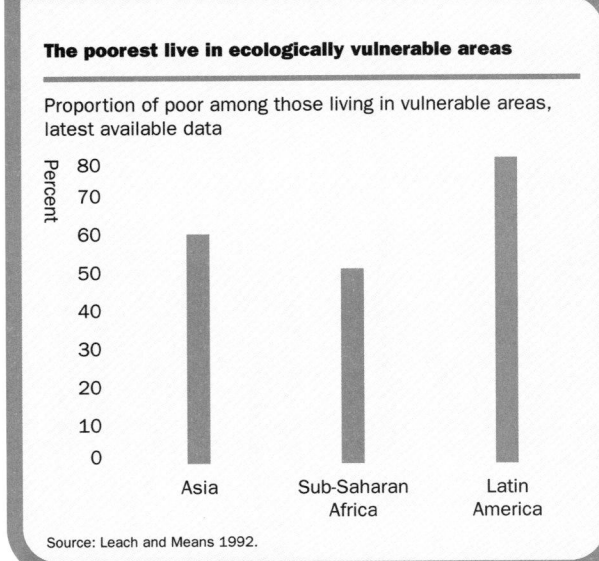

The poorest live in ecologically vulnerable areas

Proportion of poor among those living in vulnerable areas, latest available data

Source: Leach and Means 1992.

improving domestic plant and animal varieties, safeguards food security.

Degradation of those resources affects the rural poor more than others because they tend to rely on fragile natural resources for their livelihoods. At the margin of subsistence, living in ecologically vulnerable areas, the rural poor do have some assets, among them their social ties and their understanding of local conditions. What they lack is support from national institutions to nurture those assets—because the assets are often invisible to decision-makers.

while protecting natural resources for the long-term

Water in higher demand

Some countries have abundant, untapped stores of water to support growth well into the future. Others are already using most of their water, and major increases in supplies will be expensive. The situation is getting more serious: each year 80 million additional people will tap the earth's water.

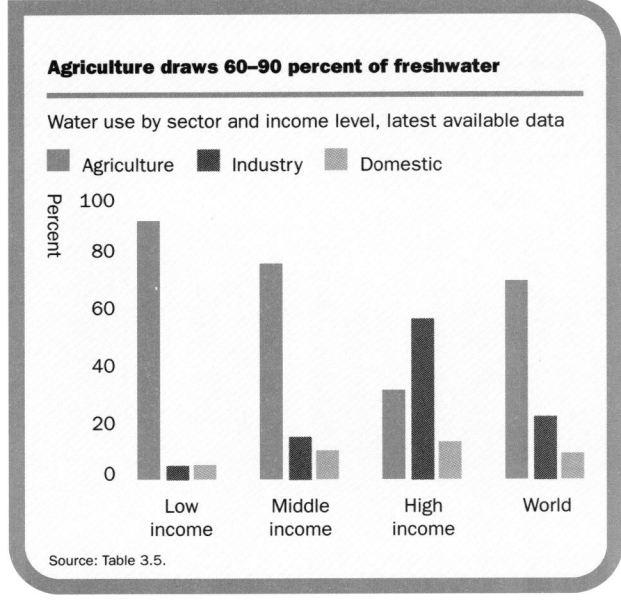

Agriculture draws 60–90 percent of freshwater

Water use by sector and income level, latest available data

■ Agriculture ■ Industry ■ Domestic

Source: Table 3.5.

In the past century global water withdrawals have increased almost tenfold. Agriculture now accounts for 60–90 percent of the withdrawals of freshwater in developing economies, but the growing amounts for industrial and domestic uses produce much more value per cubic meter (Shiklovanov 1993). Far from plentiful, rural water has to be shared by the growing cities, the burgeoning rural areas, and a thirsty environment. Needed are greater efficiency in the use of water and fair allocations to balance the limited supply with rising demand.

Demand for land, increasing

Land degradation reduces agricultural productivity and is thus a major factor affecting food security and poverty reduction in rural areas. Soil fertility declined about 13 percent between 1945 and 1990, a global average disguising far worse figures for Central America (37 percent) and Africa (25 percent). Although the global food supply is not seriously threatened in the short term, trends in Africa are of great concern.

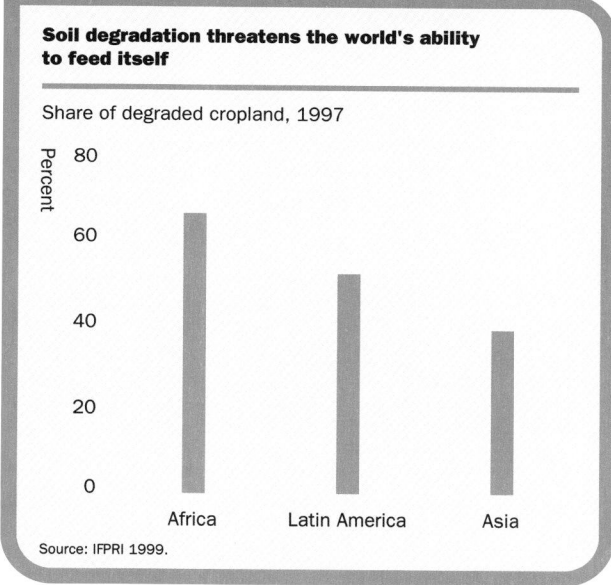

Soil degradation threatens the world's ability to feed itself

Share of degraded cropland, 1997

Source: IFPRI 1999.

Doubling food production by 2050 to meet the needs of a growing population will create more pressure, with heavy environmental costs: pesticide pollution, water table depletion, biodiversity loss, and soil degradation, all the result of inappropriate land-use systems. To manage such assaults will require institutions that allow diverse stakeholders to come together to diagnose problems, balance conflicting interests, and agree on courses of action.

sustainability of food supply and rural livelihoods.

Forests shrinking, species disappearing

Of the world's 1.2 billion extreme poor living on less than $1 a day, 90 percent depend on forests and their products. But the forests are shrinking, as is the diversity of the plants and animals they support.

At the beginning of the 20th century the earth's forested area was about 5 billion hectares. Since then it has shrunk to 3.9 billion hectares—an area roughly twice that of cropland. Caused by the growing demand for forest products and for agricultural land, the loss is concentrated in

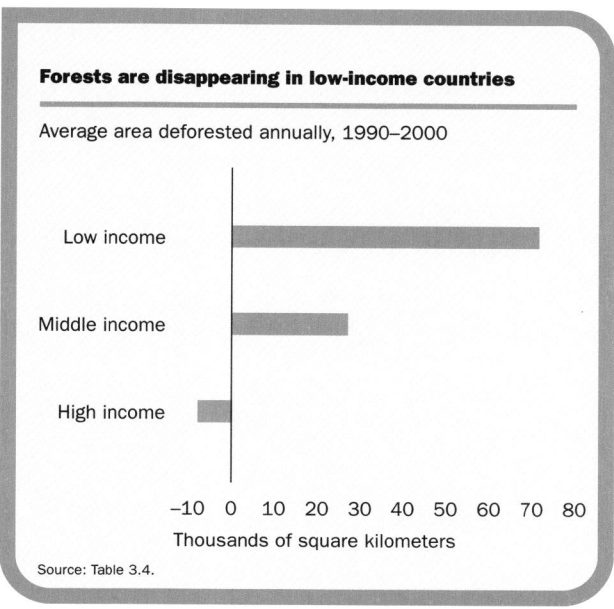

Forests are disappearing in low-income countries

Average area deforested annually, 1990–2000

Thousands of square kilometers

Source: Table 3.4.

developing countries. Low-income countries lost about 8 percent of their forest in the 1990s alone. The industrial world is actually gaining about 3.6 million hectares of forestland each year, mainly from abandoned cropland that is returning to forest on its own, as in Russia, and from the spread of commercial plantations.

But loss of biologically diverse areas may not be reversed, despite increases in protected areas. About 12 percent of the world's nearly 10,000 bird species are vulnerable or in immediate danger of extinction, as are 24 percent of the world's 4,800 mammal species and an estimated 30 percent of all fish species.

3.1 | Rural environment and land use

	Rural population			Rural population density	Land area	Land use					
	% of total		average annual % growth	people per sq. km of arable land	thousand sq. km	Arable land % of land area		Permanent cropland % of land area		Other % of land area	
	1980	2000	1980-2000	1999	1999	1980	1999	1980	1999	1980	1999
Afghanistan	84	78 ᵃ	2.2	257	652	12.1	12.1	0.2	0.2	87.7	87.6
Albania	66	61	0.8	359	27	21.4	21.1	4.3	4.5	74.4	74.5
Algeria	57	40	0.7	157	2,382	2.9	3.2	0.3	0.2	96.8	96.6
Angola	79	66	2.2	283	1,247	2.3	2.4	0.4	0.4	97.3	97.2
Argentina	17	11	-1.0	16	2,737	9.1	9.1	0.8	0.8	90.1	90.1
Armenia	34	30	0.4	233	28	..	17.6	..	2.3	..	80.1
Australia	14	15	1.7	6	7,682	5.7	6.2	0.0	0.0	94.2	93.7
Austria	35	35	0.4	205	83	18.6	16.9	1.2	1.0	80.2	82.1
Azerbaijan	47	43	0.8	200	87	..	19.9	..	3.0	..	77.1
Bangladesh	86	76	1.5	1,209	130	68.3	62.2	2.0	2.6	29.6	35.2
Belarus	44	30	-1.7	49	207	..	29.8	..	0.6	..	69.6
Belgium	5	3	-2.5	35	33 ᵇ	23.2 ᵇ	24.8 ᵇ	0.4 ᵇ	0.6 ᵇ	76.4 ᵇ	74.6 ᵇ
Benin	73	58	1.8	210	111	13.6	15.4	0.8	1.4	85.7	83.3
Bolivia	55	35	0.0	150	1,084	1.7	1.8	0.2	0.2	98.1	98.0
Bosnia and Herzegovina	65	57	-0.8	445	51	..	9.8	..	2.9	..	87.3
Botswana	85	50	0.2	233	567	0.7	0.6	0.0	0.0	99.3	99.4
Brazil	34	19	-1.3	61	8,457	4.6	6.3	1.2	1.4	94.2	92.3
Bulgaria	39	30	-1.6	59	111	34.6	38.9	3.2	1.9	62.2	59.2
Burkina Faso	92	82	1.8	265	274	10.0	12.4	0.1	0.2	89.8	87.4
Burundi	96	91	2.2	792	26	35.8	30.0	10.1	12.9	54.0	57.2
Cambodia	88	84	2.6	268	177	11.3	21.0	0.4	0.6	88.3	78.4
Cameroon	69	51	1.2	127	465	12.7	12.8	2.2	2.6	85.1	84.6
Canada	24	23	0.8	15	9,221	4.9	4.9	0.0	0.0	95.0	95.0
Central African Republic	65	59	1.9	112	623	3.0	3.1	0.1	0.1	96.9	96.8
Chad	81	76	2.4	163	1,259	2.5	2.8	0.0	0.0	97.5	97.2
Chile	19	15	0.5	118	749	5.1	2.6	0.3	0.4	94.6	96.9
China ᶜ	80	68	0.4	691	9,327	10.4	13.3	0.4	1.2	89.3	85.5
Hong Kong, China	9	0	..	0	1	7.0	5.1	1.0	1.0	92.0	93.9
Colombia	36	25	0.2	508	1,039	3.6	2.0	1.4	2.2	95.0	95.8
Congo, Dem. Rep.	71	70	3.1	518	2,267	2.9	3.0	0.4	0.5	96.6	96.5
Congo, Rep.	59	38	0.7	642	342	0.4	0.5	0.1	0.1	99.5	99.4
Costa Rica	57	48	1.7	806	51	5.5	4.4	4.4	5.5	90.1	90.1
Côte d'Ivoire	65	54	2.4	286	318	6.1	9.3	7.2	13.8	86.6	76.9
Croatia	50	42	-1.1	128	56	..	26.1	..	2.3	..	71.6
Cuba	32	25	-0.6	76	110	23.9	33.1	6.4	7.6	69.7	59.3
Czech Republic	25	25	0.0	84	77	..	40.1	..	3.1	..	56.9
Denmark	16	15	-0.2	35	42	62.3	54.1	0.3	0.2	37.4	45.7
Dominican Republic	50	35	0.2	274	48	22.1	22.1	7.2	10.3	70.6	67.5
Ecuador	53	38	0.6	302	277	5.6	5.7	3.3	5.2	91.1	89.2
Egypt, Arab Rep.	56	55	2.1	1,217	995	2.3	2.8	0.2	0.5	97.5	96.7
El Salvador	58	53	1.1	590	21	26.9	27.0	11.7	12.1	61.4	60.9
Eritrea	87	81	2.4	654	101	..	4.9	..	0.0	..	95.0
Estonia	30	31	-0.2	39	42	..	26.5	..	0.4	..	73.1
Ethiopia	90	82	2.3	520	1,000	..	10.0	..	0.7	..	89.3
Finland	40	33	-0.6	79	305	7.8	7.1	0.0	0.0	92.2	92.9
France	27	24	0.0	78	550	31.8	33.4	2.5	2.1	65.7	64.5
Gabon	50	19	-2.1	73	258	1.1	1.3	0.6	0.7	98.2	98.1
Gambia, The	80	68	2.7	442	10	15.5	19.5	0.4	0.5	84.1	80.0
Georgia	48	39	-1.1	251	70	..	11.4	..	3.8	..	84.7
Germany	17	13	-1.4	88	357	33.7	33.1	1.4	0.6	64.9	66.2
Ghana	69	62	2.4	325	228	8.4	15.8	7.5	7.5	84.2	76.7
Greece	42	40	0.2	153	129	22.5	21.4	7.9	8.6	69.6	70.0
Guatemala	63	60	2.3	488	108	11.7	12.5	4.4	5.0	83.9	82.4
Guinea	81	67	1.6	556	246	2.9	3.6	1.8	2.4	95.4	94.0
Guinea-Bissau	83	76	1.8	300	28	9.1	10.7	1.1	1.8	89.9	87.6
Haiti	76	64	1.1	905	28	19.8	20.3	12.5	12.7	67.7	67.0
Honduras	65	53	1.9	229	112	13.9	13.1	1.8	3.2	84.3	83.7

	Rural population			Rural population density	Land area	Land use					
	% of total		average annual % growth	people per sq. km of arable land	thousand sq. km	Arable land % of land area		Permanent cropland % of land area		Other % of land area	
	1980	2000	1980-2000	1999	1999	1980	1999	1980	1999	1980	1999
Hungary	43	36	-1.2	76	92	54.4	52.1	3.3	2.4	42.2	45.4
India	77	72	1.6	444	2,973	54.8	54.4	1.8	2.7	43.4	42.9
Indonesia	78	59	0.4	694	1,812	9.9	9.9	4.4	7.2	85.6	82.9
Iran, Islamic Rep.	50	38	1.1	141	1,622	8.0	10.7	0.5	1.2	91.5	88.1
Iraq	35	23	0.9	104	437	12.0	11.9	0.4	0.8	87.6	87.3
Ireland	45	41	0.1	144	69	16.1	15.6	0.0	0.0	83.9	84.3
Israel	11	9	1.1	155	21	15.8	17.0	4.3	4.3	80.0	78.7
Italy	33	33	0.0	223	294	32.2	29.1	10.0	9.8	57.7	61.2
Jamaica	53	44	0.1	661	11	12.5	16.1	9.7	9.2	77.8	74.7
Japan	24	21	-0.2	600	365	13.3	12.4	1.6	1.0	85.1	86.7
Jordan	40	26	1.8	512	89	3.4	2.7	0.4	1.6	96.2	95.6
Kazakhstan	46	44	-0.3	22	2,700	..	11.1	..	0.1	..	88.8
Kenya	84	67	1.8	499	569	6.7	7.0	0.8	0.9	92.5	92.1
Korea, Dem. Rep.	43	40	0.9	522	120	13.4	14.1	2.4	2.5	84.2	83.4
Korea, Rep.	43	18	-3.3	520	99	20.9	17.2	1.4	2.0	77.8	80.8
Kuwait	10	2	-5.2	808	18	0.1	0.3	0.0	0.1	99.9	99.6
Kyrgyz Republic	62	67	1.9	236	192	..	7.1	..	0.3	..	92.5
Lao PDR	87	77	1.9	454	231	3.4	3.8	0.1	0.3	96.5	95.9
Latvia	32	31	-0.5	40	62	..	29.8	..	0.5	..	69.7
Lebanon	26	10	-2.9	255	10	20.5	17.6	8.9	12.5	70.6	69.9
Lesotho	87	72	1.1	450	30	9.6	10.7	..	..	..	..
Liberia	65	55	1.7	892	96	1.3	2.0	2.5	2.1	96.1	96.0
Libya	31	12	-1.8	37	1,760	1.0	1.0	0.2	0.2	98.8	98.8
Lithuania	39	32	-0.6	40	65	..	45.3	..	0.9	..	53.8
Macedonia, FYR	47	38	-0.6	132	25	..	23.1	..	1.9	..	75.0
Madagascar	82	71	2.1	417	582	4.3	4.4	0.9	0.9	94.8	94.7
Malawi	91	85	2.2	458	94	16.1	19.9	0.9	1.3	83.0	78.7
Malaysia	58	43	1.1	541	329	3.0	5.5	11.6	17.6	85.4	76.9
Mali	82	70	1.7	162	1,220	1.6	3.8	0.0	0.0	98.3	96.2
Mauritania	73	42	0.0	230	1,025	0.2	0.5	0.0	0.0	99.8	99.5
Mauritius	58	59	1.1	691	2	49.3	49.3	3.4	3.0	47.3	47.8
Mexico	34	26	0.5	100	1,909	12.1	13.0	0.8	1.3	87.1	85.7
Moldova	60	54	-0.2	128	33	..	55.0	..	11.3	..	33.7
Mongolia	48	41	1.1	75	1,567	0.8	0.8	0.0	0.0	99.2	99.2
Morocco	59	44	0.5	148	446	16.9	19.0	1.1	2.1	82.0	78.8
Mozambique	87	60	0.0	339	784	3.7	4.0	0.3	0.3	96.0	95.7
Myanmar	76	72	1.5	359	658	14.6	14.5	0.7	0.9	84.8	84.6
Namibia	77	69	2.3	146	823	0.8	1.0	0.0	0.0	99.2	99.0
Nepal	94	88	2.0	686	143	16.0	20.3	0.2	0.5	83.8	79.2
Netherlands	12	11	0.1	185	34	23.3	27.0	0.9	1.0	75.7	72.0
New Zealand	17	13	-0.1	33	268	9.3	5.8	3.7	6.4	86.9	87.8
Nicaragua	47	35	1.4	72	121	9.5	20.2	1.5	2.4	89.1	77.4
Niger	87	79	2.8	168	1,267	2.8	3.9	0.0	0.0	97.2	96.1
Nigeria	73	56	1.6	250	911	30.6	31.0	2.8	2.8	66.6	66.3
Norway	30	25	-0.5	126	307	2.7	2.9	..	..	..	..
Oman	69	16	-3.4	2,595	212	0.1	0.1	0.1	0.3	99.8	99.6
Pakistan	72	63	1.9	403	771	25.9	27.5	0.4	0.8	73.7	71.6
Panama	50	42	1.1	240	74	5.8	6.7	1.6	2.1	92.5	91.2
Papua New Guinea	87	83	2.3	..	453	0.0	0.1	1.1	1.3	98.9	98.5
Paraguay	58	44	1.4	109	397	4.1	5.5	0.3	0.2	95.6	94.2
Peru	35	27	0.6	188	1,280	2.5	2.9	0.3	0.4	97.2	96.7
Philippines	63	41	0.2	566	298	17.5	18.6	14.8	15.1	67.7	66.3
Poland	42	34	-0.6	96	304	48.0	46.2	1.1	1.1	50.9	52.7
Portugal	71	36	-3.3	189	92	26.5	21.5	7.8	8.1	65.7	70.4
Puerto Rico	33	25	-0.4	2,798	9	8.3	3.9	7.3	5.2	84.3	90.9
Romania	51	44	-0.7	106	230	42.7	40.5	2.9	2.2	54.4	57.3
Russian Federation	30	27	-0.3	31	16,889	..	7.4	..	0.1	..	92.5

	Rural population			Rural population density	Land area	Land use					
	% of total		average annual % growth	people per sq. km of arable land	thousand sq. km	Arable land % of land area		Permanent cropland % of land area		Other % of land area	
	1980	2000	1980-2000	1999	1999	1980	1999	1980	1999	1980	1999
Rwanda	95	94	2.4	901	25	30.8	35.1	10.3	10.1	58.9	54.8
Saudi Arabia	34	14	-0.4	84	2,150	0.9	1.7	0.0	0.1	99.1	98.2
Senegal	64	53	1.7	222	193	12.2	11.6	0.0	0.2	87.8	88.2
Sierra Leone	76	63	1.3	653	72	6.3	6.8	0.7	0.8	93.0	92.5
Singapore	0	0	..	0	1	3.3	1.6	9.8	0.0	86.9	98.4
Slovak Republic	48	43	-0.2	158	48	..	30.4	..	2.8	..	66.8
Slovenia	52	50	0.0	577	20	..	8.5	..	1.5	..	90.0
Somalia	78	73	1.2	592	627	1.6	1.7	0.0	0.0	98.4	98.3
South Africa	52	45	1.5	129	1,221	10.2	12.1	0.7	0.8	89.1	87.1
Spain	27	22	-0.7	65	499	31.1	27.4	9.9	9.7	59.0	62.9
Sri Lanka	78	76	1.2	1,660	65	13.2	13.6	15.9	15.8	70.9	70.6
Sudan	80	64	1.3	119	2,376	5.2	7.0	0.0	0.1	94.8	92.9
Swaziland	82	74	2.5	448	17	10.8	9.8	0.2	0.7	89.0	89.5
Sweden	17	17	0.3	54	412	7.2	6.7	..	..	..	..
Switzerland	43	32	-0.8	556	40	9.9	10.5	0.5	0.6	89.6	88.9
Syrian Arab Republic	53	46	2.3	154	184	28.5	25.6	2.5	4.4	69.1	70.1
Tajikistan	66	73	2.7	611	141	..	5.2	..	0.9	..	93.9
Tanzania	85	72	2.1	640	884	3.5	4.2	1.0	1.0	95.5	94.7
Thailand	83	78	1.0	323	511	32.3	28.8	3.5	6.5	64.2	64.8
Togo	77	67	2.2	134	54	35.9	40.4	1.6	1.8	62.6	57.7
Trinidad and Tobago	37	26	-0.8	455	5	13.6	14.6	9.0	9.2	77.4	76.2
Tunisia	49	35	0.3	117	155	20.5	18.3	9.7	14.5	69.7	67.2
Turkey	56	25	-2.2	69	770	32.9	31.4	4.1	3.3	63.0	65.3
Turkmenistan	53	55	3.2	173	470	..	3.5	..	0.1	..	96.4
Uganda	91	86	2.4	368	197	20.7	25.7	8.1	8.9	71.2	65.4
Ukraine	38	32	-1.0	49	579	..	56.4	..	1.6	..	42.0
United Arab Emirates	29	14	1.6	498	84	0.2	1.0	0.1	0.6	99.7	98.4
United Kingdom	11	11	0.0	106	241	28.7	24.6	0.3	0.2	71.0	75.2
United States	26	23	0.4	36	9,159	20.6	19.3	0.2	0.2	79.2	80.5
Uruguay	15	9	-2.0	23	175	8.0	7.2	0.3	0.3	91.7	92.5
Uzbekistan	59	63	2.5	342	414	..	10.8	..	0.9	..	88.3
Venezuela, RB	21	13	-0.1	116	882	3.2	3.0	0.9	1.0	95.9	96.0
Vietnam	81	76	1.6	1,031	325	18.2	17.7	1.9	4.9	79.8	77.4
West Bank and Gaza	..	..	..	..	..	..	..	..	..	..	..
Yemen, Rep.	81	75	3.2	833	528	2.6	2.9	0.2	0.2	97.2	96.8
Yugoslavia, Fed. Rep.	54	48	-0.2	..	..	28.0	..	2.9	..	69.1	..
Zambia	60	56	2.4	105	743	6.9	7.1	0.0	0.0	93.1	92.9
Zimbabwe	78	65	1.9	252	387	6.5	8.3	0.3	0.3	93.3	91.3
World	60 w	53 w	0.9 w	524 w	130,100 s	10.2 w	10.5 w	0.9 w	1.0 w	88.9 w	88.5 w
Low income	76	68	1.6	510	32,536	11.8	13.2	1.0	1.4	87.1	85.4
Middle income	62	50	0.3	589	66,644	7.9	8.8	1.0	1.0	91.0	90.2
Lower middle income	69	58	0.5	642	43,596	8.8	9.2	1.0	0.9	90.2	89.9
Upper middle income	38	24	-0.6	184	23,048	7.0	8.0	1.1	1.3	91.9	90.7
Low & middle income	68	59	1.0	545	99,180	9.5	10.2	1.0	1.2	89.5	88.6
East Asia & Pacific	78	65	0.5	694	15,969	10.1	11.8	1.5	2.6	88.4	85.5
Europe & Central Asia	41	35	-0.4	125	23,771	37.1	11.7	3.1	0.4	59.8	87.9
Latin America & Carib.	35	25	0.0	252	20,062	5.8	6.6	1.1	1.3	93.1	92.1
Middle East & N. Africa	52	41	1.4	543	10,995	4.5	5.1	0.4	0.8	95.1	94.1
South Asia	78	72	1.6	542	4,781	42.5	42.4	1.5	2.1	56.1	55.4
Sub-Saharan Africa	77	66	1.9	377	23,603	5.5	6.5	0.7	0.9	93.8	92.6
High income	25	21	-0.1	180	30,920	12.0	11.6	0.5	0.5	87.5	87.9
Europe EMU	27	23	-0.5	140	2,537	26.2	25.1	4.6	4.4	69.2	70.5

a. Estimate does not account for recent refugee flows. b. Includes Luxembourg. c. Includes Taiwan, China.

About the data

Indicators of rural development are sparse, as few indicators are disaggregated between rural and urban areas (for some that are, see tables 2.6, 3.5, and 3.10). This table shows indicators of rural population and land use. Rural population is approximated as the midyear nonurban population.

The data in the table show that land use patterns are changing. They also indicate major differences in resource endowments and uses among countries. True comparability of the data is limited, however, by variations in definitions, statistical methods, and the quality of data collection. Countries use different definitions of rural population and land use, for example. The Food and Agriculture Organization (FAO), the primary compiler of these data, occasionally adjusts its definitions of land use categories and sometimes revises earlier data. (In 1985, for example, the FAO began to exclude from cropland, land used for shifting cultivation but currently lying fallow.) And following FAO practice,

this year's edition of the *World Development Indicators,* like the previous three, breaks down the category *cropland,* used in earlier editions, into *arable land* and *permanent cropland.* Because the data reflect changes in data reporting procedures as well as actual changes in land use, apparent trends should be interpreted with caution.

Satellite images show land use that differs from that given by ground-based measures in both area under cultivation and type of land use. Furthermore, land use data in countries such as India are based on reporting systems that were geared to the collection of tax revenue. Because taxes on land are no longer a major source of government revenue, the quality and coverage of land use data (except for cropland) have declined. Data on forest area, aggregated in the category *other,* may be particularly unreliable because of differences in definitions and irregular surveys (see *About the data* for table 3.4).

Definitions

• **Rural population** is calculated as the difference between the total population and the urban population (see *Definitions* for tables 2.1 and 3.10). • **Rural population density** is the rural population divided by the arable land area. • **Land area** is a country's total area, excluding area under inland water bodies, national claims to continental shelf, and exclusive economic zones. In most cases the definition of inland water bodies includes major rivers and lakes. (See table 1.1 for the total surface area of countries.) • **Land use** is broken into three categories. • **Arable land** includes land defined by the FAO as land under temporary crops (double-cropped areas are counted once), temporary meadows for mowing or for pasture, land under market or kitchen gardens, and land temporarily fallow. Land abandoned as a result of shifting cultivation is excluded. • **Permanent cropland** is land cultivated with crops that occupy the land for long periods and need not be replanted after each harvest, such as cocoa, coffee, and rubber. This category includes land under flowering shrubs, fruit trees, nut trees, and vines, but excludes land under trees grown for wood or timber. • **Other land** includes forest and woodland as well as logged-over areas to be forested in the near future. Also included are uncultivated land, grassland not used for pasture, wetlands, wastelands, and built-up areas—residential, recreational, and industrial lands and areas covered by roads and other fabricated infrastructure.

Table 3.1a

The 10 economies with the highest rural population density in 1999 — and the 10 with the lowest			
People per sq. km of arable land			
	Rural population density		Rural population density
Puerto Rico	2,798	United States	36
Oman	2,595	Belgium	35
Sri Lanka	1,660	Denmark	35
Egypt, Arab Rep.	1,217	New Zealand	33
Bangladesh	1,209	Russian Federation	31
Vietnam	1,031	Uruguay	23
Haiti	905	Kazakhstan	22
Rwanda	901	Argentina	16
Liberia	892	Canada	15
Yemen, Rep.	833	Australia	6

Source: Table 3.1.

Data sources

The data on urban population shares used to estimate rural population come from the United Nations Population Division's *World Urbanization Prospects: The 1999 Revision.* The total population figures are World Bank estimates. The data on land area and land use are from the FAO's electronic files and are published in its *Production Yearbook.* The FAO gathers these data from national agencies through annual questionnaires and by analyzing the results of national agricultural censuses.

3.2 | Agricultural inputs

	Arable land		Irrigated land		Land under cereal production		Fertilizer consumption		Agricultural machinery			
									Tractors per 1,000 agricultural workers		Tractors per 100 sq. km. of arable land	
	hectares per capita		% of cropland		thousand hectares		hundreds of grams per hectare of arable land					
	1979-81	1997-99	1979-81	1997-99	1979-81	1999-2001	1979-81	1997-99	1979-81	1997-99	1979-81	1997-99
Afghanistan	0.50	0.32	31.1	29.6	3,037	2,345	62	7	0	0	1	1
Albania	0.22	0.17	53.0	48.6	367	213	1,556	228	15	11	173	140
Algeria	0.37	0.26	3.4	6.8	2,968	1,903	277	152	27	38	68	121
Angola	0.41	0.24	2.2	2.1	705	888	49	10	4	3	35	34
Argentina	0.89	0.69	5.7	5.7	11,154	10,803	46	322	132	191	73	112
Armenia	..	0.13	..	51.3	..	182	..	160	..	73	..	354
Australia	2.97	2.69	3.5	4.6	15,986	16,347	269	446	751	707	75	63
Austria	0.20	0.17	0.2	0.3	1,062	839	2,615	1,774	945	1,672	2,084	2,522
Azerbaijan	..	0.21	..	74.1	..	615	..	105	..	35	..	194
Bangladesh	0.10	0.06	17.1	46.1	10,823	11,568	459	1,491	0	0	5	7
Belarus	..	0.61	..	1.8	..	2,406	..	1,417	..	111	..	140
Belgium[a]	0.08	0.08	1.7	4.6	426	334	5,323	3,766	917	1,222	1,416	1,312
Benin	0.43	0.29	0.3	0.6	525	841	11	262	0	0	1	1
Bolivia	0.35	0.24	6.6	5.9	559	780	23	34	4	4	21	29
Bosnia and Herzegovina	..	0.13	..	0.4	..	401	..	653	..	280	..	580
Botswana	0.44	0.22	0.5	0.3	153	128	32	123	9	19	54	175
Brazil	0.32	0.32	3.3	4.4	20,612	17,807	915	1,099	31	59	139	151
Bulgaria	0.43	0.52	28.3	17.7	2,110	1,905	2,334	381	66	73	161	58
Burkina Faso	0.39	0.32	0.4	0.7	2,026	2,957	26	141	0	0	0	6
Burundi	0.22	0.12	4.5	6.7	203	203	11	37	0	0	1	2
Cambodia	0.29	0.32	5.8	7.1	1,241	2,037	45	27	0	0	6	4
Cameroon	0.68	0.42	0.2	0.5	1,021	844	56	72	0	0	1	1
Canada	1.86	1.51	1.3	1.6	19,561	17,454	416	582	824	1,717	144	156
Central African Republic	0.81	0.54	..	..	194	153	5	3	0	0	0	0
Chad	0.70	0.48	0.4	0.6	907	2,000	6	40	0	0	1	0
Chile	0.34	0.13	31.1	78.4	820	580	338	2,323	43	55	90	272
China	0.10	0.10	45.1	39.0	94,647	87,077	1,494	2,911	2	1	76	60
Hong Kong, China	0.00	0.00	37.5	33.3	0	0	..	..	0	0	10	8
Colombia	0.13	0.05	7.7	20.4	1,361	1,075	812	2,848	8	6	77	103
Congo, Dem. Rep.	0.25	0.14	0.1	0.1	1,115	2,100	12	2	0	0	3	4
Congo, Rep.	0.08	0.06	0.6	0.5	19	3	27	270	2	1	49	41
Costa Rica	0.12	0.06	12.1	20.9	136	86	2,650	8,323	22	21	210	311
Côte d'Ivoire	0.24	0.19	1.0	1.0	1,008	1,621	261	306	1	1	16	13
Croatia	..	0.32	..	0.2	..	604	..	1,558	..	13	..	19
Cuba	0.27	0.33	22.9	19.5	224	202	2,024	510	78	97	259	215
Czech Republic	..	0.30	..	0.7	..	1,646	..	951	..	171	..	274
Denmark	0.52	0.44	14.5	19.6	1,818	1,515	2,453	1,763	973	1,119	708	570
Dominican Republic	0.19	0.13	11.7	17.2	149	150	572	954	3	4	20	22
Ecuador	0.20	0.13	24.8	28.8	419	904	471	1,024	6	7	40	57
Egypt, Arab Rep.	0.06	0.05	100.0	100.0	2,007	2,715	2,864	4,043	4	10	158	303
El Salvador	0.12	0.09	4.3	4.8	422	405	1,376	1,570	5	4	61	61
Eritrea	..	0.12	..	4.8	..	374	..	168	..	0	..	12
Estonia	..	0.80	..	0.4	..	337	..	260	..	538	..	453
Ethiopia	..	0.16	..	1.8	..	7,020	..	155	..	0	..	3
Finland	0.50	0.42	2.5	3.0	1,190	1,180	2,022	1,441	721	1,242	892	898
France	0.32	0.31	4.6	10.3	9,804	9,032	3,260	2,649	737	1,303	836	694
Gabon	0.42	0.28	2.4	3.0	6	17	20	6	5	7	43	46
Gambia, The	0.26	0.16	0.6	1.0	54	141	136	82	0	0	3	2
Georgia	..	0.15	..	44.2	..	375	..	467	..	21	..	138
Germany	0.15	0.14	3.7	4.0	7,692	6,951	4,249	2,485	624	959	1,340	906
Ghana	0.18	0.20	0.2	0.2	902	1,305	104	45	1	1	19	10
Greece	0.30	0.26	24.2	37.3	1,600	1,266	1,927	1,741	120	299	485	875
Guatemala	0.19	0.13	5.0	6.8	716	687	726	1,570	3	2	32	32
Guinea	0.16	0.12	7.9	6.4	708	744	16	31	0	0	2	6
Guinea-Bissau	0.34	0.26	6.0	4.9	142	132	24	17	0	0	1	1
Haiti	0.10	0.07	7.9	8.2	416	457	62	192	0	0	3	3
Honduras	0.44	0.25	4.1	4.1	421	465	163	983	5	7	21	34

	Arable land		Irrigated land		Land under cereal production		Fertilizer consumption		Agricultural machinery			
	hectares per capita		% of cropland		thousand hectares		hundreds of grams per hectare of arable land		Tractors per 1,000 agricultural workers		Tractors per 100 sq. km. of arable land	
	1979-81	1997-99	1979-81	1997-99	1979-81	1999-2001	1979-81	1997-99	1979-81	1997-99	1979-81	1997-99
Hungary	0.47	0.48	3.6	4.2	2,878	2,671	2,906	832	59	168	111	192
India	0.24	0.17	22.8	33.6	104,349	100,602	345	1,058	2	6	24	92
Indonesia	0.12	0.09	16.2	15.5	11,825	15,149	645	1,415	0	1	5	39
Iran, Islamic Rep.	0.36	0.27	35.5	39.8	8,062	7,424	430	647	17	41	57	149
Iraq	0.40	0.23	32.1	63.6	2,159	2,712	172	735	23	75	44	95
Ireland	0.33	0.29	..	..	425	279	5,373	6,391	606	1,048	1,289	1,638
Israel	0.08	0.06	49.3	45.3	129	74	2,384	3,474	294	327	809	698
Italy	0.17	0.15	19.3	24.1	5,082	4,192	2,295	2,151	370	1,115	1,117	1,966
Jamaica	0.06	0.07	10.1	9.1	4	2	1,231	1,339	9	11	208	177
Japan	0.04	0.04	56.0	54.6	2,724	2,048	4,131	3,207	209	690	2,723	4,675
Jordan	0.14	0.05	11.0	19.5	158	42	404	963	48	29	153	196
Kazakhstan	..	1.99	..	7.6	..	11,991	..	12	..	54	..	26
Kenya	0.23	0.14	0.9	1.5	1,692	1,828	160	346	1	1	17	36
Korea, Dem. Rep.	0.09	0.08	58.9	73.0	1,625	1,258	4,688	1,032	13	20	275	441
Korea, Rep.	0.05	0.04	59.6	60.7	1,689	1,174	3,920	5,323	1	60	14	908
Kuwait	0.00	0.00	83.3	90.5	0	1	4,500	1,833	3	11	220	137
Kyrgyz Republic	..	0.28	..	75.0	..	648	..	218	..	46	..	181
Lao PDR	0.24	0.17	13.3	17.8	751	742	35	79	0	1	7	12
Latvia	..	0.75	..	1.1	..	421	..	252	..	328	..	301
Lebanon	0.07	0.04	28.3	38.6	34	39	1,663	3,384	28	120	141	312
Lesotho	0.22	0.16	..	..	203	170	150	171	6	6	47	62
Liberia	0.07	0.06	0.5	0.7	203	158	363	..	0	0	24	17
Libya	0.58	0.37	10.7	21.2	538	327	357	302	101	303	134	181
Lithuania	..	0.79	..	0.3	..	975	..	521	..	381	..	332
Macedonia, FYR	..	0.29	..	8.6	..	220	..	729	..	416	..	913
Madagascar	0.28	0.18	21.5	35.1	1,309	1,374	31	29	1	1	11	14
Malawi	0.25	0.19	1.1	1.4	1,155	1,541	203	271	0	0	8	8
Malaysia	0.07	0.08	6.7	4.8	729	714	..	..	4	24	77	238
Mali	0.31	0.45	4.5	3.0	1,346	2,397	61	84	0	1	5	6
Mauritania	0.14	0.20	22.8	9.8	125	249	57	12	1	1	13	8
Mauritius	0.10	0.09	15.0	18.2	0	0	2,547	3,319	4	6	33	37
Mexico	0.34	0.26	20.3	23.8	9,356	10,952	570	706	16	20	54	69
Moldova	..	0.42	..	14.1	..	765	..	279	..	82	..	245
Mongolia	0.71	0.56	3.0	6.4	559	226	83	33	32	21	82	53
Morocco	0.39	0.32	15.0	13.1	4,414	4,904	268	369	7	10	34	49
Mozambique	0.24	0.18	2.1	3.2	1,077	1,731	107	24	1	1	20	18
Myanmar	0.28	0.21	10.4	16.7	5,133	6,817	111	173	1	1	9	10
Namibia	0.66	0.49	0.6	0.9	195	323	0	2	10	11	39	39
Nepal	0.16	0.13	22.5	38.2	2,251	3,305	98	324	0	0	10	16
Netherlands	0.06	0.06	58.5	60.0	225	213	8,620	5,374	561	596	2,238	1,712
New Zealand	0.80	0.41	5.2	8.7	193	132	1,965	4,241	619	437	367	489
Nicaragua	0.39	0.51	6.0	3.2	266	387	392	172	6	7	19	11
Niger	0.62	0.49	0.7	1.3	3,872	7,455	10	3	0	0	0	0
Nigeria	0.39	0.23	0.7	0.8	6,048	18,765	59	61	1	2	3	11
Norway	0.20	0.20	..	..	311	337	3,146	2,252	824	1,266	1,603	1,567
Oman	0.01	0.01	92.7	80.5	2	2	840	4,356	1	1	76	94
Pakistan	0.24	0.16	72.7	81.7	10,693	12,364	525	1,261	5	12	50	150
Panama	0.22	0.18	5.0	5.3	166	165	692	731	27	20	122	100
Papua New Guinea	0.01	0.01	..	..	2	3	3,827	1,700	1	1	699	193
Paraguay	0.52	0.42	3.4	2.9	307	548	44	297	14	24	45	75
Peru	0.19	0.15	32.3	28.6	732	1,189	381	602	5	5	37	36
Philippines	0.11	0.08	12.8	15.5	6,790	6,611	636	1,315	1	1	20	21
Poland	0.41	0.36	0.7	0.7	7,875	8,569	2,393	1,135	112	291	425	932
Portugal	0.25	0.19	20.1	24.6	1,099	584	1,113	1,297	72	236	351	840
Puerto Rico	0.02	0.01	27.2	49.6	1	0	..	..	..	..	..	..
Romania	0.44	0.41	21.9	29.2	6,340	5,687	1,448	325	39	92	150	177
Russian Federation	..	0.86	..	3.7	..	40,539	..	110	..	97	..	67

	Arable land		Irrigated land		Land under cereal production		Fertilizer consumption hundreds of grams per hectare of arable land		Agricultural machinery			
	hectares per capita		% of cropland		thousand hectares				Tractors per 1,000 agricultural workers		Tractors per 100 sq. km. of arable land	
	1979-81	1997-99	1979-81	1997-99	1979-81	1999-2001	1979-81	1997-99	1979-81	1997-99	1979-81	1997-99
Rwanda	0.15	0.10	0.4	0.4	239	233	3	4	0	0	1	1
Saudi Arabia	0.20	0.18	28.9	42.8	388	625	228	925	2	12	10	26
Senegal	0.42	0.25	2.6	3.1	1,216	1,360	104	116	0	0	2	2
Sierra Leone	0.14	0.10	4.1	5.4	434	235	58	23	0	0	6	2
Singapore	0.00	0.00	..	..	..	..	..	..	3	22	220	650
Slovak Republic	..	0.27	..	10.9	..	..	..	716	..	91	..	169
Slovenia	..	0.09	..	1.0	..	97	..	4,442	..	4,231	..	6,090
Somalia	0.15	0.13	13.3	18.8	638	464	9	5	1	1	17	18
South Africa	0.45	0.36	8.4	8.5	6,760	4,735	874	527	94	53	140	59
Spain	0.42	0.35	14.8	19.5	7,391	6,598	1,012	1,626	200	618	335	621
Sri Lanka	0.06	0.05	28.3	33.7	864	907	1,800	2,677	4	2	141	84
Sudan	0.64	0.56	14.4	11.5	4,447	7,068	51	41	2	2	8	6
Swaziland	0.30	0.17	34.0	38.3	70	61	1,050	327	29	25	173	174
Sweden	0.36	0.31	..	..	1,505	1,191	1,654	1,021	715	1,064	623	620
Switzerland	0.06	0.06	6.2	5.7	172	185	4,623	2,882	494	648	2,428	2,692
Syrian Arab Republic	0.60	0.31	9.6	21.6	2,642	2,977	250	754	29	67	54	195
Tajikistan	..	0.12	..	82.4	..	391	..	657	..	37	..	404
Tanzania	0.16	0.12	3.1	3.3	2,834	3,544	110	81	1	1	35	20
Thailand	0.35	0.25	16.4	26.0	10,625	11,684	177	1,102	1	10	11	147
Togo	0.77	0.52	0.3	0.3	416	796	14	77	0	0	0	0
Trinidad and Tobago	0.06	0.06	1.7	2.5	4	4	1,064	1,036	50	53	337	360
Tunisia	0.51	0.31	4.9	7.5	1,416	1,368	212	377	30	38	79	123
Turkey	0.57	0.40	9.6	15.8	13,499	13,204	529	831	38	62	169	358
Turkmenistan	..	0.33	..	..	..	732	..	651	..	80	..	307
Uganda	0.32	0.24	0.1	0.1	752	1,366	1	6	0	1	6	9
Ukraine	..	0.65	..	7.2	..	12,616	..	151	..	94	..	114
United Arab Emirates	0.01	0.03	..	57.4	0	1	2,250	4,153	6	4	106	34
United Kingdom	0.12	0.10	2.0	1.7	3,930	3,140	3,191	3,453	726	914	744	810
United States	0.83	0.64	10.8	12.5	72,639	58,055	1,092	1,127	1,230	1,546	253	271
Uruguay	0.48	0.38	5.4	13.8	614	554	564	1,041	171	173	236	262
Uzbekistan	..	0.19	..	88.3	..	1,413	..	1,912	..	59	..	380
Venezuela, RB	0.19	0.11	10.0	16.3	814	688	711	934	50	60	133	186
Vietnam	0.11	0.07	25.6	41.3	5,962	8,299	302	3,179	1	5	38	218
West Bank and Gaza	..	..	..	..	..	..	..	..	..	..	..	..
Yemen, Rep.	0.16	0.09	19.9	29.0	865	639	93	183	3	2	33	37
Yugoslavia, Fed. Rep.	0.73	..	1.9	..	4,310	2,048	1,261	..	140	..	616	..
Zambia	0.89	0.54	0.4	0.9	595	811	145	93	3	2	9	11
Zimbabwe	0.35	0.27	3.1	3.5	1,633	1,787	610	552	7	7	66	72
World	0.25 w	0.23 w	17.7 w	19.8 w	588,601 s	670,080 s	870 w	1,013 w	19 w	20 w	172 w	188 w
Low income	0.22	0.18	19.9	25.8	199,694	257,986	290	669	2	5	20	70
Middle income	0.18	0.22	23.4	20.3	233,883	279,983	985	1,111	8	11	103	126
Lower middle income	0.13	0.20	33.6	23.8	155,654	203,551	1,060	1,181	5	7	83	96
Upper middle income	0.34	0.29	10.4	12.8	78,229	76,432	888	959	39	82	137	206
Low & middle income	0.20	0.20	21.7	22.6	433,577	537,969	644	924	5	8	62	102
East Asia & Pacific	0.12	0.10	36.9	38.1	141,593	141,801	1,154	2,407	2	2	55	74
Europe & Central Asia	0.16	0.59	10.6	10.4	37,380	110,208	1,445	337	..	100	223	166
Latin America & Carib.	0.32	0.27	11.8	13.9	49,846	49,106	586	854	25	36	95	118
Middle East & N. Africa	0.29	0.20	25.8	36.4	25,653	25,677	421	715	12	24	61	122
South Asia	0.23	0.16	28.7	40.9	132,128	131,199	360	1,051	2	5	25	91
Sub-Saharan Africa	0.32	0.24	4.0	4.2	46,978	79,978	158	134	3	1	23	16
High income	0.46	0.40	9.8	11.6	155,024	132,111	1,314	1,265	519	942	387	428
Europe EMU	0.23	0.21	13.4	18.3	35,999	31,478	2,704	2,306	452	868	896	950

a. Includes Luxembourg.

About the data

Agricultural activities provide developing countries with food and revenue, but they also can degrade natural resources. Poor farming practices can cause soil erosion and loss of fertility. Efforts to increase productivity through the use of chemical fertilizers, pesticides, and intensive irrigation have environmental costs and health impacts. Excessive use of chemical fertilizers can alter the chemistry of soil. Pesticide poisoning is common in developing countries. And salinization of irrigated land diminishes soil fertility. Thus inappropriate use of inputs for agricultural production has far-reaching effects.

This table provides indicators of major inputs to agricultural production: land, fertilizers, and agricultural machinery. There is no single correct mix of inputs: appropriate levels and application rates vary by country and over time, depending on the type of crops, the climate and soils, and the production process used.

The data shown here and in table 3.3 are collected by the Food and Agriculture Organization (FAO) through annual questionnaires. The FAO tries to impose standard definitions and reporting methods, but exact consistency across countries and over time is not possible. Data on agricultural employment in particular should be used with caution. In many countries much agricultural employment is informal and unrecorded, including substantial work performed by women and children.

Fertilizer consumption measures the quantity of plant nutrients in the form of nitrogen, potassium, and phosphorous compounds available for direct application. Consumption is calculated as production plus imports minus exports. Traditional nutrients—animal and plant manures—are not included. Because some chemical compounds used for fertilizers have other industrial applications, the consumption data may overstate the quantity available for crops.

To smooth annual fluctuations in agricultural activity, the indicators in the table have been averaged over three years.

Figure 3.2

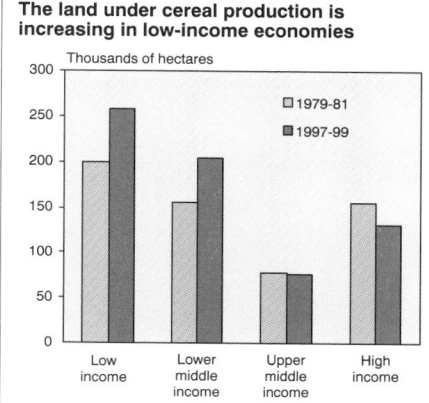

The land under cereal production is increasing in low-income economies

Thousands of hectares

1979-81
1997-99

Low income | Lower middle income | Upper middle income | High income

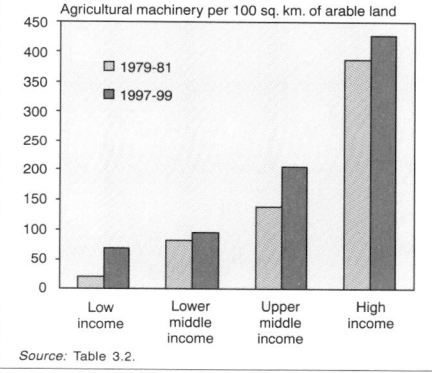

...but their use of agricultural machinery lags far behind other economies'.

Agricultural machinery per 100 sq. km. of arable land

1979-81
1997-99

Low income | Lower middle income | Upper middle income | High income

Source: Table 3.2.

Definitions

• **Arable land** includes land defined by the FAO as land under temporary crops (double-cropped areas are counted once), temporary meadows for mowing or for pasture, land under market or kitchen gardens, and land temporarily fallow. Land abandoned as a result of shifting cultivation is excluded. • **Irrigated land** refers to areas purposely provided with water, including land irrigated by controlled flooding. Cropland refers to arable land and land used for permanent crops (see table 3.1). • **Land under cereal production** refers to harvested areas, although some countries report only sown or cultivated area. • **Fertilizer consumption** measures the quantity of plant nutrients used per unit of arable land. Fertilizer products cover nitrogenous, potash, and phosphate fertilizers (including ground rock phosphate). The time reference for fertilizer consumption is the crop year (July through June). • **Agricultural machinery** refers to wheel and crawler tractors (excluding garden tractors) in use in agriculture at the end of the calendar year specified or during the first quarter of the following year.

Data sources

The data are from electronic files that the FAO makes available to the World Bank. Data on arable land, irrigated land, and land under cereal production are published in the FAO's *Production Yearbook*.

3.3 | Agricultural output and productivity

| | Crop production index | | Food production index | | Livestock production index | | Cereal yield | | Agricultural productivity | |
	1989-91 = 100		1989-91 = 100		1989-91 = 100		kilograms per hectare		Agriculture value added per worker 1995 $	
	1979-81	1998-2000	1979-81	1998-2000	1979-81	1998-2000	1979-81	1998-2000	1979-81	1998-2000
Afghanistan	..	..	..	..	..	..	1,337	1,145	..	..
Albania	..	..	..	..	..	..	2,500	2,664	1,184	1,978
Algeria	77.5	126.2	67.6	130.9	55.0	124.5	656	846	1,357	1,962
Angola	101.9	148.5	90.0	144.1	83.8	135.6	526	646	..	121
Argentina	83.5	160.0	91.7	137.5	101.1	106.7	2,184	3,448	7,148	10,243
Armenia	..	97.9	..	75.5	..	60.5	..	1,532	..	5,477
Australia	79.9	165.4	91.3	140.8	85.6	112.2	1,321	2,034	20,354	33,765
Austria	92.8	102.3	92.2	105.3	94.5	105.6	4,131	5,646	11,197	28,523
Azerbaijan	..	47.4	..	65.8	..	75.5	..	2,056	..	847
Bangladesh	80.0	117.4	79.2	119.8	81.3	137.7	1,938	2,927	217	296
Belarus	..	87.0	..	61.9	..	60.2	..	1,942	..	3,832
Belgium[a]	84.9	141.4	88.5	114.5	88.8	112.7	4,861	7,594	21,868	55,874
Benin	53.8	175.3	63.1	151.3	69.0	119.7	698	1,056	311	586
Bolivia	71.2	151.6	70.9	137.4	75.5	129.0	1,183	1,520	..	1,035
Bosnia and Herzegovina	..	..	..	..	..	..	..	3,490	..	7,970
Botswana	86.4	75.6	87.2	94.2	87.5	96.8	203	196	630	688
Brazil	75.3	122.9	69.5	137.9	67.9	150.3	1,496	2,665	2,048	4,356
Bulgaria	107.7	65.7	105.5	70.0	96.3	63.0	3,853	2,846	2,754	6,252
Burkina Faso	59.3	143.4	62.7	135.5	59.9	138.5	575	868	134	180
Burundi	79.9	89.7	79.9	90.3	82.3	81.5	1,081	1,283	177	141
Cambodia	55.2	138.2	48.9	141.3	27.3	150.5	1,025	1,875	..	403
Cameroon	86.5	130.7	79.9	129.6	61.1	118.7	849	1,551	834	1,104
Canada	77.6	129.4	79.7	128.9	88.3	131.7	2,173	3,035	14,161	36,597
Central African Republic	102.8	128.4	79.7	132.3	48.9	127.8	529	1,084	377	469
Chad	67.1	173.7	80.1	152.0	89.2	119.2	587	650	155	227
Chile	70.7	126.3	71.5	133.1	75.8	143.5	2,124	4,540	3,488	5,712
China	67.1	141.6	60.8	169.6	45.4	210.0	3,027	4,879	161	321
Hong Kong, China	133.6	59.3	99.8	49.5	194.3	44.6	1,712	..	..	..
Colombia	84.1	100.9	75.5	118.2	72.6	125.2	2,452	3,091	3,034	3,448
Congo, Dem. Rep.	73.0	89.1	72.2	92.0	77.7	103.2	807	785	241	*252*
Congo, Rep.	84.6	113.4	82.3	117.1	80.7	128.5	838	687	385	475
Costa Rica	70.7	146.8	73.1	141.3	77.2	121.5	2,498	3,543	3,139	5,140
Côte d'Ivoire	73.8	132.3	70.8	130.5	74.7	120.9	867	1,136	1,074	1,136
Croatia	..	87.2	..	69.9	..	50.2	..	4,444	..	8,839
Cuba	84.1	55.0	90.1	59.4	96.0	66.1	2,458	2,148	..	..
Czech Republic	..	89.0	..	81.9	..	75.3	..	4,092	..	5,637
Denmark	65.2	94.6	83.2	106.6	95.0	117.7	4,040	6,120	19,350	54,090
Dominican Republic	96.5	90.6	85.2	103.5	68.8	125.3	3,024	3,827	2,018	2,769
Ecuador	78.2	126.3	77.4	139.6	73.0	151.6	1,633	2,064	1,206	1,773
Egypt, Arab Rep.	75.5	142.6	68.4	151.3	67.0	159.6	4,053	7,015	721	1,240
El Salvador	120.4	108.6	90.8	119.6	88.8	123.6	1,702	2,063	1,925	1,711
Eritrea	..	180.3	..	139.4	..	110.5	..	822	..	..
Estonia	..	66.6	..	43.0	..	36.9	..	1,553	..	3,698
Ethiopia	..	121.6	..	119.9	..	116.2	..	1,141	..	138
Finland	76.3	86.3	93.8	89.7	107.5	93.0	2,511	2,763	18,547	36,557
France	87.4	111.8	93.8	107.6	97.8	105.8	4,700	7,271	19,318	53,785
Gabon	76.3	118.2	79.0	114.0	86.5	118.3	1,718	1,664	1,814	1,882
Gambia, The	79.5	114.1	82.8	115.4	94.4	114.5	1,284	1,101	325	226
Georgia	..	60.8	..	80.3	..	88.2	..	1,564	..	1,960
Germany	90.1	114.2	91.4	94.8	98.7	86.4	4,166	6,436	9,059	29,553
Ghana	67.0	173.4	68.7	162.9	79.7	101.9	807	1,306	670	558
Greece	86.8	105.8	91.2	99.3	99.9	96.8	3,090	3,486	8,600	13,400
Guatemala	89.6	121.0	69.7	124.0	76.0	127.3	1,578	1,726	2,143	2,112
Guinea	89.7	143.6	96.3	143.9	116.4	142.3	958	1,312	..	292
Guinea-Bissau	64.8	123.8	68.3	123.3	78.4	121.1	711	1,283	221	302
Haiti	103.4	86.9	101.3	95.7	100.2	128.8	1,009	922	509	349
Honduras	90.4	116.6	88.2	111.9	80.8	130.0	1,170	1,176	696	979

	Crop production index		Food production index		Livestock production index		Cereal yield		Agricultural productivity	
	1989-91 = 100		1989-91 = 100		1989-91 = 100		kilograms per hectare		Agriculture value added per worker 1995 $	
	1979-81	1998-2000	1979-81	1998-2000	1979-81	1998-2000	1979-81	1998-2000	1979-81	1998-2000
Hungary	93.3	79.3	90.7	74.3	94.1	69.6	4,519	4,507	3,390	5,016
India	70.9	123.3	68.1	125.7	62.2	133.5	1,324	2,299	272	397
Indonesia	66.2	118.6	63.3	119.2	51.0	122.4	2,837	3,915	609	736
Iran, Islamic Rep.	57.3	150.0	61.1	150.0	68.0	146.1	1,108	2,030	2,197	3,756
Iraq	74.7	83.7	78.0	78.9	81.4	64.9	832	609	..	..
Ireland	93.9	110.1	83.3	111.3	83.3	111.9	4,733	6,883	..	..
Israel	99.8	103.2	85.0	112.2	78.4	118.7	1,840	1,701	..	..
Italy	106.1	105.1	101.4	105.0	93.0	105.5	3,548	5,033	11,090	24,827
Jamaica	98.6	123.2	86.0	120.9	73.9	119.5	1,667	1,197	829	1,346
Japan	107.9	88.3	94.0	92.5	85.1	94.2	5,252	5,971	17,378	30,086
Jordan	54.7	120.4	57.5	141.2	51.5	194.2	521	1,698	1,158	1,422
Kazakhstan	..	65.7	..	61.0	..	45.3	..	975	..	1,421
Kenya	74.5	108.7	67.5	105.3	60.1	105.2	1,364	1,434	262	225
Korea, Dem. Rep.	..	..	..	..	..	..	3,694	2,987	..	..
Korea, Rep.	87.8	107.0	77.6	119.1	52.6	155.6	4,986	6,336	3,765	12,374
Kuwait	37.1	153.1	91.4	173.6	106.6	176.4	3,124	2,556	..	..
Kyrgyz Republic	..	130.6	..	115.9	..	77.7	..	2,577	..	3,528
Lao PDR	73.5	141.1	70.3	146.0	56.0	162.3	1,402	2,925	..	578
Latvia	..	69.6	..	44.3	..	34.2	..	1,981	..	2,499
Lebanon	52.0	137.7	59.2	143.1	100.5	162.9	1,307	2,428	..	29,241
Lesotho	95.1	115.9	89.1	98.6	87.7	87.6	977	974	723	540
Liberia	..	..	..	..	..	..	1,251	1,292	..	..
Libya	76.3	133.0	78.7	152.9	68.4	159.6	430	761	..	..
Lithuania	..	74.5	..	63.6	..	54.7	..	2,156	..	3,129
Macedonia, FYR	..	108.1	..	95.6	..	85.4	..	3,076	..	4,270
Madagascar	83.1	104.2	83.8	109.4	87.7	108.2	1,664	1,891	197	181
Malawi	85.7	148.8	93.2	152.7	78.2	111.9	1,161	1,514	109	140
Malaysia	75.3	111.8	55.6	135.4	41.0	152.0	2,828	2,860	3,939	6,638
Mali	54.5	142.8	76.7	125.7	94.5	122.3	804	1,163	241	283
Mauritania	62.1	149.7	86.5	105.7	89.4	99.5	384	916	299	480
Mauritius	93.3	94.2	89.7	104.0	64.0	135.6	2,536	5,094	3,087	4,977
Mexico	86.5	121.5	83.8	128.6	83.5	136.0	2,164	2,604	1,482	1,772
Moldova	..	53.7	..	44.1	..	35.4	..	2,439	..	1,297
Mongolia	44.6	36.3	88.1	89.5	93.2	93.8	573	735	*994*	1,300
Morocco	54.8	95.3	55.9	100.7	59.8	108.4	811	780	1,146	1,785
Mozambique	109.6	143.5	100.9	131.0	85.8	102.3	603	919	..	134
Myanmar	89.0	154.2	88.2	150.4	89.1	148.7	2,521	3,043	..	..
Namibia	80.1	110.4	107.2	97.0	115.6	95.5	377	285	919	1,468
Nepal	62.7	120.9	65.9	121.5	77.3	123.3	1,615	2,007	162	188
Netherlands	79.8	108.1	86.5	101.5	88.3	101.2	5,696	7,430	24,181	53,819
New Zealand	74.4	135.9	90.7	125.6	95.5	116.4	4,089	6,314	18,086	27,106
Nicaragua	124.1	134.5	117.8	140.9	139.7	136.0	1,475	1,694	1,543	1,887
Niger	90.1	151.4	97.9	141.7	109.7	125.4	440	379	222	214
Nigeria	51.4	155.5	57.2	152.3	84.3	126.0	1,265	1,206	414	672
Norway	94.5	84.8	93.8	95.9	96.2	100.5	3,634	4,002	17,013	33,305
Oman	60.4	113.8	62.5	113.8	61.6	104.0	982	2,204	..	..
Pakistan	65.6	125.6	66.4	144.4	59.5	152.3	1,608	2,261	394	630
Panama	97.1	96.5	85.6	107.3	71.3	125.4	1,524	2,217	2,122	2,632
Papua New Guinea	86.5	112.4	86.2	113.8	85.0	136.6	2,087	4,107	649	765
Paraguay	58.7	110.3	60.7	132.9	62.1	129.5	1,535	2,159	2,641	3,508
Peru	82.2	161.9	77.3	161.2	78.0	150.1	1,946	2,856	1,273	1,693
Philippines	88.2	107.8	86.1	121.3	73.7	163.0	1,611	2,434	1,347	1,328
Poland	84.6	85.6	87.9	88.0	98.0	87.0	2,345	2,885	..	1,864
Portugal	85.0	89.7	72.2	98.3	71.8	118.9	1,102	2,791	3,350	7,235
Puerto Rico	131.2	62.9	99.7	81.7	90.3	87.5	7,970	2,580	..	..
Romania	114.1	90.5	113.0	92.5	110.0	89.3	2,854	2,543	..	3,592
Russian Federation	..	66.0	..	61.8	..	52.6	..	1,387	..	2,249

	Crop production index		Food production index		Livestock production index		Cereal yield		Agricultural productivity	
	1989-91 = 100		1989-91 = 100		1989-91 = 100		kilograms per hectare		Agriculture value added per worker 1995 $	
	1979-81	1998-2000	1979-81	1998-2000	1979-81	1998-2000	1979-81	1998-2000	1979-81	1998-2000
Rwanda	84.3	88.2	85.3	91.6	81.0	108.8	1,134	930	371	235
Saudi Arabia	27.2	91.7	26.7	86.8	32.7	143.0	820	3,754	2,167	..
Senegal	77.2	102.9	74.0	114.2	65.1	138.0	690	721	336	304
Sierra Leone	80.3	81.7	84.5	87.0	84.1	112.4	1,249	1,116	367	341
Singapore	595.0	48.2	154.3	40.8	173.7	39.5	..	..	16,676	49,905
Slovak Republic	..	..	..	..	..	..	..	4,225	..	..
Slovenia	..	91.3	..	100.0	..	105.0	..	5,378	..	31,539
Somalia	..	..	..	..	..	..	474	513	..	..
South Africa	95.0	105.5	92.6	103.4	89.7	96.5	2,105	2,332	2,899	3,866
Spain	83.0	108.7	82.0	111.6	84.2	124.2	1,986	3,208	10,703	21,824
Sri Lanka	99.3	114.3	98.3	115.9	93.2	132.6	2,462	3,180	648	753
Sudan	130.2	162.9	105.1	158.4	89.3	149.9	645	514	..	..
Swaziland	72.5	90.4	80.2	91.0	96.5	83.4	1,345	1,836	1,671	1,731
Sweden	92.1	93.9	100.1	100.8	103.8	103.9	3,595	4,570	18,020	34,556
Switzerland	95.5	98.7	95.8	97.0	98.8	94.3	4,883	6,323	..	..
Syrian Arab Republic	100.4	159.6	94.2	151.1	72.2	132.5	1,156	1,333	2,206	2,890
Tajikistan	..	56.7	..	53.8	..	37.2	..	1,243	..	1,236
Tanzania	81.8	100.2	76.7	106.0	69.3	119.5	1,063	1,295	..	189
Thailand	79.2	113.4	80.3	113.6	64.9	127.3	1,911	2,478	630	909
Togo	70.4	146.6	77.1	135.9	52.0	121.9	729	933	345	538
Trinidad and Tobago	119.9	101.8	101.9	107.9	84.3	100.7	3,167	2,933	3,536	2,484
Tunisia	68.5	116.7	66.5	127.5	60.3	151.5	828	1,152	1,743	3,083
Turkey	76.6	114.8	75.8	112.5	80.4	108.1	1,869	2,196	1,860	1,886
Turkmenistan	..	78.9	..	134.0	..	136.5	..	2,346	..	1,229
Uganda	67.5	119.5	70.4	116.6	84.8	120.6	1,555	1,377	..	353
Ukraine	..	57.2	..	47.9	..	45.7	..	2,027	..	1,345
United Arab Emirates	38.9	276.2	48.8	261.6	45.3	174.1	2,224	865	..	..
United Kingdom	80.1	102.9	92.0	98.9	98.1	98.1	4,792	6,981	20,326	34,938
United States	98.6	121.9	94.5	122.9	89.0	120.0	4,151	5,794	..	..
Uruguay	86.8	151.4	87.1	137.3	85.9	121.3	1,644	3,506	5,367	8,652
Uzbekistan	..	87.9	..	116.2	..	116.4	..	2,390	..	1,035
Venezuela, RB	76.3	106.0	80.2	116.8	84.9	117.8	1,904	3,134	3,935	5,143
Vietnam	66.7	159.0	63.8	152.4	52.9	164.8	2,049	3,955	..	240
West Bank and Gaza	..	..	..	..	..	..	..	..	..	..
Yemen, Rep.	82.3	129.0	75.0	130.0	68.9	135.8	1,038	1,050	..	366
Yugoslavia, Fed. Rep.	96.3	*71.1*	94.3	*89.4*	94.2	*101.8*	3,601	*2,953*	..	..
Zambia	64.5	93.8	72.9	100.8	86.2	113.2	1,676	1,391	196	214
Zimbabwe	77.8	121.1	83.3	105.2	89.7	108.7	1,359	1,184	307	366
World	**79.1 w**	**123.6 w**	**78.8 w**	**127.9 w**	**79.6 w**	**129.4 w**	**1,608 w**	**2,083 w**	**.. w**	**.. w**
Low income	71.6	124.4	70.7	126.5	68.4	131.2	1,083	1,297	..	..
Middle income	74.5	128.2	72.0	141.4	69.3	153.7	1,789	2,343	..	..
Lower middle income	72.1	132.3	68.2	150.5	59.8	176.0	1,741	2,083	..	..
Upper middle income	80.7	117.3	79.5	122.7	82.3	122.8	1,874	2,718	..	..
Low & middle income	73.5	126.8	71.5	136.3	69.1	148.0	1,418	1,813	..	..
East Asia & Pacific	69.0	135.4	63.8	156.4	48.0	197.6	2,116	2,945	..	..
Europe & Central Asia	..	..	..	..	..	..	2,854	2,355	..	..
Latin America & Carib.	80.3	124.3	78.3	131.2	79.8	131.9	1,802	2,346	..	..
Middle East & N. Africa	66.1	131.3	64.8	134.0	64.1	136.8	925	1,354	..	..
South Asia	71.9	121.3	69.6	125.7	64.0	136.2	1,510	2,280	265	..
Sub-Saharan Africa	75.4	128.5	78.3	124.7	84.1	114.2	895	1,120	418	..
High income	93.5	115.7	92.1	112.9	91.1	109.9	3,170	3,881	..	..
Europe EMU	91.0	108.6	91.4	103.4	93.8	101.0	4,035	5,646	..	..

a. Includes Luxembourg.

About the data

The agricultural production indexes in the table are prepared by the Food and Agriculture Organization (FAO). The FAO obtains data from official and semiofficial reports of crop yields, area under production, and livestock numbers. If data are not available, the FAO makes estimates. The indexes are calculated using the Laspeyres formula: production quantities of each commodity are weighted by average international commodity prices in the base period and summed for each year. Because the FAO's indexes are based on the concept of agriculture as a single enterprise, estimates of the amounts retained for seed and feed are subtracted from the production data to avoid double counting. The resulting aggregate represents production available for any use except as seed and feed. The FAO's indexes may differ from other sources because of differences in coverage, weights, concepts, time periods, calculation methods, and use of international prices.

To ease cross-country comparisons, the FAO uses international commodity prices to value production. These prices, expressed in international dollars (equivalent in purchasing power to the U.S. dollar), are derived using a Geary-Khamis formula applied to agricultural outputs (see Inter-Secretariat Working Group on National Accounts 1993, sections 16.93–96). This method assigns a single price to each commodity so that, for example, one metric ton of wheat has the same price regardless of where it was produced. The use of international prices eliminates fluctuations in the value of output due to transitory movements of nominal exchange rates unrelated to the purchasing power of the domestic currency.

Data on cereal yield may be affected by a variety of reporting and timing differences. The FAO allocates production data to the calendar year in which the bulk of the harvest took place. But most of a crop harvested near the end of a year will be used in the following year. Cereal crops harvested for hay or harvested green for food, feed, or silage, and those used for grazing, are generally excluded. But millet and sorghum, which are grown as feed for livestock and poultry in Europe and North America, are used as food in Africa, Asia, and countries of the former Soviet Union. So some cereal crops are excluded from the data for some countries and included elsewhere, depending on their use.

Agricultural productivity is measured by value added per unit of input. (For further discussion of the calculation of value added in national accounts see *About the data* for tables 4.1 and 4.2.) Agricultural value added includes that from forestry and fishing. Thus interpretations of land productivity should be made with caution. To smooth annual fluctuations in agricultural activity, the indicators in the table have been averaged over three years.

Figure 3.3

Food production has outpaced population growth in low- and middle-income economies...

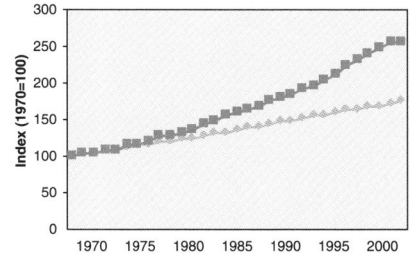

...as well as in high-income economies...

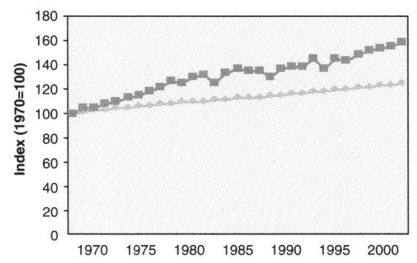

...but food production lags behind population growth in Sub-Saharan Africa

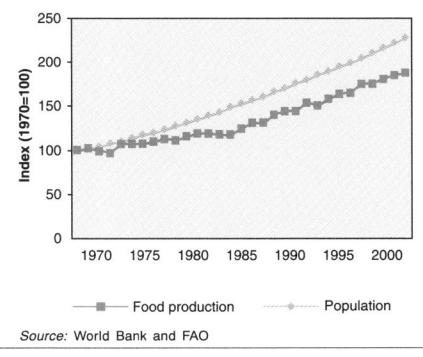

Source: World Bank and FAO

Definitions

• **Crop production index** shows agricultural production for each period relative to the base period 1989–91. It includes all crops except fodder crops. The regional and income group aggregates for the FAO's production indexes are calculated from the underlying values in international dollars, normalized to the base period 1989–91. The data in this table are three-year averages. Missing observations have not been estimated or imputed. • **Food production index** covers food crops that are considered edible and that contain nutrients. Coffee and tea are excluded because, although edible, they have no nutritive value. • **Livestock production index** includes meat and milk from all sources, dairy products such as cheese and eggs, honey, raw silk, wool, and hides and skins. • **Cereal yield**, measured in kilograms per hectare of harvested land, includes wheat, rice, maize, barley, oats, rye, millet, sorghum, buckwheat, and mixed grains. Production data on cereals refer to crops harvested for dry grain only. Cereal crops harvested for hay or harvested green for food, feed, or silage, and those used for grazing, are excluded. • **Agricultural productivity** refers to the ratio of agricultural value added, measured in constant 1995 U.S. dollars, to the number of workers in agriculture.

Data sources

The agricultural production indexes are prepared by the FAO and published annually in its *Production Yearbook*. The FAO makes these data and the data on cereal yield and agricultural employment available to the World Bank in electronic files that may contain more recent information than the published versions. For sources of agricultural value added see table 4.2.

3.4 | Deforestation and biodiversity

	Forest area		Average annual deforestation		Mammals		Birds		Higher plants[a]		Nationally protected areas	
	thousand sq. km 2000	% of total land area 2000[b]	sq. km 1990-2000	% 1990-2000	Species 1996[b]	Threatened species 2000[b]	Species 1996[b]	Threatened species 2000[b]	Species 1997[b]	Threatened species 1997[b]	thousand sq. km 1999[b]	% of total land area 1999[b]
Afghanistan	14	2.1	..	..	123	13	235	11	4,000	4	2.2	0.3
Albania	10	36.2	78	0.8	68	3	230	3	3,031	79	0.8	3.1
Algeria	21	0.9	-266	-1.3	92	13	192	6	3,164	141	58.9	2.5
Angola	698	56.0	1,242	0.2	276	18	765	15	5,185	30	81.8	6.6
Argentina	346	12.7	2,851	0.8	320	32	897	39	9,372	247	49.1	1.8
Armenia	4	12.4	-42	-1.3	..	7	..	4	..	31	2.1	7.6
Australia	1,581	20.6	..	..	252	63	649	35	15,638	2,245	542.5	7.1
Austria	39	47.0	-77	-0.2	83	9	213	3	3,100	23	24.5	29.6
Azerbaijan	11	12.6	-130	-1.3	..	13	..	8	..	28	4.8	5.5
Bangladesh	13	10.2	-165	-1.3	109	21	295	23	5,000	24	1.0	0.8
Belarus	94	45.3	-2,562	-3.2	..	5	221	3	..	1	13.0	6.3
Belgium	..	..	..	..	58	11	180	2	1,550	2	0.0	0.0
Benin	27	24.0	699	2.3	188	7	307	2	2,201	4	7.8	7.0
Bolivia	531	48.9	1,611	0.3	316	23	1,274	27	17,367	227	156.0	14.4
Bosnia and Herzegovina	23	44.6	..	..	..	10	..	3	..	64	0.3	0.5
Botswana	124	21.9	1,184	0.9	164	5	386	7	2,151	7	105.0	18.5
Brazil	5,325	63.0	22,264	0.4	394	79	1,492	113	56,215	1,358	375.1	4.4
Bulgaria	37	33.4	-204	-0.6	81	15	240	10	3,572	106	5.0	4.5
Burkina Faso	71	25.9	152	0.2	147	7	335	2	1,100	0	28.6	10.4
Burundi	1	3.7	147	9.0	107	5	451	7	2,500	1	1.5	5.7
Cambodia	93	52.9	561	0.6	123	21	307	19	..	5	28.6	16.2
Cameroon	239	51.3	2,218	0.9	297	37	690	15	8,260	89	21.0	4.5
Canada	2,446	26.5	..	..	193	14	426	8	3,270	278	907.0	9.8
Central African Republic	229	36.8	300	0.1	209	12	537	3	3,602	1	51.1	8.2
Chad	127	10.1	817	0.6	134	17	370	5	1,600	12	114.9	9.1
Chile	155	20.7	203	0.1	91	21	296	21	5,284	329	141.4	18.9
China	1,635	17.5	-18,063	-1.2	394	76	1,100	73	32,200	312	598.4	6.4
Hong Kong, China	..	..	..	..	24	1	76	11	1,984	9	0.5	..
Colombia	496	47.8	1,905	0.4	359	36	1,695	77	51,220	712	93.6	9.0
Congo, Dem. Rep.	1,352	59.6	5,324	0.4	415	40	929	28	11,007	78	101.9	4.5
Congo, Rep.	221	64.6	175	0.1	200	12	449	4	6,000	3	15.4	4.5
Costa Rica	20	38.5	158	0.8	205	14	600	13	12,119	527	7.2	14.2
Côte d'Ivoire	71	22.4	2,649	3.1	230	17	535	12	3,660	94	19.9	6.2
Croatia	18	31.9	-20	-0.1	..	9	224	4	..	6	4.2	7.5
Cuba	23	21.4	-277	-1.3	31	11	137	18	6,522	888	19.1	17.4
Czech Republic	26	34.1	-5	0.0	..	8	199	2	..	81	12.5	16.1
Denmark	5	10.7	-10	-0.2	43	5	196	1	1,450	2	13.8	32.5
Dominican Republic	14	28.4	..	..	20	5	136	15	5,657	136	15.2	31.5
Ecuador	106	38.1	1,372	1.2	302	31	1,388	62	19,362	824	120.8	43.6
Egypt, Arab Rep.	1	0.1	-20	-3.4	98	12	153	7	2,076	82	7.9	0.8
El Salvador	1	5.8	72	4.6	135	2	251	0	2,911	42	0.1	0.3
Eritrea	16	15.7	54	0.3	112	12	319	7	..	0	5.0	5.0
Estonia	21	48.7	-125	-0.6	65	5	213	3	..	2	5.0	11.8
Ethiopia	46	4.6	403	0.8	255	34	626	16	6,603	163	55.2	5.5
Finland	219	72.0	-80	0.0	60	6	248	3	1,102	6	18.7	6.1
France	153	27.9	-616	-0.4	93	18	269	5	4,630	195	74.4	13.5
Gabon	218	84.7	101	0.0	190	15	466	6	6,651	91	7.2	2.8
Gambia, The	5	48.1	-45	-1.0	108	3	280	2	974	1	0.2	2.3
Georgia	30	42.9	..	..	..	14	..	3	..	29	2.0	2.8
Germany	107	30.1	..	..	76	12	239	5	2,682	14	0.0	0.0
Ghana	63	27.8	1,200	1.7	222	13	529	8	3,725	103	11.0	4.9
Greece	36	27.9	-300	-0.9	95	14	251	7	4,992	571	4.7	3.6
Guatemala	29	26.3	537	1.7	250	6	458	6	8,681	355	18.3	16.8
Guinea	69	28.2	347	0.5	190	11	409	10	3,000	39	1.6	0.7
Guinea-Bissau	22	77.8	216	0.9	108	2	243	0	1,000	0	0.0	0.0
Haiti	1	3.2	70	5.7	..	4	75	14	5,242	100	0.1	0.4
Honduras	54	48.1	590	1.0	173	9	422	5	5,680	96	6.7	6.0

	Forest area		Average annual deforestation		Mammals		Birds		Higher plants[a]		Nationally protected areas	
	thousand sq. km 2000	% of total land area 2000[b]	sq. km 1990-2000	% 1990-2000	Species 1996[b]	Threatened species 2000[b]	Species 1996[b]	Threatened species 2000[b]	Species 1997[b]	Threatened species 1997[b]	thousand sq. km 1999[b]	% of total land area 1999[b]
Hungary	18	19.9	-72	-0.4	72	9	205	8	2,214	30	6.5	7.0
India	641	21.6	-381	-0.1	316	86	923	70	16,000	1,236	143.1	4.8
Indonesia	1,050	58.0	13,124	1.2	436	140	1,519	113	29,375	264	192.5	10.6
Iran, Islamic Rep.	73	4.5	..	..	140	23	323	13	8,000	2	83.0	5.1
Iraq	8	1.8	..	..	81	10	172	11	..	2	0.0	0.0
Ireland	7	9.6	-170	-3.0	25	5	142	1	950	1	0.7	0.9
Israel	1	6.4	-50	-4.9	92	14	180	12	2,317	32	3.3	15.8
Italy	100	34.0	-295	-0.3	90	14	234	5	5,599	311	22.0	7.5
Jamaica	3	30.0	54	1.5	24	5	113	12	3,308	744	0.0	0.1
Japan	241	66.1	-34	0.0	132	37	250	34	5,565	707	25.6	6.8
Jordan	1	1.0	..	..	71	8	141	8	2,100	9	3.0	3.4
Kazakhstan	121	4.5	-2,390	-2.2	..	18	..	15	..	71	73.4	2.7
Kenya	171	30.0	931	0.5	359	51	844	24	6,506	240	35.1	6.2
Korea, Dem. Rep.	82	68.2	..	..	..	13	115	19	2,898	4	3.2	2.6
Korea, Rep.	63	63.3	49	0.1	49	13	112	25	2,898	66	6.8	6.9
Kuwait	0	0.3	-2	-5.2	21	1	20	7	234	0	0.3	1.5
Kyrgyz Republic	10	5.2	-228	-2.6	..	7	..	4	..	34	6.9	3.6
Lao PDR	126	54.4	527	0.4	172	27	487	19	..	2	0.0	0.0
Latvia	29	47.1	-127	-0.4	83	5	217	3	1,153	0	8.1	13.0
Lebanon	0	3.5	1	0.3	54	6	154	7	3,000	5	0.0	0.5
Lesotho	0	0.5	..	..	33	3	58	7	1,591	21	0.1	0.2
Liberia	35	36.1	760	2.0	193	16	372	11	2,200	25	1.3	1.3
Libya	4	0.2	-47	-1.4	76	9	91	1	1,825	57	1.7	0.1
Lithuania	20	30.9	-48	-0.2	70	22	321	76	1,847	332	7.5	11.5
Macedonia, FYR	9	35.6	..	..	..	11	..	3	..	0	1.8	7.1
Madagascar	117	20.2	1,174	0.9	105	50	202	27	9,505	306	11.2	1.9
Malawi	26	27.6	707	2.4	195	8	521	11	3,765	61	10.6	11.3
Malaysia	193	58.7	2,377	1.2	286	47	501	37	15,500	490	15.1	4.6
Mali	132	10.8	993	0.7	137	13	397	4	1,741	15	45.3	3.7
Mauritania	3	0.3	98	2.7	61	10	273	2	1,100	3	17.5	1.7
Mauritius	0	7.9	1	0.6	4	4	27	9	750	294	0.2	7.7
Mexico	552	28.9	6,306	1.1	450	69	769	39	26,071	1,593	66.4	3.5
Moldova	3	9.9	-7	-0.2	68	3	177	5	..	5	0.5	1.4
Mongolia	106	6.8	600	0.5	134	12	390	16	2,272	0	179.9	11.5
Morocco	30	6.8	12	0.0	105	16	210	9	3,675	186	3.2	0.7
Mozambique	306	39.0	637	0.2	179	15	498	16	5,692	89	47.8	6.1
Myanmar	344	52.3	5,169	1.4	251	36	867	35	7,000	32	1.7	0.3
Namibia	80	9.8	734	0.9	154	14	469	11	3,174	75	106.2	12.9
Nepal	39	27.3	783	1.8	167	27	611	26	6,973	20	11.1	7.8
Netherlands	4	11.1	-10	-0.3	55	11	191	4	1,221	1	2.3	6.8
New Zealand	79	29.7	-390	-0.5	10	8	150	62	2,382	211	63.3	23.6
Nicaragua	33	27.0	1,172	3.0	200	6	482	5	7,590	98	9.1	7.5
Niger	13	1.0	617	3.7	131	11	299	3	1,170	0	96.9	7.7
Nigeria	135	14.8	3,984	2.6	274	25	681	9	4,715	37	30.2	3.3
Norway	89	28.9	-310	-0.4	54	10	243	2	1,715	12	20.9	6.8
Oman	0	0.0	..	..	56	9	107	10	1,204	30	34.3	16.1
Pakistan	25	3.2	304	1.1	151	18	375	17	4,950	14	37.3	4.8
Panama	29	38.6	519	1.6	218	20	732	16	9,915	1,302	14.2	19.1
Papua New Guinea	306	67.6	1,129	0.4	214	58	644	32	11,544	92	0.1	0.0
Paraguay	234	58.8	1,230	0.5	305	9	556	26	7,851	129	14.0	3.5
Peru	652	50.9	2,688	0.4	344	47	1,538	73	18,245	906	34.6	2.7
Philippines	58	19.4	887	1.4	153	50	395	67	8,931	360	14.5	4.9
Poland	93	30.6	-110	-0.1	84	15	227	4	2,450	27	29.3	9.6
Portugal	37	40.1	-570	-1.7	63	17	207	7	5,050	269	6.0	6.6
Puerto Rico	2	25.8	5	0.2	16	2	105	8	2,493	223	0.2	2.1
Romania	64	28.0	-147	-0.2	84	17	247	8	3,400	99	10.9	4.7
Russian Federation	8,514	50.4	-1,353	0.0	269	42	628	38	..	214	529.1	3.1

	Forest area		Average annual deforestation		Mammals		Birds		Higher plants[a]		Nationally protected areas	
	thousand sq. km 2000	% of total land area 2000[b]	sq. km 1990-2000	% 1990-2000	Species 1996[b]	Threatened species 2000[b]	Species 1996[b]	Threatened species 2000[b]	Species 1997[b]	Threatened species 1997[b]	thousand sq. km 1999[b]	% of total land area 1999[b]
Rwanda	3	12.4	150	3.9	151	8	513	9	2,288	0	3.6	14.7
Saudi Arabia	15	0.7	..	..	77	7	155	15	2,028	7	49.7	2.3
Senegal	62	32.2	450	0.7	155	11	384	4	2,086	31	21.8	11.3
Sierra Leone	11	14.7	361	2.9	147	11	466	10	2,090	29	0.8	1.1
Singapore	0	3.3	..	..	45	3	118	7	2,168	29	0.0	4.8
Slovak Republic	20	42.5	-69	-0.3	..	9	209	4	..	65	10.8	22.6
Slovenia	11	55.0	-22	-0.2	69	9	207	1	..	13	1.2	6.0
Somalia	75	12.0	769	1.0	171	19	422	10	3,028	103	1.8	0.3
South Africa	89	7.3	80	0.1	247	41	596	28	23,420	2,215	66.2	5.4
Spain	144	28.8	-860	-0.6	82	24	278	7	5,050	985	42.4	8.5
Sri Lanka	19	30.0	348	1.6	88	20	250	14	3,314	455	8.7	13.5
Sudan	616	25.9	9,589	1.4	267	24	680	6	3,137	10	86.4	3.6
Swaziland	5	30.3	-58	-1.2	47	4	364	5	2,715	42	0.4	2.0
Sweden	271	65.9	-6	0.0	60	8	249	2	1,750	13	36.4	8.9
Switzerland	12	30.3	-43	-0.4	75	6	193	2	3,030	30	10.6	26.9
Syrian Arab Republic	5	2.5	..	..	63	4	204	8	3,000	8	0.0	0.0
Tajikistan	4	2.8	-20	-0.5	..	9	..	7	..	50	5.9	4.2
Tanzania	388	43.9	913	0.2	316	43	822	33	10,008	436	138.2	15.6
Thailand	148	28.9	1,124	0.7	265	34	616	37	11,625	385	70.8	13.9
Togo	5	9.4	209	3.4	196	9	391	0	2,201	4	4.3	7.9
Trinidad and Tobago	3	50.5	22	0.8	100	1	260	1	2,259	21	0.3	6.0
Tunisia	5	3.3	-11	-0.2	78	11	173	5	2,196	24	0.4	0.3
Turkey	102	13.3	-220	-0.2	116	17	302	11	8,650	1,876	9.9	1.3
Turkmenistan	38	8.0	..	..	..	13	..	6	..	17	19.8	4.2
Uganda	42	21.3	913	2.0	338	19	830	13	5,406	15	19.1	9.6
Ukraine	96	16.5	-310	-0.3	..	17	263	8	..	52	9.4	1.6
United Arab Emirates	3	3.8	-78	-2.8	25	3	67	8	..	0	0.0	0.0
United Kingdom	26	10.7	-200	-0.8	50	12	230	2	1,623	18	50.0	20.7
United States	2,260	24.7	-3,880	-0.2	428	37	650	55	19,473	4,669	1,231.2	13.4
Uruguay	13	7.4	-501	-5.0	81	6	237	11	2,278	15	0.5	0.3
Uzbekistan	20	4.8	-46	-0.2	..	11	..	9	..	41	8.2	2.0
Venezuela, RB	495	56.1	2,175	0.4	305	25	1,181	24	21,073	426	322.5	36.6
Vietnam	98	30.2	-516	-0.5	213	37	535	35	10,500	341	10.0	3.1
West Bank and Gaza	..	..	..	..	..	1	..	1	..	..	..	..
Yemen, Rep.	4	0.9	92	1.8	66	4	143	12	..	149	0.0	0.0
Yugoslavia, Fed. Rep.	29	..	14	0.0	..	11	..	5	5,351	155	3.4	3.3
Zambia	312	42.0	8,509	2.4	229	12	605	11	4,747	12	63.7	8.6
Zimbabwe	190	49.2	3,199	1.5	270	12	532	10	4,440	100	30.7	7.9
World	**38,602 s**	**29.7 w**	**90,385.0 s**	**0.2 w**							**8,437.7 s**	**6.5 w**
Low income	8,802	27.1	71,466.0	0.8							1,852.8	5.7
Middle income	21,828	32.7	26,930.0	0.1							3,461.3	5.2
Lower middle income	13,881	31.8	-10,206.0	-0.1							2,119.4	4.9
Upper middle income	7,947	34.5	37,136.0	0.5							1,341.9	5.8
Low & middle income	30,630	30.9	98,396.0	0.3							5,314.1	5.4
East Asia & Pacific	4,341	27.2	7,048.0	0.2							1,122.2	7.0
Europe & Central Asia	9,464	39.7	-8,143.0	-0.1							789.9	3.3
Latin America & Carib.	9,440	47.1	45,878.0	0.5							1,477.5	7.4
Middle East & N. Africa	168	1.5	-239.0	-0.1							242.4	2.2
South Asia	782	16.3	889.0	0.1							213.3	4.5
Sub-Saharan Africa	6,436	27.3	52,963.0	0.8							1,468.8	6.2
High income	7,972	26.1	-8,011.0	-0.1							3,123.6	10.2
Europe EMU	927	37.0	-2,988.0	-0.3							198.3	7.8

a. Flowering plants only. b. Data may refer to earlier years. They are the most recent reported by the World Conservation Monitoring Center in 2000.

Deforestation and biodiversity | 3.4

About the data

The estimates of forest area are from the Food and Agriculture Organization's (FAO) *State of the World's Forests 2001,* which provides information on forest cover as of 2000 and a revised estimate of forest cover in 1990. The current survey is the latest global forest assessment and the first to use a uniform global definition of forest. According to this assessment, the global rate of net deforestation has slowed to 9 million hectares a year, a rate 20 percent lower than that previously reported.

No breakdown of forest cover between natural forest and plantation is shown in the table because of space limitations. (This breakdown is provided by the FAO only for developing countries.) For this reason the deforestation data in the table may underestimate the rate at which natural forest is disappearing in some countries.

Deforestation is a major cause of loss of biodiversity, and habitat conservation is vital for stemming this loss. Conservation efforts traditionally have focused on protected areas, which have grown substantially in recent decades. Measures of species richness are one of the most straightforward ways to indicate the importance of an area for biodiversity. The number of small plants and animals is usually estimated by sampling of plots. It is also important to know which aspects are under the most immediate threat. This, however, requires a large amount of data and time-consuming analysis. For this reason global analyses of the status of threatened species have been carried out for few groups of organisms. Only for birds has the status of all species been assessed. An estimated 45 percent of mammal species remain to be assessed. For plants the World Conservation Union's (IUCN) *1997 IUCN Red List of Threatened Plants* provides the first-ever comprehensive listing of threatened species on a global scale, the result of more than 20 years' work by botanists from around the world. Nearly 34,000 plant species, 12.5 percent of the total, are threatened with extinction.

The table shows information on protected areas, numbers of certain species, and numbers of those species under threat. The World Conservation Monitoring Centre (WCMC) compiles these data from a variety of sources. Because of differences in definitions and reporting practices, cross-country comparability is limited. Compounding these problems, available data cover different periods.

Nationally protected areas are areas of at least 1,000 hectares that fall into one of five management categories defined by the WCMC:
- Scientific reserves and strict nature reserves with limited public access.
- National parks of national or international

significance (not materially affected by human activity).
- Natural monuments and natural landscapes with unique aspects.
- Managed nature reserves and wildlife sanctuaries.
- Protected landscapes and seascapes (which may include cultural landscapes).

Designating land as a protected area does not necessarily mean that protection is in force. For small countries that may only have protected areas smaller than 1,000 hectares, this size limit in the definition will result in an underestimate of the extent and number of protected areas.

Threatened species are defined according to the IUCN's classification categories: endangered (in danger of extinction and unlikely to survive if causal factors continue operating), vulnerable (likely to move into the endangered category in the near future if causal factors continue operating), rare (not endangered or vulnerable but at risk), indeterminate (known to be endangered, vulnerable, or rare but not enough information is available to say which), out of danger (formerly included in one of the above categories but now considered relatively secure because appropriate conservation measures are in effect), and insufficiently known (suspected but not definitely known to belong to one of the above categories).

Figures on species are not necessarily comparable across countries because taxonomic concepts and coverage vary. And while the number of birds and mammals is fairly well known, it is difficult to make an accurate count of plants. Although the data in the table should be interpreted with caution, especially for numbers of threatened species (where our knowledge is very incomplete), they do identify countries that are major sources of global biodiversity and show national commitments to habitat protection.

Definitions

- **Forest area** is land under natural or planted stands of trees, whether productive or not.
- **Average annual deforestation** refers to the permanent conversion of natural forest area to other uses, including shifting cultivation, permanent agriculture, ranching, settlements, and infrastructure development. Deforested areas do not include areas logged but intended for regeneration or areas degraded by fuelwood gathering, acid precipitation, or forest fires. Negative numbers indicate an increase in forest area. • **Mammals** exclude whales and porpoises. • **Birds** are listed for countries included within their breeding or wintering ranges. • **Higher plants** refer to native vascular plant species. • **Threatened species** are the number of species classified by the IUCN as endangered, vulnerable, rare, indeterminate, out of danger, or insufficiently known. • **Nationally protected areas** are totally or partially protected areas of at least 1,000 hectares that are designated as national parks, natural monuments, nature reserves or wildlife sanctuaries, protected landscapes and seascapes, or scientific reserves with limited public access. The data do not include sites protected under local or provincial law. Total land area is used to calculate the percentage of total area protected (see table 3.1).

Data sources

The forestry data are from the FAO's *State of the World's Forests 2001.* The data on species are from the WCMC's *Biodiversity Data Sourcebook* (1994) and the IUCN's *2000 IUCN Red List of Threatened Animals* and *1997 IUCN Red List of Threatened Plants.* The data on protected areas are from the WCMC's Protected Areas Data Unit.

	Freshwater resources			Annual freshwater withdrawals					Access to improved water source			
	Internal flows billion cu.m.	Flows from other countries billion cu.m.	Total resources per capita cu.m.	billion cu.m.[b]	% of total resources[a,b]	% for agriculture[c]	% for industry[c]	% for domestic[c]	% of urban population with access		% of rural population with access	
	2000	2000	2000						1990	2000	1990	2000
Afghanistan	55	10.0	2,448	26.1	40.2	99 [d]	0 [d]	1 [d]	..	19	..	11
Albania	27	15.7	12,489	1.4	3.3	71	0	29	..	..	..	..
Algeria	14	0.4	470	4.5	31.5	60 [d]	15 [d]	25 [d]	..	98	..	88
Angola	184	..	14,009	0.5	0.3	76 [d]	10 [d]	14 [d]	..	34	..	40
Argentina	360	623.0	26,545	28.6	2.9	75	9	16	..	85	..	30
Armenia	9	1.5	2,787	2.9	27.6	66	4	30	..	..	..	..
Australia	352	0.0	18,351	15.1	4.3	33	2	65	100	100	100	100
Austria	55	29.0	10,357	2.2	2.7	9	60	31	100	100	100	100
Azerbaijan	8	21.0	3,615	16.5	56.8	70	25	5	..	..	..	..
Bangladesh	105	1,105.6	9,238	14.6	1.2	86	2	12	98	99	89	97
Belarus	37	20.8	5,797	2.7	4.7	35	43	22	..	100	..	100
Belgium	12	4.0	1,561	0.0	56.4	..	..	..	..	..	..	..
Benin	10	15.5	4,114	0.2	0.6	67 [d]	10 [d]	23 [d]	..	74	..	55
Bolivia	316	7.2	38,806	1.4	0.4	48	20	32	92	93	52	55
Bosnia and Herzegovina	36	2.0	9,429	..	..	..	..	..	..	..	..	..
Botswana	3	11.8	9,176	0.1	0.7	48 [d]	20 [d]	32 [d]	100	100	91	..
Brazil	5,418	1,900.0	42,944	54.9	0.7	61	18	21	93	95	50	54
Bulgaria	18	0.2	2,228	0.0	76.4	..	..	..	..	..	..	98
Burkina Faso	18	2.0	1,730	0.4	1.9	81 [d]	0 [d]	19 [d]	74	84	50	..
Burundi	4	..	529	0.1	2.8	64 [d]	0 [d]	36 [d]	94	96	63	..
Cambodia	121	355.6	39,613	0.5	0.1	94	1	5	..	53	..	25
Cameroon	268	0.0	18,016	0.4	0.1	35 [d]	19 [d]	46 [d]	76	82	36	42
Canada	2,740	52.0	90,797	45.1	1.6	9	80	11	100	100	99	99
Central African Republic	141	..	37,934	0.1	0.0	73 [d]	6 [d]	21 [d]	80	80	46	46
Chad	15	28.0	5,589	0.2	0.4	82 [d]	2 [d]	16 [d]	..	31	..	26
Chile	928	0.0	61,007	21.4	2.2	84	11	5	98	99	48	66
China	2,812	17.2	2,241	525.5	18.6	77	18	5	99	94	60	66
Hong Kong, China	..	..	..	..	..	..	..	..	..	..	..	..
Colombia	2,133	0.0	50,426	8.9	0.4	37	4	59	95	98	68	73
Congo, Dem. Rep.	935	313.0	24,496	0.4	0.0	23 [d]	16 [d]	61 [d]	..	89	..	26
Congo, Rep.	222	610.0	275,646	0.0	0.0	11 [d]	27 [d]	62 [d]	..	71	..	17
Costa Rica	112	..	29,494	5.8	5.1	80	7	13	..	98	..	98
Côte d'Ivoire	77	..	4,790	0.7	0.9	67 [d]	11 [d]	22 [d]	89	90	49	65
Croatia	38	33.7	16,301	0.1	1.1	..	50	50	..	..	..	..
Cuba	38	0.0	3,396	5.2	13.7	51	0	49	..	99	..	82
Czech Republic	15	1.0	1,557	2.5	15.8	2	57	41	..	..	..	..
Denmark	6	..	1,124	0.9	14.8	43	27	30	..	100	..	100
Dominican Republic	21	..	2,508	8.3	39.7	89	1	11	83	83	70	70
Ecuador	442	0.0	34,952	17.0	3.8	82	6	12	..	81	..	51
Egypt, Arab Rep.	2	66.7	1,071	55.1	80.4	86 [d]	8 [d]	6 [d]	97	96	91	94
El Salvador	18	..	2,820	0.7	4.1	46	20	34	..	88	47	61
Eritrea	3	6.0	2,148	..	..	..	..	..	..	63	..	42
Estonia	13	0.1	9,350	0.2	1.3	5	39	56	..	..	..	..
Ethiopia	110	0.0	1,711	2.2	2.0	86 [d]	3 [d]	11 [d]	77	77	13	13
Finland	107	3.0	21,248	2.4	2.2	0	82	17	100	100	100	100
France	180	11.0	3,243	40.6	21.3	12	73	15	..	..	..	..
Gabon	164	0.0	133,333	0.1	0.0	6 [d]	22 [d]	72 [d]	..	73	..	55
Gambia, The	3	5.0	6,140	0.0	0.4	91 [d]	2 [d]	7 [d]	..	80	..	53
Georgia	58	8.4	13,236	3.5	5.2	59	20	21	..	..	..	..
Germany	107	71.0	2,167	46.3	26.0	0	86	14	..	..	..	..
Ghana	30	22.9	2,756	0.3	0.6	52 [d]	13 [d]	35 [d]	83	87	43	49
Greece	54	15.0	6,534	7.0	10.2	81	3	16	..	..	..	..
Guatemala	134	0.0	11,805	1.2	0.9	74	17	9	88	97	72	88
Guinea	226	0.0	30,479	0.7	0.3	87 [d]	3 [d]	10 [d]	72	72	36	36
Guinea-Bissau	16	11.0	22,519	0.0	0.1	36 [d]	4 [d]	60 [d]	..	29	..	55
Haiti	12	..	1,520	1.0	8.1	94	1	5	55	49	42	45
Honduras	96	0.0	14,976	1.5	1.6	91	5	4	90	97	79	82

	Freshwater resources			Annual freshwater withdrawals					Access to improved water source			
	Internal flows billion cu.m.	Flows from other countries billion cu.m.	Total resources per capita cu.m.	billion cu.m.[b]	% of total resources[a,b]	% for agriculture[c]	% for industry[c]	% for domestic[c]	% of urban population with access		% of rural population with access	
	2000	2000	2000						1990	2000	1990	2000
Hungary	6	114.0	11,974	6.3	5.2	5	70	14	100	100	98	98
India	1,261	647.2	1,878	500.0	26.2	92	3	5	92	92	73	86
Indonesia	2,838	..	13,487	74.3	2.6	93	1	6	90	91	60	65
Iran, Islamic Rep.	129	..	2,018	70.0	54.5	92	2	6	95	99	75	89
Iraq	35	75.9	4,776	42.8	38.5	92	5	3	..	96	..	48
Ireland	49	3.0	13,706	1.2	2.3	10	74	16	..	..	..	..
Israel	2	0.9	449	1.7	61.1	64 [d]	7 [d]	29 [d]	..	..	..	..
Italy	161	6.8	2,903	57.5	28.6	45	37	18	..	..	..	..
Jamaica	9	..	3,570	0.9	9.6	77	7	15	..	81	..	59
Japan	430	0.0	3,389	91.4	21.3	64	17	19	..	..	..	..
Jordan	1	..	143	1.0	140.0	75	3	22	99	100	92	84
Kazakhstan	75	34.2	7,371	33.7	30.7	81	17	2	..	98	..	82
Kenya	20	10.0	1,004	2.0	6.8	76 [d]	4 [d]	20 [d]	89	87	25	31
Korea, Dem. Rep.	67	10.1	3,462	14.2	18.4	73	16	11	..	..	..	..
Korea, Rep.	65	4.9	1,476	23.7	33.9	63	11	26	..	97	..	71
Kuwait	0	0.0	0	0.5	..	60	2	37	..	..	..	..
Kyrgyz Republic	47	0.0	9,461	10.1	21.7	94	3	3	..	98	..	66
Lao PDR	190	143.1	63,175	1.0	0.3	82	10	8	..	59	..	100
Latvia	17	18.7	14,924	0.3	0.8	13	32	55	..	..	..	..
Lebanon	5	0.0	1,109	1.3	26.9	68	4	28	..	100	..	100
Lesotho	5	0.0	2,555	0.1	1.0	56 [d]	22	22 [d]	..	98	..	88
Liberia	200	32.0	74,121	0.1	0.1	60 [d]	13 [d]	27 [d]	..	..	..	..
Libya	1	0.0	151	3.9	486.3	87 [d]	4 [d]	9 [d]	72	72	68	68
Lithuania	17	7.0	6,857	3.6	14.9	3	16	81	..	..	..	..
Macedonia, FYR	6	1.0	3,447	..	..	..	..	..	..	..	..	..
Madagascar	337	0.0	21,710	19.7	5.8	99 [d]	0 [d]	1 [d]	85	85	31	31
Malawi	18	1.1	1,804	0.9	5.1	86 [d]	3 [d]	10 [d]	90	95	43	44
Malaysia	580	..	24,925	12.7	2.2	76	13	11	..	..	..	94
Mali	60	40.0	9,225	1.4	1.4	97 [d]	1 [d]	2 [d]	65	74	52	61
Mauritania	0	11.0	4,278	16.3	14.3	92	2	6	34	34	40	40
Mauritius	2	0.0	1,855	0.4	16.4	77 [d]	7 [d]	16 [d]	100	100	100	100
Mexico	409	49.0	4,675	77.8	17.0	78	5	17	92	94	61	63
Moldova	1	10.7	2,732	3.0	25.3	26	65	9	..	100	..	100
Mongolia	35	..	14,512	0.4	1.2	53	27	20	..	77	..	30
Morocco	30	0.0	1,045	11.1	36.8	92 [d]	3 [d]	5 [d]	94	100	58	58
Mozambique	100	111.0	11,927	0.6	0.3	89 [d]	2 [d]	9 [d]	..	86	..	43
Myanmar	881	165.0	21,898	4.0	0.4	90	3	7	88	88	56	60
Namibia	6	39.3	25,896	0.3	0.5	68 [d]	3 [d]	29 [d]	98	100	63	67
Nepal	198	12.0	9,122	29.0	13.8	99	0	1	96	85	63	80
Netherlands	11	80.0	5,716	7.8	8.6	34	61	5	100	100	100	100
New Zealand	327	0.0	85,361	2.0	0.6	44	10	46	100	100	..	..
Nicaragua	190	0.0	37,507	1.3	0.7	84	2	14	93	95	44	59
Niger	4	29.0	3,000	0.5	1.5	82 [d]	2 [d]	16 [d]	65	70	51	56
Nigeria	221	59.0	2,206	4.0	1.3	54 [d]	15 [d]	31 [d]	78	81	33	39
Norway	382	11.0	87,508	2.0	0.5	3	68	27	100	100	100	100
Oman	1	..	418	1.2	122.0	94	2	5	41	41	30	30
Pakistan	85	170.3	1,847	155.6	61.0	97	2	2	96	96	79	84
Panama	147	..	51,611	1.6	1.1	70	2	28	..	88	..	86
Papua New Guinea	801	..	156,140	0.1	0.0	49	22	29	88	88	32	32
Paraguay	94	..	17,103	0.4	0.5	78	7	15	80	95	47	58
Peru	1,746	144.0	73,653	19.0	1.0	86	7	7	84	87	47	51
Philippines	479	0.0	6,338	55.4	11.6	88	4	8	94	92	81	80
Poland	55	8.0	1,630	12.1	19.2	11	76	13	..	..	..	..
Portugal	37	35.0	7,194	7.3	10.1	53	40	8	..	..	..	..
Puerto Rico	..	..	..	..	..	..	..	..	..	..	..	..
Romania	49	170.0	9,762	0.0	9.0	..	..	..	..	91	..	16
Russian Federation	4,313	185.5	30,904	77.1	1.7	20	62	19	..	100	..	96

3.5 | Freshwater

	Freshwater resources			Annual freshwater withdrawals					Access to improved water source			
	Internal flows billion cu.m. 2000	Flows from other countries billion cu.m. 2000	Total resources per capita cu.m. 2000	billion cu.m.[b]	% of total resources[a,b]	% for agriculture[c]	% for industry[c]	% for domestic[c]	% of urban population with access 1990	% of urban population with access 2000	% of rural population with access 1990	% of rural population with access 2000
Rwanda	6	..	740	0.8	12.2	94[d]	1[d]	5[d]	..	60	..	40
Saudi Arabia	2	..	116	17.0	708.3	90	1	9	..	100	..	64
Senegal	26	13.0	4,134	1.5	3.5	92[d]	3[d]	5[d]	90	92	60	65
Sierra Leone	160	0.0	31,803	0.4	0.2	89[d]	4[d]	7[d]	..	23	..	31
Singapore	..	..	..	0.0	..	..	..	..	100	100	..	..
Slovak Republic	13	70.0	15,365	1.4	1.7	..	..	..	..	100	..	100
Slovenia	19	0.0	9,306	0.5	2.7	..	50	50	100	100	100	100
Somalia	6	9.7	1,789	0.8	5.2	97[d]	0[d]	3[d]	..	..	..	..
South Africa	45	5.2	1,168	13.3	26.6	72[d]	11[d]	17[d]	..	92	..	80
Spain	112	0.3	2,840	35.5	31.7	62	26	12	..	..	..	..
Sri Lanka	50	0.0	2,583	9.8	19.5	96	2	2	90	91	59	80
Sudan	35	119.0	4,953	17.8	11.6	94[d]	1[d]	5[d]	86	86	60	69
Swaziland	3	1.9	4,306	0.7	14.7	96[d]	2[d]	2[d]	..	..	..	..
Sweden	178	12.2	21,445	2.7	1.4	9	55	36	100	100	100	100
Switzerland	40	13.0	7,382	2.6	4.9	0	58	42	100	100	100	100
Syrian Arab Republic	7	37.7	2,761	14.4	32.2	94	2	4	..	94	..	64
Tajikistan	66	13.3	12,901	11.9	14.9	92	4	4	..	..	..	..
Tanzania	80	9.0	2,641	1.2	1.3	89[d]	2[d]	9[d]	80	80	42	42
Thailand	210	199.9	6,750	33.1	8.1	91	4	5	83	89	68	77
Togo	12	0.5	2,651	0.1	0.8	25[d]	13[d]	62[d]	82	85	38	38
Trinidad and Tobago	..	..	..	0.0	..	..	..	..	..	..	..	..
Tunisia	4	0.4	408	2.8	68.7	86[d]	2[d]	13[d]	94	..	61	..
Turkey	196	7.6	3,118	35.5	17.4	73[d]	11[d]	16[d]	82	82	76	84
Turkmenistan	1	59.5	11,714	23.8	39.0	98	1	1	..	..	..	..
Uganda	39	27.0	2,972	0.2	0.3	60	8	32	80	72	40	46
Ukraine	53	86.5	2,820	26.0	18.6	30	52	18	..	..	..	..
United Arab Emirates	0	0.0	69	2.1	1,055.0	67	9	24	..	..	..	..
United Kingdom	145	2.0	2,461	9.3	6.4	3	77	20	100	100	100	100
United States	2,460	18.0	8,801	447.7	18.9	27[d]	65[d]	8[d]	100	100	100	100
Uruguay	59	74.0	39,856	4.2	3.2	91	3	6	..	98	..	93
Uzbekistan	16	98.1	4,622	58.0	50.7	94	2	4	..	96	..	78
Venezuela, RB	846	..	35,002	4.1	0.5	46	10	44	..	88	..	58
Vietnam	367	524.7	11,350	54.3	6.1	86	10	4	81	81	40	50
West Bank and Gaza	..	..	..	..	..	..	..	..	..	..	..	..
Yemen, Rep.	4	..	234	2.9	71.5	92	1	7	85	85	60	64
Yugoslavia, Fed. Rep.	44	144.0	17,674	..	..	..	..	..	..	..	..	..
Zambia	80	35.8	11,498	1.7	1.5	77[d]	7[d]	16[d]	88	88	28	48
Zimbabwe	14	..	1,117	1.2	8.7	79[d]	7[d]	14[d]	99	100	68	77
World	**42,833 w**	**9,427.3**	**8,696 w**			**71 w**	**19 w**	**9 w**	**94 w**	**93 w**	**64**	**71 w**
Low income	10,449	4,903.6	6,243			90	5	5	89	88	64	70
Middle income	24,239	4,155.8	10,579			74	16	10	95	94	62	69
Lower middle income	14,755	1,253.5	7,836			76	17	7	97	95	62	69
Upper middle income	9,483	2,902.3	19,319			68	13	17	..	92	..	70
Low & middle income	34,687	9,059.4	8,505			81	11	8	93	92	63	70
East Asia & Pacific	9,445	1,420.5	..			80	14	6	96	93	60	66
Europe & Central Asia	5,232	1,134.8	13,426			57	31	11	..	..	..	..
Latin America & Carib.	13,987	2,797.2	32,905			74	9	18	92	93	56	62
Middle East & N. Africa	234	183.1	1,427			89	4	6	93	96	76	80
South Asia	1,849	1,945.1	2,800			93	2	4	93	92	75	85
Sub-Saharan Africa	3,941	1,578.7	8,379			86	4	10	81	82	37	41
High income	8,146	367.9	..			40	43	14	..	..	..	..
Europe EMU	885	258.8	3,783			34	52	14	..	..	..	..

a. River flows from other countries are included when available, but river outflows are not, because of data unreliability. b. Data refer to any year from 1980 to 1999. c. Unless otherwise noted, sectoral withdrawal shares are estimated for 1987. d. Data refer to a year other than 1987 (see *Primary data documentation*).

About the data

The data on freshwater resources are based on estimates of runoff into rivers and recharge of groundwater. These estimates are based on different sources and refer to different years, so cross-country comparisons should be made with caution. Because the data are collected intermittently, they may hide significant variations in total renewable water resources from one year to the next. The data also fail to distinguish between seasonal and geographic variations in water availability within countries. Data for small countries and countries in arid and semiarid zones are less reliable than those for larger countries and countries with greater rainfall. Finally, caution is also needed in comparing data on annual freshwater withdrawals, which are subject to variations in collection and estimation methods.

This year's table shows both internal freshwater resources and the river flows arising outside countries. Because the data on total freshwater resources include river flows entering a country while river flows out of the country are not deducted (because of data unreliability), they overestimate the availability of water from international river ways. This can be important in water-short countries, notably in the Middle East.

The data on access to an improved water source measure the share of the population with reasonable and ready access to an adequate amount of safe water for domestic purposes. An improved source can be any form of collection or piping used to make water regularly available. While information on access to an improved water source is widely used, it is extremely subjective, and such terms as *safe, improved, adequate,* and *reasonable* may have very different meanings in different countries despite official World Health Organization definitions (see *Definitions*). Even in high-income countries treated water may not always be safe to drink. While access to safe water is equated with connection to a public supply system, this does not take into account variations in the quality and cost (broadly defined) of the service once connected. Thus cross-country comparisons must be made cautiously. Changes over time within countries may result from changes in definitions or measurements.

Figure 3.5a

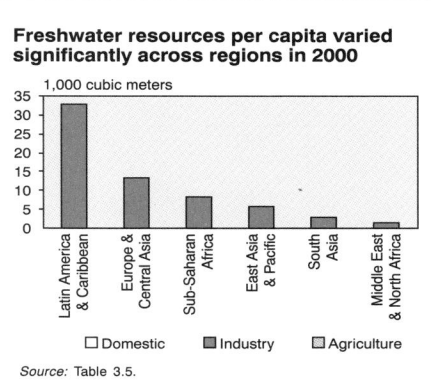

Freshwater resources per capita varied significantly across regions in 2000

Source: Table 3.5.

Figure 3.5b

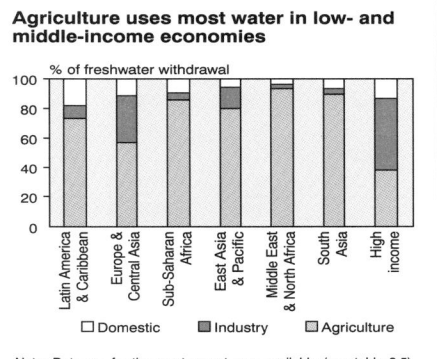

Agriculture uses most water in low- and middle-income economies

Note: Data are for the most recent year available (see table 3.5).
Source: Table 3.5.

Definitions

• **Freshwater resources** refer to total renewable resources, broken down between internal flows of rivers and groundwater from rainfall in the country, and river flows from other countries. Freshwater resources per capita are calculated using the World Bank's population estimates (see table 2.1). • **Annual freshwater withdrawals** refer to total water withdrawal, not counting evaporation losses from storage basins. Withdrawals also include water from desalination plants in countries where they are a significant source. Withdrawal data are for single years between 1980 and 1999 unless otherwise indicated. Withdrawals can exceed 100 percent of total renewable resources where extraction from nonrenewable aquifers or desalination plants is considerable or where there is significant water reuse. Withdrawals for agriculture and industry are total withdrawals for irrigation and livestock production and for direct industrial use (including withdrawals for cooling thermoelectric plants). Withdrawals for domestic uses include drinking water, municipal use or supply, and use for public services, commercial establishments, and homes. For most countries sectoral withdrawal data are estimated for 1987. • **Access to an improved water source** refers to the percentage of the population with reasonable access to an adequate amount of water from an improved source, such as a household connection, public standpipe, borehole, protected well or spring, or rainwater collection. Unimproved sources include vendors, tanker trucks, and unprotected wells and springs. Reasonable access is defined as the availability of at least 20 liters a person a day from a source within one kilometer of the dwelling.

Data sources

The data on freshwater resources and withdrawals are compiled by the World Resources Institute from various sources and published in *World Resources 1998–99* and *World Resources 2000–01* (produced in collaboration with the United Nations Environment Programme, United Nations Development Programme, and the World Bank). These are supplemented by the FAO's AQUASTAT data. The data on access to an improved water source come from the World Health Organization.

3.6 | Water pollution

	Emissions of organic water pollutants				Industry shares of emissions of organic water pollutants							
	kilograms per day		kilograms per day per worker		Primary metals %	Paper and pulp %	Chemicals %	Food and beverages %	Stone, ceramics, and glass %	Textiles %	Wood %	Other %
	1980	1999ª	1980	1999ª	1999ª	1999ª	1999ª	1999ª	1999ª	1999ª	1999ª	1999ª
Afghanistan	6,680	..	0.17	..	..	..	..	..	..	..	..	..
Albania	..	6,512	..	0.29	14.3	0.9	5.5	73.5	0.3	4.6	0.0	0.8
Algeria	60,290	45,645	0.19	0.24	23.4	2.0	5.9	59.5	0.7	7.6	0.8	0.0
Angola	..	1,472	..	0.20	7.6	3.0	9.2	65.9	0.3	5.5	4.4	4.1
Argentina	244,711	177,882	0.18	0.21	6.5	12.5	7.9	59.4	0.1	7.4	1.5	4.5
Armenia	..	10,014	..	0.25	..	..	..	..	..	..	..	..
Australia	204,333	91,544	0.18	0.21	..	..	..	..	..	..	..	..
Austria	108,416	87,294	0.16	0.14	12.2	19.6	9.7	36.5	0.3	6.1	4.5	11.1
Azerbaijan	..	45,025	..	0.17	11.6	2.5	12.0	49.0	0.2	18.1	1.0	5.6
Bangladesh	66,713	186,852	0.16	0.16	2.8	6.8	3.5	34.2	0.1	50.9	0.6	1.1
Belarus	..	..	..	..	..	..	..	..	..	..	..	..
Belgium	136,452	113,460	0.16	0.16	14.4	17.7	11.6	36.8	0.2	8.8	2.0	8.4
Benin	1,646	..	0.28	..	..	..	..	..	..	..	..	..
Bolivia	9,343	12,323	0.22	0.24	3.1	14.2	7.2	64.7	0.3	7.4	2.2	0.9
Bosnia and Herzegovina	..	8,903	..	0.18	20.5	13.1	6.6	33.3	0.2	17.6	5.8	2.8
Botswana	1,307	4,635	0.24	0.20	1.7	15.8	5.4	56.4	0.2	17.2	1.4	1.9
Brazil	866,790	629,406	0.16	0.20	17.7	12.9	9.2	44.4	0.1	9.8	1.4	4.5
Bulgaria	152,125	107,945	0.13	0.17	11.7	7.9	6.6	48.1	0.1	17.0	2.0	6.6
Burkina Faso	2,385	2,598	0.29	0.22	3.5	1.1	5.4	73.8	0.1	4.1	10.1	1.9
Burundi	769	1,644	0.22	0.24	0.0	8.3	4.7	67.8	0.1	16.7	1.6	0.9
Cambodia	..	12,078	..	0.16	0.0	3.4	3.3	59.2	0.6	24.7	5.8	3.1
Cameroon	14,569	10,810	0.29	0.20	3.3	6.2	28.0	52.6	0.0	3.7	5.8	0.4
Canada	330,241	297,370	0.18	0.17	9.5	28.8	9.7	34.3	0.1	5.5	3.9	8.2
Central African Republic	861	670	0.26	0.17	0.0	..	4.0	61.9	0.0	13.9	19.6	0.6
Chad	..	..	..	..	..	..	..	..	..	..	..	..
Chile	44,371	74,583	0.21	0.24	7.7	12.0	8.8	61.4	0.1	5.2	2.4	2.4
China	3,377,105	7,024,090	0.14	0.14	20.3	11.0	14.9	28.9	0.5	15.0	0.7	8.7
Hong Kong, China	102,002	41,639	0.11	0.18	1.3	43.4	4.3	24.2	0.1	20.9	0.3	5.4
Colombia	96,055	105,683	0.19	0.20	3.6	14.2	10.3	51.8	0.2	16.0	0.9	3.0
Congo, Dem. Rep.	..	..	..	..	..	..	..	..	..	..	..	..
Congo, Rep.	1,039	..	0.21	..	..	..	..	..	..	..	..	..
Costa Rica	..	33,975	..	0.22	1.3	9.0	6.2	63.8	0.1	15.4	1.5	2.5
Côte d'Ivoire	15,414	12,401	0.23	0.24	..	5.5	7.1	71.9	0.0	8.6	5.9	1.0
Croatia	..	48,447	..	0.17	7.2	14.4	8.6	45.2	0.2	14.6	3.8	6.0
Cuba	120,703	..	0.24	..	..	..	..	..	..	..	..	..
Czech Republic	..	158,462	..	0.14	15.6	7.0	7.9	43.6	0.3	10.4	3.9	11.4
Denmark	65,465	83,591	0.17	0.17	4.4	29.1	7.9	44.2	0.2	2.2	3.5	8.6
Dominican Republic	54,935	..	0.38	..	..	..	..	..	..	..	..	..
Ecuador	25,297	34,610	0.23	0.27	2.4	10.7	6.2	72.3	0.1	5.6	1.4	1.3
Egypt, Arab Rep.	169,146	208,104	0.19	0.18	12.0	6.9	9.8	47.7	0.3	19.1	0.6	3.5
El Salvador	9,390	22,760	0.24	0.18	2.1	10.2	8.1	43.5	0.1	34.1	0.5	1.4
Eritrea	16,754	..	..	..	..	..	..	..	..	..	..	..
Estonia	..	..	..	..	..	..	..	..	..	..	..	..
Ethiopia	..	20,449	..	0.22	1.9	10.7	4.6	59.1	0.3	21.0	1.8	0.6
Finland	92,275	61,835	0.17	0.20	9.6	42.6	3.1	31.0	0.2	3.0	4.3	6.3
France	729,776	300,964	0.14	0.10	..	..	..	..	..	..	..	..
Gabon	2,661	1,886	0.15	0.26	0.0	6.0	4.9	79.7	0.1	1.2	6.9	1.2
Gambia, The	549	832	0.30	0.34	0.0	15.3	1.9	77.9	0.1	2.6	1.9	0.2
Georgia	..	..	..	..	..	..	..	..	..	..	..	..
Germany	..	811,315	..	0.12	12.7	16.8	15.5	30.6	0.3	4.8	2.2	17.2
Ghana	15,868	14,449	0.20	0.17	9.8	16.9	10.5	39.5	0.2	9.1	12.4	1.7
Greece	65,304	57,722	0.17	0.20	6.0	12.1	8.8	54.2	0.3	13.8	1.4	3.5
Guatemala	20,856	19,253	0.25	0.28	4.9	7.2	6.1	72.8	0.1	6.9	0.8	1.0
Guinea	..	..	..	..	..	..	..	..	..	..	..	..
Guinea-Bissau	..	..	..	..	..	..	..	..	..	..	..	..
Haiti	4,734	..	0.19	..	..	..	..	..	..	..	..	..
Honduras	13,067	34,036	0.23	0.20	1.1	7.8	3.9	55.5	0.1	26.8	4.0	0.8

	Emissions of organic water pollutants				Industry shares of emissions of organic water pollutants							
	kilograms per day		kilograms per day per worker		Primary metals %	Paper and pulp %	Chemicals %	Food and beverages %	Stone, ceramics, and glass %	Textiles %	Wood %	Other %
	1980	1999ª	1980	1999ª	1999ª	1999ª	1999ª	1999ª	1999ª	1999ª	1999ª	1999ª
Hungary	201,888	140,824	0.15	0.17	8.8	10.0	8.0	50.2	0.2	13.4	1.9	7.4
India	1,422,564	1,746,562	0.21	0.19	13.4	8.0	9.2	51.0	0.2	12.9	0.3	5.0
Indonesia	214,010	676,082	0.22	0.20	2.8	7.0	7.1	55.3	0.1	21.1	4.1	2.5
Iran, Islamic Rep.	72,334	101,900	0.15	0.17	20.6	8.0	8.0	39.7	0.5	17.3	0.7	5.4
Iraq	32,986	19,617	0.19	0.16	8.8	14.1	15.1	39.4	0.7	16.7	0.3	4.8
Ireland	43,544	37,886	0.19	0.15	1.8	17.5	11.8	50.1	0.2	5.9	2.0	10.7
Israel	39,113	54,149	0.15	0.16	3.7	19.7	9.4	43.9	0.2	12.1	1.8	9.3
Italy	442,712	354,590	0.13	0.13	12.1	16.1	11.5	28.7	0.3	15.9	2.5	12.9
Jamaica	11,123	17,507	0.25	0.29	6.9	7.2	3.8	70.8	0.1	9.8	1.3	0.6
Japan	1,456,016	1,415,879	0.14	0.14	8.1	21.8	8.8	40.3	0.2	5.9	1.6	13.2
Jordan	4,146	16,142	0.17	0.18	3.9	16.2	14.5	51.4	0.5	7.2	3.3	3.0
Kazakhstan	..	..	..	..	..	..	..	..	..	..	..	..
Kenya	26,834	49,304	0.19	0.24	4.1	12.2	6.1	66.7	0.1	8.8	1.9	0.0
Korea, Dem. Rep.	..	..	..	..	..	..	..	..	..	..	..	..
Korea, Rep.	281,900	288,408	0.14	0.12	12.3	16.1	12.5	27.0	0.2	15.3	1.4	15.2
Kuwait	6,921	10,108	0.16	0.16	2.3	17.0	12.1	45.5	0.4	14.2	2.9	5.5
Kyrgyz Republic	..	20,700	..	0.16	13.7	0.2	0.9	54.8	0.4	21.0	1.0	8.0
Lao PDR	..	..	..	..	..	..	..	..	..	..	..	..
Latvia	..	25,789	..	0.21	2.8	6.7	4.3	67.5	0.1	11.2	7.3	0.0
Lebanon	14,586	..	0.20	..	..	..	..	..	..	..	..	..
Lesotho	993	3,123	0.24	0.16	1.2	4.0	0.7	39.7	0.1	51.3	0.6	2.3
Liberia	..	..	..	..	..	..	..	..	..	..	..	..
Libya	3,532	..	0.21	..	..	..	..	..	..	..	..	..
Lithuania	..	38,615	..	0.18	1.4	10.9	5.0	56.0	0.2	17.6	4.2	4.6
Macedonia, FYR	..	23,490	..	0.18	11.7	9.6	6.2	45.0	0.1	20.9	1.7	4.9
Madagascar	9,131	..	0.23	..	..	..	..	..	..	..	..	..
Malawi	12,224	11,805	0.32	0.29	0.0	16.0	3.7	70.0	0.0	7.8	1.7	0.8
Malaysia	77,215	154,926	0.15	0.11	7.9	13.7	16.1	31.5	0.3	8.6	6.6	15.3
Mali	..	..	..	..	..	..	..	..	..	..	..	..
Mauritania	..	..	..	..	..	..	..	..	..	..	..	..
Mauritius	9,224	15,677	0.21	0.16	1.1	6.6	2.6	36.1	0.1	51.5	0.7	1.2
Mexico	130,993	163,569	0.22	0.17	8.0	8.4	14.0	55.4	0.2	5.2	0.4	8.5
Moldova	..	34,234	..	0.29	0.2	4.0	1.4	81.7	0.2	10.8	1.3	0.5
Mongolia	9,254	7,939	0.19	0.18	1.8	4.3	0.9	63.1	0.3	24.6	4.9	0.0
Morocco	26,598	90,563	0.15	0.18	0.8	7.6	7.2	53.6	0.3	27.0	0.9	2.5
Mozambique	..	495	..	0.16	..	..	..	..	..	..	..	..
Myanmar	..	3,319	..	0.14	17.4	9.0	35.6	28.2	0.5	5.0	3.0	1.2
Namibia	..	7,350	..	0.35	0.0	5.0	1.6	90.4	0.1	1.2	0.9	0.8
Nepal	18,692	26,550	0.25	0.14	1.5	8.1	3.9	43.3	1.2	39.3	1.7	1.0
Netherlands	165,416	120,502	0.18	0.18	7.7	25.8	12.2	42.2	0.2	2.5	1.2	8.3
New Zealand	59,012	50,706	0.21	0.22	4.6	19.6	4.9	58.6	0.1	4.9	3.1	4.2
Nicaragua	9,647	..	0.28	..	..	..	..	..	..	..	..	..
Niger	372	..	0.19	..	..	..	..	..	..	..	..	..
Nigeria	72,082	53,646	0.17	0.18	0.9	31.2	6.5	37.4	0.2	10.6	10.4	2.9
Norway	67,897	52,616	0.19	0.21	5.7	35.4	3.3	44.4	0.1	1.6	3.4	6.1
Oman	..	5,199	..	0.17	4.6	15.2	6.7	52.1	0.8	13.4	3.6	3.5
Pakistan	75,125	100,821	0.17	0.18	11.6	7.0	8.4	39.9	0.2	30.3	0.3	2.3
Panama	8,121	12,145	0.26	0.31	1.5	11.6	5.5	75.2	0.2	5.1	0.5	0.4
Papua New Guinea	4,365	..	0.22	..	..	..	..	..	..	..	..	..
Paraguay	..	3,250	..	0.28	2.3	9.9	6.0	73.6	0.3	6.7	0.3	0.8
Peru	50,367	51,828	0.18	0.21	9.6	12.0	8.4	53.0	0.2	12.3	1.6	2.9
Philippines	182,052	204,879	0.19	0.18	5.2	9.8	7.3	54.5	0.2	16.4	2.0	4.6
Poland	580,869	412,979	0.14	0.15	14.2	4.5	6.7	50.5	0.4	12.8	1.9	9.0
Portugal	105,441	142,761	0.15	0.14	3.5	14.3	5.1	39.5	0.4	25.3	5.1	6.8
Puerto Rico	24,034	17,494	0.16	0.14	0.9	10.9	17.7	40.2	0.2	19.6	1.3	9.1
Romania	343,145	333,168	0.12	0.14	17.1	6.7	9.0	34.3	0.3	18.5	4.8	9.4
Russian Federation	..	1,485,833	..	0.16	17.7	7.4	9.3	46.8	0.3	6.9	2.1	9.5

	Emissions of organic water pollutants				Industry shares of emissions of organic water pollutants							
	kilograms per day		kilograms per day per worker		Primary metals %	Paper and pulp %	Chemicals %	Food and beverages %	Stone, ceramics, and glass %	Textiles %	Wood %	Other %
	1980	1999[a]	1980	1999[a]	1999[a]	1999[a]	1999[a]	1999[a]	1999[a]	1999[a]	1999[a]	1999[a]
Rwanda	..	..	..	..	..	..	..	..	..	..	..	..
Saudi Arabia	18,181	24,436	0.12	0.14	4.4	15.9	21.1	45.1	1.0	3.8	2.0	6.8
Senegal	9,865	10,488	0.31	0.30	0.0	6.3	8.8	78.8	0.0	4.6	0.1	1.3
Sierra Leone	1,612	4,170	0.24	0.32	..	9.6	3.0	82.3	0.1	2.0	2.2	0.8
Singapore	28,558	31,793	0.10	0.09	2.0	28.0	15.1	19.9	0.1	4.0	1.5	29.3
Slovak Republic	..	57,970	..	0.15	17.2	12.7	7.9	37.5	0.3	11.9	2.7	9.9
Slovenia	..	37,321	..	0.16	30.1	15.7	9.1	24.5	0.2	12.1	2.0	6.2
Somalia	..	..	..	..	..	..	..	..	..	..	..	..
South Africa	237,599	238,259	0.17	0.17	11.9	16.9	9.2	40.9	0.2	10.9	3.5	6.5
Spain	376,253	349,151	0.16	0.16	6.8	19.0	8.6	43.6	0.3	9.4	4.0	8.3
Sri Lanka	30,086	83,850	0.18	0.17	1.0	6.5	6.0	47.5	0.2	36.6	1.0	1.2
Sudan	..	..	..	..	..	..	..	..	..	..	..	..
Swaziland	2,826	2,009	0.26	0.23	..	79.8	0.3	..	0.1	16.5	2.0	1.2
Sweden	130,439	93,076	0.15	0.16	10.6	37.3	7.5	28.8	0.1	1.3	3.3	11.1
Switzerland	..	123,752	..	0.17	24.9	23.6	10.4	25.0	0.2	3.2	4.2	8.7
Syrian Arab Republic	36,262	15,115	0.19	0.20	4.1	1.5	3.9	69.8	0.9	19.4	0.2	0.2
Tajikistan	..	..	..	..	..	..	..	..	..	..	..	..
Tanzania	21,084	32,508	0.21	0.26	4.7	10.8	5.0	65.2	0.1	11.8	1.4	1.2
Thailand	213,271	355,819	0.22	0.16	6.1	5.3	5.3	42.2	0.2	35.4	1.5	3.9
Togo	963	..	0.27	..	..	..	..	..	..	..	..	..
Trinidad and Tobago	7,835	11,787	0.18	0.28	4.4	10.9	6.7	72.6	0.1	2.9	1.3	1.2
Tunisia	20,294	46,489	0.16	0.16	6.2	8.1	6.4	40.7	0.4	33.6	1.5	3.3
Turkey	160,173	186,275	0.20	0.16	10.7	7.0	7.6	42.9	0.3	25.5	1.0	5.1
Turkmenistan	..	..	..	..	..	..	..	..	..	..	..	..
Uganda	..	..	..	..	..	..	..	..	..	..	..	..
Ukraine	..	518,995	..	0.17	22.2	3.3	6.9	51.4	0.4	5.9	1.8	8.2
United Arab Emirates	4,524	..	0.15	..	..	..	..	..	..	..	..	..
United Kingdom	964,510	604,572	0.15	0.15	7.4	28.5	11.8	32.9	0.2	6.1	2.4	10.8
United States	2,742,993	2,529,037	0.14	0.14	8.5	32.2	10.3	28.0	0.2	5.9	2.9	11.9
Uruguay	34,270	24,896	0.21	0.25	1.4	10.8	5.9	69.5	0.1	9.5	0.7	2.0
Uzbekistan	..	..	..	..	..	..	..	..	..	..	..	..
Venezuela, RB	84,797	92,026	0.20	0.21	14.1	11.5	9.9	51.8	0.2	7.3	1.7	3.4
Vietnam	..	..	..	..	..	..	..	..	..	..	..	..
West Bank and Gaza	..	..	..	..	..	..	..	..	..	..	..	..
Yemen, Rep.	..	7,823	..	0.25	0.0	9.1	12.9	71.1	0.3	4.9	1.0	0.9
Yugoslavia, Fed. Rep.	..	117,128	..	0.16	10.3	12.3	7.8	44.9	0.3	14.5	2.1	7.9
Zambia	13,605	11,433	0.23	0.22	3.4	10.8	7.3	63.6	0.2	9.3	2.9	2.4
Zimbabwe	32,681	32,988	0.20	0.20	13.6	11.3	5.6	48.1	0.2	15.1	3.0	3.1

Note: Industry shares may not sum to 100 percent because data may be from different years.

a. Data refer to any year from 1993 to 1999.

About the data

Emissions of organic pollutants from industrial activities are a major cause of degradation of water quality. Water quality and pollution levels are generally measured in terms of concentration, or load—the rate of occurrence of a substance in an aqueous solution. Polluting substances include organic matter, metals, minerals, sediment, bacteria, and toxic chemicals. This table focuses on organic water pollution resulting from industrial activities. Because water pollution tends to be sensitive to local conditions, the national-level data in the table may not reflect the quality of water in specific locations.

The data in the table come from an international study of industrial emissions that may be the first to include data from developing countries (Hettige, Mani, and Wheeler 1998). These data have been updated through 1999 by the World Bank's Development Research Group. Unlike estimates from earlier studies based on engineering or economic models, these estimates are based on actual measurements of plant-level water pollution. The focus is on organic water pollution, measured in terms of biochemical oxygen demand (BOD), because the data for this indicator are the most plentiful and the most reliable for cross-country comparisons of emissions. BOD measures the strength of an organic waste in terms of the amount of oxygen consumed in breaking it down. A sewage overload in natural waters exhausts the water's dissolved oxygen content. Wastewater treatment, by contrast, reduces BOD.

Data on water pollution are more readily available than other emissions data because most industrial pollution control programs start by regulating emissions of organic water pollutants. Such data are fairly reliable because sampling techniques for measuring water pollution are more widely understood and much less expensive than those for air pollution.

In their study Hettige, Mani, and Wheeler (1998) used plant- and sector-level information on emissions and employment from 13 national environmental protection agencies and sector-level information on output and employment from the United Nations Industrial Development Organization (UNIDO). Their econometric analysis found that the ratio of BOD to employment in each industrial sector is about the same across countries. This finding allowed the authors to estimate BOD loads across countries and over time. The estimated BOD intensities per unit of employment were multiplied by sectoral employment numbers from UNIDO's industry database for 1980–98. The sectoral emissions estimates were then totaled to get daily emissions of organic water pollutants in kilograms per day for each country and year. The data in the table were derived by updating these estimates through 1999.

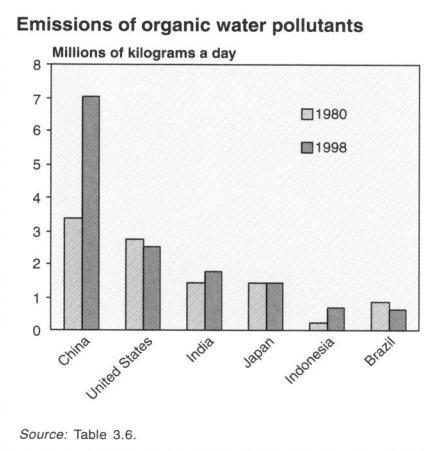

Figure 3.6a

Source: Table 3.6.

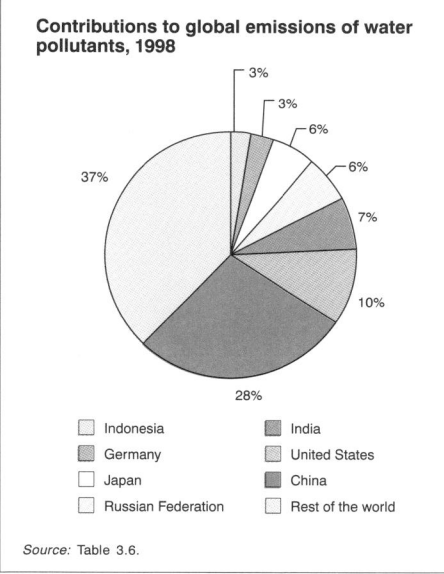

Figure 3.6b

Source: Table 3.6.

Definitions

• **Emissions of organic water pollutants** are measured in terms of biochemical oxygen demand, which refers to the amount of oxygen that bacteria in water will consume in breaking down waste. This is a standard water treatment test for the presence of organic pollutants. Emissions per worker are total emissions divided by the number of industrial workers.
• **Industry shares of emissions of organic water pollutants** refer to emissions from manufacturing activities as defined by two-digit divisions of the International Standard Industrial Classification (ISIC) revision 2: primary metals (ISIC division 37), paper and pulp (34), chemicals (35), food and beverages (31), stone, ceramics, and glass (36), textiles (32), wood (33), and other (38 and 39).

Data sources

Indicators in this table were drawn from a 1998 study by Hemamala Hettige, Muthukumara Mani, and David Wheeler, "Industrial Pollution in Economic Development: Kuznets Revisited" (available on the Web at www.worldbank.org/nipr). These indicators were then updated through 1999 by the World Bank's Development Research Group using the same methodology as the initial study. Sectoral employment numbers are from UNIDO's industry database.

3.7 | Energy production and use

	Commercial energy production		Commercial energy use			Commercial energy use per capita			Net energy imports[a]	
	thousand metric tons of oil equivalent		thousand metric tons of oil equivalent		average annual % growth	kg of oil equivalent		average annual % growth	% of commercial energy use	
	1980	1999	1980	1999	1980-99	1980	1999	1980-99	1980	1999
Afghanistan	..	..	..	..	..	..	..	..	..	..
Albania	3,428	865	3,049	1,052	-6.7	1,142	311	-7.8	-12	18
Algeria	66,741	142,883	12,088	28,280	3.6	647	944	1.1	-452	-405
Angola	11,301	43,644	4,437	7,591	2.9	628	595	-0.2	-155	-475
Argentina	38,813	81,932	41,868	63,182	2.4	1,490	1,727	0.9	7	-30
Armenia	1,263	646	1,070	1,845	..	..	485	..	..	65
Australia	86,096	212,204	70,372	107,930	2.4	4,790	5,690	1.0	-22	-97
Austria	7,561	9,520	22,823	28,432	1.6	3,022	3,513	1.1	67	67
Azerbaijan	14,821	19,037	15,001	12,574	..	..	1,575	..	..	-51
Bangladesh	6,745	14,474	8,441	17,935	4.2	99	139	1.9	20	19
Belarus	2,566	3,475	2,385	23,895	..	..	2,381	..	..	85
Belgium	7,986	13,766	46,100	58,642	1.8	4,682	5,735	1.6	83	77
Benin	1,212	1,556	1,363	1,973	1.9	394	323	-1.2	11	21
Bolivia	4,374	6,020	2,438	4,572	3.5	455	562	1.2	-79	-32
Bosnia and Herzegovina	..	705	..	2,008	..	..	518	..	..	65
Botswana	..	..	..	..	..	..	..	..	..	..
Brazil	62,372	133,654	111,471	179,701	2.7	917	1,068	1.0	44	26
Bulgaria	7,737	9,056	28,673	18,203	-2.6	3,236	2,218	-2.1	73	50
Burkina Faso	..	..	..	..	..	..	..	..	..	..
Burundi	..	..	..	..	..	..	..	..	..	..
Cambodia	..	..	..	..	..	..	..	..	..	..
Cameroon	6,707	12,109	3,676	6,103	2.5	421	419	-0.3	-82	-98
Canada	207,417	366,554	193,000	241,780	1.6	7,848	7,929	0.4	-7	-52
Central African Republic	..	..	..	..	..	..	..	..	..	..
Chad	..	..	..	..	..	..	..	..	..	..
Chile	5,801	7,668	9,662	25,348	5.7	867	1,688	4.0	40	70
China	608,625	1,056,963	592,511	1,088,349	3.8	604	868	2.4	-3	3
Hong Kong, China	39	48	5,439	17,886	5.9	1,079	2,661	4.5	99	100
Colombia	18,040	77,142	19,348	28,081	2.6	680	676	0.6	7	-175
Congo, Dem. Rep.	8,697	14,860	8,706	14,525	2.7	324	293	-0.6	0	-2
Congo, Rep.	4,024	14,079	862	720	-1.2	516	245	-4.2	-367	-1,855
Costa Rica	767	1,322	1,527	3,052	4.1	669	818	1.4	50	57
Côte d'Ivoire	2,419	5,973	3,662	6,052	2.5	447	388	-0.9	34	1
Croatia	..	3,721	..	8,156	..	..	1,864	..	..	54
Cuba	4,227	5,242	14,910	12,464	-1.8	1,536	1,117	-2.6	72	58
Czech Republic	41,208	27,952	47,254	38,584	-1.2	4,618	3,754	-1.2	13	28
Denmark	896	23,642	19,734	20,070	0.8	3,852	3,773	0.6	95	-18
Dominican Republic	1,327	1,491	3,491	7,451	3.9	613	904	2.0	62	80
Ecuador	11,745	21,730	5,180	8,750	2.7	651	705	0.3	-127	-148
Egypt, Arab Rep.	34,168	58,460	15,970	44,490	4.7	391	709	2.3	-114	-31
El Salvador	1,623	2,136	2,537	4,005	2.2	553	651	0.6	25	47
Eritrea	..	..	..	..	..	..	..	..	..	..
Estonia	6,951	2,762	6,275	4,557	..	..	3,286	..	..	39
Ethiopia	10,575	17,176	11,145	18,227	2.6	295	290	-0.1	5	6
Finland	6,912	15,402	25,413	33,372	1.7	5,317	6,461	1.3	73	54
France	46,799	127,617	187,766	255,043	2.0	3,485	4,351	1.5	75	50
Gabon	9,441	17,842	1,493	1,608	-0.3	2,158	1,342	-3.2	-532	-1,010
Gambia, The	..	..	..	..	..	..	..	..	..	..
Georgia	1,504	739	4,474	2,573	..	..	512	..	..	71
Germany	185,628	132,961	360,385	337,196	-0.2	4,602	4,108	-0.5	48	61
Ghana	3,305	5,540	4,027	7,108	3.6	375	377	0.4	18	22
Greece	3,696	9,812	15,695	26,894	3.0	1,628	2,552	2.5	76	64
Guatemala	2,503	4,566	3,754	6,074	3.0	550	548	0.4	33	25
Guinea	..	..	..	..	..	..	..	..	..	..
Guinea-Bissau	..	..	..	..	..	..	..	..	..	..
Haiti	1,877	1,578	2,099	2,067	0.2	392	265	-1.8	11	24
Honduras	1,315	1,817	1,892	3,267	3.1	530	522	0.1	30	44

	Commercial energy production		Commercial energy use			Commercial energy use per capita			Net energy imports[a]	
	thousand metric tons of oil equivalent		thousand metric tons of oil equivalent		average annual % growth	kg of oil equivalent		average annual % growth	% of commercial energy use	
	1980	1999	1980	1999	1980-99	1980	1999	1980-99	1980	1999
Hungary	14,935	11,491	28,940	25,289	-1.0	2,703	2,512	-0.7	48	55
India	222,418	409,788	242,592	480,418	3.8	353	482	1.8	8	15
Indonesia	128,996	226,378	59,933	136,121	4.8	404	658	3.0	-115	-66
Iran, Islamic Rep.	81,142	229,406	38,987	103,635	5.6	996	1,651	3.0	-108	-121
Iraq	136,643	131,754	12,030	28,802	4.6	925	1,263	1.5	-1,036	-357
Ireland	1,894	2,513	8,485	13,979	2.6	2,495	3,726	2.3	78	82
Israel	153	615	8,563	18,493	5.2	2,208	3,029	2.6	98	97
Italy	19,644	27,754	138,629	169,041	1.3	2,456	2,932	1.2	86	84
Jamaica	224	641	2,378	4,136	4.0	1,115	1,597	3.0	91	85
Japan	43,281	104,223	346,527	515,447	2.7	2,967	4,070	2.3	88	80
Jordan	1	286	1,714	4,871	5.0	786	1,028	0.5	100	94
Kazakhstan	76,799	64,668	76,799	35,439	..	..	2,374	..	0	-82
Kenya	7,891	12,129	9,791	14,690	2.2	589	499	-0.8	19	17
Korea, Dem. Rep.	29,135	54,198	31,914	58,925	4.0	1,856	2,658	2.6	9	8
Korea, Rep.	9,644	31,852	41,238	181,365	9.3	1,082	3,871	8.2	77	82
Kuwait	91,636	104,291	12,249	17,289	0.3	8,908	8,984	-0.3	-648	-503
Kyrgyz Republic	2,190	1,301	1,717	2,451	..	..	504	..	..	47
Lao PDR	..	..	..	..	..	..	..	..	..	..
Latvia	261	1,497	566	3,822	..	..	1,586	..	..	61
Lebanon	178	161	2,524	5,469	4.8	841	1,280	2.8	93	97
Lesotho	..	..	..	..	..	..	..	..	..	..
Liberia	..	..	..	..	..	..	..	..	..	..
Libya	96,550	73,420	7,193	12,254	3.9	2,364	2,370	1.2	-1,242	-499
Lithuania	..	3,540	..	7,909	..	..	2,138	..	..	55
Macedonia, FYR	..	..	..	..	..	..	..	..	..	..
Madagascar	..	..	..	..	..	..	..	..	..	..
Malawi	..	..	..	..	..	..	..	..	..	..
Malaysia	18,202	73,411	12,162	42,650	7.8	884	1,878	4.9	-50	-72
Mali	..	..	..	..	..	..	..	..	..	..
Mauritania	..	..	..	..	..	..	..	..	..	..
Mauritius	..	..	..	..	..	..	..	..	..	..
Mexico	149,359	221,771	98,898	148,991	2.1	1,464	1,543	0.2	-51	-49
Moldova	35	63	..	2,813	..	..	656	..	..	98
Mongolia	..	..	..	..	..	..	..	..	..	..
Morocco	877	615	4,778	9,931	4.2	247	352	2.1	82	94
Mozambique	7,413	7,067	8,074	6,985	-0.9	668	404	-2.6	8	..
Myanmar	9,513	13,943	9,430	12,897	1.4	280	273	-0.4	-1	-8
Namibia	..	270	..	1,108	..	..	645	..	..	76
Nepal	4,630	7,035	4,805	8,051	2.8	330	358	0.4	4	13
Netherlands	71,821	59,054	64,984	74,068	1.4	4,593	4,686	0.8	-11	20
New Zealand	5,485	15,143	9,210	18,176	3.8	2,959	4,770	2.7	40	17
Nicaragua	910	1,482	1,555	2,664	2.7	532	539	0.0	41	44
Niger	..	..	..	..	..	..	..	..	..	..
Nigeria	148,479	178,822	52,846	87,286	2.6	743	705	-0.4	-181	-105
Norway	55,716	209,765	18,792	26,606	1.8	4,593	5,965	1.3	-196	-688
Oman	15,090	54,504	996	8,469	11.3	905	3,607	6.8	-1,415	-544
Pakistan	20,997	44,091	25,472	59,830	4.7	308	444	2.1	18	26
Panama	529	704	1,821	2,347	2.2	934	835	0.2	71	70
Papua New Guinea	..	..	..	..	..	..	..	..	..	..
Paraguay	1,605	6,741	2,089	4,140	4.4	671	773	1.5	23	-63
Peru	14,655	11,659	11,700	13,101	1.0	675	519	-0.9	-25	11
Philippines	10,670	19,681	21,212	40,728	3.9	442	549	1.5	50	52
Poland	122,224	83,394	123,035	93,382	-1.4	3,458	2,416	-1.8	1	11
Portugal	1,481	1,940	10,291	23,627	4.5	1,054	2,365	4.5	86	92
Puerto Rico	..	..	..	..	..	..	..	..	..	..
Romania	52,587	27,859	65,123	36,432	-3.0	2,933	1,622	-3.1	19	24
Russian Federation	748,647	950,589	763,707	602,952	..	..	4,121	..	..	-58

	Commercial energy production		Commercial energy use			Commercial energy use per capita			Net energy imports[a]	
	thousand metric tons of oil equivalent		thousand metric tons of oil equivalent		average annual % growth	kg of oil equivalent		average annual % growth	% of commercial energy use	
	1980	1999	1980	1999	1980-99	1980	1999	1980-99	1980	1999
Rwanda	..	..	..	..	..	..	..	..	..	..
Saudi Arabia	533,071	448,735	35,357	84,907	4.4	3,773	4,204	0.3	-1,408	-429
Senegal	1,046	1,684	1,921	2,957	2.3	347	318	-0.4	46	43
Sierra Leone	..	..	..	..	..	..	..	..	..	..
Singapore	..	64	6,062	22,693	9.0	2,511	5,742	6.3	..	100
Slovak Republic	3,418	5,136	21,040	17,991	-1.3	4,221	3,335	-1.7	84	71
Slovenia	..	2,985	..	6,506	..	..	3,277	..	..	54
Somalia	..	..	..	..	..	..	..	..	..	..
South Africa	73,169	143,993	65,417	109,334	2.2	2,372	2,597	-0.1	-12	-32
Spain	15,636	30,691	68,576	118,467	3.1	1,834	3,005	2.9	77	74
Sri Lanka	3,209	4,547	4,536	7,728	2.4	308	406	1.1	29	41
Sudan	7,089	17,034	8,406	15,372	2.9	435	503	0.6	16	-11
Swaziland	..	..	..	..	..	..	..	..	..	..
Sweden	16,132	34,489	39,911	51,094	1.2	4,803	5,769	0.8	60	32
Switzerland	7,030	11,805	20,861	26,689	1.5	3,301	3,738	0.7	66	56
Syrian Arab Republic	9,502	34,205	5,348	18,049	5.5	614	1,143	2.2	-78	-90
Tajikistan	1,986	1,381	..	3,344	..	..	543	..	..	59
Tanzania	9,502	14,269	10,280	15,033	2.0	553	457	-1.0	8	5
Thailand	11,182	38,499	22,808	70,415	7.6	488	1,169	6.1	51	45
Togo	562	1,015	715	1,373	3.6	284	313	0.7	21	26
Trinidad and Tobago	13,141	16,079	3,873	8,022	3.1	3,579	6,205	2.2	-239	-100
Tunisia	6,966	7,120	3,907	7,673	3.7	612	811	1.6	-78	7
Turkey	17,077	26,903	31,452	70,326	4.6	707	1,093	2.6	46	62
Turkmenistan	8,034	26,331	7,948	13,644	..	..	2,677	..	..	-93
Uganda	..	..	..	..	..	..	..	..	..	..
Ukraine	109,708	81,923	97,893	148,389	..	..	2,973	..	..	45
United Arab Emirates	89,716	135,681	6,112	28,085	8.4	5,860	9,977	2.9	-1,368	-383
United Kingdom	196,792	281,674	201,284	230,324	1.0	3,573	3,871	0.7	2	-22
United States	1,553,263	1,687,886	1,811,650	2,269,985	1.5	7,973	8,159	0.4	14	26
Uruguay	763	961	2,641	3,232	1.5	906	976	0.8	71	70
Uzbekistan	4,615	55,109	4,821	49,383	..	..	2,024	..	..	-12
Venezuela, RB	139,392	209,707	34,962	53,406	2.4	2,317	2,253	0.0	-299	-293
Vietnam	18,364	44,858	19,573	35,209	3.1	364	454	1.1	6	-27
West Bank and Gaza	..	..	..	..	..	..	..	..	..	..
Yemen, Rep.	60	20,247	1,424	3,139	4.2	167	184	0.3	96	-545
Yugoslavia, Fed. Rep.	..	10,096	..	13,375	..	..	1,258	..	..	25
Zambia	4,198	5,784	4,551	6,190	1.3	793	626	-1.6	8	7
Zimbabwe	5,793	8,322	6,570	10,170	2.6	921	821	-0.3	12	18
World	6,907,812 t	9,714,082 t	6,929,212 t	9,635,465 t	2.9 w	1,482 w	1,671 w	1.1 w	.. w	.. w
Low income	819,980	1,359,334	674,896	1,262,983	4.9	391	567	2.6	-23	-8
Middle income	3,308,639	4,648,785	2,490,055	3,506,451	4.4	895	1,325	2.8	-33	-33
Lower middle income	1,931,423	2,962,555	1,755,632	2,308,831	5.4	660	1,146	4.0	-9	-28
Upper middle income	1,377,216	1,686,230	734,423	1,197,620	2.8	1,601	1,897	1.0	-94	-41
Low & middle income	4,128,619	6,008,119	3,164,951	4,769,434	4.5	676	979	2.6	-31	-26
East Asia & Pacific	844,331	1,559,783	810,781	1,666,659	4.5	587	920	3.0	-5	6
Europe & Central Asia	1,241,994	1,420,239	1,332,872	1,240,388	7.8	3,348	2,628	..	..	-15
Latin America & Carib.	475,362	816,043	381,870	588,053	2.4	1,071	1,171	0.6	-24	-39
Middle East & N. Africa	986,110	1,208,951	145,640	365,967	4.8	838	1,279	2.0	-580	-230
South Asia	257,999	479,935	285,846	573,962	3.9	323	441	1.8	10	16
Sub-Saharan Africa	322,823	523,168	207,942	334,405	2.3	713	671	-0.6	-57	-56
High income	2,779,193	3,705,963	3,764,261	4,866,031	1.7	4,794	5,448	1.0	26	24
Europe EMU	369,087	431,075	952,790	1,142,253	1.2	3,337	3,785	0.9	61	62

About the data

In developing countries growth in commercial energy use is closely related to growth in the modern sectors—industry, motorized transport, and urban areas—but commercial energy use also reflects climatic, geographic, and economic factors (such as the relative price of energy). Commercial energy use has been growing rapidly in low- and middle-income countries, but high-income countries still use more than five times as much on a per capita basis. Because commercial energy is widely traded, it is necessary to distinguish between its production and its use. Net energy imports show the extent to which an economy's use exceeds its domestic production. High-income countries are net energy importers; middle-income countries have been their main suppliers.

Energy data are compiled by the International Energy Agency (IEA) and the United Nations Statistics Division (UNSD). IEA data for non-OECD countries are based on national energy data adjusted to conform to annual questionnaires completed by OECD member governments. UNSD data are primarily from responses to questionnaires sent to national governments, supplemented by official national statistical publications and by data from intergovernmental organizations. When official data are not available, the UNSD prepares estimates based on the professional and commercial literature. This variety of sources affects the cross-country comparability of data.

Commercial energy use refers to the use of domestic primary energy before transformation to other end-use fuels (such as electricity and refined petroleum products). It includes energy from combustible renewables and waste, which comprises solid biomass and animal products, gas and liquid from biomass, industrial waste, and municipal waste. Biomass is defined as any plant matter used directly as fuel or converted into fuel, heat, or electricity. (The data series published in *World Development Indicators 1998* and earlier editions did not include energy from combustible renewables and waste.) All forms of commercial energy—primary energy and primary electricity—are converted into oil equivalents. To convert nuclear electricity into oil equivalents, a notional thermal efficiency of 33 percent is assumed; for hydroelectric power, 100 percent efficiency is assumed.

Figure 3.7

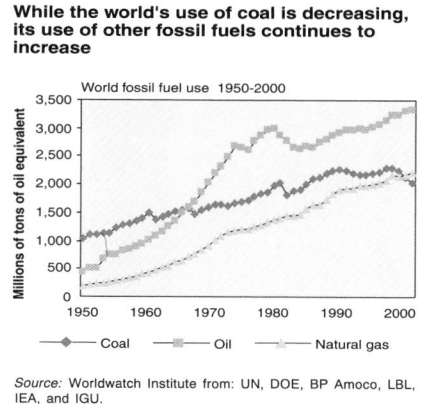

While the world's use of coal is decreasing, its use of other fossil fuels continues to increase

World fossil fuel use 1950-2000

Source: Worldwatch Institute from: UN, DOE, BP Amoco, LBL, IEA, and IGU.

Definitions

• **Commercial energy production** refers to commercial forms of primary energy—petroleum (crude oil, natural gas liquids, and oil from nonconventional sources), natural gas, and solid fuels (coal, lignite, and other derived fuels)—and primary electricity, all converted into oil equivalents (see *About the data*).
• **Commercial energy use** refers to apparent consumption, which is equal to indigenous production plus imports and stock changes, minus exports and fuels supplied to ships and aircraft engaged in international transport (see *About the data*). • **Net energy imports** are calculated as energy use less production, both measured in oil equivalents. A negative value indicates that the country is a net exporter.

Data sources

The data on commercial energy production and use are primarily from IEA electronic files and from the United Nations Statistics Division's *Energy Statistics Yearbook*. The IEA's data are published in its annual publications, *Energy Statistics and Balances of Non-OECD Countries, Energy Statistics of OECD Countries,* and *Energy Balances of OECD Countries.*

	GDP per unit of energy use		Traditional fuel use		Carbon dioxide emissions					
	PPP $ per kg oil equivalent		% of total energy use		Total million metric tons		Per capita metric tons		kg per PPP $ of GDP	
	1980	1999	1980	1997	1980	1998	1980	1998	1980	1998
Afghanistan	..	..	63.0	75.6	1.7	1.0	0.1	0.0	..	0.0
Albania	..	10.4	13.1	7.3	4.8	1.6	1.8	0.5	..	0.2
Algeria	4.9	5.4	1.9	1.5	66.1	106.6	3.5	3.6	1.1	0.7
Angola	..	4.4	64.9	69.7	5.3	5.9	0.8	0.5	..	0.2
Argentina	4.7	7.1	5.9	4.0	107.5	136.9	3.8	3.8	0.6	0.3
Armenia	..	4.9	..	0.0	..	3.4	..	0.9	..	0.4
Australia	2.1	4.4	3.8	4.4	202.8	331.5	13.8	17.7	1.4	0.7
Austria	3.5	7.2	1.2	4.7	52.4	63.9	6.9	7.9	0.7	0.3
Azerbaijan	..	1.6	..	0.0	..	38.8	..	4.9	..	2.2
Bangladesh	5.7	10.8	81.3	46.0	7.6	23.4	0.1	0.2	0.2	0.1
Belarus	..	2.9	..	0.8	..	60.5	..	6.0	..	0.9
Belgium	2.4	4.5	0.2	1.6	131.3	101.3	13.3	9.9	1.2	0.4
Benin	1.3	2.9	85.4	89.2	0.5	0.7	0.1	0.1	0.3	0.1
Bolivia	3.2	4.2	19.3	14.0	4.5	12.1	0.8	1.5	0.6	0.6
Bosnia and Herzegovina	..	..	..	10.1	..	4.7	..	1.2	..	0.0
Botswana	..	..	35.7	..	1.0	3.8	1.1	2.4	0.6	0.4
Brazil	4.4	6.7	35.5	28.7	183.4	299.6	1.5	1.8	0.4	0.3
Bulgaria	0.9	2.3	0.5	1.3	75.3	47.4	8.5	5.7	2.9	1.2
Burkina Faso	..	..	91.3	87.1	0.4	1.0	0.1	0.1	0.2	0.1
Burundi	..	..	97.0	94.2	0.1	0.2	0.0	0.0	0.1	0.1
Cambodia	..	..	100.0	89.3	0.3	0.7	0.0	0.1	..	0.0
Cameroon	2.8	3.8	51.7	69.2	3.9	1.8	0.4	0.1	0.4	0.1
Canada	1.5	3.3	0.4	4.7	420.9	467.2	17.1	15.4	1.4	0.6
Central African Republic	..	..	88.9	87.5	0.1	0.2	0.0	0.1	0.1	0.1
Chad	..	..	95.9	97.6	0.2	0.1	0.0	0.0	0.1	0.0
Chile	3.2	5.2	12.3	11.3	27.5	60.2	2.5	4.1	0.9	0.5
China	0.8	4.2	8.4	5.7	1,476.8	3,108.0	1.5	2.5	3.2	0.7
Hong Kong, China	6.4	8.4	0.9	0.7	16.3	35.8	3.2	5.4	0.5	0.3
Colombia	12.0	9.3	15.9	17.7	39.8	67.8	1.4	1.7	0.2	0.3
Congo, Dem. Rep.	3.3	2.6	73.9	91.7	3.5	2.4	0.1	0.1	0.1	0.1
Congo, Rep.	0.8	2.8	77.8	53.0	0.4	1.8	0.2	0.6	0.6	0.8
Costa Rica	5.8	10.8	26.3	54.2	2.5	5.1	1.1	1.4	0.3	0.2
Côte d'Ivoire	2.9	4.3	52.8	91.5	4.6	13.2	0.6	0.9	0.4	0.5
Croatia	..	4.1	..	3.2	..	19.8	..	4.5	..	0.6
Cuba	..	..	27.9	30.2	30.8	24.9	3.2	2.2	..	0.0
Czech Republic	..	3.5	0.6	1.6	..	118.3	..	11.5	..	0.9
Denmark	3.0	6.9	0.4	5.9	62.9	53.4	12.3	10.1	1.1	0.4
Dominican Republic	3.6	6.2	27.5	14.3	6.4	20.3	1.1	2.5	0.5	0.5
Ecuador	3.0	4.5	26.7	17.5	13.4	26.3	1.7	2.2	0.9	0.7
Egypt, Arab Rep.	3.5	4.9	4.7	3.2	45.2	105.8	1.1	1.7	0.8	0.5
El Salvador	4.3	6.8	52.9	34.5	2.1	6.1	0.5	1.0	0.2	0.2
Eritrea	..	..	..	96.0	..	0.0	..	0.0	..	0.0
Estonia	..	2.6	..	13.8	..	17.0	..	12.1	..	1.4
Ethiopia	1.4	2.2	89.6	95.9	1.8	2.0	0.0	0.0	0.1	0.1
Finland	1.8	3.6	4.3	6.5	56.9	53.3	11.9	10.3	1.3	0.5
France	2.9	5.3	1.3	5.7	482.7	369.9	9.0	6.3	0.9	0.3
Gabon	1.9	4.5	30.8	32.9	6.2	2.8	8.9	2.4	2.2	0.4
Gambia, The	..	..	72.7	78.6	0.2	0.2	0.2	0.2	0.3	0.1
Georgia	..	4.8	..	1.0	..	5.2	..	1.0	..	0.4
Germany	2.3	5.8	0.3	1.3	..	825.2	..	10.1	..	0.4
Ghana	2.8	5.0	43.7	78.1	2.4	4.4	0.2	0.2	0.2	0.1
Greece	4.8	6.0	3.0	4.5	51.7	85.2	5.4	8.1	0.7	0.6
Guatemala	4.1	6.8	54.6	62.0	4.5	9.7	0.7	0.9	0.3	0.3
Guinea	..	..	71.4	74.2	0.9	1.2	0.2	0.2	..	0.1
Guinea-Bissau	..	..	80.0	57.1	0.5	0.0	0.7	0.0	1.8	0.0
Haiti	3.6	5.5	80.7	74.7	0.8	1.3	0.1	0.2	0.1	0.1
Honduras	2.9	4.5	55.3	54.8	2.1	5.1	0.6	0.8	0.4	0.3

	GDP per unit of energy use		Traditional fuel use		Carbon dioxide emissions					
	PPP $ per kg oil equivalent		% of total energy use		Total million metric tons		Per capita metric tons		kg per PPP $ of GDP	
	1980	1999	1980	1997	1980	1998	1980	1998	1980	1998
Hungary	2.0	4.6	2.0	1.6	82.5	58.7	7.7	5.8	1.4	0.5
India	1.9	4.7	31.5	20.7	347.3	1,061.0	0.5	1.1	0.8	0.5
Indonesia	2.2	4.4	51.5	29.3	94.6	233.6	0.6	1.1	0.7	0.4
Iran, Islamic Rep.	2.9	3.4	0.4	0.7	116.1	289.9	3.0	4.7	1.0	0.9
Iraq	..	..	0.3	0.1	44.0	82.4	3.4	3.7	..	0.0
Ireland	2.3	7.0	0.0	0.2	25.2	38.3	7.4	10.3	1.3	0.5
Israel	3.6	6.1	0.0	0.0	21.1	60.3	5.4	10.1	0.7	0.6
Italy	3.9	7.7	0.8	1.0	371.9	414.9	6.6	7.2	0.7	0.3
Jamaica	1.7	2.2	5.0	6.0	8.4	11.0	4.0	4.3	2.1	1.2
Japan	3.4	6.3	0.1	1.6	920.4	1,133.5	7.9	9.0	0.8	0.4
Jordan	3.2	3.8	0.0	0.0	4.7	13.9	2.2	3.0	0.8	0.8
Kazakhstan	..	2.1	..	0.2	..	122.9	..	8.2	..	1.7
Kenya	1.1	2.1	76.8	80.3	6.2	9.1	0.4	0.3	0.6	0.3
Korea, Dem. Rep.	..	..	3.1	1.4	124.9	226.1	7.3	10.3	..	0.0
Korea, Rep.	2.8	4.1	4.0	2.4	125.1	363.7	3.3	7.8	1.1	0.6
Kuwait	1.3	1.8	0.0	0.0	24.7	49.1	18.0	26.3	1.6	1.7
Kyrgyz Republic	..	5.0	..	0.0	..	6.4	..	1.3	..	0.6
Lao PDR	..	..	72.3	88.7	0.2	0.4	0.1	0.1	..	0.1
Latvia	..	4.1	..	26.2	..	7.9	..	3.2	..	0.5
Lebanon	..	3.3	2.4	2.5	6.2	16.3	2.1	3.9	..	0.9
Lesotho	..	..	..	..	..	0.0	..	0.0	..	0.0
Liberia	..	..	62.5	89.7	2.0	0.4	1.1	0.1	..	0.0
Libya	..	..	2.3	0.9	26.9	36.4	8.8	7.2	..	0.0
Lithuania	..	3.1	..	6.3	..	15.6	..	4.2	..	0.6
Macedonia, FYR	..	..	..	6.1	..	12.4	..	6.1	..	1.4
Madagascar	..	..	78.4	84.3	1.6	1.3	0.2	0.1	0.3	0.1
Malawi	..	..	90.6	88.6	0.7	0.7	0.1	0.1	0.3	0.1
Malaysia	2.7	4.3	15.7	5.5	28.0	120.5	2.0	5.4	0.8	0.7
Mali	..	..	86.7	88.9	0.4	0.5	0.1	0.0	0.1	0.1
Mauritania	..	..	0.0	0.0	0.6	2.9	0.4	1.2	0.4	0.7
Mauritius	..	..	59.1	36.1	0.6	1.7	0.6	1.5	0.3	0.2
Mexico	3.1	5.4	5.0	4.5	252.5	374.0	3.7	3.9	0.8	0.5
Moldova	..	3.2	..	0.5	..	9.7	..	2.2	..	1.1
Mongolia	..	..	14.4	4.3	6.8	7.7	4.1	3.3	3.5	2.0
Morocco	6.8	10.0	5.2	4.0	15.9	32.0	0.8	1.2	0.5	0.3
Mozambique	0.6	2.1	43.7	91.4	3.2	1.3	0.3	0.1	0.7	0.1
Myanmar	..	..	69.3	60.5	4.8	8.2	0.1	0.2	..	0.0
Namibia	..	9.6	..	..	..	0.0	..	0.0	..	0.0
Nepal	1.5	3.5	94.2	89.6	0.5	3.0	0.0	0.1	0.1	0.1
Netherlands	2.2	5.2	0.0	1.1	153.0	163.8	10.8	10.4	1.1	0.5
New Zealand	2.9	4.0	0.2	0.8	17.6	30.0	5.6	7.9	0.6	0.4
Nicaragua	3.5	4.2	49.2	42.2	2.0	3.4	0.7	0.7	0.4	0.3
Niger	..	..	79.5	80.6	0.6	1.1	0.1	0.1	0.1	0.1
Nigeria	0.8	1.2	66.8	67.8	68.1	78.5	1.0	0.6	1.6	0.8
Norway	2.4	4.8	0.4	1.1	38.7	33.6	9.5	7.6	0.9	0.3
Oman	..	..	0.0	..	5.9	20.3	5.3	8.8	..	0.0
Pakistan	2.2	4.2	24.4	29.5	31.6	97.1	0.4	0.7	0.6	0.4
Panama	3.3	7.1	26.6	14.4	3.5	5.8	1.8	2.1	0.6	0.4
Papua New Guinea	..	..	65.4	62.5	1.8	2.3	0.6	0.5	0.5	0.2
Paraguay	4.2	5.8	62.0	49.6	1.5	4.6	0.5	0.9	0.2	0.2
Peru	4.6	8.9	15.2	24.6	23.6	27.9	1.4	1.1	0.4	0.2
Philippines	5.6	6.9	37.0	26.9	36.5	76.0	0.8	1.0	0.3	0.3
Poland	..	3.5	0.4	0.8	456.2	321.7	12.8	8.3	..	1.0
Portugal	5.6	6.9	1.2	0.9	27.1	54.6	2.8	5.5	0.5	0.4
Puerto Rico	..	..	0.0	..	14.0	17.6	4.4	4.6	..	0.0
Romania	1.6	3.8	1.3	5.7	191.8	92.4	8.6	4.1	1.9	0.7
Russian Federation	..	1.9	..	0.8	..	1,434.6	..	9.8	..	1.4

3.8 | Energy efficiency and emissions

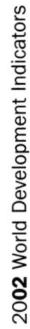

	GDP per unit of energy use		Traditional fuel use		Carbon dioxide emissions					
	PPP $ per kg oil equivalent		% of total energy use		Total million metric tons		Per capita metric tons		kg per PPP $ of GDP	
	1980	1999	1980	1997	1980	1998	1980	1998	1980	1998
Rwanda	..	..	89.8	88.3	0.3	0.5	0.1	0.1	0.1	0.1
Saudi Arabia	3.0	2.5	0.0	0.0	130.7	283.0	14.0	14.4	1.2	1.3
Senegal	2.3	4.5	50.8	56.2	2.8	3.3	0.5	0.4	0.6	0.3
Sierra Leone	..	..	90.0	86.1	0.6	0.5	0.2	0.1	0.3	0.2
Singapore	2.4	3.6	0.4	0.0	30.1	82.3	12.5	21.0	2.1	1.1
Slovak Republic	..	3.2	..	0.5	..	38.1	..	7.1	..	0.7
Slovenia	..	4.9	..	1.5	..	14.6	..	7.4	..	0.5
Somalia	..	..	78.6	..	0.6	0.0	0.1	0.0	..	0.0
South Africa	2.7	3.5	4.9	43.4	211.3	343.7	7.7	8.3	1.2	0.9
Spain	3.8	6.1	0.4	1.3	200.0	247.2	5.3	6.3	0.8	0.4
Sri Lanka	3.5	8.1	53.5	46.5	3.4	8.1	0.2	0.4	0.2	0.1
Sudan	1.4	3.2	86.9	75.1	3.3	3.6	0.2	0.1	0.3	0.1
Swaziland	..	..	..	..	0.5	0.4	0.8	0.4	0.4	0.1
Sweden	2.1	4.0	7.7	17.9	71.4	48.6	8.6	5.5	0.8	0.3
Switzerland	4.4	7.3	0.9	6.0	40.9	41.8	6.5	5.9	0.4	0.2
Syrian Arab Republic	2.6	3.0	0.0	0.0	19.3	50.6	2.2	3.3	1.4	0.9
Tajikistan	..	1.9	..	..	..	5.1	..	0.8	..	0.9
Tanzania	..	1.1	92.0	91.4	1.9	2.2	0.1	0.1	..	0.1
Thailand	3.0	5.2	40.3	24.6	40.0	192.4	0.9	3.2	0.6	0.6
Togo	4.3	4.7	35.7	71.9	0.6	0.9	0.2	0.2	0.2	0.1
Trinidad and Tobago	1.3	1.3	1.4	0.8	16.7	22.4	15.4	17.4	3.4	2.3
Tunisia	4.0	7.4	16.1	12.4	9.4	22.4	1.5	2.4	0.6	0.4
Turkey	3.6	5.9	20.5	3.1	76.3	202.0	1.7	3.2	0.7	0.5
Turkmenistan	..	1.2	..	..	..	27.9	..	5.7	..	2.1
Uganda	..	..	93.6	89.7	0.6	1.3	0.1	0.1	*0.1*	0.1
Ukraine	..	1.2	..	0.5	..	353.6	..	7.0	..	2.1
United Arab Emirates	4.4	*1.8*	*0.0*	..	36.3	88.2	34.8	32.4	1.4	1.8
United Kingdom	2.5	5.8	0.0	3.3	580.3	542.3	10.3	9.2	1.1	0.4
United States	1.6	3.9	1.3	3.8	4,626.8	5,447.6	20.4	19.8	1.6	0.6
Uruguay	5.0	9.2	11.1	21.0	5.8	5.8	2.0	1.8	0.4	0.2
Uzbekistan	..	1.1	..	0.0	..	109.2	..	4.5	..	2.1
Venezuela, RB	1.7	2.5	0.9	0.7	90.1	155.4	6.0	6.7	1.5	1.1
Vietnam	..	4.1	49.1	37.8	16.8	43.9	0.3	0.6	..	0.3
West Bank and Gaza	..	..	..	..	..	0.0	..	0.0	..	0.0
Yemen, Rep.	..	4.4	*0.0*	1.4	..	14.2	..	0.9	..	1.1
Yugoslavia, Fed. Rep.	..	..	..	1.5	102.0	0.0	10.4	0.0	..	0.0
Zambia	0.9	1.2	37.4	72.7	3.5	1.6	0.6	0.2	0.9	0.2
Zimbabwe	1.6	3.5	27.6	25.2	9.6	14.1	1.3	1.2	0.9	0.4

World	2.2 w	4.4 w	7.4 w	8.2 w	13,852.7 t	22,825.0 t	3.4 w	3.9 w	1.1 w	0.6 w
Low income	1.9	3.6	43.7	28.6	772.4	2,416.1	0.5	1.0	0.7	0.5
Middle income	2.3	4.0	9.7	7.3	4,266.1	9,211.7	2.3	3.5	1.1	0.7
Lower middle income	1.7	3.7	10.0	5.8	2,396.9	6,140.7	1.7	3.1	1.5	0.8
Upper middle income	3.3	4.7	9.2	10.4	1,869.2	3,070.9	4.2	4.9	0.8	0.6
Low & middle income	2.2	3.9	18.3	12.9	5,038.4	11,627.8	1.5	2.3	1.0	0.7
East Asia & Pacific	..	4.3	14.6	9.4	1,958.4	4,385.2	1.4	2.4	1.9	0.7
Europe & Central Asia	..	2.4	2.8	1.3	989.0	3,134.8	..	6.8	1.4	1.1
Latin America & Carib.	4.1	6.0	18.4	16.0	848.2	1,308.3	2.4	2.6	0.5	0.4
Middle East & N. Africa	3.3	3.8	1.6	1.2	498.5	1,092.9	3.0	3.9	1.0	0.8
South Asia	2.0	4.9	33.8	23.6	392.3	1,194.4	0.4	0.9	0.7	0.5
Sub-Saharan Africa	1.8	4.6	47.2	63.9	352.0	512.2	0.9	0.8	0.9	0.5
High income	2.2	4.8	1.0	3.4	8,814.2	11,197.2	12.4	12.6	1.2	0.5
Europe EMU	2.8	5.9	0.7	2.5	1,565.2	2,431.9	7.5	8.0	0.8	0.4

About the data

The ratio of GDP to energy use provides a measure of energy efficiency. To produce comparable and consistent estimates of real GDP across countries relative to physical inputs to GDP—that is, units of energy use—GDP is converted to international dollars using purchasing power parity (PPP) rates. Differences in this ratio over time and across countries, reflect in part structural changes in the economy, changes in the energy efficiency of particular sectors, and differences in fuel mixes.

The data on traditional fuel are from the United Nations Statistics Division's *Energy Statistics Yearbook.* This series differs from those published in *World Development Indicators 1999* and previous editions, which came from other sources.

Carbon dioxide (CO_2) emissions, largely a by-product of energy production and use (see table 3.7), account for the largest share of greenhouse gases, which are associated with global warming. Anthropogenic CO_2 emissions result primarily from fossil fuel combustion and cement manufacturing. In combustion, different fossil fuels release different amounts of CO_2 for the same level of energy use. Burning oil releases about 50 percent more CO_2 than burning natural gas, and burning coal releases about twice as much. Cement manufacturing releases about half a metric ton of CO_2 for each ton of cement produced.

The Carbon Dioxide Information Analysis Center (CDIAC), sponsored by the U.S. Department of Energy, calculates annual anthropogenic emissions of CO_2. These calculations are derived from data on fossil fuel consumption, based on the World Energy Data Set maintained by the United Nations Statistics Division, and from data on world cement manufacturing, based on the Cement Manufacturing Data Set maintained by the U.S. Bureau of Mines. Emissions of CO_2 are often calculated and reported in terms of their content of elemental carbon. For this table, these values were converted to the actual mass of CO_2 by multiplying the carbon mass by 3.664 (the ratio of the mass of carbon to that of CO_2).

Although the estimates of global CO_2 emissions are probably within 10 percent of actual emissions (as calculated from global average fuel chemistry and use), country estimates may have larger error bounds. Trends estimated from a consistent time series tend to be more accurate than individual values. Each year the CDIAC recalculates the entire time series from 1950 to the present, incorporating its most recent findings and the latest corrections to its database. Estimates do not include fuels supplied to ships and aircraft engaged in international transport because of the difficulty of apportioning these fuels among the countries benefiting from that transport.

Figure 3.8a

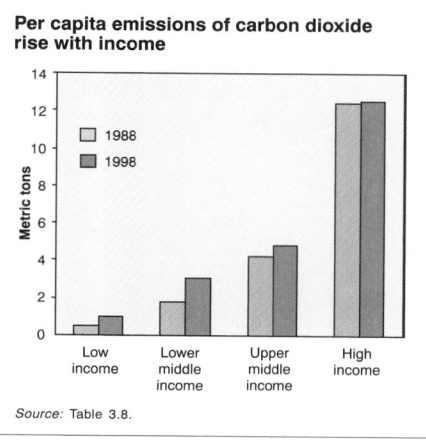

Per capita emissions of carbon dioxide rise with income

Source: Table 3.8.

Figure 3.8b

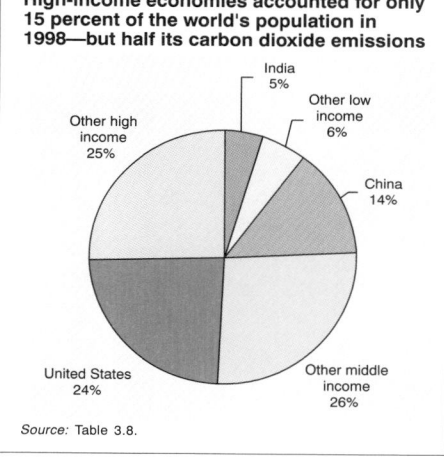

High-income economies accounted for only 15 percent of the world's population in 1998—but half its carbon dioxide emissions

Source: Table 3.8.

Definitions

• **GDP per unit of energy use** is the PPP GDP per kilogram of oil equivalent of commercial energy use. PPP GDP is gross domestic product converted to international dollars using purchasing power parity rates. An international dollar has the same purchasing power over GDP as a U.S. dollar has in the United States.
• **Traditional fuel use** includes estimates of the consumption of fuelwood, charcoal, bagasse, and animal and vegetable wastes. Total energy use comprises commercial energy use (see table 3.7) and traditional fuel use.
• **Carbon dioxide emissions** are those stemming from the burning of fossil fuels and the manufacture of cement. They include carbon dioxide produced during consumption of solid, liquid, and gas fuels and gas flaring.

Data sources

The underlying data on commercial energy production and use are from electronic files of the International Energy Agency. The data on traditional fuel use are from the United Nations Statistics Division's *Energy Statistics Yearbook.* The data on CO_2 emissions are from the Carbon Dioxide Information Analysis Center, Environmental Sciences Division, Oak Ridge National Laboratory, in the U.S. state of Tennessee.

3.9 | Sources of electricity

	Electricity production billion kwh		Sources of electricty									
			Hydropower %		Coal %		Oil %		Gas %		Nuclear power %	
	1980	1999	1980	1999	1980	1999	1980	1999	1980	1999	1980	1999
Afghanistan	..	..	..	..	..	..	..	..	..	..	..	..
Albania	3.7	5.4	79.4	97.1	..	..	20.6	2.9	..	..	..	..
Algeria	7.1	24.6	3.6	2.9	..	..	12.2	2.8	84.1	94.3	..	..
Angola	0.7	1.3	88.1	67.0	..	..	11.9	33.0	..	..	..	..
Argentina	39.7	80.7	38.1	26.8	2.1	2.2	31.6	4.9	22.0	57.0	5.9	8.8
Armenia	13.0	5.7	12.0	21.0	..	..	54.8	*0.3*	..	42.7	33.2	36.3
Australia	95.2	203.0	13.6	8.2	73.3	78.1	5.4	1.3	7.3	10.6	..	..
Austria	41.6	59.2	69.1	68.4	7.0	9.1	14.0	4.7	9.2	14.7	..	..
Azerbaijan	15.0	18.2	7.3	8.3	..	..	92.7	72.0	..	19.8	..	..
Bangladesh	2.4	14.4	24.8	5.8	..	..	26.6	9.3	48.6	85.0	..	..
Belarus	34.1	26.5	0.1	0.1	..	..	99.9	9.6	..	90.0	..	..
Belgium	53.1	83.4	0.5	0.4	29.4	15.0	34.7	1.2	11.2	23.1	23.6	58.8
Benin	0.0	0.0	..	4.3	..	..	100.0	95.7	..	..	..	..
Bolivia	1.6	3.9	68.2	46.0	..	..	10.3	3.4	20.0	49.1	..	..
Bosnia and Herzegovina	..	2.6	..	61.2	..	33.7	..	5.1	..	..	..	..
Botswana	..	..	..	..	..	..	..	..	..	..	..	..
Brazil	139.4	332.3	92.5	88.1	2.4	2.9	3.8	5.0	..	0.2	..	1.2
Bulgaria	34.8	38.0	10.7	7.2	49.2	43.4	22.5	2.4	..	5.3	17.7	41.6
Burkina Faso	..	..	..	..	..	..	..	..	..	..	..	..
Burundi	..	..	..	..	..	..	..	..	..	..	..	..
Cambodia	..	..	..	..	..	..	..	..	..	..	..	..
Cameroon	1.5	3.4	93.9	98.8	..	..	6.1	1.2	..	..	..	..
Canada	373.3	577.0	67.3	59.9	16.0	19.0	3.7	2.6	2.5	4.5	10.2	12.7
Central African Republic	..	..	..	..	..	..	..	..	..	..	..	..
Chad	..	..	..	..	..	..	..	..	..	..	..	..
Chile	11.8	38.4	67.0	37.0	16.1	35.9	14.7	9.1	1.3	15.3	..	..
China	300.6	1239.3	19.4	16.4	54.6	77.8	25.8	4.0	0.2	0.4	..	1.2
Hong Kong, China	12.6	29.5	..	..	*22.6*	56.2	100.0	0.9	..	42.9	..	..
Colombia	20.4	44.1	70.0	76.4	7.9	7.9	1.8	0.3	19.3	14.2	..	..
Congo, Dem. Rep.	4.4	5.7	95.5	99.6	..	..	4.5	0.4	..	..	..	..
Congo, Rep.	0.2	0.1	64.5	97.9	..	..	35.5	2.1	..	..	..	..
Costa Rica	2.2	6.2	95.2	83.0	..	..	4.3	2.2	..	..	..	..
Côte d'Ivoire	1.7	4.9	77.3	24.1	..	..	22.7	10.3	..	65.6	..	..
Croatia	..	12.2	..	53.8	..	4.2	..	32.3	..	9.6	..	..
Cuba	9.9	14.5	1.0	0.7	..	..	89.7	93.6	..	0.4	..	..
Czech Republic	52.7	64.2	4.6	2.6	84.8	69.9	9.6	0.7	1.1	4.7	..	20.8
Denmark	26.8	38.9	0.1	0.1	81.8	51.6	18.0	12.5	..	23.5	..	..
Dominican Republic	3.3	7.7	17.1	14.3	..	8.2	80.5	77.2	..	..	..	..
Ecuador	3.4	10.3	25.9	69.7	..	..	74.1	30.3	..	..	..	..
Egypt, Arab Rep.	18.9	68.5	51.8	22.3	..	..	27.7	28.6	20.5	49.1	..	..
El Salvador	1.5	3.8	63.7	46.6	..	..	2.7	37.0	..	..	..	..
Eritrea	..	..	..	..	..	..	..	..	..	..	..	..
Estonia	18.9	8.3	..	0.0	..	92.6	100.0	3.5	..	3.7	..	..
Ethiopia	0.7	1.7	70.2	97.3	..	..	29.8	1.2	..	..	..	..
Finland	40.7	69.4	25.1	18.4	42.6	20.9	10.8	1.3	4.2	13.7	17.2	33.1
France	256.9	519.8	26.9	13.9	27.2	6.2	18.9	2.0	2.7	1.4	23.8	75.8
Gabon	0.5	1.0	49.1	71.3	..	..	50.9	17.8	..	10.9	..	..
Gambia, The	..	..	..	..	..	..	..	..	..	..	..	..
Georgia	14.7	8.0	43.8	80.1	..	..	56.2	2.5	..	17.4	..	..
Germany	466.3	551.3	4.1	3.5	62.9	51.9	5.7	1.1	14.2	10.0	11.9	30.8
Ghana	5.3	5.2	99.2	76.4	..	..	0.8	23.6	..	..	..	..
Greece	22.7	49.4	15.0	9.3	44.8	65.6	40.1	16.5	..	7.9	..	..
Guatemala	1.8	5.2	12.9	51.3	..	..	82.9	43.3	..	..	..	..
Guinea	..	..	..	..	..	..	..	..	..	..	..	..
Guinea-Bissau	..	..	..	..	..	..	..	..	..	..	..	..
Haiti	0.3	0.7	70.1	38.4	..	..	26.1	61.6	..	..	..	..
Honduras	0.9	3.4	86.3	62.6	..	..	13.7	32.3	..	..	..	..

	Electricity production (billion kwh)		Hydropower %		Coal %		Oil %		Gas %		Nuclear power %	
	1980	1999	1980	1999	1980	1999	1980	1999	1980	1999	1980	1999
Hungary	23.9	37.2	0.5	0.5	50.4	25.9	13.9	14.3	35.2	21.1	..	37.9
India	119.3	527.3	39.0	15.4	51.2	75.2	6.4	1.1	0.8	5.5	2.5	2.5
Indonesia	8.4	84.3	16.0	11.1	..	30.1	84.0	19.0	..	36.5	..	..
Iran, Islamic Rep.	22.4	112.7	25.1	4.4	..	..	50.1	19.0	24.8	76.5	..	..
Iraq	11.4	29.7	6.1	2.0	..	..	93.9	98.0	..	..	..	..
Ireland	10.6	21.8	7.9	3.9	16.4	34.5	60.4	28.3	15.2	31.9	..	..
Israel	12.4	39.2	0.0	0.1	18.1	67.3	100.0	32.6	..	0.1	..	..
Italy	183.5	259.2	24.7	17.5	9.9	10.9	57.0	35.2	5.0	33.6	1.2	..
Jamaica	1.7	6.6	7.2	1.8	..	..	76.0	90.4	..	..	..	..
Japan	572.5	1057.0	15.4	8.2	9.6	21.2	46.2	16.6	14.2	22.1	14.4	30.0
Jordan	1.1	7.1	..	0.2	..	..	100.0	89.4	..	10.4	..	..
Kazakhstan	61.5	47.5	9.3	12.9	..	72.0	90.7	6.4	..	8.7	..	..
Kenya	1.5	4.5	71.1	72.4	..	..	28.9	19.0	..	..	..	..
Korea, Dem. Rep.	35.0	32.6	64.3	64.7	35.7	35.3	..	..	..	..	..	..
Korea, Rep.	37.2	265.0	5.3	1.6	6.7	41.1	78.7	7.0	..	11.4	9.3	38.9
Kuwait	9.0	31.6	..	..	..	..	20.1	77.3	79.9	22.7	..	..
Kyrgyz Republic	9.2	13.2	53.1	92.3	..	3.9	46.9	..	..	3.9	..	..
Lao PDR	..	..	..	..	..	..	..	..	..	..	..	..
Latvia	4.7	4.1	64.9	67.1	..	0.9	35.1	8.7	..	23.2	..	..
Lebanon	2.8	8.2	30.9	4.1	..	..	69.1	95.9	..	..	..	..
Lesotho	..	..	..	..	..	..	..	..	..	..	..	..
Liberia	..	..	..	..	..	..	..	..	..	..	..	..
Libya	4.8	20.0	..	..	..	..	100.0	100.0	..	..	..	..
Lithuania	11.7	13.1	4.0	3.2	..	..	96.0	13.8	..	7.7	..	75.4
Macedonia, FYR	..	..	..	..	..	..	..	..	..	..	..	..
Madagascar	..	..	..	..	..	..	..	..	..	..	..	..
Malawi	..	..	..	..	..	..	..	..	..	..	..	..
Malaysia	10.0	65.2	13.9	11.5	..	2.5	84.9	8.3	1.2	77.6	..	..
Mali	..	..	..	..	..	..	..	..	..	..	..	..
Mauritania	..	..	..	..	..	..	..	..	..	..	..	..
Mauritius	..	..	..	..	..	..	..	..	..	..	..	..
Mexico	67.0	192.3	25.2	17.1	0.0	9.4	57.9	47.2	15.5	17.9	..	5.2
Moldova	15.4	3.8	2.6	2.2	..	5.5	97.4	9.6	..	82.7	..	..
Mongolia	..	..	..	..	..	..	..	..	..	..	..	..
Morocco	5.2	13.9	28.9	5.9	19.5	49.7	51.6	44.4	..	..	..	..
Mozambique	0.5	6.9	65.2	99.6	17.5	..	17.3	0.4	..	0.0	..	..
Myanmar	1.5	4.8	53.5	15.9	2.0	..	31.3	16.1	13.2	68.0	..	..
Namibia	..	1.2	..	97.6	..	..	..	2.4	..	..	..	..
Nepal	0.2	1.3	94.4	90.4	..	..	5.6	9.6	..	..	..	..
Netherlands	64.8	86.7	..	0.1	13.7	25.5	38.4	7.6	39.8	56.9	6.5	4.4
New Zealand	22.6	38.1	83.6	61.7	1.9	4.8	0.2	..	7.5	25.1	..	..
Nicaragua	1.1	2.1	51.3	18.3	..	..	43.3	76.2	..	..	..	..
Niger	..	..	..	..	..	..	..	..	..	..	..	..
Nigeria	7.1	16.1	39.0	35.0	0.4	..	45.1	24.2	15.5	40.8	..	..
Norway	83.8	121.7	99.8	99.3	0.0	0.2	0.1	0.0	..	0.2	..	..
Oman	0.8	8.4	..	..	..	..	21.5	16.7	78.5	83.3	..	..
Pakistan	15.0	65.4	58.2	34.3	0.2	0.8	1.1	35.2	40.5	29.3	0.0	0.4
Panama	2.0	4.6	49.2	60.7	..	..	49.0	37.8	..	..	..	..
Papua New Guinea	..	..	..	..	..	..	..	..	..	..	..	..
Paraguay	0.8	52.0	80.0	99.9	..	..	11.1	0.0	..	..	..	..
Peru	10.0	19.1	69.8	76.3	..	..	27.4	17.6	1.7	5.3	..	..
Philippines	18.0	41.3	19.6	19.0	1.0	27.1	67.9	28.3	..	0.0	..	..
Poland	120.9	142.0	1.9	1.5	94.7	96.3	2.9	1.3	0.1	0.5	..	..
Portugal	15.2	42.9	52.7	16.9	2.3	35.2	42.9	25.6	..	18.8	..	..
Puerto Rico	..	..	..	..	..	..	..	..	..	..	..	..
Romania	67.5	50.7	18.7	36.1	31.4	29.4	9.6	7.6	40.2	16.6	..	10.2
Russian Federation	804.9	845.3	16.1	19.0	..	19.1	77.2	4.8	..	42.4	6.7	14.4

	Electricity production		Sources of electricty									
	billion kwh		Hydropower %		Coal %		Oil %		Gas %		Nuclear power %	
	1980	1999	1980	1999	1980	1999	1980	1999	1980	1999	1980	1999
Rwanda	..	..	..	..	..	..	..	..	..	..	..	..
Saudi Arabia	20.5	120.0	..	..	..	..	58.5	64.3	41.5	35.7	..	..
Senegal	0.6	1.4	..	..	..	..	100.0	98.5	..	1.5	..	..
Sierra Leone	..	..	..	..	..	..	..	..	..	..	..	..
Singapore	7.0	29.4	..	..	..	..	100.0	77.8	..	19.7	..	..
Slovak Republic	20.0	27.5	11.3	16.5	37.9	23.4	17.9	1.2	10.2	11.2	22.7	47.7
Slovenia	..	13.3	..	28.2	..	33.8	..	1.1	..	1.3	..	35.4
Somalia	..	..	..	..	..	..	..	..	..	..	..	..
South Africa	99.0	200.4	1.0	0.4	99.0	93.2	0.0	..	..	..	..	6.4
Spain	109.2	206.3	27.1	11.1	30.0	36.6	35.2	11.8	2.7	9.2	4.7	28.5
Sri Lanka	1.7	6.2	88.7	67.5	..	..	11.3	32.5	..	..	..	..
Sudan	0.8	2.1	70.0	53.1	..	..	30.0	46.9	..	..	..	..
Swaziland	..	..	..	..	..	..	..	..	..	..	..	..
Sweden	96.3	155.2	61.1	46.1	0.2	2.1	10.4	1.9	..	0.3	27.5	47.2
Switzerland	48.2	68.5	68.1	58.4	0.1	..	1.0	0.2	0.6	1.5	29.8	37.7
Syrian Arab Republic	4.0	21.1	64.7	41.1	..	..	31.9	23.8	3.4	35.1	..	..
Tajikistan	13.6	15.8	93.4	97.7	..	..	6.6	..	..	2.3	..	..
Tanzania	0.8	2.3	86.4	96.5	..	..	13.6	3.5	..	..	..	..
Thailand	14.4	90.1	8.8	3.6	9.8	18.3	81.4	17.8	9.9	59.2	..	..
Togo	0.0	0.1	13.3	3.1	..	..	86.7	96.9	..	..	..	..
Trinidad and Tobago	2.0	5.3	..	..	..	..	2.3	..	96.5	99.6	..	..
Tunisia	2.9	10.0	0.8	0.9	..	..	64.5	13.5	34.7	85.5	..	..
Turkey	23.3	116.4	48.8	29.8	25.6	31.8	25.1	6.9	..	31.2	..	..
Turkmenistan	6.7	8.9	0.1	0.1	..	..	99.9	..	..	99.9	..	..
Uganda	..	..	..	..	..	..	..	..	..	..	..	..
Ukraine	236.0	172.1	5.7	6.8	..	29.5	88.3	4.6	..	17.3	6.0	41.9
United Arab Emirates	6.3	37.1	..	..	..	..	3.7	7.9	96.3	92.1	..	..
United Kingdom	284.1	363.9	1.4	1.5	73.2	29.3	11.7	1.5	0.7	38.8	13.0	26.5
United States	2427.3	3910.2	11.5	7.4	51.2	51.8	10.8	3.1	15.3	15.7	11.0	19.9
Uruguay	4.6	7.2	76.3	76.5	..	..	23.5	23.0	..	..	..	..
Uzbekistan	33.9	45.3	14.6	12.5	..	4.8	85.4	11.4	..	71.3	..	..
Venezuela, RB	35.8	80.6	40.7	75.1	..	..	32.4	7.1	26.9	17.8	..	..
Vietnam	3.6	23.6	41.8	58.5	39.9	12.4	18.3	13.9	0.4	15.3	..	..
West Bank and Gaza	..	..	..	..	..	..	..	..	..	..	..	..
Yemen, Rep.	0.5	3.0	..	..	..	..	100.0	100.0	..	..	..	..
Yugoslavia, Fed. Rep.	..	33.4	..	40.1	..	53.8	..	3.2	..	2.9	..	..
Zambia	9.5	8.1	98.8	99.5	0.7	0.5	0.5	0.0	..	..	..	..
Zimbabwe	4.5	7.1	88.3	41.6	11.7	58.4	..	..	..	..	..	..
World	8205.6 s	14732.8 s	20.6 w	17.5 w	33.0 w	38.2 w	28.4 w	8.4 w	8.8 w	17.2 w	8.7 w	17.2 w
Low income	577.8	1112.4	27.8	22.7	13.1	44.5	53.7	8.2	1.6	16.3	3.7	7.9
Middle income	2233.8	4759.2	21.6	22.7	22.3	38.5	48.0	11.2	4.6	19.6	3.2	7.3
Lower middle income	1492.5	2911.7	18.1	19.9	13.8	42.9	60.5	8.9	3.3	21.9	4.0	5.8
Upper middle income	741.3	1847.5	28.9	27.0	39.3	31.5	22.8	14.9	7.1	16.0	1.4	9.6
Low & middle income	2811.7	5871.6	22.9	22.7	20.4	39.6	49.2	10.7	4.0	19.0	3.3	7.4
East Asia & Pacific	428.8	1846.1	21.6	14.7	42.5	61.9	34.4	6.5	0.2	9.6	0.8	6.4
Europe & Central Asia	1640.1	1763.4	13.5	17.9	13.6	30.6	65.4	5.8	2.3	30.3	5.1	15.2
Latin America & Carib.	360.9	921.0	60.2	60.1	2.1	5.2	25.7	17.7	9.8	12.6	0.6	2.3
Middle East & N. Africa	104.0	453.1	20.5	7.0	1.0	1.5	52.2	44.0	26.3	47.6	..	..
South Asia	138.5	614.6	41.6	17.9	44.1	64.6	6.3	5.3	5.9	9.9	2.2	2.2
Sub-Saharan Africa	139.3	273.4	24.0	18.1	70.8	69.9	4.4	3.6	0.8	3.6	..	4.7
High income	5393.9	8861.2	19.5	14.0	39.6	37.2	17.6	6.8	11.3	16.0	11.5	23.8
Europe EMU	1265.5	1949.8	17.0	11.6	37.3	27.2	23.2	8.6	9.8	14.1	11.7	35.8

About the data

Use of energy in general, and access to electricity in particular, are important in improving people's standard of living. But electricity generation also can damage the environment. Whether such damage occurs depends largely on how electricity is generated. For example, burning coal releases twice as much carbon dioxide—a major contributor to global warming—as does burning an equivalent amount of natural gas (see *About the data* for table 3.8). Nuclear energy does not generate carbon dioxide emissions, but it produces other dangerous waste products. The table provides information on electricity production by source. Shares may not sum to 100 percent because some sources of generated electricity (such as geothermal, solar, and wind) are not shown.

The International Energy Agency (IEA) compiles data on energy inputs used to generate electricity. IEA data for non-OECD countries are based on national energy data adjusted to conform to annual questionnaires completed by OECD member governments. In addition, estimates are sometimes made to complete major aggregates from which key data are missing, and adjustments are made to compensate for differences in definitions. The IEA makes these estimates in consultation with national statistical offices, oil companies, electricity utilities, and national energy experts.

The IEA occasionally revises its time series to reflect political changes. Since 1990, for example, it has constructed energy statistics for countries of the former Soviet Union. In addition, energy statistics for other countries have undergone continuous changes in coverage or methodology as more detailed energy accounts have become available in recent years. Breaks in series are therefore unavoidable.

Figure 3.9a

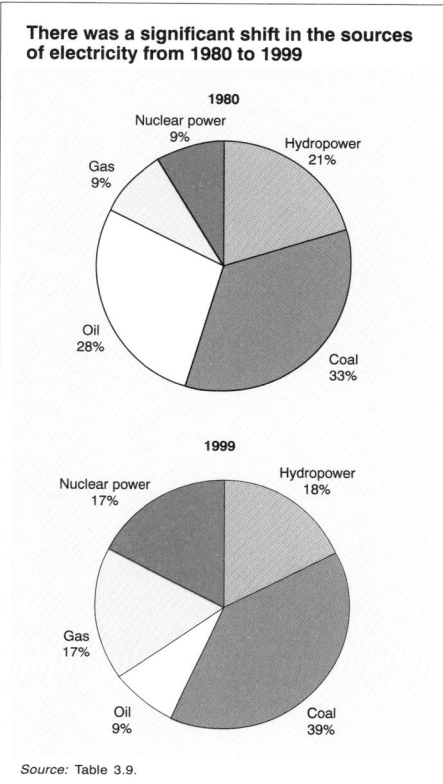

There was a significant shift in the sources of electricity from 1980 to 1999

1980
- Nuclear power 9%
- Hydropower 21%
- Gas 9%
- Oil 28%
- Coal 33%

1999
- Nuclear power 17%
- Hydropower 18%
- Gas 17%
- Oil 9%
- Coal 39%

Source: Table 3.9.

Figure 3.9b

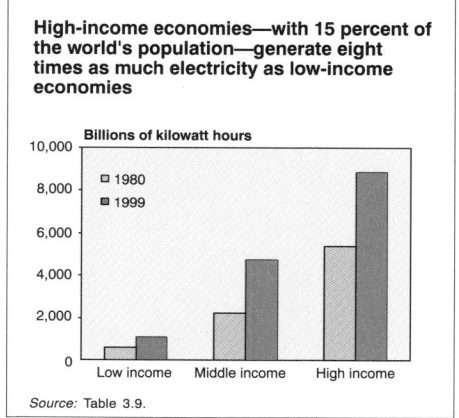

High-income economies—with 15 percent of the world's population—generate eight times as much electricity as low-income economies

Billions of kilowatt hours

□ 1980
■ 1999

Low income, Middle income, High income

Source: Table 3.9.

Definitions

• **Electricity production** is measured at the terminals of all alternator sets in a station. In addition to hydropower, coal, oil, gas, and nuclear power generation, it covers generation by geothermal, solar, wind, and tide and wave energy as well as that from combustible renewables and waste. Production includes the output of electricity plants designed to produce electricity only as well as that of combined heat and power plants. • **Sources of electricity** refer to the inputs used to generate electricity: hydropower, coal, oil, gas, and nuclear power. Hydropower refers to electricity produced by hydroelectric power plants, oil refers to crude oil and petroleum products, gas refers to natural gas but not natural gas liquids, and nuclear power refers to electricity produced by nuclear power plants.

Data sources

The data on electricity production are from the IEA's electronic files and its annual publications, *Energy Statistics and Balances of Non-OECD Countries, Energy Statistics of OECD Countries,* and *Energy Balances of OECD Countries.*

	Urban population				Population in urban agglomerations of more than one million			Population in largest city		Access to improved sanitation facilities			
	millions		% of total population		% of total population			% of urban population		Urban % of population		Rural % of population	
	1980	2000	1980	2000	1980	2000	2015	1980	2000	1990	2000	1990	2000
Afghanistan	2.5	5.8	16	22	6	10	14	39	45	..	25	..	8
Albania	0.9	1.3	34	39	..	..	..	..	..	..	..	..	..
Algeria	8.1	18.3	44	60	8	6	7	17	10	..	90	..	47
Angola	1.5	4.5	21	34	13	20	25	63	60	..	70	..	30
Argentina	23.3	33.1	83	89	42	41	40	43	38	..	89	..	48
Armenia	2.0	2.7	66	70	34	34	35	51	48	..	..	..	..
Australia	12.6	16.2	86	85	61	56	55	26	23	100	100	100	100
Austria	4.9	5.2	65	65	27	26	26	42	39	100	100	100	100
Azerbaijan	3.3	4.6	53	57	26	24	25	48	42	..	..	..	..
Bangladesh	12.3	32.1	14	25	6	13	17	26	38	78	82	27	44
Belarus	5.4	7.0	57	70	14	18	20	24	25	..	..	..	..
Belgium	9.4	10.0	95	97	12	11	11	13	11	..	..	..	..
Benin	0.9	2.7	27	42	..	..	..	..	..	46	46	6	6
Bolivia	2.4	5.4	46	65	14	18	20	30	27	77	82	28	38
Bosnia and Herzegovina	1.5	1.7	36	43	..	..	..	..	..	..	..	..	..
Botswana	0.1	0.8	15	50	..	..	..	..	..	84	..	44	..
Brazil	80.5	138.5	66	81	32	34	34	16	13	84	85	37	40
Bulgaria	5.4	5.7	61	70	12	15	16	20	21	..	..	..	..
Burkina Faso	0.6	2.1	9	19	..	..	..	44	54	88	88	14	16
Burundi	0.2	0.6	4	9	..	..	..	..	..	67	79	90	..
Cambodia	0.8	1.9	12	16	..	..	..	44	51	..	58	..	10
Cameroon	2.7	7.3	31	49	11	21	27	19	23	99	99	79	85
Canada	18.6	23.7	76	77	32	37	38	16	20	100	100	99	99
Central African Republic	0.8	1.5	35	41	..	..	..	..	..	43	43	23	23
Chad	0.8	1.8	19	24	..	..	..	40	57	70	81	4	13
Chile	9.0	12.9	81	85	33	36	37	41	43	98	98	93	93
China	192.3	405.2	20	32	13	14	17	6	3	57	68	18	24
Hong Kong, China	4.6	6.8	92	100	91	100	100	100	100	..	..	..	..
Colombia	18.2	31.7	64	75	26	32	35	20	20	95	97	53	51
Congo, Dem. Rep.	7.7	15.4	29	30	8	10	12	28	33	..	53	..	6
Congo, Rep.	0.7	1.9	41	63	27	41	43	65	65	..	14	..	..
Costa Rica	1.0	2.0	43	52	..	..	..	61	50	..	98	..	96
Côte d'Ivoire	2.8	7.4	35	46	15	21	25	44	44	78	..	30	..
Croatia	2.3	2.5	50	58	..	..	..	28	42	..	..	..	..
Cuba	6.6	8.4	68	75	20	20	20	29	27	..	96	..	91
Czech Republic	7.6	7.7	75	75	12	12	12	15	16	..	..	..	..
Denmark	4.3	4.5	84	85	27	26	26	32	31	..	..	..	..
Dominican Republic	2.9	5.4	51	65	34	61	67	50	66	66	75	52	64
Ecuador	3.7	7.9	47	62	23	32	37	29	29	..	70	..	37
Egypt, Arab Rep.	17.9	28.9	44	45	23	23	24	38	36	96	98	80	91
El Salvador	1.9	2.9	42	47	16	22	25	39	48	..	88	..	78
Eritrea	0.3	0.8	14	19	..	..	..	..	..	..	66	..	1
Estonia	1.0	0.9	70	69	..	..	..	..	..	..	93	..	..
Ethiopia	4.0	11.3	11	18	3	4	6	30	23	58	58	6	6
Finland	2.9	3.5	60	67	13	23	25	22	33	100	100	100	100
France	39.5	44.5	73	76	21	21	20	23	22	..	..	..	..
Gabon	0.3	1.0	50	81	..	..	..	..	..	..	25	..	4
Gambia, The	0.1	0.4	20	33	..	..	..	..	..	..	41	..	35
Georgia	2.6	3.0	52	61	22	26	29	42	43	..	..	..	..
Germany	64.7	71.9	83	88	39	41	43	10	9	..	..	..	..
Ghana	3.4	7.4	31	38	9	10	14	30	27	59	62	61	64
Greece	5.6	6.3	58	60	31	30	30	54	49	..	..	..	..
Guatemala	2.6	4.6	37	40	11	28	32	29	70	94	98	66	76
Guinea	0.9	2.4	19	33	12	25	32	65	75	94	94	41	41
Guinea-Bissau	0.1	0.3	17	24	..	..	..	..	..	..	88	..	34
Haiti	1.3	2.8	24	36	13	22	28	55	62	48	50	15	16
Honduras	1.2	3.0	35	47	..	..	..	33	32	85	94	..	57

	Urban population				Population in urban agglomerations of more than one million			Population in largest city		Access to improved sanitation facilities			
	millions		% of total population			% of total population		% of urban population		Urban % of population		Rural % of population	
	1980	2000	1980	2000	1980	2000	2015	1980	2000	1990	2000	1990	2000
Hungary	6.1	6.4	57	64	19	18	19	34	28	100	100	98	98
India	158.8	288.5	23	28	8	10	12	5	6	58	73	8	14
Indonesia	32.9	86.1	22	41	8	10	12	18	13	76	87	44	52
Iran, Islamic Rep.	19.4	39.2	50	62	21	23	24	26	18	86	86	74	74
Iraq	8.5	17.9	66	77	29	31	34	39	27	..	93	..	31
Ireland	1.9	2.2	55	59	..	..	..	48	44	..	..	..	..
Israel	3.4	5.7	89	91	37	35	33	41	38	..	..	..	..
Italy	37.6	38.7	67	67	24	19	21	14	11	..	..	..	..
Jamaica	1.0	1.5	47	56	..	..	..	..	..	..	98	..	65
Japan	89.0	100.0	76	79	34	38	39	25	26	..	..	..	..
Jordan	1.3	3.6	60	74	29	29	32	49	39	100	100	95	98
Kazakhstan	8.0	8.4	54	56	6	8	8	12	15	..	100	..	98
Kenya	2.7	10.0	16	33	5	8	10	32	23	94	96	81	81
Korea, Dem. Rep.	9.8	13.4	57	60	11	14	16	19	24	..	..	..	..
Korea, Rep.	21.7	38.7	57	82	40	47	45	38	26	..	76	..	..
Kuwait	1.2	1.9	90	98	60	60	55	67	61	..	..	..	..
Kyrgyz Republic	1.4	1.6	38	33	..	..	..	..	..	..	100	..	100
Lao PDR	0.4	1.2	13	24	..	..	..	..	..	..	84	..	34
Latvia	1.7	1.6	68	69	..	..	..	49	47	..	..	..	..
Lebanon	2.2	3.9	74	90	40	47	48	55	53	..	100	..	87
Lesotho	0.2	0.6	13	28	..	..	..	..	..	..	93	..	92
Liberia	0.7	1.4	35	45	..	..	..	..	..	..	..	..	..
Libya	2.1	4.6	69	88	26	34	34	38	39	97	97	96	96
Lithuania	2.1	2.5	61	68	..	..	..	..	23	..	..	..	..
Macedonia, FYR	1.0	1.3	54	62	..	..	..	..	..	..	..	..	..
Madagascar	1.6	4.6	18	30	6	10	13	33	33	70	70	25	30
Malawi	0.6	1.6	9	15	..	..	..	..	..	96	96	70	70
Malaysia	5.8	13.4	42	57	7	6	6	16	10	..	..	..	98
Mali	1.2	3.3	19	30	..	..	..	40	35	95	93	62	58
Mauritania	0.4	1.5	27	58	..	..	..	..	..	44	44	19	19
Mauritius	0.4	0.5	42	41	..	..	..	..	..	100	100	100	99
Mexico	44.8	72.9	66	74	28	28	25	31	25	85	87	28	32
Moldova	1.6	2.0	40	46	..	..	..	..	..	..	100	..	..
Mongolia	0.9	1.4	52	59	..	..	..	..	..	..	46	..	2
Morocco	8.0	16.1	41	56	15	18	20	26	22	95	100	31	42
Mozambique	1.6	7.1	13	40	6	17	21	47	43	..	69	..	26
Myanmar	8.1	13.2	24	28	7	9	11	27	32	65	65	38	39
Namibia	0.2	0.5	23	31	..	..	..	..	..	84	96	14	17
Nepal	0.9	2.7	7	12	..	..	..	..	..	68	75	16	20
Netherlands	12.5	14.2	88	89	14	14	14	8	8	100	100	100	100
New Zealand	2.6	3.3	83	87	..	..	..	30	33	..	..	..	..
Nicaragua	1.6	3.3	53	65	..	..	..	34	29	97	96	53	68
Niger	0.7	2.2	13	21	..	..	..	..	..	71	79	4	5
Nigeria	19.1	55.8	27	44	8	12	15	23	24	77	85	51	45
Norway	2.9	3.4	71	76	..	..	..	22	29	100	..	..	..
Oman	0.3	2.0	32	84	..	..	..	..	..	98	98	61	61
Pakistan	23.2	51.1	28	37	15	21	25	22	23	78	94	13	42
Panama	1.0	1.6	50	58	..	..	..	62	71	..	99	..	87
Papua New Guinea	0.4	0.9	13	17	..	..	..	..	..	92	92	80	80
Paraguay	1.3	3.1	42	56	22	23	26	52	41	92	95	87	95
Peru	11.2	18.7	65	73	25	29	30	39	40	81	90	26	40
Philippines	18.0	44.3	38	59	14	16	17	33	25	85	92	64	71
Poland	20.7	25.4	58	66	18	18	18	16	14	..	..	..	..
Portugal	2.9	6.4	29	64	19	57	68	46	59	..	..	..	..
Puerto Rico	2.1	2.9	67	75	34	35	36	51	47	..	..	..	..
Romania	10.9	12.6	49	56	9	9	10	18	16	..	86	..	10
Russian Federation	97.0	106.4	70	73	18	19	21	8	9	..	..	..	..

	Urban population				Population in urban agglomerations of more than one million			Population in largest city		Access to improved sanitation facilities			
	millions		% of total population		% of total population			% of urban population		Urban % of population		Rural % of population	
	1980	2000	1980	2000	1980	2000	2015	1980	2000	1990	2000	1990	2000
Rwanda	0.2	0.5	5	6	..	..	..	..	..	..	12	..	8
Saudi Arabia	6.2	17.8	66	86	19	25	24	16	19	..	100	..	100
Senegal	2.0	4.5	36	47	17	22	27	48	46	86	94	38	48
Sierra Leone	0.8	1.8	24	37	..	..	..	..	..	..	23	..	31
Singapore	2.4	4.0	100	100	100	89	82	100	89	100	100	..	..
Slovak Republic	2.6	3.1	52	57	..	..	..	..	..	..	100	..	100
Slovenia	0.9	1.0	48	50	..	..	..	..	..	100	..	..	..
Somalia	1.4	2.4	22	28	..	..	..	27	50	..	..	..	..
South Africa	13.3	23.5	48	55	27	32	36	12	13	..	99	..	73
Spain	27.2	30.6	73	78	20	17	18	16	13	..	..	..	..
Sri Lanka	3.2	4.6	22	24	..	..	..	..	..	93	91	79	83
Sudan	3.9	11.2	20	36	6	9	11	30	24	87	87	48	48
Swaziland	0.1	0.3	18	26	..	..	..	..	..	..	..	..	..
Sweden	6.9	7.4	83	83	17	18	18	20	21	100	100	100	100
Switzerland	3.6	4.9	57	68	..	..	..	20	20	100	100	100	100
Syrian Arab Republic	4.1	8.8	47	55	28	28	31	34	26	..	98	..	81
Tajikistan	1.4	1.7	34	28	..	..	..	..	..	..	..	..	..
Tanzania	2.7	9.4	15	28	5	12	18	30	25	97	98	86	86
Thailand	7.9	13.1	17	22	10	12	15	59	56	97	97	83	96
Togo	0.6	1.5	23	33	..	..	..	..	..	71	69	24	17
Trinidad and Tobago	0.7	1.0	63	74	..	..	..	..	..	..	..	..	..
Tunisia	3.3	6.3	52	66	18	20	21	35	30	97	..	48	..
Turkey	19.5	49.2	44	75	19	27	30	23	19	98	98	70	70
Turkmenistan	1.3	2.3	47	45	..	..	..	..	..	..	..	..	..
Uganda	1.1	3.2	9	14	..	..	..	42	38	96	96	82	72
Ukraine	30.9	33.7	62	68	14	15	17	7	8	..	..	..	..
United Arab Emirates	0.7	2.5	72	86	..	..	..	31	37	..	..	..	..
United Kingdom	50.0	53.5	89	90	25	23	23	15	14	100	100	100	100
United States	167.6	217.4	74	77	38	38	37	9	8	100	100	100	100
Uruguay	2.5	3.0	85	91	42	37	35	49	41	..	96	..	89
Uzbekistan	6.5	9.1	41	37	11	9	8	28	24	..	100	..	100
Venezuela, RB	12.0	21.1	79	87	28	29	30	21	15	..	75	..	69
Vietnam	10.3	18.8	19	24	14	13	14	34	24	86	86	70	70
West Bank and Gaza	..	..	..	..	..	..	..	..	..	..	..	..	..
Yemen, Rep.	1.6	4.3	19	25	..	..	..	15	30	80	87	27	31
Yugoslavia, Fed. Rep.	4.5	5.6	46	52	11	14	15	24	27	..	..	..	..
Zambia	2.3	4.5	40	45	9	16	22	23	37	86	99	48	64
Zimbabwe	1.6	4.5	22	35	9	14	19	39	39	98	99	51	51
World	1,759.9 s	2,847.8 s	40 w	47 w	.. w	.. w	.. w	18 w	17 w	78 w	84 w	29 w	35 w
Low income	388.2	785.1	24	32	..	..	..	16	18	68	78	25	30
Middle income	776.5	1,350.8	38	50	..	..	..	19	16	75	82	29	38
Lower middle income	486.9	859.5	31	42	..	..	..	16	13	69	79	28	35
Upper middle income	289.6	491.3	62	76	..	..	..	25	21	..	88	..	57
Low & middle income	1,164.7	2,135.9	32	41	..	..	..	18	17	72	81	27	33
East Asia & Pacific	309.8	652.4	22	35	..	..	..	15	10	64	74	28	34
Europe & Central Asia	249.3	310.1	59	65	16	18	20	15	15	..	..	..	..
Latin America & Carib.	233.4	388.7	65	75	29	32	32	27	25	85	87	39	48
Middle East & N. Africa	83.5	172.9	48	59	21	22	24	30	25	92	94	63	67
South Asia	201.0	385.0	22	28	8	12	14	9	12	63	76	12	21
Sub-Saharan Africa	87.7	226.9	23	34	..	..	..	28	29	80	81	47	41
High income	595.1	711.9	75	79	..	..	..	17	17	..	..	..	..
Europe EMU	210.1	235.3	73	77	26	27	28	17	16	..	..	..	..

About the data

The population of a city or metropolitan area depends on the boundaries chosen. For example, in 1990 Beijing, China, contained 2.3 million people in 87 square kilometers of "inner city" and 5.4 million in 158 square kilometers of "core city." The population of "inner city and inner suburban districts" was 6.3 million, and that of "inner city, inner and outer suburban districts, and inner and outer counties" was 10.8 million. (For most countries the last definition is used.)

Estimates of the world's urban population would change significantly if China, India, and a few other populous nations were to change their definition of urban centers. According to China's State Statistical Bureau, by the end of 1996 urban residents accounted for about 43 percent of China's population, while in 1994 only 20 percent of the population was considered urban. In addition to the continuous migration of people from rural to urban areas, one of the main rea-

sons for this shift was the rapid growth in the hundreds of towns reclassified as cities in recent years. Because the estimates in the table are based on national definitions of what constitutes a city or metropolitan area, cross-country comparisons should be made with caution.

To estimate urban populations, the United Nations' ratios of urban to total population were applied to the World Bank's estimates of total population (see table 2.1).

The urban population with access to improved sanitation facilities is defined as those with access to at least adequate excreta disposal facilities that can effectively prevent human, animal, and insect contact with excreta. The rural population with access is included to allow comparison of rural and urban access. This definition and the definition of urban areas vary, however, so comparisons between countries can be misleading (see *Definitions* for table 2.16).

Definitions

• **Urban population** is the midyear population of areas defined as urban in each country and reported to the United Nations (see *About the data*). • **Population in urban agglomerations of more than one million** is the percentage of a country's population living in metropolitan areas that in 1990 had a population of more than one million. • **Population in largest city** is the percentage of a country's urban population living in that country's largest metropolitan area. • **Access to improved sanitation facilities** refers to the percentage of the urban or rural population with access to at least adequate excreta disposal facilities (private or shared, but not public) that can effectively prevent human, animal, and insect contact with excreta. Improved facilities range from simple but protected pit latrines to flush toilets with a sewerage connection. To be effective, facilities must be correctly constructed and properly maintained.

Data sources

The data on urban population and the population in urban agglomerations and in the largest city come from the United Nations Population Division's *World Urbanization Prospects: The 1999 Revision.* The total population figures are World Bank estimates. The data on access to sanitation in urban and rural areas are from the World Health Organization.

Figure 3.10

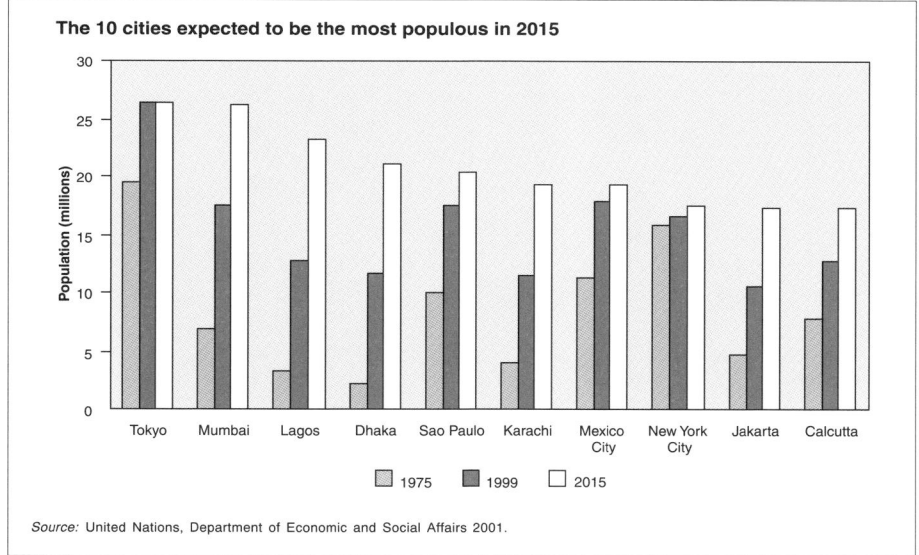

The 10 cities expected to be the most populous in 2015

Source: United Nations, Department of Economic and Social Affairs 2001.

3.11 | Urban environment

	City	Urban population	Secure tenure	House price to income ratio	Work trips by public transportation	Travel time to work	Households with access to services				Wastewater treated
			Proportion of people with secure tenure				Access to potable water	Sewerage connection	Electricity	Telephone	
		thousands 2000	% 1998[a]	1998[a]	% 1998[a]	minutes 1998[a]	% 1998[a]	% 1998[a]	% 1998[a]	% 1998[a]	% 1998[a]
Algeria	Algiers	2,562 [b]	93.2	..	..	75	..	..	..	..	80
Argentina	Buenos Aires	2,996 [b]	92.1	5.1	59	42	100	98	100	70	..
	Córdoba	132 [b]	85.0	6.8	44	32	99	40	99	80	49
	Rosario	1,248 [b]	..	5.7	..	22	98	67	93	76	1
Armenia	Yerevan	1,250 [b]	100.0	4.0	84	30	98	98	100	88	36
Bangladesh	Chittagong	2,301 [b]	..	8.1	27	45	44	..	95	..	..
	Dhaka	10,000 [b]	..	16.7	9	45	60	22	90	7	..
	Sylhet	242 [b]	..	6.0	10	50	29	0	93	40	..
	Tangail	152 [b]	85.7	13.9	..	30	12	0	90	12	..
Barbados	Bridgetown	..	99.7	4.4	..	..	98	5	99	78	7
Belize	Belize City	55 [b]	..	..	..	..	..	..	..	..	..
Bolivia	Santa Cruz de la Sierra	1,065 [c]	87.0	29.3	..	29	53	33	98	59	53
Bosnia and Herzegovina	Sarajevo	522 [c]	..	..	100	12	95	90	100	..	..
Brazil	Belem	1,638 [c]	..	..	..	..	..	..	..	..	..
	Icapui	..	91.7	4.5	..	30	88	..	90	33	..
	Maranguape	..	..	..	30	20	73	..	..	..	..
	Porto Alegre	3 [b]	..	..	..	..	99	87	100	..	..
	Recife	3,088 [b]	..	12.5	46	35	89	41	100	29	33
	Rio de Janeiro	10,192 [b]	..	..	..	..	88	80	10	..	..
	Santo Andre	1,658 [b]	80.3	23.4	43	40	98	95	100	79	..
Bulgaria	Bourgas	.. [b]	..	5.1	61	32	100	93	100	..	93
	Sofia	1,200 [b]	100.0	13.2	79	32	95	91	100	89	94
	Troyan	24 [b]	100.0	3.7	44	22	99	82	100	45	..
	Veliko Tarnovo	..	100.0	5.4	46	30	98	98	100	96	50
Burkina Faso	Bobo-Dioulasso	..	100.0	..	..	..	24	..	29	6	..
	Koudougou	..	..	..	..	..	30	..	26	7	..
	Ouagadougou	1,130 [c]	100.0	..	2	..	30	..	47	11	19
Burundi	Bujumbura	373 [b]	97.0	..	48	25	26	62	57	19	21
Cambodia	Phnom Penh	1,000 [b]	..	8.9	0	45	45	75	76	40	..
Cameroon	Douala	1,148 [b]	..	13.4	..	40	34	1	95	9	5
	Yaounde	968 [b]	..	..	42	45	34	1	95	9	24
Canada	Hull	254 [b]	100.0	..	16	..	100	100	100	100	100
Central African Republic	Bangui	..	94.0	..	66	60	31	..	18	11	0
Chad	N'Djamena	998 [c]	..	..	35	..	42	0	13	6	21
Chile	Gran Concepcion	..	..	..	57	35	100	91	95	69	6
	Santiago de Chile	5,737 [b]	..	..	60	38	100	99	99	73	3
	Tome	..	..	..	..	..	92	52	98	58	57
	Valparaiso	851 [b]	91.8	..	55	..	98	92	97	63	100
	Vina del mar	851 [b]	92.7	..	..	..	97	97	98	65	93
Colombia	Armenia	..	94.1	5.0	42	60	90	50	99	97	..
	Marinilla	170 [b]	94.5	8.5	18	15	98	93	100	65	..
	Medellin	2,901 [b]	..	..	38	35	100	99	100	87	..
Congo	Brazzaville	989 [b]	87.9	..	55	20	56	0	52	18	..
Côte d'Ivoire	Abidjan	3,201 [b]	..	14.5	..	45	26	15	41	5	45
Croatia	Zagreb	2,497 [b]	96.5	7.8	56	31	98	97	100	94	..
Cuba	Baracoa	..	96.2	..	..	..	83	3	93	32	..
	Camaguey	..	84.7	..	2	60	72	47	97	..	..
	Cienfuegos	..	96.3	4.0	..	80	100	73	100	9	2
	Ciudad Habana	..	..	8.5	58	83	100	85	100	14	..
	Pinar Del Rio	..	96.4	..	..	80	97	48	100	..	..
	Santa Clara	..	98.8	..	7	48	95	42	100	43	..
Czech Republic	Brno	..	..	..	50	25	100	96	100	69	100
	Prague	1,193 [b]	99.3	..	55	22	99	100	100	100	..
Dem. Rep. of Congo	Kinshasa	5,398 [b]	94.9	..	72	57	72	0	66	1	..
Dominican Republic	Santiago de los Caballeros	691 [b]	..	..	..	30	75	80	..	71	80
Ecuador	Ambato	286 [b]	..	..	..	..	90	81	91	87	..

	City	Urban population	Secure tenure	House price to income ratio	Work trips by public trans-portation	Travel time to work	Households with access to services				Wastewater treated
			Proportion of people with secure tenure				Access to potable water	Sewerage connection	Electricity	Telephone	
		thousands 2000	% 1998ᵃ	1998ᵃ	% 1998ᵃ	minutes 1998ᵃ	% 1998ᵃ	% 1998ᵃ	% 1998ᵃ	% 1998ᵃ	% 1998ᵃ
	Cuenca	..	91.0	4.6	..	25	97	92	97	48	82
	Guayaquil	2,317 ᵇ	45.8	3.4	89	45	70	42	..	44	9
	Manta	126 ᵇ	..	..	..	30	70	52	98	40	..
	Puyo	40 ᵇ	..	2.1	..	15	80	30	90	60	..
	Quito	1,531 ᵇ	93.8	2.4	..	33	85	70	96	55	..
	Tena	..	..	6.3	..	5	80	60	..	..	..
El Salvador	San Salvador	1,863 ᵇ	90.5	3.5	..	..	82	80	98	70	..
Estonia	Riik	..	99.5	..	..	..	92	90	98	55	..
	Tallin	397 ᶜ	98.8	6.4	..	35	98	98	100	86	100
Gabon	Libreville	523 ᶜ	..	..	80	30	55	0	95	45	44
Gambia	Banjul	50 ᵇ	91.8	11.4	55	22	23	12	24	..	..
Georgia	Tbilisi	1,310 ᶜ	100.0	9.4	..	..	..	98	100	58	..
Ghana	Accra	1,500 ᵇ	..	14.0	54	21	..	..	..	..	..
	Kumasi	780 ᵇ	77.7	13.7	51	21	65	..	95	51	..
Guatemala	Quetzaltenango	333 ᵇ	..	4.3	..	15	60	55	80	40	..
Guinea	Conakry	1,824 ᶜ	..	..	26	45	30	32	54	6	..
Indonesia	Jakarta	9,489 ᵇ	95.5	14.6	..	..	50	65	99	..	16
	Semarang	1,076 ᵇ	80.2	..	..	..	34	..	85	..	..
	Surabaya	2,373 ᵇ	97.6	3.4	18	35	41	56	89	71	..
Iraq	Baghdad	4,797 ᶜ	..	..	..	..	..	..	..	..	..
Italy	Aversa	..	..	..	..	..	..	..	..	..	90
Jamaica	Kingston	655 ᶜ	..	..	..	..	97	..	88	..	20
	Montego Bay	..	..	..	..	..	78	..	86	..	15
Jordan	Amman	1,621 ᵇ	97.3	6.1	21	25	98	81	99	62	54
Kenya	Kisumu	134 ᵇ	97.3	8.5	43	24	38	31	49	..	65
	Mombasa	..	..	..	47	20	..	..	..	..	50
	Nairobi	2,310 ᶜ	..	..	71	57	89	..	..	..	52
Korea, Rep	Hanam	124 ᵇ	..	3.7	..	..	81	68	100	100	81
	Pusan	3,843 ᵇ	100.0	4.0	39	42	98	69	100	100	69
	Seoul	10,389 ᵇ	98.6	5.7	71	60	100	99	100	..	99
Kuwait	Kuwait City	1,165 ᶜ	..	6.5	21	10	100	98	100	98	..
Kyrgyz Republic	Bishkek	60 ᵇ	94.8	..	95	35	30	23	100	20	15
Lao PDR	Vientiane	562 ᵇ	92.2	23.2	2	27	87	..	100	87	20
Latvia	Riga	775 ᶜ	97.4	15.6	..	..	95	93	100	70	..
Lebanon	Sin El Fil	.. ᵇ	..	8.3	50	10	80	30	98	80	..
Liberia	Monrovia	651 ᵇ	57.6	28.0	80	60	..	..	..	..	..
Libya	Tripoli	1,773 ᵇ	..	0.8	18	20	97	90	99	6	40
Lithuania	Vilnius	578 ᵇ	100.0	20.0	52	37	89	89	100	77	54
Madagascar	Antananarivo	1,507 ᶜ	..	..	..	..	..	..	..	..	..
Malawi	Lilongwe	765 ᶜ	..	..	27	5	65	12	50	10	..
Malaysia	Penang	..	..	7.2	55	40	99	..	100	98	20
Mauritania	Nouakchott	881 ᶜ	89.9	5.4	45	50	..	..	..	..	..
Mexico	Ciudad Juarez	1,018 ᵇ	..	..	24	23	89	77	96	45	..
Moldova	Chisinau	..	..	..	80	23	100	95	100	83	71
Mongolia	Ulaanbaatar	627 ᵇ	51.6	7.8	80	30	60	60	100	90	96
Morocco	Casablanca	3,292 ᵇ	..	..	..	30	83	93	91	..	..
	Rabat	646 ᵇ	..	..	40	20	93	97	52	..	..
Myanmar	Yangon	3,692 ᵇ	..	8.3	69	45	78	81	85	17	..
Nicaragua	Leon	..	98.8	..	..	15	78	..	84	21	..
Niger	Niamey	731 ᶜ	87.4	..	..	30	33	0	51	4	..
Nigeria	Ibadan	1,731 ᶜ	85.8	..	46	45	26	12	41	..	..
	Lagos	13,427 ᶜ	93.0	..	48	60	..	..	41	..	..
Oman	Muscat	887 ᵇ	..	..	..	20	80	90	89	53	..
Panama	Colon	132 ᵇ	..	14.2	..	15	..	..	..	..	..
Paraguay	Asuncion	1,262 ᶜ	90.2	10.7	..	25	46	8	86	17	..
Peru	Cajamarca	..	90.0	3.9	..	20	86	69	81	38	62
	Huanuco	747 ᵇ	..	30.0	..	20	57	28	80	32	..

	City	Urban population	Secure tenure	House price to income ratio	Work trips by public transportation	Travel time to work	Households with access to services				Wastewater treated
			Proportion of people with secure tenure				Access to potable water	Sewerage connection	Electricity	Telephone	
		thousands 2000	% 1998[a]	1998[a]	% 1998[a]	minutes 1998[a]	% 1998[a]	% 1998[a]	% 1998[a]	% 1998[a]	% 1998[a]
	Huaras	54 [b]	..	6.7	..	15	..	..	71	..	..
	Iquitos	347 [b]	97.3	5.6	25	10	73	60	82	62	..
	Lima	7,431 [b]	80.6	10.4	82	..	75	71	99	..	4
	Tacna	..	..	4.0	..	25	65	58	74	16	64
	Tumbes	..	..	..	..	20	60	35	80	25	..
Philippines	Cebu	2,189 [b]	95.0	13.3	..	35	41	92	80	25	..
Poland	Bydgoszcz	..	60.5	4.3	35	18	95	87	100	85	28
	Gdansk	893 [c]	..	4.4	56	20	99	94	100	56	100
	Katowice	3,487 [c]	27.8	1.7	29	36	99	94	100	75	67
	Poznan	..	65.5	5.8	51	25	95	96	100	86	78
Qatar	Doha	391 [c]	..	..	..	..	..	..	..	..	..
Russian Federation	Astrakhan	..	100.0	5.0	66	35	81	79	100	51	92
	Belgorod	..	100.0	4.0	..	25	90	89	100	51	96
	Kostroma	..	100.0	6.9	68	20	88	84	100	46	96
	Moscow	9,321 [c]	100.0	5.1	85	62	100	100	100	102	98
	Nizhny Novgorod	1,458 [c]	100.0	6.9	79	35	98	98	100	64	98
	Novomoscowsk	..	100.0	4.2	61	25	99	93	100	62	97
	Omsk	1,216 [c]	99.7	3.9	86	43	87	87	100	41	89
	Pushkin	..	100.0	9.6	60	15	99	99	100	89	100
	Surgut	..	100.0	4.5	81	57	98	98	100	50	93
	Veliky Novgorod	..	100.0	3.4	75	30	97	97	100	51	95
Rwanda	Kigali	358 [b]	..	11.4	32	45	36	20	57	6	20
Samoa	Apia	34 [b]	..	10.0	..	..	60	0	98	96	..
Singapore	Singapore	3,164 [b]	100.0	3.1	53	30	100	100	100	100	100
Slovenia	Ljubljana	273 [b]	98.9	7.8	20	30	100	100	100	97	98
Spain	Madrid	4,577 [b]	..	..	16	32	..	..	..	..	100
	Pamplona	..	..	..	..	..	100	..	100	..	79
Sweden	Amal	13 [b]	..	2.9	..	..	100	100	100	..	100
	Stockholm	736 [b]	..	6.0	48	28	100	100	100	..	100
	Umea	104 [b]	..	5.3	..	16	100	100	100	..	100
Switzerland	Basel	170 [b]	..	12.3	..	..	100	100	100	99	100
Syria	Damascus	2,335 [b]	..	10.3	33	40	98	71	95	10	3
Thailand	Bangkok	5,647 [b]	77.2	8.8	28	60	99	100	100	60	..
	Chiang Mai	499 [b]	96.5	6.8	5	30	95	60	100	75	70
Togo	Lome	663 [b]	64.0	..	40	30	..	70	51	18	..
Trinidad and Tobago	Port of Spain	..	78.6	..	44	..	..	..	..	..	..
Tunisia	Tunis	2,023 [b]	..	5.0	..	..	75	47	95	27	83
Turkey	Ankara	2,837 [b]	91.3	4.5	..	32	97	98	100	..	80
Uganda	Entebbe	65 [b]	74.0	10.4	65	20	48	13	42	0	30
	Jinja	92 [b]	82.0	15.4	49	12	65	43	55	5	30
Uruguay	Montevideo	1,670 [b]	88.0	5.6	60	45	98	79	100	75	34
West Bank and Gaza	Gaza	367 [b]	87.3	5.4	..	..	85	38	99	38	..
Yemen, Rep.	Aden	1,200 [b]	..	..	78	20	..	..	96	..	30
	Sana'a	1,200 [b]	..	..	78	20	30	9	96	..	30
Yugoslavia, Fed. Rep.	Belgrade	1,182 [b]	96.5	13.5	72	40	95	86	100	86	20
Zimbabwe	Bulawayo	900 [b]	99.4	..	75	15	100	100	98	..	80
	Chegutu	..	51.5	3.4	20	22	100	68	9	3	69
	Gweru	..	94.0	..	..	15	100	100	90	61	95
	Harare	1,634 [b]	99.9	..	32	45	100	100	88	42	..
	Mutare	149 [b]	..	..	70	20	88	88	74	4	100

a. Data are preliminary. b. Data refer to 1998 and are from UNCHS c. Data refer to 2000 and are from the United Nations Population Division's *World Urbanization Prospects: The 1999 Revision.*

About the data

Despite the importance of cities and urban agglomerations as home to almost half the world's people, data on many aspects of urban life are sparse. Compiling comparable data has been difficult, and the available indicators have been scattered among international agencies with different mandates. Even within cities it is difficult to assemble an integrated data set. Urban areas are often spread across many jurisdictions with no single agency responsible for collecting and reporting data for the entire area. Adding to the difficulties of data collection are gaps and overlaps in the data collection and reporting responsibilities of different administrative units. Creating a comprehensive, comparable international data set is further complicated by differences in the definition of an urban area and by uneven data quality.

The United Nations Global Plan of Action calls for monitoring the changing role of the world's cities and human settlements. The international agency with the mandate to assemble information on urban areas is the United Nations Centre for Human Settlements (UNCHS, or Habitat). Its Urban Indicators Programme is intended to provide data for monitoring and evaluating the performance of urban areas and for developing government policies and strategies. These data are collected through questionnaires completed by city officials in more than a hundred countries. The table shows selected indicators for more than 160 cities from the UNCHS data set. A few more indicators are included on the *World Development Indicators* CD-ROM. These data are still preliminary and are undergoing further validation.

The UNCHS selection of cities does not reflect population weights or the economic importance of cities and is therefore biased toward smaller cities. Moreover, it is based on demand for participation in the Urban Indicators Programme. As a result, the database excludes a large number of major cities. The table reflects this bias as well as the criterion of data availability for the indicators shown in the table.

The data should be used with care. Because different data collection methods and definitions may have been used, comparisons can be misleading. In addition, the definitions used here for urban population and access to potable water are more stringent than those used for tables 3.5 and 3.10 (see *Definitions*).

Definitions

• **Urban population** refers to the population of the urban agglomeration, a contiguous inhabited territory without regard to administrative boundaries. • **Secure tenure** refers to the percentage of the population protected from involuntary removal from land or residence except through due legal process including residences owned, purchased, or privately rented; residence in social housing; and subtenancy. • **House price to income ratio** is the average house price divided by the average household income. • **Work trips by public transportation** are the percentage of trips to work made by bus or minibus, tram, or train. Buses or minibuses refer to road vehicles other than cars taking passengers on a fare-paying basis. Other means of transport commonly used in developing countries, such as taxi, ferry, rickshaw, or animal, are not included. • **Travel time to work** is the average time in minutes, for all modes, for a one-way trip to work. Train and bus times include average walking and waiting times, and car times include parking and walking to the workplace. • **Households with access to services** are the percentage of households in formal settlements with access to potable water and connections to sewerage, electricity, and telephone. Households with access to potable water are those having access to safe or potable drinking water within 200 meters of the dwelling. Potable water is water that is free from contamination and safe to drink without further treatment. • **Wastewater treated** is the percentage of all wastewater undergoing some form of treatment.

Data sources

The data in the table are from the Global Urban Indicators database of the UNCHS.

Table 3.11a

House prices vary widely relative to household income					
Country	City	House price to income ratio	Country	City	House price to income ratio
Peru	Huanuco	30.0	Bulgaria	Troyan	3.7
Bolivia	Santa Cruz de la Sierra	29.3	Korea, Rep.	Hanam	3.7
Liberia	Monrovia	28.0	El Salvador	San Salvador	3.5
Brazil	Santo André	23.4	Russian Federation	Veliky Novgorod	3.4
Lao PDR	Vientiane	23.2	Zimbabwe	Chegutu	3.4
Lithuania	Vilnius	20.0	Singapore	Singapore	3.1
Bangladesh	Dhaka	16.7	Sweden	Amal	2.9
Latvia	Riga	15.6	Ecuador	Quito	2.4
Uganda	Jinja	15.4	Poland	Katowice	1.7
Indonesia	Jakarta	14.6	Libya	Tripoli	0.8

Source: Table 3.11.

3.12 | Traffic and congestion

| | Motor vehicles | | | | Passenger cars | | Two-wheelers | | Road traffic | | Fuel prices | |
| | per 1,000 people | | per kilometer of road | | per 1,000 people | | per 1,000 people | | million vehicle kilometers | | Super $ per liter | Diesel $ per liter |
	1990	2000	1990	2000	1990	2000	1990	2000	1990	2000	2000	2000
Afghanistan	..	..	..	..	..	..	..	..	..	..	..	..
Albania	11	44	3	10	2	29	3	1	..	..	0.57	0.30
Algeria	..	..	..	..	..	..	..	..	..	..	0.27	0.15
Angola	19	..	..	..	14	..	..	..	..	..	0.30	0.15
Argentina	181	181	27	30	134	140	1	..	43,119	27,458	1.07	0.52
Armenia	5	..	2	..	1	..	..	..	..	..	0.51	0.34
Australia	530	..	11	13	450	..	18	..	138,501	..	0.57	0.57
Austria	421	536	30	22	387	495	71	77	..	..	0.82	0.74
Azerbaijan	52	49	7	16	36	38	5	1	..	..	0.46	0.22
Bangladesh	1	1	0	1	0	0	1	1	..	..	0.46	0.29
Belarus	61	135	13	20	59	135	..	53	10,026	4,964	0.34	0.13
Belgium	423	497	30	35	385	448	14	25	..	158,759	0.96	0.78
Benin	3	..	2	..	2	..	34	..	..	..	0.48	0.39
Bolivia	41	..	6	8	25	..	9	..	1,139	..	0.80	0.50
Bosnia and Herzegovina	114	..	24	..	101	..	..	..	..	..	0.68	0.57
Botswana	19	70	3	11	10	30	..	1	..	..	0.42	0.39
Brazil	88	..	8	17	..	..	..	..	..	..	0.92	0.34
Bulgaria	163	266	39	60	146	233	55	63	..	..	0.70	0.58
Burkina Faso	4	..	3	..	2	..	9	..	..	..	0.68	0.46
Burundi	..	..	..	..	..	..	..	..	..	..	1.01	0.71
Cambodia	1	6	0	31	0	5	9	41	314	7,210	0.61	0.44
Cameroon	10	..	3	..	6	..	..	..	..	..	0.56	0.47
Canada	605	581	20	19	468	459	12	11	..	..	0.58	0.47
Central African Republic	1	0	0	0	1	0	0	..	1,494	..	0.81	0.65
Chad	5	..	0	..	1	..	0	..	..	..	0.68	0.60
Chile	81	135	13	25	52	88	2	2	..	..	0.64	0.47
China	5	..	4	11	1	..	3	..	..	..	0.40	0.45
Hong Kong, China	66	78	253	287	42	58	4	5	8,192	10,781	1.46	0.80
Colombia	..	51	..	19	..	43	8	12	50,945	41,587	0.49	0.35
Congo, Dem. Rep.	..	..	..	..	..	..	..	..	..	..	1.00	0.93
Congo, Rep.	18	..	3	..	12	..	..	..	..	..	0.53	0.30
Costa Rica	87	133	7	14	55	88	14	22	..	507,796	0.65	0.44
Côte d'Ivoire	23	..	6	..	15	..	..	..	..	..	0.76	0.51
Croatia	..	..	..	44	..	..	..	..	..	13,764	0.76	0.60
Cuba	37	32	16	6	18	16	19	16	..	..	0.50	0.18
Czech Republic	246	363	46	67	228	335	113	78	..	..	0.77	0.68
Denmark	368	411	27	31	320	353	9	12	36,304	45,165	1.01	0.90
Dominican Republic	75	..	48	..	21	..	..	..	..	..	0.71	0.39
Ecuador	35	46	8	14	31	41	2	2	10,306	14,449	0.31	0.18
Egypt, Arab Rep.	29	..	33	..	21	..	6	..	..	..	0.26	0.10
El Salvador	33	61	14	36	17	30	0	5	2,002	3,646	0.67	0.40
Eritrea	1	..	1	..	1	..	..	..	..	..	0.56	0.33
Estonia	211	394	22	11	154	331	66	1	..	6,412	0.60	0.55
Ethiopia	1	2	2	3	1	1	0	0	..	1,642	0.46	0.27
Finland	441	462	29	31	386	403	12	35	39,750	46,010	1.06	0.84
France	494	564	32	38	405	469	55	..	422,000	519,400	0.99	0.82
Gabon	26	..	4	..	19	..	..	..	..	..	0.53	0.37
Gambia, The	14	..	5	..	6	..	..	..	..	..	0.64	0.47
Georgia	107	63	27	15	89	49	5	1	4,620	..	0.46	0.25
Germany	405	..	53	..	386	508	18	36	446,000	589,500	0.91	0.78
Ghana	..	..	..	..	..	..	..	..	..	..	0.20	0.19
Greece	248	348	22	31	171	254	120	203	..	77,954	0.72	0.71
Guatemala	..	57	..	45	..	52	..	12	..	3,455	0.53	0.42
Guinea	4	..	1	..	2	..	..	..	..	..	0.85	0.69
Guinea-Bissau	7	..	2	..	4	..	..	..	..	..	..	..
Haiti	..	..	..	..	..	..	..	..	..	..	0.64	0.35
Honduras	22	62	9	28	..	52	..	15	3,288	..	0.62	0.46

2002 World Development Indicators

	Motor vehicles				Passenger cars		Two-wheelers		Road traffic		Fuel prices	
	per 1,000 people		per kilometer of road		per 1,000 people		per 1,000 people		million vehicle kilometers		Super $ per liter	Diesel $ per liter
	1990	2000	1990	2000	1990	2000	1990	2000	1990	2000	2000	2000
Hungary	212	272	21	15	188	238	16	14	22,898	..	0.81	0.79
India	4	8	2	3	2	5	15	27	..	..	0.60	0.39
Indonesia	16	25	10	14	7	14	34	62	..	..	0.17	0.06
Iran, Islamic Rep.	34	..	14	..	25	..	36	..	..	..	0.05	0.02
Iraq	14	..	6	..	1	..	..	..	..	..	0.03	0.01
Ireland	270	..	10	14	227	..	6	..	24,205	..	0.72	0.72
Israel	210	270	74	107	174	220	8	12	18,212	35,863	1.14	0.64
Italy	529	591	99	73	476	539	45	66	344,726	..	0.97	0.83
Jamaica	..	..	..	..	..	..	..	..	..	..	0.62	0.49
Japan	469	560	52	62	283	395	146	115	628,581	765,056	1.06	0.76
Jordan	60	..	26	..	..	..	0	..	1,098	..	0.45	0.15
Kazakhstan	76	86	8	12	50	66	..	10	18,248	3,215	0.36	0.29
Kenya	13	..	5	..	10	..	1	..	5,170	..	0.71	0.60
Korea, Dem. Rep.	..	..	..	..	..	..	..	..	..	..	0.73	0.41
Korea, Rep.	79	238	60	128	48	167	32	59	30,464	67,266	0.92	0.66
Kuwait	..	..	..	..	..	..	..	..	..	..	0.21	0.18
Kyrgyz Republic	44	39	10	10	44	39	..	..	5,220	..	0.44	0.33
Lao PDR	9	..	3	..	6	..	18	..	..	..	0.41	0.32
Latvia	135	260	6	9	106	218	76	8	3,932	..	0.67	0.58
Lebanon	321	336	183	..	300	313	13	15	..	..	0.53	0.31
Lesotho	11	..	4	..	3	..	..	..	..	..	0.50	0.47
Liberia	15	..	4	..	7	..	..	..	..	..	..	..
Libya	..	..	..	..	..	..	..	..	..	..	0.25	0.16
Lithuania	159	322	12	17	132	334	52	5	..	..	0.55	0.45
Macedonia, FYR	132	..	30	..	121	..	1	..	3,102	..	0.76	0.56
Madagascar	6	..	2	..	4	..	..	..	41,500	..	0.76	0.45
Malawi	4	..	4	..	2	..	..	..	..	..	0.69	0.68
Malaysia	124	200	26	69	101	170	167	224	..	..	0.28	0.16
Mali	4	..	2	..	2	..	..	..	..	..	0.70	0.43
Mauritania	9	..	3	..	7	..	..	..	..	..	0.67	0.40
Mauritius	60	98	35	49	44	73	54	96	..	..	..	..
Mexico	119	151	41	44	82	102	3	..	55,095	..	0.61	0.45
Moldova	53	70	17	24	48	54	45	..	..	538	0.45	0.40
Mongolia	21	30	1	2	6	17	22	11	340	40	0.38	0.38
Morocco	37	52	15	21	28	41	1	1	..	..	0.82	0.53
Mozambique	4	..	2	0	3	..	..	..	1,889	..	0.56	0.54
Myanmar	..	..	..	..	..	..	..	..	..	..	0.00	0.00
Namibia	71	0	1	2	39	..	1	..	1,896	2,706	0.47	0.44
Nepal	..	..	..	..	..	..	..	..	..	..	0.63	0.37
Netherlands	405	427	58	58	368	383	44	25	90,150	109,955	1.03	0.78
New Zealand	524	540	19	29	436	481	24	12	..	..	0.48	0.34
Nicaragua	19	10	5	8	10	3	3	2	108	523	0.62	0.54
Niger	6	..	4	5	5	..	..	..	178	240	0.68	0.48
Nigeria	33	..	21	14	12	..	5	..	..	..	0.27	0.27
Norway	458	505	22	25	380	407	48	54	..	30,148	1.19	1.15
Oman	130	..	9	..	83	..	3	..	..	..	0.31	0.29
Pakistan	6	8	4	4	4	5	8	15	18,933	218,779	0.53	0.27
Panama	75	113	18	27	60	83	2	3	..	..	0.53	0.41
Papua New Guinea	..	..	..	..	..	..	..	..	..	..	0.53	0.34
Paraguay	..	..	..	..	..	..	..	..	..	..	0.72	0.34
Peru	..	43	..	15	..	27	..	..	..	..	0.80	0.54
Philippines	10	31	4	11	7	10	6	14	6,189	9,548	0.37	0.28
Poland	168	286	18	33	138	240	36	37	59,608	138,100	0.76	0.65
Portugal	222	348	34	..	162	310	5	77	28,623	93,020	0.77	0.54
Puerto Rico	..	..	..	..	..	..	..	..	..	..	0.34	0.32
Romania	72	154	11	17	56	133	13	14	23,907	36,884	0.46	0.35
Russian Federation	87	153	14	48	65	120	..	..	..	60,950	0.33	0.29

	Motor vehicles				Passenger cars		Two-wheelers		Road traffic		Fuel prices	
	per 1,000 people		per kilometer of road		per 1,000 people		per 1,000 people		million vehicle kilometers		Super $ per liter	Diesel $ per liter
	1990	2000	1990	2000	1990	2000	1990	2000	1990	2000	2000	2000
Rwanda	2	..	1	2	1	..	..	..	..	..	0.89	0.84
Saudi Arabia	165	..	19	..	98	..	0	..	..	..	0.24	0.10
Senegal	11	..	6	8	8	..	0	..	..	..	0.73	0.52
Sierra Leone	10	3	4	2	7	2	2	0	996	529	0.00	0.00
Singapore	130	132	142	170	89	97	40	34	..	..	0.84	0.38
Slovak Republic	194	260	57	33	163	229	61	8	..	0	0.69	0.68
Slovenia	306	455	42	46	289	418	8	5	5,620	9,245	0.63	0.66
Somalia	2	..	1	0	1	..	..	..	..	..	..	..
South Africa	160	143	26	11	97	94	8	4	..	..	0.50	0.50
Spain	360	472	43	53	309	389	79	34	100,981	201,896	0.73	0.65
Sri Lanka	20	34	4	7	6	15	23	40	3,468	15,630	0.66	0.27
Sudan	9	..	21	28	8	..	..	..	..	..	0.28	0.24
Swaziland	72	70	18	17	35	34	3	3	..	..	0.47	0.44
Sweden	464	478	29	21	426	437	11	29	61,040	69,200	0.94	0.80
Switzerland	491	526	46	54	449	486	114	104	48,660	53,506	0.78	0.84
Syrian Arab Republic	26	30	10	11	10	9	..	..	..	..	0.44	0.13
Tajikistan	3	..	1	..	0	..	..	..	..	..	0.45	0.55
Tanzania	5	..	2	2	1	..	..	..	..	..	0.75	0.73
Thailand	46	..	36	..	14	..	86	..	45,769	..	0.39	0.35
Togo	24	..	11	..	16	..	8	..	..	..	0.48	0.40
Trinidad and Tobago	..	..	..	..	..	..	..	..	..	..	0.39	0.20
Tunisia	48	..	19	40	23	..	..	..	..	..	0.49	0.29
Turkey	50	85	8	14	34	63	10	15	27,041	49,846	0.88	0.66
Turkmenistan	..	..	..	..	..	..	..	..	..	..	0.02	0.02
Uganda	2	5	..	4	1	2	0	3	..	..	0.86	0.75
Ukraine	63	..	19	..	63	104	..	49	59,500	61,200	0.37	0.30
United Arab Emirates	121	..	52	..	97	..	..	..	..	..	0.25	0.26
United Kingdom	400	418	64	62	341	373	14	12	399,000	462,400	1.17	1.22
United States	758	760	30	34	573	478	17	14	2,527,441	2,653,043	0.47	0.48
Uruguay	138	174	45	63	122	158	74	110	..	..	1.19	0.53
Uzbekistan	..	..	..	..	..	..	..	..	..	..	0.43	0.28
Venezuela, RB	..	..	..	..	..	..	..	..	..	563	0.12	0.08
Vietnam	..	..	..	..	..	..	45	..	..	..	0.38	0.27
West Bank and Gaza	..	..	..	..	..	..	..	..	..	..	0.01	0.00
Yemen, Rep.	34	..	8	..	14	..	..	..	8,681	11,476	0.21	0.06
Yugoslavia, Fed. Rep.	137	190	31	36	133	176	3	..	..	..	0.56	0.56
Zambia	15	..	3	..	8	..	..	..	..	..	1.00	1.00
Zimbabwe	..	..	..	..	..	..	..	..	..	..	0.85	0.72
World	**120 w**	**176 w**			**91 w**	**141 w**					**0.61 m**	**0.45 m**
Low income	9	10			6	9					0.58	0.40
Middle income	40	65			26	49					0.55	0.41
Lower middle income	15	33			9	24					0.53	0.39
Upper middle income	116	191			93	150					0.58	0.45
Low & middle income	26	60			17	47					0.56	0.41
East Asia & Pacific	11	16			5	10					0.39	0.34
Europe & Central Asia	98	205			83	171					0.58	0.55
Latin America & Carib.	92	158			77	119					0.62	0.41
Middle East & N. Africa	58	..			32	..					0.27	0.16
South Asia	4	8			2	5					0.59	0.33
Sub-Saharan Africa	24	..			14	..					0.65	0.47
High income	536	610			414	459					0.81	0.69
Europe EMU	453	558			379	496					0.87	0.76

About the data

Traffic congestion in urban areas constrains economic productivity, damages people's health, and degrades the quality of their lives. The particulate air pollution emitted by motor vehicles—the dust and soot in exhaust—is proving to be far more damaging to human health than was once believed. (For information on suspended particulates and other air pollutants see table 3.13.)

In recent years ownership of passenger cars has increased, and the expansion of economic activity has led to the transport by road of more goods and services over greater distances (see table 5.8). These developments have increased demand for roads and vehicles, adding to urban congestion, air pollution, health hazards, traffic accidents, and injuries.

Congestion, the most visible cost of expanding vehicle ownership, is reflected in the indicators in the table. Other relevant indicators—such as average vehicle speed in major cities or the cost of traffic congestion, which takes a heavy toll on economic productivity—are not included here because data are incomplete or difficult to compare.

The data in the table—except for those on fuel prices—are compiled by the International Road Federation (IRF) through questionnaires sent to national organizations. The IRF uses a hierarchy of sources to gather as much information as possible. The primary sources are national road associations. Where such an association lacks data or does not respond, other agencies are contacted, including road directorates, ministries of transport or public works, and central statistical offices. As a result, the compiled data are of uneven quality. The coverage of each indicator may differ across countries because of differences in definitions. Comparability also is limited when time-series data are reported. Moreover, the data do not capture the quality or age of vehicles or the condition or width of roads. Thus comparisons over time and between countries should be made with caution.

The data on fuel prices are compiled by the German Agency for Technical Cooperation (GTZ) from its global network of regional offices and representatives as well as other sources, including the Allgemeiner Deutscher Automobil Club (for Europe) and a project of the Latin American Energy Organization (OLADE, for Latin America). Local prices have been converted to U.S. dollars using the exchange rate on the survey date as listed in the international monetary table of the *Financial Times*. For countries with multiple exchange rates, the market, parallel, or black market rate was used rather than the official exchange rate.

181

2002 World Development Indicators

Figure 3.12

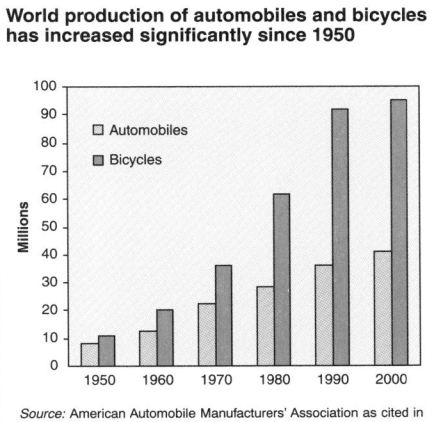

World production of automobiles and bicycles has increased significantly since 1950

Source: American Automobile Manufacturers' Association as cited in the WorldWatch Institute (2001)

Definitions

• **Motor vehicles** include cars, buses, and freight vehicles but not two-wheelers. Population figures refer to the midyear population in the year for which data are available. Roads refer to motorways, highways, main or national roads, and secondary or regional roads. A motorway is a road specially designed and built for motor traffic that separates the traffic flowing in opposite directions. • **Passenger cars** refer to road motor vehicles, other than two-wheelers, intended for the carriage of passengers and designed to seat no more than nine people (including the driver). • **Two-wheelers** refer to mopeds and motorcycles. • **Road traffic** is the number of vehicles multiplied by the average distances they travel. • **Fuel prices** refer to the pump prices of the most widely sold grade of gasoline and of diesel fuel. Prices have been converted from the local currency to U.S. dollars (see *About the data*).

Data sources

The data on vehicles and traffic are from the IRF's electronic files and its annual *World Road Statistics*. The data on fuel prices are from the GTZ's electronic files.

3.13 | Air pollution

	City	City population	Total suspended particulates	Sulfur dioxide	Nitrogen dioxide
		thousands **2000**	micrograms per cubic meter **1995**[a]	micrograms per cubic meter **1998**[b]	micrograms per cubic meter **1998**[b]
Argentina	Córdoba City	1,423	97	..	97
Australia	Melbourne	3,187	35	0	30
	Perth	1,313	45	5	19
	Sydney	3,664	54	28	81
Austria	Vienna	2,070	47	14	42
Belgium	Brussels	1,122	78	20	48
Brazil	Rio de Janeiro	10,582	139	129	..
	São Paulo	17,755	86	43	83
Bulgaria	Sofia	1,192	195	39	122
Canada	Montreal	3,448	34	10	42
	Toronto	4,651	36	17	43
	Vancouver	2,033	29	14	37
Chile	Santiago	5,538	..	29	81
China	Anshan	1,453	305	115	88
	Beijing	10,839	377	90	122
	Changchun	3,093	381	21	64
	Chengdu	3,294	366	77	74
	Chongqing	5,312	320	340	70
	Dalian	2,628	185	61	100
	Guangzhu	3,893	295	57	136
	Guiyang	2,533	330	424	53
	Harbin	2,928	359	23	30
	Jinan	2,568	472	132	45
	Kunming	1,701	253	19	33
	Lanzhou	1,730	732	102	104
	Liupanshui	2,023	408	102	..
	Nanchang	1,722	279	69	29
	Pinxiang	1,502	276	75	..
	Quingdao	2,316	..	190	64
	Shanghai	12,887	246	53	73
	Shenyang	4,828	374	99	73
	Taiyuan	2,415	568	211	55
	Tianjin	9,156	306	82	50
	Urumqi	1,643	515	60	70
	Wuhan	5,169	211	40	43
	Zhengzhou	2,070	474	63	95
	Zibo	2,675	453	198	43
Colombia	Bogotá	6,288	120	..	..
Croatia	Zagreb	810	71	31	..
Cuba	Havana	2,256	..	1	5
Czech Republic	Prague	1,226	59	14	33
Denmark	Copenhagen	1,388	61	7	54
Ecuador	Guayaquil	2,293	127	15	..
	Quito	1,754	175	22	..
Egypt, Arab Rep.	Cairo	10,552	..	69	..
Finland	Helsinki	1,167	40	4	35
France	Paris	9,624	14	14	57
Germany	Berlin	3,324	50	18	26
	Frankfurt	3,687	36	11	45
	Munich	2,294	45	8	53
Ghana	Accra	1,976	137	..	..
Greece	Athens	3,116	178	34	64
Hungary	Budapest	1,825	63	39	51
Iceland	Reykjavik	168	24	5	42
India	Ahmedabad	4,160	299	30	21
	Bangalore	5,561	123	..	..
	Calcutta	12,918	375	49	34

About the data

In many towns and cities exposure to air pollution is the main environmental threat to human health. Winter smog—made up of soot, dust, and sulfur dioxide—has long been associated with temporary spikes in the number of deaths. Long-term exposure to high levels of soot and small particles in the air also contributes to a wide range of chronic respiratory diseases and exacerbates heart disease and other conditions. Particulate pollution, on its own or in combination with sulfur dioxide, leads to an enormous burden of ill health.

Emissions of sulfur dioxide and nitrogen oxides lead to the deposition of acid rain and other acidic compounds over long distances—often more than 1,000 kilometers from their source. Acid deposition changes the chemical balance of soils and can lead to the leaching of trace minerals and nutrients critical to trees and plants. The links between forest damage and acid deposition are complex. Direct exposure to high levels of acid deposition can cause defoliation and dieback.

Where coal is the primary fuel for power plants, steel mills, industrial boilers, and domestic heating, the result is usually high levels of urban air pollution—especially particulates and sometimes sulfur dioxide—and, if the sulfur content of the coal is high, widespread acid deposition. Where coal is not an important primary fuel or is used by plants with effective dust control, the worst emissions of air pollutants stem from the combustion of petroleum products.

The data on air pollution are based on reports from urban monitoring sites. Annual means (measured in micrograms per cubic meter) are average concentrations observed at these sites. Coverage is not comprehensive because not all cities have monitoring systems. For example, data are reported for just 5 cities in Africa but for more than 87 cities in China. Pollutant concentrations are sensitive to local conditions, and even in the same city different monitoring sites may register different concentrations. Thus these data should be considered only a general indication of air quality in each city, and cross-country comparisons should be made with caution. World Health Organization (WHO) annual mean guidelines for air quality standards are 90 micrograms per cubic meter for total suspended particulates, and 50 for sulfur dioxide and nitrogen dioxide.

Air pollution | 3.13

City		City population	Total suspended particulates	Sulfur dioxide	Nitrogen dioxide
		thousands 2000	micrograms per cubic meter 1995[a]	micrograms per cubic meter 1998[b]	micrograms per cubic meter 1998[b]
	Chennai	6,002	130	15	17
	Delhi	11,695	415	24	41
	Hyderabad	6,842	152	12	17
	Kanpur	2,450	459	15	14
	Lucknow	2,568	463	26	25
	Mumbai	18,066	240	33	39
	Nagpur	2,062	185	6	13
	Pune	3,489	208		
Indonesia	Jakarta	11,018	271	..	..
Iran, Islamic Rep.	Tehran	7,225	248	209	..
Ireland	Dublin	985	..	20	..
Italy	Milan	4,251	77	31	248
	Rome	2,688	73	..	..
	Torino	1,294	151	..	..
Japan	Osaka	11,013	43	19	63
	Tokyo	26,444	49	18	68
	Yokohama	3,178	..	100	13
Kenya	Nairobi	2,310	69	..	..
Korea, Rep.	Seoul	9,888	84	44	60
	Pusan	3,830	94	60	51
	Seoul	9,888	84	44	60
	Taegu	2,675	72	81	62
Malaysia	Kuala Lumpur	1,378	85	24	..
Mexico	Mexico City	18,131	279	74	130
Netherlands	Amsterdam	1,144	40	10	58
New Zealand	Auckland	1,102	26	3	20
Norway	Oslo	970	15	8	43
Philippines	Manila	10,870	200	33	..
Poland	Lodz	1,055	..	21	43
	Warsaw	2,269	..	16	32
Portugal	Lisbon	3,826	61	8	52
Romania	Bucharest	2,054	82	10	71
Russian Federation	Moscow	9,321	100	109	..
	Omsk	1,216	100	20	34
Singapore	Singapore	3,567	..	20	30
Slovak Republic	Bratislava	460	62	21	27
South Africa	Capetown	2,993	..	21	72
	Durban	1,335	..	31	..
	Johannesburg	2,335	..	19	31
Spain	Barcelona	2,819	117	11	43
	Madrid	4,072	42	24	66
Sweden	Stockholm	1,583	9	3	20
Switzerland	Zurich	983	31	11	39
Thailand	Bangkok	7,281	223	11	23
Turkey	Ankara	3,203	57	55	46
	Istanbul	9,451	..	120	..
Ukraine	Kiev	2,670	100	14	51
United Kingdom	Birmingham	2,272	..	9	45
	London	7,640	..	25	77
	Manchester	2,252	..	26	49
United States	Chicago	6,951	..	14	57
	Los Angeles	13,140	..	9	74
	New York	16,640	..	26	79
Venezuela, RB	Caracas	3,151	53	33	57

Definitions

• **City population** is the number of residents of the city as defined by national authorities and reported to the United Nations. • **Total suspended particulates** refer to smoke, soot, dust, and liquid droplets from combustion that are in the air. Particulate levels indicate the quality of the air people are breathing and the state of a country's technology and pollution controls. • **Sulfur dioxide** (SO_2) is an air pollutant produced when fossil fuels containing sulfur are burned. It contributes to acid rain and can damage human health, particularly that of the young and the elderly. • **Nitrogen dioxide** (NO_2) is a poisonous, pungent gas formed when nitric oxide combines with hydrocarbons and sunlight, producing a photochemical reaction. These conditions occur in both natural and anthropogenic activities. NO_2 is emitted by bacteria, nitrogenous fertilizers, aerobic decomposition of organic matter in oceans and soils, combustion of fuels and biomass, motor vehicles, and industrial activities.

Data sources

The data in the table are from the WHO's Healthy Cities Air Management Information System and the World Resources Institute, which relies on various national sources as well as, among others, the United Nations Environment Programme and WHO's *Urban Air Pollution in Megacities of the World* (1992), the Organisation for Economic Co-operation and Development's *OECD Environmental Data: Compendium 1999,* the U.S. Environmental Protection Agency's *National Air Quality and Emissions Trends Report 1995,* AIRS Executive International database, and the United Nations Centre for Human Settlements' (UNCHS) Urban Indicators database.

183

2002 World Development Indicators

a. Data are for the most recent year available in 1990-95. Most are for 1995. b. Data are for the most recent year available in 1990-98. Most are for 1995.

3.14 | Government commitment

	Environmental strategy or action plan	Country environmental profile	Biodiversity assessment, strategy or action plan	Participation in treaties[a]				
				Climate change	Ozone layer	CFC control	Law of the Sea[b]	Biological diversity[b]
Afghanistan	..	..	..	..	..	..	..	..
Albania	1993	..	..	1995	2000	2000	..	1994
Algeria	2001	..	..	1994	1993	1993	1996	1995
Angola	..	..	..	2000 c	2000	2000	1994	1998
Argentina	1992	..	..	1994	1990	1990	1996	1995
Armenia	..	..	..	1994	2000	2000	..	1993
Australia	1992	..	1994	1994	1987	1989	1995	1993
Austria	..	..	..	1994	1987	1989	1995	1994
Azerbaijan	1998	..	..	1995	1996	1996	..	2000 c
Bangladesh	1991	1989	1990	1994	1990	1990	2001	1994
Belarus	..	..	..	2000 c	1986	1989	..	1993
Belgium	..	..	..	1996	1989	1989	1998	1997
Benin	1993	..	..	1994	1993	1993	1997	1994
Bolivia	1994	1986	1988	1995	1995	1995	1995	1995
Bosnia and Herzegovina	..	..	..	..	1992	1992	1994	..
Botswana	1990	1986	1991	1994	1992	1992	1994	1996
Brazil	..	..	1988	1994	1990	1990	1994	1994
Bulgaria	..	..	1994	1995	1991	1991	1996	1996
Burkina Faso	1993	1994	..	1994	1989	1989	..	1993
Burundi	1994	1981	1989	1997	1997	1997	..	1997
Cambodia	1999	..	..	1996	..	..	..	1995
Cameroon	..	1989	1989	1995	1989	1989	1994	1995
Canada	1990	..	1994	1994	1986	1988	..	1993
Central African Republic	..	..	..	1995	1993	1993	..	1995
Chad	1990	1982	..	1994	1989	1994	..	1994
Chile	..	1987	1993	1995	1990	1990	1997	1994
China	1994	..	1994	1994	1989	1991	1996	1993
Hong Kong, China	..	..	..	..	..	..	..	..
Colombia	1998	1990	1988	1995	1990	1994	..	1995
Congo, Dem. Rep.	..	1986	1990	1995	1995	1995	1994	1995
Congo, Rep.	..	..	1990	1997	1995	1995	..	1996
Costa Rica	1990	1987	1992	1994	1991	1991	1994	1994
Côte d'Ivoire	1994	..	1991	1995	1993	1993	1994	1995
Croatia	2001	1998	2000	1996	1992	1992	1994	1997
Cuba	..	..	..	1994	1992	1992	1994	1994
Czech Republic	1994	..	..	1994	1993	1993	1996	1994
Denmark	1994	..	..	1994	1988	1989	..	1994
Dominican Republic	..	1984	1995	2000	1993	1993	..	1996
Ecuador	1993	1987	1995	1994	1990	1990	..	1993
Egypt, Arab Rep.	1992	1992	1988	1995	1988	1988	1994	1994
El Salvador	1994	1985	1988	1996	1993	1993	..	1994
Eritrea	1995	..	..	1995	..	..	..	1996
Estonia	1998	..	..	1994	1997	1997	..	1994
Ethiopia	1994	..	1991	1994	1995	1995	..	1994
Finland	1995	..	..	1994	1986	1989	1996	1994
France	1990	..	..	1994	1988	1989	1996	1994
Gabon	..	..	1990	2000	1994	1994	..	2000
Gambia, The	1992	1981	1989	1994	1990	1990	1998	1994
Georgia	1998	..	..	1994	1996	1996	1996	1994
Germany	..	..	..	1994	1988	1989	1994	1994
Ghana	1992	1985	1988	1995	1989	1989	1994	1994
Greece	..	..	..	1994	1989	1989	1995	1994
Guatemala	1994	1984	1988	1996	1987	1990	1997	1995
Guinea	1994	1983	1988	1994	1992	1992	1994	1993
Guinea-Bissau	1993	..	1991	1996	..	..	1994	1996
Haiti	1999	1985	..	1996	2000	2000	1996	1996
Honduras	1993	1989	..	1996	1994	1994	1994	1995

Table 3.14a

Status of national environmental action plans

Completed

Albania	Ghana	Niger
Algeria	Grenada	Nigeria
Armenia	Guinea	Pakistan
Azerbaijan	Guinea-Bissau	Papua New Guinea
Bangladesh	Guyana	Poland
Belarus	Haiti	Romania
Benin	Honduras	Russian Federation
Bhutan	India	Rwanda
Bolivia	Indonesia	São Tomé and Principe
Botswana	Iran, Islamic Rep.	Senegal
Bulgaria	Kazakhstan	Seychelles
Burkina Faso	Kenya	Sierra Leone
Burundi	Kiribati	Slovak Republic
Cambodia	Kyrgyz Republic	Slovenia
Cameroon	Lao PDR	Solomon Islands
Cape Verde	Latvia	South Africa
China	Lebanon	Sri Lanka
Colombia	Lesotho	St. Kitts and Nevis
Comoros	Lithuania	Swaziland
Congo, Dem. Rep.	Macedonia, FYR	Syrian Arab Rep.
Congo, Rep.	Madagascar	Tanzania
Costa Rica	Malawi	Togo
Côte d'Ivoire	Maldives	Tonga
Croatia	Mali	Tunisia
Czech Republic	Mauritania	Turkey
Djibouti	Mauritius	Uganda
Egypt, Arab Rep.	Mexico	Ukraine
El Salvador	Moldova	Uruguay
Equatorial Guinea	Mongolia	Uzbekistan
Eritrea	Montserrat	Vanuatu
Estonia	Morocco	West Bank and Gaza
Ethiopia	Mozambique	Vietnam
Gabon	Namibia	Yemen, Rep.
Gambia, The	Nepal	Zambia
Georgia	Nicaragua	

Being prepared

Argentina	Ecuador	Tajikistan
Belize	Korea, Rep.	Turkmenistan
Central African Republic	Malaysia	Zimbabwe
	Paraguay	
Dominican Republic		

Note: Status is as of January 2002.

Source: World Bank regional data; World Resources Institute, International Institute for Environment and Development, and IUCN, *1996 World Directory of Country Environmental Studies.*

	Environmental strategy or action plan	Country environmental profile	Biodiversity assessment, strategy or action plan	Participation in treaties[a]				
				Climate change	Ozone layer	CFC control	Law of the Sea[b]	Biological diversity[b]
Hungary	1995	..	..	1994	1988	1989	..	1994
India	1993	1989	1994	1994	1991	1992	1995	1994
Indonesia	1993	1994	1993	1994	1992	1992	1994	1994
Iran, Islamic Rep.	..	..	..	1996	1991	1991	..	1996
Iraq	..	..	..	..	..	..	1994	..
Ireland	..	..	..	1994	1988	1989	..	1996
Israel	..	..	..	1996	1992	1992	..	1995
Italy	..	..	..	1994	1988	1989	1995	1994
Jamaica	1994	1987	..	1995	1993	1993	1994	1995
Japan	..	..	..	1994	1988	1988	1996	1993
Jordan	1991	1979	..	1994	1989	1989	1995	1994
Kazakhstan	..	..	..	1995	1998	1998	..	1994
Kenya	1994	1989	1992	1994	1989	1989	1994	1994
Korea, Dem. Rep.	..	..	..	1995	1995	1995	..	1995
Korea, Rep.	..	..	..	1994	1992	1992	1996	1995
Kuwait	..	..	..	1995	1993	1993	1994	..
Kyrgyz Republic	1995	..	..	2000 [c]	2000	2000	..	1996
Lao PDR	1995	..	..	1995	1998	1998	1998	1996
Latvia	..	..	..	1995	1995	1995	..	1996
Lebanon	..	..	..	1995	1993	1993	1995	1995
Lesotho	1989	1982	..	1995	1994	1994	..	1995
Liberia	..	..	..	..	..	..	..	..
Libya	..	..	..	1999 [c]	1990	1990	..	..
Lithuania	..	..	..	1995	1995	1995	..	1996
Macedonia, FYR	..	..	..	2000	1994	1994	1994	1997 [c]
Madagascar	1988	..	1991	1996	1997	1997	2001	1996
Malawi	1994	1982	..	1994	1991	1991	..	1994
Malaysia	1991	1979	1988	1994	1989	1989	1997	1994
Mali	..	1991	1989	1995	1995	1995	1994	1995
Mauritania	1988	1984	..	1994	1994	1994	1996	1996
Mauritius	1990	..	..	1994	1992	1992	1994	1993
Mexico	..	..	1988	1994	1987	1988	1994	1993
Moldova	..	..	..	1995	1997	1997	..	1996
Mongolia	1995	..	..	1994	1996	1996	1997	1993
Morocco	..	1980	1988	1996	1996	1996	..	1995
Mozambique	1994	..	..	1995	1994	1994	1997	1995
Myanmar	..	1982	1989	1995	1994	1994	1996	1995
Namibia	1992	..	..	1995	1993	1993	1994	1997
Nepal	1993	1983	..	1994	1994	1994	1998	1994
Netherlands	1994	..	..	1994	1988	1989	1996	1994
New Zealand	1994	..	..	1994	1987	1988	1996	1993
Nicaragua	1994	1981	..	1996	1993	1993	2000	1996
Niger	..	1985	1991	1995	1993	1993	..	1995
Nigeria	1990	..	1992	1994	1989	1989	1994	1994
Norway	..	..	1994	1994	1986	1988	1996	1993
Oman	..	1981	..	1995	1999	1999	1994	1995
Pakistan	1994	1994	1991	1994	1993	1993	1997	1994
Panama	1990	1980	..	1995	1989	1989	1996	1995
Papua New Guinea	1992	1994	1993	1994	1993	1993	1997	1993
Paraguay	..	1985	..	1994	1993	1993	1994	1994
Peru	..	1988	1988	1994	1989	1993	..	1993
Philippines	1989	1992	1989	1994	1991	1991	1994	1994
Poland	1993	..	1991	1994	1990	1990	1998	1996
Portugal	1995	..	..	1994	1989	1989	1997	1994
Puerto Rico	..	..	..	..	..	..	..	..
Romania	1995	..	..	1994	1993	1993	1997	1994
Russian Federation	1999	..	1994	1995	1986	1989	1997	1995

Table 3.14b

States that have signed the Convention on Climate Change

Antigua and Barbuda[a]	Guatemala[a]	Palau[a]
Argentina[a]	Guinea[a]	Panama[a]
Australia	Honduras[a]	Papua New Guinea
Austria	Indonesia	Paraguay[a]
Azerbaijan[a]	Ireland	Peru
Bahamas, The[a]	Israel	Philippines
Bangladesh[a]	Italy	Poland
Barbados[a]	Jamaica[a]	Portugal
Belgium	Japan	Romania[a]
Bolivia[a]	Kazakhstan	Russian Federation
Brazil	Kiribati[a]	Samoa[a]
Bulgaria	Korea, Rep.	Senegal[a]
Burundi[a]	Latvia	Seychelles
Canada	Lesotho[a]	Slovak Republic
Chile	Liechtenstein	Slovenia
China	Lithuania	Solomon Islands
Cook Islands	Luxembourg	Spain
Costa Rica[a]	Malawi[a]	St. Lucia
Croatia	Malaysia	St. Vincent and the
Cuba	Maldives[a]	Grenadines
Cyprus[a]	Mali	Sweden
Czech Republic	Malta	Switzerland
Denmark	Marshall Islands	Thailand
Ecuador[a]	Mauritius[a]	Trinidad and Tobago[a]
Egypt, Arab Rep.	Mexico[a]	Turkmenistan[a]
El Salvador[a]	Micronesia[a]	Tuvalu[a]
Equatorial Guinea[a]	Monaco	Ukraine
Estonia	Mongolia[a]	United Kingdom
Fiji[a]	Nauru	United States
Finland	Netherlands	Uruguay[a]
France	New Zealand	Uzbekistan[a]
Gambia, The[a]	Nicaragua[a]	Vanuatu[a]
Georgia[a]	Niger	Vietnam
Germany	Niue[a]	Zambia
Greece	Norway	

Note: Status is as of December 2001.
a. Ratification or accession signed.
Source: Secretariat of the United Nations Framework Convention on Climate Change.

	Environmental strategy or action plan	Country environmental profile	Biodiversity assessment, strategy or action plan	Participation in treaties[a]				
				Climate change	Ozone layer	CFC control	Law of the Sea[b]	Biological diversity[b]
Rwanda	1991	1987	..	1998	..	..	..	1996
Saudi Arabia	..	..	..	1995	1993	1993	..	..
Senegal	1984	1990	1991	1995	1993	1993	1994	1995
Sierra Leone	1994	..	..	1995	..	..	1995	1995
Singapore	1993	1988	1995	1997	1989	1989	1994	1996
Slovak Republic	..	..	..	1994	1993	1993	1996	1994
Slovenia	1994	..	..	1996	1992	1992	1994	1996
Somalia	..	..	..	..	..	..	1994	..
South Africa	1993	..	..	2000	1990	1990	1997	2000
Spain	..	..	..	1994	1988	1989	1997	1994
Sri Lanka	1994	1983	1991	1994	1990	1990	1994	1994
Sudan	..	1989	..	1994	1993	1993	1994	1996
Swaziland	..	..	..	1997			..	1995
Sweden	..	..	..	1994	1987	1988	1996	1994
Switzerland	..	..	..	1994	1988	1989	..	1995
Syrian Arab Republic	1999	1981	..	1996	1990	1990	..	1996
Tajikistan	..	..	..	1998	1996	1998	..	1997
Tanzania	1994	1989	1988	1996	1993	1993	1994	1996
Thailand	..	1992	..	1995	1989	1989	..	..
Togo	1991	..	..	1995	1991	1991	1994	1996
Trinidad and Tobago	..	..	..	1994	1989	1989	1994	1996
Tunisia	1994	1980	1988	1994	1989	1989	1994	1993
Turkey	1998	1982	..	..	1991	1991	..	1997
Turkmenistan	..	..	..	1995	1994	1994	..	1996
Uganda	1994	1982	1988	1994	1988	1988	1994	1993
Ukraine	1999	..	..	1997	1986	1988	1999	1995
United Arab Emirates	..	..	..	1996	1990	1990	..	..
United Kingdom	1995	..	1994	1994	1987	1989	1997	1994
United States	1995	..	1995	1994	1986	1988	..	1993
Uruguay	..	..	..	1994	1989	1991	1994	1994
Uzbekistan	..	..	..	1994	1993	1993	..	1995
Venezuela, RB	..	..	..	1995	1988	1989	..	1994
Vietnam	..	..	1993	1995	1994	1994	1994	1995
West Bank and Gaza	..	..	..	..	..	..	..	..
Yemen, Rep.	1996	1990	1992	1996	1996	1996	1994	1996
Yugoslavia, FR (Serb./Mont.)	..	..	..	1997	1990	1991	2001	
Zambia	1994	1988	..	1994	1990	1990	1994	1993
Zimbabwe	1987	1982	..	1994	1993	1993	1994	1995

a. The years shown refer to the year the treaty entered into force in that country. b. Convention became effective November 16, 1994. c. Ratification of the treaty.

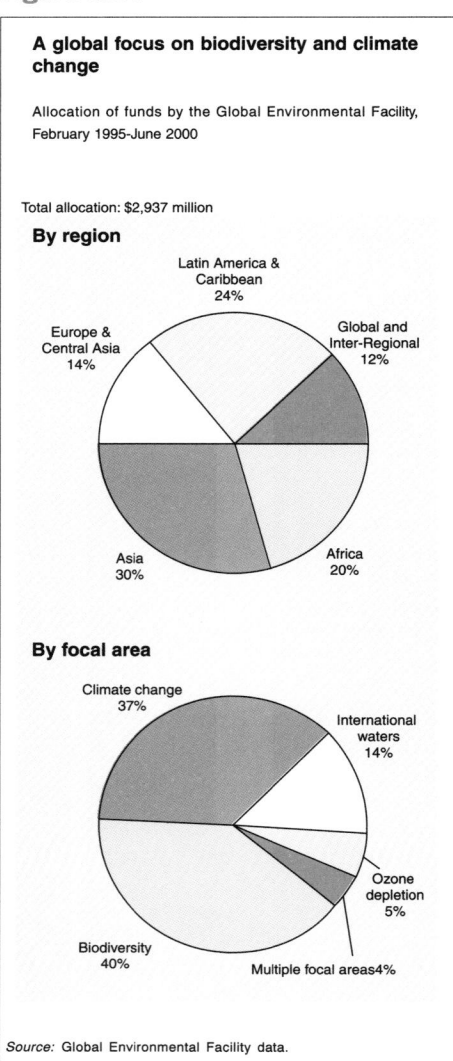

Figure 3.14

A global focus on biodiversity and climate change

Allocation of funds by the Global Environmental Facility, February 1995-June 2000

Total allocation: $2,937 million

By region

Latin America & Caribbean 24%
Global and Inter-Regional 12%
Europe & Central Asia 14%
Asia 30%
Africa 20%

By focal area

Climate change 37%
International waters 14%
Ozone depletion 5%
Biodiversity 40%
Multiple focal areas 4%

Source: Global Environmental Facility data.

ENVIRONMENT

About the data

National environmental strategies and participation in international treaties on environmental issues provide some evidence of government commitment to sound environmental management. But the signing of these treaties does not always imply ratification, nor does it guarantee that governments will comply with treaty obligations.

In many countries efforts to halt environmental degradation have failed, primarily because governments have neglected to make this issue a priority, a reflection of competing claims on scarce resources. To address this problem, many countries are preparing national environmental strategies—some focusing narrowly on environmental issues, and others integrating environmental, economic, and social concerns. Among such initiatives are conservation strategies and environmental action plans. Some countries have also prepared country environmental profiles and biological diversity strategies and profiles.

National conservation strategies—promoted by the World Conservation Union (IUCN)—provide a comprehensive, cross-sectoral analysis of conservation and resource management issues to help integrate environmental concerns with the development process. Such strategies discuss current and future needs, institutional capabilities, prevailing technical conditions, and the status of natural resources in a country.

National environmental action plans (NEAPs), supported by the World Bank and other development agencies, describe a country's main environmental concerns, identify the principal causes of environmental problems, and formulate policies and actions to deal with them (table 3.14a). The NEAP is a continuing process in which governments develop comprehensive environmental policies, recommend specific actions, and outline the investment strategies, legislation, and institutional arrangements required to implement them.

Country environmental profiles identify how national economic and other activities can stay within the constraints imposed by the need to conserve natural resources. Some profiles consider issues of equity, justice, and fairness. Biodiversity profiles—prepared by the World Conservation Monitoring Centre and the IUCN—provide basic background on species diversity, protected areas, major ecosystems and habitat types, and legislative and administrative support. In an effort to establish a scientific baseline for measuring progress in biodiversity conservation, the United Nations Environment Programme (UNEP) coordinates global biodiversity assessments.

To address global issues, many governments have also signed international treaties and agreements launched in the wake of the 1972 United Nations Conference on Human Environment in Stockholm and the 1992 United Nations Conference on Environment and Development (the Earth Summit) in Rio de Janeiro:

- The Framework Convention on Climate Change aims to stabilize atmospheric concentrations of greenhouse gases at levels that will prevent human activities from interfering dangerously with the global climate.
- The Vienna Convention for the Protection of the Ozone Layer aims to protect human health and the environment by promoting research on the effects of changes in the ozone layer and on alternative substances (such as substitutes for chlorofluorocarbons) and technologies, monitoring the ozone layer, and taking measures to control the activities that produce adverse effects.
- The Montreal Protocol for CFC Control requires that countries help protect the earth from excessive ultraviolet radiation by cutting chlorofluorocarbon consumption by 20 percent over their 1986 level by 1994 and by 50 percent over their 1986 level by 1999, with allowances for increases in consumption by developing countries.
- The United Nations Convention on the Law of the Sea, which became effective in November 1994, establishes a comprehensive legal regime for seas and oceans, establishes rules for environmental standards and enforcement provisions, and develops international rules and national legislation to prevent and control marine pollution.
- The Convention on Biological Diversity promotes conservation of biodiversity among nations through scientific and technological cooperation, access to financial and genetic resources, and transfer of ecologically sound technologies.

To help developing countries comply with their obligations under these agreements, the Global Environment Facility (GEF) was created to focus on global improvement in biodiversity, climate change, international waters, and ozone layer depletion. The UNEP, United Nations Development Programme (UNDP), and the World Bank manage the GEF according to the policies of its governing body of country representatives. The World Bank is responsible for the GEF Trust Fund and is chair of the GEF.

Definitions

- **Environmental strategies and action plans** provide a comprehensive, cross-sectoral analysis of conservation and resource management issues to help integrate environmental concerns with the development process. They include national conservation strategies, national environmental action plans, national environmental management strategies, and national sustainable development strategies. The year shown for a country refers to the year in which a strategy or action plan was adopted. • **Country environmental profiles** identify how national economic and other activities can stay within the constraints imposed by the need to conserve natural resources. The year shown for a country refers to the year in which a profile was completed. • **Biodiversity assessments, strategies, and action plans** include biodiversity profiles (see About the data). • **Participation in treaties** covers five international treaties (see About the data). • **Climate change** refers to the Framework Convention on Climate Change (signedin New York in 1992). • **Ozone layer** refers to the Vienna Convention for the Protection of the Ozone Layer (signed in 1985). • **CFC control** refers to the Montreal Protocol for CFC Control (formally, the Protocol on Substances That Deplete the Ozone Layer, signed in 1987). • **Law of the Sea** refers to the United Nations Convention on the Law of the Sea (signed in Montego Bay, Jamaica, in 1982). • **Biological diversity** refers to the Convention on Biological Diversity (signed at the Earth Summit in Rio de Janeiro in 1992). The year shown for a country refers to the year in which a treaty entered into force in that country.

Data sources

The data are from the Secretariat of the United Nations Framework Convention on Climate Change; the Ozone Secretariat of the UNEP; the World Resources Institute; the UNEP; the U.S. National Aeronautics and Space Administration's Socioeconomic Data and Applications Center (SEDAC), Center for International Earth Science Information Network (CIESIN); and the World Resources Institute, International Institute for Environment and Development, and IUCN's *1996 World Directory of Country Environmental Studies*.

	Gross national savings	Consumption of fixed capital	Net national savings	Education expenditure	Energy depletion	Mineral depletion	Net forest depletion	Carbon dioxide damage	Adjusted net savings
	% of GNI 2000	% of GNI 2000	% of GNI 2000	% of GNI 2000	% of GNI 2000	% of GNI 2000	% of GNI 2000	% of GNI 2000	% of GNI 2000
Afghanistan	..	..	..	..	..	..	..	..	..
Albania	13.7	9.0	4.7	2.8	1.4	0.0	0.0	0.3	5.9
Algeria	..	11.2	..	4.5	38.1	0.0	0.0	1.2	..
Angola	-1.8	16.1	-17.9	4.4	..	0.0	0.0	0.8	..
Argentina	13.1	12.0	1.1	3.2	2.2	0.1	0.0	0.3	1.7
Armenia	2.5	8.2	-5.7	1.8	0.0	0.0	0.0	1.1	-5.0
Australia	18.9	16.1	2.7	5.4	1.8	1.5	0.0	0.6	4.3
Austria	24.3	14.6	9.8	5.0	0.1	0.0	0.0	0.2	14.5
Azerbaijan	24.5	15.1	9.5	3.0	..	0.0	0.0	5.3	..
Bangladesh	23.3	6.1	17.2	1.7	1.2	0.0	1.0	0.4	16.3
Belarus	22.8	9.3	13.5	5.5	1.2	0.0	0.0	1.5	16.4
Belgium	23.9	14.5	9.4	3.1	0.0	0.0	0.0	0.3	12.2
Benin	10.5	7.9	2.6	2.7	0.3	0.0	1.4	0.3	3.4
Bolivia	12.9	9.4	3.5	5.5	4.6	0.7	0.0	0.9	2.9
Bosnia and Herzegovina	..	8.8	..	..	0.0	0.0	0.0	0.7	..
Botswana	12.5	11.3	1.2	7.8	0.0	0.4	0.0	0.4	8.1
Brazil	15.9	11.2	4.7	4.8	2.1	0.8	0.0	0.3	6.3
Bulgaria	11.0	9.9	1.1	3.1	0.3	0.6	0.0	2.8	0.5
Burkina Faso	24.0	7.1	16.8	1.4	0.0	0.0	1.2	0.3	16.7
Burundi	0.9	6.4	-5.5	3.1	0.0	0.2	3.0	0.2	-5.8
Cambodia	17.5	7.5	10.0	1.8	0.0	0.0	0.4	0.1	11.3
Cameroon	15.9	9.1	6.8	2.3	9.5	0.0	0.0	0.2	-0.5
Canada	25.3	13.0	12.3	6.5	4.4	0.2	0.0	0.5	13.7
Central African Republic	12.0	7.6	4.5	1.6	0.0	0.0	0.0	0.2	5.9
Chad	4.5	7.0	-2.6	2.0	0.0	0.0	0.0	0.0	-0.6
Chile	22.6	10.0	12.7	3.4	0.3	6.3	0.0	0.5	8.9
China	39.7	9.1	30.6	2.0	3.2	0.2	0.1	2.4	26.8
Hong Kong, China	32.5	12.9	19.5	2.8	0.0	0.0	0.0	0.1	22.2
Colombia	13.0	10.3	2.7	3.1	8.8	0.3	0.0	0.5	-3.8
Congo, Dem. Rep.	-4.0	7.3	-11.3	0.9	2.6	0.2	0.0	0.3	-13.5
Congo, Rep.	41.9	13.3	28.5	6.5	..	0.0	0.0	0.4	..
Costa Rica	13.4	6.2	7.2	5.1	0.0	0.0	0.5	0.3	11.6
Côte d'Ivoire	7.3	9.2	-1.9	4.5	0.0	0.0	0.9	1.0	0.8
Croatia	19.6	11.2	8.4	..	1.2	0.0	0.0	0.7	..
Cuba	..	..	..	..	..	..	..	..	..
Czech Republic	25.4	11.3	14.1	4.6	0.2	0.0	0.0	1.5	17.0
Denmark	24.5	15.2	9.2	8.2	0.8	0.0	0.0	0.2	16.4
Dominican Republic	19.6	5.4	14.2	2.1	0.0	0.7	0.0	0.6	14.9
Ecuador	32.3	10.2	22.1	3.2	29.6	0.1	0.0	1.1	-5.5
Egypt, Arab Rep.	22.9	9.6	13.2	4.4	5.5	0.0	0.0	0.8	11.3
El Salvador	14.1	10.3	3.8	2.2	0.0	0.0	0.7	0.3	5.0
Eritrea	..	5.9	..	1.4	0.0	0.0	0.0	..	..
Estonia	17.8	14.7	3.1	6.4	0.5	0.0	0.0	2.7	6.2
Ethiopia	9.1	6.3	2.8	2.7	0.0	0.0	12.4	0.3	-7.3
Finland	28.1	16.4	11.7	7.1	0.0	0.0	0.0	0.3	18.4
France	21.5	12.6	9.0	5.6	0.0	0.0	0.0	0.2	14.3
Gabon	15.0	12.7	2.3	2.1	41.6	0.0	0.0	0.4	-37.6
Gambia, The	6.3	7.9	-1.6	3.6	0.0	0.0	0.1	0.4	1.5
Georgia	9.1	16.1	-7.0	2.5	0.6	0.0	0.0	1.0	-6.1
Germany	21.1	14.9	6.2	4.4	0.1	0.0	0.0	0.3	10.2
Ghana	13.4	7.3	6.1	4.4	0.0	1.4	3.2	0.6	5.3
Greece	16.3	8.5	7.8	2.3	0.1	0.0	0.0	0.5	9.4
Guatemala	12.3	9.9	2.4	1.5	1.0	0.0	1.0	0.3	1.6
Guinea	14.0	8.2	5.8	1.5	0.0	4.0	0.7	0.3	2.2
Guinea-Bissau	..	7.4	..	2.7	0.0	0.0	0.0	0.6	..
Haiti	1.9	1.8	0.1	1.6	0.0	0.0	2.5	0.2	-1.1
Honduras	31.3	5.6	25.8	3.5	0.0	0.2	0.0	0.5	28.6

	Gross national savings	Consumption of fixed capital	Net national savings	Education expenditure	Energy depletion	Mineral depletion	Net forest depletion	Carbon dioxide damage	Adjusted net savings
	% of GNI 2000	% of GNI 2000	% of GNI 2000	% of GNI 2000	% of GNI 2000	% of GNI 2000	% of GNI 2000	% of GNI 2000	% of GNI 2000
Hungary	24.8	11.5	13.3	4.6	0.7	0.0	0.0	0.9	16.3
India	23.5	9.6	13.9	3.3	2.2	0.4	1.0	1.6	12.2
Indonesia	21.5	5.6	15.9	0.6	10.9	1.4	0.3	1.0	2.9
Iran, Islamic Rep.	34.6	9.7	24.9	3.2	38.6	0.1	0.0	1.8	-12.5
Iraq	..	..	..	..	..	..	..	..	..
Ireland	30.5	12.1	18.5	5.5	0.0	0.1	0.0	0.4	23.5
Israel	15.0	14.9	0.1	6.3	0.0	0.0	0.0	0.4	6.0
Italy	20.6	13.6	7.0	4.6	0.1	0.0	0.0	0.2	11.2
Jamaica	22.4	11.1	11.4	6.8	0.0	1.8	0.0	0.9	15.5
Japan	29.4	15.9	13.5	4.6	0.0	0.0	0.0	0.1	18.0
Jordan	21.9	10.6	11.4	5.6	0.0	0.0	0.0	1.2	15.8
Kazakhstan	21.5	10.1	11.5	4.6	40.6	0.0	0.0	5.1	-29.6
Kenya	11.3	7.9	3.4	6.1	0.0	0.0	0.9	0.5	8.1
Korea, Dem. Rep.	..	..	..	..	..	..	..	..	..
Korea, Rep.	31.3	12.1	19.2	3.4	0.0	0.0	0.0	0.6	21.9
Kuwait	42.7	6.5	36.1	4.2	48.1	0.0	0.0	0.7	-8.4
Kyrgyz Republic	4.8	8.0	-3.2	5.5	1.5	0.0	0.0	3.6	-2.9
Lao PDR	16.4	7.9	8.5	1.8	0.0	0.1	0.0	0.2	10.1
Latvia	20.2	10.7	9.5	6.2	0.0	0.0	0.0	0.8	15.0
Lebanon	-0.5	10.3	-10.8	1.6	0.0	0.0	0.0	0.6	-9.8
Lesotho	18.4	6.3	12.1	6.4	0.0	0.0	1.6	..	..
Liberia	..	..	..	..	..	..	..	..	..
Libya	..	..	..	..	..	..	..	..	..
Lithuania	15.0	10.2	4.8	5.3	0.4	0.0	0.0	0.9	8.9
Macedonia, FYR	13.8	10.0	3.8	..	0.0	0.0	0.0	2.2	..
Madagascar	7.1	7.5	-0.4	1.8	0.0	0.0	0.0	0.2	1.2
Malawi	-0.7	6.9	-7.6	3.8	0.0	0.0	4.0	0.3	-8.1
Malaysia	42.2	11.8	30.4	4.3	10.8	0.0	0.3	1.0	22.5
Mali	10.9	7.3	3.6	2.2	0.0	0.0	0.0	0.1	5.7
Mauritania	30.8	8.0	22.7	3.7	0.0	20.6	0.0	2.2	3.7
Mauritius	23.1	10.9	12.2	3.3	0.0	0.0	0.0	0.3	15.2
Mexico	20.7	10.6	10.1	4.5	5.9	0.1	0.0	0.5	8.1
Moldova	12.2	7.2	4.9	8.4	0.0	0.0	0.0	4.4	9.0
Mongolia	22.4	10.9	11.5	..	0.0	1.6	0.0	5.3	..
Morocco	23.6	9.6	14.0	4.7	0.0	0.5	0.0	0.7	17.6
Mozambique	10.1	7.7	2.5	3.7	0.0	0.0	0.0	0.2	5.9
Myanmar	..	..	..	..	..	..	..	..	..
Namibia	27.5	13.3	14.2	8.4	0.0	0.1	0.0	0.0	22.5
Nepal	22.0	2.3	19.7	2.1	0.0	0.0	4.9	0.3	16.6
Netherlands	28.7	14.6	14.1	5.1	0.5	0.0	0.0	0.3	18.4
New Zealand	18.6	11.1	7.5	6.9	1.6	0.1	0.0	0.4	12.2
Nicaragua	14.1	9.3	4.7	2.6	0.0	0.1	0.3	1.1	5.9
Niger	1.4	7.0	-5.6	3.0	0.0	0.0	3.2	0.4	-6.3
Nigeria	29.9	8.6	21.2	0.8	51.6	0.0	0.8	1.5	-31.8
Norway	36.8	16.2	20.6	6.9	7.7	0.0	0.0	0.2	19.5
Oman	..	..	..	..	..	..	..	..	..
Pakistan	12.6	7.9	4.7	2.4	3.2	0.0	0.9	1.1	1.9
Panama	22.1	7.9	14.2	4.8	0.0	0.0	0.0	0.4	18.5
Papua New Guinea	17.7	9.2	8.6	..	13.9	10.8	0.0	0.4	..
Paraguay	9.7	9.5	0.2	3.5	0.0	0.0	0.0	0.3	3.3
Peru	17.8	10.4	7.4	2.6	1.4	1.3	0.0	0.3	7.0
Philippines	28.9	8.1	20.8	2.9	0.0	0.1	0.8	0.6	22.2
Poland	20.6	11.0	9.6	5.1	0.4	0.1	0.0	1.5	12.7
Portugal	18.1	15.2	2.9	5.6	0.0	0.0	0.0	0.3	8.1
Puerto Rico	..	11.3	..	..	0.0	0.0	0.0	0.3	..
Romania	15.2	9.9	5.3	3.3	4.1	0.0	0.0	1.7	2.8
Russian Federation	35.4	10.3	25.1	3.9	38.4	0.0	0.0	4.0	-13.4

	Gross national savings	Consumption of fixed capital	Net national savings	Education expenditure	Energy depletion	Mineral depletion	Net forest depletion	Carbon dioxide damage	Adjusted net savings
	% of GNI 2000	% of GNI 2000	% of GNI 2000	% of GNI 2000	% of GNI 2000	% of GNI 2000	% of GNI 2000	% of GNI 2000	% of GNI 2000
Rwanda	14.2	7.3	6.9	3.3	0.0	0.0	3.9	0.2	6.0
Saudi Arabia	31.3	10.0	21.3	6.2	53.9	0.0	0.0	1.0	-27.3
Senegal	13.6	8.3	5.3	3.4	0.0	0.1	0.0	0.6	8.1
Sierra Leone	..	6.7	..	1.1	0.0	0.1	3.4	0.4	..
Singapore	51.5	13.3	38.2	2.3	0.0	0.0	0.0	0.6	39.9
Slovak Republic	26.9	10.9	15.9	4.3	0.1	0.0	0.0	1.3	18.8
Slovenia	24.6	12.0	12.6	5.2	0.0	0.0	0.0	0.6	17.2
Somalia	..	..	..	..	..	..	..	..	..
South Africa	15.1	13.3	1.7	6.9	1.4	0.9	0.2	1.7	4.5
Spain	23.0	12.9	10.1	4.6	0.0	0.0	0.0	0.3	14.4
Sri Lanka	21.7	5.2	16.5	2.6	0.0	0.0	0.8	0.3	18.0
Sudan	2.7	9.4	-6.7	0.9	0.0	0.1	0.0	0.3	-6.2
Swaziland	13.7	9.4	4.3	6.5	0.0	0.0	0.0	0.2	10.6
Sweden	20.8	14.1	6.7	7.5	0.0	0.1	0.0	0.1	14.0
Switzerland	33.8	14.9	19.0	4.8	0.0	0.0	0.0	0.1	23.6
Syrian Arab Republic	20.1	9.8	10.3	2.6	38.8	0.0	0.0	2.0	-27.9
Tajikistan	15.0	7.2	7.8	2.0	0.6	0.0	0.0	4.1	5.2
Tanzania	14.5	7.5	6.9	3.4	0.0	0.1	0.0	0.2	10.1
Thailand	30.3	14.9	15.4	3.5	1.3	0.0	0.3	1.0	16.2
Togo	10.2	7.6	2.6	4.3	0.0	0.1	1.2	0.5	5.2
Trinidad and Tobago	18.4	12.4	6.1	3.4	31.5	0.0	0.0	2.3	*-24.3*
Tunisia	24.6	10.0	14.7	6.6	4.7	0.0	0.2	0.7	15.6
Turkey	20.0	6.8	13.2	3.2	0.3	0.0	0.0	0.7	15.3
Turkmenistan	29.1	9.4	19.6	..	..	0.0	0.0	5.8	..
Uganda	11.4	7.5	3.9	2.2	0.0	0.0	2.3	0.1	3.7
Ukraine	24.1	19.4	4.7	6.1	7.6	0.0	0.0	7.4	-4.2
United Arab Emirates	..	11.9	..	1.7	41.9	0.0	0.0	1.0	..
United Kingdom	15.2	11.6	3.6	4.7	1.1	0.0	0.0	0.2	7.0
United States	18.0	11.9	6.1	4.7	1.1	0.0	0.0	0.4	9.3
Uruguay	11.3	11.6	-0.3	3.0	0.0	0.0	0.3	0.2	2.3
Uzbekistan	13.9	7.9	5.9	7.8	..	0.0	0.0	9.6	..
Venezuela, RB	29.0	7.2	21.8	5.0	26.4	0.3	0.0	0.9	-0.7
Vietnam	29.4	8.0	21.4	2.8	8.4	0.0	1.2	1.0	13.6
West Bank and Gaza	..	8.3	..	..	0.0	0.0	0.0	..	..
Yemen, Rep.	36.3	9.5	26.7	5.7	49.2	0.0	0.0	1.5	-18.2
Yugoslavia, Fed. Rep.	..	8.9	..	4.6	2.3	0.0	0.0	3.0	..
Zambia	..	7.9	..	2.0	0.1	2.7	0.0	0.5	..
Zimbabwe	..	8.8	..	7.5	0.4	2.6	0.0	1.4	..

World	**22.9 w**	**12.7 w**	**10.2 w**	**4.6 w**	**2.2 w**	**0.1 w**	**0.0 w**	**0.5 w**	**12.0 w**
Low income	20.7	8.7	11.9	2.8	7.2	0.5	0.9	1.5	4.7
Middle income	25.3	10.3	14.9	3.8	8.0	0.3	0.1	1.2	9.1
Lower middle income	32.4	9.7	22.7	2.9	10.1	0.2	0.1	2.0	13.1
Upper middle income	20.9	10.8	10.0	4.4	6.5	0.4	0.0	0.7	6.9
Low & middle income	24.6	10.1	14.5	3.6	7.9	0.3	0.2	1.3	8.4
East Asia & Pacific	34.0	9.9	24.1	2.5	3.2	0.2	0.1	1.7	21.3
Europe & Central Asia	25.9	10.0	15.9	4.2	12.7	0.0	..	2.3	..
Latin America & Carib.	17.0	10.6	6.4	4.2	5.1	0.6	0.0	0.4	4.4
Middle East & N. Africa	28.1	10.0	18.1	4.8	31.6	0.1	0.0	1.1	-10.0
South Asia	21.9	9.0	13.0	3.1	2.1	0.3	1.0	1.4	11.3
Sub-Saharan Africa	14.8	10.7	4.1	4.7	9.7	0.6	0.7	1.1	-3.3
High income	22.5	13.4	9.1	4.8	0.8	0.0	0.0	0.3	12.8
Europe EMU	22.0	13.8	8.2	4.7	0.1	0.0	..	0.3	..

About the data

Adjusted net savings measure the change in value of a specified set of assets, excluding capital gains. If a country's net savings are positive, and if the accounting includes a sufficiently broad range of assets, economic theory suggests that the present value of social welfare is increasing. Conversely, persistently negative adjusted net savings indicates that an economy is on an unsustainable path.

Adjusted net savings are derived from standard national accounting measures of gross national savings by making four types of adjustments. First, estimates of capital consumption of produced assets are deducted to obtain net national savings. Then current expenditures on education are added to net national savings (in standard national accounting these expenditures are treated as consumption). Next, estimates of the depletion of a variety of natural resources are deducted to reflect the decline in asset values associated with their extraction and harvest. Finally, a deduction is made for damage from carbon dioxide emissions. (In earlier editions of the *World Development Indicators* these adjustments were made to gross domestic savings and the adjusted net saving figures were referred to as "genuine savings").

Education expenditures are treated as an addition to savings effort. However, owing to the wide variability in the effectiveness of government education expenditures, these figures cannot be construed as the value of investments in human capital. The accounting for human capital is also incomplete because depreciation of human capital is not estimated.

There are gaps in the accounting of natural resource depletion and costs of pollution. Key estimates missing on the resource side include the value of fossil water extracted from aquifers, depletion and degradation of soils, and net depletion of fish stocks. The most important pollutants affecting human health and economic assets are also excluded, because no internationally comparable data are widely available on damage from particulate emissions, ground-level ozone, or sulfur oxides.

Estimates of resource depletion are based on the calculation of unit resource rents. An economic rent represents an excess return to a given factor of production—that is, in this case the returns from resource extraction or harvest are higher than the normal rate of return on capital. Natural resources give rise to rents because they are not produced; in contrast, for produced goods and services competitive forces will expand supply until economic profits are driven to zero. For each type of resource and each country, unit resource rents are derived by taking the difference between world prices and the average unit extraction or harvest costs (including a "normal" return on capital). Unit rents are then multiplied by

the physical quantity extracted or harvested in order to arrive at a depletion figure. This figure is one of a range of depletion estimates that are possible, depending on the assumptions made about future quantities, prices, and costs, and there is reason to believe that it is at the high end of the range. Some of the largest depletion estimates in the table should therefore be viewed with caution.

A positive net depletion figure for forest resources implies that the harvest rate exceeds the rate of natural growth; this is not the same as deforestation, which represents a change in land use (see *Definitions* for table 3.4). In principle, there should be an addition to savings in countries where growth exceeds harvest, but empirical estimates suggest that most of this net growth is in forested areas that cannot be exploited economically at present. Because the depletion estimates reflect only timber values, they ignore all the external and nontimber benefits associated with standing forests.

Pollution damage is calculated as the marginal social cost associated with a unit of pollution multiplied by the increase in the stock of pollutant in the receiving medium. For carbon dioxide the unit damage figure represents the present value of global damage to economic assets and to human welfare over the time the unit of pollution remains in the atmosphere.

Figure 3.15

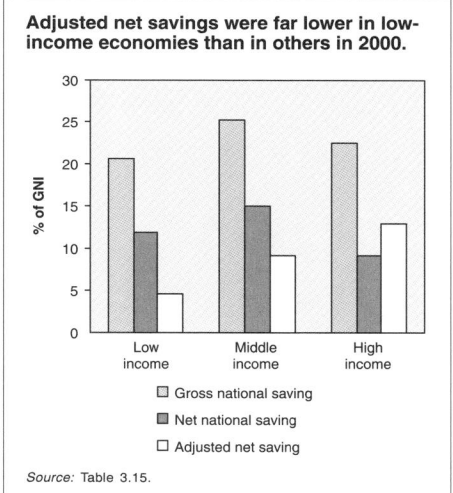

Adjusted net savings were far lower in low-income economies than in others in 2000.

% of GNI

- Low income
- Middle income
- High income

☐ Gross national saving
■ Net national saving
☐ Adjusted net saving

Source: Table 3.15.

Definitions

• **Gross national savings** are calculated as the difference between GNI and public and private consumption, plus net current transfers. • **Consumption of fixed capital** represents the replacement value of capital used up in the process of production. • **Net national savings** are equal to gross national savings less the value of consumption of fixed capital. • **Education expenditure** refers to the current operating expenditures in education, including wages and salaries and excluding capital investments in buildings and equipment. • **Energy depletion** is equal to the product of unit resource rents and the physical quantities of energy extracted. It covers crude oil, natural gas, and coal. • **Mineral depletion** is equal to the product of unit resource rents and the physical quantities of minerals extracted. It refers to bauxite, copper, iron, lead, nickel, phosphate, tin, zinc, gold, and silver. • **Net forest depletion** is calculated as the product of unit resource rents and the excess of roundwood harvest over natural growth. • **Carbon dioxide damage** is estimated to be $20 per ton of carbon (the unit damage in 1995 U.S. dollars) times the number of tons of carbon emitted. • **Adjusted net savings** are equal to net national savings plus education expenditure and minus energy depletion, mineral depletion, net forest depletion, and carbon dioxide damage.

Data sources

Gross national savings are derived from the World Bank's national accounts data files, described in the *Economy* section. Consumption of fixed capital is from the United Nations Statistics Division's *National Accounts Statistics: Main Aggregates and Detailed Tables, 1997,* extrapolated to 2000. The education expenditure data are from the United Nations Statistics Division's *Statistical Yearbook 1997,* extrapolated to 2000. The wide range of data sources and estimation methods used to arrive at resource depletion estimates are described in a World Bank working paper, "Estimating National Wealth" (Kunte and others 1998). The unit damage figure for carbon dioxide emissions is from Fankhauser (1995). The conceptual underpinnings of the savings measure appear in Hamilton and Clemens (1999).

ECONOMY

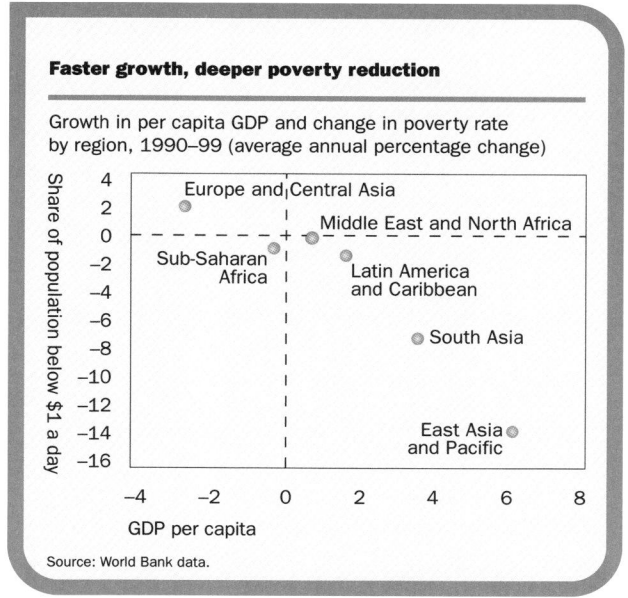

Faster growth, deeper poverty reduction

Growth in per capita GDP and change in poverty rate
by region, 1990–99 (average annual percentage change)

Source: World Bank data.

Growth and development

Without economic growth there can be no long-term poverty reduction. Economies that have achieved sustained growth—by making markets work better for poor people and building up their assets—have also succeeded in significantly reducing poverty. Economies that have not grown have experienced stagnant or increasing poverty rates. Thus the keen interest in economic growth and its predominance among the objectives of economic policy.

Experience between 1990 and 1999 illustrates the general rule. Over that decade the number of people living in developing countries on less than $1 a day fell from 1.3 billion to 1.2 billion, and the proportion of people living in extreme poverty—the poverty rate—fell from 29 percent to 23 percent. Most of these gains were made in the two fastest growing regions, East Asia and Pacific and South Asia. In Europe and Central Asia, which experienced painful economic contraction over much of the period, both the number and the proportion of people living on less than $1 a day increased. In Sub-Saharan Africa and the Middle East and North Africa the poverty rate declined slightly, but not fast enough to reduce the number of people living in extreme poverty. And in Latin America and the Caribbean, where average growth has been slow, poverty reduction has also slowed.

194

Regional growth patterns

East Asia and Pacific. Over the past 40 years East Asia and Pacific grew faster than any other developing region. Led by China, the region achieved GDP per capita growth of 5.3 percent a year. This exceptional record was interrupted by a sharp drop in growth following the financial crisis that began in 1997. In most countries recovery came quickly, but growth rates for many have not returned to the levels of the early 1990s.

Europe and Central Asia. For the transition economies of Europe and Central Asia it is hard to establish comparable time series for the pre-transition period. Since 1988 the region has experienced a sharp drop in growth from which it began to recover in the past two years. The regional average is dominated by Russia, which grew 8.9 percent in 2000 after having contracted throughout the decade. The recent growth was fueled in part by higher oil export prices. The first country to emerge from the transition recession in 1992, Poland maintained average GDP per capita growth of 4.5 percent in the 1990s, the highest among transition economies.

Latin America and the Caribbean. In Latin America and the Caribbean GDP per capita increased by about 1.6 percent a year over the period since 1960. Although the region has the highest GDP per capita in the developing world, it also includes some of the poorest countries: Guyana, Haiti, and Nicaragua. Latin America and the Caribbean has experienced greater volatility in growth than other regions, and regional growth rates have declined since the 1980s. Some of the largest and wealthiest economies—Argentina, Brazil, and Mexico—experienced growth-interrupting financial crises. Chile is Latin America's notable exception, having achieved economic stability and steady growth of 5.2 percent over the past decade.

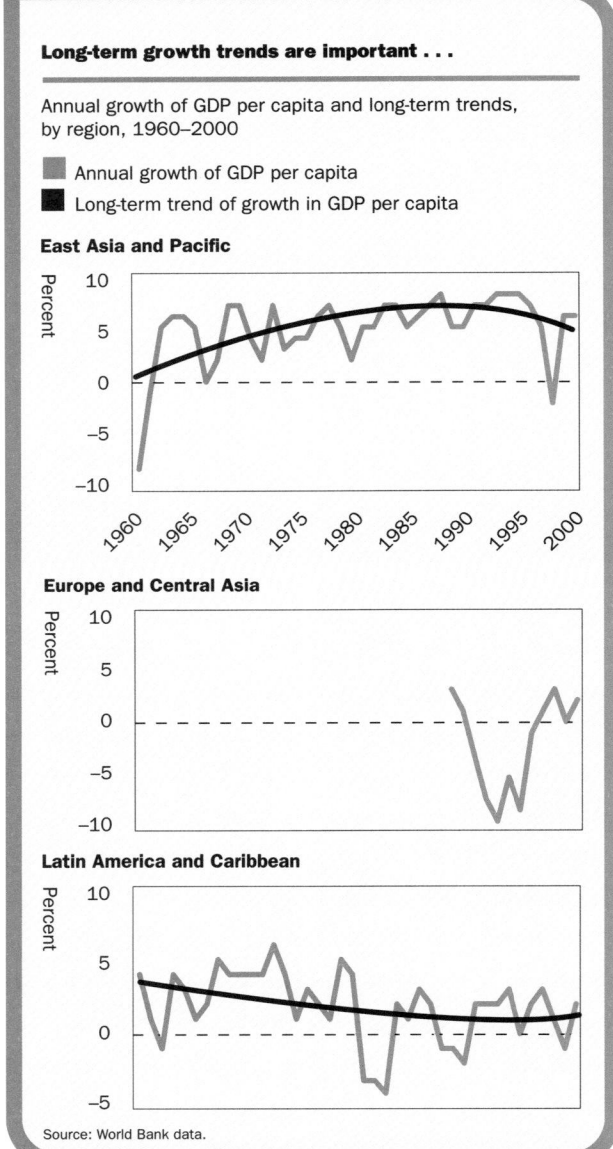

Long-term growth trends are important . . .

Annual growth of GDP per capita and long-term trends, by region, 1960–2000

Annual growth of GDP per capita
Long-term trend of growth in GDP per capita

East Asia and Pacific

Europe and Central Asia

Latin America and Caribbean

Source: World Bank data.

Regional patterns

Annual growth and trends vary

Middle East and North Africa. The Middle East and North Africa region has been unable to achieve sustained growth. Saudi Arabia, the largest economy in the region, has grown about 0.8 percent a year since the 1960s. Egypt has grown an average of 3.2 percent a year for the past 40 years, helped by large aid transfers. But 26 years after the first oil boom the region's economic fortunes are still driven by international oil prices.

South Asia. South Asia has experienced erratic growth, especially in earlier years, averaging 2.2 percent a year over the past 40 years.

More recently, strong growth in India, which opened its economy and encouraged foreign investment in the past decade, has helped to raise regional growth rates. India averaged 4.1 percent annual growth during the 1990s. Pakistan, the second largest economy in the region, grew 1.2 percent a year and Bangladesh 3.0 percent.

Sub-Saharan Africa. Sub-Saharan Africa has been nearly stagnant, with less than 0.2 percent annual growth over the same period and declining growth rates. Fourteen major African countries had negative growth. Even such resource-rich economies as Ghana, Nigeria, and Zambia, classified as lower-middle-income economies in the

1960s, have become considerably poorer, in some cases because of political instability. In South Africa, a middle-income economy, output has barely kept pace with population growth. But Botswana, another resource-rich economy, and Mauritius have done well, improving their status from low-income economies in the 1960s to upper-middle-income economies today. Both doubled their incomes in the past decade. Mozambique, a post-conflict country, has grown steadily at an average of about 5.4 percent a year since 1992. What made the difference? Although the explanation is not simple, it is probably to be found in consistent, sound economic policy, general political stability, and an openness to external markets.

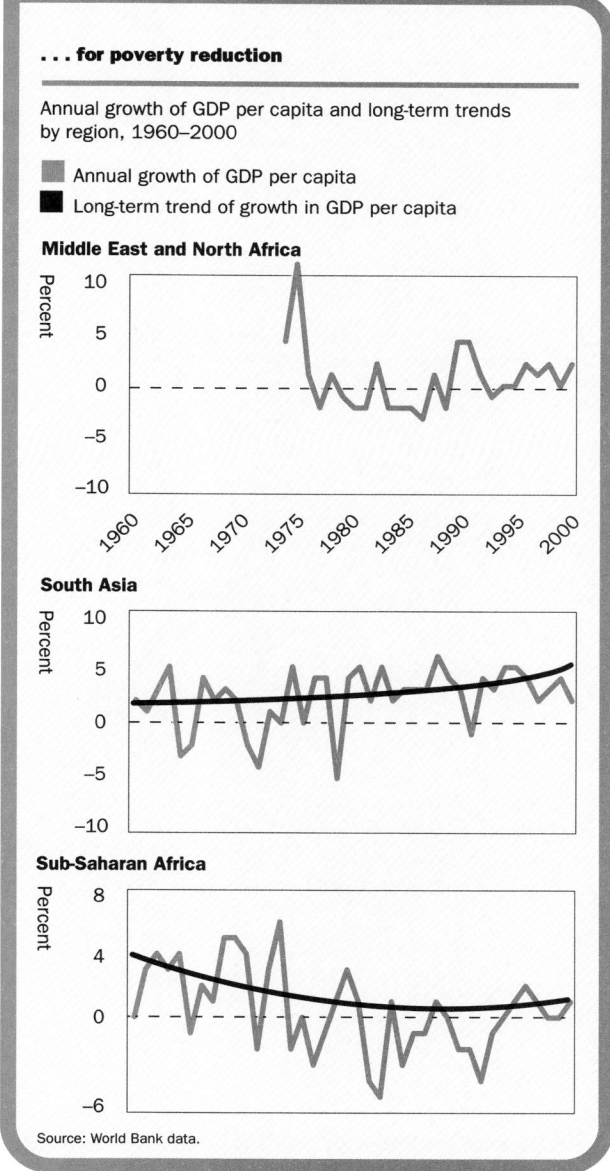

. . . for poverty reduction

Annual growth of GDP per capita and long-term trends by region, 1960–2000

Annual growth of GDP per capita
Long-term trend of growth in GDP per capita

Middle East and North Africa

South Asia

Sub-Saharan Africa

Source: World Bank data.

of economic growth

Savings rate

Savings are the difference between total output and total consumption. For the world, savings must equal investment. But some economies save more and some save less than they need. The balance between the supply of savings and the demand for investment must be met by financial flows between economies.

Sub-Saharan Africa consistently has the lowest savings rate and the smallest pool of savings.

South Asia's savings rate exceeds only Sub-Saharan Africa's. Its output is less than a third of East Asia's.

The savings rate in the *Middle East and North Africa* has been as high as 30 percent and as low as 21 percent over the past decade. *Europe and Central Asia*, with half the output of Latin America, saves at about the same rate.

In 2000 *Latin America*'s regional economy was almost the same size as East Asia's, but its total savings were considerably less. *East Asia and Pacific*, the fastest growing region in the past two decades, has maintained a high average savings rate of 37 percent of GDP.

High-income economies saved a smaller share of their output, but their total savings were more than three times those of all low- and middle-income economies combined.

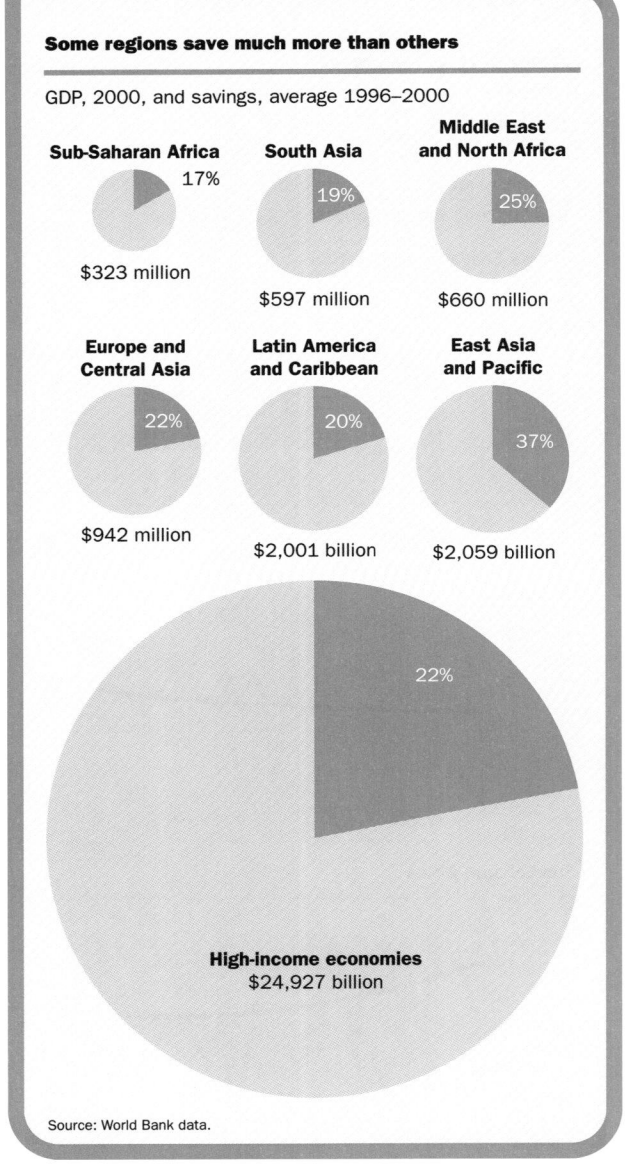

Some regions save much more than others

GDP, 2000, and savings, average 1996–2000

Sub-Saharan Africa 17%
$323 million

South Asia 19%
$597 million

Middle East and North Africa 25%
$660 million

Europe and Central Asia 22%
$942 million

Latin America and Caribbean 20%
$2,001 billion

East Asia and Pacific 37%
$2,059 billion

22%

High-income economies
$24,927 billion

Source: World Bank data.

Savings

More productive investment

Investment is needed for growth, but many countries cannot save enough from their own output to finance it. As a result, they must tap into foreign savings provided by lenders or investors. To repay them, the economy must continue to grow. So not just the quantity but also the quality of investment is important. While there is no simple formula for ensuring high-quality investment, the more open an economy is to trade and investment, the more stable its fiscal and monetary policies, the better educated its workforce, and the less prone it is to conflict, the more productive its investments will be.

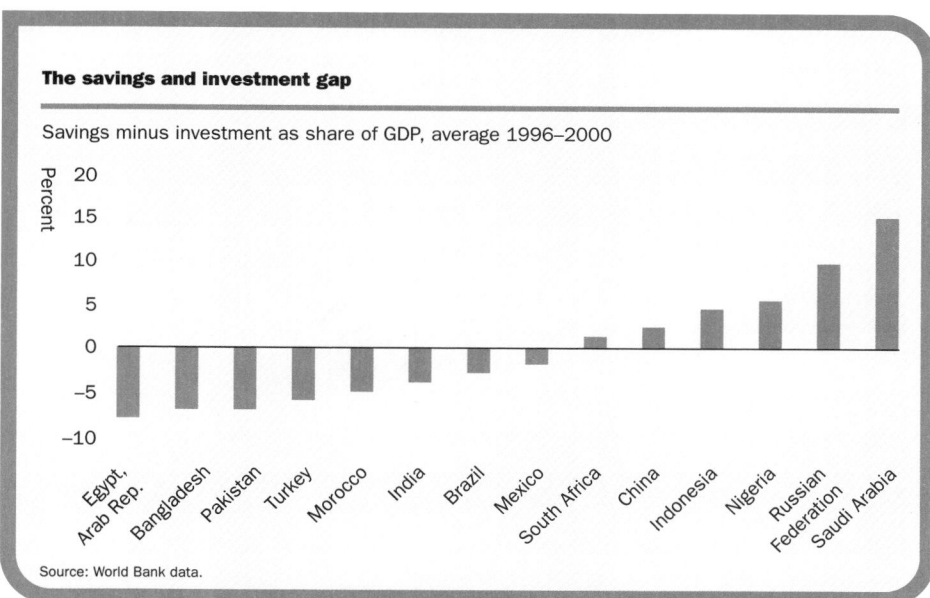

The savings and investment gap

Savings minus investment as share of GDP, average 1996–2000

Source: World Bank data.

and investment

Attracting more foreign direct investment

Foreign direct investment (FDI)—investment in a lasting interest in an enterprise—contributes to productivity by facilitating the transfer of technology, management techniques, and information about export markets. FDI has proved more stable than other forms of private sector finance, although it did fall slightly after the financial crisis in 1998. The top four recipients of FDI flows account for more than half the FDI received by developing countries.

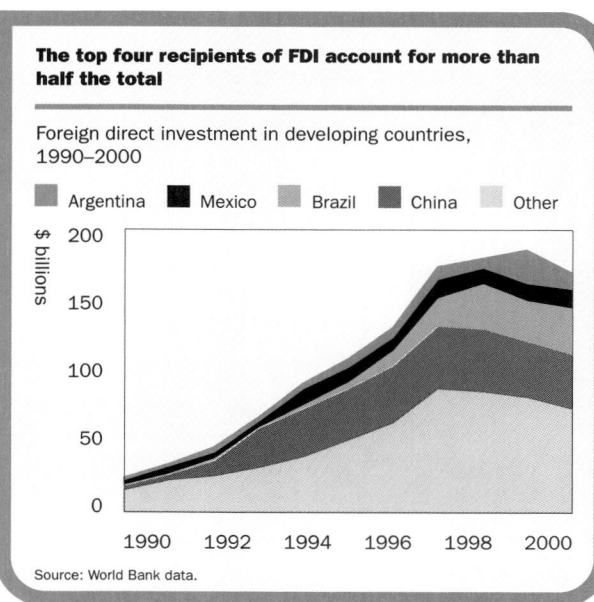

The top four recipients of FDI account for more than half the total

Foreign direct investment in developing countries, 1990–2000

Argentina   Mexico   Brazil   China   Other

Source: World Bank data.

But even the poorest countries, which have difficulty borrowing in international capital markets, attract about the same amount of FDI as middle-income countries relative to the size of their economies. Improving the investment climate to attract more foreign investment remains a key challenge for most of the developing world.

Some debt is manageable . . .

Debt problems in developing countries became a global concern in the 1980s, beginning in Latin America and spreading to other regions. The inability of several large debtors to service their debt to public and private lenders threatened to disrupt international financial markets. Weak economic performance—exacerbated by high real interest rates and weak commodity prices—contributed to the heavy indebtedness.

In 2000 the 10 largest debtors were responsible for 57 percent of the external debt of developing countries. But large, growing

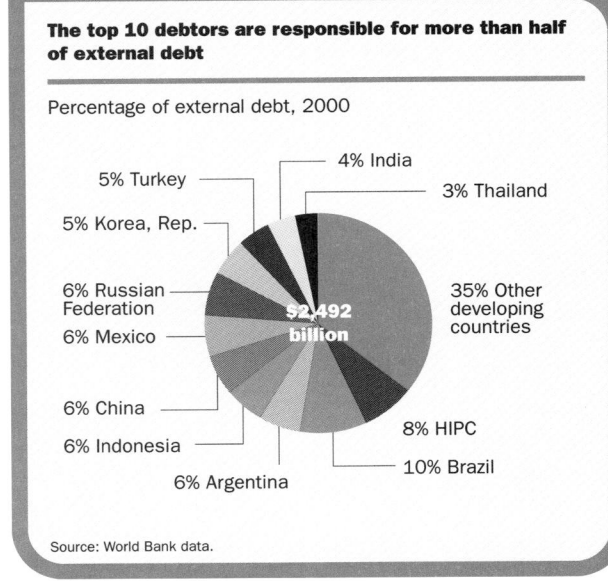

The top 10 debtors are responsible for more than half of external debt

Percentage of external debt, 2000

- 5% Turkey
- 4% India
- 3% Thailand
- 5% Korea, Rep.
- 6% Russian Federation
- 6% Mexico
- $2,492 billion
- 35% Other developing countries
- 6% China
- 6% Indonesia
- 8% HIPC
- 6% Argentina
- 10% Brazil

Source: World Bank data.

economies with robust exports can sustain large debt. Only 3 of the 10 largest debtors are classified by the World Bank as severely indebted—Argentina, Brazil, and Indonesia. Mexico, Russia, Turkey, and Thailand are classified as moderately indebted, and China, India, and the Republic of Korea as less indebted.

The heavily indebted poor countries (HIPCs) account for only 8 percent of the total external debt of developing countries—nearly all of it owed to official creditors. But they have been a cause for concern because their debt service payments are large relative to government budgets and average incomes. Relieving debt burdens and expanding the resources available for poverty reducing programs is the focus of the HIPC initiative.

Sustainable debt

. . . and some is no longer manageable

The World Bank classifies a country as severely indebted when the present value of its external debt exceeds 220 percent of its exports of goods and services (including worker remittances) or 80 percent of GNI. But experience has shown that countries are likely to experience debt service difficulties when the present value of debt exceeds 200 percent of exports. Countries that are not severely indebted but whose present value of debt exceeds 132 percent of exports

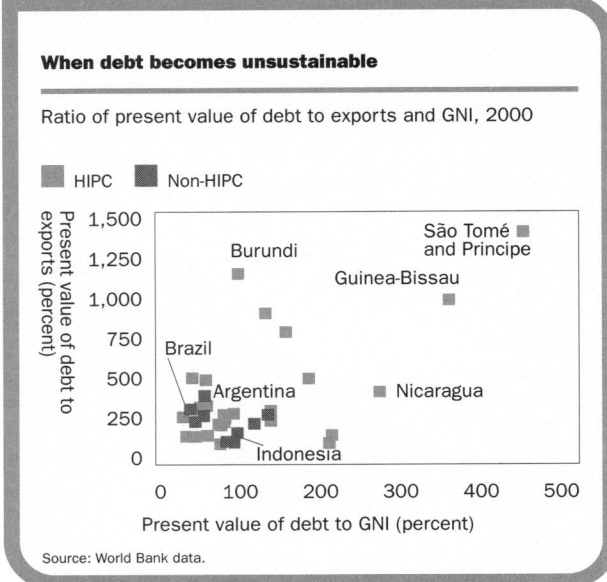

When debt becomes unsustainable

Ratio of present value of debt to exports and GNI, 2000

■ HIPC   ■ Non-HIPC

Present value of debt to exports (percent)

1,500 — São Tomé and Principe
1,250 — Burundi
1,000 — Guinea-Bissau
750 — Brazil
500 — Argentina, Nicaragua
250
0 — Indonesia

Present value of debt to GNI (percent): 0, 100, 200, 300, 400, 500

Source: World Bank data.

or 48 percent of GNI are classified as moderately indebted.

The most severely indebted countries may be eligible to apply for renegotiation of obligations to public and private creditors. The goal of debt renegotiation is to match a country's obligations to its ability to pay. But for some very poor countries traditional debt relief, such as rescheduling of bilateral debt, would not have been enough to make their debt burden sustainable. To provide further debt relief, the World Bank and IMF launched the HIPC initiative in September 1996. The enhanced HIPC initiative, begun in 1999, provides deeper, broader, and faster debt relief.

The need for debt reduction

In the HIPC initiative all creditors—including multilateral institutions and governments—participate. The goal is to channel the domestic resources freed up by debt forgiveness into reducing poverty, mainly by improving health and education services. The initiative will help to reduce debt to sustainable levels for many countries.

Little left for social services

HIPCs reaching decision point before January 2002 (dollars per capita)

	GNI	Debt service	Health expenditure	Primary education expenditure
Benin	370	12	12	43
Bolivia	990	79	69	108
Burkina Faso	210	5	9	..
Cameroon	580	38	31	..
Chad	200	3	7	13
Ethiopia	100	2	4	27
Gambia, The	340	14	13	46
Guinea	450	18	19	..
Guinea-Bissau	180	5	..	..
Guyana	860	152	..	..
Honduras	860	90	74	..
Madagascar	250	6	5	..
Malawi	170	6	11	14
Mali	240	9	11	32
Mauritania	370	38	19	47
Mozambique	210	5	8	..
Nicaragua	400	59	54	50
Niger	180	3	5	..
Rwanda	230	4	10	..
São Tomé and Principe	290	30	..	..
Senegal	490	24	8	..
Tanzania	270	6	8	..
Uganda	300	7	18	..
Zambia	300	18	23	14

Note: Data are for 2000 or latest available year.
Source: World Bank data.

As of January 2002, 24 countries, 20 in Africa and 4 in Latin America, had the present value of their debt reduced by about $22 billion—from $47 billion to $25 billion. This is expected to lower their payments of principal and interest by $1.8 billion a year in 2001–03. The arrangement brings their ratio of debt service to exports to less than 10 percent (half the developing country average). An additional 18 countries are eligible to qualify for relief under the enhanced HIPC initiative framework.

Helping the HIPCs

Growth and debt reduction

The total external debt of HIPC countries increased from the mid-1980s to the mid-1990s. But the current value of their output declined from 1988 to 1989 and again from 1991 to 1994. Only in 2000 did output once again exceed debt. Reducing debt and increasing growth will help put the HIPC countries back on track for improvements in poverty and social indicators.

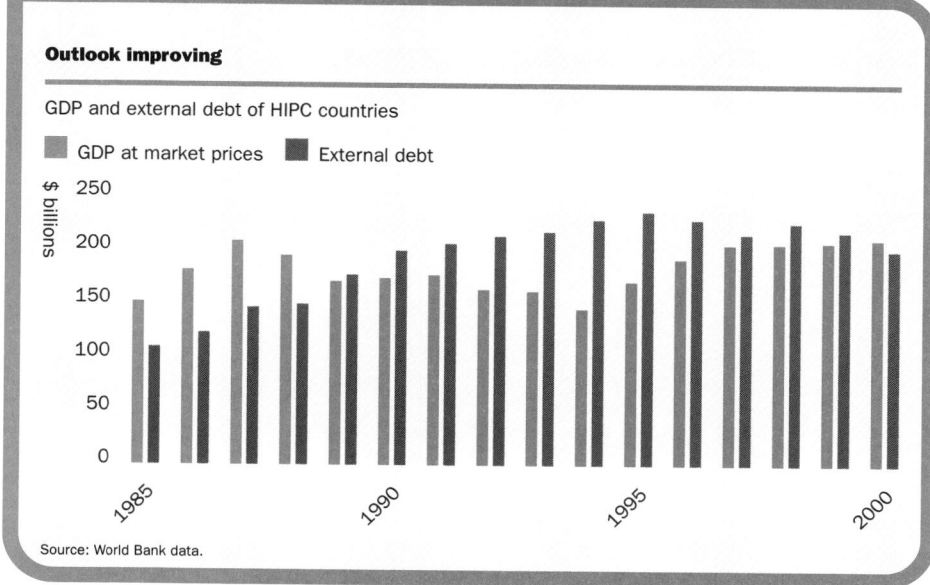

Outlook improving

GDP and external debt of HIPC countries

■ GDP at market prices ■ External debt

Source: World Bank data.

Table 4.a Recent economic performance

	Gross domestic product		Exports of goods and services		Imports of goods and services		GDP deflator		Current account balance		Gross international reserves	
	average annual % growth		average annual % growth		average annual % growth		% growth		% of GDP		$ millions	months of import coverage
	2000	2001	2000	2001	2000	2001	2000	2001	2000	2001	2001	2001
Algeria	2.4	3.6	7.4	-1.1	7.0	17.2	23.7	5.3	..	12.3	17,863	13.1
Argentina	-0.5	-1.7	2.0	5.2	-0.5	-1.8	1.1	-0.1	-3.1	-2.8	20,964	5.3
Armenia	6.0	9.6	16.6	12.7	10.0	-1.8	-1.3	4.0	-14.6	-15.2	337	4.7
Azerbaijan	11.1	8.5	17.8	16.4	8.9	25.3	13.0	3.5	-2.8	-13.5	679	2.8
Bangladesh	5.9	6.0	8.6	17.3	5.7	17.8	1.9	3.4	0.0	-2.7	1,653	1.8
Bolivia	2.4	0.0	6.1	6.1	1.3	0.2	3.7	3.5	-5.6	-4.8	1,034	5.4
Brazil	4.5	2.0	11.0	8.6	13.8	5.0	8.5	6.0	-4.1	-4.3	27,078	3.5
Bulgaria	5.8	4.5	24.2	7.9	14.6	5.3	5.6	7.0	-5.8	-6.0	3,423	4.5
Cameroon	4.2	5.3	-4.9	1.9	16.0	11.4	3.5	3.0	-1.7	-2.0	11	0.0
Chile	5.4	3.2	7.5	18.2	10.1	16.4	4.0	4.1	-1.4	-2.1	16,331	8.0
China	7.9	7.3	32.0	5.0	24.8	13.0	0.9	2.0	1.9	1.6	185,662	7.4
Colombia	2.8	1.8	5.3	1.5	5.8	18.1	10.7	11.1	0.4	-2.7	9,185	5.8
Congo, Rep.	7.9	3.1	9.1	-1.5	17.3	0.2	46.4	-12.4	..	-14.4	..	..
Costa Rica	1.7	0.6	-0.5	-4.2	-5.0	2.0	7.1	10.0	..	-5.5	1,003	1.4
Côte d'Ivoire	-2.3	-1.5	-1.9	-2.7	1.0	-1.8	-0.1	2.9	-0.1	-5.0	..	..
Croatia	3.7	4.0	8.7	7.1	4.2	10.3	6.5	5.4	-2.1	-4.4	4,422	4.6
Dominican Republic	7.8	2.0	8.7	4.4	14.5	0.1	7.7	6.0	-5.2	-2.4	850	1.1
Ecuador	2.3	4.6	-0.2	0.0	18.7	31.1	105.9	18.0	..	-0.2	1,408	2.3
Egypt, Arab Rep.	5.1	3.3	10.3	6.5	2.5	-3.8	5.8	3.1	-1.2	0.0	..	..
El Salvador	2.0	2.0	15.8	-2.6	14.8	1.6	3.9	3.7	-3.2	-6.5	1,710	4.1
Estonia	6.4	4.2	3.5	4.8	3.8	4.5	5.3	-0.5	-6.3	-5.5	1,272	2.8
Ghana	3.7	4.0	-2.3	0.3	-17.3	2.0	27.2	34.6	-7.9	-12.4	431	1.4
Guatemala	3.3	1.9	4.8	1.1	2.6	2.7	5.5	7.3	-5.5	-4.5	2,152	4.5
Honduras	4.8	2.5	14.6	-3.1	8.0	4.0	9.0	9.5	-3.4	-4.7	1,386	4.7
India	5.2	4.5	5.0	-1.6	5.0	2.9	5.3	6.0	-0.6	-1.2	42,636	6.2
Indonesia	4.8	3.3	16.1	-3.3	18.2	6.0	11.0	10.0	5.2	2.6	30,085	5.4
Iran, Islamic Rep.	5.4	5.1	11.8	-4.5	14.2	20.2	22.3	16.9	12.1	6.9	22,886	11.8
Jamaica	0.8	1.5	4.4	1.8	4.3	1.9	10.6	8.8	-3.7	-5.5	1,451	..
Jordan	3.9	3.5	2.1	14.1	13.0	12.4	-0.6	1.1	0.7	-2.7	3,226	5.7
Kazakhstan	9.6	13.2	23.9	-3.0	10.9	22.0	17.5	11.6	5.9	-5.0	2,508	2.7
Kenya	-0.2	2.0	8.6	3.1	18.1	1.4	6.8	5.0	-2.3	-8.0	743	2.2
Latvia	6.6	7.0	12.8	6.5	4.8	6.1	4.3	2.4	-6.9	-6.8	..	..
Lithuania	3.9	3.8	12.9	10.2	4.5	8.1	2.1	0.8	-6.0	-6.0	..	..
Macedonia, FYR	4.3	-4.6	19.2	..	33.0	..	8.0	6.0	-3.0	..	..	..

continues on page 202

Table 4.b Key macroeconomic indicators

	Nominal exchange rate			Real effective exchange rate		Money and quasi money		Gross domestic credit		Real interest rate		Short-term debt [a]
	local currency units per $	% change		1995=100		annual % growth		annual % growth		%	%	% of exports
	2001	2000	2001	2000	2001	2000	2001	2000	2001	2000	2001	2000
Algeria	77.8	8.7	3.3	107.7	113.2	13.2	..	-19.5	..	-11.0	9.5	1.0
Argentina	1.0	0.0	0.0	..	..	1.5	-16.5	-2.7	2.9	9.8	50.0	73.8
Armenia	561.8	5.4	1.7	108.7	91.6	38.6	15.2	12.3	-1.6	33.4	26.7	7.9
Azerbaijan	4,775.0	4.3	4.6	..	..	73.4	-10.8	13.5	-33.3	..	..	6.9
Bangladesh	57.0	5.9	5.6	..	..	19.3	15.5	13.7	17.7	13.4	15.8	3.4
Bolivia	6.8	6.7	6.7	117.9	117.7	0.4	3.4	-0.9	-3.7	29.7	20.1	23.8
Brazil	2.3	8.9	19.0	..	..	4.3	10.9	8.6	29.7	44.5	61.9	44.8
Bulgaria	2.2	7.7	5.7	120.7	128.1	28.8	..	9.8	..	5.6	..	5.8
Cameroon	744.3	8.0	5.6	95.7	100.4	19.1	17.2	-0.8	5.3	17.9	20.7	48.7
Chile	656.2	8.0	14.6	106.0	90.8	6.2	11.3	13.9	14.5	10.4	10.4	10.7
China	8.3	0.0	0.0	107.6	109.6	12.3	14.5	10.9	8.1	4.9	5.9	5.9
Colombia	2,301.3	16.7	5.2	95.6	101.1	14.8	18.9	12.1	13.2	7.3	20.7	15.9
Congo, Rep.	744.3	8.0	5.6	..	..	58.5	6.4	-28.1	16.4	-16.6	20.7	40.0
Costa Rica	341.7	6.7	7.4	106.8	114.5	18.4	8.6	22.0	3.3	16.6	23.8	12.0
Côte d'Ivoire	744.3	8.0	5.6	96.5	100.6	-1.9	2.1	-4.5	-7.2	..	..	22.9
Croatia	8.4	6.7	2.5	98.9	104.3	29.1	29.2	9.3	25.8	5.3	8.5	7.3
Dominican Republic	17.2	3.9	2.9	110.3	116.2	17.4	27.6	20.5	23.1	17.7	24.3	10.8
Ecuador	25,000.0	23.5	0.0	73.3	113.1	11.1	31.0	-6.8	30.7	-43.5	15.0	13.3
Egypt, Arab Rep.	4.5	8.2	21.7	..	..	11.6	..	11.1	..	7.0	..	19.0
El Salvador	8.8	0.0	-0.1	..	..	1.0	..	3.1	..	9.7	..	20.5
Estonia	17.7	8.1	5.2	..	..	25.7	23.0	27.2	24.4	2.2	9.4	19.2
Ghana	7,190.0	99.4	2.0	81.1	88.4	38.4	..	50.4	..	..	..	23.6
Guatemala	8.0	-1.2	3.5	..	..	35.5	9.4	13.5	-15.4	14.6	19.0	28.8
Honduras	15.9	4.4	5.2	..	..	24.4	13.0	29.8	13.3	16.4	23.4	12.5
India	48.2	7.5	3.1	..	..	15.2	14.6	16.0	12.4	7.8	12.0	4.5
Indonesia	10,400.0	35.4	8.4	..	..	15.9	13.0	26.2	8.1	6.7	19.2	30.5
Iran, Islamic Rep.	1,751.0	29.1	-22.6	297.7	360.7	22.4	26.5	12.8	15.1	..	..	12.2
Jamaica	47.3	10.0	4.1	..	..	13.0	13.2	-1.8	-20.6	11.6	19.5	16.5
Jordan	0.7	0.0	0.0	..	..	7.6	..	1.8	..	12.4	..	12.1
Kazakhstan	150.2	4.6	3.9	..	..	45.0	35.9	70.6	6.0	..	..	4.9
Kenya	79.0	7.0	-0.4	..	..	4.5	4.5	1.3	2.8	14.5	19.8	29.2
Latvia	0.6	5.2	4.9	..	..	27.0	17.8	43.1	31.8	7.2	9.3	35.8
Lithuania	4.0	0.0	0.0	..	..	16.5	21.4	-3.1	5.8	9.8	7.0	21.0
Macedonia, FYR	68.6	9.9	-2.3	72.8	74.0	21.4	..	-17.2	..	10.1	..	4.5

continues on page 203

Table 4.a Recent economic performance

2002 World Development Indicators

	Gross domestic product		Exports of goods and services		Imports of goods and services		GDP deflator		Current account balance		Gross international reserves	
	average annual % growth		average annual % growth		average annual % growth		% growth		% of GDP		$ millions	months of import coverage
	2000	2001	2000	2001	2000	2001	2000	2001	2000	2001	2001	2001
Malawi	1.7	2.8	-5.3	11.1	-18.2	6.0	24.5	28.0	-30.8	-10.8	..	..
Malaysia	8.3	1.1	26.2	3.0	16.3	1.3	4.7	3.0	..	6.2	..	..
Mauritius	8.0	5.5	5.5	6.3	0.7	5.9	0.0	12.1	-0.8	0.8	982	3.5
Mexico	6.9	0.9	16.0	-2.4	21.4	-3.4	10.9	7.0	-3.2	-3.1	39,463	2.3
Moldova	1.9	6.1	7.5	16.4	30.6	12.3	27.0	12.0	-9.4	-8.0	227	2.4
Morocco	0.9	6.5	4.4	1.4	7.8	2.3	1.6	2.5	-1.4	-0.8	7,018	6.2
Nicaragua	4.3	3.0	11.5	2.2	-8.5	0.3	11.6	8.2	-20.6	-30.5	539	3.0
Nigeria	3.8	2.9	-1.6	1.9	16.0	16.9	25.4	6.9	17.0	-4.0	..	..
Pakistan	4.4	3.4	16.0	7.2	-2.3	6.2	3.7	5.5	-3.6	-3.3	2,080	1.7
Panama	2.7	2.0	5.7	4.8	-0.8	-3.7	0.8	1.6	-9.4	-6.0	743	1.5
Papua New Guinea	0.3	3.0	2.4	2.3	..	..	15.6	7.7	-0.2	-5.9	442	1.8
Paraguay	-0.3	-0.5	-31.6	1.7	-11.7	-1.4	8.9	9.0	-4.0	-2.7	936	3.3
Peru	3.1	0.5	7.9	1.1	3.6	7.4	3.6	1.5	-3.0	-2.6	8,732	8.6
Philippines	4.0	2.5	6.6	-12.3	0.2	-6.7	6.7	8.3	12.2	7.8	16,574	4.5
Poland	4.0	1.1	6.0	..	-2.5	..	7.2	6.0	-6.3	..	28,004	6.4
Romania	1.6	4.5	23.9	11.7	29.1	21.0	45.3	35.0	-3.7	-4.7	4,591	3.4
Russian Federation	8.3	5.5	4.3	2.6	17.5	16.5	37.1	20.5	16.7	11.4	40,806	6.2
Slovak Republic	2.2	2.8	15.9	7.0	10.2	13.0	6.5	6.4	-3.6	-8.5	6,441	4.4
South Africa	3.1	2.5	8.2	3.1	7.4	9.2	6.5	6.0	-0.4	-0.3	15,532	5.1
Sri Lanka	6.0	2.5	7.2	8.3	12.9	0.9	7.1	13.5	-6.2	-4.0	1,050	1.5
Syrian Arab Republic	2.5	0.8	21.4	..	11.0	..	1.1	2.0	6.3	0.6	3,264	..
Thailand	4.3	1.6	15.4	-0.1	20.4	-2.1	1.8	2.0	7.7	4.7	30,141	4.5
Trinidad and Tobago	4.8	4.5	1.2	-2.1	16.2	14.3	9.8	3.4	..	3.7	1,849	4.3
Tunisia	4.7	5.4	6.6	6.8	9.6	6.3	2.4	2.5	-4.2	-4.3	2,442	2.7
Turkey	7.2	-6.5	10.5	10.2	33.4	-20.1	50.6	60.7	-4.9	1.3	18,938	4.1
Uganda	3.5	6.0	-0.7	10.1	6.3	6.6	3.3	5.5	-13.9	-13.4	858	5.0
Ukraine	5.8	7.0	13.8	10.2	17.5	11.5	25.3	11.3	4.7	2.8	2,980	1.7
Uruguay	-1.3	-1.2	4.0	0.8	-0.9	-6.0	3.6	5.1	-3.0	-2.9	2,800	6.8
Uzbekistan	4.0	3.8	-5.6	1.5	-6.2	8.6	44.3	42.8	2.4	-0.5	1,160	4.2
Venezuela, RB	3.2	3.3	5.8	-3.7	19.5	3.3	26.8	9.6	11.1	5.1	16,401	7.4
Zambia	3.5	5.0	4.9	26.7	7.2	21.6	18.1	24.9	0.0	-20.3	..	..
Zimbabwe	-4.9	-8.1	-16.6	-3.8	-21.6	-2.5	59.9	70.0	0.0	-1.0	..	..

Note: Data for 2001 are the latest preliminary estimates, and may differ from those in earlier World Bank publications.

Source: World Bank staff estimates.

Table 4.b Key macroeconomic indicators

	Nominal exchange rate			Real effective exchange rate		Money and quasi money		Gross domestic credit		Real interest rate		Short-term debt[a]
	local currency units per $	% change		1995=100		annual % growth		annual % growth		%	%	% of exports
	2001	2000	2001	2000	2001	2000	2001	2000	2001	2000	2001	2000
Malawi	67.3	72.4	-16.0	112.7	146.4	41.4	4.4	24.4	9.9	23.0	56.2	15.7
Malaysia	3.8	0.0	0.0	86.6	92.7	9.9	6.7	9.6	7.5	1.9	6.7	4.1
Mauritius	30.4	9.5	9.0	..	..	9.2	9.3	4.8	12.7	20.8	21.0	28.8
Mexico	9.1	0.6	-4.5	..	..	-4.2	5.7	-2.6	-3.5	6.6	13.9	9.8
Moldova	12.9	6.8	4.5	109.8	105.9	41.7	40.5	14.4	20.4	5.3	27.1	3.4
Morocco	11.6	5.3	8.9	108.2	101.6	8.4	14.7	11.2	3.4	11.6	..	2.0
Nicaragua	13.8	6.0	6.0	113.1	115.8	9.4	6.5	9.3	16.4	8.7	22.8	75.9
Nigeria	..	11.8	..	81.0	98.9	48.1	..	-25.3	..	-3.3	..	5.1
Pakistan	60.9	12.1	4.9	93.6	89.3	12.1	..	10.6	..	..	..	14.2
Panama	1.0	0.0	0.0	..	..	10.0	..	7.6	..	9.3	10.2	5.0
Papua New Guinea	3.8	13.7	22.5	92.8	83.6	5.0	-0.6	-2.1	-6.2	1.7	14.7	2.2
Paraguay	4,718.1	5.9	33.8	97.1	85.0	4.8	16.4	11.7	16.7	16.4	30.5	18.2
Peru	3.4	0.6	-2.8	..	..	-0.4	1.6	-0.3	0.3	23.4	20.4	39.3
Philippines	51.4	24.0	2.8	89.8	84.9	8.1	1.5	9.3	1.8	4.0	11.9	12.0
Poland	4.0	-0.2	-3.6	121.6	134.8	11.8	..	7.2	..	12.0	..	14.4
Romania	3,1597.0	42.0	21.9	107.1	111.2	38.0	48.8	15.5	33.4	..	..	2.9
Russian Federation	30.1	4.3	7.0	90.5	109.2	58.4	36.2	13.7	26.3	-9.2	17.0	13.4
Slovak Republic	..	12.1	..	109.3	107.9	15.2	..	8.2	..	7.9	..	8.0
South Africa	12.1	23.1	60.2	82.9	64.3	7.2	15.1	14.0	12.3	7.5	13.0	24.7
Sri Lanka	93.2	14.4	12.8	..	..	12.8	..	26.2	..	8.5	..	9.2
Syrian Arab Republic	11.2	0.0	0.0	..	..	19.0	..	-7.8	..	..	..	79.6
Thailand	44.2	15.5	2.2	..	..	3.4	2.4	-7.5	-6.1	5.9	7.3	17.3
Trinidad and Tobago	6.2	0.0	-1.0	115.4	128.8	11.7	..	-6.2	..	6.1	..	17.7
Tunisia	1.4	11.2	-2.7	100.8	99.4	14.1	11.7	27.5	20.4	..	..	9.7
Turkey	1,477,524.0	24.4	116.1	..	..	40.0	95.3	75.9	134.0	..	..	49.4
Uganda	1727.4	17.3	-2.2	96.0	103.2	18.1	..	73.9	..	19.0	21.4	14.2
Ukraine	5.3	4.0	-2.4	118.4	119.7	44.4	43.2	23.1	18.8	12.9	32.3	2.3
Uruguay	14.8	7.7	18.0	113.1	110.1	7.2	11.7	1.4	1.7	43.8	51.7	42.6
Uzbekistan	..	..	..	..	..	..	..	..	..	..	..	8.3
Venezuela, RB	763.0	7.9	9.0	161.6	176.8	23.1	13.8	15.4	34.8	-1.3	23.1	4.7
Zambia	3,830.4	58.0	-7.9	113.3	120.9	73.8	..	59.5	..	17.6	46.2	8.0
Zimbabwe	55.0	44.4	-0.1	..	..	68.9	105.6	66.4	73.0	5.2	..	26.4

Note: Data for 2001 are preliminary and may not cover the entire year.

a. More recent data on short-term debt are available on a Web site maintained by the Bank for International Settlements, the International Monetary Fund, the Organisation for Economic Co-operation and Development, and the World Bank: www.oecd.org/dac/debt.

Source: International Monetary Fund, *International Financial Statistics*; World Bank, Debtor Reporting System.

	Gross domestic product		Agriculture		Industry		Manufacturing		Services	
	average annual % growth		average annual % growth		average annual % growth		average annual % growth		average annual % growth	
	1980-90	1990-2000	1980-90	1990-2000	1980-90	1990-2000	1980-90	1990-2000	1980-90	1990-2000
Afghanistan	..	..	..	..	..	..	..	..	..	..
Albania	1.5	3.3	1.9	6.0	2.1	-0.4	..	-6.6	-0.4	3.8
Algeria	2.7	1.9	4.1	3.6	2.6	1.8	4.1	-2.1	3.0	1.9
Angola	3.4	1.3	0.5	-1.5	6.4	3.7	-11.1	-0.4	1.3	-2.0
Argentina	-0.7	4.3	0.7	3.4	-1.3	3.8	-0.8	2.8	0.0	4.5
Armenia	..	-1.9	..	0.4	..	-7.9	..	-4.3	..	6.7
Australia	3.5	4.1	3.4	3.1	2.9	3.2	1.9	2.4	4.0	4.5
Austria	2.2	2.1	1.2	4.4	1.8	2.5	..	2.3	2.6	1.8
Azerbaijan	..	-6.3	..	0.6	..	-2.8	..	-21.1	..	2.3
Bangladesh	4.3	4.8	2.7	2.9	4.9	7.3	3.0	7.2	4.4	4.5
Belarus	..	-1.6	..	-4.1	..	-1.9	..	-0.8	..	-0.5
Belgium	2.1	2.0	2.0	3.7	2.3	1.8	..	..	1.9	1.8
Benin	2.5	4.7	5.1	5.8	3.4	4.1	5.1	5.8	0.7	4.1
Bolivia	-0.2	4.0	..	3.3	..	4.0	..	..	..	4.3
Bosnia and Herzegovina	..	..	..	..	..	..	..	..	..	..
Botswana	10.3	4.7	3.3	0.8	10.2	2.9	8.7	4.1	11.7	6.9
Brazil	2.7	2.9	2.8	3.2	2.0	2.6	1.6	2.1	3.3	3.0
Bulgaria	3.4	-2.1	-2.1	0.4	5.2	-3.7	..	..	4.5	-1.3
Burkina Faso	3.6	4.9	3.1	4.2	3.8	5.9	2.0	7.0	4.6	4.6
Burundi	4.4	-2.6	3.1	-1.6	4.5	-5.6	5.7	-8.0	5.6	-2.0
Cambodia	..	4.8	..	1.9	..	8.3	..	8.2	..	6.9
Cameroon	3.4	1.7	2.2	5.6	5.9	-0.8	5.0	1.4	2.1	0.2
Canada	3.3	2.9	2.0	1.1	2.8	2.6	3.3	3.8	3.1	2.6
Central African Republic	1.4	2.0	1.6	3.9	1.4	0.8	5.0	0.0	1.0	-0.5
Chad	6.1	2.2	2.3	4.4	8.1	2.2	..	..	6.7	1.2
Chile	4.2	6.8	5.9	1.5	3.5	6.0	3.4	4.6	2.9	5.6
China	10.1	10.3	5.9	4.1	11.1	13.7	11.1	13.4	13.5	9.0
Hong Kong, China	6.9	4.0	..	..	..	..	..	..	..	..
Colombia	3.6	3.0	2.9	-2.2	5.0	1.7	3.5	-2.3	3.1	4.3
Congo, Dem. Rep.	1.6	-5.1	2.5	2.9	0.9	-11.7	1.6	-13.4	1.3	-15.2
Congo, Rep.	3.3	-0.4	3.4	1.3	5.2	2.6	6.8	-2.8	2.1	-3.9
Costa Rica	3.0	5.3	3.1	4.1	2.8	6.2	3.0	6.7	3.3	4.7
Côte d'Ivoire	0.7	3.5	0.3	3.6	4.4	5.1	3.0	3.8	-0.3	2.6
Croatia	..	0.6	..	-2.0	..	-2.5	..	-3.3	..	0.9
Cuba	..	4.2	..	5.2	..	6.6	..	6.3	..	2.5
Czech Republic	..	0.9	..	3.3	..	-0.8	..	..	..	1.8
Denmark	2.0	2.5	2.6	2.9	2.0	2.0	1.3	2.1	1.9	2.6
Dominican Republic	3.1	6.0	-1.0	3.7	3.0	7.1	2.3	4.9	4.2	5.9
Ecuador	2.0	1.8	4.4	1.7	1.2	2.7	0.0	2.1	1.7	1.3
Egypt, Arab Rep.	5.4	4.6	2.7	3.1	3.3	4.9	..	6.3	7.8	4.5
El Salvador	0.2	4.7	-1.1	1.3	0.1	5.3	-0.2	5.3	0.7	5.4
Eritrea	..	3.9	..	-1.0	..	..	..	..	..	..
Estonia	2.2	-0.5	..	-3.1	..	-3.2	..	2.5	..	1.8
Ethiopia	1.1	4.7	0.2	2.1	0.4	6.1	-0.9	6.6	3.1	7.1
Finland	3.3	2.8	-0.4	1.2	3.3	4.8	3.4	5.8	3.6	2.3
France	2.4	1.7	1.3	2.0	1.4	1.2	..	2.1	3.0	1.9
Gabon	0.9	2.8	1.2	-1.4	1.5	2.5	1.8	0.6	0.1	3.9
Gambia, The	3.6	3.1	0.9	2.7	4.7	1.1	7.8	1.0	2.7	4.3
Georgia	..	-13.0	..	1.7	..	5.1	..	3.2	..	15.6
Germany	2.3	1.5	1.7	1.7	1.1	-0.1	..	-0.4	3.1	2.4
Ghana	3.0	4.3	1.0	3.4	3.3	2.6	3.9	-3.3	5.7	5.7
Greece	0.9	2.1	-0.1	0.5	1.3	1.1	..	..	0.9	2.4
Guatemala	0.8	4.1	1.2	2.8	-0.2	4.3	0.0	2.8	0.9	4.7
Guinea	..	4.3	..	4.3	..	4.7	..	4.1	..	3.6
Guinea-Bissau	4.0	1.2	4.7	3.9	2.2	-3.1	..	-2.0	3.5	-0.6
Haiti	-0.2	-0.6	-0.1	-3.3	-1.7	1.2	-1.7	-10.8	0.9	0.2
Honduras	2.7	3.2	2.7	2.0	3.3	3.7	3.7	3.9	2.5	3.8

	Gross domestic product		Agriculture		Industry		Manufacturing		Services	
	average annual % growth		average annual % growth		average annual % growth		average annual % growth		average annual % growth	
	1980-90	1990-2000	1980-90	1990-2000	1980-90	1990-2000	1980-90	1990-2000	1980-90	1990-2000
Hungary	1.3	1.5	1.7	-2.2	0.2	3.8	..	7.9	2.1	1.4
India	5.8	6.0	3.1	3.0	6.9	6.4	7.4	7.0	7.0	8.0
Indonesia	6.1	4.2	3.6	2.1	7.3	5.2	12.8	6.7	6.5	4.0
Iran, Islamic Rep.	1.7	3.5	4.5	3.8	3.3	-3.8	4.5	4.7	-1.0	9.2
Iraq	-6.8	..	..	..	..	..	..	..	..	..
Ireland	3.2	7.3	..	..	..	..	..	..	..	..
Israel	3.5	5.1	..	..	..	..	..	..	..	..
Italy	2.5	1.6	-0.5	1.6	1.8	1.2	2.1	1.5	3.0	1.7
Jamaica	2.0	0.5	0.6	1.9	2.4	-0.5	2.7	-1.9	1.8	1.1
Japan	4.1	1.3	1.3	-3.2	4.1	-0.4	..	0.5	4.2	2.5
Jordan	2.5	5.0	6.8	-2.0	1.7	4.7	0.5	5.4	2.3	5.0
Kazakhstan	..	-4.1	..	-7.9	..	-9.0	..	..	..	2.8
Kenya	4.2	2.1	3.3	1.3	3.9	1.7	4.9	2.1	4.9	3.3
Korea, Dem. Rep.	..	..	..	..	..	..	..	..	..	..
Korea, Rep.	8.9	5.7	3.0	2.0	11.4	6.3	12.1	7.5	8.4	5.7
Kuwait	1.3	3.2	14.7	..	1.0	..	2.3	..	2.1	..
Kyrgyz Republic	..	-4.1	..	1.5	..	-10.4	..	-14.3	..	-6.4
Lao PDR	3.7	6.5	3.5	4.9	6.1	11.0	8.9	11.7	3.3	6.5
Latvia	3.5	-3.4	2.3	-7.0	4.3	-8.4	4.4	-7.8	3.3	2.5
Lebanon	..	6.0	..	1.8	..	-1.6	..	-4.3	..	4.1
Lesotho	4.5	4.1	2.8	1.8	4.9	5.9	8.5	6.6	4.0	4.4
Liberia	-1.7	..	1.2	..	-6.0	..	-5.0	..	-0.8	..
Libya	-5.7	..	..	..	..	..	..	..	..	..
Lithuania	..	-3.1	..	-1.1	..	-7.0	..	-8.5	..	-0.3
Macedonia, FYR	..	-0.8	..	0.3	..	-2.5	..	-4.4	..	0.7
Madagascar	1.1	2.0	2.5	1.4	0.9	2.4	2.1	0.6	0.3	2.5
Malawi	2.5	3.8	2.0	7.6	2.9	1.6	3.6	-2.1	3.3	3.4
Malaysia	5.3	7.0	3.4	0.3	6.8	8.6	9.3	9.8	4.9	7.2
Mali	0.8	3.8	3.3	3.2	4.3	6.6	6.8	3.0	1.9	2.9
Mauritania	1.8	4.2	1.7	5.0	4.9	2.4	-2.1	-0.5	0.4	4.9
Mauritius	6.2	5.3	2.9	-0.9	10.3	5.5	11.1	5.6	5.5	6.4
Mexico	1.1	3.1	0.8	1.8	1.1	3.8	1.5	4.4	1.4	2.9
Moldova[a]	2.8	-9.7	..	-13.7	..	-16.7	..	..	..	1.9
Mongolia	5.4	1.0	1.4	3.2	6.6	-0.5	..	..	8.4	0.1
Morocco	4.2	2.3	6.7	-0.9	3.0	3.2	4.1	2.7	4.2	2.8
Mozambique	-0.1	6.4	6.6	5.5	-4.5	14.0	..	17.6	9.1	1.7
Myanmar	0.6	6.6	0.5	5.3	0.5	10.1	-0.2	7.0	0.8	6.8
Namibia	1.3	4.1	2.5	4.1	-0.1	2.3	3.3	2.7	2.1	4.6
Nepal	4.6	4.9	4.0	2.5	8.7	7.2	9.3	9.2	3.9	6.2
Netherlands	2.3	2.8	3.5	1.6	1.5	1.6	..	..	2.6	3.1
New Zealand	1.9	3.0	3.8	2.7	1.1	2.4	..	..	2.7	3.7
Nicaragua	-1.9	3.5	-2.2	5.7	-2.3	4.2	-3.2	1.8	-1.5	1.8
Niger	-0.1	2.4	1.7	3.2	-1.7	2.0	-2.7	2.6	-0.7	1.9
Nigeria	1.6	2.4	3.3	3.5	-1.1	1.0	0.7	1.2	3.7	2.9
Norway	2.8	3.6	0.1	2.4	4.0	3.9	0.2	2.3	2.9	3.4
Oman	8.4	5.9	7.9	..	10.3	..	20.6	..	5.9	..
Pakistan	6.3	3.7	4.3	4.4	7.3	3.9	7.7	3.5	6.8	4.4
Panama	0.5	4.1	2.5	2.0	-1.3	5.4	0.4	2.8	0.7	4.0
Papua New Guinea	1.9	4.0	1.8	3.7	1.9	5.5	0.1	5.6	2.0	3.0
Paraguay	2.5	2.2	3.6	2.5	0.3	3.2	4.0	0.7	3.1	1.6
Peru	-0.1	4.7	3.0	5.8	0.1	5.4	-0.2	3.8	-0.4	4.0
Philippines	1.0	3.3	1.0	1.6	-0.9	3.3	0.2	3.0	2.8	4.1
Poland	..	4.6	..	-0.2	..	4.2	..	..	..	4.1
Portugal	3.1	2.7	2.8	-0.3	3.2	3.2	..	..	2.3	2.3
Puerto Rico	4.0	3.1	1.8	..	3.6	..	3.6	..	4.6	..
Romania	0.5	-0.7	..	-0.6	..	-0.8	..	-2.8	..	-0.5
Russian Federation	..	-4.8	..	-6.0	..	-7.6	..	..	..	-1.0

4.1 | Growth of output

	Gross domestic product		Agriculture		Industry		Manufacturing		Services	
	average annual % growth		average annual % growth		average annual % growth		average annual % growth		average annual % growth	
	1980-90	1990-2000	1980-90	1990-2000	1980-90	1990-2000	1980-90	1990-2000	1980-90	1990-2000
Rwanda	2.2	-0.2	0.5	-2.3	2.5	2.8	2.6	6.6	5.5	-0.1
Saudi Arabia	0.0	1.5	13.4	*0.7*	-2.3	*1.5*	7.5	*2.7*	1.3	*2.0*
Senegal	3.1	3.6	2.8	1.9	4.3	4.8	4.6	4.0	2.8	3.8
Sierra Leone	1.2	-4.3	3.1	-0.1	1.7	-6.2	..	5.0	-2.7	-10.3
Singapore	6.7	7.8	-5.3	-1.6	5.2	7.9	6.6	7.1	7.6	7.8
Slovak Republic	*2.0*	2.1	*1.6*	1.2	*2.0*	-2.7	..	*4.1*	*0.8*	6.5
Slovenia	..	2.7	..	*-0.1*	..	2.9	..	4.0	..	*3.9*
Somalia	2.1	..	3.3	..	1.0	..	-1.7	..	0.9	..
South Africa	1.0	2.0	2.9	0.6	0.7	1.0	1.1	1.2	2.4	2.6
Spain	3.0	2.5	1.6	-0.6	3.1	2.5	..	..	3.0	2.7
Sri Lanka	4.0	5.3	2.2	1.9	4.6	7.0	6.3	8.1	4.7	6.0
Sudan	0.4	8.1	-0.6	11.3	*1.3*	7.7	3.4	4.0	*1.9*	6.3
Swaziland	6.5	3.3	2.5	1.0	11.2	3.9	14.0	3.0	4.9	3.5
Sweden	2.5	1.9	1.4	0.0	2.8	3.4	..	..	2.4	1.7
Switzerland	2.0	0.8	..	..	..	..	..	..	..	..
Syrian Arab Republic	1.5	5.8	-0.6	5.3	6.6	9.9	..	10.8	1.6	4.6
Tajikistan	*2.0*	-10.4	*-2.8*	-5.8	*5.5*	-16.6	*5.6*	-12.6	*3.4*	-0.4
Tanzania [b]	..	2.9	..	3.2	..	3.1	..	2.7	..	2.7
Thailand	7.6	4.2	3.9	2.1	9.8	5.3	9.5	6.4	7.3	3.7
Togo	1.7	2.3	5.6	4.0	1.1	2.8	1.7	2.9	-0.3	0.4
Trinidad and Tobago	-0.8	3.0	-5.9	1.9	-5.5	3.4	-10.1	5.9	6.7	2.7
Tunisia	3.3	4.7	2.8	2.4	3.1	4.6	3.7	5.5	3.5	5.3
Turkey	5.4	3.7	1.3	1.4	7.8	4.1	7.9	4.8	4.4	3.7
Turkmenistan	..	-4.8	..	-5.7	..	-3.2	..	..	..	-5.8
Uganda	*2.9*	7.0	*2.1*	3.7	*5.0*	12.3	*3.7*	13.6	*2.8*	7.9
Ukraine	..	-9.3	..	-5.8	..	-11.4	..	-11.2	..	-1.1
United Arab Emirates	-2.1	*2.9*	9.6	..	-4.2	..	3.1	..	3.6	..
United Kingdom	3.2	2.5	2.1	-0.2	3.1	1.3	..	..	3.2	3.2
United States	3.5	3.5	..	..	..	..	..	..	..	..
Uruguay	0.5	3.4	*1.8*	2.8	*1.2*	1.1	*1.7*	-0.1	*2.4*	4.6
Uzbekistan	..	-0.5	..	0.1	..	-3.2	..	..	..	0.3
Venezuela, RB	1.1	1.6	3.1	1.4	1.7	2.9	4.4	0.9	0.5	0.4
Vietnam	*4.6*	7.9	*4.3*	4.8	..	12.1	..	..	..	7.7
West Bank and Gaza	..	2.8	..	-4.2	..	0.8	..	3.6	..	2.8
Yemen, Rep.	..	5.8	..	5.1	..	7.9	..	4.4	..	5.1
Yugoslavia, Fed. Rep.	..	*0.6*	..	..	..	..	..	..	..	..
Zambia	1.0	0.5	3.6	3.9	1.0	-4.0	4.1	1.2	-0.2	2.6
Zimbabwe	3.6	2.5	3.1	4.3	3.2	0.4	2.8	0.4	3.0	3.1

World	3.3 w	2.7 w	2.5 w	1.4 w	3.1 w	1.5 w	.. w	.. w	.. w	2.9 w
Low income	4.5	3.2	3.0	2.5	5.5	2.7	7.8	2.6	5.5	5.1
Middle income	3.3	3.6	3.5	2.0	3.6	3.9	4.6	6.2	3.6	3.9
Lower middle income	4.1	3.6	4.2	2.1	5.9	4.1	7.0	8.9	5.5	4.3
Upper middle income	2.7	3.6	2.7	1.9	2.6	3.7	3.6	*4.1*	3.0	3.7
Low & middle income	3.5	3.5	3.4	2.2	3.9	3.7	4.9	5.7	3.9	4.1
East Asia & Pacific	7.9	7.2	4.4	3.1	9.3	9.3	10.4	9.9	8.6	6.4
Europe & Central Asia	..	-1.5	..	-2.3	..	-3.8	..	..	..	*1.6*
Latin America & Carib.	1.7	3.3	2.3	2.3	1.4	3.3	1.4	*2.6*	1.9	3.4
Middle East & N. Africa	2.0	3.0	5.2	2.6	0.3	*0.9*	..	3.8	2.4	*4.5*
South Asia	5.6	5.6	3.2	3.1	6.8	6.2	7.0	6.6	6.5	7.1
Sub-Saharan Africa	1.6	2.5	2.3	2.8	1.2	1.6	1.7	1.6	2.4	2.6
High income	3.3	2.5	1.4	*0.0*	2.9	*0.7*	..	..	..	..
Europe EMU	2.4	1.9	1.1	1.3	1.6	1.0	..	*1.2*	2.9	2.2

a. Exludes data for Transnistria. b. Data cover mainland Tanzania only.

About the data

An economy's growth is measured by the change in the volume of its output or in the real incomes of persons resident in the economy. The 1993 United Nations System of National Accounts (1993 SNA) offers three plausible indicators from which to calculate growth: the volume of gross domestic product, real gross domestic income, and real gross national income. The volume of GDP is the sum of value added, measured at constant prices, by households, government, and the enterprises operating in the economy. This year's edition of the *World Development Indicators* continues to follow the practice of past editions, measuring the growth of the economy by the change in GDP measured at constant prices.

Each industry's contribution to the growth in the economy's output is measured by the growth in value added by the industry. In principle, value added in constant prices can be estimated by measuring the quantity of goods and services produced in a period, valuing them at an agreed set of base year prices, and subtracting the cost of inputs, also in constant prices. This double deflation method, recommended by the 1993 SNA and its predecessors, requires detailed information on the structure of prices of inputs and outputs.

In many industries, however, value added is extrapolated from the base year using single volume indexes of outputs or, more rarely, inputs. Particularly in the service industries, including most of government, value added in constant prices is often imputed from labor inputs, such as real wages or the number of employees. In the absence of well-defined measures of output, measuring the growth of services remains difficult.

Moreover, technical progress can lead to improvements in production and in the quality of goods and services that, if not properly accounted for, can distort measures of value added and thus of growth. When inputs are used to estimate output, as is the case for nonmarket services, unmeasured technical progress leads to underestimates of the volume of output. Similarly, unmeasured changes in the quality of goods and services produced lead to underestimates of the value of output and value added. The result can be underestimates of growth and productivity change, and overestimates of inflation. This is a highly complex issue, and only a few advanced industrial countries have so far attempted to introduce any GDP adjustments for these factors.

Informal economic activities pose a particular measurement problem, especially in developing countries, where much economic activity may go unrecorded. Obtaining a complete picture of the economy requires estimating household outputs produced for local sale and home use, barter exchanges, and illicit or deliberately unreported activity. The consistency and completeness of such estimates depends on the skill and methods of the compiling statisticians and the resources available to them.

Rebasing national accounts

When countries rebase their national accounts, they update the weights assigned to various components to better reflect the current pattern of production (or consumption). The new base year should represent normal operation of the economy—that is, it should be a year without major shocks or distortions—but the choice of base year is often constrained by the lack of data. Some developing countries have not rebased their national accounts for many years. Using an old base year can be misleading because implicit price and volume weights become progressively less relevant and useful.

To obtain comparable series of constant price data, the World Bank rescales GDP and value added by industrial origin to a common reference year, currently 1995. This process gives rise to a discrepancy between the rescaled GDP and the sum of the rescaled components. Because allocating the discrepancy would give rise to distortions in the growth rates, the discrepancy is left unallocated. As a result, the weighted average of the growth rates of the components generally will not equal the GDP growth rate.

Growth rates of GDP and its components are calculated using constant price data in the local currency. Regional and income group growth rates are calculated after converting local currencies to constant price U.S. dollars using an exchange rate in the common reference year. The growth rates in the table are annual average compound growth rates. Methods of computing growth rates and the alternative conversion factor are described in *Statistical methods*.

Changes in the System of National Accounts

Last year the *World Development Indicators* adopted the terminology of the 1993 SNA. Although most countries continue to compile their national accounts according to the System of National Accounts version 3 (referred to as the 1968 SNA), more and more are adopting the 1993 SNA. Countries that use the 1993 SNA are identified in *Primary data documentation*. Some low-income countries still use concepts from the even older 1953 SNA guidelines, including valuations such as factor cost, in describing major economic aggregates.

Definitions

• **Gross domestic product** (GDP) at purchaser prices is the sum of the gross value added by all resident producers in the economy plus any product taxes and minus any subsidies not included in the value of the products. It is calculated without making deductions for depreciation of fabricated assets or for depletion and degradation of natural resources. Value added is the net output of an industry after adding up all outputs and subtracting intermediate inputs. The industrial origin of value added is determined by the International Standard Industrial Classification (ISIC) revision 3. • **Agriculture** corresponds to ISIC divisions 1–5 and includes forestry and fishing. • **Industry** comprises mining, manufacturing (also reported as a separate subgroup), construction, electricity, water, and gas (ISIC divisions 10–45). • **Manufacturing** refers to industries belonging to divisions 15–37. • **Services** correspond to ISIC divisions 50–99. This sector is derived as a residual (from GDP less agriculture and industry) and may not properly reflect the sum of service output, including banking and financial services.

Data sources

The national accounts data for most developing countries are collected from national statistical organizations and central banks by visiting and resident World Bank missions. The data for high-income economies come from Organisation for Economic Co-operation and Development (OECD) data files; for information on the OECD's national accounts series see its *Main Economic Indicators* (monthly). The World Bank rescales constant price data to a common reference year. The complete national accounts time series is available on the *World Development Indicators 2002* CD-ROM. The United Nations Statistics Division publishes detailed national accounts for United Nations member countries in *National Accounts Statistics: Main Aggregates and Detailed Tables* and publishes updates in the *Monthly Bulletin of Statistics*.

	Gross domestic product ($ millions)		Agriculture value added (% of GDP)		Industry value added (% of GDP)		Manufacturing value added (% of GDP)		Services value added (% of GDP)	
	1990	2000	1990	2000	1990	2000	1990	2000	1990	2000
Afghanistan	..	..	..	..	..	..	..	..	..	..
Albania	2,102	3,752	36	51	48	26	42	12	16	23
Algeria	62,045	53,306	11	9	48	60	11	8	40	31
Angola	10,260	8,828	18	6	41	76	5	3	41	18
Argentina	141,352	284,960	8	5	36	28	27	18	56	68
Armenia	4,124	1,914	17	25	52	36	33	24	31	39
Australia	309,654	390,113	3	3	28	26	14	13	68	71
Austria	161,692	189,029	4	2	34	33	23	21	62	65
Azerbaijan	9,837	5,267	..	19	..	38	..	7	..	43
Bangladesh	30,129	47,106	29	25	21	24	13	15	50	51
Belarus	35,203	29,950	24	15	47	37	39	31	29	47
Belgium	197,349	226,648	2	2	33	27	..	20	65	72
Benin	1,845	2,168	36	38	13	14	8	9	51	48
Bolivia	4,868	8,281	26	22	20	15	17	13	54	63
Bosnia and Herzegovina	..	4,394	..	12	..	26	..	16	..	62
Botswana	3,766	5,285	5	4	56	44	5	5	39	52
Brazil	464,989	595,458	8	7	39	29	25	24	53	64
Bulgaria	20,726	11,995	18	15	51	28	..	17	31	58
Burkina Faso	2,765	2,192	32	35	22	17	16	12	45	48
Burundi	1,132	689	56	51	19	18	13	9	25	31
Cambodia	1,115	3,183	56	37	11	20	5	6	33	42
Cameroon	11,152	8,879	25	44	29	20	15	11	46	36
Canada	572,673	687,882	3	..	33	..	18	..	64	..
Central African Republic	1,488	963	48	55	20	20	11	9	33	26
Chad	1,739	1,407	29	39	18	14	14	11	53	47
Chile	30,323	70,545	9	11	41	34	20	16	50	56
China	354,644	1,079,948	27	16	42	51	33	35	31	33
Hong Kong, China	74,784	162,642	0	0	25	14	18	6	74	85
Colombia	40,274	81,283	17	14	38	31	21	14	45	56
Congo, Dem. Rep.	9,348	5,584	30	..	28	..	11	..	42	..
Congo, Rep.	2,799	3,215	13	5	41	71	8	3	46	24
Costa Rica	5,713	15,851	18	9	29	31	22	24	53	59
Côte d'Ivoire	10,796	9,370	32	29	23	22	21	19	44	48
Croatia	18,156	19,031	10	9	34	33	28	23	56	58
Cuba	..	..	..	7	..	46	..	37	..	47
Czech Republic	34,880	50,777	6	4	49	41	..	..	45	55
Denmark	133,361	162,343	4	3	27	26	18	17	69	71
Dominican Republic	7,074	19,669	13	11	31	34	18	17	55	55
Ecuador	10,686	13,607	13	10	38	40	19	17	49	50
Egypt, Arab Rep.	43,130	98,725	19	17	29	34	18	19	52	49
El Salvador	4,807	13,211	17	10	26	30	22	23	57	60
Eritrea	437	608	29	17	19	29	13	15	52	54
Estonia	6,760	4,969	17	6	50	27	42	16	34	67
Ethiopia	6,842	6,391	49	52	13	11	8	7	38	37
Finland	136,794	121,466	7	4	34	34	23	25	60	62
France	1,215,892	1,294,246	4	3	30	26	21	19	66	71
Gabon	5,952	4,932	7	6	43	53	6	4	50	40
Gambia, The	317	422	29	38	13	13	7	5	58	49
Georgia	12,171	3,029	32	32	33	13	24	7	35	55
Germany	1,688,568	1,872,992	2	1	38	31	28	23	60	68
Ghana	5,886	5,190	45	35	17	25	10	9	38	39
Greece	84,075	112,646	11	8	28	24	..	12	61	68
Guatemala	7,650	18,988	26	23	20	20	15	13	54	57
Guinea	2,818	3,012	24	24	33	37	5	4	43	39
Guinea-Bissau	244	215	61	59	19	12	8	10	21	29
Haiti	2,981	4,050	32	28	21	20	15	7	48	51
Honduras	3,049	5,932	22	18	26	32	16	20	51	51

	Gross domestic product		Agriculture value added		Industry value added		Manufacturing value added		Services value added	
	$ millions		% of GDP		% of GDP		% of GDP		% of GDP	
	1990	2000	1990	2000	1990	2000	1990	2000	1990	2000
Hungary	33,056	45,633	15	6	39	34	23	25	46	61
India	316,891	456,990	31	25	28	27	17	16	41	48
Indonesia	114,427	153,255	20	17	38	47	18	26	42	36
Iran, Islamic Rep.	120,404	104,904	24	19	29	22	12	16	48	59
Iraq	48,657	..	..	..	..	..	..	..	..	..
Ireland	47,301	93,865	9	4	35	36	28	28	56	60
Israel	52,490	110,386	..	..	..	..	..	..	..	..
Italy	1,102,437	1,073,960	4	3	34	30	25	21	63	68
Jamaica	4,239	7,403	6	6	43	31	20	13	50	62
Japan	3,052,058	4,841,584	2	1	39	32	27	22	58	66
Jordan	4,020	8,340	8	2	28	25	15	16	64	73
Kazakhstan	40,304	18,230	27	9	45	43	9	18	29	48
Kenya	8,533	10,357	29	20	19	19	12	13	52	61
Korea, Dem. Rep.	..	..	..	..	..	..	..	..	..	..
Korea, Rep.	252,622	457,219	9	5	43	43	29	31	48	53
Kuwait	18,428	37,783	1	..	52	..	12	..	47	..
Kyrgyz Republic	2,951	1,304	34	39	36	26	28	6	30	34
Lao PDR	865	1,709	61	53	15	23	10	17	24	24
Latvia	12,490	7,150	22	4	46	25	34	14	32	70
Lebanon	2,838	16,488	..	12	..	22	..	10	..	66
Lesotho	615	899	24	17	33	44	14	16	43	39
Liberia	..	..	..	..	..	..	..	..	..	..
Libya	..	..	..	..	..	..	..	..	..	..
Lithuania	13,254	11,314	27	8	31	33	21	21	42	59
Macedonia, FYR	4,472	3,573	9	12	46	33	36	21	46	55
Madagascar	3,081	3,878	32	35	14	13	12	..	53	52
Malawi	1,881	1,697	45	42	29	19	19	14	26	39
Malaysia	44,024	89,659	15	11	42	45	24	33	43	44
Mali	2,421	2,298	46	46	16	17	9	4	39	37
Mauritania	1,020	935	30	22	29	31	10	9	42	47
Mauritius	2,642	4,381	12	6	32	32	24	24	56	62
Mexico	262,710	574,512	8	4	28	28	21	21	64	67
Moldova[a]	10,567	1,286	31	28	39	20	..	16	30	52
Mongolia	..	969	17	33	30	19	..	5	52	48
Morocco	25,821	33,345	18	14	32	32	18	18	50	54
Mozambique	2,463	3,754	37	24	18	25	10	13	44	50
Myanmar	..	..	57	60	11	9	8	7	32	31
Namibia	2,530	3,479	11	11	35	28	13	11	54	61
Nepal	3,628	5,497	52	40	16	22	6	10	32	37
Netherlands	295,378	364,766	5	3	31	27	..	17	64	70
New Zealand	43,103	49,903	7	..	28	..	19	..	65	..
Nicaragua	1,009	2,396	31	32	21	23	17	14	48	45
Niger	2,481	1,826	35	39	16	18	7	7	49	44
Nigeria	28,472	41,085	33	30	41	46	6	4	26	25
Norway	115,453	161,769	4	2	35	43	13	..	61	55
Oman	10,535	14,962	3	..	58	..	4	..	39	..
Pakistan	40,010	61,638	26	26	25	23	17	15	49	51
Panama	5,313	9,889	9	7	15	17	9	8	76	76
Papua New Guinea	3,221	3,818	29	26	30	44	9	9	41	30
Paraguay	5,265	7,521	28	21	25	27	17	14	47	52
Peru	26,294	53,466	7	8	23	27	15	14	70	65
Philippines	44,331	74,733	22	16	34	31	25	23	44	53
Poland	58,976	157,739	8	4	50	36	..	21	42	60
Portugal	70,863	105,054	9	4	31	31	..	19	60	66
Puerto Rico	30,604	..	1	..	42	..	40	..	57	..
Romania	38,299	36,719	20	13	50	36	..	27	30	51
Russian Federation	579,068	251,106	17	7	48	39	..	..	35	54

	Gross domestic product ($ millions)		Agriculture value added (% of GDP)		Industry value added (% of GDP)		Manufacturing value added (% of GDP)		Services value added (% of GDP)	
	1990	2000	1990	2000	1990	2000	1990	2000	1990	2000
Rwanda	2,584	1,794	33	44	25	21	19	12	42	35
Saudi Arabia	104,670	173,287	6	7	50	48	8	10	43	45
Senegal	5,698	4,371	20	18	19	27	13	18	61	55
Sierra Leone	897	636	47	47	20	30	4	5	33	23
Singapore	36,670	92,252	0	0	34	34	27	26	65	66
Slovak Republic	15,485	19,121	7	4	59	31	..	22	33	65
Slovenia	12,673	18,129	6	3	46	38	35	28	49	58
Somalia	917	..	65	..	..	..	5	..	..	..
South Africa	111,997	125,887	5	3	40	31	24	19	55	66
Spain	513,522	558,558	7	4	34	31	..	20	59	66
Sri Lanka	8,032	16,305	26	20	26	27	15	17	48	53
Sudan	13,167	11,516	..	37	..	18	..	9	..	45
Swaziland	842	1,478	14	17	43	44	35	33	44	39
Sweden	238,327	227,319	3	2	32	29	..	..	64	69
Switzerland	228,415	239,764	..	2	..	30	..	..	..	68
Syrian Arab Republic	12,309	16,984	28	24	24	30	20	27	48	46
Tajikistan	4,339	991	33	19	38	26	25	23	29	55
Tanzania[b]	4,259	9,027	46	45	18	16	9	7	36	39
Thailand	85,345	122,166	12	10	37	40	27	32	50	49
Togo	1,628	1,219	34	38	23	22	10	10	44	40
Trinidad and Tobago	5,068	7,312	3	2	46	43	9	8	51	55
Tunisia	12,291	19,462	16	12	30	29	17	18	54	59
Turkey	150,721	199,937	18	16	30	25	20	15	52	59
Turkmenistan	8,129	4,404	32	27	30	50	..	40	38	23
Uganda	4,304	6,170	57	42	11	19	6	9	32	38
Ukraine	91,327	31,791	26	14	45	38	36	34	30	48
United Arab Emirates	34,132	46,481	2	..	64	..	8	..	35	..
United Kingdom	987,641	1,414,557	2	1	35	29	23	18	63	70
United States	5,750,800	9,837,406	..	..	..	..	..	..	..	..
Uruguay	9,287	19,715	9	6	35	27	28	17	56	67
Uzbekistan	23,673	7,666	33	35	33	23	..	10	34	42
Venezuela, RB	48,593	120,484	5	5	50	36	20	14	44	59
Vietnam	6,472	31,344	37	24	23	37	19	18	40	39
West Bank and Gaza	..	4,359	..	8	..	27	..	15	..	66
Yemen, Rep.	4,828	8,532	24	15	27	46	9	7	49	38
Yugoslavia, Fed. Rep.	..	8,449	..	..	..	..	..	..	..	..
Zambia	3,288	2,911	21	27	51	24	36	13	28	49
Zimbabwe	8,784	7,392	16	18	33	25	23	16	50	57
World	21,816,968 t	31,492,776 t	7 w	5 w	36 w	31 w	.. w	22 w	57 w	64 w
Low income	890,673	1,048,306	29	24	30	32	18	18	41	44
Middle income	3,518,514	5,513,236	13	9	39	36	25	25	47	55
Lower middle income	1,656,455	2,347,172	21	13	40	41	27	27	39	45
Upper middle income	1,879,581	3,170,508	9	7	39	32	24	23	52	62
Low & middle income	4,403,910	6,560,552	16	12	38	35	23	23	46	54
East Asia & Pacific	927,056	2,059,121	20	13	40	46	28	32	40	41
Europe & Central Asia	1,252,935	942,079	17	10	44	35	..	..	39	57
Latin America & Carib.	1,132,901	2,000,535	9	7	36	29	23	21	55	64
Middle East & N. Africa	401,331	659,692	15	14	39	37	12	14	47	48
South Asia	404,744	596,794	31	25	27	26	17	16	43	49
Sub-Saharan Africa	297,641	322,730	18	17	34	30	17	14	48	53
High income	17,413,841	24,927,330	..	..	..	..	..	..	..	..
Europe EMU	5,539,185	6,048,446	4	2	34	29	25	21	62	68

a. Excludes data for Transnistria. b. Data cover mainland Tanzania only.

About the data

A country's gross domestic product (GDP) represents the sum of value added by all producers in that country. Value added is the value of the gross output of producers less the value of intermediate goods and services consumed in production, before taking account of the consumption of fixed capital in the production process. Since 1968, the System of National Accounts has called for estimates of value added to be valued at either basic prices (excluding net taxes on products) or producer prices (including net taxes on products paid by the producers, but excluding sales or value added taxes). Both valuations exclude transport charges that are invoiced separately by the producers. Some countries, however, report such data at purchaser prices—the prices at which final sales are made (including transport charges)—which may affect estimates of the distribution of output. Total GDP as shown in the table and elsewhere in this book is measured at purchaser prices. Value added by industry is normally measured at basic prices. When value added is measured at producer prices, this is noted in *Primary data documentation*.

While GDP estimates based on the production approach are generally more reliable than estimates compiled from the income or expenditure side, different countries use different definitions, methods, and reporting standards. World Bank staff review the quality of national accounts data and sometimes make adjustments to increase consistency with international guidelines. Nevertheless, significant discrepancies remain between international standards and actual practice. Many statistical offices, especially those in developing countries, face severe limitations in the resources, time, training, and budgets required to produce reliable and comprehensive series of national accounts statistics.

Data problems in measuring output
Among the difficulties faced by compilers of national accounts is the extent of unreported economic activity in the informal or secondary economy. In developing countries a large share of agricultural output is either not exchanged (because it is consumed within the household) or not exchanged for money.

Agricultural production often must be estimated indirectly, using a combination of methods involving estimates of inputs, yields, and area under cultivation. This approach sometimes leads to crude approximations that can differ from the true values over time and across crops for reasons other than climatic conditions or farming techniques. Similarly, agricultural inputs that cannot easily be allocated to specific outputs are frequently "netted out" using equally crude and ad hoc approximations. For further discussion of the measurement of agricultural production see *About the data* for table 3.3.

Ideally, industrial output should be measured through regular censuses and surveys of firms. But in most developing countries such surveys are infrequent, so survey results must be extrapolated using an appropriate indicator. The choice of sampling unit, which may be the enterprise (where responses may be based on financial records) or the establishment (where production units may be recorded separately), also affects the quality of the data. Moreover, much industrial production is organized in unincorporated or owner-operated ventures that are not captured by surveys aimed at the formal sector. Even in large industries, where regular surveys are more likely, evasion of excise and other taxes and nondisclosure of income lower the estimates of value added. Such problems become more acute as countries move from state control of industry to private enterprise, because new firms enter business and growing numbers of established firms fail to report. In accordance with the System of National Accounts, output should include all such unreported activity as well as the value of illegal activities and other unrecorded, informal, or small-scale operations. Data on these activities need to be collected using techniques other than conventional surveys of firms.

In industries dominated by large organizations and enterprises, such as public utilities, data on output, employment, and wages are usually readily available and reasonably reliable. But in the service industry, the many self-employed workers and one-person businesses are sometimes difficult to locate, and they have little incentive to respond to surveys, let alone report their full earnings. Compounding these problems are the many forms of economic activity that go unrecorded, including the work that women and children do for little or no pay. For further discussion of the problems of using national accounts data see Srinivasan (1994) and Heston (1994).

Dollar conversion
To produce national accounts aggregates that are measured in the same standard monetary units, the value of output must be converted to a single common currency. The World Bank conventionally uses the U.S. dollar and applies the average official exchange rate reported by the International Monetary Fund for the year shown. An alternative conversion factor is applied if the official exchange rate is judged to diverge by an exceptionally large margin from the rate effectively applied to transactions in foreign currencies and traded products.

Definitions

• **Gross domestic product** (GDP) at purchaser prices is the sum of the gross value added by all resident producers in the economy plus any product taxes and minus any subsidies not included in the value of the products. It is calculated without making deductions for depreciation of fabricated assets or for depletion and degradation of natural resources. • **Value added** is the net output of an industry after adding up all outputs and subtracting intermediate inputs. The industrial origin of value added is determined by the International Standard Industrial Classification (ISIC) revision 3. • **Agriculture** corresponds to ISIC divisions 1–5 and includes forestry and fishing. • **Industry** comprises mining, manufacturing (also reported as a separate subgroup), construction, electricity, water, and gas (ISIC divisions 10–45). • **Manufacturing** refers to industries belonging to divisions 15–37. • **Services** correspond to ISIC divisions 50–99. This sector is derived as a residual (from GDP less agriculture and industry) and may not properly reflect the sum of service output, including banking and financial services.

Data sources

The national accounts indicators for most developing countries are collected from national statistical organizations and central banks by visiting and resident World Bank missions. The data for high-income economies come from Organisation for Economic Co-operation and Development (OECD) data files; see the OECD's *Main Economic Indicators* (monthly). The United Nations Statistics Division publishes detailed national accounts for United Nations member countries in *National Accounts Statistics: Main Aggregates and Detailed Tables* and publishes updates in the *Monthly Bulletin of Statistics*.

	Value added in manufacturing		Food, beverages, and tobacco		Textiles and clothing		Machinery and transport equipment		Chemicals		Other manufacturing[a]	
	$ millions		% of total		% of total		% of total		% of total		% of total	
	1990	1999	1990	1999	1990	1999	1990	1999	1990	1999	1990	1999
Afghanistan	..	..	..	..	..	..	..	..	..	..	..	..
Albania	878	436	24	..	33	..	..	..	..	..	44	..
Algeria	6,452	4,242	13	33	17	8	..	..	..	..	70	59
Angola	513	198	..	..	..	..	..	..	..	..	..	..
Argentina	37,868	48,169	20	30	10	7	13	15	12	12	46	36
Armenia	1,243	390	..	..	..	..	..	..	..	..	..	..
Australia	39,593	49,484	18	..	6	..	20	..	7	..	49	..
Austria	33,386	39,402	15	15	7	4	28	33	8	8	43	41
Azerbaijan	..	334	..	..	..	..	..	..	..	..	..	..
Bangladesh	3,839	6,858	24	..	38	..	7	..	17	..	14	..
Belarus	13,437	7,560	..	..	..	..	..	..	..	..	..	..
Belgium	..	43,421	17	19	7	6	..	..	13	17	62	59
Benin	145	207	..	..	..	..	..	..	..	..	..	..
Bolivia	826	1,154	28	34	5	4	1	1	3	5	63	55
Bosnia and Herzegovina	..	697	12	..	15	..	18	..	7	..	48	..
Botswana	184	251	51	..	12	..	..	..	..	..	36	..
Brazil	90,052	102,597	14	..	12	..	27	..	..	..	48	..
Bulgaria	..	1,799	22	20	9	10	19	5	5	..	45	65
Burkina Faso	423	316	..	..	..	..	..	..	..	..	..	..
Burundi	134	60	83	..	9	..	..	..	2	..	7	..
Cambodia	58	178	..	..	..	..	..	..	..	..	..	..
Cameroon	1,581	1,057	61	35	-13	9	1	3	5	6	46	47
Canada	88,928	104,211	15	13	6	4	26	33	10	9	44	41
Central African Republic	154	89	57	..	6	..	2	..	6	..	28	..
Chad	239	181	..	..	..	..	..	..	..	..	..	..
Chile	5,613	10,396	25	32	7	4	5	5	10	13	52	46
China	116,573	333,407	15	16	15	12	24	28	13	11	34	32
Hong Kong, China	12,626	8,478	8	11	36	21	21	24	2	3	33	40
Colombia	8,034	10,848	31	31	15	12	9	8	14	16	31	34
Congo, Dem. Rep.	1,029	..	..	..	..	..	..	..	..	..	..	..
Congo, Rep.	234	129	..	..	..	..	..	..	..	..	..	..
Costa Rica	1,107	4,135	47	46	8	6	7	9	9	13	30	26
Côte d'Ivoire	2,257	2,209	..	42	..	10	..	3	..	12	..	33
Croatia	4,770	3,694	22	..	15	..	20	..	8	..	36	..
Cuba	..	..	..	..	..	..	..	..	..	..	..	..
Czech Republic	..	..	..	..	..	..	..	..	..	..	..	..
Denmark	20,757	26,044	22	..	4	..	24	..	12	..	39	..
Dominican Republic	1,270	2,921	..	..	..	..	..	..	..	..	..	..
Ecuador	2,068	4,036	22	24	10	3	5	3	8	3	56	68
Egypt, Arab Rep.	7,296	16,286	19	18	15	12	9	13	14	14	43	43
El Salvador	1,044	2,805	36	29	14	28	4	3	24	16	22	24
Eritrea	49	88	..	..	..	..	..	..	..	..	..	..
Estonia	2,679	705	..	..	..	..	..	..	..	..	..	..
Ethiopia	497	419	62	52	21	18	1	2	2	4	14	23
Finland	27,533	27,799	13	8	4	2	24	21	8	2	52	66
France	228,104	242,127	13	..	6	..	31	..	9	..	41	..
Gabon	332	225	45	..	2	..	1	..	7	..	45	..
Gambia, The	18	19	..	..	..	..	..	..	..	..	..	..
Georgia	2,789	192	..	..	..	..	..	..	..	..	..	..
Germany	456,313	439,770	..	..	..	..	..	..	..	..	..	..
Ghana	575	702	..	..	..	..	..	..	..	..	..	..
Greece	..	13,161	22	26	20	12	12	15	10	13	36	34
Guatemala	1,151	2,442	..	..	..	..	..	..	..	..	..	..
Guinea	126	138	..	..	..	..	..	..	..	..	..	..
Guinea-Bissau	19	23	..	..	..	..	..	..	..	..	..	..
Haiti	446	282	51	46	9	19	..	..	..	..	40	34
Honduras	443	909	45	42	10	22	3	2	5	5	36	29

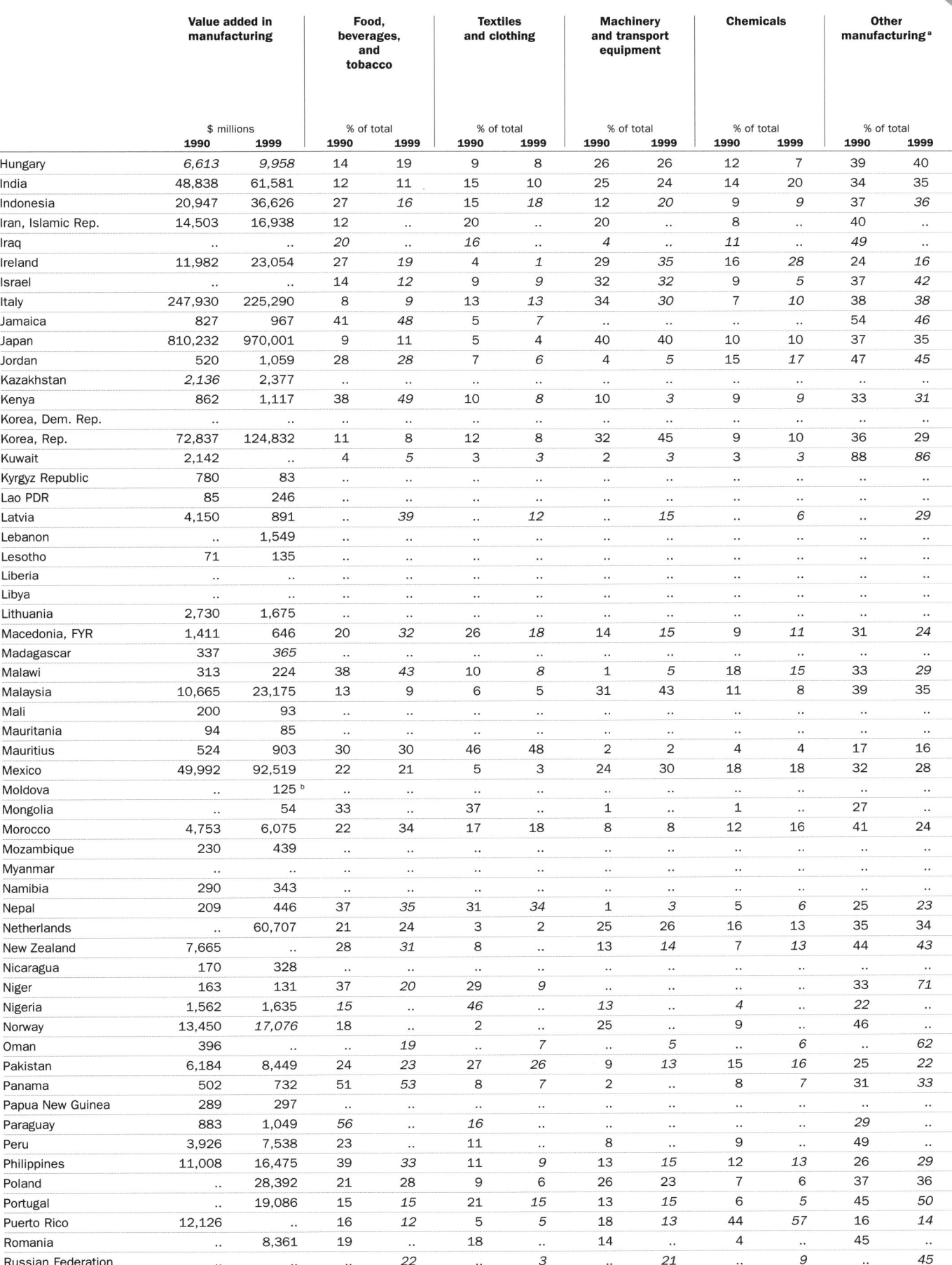

	Value added in manufacturing		Food, beverages, and tobacco		Textiles and clothing		Machinery and transport equipment		Chemicals		Other manufacturing [a]	
	$ millions		% of total		% of total		% of total		% of total		% of total	
	1990	1999	1990	1999	1990	1999	1990	1999	1990	1999	1990	1999
Hungary	6,613	9,958	14	19	9	8	26	26	12	7	39	40
India	48,838	61,581	12	11	15	10	25	24	14	20	34	35
Indonesia	20,947	36,626	27	16	15	18	12	20	9	9	37	36
Iran, Islamic Rep.	14,503	16,938	12	..	20	..	20	..	8	..	40	..
Iraq	..	..	20	..	16	..	4	..	11	..	49	..
Ireland	11,982	23,054	27	19	4	1	29	35	16	28	24	16
Israel	..	..	14	12	9	9	32	32	9	5	37	42
Italy	247,930	225,290	8	9	13	13	34	30	7	10	38	38
Jamaica	827	967	41	48	5	7	..	..	..	..	54	46
Japan	810,232	970,001	9	11	5	4	40	40	10	10	37	35
Jordan	520	1,059	28	28	7	6	4	5	15	17	47	45
Kazakhstan	2,136	2,377	..	..	..	..	..	..	..	..	..	..
Kenya	862	1,117	38	49	10	8	10	3	9	9	33	31
Korea, Dem. Rep.	..	..	..	..	..	..	..	..	..	..	..	..
Korea, Rep.	72,837	124,832	11	8	12	8	32	45	9	10	36	29
Kuwait	2,142	..	4	5	3	3	2	3	3	3	88	86
Kyrgyz Republic	780	83	..	..	..	..	..	..	..	..	..	..
Lao PDR	85	246	..	..	..	..	..	..	..	..	..	..
Latvia	4,150	891	..	39	..	12	..	15	..	6	..	29
Lebanon	..	1,549	..	..	..	..	..	..	..	..	..	..
Lesotho	71	135	..	..	..	..	..	..	..	..	..	..
Liberia	..	..	..	..	..	..	..	..	..	..	..	..
Libya	..	..	..	..	..	..	..	..	..	..	..	..
Lithuania	2,730	1,675	..	..	..	..	..	..	..	..	..	..
Macedonia, FYR	1,411	646	20	32	26	18	14	15	9	11	31	24
Madagascar	337	365	..	..	..	..	..	..	..	..	..	..
Malawi	313	224	38	43	10	8	1	5	18	15	33	29
Malaysia	10,665	23,175	13	9	6	5	31	43	11	8	39	35
Mali	200	93	..	..	..	..	..	..	..	..	..	..
Mauritania	94	85	..	..	..	..	..	..	..	..	..	..
Mauritius	524	903	30	30	46	48	2	2	4	4	17	16
Mexico	49,992	92,519	22	21	5	3	24	30	18	18	32	28
Moldova	..	125 [b]	..	..	..	..	..	..	..	..	..	..
Mongolia	..	54	33	..	37	..	1	..	1	..	27	..
Morocco	4,753	6,075	22	34	17	18	8	8	12	16	41	24
Mozambique	230	439	..	..	..	..	..	..	..	..	..	..
Myanmar	..	..	..	..	..	..	..	..	..	..	..	..
Namibia	290	343	..	..	..	..	..	..	..	..	..	..
Nepal	209	446	37	35	31	34	1	3	5	6	25	23
Netherlands	..	60,707	21	24	3	2	25	26	16	13	35	34
New Zealand	7,665	..	28	31	8	..	13	14	7	13	44	43
Nicaragua	170	328	..	..	..	..	..	..	..	..	..	..
Niger	163	131	37	20	29	9	..	..	..	..	33	71
Nigeria	1,562	1,635	15	..	46	..	13	..	4	..	22	..
Norway	13,450	17,076	18	..	2	..	25	..	9	..	46	..
Oman	396	..	..	19	..	7	..	5	..	6	..	62
Pakistan	6,184	8,449	24	23	27	26	9	13	15	16	25	22
Panama	502	732	51	53	8	7	2	..	8	7	31	33
Papua New Guinea	289	297	..	..	..	..	..	..	..	..	..	..
Paraguay	883	1,049	56	..	16	..	..	..	..	..	29	..
Peru	3,926	7,538	23	..	11	..	8	..	9	..	49	..
Philippines	11,008	16,475	39	33	11	9	13	15	12	13	26	29
Poland	..	28,392	21	28	9	6	26	23	7	6	37	36
Portugal	..	19,086	15	15	21	15	13	15	6	5	45	50
Puerto Rico	12,126	..	16	12	5	5	18	13	44	57	16	14
Romania	..	8,361	19	..	18	..	14	..	4	..	45	..
Russian Federation	..	..	..	22	..	3	..	21	..	9	..	45

	Value added in manufacturing $ millions		Food, beverages, and tobacco % of total		Textiles and clothing % of total		Machinery and transport equipment % of total		Chemicals % of total		Other manufacturing[a] % of total	
	1990	1999	1990	1999	1990	1999	1990	1999	1990	1999	1990	1999
Rwanda	473	223	..	..	..	..	..	..	..	..	..	..
Saudi Arabia	7,962	*12,550*	..	..	..	..	..	..	..	..	..	..
Senegal	747	802	60	*44*	3	*5*	5	*3*	9	*26*	23	*21*
Sierra Leone	31	28	..	..	..	..	..	..	..	..	..	..
Singapore	9,937	21,017	4	4	3	1	53	60	10	11	29	25
Slovak Republic	..	4,305	..	..	..	..	..	..	..	..	..	..
Slovenia	*4,008*	4,729	12	*12*	15	*10*	16	*16*	9	*11*	48	*51*
Somalia	41	..	..	..	..	..	..	..	..	..	..	..
South Africa	24,040	22,253	14	15	8	7	18	20	9	10	50	48
Spain	..	*104,997*	18	..	8	..	25	..	10	..	39	..
Sri Lanka	1,077	2,309	50	..	24	..	4	..	4	..	17	..
Sudan	..	749	..	..	..	..	..	..	..	..	..	..
Swaziland	246	331	69	..	8	..	1	..	0	..	22	..
Sweden	..	*51,419*	10	8	2	1	33	38	9	11	47	43
Switzerland	..	..	10	*9*	4	*3*	34	*27*	..	..	53	*60*
Syrian Arab Republic	2,508	4,291	35	*27*	29	*24*	..	..	..	..	36	*49*
Tajikistan	1,078	207	..	..	..	..	..	..	..	..	..	..
Tanzania[c]	361	583	51	..	3	..	7	..	11	..	28	..
Thailand	23,217	37,959	24	..	30	..	19	..	2	..	26	..
Togo	162	122	..	..	..	..	..	..	..	..	..	..
Trinidad and Tobago	438	552	31	..	3	..	3	..	19	..	44	..
Tunisia	2,075	3,748	19	*20*	20	*28*	5	*7*	4	*8*	52	*36*
Turkey	26,896	23,989	16	*13*	15	*17*	16	*18*	10	*10*	43	*42*
Turkmenistan	..	1,063	..	..	..	..	..	..	..	..	..	..
Uganda	230	508	..	..	..	..	..	..	..	..	..	..
Ukraine	31,489	8,600	..	..	..	..	..	..	..	..	..	..
United Arab Emirates	2,643	..	..	..	..	..	..	..	..	..	..	..
United Kingdom	203,865	238,975	13	12	5	5	32	29	11	11	38	43
United States	..	..	12	9	5	3	31	46	12	10	40	32
Uruguay	2,597	3,445	31	*38*	18	*12*	9	*5*	10	*9*	32	*36*
Uzbekistan	..	787	..	..	..	..	..	..	..	..	..	..
Venezuela, RB	9,809	13,938	17	*28*	5	*5*	5	*10*	9	*12*	64	*45*
Vietnam	1,219	5,045	..	..	..	..	..	..	..	..	..	..
West Bank and Gaza	..	570	..	..	..	..	..	..	..	..	..	..
Yemen, Rep.	449	595	..	..	..	..	..	..	..	..	..	..
Yugoslavia, Fed. Rep.	..	..	..	*28*	..	*9*	..	*17*	..	*10*	..	*35*
Zambia	1,048	339	44	..	11	..	7	..	9	..	29	..
Zimbabwe	1,799	797	28	*34*	19	*15*	9	*7*	6	*5*	38	*39*

World	**4,617,236 w**	**5,397,733 w**
Low income	150,714	150,986
Middle income	693,897	1,200,241
Lower middle income	303,274	648,001
Upper middle income	379,852	560,402
Low & middle income	851,662	1,350,094
East Asia & Pacific	259,745	584,052
Europe & Central Asia	..	..
Latin America & Carib.	*254,376*	330,258
Middle East & N. Africa	45,996	77,249
South Asia	61,115	80,947
Sub-Saharan Africa	42,947	39,088
High income	..	4,048,461
Europe EMU	*1,233,700*	1,241,073

a. Includes unallocated data. b. Excludes data for Transinistria. c. Data cover mainland Tanzania only.

About the data

The data on the distribution of manufacturing value added by industry are provided by the United Nations Industrial Development Organization (UNIDO). UNIDO obtains data on manufacturing value added from a variety of national and international sources, including the United Nations Statistics Division, the World Bank, the Organisation for Economic Co-operation and Development, and the International Monetary Fund. To improve comparability over time and across countries, UNIDO supplements these data with information from industrial censuses, statistics supplied by national and international organizations, unpublished data that it collects in the field, and estimates by the UNIDO Secretariat. Nevertheless, coverage may be less than complete, particularly for the informal sector. To the extent that direct information on inputs and outputs is not available, estimates may be used that may result in errors in industry totals. Moreover, countries use different reference periods (calendar or fiscal year) and valuation methods (basic, producer, or purchaser prices) to estimate value added. (See also *About the data* for table 4.2.)

The data on manufacturing value added in U.S. dollars are from the World Bank's national accounts files. These figures may differ from those used by UNIDO to calculate the shares of value added by industry. Thus estimates of value added in a particular industry group calculated by applying the shares to total value added will not match those from UNIDO sources in part because of exchange rate differences.

The classification of manufacturing industries in the table accords with the United Nations International Standard Industrial Classification (ISIC) either revision 2 or revision 3. First published in 1948, the ISIC has its roots in the work of the League of Nations Committee of Statistical Experts. The committee's efforts, interrupted by the Second World War, were taken up by the United Nations Statistical Commission, which at its first session appointed a committee on industrial classification. The latest revision, ISIC revision 3, was completed in 1989 and many countries have now switched to it. However, revision 2 is still widely used for compiling cross-country data and concordances matching ISIC categories to national systems of classification and to related systems such as the Standard International Trade Classification (SITC) which are readily available.

In establishing a classification system, compilers must define both the types of activities to be described and the organizational units whose activities are to be reported. There are many possibilities and the choices made affect how the resulting statistics can be interpreted and how useful they are in analyzing economic behavior. The ISIC emphasizes commonalities in the production process and is explicitly not intended to measure outputs (for which there is a newly developed Central Product Classification). Nevertheless, the ISIC views an activity as defined by "a process resulting in a homogeneous set of products" (United Nations 1990 [ISIC, series M, no. 4, rev. 3], p. 9). Firms typically use a multitude of processes to produce a final product. For example, an automobile manufacturer engages in forging, welding, and painting as well as advertising, accounting, and many other service activities. In some cases, the processes may be carried out by different technical units within the larger enterprise, but collecting data at such a detailed level is not practical. Nor would it be useful to record production data at the very highest level of a large, multiplant, multiproduct firm. The ISIC has therefore adopted as the definition of an establishment "an enterprise or part of an enterprise which independently engages in one, or predominantly one, kind of economic activity at or from one location . . . for which data are available . . ." (United Nations 1990, p. 25). By design, this definition matches the reporting unit required for the production accounts of the United Nations System of National Accounts.

Definitions

• **Value added in manufacturing** is the sum of gross output less the value of intermediate inputs used in production for industries classified in ISIC major division 3. • **Food, beverages, and tobacco** comprise ISIC division 31. • **Textiles and clothing** comprise ISIC division 32. • **Machinery and transport equipment** comprise ISIC groups 382–84. • **Chemicals** comprise ISIC groups 351 and 352. • **Other manufacturing** includes wood and related products (ISIC division 33), paper and related products (ISIC division 34), petroleum and related products (ISIC groups 353–56), basic metals and mineral products (ISIC divisions 36 and 37), fabricated metal products and professional goods (ISIC groups 381 and 385), and other industries (ISIC group 390). When data for textiles and clothing, machinery and transport equipment, or chemicals are shown in the table as not available, they are included in other manufacturing.

Data sources

The data on value added in manufacturing in U.S. dollars are from the World Bank's national accounts files. The data used to calculate shares of value added by industry are provided to the World Bank in electronic files by UNIDO. The most recent published source is UNIDO's *International Yearbook of Industrial Statistics 2001*. The ISIC system is described in the United Nations' *International Standard Industrial Classification of All Economic Activities, Third Revision* (1990). The discussion of the ISIC draws on Jacob Ryten's paper "Fifty Years of ISIC: Historical Origins and Future Perspectives" (1998).

Figure 4.3

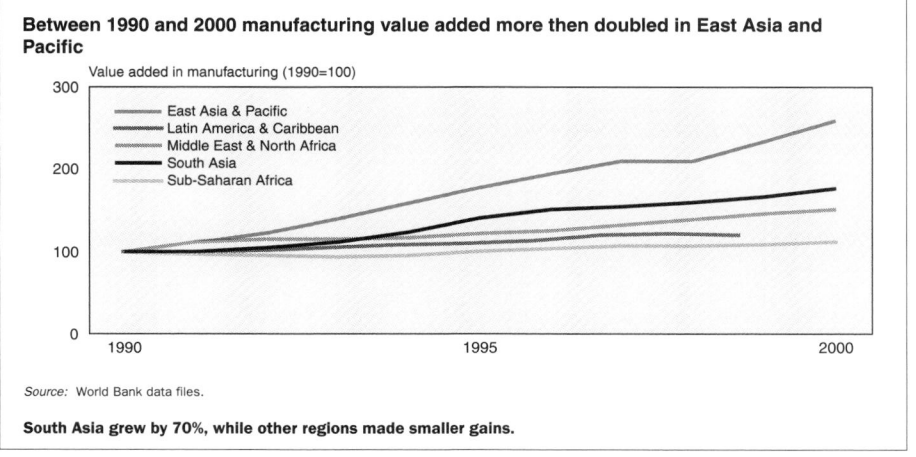

Between 1990 and 2000 manufacturing value added more then doubled in East Asia and Pacific

Value added in manufacturing (1990=100)

- East Asia & Pacific
- Latin America & Caribbean
- Middle East & North Africa
- South Asia
- Sub-Saharan Africa

Source: World Bank data files.

South Asia grew by 70%, while other regions made smaller gains.

	Export volume		Import volume		Export value		Import value		Net barter terms of trade	
	average annual % growth		average annual % growth		average annual % growth		average annual % growth		1995 = 100	
	1980-90	1990-99	1980-90	1990-99	1980-90	1990-99	1980-90	1990-99	1990	1999
Afghanistan	-9.8	-4.7	0.0	1.8	-10.4	-5.2	1.8	1.8	99	96
Albania[a]	..	..	..	..	..	14.3	..	19.9	..	..
Algeria	3.6	3.8	-4.5	2.1	-4.3	0.7	-2.7	1.8	127	106
Angola	5.9	-1.2	1.0	0.1	6.3	-1.1	-0.7	2.3	137	85
Argentina	5.0	9.9	-6.8	19.5	2.2	11.0	-6.5	20.3	97	98
Armenia[a]	..	..	..	..	..	11.4	..	24.5	..	..
Australia[a]	6.3	7.5	5.9	9.3	6.7	5.1	6.3	6.8	117	95
Austria[a]	..	..	..	..	10.3	6.1	8.7	4.5	..	..
Azerbaijan[a]	..	..	..	..	..	-6.4	..	4.0	..	..
Bangladesh	1.0	14.9	-4.3	20.5	7.8	11.3	3.6	10.7	74	97
Belarus[a]	..	..	..	..	..	17.2	..	18.0	..	..
Belgium[a,b]	4.5	6.3	4.0	5.4	7.8	6.3	6.5	4.4	100	99
Benin	3.6	7.6	-10.0	9.2	9.8	9.3	-4.8	10.9	100	82
Bolivia	3.1	2.5	-1.3	10.0	-2.0	4.3	-0.4	11.0	115	110
Bosnia and Herzegovina	..	..	..	..	..	..	..	..	..	..
Botswana	11.4	8.6	11.1	1.7	18.9	4.7	10.9	2.1	110	69
Brazil	6.2	4.5	0.8	19.1	5.2	6.1	-1.8	14.2	60	95
Bulgaria[a]	..	..	..	..	-12.3	2.5	-14.1	5.1	..	..
Burkina Faso	-0.3	14.8	3.8	4.4	8.0	15.3	4.4	4.5	91	85
Burundi	3.5	6.9	1.0	1.1	2.5	-3.5	2.2	-7.9	79	72
Cambodia	..	..	..	..	..	..	..	..	..	..
Cameroon	7.3	1.8	4.9	4.6	1.4	-1.1	0.1	2.1	89	77
Canada[a]	6.4	9.1	7.5	9.0	6.7	8.1	7.8	7.4	100	97
Central African Republic	-1.9	26.7	4.3	9.4	1.6	9.9	7.8	5.3	123	56
Chad	8.5	4.9	10.7	3.6	9.5	3.9	12.5	4.5	116	100
Chile	9.2	10.3	-2.9	11.4	8.0	8.6	2.6	10.8	84	73
China[†]	13.3	10.5	15.8	9.1	12.8	14.6	13.5	12.6	101	103
Hong Kong, China	11.1	8.8	9.2	9.5	16.7	8.9	14.9	9.6	101	102
Colombia	7.7	4.7	-2.1	10.6	7.7	7.3	-0.1	12.3	94	102
Congo, Dem. Rep.	10.6	-4.9	29.6	-14.0	3.6	-3.0	19.1	-8.0	109	78
Congo, Rep.	7.2	6.6	3.6	8.7	2.1	6.9	5.3	6.0	83	84
Costa Rica	3.7	14.3	5.2	15.8	4.7	18.4	4.4	15.0	71	102
Côte d'Ivoire	2.6	5.7	-2.1	5.0	1.8	7.2	-1.5	5.5	82	95
Croatia[a]	..	..	..	..	..	1.2	..	10.1	..	..
Cuba	-1.1	-8.9	-0.4	-1.1	-0.9	-8.9	1.7	-2.0	96	90
Czech Republic[a]	..	..	..	..	..	10.5	..	11.4	..	..
Denmark[a]	4.1	5.3	3.1	6.1	8.5	4.1	6.3	4.8	100	100
Dominican Republic	-0.9	3.7	0.8	13.4	-2.0	4.9	3.4	14.1	97	104
Ecuador	7.1	7.7	-1.9	7.2	-0.3	7.3	-1.4	9.7	141	106
Egypt, Arab Rep.	13.5	-2.8	8.0	2.4	7.3	-1.0	12.8	5.1	86	91
El Salvador	-4.6	2.4	4.5	7.6	-4.6	10.7	2.4	11.4	69	87
Eritrea	..	..	..	..	..	..	..	..	..	..
Estonia[a]	..	..	..	..	..	24.3	..	29.1	..	..
Ethiopia	-0.4	7.2	3.6	2.0	-1.2	13.0	4.3	8.8	89	94
Finland[a]	2.3	9.2	4.4	4.3	7.4	7.9	6.9	4.5	100	95
France[a]	3.7	6.0	3.7	5.1	7.6	4.7	6.5	3.3	97	99
Gabon	-3.0	-15.5	-5.6	-1.3	0.0	-14.9	2.5	0.2	102	99
Gambia, The	..	..	..	..	..	..	..	..	..	..
Georgia	..	..	..	..	..	..	..	..	..	..
Germany[a, c]	4.4	5.9	4.9	4.3	9.1	4.2	7.2	3.5	102	100
Ghana	-15.3	9.1	-17.5	7.2	-0.2	10.8	2.8	9.1	103	98
Greece[a]	5.0	8.9	6.3	9.0	5.9	3.1	6.6	2.1	108	102
Guatemala	-1.1	8.4	0.1	10.3	-2.2	10.5	0.5	11.6	98	87
Guinea	..	8.4	..	0.4	3.9	4.7	9.9	0.5	135	92
Guinea-Bissau	-2.0	15.4	-0.3	-3.8	4.1	13.4	5.2	-1.8	143	100
Haiti	-0.3	3.6	-4.6	13.5	-1.3	3.2	-2.8	14.3	116	95
Honduras	4.0	2.9	1.6	13.0	1.5	8.3	0.6	14.2	81	110
† Data for Taiwan, China	16.7	2.8	17.8	4.6	15.2	6.9	12.3	8.3	102	108

	Export volume		Import volume		Export value		Import value		Net barter terms of trade	
	average annual % growth		average annual % growth		average annual % growth		average annual % growth		1995 = 100	
	1980-90	1990-99	1980-90	1990-99	1980-90	1990-99	1980-90	1990-99	1990	1999
Hungary[a]	3.4	7.8	1.4	10.0	1.4	11.8	0.1	12.9	100	108
India	-3.1	5.3	-2.9	7.7	7.4	9.6	4.2	9.9	79	99
Indonesia	8.1	8.0	1.8	4.2	-0.8	8.0	2.6	3.0	102	110
Iran, Islamic Rep.	16.9	-2.6	-2.4	-8.4	7.3	-2.6	0.2	-6.8	169	146
Iraq	2.3	20.4	-4.5	5.1	-4.0	16.7	-2.2	5.2	132	109
Ireland[a]	9.3	14.8	4.7	11.0	12.7	14.0	7.1	10.9	107	99
Israel[a]	6.9	9.1	5.8	8.9	8.2	10.7	5.9	8.7	97	112
Italy[a]	4.4	5.7	5.4	4.0	8.7	5.3	6.9	2.9	98	108
Jamaica	1.5	4.5	2.9	7.7	1.2	2.6	2.7	7.3	105	88
Japan[a]	5.1	1.9	6.5	5.2	9.1	4.0	5.0	4.3	73	102
Jordan	7.7	4.7	1.2	3.7	6.0	7.3	-1.9	5.0	80	90
Kazakhstan[a]	..	..	..	..	..	10.9	..	1.3	..	..
Kenya	1.7	3.9	2.4	8.2	-1.0	7.8	1.8	6.6	68	107
Korea, Dem. Rep.	..	..	..	..	..	..	..	..	..	..
Korea, Rep.	11.5	15.3	11.0	9.5	14.9	10.1	11.8	6.6	98	82
Kuwait	-2.2	16.4	-6.3	7.9	-7.7	16.9	-4.1	7.2	94	99
Kyrgyz Republic[a]	..	..	..	..	..	7.8	..	11.1	..	..
Lao PDR[a]	..	..	..	..	11.2	18.3	6.4	15.6	..	..
Latvia[a]	..	6.4	..	..	..	12.9	..	23.6	..	..
Lebanon	-5.2	1.9	-7.5	12.1	-5.2	4.2	-5.5	12.8	104	114
Lesotho	6.3	14.0	3.5	3.4	3.7	13.4	3.3	1.9	97	96
Liberia	-3.5	6.9	-7.5	7.4	-3.1	4.6	-7.2	6.5	112	98
Libya	0.0	-4.1	-6.5	-1.8	-7.3	-4.5	-4.4	0.2	145	123
Lithuania[a]	..	..	..	..	..	10.3	..	17.6	..	..
Macedonia, FYR[a]	..	..	..	..	..	2.8	..	6.4	..	..
Madagascar	-3.0	-6.8	-3.7	-3.2	-1.0	-2.9	-1.8	-1.5	87	97
Malawi	2.4	4.3	-0.1	-1.5	2.0	2.5	3.2	0.6	141	100
Malaysia	14.3	15.8	5.8	11.2	8.6	12.7	7.6	9.9	102	88
Mali	4.3	10.7	3.0	5.9	6.2	6.7	2.8	4.6	122	90
Mauritania	3.9	6.6	-3.2	7.4	8.1	3.0	-2.0	4.0	96	102
Mauritius	10.3	4.4	11.2	3.6	14.3	4.1	12.9	4.6	109	96
Mexico	15.4	15.4	1.0	12.4	5.8	16.0	6.3	13.8	109	102
Moldova[a]	..	..	..	..	..	9.0	..	11.7	..	..
Mongolia	..	..	..	..	5.0	-3.0	5.5	-1.9	..	..
Morocco	5.7	8.0	3.1	6.8	6.2	8.8	3.6	5.5	94	117
Mozambique	-9.5	16.4	-2.7	-2.5	-9.7	8.1	0.2	0.2	161	76
Myanmar	-3.0	13.7	-6.4	15.3	-7.6	13.5	-5.0	25.1	116	51
Namibia[a]	..	..	..	..	..	..	..	..	..	..
Nepal[a]	..	..	..	..	8.1	9.2	6.7	10.1	..	..
Netherlands[a]	4.6	7.1	4.5	6.9	4.6	6.0	4.4	5.7	98	96
New Zealand[a]	3.5	4.6	4.3	6.2	6.2	4.3	5.5	6.4	103	98
Nicaragua	-4.8	10.3	-3.4	9.6	-5.8	10.5	-3.1	11.9	119	81
Niger	-5.1	3.7	-5.2	-3.0	-5.4	0.2	-3.5	0.1	137	78
Nigeria	-4.4	3.4	-21.4	5.1	-8.4	0.5	-15.6	5.9	161	108
Norway[a]	4.1	7.2	3.4	7.4	5.3	4.1	6.3	4.5	112	111
Oman	7.0	4.6	-1.7	4.5	3.4	3.6	0.7	6.8	159	132
Pakistan	-0.3	-2.4	-5.3	-0.5	8.1	4.6	3.0	3.4	91	116
Panama	-0.6	5.8	-6.8	8.8	-0.5	10.1	-3.6	9.6	69	106
Papua New Guinea	1.4	-7.9	..	..	4.8	3.8	1.3	-0.3	..	..
Paraguay	13.0	1.2	10.2	5.8	11.8	3.9	4.3	7.3	87	88
Peru	2.7	9.0	-2.0	12.3	-1.5	9.3	1.4	12.6	93	83
Philippines	-7.4	17.0	-7.8	13.7	3.9	19.1	2.9	13.6	90	121
Poland[a]	4.8	8.6	1.4	19.6	1.4	10.0	-3.1	20.1	86	94
Portugal[a]	..	..	..	..	15.0	6.1	10.3	5.5	..	..
Puerto Rico	..	..	..	..	..	..	..	..	..	..
Romania[a]	..	..	..	..	-4.0	8.4	-3.8	6.6	..	..
Russian Federation[a]	..	..	..	..	..	9.3	..	6.8	..	..

	Export volume		Import volume		Export value		Import value		Net barter terms of trade	
	average annual % growth		average annual % growth		average annual % growth		average annual % growth		1995 = 100	
	1980-90	**1990-99**	**1980-90**	**1990-99**	**1980-90**	**1990-99**	**1980-90**	**1990-99**	**1990**	**1999**
Rwanda	3.3	-7.7	2.3	2.5	-0.3	-3.8	3.3	-1.3	38	88
Saudi Arabia	-6.4	2.6	-8.4	-1.4	-13.4	1.2	-6.1	0.6	169	132
Senegal	1.2	5.1	0.5	4.3	3.6	4.5	1.4	3.6	109	102
Sierra Leone	-1.0	-34.3	-6.3	-7.3	-2.4	-31.8	-8.7	-6.2	63	67
Singapore	13.5	13.5	10.1	9.9	9.8	10.4	8.0	8.3	111	99
Slovak Republic[a]	..	..	..	..	..	*10.4*	..	*12.5*	..	..
Slovenia[a]	..	..	..	..	..	9.4	..	10.4	..	..
Somalia	-1.6	1.8	-16.7	13.5	-1.1	0.6	-15.0	12.4	99	94
South Africa[a, d]	3.3	*7.4*	-0.8	*7.7*	0.7	2.5	-1.3	6.6	98	*100*
Spain[a]	..	..	..	..	10.7	9.3	10.6	5.9	96	102
Sri Lanka	-4.1	3.3	-6.6	2.8	5.4	12.0	2.2	9.7	83	92
Sudan	-3.1	15.7	-7.7	14.7	-2.5	10.0	-6.4	13.2	123	81
Swaziland	7.6	1.5	2.1	-4.6	4.6	7.0	-0.6	5.6	116	80
Sweden[a]	4.3	0.6	5.0	1.1	8.0	6.5	6.6	4.5	99	95
Switzerland[a]	..	..	..	..	9.4	3.0	8.9	1.9	..	..
Syrian Arab Republic	8.6	-0.6	-10.0	4.7	4.4	-0.5	-6.8	5.0	132	126
Tajikistan	..	..	..	..	..	..	..	..	..	..
Tanzania	-3.5	5.4	-2.1	-7.0	-5.1	8.3	-0.6	0.1	102	64
Thailand	11.2	4.1	8.8	-2.3	14.6	11.0	12.8	5.3	103	94
Togo	-1.2	8.9	0.7	6.4	1.2	8.5	1.9	6.0	127	124
Trinidad and Tobago	-11.0	3.1	-20.5	10.9	-9.4	4.7	-12.3	12.0	116	122
Tunisia	4.9	5.2	1.7	4.0	3.5	6.5	2.7	5.7	103	102
Turkey	..	11.0	..	11.1	14.3	9.9	9.3	10.3	104	104
Turkmenistan	..	..	..	..	..	..	..	..	..	..
Uganda	-5.4	18.3	-6.1	24.7	-4.0	18.5	4.3	23.6	74	57
Ukraine[a]	..	..	..	..	..	7.5	..	9.2	..	..
United Arab Emirates	8.8	8.8	-1.3	8.8	-0.8	7.9	0.6	11.2	172	143
United Kingdom[a]	4.5	6.2	6.7	6.1	5.8	5.7	8.4	5.4	101	104
United States[a]	3.5	6.7	7.2	8.9	5.6	7.4	8.3	9.0	98	101
Uruguay	4.3	6.5	1.3	12.1	4.4	6.1	-1.3	11.7	100	95
Uzbekistan	..	..	..	..	..	..	..	..	..	..
Venezuela, RB	3.5	5.7	-3.9	4.2	-4.4	3.5	-3.2	5.1	141	107
Vietnam	..	..	..	..	..	..	..	..	..	..
West Bank and Gaza	..	..	..	..	..	..	..	..	..	..
Yemen, Rep.[a]	..	..	..	..	..	*21.6*	..	*-2.1*	..	..
Yugoslavia, Fed. Rep.	..	..	..	..	..	..	..	..	..	..
Zambia	-0.1	5.0	2.1	0.8	1.2	-2.5	0.0	-1.4	109	46
Zimbabwe	4.0	8.2	3.5	9.2	2.8	2.9	-0.3	4.1	100	100

a. Data are from the International Monetary Fund's International Financial Statistics database. b. Includes Luxembourg. c. Data prior to 1990 refer to the Federal Republic of Germany before unification. d. Data refer to the South African Customs Union (Botswana, Lesotho, Namibia, South Africa and Swaziland).

About the data

Data on international trade in goods are recorded in each country's balance of payments and by customs services. While the balance of payments focuses on the financial transactions that accompany trade, customs data record the direction of trade and the physical quantities and value of goods entering or leaving the customs area. Customs data may differ from those recorded in the balance of payments because of differences in valuation and the time of recording. The 1993 System of National Accounts and the fifth edition of the International Monetary Fund's (IMF) *Balance of Payments Manual* (1993) have attempted to reconcile the definitions and reporting standards for international trade statistics, but differences in sources, timing, and national practices limit comparability. Real growth rates derived from trade volume indexes and terms of trade based on unit price indexes may therefore differ from those derived from national accounts aggregates.

Trade in goods, or merchandise trade, includes all goods that add to or subtract from an economy's material resources. Thus the total supply of goods in an economy is made up of gross output plus imports less exports. Currency in circulation, titles of ownership, and securities are excluded, but monetary gold is included. Trade data are collected on the basis of a country's customs area, which in most cases is the same as its geographic area. Goods provided as part of foreign aid are included, but goods destined for extraterritorial agencies (such as embassies) are not.

Collecting and tabulating trade statistics is difficult. Some developing countries lack the capacity to report timely data; this is a problem especially for countries that are landlocked and where territorial boundaries are porous. As a result, it is necessary to estimate their trade from the data reported by their partners. Other countries that belong to common customs unions may need to collect their data by direct inquiry from companies. (For further discussion of the use of partner country reports see *About the data* for table 6.2.) In some cases economic or political concerns may lead national authorities to suppress or misrepresent data on certain trade flows, such as oil, military equipment, or the exports of a dominant producer. In other cases reported trade data may be distorted by deliberate under- or overinvoicing to effect capital transfers or avoid taxes. And in some regions smuggling and black market trading result in unreported trade flows.

By international agreement, customs data are reported to the United Nations Statistics Division, which maintains the Commodity Trade (COMTRADE) database. The United Nations Conference on Trade and Development (UNCTAD) compiles a variety of international trade statistics, including price and volume indexes, based on the COMTRADE data. The IMF and the World Trade Organization also compile data on trade prices and volumes. The growth rates and terms of trade for low- and middle-income economies shown in this table were calculated from index numbers compiled by UNCTAD. Volume measures for high-income economies were derived by deflating the value of trade using deflators from the IMF's *International Financial Statistics*. In some cases price and volume indexes from different sources may vary significantly as a result of differences in estimation procedures. All indexes are rescaled to a 1995 base year. Terms of trade were computed from the same indicators.

The terms of trade measure the relative prices of a country's exports and imports. There are a number of ways to calculate terms of trade. The most common is the net barter, or commodity, terms of trade, constructed as the ratio of the export price index to the import price index. When the net barter terms of trade increase, a country's exports are becoming more valuable or its imports cheaper.

Definitions

- **Growth rates of export and import volumes** are average annual growth rates calculated for low- and middle-income economies from UNCTAD's quantum index series and for high-income economies from export and import data deflated by the IMF's trade price deflators.
- **Growth rates of export and import values** are average annual growth rates calculated from UNCTAD's value indexes or from current values of merchandise exports and imports.
- **Net barter terms of trade** are calculated as the ratio of the export price index to the corresponding import price index measured relative to the base year 1995.

Data sources

The main source of trade data for developing countries is UNCTAD's annual *Handbook of International Trade and Development Statistics*. The IMF's *International Financial Statistics* includes data on the export and import values and deflators for high-income and selected developing economies.

4.5 | Structure of merchandise exports

	Merchandise exports		Food		Agricultural raw materials		Fuels		Ores and metals		Manufactures	
	$ millions		% of total		% of total		% of total		% of total		% of total	
	1990	2000	1990	2000	1990	2000	1990	2000	1990	2000	1990	2000
Afghanistan	235	130	..	..	..	..	..	..	..	..	..	..
Albania	230	260	..	7	..	6	..	2	..	4	..	82
Algeria	12,930	19,550	0	0	0	0	96	97	0	0	3	2
Angola	3,910	7,858	0	..	0	..	93	..	6	..	0	..
Argentina	12,353	26,298	56	44	4	2	8	18	2	3	29	32
Armenia	..	300	..	14	..	5	..	11	..	22	..	43
Australia	39,752	63,869	20	21	10	6	18	22	16	17	16	29
Austria	41,265	63,903	3	5	4	3	1	1	3	3	88	83
Azerbaijan	..	1,750	..	3	..	2	..	85	..	2	..	8
Bangladesh	1,671	6,500	14	7	7	2	1	0	..	0	77	91
Belarus	..	7,380	..	7	..	4	..	20	..	1	..	67
Belgium[a]	117,703	193,998	9	10	2	1	3	2	4	3	77	78
Benin	288	376	..	15	..	80	..	1	..	0	..	3
Bolivia	926	1,214	19	30	8	3	25	13	44	25	5	29
Bosnia and Herzegovina	276	1,030	..	..	..	..	..	..	..	..	..	..
Botswana	1,784	2,670	..	..	..	..	..	..	..	..	..	..
Brazil	31,414	55,086	28	23	3	5	2	2	14	10	52	59
Bulgaria	5,030	4,725	..	10	..	3	..	12	..	13	..	57
Burkina Faso	152	228	..	..	..	..	..	..	..	..	..	..
Burundi	75	49	..	91	..	8	..	..	..	1	..	0
Cambodia	86	700	..	..	..	..	..	..	..	..	..	..
Cameroon	2,002	1,880	20	23	14	28	50	35	7	6	9	5
Canada	127,629	276,635	9	6	9	6	10	13	9	4	59	64
Central African Republic	120	170	..	..	..	..	..	..	..	..	..	..
Chad	188	183	..	..	..	..	..	..	..	..	..	..
Chile	8,372	18,158	24	25	9	10	1	1	55	45	11	16
China[†]	62,091	249,297	13	5	3	1	8	3	2	2	72	88
Hong Kong, China[b]	82,390	202,440	3	2	0	0	0	0	1	2	95	95
Colombia	6,766	13,040	33	19	4	5	37	41	0	1	25	34
Congo, Dem. Rep.	999	450	..	..	..	..	..	..	..	..	..	..
Congo, Rep.	981	2,500	..	..	..	..	..	..	..	..	..	..
Costa Rica	1,448	5,865	58	30	5	3	1	1	1	1	27	66
Côte d'Ivoire	3,072	4,029	..	50	..	14	..	21	..	0	..	14
Croatia	4,597	4,390	13	9	6	5	9	11	5	3	68	73
Cuba	5,100	1,635	..	..	..	..	..	..	..	..	..	..
Czech Republic	12,170	29,000	..	4	..	2	..	3	..	2	..	88
Denmark	36,870	49,631	27	20	3	3	3	7	1	1	60	64
Dominican Republic	2,170	5,700	21	..	0	..	0	..	0	..	78	..
Ecuador	2,714	4,846	44	37	1	4	52	49	0	0	2	10
Egypt, Arab Rep.	2,585	4,689	10	9	10	8	29	37	9	4	42	37
El Salvador	582	2,933	57	42	1	1	2	5	3	2	38	48
Eritrea	..	..	..	..	..	..	..	..	..	..	..	..
Estonia	..	3,175	..	8	..	9	..	4	..	6	..	73
Ethiopia	298	..	..	71	..	19	..	..	..	1	..	10
Finland	26,571	45,635	2	2	10	6	1	3	4	3	83	85
France	216,588	298,127	16	11	2	1	2	3	3	2	77	81
Gabon	2,204	3,350	..	..	..	..	..	..	..	..	..	..
Gambia, The	40	7	..	90	..	4	..	0	..	0	..	5
Georgia	..	330	..	..	..	..	..	..	..	..	..	..
Germany	421,100	551,505	5	4	1	1	1	1	3	2	89	85
Ghana	897	1,670	51	48	15	10	9	8	17	19	8	15
Greece	8,105	10,229	30	28	3	4	7	10	7	7	54	50
Guatemala	1,163	2,650	67	56	6	4	2	6	0	2	24	32
Guinea	19	80	..	3	..	3	..	0	..	63	..	30
Guinea-Bissau	68	90	..	..	..	..	..	..	..	..	..	..
Haiti	160	164	14	..	1	..	0	..	0	..	85	..
Honduras	831	1,322	82	59	4	4	1	0	4	4	9	33
† Data for Taiwan, China	67,142	148,370	4	1	2	1	1	1	1	1	93	95

	Merchandise exports		Food		Agricultural raw materials		Fuels		Ores and metals		Manufactures	
	$ millions		% of total		% of total		% of total		% of total		% of total	
	1990	2000	1990	2000	1990	2000	1990	2000	1990	2000	1990	2000
Hungary	10,000	28,090	23	7	3	1	3	2	6	2	63	86
India	17,975	42,295	16	14	4	1	3	0	5	2	71	79
Indonesia	25,675	62,124	11	9	5	4	44	25	4	5	35	57
Iran, Islamic Rep.	16,870	30,017	..	3	..	0	..	89	..	1	..	7
Iraq	12,380	19,300	..	..	..	..	..	..	..	..	..	..
Ireland	23,743	79,868	22	8	2	0	1	0	1	0	70	86
Israel	12,080	31,338	8	3	3	1	1	1	2	1	87	94
Italy	170,304	237,750	6	6	1	1	2	2	1	1	88	88
Jamaica	1,135	1,296	19	23	0	0	1	0	10	4	69	73
Japan	287,581	479,249	1	0	1	0	0	0	1	1	96	94
Jordan	1,064	1,897	11	16	0	0	0	0	38	15	51	69
Kazakhstan	..	9,140	..	7	..	1	..	54	..	18	..	20
Kenya	1,031	1,734	49	59	6	9	13	8	3	3	29	21
Korea, Dem. Rep.	1,857	655	..	..	..	..	..	..	..	..	..	..
Korea, Rep.	65,016	172,268	3	2	1	1	1	5	1	1	94	91
Kuwait	7,042	19,544	1	0	0	0	93	79	0	0	6	20
Kyrgyz Republic	..	505	..	16	..	6	..	12	..	6	..	20
Lao PDR	78	320	..	..	..	..	..	..	..	..	..	..
Latvia	..	1,865	..	6	..	29	..	2	..	6	..	56
Lebanon	494	714	..	..	..	..	..	..	..	..	..	..
Lesotho	59	200	..	..	..	..	..	..	..	..	..	..
Liberia	330	500	..	..	..	..	..	..	..	..	..	..
Libya	13,877	14,200	0	..	0	..	94	..	0	..	5	..
Lithuania	..	3,810	..	12	..	5	..	21	..	2	..	60
Macedonia, FYR	1,199	1,365	..	19	..	2	..	2	..	9	..	66
Madagascar	319	260	73	36	4	6	1	2	8	4	14	50
Malawi	417	350	93	..	2	..	0	..	0	..	5	..
Malaysia	29,416	98,237	12	6	14	3	18	10	2	1	54	80
Mali	359	550	36	..	62	..	..	..	0	..	2	..
Mauritania	469	300	..	..	..	..	..	..	..	..	..	..
Mauritius	1,194	1,493	32	18	1	1	1	0	0	0	66	81
Mexico	40,711	166,424	12	5	2	1	38	10	6	1	43	83
Moldova	..	470	..	62	..	3	..	0	..	1	..	33
Mongolia	660	355	..	..	..	..	..	..	..	..	..	..
Morocco	4,265	7,417	26	21	3	2	4	4	15	9	52	64
Mozambique	126	235	..	52	..	11	..	25	..	2	..	10
Myanmar	325	1,391	51	..	36	..	0	..	2	..	10	..
Namibia	1,085	1,455	..	..	..	..	..	..	..	..	..	..
Nepal	210	804	13	21	3	0	..	0	0	2	83	77
Netherlands	131,775	212,507	20	15	4	3	10	10	3	2	59	70
New Zealand	9,488	13,267	47	46	18	14	4	2	6	5	23	28
Nicaragua	330	625	77	88	14	2	0	2	1	0	8	8
Niger	282	290	..	29	..	1	..	0	..	67	..	2
Nigeria	13,670	20,100	1	0	1	0	97	100	0	0	1	0
Norway	34,047	60,038	7	6	2	1	48	64	10	6	33	18
Oman	5,508	11,328	1	4	0	0	92	83	1	1	5	12
Pakistan	5,589	9,173	9	11	10	3	1	1	0	0	79	85
Panama	340	859	75	74	1	1	0	7	1	2	21	16
Papua New Guinea	1,144	1,980	22	15	9	2	0	29	58	51	10	2
Paraguay	959	852	52	65	38	15	0	0	0	0	10	19
Peru	3,230	7,002	21	30	3	3	10	7	47	39	18	20
Philippines	8,068	39,783	19	5	2	1	2	1	8	2	38	92
Poland	14,320	31,650	13	8	3	2	11	5	9	5	59	80
Portugal	16,417	23,323	7	7	6	3	3	2	3	2	80	85
Puerto Rico	..	..	..	..	..	..	..	..	..	..	..	..
Romania	4,960	10,365	1	3	3	5	18	7	4	7	73	77
Russian Federation	40,000	105,200	..	1	..	3	..	51	..	9	..	22

4.5 Structure of merchandise exports

	Merchandise exports ($ millions)		Food (% of total)		Agricultural raw materials (% of total)		Fuels (% of total)		Ores and metals (% of total)		Manufactures (% of total)	
	1990	2000	1990	2000	1990	2000	1990	2000	1990	2000	1990	2000
Rwanda	110	53	..	..	..	..	..	..	..	..	..	..
Saudi Arabia	44,417	84,060	1	1	0	0	92	92	0	0	7	7
Senegal	761	960	53	59	3	2	12	3	9	5	23	30
Sierra Leone	138	13	..	..	..	..	..	..	..	..	..	..
Singapore[b]	52,752	137,875	5	2	3	0	18	10	2	1	72	86
Slovak Republic	6,355	11,905	..	4	..	2	..	5	..	3	..	85
Slovenia	6,681	8,733	7	4	2	2	3	1	3	4	86	90
Somalia	150	110	..	..	..	..	..	..	..	..	..	..
South Africa[c]	23,549	29,983	8	9	4	3	7	10	11	11	22	54
Spain	55,642	113,747	15	14	2	1	5	4	2	2	75	78
Sri Lanka	1,983	5,134	34	21	6	2	1	0	2	0	54	75
Sudan	374	1,807	61	67	38	27	..	..	0	0	1	3
Swaziland	556	900	..	..	..	..	..	..	..	..	..	..
Sweden	57,540	86,933	2	2	7	1	3	3	3	3	83	85
Switzerland	63,784	81,534	3	3	1	1	0	0	3	6	94	91
Syrian Arab Republic	4,212	4,250	14	9	4	5	45	76	1	1	36	8
Tajikistan	..	780	..	..	..	..	..	..	..	..	..	..
Tanzania	415	663	..	70	..	13	..	0	..	1	..	15
Thailand	23,070	69,057	29	14	5	3	1	3	1	1	63	76
Togo	268	340	23	20	21	23	0	1	45	26	9	31
Trinidad and Tobago	2,080	4,600	5	6	0	0	67	65	1	0	27	29
Tunisia	3,526	5,850	11	9	1	1	17	12	2	2	69	77
Turkey	12,959	26,572	22	13	3	1	2	1	4	3	68	81
Turkmenistan	..	2,700	..	0	..	10	..	81	..	0	..	7
Uganda	147	380	..	67	..	14	..	8	..	5	..	6
Ukraine	..	14,575	..	..	..	..	..	..	..	..	..	..
United Arab Emirates	20,730	39,900	8	..	1	..	5	..	39	..	46	..
United Kingdom	185,172	284,090	7	5	1	0	8	9	3	2	79	82
United States	393,592	781,125	11	7	4	2	3	2	3	2	74	83
Uruguay	1,693	2,295	40	47	21	9	0	2	0	0	39	42
Uzbekistan	..	3,010	..	..	..	..	..	..	..	..	..	..
Venezuela, RB	17,497	31,802	2	1	0	0	80	86	7	3	10	9
Vietnam	2,404	14,450	..	..	..	..	..	..	..	..	..	..
West Bank and Gaza	..	..	..	..	..	..	..	..	..	..	..	..
Yemen, Rep.	692	4,200	75	5	10	1	8	93	7	0	1	1
Yugoslavia, Fed. Rep.	2,929	1,727	7	..	4	..	2	..	7	..	79	..
Zambia	1,309	800	..	..	..	..	..	..	..	..	..	..
Zimbabwe	1,726	1,670	44	47	7	13	1	1	16	11	31	28
World	3,432,703 t	6,355,992 t	10 w	7 w	3 w	2 w	8 w	8 w	4 w	3 w	74 w	78 w
Low income	99,107	217,485	15	17	4	4	28	21	4	3	48	53
Middle income	603,553	1,526,414	15	8	4	2	19	21	5	4	54	63
Lower middle income	237,296	655,579	18	8	4	2	12	23	4	5	59	59
Upper middle income	366,521	870,835	13	9	4	2	23	19	6	4	51	65
Low & middle income	702,386	1,743,942	15	9	4	2	20	21	5	4	54	61
East Asia & Pacific	220,936	711,644	12	6	5	2	10	7	2	2	68	83
Europe & Central Asia[d]	125,115	306,069	..	5	..	3	..	26	..	6	..	53
Latin America & Carib.	143,146	356,115	26	21	4	3	24	18	12	9	34	48
Middle East & N. Africa	126,606	213,202	3	3	1	0	79	80	3	2	15	14
South Asia	27,790	64,252	16	15	5	1	2	0	4	2	71	80
Sub-Saharan Africa	66,402	92,560	13	17	3	4	28	28	7	8	20	36
High income	2,729,693	4,612,427	8	6	3	2	5	4	3	2	79	82
Europe EMU	1,229,887	1,823,399	10	8	2	1	3	3	2	2	81	82

Note: Components may not sum to 100 percent because of unclassified trade.

a. Includes Luxembourg. b. Includes re-exports. c. Data on total merchandise exports for 1990 refer to the South African Customs Union (Botswana, Lesotho, Namibia, South Africa, and Swaziland); those for 2000 refer to South Africa only. Data on export commodity shares refer to the South African Customs Union. d. Data for 2000 include the intratrade of the Baltic states and the Commonwealth of Independent States.

About the data

Data on merchandise trade come from customs reports of goods entering an economy or from reports of the financial transactions related to merchandise trade recorded in the balance of payments. Because of differences in timing and definitions, estimates of trade flows from customs reports are likely to differ from those based on the balance of payments. Moreover, several international agencies process trade data, each making estimates to correct for unreported or misreported data, and this leads to other differences in the available data.

The most detailed source of data on international trade in goods is the Commodity Trade (COMTRADE) database maintained by the United Nations Statistics Division. The International Monetary Fund (IMF) also collects customs-based data on exports and imports of goods. The value of exports is recorded as the cost of the goods delivered to the frontier of the exporting country for shipment—the f.o.b. (free on board) value. Many countries report trade data in U.S. dollars. When countries report in local currency, the United Nations Statistics Division applies the average official exchange rate for the period shown.

Countries may report trade according to the general or special system of trade (see *Primary data documentation*). Under the general system, exports comprise outward-moving goods that are (a) goods wholly or partly produced in the country; (b) foreign goods, neither transformed nor declared for domestic consumption in the country, that move outward from customs storage; and (c) goods previously included as imports for domestic consumption but subsequently exported without transformation. Under the special system exports comprise categories a and c. In some compilations categories b and c are classified as re-exports. Because of differences in reporting practices, data on exports may not be fully comparable across economies.

The data on total exports of goods (merchandise) in this table come from the World Trade Organization (WTO). The WTO uses two main sources, national statistical offices and the IMF's *International Financial Statistics*. It supplements these with

the COMTRADE database and publications or databases of regional organizations, specialized agencies, and economic groups (such as the Commonwealth of Independent States, the Economic Commission for Latin America and the Caribbean, Eurostat, the Food and Agriculture Organization, the Organisation for Economic Co-operation and Development, and the Organization of Petroleum Exporting Countries). It also consults private sources, such as country reports of the Economist Intelligence Unit and press clippings. In recent years country Web sites and direct contacts through email have helped to improve the collection of up-to-date statistics for many countries, reducing the proportion of estimated figures. The WTO database now covers most of the major traders in Africa, Asia, and Latin America, which together with the high-income countries account for nearly 90 percent of total world trade. There has also been a remarkable improvement in the availability of recent, reliable, and standardized figures for countries in Europe and Central Asia.

The shares of exports by major commodity group were estimated by World Bank staff from the COMTRADE database. The values of total exports reported here have not been fully reconciled with the estimates of exports of goods and services from the national accounts (shown in table 4.9) or those from the balance of payments (table 4.15).

The classification of commodity groups is based on the Standard International Trade Classification (SITC) revision 1. Most countries now report using later revisions of the SITC or the Harmonized System. Concordance tables are used to convert data reported in one system of nomenclature to another. The conversion process may introduce some errors of classification, but conversions from later to early systems are generally reliable. Shares may not sum to 100 percent because of unclassified trade.

Definitions

• **Merchandise exports** show the f.o.b. value of goods provided to the rest of the world valued in U.S. dollars. • **Food** comprises the commodities in SITC sections 0 (food and live animals), 1 (beverages and tobacco), and 4 (animal and vegetable oils and fats) and SITC division 22 (oil seeds, oil nuts, and oil kernels). • **Agricultural raw materials** comprise SITC section 2 (crude materials except fuels) excluding divisions 22, 27 (crude fertilizers and minerals excluding coal, petroleum, and precious stones), and 28 (metalliferous ores and scrap). • **Fuels** comprise SITC section 3 (mineral fuels). • **Ores and metals** comprise the commodities in SITC divisions 27, 28, and 68 (nonferrous metals). • **Manufactures** comprise the commodities in SITC sections 5 (chemicals), 6 (basic manufactures), 7 (machinery and transport equipment), and 8 (miscellaneous manufactured goods), excluding division 68.

Data sources

The WTO publishes data on world trade in its *Annual Report*. Estimates of total exports of goods are also published in the IMF's *International Financial Statistics* and *Direction of Trade Statistics* and in the United Nations Statistics Division's *Monthly Bulletin of Statistics*. The United Nations Conference on Trade and Development (UNCTAD) publishes data on the structure of exports and imports in its *Handbook of International Trade and Development Statistics*. Tariff line records of exports and imports are compiled in the United Nations Statistics Division's COMTRADE database.

Figure 4.5

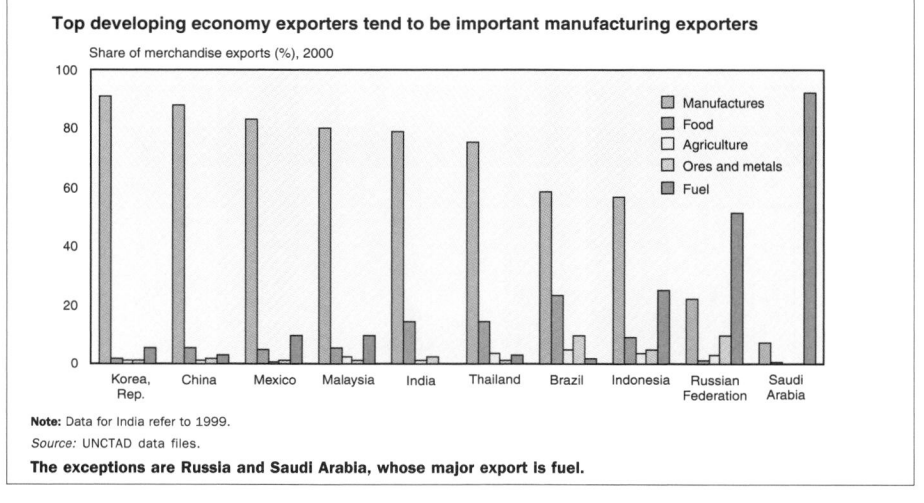

Top developing economy exporters tend to be important manufacturing exporters

Share of merchandise exports (%), 2000

Manufactures
Food
Agriculture
Ores and metals
Fuel

Korea, Rep. China Mexico Malaysia India Thailand Brazil Indonesia Russian Federation Saudi Arabia

Note: Data for India refer to 1999.

Source: UNCTAD data files.

The exceptions are Russia and Saudi Arabia, whose major export is fuel.

4.6 | Structure of merchandise imports

	Merchandise imports $ millions		Food % of total		Agricultural raw materials % of total		Fuels % of total		Ores and metals % of total		Manufactures % of total	
	1990	2000	1990	2000	1990	2000	1990	2000	1990	2000	1990	2000
Afghanistan	936	450	..	..	..	..	..	..	..	..	..	..
Albania	380	1,080	..	22	..	1	..	9	..	2	..	67
Algeria	9,780	9,152	24	28	5	3	1	1	2	1	68	67
Angola	1,578	3,400	..	..	..	..	..	..	..	..	..	..
Argentina	4,076	25,149	4	5	4	1	8	4	6	2	78	87
Armenia	..	885	..	25	..	1	..	21	..	1	..	52
Australia	42,032	71,531	5	5	2	1	5	8	1	1	80	84
Austria	49,146	68,627	5	6	3	3	6	6	4	3	81	82
Azerbaijan	..	1,390	..	19	..	2	..	5	..	4	..	71
Bangladesh	3,618	8,360	19	15	5	5	16	7	3	2	56	69
Belarus	..	8,485	..	12	..	2	..	31	..	4	..	50
Belgium[a]	119,702	183,204	..	9	..	2	..	9	..	4	..	76
Benin	265	602	..	25	..	5	..	21	..	1	..	49
Bolivia	687	1,760	12	14	2	2	1	5	1	1	85	79
Bosnia and Herzegovina	360	2,810	..	..	..	..	..	..	..	..	..	..
Botswana	1,946	2,240	..	..	..	..	..	..	..	..	..	..
Brazil	22,524	58,532	9	7	3	2	27	15	5	3	56	73
Bulgaria	5,100	6,440	8	5	3	1	36	5	4	6	49	59
Burkina Faso	536	545	..	..	..	..	..	..	..	..	..	..
Burundi	231	148	..	23	..	2	..	12	..	2	..	60
Cambodia	164	580	..	..	..	..	..	..	..	..	..	..
Cameroon	1,400	1,360	19	19	0	2	2	16	1	1	78	61
Canada	123,244	244,786	6	5	2	1	6	5	3	2	81	84
Central African Republic	154	110	..	..	..	..	..	..	..	..	..	..
Chad	285	290	..	..	..	..	..	..	..	..	..	..
Chile	7,678	18,070	4	7	2	1	16	18	1	1	75	71
China[†]	53,345	225,097	9	4	6	5	2	9	3	6	80	76
Hong Kong, China	84,725	214,200	8	4	2	1	2	2	2	2	85	91
Colombia	5,590	11,539	7	12	4	3	6	2	3	2	77	80
Congo, Dem. Rep.	887	320	..	..	..	..	..	..	..	..	..	..
Congo, Rep.	621	890	..	..	..	..	..	..	..	..	..	..
Costa Rica	1,990	6,372	8	7	2	1	10	8	2	2	66	82
Côte d'Ivoire	2,097	3,084	..	17	..	1	..	34	..	1	..	46
Croatia	4,500	7,911	12	8	4	2	10	15	4	2	64	73
Cuba	4,600	4,900	..	..	..	..	..	..	..	..	..	..
Czech Republic	12,880	32,180	..	5	..	2	..	10	..	4	..	80
Denmark	33,333	44,322	12	11	3	3	7	6	2	2	73	76
Dominican Republic	3,006	9,800	..	..	..	..	..	..	..	..	..	..
Ecuador	1,861	3,465	9	9	3	3	2	7	2	2	84	77
Egypt, Arab Rep.	9,216	14,010	32	23	7	4	3	6	2	3	56	59
El Salvador	1,263	4,888	14	16	3	2	15	16	4	1	63	65
Eritrea	..	..	..	..	..	..	..	..	..	..	..	..
Estonia	..	4,255	..	10	..	3	..	7	..	4	..	76
Ethiopia	1,081	..	..	7	..	1	..	20	..	1	..	71
Finland	27,001	33,903	5	5	2	2	12	12	4	6	76	73
France	234,436	305,423	10	8	3	2	10	10	4	3	74	77
Gabon	918	1,030	..	..	..	..	..	..	..	..	..	..
Gambia, The	199	200	..	44	..	2	..	6	..	1	..	46
Georgia	..	725	..	..	..	..	..	..	..	..	..	..
Germany	355,686	502,827	10	7	3	2	8	9	4	4	72	69
Ghana	1,205	3,075	11	13	1	2	17	21	0	1	70	62
Greece	19,777	26,336	15	13	3	2	8	6	3	2	70	76
Guatemala	1,649	4,770	10	12	2	2	17	13	2	1	69	72
Guinea	723	1,130	..	24	..	1	..	25	..	1	..	49
Guinea-Bissau	68	90	..	..	..	..	..	..	..	..	..	..
Haiti	332	1,036	..	..	..	..	..	..	..	..	..	..
Honduras	935	2,885	10	16	1	1	16	13	1	1	71	68
† Data for Taiwan, China	54,831	140,010	7	4	5	2	11	9	6	5	69	79

2002 World Development Indicators

	Merchandise imports		Food		Agricultural raw materials		Fuels		Ores and metals		Manufactures	
	$ millions		% of total		% of total		% of total		% of total		% of total	
	1990	2000	1990	2000	1990	2000	1990	2000	1990	2000	1990	2000
Hungary	10,340	32,080	8	3	4	1	14	5	4	3	70	84
India	23,642	50,455	3	7	4	3	27	31	8	5	51	51
Indonesia	21,837	33,515	5	10	5	7	9	18	4	3	77	61
Iran, Islamic Rep.	15,716	15,220	..	19	..	3	..	2	..	2	..	73
Iraq	7,660	13,700	..	..	..	..	..	..	..	..	..	..
Ireland	20,669	50,870	11	6	2	1	6	4	2	1	76	82
Israel	16,793	38,130	8	5	2	1	9	10	3	2	77	81
Italy	181,968	236,461	12	9	6	4	11	10	5	4	64	69
Jamaica	1,859	3,216	15	15	1	2	20	18	1	1	61	61
Japan	235,368	379,511	15	13	7	3	25	20	9	6	44	57
Jordan	2,600	4,539	26	21	2	2	18	5	1	2	51	66
Kazakhstan	..	5,050	..	9	..	1	..	12	..	3	..	75
Kenya	2,125	3,105	9	14	3	2	20	22	2	1	66	60
Korea, Dem. Rep.	2,930	900	..	..	..	..	..	..	..	..	..	..
Korea, Rep.	69,844	160,481	6	5	8	3	16	24	7	6	63	62
Kuwait	3,972	7,622	17	17	1	1	1	1	2	2	79	79
Kyrgyz Republic	..	555	..	14	..	1	..	20	..	2	..	64
Lao PDR	201	580	..	..	..	..	..	..	..	..	..	..
Latvia	..	3,190	..	12	..	2	..	12	..	2	..	71
Lebanon	2,529	6,228	..	..	..	..	..	..	..	..	..	..
Lesotho	672	700	..	..	..	..	..	..	..	..	..	..
Liberia	220	290	..	..	..	..	..	..	..	..	..	..
Libya	5,336	7,740	23	..	2	..	0	..	1	..	74	..
Lithuania	..	5,455	..	10	..	3	..	22	..	2	..	61
Macedonia, FYR	1,206	2,220	..	15	..	2	..	9	..	3	..	49
Madagascar	571	700	11	14	1	1	17	24	1	0	69	60
Malawi	581	590	9	20	1	1	11	10	1	1	78	68
Malaysia	29,258	82,210	7	4	1	1	5	5	4	3	82	85
Mali	619	690	26	..	1	..	19	..	1	..	53	..
Mauritania	388	340	..	..	..	..	..	..	..	..	..	..
Mauritius	1,618	2,081	12	14	3	2	8	12	1	1	76	70
Mexico	43,548	182,635	15	5	4	1	4	3	3	2	75	87
Moldova	..	775	..	13	..	2	..	32	..	1	..	51
Mongolia	924	550	..	..	..	..	..	..	..	..	..	..
Morocco	6,800	11,484	10	14	6	3	17	18	6	3	61	63
Mozambique	878	1,100	..	..	..	..	..	..	..	..	..	..
Myanmar	270	2,369	13	..	1	..	5	..	0	..	81	..
Namibia	1,163	1,510	..	..	..	..	..	..	..	..	..	..
Nepal	686	1,573	15	17	7	5	9	12	2	3	67	63
Netherlands	126,098	197,982	13	10	2	2	10	11	3	3	71	74
New Zealand	9,501	13,906	7	8	1	1	8	10	3	2	81	79
Nicaragua	638	1,792	19	16	1	1	19	18	1	1	59	65
Niger	388	445	..	39	..	4	..	15	..	2	..	41
Nigeria	5,627	12,910	6	20	1	1	0	1	2	2	67	76
Norway	27,231	34,408	6	6	2	2	4	4	6	5	82	81
Oman	2,681	5,040	19	22	1	1	4	2	1	3	69	70
Pakistan	7,546	11,048	17	14	4	3	21	33	4	2	54	47
Panama	1,539	3,379	12	12	1	0	16	19	1	1	70	68
Papua New Guinea	1,193	1,120	18	18	0	1	7	22	1	1	73	58
Paraguay	1,352	2,193	8	17	0	1	14	14	1	1	77	68
Peru	3,470	8,797	24	12	2	2	12	16	1	1	61	70
Philippines	13,041	33,808	10	8	2	1	15	12	3	3	53	76
Poland	11,570	48,940	8	6	3	2	22	11	4	3	63	78
Portugal	25,263	38,240	12	11	4	3	11	10	2	2	71	73
Puerto Rico	..	..	..	..	..	..	..	..	..	..	..	..
Romania	7,600	13,055	12	7	4	1	38	12	6	4	39	76
Russian Federation	33,100	45,500	..	15	..	2	..	3	..	3	..	42

	Merchandise imports ($ millions)		Food (% of total)		Agricultural raw materials (% of total)		Fuels (% of total)		Ores and metals (% of total)		Manufactures (% of total)	
	1990	2000	1990	2000	1990	2000	1990	2000	1990	2000	1990	2000
Rwanda	288	213	..	..	..	..	..	..	..	..	..	..
Saudi Arabia	24,069	30,300	15	18	1	1	0	0	3	3	81	76
Senegal	1,219	1,525	29	24	2	2	16	20	2	1	51	52
Sierra Leone	149	149	..	..	..	..	..	..	..	..	..	..
Singapore	60,899	134,545	6	3	2	0	16	12	2	2	73	82
Slovak Republic	6,670	12,670	..	7	..	2	..	13	..	3	..	76
Slovenia	6,142	10,107	9	6	4	4	11	9	4	5	67	76
Somalia	95	200	..	..	..	..	..	..	..	..	..	..
South Africa[b]	18,399	29,695	5	5	2	1	1	14	2	2	77	70
Spain	87,715	153,516	11	9	3	2	12	12	4	3	71	73
Sri Lanka	2,685	6,823	19	15	2	1	13	6	1	1	65	77
Sudan	618	1,500	13	15	1	1	20	10	0	1	66	72
Swaziland	663	1,040	..	..	..	..	..	..	..	..	..	..
Sweden	54,264	72,788	6	6	2	1	9	9	3	3	79	74
Switzerland	69,681	83,584	6	6	2	1	5	5	3	6	84	83
Syrian Arab Republic	2,400	3,860	31	19	2	3	3	4	1	2	62	65
Tajikistan	..	675	..	..	..	..	..	..	..	..	..	..
Tanzania	1,027	1,524	..	16	..	2	..	8	..	1	..	72
Thailand	33,379	61,924	5	4	5	3	9	12	4	3	75	77
Togo	581	550	22	18	1	2	8	19	1	2	67	59
Trinidad and Tobago	1,262	3,250	19	8	1	1	11	32	6	2	62	56
Tunisia	5,542	8,560	11	8	4	3	9	11	4	2	72	76
Turkey	22,302	53,499	8	4	4	4	21	14	5	4	61	70
Turkmenistan	..	1,400	..	12	..	0	..	1	..	1	..	80
Uganda	213	1,650	..	14	..	2	..	17	..	2	..	65
Ukraine	..	13,955	..	..	..	..	..	..	..	..	..	..
United Arab Emirates	11,199	31,930	14	..	1	..	3	..	4	..	77	..
United Kingdom	222,977	336,979	10	8	3	2	6	4	4	3	75	82
United States	516,987	1,257,636	6	4	2	1	13	11	3	2	73	77
Uruguay	1,343	3,466	7	11	4	3	18	15	2	1	69	69
Uzbekistan	..	2,810	..	..	..	..	..	..	..	..	..	..
Venezuela, RB	7,335	16,085	11	12	4	2	3	4	4	2	77	81
Vietnam	2,752	15,635	..	..	..	..	..	..	..	..	..	..
West Bank and Gaza	..	..	..	..	..	..	..	..	..	..	..	..
Yemen, Rep.	1,571	2,880	27	35	1	2	40	6	1	1	31	55
Yugoslavia, Fed. Rep.	4,634	3,698	12	..	5	..	17	..	3	..	63	..
Zambia	1,220	780	..	..	..	..	..	..	..	..	..	..
Zimbabwe	1,847	1,650	4	9	3	2	16	12	2	3	73	75

World	3,516,422 t	6,565,299 t	9 w	7 w	3 w	2 w	11 w	10 w	4 w	3 w	71 w	74 w
Low income	103,409	201,545	7	14	3	5	17	19	4	3	64	57
Middle income	558,998	1,414,536	9	7	4	2	11	11	4	3	70	72
Lower middle income	243,482	572,247	11	9	5	3	8	9	3	4	71	69
Upper middle income	316,575	842,282	8	6	4	2	13	13	4	3	70	74
Low & middle income	662,742	1,616,357	9	8	4	3	11	12	4	3	70	71
East Asia & Pacific	230,644	620,409	7	5	5	3	9	14	4	4	73	72
Europe & Central Asia[c]	136,653	311,688	..	9	..	2	..	9	..	3	..	65
Latin America & Carib.	120,526	381,064	11	8	3	2	13	10	3	2	69	78
Middle East & N. Africa	99,827	137,575	19	18	3	2	6	6	3	2	68	70
South Asia	39,329	79,318	9	10	4	4	23	26	6	4	54	54
Sub-Saharan Africa	56,179	85,932	..	10	..	2	..	14	..	2	..	68
High income	2,846,174	4,949,031	9	7	3	2	11	10	4	3	72	75
Europe EMU	1,253,828	1,804,630	11	8	3	2	9	10	4	3	72	73

Note: Components may not sum to 100 percent because of unclassified trade.

a. Includes Luxembourg. b. Data on total merchandise imports for 1990 refer to the South African Customs Union (Botswana, Lesotho, Namibia, South Africa, and Swaziland); those for 2000 refer to South Africa only. Data on import commodity shares refer to the South African Customs Union. c. Data for 2000 include the intratrade of the Baltic states and the Commonwealth of Independent States.

About the data

Data on imports of goods are derived from the same sources as data on exports. In principle, world exports and imports should be identical. Similarly, exports from an economy should equal the sum of imports by the rest of the world from that economy. But differences in timing and definitions result in discrepancies in reported values at all levels. For further discussion of indicators of merchandise trade see *About the data* for tables 4.4 and 4.5.

The value of imports is generally recorded as the cost of the goods when purchased by the importer plus the cost of transport and insurance to the frontier of the importing country—the c.i.f. (cost, insurance, and freight) value, corresponding to the landed cost at the point of entry of foreign goods into the country. A few countries, including Australia, Canada, and the United States, collect import data on an f.o.b. (free on board) basis and adjust them for freight and insurance costs. Many countries collect and report trade data in U.S. dollars. When countries report in local currency, the United Nations Statistics Division applies the average official exchange rate for the period shown.

Countries may report trade according to the general or special system of trade (see *Primary data documentation*). Under the general system imports include goods imported for domestic consumption and imports into bonded warehouses and free trade zones. Under the special system imports comprise goods imported for domestic consumption (including transformation and repair) and withdrawals for domestic consumption from bonded warehouses and free trade zones. Goods transported through a country en route to another are excluded.

The data on total imports of goods (merchandise) in this table come from the World Trade Organization (WTO). The WTO uses two main sources, national statistical offices and the International Monetary Fund's (IMF) *International Financial Statistics*. It supplements these sources with the Commodity Trade (COMTRADE) database maintained by the United Nations Statistics Division and publications or databases of regional organizations, specialized agencies, and economic groups (such as the Commonwealth of Independent States, the Economic Commission for Latin America and the Caribbean, Eurostat, the Food and Agriculture Organization, the Organisation for Economic Co-operation and Development, and the Organization of Petroleum Exporting Countries). It also consults private sources, such as country reports of the Economist Intelligence Unit, and press clippings. In recent years country Web sites and direct contacts through email have helped to improve the collection of up-to-date statistics for many countries, reducing the proportion of estimated figures. The WTO database now covers most of the major traders

in Africa, Asia, and Latin America, which together with the high-income countries account for nearly 90 percent of total world trade. There has also been a remarkable improvement in the availability of recent, reliable, and standardized figures for countries in Europe and Central Asia.

The shares of imports by major commodity group were estimated by World Bank staff from the COMTRADE database. The values of total imports reported here have not been fully reconciled with the estimates of imports of goods and services from the national accounts (shown in table 4.9) or those from the balance of payments (table 4.15).

The classification of commodity groups is based on the Standard International Trade Classification (SITC) revision 1. Most countries now report using later revisions of the SITC or the Harmonized System. Concordance tables are used to convert data reported in one system of nomenclature to another. The conversion process may introduce some errors of classification, but conversions from later to early systems are generally reliable. Shares may not sum to 100 percent because of unclassified trade.

Figure 4.6

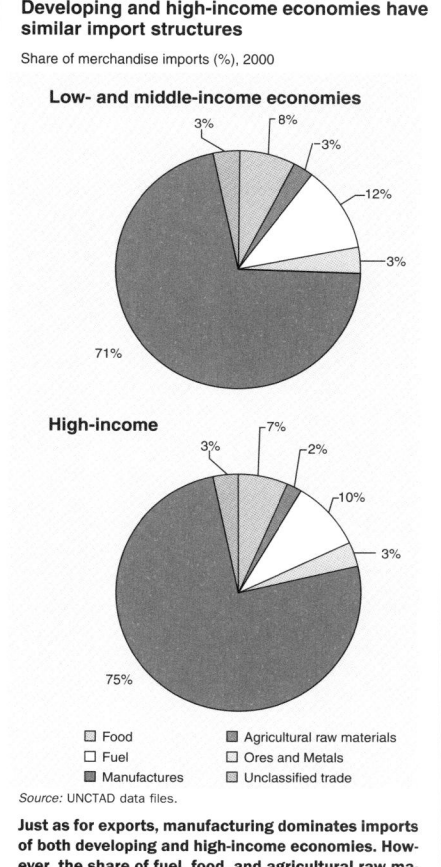

Developing and high-income economies have similar import structures

Share of merchandise imports (%), 2000

Low- and middle-income economies

3% — 8%
— 3%
— 12%
— 3%
71%

High-income

3% — 7%
— 2%
— 10%
— 3%
75%

☐ Food ▨ Agricultural raw materials
☐ Fuel ☐ Ores and Metals
▨ Manufactures ▨ Unclassified trade

Source: UNCTAD data files.

Just as for exports, manufacturing dominates imports of both developing and high-income economies. However, the share of fuel, food, and agricultural raw materials imports by developing economies are slightly higher than in high-income economies.

Definitions

• **Merchandise imports** show the c.i.f. value of goods purchased from the rest of the world valued in U.S. dollars. • **Food** comprises the commodities in SITC sections 0 (food and live animals), 1 (beverages and tobacco), and 4 (animal and vegetable oils and fats) and SITC division 22 (oil seeds, oil nuts, and oil kernels). • **Agricultural raw materials** comprise SITC section 2 (crude materials except fuels) excluding divisions 22, 27 (crude fertilizers and minerals excluding coal, petroleum, and precious stones), and 28 (metalliferous ores and scrap). • **Fuels** comprise SITC section 3 (mineral fuels). • **Ores and metals** comprise the commodities in SITC divisions 27, 28, and 68 (nonferrous metals). • **Manufactures** comprise the commodities in SITC sections 5 (chemicals), 6 (basic manufactures), 7 (machinery and transport equipment), and 8 (miscellaneous manufactured goods), excluding division 68.

Data sources

The WTO publishes data on world trade in its *Annual Report*. Estimates of total imports of goods are also published in the IMF's *International Financial Statistics* and *Direction of Trade Statistics* and in the United Nations Statistics Division's *Monthly Bulletin of Statistics*. The United Nations Conference on Trade and Development (UNCTAD) publishes data on the structure of exports and imports in its *Handbook of International Trade and Development Statistics*. Tariff line records of exports and imports are compiled in the United Nations Statistics Division's COMTRADE database.

4.7 | Structure of service exports

	Commercial service exports		Transport		Travel		Others	
	$ millions		% of total services		% of total services		% of total services	
	1990	**2000**	**1990**	**2000**	**1990**	**2000**	**1990**	**2000**
Afghanistan	..	..	..	..	..	..	..	..
Albania	32	429	20.0	4.0	11.1	90.8	68.9	5.2
Algeria	479	..	41.7	..	13.4	..	44.9	..
Angola	65	*155*	48.8	*30.4*	20.6	*0.0*	30.7	*69.6*
Argentina	2,264	4,374	51.1	22.9	39.9	66.4	9.1	10.7
Armenia	..	*129*	..	*41.0*	..	*23.9*	..	*35.0*
Australia	9,833	17,895	35.5	24.2	43.2	47.2	21.4	28.6
Austria	22,755	30,043	6.4	14.5	59.0	33.3	34.6	52.3
Azerbaijan	..	234	..	50.9	..	26.9	..	22.2
Bangladesh	296	283	12.9	32.3	6.4	17.8	80.6	49.9
Belarus	..	982	..	65.3	..	1.9	..	32.8
Belgium[a]	26,646	42,508	27.5	24.8	14.0	17.5	58.5	57.7
Benin	109	*155*	33.4	*12.9*	50.2	*60.5*	16.4	*26.7*
Bolivia	133	207	35.8	24.1	43.6	33.0	20.6	42.9
Bosnia and Herzegovina	..	..	..	..	..	..	..	..
Botswana	183	*346*	20.4	*27.7*	64.1	*67.7*	15.5	*4.7*
Brazil	3,706	8,846	36.4	14.6	37.3	20.5	26.3	64.9
Bulgaria	837	2,129	27.5	29.7	38.2	50.5	34.2	19.9
Burkina Faso	34	..	37.1	..	34.1	..	28.9	..
Burundi	7	2	38.7	42.8	51.4	36.6	9.9	20.6
Cambodia	*50*	159	0.0	43.6	*100.0*	40.4	*0.0*	16.1
Cameroon	369	..	42.6	..	14.4	..	43.0	..
Canada	18,350	36,287	23.0	20.1	34.7	29.5	42.3	50.4
Central African Republic	17	..	50.9	..	16.0	..	33.1	..
Chad	23	..	18.4	..	34.1	..	47.5	..
Chile	1,786	3,843	40.0	43.3	29.8	24.8	30.3	32.0
China	5,748	30,146	47.1	12.2	30.2	53.8	22.7	34.0
Hong Kong, China	..	41,331	..	..	..	..	..	..
Colombia	1,548	1,994	31.3	29.9	26.2	51.6	42.5	18.6
Congo, Dem. Rep.	..	..	..	..	..	..	..	..
Congo, Rep.	65	..	53.9	..	12.9	..	33.1	..
Costa Rica	583	*1,503*	16.3	*16.3*	48.9	*67.9*	34.8	*15.8*
Côte d'Ivoire	425	369	62.4	20.3	12.1	15.5	25.5	64.2
Croatia	..	4,084	..	13.6	..	67.5	..	18.8
Cuba	..	..	..	..	..	..	..	..
Czech Republic	..	6,638	..	20.9	..	43.1	..	36.0
Denmark	12,731	20,438	32.5	53.0	26.2	19.5	41.3	27.5
Dominican Republic	1,086	3,142	5.6	2.3	66.8	91.0	27.5	6.7
Ecuador	508	793	47.6	*37.6*	37.0	*45.0*	15.4	*17.4*
Egypt, Arab Rep.	4,812	9,687	50.1	27.3	22.9	44.9	27.1	27.8
El Salvador	301	649	26.2	35.3	25.2	33.5	48.6	31.2
Eritrea	..	..	..	..	..	..	..	..
Estonia	*200*	1,495	*74.7*	48.5	*13.7*	33.8	*11.6*	17.8
Ethiopia	261	387	80.6	55.7	2.1	14.7	17.3	29.7
Finland	4,562	6,002	38.4	27.3	25.8	23.4	35.7	49.3
France	74,948	81,153	21.7	23.9	27.0	38.1	51.3	38.0
Gabon	214	*249*	33.4	*60.9*	1.4	*6.0*	65.2	*33.2*
Gambia, The	53	..	8.8	..	87.9	..	3.3	..
Georgia	..	206	..	49.7	..	46.9	..	3.5
Germany	51,605	80,480	28.6	24.7	27.9	21.9	43.5	53.4
Ghana	79	490	49.2	20.1	5.6	68.3	45.2	11.6
Greece	6,514	19,181	4.9	41.3	39.7	48.1	55.4	10.6
Guatemala	313	735	7.4	11.2	37.6	65.6	55.0	23.2
Guinea	91	*36*	14.2	*53.7*	32.6	*4.7*	53.3	*41.6*
Guinea-Bissau	4	..	5.4	..	0.0	..	94.6	..
Haiti	43	*178*	19.8	*2.0*	78.9	*63.7*	1.3	*34.3*
Honduras	121	412	35.1	11.5	24.0	59.4	40.9	29.0

| | Commercial service exports | | Transport | | Travel | | Others | |
| | $ millions | | % of total services | | % of total services | | % of total services | |
	1990	2000	1990	2000	1990	2000	1990	2000
Hungary	2,677	6,204	1.6	10.4	36.8	55.1	61.6	34.5
India	4,610	17,670	20.8	10.6	33.8	17.9	45.4	71.4
Indonesia	2,488	5,060	2.8	0.0	86.5	98.3	10.7	1.7
Iran, Islamic Rep.	343	1,357	10.5	49.4	8.2	36.9	81.3	13.6
Iraq	..	..	..	..	..	..	..	..
Ireland	3,286	16,638	31.1	8.1	44.4	15.9	24.5	75.9
Israel	4,546	14,260	30.8	17.4	30.7	26.8	38.5	55.8
Italy	48,579	55,558	21.0	16.0	33.9	49.5	45.2	34.6
Jamaica	976	1,988	18.0	16.5	77.0	67.0	5.0	16.4
Japan	41,384	68,303	40.4	37.5	7.9	4.9	51.7	57.6
Jordan	1,430	1,689	26.0	17.7	35.7	47.1	38.3	35.2
Kazakhstan	..	987	..	54.9	..	36.1	..	9.0
Kenya	774	701	32.0	58.6	60.2	36.7	7.8	4.7
Korea, Dem. Rep.	..	..	..	..	..	..	..	..
Korea, Rep.	9,155	28,910	34.7	44.5	34.5	23.6	30.7	31.9
Kuwait	1,054	1,793	87.5	89.6	12.5	5.5	0.0	4.9
Kyrgyz Republic	..	57	..	29.2	..	26.8	..	44.0
Lao PDR	11	101	74.8	17.9	24.3	80.8	0.9	1.4
Latvia	290	1,193	94.9	66.7	2.5	11.0	2.6	22.3
Lebanon	..	..	..	..	..	..	..	..
Lesotho	34	36	14.1	1.5	51.2	67.2	34.7	31.3
Liberia	..	..	..	..	..	..	..	..
Libya	83	46	83.8	37.9	7.7	53.9	8.5	8.2
Lithuania	..	1,052	..	46.7	..	37.2	..	16.1
Macedonia, FYR	..	281	..	41.3	..	13.3	..	45.4
Madagascar	129	314	32.1	16.4	31.3	38.6	36.6	45.0
Malawi	37	..	46.1	..	42.6	..	11.3	..
Malaysia	3,769	11,800	31.8	21.1	44.7	30.4	23.5	48.5
Mali	71	..	31.0	..	54.3	..	14.7	..
Mauritania	14	24	35.3	2.6	64.7	82.7	0.0	14.7
Mauritius	478	1,067	32.9	20.9	51.1	50.8	15.9	28.3
Mexico	7,222	13,567	12.4	10.1	76.5	61.1	11.1	28.8
Moldova	..	158	..	50.8	..	29.3	..	19.9
Mongolia	48	73	41.8	39.4	10.4	48.6	47.8	12.0
Morocco	1,871	2,853	9.6	17.0	68.4	71.5	22.0	11.5
Mozambique	103	325	61.3	20.4	0.0	..	38.7	79.6
Myanmar	93	509	10.3	16.6	20.9	33.4	68.8	50.0
Namibia	106	315	0.0	0.0	81.0	91.4	19.0	8.6
Nepal	166	410	3.6	15.0	65.6	38.5	30.8	46.5
Netherlands	28,478	51,493	45.4	38.4	14.6	14.0	40.0	47.6
New Zealand	2,415	4,270	43.4	28.9	42.7	52.9	13.9	18.2
Nicaragua	34	265	19.2	9.9	35.5	48.5	45.3	41.5
Niger	22	..	5.2	..	59.5	..	35.3	..
Nigeria	965	980	3.9	12.0	2.5	5.5	93.6	82.5
Norway	12,452	14,969	68.7	63.6	12.6	12.6	18.7	23.8
Oman	68	283	15.3	6.4	84.7	78.0	0.0	15.6
Pakistan	1,218	1,284	59.3	65.4	12.0	6.3	28.7	28.3
Panama	907	1,806	64.9	54.7	18.9	26.0	16.2	19.2
Papua New Guinea	198	248	11.2	4.3	12.0	2.4	76.8	93.3
Paraguay	404	568	18.3	12.0	21.1	17.7	60.5	70.3
Peru	714	1,463	43.4	16.2	30.4	62.3	26.2	21.5
Philippines	2,897	4,133	8.5	21.6	16.1	56.4	75.4	22.0
Poland	3,200	10,390	57.3	23.5	11.2	54.6	31.5	21.9
Portugal	5,054	8,317	15.6	17.1	70.4	63.2	14.0	19.8
Puerto Rico	..	..	..	..	..	..	..	..
Romania	610	1,740	50.5	37.5	17.4	20.6	32.2	41.9
Russian Federation	..	9,632	..	33.9	..	39.9	..	26.3

	Commercial service exports		Transport		Travel		Others	
	$ millions		% of total services		% of total services		% of total services	
	1990	**2000**	**1990**	**2000**	**1990**	**2000**	**1990**	**2000**
Rwanda	31	39	56.1	31.5	32.8	60.3	11.0	8.3
Saudi Arabia	3,031	4,785	..	..	..	..	..	..
Senegal	356	*351*	19.1	*10.1*	42.7	*49.4*	38.1	*40.4*
Sierra Leone	45	..	9.7	..	76.2	..	14.1	..
Singapore	12,719	26,960	17.5	19.8	36.6	21.4	45.9	58.8
Slovak Republic	..	2,218	..	44.9	..	19.5	..	35.6
Slovenia	*1,219*	1,881	*22.6*	26.2	*55.0*	50.8	*22.4*	23.0
Somalia	..	..	..	..	..	..	..	..
South Africa	3,290	4,930	21.6	24.0	55.8	54.9	22.7	21.1
Spain	27,649	53,041	17.2	14.6	67.2	58.3	15.6	27.0
Sri Lanka	425	915	39.7	43.7	30.2	27.1	30.1	29.2
Sudan	134	24	14.1	62.8	15.7	22.3	70.2	14.9
Swaziland	102	72	24.5	21.1	29.2	46.8	46.3	32.1
Sweden	13,453	20,014	35.8	21.8	21.7	20.3	42.6	57.9
Switzerland	18,233	26,203	16.3	17.3	40.6	29.4	43.0	53.3
Syrian Arab Republic	740	1,481	29.7	16.6	43.3	73.1	27.0	10.3
Tajikistan	..	..	..	..	..	..	..	..
Tanzania	131	615	19.9	9.2	36.4	61.3	43.6	29.5
Thailand	6,292	13,785	21.1	23.6	68.7	54.3	10.2	22.1
Togo	114	*54*	26.9	*23.7*	50.7	*12.8*	22.3	*63.5*
Trinidad and Tobago	322	*574*	50.7	*35.2*	29.4	*35.0*	19.9	*29.9*
Tunisia	1,575	2,602	23.0	22.8	64.8	64.7	12.2	12.5
Turkey	7,882	19,232	11.7	15.4	40.9	39.7	47.4	44.9
Turkmenistan	..	..	..	..	..	..	..	..
Uganda	..	*182*	..	*13.4*	..	*82.0*	..	*4.6*
Ukraine	..	3,800	..	76.8	..	10.4	..	12.8
United Arab Emirates	..	..	..	..	..	..	..	..
United Kingdom	53,830	115,658	25.5	18.2	29.3	21.7	45.2	60.1
United States	132,880	272,110	28.1	18.7	37.9	35.8	34.0	45.5
Uruguay	460	1,326	36.9	27.9	51.8	49.2	11.3	22.9
Uzbekistan	..	..	..	..	..	..	..	..
Venezuela, RB	1,121	1,067	40.9	34.8	44.2	61.7	14.9	3.5
Vietnam	..	2,702	..	..	..	..	..	..
West Bank and Gaza	..	..	..	..	..	..	..	..
Yemen, Rep.	82	*141*	27.2	*18.4*	48.8	*43.3*	24.0	*38.3*
Yugoslavia, Fed. Rep.	..	..	..	..	..	..	..	..
Zambia	94	..	68.9	..	13.5	..	17.5	..
Zimbabwe	253	..	44.3	..	25.3	..	30.4	..
World	**750,361 s**	**1,430,843 s**	**28.1 w**	**23.2 w**	**34.1 w**	**32.1 w**	**37.8 w**	**44.7 w**
Low income	14,027	36,100	25.0	18.8	38.1	32.6	36.9	48.6
Middle income	88,902	225,049	29.3	23.8	42.8	44.5	27.9	31.8
Lower middle income	35,373	98,116	29.9	20.7	42.0	53.3	28.1	26.0
Upper middle income	53,529	126,932	28.8	25.6	43.5	39.1	27.7	35.3
Low & middle income	102,929	261,149	28.7	23.2	42.2	43.2	29.1	33.5
East Asia & Pacific	31,204	85,404	28.6	24.2	44.4	43.9	27.0	31.9
Europe & Central Asia	15,237	73,142	25.0	26.5	35.8	40.7	39.3	32.8
Latin America & Carib.	25,313	48,444	28.3	20.2	51.3	49.9	20.4	29.9
Middle East & N. Africa	14,872	23,880	34.4	24.4	38.5	53.1	27.1	22.5
South Asia	6,816	20,908	27.9	11.0	30.1	19.0	42.0	70.0
Sub-Saharan Africa	9,487	9,371	32.1	24.1	38.6	54.8	29.3	21.1
High income	647,432	1,169,694	28.0	23.2	32.8	29.7	39.2	47.1
Europe EMU	300,074	458,079	24.7	22.5	34.5	33.7	40.8	43.8

a. Includes Luxembourg.

About the data

Balance of payments statistics, the main source of information on international trade in services, have many weaknesses. Some large economies—such as the former Soviet Union—did not report data on trade in services until recently. Disaggregation of important components may be limited, and it varies significantly across countries. There are inconsistencies in the methods used to report items. And the recording of major flows as net items is common (for example, insurance transactions are often recorded as premiums less claims). These factors contribute to a downward bias in the value of the service trade reported in the balance of payments.

Efforts are being made to improve the coverage, quality, and consistency of these data. Eurostat and the Organisation for Economic Co-operation and Development, for example, are working together to improve the collection of statistics on trade in services in member countries. In addition, the International Monetary Fund (IMF) has implemented the new classification of trade in services introduced in the fifth edition of its *Balance of Payments Manual* (1993).

Still, difficulties in capturing all the dimensions of international trade in services mean that the record is likely to remain incomplete. Cross-border intrafirm service transactions, which are usually not captured in the balance of payments, are increasing rapidly as foreign direct investment expands and electronic networks become pervasive. One example of such transactions is transnational corporations' use of mainframe computers around the clock for data processing, exploiting time zone differences between their home country and the host countries of their affiliates. Another important dimension of service trade not captured by conventional balance of payments statistics is establishment trade—sales in the host country by foreign affiliates. By contrast, cross-border intrafirm transactions in merchandise may be reported as exports or imports in the balance of payments.

The data on exports of services in this table, and on imports of services in table 4.8, unlike those in editions before 2000, include only commercial services and exclude the category "government services not included elsewhere." The data are compiled by the IMF based on returns from national sources.

Data on total trade in goods and services from the IMF's Balance of Payments database are shown in table 4.15.

Figure 4.7

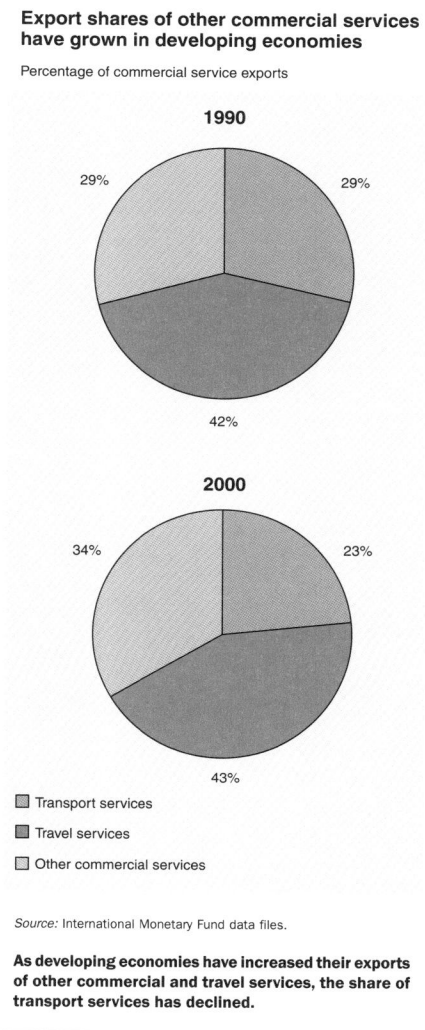

Export shares of other commercial services have grown in developing economies

Percentage of commercial service exports

1990

29%   29%

42%

2000

34%   23%

43%

☐ Transport services
☐ Travel services
☐ Other commercial services

Source: International Monetary Fund data files.

As developing economies have increased their exports of other commercial and travel services, the share of transport services has declined.

Definitions

• **Commercial service exports** are total service exports minus exports of government services not included elsewhere. International transactions in services are defined by the IMF's *Balance of Payments Manual* (1993) as the economic output of intangible commodities that may be produced, transferred, and consumed at the same time. Definitions may vary among reporting economies. • **Transport** covers all transport services (sea, air, land, internal waterway, space, and pipeline) performed by residents of one economy for those of another and involving the carriage of passengers, movement of goods (freight), rental of carriers with crew, and related support and auxiliary services. Excluded are freight insurance, which is included in insurance services; goods procured in ports by nonresident carriers and repairs of transport equipment, which are included in goods; repairs of railway facilities, harbors, and airfield facilities, which are included in construction services; and rental of carriers without crew, which is included in other services. • **Travel** covers goods and services acquired from an economy by travelers in that economy for their own use during visits of less than one year for business or personal purposes. Travel services include the goods and services consumed by travelers, such as meals, lodging, and transport, including car rental (within the economy visited). • **Other commercial services** include such activities as insurance and financial services, international telecom-munications, and postal and courier services; computer data; news-related service transactions between residents and non-residents; construction services; royalties and license fees; miscellaneous business, professional, and technical services; and personal, cultural, and recreational services.

Data sources

The data on exports of commercial services are from the IMF. The IMF publishes balance of payments data in its *International Financial Statistics* and *Balance of Payments Statistics Yearbook.*

4.8 | Structure of service imports

	Commercial service imports		Transport		Travel		Other	
	$ millions		% of total		% of total		% of total	
	1990	**2000**	**1990**	**2000**	**1990**	**2000**	**1990**	**2000**
Afghanistan	..	..	..	..	..	..	..	..
Albania	29	413	26.3	22.7	0.0	65.9	73.7	11.4
Algeria	1,155	..	58.1	..	12.9	..	29.0	..
Angola	1,288	*2,193*	38.3	*18.0*	3.0	*5.8*	58.7	*76.2*
Argentina	2,876	8,612	32.6	28.1	40.7	51.4	26.7	20.5
Armenia	..	*183*	..	*58.5*	..	*20.1*	..	*21.4*
Australia	13,388	17,654	33.9	35.6	31.5	34.2	34.7	30.2
Austria	14,104	29,102	8.4	10.3	54.9	29.1	36.7	60.7
Azerbaijan	..	475	..	30.3	..	27.7	..	42.0
Bangladesh	554	1,523	71.1	66.5	14.1	19.0	14.9	14.5
Belarus	..	421	..	20.3	..	31.7	..	48.1
Belgium[a]	25,924	38,277	23.3	21.7	21.1	26.5	55.6	51.8
Benin	113	*213*	46.9	*67.3*	12.8	*12.0*	40.3	*20.7*
Bolivia	291	451	61.7	59.9	20.6	17.1	17.7	23.0
Bosnia and Herzegovina	..	..	..	..	..	..	..	..
Botswana	371	*511*	57.5	*42.4*	15.0	*28.0*	27.5	*29.7*
Brazil	6,733	15,869	44.4	29.0	22.4	24.5	33.2	46.5
Bulgaria	600	1,660	40.5	44.1	31.5	32.4	28.0	23.5
Burkina Faso	196	..	64.7	..	16.6	..	18.7	..
Burundi	59	34	62.6	55.7	29.0	39.7	8.4	4.5
Cambodia	*64*	237	*24.5*	60.1	..	8.1	*75.5*	31.8
Cameroon	1,018	..	45.3	..	27.5	..	27.3	..
Canada	27,479	41,306	21.1	22.3	39.8	29.4	39.2	48.2
Central African Republic	166	..	49.7	..	30.6	..	19.6	..
Chad	223	..	45.1	..	31.2	..	23.7	..
Chile	1,983	4,336	47.4	55.9	21.5	19.4	31.1	24.7
China	4,113	35,858	78.9	29.0	11.4	36.6	9.7	34.4
Hong Kong, China	..	25,420	..	..	..	..	..	..
Colombia	1,683	3,234	34.9	40.6	27.0	32.7	38.1	26.7
Congo, Dem. Rep.	..	..	..	..	..	..	..	..
Congo, Rep.	748	..	18.4	..	15.2	..	66.5	..
Costa Rica	540	*1,164*	41.2	*37.8*	28.8	*36.9*	30.0	*25.3*
Côte d'Ivoire	1,518	1,131	32.1	45.0	11.1	20.0	56.8	35.0
Croatia	..	1,827	..	20.7	..	31.1	..	48.2
Cuba	..	..	..	..	..	..	..	..
Czech Republic	..	5,341	..	13.4	..	23.5	..	63.1
Denmark	10,106	17,937	38.3	51.2	36.5	28.1	25.2	20.7
Dominican Republic	435	1,340	40.0	61.8	33.1	23.1	26.9	15.1
Ecuador	755	1,212	41.6	*32.4*	23.2	*21.4*	35.2	*46.2*
Egypt, Arab Rep.	3,327	7,161	44.0	30.9	3.9	15.0	52.1	54.1
El Salvador	296	931	45.9	42.6	20.5	18.3	33.5	39.1
Eritrea	..	..	..	..	..	..	..	..
Estonia	*123*	868	*76.3*	48.4	*15.4*	23.5	*8.3*	28.2
Ethiopia	348	480	76.5	59.6	3.3	15.4	20.3	25.1
Finland	7,432	8,231	26.1	31.4	37.2	22.5	36.6	46.1
France	59,560	61,520	29.4	31.8	20.7	29.1	49.9	39.1
Gabon	984	*854*	23.2	*33.7*	13.9	*10.7*	62.9	*55.6*
Gambia, The	35	..	65.1	..	23.1	..	11.8	..
Georgia	..	216	..	41.2	..	51.0	..	7.8
Germany	79,214	132,593	21.6	19.1	42.8	35.5	35.6	45.4
Ghana	226	527	55.1	53.7	5.9	19.0	39.0	27.3
Greece	2,756	10,918	34.0	37.4	39.5	41.7	26.5	20.8
Guatemala	363	802	41.0	52.6	27.4	22.6	31.6	24.8
Guinea	243	*236*	57.5	*42.6*	12.2	*10.0*	30.3	*47.4*
Guinea-Bissau	17	..	54.5	..	19.8	..	25.6	..
Haiti	71	*370*	47.9	*88.1*	52.1	*9.9*	0.0	*2.1*
Honduras	213	565	45.4	53.2	17.6	17.5	37.0	29.2

	Commercial service imports		Transport		Travel		Other	
	$ millions		% of total		% of total		% of total	
	1990	**2000**	**1990**	**2000**	**1990**	**2000**	**1990**	**2000**
Hungary	2,264	4,409	8.8	11.7	25.9	24.8	65.3	63.5
India	5,943	19,601	57.5	41.1	6.6	13.1	35.9	45.8
Indonesia	5,898	14,755	47.4	27.2	14.2	21.7	38.4	51.1
Iran, Islamic Rep.	3,703	1,577	47.3	72.4	9.2	13.0	43.5	14.6
Iraq	..	..	..	..	..	..	..	..
Ireland	5,145	28,692	24.3	9.0	22.6	9.1	53.1	81.9
Israel	4,825	12,149	39.6	39.4	29.7	23.1	30.7	37.5
Italy	46,602	55,204	23.7	24.9	22.1	28.4	54.2	46.7
Jamaica	667	1,400	47.9	41.1	17.0	14.9	35.1	44.0
Japan	84,281	115,686	30.8	30.3	27.9	27.6	41.4	42.1
Jordan	1,118	1,485	52.0	38.6	30.1	23.9	17.9	37.5
Kazakhstan	..	2,146	..	23.0	..	19.0	..	58.0
Kenya	598	665	66.2	51.3	6.4	19.8	27.4	28.9
Korea, Dem. Rep.	..	..	..	..	..	..	..	..
Korea, Rep.	10,050	32,998	39.8	33.0	27.5	21.6	32.7	45.4
Kuwait	2,805	4,078	31.9	37.7	65.5	60.1	2.6	2.2
Kyrgyz Republic	..	145	..	48.2	..	10.8	..	41.0
Lao PDR	25	49	73.0	10.7	0.0	24.2	27.0	65.1
Latvia	120	710	82.3	33.3	10.9	35.0	6.8	31.8
Lebanon	..	..	..	..	..	..	..	..
Lesotho	48	41	67.9	77.1	24.7	22.9	7.3	0.0
Liberia	..	..	..	..	..	..	..	..
Libya	926	824	41.9	45.7	45.7	45.3	12.4	9.0
Lithuania	..	655	..	33.7	..	38.6	..	27.6
Macedonia, FYR	..	350	..	48.6	..	9.8	..	41.6
Madagascar	172	395	43.5	48.3	23.4	29.2	33.0	22.5
Malawi	268	..	81.8	..	5.9	..	12.3	..
Malaysia	5,394	14,622	46.9	32.3	26.9	13.5	26.2	54.2
Mali	352	..	57.4	..	15.8	..	26.8	..
Mauritania	126	130	76.9	37.4	18.3	32.8	4.8	29.8
Mauritius	407	732	51.6	33.6	23.0	24.8	25.4	41.5
Mexico	10,063	16,790	25.0	11.8	54.9	33.2	20.2	55.0
Moldova	..	199	..	31.0	..	39.1	..	29.9
Mongolia	155	140	56.2	61.3	0.8	29.2	43.0	9.5
Morocco	940	1,512	58.3	41.0	19.9	28.1	21.9	30.9
Mozambique	206	439	57.7	27.0	0.0	..	42.3	73.0
Myanmar	72	499	35.4	51.5	22.6	5.0	42.0	43.5
Namibia	341	449	46.9	33.4	17.9	19.7	35.2	46.9
Nepal	159	193	40.8	33.5	28.5	37.9	30.7	28.5
Netherlands	28,995	51,589	37.7	28.3	25.4	23.6	36.9	48.1
New Zealand	3,251	4,449	40.6	32.2	29.5	34.4	30.0	33.4
Nicaragua	73	323	70.7	46.0	20.1	24.3	9.3	29.8
Niger	209	..	68.3	..	10.4	..	21.4	..
Nigeria	1,901	3,311	33.6	19.8	30.3	18.7	36.1	61.4
Norway	12,247	14,466	44.6	38.1	30.0	30.6	25.3	31.3
Oman	719	1,501	36.6	32.4	6.5	22.7	56.9	44.9
Pakistan	1,863	2,109	67.0	71.9	23.1	11.9	9.9	16.2
Panama	666	1,098	66.6	60.4	14.8	18.5	18.6	21.1
Papua New Guinea	393	728	35.6	24.9	12.8	7.3	51.5	67.9
Paraguay	361	394	61.6	60.0	19.8	24.5	18.6	15.5
Peru	1,070	2,210	43.5	38.6	27.6	24.0	29.0	37.3
Philippines	1,721	6,066	56.9	44.1	6.4	16.6	36.6	39.3
Poland	2,847	8,866	52.4	17.3	14.9	37.4	32.8	45.3
Portugal	3,772	6,412	48.4	31.8	23.0	34.8	28.6	33.4
Puerto Rico	..	..	..	..	..	..	..	..
Romania	787	1,976	65.5	33.1	13.1	21.5	21.4	45.3
Russian Federation	..	17,352	..	13.4	..	58.9	..	27.6

	Commercial service imports		Transport		Travel		Other	
	$ millions		% of total		% of total		% of total	
	1990	2000	1990	2000	1990	2000	1990	2000
Rwanda	96	104	69.0	72.4	23.7	19.1	7.3	8.5
Saudi Arabia	12,694	10,942	18.1	20.5	0.0	0.0	81.9	79.5
Senegal	368	419	60.1	60.4	12.4	12.9	27.5	26.8
Sierra Leone	67	..	29.5	..	32.7	..	37.8	..
Singapore	8,575	21,300	41.0	37.6	21.0	23.4	38.0	39.0
Slovak Republic	..	1,779	..	24.4	..	16.6	..	59.0
Slovenia	1,034	1,435	42.5	24.4	27.3	35.8	30.3	39.8
Somalia	..	..	..	..	..	..	..	..
South Africa	3,593	5,449	40.2	44.4	31.5	36.8	28.3	18.8
Spain	15,197	30,818	30.8	26.1	28.0	17.8	41.2	56.1
Sri Lanka	620	1,592	64.2	61.6	11.9	15.1	23.9	23.3
Sudan	202	632	31.9	87.9	25.4	8.8	42.7	3.4
Swaziland	171	170	6.1	14.3	20.6	21.5	73.4	64.2
Sweden	16,959	23,367	23.2	15.6	37.1	34.4	39.7	50.0
Switzerland	11,093	15,369	33.7	34.0	53.0	41.6	13.4	24.3
Syrian Arab Republic	702	1,468	54.5	47.5	35.5	45.6	10.1	6.9
Tajikistan	..	..	..	..	..	..	..	..
Tanzania	288	670	58.0	33.5	7.9	50.3	34.1	16.2
Thailand	6,160	15,329	58.0	44.1	23.3	18.1	18.7	37.8
Togo	217	130	56.9	73.0	18.4	2.0	24.7	25.0
Trinidad and Tobago	460	235	51.7	52.7	26.6	28.5	21.8	18.7
Tunisia	682	1,089	51.4	50.2	26.2	24.1	22.4	25.7
Turkey	2,794	7,620	32.2	36.0	18.6	22.5	49.2	41.5
Turkmenistan	..	..	..	..	..	..	..	..
Uganda	195	745	58.3	34.1	0.0	18.9	41.7	47.0
Ukraine	..	2,590	..	15.1	..	18.1	..	66.8
United Arab Emirates	..	..	..	..	..	..	..	..
United Kingdom	44,713	92,308	33.2	26.8	41.1	46.3	25.6	26.9
United States	97,950	201,060	36.3	32.5	38.9	33.2	24.8	34.3
Uruguay	363	855	48.2	50.3	30.7	32.9	21.1	16.8
Uzbekistan	..	..	..	..	..	..	..	..
Venezuela, RB	2,390	4,056	33.5	40.8	42.8	42.3	23.7	16.9
Vietnam	..	3,252	..	..	..	..	..	..
West Bank and Gaza	..	..	..	..	..	..	..	..
Yemen, Rep.	639	672	27.6	40.0	9.9	20.3	62.5	39.7
Yugoslavia, Fed. Rep.	..	..	..	..	..	..	..	..
Zambia	370	..	76.8	..	14.6	..	8.6	..
Zimbabwe	460	..	51.8	..	14.4	..	33.8	..
World	**774,558 s**	**1,399,541 s**	**32.5 w**	**28.0 w**	**31.7 w**	**30.9 w**	**35.8 w**	**41.2 w**
Low income	27,885	51,237	50.7	35.0	14.0	17.4	35.3	47.6
Middle income	103,290	245,594	41.6	32.5	21.9	29.3	36.5	38.2
Lower middle income	33,346	110,498	42.6	30.8	12.1	35.2	45.3	34.0
Upper middle income	69,944	135,097	40.7	33.5	29.9	25.6	29.4	40.9
Low & middle income	131,175	296,831	43.5	32.8	20.3	27.7	36.2	39.5
East Asia & Pacific	34,357	108,994	51.2	33.0	20.9	24.5	27.8	42.5
Europe & Central Asia	9,321	60,019	24.8	20.1	8.6	34.6	66.6	45.3
Latin America & Carib.	32,861	65,290	37.2	38.1	35.8	33.0	26.9	28.9
Middle East & N. Africa	27,080	25,933	55.7	37.0	13.3	19.1	31.0	43.9
South Asia	9,176	25,126	60.7	44.2	11.2	13.5	28.2	42.2
Sub-Saharan Africa	18,380	11,470	45.8	45.0	18.0	35.4	36.1	19.6
High income	643,383	1,102,710	30.1	26.8	34.2	31.6	35.7	41.6
Europe EMU	288,701	463,840	26.8	22.0	31.4	28.2	41.8	49.8

a. Includes Luxembourg.

About the data

Trade in services differs from trade in goods because services are produced and consumed at the same time. Thus services to a traveler may be consumed in the producing country (for example, use of a hotel room) but are classified as imports of the traveler's country. In other cases services may be supplied from a remote location; for example, insurance services may be supplied from one location and consumed in another. For further discussion of the problems of measuring trade in services see *About the data* for table 4.7.

The data on exports of services in table 4.7 and on imports of services in this table, unlike those in editions before 2000, include only commercial services and exclude the category "government services not included elsewhere." The data are compiled by the International Monetary Fund (IMF) based on returns from national sources.

Definitions

• **Commercial service imports** are total service imports minus imports of government services not included elsewhere. International transactions in services are defined by the IMF's *Balance of Payments Manual* (1993) as the economic output of intangible commodities that may be produced, transferred, and consumed at the same time. Definitions may vary among reporting economies. • **Transport** covers all transport services (sea, air, land, internal waterway, space, and pipeline) performed by residents of one economy for those of another and involving the carriage of passengers, movement of goods (freight), rental of carriers with crew, and related support and auxiliary services. Excluded are freight insurance, which is included in insurance services; goods procured in ports by nonresident carriers, and repairs of transport equipment, which are included in goods; repairs of railway facilities, harbors, and airfield facilities, which are included in construction services; and rental of carriers without crew, which is included in other services. • **Travel** covers goods and services acquired from an economy by travelers in that economy for their own use during visits of less than one year for business or personal purposes. Travel services include the goods and services consumed by travelers, such as meals, lodging, and transport, including car hire rental (within the economy visited). • **Other commercial services** include such activities as insurance and financial services, international telecommunications, and postal and courier services; computer data; news-related service transactions between residents and nonresidents; construction services; royalties and license fees; miscellaneous business, professional, and technical services; and personal, cultural, and recreational services.

Data sources

The data on imports of commercial services come from the IMF. The IMF publishes balance of payments data in its *International Financial Statistics* and *Balance of Payments Statistics Yearbook*.

Figure 4.8

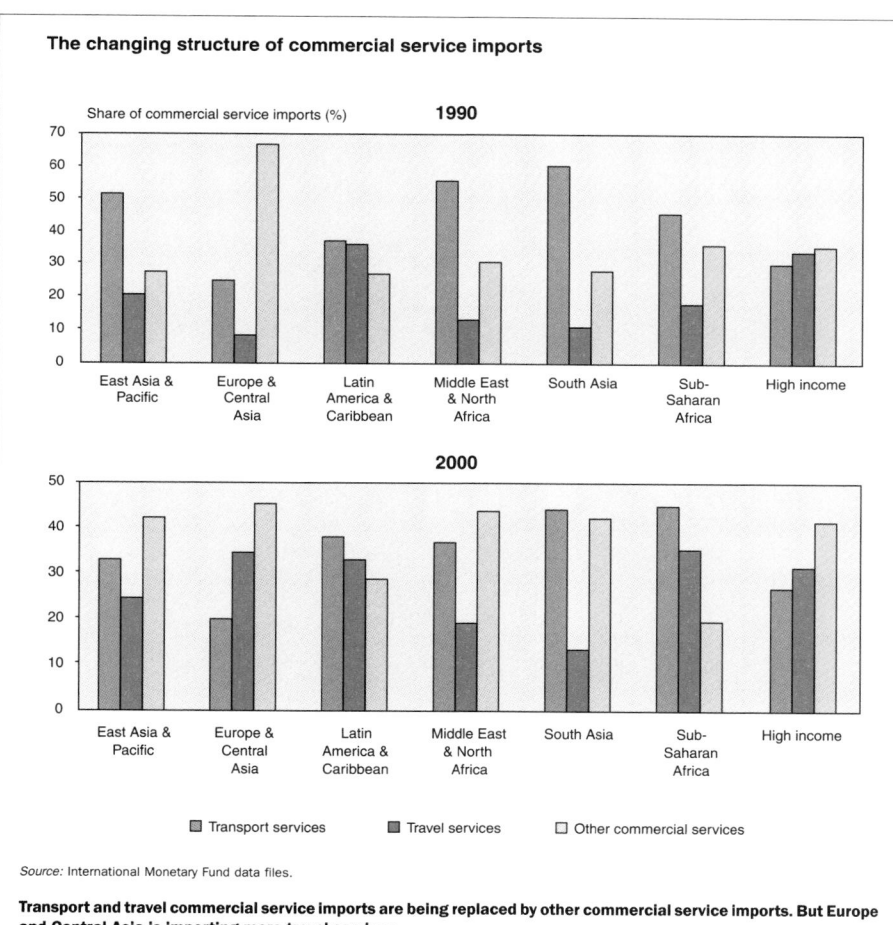

The changing structure of commercial service imports

Share of commercial service imports (%)

1990

East Asia & Pacific · Europe & Central Asia · Latin America & Caribbean · Middle East & North Africa · South Asia · Sub-Saharan Africa · High income

2000

East Asia & Pacific · Europe & Central Asia · Latin America & Caribbean · Middle East & North Africa · South Asia · Sub-Saharan Africa · High income

■ Transport services   ■ Travel services   □ Other commercial services

Source: International Monetary Fund data files.

Transport and travel commercial service imports are being replaced by other commercial service imports. But Europe and Central Asia is importing more travel services.

4.9 | Structure of demand

	Household final consumption expenditure		General government final consumption expenditure		Gross capital formation		Exports of goods and services		Imports of goods and services		Gross domestic savings	
	% of GDP		% of GDP		% of GDP		% of GDP		% of GDP		% of GDP	
	1990	2000	1990	2000	1990	2000	1990	2000	1990	2000	1990	2000
Afghanistan	..	..	..	..	..	..	..	..	..	..	..	..
Albania	61	92	19	11	29	19	15	19	23	40	21	-3
Algeria	57	42	16	14	29	24	23	42	25	22	27	44
Angola	36	17	34	39	12	28	39	90	21	74	30	44
Argentina	77	71	3	14	14	16	10	11	5	11	20	15
Armenia	46	96	18	12	47	19	35	23	46	51	36	-8
Australia	59	60	19	19	22	24	17	20	17	22	22	22
Austria	55	57	19	20	25	24	40	45	38	46	26	24
Azerbaijan	..	59	..	12	..	26	..	41	..	38	..	28
Bangladesh	86	78	4	5	17	23	6	14	14	19	10	18
Belarus	47	59	24	20	27	23	46	68	44	69	29	21
Belgium	55	54	20	21	22	22	71	88	69	85	24	25
Benin	87	82	11	12	14	20	14	15	26	29	2	6
Bolivia	77	74	12	16	13	18	23	18	24	25	11	11
Bosnia and Herzegovina	..	110	..	.. ª	..	20	..	27	..	58	..	-10
Botswana	39	58	24	28	32	20	55	28	50	33	37	14
Brazil	59	63	19	18	20	21	8	11	7	12	21	19
Bulgaria	60	71	18	18	26	17	33	58	37	64	22	11
Burkina Faso	77	76	15	15	21	28	13	11	26	30	8	9
Burundi	95	93	11	13	15	9	8	9	28	24	-5	-6
Cambodia	91	92	7	.. ª	8	15	6	40	13	47	2	8
Cameroon	67	69	13	10	18	16	20	31	17	27	21	20
Canada	57	58	23	19	21	20	26	44	26	41	21	23
Central African Republic	86	81	15	11	12	11	15	13	28	16	-1	8
Chad	89	91	10	8	16	17	13	17	29	32	0	1
Chile	62	63	10	12	25	23	35	32	31	31	28	25
China	50	47	12	13	35	37	18	26	14	23	38	40
Hong Kong, China	57	58	7	10	27	28	134	150	126	145	36	32
Colombia	66	67	9	19	19	12	21	22	15	20	24	14
Congo, Dem. Rep.	79	..	12	..	9	..	30	..	29	..	9	..
Congo, Rep.	62	28	14	11	16	24	54	79	46	42	24	61
Costa Rica	61	67	18	13	27	17	35	48	41	46	21	19
Côte d'Ivoire	72	71	17	10	7	12	32	46	27	39	11	19
Croatia	74	57	24	26	14	22	78	45	86	51	-21	16
Cuba	..	70	..	23	..	10	..	16	..	18	..	7
Czech Republic	49	54	23	20	25	30	45	71	43	75	28	26
Denmark	49	48	26	25	20	22	36	42	31	37	25	27
Dominican Republic	80	78	5	8	25	24	34	30	44	39	15	14
Ecuador	69	62	9	9	17	17	33	42	27	31	23	28
Egypt, Arab Rep.	73	73	11	10	29	24	20	16	33	23	16	17
El Salvador	89	88	10	10	14	17	19	28	31	43	1	2
Eritrea	98	132	33	.. ª	5	38	20	16	57	86	-31	-32
Estonia	62	58	16	21	30	26	60	84	54	88	22	21
Ethiopia	74	78	19	23	12	14	8	15	12	31	7	-1
Finland	51	50	22	21	29	20	23	42	24	32	27	30
France	55	55	22	23	23	21	21	29	22	27	22	22
Gabon	50	62	13	10	22	26	46	37	31	35	37	28
Gambia, The	76	83	14	13	22	17	60	48	72	61	11	4
Georgia	65	82	10	13	31	15	40	37	46	47	25	5
Germany	55	58	19	19	22	23	29	33	25	33	26	23
Ghana	85	81	9	15	14	24	17	49	26	70	5	3
Greece	72	71	15	15	23	22	18	20	28	29	13	14
Guatemala	84	84	7	7	14	17	21	20	25	28	10	9
Guinea	73	77	9	6	18	22	31	26	31	31	18	17
Guinea-Bissau	87	95	10	14	30	18	10	32	37	58	3	-9
Haiti	93	100	8	7	12	11	16	12	29	27	-1	-4
Honduras	66	66	14	13	23	35	36	42	40	56	20	21

	Household final consumption expenditure		General government final consumption expenditure		Gross capital formation		Exports of goods and services		Imports of goods and services		Gross domestic savings	
	% of GDP		% of GDP		% of GDP		% of GDP		% of GDP		% of GDP	
	1990	2000	1990	2000	1990	2000	1990	2000	1990	2000	1990	2000
Hungary	61	64	11	10	25	31	31	63	29	67	28	26
India	66	65	12	13	25	24	7	14	10	17	22	21
Indonesia	59	67	9	7	31	18	25	39	24	31	32	26
Iran, Islamic Rep.	62	52	11	14	29	20	22	35	24	21	27	34
Iraq	..	..	..	..	..	..	..	..	..	..	..	..
Ireland	58	*49*	16	*14*	21	*23*	57	*88*	52	*74*	26	*37*
Israel	56	59	30	29	25	19	35	40	45	47	14	12
Italy	58	60	20	18	22	20	20	28	20	27	22	22
Jamaica	62	68	14	16	28	27	52	44	56	55	24	16
Japan	53	*56*	13	*16*	33	*26*	10	*10*	9	*8*	34	*28*
Jordan	74	81	25	25	32	20	62	42	93	69	1	-6
Kazakhstan	*52*	63	*18*	11	*32*	14	*74*	59	*75*	47	*30*	25
Kenya	67	78	19	18	20	13	26	26	31	36	14	4
Korea, Dem. Rep.	..	..	..	..	..	..	..	..	..	..	..	..
Korea, Rep.	53	58	10	10	38	29	29	45	30	42	37	31
Kuwait	57	41	39	22	18	11	45	57	58	31	4	37
Kyrgyz Republic	71	77	25	19	24	16	29	43	50	55	4	4
Lao PDR	..	82	..	5	..	24	..	36	..	48	..	13
Latvia	53	63	9	19	40	27	48	46	49	54	39	19
Lebanon	140	88	25	19	18	18	18	13	100	38	-64	-7
Lesotho	139	101	14	18	53	40	17	28	122	88	-53	-20
Liberia	..	..	..	..	..	..	..	..	..	..	..	..
Libya	..	..	..	..	..	..	..	..	..	..	..	..
Lithuania	57	64	19	21	33	21	52	45	61	52	24	14
Macedonia, FYR	72	82	19	18	19	17	26	45	36	62	9	0
Madagascar	86	87	8	7	17	16	17	25	27	35	6	6
Malawi	72	82	15	17	23	13	24	26	33	38	13	1
Malaysia	52	43	14	11	32	26	75	125	72	104	34	47
Mali	80	79	14	13	23	23	17	25	34	40	6	7
Mauritania	69	68	26	17	20	30	46	41	61	57	5	15
Mauritius	65	66	12	12	31	26	65	64	72	67	24	22
Mexico	70	68	8	11	23	23	19	31	20	33	22	21
Moldova[b]	*58*	89	*15*	16	25	22	49	50	51	77	23	-5
Mongolia	58	66	32	20	38	30	24	65	53	82	9	14
Morocco	65	63	15	19	25	24	26	31	32	37	19	18
Mozambique	101	79	12	12	16	34	8	15	36	39	-12	10
Myanmar	89	87	..[a]	..[a]	13	*13*	3	*0*	5	*1*	11	*13*
Namibia	46	*54*	28	*29*	35	24	47	*49*	56	*56*	26	*17*
Nepal	83	75	9	9	18	24	11	24	21	32	8	16
Netherlands	49	*50*	23	*23*	24	*22*	59	*61*	55	*56*	28	*27*
New Zealand	63	*64*	17	*16*	19	*21*	28	*32*	27	*33*	20	*20*
Nicaragua	59	88	43	19	19	34	25	40	46	81	-2	-7
Niger	84	84	15	13	8	11	15	15	22	23	1	3
Nigeria	56	45	15	21	15	23	43	52	29	41	29	34
Norway	49	43	21	19	23	22	41	47	34	30	30	38
Oman	27	..	38	..	13	..	53	..	31	..	35	..
Pakistan	74	77	15	11	19	16	16	16	23	19	11	12
Panama	60	61	18	15	17	30	38	33	34	39	21	24
Papua New Guinea	59	*66*	25	*13*	24	*18*	41	*45*	49	*42*	16	*21*
Paraguay	77	83	6	10	23	22	33	20	39	35	17	7
Peru	74	71	8	11	16	20	16	16	14	18	18	18
Philippines	72	63	10	13	24	18	28	56	33	50	18	24
Poland	48	64	19	16	26	27	29	27	22	34	33	20
Portugal	62	63	16	20	28	28	33	31	40	43	21	16
Puerto Rico	..	..	..	..	..	..	..	..	..	..	..	..
Romania	66	74	13	13	30	19	17	34	26	40	21	14
Russian Federation	49	46	21	16	30	17	18	46	18	25	30	38

4.9 | Structure of demand

2002 World Development Indicators

	Household final consumption expenditure		General government final consumption expenditure		Gross capital formation		Exports of goods and services		Imports of goods and services		Gross domestic savings	
	% of GDP		% of GDP		% of GDP		% of GDP		% of GDP		% of GDP	
	1990	2000	1990	2000	1990	2000	1990	2000	1990	2000	1990	2000
Rwanda	84	88	10	12	15	15	6	8	14	24	6	-1
Saudi Arabia	40	33	31	27	20	16	46	50	36	26	30	40
Senegal	76	79	15	10	14	20	25	31	30	40	9	11
Sierra Leone	82	91	10	17	9	8	24	17	25	33	8	-8
Singapore	46	40	10	10	37	31	202	180	195	161	44	50
Slovak Republic	54	53	22	19	33	30	27	74	36	76	24	28
Slovenia	55	55	19	21	17	28	84	59	74	63	26	24
Somalia	112	..	..ᵃ	..	16	..	10	..	38	..	-12	..
South Africa	63	64	20	18	12	15	24	29	19	26	18	18
Spain	60	59	17	17	27	26	16	30	20	32	23	24
Sri Lanka	76	72	10	10	23	28	29	40	38	51	14	17
Sudan	..	85	..	..ᵃ	..	14	..	17	..	16	..	15
Swaziland	62	75	18	20	20	20	76	66	76	81	21	4
Sweden	49	50	28	26	23	18	30	47	29	42	24	23
Switzerland	57	61	14	14	28	20	36	42	36	37	29	25
Syrian Arab Republic	69	62	14	13	17	21	28	38	28	35	17	24
Tajikistan	74	76	9	8	25	20	28	81	35	85	17	16
Tanzaniaᶜ	81	84	18	7	26	18	13	15	37	23	1	9
Thailand	57	60	9	9	41	23	34	67	42	59	34	31
Togo	71	83	14	11	27	21	33	36	45	50	15	6
Trinidad and Tobago	59	56	12	12	13	19	45	65	29	52	29	32
Tunisia	58	60	16	16	32	27	44	44	51	48	25	24
Turkey	69	69	11	14	24	24	13	24	18	31	20	17
Turkmenistan	49	34	23	16	40	40	..	63	..	53	28	49
Uganda	92	87	8	11	13	18	7	10	19	26	1	3
Ukraine	57	58	17	19	27	19	28	61	29	57	26	23
United Arab Emirates	39	..	16	..	20	..	65	..	40	..	45	..
United Kingdom	63	65	20	19	20	18	24	27	27	29	18	16
United States	67	68	17	14	18	21	10	11	11	13	16	18
Uruguay	70	75	12	13	12	14	24	19	18	21	18	12
Uzbekistan	61	64	25	20	32	11	29	44	48	39	13	17
Venezuela, RB	62	63	8	7	10	18	39	29	20	17	29	30
Vietnam	86	69	8	6	13	27	26	..	33	..	6	25
West Bank and Gaza	..	92	..	32	..	33	..	14	..	71	..	-24
Yemen, Rep.	74	58	17	14	15	19	14	50	20	41	9	28
Yugoslavia, Fed. Rep.	..	79	..	25	..	14	..	32	..	50	..	-4
Zambia	64	86	19	11	17	18	36	31	37	46	17	3
Zimbabwe	63	63	19	24	17	13	23	30	23	31	17	12
World	**59 w**	**61 w**	**17 w**	**17 w**	**24 w**	**22 w**	**20 w**	**23 w**	**20 w**	**23 w**	**24 w**	**23 w**
Low income	66	67	12	12	24	20	17	28	20	28	21	20
Middle income	59	59	14	15	26	24	21	32	20	29	27	26
Lower middle income	56	54	13	14	31	26	22	36	22	30	30	32
Upper middle income	61	62	15	15	23	22	21	29	19	28	24	23
Low & middle income	60	60	14	14	26	23	21	31	20	29	26	26
East Asia & Pacific	54	54	11	11	35	30	26	42	26	37	35	35
Europe & Central Asia	55	58	18	16	28	21	23	44	24	39	26	26
Latin America & Carib.	65	66	13	15	19	20	14	17	12	18	21	19
Middle East & N. Africa	57	51	20	18	24	20	33	38	35	28	23	30
South Asia	69	68	12	12	24	23	9	15	13	18	20	20
Sub-Saharan Africa	66	66	17	17	15	17	27	32	26	32	16	17
High income	59	61	18	17	23	22	20	22	20	22	24	22
Europe EMU	56	57	20	20	23	22	28	34	28	33	24	23

a. Data on general government final consumption expenditure are not available separately; they are included in household final consumption expenditure. b. Excludes data for Transnistria. c. Data cover mainland Tanzania only.

About the data

Gross domestic product (GDP) from the expenditure side is made up of household final consumption expenditure, general government final consumption expenditure, gross capital formation (private and public investment in fixed assets and changes in inventories), and net exports (exports minus imports) of goods and services. Such expenditures are recorded in purchaser prices and include net taxes on products.

Because policymakers have tended to focus on fostering the growth of output, and because data on production are easier to collect than data on spending, many countries generate their primary estimate of GDP using the production approach. Moreover, many countries do not estimate all the separate components of national expenditures but instead derive some of the main aggregates indirectly using GDP (based on the production approach) as the control total.

Household final consumption expenditure (private consumption in the terminology of the 1968 System of National Accounts, or SNA) is often estimated as a residual, by subtracting from GDP all other known expenditures. The resulting aggregate may incorporate fairly large discrepancies. When household consumption is calculated separately, the household surveys on which many of the estimates are based tend to be one-year studies with limited coverage. Thus the estimates quickly become outdated and must be supplemented by price- and quantity-based statistical estimating procedures. Complicating the issue, in many developing countries the distinction between cash outlays for personal business and those for household use may be blurred. The *World Development Indicators* includes in household consumption the expenditures of nonprofit institutions serving households.

General government final consumption expenditure (general government consumption in the 1968 SNA) includes expenditures on goods and services for individual consumption as well as those on services for collective consumption. Defense expenditures, including those on capital outlays—with certain exceptions—are treated as current spending.

Gross capital formation (gross domestic investment in the 1968 SNA) consists of outlays on additions to the economy's fixed assets plus net changes in the level of inventories. It is generally obtained from reports by industry of acquisition and distinguishes only the broad categories of capital formation. The 1993 System of National Accounts recognizes a third category of capital formation: net acquisition of valuables. Included in gross capital formation under the 1993 SNA guidelines are capital outlays on defense establishments that may be used by the general public, such as schools, airfields, and hospitals. These expenses were treated as consumption in the earlier version of

the SNA. Data on capital formation may be estimated from direct surveys of enterprises and administrative records or based on the commodity flow method using data from production, trade, and construction activities. The quality of data on fixed capital formation by government depends on the quality of government accounting systems (which tend to be weak in developing countries). Measures of fixed capital formation by households and corporations—particularly capital outlays by small, unincorporated enterprises—are usually very unreliable.

Estimates of changes in inventories are rarely complete but usually include the most important activities or commodities. In some countries these estimates are derived as a composite residual along with household final consumption expenditure. According to national accounts conventions, adjustments should be made for appreciation of the value of inventory holdings due to price changes, but this is not always done. In highly inflationary economies this element can be substantial.

Data on exports and imports are compiled from customs reports and balance of payments data. Although the data on exports and imports from the payments side provide reasonably reliable records of cross-border transactions, they may not adhere strictly to the appropriate definitions of valuation and timing used in the balance of payments or correspond with the change-of-ownership criterion. This issue has assumed greater significance with the increasing globalization of international business. Neither customs nor balance of payments data usually capture the illegal transactions that occur in many countries. Goods carried by travelers across borders in legal but unreported shuttle trade may further distort trade statistics.

Domestic savings, a concept used by the World Bank, represent the difference between GDP and total consumption. Domestic savings also satisfy the fundamental identity: exports minus imports equal domestic savings minus capital formation. Domestic savings differ from savings as defined in the national accounts; this SNA concept represents the difference between disposable income and consumption.

For further discussion of the problems in building and maintaining national accounts see Srinivasan (1994), Heston (1994), and Ruggles (1994). For a classic analysis of the reliability of foreign trade and national income statistics see Morgenstern (1963).

Definitions

• **Household final consumption expenditure** is the market value of all goods and services, including durable products (such as cars, washing machines, and home computers), purchased by households. It excludes purchases of dwellings but includes imputed rent for owner-occupied dwellings. It also includes payments and fees to governments to obtain permits and licenses. Here, household consumption expenditure includes the expenditures of nonprofit institutions serving households, even when reported separately by the country. In practice, household consumption expenditure may include any statistical discrepancy in the use of resources relative to the supply of resources. • **General government final consumption expenditure** includes all government current expenditures for purchases of goods and services (including compensation of employees). It also includes most expenditures on national defense and security, but excludes government military expenditures that are part of government capital formation. • **Gross capital formation** consists of outlays on additions to the fixed assets of the economy plus net changes in the level of inventories. Fixed assets include land improvements (fences, ditches, drains, and so on); plant, machinery, and equipment purchases; and the construction of roads, railways, and the like, including schools, offices, hospitals, private residential dwellings, and commercial and industrial buildings. Inventories are stocks of goods held by firms to meet temporary or unexpected fluctuations in production or sales, and "work in progress." According to the 1993 SNA, net acquisitions of valuables are also considered capital formation. • **Exports and imports of goods and services** represent the value of all goods and other market services provided to, or received from, the rest of the world. They include the value of merchandise, freight, insurance, transport, travel, royalties, license fees, and other services, such as communication, construction, financial, information, business, personal, and government services. They exclude labor and property income (factor services in the 1968 SNA) as well as transfer payments. • **Gross domestic savings** are calculated as GDP less total consumption.

Data sources

The national accounts indicators for most developing countries are collected from national statistical organizations and central banks by visiting and resident World Bank missions. The data for high-income economies come from OECD data files (see the OECD's *National Accounts, 1988–1999,* volumes 1 and 2). The United Nations Statistics Division publishes detailed national accounts for United Nations member countries in *National Accounts Statistics: Main Aggregates and Detailed Tables* and updates in the *Monthly Bulletin of Statistics.*

4.10 | Growth of consumption and investment

	Household final consumption expenditure				Household final consumption expenditure per capita		General government final consumption expenditure		Gross capital formation	
	$ millions		average annual % growth		average annual % growth		average annual % growth		average annual % growth	
	1990	2000	1980-90	1990-2000	1980-90	1990-2000	1980-90	1990-2000	1980-90	1990-2000
Afghanistan	..	..	..	..	..	..	..	..	..	..
Albania	1,271	3,453	..	4.6	..	3.9	..	-1.1	-0.3	22.0
Algeria	35,265	22,219	1.4	0.8	-1.6	-1.1	0.7	3.6	-1.8	-0.5
Angola	3,674	1,461	-0.1	-3.8	..	..	6.7	-2.0	-5.1	10.8
Argentina	109,038	202,101	..	2.8	..	1.5	..	1.8	-5.2	7.3
Armenia	2,005	1,821	..	-0.5	..	-1.1	..	-1.7	..	-2.3
Australia	181,421	240,855	3.0	3.7	1.5	2.5	3.7	2.9	3.2	6.6
Austria	89,789	118,889	2.4	2.3	2.3	1.8	1.4	2.1	2.3	2.1
Azerbaijan	..	3,130	..	6.4	..	5.4	..	5.4	..	5.6
Bangladesh	25,952	36,579	4.5	3.6	1.8	1.8	5.0	4.7	1.4	9.2
Belarus	16,667	17,075	..	-0.5	..	-0.3	..	-1.8	..	-7.8
Belgium	109,445	121,992	1.9	1.6	1.8	1.3	1.1	1.5	3.4	2.6
Benin	1,602	1,774	1.9	4.3	-1.2	1.4	0.5	4.0	-5.3	5.6
Bolivia	3,741	6,100	1.2	3.6	-0.9	1.2	-3.8	3.5	1.0	8.5
Bosnia and Herzegovina	..	..	..	..	..	..	..	..	..	..
Botswana	1,473	2,940	5.9	6.2	2.4	3.6	13.6	5.2	13.8	-0.7
Brazil	275,753	372,502	1.2	5.7	-0.7	4.2	7.3	-1.7	3.3	3.4
Bulgaria	12,401	8,658	3.1	-2.9	3.2	-2.3	5.1	-9.4	2.3	-4.1
Burkina Faso	2,141	1,670	2.6	4.4	0.1	2.0	6.2	-0.7	8.6	7.2
Burundi	1,070	684	3.4	-1.7	0.5	-3.8	3.2	-2.1	6.9	-0.4
Cambodia	1,016	2,705	..	1.5	..	..	..	-0.8	..	13.4
Cameroon	7,432	6,169	3.5	2.9	0.6	0.4	6.8	0.7	-2.6	0.7
Canada	323,850	366,938	3.3	2.5	2.1	1.5	2.5	-0.1	5.2	4.7
Central African Republic	1,274	781	1.5	..	..	..	-1.7	..	10.0	..
Chad	1,482	1,277	5.3	0.5	2.8	-2.5	14.5	-0.4	..	1.3
Chile	18,759	44,671	2.0	7.4	0.3	5.8	0.4	3.9	6.4	8.9
China	174,249	521,114	8.8	8.5	7.2	7.4	9.8	9.4	10.8	11.6
Hong Kong, China	42,422	94,492	6.7	3.7	5.3	1.7	5.0	3.9	4.0	5.4
Colombia	26,357	54,742	2.6	2.6	0.5	0.7	4.2	9.5	1.4	2.1
Congo, Dem. Rep.	7,398	..	3.4	-6.6	0.1	-9.7	0.0	-16.1	-5.1	-2.6
Congo, Rep.	1,746	906	3.3	0.5	0.4	-2.5	2.5	-10.8	-12.6	0.6
Costa Rica	3,502	10,677	3.6	5.0	0.6	2.7	1.1	1.9	4.6	4.7
Côte d'Ivoire	7,766	6,692	1.5	2.3	-2.1	-0.8	-0.1	1.4	-10.4	11.8
Croatia	13,527	10,877	..	2.6	..	3.8	..	1.1	..	8.4
Cuba	..	..	..	2.6	..	..	..	1.9	..	16.9
Czech Republic	17,195	27,631	..	2.8	..	2.8	..	-1.8	..	5.0
Denmark	65,430	77,619	1.4	2.4	1.4	2.0	0.9	2.3	4.7	5.3
Dominican Republic	5,633	15,268	3.9	5.3	1.7	3.5	-3.2	15.1	4.5	5.6
Ecuador	7,323	8,446	1.9	1.3	-0.7	-0.8	-1.4	-1.8	-3.8	-0.5
Egypt, Arab Rep.	30,933	72,027	4.6	4.4	2.0	2.4	3.1	3.0	0.0	6.3
El Salvador	4,273	11,623	0.8	5.1	-0.2	2.9	0.1	3.0	2.2	7.1
Eritrea	430	459	..	..	..	..	..	..	..	..
Estonia	4,074	2,685	..	0.4	..	1.9	..	4.6	..	-1.4
Ethiopia	5,081	4,974	0.2	3.0	-2.8	0.7	4.5	8.8	2.1	9.7
Finland	68,939	59,752	3.9	2.0	3.4	1.6	3.2	0.9	3.4	1.5
France	672,960	708,622	2.2	1.3	1.7	0.9	2.6	1.8	3.3	1.2
Gabon	2,961	3,040	1.5	1.2	-1.5	-1.5	-0.6	5.4	-5.7	3.8
Gambia, The	240	350	-2.4	4.3	-5.9	0.9	1.7	-2.8	0.0	3.3
Georgia	8,228	2,485	..	..	..	..	..	..	..	..
Germany	941,915	1,087,707	2.2	1.6	2.1	1.3	1.5	1.2	2.0	1.7
Ghana	5,016	4,224	2.8	4.1	-0.8	1.7	2.4	5.4	3.3	2.3
Greece	60,164	88,745	2.0	2.1	1.5	1.7	1.1	1.3	-0.7	3.3
Guatemala	6,398	16,041	1.1	4.2	-1.4	1.5	2.6	4.7	-1.8	6.0
Guinea	2,068	2,330	..	3.6	..	1.0	..	4.7	..	2.8
Guinea-Bissau	212	205	0.8	2.7	-1.5	0.4	7.2	1.9	12.9	-10.6
Haiti	2,785	3,860	0.9	..	..	..	-4.4	..	-0.6	-1.3
Honduras	2,026	3,930	2.7	2.7	-0.5	-0.1	3.3	1.7	2.9	7.5

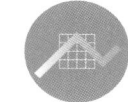

	Household final consumption expenditure			Household final consumption expenditure per capita		General government final consumption expenditure		Gross capital formation	
	$ millions		average annual % growth	average annual % growth		average annual % growth		average annual % growth	
	1990	2000	1980-90	1990-2000	1980-90	1990-2000	1980-90	1990-2000	1980-90	1990-2000

	1990	2000	1980-90	1990-2000	1980-90	1990-2000	1980-90	1990-2000	1980-90	1990-2000
Hungary	20,290	29,094	1.3	-0.3	1.7	0.0	1.9	0.9	-0.9	9.5
India	208,896	298,779	5.8	4.8	3.6	3.0	4.2	6.9	6.6	7.9
Indonesia	67,388	103,066	5.6	6.5	3.7	4.7	4.6	0.1	7.2	-0.6
Iran, Islamic Rep.	74,476	54,312	2.8	3.1	-0.6	1.5	-5.0	6.4	-2.5	2.8
Iraq	..	..	..	..	..	..	..	..	..	..
Ireland	27,957	45,806	2.2	5.1	1.9	4.3	-0.3	3.6	-0.4	8.9
Israel	32,112	65,189	5.4	6.3	3.6	3.4	0.5	2.9	2.2	4.9
Italy	634,194	649,183	2.9	1.5	2.8	1.3	2.9	0.1	2.1	1.3
Jamaica	2,637	5,029	4.5	-1.1	3.3	-1.9	6.2	2.7	-0.1	4.4
Japan	1,617,071	2,533,095	3.6	1.7	3.0	1.4	3.4	2.9	5.5	-0.1
Jordan	2,978	6,728	1.9	5.0	-1.9	1.0	1.9	5.1	-1.9	-0.6
Kazakhstan	14,148	11,677	..	-7.7	..	-6.7	..	-7.3	..	-16.4
Kenya	5,309	8,186	4.6	3.0	1.1	0.4	2.6	8.4	0.4	3.9
Korea, Dem. Rep.	..	..	..	..	..	..	..	..	..	..
Korea, Rep.	132,113	261,913	7.9	4.9	6.7	3.9	5.2	3.0	12.0	1.4
Kuwait	10,459	15,384	-1.4	..	..	..	2.2	..	-4.5	..
Kyrgyz Republic	2,103	1,017	..	-6.0	..	-7.0	..	-8.9	..	-5.0
Lao PDR	..	882	..	..	..	..	..	..	..	..
Latvia	6,578	4,471	2.9	-4.8	2.3	-3.6	5.0	8.0	3.4	-1.1
Lebanon	3,961	14,480	..	3.2	..	1.4	..	4.3	..	8.8
Lesotho	855	909	3.6	0.7	1.4	-1.2	3.2	6.3	5.0	1.5
Liberia	..	..	1.2	..	..	..	1.3	..	-16.7	..
Libya	..	..	..	..	..	..	..	..	..	..
Lithuania	7,527	7,280	..	2.4	..	2.5	..	3.8	..	9.9
Macedonia, FYR	3,021	2,945	..	2.5	..	1.8	..	1.2	..	0.7
Madagascar	2,649	3,349	-0.6	2.4	-3.3	-0.5	0.5	0.4	4.9	2.2
Malawi	1,345	1,392	1.5	5.4	-1.7	3.4	6.3	-3.3	-2.8	-8.5
Malaysia	22,806	38,211	3.3	2.2	0.4	3.7	2.7	8.7	3.1	5.2
Mali	1,933	1,826	1.0	2.8	-1.5	0.3	7.9	5.2	3.6	-0.7
Mauritania	705	633	1.4	3.7	-1.1	0.8	-3.8	-0.5	6.9	9.9
Mauritius	1,707	2,889	6.7	4.8	5.8	3.6	3.3	4.3	9.0	3.5
Mexico	182,791	388,054	1.1	2.4	-1.0	0.7	2.4	1.8	-3.3	4.6
Moldova	2,328	1,147	..	6.9	..	7.1	..	-5.4	..	-15.5
Mongolia	..	643	..	..	..	..	..	..	..	..
Morocco	16,833	20,883	4.3	3.0	2.0	1.2	2.1	3.3	1.2	2.0
Mozambique	2,481	2,964	-1.4	4.3	-2.9	1.9	-2.6	1.4	3.8	10.8
Myanmar	..	..	0.6	3.9	..	..	..	..	-4.1	15.4
Namibia	1,280	1,995	1.3	4.4	-2.0	2.0	3.7	3.1	-2.9	3.9
Nepal	3,028	4,112	4.5	4.0	2.2	1.6	7.2	5.7	6.0	7.0
Netherlands	144,279	197,321	1.6	2.6	1.1	2.0	2.0	1.9	3.1	2.6
New Zealand	27,300	35,260	2.0	3.0	1.1	1.8	1.5	2.0	2.7	7.1
Nicaragua	592	2,102	-3.6	5.8	-6.2	2.9	3.4	-1.8	-4.8	11.8
Niger	2,079	1,540	0.0	2.9	-3.1	-0.6	4.4	0.7	-7.1	4.2
Nigeria	15,816	18,669	-2.6	-3.7	-5.5	-6.4	-3.5	5.6	-8.5	8.3
Norway	57,047	69,082	2.2	3.3	1.9	2.7	2.3	2.4	0.7	5.2
Oman	2,810	..	..	..	..	..	..	..	25.5	..
Pakistan	29,512	47,401	4.3	4.9	1.6	2.3	10.3	0.7	5.8	1.8
Panama	3,022	6,018	2.1	3.8	0.0	2.0	1.2	2.1	-8.9	11.2
Papua New Guinea	1,902	2,358	0.4	4.9	-2.1	2.2	-0.1	2.2	-0.9	1.3
Paraguay	4,063	6,226	2.4	3.6	-0.7	1.0	1.5	6.4	-0.8	0.2
Peru	19,376	37,742	0.7	4.0	-1.5	2.2	-0.9	5.2	-3.8	7.4
Philippines	31,566	49,007	2.6	3.7	0.2	1.5	0.6	3.4	-2.1	3.1
Poland	28,281	101,013	..	6.2	..	6.1	..	2.3	..	10.6
Portugal	43,985	66,484	2.5	3.2	2.4	3.0	5.0	2.8	3.0	5.2
Puerto Rico	19,827	..	3.5	..	..	..	5.1	..	6.9	..
Romania	25,232	27,120	..	0.7	..	1.0	..	1.1	..	-5.2
Russian Federation	282,978	114,596	..	-0.7	..	-0.5	..	-2.3	..	-18.3

4.10 | Growth of consumption and investment

	Household final consumption expenditure				Household final consumption expenditure per capita		General government final consumption expenditure		Gross capital formation	
	$ millions		average annual % growth		average annual % growth		average annual % growth		average annual % growth	
	1990	2000	1980-90	1990-2000	1980-90	1990-2000	1980-90	1990-2000	1980-90	1990-2000
Rwanda	2,162	1,586	1.4	1.6	-1.6	-0.3	5.2	-2.4	4.3	2.6
Saudi Arabia	41,621	56,919	..	..	..	..	..	..	..	..
Senegal	4,353	3,444	2.1	3.6	-0.8	0.9	3.3	-0.1	5.2	5.0
Sierra Leone	734	581	0.1	-2.4	-2.0	-4.7	0.0	-1.8	-1.1	-4.9
Singapore	17,019	36,871	5.8	5.7	3.9	2.6	6.6	8.6	3.1	7.6
Slovak Republic	8,350	10,207	3.8	0.5	3.5	0.3	4.8	1.3	0.3	7.8
Slovenia	6,917	9,956	..	3.8	..	3.9	..	3.2	..	10.7
Somalia	..	..	1.3	..	..	..	7.0	..	-2.6	..
South Africa	70,283	80,091	2.4	2.6	-0.2	0.6	3.5	0.5	-5.3	2.7
Spain	308,803	331,606	2.5	2.1	2.2	2.0	5.4	2.3	5.7	2.6
Sri Lanka	6,143	11,806	4.0	3.8	2.5	2.5	7.3	8.8	0.6	6.4
Sudan	..	..	0.0	..	..	..	-0.5	..	-1.8	9.5
Swaziland	521	1,111	4.6	3.9	1.4	0.8	2.9	5.8	1.6	2.6
Sweden	116,247	114,681	2.2	1.1	1.9	0.8	1.6	0.3	4.7	1.7
Switzerland	130,900	158,369	1.6	0.9	1.1	0.2	3.1	0.7	3.9	0.7
Syrian Arab Republic	8,458	11,626	3.6	2.2	0.2	-0.8	-3.6	2.0	-5.3	4.3
Tajikistan	3,202	752	4.0	-7.3	0.9	-8.7	4.1	-14.2	-6.8	-14.6
Tanzania[a]	3,526	7,604	..	2.0	..	-0.8	..	-8.3	..	-1.4
Thailand	48,270	71,625	5.9	3.6	4.1	2.8	4.2	5.1	9.5	-4.1
Togo	1,158	1,012	4.7	3.6	1.3	0.8	-1.2	-1.7	2.7	-0.2
Trinidad and Tobago	2,975	4,219	-1.3	0.3	-2.5	-0.3	-1.7	0.7	-10.1	15.5
Tunisia	7,152	11,773	2.9	4.3	0.3	2.6	3.8	4.1	-1.8	3.6
Turkey	103,378	137,646	..	3.7	..	2.2	..	4.6	..	4.0
Turkmenistan	4,065	1,513	..	..	..	..	..	..	..	1.9
Uganda	4,002	5,390	2.6	7.6	0.0	4.3	2.0	6.4	8.0	9.3
Ukraine	52,131	18,518	..	-7.1	..	-6.6	..	-4.2	..	-18.5
United Arab Emirates	12,726	..	4.6	..	..	..	-3.9	..	-8.7	..
United Kingdom	617,733	925,496	4.0	2.8	3.8	2.5	0.8	1.1	6.4	4.2
United States	3,831,500	6,268,600	3.8	3.4	2.9	2.1	3.3	0.4	4.0	7.5
Uruguay	6,525	14,694	0.7	5.0	0.1	4.3	1.8	2.1	-6.6	6.3
Uzbekistan	13,321	4,884	..	..	..	..	..	..	..	..
Venezuela, RB	30,171	75,986	1.3	0.4	-1.2	-1.7	2.0	-0.3	-5.3	4.4
Vietnam	5,597	20,846	..	9.1	..	7.2	..	10.9	..	20.2
West Bank and Gaza	..	4,019	..	2.5	..	-1.7	..	12.6	..	3.8
Yemen, Rep.	3,561	4,930	..	3.0	..	-0.4	..	2.3	..	9.6
Yugoslavia, Fed. Rep.	..	6,688	..	..	..	..	..	..	..	..
Zambia	2,078	2,761	1.8	-2.8	-1.3	-5.3	-3.4	-6.6	-4.3	5.2
Zimbabwe	5,543	4,504	3.7	0.0	0.0	-2.0	4.7	-2.2	3.6	-3.4

World	12,910,826 t	18,821,092 t	3.3 w	2.7 w	1.6 w	1.2 w	2.9 w	1.5 w	3.9 w	2.8 w
Low income	574,483	702,729	4.2	3.6	1.9	1.6	4.0	2.8	4.4	1.6
Middle income	2,015,476	3,228,520	3.3	3.9	1.6	2.6	5.0	2.0	2.6	2.0
Lower middle income	897,553	1,284,732	4.6	3.6	2.9	2.4	3.7	4.3	4.7	0.0
Upper middle income	1,130,065	1,944,018	2.5	4.1	0.6	2.6	5.5	0.7	1.4	4.2
Low & middle income	2,584,252	3,929,051	3.5	3.8	1.5	2.2	4.8	2.1	2.8	2.0
East Asia & Pacific	496,327	1,095,144	6.9	6.3	5.2	5.0	5.9	6.2	9.3	5.9
Europe & Central Asia	672,345	562,238	..	0.7	..	0.5	..	-0.6	..	-8.1
Latin America & Carib.	737,633	1,321,356	1.3	4.0	-0.6	2.3	5.6	0.1	-0.3	4.6
Middle East & N. Africa	220,686	341,201	..	..	..	..	..	..	..	..
South Asia	277,595	404,700	5.4	4.7	3.1	2.7	5.2	6.0	5.8	7.3
Sub-Saharan Africa	192,381	206,155	1.6	2.1	-1.3	-0.5	2.7	1.5	-3.9	3.4
High income	10,324,580	15,115,577	3.3	2.5	2.7	1.7	2.7	1.4	4.1	3.0
Europe EMU	3,116,888	3,450,141	2.3	1.7	2.1	1.4	2.3	1.4	2.7	1.9

a. Data cover mainland Tanzania only.

2002 World Development Indicators

About the data

Measures of growth in consumption and capital formation are subject to two kinds of inaccuracy. The first stems from the difficulty of measuring expenditures at current price levels, as described in *About the data* for table 4.9. The second arises in deflating current price data to measure volume growth, where results depend on the relevance and reliability of the price indexes and weights used. Measuring price changes is more difficult for investment goods than for consumption goods because of the one-time nature of many investments and because the rate of technological progress in capital goods makes capturing change in quality difficult. (An example is computers—prices have fallen as quality has improved.) Several countries estimate capital formation from the supply side, identifying capital goods entering an economy directly from detailed production and international trade statistics. This means that the price indexes used in deflating production and international trade, reflecting delivered or offered prices, will determine the deflator for capital formation expenditures on the demand side.

The data in the table on household final consumption expenditure (private consumption in the 1968 System of National Accounts), in current U.S. dollars, are converted from national currencies using official exchange rates or an alternative conversion factor as noted in *Primary data documentation*. (For a discussion of alternative conversion factors, see *Statistical methods*.) Growth rates of household final consumption expenditure, household final consumption expenditure per capita, general government final consumption expenditure, and gross capital formation are estimated using constant price data. (Consumption and capital formation as shares of GDP are shown in table 4.9.)

To obtain government consumption in constant prices, countries may deflate current values by applying a wage (price) index or extrapolate from the change in government employment. Neither technique captures improvements in productivity or changes in the quality of government services. Deflators for household consumption are usually calculated on the basis of the consumer price index. Many countries estimate household consumption as a residual that includes statistical discrepancies accumulated from other domestic sources including stock changes; thus these estimates lack detailed breakdowns of expenditures.

Figure 4.10

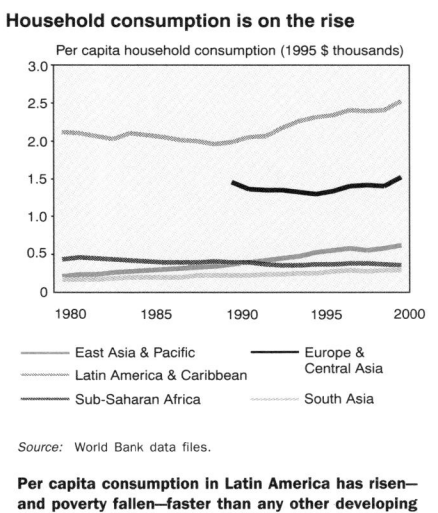

Household consumption is on the rise

Per capita household consumption (1995 $ thousands)

Legend:
— East Asia & Pacific
······ Latin America & Caribbean
— Sub-Saharan Africa
— Europe & Central Asia
— South Asia

Source: World Bank data files.

Per capita consumption in Latin America has risen—and poverty fallen—faster than any other developing region.

Definitions

• **Household final consumption expenditure** is the market value of all goods and services, including durable products (such as cars, washing machines, and home computers), purchased by households. It excludes purchases of dwellings but includes imputed rent for owner-occupied dwellings. It also includes payments and fees to governments to obtain permits and licenses. The *World Development Indicators* includes in household consumption expenditure the expenditures of nonprofit institutions serving households, even when reported separately by the country. In practice, household consumption expenditure may include any statistical discrepancy in the use of resources relative to the supply of resources. • **General government final consumption expenditure** includes all government current expenditures for purchases of goods and services (including compensation of employees). It also includes most expenditures on national defense and security, but excludes government military expenditures that have potential wider public use and are part of government capital formation. • **Gross capital formation** consists of outlays on additions to the fixed assets of the economy plus net changes in the level of inventories. Fixed assets include land improvements (fences, ditches, drains, and so on); plant, machinery, and equipment purchases; and the construction of roads, railways, and the like, including schools, offices, hospitals, private residential dwellings, and commercial and industrial buildings. Inventories are stocks of goods held by firms to meet temporary or unexpected fluctuations in production or sales, and "work in progress." According to the 1993 SNA, net acquisitions of valuables are also considered capital formation.

Data sources

The national accounts indicators for most developing countries are collected from national statistical organizations and central banks by visiting and resident World Bank missions. Data for high-income economies come from Organisation for Economic Co-operation and Development (OECD) data files (see the OECD's *National Accounts, 1988–1999*, volumes 1 and 2). The United Nations Statistics Division publishes detailed national accounts for United Nations member countries in *National Accounts Statistics: Main Aggregates and Detailed Tables* and publishes updates in the *Monthly Bulletin of Statistics*.

4.11 | Central government finances

	Current revenue [a]		Total expenditure		Overall budget balance (including grants)		Financing from abroad		Domestic financing		Debt and interest payments	
	% of GDP		% of GDP		% of GDP		% of GDP		% of GDP		Total debt % of GDP	Interest % of current revenue
	1990	1999	1990	1999	1990	1999	1990	1999	1990	1999	1999	1999
Afghanistan	..	..	..	..	..	..	..	..	..	..	..	..
Albania	..	19.3	..	29.8	..	-8.5	..	2.5	..	6.0	46.4	40.3
Algeria	..	30.0	..	30.4	..	-0.4	..	..	..	..	62.0	13.3
Angola	..	..	..	..	..	..	..	..	..	..	..	..
Argentina	10.4	14.0	10.6	17.0	-0.4	-2.9	0.2	4.0	0.2	-1.1	..	20.6
Armenia	..	..	..	..	..	..	..	..	..	..	..	..
Australia	24.9	23.8	23.3	23.4	2.0	1.4	0.2	-0.5	-2.2	-0.9	15.3	5.3
Austria	34.0	37.3	37.6	40.3	-4.4	..	0.5	..	3.9	..	62.3	8.9
Azerbaijan	..	17.7	..	22.7	..	-2.6	..	..	..	..	..	2.5
Bangladesh	..	9.3	..	12.7	..	-2.8	..	0.1	..	2.7	40.1	15.7
Belarus	30.9	28.7	37.3	30.9	-4.8	-2.0	2.7	-0.8	2.4	2.8	20.2	2.2
Belgium	42.7	43.8	47.8	45.7	-5.5	-1.8	-0.3	-0.9	5.8	2.7	114.7	16.7
Benin	..	..	..	..	..	..	..	..	..	..	..	..
Bolivia	13.7	16.7	16.4	23.1	-1.7	-2.3	0.7	1.6	1.0	0.7	56.1	7.8
Bosnia and Herzegovina	..	..	..	..	..	..	..	..	..	..	..	..
Botswana	51.1	..	33.8	..	11.3	..	0.0	..	-11.4	..	..	..
Brazil	22.8	24.9	34.9	26.8	-5.8	-7.8	..	..	..	..	..	15.4
Bulgaria	47.1	34.6	55.1	35.7	-8.3	1.5	-0.8	0.8	9.1	-2.3	52.8	11.3
Burkina Faso	11.0	..	15.0	..	-1.3	..	..	..	..	..	..	..
Burundi	18.2	17.9	28.7	26.1	-3.3	-4.7	4.9	3.3	-1.6	1.5	183.9	13.2
Cambodia	..	..	..	..	..	..	..	..	..	..	..	..
Cameroon	15.4	16.0	21.2	15.9	-5.9	0.1	5.2	0.2	1.2	-0.3	104.6	19.2
Canada	21.6	22.2	26.2	21.4	-4.8	1.0	0.2	0.4	4.6	-1.3	69.0	15.0
Central African Republic	..	..	..	..	..	..	..	..	..	..	..	..
Chad	6.7	..	21.8	..	-4.7	..	5.0	..	-0.3	..	..	..
Chile	20.6	22.4	20.4	23.9	0.8	-1.5	0.9	0.5	-2.5	0.9	15.0	1.6
China	6.3	7.2	10.1	10.9	-1.9	-2.9	0.8	-0.1	1.1	3.0	12.7	..
Hong Kong, China	..	..	..	..	..	..	..	..	..	..	..	..
Colombia	12.6	12.6	11.6	19.1	3.9	-7.1	..	2.2	..	5.0	29.8	26.8
Congo, Dem. Rep.	10.1	0.1	18.8	0.1	-6.5	0.0	0.0	0.0	6.5	0.0	160.4	4.6
Congo, Rep.	22.5	26.8	35.6	32.8	-14.1	-5.6	..	5.9	..	-0.3	283.7	43.4
Costa Rica	23.0	20.0	25.6	21.5	-3.1	-1.5	0.3	1.5	2.8	0.0	36.3	18.3
Côte d'Ivoire	22.0	20.6	24.5	22.4	-2.9	-0.2	4.0	1.7	0.4	-1.5	112.5	20.2
Croatia	33.0	42.8	37.6	48.3	-4.6	-2.0	0.0	3.2	4.7	-1.3	..	3.6
Cuba	..	..	..	..	..	..	..	..	..	..	..	..
Czech Republic	..	33.1	..	35.5	..	-1.6	..	-0.4	..	2.0	12.9	2.8
Denmark	37.8	37.4	39.0	36.0	-0.7	0.5	..	..	..	..	63.7	11.2
Dominican Republic	12.0	16.3	11.7	17.0	0.6	-0.5	0.0	-0.1	-0.6	0.6	20.7	3.9
Ecuador	18.2	..	14.5	..	3.7	..	..	..	..	..	..	..
Egypt, Arab Rep.	23.0	26.3	27.8	30.6	-5.7	-2.0	-0.7	-0.6	6.4	2.6	..	23.0
El Salvador	..	14.4	..	16.3	..	-2.2	..	1.4	..	0.8	29.2	9.3
Eritrea	..	..	..	..	..	..	..	..	..	..	..	..
Estonia	26.2	30.8	23.7	35.6	0.4	-0.2	0.0	-0.5	-0.4	0.6	4.7	0.8
Ethiopia	17.4	..	27.2	..	-9.8	..	2.8	..	7.0	..	..	..
Finland	30.6	32.0	30.3	33.4	0.2	-0.3	0.7	-1.1	-0.8	1.4	61.1	14.3
France	39.7	41.4	41.8	46.2	-2.1	-3.5	1.1	..	1.0	..	..	7.4
Gabon	20.6	..	20.2	..	3.2	..	2.7	..	-5.8	..	..	..
Gambia, The	19.4	..	23.6	..	-0.8	..	..	..	..	..	..	..
Georgia	..	11.5	..	15.0	..	-4.4	..	2.6	..	1.9	72.0	22.7
Germany	25.6	31.3	26.3	32.6	-1.4	-0.9	0.5	0.6	1.0	-0.1	19.9	7.3
Ghana	12.5	..	13.2	..	0.2	..	1.3	..	-1.5	..	..	..
Greece	27.8	23.5	52.2	30.9	-22.9	-4.4	1.6	2.4	21.3	2.0	113.2	38.4
Guatemala	..	..	..	..	..	..	..	..	..	..	..	..
Guinea	16.0	11.8	22.9	21.2	-3.3	-2.4	4.1	2.3	-0.8	0.2	..	37.1
Guinea-Bissau	..	..	..	..	..	..	..	..	..	..	..	..
Haiti	..	8.9	..	11.5	..	-1.4	..	-0.4	..	1.8	..	9.3
Honduras	..	..	..	..	..	..	..	..	..	..	..	..

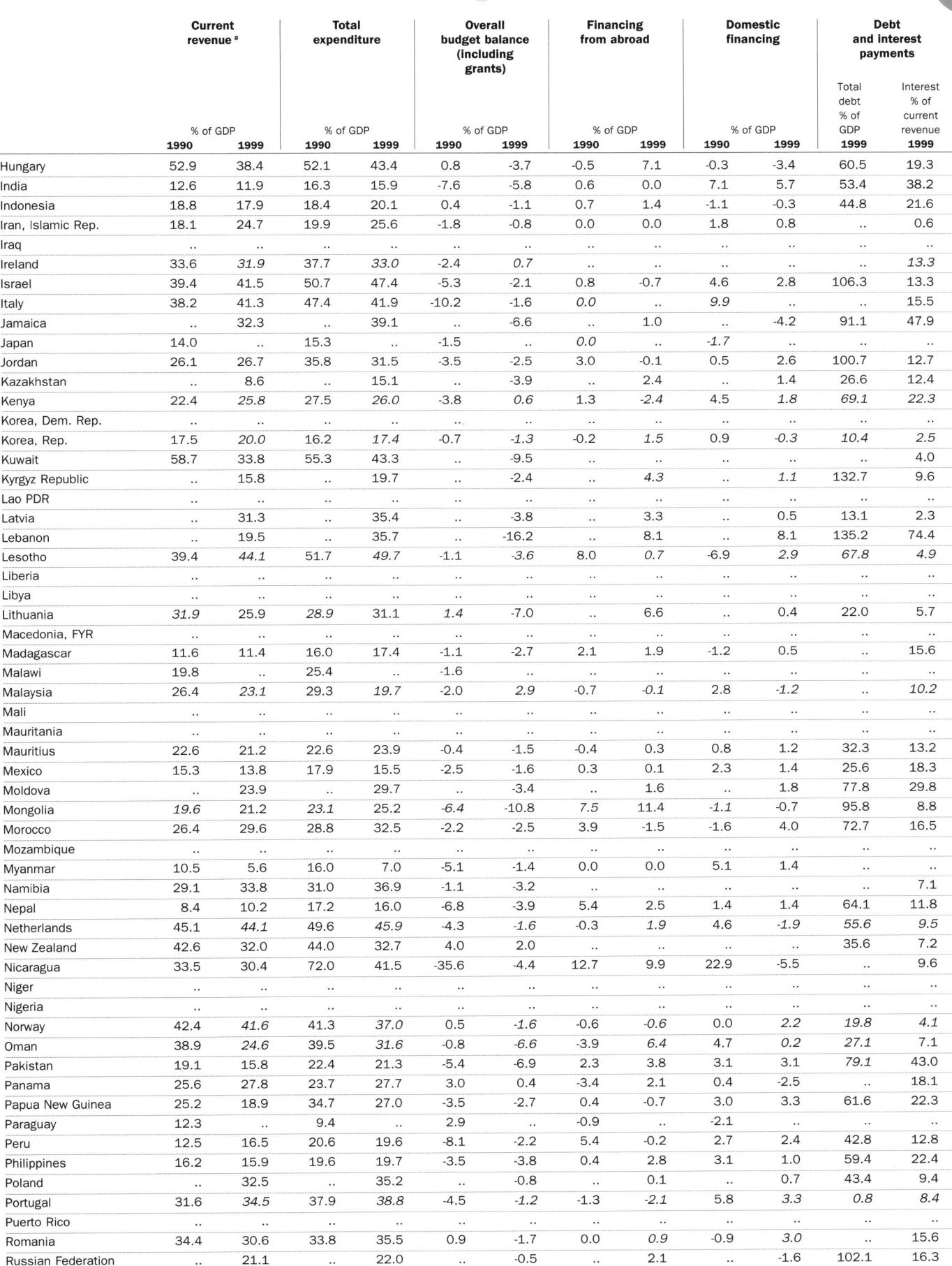
	Current revenue [a]		Total expenditure		Overall budget balance (including grants)		Financing from abroad		Domestic financing		Debt and interest payments	
	% of GDP		% of GDP		% of GDP		% of GDP		% of GDP		Total debt % of GDP	Interest % of current revenue
	1990	1999	1990	1999	1990	1999	1990	1999	1990	1999	1999	1999
Hungary	52.9	38.4	52.1	43.4	0.8	-3.7	-0.5	7.1	-0.3	-3.4	60.5	19.3
India	12.6	11.9	16.3	15.9	-7.6	-5.8	0.6	0.0	7.1	5.7	53.4	38.2
Indonesia	18.8	17.9	18.4	20.1	0.4	-1.1	0.7	1.4	-1.1	-0.3	44.8	21.6
Iran, Islamic Rep.	18.1	24.7	19.9	25.6	-1.8	-0.8	0.0	0.0	1.8	0.8	..	0.6
Iraq	..	..	..	..	..	..	..	..	..	..	..	..
Ireland	33.6	_31.9_	37.7	_33.0_	-2.4	_0.7_	..	..	..	..	..	_13.3_
Israel	39.4	41.5	50.7	47.4	-5.3	-2.1	0.8	-0.7	4.6	2.8	106.3	13.3
Italy	38.2	41.3	47.4	41.9	-10.2	-1.6	_0.0_	..	9.9	..	..	15.5
Jamaica	..	32.3	..	39.1	..	-6.6	..	1.0	..	-4.2	91.1	47.9
Japan	14.0	..	15.3	..	-1.5	..	_0.0_	..	-1.7	..	..	..
Jordan	26.1	26.7	35.8	31.5	-3.5	-2.5	3.0	-0.1	0.5	2.6	100.7	12.7
Kazakhstan	..	8.6	..	15.1	..	-3.9	..	2.4	..	1.4	26.6	12.4
Kenya	22.4	_25.8_	27.5	_26.0_	-3.8	_0.6_	1.3	_-2.4_	4.5	_1.8_	_69.1_	_22.3_
Korea, Dem. Rep.	..	..	..	..	..	..	..	..	..	..	..	..
Korea, Rep.	17.5	_20.0_	16.2	_17.4_	-0.7	_-1.3_	-0.2	_1.5_	0.9	_-0.3_	_10.4_	_2.5_
Kuwait	58.7	33.8	55.3	43.3	..	-9.5	..	..	..	..	..	4.0
Kyrgyz Republic	..	15.8	..	19.7	..	-2.4	..	_4.3_	..	_1.1_	132.7	9.6
Lao PDR	..	..	..	..	..	..	..	..	..	..	..	..
Latvia	..	31.3	..	35.4	..	-3.8	..	3.3	..	0.5	13.1	2.3
Lebanon	..	19.5	..	35.7	..	-16.2	..	8.1	..	8.1	135.2	74.4
Lesotho	39.4	_44.1_	51.7	_49.7_	-1.1	_-3.6_	8.0	_0.7_	-6.9	_2.9_	_67.8_	_4.9_
Liberia	..	..	..	..	..	..	..	..	..	..	..	..
Libya	..	..	..	..	..	..	..	..	..	..	..	..
Lithuania	_31.9_	25.9	_28.9_	31.1	_1.4_	-7.0	..	6.6	..	0.4	22.0	5.7
Macedonia, FYR	..	..	..	..	..	..	..	..	..	..	..	..
Madagascar	11.6	11.4	16.0	17.4	-1.1	-2.7	2.1	1.9	-1.2	0.5	..	15.6
Malawi	19.8	..	25.4	..	-1.6	..	..	..	..	..	..	..
Malaysia	26.4	_23.1_	29.3	_19.7_	-2.0	_2.9_	-0.7	_-0.1_	2.8	_-1.2_	..	_10.2_
Mali	..	..	..	..	..	..	..	..	..	..	..	..
Mauritania	..	..	..	..	..	..	..	..	..	..	..	..
Mauritius	22.6	21.2	22.6	23.9	-0.4	-1.5	-0.4	0.3	0.8	1.2	32.3	13.2
Mexico	15.3	13.8	17.9	15.5	-2.5	-1.6	0.3	0.1	2.3	1.4	25.6	18.3
Moldova	..	23.9	..	29.7	..	-3.4	..	1.6	..	1.8	77.8	29.8
Mongolia	_19.6_	21.2	_23.1_	25.2	_-6.4_	-10.8	_7.5_	11.4	_-1.1_	-0.7	95.8	8.8
Morocco	26.4	29.6	28.8	32.5	-2.2	-2.5	3.9	-1.5	-1.6	4.0	72.7	16.5
Mozambique	..	..	..	..	..	..	..	..	..	..	..	..
Myanmar	10.5	5.6	16.0	7.0	-5.1	-1.4	0.0	0.0	5.1	1.4	..	..
Namibia	29.1	33.8	31.0	36.9	-1.1	-3.2	..	..	..	..	..	7.1
Nepal	8.4	10.2	17.2	16.0	-6.8	-3.9	5.4	2.5	1.4	1.4	64.1	11.8
Netherlands	45.1	_44.1_	49.6	_45.9_	-4.3	_-1.6_	-0.3	_1.9_	4.6	_-1.9_	_55.6_	_9.5_
New Zealand	42.6	32.0	44.0	32.7	4.0	2.0	..	..	..	..	35.6	7.2
Nicaragua	33.5	30.4	72.0	41.5	-35.6	-4.4	12.7	9.9	22.9	-5.5	..	9.6
Niger	..	..	..	..	..	..	..	..	..	..	..	..
Nigeria	..	..	..	..	..	..	..	..	..	..	..	..
Norway	42.4	_41.6_	41.3	_37.0_	0.5	_-1.6_	-0.6	_-0.6_	0.0	_2.2_	_19.8_	_4.1_
Oman	38.9	_24.6_	39.5	_31.6_	-0.8	_-6.6_	-3.9	_6.4_	4.7	_0.2_	_27.1_	_7.1_
Pakistan	19.1	15.8	22.4	21.3	-5.4	-6.9	2.3	3.8	3.1	3.1	_79.1_	43.0
Panama	25.6	27.8	23.7	27.7	3.0	0.4	-3.4	2.1	0.4	-2.5	..	18.1
Papua New Guinea	25.2	18.9	34.7	27.0	-3.5	-2.7	0.4	-0.7	3.0	3.3	61.6	22.3
Paraguay	12.3	..	9.4	..	2.9	..	-0.9	..	-2.1	..	..	..
Peru	12.5	16.5	20.6	19.6	-8.1	-2.2	5.4	-0.2	2.7	2.4	42.8	12.8
Philippines	16.2	15.9	19.6	19.7	-3.5	-3.8	0.4	2.8	3.1	1.0	59.4	22.4
Poland	..	32.5	..	35.2	..	-0.8	..	0.1	..	0.7	43.4	9.4
Portugal	31.6	_34.5_	37.9	_38.8_	-4.5	_-1.2_	-1.3	_-2.1_	5.8	_3.3_	_0.8_	_8.4_
Puerto Rico	..	..	..	..	..	..	..	..	..	..	..	..
Romania	34.4	30.6	33.8	35.5	0.9	-1.7	0.0	_0.9_	-0.9	_3.0_	..	15.6
Russian Federation	..	21.1	..	22.0	..	-0.5	..	2.1	..	-1.6	102.1	16.3

	Current revenue [a]		Total expenditure		Overall budget balance (including grants)		Financing from abroad		Domestic financing		Debt and interest payments	
	% of GDP		% of GDP		% of GDP		% of GDP		% of GDP		Total debt % of GDP	Interest % of current revenue
	1990	1999	1990	1999	1990	1999	1990	1999	1990	1999	1999	1999
Rwanda	10.8	..	18.9	..	-5.3	..	2.5	..	2.8	..	..	..
Saudi Arabia	..	..	..	..	..	..	..	..	..	..	..	..
Senegal	..	..	..	..	..	..	..	..	..	..	..	..
Sierra Leone	4.0	7.1	6.0	20.9	-1.8	-8.5	0.4	1.1	1.4	7.4	247.4	81.8
Singapore	26.9	27.1	21.4	18.5	10.8	7.0	-0.1	0.0	-10.7	-7.0	90.4	2.2
Slovak Republic	..	36.8	..	37.2	..	-3.3	..	3.5	..	-0.3	28.8	8.5
Slovenia	39.8	39.7	38.6	40.5	0.3	-0.7	0.1	1.7	-0.4	-0.9	24.5	3.5
Somalia	..	..	..	..	..	..	..	..	..	..	..	..
South Africa	26.3	28.2	30.1	30.6	-4.1	-2.0	0.0	1.3	4.1	0.7	49.1	19.7
Spain	29.1	28.7	32.4	32.8	-3.1	-2.9	0.7	1.7	2.4	1.1	55.4	14.1
Sri Lanka	21.0	17.7	28.4	24.2	-7.8	-6.9	3.6	0.1	4.2	6.8	95.1	31.7
Sudan	..	8.5	..	9.0	..	-1.0	..	0.2	..	0.8	9.2	9.4
Swaziland	34.2	31.0	26.7	34.2	0.0	-1.6	-0.3	-1.2	0.2	2.8	26.3	2.7
Sweden	42.6	39.6	39.3	39.5	1.0	0.1	-0.3	-5.6	-0.7	5.4	..	11.4
Switzerland	20.8	24.0	23.3	27.6	-0.9	0.3	0.0	0.0	0.9	-0.3	26.3	4.0
Syrian Arab Republic	21.9	22.8	21.8	23.5	0.3	-0.7	..	1.7	..	-1.0	..	..
Tajikistan	..	10.2	..	12.4	..	-0.8	..	2.4	..	-1.7	..	4.3
Tanzania	..	..	..	..	..	..	..	..	..	..	..	..
Thailand	18.5	16.0	14.1	25.1	4.6	-10.4	-1.5	1.2	-3.1	9.3	20.8	6.1
Togo	..	..	..	..	..	..	..	..	..	..	..	..
Trinidad and Tobago	..	..	..	..	..	..	..	..	..	..	..	..
Tunisia	30.7	28.8	34.6	31.6	-5.4	-2.3	1.8	1.4	3.6	0.9	60.9	11.7
Turkey	13.7	25.5	17.4	38.1	-3.0	-13.0	0.0	1.2	3.0	11.9	53.5	54.2
Turkmenistan	..	..	..	..	..	..	..	..	..	..	..	..
Uganda	..	11.2	..	16.6	..	-0.6	..	..	..	..	52.4	..
Ukraine	..	23.3	..	26.0	..	-2.1	..	-0.1	..	2.2	9.4	9.9
United Arab Emirates	1.6	3.5	11.5	11.2	0.4	-0.3	0.0	0.0	-0.4	0.3	..	0.0
United Kingdom	36.1	36.4	37.5	36.4	0.6	0.0	0.2	-0.4	-0.8	0.3	49.8	7.7
United States	18.9	20.6	22.7	19.3	-3.8	1.3	0.2	0.7	3.6	-2.0	39.3	12.7
Uruguay	23.8	27.7	23.3	32.1	0.3	-3.7	1.4	2.6	-1.7	1.2	..	7.2
Uzbekistan	..	..	..	..	..	..	..	..	..	..	..	..
Venezuela, RB	23.7	17.2	20.7	19.4	0.0	-2.4	1.0	-1.0	-1.0	3.4	..	15.4
Vietnam	..	18.8	..	21.2	..	-1.6	..	1.2	..	0.4	..	3.1
West Bank and Gaza	..	..	..	..	..	..	..	..	..	..	..	..
Yemen, Rep.	18.9	24.5	27.8	27.4	-8.8	-3.6	3.2	1.3	5.6	2.2	..	9.8
Yugoslavia, Fed. Rep.	..	..	..	..	..	..	..	..	..	..	..	..
Zambia	..	..	..	..	..	..	..	..	..	..	..	..
Zimbabwe	24.1	29.4	27.3	35.7	-5.3	-5.0	0.9	-0.1	4.4	5.1	58.1	24.2
World	22.5 w	24.2 w	25.5 w	25.2 w	-2.8 w	-1.0 w	0.6 m	0.4 m	1.0 m	0.5 m	.. m	11.5 m
Low income	15.4	15.0	18.3	18.4	-4.8	-3.8	..	..	..	..	..	..
Middle income	17.4	18.8	21.5	22.1	-2.5	-4.3	0.3	1.2	0.4	0.9	42.8	12.6
Lower middle income	12.6	14.9	15.0	18.5	-1.3	-3.1	..	0.9	..	1.2	52.8	12.0
Upper middle income	19.9	22.6	25.0	25.2	-3.1	-4.9	0.0	1.3	0.8	0.7	29.2	14.3
Low & middle income	17.1	18.1	21.1	21.4	-2.8	-4.3	..	1.3	..	0.9	..	12.8
East Asia & Pacific	13.2	10.8	14.4	15.0	-0.8	-3.7	0.2	1.2	2.0	1.2	55.7	9.9
Europe & Central Asia	..	25.9	..	30.1	..	-3.5	..	2.1	..	0.6	43.4	9.5
Latin America & Carib.	18.8	20.0	25.6	21.9	-3.5	-4.8	0.3	1.4	-1.3	0.8	..	12.8
Middle East & N. Africa	..	..	..	..	..	..	1.8	2.0	3.6	1.9	..	12.2
South Asia	13.8	12.5	17.6	16.7	-7.3	-5.7	3.0	0.1	3.6	3.1	58.7	31.7
Sub-Saharan Africa	24.0	23.8	27.7	26.9	-3.5	-2.3	..	..	..	..	..	..
High income	23.7	28.0	26.5	29.5	-2.8	-1.0	0.2	0.0	1.0	0.0	42.7	7.5
Europe EMU	33.1	35.2	36.6	38.1	-3.9	-2.3	0.6	1.0	3.1	0.7	55.6	9.3

a. Excluding grants.

About the data

Tables 4.11–4.13 present an overview of the size and role of central governments relative to national economies. The International Monetary Fund's (IMF) *Manual on Government Finance Statistics* describes the government as the sector of the economy responsible for "implementation of public policy through the provision of primarily nonmarket services and the transfer of income, supported mainly by compulsory levies on other sectors" (1986, p. 3). The definition of government generally excludes nonfinancial public enterprises and public financial institutions (such as the central bank).

Units of government meeting this definition exist at many levels, from local administrative units to the highest level of national government. Inadequate statistical coverage precludes the presentation of subnational data, however, making cross-country comparisons potentially misleading.

Central government can refer to one of two accounting concepts: consolidated or budgetary. For most countries, central government finance data have been consolidated into one account, but for others only budgetary central government accounts are available. Countries reporting budgetary data are noted in *Primary data documentation*. Because budgetary accounts do not necessarily include all central government units, the picture they provide of central government activities is usually incomplete. A key issue is the failure to include the quasi-fiscal operations of the central bank. Central bank losses arising from monetary operations and subsidized financing can result in sizable quasi-fiscal deficits. Such deficits may also result from the operations of other financial intermediaries, such as public development finance institutions. Also missing from the data are governments' contingent liabilities for unfunded pension and national insurance plans.

Data on government revenues and expenditures are collected by the IMF through questionnaires distributed to member governments and by the Organisation for Economic Co-operation and Development. Despite the IMF's efforts to systematize and standardize the collection of public finance data, statistics on public finance are often incomplete, untimely, and not comparable across countries.

Government finance statistics are reported in local currency. The indicators here are shown as percentages of GDP. Many countries report government finance data according to fiscal years; see *Primary data documentation* for the timing of these years. For further discussion of government finance statistics, see *About the data* for tables 4.12 and 4.13.

Definitions

• **Current revenue** includes all revenue from taxes and current nontax revenues (other than grants) such as fines, fees, recoveries, and income from property or sales. • **Total expenditure** includes nonrepayable current and capital expenditures. It does not include government lending or repayments to the government or government acquisition of equity for public policy purposes. • **Overall budget balance** is current and capital revenue and official grants received, less total expenditure and lending minus repayments. • **Financing from abroad** (obtained from nonresidents) and **domestic financing** (obtained from residents) refer to the means by which a government provides financial resources to cover a budget deficit or allocates financial resources arising from a budget surplus. The data include all government liabilities—other than those for currency issues or demand, time, or savings deposits with government—or claims on others held by government, and changes in government holdings of cash and deposits. They exclude government guarantees of the debt of others. • **Debt** is the entire stock of direct government, fixed term contractual obligations to others outstanding on a particular date. It includes domestic debt (such as debt held by monetary authorities, deposit money banks, nonfinancial public enterprises, and households) and foreign debt (such as debt to international development institutions and foreign governments). It is the gross amount of government liabilities not reduced by the amount of government claims against others. Because debt is a stock rather than a flow, it is measured as of a given date, usually the last day of the fiscal year. • **Interest payments** include interest payments on government debt—including long-term bonds, long-term loans, and other debt instruments—to both domestic and foreign residents.

Data sources

The data on central government finances are from the IMF's *Government Finance Statistics Yearbook, 2001* and IMF data files. Each country's accounts are reported using the system of common definitions and classifications in the IMF's *Manual on Government Finance Statistics* (1986). See these sources for complete and authoritative explanations of concepts, definitions, and data sources.

Figure 4.11

Some developing countries are spending a large proportion of their current revenue on interest payments

Central government interest payments as % of current revenue

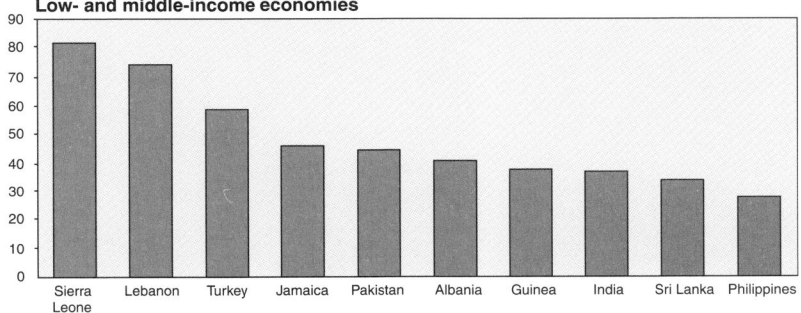

Low- and middle-income economies

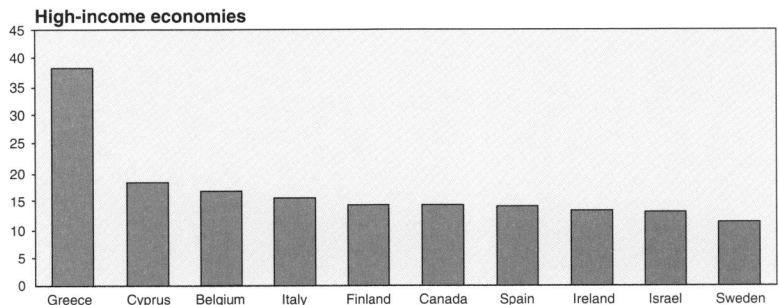

High-income economies

Note: Data refer to the most recent year available in 1998-2000 for low- and middle-income economies and in 1997-2000 for high-income economies.

Source: International Monetary Fund, Government Finance Statistics data files.

With the exception of Greece, governments of high-income economies spend less than 20 percent of their current revenue on interest payments.

4.12 | Central government expenditures

	Goods and services		Wages and salaries[a]		Interest payments		Subsidies and other current transfers		Capital expenditure	
	% of total expenditure		% of total expenditure		% of total expenditure		% of total expenditure		% of total expenditure	
	1990	1999	1990	1999	1990	1999	1990	1999	1990	1999
Afghanistan	..	..	..	..	..	..	..	..	..	..
Albania	..	17	..	9	..	26	..	42	..	16
Algeria	..	35	..	24	..	13	..	32	..	19
Angola	..	..	..	..	..	..	..	..	..	..
Argentina	30	20	23	15	8	17	57	57	5	6
Armenia	..	..	..	..	..	..	..	..	..	..
Australia	27	27	2	3	8	5	56	61	9	5
Austria	25	25	10	10	9	8	57	61	9	5
Azerbaijan	..	31	..	11	..	2	..	50	..	17
Bangladesh	..	27	..	18	..	11	..	25	..	23
Belarus	37	21	2	8	2	2	46	54	16	23
Belgium	19	19	14	13	21	16	56	60	5	5
Benin	..	..	..	..	..	..	..	..	..	..
Bolivia	63	38	36	23	6	6	16	41	15	16
Bosnia and Herzegovina	..	..	..	..	..	..	..	..	..	..
Botswana	51	..	23	..	2	..	25	..	21	..
Brazil	16	22	9	12	78	14	39	62	2	2
Bulgaria	35	33	3	8	10	11	52	45	3	11
Burkina Faso	60	..	51	..	6	..	11	..	23	..
Burundi	34	50	22	30	5	9	10	11	51	23
Cambodia	..	..	..	..	..	..	..	..	..	..
Cameroon	51	52	39	32	5	19	13	15	26	14
Canada	21	18	9	8	20	16	57	65	2	2
Central African Republic	..	..	..	..	..	..	..	..	..	..
Chad	41	..	28	..	2	..	3	..	56	..
Chile	28	28	18	20	10	1	51	54	11	16
China	..	..	..	..	..	..	..	..	..	..
Hong Kong, China	..	..	..	..	..	..	..	..	..	..
Colombia	26	19	18	14	10	18	42	41	22	22
Congo, Dem. Rep.	73	78	23	49	7	3	4	18	16	2
Congo, Rep.	56	39	49	21	22	35	20	7	2	19
Costa Rica	57	47	43	36	12	17	20	26	11	10
Côte d'Ivoire	69	45	38	27	1	19	30	9	0	26
Croatia	54	45	22	24	0	3	42	41	3	11
Cuba	..	..	..	..	..	..	..	..	..	..
Czech Republic	..	14	..	8	..	3	..	74	..	9
Denmark	20	21	12	12	15	12	61	64	3	3
Dominican Republic	39	47	29	35	4	4	13	19	44	27
Ecuador	42	..	38	..	23	..	16	..	18	..
Egypt, Arab Rep.	42	41	23	20	14	20	26	15	17	24
El Salvador	..	78	..	47	..	8	..	3	..	18
Eritrea	..	..	..	..	..	..	..	..	..	..
Estonia	25	44	8	13	0	1	73	47	8	8
Ethiopia	77	..	40	..	5	..	9	..	16	..
Finland	20	18	10	7	3	14	70	63	7	5
France	26	24	17	16	5	7	63	65	6	4
Gabon	63	..	37	..	0	..	6	..	32	..
Gambia, The	41	..	21	..	16	..	9	..	34	..
Georgia	..	42	..	11	..	18	..	36	..	4
Germany	32	31	8	8	5	7	58	57	5	4
Ghana	50	..	32	..	11	..	20	..	19	..
Greece	31	34	21	28	20	29	41	20	8	17
Guatemala	..	..	..	..	..	..	..	..	..	..
Guinea	37	29	18	19	7	21	4	8	53	36
Guinea-Bissau	..	..	..	..	..	..	..	..	..	..
Haiti	..	67	..	37	..	7	..	7	..	19
Honduras	..	..	..	..	..	..	..	..	..	..

	Goods and services		Wages and salaries[a]		Interest payments		Subsidies and other current transfers		Capital expenditure	
	% of total expenditure		% of total expenditure		% of total expenditure		% of total expenditure		% of total expenditure	
	1990	1999	1990	1999	1990	1999	1990	1999	1990	1999
Hungary	27	16	6	8	6	17	64	58	4	8
India	24	23	11	11	22	29	43	39	11	9
Indonesia	23	18	16	9	13	19	21	39	43	24
Iran, Islamic Rep.	53	64	40	50	0	1	22	10	25	26
Iraq	..	..	..	..	..	..	..	..	..	..
Ireland	19	*18*	14	*13*	21	*13*	54	*61*	7	*9*
Israel	38	33	14	15	18	12	37	49	6	6
Italy	17	20	13	16	21	15	54	59	8	6
Jamaica	..	52	..	30	..	40	..	1	..	8
Japan	14	..	..	..	19	..	54	..	13	..
Jordan	55	65	44	47	18	11	11	8	16	16
Kazakhstan	..	30	..	10	..	7	..	55	..	8
Kenya	51	..	31	..	19	*22*	10	..	20	*7*
Korea, Dem. Rep.	..	..	..	..	..	..	..	..	..	..
Korea, Rep.	35	*27*	13	*13*	4	*3*	46	*49*	15	*22*
Kuwait	62	58	31	35	0	3	20	26	18	13
Kyrgyz Republic	..	69	..	26	..	8	..	13	..	10
Lao PDR	..	..	..	..	..	..	..	..	..	..
Latvia	..	25	..	12	..	2	..	65	..	8
Lebanon	..	30	..	23	..	41	..	12	..	17
Lesotho	40	*76*	22	*35*	11	*4*	5	*0*	45	*19*
Liberia	..	..	..	..	..	..	..	..	..	..
Libya	..	..	..	..	..	..	..	..	..	..
Lithuania	*12*	45	*6*	15	..	5	*67*	35	*20*	16
Macedonia, FYR	..	..	..	..	..	..	..	..	..	..
Madagascar	37	34	25	23	9	10	9	7	43	38
Malawi	54	..	23	..	14	..	8	..	24	..
Malaysia	41	*42*	26	*26*	20	*12*	16	*24*	24	*23*
Mali	..	..	..	..	..	..	..	..	..	..
Mauritania	..	..	..	..	..	..	..	..	..	..
Mauritius	47	46	37	35	15	12	22	29	17	14
Mexico	25	24	18	17	45	16	17	49	14	11
Moldova	..	16	..	7	..	24	..	54	..	6
Mongolia	*30*	33	*7*	11	*1*	7	*56*	47	*13*	13
Morocco	48	46	35	36	16	15	8	16	28	22
Mozambique	..	..	..	..	..	..	..	..	..	..
Myanmar	..	..	..	..	..	..	..	..	29	47
Namibia	73	66	46	46	1	7	10	15	15	12
Nepal	..	..	..	..	..	7	..	..	..	..
Netherlands	15	*15*	9	*9*	9	*9*	70	*72*	6	*3*
New Zealand	19	52	12	..	15	7	64	38	2	3
Nicaragua	43	32	23	16	0	7	14	20	4	42
Niger	..	..	..	..	..	..	..	..	..	..
Nigeria	..	..	..	..	..	..	..	..	..	..
Norway	19	*21*	8	*8*	6	*5*	69	*70*	5	*5*
Oman	76	76	22	30	6	5	7	6	11	12
Pakistan	44	49	..	4	25	32	20	8	12	11
Panama	64	50	49	36	8	18	26	24	2	8
Papua New Guinea	61	51	34	30	11	16	18	27	11	7
Paraguay	54	..	36	..	10	..	19	..	17	..
Peru	30	37	17	18	37	11	25	35	8	17
Philippines	44	53	29	28	34	18	7	19	16	10
Poland	..	15	..	8	..	9	..	72	..	4
Portugal	38	*41*	27	*32*	18	*7*	33	*38*	12	*13*
Puerto Rico	..	..	..	..	..	..	..	..	..	..
Romania	26	35	12	14	0	13	57	44	17	8
Russian Federation	..	33	..	12	..	16	..	45	..	7

	Goods and services		Wages and salaries[a]		Interest payments		Subsidies and other current transfers		Capital expenditure	
	% of total expenditure		% of total expenditure		% of total expenditure		% of total expenditure		% of total expenditure	
	1990	1999	1990	1999	1990	1999	1990	1999	1990	1999
Rwanda	53	..	29	..	5	..	16	..	33	..
Saudi Arabia	..	..	..	..	..	..	..	..	..	..
Senegal	..	..	..	..	..	..	..	..	..	..
Sierra Leone	77	60	35	46	18	28	1	6	8	11
Singapore	51	56	27	27	14	3	12	9	24	32
Slovak Republic	..	23	..	13	..	8	..	59	..	9
Slovenia	40	39	20	22	1	3	52	50	7	8
Somalia	..	..	..	..	..	..	..	..	..	..
South Africa	53	25	23	16	14	18	23	52	10	5
Spain	19	16	13	11	9	12	63	68	9	4
Sri Lanka	33	37	17	22	23	23	23	18	21	23
Sudan	..	74	..	34	..	9	..	7	..	10
Swaziland	62	59	42	34	3	2	11	17	24	22
Sweden	15	18	6	6	11	11	72	69	2	2
Switzerland	31	29	5	5	3	3	61	63	5	5
Syrian Arab Republic	..	..	..	..	..	..	..	..	27	38
Tajikistan	..	51	..	6	..	4	..	26	..	19
Tanzania	..	..	..	..	..	..	..	..	..	..
Thailand	60	41	35	25	13	4	9	7	18	49
Togo	..	..	..	..	..	..	..	..	..	..
Trinidad and Tobago	..	..	..	..	..	..	..	..	..	..
Tunisia	34	40	28	35	10	11	35	28	22	22
Turkey	52	32	38	24	18	36	16	25	13	7
Turkmenistan	..	..	..	..	..	..	..	..	..	..
Uganda	..	..	..	..	..	..	..	..	..	41
Ukraine	..	24	..	11	..	9	..	61	..	6
United Arab Emirates	88	78	33	35	0	0	10	18	1	4
United Kingdom	30	29	13	6	9	8	52	59	10	4
United States	28	21	10	8	15	14	49	61	8	5
Uruguay	35	34	20	16	8	6	50	54	7	6
Uzbekistan	..	..	..	..	..	..	..	..	..	..
Venezuela, RB	31	24	23	19	16	14	37	47	16	16
Vietnam	..	..	..	..	..	3	..	..	..	35
West Bank and Gaza	..	..	..	..	..	..	..	..	..	..
Yemen, Rep.	64	54	55	39	8	9	6	18	33	17
Yugoslavia, Fed. Rep.	..	..	..	..	..	..	..	..	..	..
Zambia	..	..	..	..	..	..	..	..	..	..
Zimbabwe	56	48	37	36	16	20	18	26	10	6
World	39 m	35 m	23 m	18 m	10 m	10 m	23 m	35 m	13 m	11 m
Low income	..	..	..	..	..	..	..	..	..	..
Middle income	42	37	25	22	10	11	23	35	16	12
Lower middle income	45	40	28	24	10	11	20	27	17	16
Upper middle income	38	29	23	18	11	13	26	48	11	9
Low & middle income	..	37	..	21	..	11	..	27	..	14
East Asia & Pacific	41	..	27	..	10	10	19	24	18	24
Europe & Central Asia	..	32	..	11	..	8	..	48	..	8
Latin America & Carib.	35	37	23	20	10	11	25	35	11	16
Middle East & N. Africa	53	50	35	35	10	11	11	14	23	18
South Asia	33	32	..	14	23	23	23	21	12	17
Sub-Saharan Africa	53	..	31	..	7	..	10	..	20	..
High income	25	29	13	11	11	7	56	59	7	5
Europe EMU	23	30	13	10	9	9	57	58	7	5

Note: Components include expenditures financed by grants in kind and other cash adjustments to total expenditure.

a. Part of goods and services.

About the data

Government expenditures include all non-repayable payments, whether current or capital, requited or unrequited. Total central government expenditure as presented in the International Monetary Fund's (IMF) *Government Finance Statistics Yearbook* is a more limited measure of general government consumption than that shown in the national accounts (see table 4.10) because it excludes consumption expenditures by state and local governments. At the same time, the IMF's concept of central government expenditure is broader than the national accounts definition because it includes government gross capital formation and transfer payments.

Expenditures can be measured either by function (education, health, defense) or by economic type (wages and salaries, interest payments, purchases of goods and services). Functional data are often incomplete, and coverage varies by country because functional responsibilities stretch across levels of government for which

no data are available. Defense expenditures, which are usually the central government's responsibility, are shown in table 5.7. For more information on education expenditures see table 2.11; for more on health expenditures see table 2.15.

The classification of expenditures by economic type can also be problematic. For example, the distinction between current and capital expenditure may be arbitrary, and subsidies to state-owned enterprises or banks may be disguised as capital financing. Subsidies may also be hidden in special contractual pricing for goods and services.

Expenditure shares may not sum to 100 percent because expenditures financed by grants in kind and other cash adjustments (which may be positive or negative) are not shown.

For further discussion of government finance statistics see *About the data* for tables 4.11 and 4.13.

Definitions

• **Total expenditure of the central government** includes both current and capital (development) expenditures and excludes lending minus repayments. • **Goods and services** include all government payments in exchange for goods and services, whether in the form of wages and salaries to employees or other purchases of goods and services. • **Wages and salaries** consist of all payments in cash, but not in kind (such as food rations and housing) to employees in return for services rendered, before deduction of withholding taxes and employee contributions to social security and pension funds. • **Interest payments** are payments made to domestic sectors and to nonresidents for the use of borrowed money. (Repayment of principal is shown as a financing item, and commission charges are shown as purchases of services.) Interest payments do not include payments by government as guarantor or surety of interest on the defaulted debts of others, which are classified as government lending. • **Subsidies and other current transfers** include all unrequited, nonrepayable transfers on current account to private and public enterprises, and the cost to the public of covering the cash operating deficits on sales to the public by departmental enterprises. • **Capital expenditure** is spending to acquire fixed capital assets, land, intangible assets, government stocks, and nonmilitary, nonfinancial assets. Also included are capital grants.

Data sources

The data on central government expenditures are from the IMF's *Government Finance Statistics Yearbook, 2001* and IMF data files. Each country's accounts are reported using the system of common definitions and classifications in the IMF's *Manual on Government Finance Statistics* (1986). See these sources for complete and authoritative explanations of concepts, definitions, and data sources.

Figure 4.12

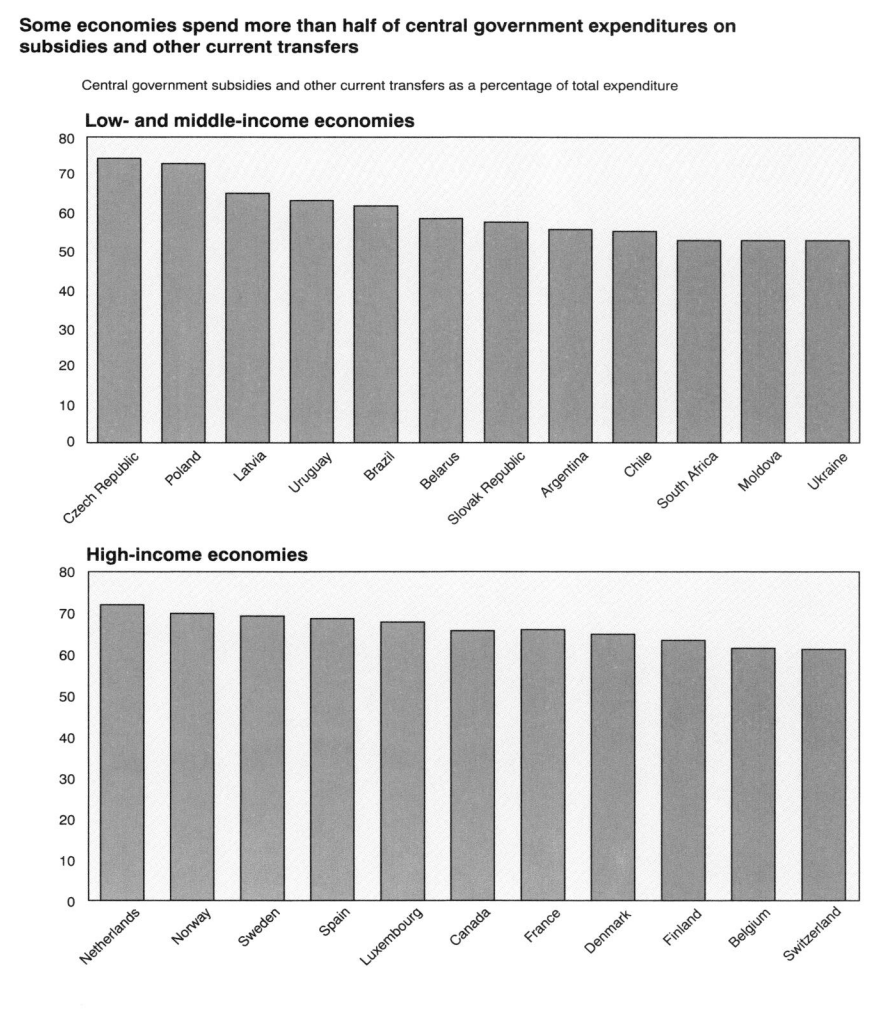

Some economies spend more than half of central government expenditures on subsidies and other current transfers

Central government subsidies and other current transfers as a percentage of total expenditure

Low- and middle-income economies

(Czech Republic, Poland, Latvia, Uruguay, Brazil, Belarus, Slovak Republic, Argentina, Chile, South Africa, Moldova, Ukraine)

High-income economies

(Netherlands, Norway, Sweden, Spain, Luxembourg, Canada, France, Denmark, Finland, Belgium, Switzerland)

Note: For developing economes data refer to the most recent year available in 1998-2000, and for high-income economies in 1997-2000.

Source: International Monetary Fund, Government Finance Statistics data files.

4.13 | Central government revenues

	Taxes on income, profits, and capital gains		Social security taxes		Taxes on goods and services		Taxes on international trade		Other taxes		Nontax revenue	
	% of total current revenue		% of total current revenue		% of total current revenue		% of total current revenue		% of total current revenue		% of total current revenue	
	1990	1999	1990	1999	1990	1999	1990	1999	1990	1999	1990	1999
Afghanistan	..	..	..	..	..	..	..	..	..	..	..	..
Albania	..	7	..	14	..	40	..	15	..	1	..	23
Algeria	..	67	..	0	..	10	..	14	..	1	..	8
Angola	..	..	..	..	..	..	..	..	..	..	..	..
Argentina	2	16	44	24	20	42	14	6	10	1	10	11
Armenia	..	..	..	..	..	..	..	..	..	..	..	..
Australia	65	68	0	0	21	21	4	3	2	2	8	8
Austria	19	25	37	40	25	25	1	0	9	4	9	6
Azerbaijan	..	22	..	22	..	40	..	9	..	2	..	5
Bangladesh	..	11	..	0	..	40	..	23	..	1	..	25
Belarus	12	11	32	34	40	38	5	7	9	3	2	8
Belgium	35	37	35	33	24	25	0	0	3	3	3	2
Benin	..	..	..	..	..	..	..	..	..	..	..	..
Bolivia	5	9	9	12	31	44	7	6	11	13	38	16
Bosnia and Herzegovina	..	..	..	..	..	..	..	..	..	..	..	..
Botswana	39	..	0	..	2	..	13	..	0	..	46	..
Brazil	20	20	31	34	24	21	2	3	6	4	16	17
Bulgaria	30	13	23	23	18	33	2	3	1	4	27	23
Burkina Faso	23	..	0	..	30	..	33	..	7	..	8	..
Burundi	21	21	6	7	37	44	24	20	1	1	10	6
Cambodia	..	..	..	..	..	..	..	..	..	..	..	..
Cameroon	18	21	6	0	21	26	14	28	4	4	28	20
Canada	51	54	16	20	17	16	3	1	0	0	13	9
Central African Republic	..	..	..	..	..	..	..	..	..	..	..	..
Chad	19	..	0	..	39	..	24	..	10	..	8	..
Chile	12	17	8	7	43	47	12	7	3	4	21	18
China	31	6	0	0	18	75	14	10	0	4	37	6
Hong Kong, China	..	..	..	..	..	..	..	..	..	..	..	..
Colombia	29	34	0	0	30	39	20	7	1	5	19	14
Congo, Dem. Rep.	27	29	1	0	18	17	46	33	1	9	7	12
Congo, Rep.	26	8	0	0	16	15	21	6	2	1	35	71
Costa Rica	10	15	29	29	27	39	23	6	1	0	14	11
Côte d'Ivoire	16	22	7	6	27	18	29	47	11	4	9	3
Croatia	17	11	52	32	24	43	3	7	0	1	3	5
Cuba	..	..	..	..	..	..	..	..	..	..	..	..
Czech Republic	..	14	..	44	..	36	..	2	..	1	..	3
Denmark	37	38	4	4	41	42	0	0	3	4	15	12
Dominican Republic	21	18	4	4	23	30	40	40	1	2	10	7
Ecuador	62	..	0	..	22	..	13	..	1	..	2	..
Egypt, Arab Rep.	19	22	15	0	14	17	14	13	11	12	27	37
El Salvador	..	23	..	12	..	40	..	8	..	4	..	12
Eritrea	..	..	..	..	..	..	..	..	..	..	..	..
Estonia	27	19	28	34	41	40	1	0	1	0	2	7
Ethiopia	29	..	0	..	25	..	15	..	2	..	30	..
Finland	31	29	9	10	47	44	1	0	3	2	9	13
France	17	20	44	42	28	29	0	0	3	4	7	6
Gabon	24	..	1	..	23	..	18	..	2	..	32	..
Gambia, The	13	..	0	..	37	..	43	..	1	..	6	..
Georgia	..	10	..	17	..	55	..	4	..	0	..	14
Germany	16	15	53	48	24	20	0	0	0	0	6	16
Ghana	23	..	0	..	30	..	39	..	0	..	8	..
Greece	22	39	29	2	43	55	0	0	8	8	8	7
Guatemala	..	..	..	..	..	..	..	..	..	..	..	..
Guinea	9	10	0	1	15	5	47	77	0	4	28	4
Guinea-Bissau	..	..	..	..	..	..	..	..	..	..	..	..
Haiti	..	..	..	..	..	..	..	..	..	..	..	..
Honduras	..	..	..	..	..	..	..	..	..	..	..	..

	Taxes on income, profits, and capital gains		Social security taxes		Taxes on goods and services		Taxes on international trade		Other taxes		Nontax revenue	
	% of total current revenue		% of total current revenue		% of total current revenue		% of total current revenue		% of total current revenue		% of total current revenue	
	1990	1999	1990	1999	1990	1999	1990	1999	1990	1999	1990	1999
Hungary	18	19	29	30	31	33	6	3	0	2	16	12
India	15	25	0	0	36	28	29	21	0	0	20	26
Indonesia	62	59	0	2	24	28	6	3	3	0	5	8
Iran, Islamic Rep.	10	15	8	8	4	16	13	25	4	1	60	34
Iraq	..	..	..	..	..	..	..	..	..	..	..	..
Ireland	37	42	15	13	38	37	0	0	3	4	7	4
Israel	36	36	9	14	33	31	2	1	4	4	14	14
Italy	37	36	29	30	29	24	0	0	2	3	3	7
Jamaica	..	27	..	0	..	30	..	7	..	7	..	28
Japan	69	..	0	..	17	..	1	..	7	..	5	..
Jordan	16	10	0	0	21	30	27	20	7	8	29	32
Kazakhstan	..	16	..	2	..	63	..	7	..	3	..	9
Kenya	30	31	0	0	43	37	16	14	1	0	10	18
Korea, Dem. Rep.	..	..	..	..	..	..	..	..	..	..	..	..
Korea, Rep.	34	27	5	9	35	34	12	6	5	10	9	14
Kuwait	1	1	0	6	0	0	2	3	0	0	97	90
Kyrgyz Republic	..	15	..	0	..	58	..	4	..	0	..	23
Lao PDR	..	..	..	..	..	..	..	..	..	..	..	..
Latvia	..	13	..	34	..	40	..	1	..	0	..	12
Lebanon	..	11	..	0	..	20	..	28	..	13	..	28
Lesotho	11	18	0	0	21	12	57	48	0	0	11	22
Liberia	..	..	..	..	..	..	..	..	..	..	..	..
Libya	..	..	..	..	..	..	..	..	..	..	..	..
Lithuania	20	13	28	31	40	49	1	2	3	0	8	5
Macedonia, FYR	..	..	..	..	..	..	..	..	..	..	..	..
Madagascar	13	15	0	0	19	25	48	56	2	1	18	3
Malawi	37	..	0	..	33	..	16	..	1	..	13	..
Malaysia	31	36	1	1	20	26	18	13	3	5	28	18
Mali	..	..	..	..	..	..	..	..	..	..	..	..
Mauritania	..	..	..	..	..	..	..	..	..	..	..	..
Mauritius	14	12	4	5	21	37	46	26	6	6	9	14
Mexico	31	37	13	11	56	58	6	4	2	1	11	11
Moldova	..	5	..	26	..	50	..	8	..	0	..	11
Mongolia	24	7	14	20	31	41	17	5	0	1	15	27
Morocco	24	24	4	5	38	36	18	16	4	3	13	16
Mozambique	..	..	..	..	..	..	..	..	..	..	..	..
Myanmar	18	17	0	0	28	28	14	4	0	0	41	51
Namibia	34	32	0	0	25	27	27	31	1	1	13	8
Nepal	11	17	0	0	36	35	31	27	5	4	17	17
Netherlands	31	25	35	41	22	23	0	0	3	5	9	7
New Zealand	53	61	0	0	27	29	2	2	3	1	15	7
Nicaragua	17	12	9	13	35	58	19	7	8	0	13	9
Niger	..	..	..	..	..	..	..	..	..	..	..	..
Nigeria	..	..	..	..	..	..	..	..	..	..	..	..
Norway	16	21	24	23	34	38	1	1	1	1	24	17
Oman	23	19	0	0	1	2	2	6	1	3	73	71
Pakistan	9	23	0	0	30	29	31	14	0	18	30	17
Panama	17	19	20	18	17	..	12	..	3	4	31	35
Papua New Guinea	37	50	0	0	14	11	25	32	3	4	20	3
Paraguay	9	..	0	..	21	..	20	..	24	..	25	..
Peru	5	21	7	8	50	50	17	10	19	2	7	17
Philippines	28	39	0	0	31	29	25	18	3	5	13	9
Poland	..	19	..	29	..	38	..	3	..	1	..	11
Portugal	23	27	25	25	34	36	2	0	4	2	12	10
Puerto Rico	..	..	..	..	..	..	..	..	..	..	..	..
Romania	19	16	23	34	33	33	1	5	15	1	10	12
Russian Federation	..	10	..	32	..	35	..	9	..	1	..	14

	Taxes on income, profits, and capital gains		Social security taxes		Taxes on goods and services		Taxes on international trade		Other taxes		Nontax revenue	
	% of total current revenue		% of total current revenue		% of total current revenue		% of total current revenue		% of total current revenue		% of total current revenue	
	1990	1999	1990	1999	1990	1999	1990	1999	1990	1999	1990	1999
Rwanda	18	..	7	..	34	..	26	..	4	..	12	..
Saudi Arabia	..	..	..	..	..	..	..	..	..	..	..	..
Senegal	..	..	..	..	..	..	..	..	..	..	..	..
Sierra Leone	31	26	0	0	23	22	40	49	0	0	5	4
Singapore	26	26	0	0	16	17	2	1	14	11	43	45
Slovak Republic	..	21	..	29	..	28	..	4	..	1	..	17
Slovenia	12	13	47	35	27	41	8	3	0	4	5	4
Somalia	..	..	..	..	..	..	..	..	..	..	..	..
South Africa	51	52	2	2	34	33	4	3	2	2	8	8
Spain	32	30	38	39	22	25	2	0	0	0	5	6
Sri Lanka	11	14	0	0	46	52	29	14	5	4	10	15
Sudan	..	15	..	0	..	35	..	29	..	1	..	20
Swaziland	30	27	0	0	11	13	47	48	2	5	10	7
Sweden	18	14	31	33	29	27	1	0	9	15	13	11
Switzerland	15	13	51	51	23	25	1	1	3	3	7	7
Syrian Arab Republic	31	34	0	0	31	17	7	12	7	6	24	31
Tajikistan	..	7	..	17	..	59	..	13	..	2	..	2
Tanzania	..	..	..	..	..	..	..	..	..	..	..	..
Thailand	24	29	0	2	41	45	22	9	4	1	8	13
Togo	..	..	..	..	..	..	..	..	..	..	..	..
Trinidad and Tobago	..	..	..	..	..	..	..	..	..	..	..	..
Tunisia	13	19	13	17	19	37	28	12	5	4	22	10
Turkey	43	38	0	0	32	38	6	1	3	6	15	17
Turkmenistan	..	..	..	..	..	..	..	..	..	..	..	..
Uganda	..	16	..	0	..	64	..	10	..	3	..	6
Ukraine	..	11	..	39	..	37	..	4	..	3	..	6
United Arab Emirates	0	0	2	1	36	51	0	0	0	0	62	48
United Kingdom	39	40	17	17	28	31	0	0	7	7	9	5
United States	52	56	35	32	3	4	2	1	1	1	8	6
Uruguay	7	15	27	27	36	43	10	4	12	6	5	10
Uzbekistan	..	..	..	..	..	..	..	..	..	..	..	..
Venezuela, RB	64	22	4	4	3	30	7	10	0	8	22	26
Vietnam	..	22	..	0	..	35	..	20	..	9	..	14
West Bank and Gaza	..	..	..	..	..	..	..	..	..	..	..	..
Yemen, Rep.	26	18	0	0	10	9	17	10	5	2	43	61
Yugoslavia, Fed. Rep.	..	..	..	..	..	..	..	..	..	..	..	..
Zambia	..	..	..	..	..	..	..	..	..	..	..	..
Zimbabwe	45	43	0	0	26	24	17	20	1	2	10	10
World	23 m	18 m	4 m	6 m	27 m	35 m	13 m	7 m	3 m	2 m	13 m	11 m
Low income	..	..	..	..	..	..	..	..	..	..	..	..
Middle income	22	19	4	8	25	37	14	7	3	3	16	12
Lower middle income	23	18	0	4	24	36	19	10	4	3	20	12
Upper middle income	22	19	7	21	26	38	11	4	3	2	15	12
Low & middle income	21	17	1	5	26	36	17	9	3	2	15	12
East Asia & Pacific	31	25	0	0	26	32	16	9	3	2	17	11
Europe & Central Asia	..	14	..	30	..	39	..	4	..	1	..	11
Latin America & Carib.	17	19	9	11	27	42	13	7	3	4	14	13
Middle East & N. Africa	21	18	2	0	17	18	15	15	5	3	28	30
South Asia	11	17	0	0	36	35	30	21	3	4	18	17
Sub-Saharan Africa	23	..	0	..	25	..	27	..	1	..	10	..
High income	31	26	17	20	28	25	1	1	3	3	9	8
Europe EMU	27	27	32	31	29	26	0	0	3	3	8	7

Note: Components may not sum to 100 percent as a result of adjustments to tax revenue.

About the data

The International Monetary Fund (IMF) classifies government transactions as receipts or payments and according to whether they are repayable or nonrepayable. If nonrepayable, they are classified as capital (meant to be used in production for more than a year) or current, and as requited (involving payment in return for a benefit or service) or unrequited. Revenues include all nonrepayable receipts (other than grants), the most important of which are taxes. Grants are unrequited, nonrepayable, noncompulsory receipts from other governments or from international organizations. Transactions are generally recorded on a cash rather than an accrual basis. Measuring the accumulation of arrears on revenues or payments on an accrual basis would typically result in a higher deficit. Transactions within a level of government are not included, but transactions between levels are included. In some instances, the government budget may include transfers used to finance the deficits of autonomous, extrabudgetary agencies.

The IMF's *Manual on Government Finance Statistics* (1986) describes taxes as compulsory, unrequited payments made to governments by individuals, businesses, or institutions. Taxes traditionally have been classified as either direct (those levied directly on the income or profits of individuals and corporations) or indirect (sales and excise taxes and duties levied on goods and services). This distinction may be a useful simplification, but it has no particular analytical significance, except with respect to the capacity to fix tax rates.

Social security taxes do not reflect compulsory payments made by employers to provident funds or other agencies with a similar purpose. Similarly, expenditures from such funds are not reflected in government expenditure (see table 4.12). The revenue shares shown in this table may not sum to 100 percent because adjustments to tax revenues are not shown.

For further discussion of taxes and tax policies see *About the data* for table 5.5. For further discussion of government revenues and expenditures see *About the data* for tables 4.11 and 4.12.

Definitions

• **Taxes on income, profits, and capital gains** are levied on the actual or presumptive net income of individuals, on the profits of enterprises, and on capital gains, whether realized or not, on land, securities, or other assets. Intragovernmental payments are eliminated in consolidation. • **Social security taxes** include employer and employee social security contributions and those of self-employed and unemployed people. • **Taxes on goods and services** include general sales and turnover, or value added taxes, selective excises on goods, selective taxes on services, taxes on the use of goods or property, and profits of fiscal monopolies. • **Taxes on international trade** include import duties, export duties, profits of export or import monopolies, exchange profits, and exchange taxes. • **Other taxes** include employer payroll or labor taxes, taxes on property, and taxes not allocable to other categories. They may include negative values that are adjustments (for example, for taxes collected on behalf of state and local governments and not allocable to individual tax categories). • **Nontax revenue** includes requited, nonrepayable receipts for public purposes, such as fines, administrative fees, or entrepreneurial income from government ownership of property, and voluntary, unrequited, nonrepayable receipts other than from government sources. It does not include proceeds of grants and borrowing, funds arising from the repayment of previous lending by governments, incurrence of liabilities, and proceeds from the sale of capital assets.

Data sources

The data on central government revenues are from the IMF's *Government Finance Statistics Yearbook, 2001* and IMF data files. Each country's accounts are reported using the system of common definitions and classifications in the IMF's *Manual on Government Finance Statistics* (1986). The IMF receives additional information from the Organisation for Economic Co-operation and Development on the tax revenues of some of its members. See the IMF sources for complete and authoritative explanations of concepts, definitions, and data sources.

Figure 4.13

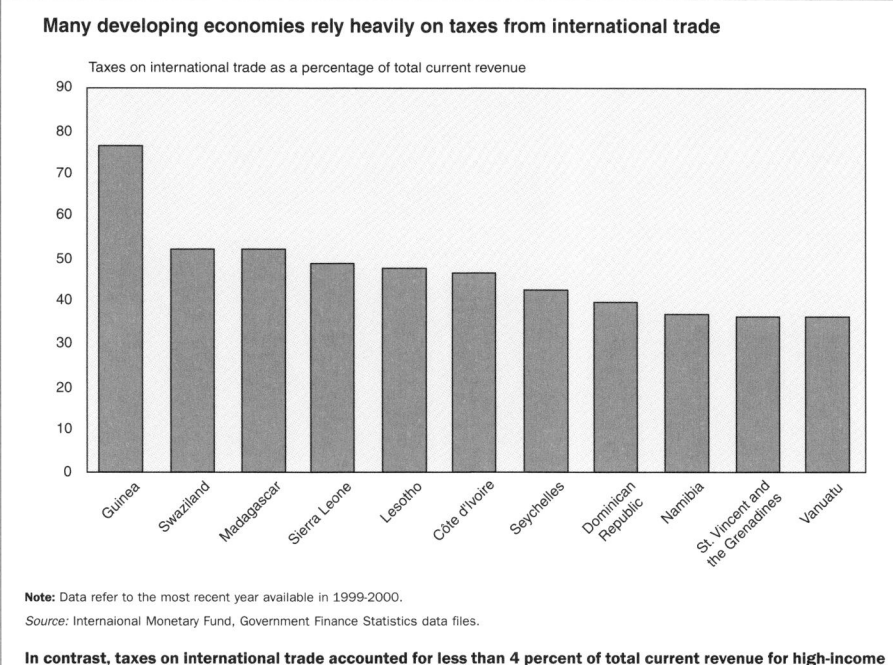

Many developing economies rely heavily on taxes from international trade

Taxes on international trade as a percentage of total current revenue

Note: Data refer to the most recent year available in 1999-2000.

Source: Internaional Monetary Fund, Government Finance Statistics data files.

In contrast, taxes on international trade accounted for less than 4 percent of total current revenue for high-income economies (with the exception of the Bahamas).

4.14 | Monetary indicators and prices

	Money and quasi money		Claims on private sector		Claims on governments and other public entities		GDP implicit deflator		Consumer price index		Food price index	
	annual % growth of M2		annual growth as % of M2		annual growth as % of M2		average annual % growth		average annual % growth		average annual % growth	
	1990	2000	1990	2000	1990	2000	1980-90	1990-2000	1980-90	1990-2000	1980-90	1990-2000
Afghanistan	..	..	..	..	..	..	..	..	..	..	..	..
Albania	..	12.0	..	2.1	..	6.1	-0.4	39.2	..	27.8	..	31.2
Algeria	11.4	13.2	12.2	4.9	3.2	-26.0	8.3	18.1	9.1	19.5	6.9	18.4
Angola	..	309.0	..	35.6	..	-410.1	5.9	740.6	..	708.7	..	1,216.8
Argentina	1,113.3	1.5	1,444.7	-2.9	1,573.2	0.7	391.1	5.2	390.6	8.9	279.3	8.1
Armenia	..	38.6	..	17.5	..	-5.5	..	212.5	..	72.0	..	23.7
Australia	12.8	3.8	15.3	13.8	-2.2	-1.9	7.2	1.5	7.9	2.1	7.3	4.3
Austria[a]	..	..	..	..	..	..	3.3	2.0	3.2	2.2	2.6	1.5
Azerbaijan	..	73.4	..	37.5	..	-25.5	..	199.1	..	170.8	1.5	201.8
Bangladesh	10.4	19.3	9.2	9.8	-0.2	4.6	9.5	4.0	..	5.5	10.4	4.3
Belarus	..	219.3	..	104.5	..	122.7	..	355.1	..	336.7	2.4	373.3
Belgium[a]	..	..	..	..	..	..	4.1	1.9	2.9	1.6	4.0	7.6
Benin	28.6	26.0	-1.3	8.5	12.4	0.9	1.7	8.3	..	8.7	..	7.1
Bolivia	52.8	0.4	40.8	-3.9	18.0	2.8	327.0	8.5	322.5	8.7	322.0	8.5
Bosnia and Herzegovina	..	..	..	..	..	..	..	2.3	..	..	..	..
Botswana	-14.0	1.4	12.6	11.4	-52.4	-56.5	13.6	9.7	10.0	10.4	10.7	10.8
Brazil	1,289.2	4.3	1,566.4	23.1	3,093.6	-15.0	284.0	207.7	285.6	199.5	238.2	194.2
Bulgaria	53.8	28.8	1.9	5.8	84.5	0.6	1.8	102.8	6.3	117.5	..	123.0
Burkina Faso	-0.5	6.2	3.6	8.3	-1.5	5.3	3.3	3.8	1.0	5.5	-0.5	6.7
Burundi	9.6	4.3	15.4	33.6	-6.9	-19.9	4.4	12.3	7.1	16.1	6.1	6.7
Cambodia	..	26.9	..	9.4	..	-7.4	..	24.6	..	6.3	..	6.6
Cameroon	-1.7	19.1	0.9	7.4	-3.0	-8.2	5.6	5.1	8.7	6.5	3.9	3.3
Canada	7.8	14.0	9.2	12.2	0.6	1.8	4.5	1.4	5.3	1.7	4.6	1.5
Central African Republic	-3.7	2.4	-1.6	2.9	2.3	0.6	7.9	4.6	3.2	5.9	2.0	5.5
Chad	-2.4	18.5	1.3	0.4	-17.3	19.3	1.4	7.1	0.6	8.1	..	7.1
Chile	23.5	6.2	21.4	14.7	16.4	4.6	20.7	7.3	20.6	8.9	20.8	8.3
China	28.9	12.3	26.5	9.4	1.5	0.2	5.9	7.1	..	8.6	8.8	..
Hong Kong, China	8.5	9.3	7.9	1.7	-1.0	0.4	7.7	4.1	..	5.8	6.8	4.7
Colombia	33.0	14.8	8.7	2.8	-5.1	7.6	24.8	21.1	22.7	20.6	24.5	18.3
Congo, Dem. Rep.	195.4	..	18.0	..	429.7	..	62.9	1,423.1	57.1	2,089.0	..	..
Congo, Rep.	18.5	58.5	5.1	-23.0	-12.6	-13.3	0.5	10.6	0.9	9.2	4.1	11.2
Costa Rica	27.5	18.4	7.3	17.4	8.2	0.8	23.6	17.2	23.0	15.6	23.0	14.0
Côte d'Ivoire	-2.6	-1.9	-3.9	2.9	-3.0	-7.6	2.8	7.5	5.4	7.2	6.0	..
Croatia	..	29.1	..	7.3	..	4.1	..	86.2	304.1	86.3	246.3	103.0
Cuba	..	..	..	..	..	..	..	1.1	..	..	..	..
Czech Republic	..	16.0	..	-4.1	..	3.3	..	11.5	..	7.8	..	11.4
Denmark	6.5	-0.9	3.0	2.3	-3.1	-1.0	5.8	2.2	5.6	2.1	4.8	2.0
Dominican Republic	42.5	17.4	19.1	16.9	0.7	1.0	21.6	9.4	22.4	8.7	25.2	11.7
Ecuador	48.9	11.1	17.2	8.5	-27.4	-18.3	36.4	37.1	35.8	37.1	43.0	36.7
Egypt, Arab Rep.	28.7	11.6	6.3	7.2	25.3	6.1	13.7	8.2	17.4	8.8	19.0	7.5
El Salvador	32.4	1.0	8.8	-0.3	9.6	2.8	16.3	7.4	19.6	8.5	21.4	9.8
Eritrea	..	..	..	..	..	..	..	9.4	..	..	..	..
Estonia	76.5	25.7	27.6	8.8	-6.8	-3.5	2.3	53.1	..	21.6	..	48.6
Ethiopia	18.5	14.2	0.3	3.3	21.7	18.0	4.6	7.0	4.0	5.3	3.7	6.5
Finland[a]	..	..	..	..	..	..	6.7	1.9	6.2	1.5	5.8	7.2
France[a]	..	..	..	..	..	..	5.8	1.5	5.8	1.6	5.7	10.8
Gabon	3.3	18.3	0.7	6.2	-20.6	-43.4	1.8	6.2	5.1	5.7	2.8	4.8
Gambia, The	8.4	34.8	7.8	4.2	-35.4	2.9	17.9	4.1	20.0	4.0	20.4	4.4
Georgia	..	39.4	..	23.3	..	20.1	1.9	387.5	..	24.7	..	..
Germany[a]	..	..	..	..	..	..	2.4	2.0	2.2 [b]	2.2	..	2.3
Ghana	13.3	38.4	4.9	35.6	-0.8	59.8	42.1	26.7	39.1	28.4	33.1	25.9
Greece[a]	..	..	..	..	..	..	19.3	9.2	18.7	9.0	18.0	49.9
Guatemala	25.8	35.5	15.0	7.4	0.5	1.5	14.6	10.3	14.0	10.1	14.6	9.7
Guinea	-17.4	514.1	13.1	-6.1	2.9	1.1	..	5.1	..	..	..	9.1
Guinea-Bissau	574.6	60.8	90.5	5.5	460.7	16.2	57.4	32.5	..	34.0	..	..
Haiti	2.5	20.1	-0.6	8.2	0.4	16.9	7.5	20.3	5.2	21.9	4.1	19.2
Honduras	21.4	24.4	13.0	11.5	-10.5	6.1	5.7	18.8	6.3	17.3	5.1	19.0

	Money and quasi money		Claims on private sector		Claims on governments and other public entities		GDP implicit deflator		Consumer price index		Food price index	
	annual % growth of M2		annual growth as % of M2		annual growth as % of M2		average annual % growth		average annual % growth		average annual % growth	
	1990	2000	1990	2000	1990	2000	1980-90	1990-2000	1980-90	1990-2000	1980-90	1990-2000
Hungary	29.2	12.2	23.0	19.1	69.7	-1.2	8.9	19.3	9.6	20.3	9.5	19.5
India	15.1	15.2	5.9	9.9	10.5	4.7	8.1	8.0	8.6	9.1	8.4	9.2
Indonesia	44.6	15.9	66.9	7.0	-6.7	20.7	8.6	15.5	8.3	13.7	8.6	17.1
Iran, Islamic Rep.	18.0	22.4	14.7	15.8	5.8	-1.9	14.4	26.2	18.2	26.0	16.3	28.7
Iraq	..	..	..	..	..	..	10.3	..	..	..	14.3	..
Ireland[a]	..	..	..	..	..	..	6.6	3.5	6.8	2.3	10.5	27.9
Israel	19.4	8.0	18.5	10.7	4.9	-4.8	101.1	10.0	101.7	9.7	102.4	8.4
Italy[a]	..	..	..	..	..	..	10.0	3.8	9.1	3.7	8.2	19.2
Jamaica	21.5	13.0	12.5	13.7	-16.0	-15.7	18.6	24.1	15.1	23.5	16.2	5.3
Japan	8.2	1.1	9.7	-1.8	1.5	3.8	1.8	0.1	1.7	0.7	1.6	0.6
Jordan	8.3	7.6	4.7	2.9	1.0	-1.5	4.3	3.2	5.7	3.5	4.7	3.9
Kazakhstan	..	45.0	..	58.5	..	-3.2	..	204.7	..	67.8	..	246.0
Kenya	20.1	4.5	8.0	2.3	21.5	-1.7	9.1	13.9	11.1	15.1	..	15.2
Korea, Dem. Rep.	..	..	..	..	..	..	..	..	..	..	..	..
Korea, Rep.	17.2	25.4	36.1	21.9	-1.2	-1.5	6.5	5.0	4.9	5.1	5.0	5.3
Kuwait	0.7	6.3	3.3	3.1	-3.1	-6.6	-2.8	3.0	2.9	2.0	1.2	2.6
Kyrgyz Republic	..	11.7	..	3.5	..	7.2	..	110.2	..	23.1	..	70.7
Lao PDR	7.8	46.0	3.6	22.4	7.0	3.2	37.6	27.0	..	28.2	..	..
Latvia	..	27.0	..	18.5	..	13.9	0.0	49.2	..	29.2	..	25.0
Lebanon	55.1	9.8	27.6	2.9	18.5	10.5	..	17.4	..	..	..	..
Lesotho	8.4	1.4	6.8	1.5	-14.9	13.3	12.1	9.9	13.6	9.8	13.2	13.0
Liberia	19.6	18.3	16.1	-10.0	29.5	196.9	1.8	..	..	..	..	..
Libya	19.0	3.1	2.0	0.2	15.0	-2.0	0.2	..	..	..	..	..
Lithuania	..	16.5	..	-3.7	..	2.2	..	75.2	..	32.6	..	55.6
Macedonia, FYR	..	21.4	..	-3.9	..	-14.5	..	79.3	..	13.0	242.1	89.0
Madagascar	4.5	17.2	23.8	9.9	-14.8	-0.3	17.1	19.1	16.6	18.7	15.7	19.1
Malawi	11.1	41.4	15.8	14.6	-12.8	-2.7	15.1	33.5	16.9	33.8	16.3	36.0
Malaysia	10.6	9.9	20.8	7.9	-1.2	1.5	1.7	3.9	2.6	3.6	1.3	5.1
Mali	-4.9	12.2	0.1	-1.5	-13.4	-5.0	4.5	7.1	..	5.2	..	..
Mauritania	11.5	16.1	20.2	41.1	1.5	-64.3	8.4	5.9	7.1	6.1	..	6.2
Mauritius	21.2	9.2	10.8	9.3	0.8	-4.8	9.5	5.9	6.9	6.9	7.4	6.7
Mexico	81.9	-4.2	48.5	-3.4	13.6	-0.1	71.5	18.9	73.8	19.4	73.1	19.3
Moldova	358.0	41.7	53.3	22.8	469.1	-2.2	..	120.2	..	18.9	..	64.4
Mongolia	31.6	17.6	40.2	2.0	38.5	-6.5	-1.6	58.4	..	53.7	..	..
Morocco	21.5	8.4	12.4	7.6	-4.9	3.6	7.1	2.8	7.0	3.8	6.7	4.8
Mozambique	37.2	38.4	22.0	18.2	-5.1	3.8	38.3	32.6	..	34.9	24.4	..
Myanmar	37.7	42.4	12.8	13.9	24.2	27.6	12.2	26.4	11.5	25.9	11.9	28.4
Namibia	30.3	13.0	15.4	14.9	-4.2	-1.1	13.7	9.5	12.6	9.9	14.9	9.8
Nepal	18.5	18.8	5.7	10.7	7.3	2.9	11.1	8.2	10.2	8.6	10.1	9.8
Netherlands[a]	..	..	..	..	..	..	1.6	1.9	2.0	2.4	1.2	5.1
New Zealand	12.5	2.3	4.2	7.8	-1.7	-0.9	10.7	1.5	11.0	1.8	9.9	1.3
Nicaragua	7,677.8	9.4	4,932.9	11.1	12,679.2	10.1	422.3	33.5	535.7	35.1	..	..
Niger	-4.1	12.4	-5.1	14.8	1.4	-14.1	1.9	6.0	0.7	6.1	-1.5	9.8
Nigeria	32.7	48.1	7.8	19.3	27.1	-41.4	16.7	28.9	21.5	32.5	21.6	37.6
Norway	5.6	8.7	5.0	18.0	-0.6	-30.5	5.6	2.8	7.4	2.2	7.8	2.0
Oman	10.0	6.0	9.6	1.1	-10.9	10.1	-3.6	-2.9	..	0.1	..	0.3
Pakistan	11.6	12.1	5.9	8.7	7.7	2.6	6.7	10.2	6.3	9.7	6.6	10.1
Panama	36.6	10.0	0.8	9.6	-25.7	0.3	1.9	1.9	1.4	1.1	1.9	1.0
Papua New Guinea	4.3	5.0	-0.9	3.8	8.8	-5.9	5.3	7.9	5.6	9.3	4.6	8.9
Paraguay	54.4	4.8	32.0	3.3	-9.2	4.0	24.4	12.5	21.9	13.1	24.9	12.5
Peru	6,384.9	-0.4	2,123.7	-2.7	2,129.5	2.6	220.2	26.8	246.1	27.3	..	24.9
Philippines	22.4	8.1	15.6	3.5	3.4	3.6	14.9	8.4	13.4	8.2	14.1	7.5
Poland	160.1	11.8	20.8	12.5	75.6	-5.9	..	23.4	50.9	25.3	52.4	21.9
Portugal[a]	..	..	..	..	..	..	18.0	5.3	17.1	4.5	16.9	33.2
Puerto Rico	..	..	..	..	..	..	3.5	3.7	..	..	2.8	9.6
Romania	26.4	38.0	..	10.1	0.0	-0.4	2.5	98.0	..	100.5	1.8	95.8
Russian Federation	..	58.4	..	35.1	..	-14.5	..	162.0	..	99.1	..	143.3

2002 World Development Indicators

	Money and quasi money		Claims on private sector		Claims on governments and other public entities		GDP implicit deflator		Consumer price index		Food price index	
	annual % growth of M2		annual growth as % of M2		annual growth as % of M2		average annual % growth		average annual % growth		average annual % growth	
	1990	2000	1990	2000	1990	2000	1980-90	1990-2000	1980-90	1990-2000	1980-90	1990-2000
Rwanda	5.6	15.6	-10.0	10.3	26.8	-11.3	4.0	14.6	3.9	16.2	6.6	..
Saudi Arabia	4.6	4.5	-4.5	3.3	4.2	-4.1	-4.9	2.2	-0.8	1.0	-0.4	1.0
Senegal	-4.8	10.7	-8.4	19.1	-5.3	-3.9	6.5	4.6	6.2	5.4	5.3	5.8
Sierra Leone	74.0	12.1	4.9	1.6	228.7	54.9	62.8	28.9	72.4	29.3	71.0	..
Singapore	20.0	-2.0	13.7	5.1	-4.9	-1.6	1.9	1.3	1.6	1.7	0.9	1.8
Slovak Republic	..	15.2	..	-5.5	..	13.2	1.8	10.6	..	8.4	1.6	8.8
Slovenia	123.0	18.0	96.1	13.3	-10.4	4.9	..	20.4	..	24.6	252.3	26.4
Somalia	..	..	..	..	..	..	49.7	..	..	..	..	..
South Africa	11.4	7.2	13.7	17.4	1.8	0.2	15.5	9.6	14.8	8.7	15.1	10.0
Spainª	..	..	..	..	..	..	9.3	3.9	9.0	3.8	9.3	16.8
Sri Lanka	21.1	12.8	16.2	9.2	6.8	12.2	11.0	9.1	10.9	9.9	10.9	10.4
Sudan	48.8	36.9	12.6	11.0	29.4	18.4	41.0	60.8	37.6	81.1	38.0	..
Swaziland	0.6	-6.6	20.5	3.9	-13.2	-8.5	10.1	12.6	14.6	9.4	..	..
Sweden	0.8	1.9	13.4	12.4	-12.2	2.1	7.3	2.1	7.0	1.9	8.2	-0.5
Switzerland	0.8	-16.9	11.7	-1.2	1.0	2.1	3.4	1.3	2.9	1.6	3.1	0.5
Syrian Arab Republic	26.1	19.0	3.4	0.3	11.4	-4.5	15.3	6.7	23.2	6.7	24.5	5.4
Tajikistan	..	..	..	..	..	..	2.5	235.2	..	..	..	..
Tanzania	41.9	14.8	22.6	2.6	80.6	0.6	..	21.5	31.0	20.9	30.2	56.7
Thailand	26.7	3.4	30.0	-16.0	-4.0	0.8	3.9	4.2	3.5	4.9	2.7	5.9
Togo	9.5	15.2	1.8	0.5	6.9	-0.5	4.8	7.1	2.5	8.5	1.2	..
Trinidad and Tobago	6.2	11.7	2.7	8.8	-1.9	-14.0	2.4	5.5	10.7	5.7	14.6	13.3
Tunisia	7.6	14.1	5.9	23.7	1.8	5.6	7.4	4.5	7.4	4.4	8.3	4.4
Turkey	53.2	40.0	42.9	29.4	2.2	38.1	45.2	76.3	44.9	79.9	..	83.4
Turkmenistan	..	22.6	..	0.3	..	82.3	..	407.5	..	..	..	..
Uganda	60.2	18.1	..	5.1	-0.9	32.9	113.8	12.4	102.5	10.5	..	13.4
Ukraine	..	44.4	..	32.7	..	2.2	..	271.3	..	200.4	2.0	203.9
United Arab Emirates	-8.2	15.3	1.3	8.7	-4.8	-9.4	0.8	2.3	..	..	..	..
United Kingdom	10.5	11.3	13.1	17.5	1.1	-2.4	5.7	2.9	5.8	2.9	4.6	1.8
United States	4.9	7.0	1.1	11.6	0.6	1.9	3.8	2.1	4.2	2.7	3.8	3.6
Uruguay	118.5	7.2	56.2	5.1	25.8	-5.3	62.7	31.1	61.1	33.9	62.0	30.9
Uzbekistan	..	..	..	..	..	..	..	246.6	..	..	..	..
Venezuela, RB	64.9	23.1	17.6	14.5	45.3	-5.6	19.3	45.5	20.9	20.9	29.7	48.4
Vietnam	..	35.4	..	29.6	..	-2.4	210.8	15.4	..	4.1	..	..
West Bank and Gaza	..	..	..	..	..	..	..	8.9	..	..	..	..
Yemen, Rep.	11.3	25.3	1.4	3.6	10.2	-46.2	..	21.9	..	32.6	2.6	..
Yugoslavia, Fed. Rep.	..	..	..	..	..	..	..	49.1	..	..	..	45.5
Zambia	47.9	73.8	22.8	22.0	195.2	169.3	42.2	51.4	72.5	80.8	42.8	73.0
Zimbabwe	15.1	68.9	13.5	46.0	5.0	53.4	11.6	25.5	13.8	27.0	14.6	34.1

a. As members of the European Monetary Union, these countries share a single currency, the euro. b. Data prior to 1990 refer to the Federal Republic of Germany before unification.

About the data

Money and the financial accounts that record the supply of money lie at the heart of a country's financial system. There are several commonly used definitions of the money supply. The narrowest, M1, encompasses currency held by the public and demand deposits with banks. M2 includes M1 plus time and savings deposits with banks that require a notice for withdrawal. M3 includes M2 as well as various money market instruments, such as certificates of deposit issued by banks, bank deposits denominated in foreign currency, and deposits with financial institutions other than banks. However defined, money is a liability of the banking system, distinguished from other bank liabilities by the special role it plays as a medium of exchange, a unit of account, and a store of value.

The banking system's assets include its net foreign assets and net domestic credit. Net domestic credit includes credit to the private sector and general government, and credit extended to the nonfinancial public sector in the form of investments in short- and long-term government securities and loans to state enterprises; liabilities to the public and private sectors in the form of deposits with the banking system are netted out. Net domestic credit also includes credit to banking and nonbank financial institutions.

Domestic credit is the main vehicle through which changes in the money supply are regulated, with central bank lending to the government often playing the most important role. The central bank can regulate lending to the private sector in several ways—for example, by adjusting the cost of the refinancing facilities it provides to banks, by changing market interest rates through open market operations, or by controlling the availability of credit through changes in the reserve requirements imposed on banks and ceilings on the credit provided by banks to the private sector.

Monetary accounts are derived from the balance sheets of financial institutions—the central bank, commercial banks, and nonbank financial intermediaries. Although these balance sheets are usually reliable, they are subject to errors of classification, valuation, and timing and to differences in accounting practices. For example, whether interest income is recorded on an accrual or a cash basis can make a substantial difference, as can the treatment of non-performing assets. Valuation errors typically arise with respect to foreign exchange transactions, particularly in countries with flexible exchange rates or in those that have undergone a currency devaluation during the reporting period. The valuation of financial derivatives and the net liabilities of the banking system can also be difficult.

The quality of commercial bank reporting also may be adversely affected by delays in reports from bank branches, especially in countries where branch accounts are not computerized. Thus the data in the balance sheets of commercial banks may be based on preliminary estimates subject to constant revision. This problem is likely to be even more serious for non-bank financial intermediaries.

Controlling inflation is one of the primary goals of monetary policy and is intimately linked to the growth in money supply. Inflation is measured by the rate of increase in a price index, but actual price change can also be negative. Which index is used depends on which set of prices in the economy is being examined. The GDP deflator reflects changes in prices for total gross domestic product. The most general measure of the overall price level, it takes into account changes in government consumption, capital formation (including inventory appreciation), international trade, and the main component, household final consumption expenditure. The GDP deflator is usually derived implicitly as the ratio of current to constant price GDP, resulting in a Paasche index. It is defective as a general measure of inflation for use in policy because of the long lags in deriving estimates and because it is often only an annual measure.

Consumer price indexes are more current and produced more frequently. They are also constructed explicitly, based on surveys of the cost of a defined basket of consumer goods and services. Nevertheless, consumer price indexes should be interpreted with caution. The definition of a household, and the geographic (urban or rural) and income group coverage of consumer price surveys, can vary widely across countries, as can the basket of goods chosen. In addition, the weights are derived from household expenditure surveys, which, for budgetary reasons, tend to be conducted infrequently in developing countries, leading to poor comparability over time. Although a useful indicator for measuring consumer price inflation within a country, consumer price indexes are of less value in making comparisons across countries. Like consumer price indexes, food price indexes should be interpreted with caution because of the high variability across countries in the items covered.

The least-squares method is used to calculate the growth rates of the GDP implicit deflator, consumer price index, and food price index.

Definitions

• **Money and quasi money** comprise the sum of currency outside banks, demand deposits other than those of the central government, and the time, savings, and foreign currency deposits of resident sectors other than the central government. This definition of the money supply is frequently called M2; it corresponds to lines 34 and 35 in the International Monetary Fund's (IMF) *International Financial Statistics* (IFS). The change in money supply is measured as the difference in end-of-year totals relative to M2 in the preceding year. • **Claims on private sector** (IFS line 32d) include gross credit from the financial system to individuals, enterprises, nonfinancial public entities not included under net domestic credit, and financial institutions not included elsewhere. • **Claims on govern-ments and other public entities** (IFS line 32an + 32b + 32bx + 32c) usually comprise direct credit for specific purposes, such as financing the government budget deficit, loans to state enterprises, advances against future credit authorizations, and purchases of treasury bills and bonds, net of deposits by the public sector. Public sector deposits with the banking system also include sinking funds for the service of debt and temporary deposits of government revenues. • **GDP implicit deflator** measures the average annual rate of price change in the economy as a whole for the periods shown. • **Consumer price index** reflects changes in the cost to the average consumer of acquiring a basket of goods and services that may be fixed or change at specified intervals, such as yearly. The Laspeyres formula is generally used. • **Food price index** is a subindex of the consumer price index.

Data sources

The monetary, financial, and consumer price index data in this table are published by the IMF in its monthly *International Financial Statistics* and annual *International Financial Statistics Yearbook*. The IMF collects data on the financial systems of its member countries. The World Bank receives data from the IMF in electronic files that may contain more recent revisions than the published sources. The GDP deflator data are from the World Bank's national accounts files. The food price index data are from the United Nations Statistics Division's *Statistical Yearbook* and *Monthly Bulletin of Statistics*. The discussion of monetary indicators draws from an IMF publication by Marcello Caiola, *A Manual for Country Economists* (1995).

4.15 | Balance of payments current account

	Goods and services				Net income		Net current transfers		Current account balance		Gross international reserves	
	Exports $ millions		Imports $ millions		$ millions		$ millions		$ millions		$ millions	
	1990	2000	1990	2000	1990	2000	1990	2000	1990	2000	1990	2000
Afghanistan	..	..	..	..	..	..	..	..	..	..	638	..
Albania	354	704	485	1,499	-2	107	15	533	-118	-156	..	383
Algeria	13,462	22,359	10,106	9,842	-2,268	-3,075	333	..	1,420	..	2,703	13,556
Angola	3,992	7,945	3,385	6,195	-765	-1,843	-77	89	-236	-4	..	1,198
Argentina	14,800	30,945	6,846	32,722	-4,400	-7,482	998	289	4,552	-8,970	6,222	25,152
Armenia	..	447	..	966	..	53	..	188	..	-278	1	331
Australia	49,843	82,387	53,056	86,777	-13,176	-10,926	439	0	-15,950	-15,316	19,319	18,822
Austria	63,694	94,907	61,580	96,597	-942	-2,265	-6	-1,249	1,166	-5,205	17,228	17,649
Azerbaijan	..	2,146	..	2,023	..	-346	..	73	..	-150	0	680
Bangladesh	1,903	6,611	4,156	9,060	-122	-221	802	2,672	-1,573	2	660	1,516
Belarus	3,661	7,980	3,557	8,257	-1	-42	79	157	182	-162	..	350
Belgiumª	138,605	210,725	135,098	202,898	2,316	8,219	-2,197	-4,202	3,627	11,844	61,284	53,620
Benin	364	522	454	782	-25	-19	97	111	-18	-168	69	458
Bolivia	977	1,454	1,086	2,078	-249	-225	159	385	-199	-464	511	1,038
Bosnia and Herzegovina	..	..	..	..	..	..	..	..	..	..	..	..
Botswana	2,005	3,044	1,987	2,512	-106	-266	69	252	-19	517	3,331	6,318
Brazil	35,170	64,469	28,184	72,739	-11,608	-17,884	799	1,522	-3,823	-24,632	9,200	33,008
Bulgaria	6,950	7,000	8,027	7,669	-758	-321	125	290	-1,710	-701	670	3,625
Burkina Faso	349	259	758	635	0	-39	332	350	-77	-65	305	244
Burundi	89	55	318	151	-15	-12	174	59	-69	-49	112	38
Cambodia	314	1,497	507	1,769	-21	-52	120	305	-93	-19	..	502
Cameroon	2,251	2,719	1,931	2,376	-478	-593	-39	97	-196	-153	37	212
Canada	149,538	321,693	149,118	286,386	-19,388	-18,267	-796	974	-19,764	18,014	23,530	32,249
Central African Republic	220	110	410	149	-22	-12	123	51	-89	0	123	133
Chad	271	279	488	478	-21	-10	192	51	-46	-158	132	111
Chile	10,221	22,090	9,166	21,209	-1,737	-2,409	198	537	-485	-991	6,784	14,749
China†	57,374	279,562	46,706	250,688	1,055	-14,666	274	6,311	11,997	20,518	34,476	171,763
Hong Kong, China	100,413	244,004	94,084	236,311	0	2,766	..	-1,632	6,329	8,827	24,656	107,560
Colombia	8,679	15,678	6,858	14,385	-2,305	-2,577	1,026	1,590	542	306	4,869	9,006
Congo, Dem. Rep.	2,557	..	2,497	..	-770	-754	-27	..	-738	-583	261	..
Congo, Rep.	1,488	2,714	1,282	1,332	-460	-839	3	..	-251	..	10	222
Costa Rica	1,963	7,628	2,346	7,265	-233	-1,176	192	102	-424	-649	525	1,318
Côte d'Ivoire	3,503	4,408	3,445	3,391	-1,091	-660	-181	-370	-1,214	-13	21	668
Croatia	..	8,651	..	9,597	..	-311	..	858	..	-399	167	3,524
Cuba	..	..	..	..	..	..	..	..	..	..	..	..
Czech Republic	..	35,746	..	37,528	..	-752	..	298	..	-2,236	..	13,142
Denmark	48,902	71,141	41,415	61,883	-5,708	-3,561	-408	-3,190	1,372	2,507	11,226	15,696
Dominican Republic	1,832	8,964	2,233	10,852	-249	-1,041	371	1,902	-280	-1,026	69	630
Ecuador	3,262	5,987	2,519	4,998	-1,210	-1,412	107	1,352	-360	928	1,009	1,179
Egypt, Arab Rep.	9,151	15,975	13,710	22,756	-912	932	4,836	4,679	-634	-1,171	3,620	13,785
El Salvador	973	3,645	1,624	5,642	-132	-250	631	1,829	-152	-418	595	2,051
Eritrea	88	96	278	499	..	0	171	196	-19	-208	..	..
Estonia	664	4,791	711	5,040	-13	-204	97	138	36	-315	198	923
Ethiopia	672	984	1,069	1,960	-67	-60	220	701	-244	-335	55	312
Finland	31,180	51,764	33,456	40,366	-3,735	-1,913	-952	-631	-6,962	8,854	10,415	8,897
France	285,389	377,274	283,238	357,030	-3,896	13,710	-8,199	-13,526	-9,944	20,428	68,291	63,728
Gabon	2,730	3,023	1,812	1,868	-617	-699	-134	-71	168	385	279	190
Gambia, The	168	262	192	321	-11	-5	59	15	23	-48	55	109
Georgia	..	1,136	..	1,410	..	13	..	100	..	-162	..	109
Germany	474,713	633,052	423,497	625,892	20,832	-988	-23,745	-24,878	48,303	-18,707	104,547	87,497
Ghana	983	2,403	1,506	3,339	-111	-108	411	631	-223	-413	309	309
Greece	13,018	29,440	19,564	41,727	-1,709	-885	4,718	3,352	-3,537	-9,820	4,721	14,594
Guatemala	1,568	3,892	1,812	5,584	-196	-226	227	868	-213	-1,049	362	1,806
Guinea	829	843	953	919	-149	-79	70	-10	-203	-165	80	148
Guinea-Bissau	26	70	88	106	-22	-13	39	..	-45	..	18	67
Haiti	318	530	515	1,333	-18	-21	193	223	-22	-38	10	184
Honduras	1,032	2,501	1,127	3,275	-237	-138	280	708	-51	-204	47	1,319
† Data for Taiwan, China	74,175	167,907	67,015	160,457	4,361	4,468	-601	-2,602	10,920	9,316	77,653	110,139

	Goods and services				Net income		Net current transfers		Current account balance		Gross international reserves	
	Exports $ millions		Imports $ millions		$ millions		$ millions		$ millions		$ millions	
	1990	**2000**	**1990**	**2000**	**1990**	**2000**	**1990**	**2000**	**1990**	**2000**	**1990**	**2000**
Hungary	12,035	31,618	11,017	31,948	-1,427	-1,574	787	410	379	-1,494	1,185	11,217
India	23,028	63,764	31,485	75,656	-3,753	-3,821	2,068	12,798	-10,142	-2,915	5,637	41,059
Indonesia	29,295	70,619	27,511	55,377	-5,190	-9,072	418	1,816	-2,988	7,986	8,657	29,353
Iran, Islamic Rep.	19,741	29,727	22,292	17,503	378	-200	2,500	621	327	12,645	..	..
Iraq	..	..	..	..	..	..	..	..	..	..	..	..
Ireland	26,786	90,221	24,576	76,762	-4,955	-15,002	2,384	949	-361	-593	5,362	5,408
Israel	17,312	45,179	20,228	46,534	-1,975	-6,663	5,060	6,602	170	-1,416	6,598	23,281
Italy	219,971	294,852	218,573	284,191	-14,712	-12,003	-3,164	-4,328	-16,479	-5,670	88,595	47,201
Jamaica	2,217	3,580	2,390	4,340	-430	-336	291	821	-312	-275	168	1,054
Japan	323,692	528,751	297,306	459,660	22,492	57,623	-4,800	-9,831	44,078	116,883	87,828	361,639
Jordan	2,511	3,536	3,754	5,796	-215	-27	1,046	2,345	-411	59	1,139	3,441
Kazakhstan	5,758	10,751	5,862	8,705	-175	-1,179	168	207	-111	1,074	..	2,099
Kenya	2,228	2,741	2,705	3,768	-418	-133	368	922	-527	-238	236	898
Korea, Dem. Rep.	..	..	..	..	..	..	..	..	..	..	..	..
Korea, Rep.	73,295	205,645	76,360	192,499	-87	-2,421	1,149	680	-2,003	11,405	14,916	96,251
Kuwait	8,268	21,617	7,169	11,785	7,738	6,918	-4,951	-1,884	3,886	14,865	2,929	7,779
Kyrgyz Republic	..	573	..	651	..	-80	..	82	..	-77	..	262
Lao PDR	102	501	212	613	-1	-49	56	240	-55	90	8	144
Latvia	1,090	3,270	997	3,886	2	24	96	97	191	-494	..	919
Lebanon	511	2,141	2,836	6,228	622	932	1,818	90	115	-3,065	4,210	8,475
Lesotho	100	254	754	770	433	226	286	139	65	-151	72	418
Liberia	..	..	..	..	..	..	..	..	..	..	1	0
Libya	11,469	6,813	8,960	4,914	174	289	-481	-204	2,201	1,984	7,225	13,730
Lithuania	..	5,109	..	5,833	..	-194	..	243	..	-675	107	1,363
Macedonia, FYR	..	1,620	..	2,233	..	-45	..	551	..	-107	..	460
Madagascar	471	1,188	809	1,520	-161	-42	234	113	-265	-260	92	285
Malawi	443	487	549	934	-80	-83	99	6	-86	-523	142	250
Malaysia	32,665	111,261	31,765	94,024	-1,872	-9,282	102	-1,728	-870	12,606	10,659	29,844
Mali	420	705	830	1,060	-37	-28	225	..	-221	..	198	381
Mauritania	471	372	520	428	-46	-19	86	165	-10	90	59	228
Mauritius	1,722	2,630	1,916	2,699	-23	-28	97	64	-119	-33	761	914
Mexico	48,805	180,210	51,915	191,895	-8,316	-13,466	3,975	6,994	-7,451	-18,157	10,217	35,577
Moldova	..	640	..	990	..	72	..	157	..	-121	0	230
Mongolia	493	607	1,096	772	-44	-3	7	74	-640	-52	23	202
Morocco	6,239	10,453	7,783	12,538	-988	-873	2,336	2,483	-196	-475	2,338	5,017
Mozambique	229	689	996	1,492	-97	-192	448	231	-415	-764	233	744
Myanmar	641	1,840	1,182	2,787	-61	-70	77	366	-526	-651	410	286
Namibia	1,220	1,745	1,584	1,889	37	-42	354	390	28	204	50	260
Nepal	379	1,279	761	1,782	71	34	60	175	-251	-293	354	989
Netherlands	159,304	258,951	147,652	240,624	-620	1,631	-2,943	-6,193	8,089	13,764	34,401	17,688
New Zealand	11,683	17,810	11,699	17,358	-1,576	-3,428	138	242	-1,453	-2,734	4,129	3,329
Nicaragua	392	953	682	1,986	-217	-201	202	741	-305	-493	166	493
Niger	533	282	728	424	-54	-15	14	-10	-236	-168	226	80
Nigeria	14,550	23,047	6,909	14,124	-2,738	-3,287	85	1,348	4,988	6,983	4,129	6,485
Norway	47,078	75,176	38,911	49,187	-2,700	-1,533	-1,476	-1,471	3,992	22,986	15,788	20,489
Oman	5,577	11,602	3,342	6,094	-254	-705	-874	-1,456	1,106	3,347	1,784	2,460
Pakistan	6,217	9,575	9,351	11,762	-966	-2,018	2,210	1,997	-1,890	-2,208	1,046	2,087
Panama	4,438	7,666	4,193	8,164	-255	-612	219	177	209	-933	344	723
Papua New Guinea	1,381	2,233	1,509	1,927	-103	-305	156	-9	-76	-8	427	326
Paraguay	2,514	2,801	2,169	3,307	2	32	43	175	390	-299	675	770
Peru	4,120	8,598	4,087	9,704	-1,733	-1,541	281	1,019	-1,419	-1,628	1,891	8,676
Philippines	11,430	41,468	13,967	36,465	-872	3,645	714	433	-2,695	9,081	2,036	15,035
Poland	19,037	46,294	15,095	57,210	-3,386	-1,461	2,511	2,380	3,067	-9,997	4,674	27,469
Portugal	21,554	33,166	27,146	45,544	-96	-2,041	5,507	3,406	-181	-11,012	20,579	14,262
Puerto Rico	..	..	..	..	..	..	..	..	..	..	..	..
Romania	6,380	12,133	9,901	14,071	161	-281	106	860	-3,254	-1,359	1,374	4,848
Russian Federation	53,883	115,200	48,915	62,290	-4,500	-11,154	0	90	468	41,846	..	27,656

	Goods and services				Net income		Net current transfers		Current account balance		Gross international reserves	
	Exports $ millions		Imports $ millions		$ millions		$ millions		$ millions		$ millions	
	1990	2000	1990	2000	1990	2000	1990	2000	1990	2000	1990	2000
Rwanda	145	131	359	403	-17	-15	145	281	-86	-7	44	191
Saudi Arabia	47,445	82,369	43,939	53,003	7,979	480	-15,637	-15,511	-4,152	14,336	13,437	20,847
Senegal	1,453	1,337	1,840	1,732	-129	-113	153	197	-363	-310	22	384
Sierra Leone	210	87	215	240	-71	-24	7	..	-69	..	5	51
Singapore	67,489	165,971	64,953	148,939	1,006	6,123	-421	-1,359	3,122	21,797	27,748	80,132
Slovak Republic	..	14,137	..	14,596	..	-355	..	120	..	-694	..	4,376
Slovenia	7,900	10,694	6,930	11,397	-38	-25	46	115	978	-612	112	3,196
Somalia	70	..	322	..	..	..	..	..	..	..	..	..
South Africa	27,742	36,522	21,016	32,818	-4,271	-3,247	-321	-926	2,134	-469	2,583	7,702
Spain	83,595	168,463	100,870	178,987	-3,533	-8,311	2,799	1,578	-18,009	-17,257	57,238	35,607
Sri Lanka	2,293	6,378	2,965	8,105	-167	-299	541	984	-298	-1,042	447	1,211
Sudan	532	1,892	1,453	1,921	-784	-1,264	407	319	-1,299	-974	11	189
Swaziland	658	885	768	1,098	59	77	102	96	51	-40	216	352
Sweden	70,560	107,683	70,490	95,656	-4,473	-2,063	-1,936	-3,348	-6,339	6,617	20,324	16,499
Switzerland	96,927	120,743	96,388	108,386	8,746	23,999	-2,329	-3,815	6,955	32,542	61,284	53,620
Syrian Arab Republic	5,030	6,846	2,955	5,390	-401	-879	88	485	1,762	1,062	..	..
Tajikistan	185	800	238	839	0	-55	..	33	-53	-61	..	56
Tanzania	538	1,280	1,474	2,010	-185	-80	562	511	-559	-298	193	974
Thailand	29,229	81,817	35,870	71,652	-853	-1,381	213	586	-7,281	9,369	14,258	32,665
Togo	663	438	847	614	-32	-25	132	95	-84	-106	358	152
Trinidad and Tobago	2,289	4,769	1,427	3,823	-397	-610	-6	22	459	-644	513	1,403
Tunisia	5,203	8,607	6,039	9,311	-455	-942	828	824	-463	-821	867	1,871
Turkey	21,042	51,148	25,652	62,190	-2,508	-4,002	4,493	5,225	-2,625	-9,819	7,626	23,515
Turkmenistan	1,238	2,774	857	2,350	0	-177	66	166	447	412	..	1,513
Uganda	246	626	676	1,985	-77	-15	78	513	-429	-860	44	808
Ukraine	..	19,522	..	18,116	..	-942	..	1,017	..	1,481	469	1,477
United Arab Emirates	..	..	..	..	..	..	..	..	..	..	4,891	13,632
United Kingdom	239,226	401,385	264,090	425,075	-5,154	9,098	-8,794	-13,248	-38,811	-27,840	43,146	48,193
United States	535,260	1,065,740	616,120	1,441,500	28,560	-14,780	-26,660	-54,150	-78,960	-444,690	173,094	128,400
Uruguay	2,158	3,733	1,659	4,216	-321	-176	8	66	186	-593	1,446	2,776
Uzbekistan	..	3,383	..	2,962	..	-251	..	13	..	184	..	1,242
Venezuela, RB	18,806	34,272	9,451	19,746	-774	-1,204	-302	-211	8,279	13,111	12,733	15,899
Vietnam	1,913	17,107	1,901	17,344	-412	-597	49	1,341	-351	507	..	3,417
West Bank and Gaza	..	..	..	..	..	..	..	..	..	..	..	..
Yemen, Rep.	1,490	4,305	2,170	3,150	-372	-514	1,790	1,422	739	2,063	441	2,914
Yugoslavia, Fed. Rep.	..	..	..	..	..	..	..	..	..	..	..	..
Zambia	1,360	936	1,897	1,167	-437	-411	380	..	-594	..	201	245
Zimbabwe	2,012	2,101	2,001	1,991	-263	-242	112	..	-140	..	295	321

World	4,252,055 t	7,820,225 t	4,257,973 t	7,848,991 t
Low income	130,306	274,302	147,914	275,884
Middle income	699,866	1,771,709	664,038	1,641,764
Lower middle income	268,479	747,156	274,866	654,664
Upper middle income	430,021	1,024,328	390,689	986,006
Low & middle income	829,051	2,046,020	811,098	1,917,665
East Asia & Pacific	239,776	817,861	240,892	730,851
Europe & Central Asia	187,852	392,525	187,180	372,245
Latin America & Carib.	169,120	417,454	146,270	436,649
Middle East & N. Africa	132,144	213,961	132,549	162,895
South Asia	34,113	88,259	49,041	107,198
Sub-Saharan Africa	81,284	116,295	74,679	106,577
High income	3,419,212	5,774,700	3,432,886	5,933,098
Europe EMU	1,530,965	2,256,837	1,495,268	2,215,062

a. Includes Luxembourg.

About the data

The balance of payments records an economy's transactions with the rest of the world. Balance of payments accounts are divided into two groups: the current account, which records transactions in goods, services, income, and current transfers; and the capital and financial account, which records capital transfers, acquisition or disposal of nonproduced, nonfinancial assets, and transactions in financial assets and liabilities. This table presents data from the current account with the addition of gross international reserves.

The balance of payments is a double-entry accounting system that shows all flows of goods and services into and out of a country; all transfers that are the counterpart of real resources or financial claims provided to or by the rest of the world without a quid pro quo, such as donations and grants; and all changes in residents' claims on, and liabilities to, nonresidents that arise from economic transactions. All transactions are recorded twice—once as a credit and once as a debit. In principle the net balance should be zero, but in practice the accounts often do not balance. In these cases a balancing item, net errors and omissions, is included.

Discrepancies may arise in the balance of payments because there is no single source for balance of payments data and therefore no way to ensure that the data are fully consistent. Sources include customs data, monetary accounts of the banking system, external debt records, information provided by enterprises, surveys to estimate service transactions, and foreign exchange records. Differences in collection methods—such as in timing, definitions of residence and ownership, and the exchange rate used to value transactions—contribute to net errors and omissions. In addition, smuggling and other illegal or quasi-legal transactions may be unrecorded or misrecorded. For further discussion of issues relating to the recording of data on trade in goods and services see *About the data* for tables 4.4–4.8.

The concepts and definitions underlying the data in the table are based on the fifth edition of the International Monetary Fund's (IMF) *Balance of Payments Manual* (1993). The fifth edition redefined as capital transfers some transactions previously included in the current account, such as debt forgiveness, migrants' capital transfers, and foreign aid to acquire capital goods. Thus the current account balance now reflects more accurately net current transfer receipts in addition to transactions in goods, services (previously nonfactor services), and income (previously factor income). Many countries maintain their data collection systems according to the fourth edition. Where necessary, the IMF converts data reported in such systems to conform to the fifth edition (see *Primary data documentation*). Values are in U.S. dollars

converted at market exchange rates.

The data in this table come from the IMF's Balance of Payments and International Financial Statistics databases, supplemented by estimates by World Bank staff for countries whose national accounts are recorded in fiscal years (see *Primary data documentation*) and countries for which the IMF does not collect balance of payments statistics. In addition, World Bank staff make estimates of missing data for the most recent year.

Figure 4.15

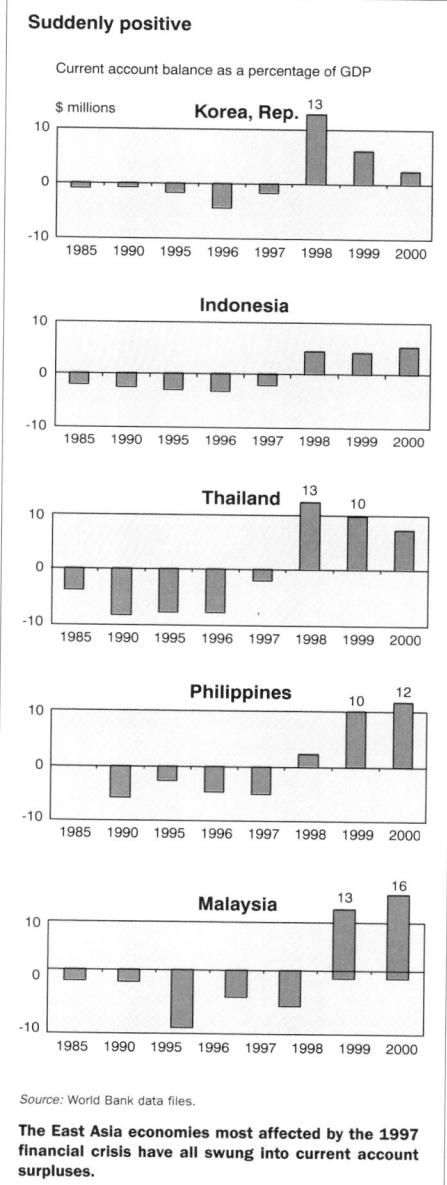

Suddenly positive

Current account balance as a percentage of GDP

Source: World Bank data files.

The East Asia economies most affected by the 1997 financial crisis have all swung into current account surpluses.

Definitions

• **Exports and imports of goods and services** comprise all transactions between residents of a country and the rest of the world involving a change in ownership of general merchandise, goods sent for processing and repairs, nonmonetary gold, and services. • **Net income** refers to receipts and payments of employee compensation to nonresident workers, and investment income (receipts and payments on direct investment, portfolio investment, and other investments, and receipts on reserve assets). Income derived from the use of intangible assets is recorded under business services. • **Net current transfers** are recorded in the balance of payments whenever an economy provides or receives goods, services, income, or financial items without a quid pro quo. All transfers not considered to be capital are current. • **Current account balance** is the sum of net exports of goods and services, net income, and net current transfers. • **Gross international reserves** comprise holdings of monetary gold, special drawing rights, reserves of IMF members held by the IMF, and holdings of foreign exchange under the control of monetary authorities. The gold component of these reserves is valued at year-end (31 December) London prices ($385 an ounce in 1990 and $274.45 an ounce in 2000).

Data sources

More information about the design and compilation of the balance of payments can be found in the IMF's *Balance of Payments Manual*, fifth edition (1993), *Balance of Payments Textbook* (1996a), and *Balance of Payments Compilation Guide* (1995). The balance of payments data are published in the IMF's *Balance of Payments Statistics Yearbook* and *International Financial Statistics*. The World Bank exchanges data with the IMF through electronic files that in most cases are more timely and cover a longer period than the published sources. The IMF's International Financial Statistics and Balance of Payments databases are available on CD-ROM.

	Total external debt $ millions		Long-term debt $ millions		Public and publicly guaranteed debt				Private nonguaranteed external debt $ millions		Use of IMF credit $ millions	
					Total $ millions		IBRD loans and IDA credits $ millions					
	1990	2000	1990	2000	1990	2000	1990	2000	1990	2000	1990	2000
Afghanistan	..	..	..	..	..	..	..	..	..	..	..	..
Albania	349	784	36	659	36	644	0	346	0	15	0	88
Algeria	27,877	25,002	26,416	23,062	26,416	23,062	1,208	1,425	0	0	670	1,718
Angola	8,594	10,146	7,605	8,758	7,605	8,758	0	226	0	0	0	0
Argentina	62,232	146,172	48,676	112,801	46,876	86,599	2,609	8,789	1,800	26,202	3,083	5,056
Armenia	..	898	..	678	..	658	..	397	..	20	..	176
Australia	..	..	..	..	..	..	..	..	..	..	..	..
Austria	..	..	..	..	..	..	..	..	..	..	..	..
Azerbaijan	..	1,184	..	692	..	594	..	216	..	99	..	336
Bangladesh	12,439	15,609	11,657	15,098	11,657	15,098	4,159	6,455	0	0	626	216
Belarus	..	851	..	693	..	692	..	105	..	1	..	114
Belgium	..	..	..	..	..	..	..	..	..	..	..	..
Benin	1,292	1,598	1,218	1,443	1,218	1,443	326	578	0	0	18	84
Bolivia	4,275	5,762	3,864	5,140	3,687	4,120	587	1,096	177	1,020	257	220
Bosnia and Herzegovina	..	2,828	..	2,575	..	2,569	..	959	..	7	..	105
Botswana	561	413	556	398	556	398	169	25	0	0	0	0
Brazil	119,964	237,953	94,427	205,210	87,756	92,590	8,427	7,377	6,671	112,620	1,821	1,768
Bulgaria	10,890	10,026	9,834	8,282	9,834	7,513	0	824	0	769	0	1,322
Burkina Faso	834	1,332	750	1,135	750	1,135	282	592	0	0	0	112
Burundi	907	1,100	851	1,028	851	1,028	398	600	0	0	43	7
Cambodia	1,854	2,357	1,688	2,180	1,688	2,180	0	207	0	0	27	73
Cameroon	6,676	9,241	5,595	7,674	5,365	7,357	889	987	230	317	121	235
Canada	..	..	..	..	..	..	..	..	..	..	..	..
Central African Republic	698	872	624	810	624	810	265	391	0	0	37	22
Chad	524	1,116	464	1,009	464	1,009	186	515	0	0	31	78
Chile	19,226	36,978	14,687	34,447	10,425	5,210	1,874	816	4,263	29,236	1,156	0
China	55,301	149,800	45,515	132,625	45,515	104,709	5,881	19,889	0	27,916	469	0
Hong Kong, China	..	..	..	..	..	..	..	..	..	..	..	..
Colombia	17,222	34,081	15,784	31,210	14,671	20,950	3,874	1,927	1,113	10,259	0	0
Congo, Dem. Rep.	10,274	11,645	9,010	7,842	9,010	7,842	1,161	1,269	0	0	521	391
Congo, Rep.	4,947	4,887	4,200	3,757	4,200	3,757	239	224	0	0	11	41
Costa Rica	3,756	4,466	3,367	3,510	3,063	3,274	412	123	304	236	11	0
Côte d'Ivoire	17,251	12,138	13,223	10,546	10,665	9,063	1,920	1,965	2,558	1,482	431	549
Croatia	..	12,120	..	11,264	..	7,685	..	395	..	3,578	..	158
Cuba	..	..	..	..	..	..	..	..	..	..	..	..
Czech Republic	6,383	21,299	3,983	12,282	3,983	8,132	0	260	0	4,151	0	0
Denmark	..	..	..	..	..	..	..	..	..	..	..	..
Dominican Republic	4,372	4,598	3,518	3,368	3,419	3,368	258	306	99	0	72	52
Ecuador	12,107	13,281	10,029	12,151	9,865	11,366	848	861	164	785	265	148
Egypt, Arab Rep.	33,017	28,957	28,438	24,852	27,438	24,279	2,401	1,905	1,000	573	125	0
El Salvador	2,149	4,023	1,938	2,886	1,913	2,775	164	325	26	111	0	0
Eritrea	..	311	..	298	..	298	..	85	..	0	..	0
Estonia	..	3,280	..	2,317	..	206	..	71	..	2,111	..	19
Ethiopia	8,630	5,481	8,479	5,325	8,479	5,325	851	1,779	0	0	6	77
Finland	..	..	..	..	..	..	..	..	..	..	..	..
France	..	..	..	..	..	..	..	..	..	..	..	..
Gabon	3,983	3,995	3,150	3,512	3,150	3,512	69	64	0	0	140	89
Gambia, The	369	471	308	425	308	425	102	171	0	0	45	18
Georgia	..	1,633	..	1,311	..	1,271	..	347	..	40	..	278
Germany	..	..	..	..	..	..	..	..	..	..	..	..
Ghana	3,881	6,657	2,816	5,786	2,783	5,529	1,423	3,140	33	257	745	293
Greece	..	..	..	..	..	..	..	..	..	..	..	..
Guatemala	3,080	4,622	2,605	3,287	2,478	3,146	293	296	127	142	67	0
Guinea	2,476	3,388	2,253	2,940	2,253	2,940	420	982	0	0	52	113
Guinea-Bissau	692	942	630	818	630	818	146	228	0	0	5	25
Haiti	910	1,169	772	1,040	772	1,040	324	480	0	0	38	39
Honduras	3,718	5,487	3,487	4,897	3,420	4,337	635	989	66	560	32	216

	Total external debt $ millions		Long-term debt $ millions		Public and publicly guaranteed debt Total $ millions		IBRD loans and IDA credits $ millions		Private nonguaranteed external debt $ millions		Use of IMF credit $ millions	
	1990	2000	1990	2000	1990	2000	1990	2000	1990	2000	1990	2000
Hungary	21,202	29,415	17,931	25,263	17,931	14,251	1,512	582	0	11,012	330	0
India	83,628	100,367	72,462	96,903	70,974	87,598	20,996	27,866	1,488	9,305	2,623	0
Indonesia	69,872	141,803	58,242	108,330	47,982	69,161	10,385	12,428	10,261	39,169	494	10,838
Iran, Islamic Rep.	9,020	7,953	1,797	4,275	1,797	3,812	86	481	0	463	0	0
Iraq	..	..	..	..	..	..	..	..	..	..	..	..
Ireland	..	..	..	..	..	..	..	..	..	..	..	..
Israel	..	..	..	..	..	..	..	..	..	..	..	..
Italy	..	..	..	..	..	..	..	..	..	..	..	..
Jamaica	4,674	4,287	3,970	3,475	3,937	3,373	672	415	34	103	357	60
Japan	..	..	..	..	..	..	..	..	..	..	..	..
Jordan	8,177	8,226	7,043	7,055	7,043	7,055	593	856	0	0	94	462
Kazakhstan	..	6,664	..	6,131	..	3,602	..	1,057	..	2,529	..	0
Kenya	7,058	6,295	5,642	5,355	4,762	5,180	2,056	2,309	880	175	482	127
Korea, Dem. Rep.	..	..	..	..	..	..	..	..	..	..	..	..
Korea, Rep.	34,968	134,417	24,168	88,141	18,768	46,941	3,337	8,097	5,400	41,200	0	5,814
Kuwait	..	..	..	..	..	..	..	..	..	..	..	..
Kyrgyz Republic	..	1,829	..	1,512	..	1,224	..	377	..	288	..	188
Lao PDR	1,768	2,499	1,758	2,449	1,758	2,449	131	403	0	0	8	42
Latvia	..	3,379	..	2,074	..	827	..	242	..	1,247	..	35
Lebanon	1,779	10,311	358	7,770	358	7,034	34	248	0	736	0	0
Lesotho	396	716	378	698	378	698	112	242	0	0	15	11
Liberia	1,849	2,032	1,116	1,040	1,116	1,040	248	230	0	0	322	292
Libya	..	..	..	..	..	..	..	..	..	..	..	..
Lithuania	..	4,855	..	3,549	..	2,188	..	253	..	1,361	..	192
Macedonia, FYR	..	1,465	..	1,304	..	1,165	..	365	..	140	..	81
Madagascar	3,704	4,701	3,335	4,295	3,335	4,295	797	1,378	0	0	144	104
Malawi	1,558	2,716	1,385	2,555	1,382	2,555	854	1,601	3	0	115	83
Malaysia	15,328	41,797	13,422	37,156	11,592	19,090	1,102	812	1,830	18,067	0	0
Mali	2,467	2,956	2,336	2,645	2,336	2,645	498	957	0	0	69	176
Mauritania	2,096	2,500	1,789	2,150	1,789	2,150	264	450	0	0	70	98
Mauritius	984	2,374	910	1,608	762	889	195	99	148	718	22	0
Mexico	104,442	150,288	81,809	131,356	75,974	81,550	11,030	11,444	5,835	49,806	6,551	0
Moldova	..	1,233	..	1,051	..	854	..	294	..	197	..	154
Mongolia	..	859	..	795	..	795	0	137	..	0	0	50
Morocco	24,458	17,944	23,301	17,688	23,101	15,792	3,138	2,864	200	1,896	750	0
Mozambique	4,650	7,135	4,231	6,346	4,211	4,598	268	760	19	1,747	74	220
Myanmar	4,695	6,046	4,466	5,360	4,466	5,360	716	802	0	0	0	0
Namibia	..	..	..	..	..	..	..	..	..	..	..	..
Nepal	1,640	2,823	1,572	2,784	1,572	2,784	668	1,134	0	0	44	12
Netherlands	..	..	..	..	..	..	..	..	..	..	..	..
New Zealand	..	..	..	..	..	..	..	..	..	..	..	..
Nicaragua	10,745	7,019	8,313	5,860	8,313	5,602	299	659	0	258	0	169
Niger	1,726	1,638	1,487	1,481	1,226	1,413	461	723	261	68	85	74
Nigeria	33,439	34,134	31,935	32,950	31,545	32,735	3,321	2,268	391	215	0	0
Norway	..	..	..	..	..	..	..	..	..	..	..	..
Oman	2,736	6,267	2,400	4,968	2,400	2,673	52	3	0	2,296	0	0
Pakistan	20,663	32,091	16,643	29,043	16,506	27,140	3,922	6,922	138	1,903	836	1,529
Panama	6,506	7,056	3,856	6,503	3,856	5,723	462	283	0	780	272	90
Papua New Guinea	2,594	2,604	2,461	2,515	1,523	1,502	349	336	938	1,014	61	39
Paraguay	2,105	3,091	1,732	2,511	1,713	2,061	320	230	19	450	0	0
Peru	20,064	28,560	13,959	24,045	13,629	19,205	1,188	2,590	330	4,841	755	558
Philippines	30,580	50,063	25,241	42,083	24,040	33,429	4,044	3,834	1,201	8,654	912	2,032
Poland	49,364	63,561	39,261	56,457	39,261	30,784	55	2,229	0	25,672	509	0
Portugal	..	..	..	..	..	..	..	..	..	..	..	..
Puerto Rico	..	..	..	..	..	..	..	..	..	..	..	..
Romania	1,140	10,224	230	9,410	223	6,430	0	1,898	7	2,980	0	453
Russian Federation	59,340	160,300	47,540	133,158	47,540	111,419	0	6,844	0	21,739	0	11,613

| | Total external debt $ millions | | Long-term debt $ millions | | Public and publicly guaranteed debt | | | | Private nonguaranteed external debt $ millions | | Use of IMF credit $ millions | |
| | | | | | Total $ millions | | IBRD loans and IDA credits $ millions | | | | | |
	1990	2000	1990	2000	1990	2000	1990	2000	1990	2000	1990	2000
Rwanda	712	1,271	664	1,147	664	1,147	340	692	0	0	0	86
Saudi Arabia	..	..	..	..	..	..	..	..	..	..	..	..
Senegal	3,736	3,372	3,000	2,971	2,940	2,958	835	1,331	60	13	314	255
Sierra Leone	1,151	1,273	604	969	604	969	92	354	0	0	108	174
Singapore	..	..	..	..	..	..	..	..	..	..	..	..
Slovak Republic	2,008	9,462	1,505	8,304	1,505	4,883	0	184	0	3,421	0	0
Slovenia	..	..	..	..	..	..	..	..	..	..	..	..
Somalia	2,370	2,561	1,926	1,825	1,926	1,825	419	396	0	0	159	146
South Africa	..	24,861	..	15,308	..	9,088	0	3	..	6,220	0	0
Spain	..	..	..	..	..	..	..	..	..	..	..	..
Sri Lanka	5,863	9,065	5,049	8,200	4,947	8,035	946	1,624	102	165	410	161
Sudan	14,762	15,741	9,651	9,143	9,155	8,647	1,048	1,168	496	496	956	625
Swaziland	254	262	249	198	249	198	44	14	0	0	0	0
Sweden	..	..	..	..	..	..	..	..	..	..	..	..
Switzerland	..	..	..	..	..	..	..	..	..	..	..	..
Syrian Arab Republic	17,259	21,657	15,108	15,930	15,108	15,930	523	54	0	0	0	0
Tajikistan	..	1,170	..	995	..	626	..	143	..	370	..	111
Tanzania	6,454	7,445	5,796	6,353	5,784	6,325	1,493	2,604	12	28	140	324
Thailand	28,095	79,675	19,771	61,733	12,460	29,418	2,530	3,030	7,311	32,316	1	3,062
Togo	1,281	1,435	1,081	1,232	1,081	1,232	398	604	0	0	87	70
Trinidad and Tobago	2,512	2,467	2,055	1,606	1,782	1,496	41	89	273	110	329	0
Tunisia	7,690	10,610	6,880	9,669	6,662	8,869	1,406	1,250	218	800	176	32
Turkey	49,424	116,209	39,924	83,121	38,870	55,293	6,429	3,734	1,054	27,828	0	4,176
Turkmenistan	..	..	..	..	..	..	..	28	..	..	..	0
Uganda	2,583	3,408	2,161	2,997	2,161	2,997	969	2,115	0	0	282	316
Ukraine	..	12,166	..	9,646	..	8,139	..	1,991	..	1,507	..	2,073
United Arab Emirates	..	..	..	..	..	..	..	..	..	..	..	..
United Kingdom	..	..	..	..	..	..	..	..	..	..	..	..
United States	..	..	..	..	..	..	..	..	..	..	..	..
Uruguay	4,415	8,196	3,114	6,131	3,045	5,597	359	552	69	534	101	149
Uzbekistan	..	4,340	..	3,931	..	3,578	..	217	..	354	..	127
Venezuela, RB	33,170	38,196	28,159	36,230	24,509	27,628	974	972	3,650	8,602	3,012	203
Vietnam	23,270	12,787	21,378	11,546	21,378	11,546	59	1,113	0	0	112	316
West Bank and Gaza	..	..	..	..	..	..	..	..	..	..	..	..
Yemen, Rep.	6,352	5,615	5,160	4,524	5,160	4,524	602	1,216	0	0	0	317
Yugoslavia, Fed. Rep.[a]	17,792	11,960	16,802	6,685	12,942	6,074	2,433	1,097	3,860	611	467	152
Zambia	6,916	5,730	4,554	4,513	4,552	4,448	813	1,848	2	65	949	1,138
Zimbabwe	3,247	4,002	2,649	3,158	2,464	2,948	449	853	185	211	7	281

World	.. s		.. s		.. s		.. s		.. s		.. s	
Low income	418,586	550,548	357,322	471,077	340,308	412,834	66,693	100,470	17,015	58,243	11,250	23,580
Middle income[b]	1,039,801	1,941,427	822,006	1,576,622	773,507	1,077,611	73,946	108,622	48,498	499,009	23,400	40,683
Lower middle income	470,037	779,736	386,402	652,075	369,306	528,573	34,782	61,176	17,096	123,502	6,058	23,048
Upper middle income[b]	567,807	1,156,041	434,963	921,959	403,561	546,822	39,164	47,303	31,402	375,137	17,343	17,524
Low & middle income[b]	1,458,389	2,491,975	1,179,328	2,047,696	1,113,815	1,490,445	140,639	209,093	65,513	557,251	34,651	64,262
East Asia & Pacific	273,983	632,953	222,722	502,238	195,687	333,852	28,644	51,211	27,035	168,386	2,085	22,266
Europe & Central Asia	219,850	499,344	177,688	396,428	172,767	284,369	10,429	25,455	4,921	112,060	1,305	21,951
Latin America & Carib.	474,720	774,419	379,206	661,735	354,155	415,077	35,841	40,904	25,051	246,658	18,297	8,846
Middle East & N. Africa	183,471	203,785	137,762	153,794	136,260	147,031	10,074	10,351	1,502	6,763	1,815	2,542
South Asia	129,481	165,679	112,573	157,724	110,845	146,351	30,717	44,073	1,727	11,372	4,537	1,918
Sub-Saharan Africa	176,883	215,794	149,377	175,777	144,101	163,765	24,935	37,098	5,276	12,012	6,612	6,739
High income												
Europe EMU												

a. Data for 1990 refer to the former Socialist Federal Republic of Yugoslavia. Data for 2000 are estimates and reflect borrowings by the former Socialist Federal Republic of Yugoslavia that are not yet allocated to the successor republics. b. Includes data for Gibraltar not included in other tables.

About the data

Data on the external debt of low- and middle-income economies are gathered by the World Bank through its Debtor Reporting System. World Bank staff calculate the indebtedness of developing countries using loan-by-loan reports submitted by these countries on long-term public and publicly guaranteed borrowing, along with information on short-term debt collected by the countries or collected from creditors through the reporting systems of the Bank for International Settlements and the Organisation for Economic Co-operation and Development. These data are supplemented by information on loans and credits from major multilateral banks, loan statements from official lending agencies in major creditor countries, and estimates from World Bank and International Monetary Fund (IMF) staff. In addition, the table includes data on private nonguaranteed debt for 79 countries either reported to the World Bank or estimated by Bank staff.

The coverage, quality, and timeliness of debt data vary across countries. Coverage varies for both debt instruments and borrowers. With the widening spectrum of debt instruments and investors and the expansion of private nonguaranteed borrowing, comprehensive coverage of long-term external debt becomes more complex. Reporting countries differ in their capacity to monitor debt, especially private nonguaranteed debt. Even data on public and publicly- guaranteed debt are affected by coverage and accuracy in reporting—again because of monitoring capacity and sometimes because of unwillingness to provide information. A key part often underreported is military debt.

Because debt data are normally reported in the currency of repayment, they have to be converted into U.S. dollars to produce summary tables. Stock figures (amount of debt outstanding) are converted using end-period exchange rates, as published in the IMF's *International Financial Statistics* (line ae). Flow figures are converted at annual average exchange rates (line rf). Projected debt service is converted using end-period exchange rates. Debt repayable in multiple currencies, goods, or services and debt with a provision for maintenance of value of the currency of repayment are shown at book value.

Because flow data are converted at annual average exchange rates and stock data at year-end exchange rates, year-to-year changes in debt outstanding and disbursed are sometimes not equal to net flows (disbursements less principal repayments); similarly, changes in debt outstanding, including undisbursed debt, differ from commitments less repayments. Discrepancies are particularly significant when exchange rates have moved sharply during the year. Cancellations and reschedulings of other liabilities into long-term public debt also contribute to the differences.

Variations in reporting rescheduled debt also affect cross-country comparability. For example, rescheduling under the auspices of the Paris Club of official creditors may be subject to lags between the completion of the general rescheduling agreement and the completion of the specific, bilateral agreements that define the terms of the rescheduled debt. Other areas of inconsistency include country treatment of arrears and of nonresident national deposits denominated in foreign currency.

Definitions

• **Total external debt** is debt owed to nonresidents repayable in foreign currency, goods, or services. It is the sum of public, publicly guaranteed, and private nonguaranteed long-term debt, use of IMF credit, and short-term debt. Short-term debt includes all debt having an original maturity of one year or less and interest in arrears on long-term debt. • **Long-term debt** is debt that has an original or extended maturity of more than one year. It has three components: public, publicly guaranteed, and private nonguaranteed debt. • **Public and publicly guaranteed debt** comprises long-term external obligations of public debtors, including the national government and political subdivisions (or an agency of either) and autonomous public bodies, and external obligations of private debtors that are guaranteed for repayment by a public entity. • **IBRD loans and IDA credits** are extended by the World Bank Group. The International Bank for Reconstruction and Development (IBRD) lends at market rates. Credits from the International Development Association (IDA) are at concessional rates. • **Private nonguaranteed external debt** comprises long-term external obligations of private debtors that are not guaranteed for repayment by a public entity. • **Use of IMF credit** denotes repurchase obligations to the IMF for all uses of IMF resources (excluding those resulting from drawings on the reserve tranche). These obligations, shown for the end of the year specified, comprise purchases outstanding under the credit tranches, including enlarged access resources, and all special facilities (the buffer stock, compensatory financing, extended fund, and oil facilities), trust fund loans, and operations under the structural adjustment and enhanced structural adjustment facilities.

Data sources

The main sources of external debt information are reports to the World Bank through its Debtor Reporting System from member countries that have received IBRD loans or IDA credits. Additional information has been drawn from the files of the World Bank and the IMF. Summary tables of the external debt of developing countries are published annually in the World Bank's *Global Development Finance* and on its *Global Development Finance* CD-ROM.

4.17 | External debt management

	Indebtness classfication[a]	Present value of debt		Total debt service				Public and publicly guaranteed debt service		Short-term debt	
		% of GNI	% of exports of goods and services	% of GNI		% of exports of goods and services		% of central government current revenue		% of total debt	
	2000	2000	2000	1990	2000	1990	2000	1990	2000	1990	2000
Afghanistan	..	..	..	..	..	..	..	..	..	..	..
Albania	L	13	36	0.1	0.7	0.9	2.0	..	..	89.8	4.7
Algeria	M	50	112	14.7	8.8	63.4	19.6	..	..	2.8	0.9
Angola	S	203	121	4.0	25.4	8.1	15.1	..	..	11.5	13.7
Argentina	S	56	404	4.6	9.9	37.0	71.3	32.5	41.1	16.8	19.4
Armenia	L	31	106	..	2.2	..	7.6	..	..	..	4.9
Australia	..	..	..	..	..	..	..	..	..	..	..
Austria	..	..	..	..	..	..	..	..	..	..	..
Azerbaijan	L	20	44	..	3.7	..	8.0	..	..	..	13.2
Bangladesh	L	20	111	2.5	1.7	27.4	9.1	..	..	1.3	1.9
Belarus	L	3	10	..	0.8	..	2.9	..	5.5	..	5.1
Belgium	..	..	..	..	..	..	..	..	..	..	..
Benin	S	45 [b]	161 [b]	2.1	3.6	8.2	12.6	..	..	4.3	4.5
Bolivia	M	34 [b]	162 [b]	8.3	8.2	38.6	39.1	41.3	18.8	3.6	7.0
Bosnia and Herzegovina	M	49	..	7.2	..	..	..	..	..	..	5.2
Botswana	L	6	9	2.9	1.3	4.4	1.8	5.5	..	1.0	3.7
Brazil	S	39	323	1.8	11.0	22.2	90.7	3.9	..	19.8	13.0
Bulgaria	M	82	131	7.2	10.2	19.4	16.2	12.9	15.8	9.7	4.2
Burkina Faso	M	31 [b]	210 [b]	1.2	2.5	6.8	17.3	9.1	..	10.1	6.3
Burundi	S	96	1,118	3.8	3.2	43.4	37.2	..	..	1.5	5.9
Cambodia	M	62	127	2.7	1.0	..	2.0	..	..	7.5	4.4
Cameroon	S	75	228	4.9	6.8	22.5	20.5	16.8	..	14.4	14.4
Canada	..	..	..	..	..	..	..	..	..	..	..
Central African Republic	S	57	497	2.0	1.5	13.2	12.9	..	..	5.4	4.7
Chad	S	42	207	0.7	1.9	4.4	9.3	5.6	..	5.7	2.6
Chile	M	51	147	9.7	9.0	25.9	26.0	25.6	6.7	17.6	6.8
China	L	13	46	2.0	2.0	11.7	7.4	23.9	..	16.8	11.5
Hong Kong, China	..	..	..	..	..	..	..	..	..	..	..
Colombia	M	42	185	10.2	6.6	40.9	28.6	61.2	..	8.4	8.4
Congo, Dem. Rep.	S	..	..	4.1	..	13.5	..	14.5	..	7.2	29.3
Congo, Rep.	S	206	169	22.9	1.9	35.3	1.6	..	1.4	14.9	22.3
Costa Rica	L	31	56	9.2	4.4	23.9	8.2	32.8	16.9	10.0	21.4
Côte d'Ivoire	S	134 [b]	254 [b]	13.7	11.8	35.4	22.4	22.1	..	20.8	8.6
Croatia	M	65	127	..	13.0	..	25.5	..	16.9	..	5.8
Cuba	..	..	..	..	..	..	..	..	..	..	..
Czech Republic	L	43	57	..	9.5	..	12.7	..	15.6	37.6	42.3
Denmark	..	..	..	..	..	..	..	..	..	..	..
Dominican Republic	L	23	40	3.4	2.8	10.4	4.8	16.1	..	17.9	25.6
Ecuador	S	106	178	11.1	10.3	32.5	17.3	45.0	..	15.0	7.4
Egypt, Arab Rep.	L	23	107	7.3	1.8	22.5	8.4	16.5	..	13.5	14.2
El Salvador	L	29	68	4.4	2.9	15.3	6.7	..	12.5	9.8	28.3
Eritrea	L	27	63	..	0.5	..	1.1	..	..	..	4.2
Estonia	M	66	62	..	9.3	..	8.7	..	2.4	..	28.8
Ethiopia	S	52	326	3.5	2.2	34.9	13.9	13.4	..	1.7	1.4
Finland	..	..	..	..	..	..	..	..	..	..	..
France	..	..	..	..	..	..	..	..	..	..	..
Gabon	S	91	125	3.3	11.0	6.4	15.0	7.6	..	17.4	9.9
Gambia, The	M	64	99	12.9	4.5	22.2	7.0	49.1	..	4.3	5.8
Georgia	L	42	104	..	3.8	..	9.5	..	25.8	..	2.7
Germany	..	..	..	..	..	..	..	..	..	..	..
Ghana	M	78 [b]	160 [b]	6.4	9.4	36.9	19.3	26.2	..	8.2	8.7
Greece	..	..	..	..	..	..	..	..	..	..	..
Guatemala	L	23	93	2.9	2.3	12.6	9.4	..	..	13.3	28.9
Guinea	S	80	269	6.3	4.5	20.0	15.3	33.0	..	6.9	9.9
Guinea-Bissau	S	345	970	3.6	3.1	31.0	8.6	..	..	8.2	10.5
Haiti	M	17	133	1.2	1.0	11.0	8.0	..	11.3	11.1	7.7
Honduras	M	54	104	13.7	10.0	35.3	19.3	..	..	5.4	6.8

	Indebtness classfication[a]	Present value of debt		Total debt service				Public and publicly guaranteed debt service		Short-term debt	
		% of GNI	% of exports of goods and services	% of GNI		% of exports of goods and services		% of central government current revenue		% of total debt	
	2000	2000	2000	1990	2000	1990	2000	1990	2000	1990	2000
Hungary	M	63	85	13.4	18.0	34.3	24.4	21.4	20.4	13.9	14.1
India	L	16	91	2.6	2.2	32.4	12.8	14.5	13.6	10.2	3.5
Indonesia	S	95	182	9.1	13.2	33.3	25.3	34.4	..	15.9	16.0
Iran, Islamic Rep.	L	7	25	0.5	3.3	3.2	11.4	0.3	4.4	80.1	46.2
Iraq	..	..	..	..	..	..	..	..	..	..	..
Ireland	..	..	..	..	..	..	..	..	..	..	..
Israel	..	..	..	..	..	..	..	..	..	..	..
Italy	..	..	..	..	..	..	..	..	..	..	..
Jamaica	M	62	95	17.7	9.2	26.9	14.1	..	19.5	7.4	17.5
Japan	..	..	..	..	..	..	..	..	..	..	..
Jordan	S	92	130	16.4	8.0	20.3	11.4	52.1	26.7	12.7	8.6
Kazakhstan	L	39	61	..	10.8	..	16.8	..	20.1	..	8.0
Kenya	M	46	168	9.8	4.7	35.4	17.3	26.6	..	13.2	12.9
Korea, Dem. Rep.	..	..	..	..	..	..	..	..	..	..	..
Korea, Rep.	L	28	61	3.3	5.1	10.8	10.9	10.5	..	30.9	30.1
Kuwait	..	..	..	..	..	..	..	..	..	..	..
Kyrgyz Republic	S	115 [b]	237 [b]	..	14.2	..	29.3	..	20.4	..	7.1
Lao PDR	S	72	234	1.1	2.5	8.7	8.1	..	..	0.1	0.3
Latvia	L	46	94	..	7.8	..	15.8	..	6.4	..	37.6
Lebanon	M	61	..	2.9	10.5	3.3	..	..	..	79.9	24.6
Lesotho	L	45	95	2.3	5.7	4.2	12.1	9.4	..	0.7	1.0
Liberia	S	..	..	..	..	..	..	..	..	22.2	34.4
Libya	..	..	..	..	..	..	..	..	..	..	..
Lithuania	L	43	90	..	8.1	..	17.1	..	16.0	..	22.9
Macedonia, FYR	L	36	72	..	4.6	..	9.3	..	..	..	5.4
Madagascar	S	79	247	7.6	2.4	45.5	7.7	42.9	17.3	6.1	6.4
Malawi	S	90 [b]	297 [b]	7.2	3.5	29.3	11.7	27.2	..	3.7	2.9
Malaysia	M	52	38	10.3	7.2	12.6	5.3	31.4	..	12.4	11.1
Mali	M	59 [b]	167 [b]	2.8	4.3	12.3	12.1	..	..	2.5	4.6
Mauritania	S	134	314	13.6	11.0	29.9	25.9	..	..	11.3	10.1
Mauritius	M	54	88	5.9	12.7	8.8	20.8	13.5	45.7	5.3	32.3
Mexico	L	28	81	4.5	10.4	20.7	30.2	19.5	..	15.4	12.6
Moldova	M	84	140	..	10.0	..	16.7	..	20.7	..	2.2
Mongolia	M	59	91	..	3.1	..	4.7	..	7.7	..	1.6
Morocco	L	49	124	7.2	10.3	21.5	25.9	21.3	..	1.7	1.4
Mozambique	M	33 [b]	151 [b]	3.4	2.5	26.2	11.4	..	..	7.4	8.0
Myanmar	S	..	235	..	..	9.0	4.7	2.2	..	4.9	11.3
Namibia	..	..	..	..	..	..	..	..	..	7.4	8.0
Nepal	L	27	102	1.9	1.8	13.4	6.5	18.2	16.3	1.5	0.9
Netherlands	..	..	..	..	..	..	..	..	..	..	..
New Zealand	..	..	..	..	..	..	..	..	..	..	..
Nicaragua	S	263 [b]	425 [b]	1.6	14.2	3.9	23.0	2.6	22.6	22.6	14.1
Niger	S	58 [b]	344 [b]	4.1	1.6	17.4	9.4	..	..	8.9	5.1
Nigeria	S	74	117	13.0	2.7	22.6	4.3	..	..	4.5	3.5
Norway	..	..	..	..	..	..	..	..	..	..	..
Oman	L	..	50	7.8	..	12.3	7.3	17.4	8.2	12.3	20.7
Pakistan	S	45	249	4.9	4.8	23.0	26.8	18.1	18.0	15.4	4.7
Panama	M	78	79	6.8	9.9	6.2	10.0	10.4	..	36.6	6.6
Papua New Guinea	M	60	97	17.9	8.3	37.2	13.5	33.2	..	2.8	1.9
Paraguay	L	39	93	6.0	4.4	12.2	10.4	46.8	..	17.7	18.8
Peru	S	55	283	1.9	8.3	10.8	42.8	4.9	24.0	26.7	13.9
Philippines	M	64	103	8.1	8.5	27.0	13.6	39.5	36.9	14.5	11.9
Poland	L	37	118	1.7	6.6	4.9	20.9	..	6.9	19.4	11.2
Portugal	..	..	..	..	..	..	..	..	..	..	..
Puerto Rico	..	..	..	..	..	..	..	..	..	..	..
Romania	L	28	80	0.0	6.4	0.3	18.8	0.0	..	79.8	3.5
Russian Federation	M	62	128	2.0	4.9	..	10.1	..	7.8	19.9	9.7

	Indebtness classfication[a]	Present value of debt		Total debt service				Public and publicly guaranteed debt service		Short-term debt	
		% of GNI	% of exports of goods and services	% of GNI		% of exports of goods and services		% of central government current revenue		% of total debt	
	2000	2000	2000	1990	2000	1990	2000	1990	2000	1990	2000
Rwanda	S	41	509	0.8	2.0	14.0	24.7	5.4	..	6.6	3.0
Saudi Arabia	..	..	..	..	..	..	..	..	..	..	..
Senegal	M	56	153	5.9	5.3	20.0	14.4	..	..	11.3	4.4
Sierra Leone	S	128	892	2.7	6.9	10.1	48.0	30.6	..	38.1	10.3
Singapore	..	..	..	..	..	..	..	..	..	..	..
Slovak Republic	L	48	63	2.1	13.8	..	18.0	..	11.8	25.0	12.2
Slovenia	..	..	..	..	..	..	..	..	..	..	..
Somalia	S	..	..	1.3	..	15.2	..	..	..	12.0	23.1
South Africa	L	19	61	..	3.1	..	10.0	..	6.3	..	38.4
Spain	..	..	..	..	..	..	..	..	..	..	..
Sri Lanka	L	44	91	4.9	4.6	13.8	9.6	16.8	21.6	6.9	7.8
Sudan	S	152	781	0.4	0.6	7.5	3.2	..	..	28.1	37.9
Swaziland	L	14	21	5.3	1.6	5.7	2.3	16.0	5.1	1.8	24.2
Sweden	..	..	..	..	..	..	..	..	..	..	..
Switzerland	..	..	..	..	..	..	..	..	..	..	..
Syrian Arab Republic	S	131	290	9.9	2.2	21.8	4.8	21.2	..	12.5	26.4
Tajikistan	S	100	118	..	9.3	..	10.9	..	24.3	..	5.5
Tanzania[c]	S	50	335	4.4	2.4	32.9	16.2	..	..	8.0	10.3
Thailand	M	64	89	6.3	11.6	16.9	16.3	20.7	23.5	29.6	18.7
Togo	M	85	209	5.4	2.5	11.9	6.1	..	..	8.8	9.3
Trinidad and Tobago	L	38	53	9.7	7.5	19.3	10.3	..	..	5.1	34.9
Tunisia	M	57	112	12.0	10.2	24.5	20.2	32.2	31.5	8.2	8.6
Turkey	M	57	196	4.9	10.5	29.4	36.1	30.9	18.0	19.2	24.9
Turkmenistan	M	..	..	..	..	..	..	..	..	..	..
Uganda	M	16 [b]	146 [b]	3.4	2.6	58.9	23.7	..	15.6	5.4	2.8
Ukraine	L	37	58	..	11.9	..	18.6	..	21.0	..	3.7
United Arab Emirates	..	..	..	..	..	..	..	..	..	..	..
United Kingdom	..	..	..	..	..	..	..	..	..	..	..
United States	..	..	..	..	..	..	..	..	..	..	..
Uruguay	M	42	183	11.0	6.8	40.8	29.2	32.0	18.5	27.2	23.4
Uzbekistan	M	57	125	..	12.1	..	26.4	..	..	..	6.5
Venezuela, RB	M	32	104	10.6	4.9	23.2	15.7	36.2	18.2	6.0	4.6
Vietnam	L	36	64	..	4.2	8.9	7.5	..	22.0	7.7	7.2
West Bank and Gaza	..	..	..	..	..	..	..	..	..	..	..
Yemen, Rep.	M	57	72	3.5	3.0	5.6	3.8	..	..	18.8	13.8
Yugoslavia, Fed. Rep.	L	142	..	..	2.1	..	..	..	..	2.9	42.8
Zambia	S	179	505	6.7	6.7	14.9	18.7	..	..	20.4	1.4
Zimbabwe	M	50	169	5.5	6.6	23.1	22.1	17.4	..	18.2	14.1

World				.. w	.. w	.. w	.. w			.. w	.. w
Low income				4.8	4.9	23.0	15.7			11.9	10.2
Middle income				3.9	6.6	17.2 [d]	18.5 [d]			18.7	16.7
Lower middle income				3.7	4.2	20.4	11.3			16.5	13.4
Upper middle income				4.0	8.4	14.9 [d]	24.1 [d]			20.3	18.7
Low & middle income				4.0	6.3	18.1 [d]	18.1 [d]			16.8	15.2
East Asia & Pacific				4.4	4.6	15.7	10.8			17.9	17.1
Europe & Central Asia				2.9	8.1	..	18.1			18.6	16.2
Latin America & Carib.				4.2	9.5	24.4	38.7			16.3	13.4
Middle East & N. Africa				5.1	4.0	15.0	10.5			23.9	23.3
South Asia				2.9	2.4	28.7	13.8			9.6	3.6
Sub-Saharan Africa				..	4.2	12.8	10.2			11.8	15.4
High income											
Europe EMU											

a. S = severely indebted, M = moderately indebted, L = less indebted. b. Data are from debt sustainability analyses undertaken as part of the Heavily Indebted Poor Countries (HIPC) Initiative. Present value estimates for these countries are for public and publicly guaranteed debt only, and export figures exclude workers' remittances. c. Data refer to mainland Tanzania only. d. Includes data for Gibraltar not included in other tables.

About the data

The indicators in the table measure the relative burden on developing countries of servicing external debt. The present value of external debt provides a measure of future debt service obligations that can be compared with the current value of indicators such as gross national income, or GNI (gross national product, or GNP, in the 1968 System of National Accounts), and exports of goods and services. This table shows the present value of total debt service both as a percentage of GNI in 2000 and as a percentage of exports in 2000. The ratios compare total debt service obligations with the size of the economy and its ability to obtain foreign exchange through exports. Because workers' remittances are an important source of foreign exchange for many countries, they are included in the value of exports used to calculate debt indicators. Public and publicly-guaranteed debt service is compared with the size of the central government budget. The ratios shown here may differ from those published elsewhere because estimates of exports and GNI have been revised to incorporate data available as of 1 February 2002.

The present value of external debt is calculated by discounting the debt service (interest plus amortization) due on long-term external debt over the life of existing loans. Short-term debt is included at its face value. The data on debt are in U.S. dollars converted at official exchange rates (see *About the data* for table 4.16). The discount rate applied to long-term debt is determined by the currency of repayment of the loan and is based on reference rates for commercial interest established by the Organisation for Economic Co-operation and Development. Loans from the International Bank for Reconstruction and Development (IBRD) and credits from the International Development

Association (IDA) are discounted using an SDR (special drawing rights) reference rate, as are obligations to the International Monetary Fund (IMF). When the discount rate is greater than the interest rate of the loan, the present value is less than the nominal sum of future debt service obligations.

The ratios in the table are used to assess the sustainability of a country's debt service obligations, but there are no absolute rules that determine what values are too high. Empirical analysis of the experience of developing countries and their debt service performance has shown that debt service difficulties become increasingly likely when the ratio of the present value of debt to exports reaches 200 percent. Still, what constitutes a sustainable debt burden varies from one country to another. Countries with fast-growing economies and exports are likely to be able to sustain higher debt levels.

The World Bank classifies countries by their level of indebtedness for the purpose of developing debt management strategies. The most severely indebted countries may be eligible for debt relief under special program, such as the Debt Initiative for Heavily Indebted Poor Countries (HIPCs). Indebted countries may also apply to the Paris and London Clubs for renegotiation of obligations to public and private creditors. In 2000 countries with a present value of debt service greater than 220 percent of exports or 80 percent of GNI were classified as severely indebted; countries that were not severely indebted but whose present value of debt service exceeded 132 percent of exports or 48 percent of GNI were classified as moderately indebted; and countries that did not fall into the above two groups were classified as less indebted.

Definitions

• **Indebtedness** is assessed on a three-point scale: severely indebted (S), moderately indebted (M), and less indebted (L). • **Present value of debt** is the sum of short-term external debt plus the discounted sum of total debt service payments due on public, publicly guaranteed, and private nonguaranteed long-term external debt over the life of existing loans. • **Total debt service** is the sum of principal repayments and interest actually paid in foreign currency, goods, or services on long-term debt, interest paid on short-term debt, and repayments (repurchases and charges) to the IMF. • **Public and publicly guaranteed debt service** is the sum of principal repayments and interest actually paid on long-term obligations of public debtors and long-term private obligations guaranteed by a public entity. • **Short-term debt** includes all debt having an original maturity of one year or less and interest in arrears on long-term debt.

Data sources

The main sources of external debt information are reports to the World Bank through its Debtor Reporting System from member countries that have received IBRD loans or IDA credits. Additional information has been drawn from the files of the World Bank and the IMF. The data on GNI and exports of goods and services are from the World Bank's national accounts files. Summary tables of the external debt of developing countries are published annually in the World Bank's *Global Development Finance* and on its *Global Development Finance* CD-ROM.

Figure 4.17

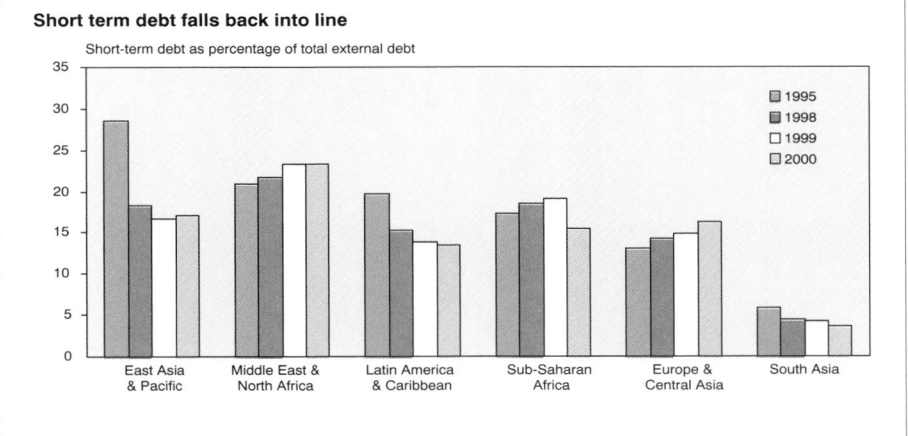

Short term debt falls back into line

Short-term debt as percentage of total external debt

Legend: 1995, 1998, 1999, 2000

Regions: East Asia & Pacific, Middle East & North Africa, Latin America & Caribbean, Sub-Saharan Africa, Europe & Central Asia, South Asia

Source: World Bank data files.

East Asian countries relied too heavily on short-term debt, which helped to precipitate the 1997 financial crisis. Since then, they have reduced the share of short-term debt in their borrowing to a level similar to most other developing regions.

STATES AND MARKETS

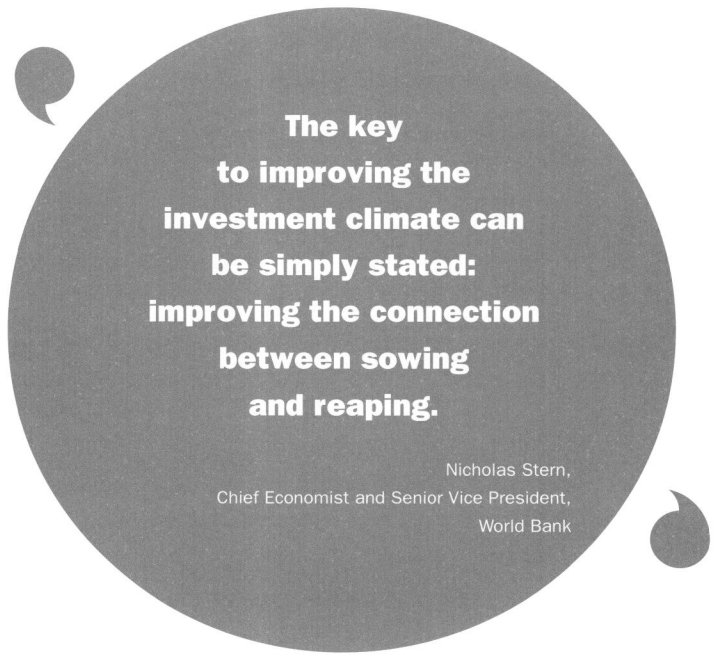

The key
to improving the
investment climate can
be simply stated:
improving the connection
between sowing
and reaping.

Nicholas Stern,
Chief Economist and Senior Vice President,
World Bank

A good investment climate promotes growth and reduces poverty

People rise from poverty when countries act on two pillars of development: building a good investment climate in which private entrepreneurs will invest, generate jobs, and produce efficiently, and empowering poor people and investing in them so that they can participate in economic growth.

What's a good investment climate? Start with sound macroeconomic management and trade and investment policies that promote openness and raise productivity and growth. Add the elements of good governance, such as regulation of industry, promotion of competition, and prevention of corruption. Then set all that on a foundation of basic infrastructure and effective basic services, such as health and education.

The case for creating a good investment climate is simple: an economy needs a predictable environment for people, ideas, and money to work together productively and efficiently. The role of government is to provide ample room for entrepreneurs to invest in agriculture, industry, and services. That allows private firms—small and large, domestic and foreign—operating in competitive markets to be the engine of growth and job creation, providing opportunities to escape poverty.

Countries should focus first on improving the investment climate for domestic entrepreneurs. An improved climate will also attract foreign investors. In today's globalizing world, countries with a good investment climate get more foreign investment—an important conduit for new technology, management experience, and access to markets—and enjoy faster growth and more poverty reduction.

Good governance and strong institutions

Good governance and strong institutions can create an environment that encourages markets and entrepreneurs to flourish. Too often, however, corrupt or ineffective government bureaucracies administer regulations and enforce laws selectively, raising the cost of doing business. Consumers must then pay more for goods and services.

So, what can governments do to improve productivity and

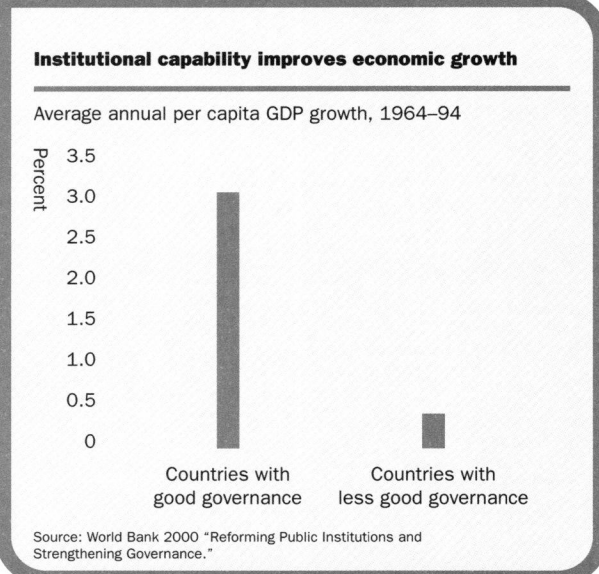

Institutional capability improves economic growth

Average annual per capita GDP growth, 1964–94

Source: World Bank 2000 "Reforming Public Institutions and Strengthening Governance."

employment? They can streamline cumbersome regulations, such as the red tape that controls business startups and liquidation of failing businesses. They can promote more flexible labor regulation, providing safety nets for displaced workers. And they can strengthen their legal and judicial systems.

Countries with good governance grow faster than countries with less good governance. Between 1964 and 1994 GDP per capita rose an average of 3 percent a year in countries with good governance, more than seven times the 0.4 percent a year in those with low capabilities and poor policies.

What makes for a good investment climate?

Openness and integration with the global economy

A stable economy—with low inflation, steady growth, and balanced government spending and revenues—is an important part of a good investment climate. So is social and political stability.

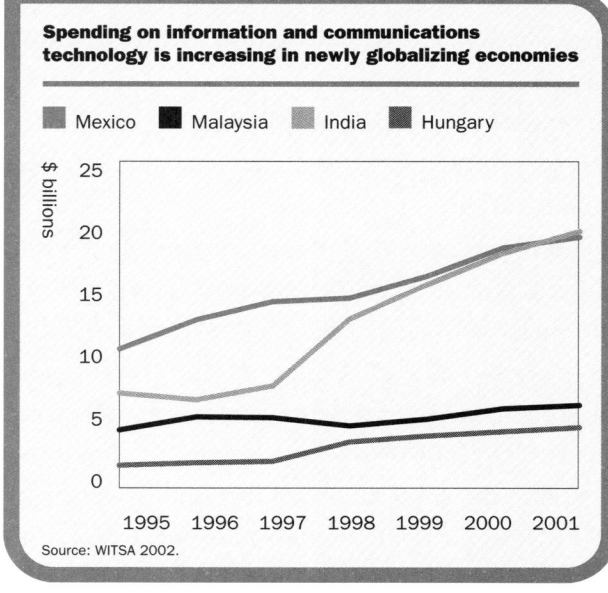

Spending on information and communications technology is increasing in newly globalizing economies

Mexico   Malaysia   India   Hungary

Source: WITSA 2002.

Openness to the global economy brings greater trade and private capital flows. It also brings new technologies, such as those for information and communications, which benefit consumers and businesses by improving labor skills and increasing business efficiency.

High-quality infrastructure

High-quality infrastructure and other business support services help determine the success of manufacturing and agricultural businesses.

So if reliable and affordable power, telecommunications, transport, and water are not available, entrepreneurs will not be inclined to do business in a region or a country. Small and medium-size enterprises are especially at a disadvantage, since they often cannot afford the high cost of generating their own power when blackouts occur.

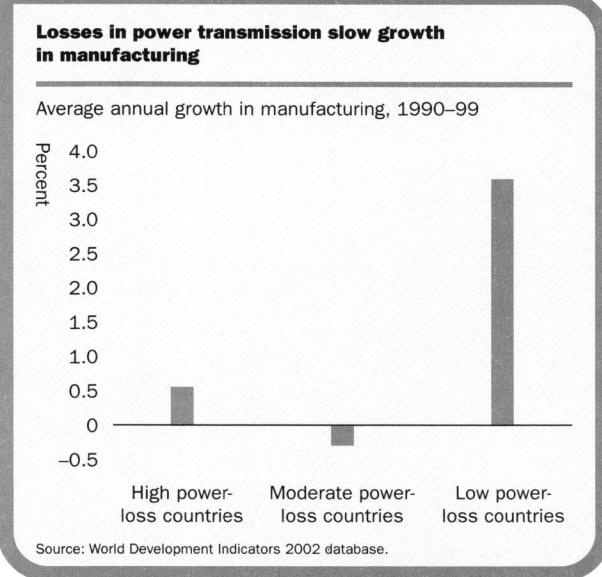

Losses in power transmission slow growth in manufacturing

Average annual growth in manufacturing, 1990–99

Source: World Development Indicators 2002 database.

In competitive environments private firms can improve the provision of infrastructure and other support services. But they have to be regulated well. One way to encourage firms to provide these services is to remove long-standing (and usually unjustified) barriers to their doing so.

Good governance, openness, high-quality infrastructure

Assessing the investment climate

Surveys of private enterprises can inform governments and build public support for reform. The Business Environment and Enterprise Performance Survey (BEEPS), developed by the World Bank and the European Bank for Reconstruction and Development (EBRD), examined a wide range of interactions between firms and the state for more than 4,000 firms in 22 transition economies in 1999–2000.

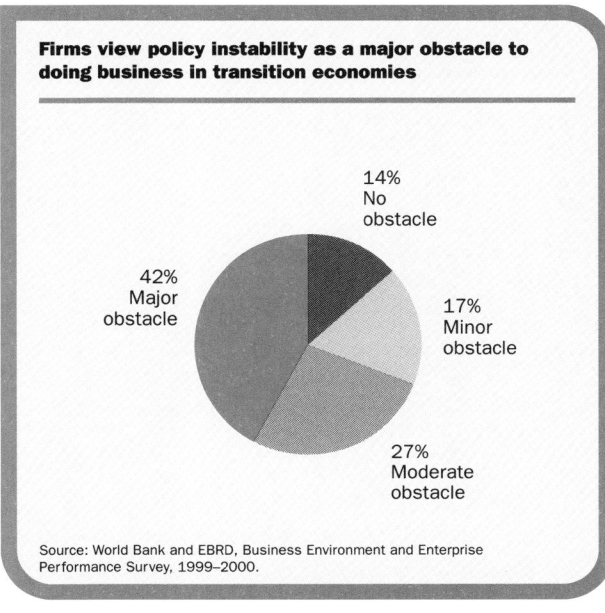

Firms view policy instability as a major obstacle to doing business in transition economies

14% No obstacle

17% Minor obstacle

27% Moderate obstacle

42% Major obstacle

Source: World Bank and EBRD, Business Environment and Enterprise Performance Survey, 1999–2000.

Based on face-to-face interviews with firm managers and owners, BEEPS generated comparative measures in such areas as corruption, state capture, lobbying, and the quality of the business environment. These measures were then related to firm characteristics and performance. For example, 42 percent of surveyed firms view political instability as a major obstacle.

A dynamic economy needs the private sector to create jobs

Private firms are a powerful source of job creation, and their growth brings more growth to the entire economy—the biggest factor in poverty reduction. For a range of developing countries, the private sector provides many more of the new jobs than does the public sector. In fact, most poor people work in the private sector—formal and informal.

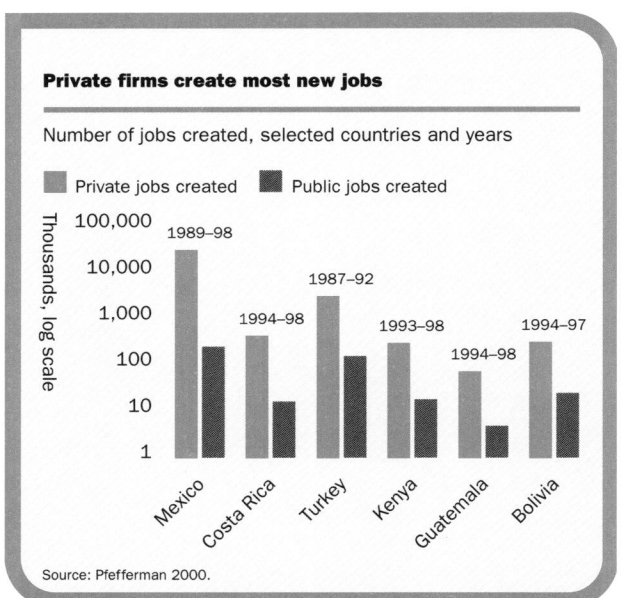

Private firms create most new jobs

Number of jobs created, selected countries and years

Source: Pfefferman 2000.

Building a good investment climate

High-quality infrastructure is key to long-term sustainable growth

Investment in infrastructure—whether in power, transport, telecommunications, housing, or water and sanitation—enables businesses and communities to grow. It also helps people stay healthy, learn new skills, and earn a better living.

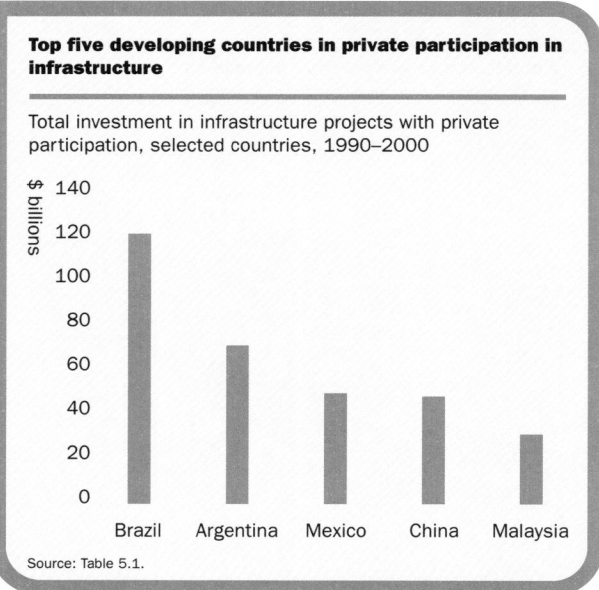

Top five developing countries in private participation in infrastructure

Total investment in infrastructure projects with private participation, selected countries, 1990–2000

Source: Table 5.1.

Private participation in infrastructure can improve access to basic infrastructure services, providing a key to poverty reduction. In developing countries private participation in infrastructure is mainly in telecommunications and energy.

Brazil, Argentina, Mexico, China, and Malaysia had the highest private participation in infrastructure projects in developing economies in the 1990s.

Smaller enterprises make the economy flourish

A recent World Bank survey of more than 10,000 firms in 80 countries found that small and medium-size firms were at a competitive disadvantage to larger ones. Smaller firms lacked the resources and political clout to struggle against corruption, burdensome taxation and regulation, and unreliable power supplies.

Helping those smaller enterprises thrive can improve people's lives and reduce poverty. Why? Because most poor people in the developing world work in small and medium-size enterprises, including farms. For many of these workers the issue is more one of accessing their local markets than one of technology. In fact, most poor people (70 percent) live in rural areas, and their escape from poverty lies in their ability to better market their agricultural products and to develop off-farm employment activities. Improving the investment climate will also benefit small enterprises in the developing world's cities, where the population is expected to double from around 2 billion to 3.8 billion over the next 30 years.

The Mekong Project Development Facility was launched in 1997 to support the establishment and growth of smaller enterprises in Vietnam, Cambodia, and the Lao People's Democratic Republic. These projects are effective in reducing poverty. For example, in 2000 the Hagar Project in Cambodia helped 6,100 women learn new skills such as handicraft production to provide income-generating opportunities.

is crucial for strong growth

A knowledge economy makes investment and labor more effective

The global knowledge revolution, led by information and communications technology, is at the doorstep of all countries. But the door has to be open to turn ideas and technologies into competitive businesses that create jobs and help economies grow.

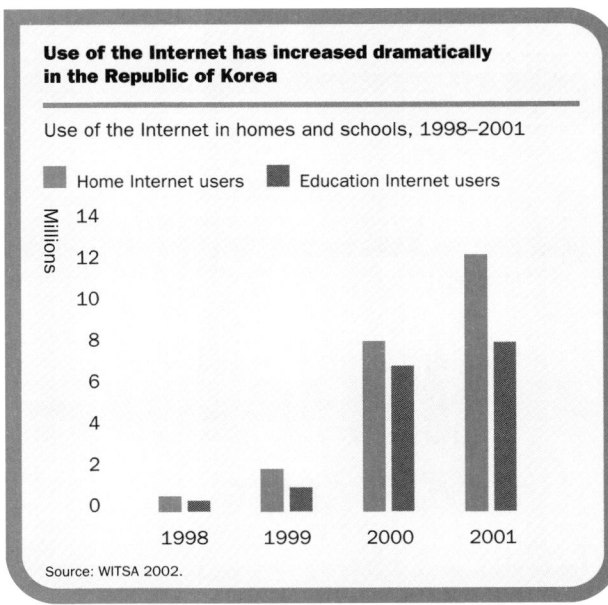

Use of the Internet has increased dramatically in the Republic of Korea

Use of the Internet in homes and schools, 1998–2001

■ Home Internet users ■ Education Internet users

Millions

14
12
10
8
6
4
2
0

1998   1999   2000   2001

Source: WITSA 2002.

One important aspect of a knowledge economy is ensuring access for all to computers and the Internet. In April 2000 the Republic of Korea decided to eliminate the digital divide—the gap between those with access to information and communications technology and those without. So far the government has distributed personal computers to 80 percent of teachers, and 96 percent of central government officials have email accounts. Computer training has also been offered to 300,000 housewives and 9,000 farmers and fishers.

A good investment climate helps reduce poverty

A good investment climate does more than reward entrepreneurs and generate strong growth. It is also associated with poverty reduction. But for growth to help poor people, they need to participate in the growth process.

What does it take to increase the participation of poor people in the economy? Invest in areas that empower them to improve their standard of living and shape their own lives: education, health

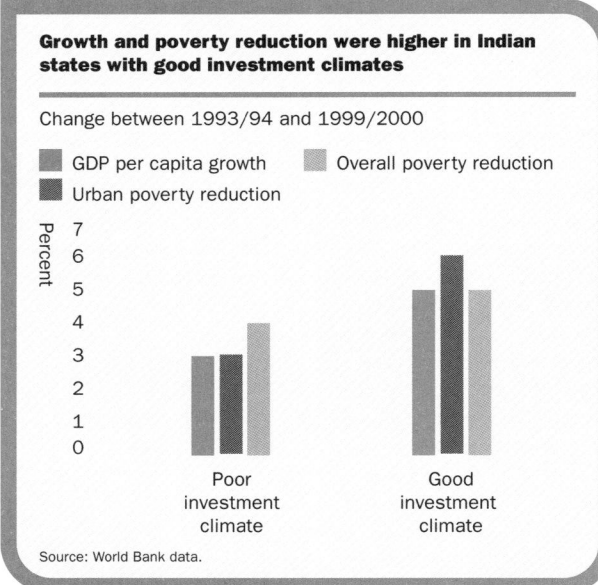

Growth and poverty reduction were higher in Indian states with good investment climates

Change between 1993/94 and 1999/2000

- GDP per capita growth
- Urban poverty reduction
- Overall poverty reduction

Source: World Bank data.

services, social protection, and participatory processes. As healthier, more educated people participate in the economy, productivity and growth increase, leading to greater poverty reduction.

A recent investment climate survey covering 10 Indian states found that growth and poverty reduction were higher in the "good investment climate states" between 1993/94 and 1999/2000 than in "poor investment climate" states.

Improving the investment climate

Empowerment and poverty reduction

Increasing income is not the whole story of poverty reduction, for poverty has other human dimensions that are equally important to address: lack of voice and participation in society, vulnerability to health risks and violence, and lack of educational opportunities. Investing in poor people and the education and health services they need can thus enable them to shape their lives and participate as full citizens in their communities.

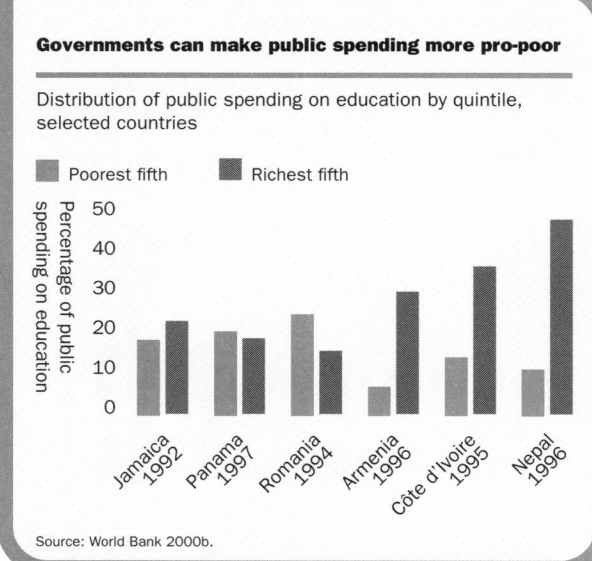

Governments can make public spending more pro-poor

Distribution of public spending on education by quintile, selected countries

- Poorest fifth
- Richest fifth

Jamaica 1992, Panama 1997, Romania 1994, Armenia 1996, Côte d'Ivoire 1995, Nepal 1996

Source: World Bank 2000b.

What can governments do to help the poor? They can shift spending to strengthen public services for poor people.

In some countries spending on education is well distributed across all income levels. But in others it is unevenly distributed. In Jamaica, Panama, and Romania the poorest and richest fifths of the population receive about the same shares of public spending on education. But in Armenia, Côte d'Ivoire, and Nepal the richest fifth receives two to four times as much.

Private provision of infrastructure and social services

Poor people in developing countries usually have inadequate access to water, power, transport systems, and social services such as health and education. And when they do have access, the services are often low in quality or more expensive than those provided to better-off people. For example, poor people who have to buy water from vendors pay 10–40 times more than richer people who have water supplied by pipes to their homes.

Examples of successful small private service providers

• In Cambodia hundreds of small private providers have improved the access of poor households to electricity. These small private providers supply power to more than 115,000 customers, or about a third of the country's customers.

• In Paraguay small water companies supplying customers in urban perimeters have increased access to piped water at prices only slightly higher than those of public water suppliers.

In recent years improvements in technology have made smaller scale provision of infrastructure services feasible. But for the private sector to supply these services, an effective regulatory system has to ensure that the price and quality of services meet appropriate standards.

benefits the poor

Microcredit

Large, formal financial institutions seldom lend to the poor. But poor people need financial services to invest in businesses and homes. Many microfinance institutions around the world are beginning to meet the demand for reliable financial services for the poor. It is estimated that 500 million people worldwide need access to microfinance, which now reaches only about 12.5 million.

Informal microfinancing has been around for a long time in the form of family loans and savings clubs. In 1995 the Consultative Group to Assist the Poorest (CGAP) was

formed to increase the quality and quantity of microfinance institutions, which often serve the very poorest people in a community, with loans as small as $50. The Consultative Group focuses on five main areas:
• Supporting the development of microfinance institutions.
• Supporting changes in the practices of member donors to improve their microfinance operations.
• Increasing the poverty outreach of microfinance institutions.
• Improving the legal and regulatory framework for microfinance institutions.
• Facilitating the commercialization of the industry.

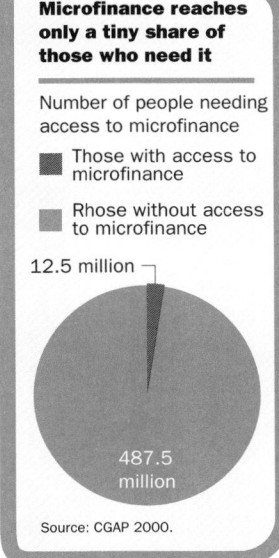

Microfinance reaches only a tiny share of those who need it

Number of people needing access to microfinance
▆ Those with access to microfinance
▆ Rhose without access to microfinance

12.5 million

487.5 million

Source: CGAP 2000.

Microcredit for poor women

Nirdan, an NGO in Nepal, has about 17,000 active loans and 33,000 savings accounts, all for poor women. It makes small loans to small groups of women, who are jointly liable for the loans.

5.1 | Private sector development

	Private fixed investment		Domestic credit to private sector		Investment in infrastructure projects with private participation [a]							
	% of gross domestic fixed investment		% of GDP		Telecommunications $ millions		Energy $ millions		Transport $ millions		Water and sanitation $ millions	
	1990	1999	1990	2000	1990-94	1995-2000	1990-94	1995-2000	1990-94	1995-2000	1990-94	1995-2000
Afghanistan	..	..	..	..	..	..	..	..	..	..	..	..
Albania	..	..	..	4.5	..	102.2	..	..	..	..	..	..
Algeria	..	..	44.4	6.1	..	..	..	..	..	..	..	..
Angola	..	..	..	2.1	..	..	..	..	..	..	..	..
Argentina	67.4	89.9	15.6	23.8	9,262.0	12,991.3	9,899.9	13,694.4	5,373.9	8,965.5	4,075.0	4,172.5
Armenia	..	..	40.4	10.6	..	442.0	..	..	..	..	..	..
Australia	88.4 [b]	90.4 [b]	64.4	87.9	..	..	..	..	..	..	..	..
Austria	..	92.3	91.6	..	..	..	..	..	..	..	..	..
Azerbaijan	..	86.7	9.4	5.9	14.0	127.6	..	..	..	..	..	..
Bangladesh	57.5	69.7	16.7	24.7	116.0	543.4	..	1,040.2	..	..	..	..
Belarus	..	..	..	8.9	10.0	15.0	..	500.0	..	..	..	..
Belgium	92.8 [b]	91.4 [b]	8.1	6.7	..	..	..	..	..	..	..	..
Benin	44.7	60.1	20.3	12.6	..	90.4	..	..	..	..	..	..
Bolivia	39.4	61.6	24.0	59.5	20.0	670.4	..	941.6	..	163.2	..	682.0
Bosnia and Herzegovina	..	..	..	..	..	..	..	..	..	..	..	..
Botswana	..	..	9.4	16.1	..	80.0	..	..	..	..	..	..
Brazil	76.7 [b]	86.2 [b]	38.9	37.6	..	53,692.4	212.0	40,048.1	328.1	19,545.9	2.5	2891.4
Bulgaria	3.6	50.3	7.2	14.6	37.5	207.9	..	..	..	..	..	152.0
Burkina Faso	..	..	19.0	14.0	..	..	..	5.6	..	..	..	..
Burundi	..	..	13.7	23.5	0.5	15.6	..	..	..	..	..	..
Cambodia	89.5	60.7	..	7.3	30.1	104.8	..	89.0	..	120.0	..	..
Cameroon	..	..	26.7	9.3	..	72.7	..	..	30.8	95.0	..	..
Canada	86.3 [b]	89.4 [b]	76.1	80.1	..	..	..	..	..	..	..	..
Central African Republic	..	..	7.2	4.5	..	1.1	..	..	..	..	0.7	..
Chad	..	62.5	7.3	3.4	..	2.0	..	..	..	..	..	..
Chile	79.3	68.3	47.2	68.0	95.9	993.9	1,326.2	5,604.1	120.4	3,803.0	127.6	3,719.9
China	33.9 [c]	46.6 [c]	87.7	124.6	..	5,970.0	5,459.1	15,001.2	5,910.5	13,137.9	42.8	796.7
Hong Kong, China	..	..	165.1	158.7	..	..	..	..	..	..	..	..
Colombia	61.5	39.2	30.8	27.7	1,354.7	1,494.8	540.0	7,035.4	813.0	1,743.9	..	272.0
Congo, Dem. Rep.	..	..	1.8	..	..	45.0	..	..	..	..	..	..
Congo, Rep.	..	..	15.7	4.8	..	70.3	..	325.0	..	..	..	..
Costa Rica	78.9	76.8	15.8	24.1	..	..	18.2	301.2	..	185.0	..	..
Côte d'Ivoire	57.8	74.1	36.5	17.2	..	802.4	109.6	260.6	..	178.0	..	..
Croatia	..	77.3	..	36.2	..	978.0	..	368.5	..	672.2	..	..
Cuba	..	..	..	..	371.0	..	..	165.0	..	..	..	600.0
Czech Republic	86.4	82.0	..	49.7	41.0	7,634.9	356.0	944.1	..	390.4	16.0	36.9
Denmark	91.8 [b]	91.7 [b]	52.2	34.4	..	..	..	..	..	..	..	..
Dominican Republic	73.0	76.3	27.5	34.9	5.0	163.0	87.5	1,556.3	..	633.9	..	..
Ecuador	67.0	49.5	13.2	33.4	27.6	716.4	..	310.0	12.5	686.8	..	..
Egypt, Arab Rep.	62.2	65.2	30.6	59.3	..	2,297.7	..	1,376.0	..	492.2	..	..
El Salvador	81.4	80.7	20.1	41.3	..	651.5	..	975.2	..	..	..	..
Eritrea	..	..	..	..	..	..	..	..	..	..	..	..
Estonia	95.0	83.5	20.2	26.3	136.1	704.6	..	26.5	..	15.8	..	81.0
Ethiopia	..	..	19.5	29.0	..	..	..	..	..	..	..	..
Finland	86.9 [b]	84.5 [b]	86.7	52.3	..	..	..	..	..	..	..	..
France	..	..	96.1	..	..	..	..	..	..	..	..	..
Gabon	..	..	13.0	8.9	..	20.7	..	624.8	..	46.7	..	624.8
Gambia, The	66.8	67.9	11.0	12.5	..	..	..	..	..	..	..	..
Georgia	..	..	..	8.8	11.6	53.8	..	65.0	..	..	..	..
Germany	..	..	89.7	120.3	..	..	..	..	..	..	..	..
Ghana	..	..	4.9	14.1	20.0	441.1	..	..	..	10.0	..	..
Greece	..	83.9 [b]	36.3	53.0	..	..	..	..	..	..	..	..
Guatemala	79.9	82.9	14.2	20.1	..	1,463.3	100.0	1,273.2	..	33.8	..	..
Guinea	..	..	3.5	4.0	..	120.3	..	36.4	..	..	..	..
Guinea-Bissau	28.1	32.0	22.0	7.9	..	..	23.2	..	..	..	23.2	..
Haiti	57.8	51.8	12.1	15.6	..	1.5	..	..	..	..	..	..
Honduras	..	..	31.1	41.3	..	38.1	70.0	112.1	..	130.5	..	..

	Private fixed investment		Domestic credit to private sector		Investment in infrastructure projects with private participation [a]							
	% of gross domestic fixed investment		% of GDP		Telecommunications $ millions		Energy $ millions		Transport $ millions		Water and sanitation $ millions	
	1990	1999	1990	2000	1990-94	1995-2000	1990-94	1995-2000	1990-94	1995-2000	1990-94	1995-2000
Hungary	..	..	46.6	30.9	1,623.2	7,072.1	..	3,872.1	1086.0	135.0	..	170.5
India	60.8	70.1	25.2	29.0	96.7	10,063.6	2,139.2	9,683.8	126.9	1,055.7	..	216.0
Indonesia	69.7	61.0	46.9	20.9	1,119.0	9,602.7	352.5	9,817.1	709.8	2,223.1	3.8	882.8
Iran, Islamic Rep.	53.8	58.6	32.5	30.7	..	28.0	..	..	..	..	..	..
Iraq	..	..	..	..	..	..	..	..	..	..	..	..
Ireland	88.8 [b]	88.7 [b]	47.6	108.6	..	..	..	..	..	..	..	..
Israel	..	..	57.6	86.9	..	..	..	..	..	..	..	..
Italy	..	..	56.5	77.6	..	..	..	..	..	..	..	..
Jamaica	..	..	39.0	32.9	..	44.5	246.0	43.0	30.0	..	..	..
Japan	84.2 [b]	78.5 [b]	195.2	187.7	..	..	..	..	..	..	..	..
Jordan	..	..	72.3	77.6	43.0	549.9	..	..	..	182.0	..	55.0
Kazakhstan	..	88.1	..	13.1	30.0	1,743.5	..	2,411.7	..	..	..	40.0
Kenya	54.6	67.1	32.8	30.1	..	107.0	..	171.5	..	53.4	..	..
Korea, Dem. Rep.	..	..	..	..	..	..	..	..	..	..	..	..
Korea, Rep.	86.8	78.7	65.5	101.9	2,379.0	17,050.9	..	2,688.2	..	6,268.3	..	..
Kuwait	..	..	52.1	51.9	..	..	..	..	..	..	..	..
Kyrgyz Republic	..	..	..	4.4	..	94.0	..	..	..	..	..	..
Lao PDR	..	..	1.0	9.0	..	160.8	..	535.5	..	..	..	..
Latvia	..	..	..	18.6	180.0	782.0	..	154.0	..	75.0	..	..
Lebanon	..	..	79.4	92.0	50.0	323.0	..	..	..	200.0	..	..
Lesotho	..	..	15.8	14.2	..	16.5	..	..	..	..	..	..
Liberia	..	..	..	..	..	..	..	..	..	..	..	..
Libya	..	..	..	..	..	..	..	..	..	..	..	..
Lithuania	..	63.6	..	11.5	30.0	1,222.3	..	20.0	..	..	..	..
Macedonia, FYR	..	..	..	17.9	..	..	..	..	..	..	..	..
Madagascar	46.5	52.9	16.9	9.2	5.0	10.1	..	..	..	..	..	..
Malawi	51.8	17.6	12.3	6.2	..	34.7	..	..	..	6.0	..	..
Malaysia	64.6	50.6	69.4	135.5	1,618.0	3,615.3	5,709.5	2,101.1	2,768.6	9,228.7	3,976.7	1,115.5
Mali	..	..	12.8	17.5	..	..	0.1	697.3	..	..	0.1	697.3
Mauritania	68.9	36.7	43.5	26.7	..	28.1	..	..	..	..	..	..
Mauritius	62.8	78.7	33.2	61.4	..	..	..	109.3	..	42.6	..	..
Mexico	76.1	89.9	17.5	13.2	15,840.0	13,386.8	..	4,560.1	7,583.7	5,630.2	295.1	276.5
Moldova	..	..	5.9	12.7	..	84.6	..	85.3	..	..	..	..
Mongolia	..	..	19.0	8.1	..	35.2	..	..	..	..	..	..
Morocco	65.6	71.1	34.0	58.6	..	3,375.0	2,300.0	5,819.9	..	..	..	4,050.9
Mozambique	..	..	17.6	18.7	..	29.0	..	..	..	..	..	0.6
Myanmar	..	..	4.7	8.6	..	4.0	..	..	..	50.0	..	..
Namibia	61.4	55.4	21.0	44.7	..	22.0	..	5.0	..	..	..	..
Nepal	..	..	12.8	30.7	..	..	131.4	137.2	..	..	..	..
Netherlands	..	..	79.7	..	..	..	..	..	..	..	..	..
New Zealand	..	..	76.9	117.7	..	..	..	..	..	..	..	..
Nicaragua	54.7	51.6	112.6	54.5	6.6	24.5	..	347.4	..	104.0	..	..
Niger	..	..	12.3	4.7	..	11.5	..	..	..	..	..	..
Nigeria	..	..	9.4	13.9	..	117.7	..	..	..	..	..	..
Norway	83.5 [b]	83.8 [b]	82.2	78.8	..	..	..	..	..	..	..	..
Oman	..	..	22.9	44.6	..	..	204.5	183.0	..	106.1	..	..
Pakistan	51.7	62.3	27.7	29.4	581.5	133.5	1,638.7	5,054.3	..	418.3	..	..
Panama	86.9	88.8	46.7	119.7	..	1,429.2	..	1,064.9	169.9	1,046.0	..	25.0
Papua New Guinea	79.6	77.1	28.6	15.8	..	..	..	50.0	..	..	..	818.0
Paraguay	87.4	64.3	15.8	25.7	33.2	199.3	..	..	..	58.0	..	..
Peru	80.0	77.8	11.8	25.9	1,645.0	5,378.2	451.2	3,322.9	6.6	86.8	..	..
Philippines	81.7	69.2	22.3	44.5	591.8	5,539.6	4,502.1	9,272.3	..	3,088.8	..	5,820.0
Poland	41.3	62.1	3.1	26.0	273.0	9,899.6	..	1,052.6	3.1	705.9	..	22.1
Portugal	..	..	49.5	141.0	..	..	..	..	..	..	..	..
Puerto Rico	..	..	..	..	..	..	..	..	..	..	..	..
Romania	9.7	51.4	..	7.2	5.0	2,326.3	..	100.0	..	23.4	..	1,025.0
Russian Federation	..	..	..	12.3	452.6	6,328.2	1,100.0	2,281.3	..	515.4	..	108.0

	Private fixed investment		Domestic credit to private sector		Investment in infrastructure projects with private participation [a]							
	% of gross domestic fixed investment		% of GDP		Telecommunications $ millions		Energy $ millions		Transport $ millions		Water and sanitation $ millions	
	1990	1999	1990	2000	1990-94	1995-2000	1990-94	1995-2000	1990-94	1995-2000	1990-94	1995-2000
Rwanda	..	..	6.9	10.1	..	15.0	..	..	..	..	..	..
Saudi Arabia	..	..	61.0	57.1	..	..	..	..	..	..	..	..
Senegal	..	..	26.5	20.0	..	343.3	..	159.0	..	..	..	3.7
Sierra Leone	..	..	2.4	2.1	..	..	..	..	..	..	..	..
Singapore	..	..	97.4	110.0	..	..	..	..	..	..	..	..
Slovak Republic	..	..	..	31.0	109.2	1,451.5	..	..	..	..	..	..
Slovenia	..	..	34.9	38.1	..	..	..	..	..	..	..	..
Somalia	..	..	..	..	..	..	..	..	..	..	..	..
South Africa	65.6	69.0	81.0	141.9	542.2	7,818.3	..	18.9	..	1,390.1	..	209.3
Spain	..	..	79.6	101.6	..	..	..	..	..	..	..	..
Sri Lanka	..	..	19.6	28.9	43.6	1,390.6	..	265.0	..	240.0	..	..
Sudan	..	..	4.8	2.4	..	6.0	..	..	..	..	..	..
Swaziland	..	..	21.7	14.2	..	10.0	..	..	..	..	..	..
Sweden	..	..	128.4	46.0	..	..	..	..	..	..	..	..
Switzerland	..	..	167.9	165.2	..	..	..	..	..	..	..	..
Syrian Arab Republic	..	..	7.5	9.0	..	..	..	..	..	..	..	..
Tajikistan	..	..	..	..	..	1.0	..	..	..	..	..	..
Tanzania	..	..	13.9	4.6	1.8	66.9	6.0	150.0	..	23.0	..	..
Thailand	84.8	67.7	83.4	108.8	3,664.0	4,143.7	674.8	6,990.4	695.9	1,759.4	..	260.5
Togo	..	..	22.6	17.0	..	5.0	..	..	..	..	..	..
Trinidad and Tobago	85.2	67.8	44.7	45.5	47.0	146.7	..	207.0	..	..	..	120.0
Tunisia	64.1	52.2	55.1	66.2	..	..	627.0	265.0	..	..	..	..
Turkey	69.2	72.0	16.7	23.7	74.0	7,794.7	718.0	6,567.2	..	724.8	..	942.0
Turkmenistan	..	..	..	1.5	..	..	..	..	..	..	..	..
Uganda	..	..	4.0	6.3	16.0	129.8	..	..	..	..	..	..
Ukraine	..	..	2.6	10.6	90.0	1,154.9	..	..	..	..	..	..
United Arab Emirates	..	..	37.4	60.0	..	..	..	..	..	..	..	..
United Kingdom	87.3 [b]	93.6 [b]	116.0	135.1	..	..	..	..	..	..	..	..
United States	..	..	93.1	143.5	..	..	..	..	..	..	..	..
Uruguay	68.0	72.5	32.4	51.3	13.0	63.7	..	246.0	96.0	20.0	10.0	..
Uzbekistan	..	34.0	..	..	2.5	357.4	..	..	..	..	..	..
Venezuela, RB	34.8	56.1	25.4	12.1	4,185.7	5,574.0	..	133.0	100.0	268.0	..	25.0
Vietnam	..	..	2.5	35.1	..	..	..	435.5	10.0	70.0	..	208.8
West Bank and Gaza	..	..	..	..	..	155.0	..	150.0	..	..	..	..
Yemen, Rep.	..	..	6.1	5.5	25.0	..	..	..	..	190.0	..	..
Yugoslavia, Fed. Rep.	..	87.7	..	..	..	1,929.5	..	..	..	..	..	..
Zambia	..	..	8.9	9.5	..	57.8	..	289.4	..	..	..	..
Zimbabwe	..	..	23.0	25.2	..	46.0	..	1,180.0	18.0	70.0	..	..
World	78.1 w	.. w	97.1 w	119.5 w	.. s	.. s	.. s	.. s	.. s	.. s	.. s	
Low income	48.1	53.7	26.5	23.9	2,136.3	25,684.6	4,400.7	30,576.0	895.5	4,666.5	27.8	2,020.1
Middle income	72.2	74.8	45.4	61.1	44,913.0	201,894.1	34,676.5	145,020.8	25,098.2	82,513.2	8,545.7	29,160.4
Lower middle income	..	..	..	78.4	8,623.7	49,147.5	16,226.6	60,579.5	7,468.5	23,123.0	42.8	14,728.0
Upper middle income	73.8	77.9	38.9	48.4	36,289.3	152,746.6	18,449.9	84,441.4	17,629.7	59,390.2	8,502.9	14,432.4
Low & middle income	64.5	66.9	41.6	55.3	47,049.3	227,578.7	39,077.2	175,596.8	25,993.7	87,179.7	8,573.5	31,180.5
East Asia & Pacific	63.3	50.2	71.4	106.1	9,433.9	46,365.0	16,698.0	46,980.3	10,094.8	35,946.2	4,023.3	9902.3
Europe & Central Asia	..	..	..	20.7	3,119.7	52,507.6	2,174.0	18,448.3	1,089.1	3,257.9	16.0	2577.5
Latin America & Carib.	74.3	79.8	28.4	27.5	32,954.4	99,165.1	13,025.5	82,102.2	14,634.1	43,104.5	4,510.2	12,784.3
Middle East & N. Africa	..	..	41.6	47.0	118.0	6,728.6	3,131.5	7,793.9	..	1,220.3	..	4,105.9
South Asia	55.9	71.8	24.6	28.7	837.8	12,131.1	3,909.3	16,180.5	126.9	1,714.0	..	216.0
Sub-Saharan Africa	..	..	42.5	66.0	585.5	10,681.3	138.9	4,091.6	48.8	1,936.8	24.0	1,594.5
High income	81.9	..	107.8	136.3	..	..	..	..	..	..	..	..
Europe EMU	..	..	78.4	97.7	..	..	..	..	..	..	..	..

a. Data refer to total for the period shown. For differences in concepts and definitions between proceeds from privatization and Investment in infrastructure projects with private participation see *About the data*. b. Data refer to investment by both private and public corporations. c. Data refer to investment by individuals, shareholding units, jointly owned units, collectively owned units, foreign-funded units, and units in Hong Kong, China; Macao, China; and Taiwan, China.

About the data

Private sector development, that is, tapping private sector initiative for socially useful purposes, is critical for poverty reduction. Private initiative, especially in competitive markets, has tremendous potential to contribute to growth in parallel with public sector efforts. Private markets are the engine of productivity growth, creating productive jobs and higher incomes, and along with the complementary government role of regulation, funding, and provision, private initiative can help to provide the basic services and conditions that empower the poor by improving infrastructure, health and education. More than 130 developing countries introduced private participation in at least one infrastructure sector between 1990 and 2000 involving over 2,330 projects with investment commitments of $693 billion.

Private fixed investment consists of outlays for additions to fixed assets—improvements to land, construction of infrastructure and buildings, and purchases of plant, machinery, and equipment—by the private sector. When direct estimates of private investment are unavailable, private fixed investment is estimated as the difference between total gross fixed investment and consolidated public investment. Total investment may be estimated directly from surveys of enterprises and administrative records, or indirectly using the commodity flow method. Consolidated measures of public investment may omit important subnational units of government and in some cases may include financial as well as physical capital investment. As the difference between two estimated quantities, private fixed investment may be undervalued or overvalued and subject to large errors over time. When private domestic investment accounts for a large share of total investment, it may reflect a highly competitive and efficient private sector—or one that is subsidized and protected.

This concept of private investment is the one used by the International Finance Corporation (IFC) in its *Trends in Private Investment in Developing Countries 2001*, the source of data for most countries in the table. But for other countries, most notably members of the Organisation for Economic Co-operation and Development (OECD), the concepts and definitions of the 1993 System of National Accounts (SNA) are used. Since IFC data conform to the concepts and definitions of the 1968 SNA, the data are not strictly comparable. While the IFC data on private investment represent only the capital expenditure decisions of the private sector, in the 1993 SNA the term *fixed capital formation by households and corporations* includes capital expenditures by both private and public corporations. Countries reporting on this basis are footnoted in the table. (For further discussion on measuring gross capital formation see *About the data* for table 4.9.)

The data on domestic credit to the private sector are taken from the banking survey of the International Monetary Fund's (IMF) *International Financial Statistics* or, when data are unavailable, from its monetary survey. The monetary survey includes monetary authorities (the central bank) and deposit money banks. In addition to these, the banking survey includes other banking institutions, such as savings and loan institutions, finance companies, and development banks. In some cases credit to the private sector may include credit to state-owned or partially state-owned enterprises.

Private participation in infrastructure has made important contributions to easing fiscal restraints and to improving the efficiency of infrastructure services and in extending their delivery to poor people. The privatization trend in infrastructure that began in the 1970s and 1980s took off in the 1990s. Developing countries have been at the head of this wave, pioneering better approaches to providing infrastructure services and reaping the benefits of increased competition and customer focus.

The data on investment in infrastructure projects with private participation refer to all investment (public and private) in projects in which a private company assumes operating risk during the operating period or assumes development and operating risk during the contract period. Foreign state-owned companies are considered private entities for the purposes of this measure. The data are from the World Bank's PPI Project Database, which tracks about 2,330 projects, newly owned or managed by private companies, that reached financial closure in low- and middle-income economies in 1990–2000. For more information go to www.worldbank.org/html/fpd/privatesector/PPIDBweb/Intro.htm.

Definitions

• **Private fixed investment** covers gross outlays by the private sector (including private nonprofit agencies) on additions to its fixed domestic assets. Gross domestic fixed investment includes similar outlays by the public sector. No allowance is made for the depreciation of assets. • **Domestic credit to private sector** refers to financial resources provided to the private sector—such as through loans, purchases of nonequity securities, and trade credits and other accounts receivable—that establish a claim for repayment. For some countries these claims include credit to public enterprises. • **Investment in infrastructure projects with private participation** covers infrastructure projects in telecommunications, energy (electricity and natural gas transmission and distribution), transport, and water and sanitation that have reached financial closure and directly or indirectly serve the public. Movable assets, incinerators, standalone solid waste projects, and small projects such as windmills are excluded. The types of projects included are operations and management contracts, operations and management contracts with major capital expenditure, greenfield projects (in which a private entity or a public-private joint venture builds and operates a new facility), and divestiture.

Data sources

The data on private investment are from the International Finance Corporation's *Trends in Private Investment in Developing Countries 2001*, OECD data files (see OECD, *National Accounts, 1960–99*, volumes 1 and 2), and World Bank estimates. The data on domestic credit are from the IMF's *International Financial Statistics*. The data on investment in infrastructure projects with private participation are from the World Bank's Private Participation in Infrastructure (PPI) Project Database (www.worldbank.org/html/fpd/ privatesector/PPIDBweb/Intro.htm).

5.2 | Investment climate

	Foreign direct investment		Entry and exit regulation [a]			Composite ICRG risk rating [b]	Institutional Investor credit rating [b]	Euromoney country credit-worthiness rating [b]	Moody's sovereign long-term debt rating [b]		Standard & Poor's sovereign long-term debt rating [b]	
	% of gross capital formation		Entry	Repatriation of					Foreign currency	Domestic currency	Foreign currency	Domestic currency
				income	capital	December	September	September	January	January	January	January
	1990	2000	2000	2000	2000	2001	2001	2001	2002	2002	2002	2002
Afghanistan	..	..	..	..	..	..	5.9	1.3	..	..	..	..
Albania	0.0	20.5	..	..	..	62.5	12.1	26.5	..	..	..	..
Algeria	0.0	0.1	..	..	..	62.3	30.6	38.6	..	..	..	..
Angola	-27.9	68.1	..	..	..	50.5	12.1	20.1	..	..	..	..
Argentina	9.3	25.7	F	F	F	64.8	34.7	43.4	Ca	Ca	SD	SD
Armenia	..	38.2	..	..	..	59.8	..	30.5	..	..	..	..
Australia	11.9	5.8	..	..	..	81.5	80.4	88.4	Aa2	Aaa	AA+	AAA
Austria	1.6	6.0	..	..	..	86.5	87.7	92.4	Aaa	Aaa	AAA	AAA
Azerbaijan	..	9.6	..	..	..	68.5	..	32.3	..	..	..	..
Bangladesh	0.1	2.6	F	F	F	60.5	26.4	36.5	..	..	..	..
Belarus	..	1.3	..	..	..	61.3	12.5	24.4	..	..	..	..
Belgium	13.6	36.7	..	..	..	84.0	86.6	90.5	Aa1	Aa1	AA+	AA+
Benin	0.4	7.0	..	..	..	..	18.5	25.1	..	..	..	..
Bolivia	4.4	48.6	..	..	..	66.3	30.8	39.3	B1	B1	B+	BB
Bosnia and Herzegovina	..	0.0	..	..	..	..	..	23.9	..	..	..	..
Botswana	8.0	3.7	F	F	F	78.5	56.7	60.7	A2	A1	A	A+
Brazil	1.1	26.9	F	F	F	62.5	42.1	48.7	B1	B1	BB-	BB+
Bulgaria	0.1	50.4	F	F	F	72.3	36.6	44.5	B2	B1	BB-	BB
Burkina Faso	0.0	1.7	..	..	..	60.5	16.1	29.3	..	..	..	..
Burundi	0.6	19.0	..	..	..	..	10.5	22.8	..	..	..	..
Cambodia	0.0	26.3	..	..	..	..	..	26.9	..	..	..	..
Cameroon	-5.7	2.1	..	..	..	64.0	17.0	29.7	..	..	..	..
Canada	6.4	19.7	..	..	..	84.8	87.2	89.9	Aa1	Aa1	AA+	AAA
Central African Republic	0.5	4.8	..	..	..	..	..	24.2	..	..	..	..
Chad	0.0	6.3	..	..	..	..	11.9	23.1	..	..	..	..
Chile	7.7	22.2	R	F	F	76.3	64.2	64.6	Baa1	A1	A-	AA
China	2.8	9.5	S	F	F	74.3	57.4	60.7	A3	..	BBB	..
Hong Kong, China	..	..	..	..	..	83.3	65.2	80.4	A3	Aa3	A+	AA-
Colombia	6.7	23.9	A	F	F	58.8	38.8	48.4	Ba2	Baa2	BB	BBB
Congo, Dem. Rep.	-1.4	..	..	..	..	50.3	7.5	6.5	..	..	..	..
Congo, Rep.	0.0	1.8	..	..	..	57.5	8.7	23.4	..	..	..	..
Costa Rica	10.4	15.1	..	..	..	74.0	44.1	50.7	Ba1	Ba1	BB	BB+
Côte d'Ivoire	6.6	9.2	F	F	F	57.5	18.5	29.5	..	..	..	..
Croatia	..	22.1	F	F	F	75.0	43.9	53.5	Baa3	Baa1	BBB-	BBB+
Cuba	..	..	..	..	..	64.5	13.7	6.7	Caa1	..	..	..
Czech Republic	2.4	30.4	F	F	F	75.8	60.5	63.0	Baa1	A1	A-	AA-
Denmark	4.2	95.4	..	..	..	87.3	88.4	94.7	Aaa	Aaa	AAA	AAA
Dominican Republic	7.5	20.4	..	..	..	70.3	35.0	41.9	Ba2	Ba2	BB-	BB-
Ecuador	6.7	31.1	F	F	F	60.8	19.0	30.1	Caa2	Caa1	CCC+	CCC+
Egypt, Arab Rep.	5.9	5.2	F	F	F	68.8	47.1	52.6	Ba1	Baa1	BBB-	BBB+
El Salvador	0.3	8.3	..	..	..	73.5	41.9	49.1	Baa3	Baa2	BB+	BB+
Eritrea	..	15.2	..	..	..	..	..	21.4	..	..	..	..
Estonia	7.2	30.2	F	F	F	75.0	55.0	59.3	Baa1	A1	A-	A-
Ethiopia	1.5	5.5	..	..	..	60.5	14.7	25.8	..	..	..	..
Finland	2.0	38.0	..	..	..	88.3	85.9	92.3	Aaa	Aaa	AA+	AA+
France	4.6	16.2	..	..	..	81.0	92.0	92.3	Aaa	Aaa	AAA	AAA
Gabon	5.7	11.6	..	..	..	69.3	21.0	30.8	..	..	..	..
Gambia, The	0.0	19.2	..	..	..	68.8	..	27.3	..	..	..	..
Georgia	0.0	29.8	..	..	..	..	15.4	25.6	..	..	..	..
Germany	0.7	44.6	..	..	..	83.8	92.8	92.2	Aaa	Aaa	AAA	AAA
Ghana	1.8	8.9	F	F	F	59.5	25.4	35.2	..	..	..	..
Greece	5.2	2.0	F	F	F	74.0	71.2	82.0	A2	A2	A	A
Guatemala	4.6	7.2	..	..	..	70.3	31.4	42.3	Ba2	Ba1	BB	BB+
Guinea	3.6	9.5	..	..	..	61.8	15.8	23.9	..	..	..	..
Guinea-Bissau	2.7	7.9	..	..	..	48.0	..	20.7	..	..	..	..
Haiti	2.2	3.0	..	..	..	57.3	12.1	25.0	..	..	..	..
Honduras	6.3	13.6	..	..	..	64.8	22.5	36.6	B2	B2	..	..

	Foreign direct investment		Entry and exit regulation [a]			Composite ICRG risk rating [b]	Institutional Investor credit rating [b]	Euromoney country credit-worthiness rating [b]	Moody's sovereign long-term debt rating [b]		Standard & Poor's sovereign long-term debt rating [b]	
	% of gross capital formation		Entry	Repatriation of					Foreign currency	Domestic currency	Foreign currency	Domestic currency
				income	capital	December	September	September	January	January	January	January
	1990	2000	2000	2000	2000	2001	2001	2001	2002	2002	2002	2002
Hungary	0.0	12.1	F	F	F	76.0	62.0	70.2	A3	A1	A-	A+
India	0.2	2.1	A	F	F	65.3	47.4	55.0	Ba2	Ba2	BB	BBB-
Indonesia	3.1	-16.6	R	RS	RS	56.3	21.6	33.4	B3	B3	CCC	B-
Iran, Islamic Rep.	-1.1	0.2	..	..	..	69.3	31.5	41.3	B2	Ba2	..	..
Iraq	..	..	..	..	..	47.3	9.0	3.3	..	..	..	..
Ireland	6.3	*85.4*	..	..	..	88.8	83.8	91.1	Aaa	Aaa	AAA	AAA
Israel	1.1	20.6	F	F	F	67.8	60.0	72.0	A2	A2	A-	AA-
Italy	2.6	6.0	..	..	..	81.8	82.9	87.5	Aa3	Aa3	AA	AA
Jamaica	11.7	23.0	R	F	F	70.3	27.8	39.8	Ba3	Baa3	B+	BB-
Japan	0.2	*1.1*	..	..	..	84.3	86.2	89.9	Aa1	Aa3	AA	AA
Jordan	3.0	33.0	F	F	F	71.0	38.8	46.5	Ba3	Ba3	BB-	BBB-
Kazakhstan	*1.2*	49.2	..	..	..	72.0	33.9	43.6	Ba2	Ba1	BB	BB+
Kenya	3.4	8.4	R	F	F	61.0	21.7	35.8	..	..	..	..
Korea, Dem. Rep.	..	..	..	..	..	47.5	7.0	3.9	..	..	..	..
Korea, Rep.	0.8	7.1	R	F	F	79.3	61.7	62.4	Baa2	Baa1	BBB+	A+
Kuwait	..	0.4	..	..	..	84.0	63.6	75.8	Baa1	..	A	A+
Kyrgyz Republic	*0.0*	-1.1	..	..	..	..	17.5	25.1	..	..	..	..
Lao PDR	..	20.6	..	..	..	..	..	25.0	..	..	..	..
Latvia	*1.1*	21.0	F	F	F	76.0	48.0	52.6	Baa2	A2	BBB	A-
Lebanon	1.2	10.0	F	F	F	56.8	31.6	44.7	B2	B3	B	B
Lesotho	5.2	32.5	..	..	..	..	23.9	34.5	..	..	..	..
Liberia	..	..	..	..	..	49.8	7.6	12.5	..	..	..	..
Libya	..	..	..	..	..	73.8	31.3	18.0	..	..	..	..
Lithuania	*0.0*	16.2	F	F	F	74.0	45.5	50.6	Ba1	Baa1	BBB-	BBB+
Macedonia, FYR	..	29.4	..	..	..	..	..	25.4	..	..	..	..
Madagascar	4.2	13.3	..	..	..	67.0	..	27.9	..	..	..	..
Malawi	0.0	20.3	..	..	..	60.0	17.9	26.1	..	..	..	..
Malaysia	16.4	7.2	R	F	D	76.0	56.4	59.8	Baa2	A3	BBB	A
Mali	-1.3	14.6	..	..	..	57.8	16.1	28.9	..	..	..	..
Mauritania	3.4	1.8	..	..	..	..	..	22.1	..	..	..	..
Mauritius	5.0	23.6	R	F	F	..	53.9	57.4	Baa2	A2	..	..
Mexico	4.3	9.9	F	F	F	70.8	55.3	60.4	Baa3	Baa1	BB+	BBB+
Moldova	*0.0*	44.7	..	..	..	63.8	16.2	26.0	Caa1	Caa1	..	..
Mongolia	..	10.4	..	..	..	64.3	..	28.4	..	..	B	B
Morocco	2.5	0.1	F	F	F	71.8	45.4	55.2	Ba1	Ba1	BB	BBB
Mozambique	2.3	11.0	..	..	..	59.0	18.1	30.0	..	..	..	..
Myanmar	..	..	..	..	..	62.0	13.4	23.9	..	..	..	..
Namibia	..	..	F	F	F	76.3	39.1	22.8	..	..	..	..
Nepal	0.9	0.3	..	..	..	..	27.5	30.1	..	..	..	..
Netherlands	15.2	*48.1*	..	..	..	87.0	92.6	93.2	Aaa	Aaa	AAA	AAA
New Zealand	21.3	*12.5*	..	..	..	80.3	75.9	85.2	Aa2	Aaa	AA+	AAA
Nicaragua	0.0	30.8	..	..	..	57.8	18.9	28.7	B2	B2	..	..
Niger	-0.5	7.7	..	..	..	59.5	13.1	28.2	..	..	..	..
Nigeria	14.0	11.6	R	F	F	57.3	18.3	28.8	..	..	..	..
Norway	3.7	16.4	..	..	..	92.3	90.0	95.3	Aaa	Aaa	AAA	AAA
Oman	10.2	..	F	F	F	81.8	55.4	60.7	Baa2	Baa2	BBB	BBB+
Pakistan	3.2	3.2	F	F	F	56.0	18.1	34.5	Caa1	Caa1	B-	B+
Panama	14.8	20.2	..	..	..	71.5	46.4	52.7	Ba1	..	BB	BB
Papua New Guinea	19.7	*46.3*	..	..	..	61.8	28.5	37.3	B1	B1	B	BB-
Paraguay	6.3	4.9	..	..	..	63.0	28.9	38.8	B2	B1	B	BB-
Peru	0.9	6.3	F	F	F	68.8	34.7	47.9	Ba3	Baa3	BB-	BB+
Philippines	5.0	15.2	S	F	F	70.0	43.5	53.1	Ba1	Baa3	BB+	BBB+
Poland	0.6	22.3	F	F	F	75.3	59.2	59.6	Baa1	A2	BBB+	A+
Portugal	13.2	21.1	..	..	..	78.3	79.8	84.7	Aa2	Aa2	AA	AA
Puerto Rico	..	..	..	..	..	..	..	..	..	..	..	..
Romania	0.0	14.4	F	F	F	64.3	29.1	40.5	B2	B2	B	B+
Russian Federation	0.0	6.3	F	F	F	69.5	26.8	37.4	Ba3	Ba2	B+	B+

5.2 | Investment climate

	Foreign direct investment		Entry and exit regulation [a]			Composite ICRG risk rating [b]	Institutional Investor credit rating [b]	Euromoney country credit-worthiness rating [b]	Moody's sovereign long-term debt rating [b]		Standard & Poor's sovereign long-term debt rating [b]	
	% of gross capital formation		Entry	Repatriation of					Foreign currency	Domestic currency	Foreign currency	Domestic currency
	1990	2000	2000	income 2000	capital 2000	December 2001	September 2001	September 2001	January 2002	January 2002	January 2002	January 2002
Rwanda	2.1	5.2	..	..	..	..	..	21.4	..	..	..	..
Saudi Arabia [c]	..	..	C	RS	RS	77.3	58.8	67.2	Baa3	Ba1	..	..
Senegal	7.2	12.3	..	..	..	66.3	23.7	32.5	..	..	B+	B+
Sierra Leone	37.9	2.0	..	..	..	48.5	8.3	24.0	..	..	..	..
Singapore	41.5	22.1	..	..	..	89.3	84.8	90.5	Aa1	Aaa	AAA	AAA
Slovak Republic	0.0	35.7	F	F	F	73.3	47.7	53.7	Baa3	A3	BBB-	A-
Slovenia	5.0	3.5	R	F	F	78.8	64.9	73.8	A2	Aa3	A	AA
Somalia	4.2	..	..	..	..	43.5	..	11.0	..	..	..	..
South Africa	..	5.1	F	F	F	68.8	49.5	57.7	Baa2	A2	BBB-	A-
Spain	10.2	24.9	..	..	..	80.5	82.8	87.8	Aaa	Aaa	AA+	AA+
Sri Lanka	2.4	3.8	R	RS	F	57.0	33.9	39.0	..	..	..	..
Sudan	..	23.8	..	..	..	54.0	9.1	22.8	..	..	..	..
Swaziland	17.8	-15.1	..	..	..	..	27.0	34.3	..	..	..	..
Sweden	3.6	54.4	..	..	..	84.3	85.7	92.6	Aa1	Aaa	AA+	AAA
Switzerland	9.3	23.1	..	..	..	92.5	93.8	98.2	Aaa	Aaa	AAA	AAA
Syrian Arab Republic	3.5	3.2	..	..	..	71.5	22.0	36.4	..	..	..	..
Tajikistan	0.0	12.2	..	..	..	..	11.9	25.1	..	..	..	..
Tanzania	0.0	12.1	..	..	..	57.5	20.6	31.7	..	..	..	..
Thailand	6.9	12.2	R	F	F	73.8	50.0	56.7	Baa3	Baa1	BBB-	A-
Togo	0.0	12.0	..	..	..	61.0	14.6	25.6	..	..	..	..
Trinidad and Tobago	17.1	46.5	R	F	F	73.5	49.2	52.8	Baa3	Baa1	BBB-	BBB+
Tunisia	1.9	14.1	F	F	F	72.8	50.8	56.8	Baa3	Baa2	BBB	A
Turkey	1.9	2.1	F	F	F	48.5	34.4	43.7	B1	B3	B-	B-
Turkmenistan	..	10.0	..	..	..	..	16.6	25.5	B2	..	..	..
Uganda	0.0	19.6	..	..	..	62.5	21.4	34.6	..	..	..	..
Ukraine	0.0	10.0	F	F	F	66.8	17.5	30.0	Caa1	Caa1	B	B
United Arab Emirates	..	..	..	..	..	82.5	68.3	79.3	A2	..	..	..
United Kingdom	16.8	52.9	..	..	..	83.5	91.5	92.1	Aaa	Aaa	AAA	AAA
United States	4.8	15.8	..	..	..	79.0	91.6	93.5	Aaa	Aaa	AAA	AAA
Uruguay	0.0	10.9	..	..	..	74.3	49.5	57.0	Baa3	Baa3	BBB-	BBB+
Uzbekistan	1.5	11.8	..	..	..	..	16.7	28.3	..	..	..	..
Venezuela, RB	9.1	21.1	F	F	F	66.8	33.3	44.7	B2	B3	B	..
Vietnam	1.9	15.1	..	..	..	69.5	30.0	40.7	B1	..	..	..
West Bank and Gaza	..	..	..	..	..	..	..	..	..	..	..	..
Yemen, Rep.	-18.6	-12.3	..	..	..	65.3	..	30.1	..	..	..	..
Yugoslavia, Fed. Rep.	..	0.0	..	..	..	46.0	12.2	16.7	..	..	..	..
Zambia	35.7	37.6	..	..	..	53.5	16.0	26.5	..	..	..	..
Zimbabwe	-0.8	8.5	R	F	F	39.0	13.0	23.2	..	..	..	..

World	4.1 w	14.0 w				69.1 m	33.9 m	38.8 m				
Low income	1.3	3.4				59.8	16.2	26.5				
Middle income	2.5	12.2				70.3	38.8	45.6				
Lower middle income	1.9	9.5				69.4	31.5	39.5				
Upper middle income	3.3	14.6				73.8	49.5	57.2				
Low & middle income	2.3	10.9				64.8	27.0	32.5				
East Asia & Pacific	3.5	8.2				69.5	36.8	37.3				
Europe & Central Asia	0.4	13.6				70.8	29.1	32.3				
Latin America & Carib.	3.8	19.1				67.8	34.7	44.1				
Middle East & N. Africa	2.2	2.7				71.0	35.2	44.7				
South Asia	0.5	2.3				58.8	27.0	35.5				
Sub-Saharan Africa	..	12.2				59.5	17.5	26.3				
High income	4.5	14.2				83.7	85.3	90.2				
Europe EMU	4.5	27.2				83.8	85.9	91.1				

a. Entry and exit regulations are classified as free (F), relatively free (R), delayed (D), special classes of shares (S), authorized investors only (A), restricted (RS) and closed (C). For explanations of the terms see *About the data*. b. This copyrighted material is reprinted with permission from the following data providers: PRS Group, 6320 Fly Road, Suite 102, PO Box 248, East Syracuse, NY 13057; Institutional Investor Inc., 488 Madison Avenue, New York, NY 13057; Euromoney Publications PLC, Nestor House, Playhouse Yard, London EC4V 5EX, UK; Moody's Investors Service, 99 Church Street, New York, NY 10007; and Standard & Poor's Rating Services, The McGraw-Hill Companies, Inc., 1221 Avenue of the Americas, New York, NY 10020. Prior written consent from the original data providers cited must be obtained for third-party use of these data. c. Foreigners are barred from investing directly in the Saudi stock market, but they may invest indirectly through mutual funds.

About the data

As investment portfolios become increasingly global, investors as well as governments seeking to attract investment must have a good understanding of trends in foreign direct investment and country risk. This table presents information on foreign direct investment, country risk and creditworthiness ratings from several major international rating services, and information on the regulation of entry to and exit from emerging stock markets reported by Standard & Poor's.

The statistics on foreign direct investment are based on balance of payments data reported by the International Monetary Fund (IMF), supplemented by data on net foreign direct investment reported by the Organisation for Economic Co-operation and Development and official national sources. (For a detailed discussion of data on foreign direct investment see *About the data* for table 6.7.)

Entry and exit restrictions on investments are among the mechanisms by which countries attempt to reduce the risk to their economies associated with foreign investment. Yet such restrictions may increase the risk or uncertainty perceived by investors. Many countries close industries considered strategic to foreign or nonresident investors. And national law or corporate policy may limit foreign investment in a company or in certain classes of stocks.

The entry and exit regulations summarized in the table refer to "new money" investment by foreign institutions; other regulations may apply to capital invested through debt conversion schemes or to capital from other sources. The regulations reflected here are formal ones. But even formal regulations may have very different effects in different countries because of differences in the bureaucratic culture, the speed with which applications are processed, and the extent of red tape. The regulations on entry are evaluated using the terms *free* (no significant restrictions), *relatively free* (some registration procedures required to ensure repatriation rights), *special classes* (foreigners restricted to certain classes of stocks designated for foreign investors), *authorized investors only* (only approved foreign investors may buy stocks), and *closed* (closed or access severely restricted, as for nonresident nationals only). Regulations on repatriation of income and capital are evaluated as *free* (repatriation done routinely) or *restricted* (repatriation requires registration with or permission of a government agency that may restrict the timing of exchange release).

Most risk ratings are numerical or alphabetical indexes, with a higher number or a letter closer to the beginning of the alphabet meaning lower risk (a good prospect). (For more on the rating processes of the rating agencies see the *Data sources*.) Risk ratings may be highly subjective, reflecting external perceptions that do not always capture the actual situation in a coun-

try. But these subjective perceptions are the reality that policy-makers face. Countries not rated by credit risk rating agencies typically do not attract registered flows of private capital. The risk ratings presented here are included for their analytical usefulness and are not endorsed by the World Bank.

The PRS Group's *International Country Risk Guide* (ICRG) collects information on 22 components of risk, groups it into three major categories (political, financial, and economic), and converts it into a single numerical risk assessment ranging from 0 to 100. Ratings below 50 indicate very high risk, and those above 80 very low risk. Ratings are updated monthly.

Institutional Investor country credit ratings are based on information provided by leading international banks. Responses are weighted using a formula that gives more importance to responses from banks with greater worldwide exposure and more sophisticated country analysis systems. Countries are rated on a scale of 0 to 100 (highest risk to lowest), and ratings are updated every six months.

Euromoney country creditworthiness ratings are based on nine weighted categories (covering debt, economic performance, political risk, and access to financial and capital markets) that assess country risk. The ratings, also on a scale of 0 to 100 (highest risk to lowest), are based on polls of economists and political analysts supplemented by quantitative data such as debt ratios and access to capital markets.

Moody's sovereign long-term debt ratings are opinions of the ability of entities to honor senior unsecured financial obligations and contracts denominated in foreign currency (foreign currency issuer ratings) or in their domestic currency (domestic currency issuer ratings).

Standard & Poor's ratings of sovereign long-term foreign and domestic currency debt are based on current information furnished by obligors or obtained by Standard & Poor's from other sources it considers reliable. A Standard & Poor's issuer credit rating (one form of which is a sovereign credit rating) is a current opinion of an obligor's capacity and willingness to pay its financial obligations as they come due (its creditworthiness). This opinion does not apply to any specific financial obligation, as it does not take into account the nature and provisions of obligations, their standing in bankruptcy or liquidation, statutory preferences, or the legality and enforceability of obligations.

Definitions

• **Foreign direct investment** is net inflows of investment to acquire a lasting management interest (10 percent or more of voting stock) in an enterprise operating in an economy other than that of the investor. It is the sum of equity capital, reinvestment of earnings, other long-term capital, and short-term capital as shown in the balance of payments. Gross capital formation (gross domestic investment in previous editions) is the sum of gross fixed capital formation, changes in inventories, and acquisitions less disposals of valuables. • **Regulations on entry to emerging stock markets** are assessed on a scale from free to closed (see *About the data*). • **Regulations on repatriation of income** (dividends, interest, and realized capital gains) and repatriation of capital from emerging stock markets are evaluated as free or restricted (see *About the data*). • **Composite International Country Risk Guide (ICRG) risk rating** is an overall index, ranging from 0 to 100, based on 22 components of risk. • **Institutional Investor credit rating** ranks, from 0 to 100, the chances of a country's default. • **Euromoney country creditworthiness rating** ranks, from 0 to 100, the risk of investing in an economy. • **Moody's sovereign foreign and domestic currency long-term debt rating** assesses the risk of lending to governments. An entity's ability to meet its senior financial obligations is rated from Aaa (offering exceptional financial security) to C (usually in default, with potential recovery values low). Modifiers 1–3 are applied to ratings from Aa to B, with 1 indicating a high ranking in the rating category. • **Standard & Poor's sovereign foreign and domestic currency long-term debt rating** ranges from AAA (extremely strong capacity to meet financial commitments) through CC (currently highly vulnerable). Ratings from AA to CCC may be modified by a plus or minus sign to show relative standing in the category. An obligor rated SD (selective default) has failed to pay one or more financial obligations when due.

Data sources

The data on foreign direct investment are based on estimates compiled by the IMF in its *Balance of Payments Statistics Yearbook*, supplemented by World Bank staff estimates. The data on entry and exit regulations are from Standard & Poor's *Emerging Stock Markets Factbook 2001*. The country risk and credit-worthiness ratings are from the PRS Group's monthly *International Country Risk Guide* (Web site: www.ICRGonline.com), the monthly *Institutional Investor*, the monthly *Euromoney*, Moody's Investors Service's *Sovereign, Subnational and Sovereign-Guaranteed Issuers,* and Standard & Poor's Sovereign List in *Credit Week*.

5.3 | Stock markets

	Market capitalization				Value traded		Turnover ratio		Listed domestic companies		S&P/IFC Investable Index	
	$ millions		% of GDP		% of GDP		value of shares traded as % of capitalization				% change in price index	
	1990	2001	1990	2000	1990	2000	1990	2001	1990	2001	2000	2001
Afghanistan	..	..	..	..	..	..	..	..	..	..	..	..
Albania	..	..	..	..	..	..	..	..	..	..	..	..
Algeria	..	..	..	..	..	..	..	..	..	..	..	..
Angola	..	..	..	..	..	..	..	..	..	..	..	..
Argentina	3,268	192,499	2.3	58.3	0.6	2.1	33.6	0.2	179	111	-25.1	-31.7
Armenia	..	25	..	1.4	..	0.1	..	4.6	..	95	..	..
Australia	108,879	372,794	35.2	95.6	13.0	58.0	31.6	56.5	1,089	1,330	..	..
Austria	11,476	29,935	7.1	15.8	11.5	5.0	110.3	29.8	97	97	..	..
Azerbaijan	..	4	..	0.1	..	..	..	..	..	2	..	..
Bangladesh	321	1,145	1.1	2.5	0.0	1.6	1.5	3.0	134	230	28.5 a	-20.7 a
Belarus	..	..	..	..	..	..	..	..	..	..	..	..
Belgium	65,449	182,481	33.2	80.5	3.3	16.8	..	20.7	182	174	..	..
Benin	..	..	..	..	..	..	..	..	..	..	..	..
Bolivia	..	116	..	1.4	..	0.0	..	1.0	..	18	..	..
Bosnia and Herzegovina	..	..	..	..	..	..	..	..	..	..	..	..
Botswana	261	1,269	6.7	18.5	0.2	0.9	6.1	0.5	9	16	-6.9 a	43.9 a
Brazil	16,354	186,238	3.5	38.0	1.2	17.0	23.6	3.1	581	428	-10.3	-22.5
Bulgaria	..	505	..	5.1	..	0.5	..	1.0	..	399	-30.0 a	-7.5 a
Burkina Faso	..	..	..	..	..	..	..	..	..	..	..	..
Burundi	..	..	..	..	..	..	..	..	..	..	..	..
Cambodia	..	..	..	..	..	..	..	..	..	..	..	..
Cameroon	..	..	..	..	..	..	..	..	..	..	..	..
Canada	241,920	841,385	42.2	122.3	12.4	92.3	26.7	77.3	1,144	3,977	..	..
Central African Republic	..	..	..	..	..	..	..	..	..	..	..	..
Chad	..	..	..	..	..	..	..	..	..	..	..	..
Chile	13,645	56,310	45.0	85.6	2.6	8.6	6.3	0.5	215	249	-15.2	-8.3
China	2,028	523,952	0.5	53.8	0.2	66.8	158.9	4.7	14	1,160	-9.8	-19.5
Hong Kong, China	83,397	623,398	111.5	383.3	46.3	232.3	43.1	61.3	284	779	..	..
Colombia	1,416	13,217	3.5	11.8	0.2	0.5	5.6	0.3	80	123	-43.8	25.2
Congo, Dem. Rep.	..	..	..	..	..	..	..	..	..	..	..	..
Congo, Rep.	..	..	..	..	..	..	..	..	..	..	..	..
Costa Rica	475	2,303	5.5	14.7	0.1	1.4	5.8	12.0	82	22	..	..
Côte d'Ivoire	549	1,165	5.1	12.6	0.2	0.4	3.4	0.1	23	38	-25.6 a	-2.4 a
Croatia	..	3,319	..	14.4	..	1.0	..	0.3	2	62	10.9 a	-3.5 a
Cuba	..	..	..	..	..	..	..	..	..	..	..	..
Czech Republic	..	9,331	..	21.7	..	13.0	..	3.7	..	94	-0.6	-13.7
Denmark	39,063	107,666	29.3	66.3	8.3	56.4	28.0	86.0	258	225	..	..
Dominican Republic	..	141	..	0.8	..	..	..	..	..	6	..	..
Ecuador	69	1,417	0.5	5.2	..	0.1	0.0	0.3	65	31	33.0 a	85.4 a
Egypt, Arab Rep.	1,765	24,335	4.1	29.1	0.3	11.3	..	0.7	573	1,110	-45.6	-45.5
El Salvador	..	2,672	..	17.2	..	0.4	..	3.0	..	39	..	..
Eritrea	..	..	..	..	..	..	..	..	..	..	..	..
Estonia	..	1,483	..	37.1	..	6.6	..	0.9	..	17	4.5 a	-3.7 a
Ethiopia	..	..	..	..	..	..	..	..	..	..	..	..
Finland	22,721	293,635	16.6	241.7	2.9	170.1	..	64.3	73	154	..	..
France	314,384	1,446,634	25.9	111.8	9.6	83.7	..	74.1	578	808	..	..
Gabon	..	..	..	..	..	..	..	..	..	..	..	..
Gambia, The	..	..	..	..	..	..	..	..	..	..	..	..
Georgia	..	..	..	..	..	..	..	..	..	..	..	..
Germany	355,073	1,270,243	21.0	67.8	29.7	57.1	139.3	79.1	413	1,022	..	..
Ghana	76	528	1.2	9.7	..	0.2	0.0	0.1	13	22	-50.9 a	4.5 a
Greece	15,228	86,538	18.1	98.4	4.7	84.4	36.3	3.1	145	338	-44.6	-31.2
Guatemala	..	215	..	1.2	..	0.0	..	2.9	..	5	..	..
Guinea	..	..	..	..	..	..	..	..	..	..	..	..
Guinea-Bissau	..	..	..	..	..	..	..	..	..	..	..	..
Haiti	..	..	..	..	..	..	..	..	..	..	..	..
Honduras	40	..	1.3	8.7	0.0	..	0.0	..	26	71	..	..

	Market capitalization				Value traded		Turnover ratio		Listed domestic companies		S&P/IFC Investable Index	
	$ millions		% of GDP		% of GDP		value of shares traded as % of capitalization				% change in price index	
	1990	2001	1990	2000	1990	2000	1990	2001	1990	2001	2000	2001
Hungary	505	10,367	1.5	26.3	0.3	26.6	6.3	3.8	21	57	-28.2	-10.3
India	38,567	110,396	12.2	32.4	6.9	48.4	65.9	15.8	2,435	5,795	-31.1	-19.9
Indonesia	8,081	23,006	7.1	17.5	3.5	9.3	75.8	2.8	125	316	-61.0	-18.5
Iran, Islamic Rep.	34,282	21,830	..	21.9	..	2.3	30.4	12.4	97	295	..	..
Iraq	..	..	..	..	..	..	..	..	..	..	..	..
Ireland	..	81,882	..	87.2	..	15.4	..	19.2	..	76	..	..
Israel	3,324	55,964	6.3	58.1	10.5	21.2	95.8	2.7	216	636	14.7	-16.4
Italy	148,766	768,364	13.5	71.5	3.9	72.5	26.8	104.0	220	291	..	..
Jamaica	911	4,703	21.5	48.4	0.8	1.0	3.4	0.1	44	42	45.6 [a]	4.3 [a]
Japan	2,917,679	3,157,222	95.6	65.2	52.5	55.6	43.8	69.9	2,071	2,561	-27.2 [b]	-33.4 [b]
Jordan	2,001	6,316	49.8	59.3	10.1	5.0	20.0	1.3	105	161	-24.5	31.4
Kazakhstan	..	2,260	..	13.4	..	0.1	..	1.2	..	17	..	..
Kenya	453	1,050	5.3	12.4	0.1	0.5	2.2	0.2	54	57	-8.1 [a]	-22.7 [a]
Korea, Dem. Rep.	..	..	..	..	..	..	..	..	..	..	..	..
Korea, Rep.	110,594	220,046	43.8	32.5	30.1	121.3	61.3	33.3	669	1,409	-57.1	51.2
Kuwait	..	20,772	..	55.0	..	11.1	..	21.3	..	77	..	..
Kyrgyz Republic	..	..	..	..	..	..	..	..	..	..	..	..
Lao PDR	..	..	..	..	..	..	..	..	..	..	..	..
Latvia	..	697	..	7.9	..	3.2	..	0.2	..	63	41.2 [a]	60.1 [a]
Lebanon	..	1,243	..	9.6	..	0.7	..	0.5	..	12	-18.6 [a]	-29.2 [a]
Lesotho	..	..	..	..	..	..	..	..	..	..	..	..
Liberia	..	..	..	..	..	..	..	..	..	..	..	..
Libya	..	..	..	..	..	..	..	..	..	..	..	..
Lithuania	..	1,199	..	14.0	..	1.8	..	2.0	..	54	4.9 [a]	-23.6 [a]
Macedonia, FYR	..	8	..	0.2	..	0.7	..	348.3	..	2	..	..
Madagascar	..	..	..	..	..	..	..	..	..	..	..	..
Malawi	..	..	..	..	..	..	..	..	..	..	..	..
Malaysia	48,611	120,007	110.4	130.4	24.7	65.2	24.6	2.1	282	809	-23.3	4.2
Mali	..	..	..	..	..	..	..	..	..	..	..	..
Mauritania	..	1,091	..	..	..	..	..	0.4	..	40	..	..
Mauritius	268	1,063	10.1	30.4	0.2	1.7	1.9	0.3	13	40	-19.4 [a]	-21.8 [a]
Mexico	32,725	121,403	12.5	21.8	4.6	7.9	44.0	1.7	199	168	-21.5	12.8
Moldova	..	38	..	3.2	..	0.3	..	97.9	..	58	..	..
Mongolia	..	32	..	3.5	..	3.9	..	7.3	..	418	..	..
Morocco	966	9,087	3.7	32.7	0.2	3.3	..	1.2	71	55	-19.1	-17.3
Mozambique	..	..	..	..	..	..	..	..	..	..	..	..
Myanmar	..	..	..	..	..	..	..	..	..	..	..	..
Namibia	21	151	0.7	8.9	..	0.6	0.0	0.0	3	13	-37.8 [a]	-31.0 [a]
Nepal	..	418	..	8.3	..	0.5	..	6.9	..	108	..	..
Netherlands	119,825	640,456	40.6	175.6	13.6	185.7	29.0	101.4	260	234	..	..
New Zealand	8,835	18,613	20.5	37.3	4.5	21.6	17.3	45.9	171	144	..	..
Nicaragua	..	..	..	..	..	..	..	..	..	..	..	..
Niger	..	..	..	..	..	..	..	..	..	..	..	..
Nigeria	1,372	5,404	4.8	10.3	0.0	0.6	0.9	0.6	131	194	-10.3 [a]	25.1 [a]
Norway	26,130	65,034	22.6	40.2	12.1	37.2	54.4	93.4	112	191	..	..
Oman	1,061	2,606	9.4	29.4	0.9	13.0	12.3	2.0	55	91	7.2 [a]	-27.0 [a]
Pakistan	2,850	4,944	7.1	10.7	0.6	53.5	8.7	8.0	487	747	-16.7	-32.8
Panama	226	3,584	3.4	37.5	0.0	0.5	0.9	1.5	13	31	..	..
Papua New Guinea	..	..	..	..	..	..	..	..	..	..	..	..
Paraguay	..	423	..	5.5	..	0.2	..	3.5	..	55	..	..
Peru	812	11,134	3.1	19.8	0.4	2.8	19.3	0.5	294	207	-28.1	14.2
Philippines	5,927	41,523	13.4	69.0	2.7	11.0	13.6	0.5	153	232	-43.6	-29.9
Poland	144	26,017	0.2	19.8	0.0	9.3	89.7	1.9	9	230	-3.5	-24.9
Portugal	9,201	60,681	13.0	57.8	2.4	51.8	16.9	85.5	181	109	38.4	..
Puerto Rico	..	..	..	..	..	..	..	..	..	..	..	..
Romania	..	2,124	..	2.9	..	0.6	..	0.8	..	5,140	-25.3 [a]	-25.3 [a]
Russian Federation	244	76,198	0.0	15.5	..	8.1	..	3.1	13	236	-32.2	52.4

5.3 Stock markets

	Market capitalization				Value traded		Turnover ratio		Listed domestic companies		S&P/IFC Investable Index	
	$ millions		% of GDP		% of GDP		value of shares traded as % of capitalization				% change in price index	
	1990	2001	1990	2000	1990	2000	1990	2001	1990	2001	2000	2001
Rwanda	..	..	..	..	..	..	..	..	..	..	..	..
Saudi Arabia	48,213	73,199	40.8	38.8	1.9	10.0	..	1.7	59	76	42.3 [a]	3.7 [a]
Senegal	..	..	..	..	..	..	..	..	..	..	..	..
Sierra Leone	..	..	..	..	..	..	..	..	..	..	..	..
Singapore	34,308	152,827	93.6	165.7	55.3	99.2	..	52.1	150	418	..	..
Slovak Republic	..	665	..	3.9	..	4.7	..	17.7	..	844	0.4	21.3
Slovenia	..	2,839	..	14.1	..	2.6	..	3.4	24	38	-9.5 [a]	2.0 [a]
Somalia	..	..	..	..	..	..	..	..	..	..	..	..
South Africa	137,540	139,750	122.8	162.8	7.3	61.6	..	3.6	732	542	-17.3	-22.1
Spain	111,404	504,219	21.7	90.3	8.0	176.5	..	210.7	427	1,019	..	..
Sri Lanka	917	1,332	11.4	6.6	0.5	0.9	5.8	3.8	175	238	-41.7	36.5
Sudan	..	..	..	..	..	..	..	..	..	..	..	..
Swaziland	17	95	2.0	7.0	..	0.0	..	0.2	1	7	..	..
Sweden	97,929	328,339	41.1	144.4	7.4	171.6	14.9	111.2	258	292	..	..
Switzerland	160,044	792,316	70.1	330.5	29.6	254.1	..	82.0	182	252	..	..
Syrian Arab Republic	..	..	..	..	..	..	..	..	..	..	..	..
Tajikistan	..	..	..	..	..	..	..	..	..	..	..	..
Tanzania	..	181	..	2.1	..	0.1	..	3.4	..	4	..	..
Thailand	23,896	36,340	28.0	24.1	26.8	19.0	92.6	11.5	214	449	-54.1	3.0
Togo	..	..	..	..	..	..	..	..	..	..	..	..
Trinidad and Tobago	696	5,035	13.7	59.2	1.1	1.9	10.0	0.7	30	31	8.5 [a]	1.6 [a]
Tunisia	533	2,303	4.3	14.5	0.2	3.2	3.3	1.8	13	46	9.0 [a]	-29.0 [a]
Turkey	19,065	47,150	12.6	34.8	3.9	89.6	42.5	15.3	110	310	-51.2	-30.2
Turkmenistan	..	..	..	..	..	..	..	..	..	..	..	..
Uganda	..	..	..	..	..	..	..	..	..	..	..	..
Ukraine	..	1,365	..	5.9	..	0.9	..	1.6	..	131	75.2 [a]	-36.3 [a]
United Arab Emirates	..	23,262	..	71.6	..	..	..	..	..	54	..	..
United Kingdom	848,866	2,576,992	85.9	182.2	28.2	129.7	33.4	66.6	1,701	1,904	-10.2 [c]	-18.3 [c]
United States	3,059,434	15,104,037	53.2	153.5	30.5	323.9	53.4	200.8	6,599	7,524	-10.1 [d]	-13.0 [d]
Uruguay	..	168	..	0.8	..	0.0	..	0.9	36	17	..	..
Uzbekistan	..	119	..	1.4	..	0.4	..	..	..	4	..	..
Venezuela, RB	8,361	6,216	17.2	6.7	4.6	0.6	43.0	0.5	76	63	18.7	-20.1
Vietnam	..	..	..	..	..	..	..	..	..	..	..	..
West Bank and Gaza	..	848	..	19.8	..	3.5	..	20.9	..	22	..	..
Yemen, Rep.	..	..	..	..	..	..	..	..	..	..	..	..
Yugoslavia, Fed. Rep.	..	10,817	..	109.9	..	0.1	..	0.0	..	16	..	..
Zambia	..	291	..	9.4	..	0.5	..	4.7	..	8	..	..
Zimbabwe	2,395	7,972	27.3	32.9	0.6	3.8	2.9	1.6	57	72	-24.6	134.3

	Market capitalization				Value traded		Turnover ratio		Listed domestic companies			
World	9,399,659 s	32,189,220 s	48.0 w	105.1 w	28.5 w	153.8 w	57.2 w	122.3 w	25,424 s	48,645 s		
Low income	54,588	194,186	9.8	23.6	4.7	32.8	53.8	121.3	3,446	7,733		
Middle income	430,288	2,049,260	21.2	41.2	8.0	37.7	78.3	84.9	4,900	15,364		
Lower middle income	39,161	777,998	5.3	40.3	..	40.9	..	101.0	1,723	10,142		
Upper middle income	391,127	1,271,262	25.8	41.8	8.1	35.7	37.1	74.7	3,177	5,222		
Low & middle income	484,876	2,243,446	19.9	38.7	7.6	37.0	70.7	90.1	8,346	23,097		
East Asia & Pacific	197,109	954,452	21.3	48.3	13.2	69.8	117.2	148.9	1,443	3,486		
Europe & Central Asia	19,065	173,932	2.1	20.5	..	27.8	..	83.1	110	8,220		
Latin America & Carib.	78,188	614,691	7.6	34.0	2.1	8.9	29.7	26.9	1,734	1,567		
Middle East & N. Africa	5,265	126,253	27.8	34.8	1.5	7.2	..	22.3	817	1,596		
South Asia	42,655	156,905	10.8	27.0	5.6	43.8	54.0	161.6	3,231	7,159		
Sub-Saharan Africa	142,594	217,212	51.9	102.3	..	36.8	..	22.5	1,011	1,069		
High income	8,914,783	29,945,774	51.7	120.6	31.4	181.1	59.5	129.9	17,078	25,548		
Europe EMU	1,183,983	5,423,384	21.6	89.9	14.2	83.1	..	90.6	2,630	4,367		

Note: Because aggregates for market capitalization are unavailable for 2001, those shown refer to 2000.
a. Data refer to the S&P/IFC Global index. b. Data refer to the Nikkei 225 index. c. Data refer to the FT 100 index. d. Data refer to the S&P 500 index.

Stock markets | 5.3

About the data

Financial market development is closely related to an economy's overall development. Well-functioning financial systems provide good and easily accessible information, which lowers transactions costs, which in turn improves resource allocation and economic growth. Both banking systems and stock markets enhance growth, which is the main factor in poverty reduction. At low levels of economic development commercial banks tend to dominate the financial system. In higher-income economies domestic stock markets tend to become more active and efficient relative to domestic banks. The structure and development of a country's financial system are also determined by aspects of the legal, regulatory, tax, and macroeconomic environment.

The stock market indicators presented in the table include measures of size (market capitalization and number of listed domestic companies) and liquidity (value traded as a percentage of GDP, and turnover ratio). The comparability of such indicators between countries may be limited by conceptual and statistical weaknesses, such as inaccurate reporting and differences in accounting standards. The percentage change in stock market prices in U.S. dollars, from the Standard & Poor's Investable (S&P/IFCI) and Global (S&P/IFCG) country indexes, is an important measure of overall performance. Regulatory and institutional factors that can affect investor confidence, such as the existence of a securities and exchange commission and the quality of investor protection laws, may influence the functioning of stock markets but are not included in this table.

Stock market size can be measured in a number of ways, each of which may produce a different ranking among countries. Market capitalization shows the overall size of the stock market in U.S. dollars and as a percentage of GDP. The number of listed domestic companies is another measure of market size. Market size is positively correlated with the ability to mobilize capital and diversify risk.

Market liquidity, the ability to easily buy and sell securities, is measured by dividing the total value traded by GDP. This indicator complements the market capitalization ratio by showing whether market size is matched by trading. The turnover ratio—the value of shares traded as a percentage of market capitalization—is also a measure of liquidity, as well as of transactions costs. (High turnover indicates low transactions costs.) The turnover ratio complements the ratio of value traded to GDP, because the turnover ratio is related to the size of the market and the value traded ratio to the size of the economy. A small, liquid market will have a high turnover ratio but a low value traded ratio. Liquidity is an important attribute of stock markets because, in theory, liquid markets improve the allocation of capital and enhance prospects

for long-term economic growth. A more comprehensive measure of liquidity would include trading costs and the time and uncertainty in finding a counterpart in settling trades.

Standard & Poor's maintains a series of indexes for investors interested in investing in stock markets in developing countries. At the core of the Standard & Poor's family of emerging market indexes, the S&P/IFCG indexes are intended to represent the most active stocks in the markets they cover and to be the broadest possible indicator of market movements. The S&P/IFCI indexes, which apply the same calculation methodology as the S&P/IFCG indexes, are designed to measure the returns foreign portfolio investors might receive from investing in emerging market stocks that are legally and practically open to foreign portfolio investment. The EMDB covers 54 markets, providing regular updates on more than 2,200 stocks; the S&P/IFCG indexes include 34 markets and more than 1,900 stocks; the S&P/IFCI indexes cover 30 markets and close to 1,200 stocks. They are widely used benchmarks for international portfolio management. See Standard & Poor's (2001b) for further information on the indexes.

Because markets included in Standard & Poor's emerging markets category vary widely in level of development, it is best to look at the entire category to identify the most significant market trends. And it is useful to remember that stock market trends may be distorted by currency conversions, especially when a currency has registered a significant devaluation.

Definitions

• **Market capitalization** (also known as market value) is the share price times the number of shares outstanding. • **Value traded** refers to the total value of shares traded during the period. • **Turnover ratio** is the total value of shares traded during the period divided by the average market capitalization for the period. Average market capitalization is calculated as the average of the end-of-period values for the current period and the previous period. • **Listed domestic companies** are the domestically incorporated companies listed on the country's stock exchanges at the end of the year. This indicator does not include investment companies, mutual funds, or other collective investment vehicles. • **S&P/IFC Investable index** price change is the U.S. dollar price change in the stock markets covered by the S&P/IFCI country index, supplemented by the S&P/IFCG country index.

Data sources

The data on stock markets are from Standard & Poor's *Emerging Stock Markets Factbook 2001*, supplemented by other data from Standard & Poor's. The firm collects data through an annual survey of the world's stock exchanges, supplemented by information provided by its network of correspondents and by Reuters. The GDP data are from the World Bank's national accounts data files. *About the data* is based on Demirgüç-Kunt and Levine (1996a) and Beck and Levine (2001).

Figure 5.3

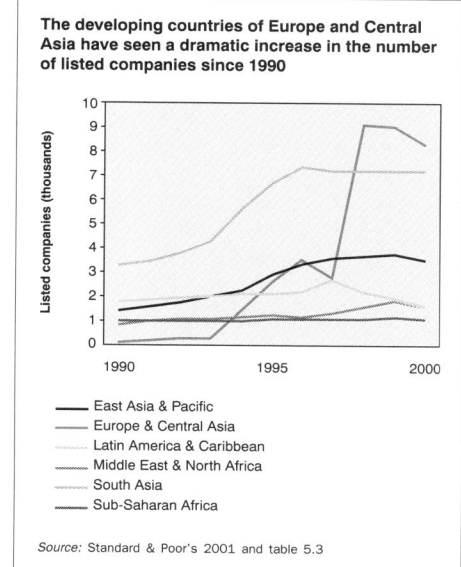

The developing countries of Europe and Central Asia have seen a dramatic increase in the number of listed companies since 1990

- East Asia & Pacific
- Europe & Central Asia
- Latin America & Caribbean
- Middle East & North Africa
- South Asia
- Sub-Saharan Africa

Source: Standard & Poor's 2001 and table 5.3

2002 World Development Indicators

	Domestic credit provided by banking sector		Liquid liabilities		Quasi-liquid liabilities		Ratio of bank liquid reserves to bank assets		Interest rate spread		Spread over LIBOR	
									Lending minus deposit rate percentage points		Lending rate minus LIBOR percentage points	
	% of GDP		% of GDP		% of GDP		%					
	1990	2000	1990	2000	1990	2000	1990	2000	1990	2000	1990	2000
Afghanistan	..	..	..	..	..	..	..	..	..	..	..	..
Albania	..	48.3	..	60.8	..	37.8	..	12.0	2.1	13.8	16.7	15.6
Algeria	74.5	32.0	73.5	41.4	24.8	15.4	1.3	3.0	..	2.5	..	3.5
Angola	..	-15.3	..	18.2	..	12.2	..	17.7	..	63.6	..	96.6
Argentina	32.4	34.4	11.5	31.9	7.1	24.9	7.4	2.5	..	2.7	..	4.6
Armenia	58.7	11.5	79.9	14.7	42.9	7.8	13.6	7.0	..	13.5	..	25.0
Australia	71.7	91.7	55.1	66.5	43.4	46.0	1.5	0.6	4.5	4.7	9.9	2.3
Austria	121.4	..	..	..	..	..	2.1	..	..	3.4	..	0.2
Azerbaijan	57.2	9.6	33.5	16.3	11.6	9.6	4.5	9.3	..	..	..	..
Bangladesh	23.9	35.3	23.4	34.7	16.8	25.5	12.8	7.6	4.0	6.9	7.7	9.0
Belarus	..	19.2	..	17.7	..	12.1	..	7.7	..	30.1	..	61.1
Belgium	8.6	7.3	7.0	5.3	5.7	3.7	1.1	0.8	-0.9	1.3	-0.9	-2.2
Benin	22.4	8.8	26.7	31.1	5.9	7.4	29.3	10.0	9.0	..	7.7	..
Bolivia	30.7	64.7	24.5	54.6	18.0	46.8	18.8	5.8	18.0	23.6	33.5	28.1
Bosnia and Herzegovina	..	..	..	..	..	..	..	..	..	..	..	..
Botswana	-46.4	-71.9	22.1	27.2	13.7	20.1	11.0	3.6	1.8	5.2	-0.4	8.8
Brazil	89.8	50.9	26.4	29.2	18.5	22.4	6.7	7.6	..	39.6	..	50.3
Bulgaria	118.5	18.3	71.9	35.0	53.6	20.7	10.2	6.6	8.9	8.4	42.4	5.0
Burkina Faso	13.7	16.9	21.3	24.9	7.5	7.5	12.7	4.6	9.0	..	7.7	..
Burundi	23.2	30.1	18.2	19.9	6.5	6.1	2.8	3.0	..	..	4.0	9.2
Cambodia	..	7.4	..	15.0	..	10.6	..	47.3	..	10.5	..	10.8
Cameroon	31.2	16.3	22.6	17.3	10.1	6.4	3.4	15.4	11.0	17.0	10.2	15.5
Canada	82.5	89.2	74.5	75.0	59.9	52.8	1.6	0.7	1.3	1.6	5.7	0.7
Central African Republic	12.9	11.4	15.3	16.2	1.8	1.3	2.8	1.7	11.0	17.0	10.2	15.5
Chad	11.5	12.2	14.6	12.2	0.6	0.8	3.3	12.9	11.0	17.0	10.2	15.5
Chile	73.0	74.7	40.7	50.3	32.8	40.0	3.8	3.1	8.5	5.6	40.6	8.3
China	90.0	132.7	79.2	152.1	41.4	91.1	15.7	12.7	0.7	3.6	1.0	-0.7
Hong Kong, China	156.3	141.4	181.7	236.8	166.8	222.3	0.1	0.3	3.3	4.7	1.7	3.0
Colombia	35.9	36.5	29.8	32.8	19.3	22.8	26.3	5.9	8.8	6.6	36.9	12.3
Congo, Dem. Rep.	25.3	..	12.9	..	2.1	..	48.5	..	..	..	..	158.5
Congo, Rep.	29.1	8.7	22.0	14.6	6.1	1.1	2.0	43.1	11.0	17.0	10.2	15.5
Costa Rica	29.9	32.7	42.7	36.9	30.0	23.9	68.5	18.9	11.4	11.5	24.2	18.4
Côte d'Ivoire	44.5	25.6	28.8	24.6	10.9	7.3	2.1	3.9	9.0	..	7.7	..
Croatia	..	45.7	..	46.1	..	34.6	..	10.7	499.3	8.3	1,153.9	5.5
Cuba	..	..	..	..	..	..	..	..	..	..	..	..
Czech Republic	..	57.3	..	73.8	..	48.3	..	18.4	..	3.7	..	0.6
Denmark	63.0	56.7	59.0	55.3	29.4	24.3	1.1	8.1	6.2	4.9	5.8	1.5
Dominican Republic	31.5	38.5	28.4	34.7	13.1	23.7	31.1	27.5	15.2	9.1	29.3	20.3
Ecuador	15.0	39.9	20.4	31.3	11.3	21.3	22.6	3.8	-6.0	8.9	29.2	9.7
Egypt, Arab Rep.	106.8	100.2	87.9	83.9	60.7	65.4	17.1	15.9	7.0	3.8	10.7	6.7
El Salvador	32.0	42.3	30.6	46.2	19.6	37.9	33.4	29.8	3.2	4.6	12.9	7.4
Eritrea	..	..	..	..	..	..	..	..	..	..	..	..
Estonia	66.7	40.0	136.0	39.3	95.2	14.6	43.1	19.9	..	3.9	26.6	1.1
Ethiopia	67.0	61.7	42.2	42.5	12.6	20.6	24.0	13.6	3.6	4.2	-2.3	4.4
Finland	83.1	55.8	54.4	48.1	..	..	4.1	2.5	4.1	4.0	3.3	-0.9
France	104.4	..	..	..	..	..	1.0	..	6.1	4.1	2.3	0.2
Gabon	20.0	12.9	17.8	15.0	6.6	5.9	2.0	12.8	11.0	17.0	10.2	15.5
Gambia, The	3.4	13.8	20.7	36.8	8.8	18.5	8.8	10.1	15.2	11.5	18.2	17.5
Georgia	..	21.9	..	10.5	..	4.3	..	13.7	..	22.6	..	26.2
Germany	103.4	147.5	68.9	78.1	..	..	3.2	1.4	4.5	6.2	3.3	3.1
Ghana	13.2	40.8	14.1	20.1	3.4	10.5	20.2	4.8	..	..	..	..
Greece	99.3	101.8	..	..	..	..	13.8	25.2	8.1	6.2	19.3	5.8
Guatemala	17.4	16.9	21.2	28.6	11.8	15.8	31.8	15.6	5.1	10.7	15.0	14.4
Guinea	6.0	8.9	0.8	11.6	0.8	2.1	6.2	17.8	0.2	11.9	12.9	12.8
Guinea-Bissau	77.5	18.1	68.9	42.7	4.4	0.7	10.8	45.5	13.1	..	37.4	..
Haiti	32.9	31.5	31.4	37.0	15.9	25.4	74.9	37.3	..	13.2	..	18.6
Honduras	40.9	31.5	33.6	52.1	18.8	38.5	6.6	18.0	8.3	10.9	8.7	20.3

	Domestic credit provided by banking sector		Liquid liabilities		Quasi-liquid liabilities		Ratio of bank liquid reserves to bank assets		Interest rate spread		Spread over LIBOR	
									Lending minus deposit rate percentage points		Lending rate minus LIBOR percentage points	
	% of GDP		% of GDP		% of GDP		%					
	1990	2000	1990	2000	1990	2000	1990	2000	1990	2000	1990	2000
Hungary	105.5	53.9	43.8	46.3	19.0	27.8	11.0	10.8	4.1	3.0	20.5	6.1
India	51.5	53.4	43.1	56.1	28.1	39.3	14.8	8.0	..	..	8.2	5.8
Indonesia	45.5	66.2	40.4	57.5	29.1	45.3	4.5	8.1	3.3	6.0	12.5	11.9
Iran, Islamic Rep.	70.8	49.3	57.6	42.9	31.1	23.8	66.0	41.0	..	..	..	..
Iraq	..	..	..	..	..	..	..	..	..	..	..	..
Ireland	55.2	110.2	44.5	..	..	..	4.8	1.4	5.0	4.7	3.0	-1.8
Israel	106.2	86.5	70.2	97.5	63.6	90.6	11.9	13.6	12.0	4.2	18.1	6.3
Italy	89.4	98.5	70.5	..	..	..	12.0	0.7	7.3	4.4	5.8	-0.3
Jamaica	34.8	38.0	51.0	47.3	37.8	32.3	37.4	19.0	6.6	11.7	22.2	16.8
Japan	259.7	310.5	182.4	189.9	155.3	142.4	1.5	1.4	3.4	2.0	-1.4	-4.5
Jordan	117.9	90.6	131.2	113.1	77.8	79.0	20.5	29.0	2.2	4.8	2.0	5.3
Kazakhstan	..	14.1	..	15.3	..	6.2	..	5.4	..	..	..	..
Kenya	52.9	48.2	43.3	46.1	29.3	31.0	9.9	8.3	5.1	14.2	10.4	15.8
Korea, Dem. Rep.	..	..	..	..	..	..	..	..	..	..	..	..
Korea, Rep.	65.7	104.0	54.6	97.9	45.7	88.8	6.3	2.0	0.0	0.6	1.7	2.0
Kuwait	243.0	82.2	192.2	70.4	153.9	57.8	1.2	1.0	0.4	3.0	4.1	2.3
Kyrgyz Republic	..	12.6	..	11.9	..	4.5	..	18.7	..	33.5	..	45.4
Lao PDR	5.1	10.7	7.2	16.7	3.1	14.2	3.4	28.1	..	20.0	..	25.5
Latvia	..	24.2	..	30.4	..	12.8	..	5.8	..	7.5	..	5.3
Lebanon	132.6	183.3	193.7	198.1	170.9	188.5	3.9	12.7	23.1	6.9	31.6	11.6
Lesotho	32.8	3.7	39.2	27.3	22.6	10.7	23.0	23.6	7.4	12.2	12.1	10.6
Liberia	..	..	..	..	..	..	64.9	70.9	..	14.3	..	14.0
Libya	..	..	..	..	..	..	26.4	30.5	1.5	4.0	-1.3	0.5
Lithuania	..	14.4	..	23.1	..	10.6	..	12.0	..	8.3	..	5.6
Macedonia, FYR	..	14.5	..	19.4	..	9.9	..	7.9	..	7.7	..	12.4
Madagascar	26.2	15.2	17.8	26.8	5.3	11.5	8.5	20.1	5.3	11.5	17.5	20.0
Malawi	19.7	8.7	21.1	18.3	11.7	9.3	32.8	15.2	8.9	19.9	12.7	46.6
Malaysia	75.7	143.4	64.4	130.0	43.0	106.4	5.9	14.0	1.3	3.4	-1.1	0.2
Mali	13.7	15.0	20.5	24.9	5.5	7.1	50.8	17.7	9.0	..	7.7	..
Mauritania	54.7	-2.7	28.5	14.8	7.0	3.9	6.1	4.3	5.0	..	1.7	..
Mauritius	45.1	74.8	63.3	83.1	49.1	71.5	8.8	5.1	5.4	11.2	9.7	14.2
Mexico	36.6	25.4	22.8	23.6	16.4	15.3	4.2	5.8	..	12.0	..	11.7
Moldova	62.8	25.3	70.3	22.4	35.4	9.7	8.3	13.3	..	8.9	..	27.2
Mongolia	73.4	10.5	56.2	24.8	14.7	12.3	2.0	18.1	..	16.5	..	23.7
Morocco	60.1	92.1	61.0	82.6	18.4	21.5	11.3	6.3	0.5	8.2	0.7	6.8
Mozambique	15.6	11.2	26.5	30.4	5.2	15.9	61.5	8.5	..	9.3	..	12.5
Myanmar	32.8	26.8	27.9	25.7	7.8	9.9	271.8	23.4	2.1	5.5	-0.3	8.7
Namibia	18.8	48.0	22.6	45.0	13.2	21.1	4.4	3.2	10.6	7.9	17.4	8.7
Nepal	28.9	43.2	32.2	51.5	18.5	34.9	12.7	10.6	2.5	3.5	6.1	2.9
Netherlands	103.2	..	..	..	..	..	0.3	..	8.4	1.9	3.4	-1.7
New Zealand	81.6	117.8	77.9	89.1	64.8	74.9	0.8	0.5	4.4	3.9	7.7	3.7
Nicaragua	206.6	141.9	56.9	64.2	23.1	52.9	20.2	15.4	12.5	11.9	13.7	14.8
Niger	16.2	9.0	19.8	8.0	8.3	2.1	42.9	9.9	9.0	..	7.7	..
Nigeria	23.7	11.3	23.6	24.8	10.3	9.2	11.6	15.4	5.5	9.6	17.0	14.7
Norway	89.5	55.8	59.9	50.9	27.0	11.2	0.5	2.2	4.6	1.5	5.9	1.7
Oman	16.6	44.7	28.9	37.0	19.3	28.3	6.9	3.6	1.4	2.4	1.4	3.5
Pakistan	50.9	49.0	39.8	47.5	10.0	20.0	8.9	6.2	..	..	..	..
Panama	52.7	110.8	41.1	86.9	33.0	75.1	..	..	3.6	3.1	3.7	3.6
Papua New Guinea	35.7	25.9	35.2	29.7	24.0	16.7	3.2	8.0	6.9	3.0	7.2	11.0
Paraguay	14.9	27.2	22.3	36.7	13.7	26.9	31.0	22.7	8.1	11.1	22.7	20.3
Peru	20.2	25.9	24.8	32.1	11.8	20.8	22.0	21.6	2,335.0	14.6	4,766.2	21.4
Philippines	26.9	68.0	37.0	66.5	28.4	54.7	20.9	7.4	4.6	2.6	15.8	4.4
Poland	19.5	37.8	34.0	43.0	17.2	30.9	20.6	4.6	462.5	5.8	495.9	13.5
Portugal	70.0	142.8	..	..	..	..	29.0	3.6	7.8	2.8	13.5	-0.2
Puerto Rico	..	..	..	..	..	..	..	..	..	..	..	..
Romania	79.7	14.1	60.4	23.2	32.7	17.7	1.2	36.4	..	..	..	..
Russian Federation	..	24.0	..	22.1	..	9.6	..	15.4	..	17.9	..	17.9

	Domestic credit provided by banking sector		Liquid liabilities		Quasi-liquid liabilities		Ratio of bank liquid reserves to bank assets		Interest rate spread		Spread over LIBOR	
									Lending minus deposit rate percentage points		Lending rate minus LIBOR percentage points	
	% of GDP		% of GDP		% of GDP		%					
	1990	2000	1990	2000	1990	2000	1990	2000	1990	2000	1990	2000
Rwanda	17.1	12.6	14.9	16.3	7.0	7.3	4.3	9.9	6.3	..	4.9	..
Saudi Arabia	58.7	68.4	47.9	48.6	21.9	23.0	5.6	4.7	..	..	..	..
Senegal	33.8	25.1	22.9	25.4	9.7	10.5	14.1	6.4	9.0	..	7.7	..
Sierra Leone	26.3	54.4	13.1	16.4	2.6	5.8	64.1	14.7	12.0	17.0	44.2	19.7
Singapore	75.6	89.6	123.4	107.5	100.5	86.5	3.7	2.5	2.7	4.1	-1.0	-0.7
Slovak Republic	..	59.9	..	67.8	..	46.8	..	5.7	..	6.4	..	8.4
Slovenia	36.8	47.1	34.2	49.7	25.8	40.1	2.7	3.5	142.0	5.7	818.6	9.2
Somalia	..	..	..	..	..	..	..	22.3	..	..	..	..
South Africa	97.8	162.6	44.6	46.3	27.2	15.9	3.3	2.7	2.1	5.3	12.7	8.0
Spain	106.2	119.8	..	..	..	..	8.7	1.0	5.4	2.2	7.7	-1.4
Sri Lanka	43.1	44.4	35.2	46.6	22.9	37.2	9.9	7.6	-6.4	7.0	4.7	9.6
Sudan	20.4	8.6	20.1	11.7	2.9	3.8	79.5	36.4	..	..	..	..
Swaziland	7.9	-4.1	29.6	22.2	20.8	15.2	21.5	7.2	5.6	7.5	6.2	7.5
Sweden	140.3	79.3	52.3	44.8	..	..	1.8	0.4	6.8	3.7	8.4	-0.7
Switzerland	179.0	179.2	145.2	130.9	118.6	91.3	1.1	0.8	-0.9	1.3	-0.9	-2.2
Syrian Arab Republic	56.6	27.6	54.7	66.2	10.5	22.9	46.0	5.8	..	..	..	..
Tajikistan	..	..	..	..	..	..	..	..	..	..	..	..
Tanzania	34.6	12.1	19.9	19.7	6.3	10.1	5.3	15.0	..	14.2	..	15.0
Thailand	91.1	121.7	74.9	115.2	66.0	101.2	3.1	1.9	2.2	4.5	6.1	1.3
Togo	21.3	23.8	36.1	28.4	19.1	8.0	59.0	6.2	9.0	..	7.7	..
Trinidad and Tobago	58.5	47.3	54.6	57.2	42.7	45.6	13.5	14.4	6.9	8.3	4.6	10.0
Tunisia	62.5	73.2	51.5	57.8	26.7	33.9	1.6	2.6	..	..	..	..
Turkey	19.4	53.7	24.1	44.9	16.4	39.6	16.3	7.1	..	..	..	..
Turkmenistan	..	30.5	..	14.9	..	5.1	..	4.1	..	..	..	..
Uganda	17.8	12.2	7.6	16.2	1.4	7.5	15.2	12.4	7.4	13.1	30.4	16.4
Ukraine	83.2	23.4	50.1	18.1	9.0	6.1	49.0	17.9	..	27.8	..	35.0
United Arab Emirates	34.7	59.9	46.3	57.9	37.7	41.6	4.4	11.5	..	..	..	..
United Kingdom	121.4	136.1	..	..	..	..	0.5	0.4	2.2	2.7	6.4	-0.6
United States	110.9	161.7	65.5	62.1	49.4	47.5	2.3	1.1	..	..	1.7	2.7
Uruguay	46.7	54.3	58.1	51.3	51.5	45.4	31.1	11.1	76.6	36.9	166.1	42.5
Uzbekistan	..	..	..	..	..	..	..	..	..	..	..	..
Venezuela, RB	37.4	14.3	38.8	18.9	29.4	9.1	21.9	29.5	7.7	8.9	27.2	18.7
Vietnam	4.7	35.0	22.7	44.4	9.3	23.9	13.3	9.1	..	6.9	..	4.0
West Bank and Gaza	..	..	..	..	..	..	..	..	..	..	..	..
Yemen, Rep.	60.6	5.2	55.1	34.1	10.4	16.1	121.2	18.8	..	3.8	..	16.6
Yugoslavia, Fed. Rep.	..	..	..	..	..	..	..	..	..	..	..	..
Zambia	67.8	79.1	21.8	26.8	10.6	18.3	33.7	13.1	9.5	18.6	26.8	32.3
Zimbabwe	41.7	48.3	41.8	34.5	30.3	17.6	12.2	8.7	2.9	18.0	3.4	61.7
World	**120.7 w**	**152 w**	**82.8 w**	**92.0 w**	**.. w**	**68.1 w**	**9.9 m**	**8.5 m**				
Low income	44.6	45.9	37.1	46.8	22.2	31.2	13.5	13.2				
Middle income	65.1	72.9	44.7	69.4	28.0	47.1	19.7	7.8				
Lower middle income	..	90.3	..	98.6	..	61.1	19.7	7.9				
Upper middle income	60.5	60.2	33.8	48.0	23.5	36.9	8.1	7.6				
Low & middle income	61.0	68.7	43.1	65.8	26.9	44.7	13.2	10.7				
East Asia & Pacific	73.4	116.4	63.9	123.9	42.7	85.6	5.9	10.9				
Europe & Central Asia	..	36.4	..	36.2	..	24.7	..	10.7				
Latin America & Carib.	59.3	37.8	25.4	29.6	17.7	21.4	22.3	15.5				
Middle East & N. Africa	69.3	70.0	61.6	61.8	30.3	36.7	14.2	9.5				
South Asia	48.9	51.1	41.0	53.1	25.2	36.0	12.7	7.6				
Sub-Saharan Africa	56.8	76.6	32.5	34.2	17.2	14.0	11.9	10.1				
High income	132.3	173.8	92.5	101.8	..	76.9	1.8	1.1				
Europe EMU	96.8	118.1	..	..	..	..	4.1	1.3				

Financial depth and efficiency 5.4

About the data

The organization and performance of financial activities in a country affect economic growth through their impact on how businesses raise and manage funds. Savers accumulate claims on financial institutions, which pass these funds to their final users. But even if a country has savings, growth may not materialize because the markets are not perfect and the financial system can fail to direct those savings where they can be invested most efficiently. Households and institutions save and invest independently. The financial system's role is to intermediate between them and to cycle available funds to where they are needed. This is accomplished through established payments systems, available price information, a way to manage uncertainty and control risk, and mechanisms to deal with problems of asymmetric information between parties to a financial transaction. As an economy develops, this indirect lending by savers to investors becomes more efficient and gradually increases financial assets relative to GDP.

As more specialized savings and financial institutions emerge, more financing instruments become available, spreading risks and reducing costs to liability holders. As securities markets mature, savers can invest their resources directly in financial assets issued by firms. There are big differences in financial systems across countries; banks, nonbanks, and stock markets are larger, more active, and more efficient in richer countries.

The ratio of domestic credit provided by the banking sector to GDP is used to measure the growth of the banking system because it reflects the extent to which savings are financial. In a few countries governments may hold international reserves as deposits in the banking system rather than in the central bank. Since the claims on the central government are a net item (claims of central government minus central government deposits), this net figure may be negative, resulting in a negative figure for domestic credit provided by the banking sector.

Liquid liabilities include bank deposits of generally less than one year plus currency. Their ratio to GDP indicates the relative size of these readily available forms of money—money that the owners can use to buy goods and services without incurring any cost. This is a general indicator of the size of financial intermediaries relative to the size of the economy, or an overall measure of financial sector development. Quasi-liquid liabilities are long-term deposits and assets—such as certificates of deposit, commercial paper, and bonds—that can be converted into currency or demand deposits, but at a cost. The ratio of bank liquid reserves to bank assets captures the banking system's liquidity. In countries whose banking system is liquid, adverse macroeconomic conditions should be less likely to lead to banking and financial crises. Data on domestic credit and liquid and quasi-liquid liabilities are cited on an end-of-year basis.

No less important than the size and structure of the financial sector is its efficiency, as indicated by the margin between the cost of mobilizing liabilities and the earnings on assets—or the interest rate spread. A narrowing of the interest rate spread reduces transactions costs, which lowers the overall cost of investment and is therefore crucial to economic growth. Interest rates reflect the responsiveness of financial institutions to competition and price incentives. The interest rate spread, also known as the intermediation margin, is a summary measure of a banking system's efficiency. To the extent that information about interest rates is inaccurate, banks do not monitor all bank managers, or the government sets deposit and lending rates, the interest rate spread may not be a reliable measure of efficiency. The spread over LIBOR reflects the differential between a country's lending rate and the London interbank offered rate (ignoring expected changes in the exchange rate). Interest rates are expressed as annual averages.

In some countries financial markets are distorted by restrictions on foreign investment, selective credit controls, and controls on deposit and lending rates. Interest rates may reflect the diversion of resources to finance the public sector deficit through statutory reserve requirements and direct borrowing from the banking system. And where state-owned banks dominate the financial sector, noncommercial considerations may unduly influence credit allocation. The indicators in the table provide quantitative assessments of each country's financial sector, but qualitative assessments of policies, laws, and regulations are needed to analyze overall financial conditions. Recent international financial crises highlight the risks of weak financial intermediation, poor corporate governance, and deficient government policies, including procyclical macroeconomic policy responses to large capital inflows.

The accuracy of financial data depends on the quality of accounting systems, which are weak in some developing economies. Some of the indicators in the table are highly correlated, particularly the ratios of domestic credit, liquid liabilities, and quasi-liquid liabilities to GDP, because changes in liquid and quasi-liquid liabilities flow directly from changes in domestic credit. Moreover, the precise definition of the financial aggregates presented varies by country.

The indicators reported here do not capture the activities of the informal sector, which remains an important source of finance in developing economies. Personal credit or credit extended through community-based pooling of assets may be the only source of credit available to small farmers, small businesses, or home-based producers. And in financially repressed economies the rationing of formal credit forces many borrowers and lenders to turn to the informal market, which is very expensive, or to self-financing and family savings.

Definitions

• **Domestic credit provided by banking sector** includes all credit to various sectors on a gross basis, with the exception of credit to the central government, which is net. The banking sector includes monetary authorities, deposit money banks, and other banking institutions for which data are available (including institutions that do not accept transferable deposits but do incur such liabilities as time and savings deposits). Examples of other banking institutions include savings and mortgage loan institutions and building and loan associations. • **Liquid liabilities** are also known as broad money, or M3. They are the sum of currency and deposits in the central bank (M0), plus transferable deposits and electronic currency (M1), plus time and savings deposits, foreign currency transferable deposits, certificates of deposit, and securities repurchase agreements (M2), plus travelers checks, foreign currency time deposits, commercial paper, and shares of mutual funds or market funds held by residents. • **Quasi-liquid liabilities** are the M3 money supply less M1. • **Ratio of bank liquid reserves to bank assets** is the ratio of domestic currency holdings and deposits with the monetary authorities to claims on other governments, nonfinancial public enterprises, the private sector, and other banking institutions. • **Interest rate spread** is the interest rate charged by banks on loans to prime customers minus the interest rate paid by commercial or similar banks for demand, time, or savings deposits. • **Spread over LIBOR** (London interbank offered rate) is the interest rate charged by banks on short-term loans in local currency to prime customers minus LIBOR. LIBOR is the most commonly recognized international interest rate and is quoted in several currencies. The average three-month LIBOR on U.S. dollar deposits is used here.

Data sources

The data on credit, liabilities, bank reserves, and interest rates are collected from central banks and finance ministries and reported in the print and electronic editions of the International Monetary Fund's *International Financial Statistics.*

5.5 | Tax policies

	Tax revenue	Taxes on income, profits, and capital gains		Domestic taxes on goods and services		Export duties		Import duties		Highest marginal tax rate[a]		
	% of GDP	% of total taxes		% of value added in industry and services		% of tax revenue		% of tax revenue		Individual rate %	on income over $	Corporate rate %
	2000	1990	2000	1990	2000	1990	2000	1990	2000	2000	2000	2000
Afghanistan	..	..	..	..	..	..	..	..	..	..	..	..
Albania	14.8	..	9.4	..	16.9	..	0.0	..	19.3	..	..	..
Algeria	27.6	..	72.3	..	3.7	..	0.0	..	15.3	..	..	..
Angola	..	..	..	..	..	..	..	..	..	..	..	..
Argentina	12.9	2.7	18.7	2.2	6.7	9.3	0.1	2.6	5.2	35	120,000	35
Armenia	..	..	..	..	..	..	..	..	..	..	..	..
Australia	21.9	70.9	72.8	5.8	5.4	0.1	0.0	4.4	2.8	47	33,324	34
Austria	35.0	20.8	27.0	10.0	10.6	0.0	..	1.6	..	50	47,900	34
Azerbaijan	16.7	..	23.1	..	8.9	..	0.0	..	9.0	35	12,987	27
Bangladesh	7.0	..	14.5	..	5.0	..	0.0	..	30.0	..	..	..
Belarus	26.8	12.1	11.7	17.1	15.4	3.6	..	0.4	..	..	..	..
Belgium	43.0	17.0	13.9	10.4	..	0.0	0.0	6.9	1.2	55	56,433	39
Benin	..	..	..	..	..	..	..	..	..	..	..	..
Bolivia	14.2	7.9	9.9	5.8	11.1	0.0	0.0	11.1	7.1	13	0	25
Bosnia and Herzegovina	..	..	..	..	..	..	..	..	..	..	..	..
Botswana	..	71.7	..	1.0	..	0.0	..	24.7	..	25	14,920	15
Brazil	20.6	24.5	24.4	7.1	6.7	0.0	0.0	2.5	3.5	28	11,077	15
Bulgaria	28.9	40.6	15.9	10.4	18.2	0.0	0.0	2.5	3.0	38	8,094	20
Burkina Faso	..	24.7	..	4.9	..	1.1	..	33.1	..	..	..	..
Burundi	16.7	23.4	22.5	16.6	17.0	3.1	0.0	23.2	16.4	..	..	..
Cambodia	..	..	..	..	..	..	..	..	..	20	38,412	20
Cameroon	12.8	25.1	26.0	4.3	6.9	1.7	3.9	18.9	31.6	60	10,726	39
Canada	20.1	59.3	58.4	4.2	..	0.0	0.0	3.2	1.4	29	40,038	38
Central African Republic	..	..	..	..	..	..	..	..	..	..	..	..
Chad	..	20.3	..	3.9	..	..	..	..	..	..	..	..
Chile	19.0	15.8	22.9	10.4	12.7	..	..	..	..	45	5,529	15
China	6.8	49.8	6.8	1.5	6.5	0.0	0.0	22.1	6.6	45	12,089	30
Hong Kong, China	..	..	..	..	..	..	..	..	..	17	13,462	16
Colombia	10.8	36.4	39.9	4.8	6.2	2.0	0.0	22.5	8.5	35	34,375	35
Congo, Dem. Rep.	..	28.5	33.1	2.6	..	4.1	1.7	45.1	35.9	60	1,500	40
Congo, Rep.	6.0	40.2	11.3	4.1	4.1	0.0	0.0	32.3	22.9	50	14,210	45
Costa Rica	18.8	11.5	14.5	8.7	10.1	8.0	0.2	18.2	4.5	25	16,746	30
Côte d'Ivoire	20.1	18.1	22.7	8.9	5.1	3.7	13.1	28.4	34.7	10	3,432	35
Croatia	38.4	17.4	9.5	9.6	25.0	0.0	0.0	3.6	6.4	35	5,437	..
Cuba	..	..	..	..	..	..	..	..	..	..	..	..
Czech Republic	32.2	..	13.8	..	13.7	..	0.0	..	2.2	32	8,587	31
Denmark	31.5	43.5	40.2	18.9	19.3	0.0	0.0	0.1	0.0	59	..	30
Dominican Republic	15.2	23.8	19.5	3.1	5.5	0.1	0.0	41.4	40.0	25	15,165	25
Ecuador	..	62.9	..	4.5	..	0.3	..	12.1	..	25	11,201	25
Egypt, Arab Rep.	..	26.4	..	4.1	..	0.0	..	18.9	..	32	12,987	40
El Salvador	13.2	..	24.2	..	7.2	..	0.0	..	8.1	30	22,857	25
Eritrea	..	..	..	..	..	..	..	..	..	..	..	..
Estonia	28.3	27.5	15.8	14.8	15.9	0.0	0.0	0.8	0.1	26	..	35
Ethiopia	..	40.9	..	9.1	..	2.8	..	18.0	..	..	..	..
Finland	27.8	34.5	33.6	17.7	16.9	0.0	0.0	1.0	0.0	37	50,940	29
France	..	18.7	..	13.1	..	0.0	..	0.0	..	..	..	33
Gabon	..	35.9	..	5.0	..	2.8	..	23.4	..	50	31,462	35
Gambia, The	..	13.7	..	12.2	..	0.2	..	45.6	..	..	..	..
Georgia	10.0	..	8.8	..	9.8	..	0.0	..	7.4	..	..	..
Germany	26.3	17.5	17.3	6.8	7.1	0.0	0.0	0.0	0.0	53	54,617	25
Ghana	..	25.1	..	6.8	..	12.4	..	28.7	..	30	7,059	33
Greece	21.9	23.3	41.6	14.5	16.0	0.0	0.0	0.1	0.1	43	46,625	35
Guatemala	..	..	..	..	..	..	..	..	..	31	38,155	31
Guinea	11.3	12.6	10.1	3.2	0.9	51.7	0.2	11.2	42.9	..	..	..
Guinea-Bissau	..	..	..	..	..	..	..	..	..	..	..	..
Haiti	..	..	..	..	..	..	..	..	..	..	..	..
Honduras	..	..	..	..	..	..	..	..	..	25	32,916	15

	Tax revenue	Taxes on income, profits, and capital gains		Domestic taxes on goods and services		Export duties		Import duties		Highest marginal tax rate[a]		
	% of GDP	% of total taxes		% of value added in industry and services		% of tax revenue		% of tax revenue		Individual rate %	on income over $	Corporate rate %
	2000	1990	2000	1990	2000	1990	2000	1990	2000	2000	2000	2000
Hungary	32.8	21.2	23.4	22.6	15.3	1.3	0.0	5.6	3.3	40	3,512	18
India	9.6	18.6	35.8	7.4	5.2	0.1	0.1	35.8	26.7	30	3,222	40
Indonesia	16.5	65.4	64.5	5.6	6.2	0.1	0.5	6.6	2.3	35	20,949	30
Iran, Islamic Rep.	9.2	24.7	41.7	1.0	1.8	0.0	0.0	18.6	14.4	54	174,583	54
Iraq	..	..	..	..	..	..	..	..	..	..	..	..
Ireland	..	39.7	..	15.5	..	0.0	..	0.0	..	42	23,912	32
Israel	37.7	42.4	45.7	..	..	0.0	0.0	1.4	0.8	50	54,647	36
Italy	38.5	37.7	38.8	12.7	11.6	0.0	0.0	0.0	0.0	46	64,207	36
Jamaica	23.3	..	43.1	..	9.8	..	0.0	..	9.3	25	2,327	33
Japan	..	73.0	..	2.4	..	0.0	..	1.4	..	37	156,863	30
Jordan	19.8	22.9	13.7	6.8	10.7	0.0	0.0	34.7	23.7	..	..	..
Kazakhstan	10.2	..	31.2	..	6.3	..	0.0	..	4.7	30	..	30
Kenya	21.2	32.9	37.9	15.9	15.2	0.0	0.0	17.8	16.8	30	5,612	30
Korea, Dem. Rep.	..	..	..	..	..	..	..	..	..	..	..	..
Korea, Rep.	..	37.5	..	6.7	..	0.0	..	13.0	..	40	63,507	28
Kuwait	3.4	19.5	8.2	0.0	..	0.0	0.0	76.8	0.0	0	..	0
Kyrgyz Republic	12.3	..	18.0	..	17.2	..	..	..	..	..	..	30
Lao PDR	..	..	..	..	..	..	..	..	..	40	658	..
Latvia	25.3	..	13.5	..	14.0	..	0.0	..	1.3	25	..	25
Lebanon	14.1	..	15.1	..	4.9	..	..	..	39.0	..	..	..
Lesotho	34.4	12.7	23.2	13.0	7.4	0.2	..	63.6	..	..	..	..
Liberia	..	..	..	..	..	..	..	..	..	..	..	..
Libya	..	..	..	..	..	..	..	..	..	..	..	..
Lithuania	22.8	22.2	12.9	16.4	14.1	..	0.0	..	1.4	33	..	24
Macedonia, FYR	..	..	..	..	..	..	..	..	..	..	..	..
Madagascar	11.3	15.7	15.7	3.6	5.5	8.5	0.0	50.1	53.5	..	..	..
Malawi	..	42.5	..	13.9	..	0.0	..	18.7	..	38	948	38
Malaysia	..	42.5	..	6.3	..	9.7	..	15.1	..	29	39,474	28
Mali	..	..	..	..	..	..	..	..	..	..	..	..
Mauritania	..	..	..	..	..	..	..	..	..	..	..	..
Mauritius	19.1	15.2	13.1	6.4	10.0	4.6	0.0	45.7	31.5	25	894	15
Mexico	12.3	34.2	41.1	10.2	9.2	0.1	0.0	6.9	4.8	40	258,269	35
Moldova	21.1	..	4.1	..	19.7	..	0.0	..	4.1	..	..	..
Mongolia	21.5	28.2	16.0	9.3	15.7	0.0	2.3	19.6	7.7	..	..	..
Morocco	25.0	27.3	28.5	12.1	12.7	0.3	0.0	20.3	18.8	44	5,758	35
Mozambique	..	..	..	..	..	..	..	..	..	20	640	35
Myanmar	2.8	29.8	35.1	6.8	3.8	0.0	0.0	23.3	8.9	30	..	30
Namibia	29.5	39.4	35.3	9.0	11.8	3.6	..	26.9	..	36	25,641	35
Nepal	8.7	13.0	21.0	6.6	6.5	0.4	1.3	37.0	31.1	..	..	..
Netherlands	..	33.6	..	11.4	..	0.0	..	0.0	..	52	43,091	35
New Zealand	29.0	62.2	66.3	13.4	..	0.0	0.0	2.5	2.0	39	26,584	33
Nicaragua	27.6	20.0	14.1	16.9	24.7	0.0	0.0	21.3	7.8	25	31,545	25
Niger	..	..	..	..	..	..	..	..	..	..	..	..
Nigeria	..	..	..	..	..	..	..	..	..	25	1,553	30
Norway	34.5	21.7	25.6	17.0	18.7	0.1	0.0	0.6	0.7	28	6,835	28
Oman	6.4	87.6	79.8	0.3	..	0.0	0.0	7.8	8.4	0	..	12
Pakistan	12.1	12.8	28.1	8.6	7.9	0.0	0.0	44.4	16.0	35	17,271	..
Panama	18.2	24.4	29.3	4.8	..	1.3	0.0	15.8	..	30	200,000	30
Papua New Guinea	18.4	47.0	51.3	5.0	2.9	2.1	5.1	29.3	27.8	47	31,066	25
Paraguay	..	12.4	..	3.6	..	0.0	..	18.8	..	0	..	30
Peru	13.3	5.8	24.7	6.7	9.0	7.6	0.0	9.9	11.5	20	45,957	30
Philippines	13.9	32.5	44.3	6.4	5.0	0.0	0.0	28.4	20.7	32	10,000	32
Poland	28.0	..	20.9	..	13.9	..	0.0	..	2.6	40	17,908	28
Portugal	31.1	25.7	29.6	13.2	15.1	0.0	0.0	2.6	0.0	40	46,967	34
Puerto Rico	..	..	..	..	..	..	..	..	..	33	50,000	20
Romania	27.0	21.0	18.1	15.3	13.2	0.0	0.0	0.6	5.6	40	2,359	25
Russian Federation	21.6	..	13.7	..	9.4	..	10.8	..	4.2	13	6,036	35

	Tax revenue	Taxes on income, profits, and capital gains		Domestic taxes on goods and services		Export duties		Import duties		Highest marginal tax rate[a]		
	% of GDP	% of total taxes		% of value added in industry and services		% of tax revenue		% of tax revenue		Individual rate %	on income over $	Corporate rate %
	2000	1990	2000	1990	2000	1990	2000	1990	2000	2000	2000	2000
Rwanda	..	20.0	..	5.6	..	7.4	..	20.7	..	..	..	..
Saudi Arabia	..	..	..	..	..	..	..	..	..	0	..	30
Senegal	..	..	..	..	..	..	..	..	..	50	22,469	35
Sierra Leone	6.8	33.0	26.9	1.9	2.8	0.4	0.0	41.3	49.8	..	..	..
Singapore	15.5	44.6	50.2	4.3	4.8	0.0	0.0	3.5	2.5	28	400,000	26
Slovak Republic	31.1	..	21.7	..	11.8	..	0.0	..	4.7	42	24,115	29
Slovenia	36.7	12.3	14.9	12.7	17.6	..	0.0	..	2.6	42	..	25
Somalia	..	..	..	..	..	..	..	..	..	..	..	..
South Africa	25.9	55.0	55.7	10.3	10.5	0.0	0.0	3.9	3.2	45	15,000	30
Spain	..	34.0	..	7.6	..	0.0	..	1.7	..	40	67,744	35
Sri Lanka	14.5	12.0	15.1	14.7	13.7	4.2	0.0	27.4	13.1	35	3,630	35
Sudan	6.8	..	18.3	..	5.1	..	0.8	..	35.5	..	..	..
Swaziland	27.5	33.2	26.4	5.4	6.8	2.0	0.0	50.5	54.7	39	5,089	30
Sweden	35.1	20.6	15.5	14.5	12.3	0.0	0.0	0.6	0.0	31	27,198	28
Switzerland	22.3	17.0	13.9	..	6.0	0.0	0.0	6.9	1.2	..	..	45
Syrian Arab Republic	15.7	40.2	48.9	9.6	5.5	1.3	3.1	8.2	13.6	..	..	..
Tajikistan	9.7	..	3.4	..	7.9	..	0.0	..	14.7	..	..	..
Tanzania	..	..	..	..	..	..	..	..	..	30	8,000	30
Thailand	14.1	26.2	34.0	8.8	7.7	0.2	0.3	23.7	12.3	37	92,829	30
Togo	..	..	..	..	..	..	..	..	..	..	..	..
Trinidad and Tobago	..	..	..	..	..	..	..	..	..	35	8,012	35
Tunisia	26.0	16.0	22.3	7.1	12.5	0.4	0.1	35.1	12.5	..	..	..
Turkey	22.0	51.2	37.4	5.9	16.0	0.0	0.0	7.3	1.7	40	104,353	30
Turkmenistan	..	..	..	..	..	..	..	..	..	..	..	..
Uganda	10.3	..	18.0	..	12.9	..	0.0	..	11.0	30	2,795	30
Ukraine	22.1	..	15.2	..	12.2	..	0.0	..	4.1	40	3,754	30
United Arab Emirates	1.8	0.0	0.0	0.6	..	..	..	..	..	0	..	20
United Kingdom	34.6	43.2	41.8	11.3	13.0	0.0	0.0	0.0	0.0	40	43,815	30
United States	20.1	56.1	61.3	..	..	0.0	0.0	1.7	1.0	40	297,350	35
Uruguay	24.9	7.1	16.9	9.4	10.2	0.6	0.1	8.1	3.0	0	..	30
Uzbekistan	..	..	..	..	..	..	..	..	..	36	603	26
Venezuela, RB	12.9	82.2	42.9	0.8	4.9	0.0	0.0	7.1	11.3	34	99,445	34
Vietnam	14.9	..	32.0	..	8.0	..	0.0	..	20.7	50	5,695	32
West Bank and Gaza	..	..	..	..	..	..	..	..	..	..	..	..
Yemen, Rep.	9.7	44.9	45.9	2.5	2.7	0.0	0.0	29.2	25.9	..	..	..
Yugoslavia, Fed. Rep.	..	..	..	..	..	..	..	..	..	..	..	..
Zambia	..	..	..	..	..	..	..	..	..	30	524	35
Zimbabwe	..	49.7	..	8.4	..	0.0	..	18.8	..	53	14,756	30

a. These data are from PricewaterhouseCoopers's *Individual Taxes: Worldwide Summaries 2001-2002* and *Corporate Taxes: Worldwide Summaries 2001-2002*, copyright 2001 by PricewaterhouseCoopers by permission of John Wiley and Sons, Inc.

About the data

Tax revenue is the main source of revenue for many governments. The sources of the tax revenue received by governments and the relative contributions of these sources are determined by policy choices about where and how to impose taxes and by changes in the structure of the economy. Tax policy may reflect concerns about distributional effects, economic efficiency (including corrections for externalities), and the practical problems of administering a tax system. There is no ideal level of taxation. But taxes influence incentives and thus the behavior of economic actors and the country's competitiveness.

Taxes are compulsory transfers received by the government sector from individuals, businesses, or institutions. They include fees that are clearly out of all proportion to the costs of providing services, but exclude compulsory social contributions, fines, and penalties. They are considered unrequited because governments provide nothing specifically in return for them, although taxes typically are used to provide goods or services to individuals or communities on a collective basis.

The level of taxation is typically measured by tax revenue as a share of GDP. Comparing levels of taxation across countries provides a quick overview of the fiscal obligations and incentives facing the private sector. In this table tax data measured in local currencies are normalized by scaling variables in the same units to ease cross-country comparisons. The table refers only to central government data, which may significantly understate the total tax burden, particularly in countries where provincial and municipal governments are large or have considerable tax authority.

Low ratios of tax collections to GDP may reflect weak administration and large-scale tax avoidance or evasion. They may also reflect the presence of a sizable parallel economy with unrecorded and undisclosed incomes. Tax collection ratios tend to rise with income, with higher-income countries relying on taxes to finance a much broader range of social services and social security than lower-income countries are able to provide.

As countries develop, their capacity to tax residents directly typically expands and indirect taxes become less important as a source of revenue. Thus the share of taxes on income, profits, and capital gains is one measure of an economy's (and tax system's) level of development. In the early stages of development governments tend to rely on indirect taxes because the administrative costs of collecting them are relatively low. The two main indirect taxes are international trade taxes (including customs revenues) and domestic taxes on goods and services. The table shows these domestic taxes as a percentage of value added in industry and services. Agriculture and mining are excluded from the denominator because indirect taxes on goods originating from these sectors are usually negligible. What is missing here is a measure of the uniformity of these taxes across industries and along the value added chain of production. Without such data no clear inferences can be drawn about how neutral a tax system is between subsectors. "Surplus" revenues raised by some governments by charging higher prices for goods produced under monopoly by state-owned enterprises are not counted as tax revenues. Similarly, losses from charging below-market prices for products are rarely identified as subsidies.

Export and import duties are shown separately because the burden they impose on the economy (and thus growth) is likely to be large. Export duties, typically levied on primary (particularly agricultural) products, often take the place of direct taxes on income and profits, but they reduce the incentive to export and encourage a shift to other products. High import duties penalize consumers, create protective barriers—which promote higher-priced output and inefficient production—and implicitly tax exports. By contrast, lower trade taxes enhance openness—to foreign competition, knowledge, technologies, and resources—energizing development in many ways. The economies growing fastest over the past 15 years have not relied on tax revenues from imports. Seeing this pattern, many developing countries have lowered tariffs over the past decade, a trend that is expected to continue. In some countries, such as members of the European Union, most customs duties are collected by a supranational authority; these revenues are not reported in the individual countries' accounts.

The tax revenues collected by governments are the outcomes of systems that are often complex, containing many exceptions, exemptions, penalties, and other inducements that affect the incidence of taxes and thus influence the decisions of workers, managers, and entrepreneurs. A potentially important influence on both domestic and international investors is a tax system's progressivity, as reflected in the highest marginal tax rate on individual and corporate income. Figures for individual marginal tax rates generally refer to employment income. For some countries the highest marginal tax rate is also the basic or flat rate, and other surtaxes, deductions, and the like may apply.

Definitions

- **Tax revenue** comprises compulsory transfers to the central government for public purposes. Compulsory transfers such as fines, penalties, and most social security contributions are excluded. Refunds and corrections of erroneously collected tax revenue are treated as negative revenue. • **Taxes on income, profits, and capital gains** are levied on wages, salaries, tips, fees, commissions and other compensation for labor services; interest, dividends, rent, and royalties; capital gains and losses; and profits of businesses, estates, and trusts. Social security contributions based on gross pay, payroll, or number of employees are not included, but taxable portions of social security, pension, and other retirement account distributions are included. • **Domestic taxes on goods and services** include all taxes and duties levied by central governments on the production, extraction, sale, transfer, leasing, or delivery of goods and rendering of services, or on the use of goods or permission to use goods or perform activities. These include value added taxes, general sales taxes, single-stage and multistage taxes (where "stage" refers to stage of production or distribution), excise taxes, and motor vehicle taxes, and taxes on the extraction, processing, or production of minerals or other products. • **Export duties** include all levies collected on goods at the point of export. Rebates on exported goods that are repayments of previously paid general consumption taxes, excise taxes, or import duties are deducted from the gross amounts receivable from the respective taxes, not from amounts receivable in this category. • **Import duties** comprise all levies collected on goods at the point of entry into the country. The levies may be imposed for revenue or protection purposes and may be determined on a specific or ad valorem basis, as long as they are restricted to imported products. • **Highest marginal tax rate** is the highest rate shown on the schedule of tax rates applied to the annual taxable income of individuals and corporations. Also presented are the income levels above which the highest marginal tax rates for individuals apply.

Data sources

The definitions used here are from the International Monetary Fund's (IMF) *Manual on Government Finance Statistics* (2001). The data on tax revenues are from print and electronic editions of the IMF's *Government Finance Statistics Yearbook*. The data on individual and corporate tax rates are from PricewaterhouseCoopers's *Individual Taxes: Worldwide Summaries 2001-02* and *Corporate Taxes: Worldwide Summaries 2001-02*.

300

	Exchange rate arrangements [a]		Official exchange rate	Purchasing power parity conversion factor		PPP conversion factor/ official exchange rate	Real effective exchange rate	Interest rate			Key agricultural producer prices	
			local currency units to $	local currency units to international $		ratio	1995=100	Deposit %	Lending %	Real %	Wheat $ per metric ton	Maize $ per metric ton
	Classification 2000	Structure 2000	2000	1990	2000	2000	2000	2000	2000	2000	1998	1998
Afghanistan	..	..	3,000.0	0.0	..	..	..	..	..	..	33	31
Albania	IF	U	143.7	1.8	45.1	0.3	..	8.3	22.1	23.6	..	..
Algeria	MF	U	75.3	4.9	24.9	0.3	107.7	7.5	10.0	-11.0	337	..
Angola	IF	U	10.0	0.0	3.1	0.3	..	39.6	103.2	-59.5	..	..
Argentina	CB	U	1.0	0.3	0.6	0.6	..	8.3	11.1	9.8	85	56
Armenia	IF	U	539.5	0.0	106.1	0.2	108.7	18.1	31.6	33.4	..	..
Australia	IF	U	1.7	1.4	1.4	0.8	94.5	4.1	8.8	5.1	127	128
Austria	EA/Euro	U	14.9 [b]	12.8	13.0	0.9	90.3	2.2	5.6	4.7	117	117
Azerbaijan	MF	U	4,474.2	0.1	997.1	0.2	..	..	..	..	204	132
Bangladesh	P	U	52.1	9.1	11.3	0.2	..	8.6	15.5	13.4	172	173
Belarus	MF	M	876.8	0.0	120.9	0.1	..	37.5	67.7	-41.2	..	..
Belgium	EA/Euro	U	43.8 [b]	34.1	35.6	0.8	87.3	3.0	4.3	3.0	..	..
Benin	EA/FF	U	712.0	151.0	248.5	0.3	..	3.5	..	..	..	285
Bolivia	P	U	6.2	1.3	2.5	0.4	117.9	11.0	34.6	29.7	195	119
Bosnia and Herzegovina	CB	U	2.1	0.0	..	..	..	..	14.7	30.5	..	..
Botswana	P	D	5.1	1.1	2.3	0.5	..	10.1	15.3	3.3	90	110
Brazil	IF	U	1.8	0.0	0.8	0.5	..	17.2	56.8	44.5	164	125
Bulgaria	CB	U	2.1	0.0	0.6	0.3	120.7	3.1	11.5	5.6	..	..
Burkina Faso	EA/FF	U	712.0	133.3	141.8	0.2	..	3.5	..	..	..	148
Burundi	MF	D	720.7	49.2	123.4	0.2	93.1	..	15.8	-5.8	156	357
Cambodia	MF	D	3,840.8	66.8	703.4	0.2	..	6.8	17.3	15.6	..	158
Cameroon	EA/FF	U	712.0	184.9	230.0	0.3	95.7	5.0	22.0	17.9	79	120
Canada	IF	U	1.5	1.2	1.2	0.8	99.5	5.7	7.3	3.6	87	78
Central African Republic	EA/FF	U	712.0	129.7	157.4	0.2	89.8	5.0	22.0	18.1	..	469
Chad	EA/FF	U	712.0	107.5	149.5	0.2	..	5.0	22.0	18.0	258	271
Chile	IF	U	535.5	141.7	263.7	0.5	106.0	9.2	14.8	10.4	201	148
China	P	U	8.3	1.2	1.8	0.2	107.6	2.3	5.8	4.9	134	109
Hong Kong, China	CB	U	7.8	6.1	7.4	1.0	..	4.8	9.5	17.2	..	..
Colombia	IF	U	2,087.9	80.4	642.1	0.3	95.6	12.1	18.8	7.3	261	156
Congo, Dem. Rep.	IF	U	21.8	0.0	0.2	0.0	264.7	..	165.0	12.2	..	..
Congo, Rep.	EA/FF	U	712.0	449.7	919.0	1.3	..	5.0	22.0	-16.6	..	238
Costa Rica	P	U	308.2	32.4	148.5	0.5	106.8	13.4	24.9	16.6	..	179
Côte d'Ivoire	EA/FF	U	712.0	160.5	255.6	0.4	96.5	3.5	..	..	..	133
Croatia	MF	U	8.3	0.0	4.4	0.5	98.9	3.7	12.1	5.3	..	..
Cuba	..	..	..	0.0	..	..	..	..	..	..	..	..
Czech Republic	MF	U	38.6	0.0	13.6	0.4	114.8	3.4	7.2	6.3	..	..
Denmark	P	U	8.1	8.2	8.9	1.1	93.5	3.2	8.1	4.3	127	..
Dominican Republic	MF	D	16.4	2.5	6.4	0.4	110.3	17.7	26.8	17.7	..	226
Ecuador	EA/Other	U	24,988.4	287.4	8,394.4	0.3	73.3	7.4	16.3	-43.5	185	203
Egypt, Arab Rep.	P	M	3.5	0.7	1.5	0.4	..	9.5	13.2	7.0	189	158
El Salvador	P	U	8.8	2.4	4.1	0.5	..	9.3	14.0	9.7	..	220
Eritrea	P	U	..	0.0	1.7	..	..	..	..	..	..	..
Estonia	CB	U	17.0	0.1	6.1	0.4	..	3.8	7.6	2.2	..	..
Ethiopia	MF	U	8.2	0.7	1.2	0.1	..	6.7	10.9	9.3	205	128
Finland	EA/Euro	U	6.5 [b]	5.9	6.1	0.9	87.1	1.6	5.6	2.7	159	..
France	EA/Euro	U	7.1 [b]	6.5	6.5	0.9	88.4	2.6	6.7	5.7	126	119
Gabon	EA/FF	U	712.0	330.7	457.7	0.6	89.7	5.0	22.0	-5.0	..	163
Gambia, The	IF	U	12.8	1.8	2.5	0.2	95.0	12.5	24.0	19.5	..	241
Georgia	IF	U	2.0	0.0	0.4	0.2	135.7	10.2	32.8	28.6	796	724
Germany	EA/Euro	U	2.1 [b]	1.9	1.9	0.9	84.6	3.4	9.6	10.1	124	139
Ghana	IF	U	5,455.1	92.7	716.2	0.1	81.1	28.6	..	..	..	242
Greece	EA/Euro	U	365.4 [b]	114.4	236.2	0.6	96.3	6.1	12.3	9.2	220	171
Guatemala	MF	U	7.8	1.4	3.4	0.4	..	10.2	20.9	14.6	234	156
Guinea	IF	U	1,746.9	212.7	358.0	0.2	..	7.5	19.4	10.2	..	226
Guinea-Bissau	EA/FF	U	712.0	12.6	169.4	0.2	..	3.5	..	..	..	..
Haiti	IF	U	21.2	1.4	6.8	0.3	..	11.9	25.1	9.1	..	271
Honduras	P	U	14.8	1.2	5.6	0.4	..	15.9	26.8	16.4	51	264

	Exchange rate arrangements [a]		Official exchange rate	Purchasing power parity conversion factor		PPP conversion factor/ official exchange rate	Real effective exchange rate	Interest rate			Key agricultural producer prices	
			local currency units to $	local currency units to international $		ratio	1995=100	Deposit %	Lending %	Real %	Wheat $ per metric ton	Maize $ per metric ton
	Classification 2000	Structure 2000	2000	1990	2000	2000	2000	2000	2000	2000	1998	1998
Hungary	P	U	282.2	21.3	103.5	0.4	109.7	9.6	12.6	4.8	113	92
India	MF	U	44.9	4.8	8.7	0.2	..	..	12.3	6.7	142	95
Indonesia	IF	U	8,421.8	606.2	2,015.6	0.2	..	12.5	18.5	6.7	..	87
Iran, Islamic Rep.	P	D	1,764.4	173.7	1,429.4	0.8	297.7	..	..	..	289	297
Iraq	P	U	0.3	0.0	..	..	..	..	..	..	..	..
Ireland	EA/Euro	U	0.9 [b]	0.6	0.7	0.8	91.2	0.1	4.8	-0.5	114	..
Israel	P	U	4.1	1.7	3.6	0.9	114.2	8.6	12.9	10.7	149	1,330
Italy	EA/Euro	U	2,101.6 [b]	1,335.4	1,655.9	0.8	106.4	1.8	6.3	3.9	181	161
Jamaica	MF	U	42.7	3.9	33.5	0.8	..	11.6	23.3	11.6	..	1,182
Japan	IF	U	107.8	177.2	153.7	1.4	95.6	0.1	2.1	2.2	1,295	1,082
Jordan	P	U	0.7	0.3	0.3	0.4	..	7.0	11.8	12.4	379	223
Kazakhstan	MF	U	142.1	0.0	29.7	0.2	..	..	..	..	72	85
Kenya	MF	U	76.2 [b]	8.6	25.6	0.3	..	8.1	22.3	14.5	262	151
Korea, Dem. Rep.	..	..	..	0.0	..	..	..	..	..	..	..	..
Korea, Rep.	IF	U	1,131.0	469.7	629.3	0.6	..	7.9	8.5	10.3	494	398
Kuwait	P	U	0.3	0.0	0.4	1.2	..	5.9	8.9	..	..	..
Kyrgyz Republic	MF	U	47.7	0.0	4.7	0.1	..	18.4	51.9	25.0	18	34
Lao PDR	MF	D	7,887.6	164.7	1,621.2	0.2	..	12.0	32.0	6.6	..	96
Latvia	P	U	0.6	0.0	0.3	0.4	..	4.4	11.9	7.2	..	..
Lebanon	P	U	1,507.5	290.2	1,333.0	0.9	..	11.2	18.2	18.6	283	304
Lesotho	P	U	6.9	0.9	1.5	0.2	78.0	4.9	17.1	10.4	195	137
Liberia	IF	U	41.0	0.0	..	..	..	6.2	20.5	..	..	..
Libya	P	D	0.5	0.0	..	..	..	3.0	7.0	..	897	889
Lithuania	CB	U	4.0	0.0	1.7	0.4	..	3.9	12.1	9.8	..	..
Macedonia, FYR	P	U	65.9	0.1	22.8	0.3	72.8	11.2	18.9	10.1	..	..
Madagascar	IF	U	6,767.5	484.1	2,012.3	0.3	..	15.0	26.5	18.1	102	192
Malawi	IF	U	59.5	1.4	15.9	0.3	112.7	33.3	53.1	23.0	64	35
Malaysia	P	U	3.8	1.4	1.6	0.4	86.6	3.4	6.8	1.9	..	98
Mali	EA/FF	U	712.0	133.8	189.4	0.3	..	3.5	..	..	124	128
Mauritania	MF	U	238.9	35.3	50.0	0.2	..	..	..	..	197	223
Mauritius	IF	U	26.2	6.6	9.7	0.4	..	9.6	20.8	20.8	..	208
Mexico	IF	U	9.5	1.4	6.2	0.7	..	6.3	18.2	6.6	141	146
Moldova	IF	U	12.4	0.0	1.8	0.1	109.8	24.9	33.8	5.3	..	..
Mongolia	IF	U	1,076.7	2.6	244.1	0.2	..	13.8	30.3	16.7	..	..
Morocco	P	U	10.6	3.1	3.5	0.3	108.2	5.2	13.3	11.6	255	205
Mozambique	IF	U	15,447.1	316.6	3,900.2	0.3	..	9.7	19.0	6.6	21	13
Myanmar	P	D	6.5	0.0	..	..	..	9.8	15.3	-5.3	..	..
Namibia	P	U	6.9	1.1	2.1	0.3	..	7.4	15.3	5.3	183	154
Nepal	P	U	71.1	6.5	12.4	0.2	..	6.0	9.5	5.0	119	106
Netherlands	EA/Euro	U	2.4 [b]	2.1	2.1	0.9	89.9	2.9	4.8	2.2	118	232
New Zealand	IF	U	2.2	1.5	1.4	0.6	83.3	6.4	10.2	7.4	153	131
Nicaragua	P	U	12.7	0.0	2.5	0.2	113.1	9.4	21.4	8.7	..	189
Niger	EA/FF	U	712.0	118.8	160.9	0.2	..	3.5	..	..	372	582
Nigeria	MF	D	101.7	3.5	36.8	0.4	81.0	11.7	21.3	-3.3	1,555	1,201
Norway	MF	U	8.8	8.7	10.6	1.2	96.1	6.7	8.2	-6.9	528	..
Oman	P	U	0.4	0.0	..	..	..	7.6	10.1	..	..	..
Pakistan	MF	U	53.6	5.7	12.0	0.2	93.6	..	..	..	125	19
Panama	EA/Other	U	1.0	0.6	0.6	0.6	..	7.1	10.2	9.3	..	265
Papua New Guinea	IF	U	2.8	0.5	0.9	0.3	92.8	14.5	17.5	1.7	..	84
Paraguay	MF	U	3,486.4	391.3	1,078.0	0.3	97.1	15.7	26.8	16.4	109	121
Peru	IF	U	3.5	0.1	1.5	0.4	..	13.3	27.9	23.4	242	246
Philippines	IF	U	44.2	5.3	11.0	0.2	89.8	8.3	10.9	4.0	..	138
Poland	IF	U	4.3	0.3	2.0	0.5	121.6	14.2	20.0	12.0	164	146
Portugal	EA/Euro	U	217.6 [b]	91.3	132.1	0.6	96.4	*2.4*	*5.2*	*1.8*	147	144
Puerto Rico	..	..	..	0.0	..	..	..	..	..	..	..	..
Romania	MF	U	21,708.7	5.9	5,527.7	0.3	107.1	..	..	..	93	73
Russian Federation	MF	M	28.1	0.0	5.8	0.2	90.5	6.5	24.4	-9.2	..	..

	Exchange rate arrangements [a]		Official exchange rate	Purchasing power parity conversion factor		PPP conversion factor/ official exchange rate	Real effective exchange rate	Interest rate			Key agricultural producer prices	
			local currency units to $	local currency units to international $		ratio	1995=100	Deposit %	Lending %	Real %	Wheat $ per metric ton	Maize $ per metric ton
	Classification 2000	Structure 2000	2000	1990	2000	2000	2000	2000	2000	2000	1998	1998
Rwanda	MF	U	389.7	32.3	87.2	0.2	..	8.9	..	..	226	145
Saudi Arabia	P	U	3.7	2.6	2.8	0.7	108.7	6.7	..	..	387	478
Senegal	EA/FF	U	712.0	176.6	216.4	0.3	..	3.5	..	..	..	135
Sierra Leone	IF	D	2,092.1	38.0	539.3	0.3	105.3	9.2	26.3	22.6	..	33
Singapore	MF	U	1.7	1.7	1.7	1.0	95.5	1.7	5.8	3.9	..	..
Slovak Republic	MF	U	46.0	5.8	14.6	0.3	109.3	8.4	14.9	7.9	101	89
Slovenia	MF	U	222.7	0.0	116.9	0.5	..	10.0	15.8	9.5	198	160
Somalia	IF	D	..	0.0	..	..	..	..	..	..	..	..
South Africa	IF	U	6.9	1.0	2.2	0.3	82.9	9.2	14.5	7.5	146	103
Spain	EA/Euro	U	180.6 b	104.9	131.3	0.7	94.2	3.0	5.2	1.7	157	154
Sri Lanka	MF	U	77.0	9.3	18.4	0.2	..	9.2	16.2	8.5	..	218
Sudan	MF	U	257.1	0.8	53.0	0.2	..	..	..	..	248	117
Swaziland	P	U	6.9	0.8	2.0	0.3	..	6.5	14.0	2.1	188	128
Sweden	IF	U	9.2	9.0	9.7	1.1	95.1	2.2	5.8	5.0	126	..
Switzerland	IF	U	1.7	2.0	2.0	1.2	87.3	3.0	4.3	3.0	525	368
Syrian Arab Republic	P	M	11.2	10.0	14.8	1.3	..	..	..	..	884	823
Tajikistan	IF	U	2.1	0.0	0.3	0.1	..	..	..	..	..	..
Tanzania	IF	U	800.4	71.9	410.4	0.5	..	7.4	21.6	11.5	348	348
Thailand	IF	U	40.1	10.2	12.6	0.3	..	3.3	7.8	5.9	..	87
Togo	EA/FF	U	712.0	91.7	133.0	0.2	98.8	3.5	..	..	..	216
Trinidad and Tobago	P	U	6.3	2.9	4.2	0.7	115.4	8.2	16.5	6.1	..	349
Tunisia	MF	U	1.4	0.3	0.4	0.3	100.8	..	..	..	284	..
Turkey	IF	U	625,218.5	1,448.4	274,484.1	0.4	..	47.2	..	..	133	126
Turkmenistan	P	D	5,200.0	0.0	1,113.4	0.2	..	..	..	..	..	..
Uganda	IF	U	1,644.5	113.0	347.6	0.2	96.0	9.8	22.9	19.0	681	358
Ukraine	MF	U	5.4	0.0	0.9	0.2	118.4	13.7	41.5	12.9	..	..
United Arab Emirates	P	U	3.7	3.4	3.5	1.0	..	..	..	..	..	..
United Kingdom	IF	U	0.7	0.6	0.7	1.0	131.9	4.5	6.0	4.1	118	176
United States	IF	U	1.0	1.0	1.0	1.0	125.2	..	9.2	7.0	99	61
Uruguay	P	U	12.1	0.6	8.1	0.7	113.1	12.1	49.1	43.8	119	125
Uzbekistan	MF	M	236.6	0.0	52.9	0.2	..	..	..	..	..	..
Venezuela, RB	P	U	680.0	23.1	585.0	0.9	161.6	16.3	25.2	-1.3	123	445
Vietnam	P	U	14,167.8	0.0	2,833.3	0.2	..	3.7	10.6	5.0	..	..
West Bank and Gaza	..	..	..	0.0	..	..	..	..	..	..	..	..
Yemen, Rep.	IF	U	161.7	18.8	88.3	0.5	..	14.0	22.0	-5.1	191	221
Yugoslavia, Fed. Rep.	MF	U	..	0.0	..	..	..	..	..	..	..	..
Zambia	IF	U	3,110.8	17.4	1,150.9	0.4	113.3	20.2	38.8	17.6	211	79
Zimbabwe	P	U	44.4	0.9	9.6	0.2	..	50.2	68.2	5.2	211	122

a. Exchange rate arrangements are given for the end of the year in 2000. Exchange rate classifications include independent floating (IF), managed floating (MF), pegged (P), currency board (CB), and several exchange arrangements (euro means that the euro is used, FF that the currency is pegged to the French franc, and other that the currency of another country is used as legal tender). Exchange rate structures include dual exchange rates (D), multiple exchange rates (M), and unitary rate (U). b. On January 1, 1999 the euro was established as the sole currency of 11 European countries, later joined by Greece in January, 2001. However, the old national currencies, now effectively sub-units of the euro, with irrevocably fixed conversion rates, remained in use until early 2002. The World Development Indicators uses the old national currencies and the exchange rates to the U.S. dollar derived from the euro-dollar rate. The average euro-dollar exchange rate in 2000 was 1.085.

About the data

In a market-based economy the choices households, producers, and governments make about the allocation of resources are influenced by relative prices, including the real exchange rate, real wages, real interest rates, and commodity prices. Relative prices also reflect, to a large extent, the choices of these agents. Thus relative prices convey vital information about the interaction of economic agents in an economy and with the rest of the world.

The exchange rate is the price of one currency in terms of another. Official exchange rates and exchange rate arrangements are established by governments (other exchange rates fully recognized by governments include market rates, which are determined largely by legal market forces, and, for countries maintaining multiple exchange arrangements, principal rates, secondary rates, and tertiary rates).

Real effective exchange rates are derived by deflating a trade-weighted average of the nominal exchange rates that apply between trading partners. For most high-income countries the weights are based on trade in manufactured goods with other high-income countries during 1989–91, and an index of relative, normalized unit labor costs is used as the deflator. (Normalization smooths a time series by removing short-term fluctuations while retaining changes of a large amplitude over the longer economic cycle.) For other countries the weights prior to 1990 take into account trade in manufactured and primary products during 1980–82, the weights from January 1990 onward take into account trade during 1988–90, and an index of relative changes in consumer prices is used as the deflator. An increase in the real effective exchange rate represents an appreciation of the local currency. Because of conceptual and data limitations, changes in real effective exchange rates should be interpreted with caution.

The official or market exchange rate is often used to compare prices in different currencies. But because market imperfections are extensive and exchange rates reflect at best the relative prices of tradable goods, the volume of goods and services that a U.S. dollar buys in the United States may not correspond to what a U.S. dollar converted to another country's currency at the official exchange rate would buy in that country. The alternative approach is to convert national currency estimates of gross national income to a common currency by using conversion factors that reflect equivalent purchasing power. Purchasing power parity (PPP) conversion factors are based on price and expenditure surveys conducted by the International Comparison Programme (ICP) and represent the conversion factors applied to equalize price levels across countries. See *About the data* for table 1.1 for further discussion of the PPP conversion factor.

Many interest rates coexist in an economy, reflecting competitive conditions, the terms governing loans and deposits, and differences in the position and status of creditors and debtors. In some economies interest rates are set by regulation or administrative fiat. In economies with imperfect markets, or where reported nominal rates are not indicative of effective rates, it may be difficult to obtain data on interest rates that reflect actual market transactions. Deposit and lending rates are collected by the International Monetary Fund (IMF) as representative interest rates offered by banks to resident customers. The terms and conditions attached to these rates differ by country, however, limiting their comparability. Real interest rates are calculated by adjusting nominal rates by an estimate of the inflation rate in the economy. A negative real interest rate indicates a loss in the purchasing power of the principal. The real interest rates in the table are calculated as $(i - P)/(1 + P)$, where i is the nominal interest rate and P is the inflation rate (as measured by the GDP deflator).

The table also shows prices for two key agricultural commodities, wheat and maize. The prices received by farmers, used here, are important determinants of the type and volume of agricultural production. In theory these prices should refer to national average farmgate, or first-point-of-sale, transactions. But depending on the country's institutional arrangements—whether it relies on market wholesale prices, government fixed prices, or support prices—the data may not always refer to the same selling points. These data come from the Food and Agriculture Organization (FAO), with most originating from official national publications or FAO questionnaires. As the data show, the prices received by farmers are often not equalized across international markets (even after adjusting for freight, transport, and insurance costs and for differences in quality). Market imperfections such as taxes, subsidies, and trade barriers drive a wedge between domestic and international prices.

Definitions

- **Exchange rate arrangements** describe the arrangement that an IMF member country has furnished to the IMF under article IV, section 2(a) of the IMF's Articles of Agreement. *Exchange rate classification* indicates how the exchange rate is determined in the main market when there is more than one market: floating (managed or independent), pegged (conventional, within horizontal bands, crawling peg, or crawling band), currency board (implicit legislative commitment to exchange domestic currency for a specified foreign currency at a fixed exchange rate), and exchange arrangement (country uses the euro, currency is pegged to the French franc, or another country's currency is used as legal tender). *Exchange rate structure* shows whether countries have a unitary exchange rate or dual or multiple rates.
- **Official exchange rate** refers to the exchange rate determined by national authorities or to the rate determined in the legally sanctioned exchange market. It is calculated as an annual average based on monthly averages (local currency units relative to the U.S. dollar). • **Purchasing power parity conversion factor** is the number of units of a country's currency required to buy the same amount of goods and services in the domestic market as a U.S. dollar would buy in the United States. • **Real effective exchange rate** is the nominal effective exchange rate (a measure of the value of a currency against a weighted average of several foreign currencies) divided by a price deflator or index of costs. • **Deposit interest rate** is the rate paid by commercial or similar banks for demand, time, or savings deposits. • **Lending interest rate** is the rate charged by banks on loans to prime customers. • **Real interest rate** is the lending interest rate adjusted for inflation as measured by the GDP deflator. • **Key agricultural producer prices** are domestic producer prices converted to U.S. dollars using the official exchange rate.

Data sources

The information on exchange rate arrangements is from the IMF's *Exchange Arrangements and Exchange Restrictions Annual Report, 2000*. The official and real effective exchange rates and deposit and lending rates are from the IMF's *International Financial Statistics*. PPP conversion factors are from the World Bank. The agricultural price data are from the FAO's *Production Yearbook*. The real interest rates are calculated using World Bank data on the GDP deflator.

5.7 | Defense expenditures and trade in arms

	Military expenditures				Armed forces personnel				Arms trade			
	% of GNI		% of central government expenditure		Total thousands		% of labor force		Exports % of total exports		Imports % of total imports	
	1992	**1999**	**1992**	**1999**	**1992**	**1999**	**1992**	**1999**	**1992**	**1999**	**1992**	**1999**
Afghanistan	..	..	..	..	45	..	0.6	..	0.0	0.0	0.0	..
Albania	4.9	1.3	10.0	4.5	65	18	4.2	1.1	0.0	0.0	0.0	2.6
Algeria	1.8	4.0	5.9	12.6	126	120	1.6	1.2	0.0	0.0	0.1	4.1
Angola	16.6	21.2	*24.6*	41.1	128	100	2.7	1.7	0.0	0.0	1.5	7.3
Argentina	1.9	1.6	16.1	9.1	65	73	0.5	0.5	0.0	0.0	0.3	0.4
Armenia	*3.5*	5.8	..	20.2	20	50	1.1	2.6	0.0	0.0	0.0	1.3
Australia	2.4	1.8	9.3	7.6	68	55	0.8	0.6	0.1	1.0	2.1	1.6
Austria	0.9	0.8	2.4	1.5	44	49	1.2	1.3	0.2	0.0	0.1	0.0
Azerbaijan	5.8	6.6	*18.0*	24.4	43	75	1.4	2.1	0.0	0.0	0.0	1.2
Bangladesh	1.3	1.3	11.2	10.1	107	110	0.2	0.2	0.0	0.0	1.1	1.0
Belarus	1.9	1.3	4.9	4.1	102	65	1.9	1.2	0.0	5.2	0.0	0.0
Belgium	1.8	1.4	3.7	3.1	79	42	1.9	1.0	0.3	0.0	0.2	0.2
Benin	1.3	1.4	6.3	8.3	7	8	0.3	0.3	0.0	0.0	0.0	0.8
Bolivia	2.2	1.8	10.6	8.0	32	33	1.2	1.0	0.0	0.0	0.9	0.6
Bosnia and Herzegovina	*19.0*	4.5	..	24.3	60	30	..	1.7	0.0	0.0	0.0	6.2
Botswana	4.2	4.7	10.3	9.8	7	8	1.2	1.1	0.0	0.0	1.1	1.8
Brazil	1.1	1.9	3.5	*5.5*	296	300	0.4	0.4	0.5	0.0	0.9	0.3
Bulgaria	3.3	3.0	7.9	8.7	99	70	2.3	1.7	3.1	5.1	0.0	0.2
Burkina Faso	2.4	1.6	11.5	5.9	9	9	0.2	0.2	0.0	0.0	1.1	0.0
Burundi	3.6	7.0	10.5	26.7	13	40	0.4	1.1	0.0	0.0	0.0	0.0
Cambodia	4.9	4.0	*30.6*	26.0	135	60	2.7	1.0	0.0	0.0	0.0	0.3
Cameroon	1.8	1.8	9.2	10.6	12	15	0.2	0.3	0.0	0.0	0.0	0.4
Canada	1.8	1.4	6.2	5.9	82	60	0.5	0.4	0.7	0.2	0.6	0.5
Central African Republic	2.0	2.8	8.3	15.4	4	3	0.3	0.2	0.0	0.0	0.0	0.0
Chad	3.7	2.4	17.3	12.7	38	30	1.3	0.8	0.0	0.0	4.1	3.2
Chile	2.3	3.0	10.5	12.3	92	88	1.8	1.4	0.0	0.1	1.0	0.7
China	2.8	2.3	32.7	22.2	3,160	2,400	0.5	0.3	1.3	0.2	1.6	0.4
Hong Kong, China	..	..	..	..	..	..	..	..	..	..	..	..
Colombia	2.4	3.2	14.7	15.9	139	155	0.9	0.9	0.0	0.0	1.7	0.6
Congo, Dem. Rep.	3.0	14.4	16.1	..	45	55	0.3	0.3	0.0	0.0	0.0	8.9
Congo, Rep.	5.7	3.5	13.5	8.4	10	10	1.0	0.8	0.0	0.0	0.0	0.0
Costa Rica	1.1	0.5	5.5	2.0	8	10	0.6	0.7	0.0	0.0	0.2	0.0
Côte d'Ivoire	1.5	0.8	4.3	3.4	15	15	0.3	0.2	0.0	0.0	0.0	0.0
Croatia	7.5	3.3 [a]	19.3	9.8 [a]	103	60	4.6	2.9	0.0	0.2	0.0	0.1
Cuba	*2.4*	1.9	..	..	175	50	3.5	0.9	0.0	0.0	4.5	0.0
Czech Republic	*2.4*	2.3	*6.7*	6.3	*107*	54	*1.9*	0.9	*1.5*	0.3	*0.0*	0.7
Denmark	2.0	1.6	4.8	4.2	28	27	1.0	0.9	0.0	0.0	0.5	0.7
Dominican Republic	0.9	0.7	6.3	4.4	22	30	0.7	0.8	0.0	0.0	0.2	0.3
Ecuador	3.5	3.7	20.6	16.2	57	58	1.5	1.2	0.0	0.0	1.2	0.7
Egypt, Arab Rep.	3.5	2.7	8.5	*9.3*	424	430	2.2	1.8	0.7	0.0	19.2	4.4
El Salvador	2.1	0.9	16.8	8.8	49	15	2.4	0.6	0.0	0.0	4.1	0.3
Eritrea	*17.3*	27.4	*34.6*	*51.1*	*55*	215	*3.2*	10.8	*0.0*	..	*0.0*	33.5
Estonia	0.5	1.5	2.2	4.5	3	7	0.4	0.9	0.0	0.0	1.2	0.2
Ethiopia	3.7	8.8	20.0	29.1	120	300	0.5	1.1	0.0	0.0	0.0	20.5
Finland	2.2	1.4	4.3	*4.5*	33	35	1.3	1.3	0.0	0.1	2.1	1.3
France	3.4	2.7	7.6	5.9	522	421	2.1	1.6	0.9	1.0	0.2	0.3
Gabon	3.1	2.4	10.1	7.3	7	7	1.5	1.3	0.0	0.0	0.0	0.0
Gambia, The	1.0	1.3	5.6	5.4	1	1	0.2	0.2	0.0	0.0	2.3	0.0
Georgia	2.7	1.2	..	7.0	*25*	14	*0.9*	0.6	0.0	6.2	0.0	1.0
Germany	2.1	1.6	6.2	4.7	442	331	1.1	0.8	0.3	0.3	0.6	0.3
Ghana	0.8	0.8	4.6	3.1	7	7	0.1	0.1	0.0	0.0	0.0	0.0
Greece	4.2	4.7	15.5	16.4	208	204	4.8	4.5	0.2	0.9	3.9	7.5
Guatemala	1.5	0.7	14.0	5.0	44	30	1.4	0.7	0.0	0.0	0.2	0.0
Guinea	1.4	1.6	7.0	7.4	15	12	0.5	0.3	0.0	0.0	0.0	0.0
Guinea-Bissau	3.2	2.7	7.6	6.1	11	7	2.3	1.3	0.0	0.0	0.0	0.0
Haiti	1.4	..	14.7	..	8	0	0.3	0.0	0.0	0.0	0.0	0.0
Honduras	1.4	0.7	5.5	2.6	17	8	0.9	0.3	0.0	0.0	2.9	0.4

	Military expenditures				Armed forces personnel				Arms trade			
	% of GNI		% of central government expenditure		Total thousands		% of labor force		Exports % of total exports		Imports % of total imports	
	1992	1999	1992	1999	1992	1999	1992	1999	1992	1999	1992	1999
Hungary	2.1	1.7	3.9	3.9	78	51	1.6	1.1	0.4	0.0	0.0	0.3
India	2.4	2.5	12.4	14.6	1,270	1,300	0.3	0.3	0.0	0.0	2.9	1.6
Indonesia	1.4	1.1	7.2	5.3	283	296	0.3	0.3	0.1	0.2	0.4	1.9
Iran, Islamic Rep.	3.0	2.9	14.9	11.2	528	460	3.2	2.4	0.1	0.1	3.3	0.9
Iraq	8.3	5.5	..	..	407	420	8.2	6.7	0.0	0.0	0.0	0.1
Ireland	1.4	1.0	3.2	2.6	13	14	1.0	0.9	0.0	0.0	0.1	0.1
Israel	11.7	8.8	23.3	18.5	181	173	8.8	6.6	6.2	2.3	10.3	7.2
Italy	2.1	2.0	3.9	4.7	471	391	1.9	1.5	0.3	0.2	0.2	0.3
Jamaica	1.0	0.8	3.0	2.1	3	3	0.2	0.2	0.0	0.0	0.6	0.3
Japan	1.0	1.0	4.5	6.1	242	240	0.4	0.4	0.0	0.0	0.9	1.0
Jordan	8.5	9.2	27.3	27.5	100	102	9.8	7.3	0.0	0.0	1.2	1.9
Kazakhstan	2.9	0.9	14.2	5.3	15	33	0.2	0.5	0.0	0.2	0.0	4.3
Kenya	3.0	1.9	11.5	7.1	24	24	0.2	0.2	0.0	0.0	1.1	0.2
Korea, Dem. Rep.	25.0	18.8	28.5	..	1,200	1,000	11.3	8.6	13.1	22.4	7.9	2.5
Korea, Rep.	3.6	2.9	19.8	11.0	750	665	3.6	2.8	0.1	0.0	1.5	1.8
Kuwait	77.0	7.7	96.3	20.8	12	21	2.1	2.7	0.2	0.0	13.8	9.5
Kyrgyz Republic	0.7	2.4	3.2	14.0	12	12	0.6	0.6	0.0	0.0	0.0	0.0
Lao PDR	9.0	2.0	21.6	11.1	37	50	1.7	2.0	0.0	0.0	3.7	0.0
Latvia	1.6	0.9	4.3	2.5	5	5	0.3	0.4	0.0	0.0	0.0	0.2
Lebanon	4.0	4.0	18.5	11.0	37	58	3.1	3.9	0.0	0.0	0.0	0.2
Lesotho	3.1	2.6	10.5	6.5	2	2	0.3	0.2	0.0	0.0	0.0	0.0
Liberia	..	1.2	..	8.3	2	..	0.2	..	0.0	0.0	0.0	0.0
Libya	7.6	..	16.4	..	85	85	6.6	5.8	0.1	0.8	1.7	0.2
Lithuania	0.7	1.3	2.5	3.9	10	12	0.5	0.6	0.0	0.0	0.0	0.4
Macedonia, FYR	2.0	2.5	..	10.4	10	16	1.1	1.7	0.0	0.0	0.0	1.1
Madagascar	1.1	1.2	5.4	7.4	21	20	0.4	0.3	0.0	0.0	0.0	0.0
Malawi	1.1	0.6	3.9	2.2	10	5	0.2	0.1	0.0	0.0	0.0	0.0
Malaysia	3.2	2.3	10.3	9.3	128	95	1.7	1.0	0.0	0.0	0.6	1.4
Mali	2.3	2.3	9.4	8.7	12	10	0.3	0.2	0.0	0.0	0.0	0.0
Mauritania	3.5	4.0	13.3	18.9	16	11	1.7	0.9	0.0	0.0	0.0	0.0
Mauritius	0.4	0.2	1.5	0.9	1	2	0.2	0.4	0.0	0.0	0.3	0.0
Mexico	0.5	0.6	4.6	3.8	175	255	0.5	0.6	0.0	0.0	0.5	0.1
Moldova	0.5	0.5	1.5	1.6	9	11	0.4	0.5	0.0	2.1	0.8	0.0
Mongolia	2.6	2.1	9.3	5.9	21	20	2.1	1.7	0.0	0.0	0.0	0.0
Morocco	4.5	4.3	14.3	13.5	195	195	2.1	1.7	0.0	0.0	1.4	1.3
Mozambique	6.0	2.5	17.0	9.1	50	8	0.6	0.1	0.0	0.0	0.6	0.4
Myanmar	8.3	7.8	74.3	..	286	345	1.3	1.4	0.0	0.0	23.0	13.6
Namibia	2.3	2.9	5.6	7.2	8	3	1.3	0.4	0.0	0.0	0.0	1.3
Nepal	1.0	0.8	6.0	5.7	35	35	0.4	0.3	0.0	0.0	0.0	0.0
Netherlands	2.3	1.8	4.6	5.9	90	54	1.3	0.7	0.1	0.1	0.4	0.4
New Zealand	1.6	1.2	4.0	3.5	11	10	0.6	0.5	0.0	0.0	1.2	4.0
Nicaragua	3.1	1.2	7.6	2.9	15	12	1.0	0.6	13.5	0.0	0.6	0.0
Niger	1.3	1.2	7.9	6.4	5	6	0.1	0.1	0.0	0.0	0.0	0.0
Nigeria	1.1	1.6	6.5	8.1	76	77	0.2	0.2	0.0	0.0	1.9	0.0
Norway	3.1	2.2	6.4	5.0	36	33	1.7	1.4	0.1	0.0	1.7	1.4
Oman	20.5	15.3	40.2	36.3	35	38	6.7	6.1	0.0	0.0	0.3	0.6
Pakistan	7.0	5.9	27.9	27.9	580	590	1.4	1.2	0.4	0.1	6.6	9.7
Panama	1.3	1.4	5.7	5.1	11	13	1.1	1.1	2.0	0.0	0.5	0.1
Papua New Guinea	1.4	1.1	4.2	3.7	4	4	0.2	0.2	0.0	0.0	4.0	0.0
Paraguay	1.8	1.1	13.2	3.9	16	17	1.0	0.8	0.0	0.0	0.7	0.6
Peru	2.2	2.4	11.1	12.3	112	115	1.4	1.2	0.0	0.0	1.4	0.4
Philippines	1.9	1.4	10.2	7.3	107	107	0.4	0.3	0.0	0.0	1.8	0.3
Poland	2.3	2.1	5.5	6.1	270	187	1.4	0.9	0.2	0.1	0.0	0.1
Portugal	2.6	2.1	6.4	5.4	80	71	1.6	1.4	0.1	0.0	0.6	0.2
Puerto Rico	..	..	..	..	..	..	..	..	..	..	..	..
Romania	3.3	1.6	7.9	4.7	172	170	1.6	1.6	0.5	0.5	0.6	1.9
Russian Federation	8.0	5.6	28.0	22.4	1,900	900	2.5	1.2	5.8	4.2	0.0	1.1

	Military expenditures				Armed forces personnel				Arms trade			
	% of GNI		% of central government expenditure		Total thousands		% of labor force		Exports % of total exports		Imports % of total imports	
	1992	1999	1992	1999	1992	1999	1992	1999	1992	1999	1992	1999
Rwanda	4.4	4.5	21.7	22.7	30	40	0.8	0.9	0.0	0.0	0.0	11.9
Saudi Arabia	27.2	14.9	72.5	43.2	172	190	3.1	2.9	0.0	0.0	25.2	27.5
Senegal	2.8	1.7	13.5	8.2	18	13	0.5	0.3	0.0	0.0	1.0	0.0
Sierra Leone	3.5	3.0	17.7	13.5	8	3	0.5	0.2	0.0	0.0	6.8	12.3
Singapore	5.2	4.8	26.1	20.5	56	60	3.4	3.0	0.0	0.0	0.4	0.9
Slovak Republic	*2.1*	1.8	*5.1*	4.4	*33*	36	*1.2*	1.2	*0.7*	0.1	*3.5*	0.2
Slovenia	2.4	1.4	6.0	3.4	15	10	1.5	1.0	0.0	0.0	0.0	0.1
Somalia	..	..	..	..	..	..	..	..	0.0	0.0	0.0	0.0
South Africa	3.0	1.5	8.9	5.0	75	68	0.5	0.4	0.4	0.1	1.3	0.2
Spain	1.5	1.3	4.3	6.1	198	155	1.2	0.9	0.3	0.1	0.4	0.5
Sri Lanka	3.7	4.7	13.2	18.4	110	110	1.5	1.3	0.0	0.0	0.3	0.7
Sudan	9.8	4.8	64.0	46.8	82	105	0.8	0.9	0.0	0.0	13.4	0.7
Swaziland	1.9	1.5	6.3	4.6	3	3	1.1	0.8	0.0	0.0	0.0	0.0
Sweden	2.5	2.3	5.3	5.5	70	52	1.5	1.1	1.5	0.8	0.3	0.3
Switzerland	1.8	1.2	7.2	*5.1*	31	39	0.8	1.0	1.2	0.1	0.7	1.5
Syrian Arab Republic	9.2	7.0	39.0	25.1	408	310	11.0	6.2	0.6	0.0	11.2	5.5
Tajikistan	0.3	1.3	0.7	9.4	3	7	0.1	0.3	0.0	0.0	0.0	0.0
Tanzania	2.0	1.4	10.0	10.1	46	35	0.3	0.2	0.0	0.0	0.3	0.3
Thailand	2.6	1.7	17.0	6.1	283	300	0.9	0.8	0.0	0.0	1.2	0.7
Togo	2.9	1.8	13.2	9.4	8	11	0.5	0.6	0.0	0.0	0.0	0.0
Trinidad and Tobago	1.5	1.4	*4.8*	5.5	2	2	0.4	0.4	0.0	0.0	0.0	0.0
Tunisia	2.4	1.8	7.1	5.4	35	35	1.1	0.9	0.0	0.0	0.3	0.1
Turkey	3.8	5.3	18.8	13.9	704	789	2.7	2.6	0.1	0.3	6.6	7.9
Turkmenistan	..	3.4	..	16.0	28	15	1.7	0.7	1.4	0.0	0.0	1.0
Uganda	2.4	2.3	11.7	13.9	70	50	0.8	0.5	0.0	0.0	2.0	2.2
Ukraine	1.9	3.0	..	8.2	430	340	1.6	1.3	0.0	4.7	0.0	0.1
United Arab Emirates	5.6	4.1	50.1	39.6	55	65	5.2	4.7	0.0	0.0	4.2	3.8
United Kingdom	3.8	2.5	9.1	6.9	293	218	1.0	0.7	3.3	1.9	1.3	0.8
United States	4.8	3.0	21.1	15.7	1,920	1,490	1.5	1.0	5.6	4.7	0.3	0.2
Uruguay	2.1	1.3	8.0	4.1	25	24	1.8	1.6	0.0	0.0	0.5	0.3
Uzbekistan	2.7	1.7	6.0	5.3	40	60	0.5	0.6	0.0	0.4	0.0	0.0
Venezuela, RB	1.4	1.4	6.3	7.1	75	75	1.0	0.8	0.0	0.0	0.9	2.2
Vietnam	3.4	*2.5*	14.5	*11.6*	857	485	2.4	1.2	0.4	0.0	0.4	0.6
West Bank and Gaza	..	..	..	..	..	..	..	..	..	..	..	..
Yemen, Rep.	9.8	6.1	29.8	18.0	64	69	1.5	1.3	0.0	0.0	0.2	1.5
Yugoslavia, Fed. Rep.	..	5.0	..	..	137	105	2.8	2.1	0.0	..	0.0	..
Zambia	3.3	1.0	9.3	3.5	16	17	0.5	0.4	0.0	0.0	0.0	0.0
Zimbabwe	3.8	5.0	10.1	12.1	48	40	1.0	0.7	0.3	0.0	4.1	0.5
World	3.2 w	2.3 w	12.2 w	10.0 w	24,533 t	21,198 t	0.9 w	0.7 w	1.2 w	1.0 w	1.1 w	0.9 w
Low income	2.6	2.5	11.8	13.8	6,485	6,254	0.7	0.6	0.1	0.5	2.0	1.9
Middle income	4.0	2.7	21.1	15.8	12,383	10,220	1.0	0.7	0.8	0.4	2.8	1.7
Lower middle income	4.3	2.7	23.7	17.2	9,172	6,971	0.9	0.6	1.7	0.9	2.1	0.8
Upper middle income	3.8	2.8	19.3	*12.3*	3,211	3,249	1.4	1.2	0.1	0.0	3.3	2.2
Low & middle income	3.7	2.7	19.7	15.4	18,868	16,474	0.9	0.7	0.7	0.4	2.6	1.7
East Asia & Pacific	2.8	2.3	22.8	16.8	7,256	5,831	0.8	0.6	0.4	0.1	1.3	1.0
Europe & Central Asia	5.2	3.7	21.6	11.7	4,303	3,192	2.0	1.3	2.9	1.8	1.4	1.7
Latin America & Carib.	1.3	1.5	5.7	*7.3*	1,443	1,371	0.8	0.6	0.2	0.0	0.7	0.3
Middle East & N. Africa	14.5	7.0	49.0	28.5	2,631	2,529	3.3	2.6	0.1	0.1	10.7	8.4
South Asia	3.0	2.8	14.9	15.7	2,152	2,153	0.4	0.4	0.1	0.0	3.3	2.4
Sub-Saharan Africa	2.9	2.2	9.1	8.9	1,083	1,398	0.5	0.5	0.2	0.1	1.3	1.4
High income	3.1	2.3	11.1	9.1	5,665	4,724	1.3	1.0	1.4	1.2	0.7	0.6
Europe EMU	2.3	1.9	5.7	5.2	2,181	1,768	1.6	1.3	0.4	0.3	0.4	0.4

Note: Data for some countries are based on partial or uncertain data or rough estimates; see U.S. Department of State (2002).

a. Data from national source.

About the data

Although national defense is an important function of government and security from external threats contributes to economic development, high levels of defense spending burden the economy and may impede growth. Comparisons of defense spending between countries should take into account the many factors that influence perceptions of vulnerability and risk, including historical and cultural traditions, the length of borders that need defending, the quality of relations with neighbors, and the role of the armed forces in the body politic.

Data on defense spending from governments are often incomplete and unreliable. Even in countries where parliaments vigilantly review government budgets and spending, defense spending and trade in arms often do not receive close scrutiny. For a detailed critique of the quality of such data see Ball (1984) and Happe and Wakeman-Linn (1994).

The International Monetary Fund's (IMF) *Government Finance Statistics Yearbook* is the primary source of data on defense spending. It uses a consistent definition of defense spending based on the United Nations' classification of the functions of government and the North Atlantic Treaty Organization (NATO) definition. The IMF checks data on defense spending for broad consistency with other macroeconomic data reported to it but is not always able to verify the accuracy and completeness of the data. Moreover, country coverage is affected by delays or failure to report data. Thus most researchers supplement the IMF's data with assessments by other organizations. However, these organizations rely heavily on reporting by governments, on confidential intelligence estimates of varying quality, on sources that they do not or cannot reveal, and on one another's publications. The data in this table are the latest available from the U.S. Department of State's Bureau of Verification and Compliance (formerly the Bureau of Arms Control).

Definitions of military spending differ depending on whether they cover civil defense, reserves and auxiliary forces, police and paramilitary forces, dual-purpose forces such as military and civilian police, military grants in kind, pensions for military personnel, and social security contributions paid by one part of government to another. Official government data may omit parts of military spending, disguise financing through extrabudgetary accounts or unrecorded use of foreign exchange receipts, or fail to include military assistance or secret military equipment imports. Current spending is more likely to be reported than capital spending. In some cases a more accurate estimate of military spending can be obtained by adding the value of estimated arms imports and nominal military expenditures. This method may understate or overstate spending in a particular year, however, because payments for arms may not coincide with deliveries.

The data on armed forces refer to military personnel on active duty, including paramilitary forces. These data exclude civilians in the defense establishment and so are not consistent with the data on military spending on personnel. Moreover, because they exclude payments to personnel not on active duty, they underestimate the share of the labor force working for the defense establishment. Because governments rarely report the size of their armed forces, such data typically come from intelligence sources. The Bureau of Verification and Compliance attributes its data to unspecified U.S. government sources.

The Standard International Trade Classification does not clearly distinguish trade in military goods. For this and other reasons, customs-based data on trade in arms are of little use, so most compilers rely on trade publications, confidential government information on third-country trade, and other sources. The construction of defense production facilities and the licensing fees paid for the production of arms are included in trade data when they are specified in military transfer agreements. Grants in kind are usually included as well. Definitional issues include treatment of dual-use equipment such as aircraft, use of military establishments such as schools and hospitals by civilians, and purchases by nongovernmental buyers. Bureau of Verification and Compliance data do not include arms supplied to subnational groups. Valuation problems arise when data are reported in volume terms and the purchase price must be estimated. Differences between sources may reflect reporting lags or differences in the period covered. Most compilers revise their time-series data regularly, so estimates for the same year may not be consistent between publication dates.

The data on U.S. arms exports were substantially revised upward in the 2000 edition of the *World Development Indicators,* based on data from the most recent edition of the Bureau of Verification and Compliance's *World Military Expenditures and Arms Transfers* (U.S. Department of State 1999). Revisions were made in commercial arms sales made directly by U.S. firms to foreign importers under authorization of the U.S. Department of State in accordance with U.S. regulations on international traffic in arms. Under the previous methodology the commercial arms component was represented by preliminary data on the deliveries made under approved export licenses. But because of weaknesses in data reporting, the extent to which authorized exports matched actual exports was uncertain. The new methodology assumes that deliveries constitute 50 percent of total authorizations by country. These deliveries are then distributed in a fixed pattern over the years of the license.

Definitions

• **Military expenditures** for NATO countries are based on the NATO definition, which covers military-related expenditures of the defense ministry (including recruiting, training, construction, and the purchase of military supplies and equipment) and other ministries. Civilian-type expenditures of the defense ministry are excluded. Military assistance is included in the expenditures of the donor country, and purchases of military equipment on credit are included at the time the debt is incurred, not at the time of payment. Data for other countries generally cover expenditures of the ministry of defense (excluded are expenditures on public order and safety, which are classified separately). • **Armed forces personnel** refer to active duty military personnel, including paramilitary forces if those forces resemble regular units in their organization, equipment, training, or mission. • **Arms trade** comprises exports and imports of military equipment usually referred to as "conventional," including weapons of war, parts thereof, ammunition, support equipment, and other commodities designed for military use. See *About the data* for more details.

Data sources

The data on military expenditures, armed forces, and arms trade are from the Bureau of Verification and Compliance's *World Military Expenditures and Arms Transfers 2000* (U.S. Department of State 2002).

5.8 | Transport infrastructure

	Roads			Railways			Air		
	Total road network km 1995-2000ᵃ	Paved roads % 1995-2000ᵃ	Goods hauled million ton-km 1995-2000ᵃ	Passenger-km per $ million of PPP GDP 1995-2000ᵃ	Goods transported ton-km per $ million of PPP GDP 1995-2000ᵃ	Diesel locomotives available (%) 1995-2000ᵃ	Aircraft departures thousands 2000	Passengers carried thousands 2000	Air freight millions ton-km 2000
Afghanistan	21,000	13.3	..	..	..	..	3	150	8
Albania	18,000	39.0	1,830	9,196	1,941	..	5	149	0
Algeria	104,000	68.9	..	11,146	..	85	37	2,995	12
Angola	51,429	10.4	..	..	..	..	4	235	61
Argentina	215,471	29.4	..	28,665	..	..	196	9,262	295
Armenia	15,918	96.3	40	6,232	49,717	30	4	298	9
Australia	811,603	38.7	..	..	..	..	351	32,223	1,860
Austria	200,000	100.0	16,100	41,307	75,075	89	148	7,263	444
Azerbaijan	24,981	92.3	3,513	..	..	..	8	546	47
Bangladesh	207,486	9.5	..	22,570	4,706	81	6	1,331	194
Belarus	74,385	89.0	8,982	202,576	463,691	93	6	211	2
Belgium	148,216	78.2	35,000	32,012	30,522	86	226	10,738	1,016
Benin	6,787	20.0	..	..	..	..	2	77	12
Bolivia	53,790	6.5	..	6,460	..	..	22	1,757	15
Bosnia and Herzegovina	21,846	52.3	..	..	..	..	5	69	1
Botswana	10,217	55.0	..	..	..	..	7	166	0
Brazil	1,724,929	5.5	..	865	31,150	..	723	31,845	1,523
Bulgaria	37,286	94.0	168	96,104	122,533	37	12	515	6
Burkina Faso	12,506	16.0	..	..	..	..	3	144	12
Burundi	14,480	7.1	..	..	..	..	1	12	0
Cambodia	12,323	16.2	412	..	77,235	..	..	..	..
Cameroon	34,300	12.5	..	14,371	40,811	71	6	273	50
Canada	901,903	35.3	82,500	1,945	429,555	..	316	25,778	1,806
Central African Republic	23,810	2.7	60	..	..	..	2	77	12
Chad	33,400	0.8	..	..	..	..	2	77	12
Chile	79,814	19.4	..	4,907	7,802	65	88	5,175	1,312
China	1,402,698	22.4	612,940	82,693	260,427	82	573	61,892	3,900
Hong Kong, China	1,831	100.0	..	..	..	..	78	14,393	4,841
Colombia	112,988	14.4	31	62	1,948	32	197	8,537	595
Congo, Dem. Rep.	157,000	..	..	700	..	9	..	..	..
Congo, Rep.	12,800	9.7	..	36,264	..	35	6	128	12
Costa Rica	35,892	22.0	3,070	..	..	50	27	861	79
Côte d'Ivoire	50,400	9.7	..	6,512	21,081	53	7	262	12
Croatia	28,123	84.6	1,090	34,782	58,859	63	17	929	3
Cuba	60,858	49.0	..	..	..	56	12	1,007	49
Czech Republic	55,408	100.0	39,036	53,029	138,506	86	40	2,228	32
Denmark	71,591	100.0	11,696	40,275	11,786	..	152	5,923	199
Dominican Republic	12,600	49.4	..	..	..	..	0	11	0
Ecuador	43,197	18.9	4,176	..	..	..	17	1,181	15
Egypt, Arab Rep.	64,000	78.1	31,500	317,220	16,164	80	47	4,522	278
El Salvador	10,029	19.8	..	..	..	..	37	1,960	31
Eritrea	4,010	21.8	..	..	..	..	..	..	..
Estonia	51,411	20.1	3,689	19,842	486,631	80	9	278	1
Ethiopia	31,571	12.0	0	..	..	..	27	945	78
Finland	77,900	64.5	26,500	29,933	87,619	89	125	6,416	266
France	894,000	100.0	245,400	50,392	42,145	93	789	51,927	5,227
Gabon	8,464	9.9	..	11,254	65,276	89	8	442	55
Gambia, The	2,700	35.4	..	..	..	..	..	..	..
Georgia	20,362	93.5	475	44,361	200,857	34	2	118	2
Germany	230,735	99.1	226,982	31,471	38,962	92	743	59,362	7,128
Ghana	39,409	29.6	..	6,221	..	..	5	314	40
Greece	117,000	91.8	17,000	11,850	2,101	55	99	7,099	129
Guatemala	14,118	34.5	..	..	..	..	7	506	3
Guinea	30,500	16.5	..	..	..	..	1	61	1
Guinea-Bissau	4,400	10.3	..	..	..	..	1	20	0
Haiti	4,160	24.3	..	..	..	..	..	..	..
Honduras	13,603	20.4	..	..	..	..	..	..	..

	Roads			Railways			Air		
	Total road network km 1995-2000[a]	Paved roads % 1995-2000[a]	Goods hauled million ton-km 1995-2000[a]	Passenger-km per $ million of PPP GDP 1995-2000[a]	Goods transported ton-km per $ million of PPP GDP 1995-2000[a]	Diesel locomotives available (%) 1995-2000[a]	Aircraft departures thousands 2000	Passengers carried thousands 2000	Air freight millions ton-km 2000
Hungary	188,203	43.4	14	94,085	72,243	79	32	2,062	51
India	3,319,644	45.7	958	195,355	136,165	86	199	17,339	545
Indonesia	342,700	46.3	..	28,490	8,725	83	153	9,485	423
Iran, Islamic Rep.	167,157	56.3	..	18,506	43,629	47	83	8,830	71
Iraq	45,550	84.3	..	..	..	..	..	..	0
Ireland	92,500	94.1	5,900	18,714	4,599	74	146	14,014	168
Israel	16,281	100.0	..	3,243	9,132	92	45	4,073	886
Italy	479,688	100.0	219,800	38,135	18,054	79	375	30,586	1,748
Jamaica	18,700	70.1	..	..	..	..	24	1,918	48
Japan	1,161,894	46.0	307,149	77,409	7,608	81	642	108,413	8,549
Jordan	7,245	100.0	..	..	35,549	91	16	1,282	204
Kazakhstan	81,331	94.7	4,506	177,393	1,474,814	..	8	461	12
Kenya	63,942	12.1	..	13,457	44,821	64	29	1,557	77
Korea, Dem. Rep.	31,200	6.4	..	..	..	..	1	86	2
Korea, Rep.	86,990	74.5	74,504	46,461	19,459	90	227	34,331	7,774
Kuwait	4,450	80.6	..	..	..	..	18	2,123	243
Kyrgyz Republic	18,500	91.1	1,220	..	..	..	6	243	4
Lao PDR	21,716	13.8	..	..	..	..	6	211	2
Latvia	73,202	38.6	4,789	108,396	770,302	88	9	224	0
Lebanon	7,300	84.9	..	..	..	..	10	806	85
Lesotho	5,940	18.3	..	..	..	..	0	1	0
Liberia	10,600	6.2	..	..	..	..	..	..	..
Libya	83,200	57.2	..	..	..	..	7	609	0
Lithuania	75,243	91.3	7,769	28,379	328,042	88	10	284	2
Macedonia, FYR	8,684[a]	63.8	1,210	15,959	40,430	40	8	611	1
Madagascar	49,827	11.6	..	..	..	..	22	667	33
Malawi	28,400	18.5	..	0	11,535	..	5	116	1
Malaysia	65,877	75.8	..	8,221	7,203	65	169	16,561	1,864
Mali	15,100	12.1	..	30,578	35,377	..	2	77	12
Mauritania	7,660	11.3	..	..	..	..	4	185	13
Mauritius	1,926	97.0	..	..	..	..	12	949	183
Mexico	329,532	32.8	197,958	2,578	61,435	77	291	21,001	318
Moldova	12,657	87.0	952	..	..	..	4	135	1
Mongolia	49,250	3.5	126	253,483	684,165	..	6	254	8
Morocco	57,707	56.4	3,035	18,176	52,224	69	45	3,671	63
Mozambique	30,400	18.7	110	..	..	..	7	260	7
Myanmar	28,200	12.2	..	..	..	60	12	600	7
Namibia	66,467	8.3	..	5,607	133,970	89	6	245	75
Nepal	13,223	30.8	..	..	..	..	12	643	17
Netherlands	116,500	90.0	32,700	41,134	9,712	93	225	20,794	4,254
New Zealand	92,053	62.8	..	..	51,030	90	215	9,888	817
Nicaragua	19,032	11.0	..	..	..	..	1	61	1
Niger	10,100	7.9	..	..	..	..	2	77	12
Nigeria	194,394	30.9	..	512	4,915	63	9	415	10
Norway	91,454	76.0	12,796	..	..	..	363	15,157	201
Oman	32,800	30.0	..	..	..	..	19	2,120	157
Pakistan	254,410	43.0	96,802	81,899	17,118	85	74	6,252	339
Panama	11,400	34.6	..	..	..	..	25	1,117	22
Papua New Guinea	19,600	3.5	..	..	..	..	27	1,129	22
Paraguay	29,500	9.5	..	..	..	..	8	266	0
Peru	72,900	12.8	..	1,397	4,640	..	46	2,125	35
Philippines	201,994	21.0	..	915	4	..	44	5,444	241
Poland	364,656	68.3	72,843	77,593	171,756	55	49	2,373	76
Portugal	68,732	86.0	14,200	30,125	13,406	84	110	6,563	225
Puerto Rico	14,400	100.0	..	..	..	..	..	..	..
Romania	198,603	49.5	13,457	97,692	135,241	85	21	1,186	12
Russian Federation	532,393	67.4	139	129,048	1,102,493	..	315	17,688	1,041

2002 World Development Indicators

	Roads			Railways			Air		
	Total road network km 1995-2000[a]	Paved roads % 1995-2000[a]	Goods hauled million ton-km 1995-2000[a]	Passenger-km per $ million of PPP GDP 1995-2000[a]	Goods transported ton-km per $ million of PPP GDP 1995-2000[a]	Diesel locomotives available (%) 1995-2000[a]	Aircraft departures thousands 2000	Passengers carried thousands 2000	Air freight millions ton-km 2000
Rwanda	12,000	8.3	..	..	..	..	..	..	..
Saudi Arabia	151,470	30.1	..	998	3,811	80	109	12,567	1,000
Senegal	14,576	29.3	..	6,609	37,365	55	2	98	12
Sierra Leone	11,330	7.9	..	..	..	..	0	18	0
Singapore	3,066	100.0	..	..	..	..	71	16,704	6,005
Slovak Republic	42,717	86.7	8,474	57,115	215,427	87	3	116	0
Slovenia	20,177	99.9	4,407	21,848	89,048	..	12	628	4
Somalia	22,100	11.8	..	..	..	..	..	..	..
South Africa	362,099	20.3	..	25,701	283,106	96	110	8,000	688
Spain	663,795	99.0	98,145	26,047	16,714	83	479	39,559	872
Sri Lanka	96,695	95.0	30	59,310	1,865	70	5	1,756	256
Sudan	11,900	36.3	..	..	..	42	8	408	35
Swaziland	3,247	..	..	..	..	..	0	0	0
Sweden	212,402	78.4	32,000	36,988	96,543	..	248	13,354	289
Switzerland	71,011	..	22,000	..	..	..	288	17,216	1,937
Syrian Arab Republic	43,381	23.1	..	5,688	28,030	100	14	750	21
Tajikistan	27,767	82.7	..	..	..	..	4	156	3
Tanzania	88,200	4.2	..	73,054	73,054	72	6	182	3
Thailand	64,600	97.5	..	26,781	7,923	94	102	17,392	1,713
Togo	7,520	31.6	..	..	..	..	2	77	12
Trinidad and Tobago	8,320	51.1	..	..	..	..	26	1,254	24
Tunisia	18,997	64.8	..	21,247	41,961	71	20	1,908	21
Turkey	385,960	34.0	150,974	14,726	20,238	78	114	11,513	375
Turkmenistan	24,000	81.2	..	..	..	..	22	1,284	12
Uganda	27,000	6.7	..	1,366	4,924	..	3	187	23
Ukraine	169,491	96.7	18,206	296,128	941,037	87	28	963	11
United Arab Emirates	1,088	100.0	..	..	..	..	48	6,871	1,428
United Kingdom	371,913	100.0	150,700	..	..	75	872	70,361	5,161
United States	6,304,193	58.8	1,534,430	1,020	350,942	..	8,766[b]	655,649[b]	30,131[b]
Uruguay	8,983	90.0	..	6,931	6,126	..	9	617	14
Uzbekistan	81,600	87.3	..	42,559	304,816	..	30	1,656	75
Venezuela, RB	96,155	33.6	..	0	342	65	139	4,295	33
Vietnam	93,300	25.1	..	18,843	9,807	95	28	2,881	116
West Bank and Gaza	..	..	..	..	..	..	..	..	..
Yemen, Rep.	67,000	11.5	..	..	..	..	11	844	32
Yugoslavia, Fed. Rep.	49,805	62.3	630	..	..	..	..	..	..
Zambia	66,781	..	..	24,892	74,141	67	6	89	0
Zimbabwe	18,338	47.4	..	..	145,373	61	14	606	159
World		45.1 m			21,392 s	1,646,775 s			
Low income		16.5			797	52,007			
Middle income		52.3			4,466	329,757			
Lower middle income		56.3			1,897	155,078			
Upper middle income		47.3			2,569	174,679			
Low & middle income		32.2			5,263	381,764			
East Asia & Pacific		23.8			1,437	151,301			
Europe & Central Asia		91.3			770	46,295			
Latin America & Carib.		29.4			1,952	95,983			
Middle East & N. Africa		66.3			440	42,285			
South Asia		36.9			305	27,793			
Sub-Saharan Africa		12.3			360	18,107			
High income		92.9			16,129	1,265,012			
Europe EMU		92.9			3,500	255,191			

a. Data are for the latest year available in the period shown. b. Data cover only those carriers designated by the U.S. Department of Transportation as major and national air carriers.

About the data

Transport infrastructure—highways, railways, ports and waterways, and airports and air traffic control systems—and the services that flow from it are crucial to the activities of households, producers, and governments. Because performance indicators vary significantly by transport mode and by focus (whether physical infrastructure or the services flowing from that infrastructure), highly specialized and carefully specified indicators are required. The table provides selected indicators of the size and extent of roads, railways, and air transport systems and the volume of freight and passengers carried.

Data for most transport sectors are not internationally comparable. Unlike for demographic statistics, national income accounts, and international trade data, the collection of infrastructure data has not been "internationalized." Data on roads are collected by the International Road Federation (IRF), and data on air transport by the International Civil Aviation Organization (ICAO). National road associations are the primary source of IRF data; in countries where such an association is lacking or does not respond, other agencies are contacted, such as road directorates, ministries of transport or public works, or central statistical offices. As a result, the compiled data are of uneven quality.

Even when data are available, they are often of limited value because of incompatible definitions, inappropriate geographical units of observation, lack of timeliness, and variations in the nature of the terrain. Data on passengers carried, for example, may be distorted because of "ticketless" travel or breaks in journeys; in such cases, the statistics may report the number of passenger-kilometers for two passengers rather than one. Measurement problems are compounded because the mix of transported commodities changes over time, and in some cases shorter-haul traffic has been excluded from intercity traffic. Finally, the quality of transport service (reliability, transit time, and condition of goods delivered) is rarely measured but may be as important as quantity in assessing an economy's transport system. Serious efforts are needed to create international databases whose comparability and accuracy can be gradually improved.

The air transport data represent the total (international and domestic) scheduled traffic carried by the air carriers registered in a country. Countries submit air transport data to ICAO on the basis of standard instructions and definitions issued by ICAO. In many cases, however, the data include estimates by ICAO for nonreporting carriers. Where possible, these estimates are based on previous submissions supplemented by information published by the air carriers, such as flight schedules. The data represent the air traffic carried on scheduled services, but changes in air transport regulations in Europe have made it more difficult to classify traffic as scheduled or nonscheduled. Thus, recent increases shown for some European countries may be due to changes in the classification of air traffic rather than actual growth. For countries with few air carriers or only one, the addition or discontinuation of a home-based air carrier may cause significant changes in air traffic.

Figure 5.8

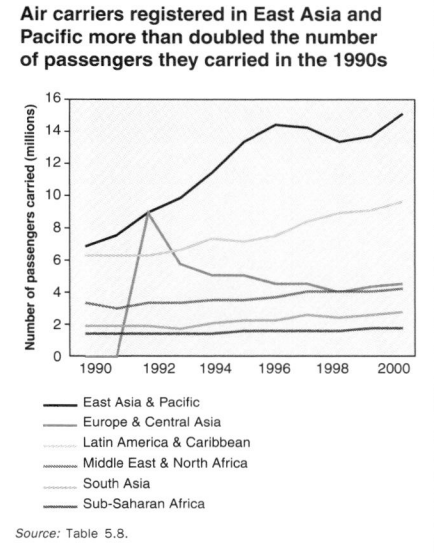

Air carriers registered in East Asia and Pacific more than doubled the number of passengers they carried in the 1990s

East Asia & Pacific
Europe & Central Asia
Latin America & Caribbean
Middle East & North Africa
South Asia
Sub-Saharan Africa

Source: Table 5.8.

Definitions

• **Total road network** includes motorways, highways, and main or national roads, secondary or regional roads, and all other roads in a country. • **Paved roads** are those surfaced with crushed stone (macadam) and hydrocarbon binder or bituminized agents, with concrete, or with cobblestones, as a percentage of all the country's roads, measured in length. • **Goods hauled by road** are the volume of goods transported by road vehicles, measured in millions of metric tons times kilometers traveled. • **Railway passengers** refer to the total number of passengers transported times kilometers traveled per million dollars of GDP, measured in purchasing power parity (PPP) terms (for a discussion of PPP see *About the data* for table 1.1). • **Goods transported by rail** are the tonnage of goods transported times kilometers traveled per million dollars of GDP, measured in purchasing power parity (PPP) terms. • **Diesel locomotives available** are those in service as a percentage of all diesel locomotives. • **Aircraft departures** are the number of domestic and international takeoffs of air carriers registered in the country. • **Air passengers carried** include both domestic and international aircraft passengers of air carriers registered in the country. • **Air freight** is the sum of the metric tons of freight, express, and diplomatic bags carried on each flight stage (the operation of an aircraft from takeoff to its next landing) multiplied by the stage distance by air carriers registered in the country.

Data sources

The data on roads are from the International Road Federation's *World Road Statistics* and from Eurostat (europa.eu.int/eurostat.html). The railway data are from a database maintained by the World Bank's Transportation, Water, and Urban Development Department, Transport Division. The air transport data are from the International Civil Aviation Organization's *Civil Aviation Statistics of the World* and ICAO staff estimates.

5.9 | Power and communications

	Electric power		Telephone mainlines[a]							Mobile phones[a]	International telecommunications[a]	
	Consumption per capita kwh 1999	Transmission and distribution losses % of output 1999	per 1,000 people 2000	In largest city per 1,000 people 2000	Waiting list thousands 2000	Waiting time years 2000	per employee 2000	Revenue per line $ 2000	Cost of local call $ per 3 minutes 2000	per 1,000 people 2000	Outgoing traffic minutes per subscriber 2000	Cost of call to U.S. $ per 3 minutes 2000
Afghanistan	..	..	1	10	..	..	..	..	..	0	..	..
Albania	783	57	39	93	98.5	4.5	34	424	0.02	8	469	4.59
Algeria	581	19	57	70	646.0	5.4	98	174	0.01	3	86	4.70
Angola	84	15	5	21	21.1	8.5	33	1,839	0.05	2	509	5.13
Argentina	1,938	15	213	247	58.2	0.2	406	1,267	0.09	163	56	2.80
Armenia	957	25	152	212	80.4	..	69	118	0.11	5	59	..
Australia	8,884	8	525	516	0.0	0.0	170	1,458	0.12	447	136	0.54
Austria	6,176	8	467	..	0.0	0.0	207	1,250	0.15	762	300	1.60
Azerbaijan	1,750	13	104	228	60.7	1.3	80	98	0.28	56	35	6.89
Bangladesh	89	16	4	24	135.1	3.3	30	558	0.03	1	91	4.14
Belarus	2,704	13	269	1,228	401.4	2.7	103	61	..	5	65	6.10
Belgium	7,286	5	498	..	..	..	223	932	0.13	525	305	2.00
Benin	53	98	8	21	23.0	4.5	52	1,062	0.09	9	321	6.90
Bolivia	390	18	61	115	7.5	0.2	103	826	0.09	70	65	3.70
Bosnia and Herzegovina	540	22	103	480	..	2.2	225	440	0.02	30	228	2.96
Botswana	..	..	93	..	..	0.5	71	974	0.02	123	323	3.60
Brazil	1,811	17	182	..	..	0.5	157	823	0.03	136	21	1.80
Bulgaria	2,899	17	350	564	242.0	3.6	112	135	0.00	90	38	..
Burkina Faso	..	..	4	36	12.3	2.2	41	981	0.08	2	202	11.00
Burundi	..	..	3	54	10.0	7.3	32	496	0.02	2	149	7.30
Cambodia	..	..	2	16	..	..	45	722	0.02	10	319	..
Cameroon	184	21	6	38	50.0	6.2	42	729	0.05	10	293	3.39
Canada	15,260	7	677	..	0.0	0.0	239	1,002	..	285	347	1.20
Central African Republic	..	..	3	..	1.8	>10.0	23	1,056	0.48	1	478	8.00
Chad	..	..	1	8	0.6	0.5	23	2,200	0.16	1	293	..
Chile	2,309	5	221	318	10.3	0.0	243	754	0.12	222	64	2.90
China	759	7	112	294	..	0.0	159	256	..	66	11	6.70
Hong Kong, China	5,178	13	583	583	0.0	0.0	102	1,845	0.00	809	801	2.62
Colombia	772	24	169	322	1,155.0	2.0	151	378	0.03	53	40	2.20
Congo, Dem. Rep.	43	4	0	..	..	..	..	..	..	0	..	..
Congo, Rep.	48	91	7	..	..	..	..	..	..	24	..	..
Costa Rica	1,426	8	249	..	34.7	0.3	213	296	0.02	52	81	1.93
Côte d'Ivoire	..	..	18	57	31.7	0.8	96	1,923	0.05	30	163	7.86
Croatia	2,674	17	365	..	..	0.9	151	474	0.03	231	198	..
Cuba	973	18	44	86	..	..	29	1,432	0.09	1	74	7.30
Czech Republic	4,682	8	378	676	32.0	0.2	164	660	0.13	424	93	0.97
Denmark	6,030	5	720	..	0.0	0.0	180	1,089	0.10	631	183	1.77
Dominican Republic	646	27	105	..	..	..	202	..	..	82	237	3.90
Ecuador	620	23	100	109	..	..	181	400	0.08	38	91	4.90
Egypt, Arab Rep.	900	12	86	173	1,300.0	1.9	100	498	0.01	21	34	3.33
El Salvador	568	13	100	..	..	..	148	897	0.06	118	222	2.40
Eritrea	..	..	8	43	20.5	7.2	67	522	0.02	0	95	5.91
Estonia	3,435	18	363	422	24.6	1.4	172	553	0.08	387	149	1.62
Ethiopia	21	10	4	52	196.9	7.8	32	360	0.02	0	59	7.15
Finland	14,366	4	550	..	0.0	0.0	118	1,406	0.12	720	164	1.07
France	6,392	6	579	..	0.0	0.0	200	813	0.10	493	129	1.00
Gabon	700	10	32	..	..	>10.0	37	1,801	0.15	98	567	..
Gambia, The	..	..	26	81	16.9	6.0	31	807	0.30	4	220	..
Georgia	1,312	19	139	233	104.8	2.2	76	47	..	34	60	2.88
Germany	5,690	4	611	686	0.0	0.0	210	1,012	0.09	586	184	0.34
Ghana	204	1	12	54	..	..	63	387	0.03	6	185	1.69
Greece	3,854	7	532	732	14.1	0.2	289	824	0.07	557	140	0.69
Guatemala	341	20	57	..	..	..	128	411	0.08	61	193	0.80
Guinea	..	..	8	19	1.7	0.1	75	449	0.10	5	289	9.04
Guinea-Bissau	..	..	9	109	5.1	4.4	45	..	..	0	272	..
Haiti	40	53	9	..	..	>10.0	20	..	..	3	204	7.10
Honduras	449	22	46	99	169.7	7.8	50	1,025	0.06	24	144	4.20

	Electric power		Telephone mainlines[a]							Mobile phones[a]	International telecommunications[a]	
	Consumption per capita kwh 1999	Transmission and distribution losses % of output 1999	per 1,000 people 2000	In largest city per 1,000 people 2000	Waiting list thousands 2000	Waiting time years 2000	per employee 2000	Revenue per line $ 2000	Cost of local call $ per 3 minutes 2000	per 1,000 people 2000	Outgoing traffic minutes per subscriber 2000	Cost of call to U.S. $ per 3 minutes 2000
Hungary	2,874	13	372	581	27.4	0.1	182	845	0.09	302	56	1.28
India	379	21	32	131	3,680.6	0.8	63	138	0.01	4	16	4.20
Indonesia	345	12	31	232	..	..	177	353	0.02	17	38	4.20
Iran, Islamic Rep.	1,407	15	149	..	1,203.5	1.2	200	210	0.01	15	24	7.65
Iraq	1,303	..	29	75	..	..	..	..	..	0	29	..
Ireland	5,011	8	420	..	..	..	91	1,653	0.17	658	786	1.54
Israel	5,689	3	482	..	..	0.3	253	1,735	0.05	702	324	3.30
Italy	4,535	7	474	..	0.0	0.0	358	1,247	0.12	737	101	1.40
Jamaica	2,294	10	199	..	209.1	6.5	175	949	..	142	144	5.20
Japan	7,443	3	586	554	0.0	0.0	462	1,641	0.07	526	35	1.67
Jordan	1,207	11	93	232	29.7	0.3	103	..	0.02	58	275	..
Kazakhstan	2,448	17	113	224	172.4	>10.0	60	147	..	12	57	2.68
Kenya	126	20	10	78	134.1	8.1	16	955	0.04	4	75	7.35
Korea, Dem. Rep.	..	..	46	..	..	..	..	..	..	0	..	..
Korea, Rep.	5,160	4	464	1,134	0.0	0.0	316	941	0.03	567	48	1.93
Kuwait	14,011	..	244	47	0.0	0.0	61	841	0.00	249	340	5.41
Kyrgyz Republic	1,512	27	77	158	58.1	6.9	52	60	..	2	62	9.84
Lao PDR	..	..	8	..	5.9	1.1	36	634	0.01	2	207	9.20
Latvia	1,851	27	303	526	19.2	3.3	170	305	0.11	166	79	2.05
Lebanon	1,778	18	195	96	..	..	114	919	0.07	212	124	4.45
Lesotho	..	..	10	64	19.0	>10.0	33	454	0.01	10	1,665	..
Liberia	..	..	2	..	..	>10.0	..	..	..	0	791	..
Libya	3,876	..	108	116	80.0	1.2	43	..	..	7	78	..
Lithuania	1,769	10	321	412	41.6	0.9	197	189	0.06	142	33	3.10
Macedonia, FYR	..	..	255	..	..	1.2	128	376	0.01	57	188	4.13
Madagascar	..	..	3	9	0.3	0.1	20	1,471	0.08	4	169	8.98
Malawi	..	..	4	37	25.0	9.1	9	892	0.03	5	241	..
Malaysia	2,474	8	199	282	..	0.7	187	596	0.02	213	193	2.37
Mali	..	..	3	22	..	..	28	1,559	0.07	1	368	12.64
Mauritania	..	..	7	18	47.8	>10.0	26	1,341	0.08	3	480	..
Mauritius	..	..	235	319	18.9	1.0	153	515	0.03	151	123	4.00
Mexico	1,570	14	125	142	137.3	0.1	133	1,065	0.14	142	153	3.01
Moldova	620	26	133	320	124.3	5.5	79	86	0.01	32	73	4.10
Mongolia	..	..	56	101	39.6	2.6	29	358	0.01	45	35	5.65
Morocco	430	4	50	115	5.0	0.1	98	591	0.07	83	172	4.50
Mozambique	53	10	4	..	21.3	3.2	37	1,315	0.06	3	265	..
Myanmar	71	25	6	29	93.2	5.3	34	59	0.01	0	44	..
Namibia	..	..	63	181	2.4	0.7	66	854	0.05	47	561	4.28
Nepal	47	23	12	..	283.4	6.7	57	263	0.01	0	98	..
Netherlands	5,993	5	618	..	0.0	0.0	169	1,130	0.13	670	286	0.30
New Zealand	8,426	12	500	..	0.0	0.0	358	1,307	0.00	563	340	0.90
Nicaragua	268	26	31	74	108.4	9.1	65	637	0.08	18	339	3.20
Niger	..	..	2	21	..	..	14	844	0.10	0	191	9.03
Nigeria	85	32	4	11	42.0	1.4	36	3,763	..	0	144	..
Norway	24,248	8	532	823	0.0	0.0	104	1,912	0.13	751	234	0.40
Oman	2,880	17	89	..	..	0.5	109	1,734	0.07	65	518	..
Pakistan	321	30	22	62	298.0	1.8	55	364	0.01	2	32	3.60
Panama	1,310	19	151	284	..	..	78	1,019	0.06	145	121	4.36
Papua New Guinea	..	..	13	..	..	..	36	1,031	..	2	368	..
Paraguay	789	3	50	..	20.1	0.7	46	685	0.06	149	129	6.10
Peru	654	12	64	..	29.6	1.2	258	850	0.06	48	68	2.40
Philippines	454	15	40	142	..	..	230	623	0.00	84	45	4.80
Poland	2,388	10	282	199	926.0	0.8	159	646	0.08	174	62	2.92
Portugal	3,616	8	430	..	25.6	0.2	234	1,155	0.10	665	118	0.89
Puerto Rico	..	..	332	..	..	..	226	897	..	237	..	0.87
Romania	1,511	13	175	368	640.0	3.8	92	222	0.11	112	43	2.49
Russian Federation	4,050	11	218	463	6,533.0	5.1	75	161	0.01	22	29	6.12

5.9 Power and communications

2002 World Development Indicators

	Electric power		Telephone mainlines[a]							Mobile phones[a]	International telecommunications[a]	
	Consumption per capita kwh 1999	Transmission and distribution losses % of output 1999	per 1,000 people 2000	In largest city per 1,000 people 2000	Waiting list thousands 2000	Waiting time years 2000	per employee 2000	Revenue per line $ 2000	Cost of local call $ per 3 minutes 2000	per 1,000 people 2000	Outgoing traffic minutes per subscriber 2000	Cost of call to U.S. $ per 3 minutes 2000
Rwanda	..	..	2	43	8.0	4.0	57	1,035	0.03	5	306	..
Saudi Arabia	4,710	8	137	253	927.4	2.6	124	1,503	0.01	64	324	5.20
Senegal	114	17	22	58	24.6	0.8	140	861	0.10	26	243	2.23
Sierra Leone	..	..	4	18	25.0	>10.0	19	..	0.03	2	279	..
Singapore	6,641	4	484	484	0.0	0.0	222	1,245	0.02	684	538	0.68
Slovak Republic	4,216	7	314	670	69.3	0.7	112	460	0.10	205	96	1.13
Slovenia	5,218	5	386	..	1.4	0.1	207	442	0.04	612	199	0.81
Somalia	..	..	2	11	..	..	..	..	..	0	..	..
South Africa	3,776	8	114	..	..	1.1	113	1,369	0.09	190	100	1.98
Spain	4,497	10	421	485	4.3	0.0	415	1,528	0.09	609	150	1.88
Sri Lanka	255	21	41	284	269.5	1.9	64	506	0.04	23	55	3.05
Sudan	46	31	12	46	405.0	4.4	138	3,386	0.23	1	83	..
Swaziland	..	..	32	115	17.0	7.2	64	925	0.04	33	831	..
Sweden	14,138	7	682	..	0.0	0.0	211	1,205	..	717	209	0.90
Switzerland	7,291	6	727	..	0.0	0.0	211	1,593	0.11	644	458	1.00
Syrian Arab Republic	863	..	103	141	3,025.8	>10.0	79	949	0.02	2	101	20.04
Tajikistan	2,163	13	36	131	10.3	..	44	32	0.01	0	29	8.16
Tanzania	55	22	5	31	29.6	1.3	47	812	0.08	5	75	13.30
Thailand	1,352	8	92	384	415.2	1.6	169	579	0.07	50	64	2.50
Togo	..	..	9	35	16.8	2.9	49	912	0.09	11	240	7.90
Trinidad and Tobago	3,527	8	231	200	10.0	0.5	98	808	0.03	103	243	3.30
Tunisia	911	10	90	96	83.7	0.9	129	445	0.02	6	165	..
Turkey	1,396	19	280	388	417.7	0.5	254	291	0.11	246	40	3.30
Turkmenistan	944	13	82	155	58.6	8.5	48	104	..	2	46	..
Uganda	..	..	3	37	9.2	3.6	25	1,549	0.13	8	183	..
Ukraine	2,306	18	199	418	2,654.9	7.9	80	82	0.00	16	38	..
United Arab Emirates	10,643	9	391	347	0.3	0.0	122	1,853	0.00	548	1,102	3.51
United Kingdom	5,384	8	589	..	0.0	0.0	170	1,508	0.17	727	227	1.10
United States	11,994	8	700	..	0.0	0.0	172	1,466	0.00	398	153	..
Uruguay	1,871	19	278	336	0.0	0.0	169	837	0.17	132	90	4.88
Uzbekistan	1,650	9	67	248	33.1	0.9	64	137	0.01	2	46	13.95
Venezuela, RB	2,493	23	108	..	..	..	137	1,385	0.10	217	72	5.20
Vietnam	252	15	32	133	..	..	..	425	0.02	10	22	..
West Bank and Gaza	..	..	..	..	..	0.7	..	..	0.04	..	..	..
Yemen, Rep.	110	26	19	77	159.5	3.8	66	271	0.01	2	105	4.45
Yugoslavia, Fed. Rep.	..	..	226	462	131.0	1.8	160	147	0.01	123	119	12.08
Zambia	540	11	8	24	13.3	6.7	26	565	0.06	9	160	2.57
Zimbabwe	894	17	18	70	158.9	>10.0	54	427	0.04	23	275	4.36

World	2,108 w	9 w	163 w	222 w	.. w	1.1 m	221 m	1,029 m	0.06 m	123 m	144 m	4.00 m
Low income	358	19	23	117	8,880.0	4.4	74	199	0.03	5	155	..
Middle income	1,393	11	139	286	..	1.0	164	840	0.06	93	93	4.36
Lower middle income	1,066	10	116	290	..	1.9	138	846	0.06	58	86	4.70
Upper middle income	2,427	12	213	..	..	0.5	209	830	0.08	201	94	2.37
Low & middle income	923	12	84	194	..	1.9	151	816	0.05	51	100	4.70
East Asia & Pacific	816	7	101	270	..	1.2	179	365	0.02	70	48	5.30
Europe & Central Asia	2,679	13	222	449	13,617.1	1.8	137	1,703	0.08	92	60	2.94
Latin America & Carib.	1,470	16	148	..	..	0.5	189	889	0.06	123	106	3.20
Middle East & N. Africa	1,289	12	92	127	6,294.6	1.2	138	486	0.01	30	139	..
South Asia	337	22	27	118	4,364.0	1.9	61	175	0.01	3	55	3.60
Sub-Saharan Africa	435	11	14	33	1,294.7	4.4	97	1,266	0.06	17	241	..
High income	8,496	7	604	..	66.0	0.0	246	1,321	0.09	532	234	1.78
Europe EMU	5,550	6	534	..	14.1	0.0	267	1,077	0.10	611	174	1.67

a. Data are from the International Telecommunication Union's (ITU) *World Telecommunication Development Report 2001*. Please cite the ITU for third-party use of these data.

About the data

The quality of an economy's infrastructure, including power, communications, and transport, are important elements in both domestic and foreign investors' decisions to invest. Competition in the marketplace, with sound regulation, is lowering costs and improving the quality of and access to telecommunications services around the globe.

An economy's production and consumption of electricity is a basic indicator of its size and level of development. Although a few countries export electric power, most production is for domestic consumption. Expanding the supply of electricity to meet the growing demand of increasingly urbanized and industrialized economies without incurring unacceptable social, economic, and environmental costs is one of the great challenges facing developing countries.

Data on electric power production and consumption are collected from national energy agencies by the International Energy Agency (IEA) and adjusted by the IEA to meet international definitions (for data on electricity production see table 3.9). Electricity consumption is equivalent to production less power plants' own use and transmission, distribution, and transformation losses. It includes consumption by auxiliary stations, losses in transformers that are considered integral parts of those stations, and electricity produced by pumping installations. It covers electricity generated by primary sources of energy—coal, oil, gas, nuclear, hydro, geothermal, wind, tide and wave, and combustible renewables—where data are available. Neither production nor consumption data capture the reliability of supplies, including breakdowns, load factors, and frequency of outages.

Over the past decade new financing and technology along with privatization and liberalization have spurred dramatic growth in telecommunications in many countries. The table presents some common performance indicators for telecommunications, including measures of supply and demand, service quality, productivity, economic and financial performance, and tariffs. The quality of data varies among reporting countries as a result of differences in regulatory obligations for the provision of data.

Demand for telecommunications is often measured by the sum of telephone mainlines and registered applicants for new connections. (A mainline is normally identified by a unique number that is the one billed.) In some countries the list of registered applicants does not reflect real current pending demand, which is often hidden or suppressed, reflecting an extremely short supply that has discouraged potential applicants from applying for telephone service. And in some cases waiting lists may overstate demand because applicants have placed their names on the list several times to improve their chances. Waiting time is calculated by dividing the number of applicants on the waiting list by the average number of mainlines added each year over the past three years. The number of mainlines no longer reflects a telephone system's full capacity because mobile telephones—whose use has been expanding rapidly in most countries, rich and poor—provide an alternative point of access.

The table includes four measures of efficiency in telecommunications: waiting list, waiting time, mainlines per employee, and revenue per mainline. Caution should be used in interpreting the estimates of mainlines per employee because firms often subcontract part of their work. The cross-country comparability of revenue per mainline may also be limited because, for example, some countries do not require telecommunications providers to submit financial information; the data usually do not include revenues from cellular and mobile phones or radio, paging, and data services; and there are definitional and accounting differences between countries.

Figure 5.9

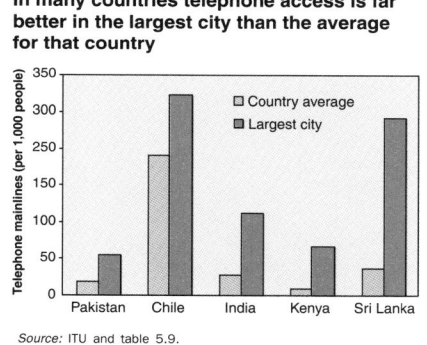

In many countries telephone access is far better in the largest city than the average for that country

Source: ITU and table 5.9.

Definitions

• **Electric power consumption** measures the production of power plants and combined heat and power plants less transmission, distribution, and transformation losses and own use by heat and power plants. • **Electric power transmission and distribution losses** are losses in transmission between sources of supply and points of distribution and in distribution to consumers, including pilferage. • **Telephone mainlines** are telephone lines connecting a customer's equipment to the public switched telephone network. Data are presented for the entire country and for the largest city. • **Waiting list** shows the number of applications for a connection to a mainline that have been held up by a lack of technical capacity. • **Waiting time** is the approximate number of years applicants must wait for a telephone line. • **Mainlines per employee** are calculated by dividing the number of mainlines by the number of telecommunications staff (with part-time staff converted to full-time equivalents) employed by telecommunications enterprises providing public telecommunications services. • **Revenue per line** is the revenue received by firms per mainline for providing telecommunications services. • **Cost of local call** is the cost of a three-minute, peak rate, fixed-line call within the same exchange area using the subscriber's equipment (that is, not from a public phone). • **Mobile phones** refer to users of portable telephones subscribing to an automatic public mobile telephone service using cellular technology that provides access to the public switched telephone network, per 1,000 people. • **Outgoing traffic** is the telephone traffic, measured in minutes per subscriber, that originates in the country and has a destination outside the country. • **Cost of call to U.S.** is the cost of a three-minute peak rate call from the country to the United States.

Data sources

The data on electricity consumption and losses are from the IEA's *Energy Statistics and Balances of Non-OECD Countries 1998–99*, the IEA's *Energy Statistics of OECD Countries 1998–99*, and the United Nations Statistics Division's *Energy Statistics Yearbook*. The telecommunications data are from the International Telecommunication Union's (ITU) *World Telecommunication Development Report 2001*.

5.10 | The information age

316

	Daily newspapers	Radios	Television[a]		Personal computers[a]	Personal computers installed in education	Internet	Monthly off-peak access charges[a]			Information and communications technology expenditures	
	per 1,000 people 1998	per 1,000 people 2000	Sets per 1,000 people 2000	Cable subscribers per 1,000 people 2000	per 1,000 people 2000	Total 2000	Users thousands[a] 2000	Service provider charge $ 2001	Telephone usage charge $ 2001	Secure servers 2001	% of GDP 2000	per capita 2000
Afghanistan	5	114	14	..	..	..	..	..	..	..	..	..
Albania	35	243	123	..	6.4	..	4	19	0.20	1	..	..
Algeria	27	244	110	..	6.5	..	50	27	0.17	..	..	..
Angola	11	74	19	..	1.1	..	30	20	0.57	..	..	..
Argentina	37	681	293	163.1	51.3	122,881	2,500	78	0.47	238	4.1	317
Armenia	6	225	244	0.9	7.1	..	50	42	0.78	1	..	..
Australia	293	1,908	738	68.0	464.6	610,745	6,600	13	2.60	3,422	9.7	1,922
Austria	296	753	536	123.4	276.5	128,606	2,100	..	17.21	669	7.2	1,697
Azerbaijan	27	22	259	0.3	..	..	12	..	2.15	1	..	..
Bangladesh	53	49	7	..	1.5	..	100	17	0.33	1	..	..
Belarus	155	299	342	33.2	..	..	180	15	54.25	4	..	..
Belgium	160	793	541	372.9	344.5	167,526	2,326	..	27.52	342	8.0	1,769
Benin	2	439	45	..	1.6	..	15	129	0.93	1	..	..
Bolivia	992	676	119	9.6	16.8	..	120	..	..	5	..	..
Bosnia and Herzegovina	152	243	111	..	..	..	20	19	0.13	..	..	..
Botswana	27	155	25	..	37.0	..	15	15	0.14	..	..	..
Brazil	43	433	343	13.7	44.1	690,196	5,000	..	..	1,028	8.4	289
Bulgaria	257	543	449	130.1	43.9	20,936	430	8	0.02	18	4.1	61
Burkina Faso	1	35	12	..	1.3	..	10	29	0.84	..	..	..
Burundi	0	220	30	..	..	..	3	..	0.18	..	..	..
Cambodia	2	119	8	..	1.1	..	6	104	0.30	2	..	..
Cameroon	7	163	34	..	3.3	..	40	77	0.56	..	..	..
Canada	159	1,047	..	259.4	390.2	893,745	12,700	12	0.00	5,055	8.4	1,911
Central African Republic	2	80	6	..	1.7	..	2	166	1.40	..	..	..
Chad	0	236	1	..	1.3	..	3	..	..	..	..	..
Chile	98	354	242	44.9	82.3	108,907	2,537	..	..	141	7.8	360
China	..	339	293	61.1	15.9	1,539,843	22,500	7	0.14	184	5.4	46
Hong Kong, China	792	684	493	78.6	350.6	127,491	2,601	18	0.00	538	8.8	2,085
Colombia	46	544	282	13.6	35.4	108,209	878	..	0.25	71	12.0	228
Congo, Dem. Rep.	3	386	2	..	..	..	1	95	..	..	..	..
Congo, Rep.	8	123	13	..	3.5	..	1	..	..	..	..	..
Costa Rica	91	816	231	19.1	149.1	..	250	16	0.10	56	..	..
Côte d'Ivoire	16	137	60	..	6.1	..	40	183	0.25	1	..	..
Croatia	114	340	293	38.0	80.7	..	250	20	0.42	61	..	..
Cuba	118	353	250	..	10.7	..	60	..	..	2	..	..
Czech Republic	254	803	508	93.2	122.0	96,539	1,000	..	11.60	273	9.3	453
Denmark	304	1,349	807	264.8	431.5	145,118	1,950	21	0.00	396	9.2	2,778
Dominican Republic	156	181	97	..	..	..	55	18	0.00	8	..	..
Ecuador	43	418	218	25.7	21.7	..	180	..	..	11	..	..
Egypt, Arab Rep.	35	339	189	..	22.1	41,443	450	9	0.14	11	2.4	36
El Salvador	28	478	201	49.7	19.1	..	50	26	0.62	7	..	..
Eritrea	..	444	26	..	1.6	..	5	23	0.21	..	..	..
Estonia	176	1,096	591	90.3	152.9	..	392	..	0.57	80	..	..
Ethiopia	0	189	6	..	0.9	..	10	94	0.24	3	..	..
Finland	455	1,623	692	183.5	396.1	181,259	1,927	..	10.62	498	7.8	1,835
France	201	950	628	45.2	304.3	759,726	8,500	20	0.00	1,641	8.7	1,916
Gabon	30	501	326	8.4	9.8	..	15	35	1.26	1	..	..
Gambia, The	2	396	3	..	11.5	..	4	18	2.70	..	..	..
Georgia	..	556	474	2.7	..	..	23	20	0.00	10	..	..
Germany	305	948	586	246.8	336.0	961,501	24,000	13	0.00	5,156	7.9	1,798
Ghana	14	710	118	..	3.0	..	30	36	0.38	1	..	..
Greece	23	478	488	..	70.5	68,329	1,000	15	5.40	116	6.1	659
Guatemala	33	79	61	..	11.4	..	80	..	..	12	..	..
Guinea	..	52	44	..	3.7	..	8	58	0.86	..	..	..
Guinea-Bissau	5	44	..	..	..	..	3	..	..	..	..	..
Haiti	3	55	5	..	..	..	6	..	..	1	..	..
Honduras	55	412	96	7.7	10.8	..	40	15	0.61	4	..	..

	Daily newspapers	Radios	Television[a]		Personal computers[a]	Personal computers installed in education	Internet		Monthly off-peak access charges[a]			Information and communications technology expenditures	
	per 1,000 people 1998	per 1,000 people 2000	Sets per 1,000 people 2000	Cable subscribers per 1,000 people 2000	per 1,000 people 2000	Total 2000	Users thousands[a] 2000	Service provider charge $ 2001	Telephone usage charge $ 2001	Secure servers 2001	% of GDP 2000	per capita 2000
Hungary	46	690	437	157.6	85.3	66,841	1,480	13	13.59	127	8.7	431
India	48	121	78	38.5	4.5	161,014	5,000	10	0.18	122	3.8	18
Indonesia	23	157	149	0.2	9.9	46,483	2,000	12	0.20	60	2.2	16
Iran, Islamic Rep.	28	281	163	..	62.8	..	250	..	..	1	..	..
Iraq	19	222	83	..	..	..	..	..	..	..	..	..
Ireland	150	695	399	176.9	359.1	45,138	784	..	16.45	350	6.7	1,676
Israel	290	526	335	185.0	253.6	..	1,270	11	0.18	301	7.4	..
Italy	104	878	494	1.0	179.8	720,911	13,200	..	17.62	1,041	5.7	1,068
Jamaica	62	784	194	98.9	46.6	..	80	49	..	5	..	..
Japan	578	956	725	147.4	315.2	1,918,000	47,080	17	27.67	5,153	8.3	3,118
Jordan	77	372	84	0.2	22.5	..	127	24	0.42	2	..	..
Kazakhstan	..	422	241	..	..	..	100	1	0.02	8	..	..
Kenya	10	223	25	..	4.9	..	200	66	0.46	1	..	..
Korea, Dem. Rep.	208	154	54	..	..	..	..	..	..	..	..	..
Korea, Rep.	393	1,033	364	177.4	237.9	405,492	19,040	8	0.00	345	6.6	641
Kuwait	374	624	486	..	130.6	..	150	32	0.00	4	..	..
Kyrgyz Republic	15	111	49	..	..	..	52	10	0.00	2	..	..
Lao PDR	4	148	10	..	2.6	..	6	50	0.17	..	..	..
Latvia	247	695	789	76.7	140.3	..	150	29	0.82	43	..	..
Lebanon	107	687	335	5.9	50.1	..	300	60	0.36	19	..	..
Lesotho	8	53	16	..	..	..	4	12	0.17	..	..	..
Liberia	12	274	25	..	..	..	1	..	..	..	..	..
Libya	15	273	137	..	..	..	10	108	0.20	..	..	..
Lithuania	29	500	422	89.2	64.9	..	225	45	0.38	43	..	..
Macedonia, FYR	..	205	282	..	..	..	50	12	0.04	..	..	..
Madagascar	5	216	24	..	2.2	..	30	66	0.44	..	..	..
Malawi	3	499	3	0.0	1.2	..	15	..	0.25	..	..	..
Malaysia	158	420	168	..	103.1	100,706	3,700	5	0.24	146	6.8	259
Mali	1	56	14	..	1.2	..	19	70	0.72	1	..	..
Mauritania	0	149	96	..	9.4	..	5	29	0.76	1	..	..
Mauritius	71	379	268	..	100.5	..	87	23	0.38	12	..	..
Mexico	98	330	283	23.1	50.6	395,813	2,712	11	0.00	259	3.2	189
Moldova	154	758	297	11.8	14.5	..	53	33	0.17	3	..	..
Mongolia	..	154	65	..	12.6	..	30	52	0.17	1	..	..
Morocco	26	243	166	..	12.3	..	200	26	0.75	5	..	..
Mozambique	3	44	5	..	3.0	..	30	..	..	..	..	..
Myanmar	9	66	7	..	1.1	..	7	..	..	..	..	..
Namibia	19	141	38	..	34.2	..	30	..	..	3	..	..
Nepal	..	39	7	2.9	3.0	..	50	16	0.07	..	..	..
Netherlands	306	980	538	387.8	394.1	624,592	3,900	..	16.40	798	9.4	2,198
New Zealand	207	997	522	4.4	360.2	189,785	830	11	0.00	609	13.6	1,771
Nicaragua	30	270	69	10.8	8.9	..	50	30	0.54	6	..	..
Niger	0	121	37	..	0.5	..	5	63	0.53	..	..	..
Nigeria	24	200	68	..	6.6	..	200	44	0.57	1	..	..
Norway	585	915	669	183.6	490.5	144,078	2,200	11	20.64	369	6.9	2,445
Oman	..	621	563	..	31.5	..	90	19	0.79	2	..	..
Pakistan	30	105	131	0.1	4.2	..	134	13	0.20	6	..	..
Panama	62	300	194	..	37.0	..	90	..	..	29	..	..
Papua New Guinea	14	86	17	..	..	..	135	34	2.52	..	..	..
Paraguay	43	182	218	17.8	12.7	..	40	..	..	4	..	..
Peru	0	273	148	13.6	40.9	..	2,500	..	..	35	..	..
Philippines	82	161	144	13.1	19.3	66,336	2,000	24	0.00	68	3.8	38
Poland	108	523	400	92.6	68.9	219,416	2,800	..	18.39	326	5.9	248
Portugal	32	304	630	92.3	299.3	48,511	2,500	..	13.00	138	7.1	743
Puerto Rico	126	742	330	72.1	..	..	400	43	1.30	63	..	..
Romania	300	334	381	157.7	31.9	32,414	800	15	0.37	53	2.3	38
Russian Federation	105	418	421	..	42.9	424,284	3,100	15	0.14	285	3.7	63

	Daily newspapers	Radios	Television[a]		Personal computers[a]	Personal computers installed in education	Internet				Information and communications technology expenditures	
			Sets	Cable subscribers			Users thousands[a]	Service provider charge $	Monthly off-peak access charges[a] Telephone usage charge $	Secure servers	% of GDP	per capita
	per 1,000 people 1998	per 1,000 people 2000	per 1,000 people 2000	per 1,000 people 2000	per 1,000 people 2000	Total 2000	2000	2001	2001	2001	2000	2000
Rwanda	0	76	0	..	..	..	5	38	0.36	1	..	..
Saudi Arabia	326	326	264	4.0	60.2	..	200	31	0.13	11	..	..
Senegal	5	141	40	..	16.8	..	40	14	0.53	1	..	..
Sierra Leone	4	259	13	..	..	..	5	..	..	1	..	..
Singapore	298	672	304	63.5	483.1	120,000	1,200	..	0.12	525	9.7	2,104
Slovak Republic	174	965	407	139.7	136.9	26,461	650	9	0.54	79	7.5	291
Slovenia	171	405	368	161.1	275.9	26,091	300	29	0.31	102	5.2	476
Somalia	1	60	14	..	..	..	0	..	..	..	..	..
South Africa	32	338	127	..	61.8	317,298	2,400	9	0.33	521	8.6	256
Spain	100	333	591	11.8	142.9	271,837	5,388	17	0.00	938	5.1	731
Sri Lanka	29	208	111	0.3	7.1	..	122	6	0.05	6	..	..
Sudan	26	464	273	0.0	3.2	..	30	3	2.33	..	..	..
Swaziland	26	162	119	..	..	..	10	12	0.24	1	..	..
Sweden	432	932	574	199.3	506.7	484,398	4,048	2	21.35	1,033	10.4	2,674
Switzerland	369	1,002	548	358.1	499.7	154,413	2,134	..	30.87	1,079	10.3	3,482
Syrian Arab Republic	20	276	67	0.0	15.4	..	30	..	..	1	..	..
Tajikistan	20	141	326	..	..	..	3	..	..	..	..	..
Tanzania	4	281	20	..	2.8	..	115	69	0.79	..	..	..
Thailand	64	235	284	2.5	24.3	225,832	2,300	9	0.75	116	3.6	71
Togo	4	265	32	..	21.6	..	100	8	0.75	..	..	..
Trinidad and Tobago	123	532	340	..	61.8	..	100	1	0.37	12	..	..
Tunisia	31	158	198	..	22.9	..	100	25	0.22	4	..	..
Turkey	111	573	449	13.4	38.1	107,991	2,000	1	4.10	219	4.8	149
Turkmenistan	..	256	196	..	..	..	6	..	..	..	..	..
Uganda	2	127	27	0.0	2.7	..	40	30	0.82	1	..	..
Ukraine	101	889	456	52.3	17.6	..	300	7	0.04	44	..	..
United Arab Emirates	156	318	292	..	153.5	..	735	13	0.00	31	..	..
United Kingdom	329	1,432	1	56.9	337.8	1,613,403	18,000	14	0.00	6,467	9.1	2,187
United States	213	2,118	854	252.1	585.2	13,426,248	95,354	5	3.50	78,126	8.1	2,926
Uruguay	293	603	530	125.9	104.9	..	370	..	..	37	..	..
Uzbekistan	3	456	276	3.0	..	..	120	77	0.10	1	..	..
Venezuela, RB	206	294	185	40.2	45.5	92,655	950	27	..	92	3.9	196
Vietnam	4	109	185	..	8.8	21,027	200	20	0.25	6	6.5	25
West Bank and Gaza	..	..	..	..	..	..	..	..	0.28	..	..	..
Yemen, Rep.	15	65	283	..	1.9	..	15	45	0.09	..	..	..
Yugoslavia, Fed. Rep.	107	297	282	..	22.6	..	400	..	0.13	7	..	..
Zambia	12	145	134	..	6.7	..	20	19	0.31	..	..	..
Zimbabwe	18	362	30	0.0	11.9	..	50	46	0.34	1	..	..
World	.. w	419 w	254 w	68.6 w	78.3 w		366,470 s	18 w	0.34 w	121,223 s		
Low income	42	156	91	..	5.1		9,337	33	0.35	279		
Middle income	..	362	275	52.6	33.1		87,311	17	0.33	5,294		
Lower middle income	..	330	260	54.4	21.1		37,918	18	0.22	1,050		
Upper middle income	91	463	319	46.7	69.9		49,393	15	0.40	4,244		
Low & middle income	..	265	185	42.5	20.1		96,649	23	0.34	5,573		
East Asia & Pacific	..	306	252	52.4	21.7		51,943	20	0.20	940		
Europe & Central Asia	102	448	380	..	45.4		14,648	15	0.37	1,694		
Latin America & Carib.	71	413	269	20.1	43.6		19,086	..	..	2,185		
Middle East & N. Africa	33	277	172	..	31.2		1,864	27	0.22	67		
South Asia	8	112	75	37.8	4.2		5,413	13	0.18	135		
Sub-Saharan Africa	12	198	59	..	9.2		3,695	36	0.53	552		
High income	285	1,280	641	173.8	392.7		269,821	11	1.46	115,650		
Europe EMU	209	811	568	127.2	267.3		65,863	..	13.00	11,741		

a. Data are from the International Telecommunication Union's (ITU) *World Telecommunication Development Report 2001*. Please cite the ITU for third-party use of these data.

About the data

The digital and information revolution has changed the way the world learns, communicates, does business, and treats illnesses. New information and communications technologies offer vast opportunities for progress in all walks of life in all countries—opportunities for economic growth, improved health, better service delivery, learning through distance education, and social and cultural advances.

The table includes indicators of the penetration of the information economy—newspapers, radios, television sets, personal computers, and Internet users—as well as some of the economics of the information age—Internet access charges, the number of secure servers, and spending on information and communications technology.

The data on the number of daily newspapers in circulation and radio receivers in use are from statistical surveys carried out by the United Nations Educational, Scientific, and Cultural Organization (UNESCO). In some countries definitions, classifications, and methods of enumeration do not entirely conform to UNESCO standards. For example, newspaper circulation data should refer to the number of copies distributed, but in some cases the figures reported are the number of copies printed. In addition, many countries impose radio and television license fees to help pay for public broadcasting, discouraging radio and television owners from declaring ownership. Because of these and other data collection problems, estimates of the number of newspapers and radios vary widely in reliability and should be interpreted with caution.

The data for other electronic communications and information technology are from the International Telecommunication Union (ITU), the Internet Software Consortium, Netcraft, and the World Information Technology and Services Alliance. The ITU collects data on television sets and cable television subscribers through annual questionnaires sent to national broadcasting authorities and industry associations. Some countries require that television sets be registered. To the extent that households do not register their televisions or do not register all of their televisions, the data on licensed sets may understate the true number.

Because of different regulatory requirements for the provision of data, complete measurement of the telecommunications sector is not possible. Telecommunications data are compiled through annual questionnaires sent to telecommunications authorities and operating companies. The data are supplemented by annual reports and statistical yearbooks of telecommunications ministries, regulators, operators, and industry associations. In some cases estimates are derived from ITU documents or other references.

The estimates of personal computers are derived from an annual questionnaire, supplemented by other sources. In many countries mainframe computers are used extensively, and thousands of users can be connected to a single mainframe computer; thus the number of personal computers understates the total use of computers.

Data on Internet users are based on estimates derived from reported counts of Internet service provider (ISP) subscribers or calculated by multiplying the number of hosts by an estimated multiplier. Internet hosts are computers connected directly to the world-wide network, each allowing many computer users to access the Internet. This method may undercount the number of people actually using the Internet, particularly in developing countries where many commercial subscribers rent computers connected to the Internet. Although survey methods used to estimate the number of Internet hosts have improved in recent years, some measurement problems remain (see Zook 2000). For detailed analysis of Internet trends by country, it is best to use the original source data.

The table shows both the off-peak ISP charge and the telephone usage charge for being logged on to the Internet. Some countries have peak rates that are higher.

The number of secure servers, from the Netcraft Secure Server Survey, gives an indication of how many companies are conducting encrypted transactions over the Internet.

The data on information and communications technology expenditures cover the world's 55 largest buyers of such technology among countries and regions, accounting for 98 percent of global spending.

Definitions

• **Daily newspapers** refer to those published at least four times a week. • **Radios** refer to radio receivers in use for broadcasts to the general public. • **Television sets** refer to those in use. • **Cable television subscribers** are households that subscribe to a multichannel television service delivered by a fixed line connection. Some countries also report subscribers to pay television using wireless technology or those cabled to community antenna systems. • **Personal computers** are self-contained computers designed to be used by a single individual. • **Personal computers installed in education** include PC shipments installed in education establishments, whether primary or secondary schools or universities. • **Internet users** are people with access to the worldwide network. • **Internet service provider charge** shows the costs associated with 30 off-peak hours of dial-up Internet access per month. It is the monthly Internet subscription rate plus extra charges once free hours have been used up. Some countries have peak rates that are higher. • **Telephone usage charge** refers to the amount payable to the telephone company for 30 off-peak hours of local telephone use while logged on to the Internet. Excluded is the monthly telephone line tariff. If a special Internet telephone tariff exists, it is used instead. Some countries have peak rates that are higher. • **Secure servers** are servers using encryption technology in Internet transactions. • **Information and communications technology expenditures** include external spending on information technology ("tangible" spending on information technology products purchased by businesses, households, governments, and education institutions from vendors or organizations outside the purchasing entity), internal spending on information technology ("intangible" spending on internally customized software, capital depreciation, and the like), and spending on telecommunications and other office equipment.

Data sources

The data on newspapers and radios are compiled by UNESCO's Institute for Statistics. The data on television sets, cable television subscribers, personal computers, Internet users, and Internet access charges are from the ITU. They are reported in the ITU's *World Telecommunication Development Report 2001, Challenges to the Network: Internet for Development* (1999*)*, and the *World Telecommunications Indicators Database* (2000b). The data on secure servers are from Netcraft (www.netcraft.com/). The data on PCs installed in education and on information and communications technology expenditures are from *Digital Planet 2002: The Global Information Economy* by the World Information Technology and Services Alliance (WITSA), which uses data from the International Data Corporation.

5.11 | Science and technology

	Scientists and engineers in R&D	Technicians in R&D	Science and engineering students	Science and technical journal articles	Expenditures for R&D	High-technology exports		Royalty and license fees		Patent applications filed [a]		Trademark applications filed [b]
	per million people 1990-2000[c]	per million people 1990-2000[c]	% of total tertiary level students 1987-1997[c]	1997	% of GNI 1989-2000[c]	$ millions 2000	% of manufactured exports 2000	Receipts $ millions 2000	Payments $ millions 2000	Residents 1999	Non-residents 1999	Total 1999
Afghanistan	..	..	10	0	..	..	..	..	..	..	..	..
Albania	..	..	19	10	..	2	1	..	..	0	89,519	2,035
Algeria	..	..	58	139	..	15	4	..	..	34	248	4,252
Angola	..	..	24	2	..	..	..	3	2	..	..	..
Argentina	711	156	28	2,119	0.48	767	9	13	458	899	5,558	65,243
Armenia	1,308	238	29	178	0.18	4	5	..	..	109	40,163	3,273
Australia	3,320	792	24	11,793	1.71	2,734	15	343	999	9,537	53,818	58,789
Austria	1,605	801	33	3,432	1.64	6,600	14	162	547	3,075	159,046	18,697
Azerbaijan	2,735	184	37	71	..	6	4	..	..	0	40,042	2,091
Bangladesh	51	32	47	130	..	4	0	0	4	32	184	..
Belarus	2,296	271	48	548	0.57	180	4	1	2	1,002	40,790	5,511
Belgium	2,307	2,195	41	4,717	1.55	15,274	10	783	900	1,786	119,195	..
Benin	174	53	18	19	..	0	0	..	1	..	..	..
Bolivia	171	154	30	27	..	158	..	2	5	..	..	..
Bosnia and Herzegovina	..	..	..	8	..	..	..	..	..	23	41,201	4,009
Botswana	..	..	37	33	..	..	..	0	6	0	54	..
Brazil	168	58	27	3,908	0.77	5,979	19	126	1,415	1,957	50,338	..
Bulgaria	1,289	466	27	896	0.00	..	..	4	10	302	42,650	8,776
Burkina Faso	17	16	18	20	..	..	..	..	..	..	..	..
Burundi	21	32	20	11	0.31	..	..	0	0	..	..	..
Cambodia	..	..	13	3	..	..	..	..	..	..	..	1,303
Cameroon	..	..	45	73	..	1	1	..	..	..	..	..
Canada	3,009	1,171	16	19,910	1.68	32,702	19	1,374	3,267	5,197	64,580	40,365
Central African Republic	47	27	30	5	0.02	..	..	..	..	..	..	..
Chad	..	..	14	2	..	..	..	..	..	..	..	..
Chile	370	..	42	850	0.56	100	3	102	44	..	..	..
China	459	187	43	9,081	0.06	40,837	19	80	1,281	146	52,202	165,122
Hong Kong, China	93	100	36	2,080	..	5,155	23	..	..	42	5,998	19,885
Colombia	..	..	28	208	..	328	7	4	71	68	1,615	12,788
Congo, Dem. Rep.	..	..	..	15	..	..	..	..	..	..	..	..
Congo, Rep.	34	37	48	8	..	..	..	..	..	..	..	..
Costa Rica	533	..	20	73	0.06	1,856	..	1	31	0	9,105	..
Côte d'Ivoire	..	..	31	31	..	..	..	0	11	..	..	..
Croatia	1,494	708	30	544	1.18	272	8	..	..	267	40,012	6,497
Cuba	1,611	1,121	16	148	..	..	..	..	..	111	40,928	4,307
Czech Republic	1,317	682	28	2,024	1.27	2,089	8	44	82	618	44,691	17,923
Denmark	3,240	2,643	25	3,950	1.94	6,527	21	..	..	3,339	158,225	11,537
Dominican Republic	..	..	35	6	..	..	..	..	30	..	..	..
Ecuador	140	17	27	39	..	27	6	..	62	15	475	..
Egypt, Arab Rep.	493	366	12	1,108	1.93	3	0	59	401	536	1,146	3,009
El Salvador	19	303	59	3	2.20	39	6	2	20	..	..	..
Eritrea	..	..	30	0	..	..	..	..	..	..	..	..
Estonia	2,164	540	27	222	0.78	830	30	2	8	14	41,742	4,660
Ethiopia	..	..	26	103	..	0	0	..	0	0	12	..
Finland	..	..	39	3,897	..	10,532	27	1,138	547	2,644	156,389	9,464
France	2,686	2,878	37	26,509	2.21	59,397	24	2,310	2,051	20,998	117,457	100,560
Gabon	..	..	29	16	..	..	..	..	..	..	..	..
Gambia, The	..	..	..	25	..	0	17	..	..	0	79,703	..
Georgia	..	..	39	128	..	..	..	..	..	273	41,687	2,574
Germany	2,873	1,362	47	36,233	2.31	82,958	18	2,821	5,454	74,232	146,529	85,770
Ghana	..	..	32	78	..	32	14	..	0	0	80,028	..
Greece	1,045	314	26	2,123	0.48	452	9	5	203	72	119,702	8,714
Guatemala	..	..	..	15	0.16	68	8	..	..	7	224	8,953
Guinea	..	..	34	3	..	..	..	..	0	..	..	..
Guinea-Bissau	..	..	0	3	..	..	..	..	..	0	1	..
Haiti	..	..	..	2	..	..	..	..	..	1	5	1,456
Honduras	..	..	24	10	..	6	2	0	10	8	148	5,045

	Scientists and engineers in R&D	Technicians in R&D	Science and engineering students	Science and technical journal articles	Expenditures for R&D	High-technology exports		Royalty and license fees		Patent applications filed [a]		Trademark applications filed [b]
	per million people	per million people	% of total tertiary level students		% of GNI	$ millions	% of manufactured exports	Receipts $ millions	Payments $ millions	Residents	Non-residents	Total
	1990-2000c	1990-2000c	1987-1997c	1997	1989-2000c	2000	2000	2000	2000	1999	1999	1999
Hungary	1,249	485	32	1,717	0.71	6,402	26	112	257	787	44,187	13,862
India	158	115	25	8,439	0.62	1,245	4	83	306	14	38,348	66,378
Indonesia	..	..	39	123	0.07	5,698	16	..	..	0	42,503	..
Iran, Islamic Rep.	590	174	39	332	0.49	38	2	0	0	366	177	..
Iraq	..	..	41	35	..	..	..	..	..	..	..	..
Ireland	2,132	589	31	1,118	1.54	31,278	48	504	7,899	1,226	119,569	4,518
Israel	1,570	518	49	5,321	3.69	7,418	25	500	349	2,728	46,686	8,759
Italy	1,322	806	30	16,405	1.04	19,306	9	563	1,198	9,613	118,647	44,906
Jamaica	..	..	64	49	..	1	0	6	41	..	..	..
Japan	4,960	663	21	43,891	2.80	127,368	28	10,227	11,007	361,094	81,151	121,861
Jordan	..	..	26	177	..	53	8	..	..	0	0	..
Kazakhstan	..	..	20	119	0.33	183	10	0	11	1,358	40,470	3,898
Kenya	..	..	19	235	..	13	4	7	77	28	80,516	2,705
Korea, Dem. Rep.	..	..	..	0	..	..	..	..	..	0	40,391	2,188
Korea, Rep.	2,139	574	32	4,619	2.70	53,950	35	688	3,221	56,214	76,913	87,332
Kuwait	214	65	29	173	..	35	1	0	0	..	..	..
Kyrgyz Republic	574	48	14	9	0.20	5	5	1	1	60	40,131	2,428
Lao PDR	..	..	20	2	..	..	..	..	..	..	..	609
Latvia	1,090	301	23	141	0.40	42	4	2	12	94	90,182	5,959
Lebanon	..	..	30	81	..	..	..	..	..	..	..	..
Lesotho	..	..	19	2	..	..	..	12	0	0	80,315	9
Liberia	..	..	18	1	..	..	..	..	..	0	41,120	1,216
Libya	361	493	..	12	..	..	..	..	..	..	..	..
Lithuania	2,031	632	31	198	..	95	4	0	12	86	90,331	6,284
Macedonia, FYR	387	29	47	49	0.35	7	1	3	6	64	89,361	3,921
Madagascar	12	37	25	..	0.18	4	3	1	11	9	41,237	510
Malawi	..	..	27	38	..	..	..	..	..	1	80,430	665
Malaysia	154	44	27	304	0.42	39,964	59	0	0	179	6,272	..
Mali	..	..	12	12	..	..	..	..	..	..	..	..
Mauritania	..	..	41	2	..	..	..	0	0	..	..	..
Mauritius	360	157	14	2	0.17	12	1	0	1	3	12	..
Mexico	213	73	32	1,915	0.36	31,053	22	43	407	468	49,532	46,146
Moldova	334	1,665	52	111	0.79	5	3	1	2	256	40,199	3,290
Mongolia	468	92	24	13	0.07	..	..	1	..	0	41,240	2,800
Morocco	..	..	41	271	..	604	12	38	210	0	3,649	3,281
Mozambique	..	..	42	9	..	1	2	..	0	..	..	1,308
Myanmar	..	..	56	3	..	..	..	0	0	..	..	..
Namibia	..	..	4	7	..	..	..	6	3	..	..	..
Nepal	..	..	13	35	..	0	0	..	..	..	..	..
Netherlands	2,490	1,464	39	11,008	2.01	44,439	35	2,176	2,565	6,395	117,118	..
New Zealand	2,197	732	20	2,308	1.21	365	10	49	308	1,650	45,990	16,576
Nicaragua	..	..	33	11	..	2	5	..	..	9	136	..
Niger	..	..	32	25	..	0	5	..	..	..	..	..
Nigeria	..	..	42	405	..	17	13	..	..	..	..	..
Norway	4,095	1,836	26	2,501	1.68	1,895	17	131	391	1,731	48,931	13,588
Oman	..	..	13	53	..	43	4	..	..	..	..	..
Pakistan	78	14	32	232	..	30	0	6	28	..	..	7,762
Panama	..	..	29	37	..	0	0	0	30	..	..	..
Papua New Guinea	..	..	10	31	..	34	42	..	..	..	..	..
Paraguay	..	..	20	4	..	5	3	203	2	..	..	..
Peru	229	1	34	63	0.00	35	3	0	57	48	944	..
Philippines	156	22	14	159	0.21	8,465	59	7	197	144	3,217	10,070
Poland	1,460	463	28	4,019	0.73	838	3	34	554	2,286	45,194	25,054
Portugal	1,583	166	36	1,085	0.63	1,045	5	21	255	133	159,533	15,782
Puerto Rico	..	..	..	..	..	..	..	..	..	..	..	..
Romania	1,393	584	21	751	0.79	445	6	3	45	1,069	90,235	9,060
Russian Federation	3,397	550	50	17,147	1.08	3,082	14	91	31	20,131	47,745	28,966

5.11 | Science and technology

	Scientists and engineers in R&D	Technicians in R&D	Science and engineering students	Science and technical journal articles	Expenditures for R&D	High-technology exports		Royalty and license fees		Patent applications filed [a]		Trademark applications filed [b]
	per million people 1990-2000c	per million people 1990-2000c	% of total tertiary level students 1987-1997c	1997	% of GNI 1989-2000c	$ millions 2000	% of manufactured exports 2000	Receipts $ millions 2000	Payments $ millions 2000	Residents 1999	Non-residents 1999	Total 1999
Rwanda	..	6	28	5	..	..	..	0	1	0	4	129
Saudi Arabia	..	..	17	613	..	22	0	0	0	72	1,144	..
Senegal	2	3	21	58	..	34	13	2	5	..	..	..
Sierra Leone	..	..	17	8	..	..	..	..	..	0	72,449	1,112
Singapore	2,182	283	..	1,164	1.13	73,643	63	..	..	374	51,121	15,753
Slovak Republic	1,706	790	40	950	0.98	382	4	16	58	222	42,857	9,913
Slovenia	2,161	877	26	517	1.47	368	5	12	49	292	90,680	7,420
Somalia	..	..	18	1	..	..	..	..	..	..	..	..
South Africa	992	303	29	1,927	0.62	21	1	62	142	116	26,354	..
Spain	1,562	456	31	11,210	0.84	6,727	8	403	1,681	3,394	159,696	85,742
Sri Lanka	188	45	34	61	..	109	3	..	..	0	41,263	..
Sudan	..	..	16	43	..	0	0	0	0	2	80,424	1,281
Swaziland	..	..	17	6	..	..	..	0	36	0	40,673	872
Sweden	4,507	404	38	8,219	3.76	25,739	22	1,275	900	9,122	155,929	15,562
Switzerland	3,058	1,399	34	6,935	2.55	14,260	19	..	..	6,412	155,991	11,061
Syrian Arab Republic	29	24	23	57	..	2	1	..	..	..	..	..
Tajikistan	660	..	17	29	..	..	..	..	..	38	40,103	2,270
Tanzania	..	..	37	89	..	6	6	0	4	0	14,467	2
Thailand	102	75	18	356	0.10	13,949	32	9	710	477	4,594	22,439
Togo	102	65	35	7	..	0	0	0	1	..	..	..
Trinidad and Tobago	145	258	58	41	0.14	11	1	0	0	0	41,238	1,196
Tunisia	124	57	33	188	0.30	124	3	9	3	..	..	..
Turkey	303	38	45	2,116	0.48	1,084	5	..	..	325	43,508	26,372
Turkmenistan	..	..	..	7	..	8	5	..	..	44	40,070	742
Uganda	25	15	17	46	0.76	2	10	..	0	0	80,421	..
Ukraine	2,121	595	42	2,163	0.97	..	..	1	663	5,415	42,858	9,578
United Arab Emirates	..	..	24	127	..	..	..	..	..	0	24,218	..
United Kingdom	2,678	1,014	34	38,530	1.81	72,616	32	7,361	6,126	31,326	161,549	70,880
United States	4,103	..	19	166,829	2.55	197,033	34	38,030	16,100	156,393	138,313	260,766
Uruguay	..	..	32	110	..	20	2	0	11	27	525	9,741
Uzbekistan	1,754	312	..	261	..	..	..	..	..	769	41,596	3,256
Venezuela, RB	194	32	26	429	0.34	80	3	0	0	201	2,323	..
Vietnam	274	..	..	106	..	..	..	..	..	37	42,175	6,518
West Bank and Gaza	..	..	..	..	..	..	..	..	..	..	..	..
Yemen, Rep.	..	..	5	10	..	..	0	..	..	..	..	..
Yugoslavia, Fed. Rep.	2,389	515	47	492	1.34	..	..	..	..	340	41,744	5,336
Zambia	..	..	16	23	..	..	..	..	..	5	87	959
Zimbabwe	..	..	24	100	..	9	2	..	..	1	80,167	14
World	.. w	.. w	35 w	512,637 s	2.12 w	1,003,791 s	20 w	72,194 s	74,051 s	810,407 s		6,177,807 s
Low income	..	..	28	13,565	..	5,766	7	105	1,108	7,027		1,342,958
Middle income	818	255	39	61,733	..	150,982	16	1,768	9,956	90,268		1,578,263
Lower middle income	787	229	41	32,967	..	45,591	14	526	3,265	25,996		931,209
Upper middle income	593	218	33	28,767	0.99	105,391	17	1,242	6,691	64,272		647,054
Low & middle income	..	..	35	75,298	..	156,748	16	1,873	11,064	97,295		2,921,221
East Asia & Pacific	496	193	43	14,817	0.88	100,485	25	784	5,409	56,541		298,643
Europe & Central Asia	2,212	478	44	34,905	0.83	15,567	10	313	1,753	35,952		1,373,268
Latin America & Carib.	287	..	30	10,075	0.58	40,497	16	501	2,666	3,618		284,873
Middle East & N. Africa	..	..	29	3,106	..	..	1	106	614	1,008		6,364
South Asia	158	114	24	8,896	0.62	..	3	87	338	14		79,611
Sub-Saharan Africa	..	..	29	3,499	..	..	8	82	283	162		878,462
High income	3,344	..	25	437,339	2.30	847,043	22	70,321	62,988	713,112		3,256,586
Europe EMU	2,141	951	38	117,764	1.97	277,585	16	11,019	23,422	123,795		1,652,255

a. Other patent applications filed in 1999 include those filed under the auspices of the African Intellectual Proprty Organization (30 by residents, 41,068 by non-residents, African Regional Industrial Property Organization (7 by residents, 40,720 by nonresidents), European Patent Office (55,947 by residents, 65,869 by nonresidents) and Eurasian Patent Organization (366 by residents, 41,476 by nonresidents). The original information was provided by the World Intellectual Property Organization (WIPO). The International Bureau of WIPO assumes no liability or responsibility with respect to the transformation of these data. b. Other trademark applications filed in 1999 include those filed under the auspices of the African Intellectual Property Organization (1730), African Regional Industrial Property Organization (15), and the Office for Harmonization in the Internal Market (41,255). The original information was provided by the World Intellectual Property Organization (WIPO). The International Bureau of WIPO assumes no liability or responsibility with respect to the transformation of these data. c. Data are for the latest year available; see *Primary data documentation* for the year.

About the data

Technological innovation, often fueled by government-led research and development (R&D), has been the driving force for industrial growth around the world. The best opportunities to improve living standards—including new ways of reducing poverty—will come from science and technology.

Science is advancing rapidly in virtually all fields, particularly biotechnology, and playing a growing economic role: countries unable to access, generate, and apply relevant scientific knowledge will fall even further behind. And there is greater appreciation of the need for high-quality scientific input into public policy issues such as regional and global environmental concerns.

Science and technology cover a range of issues too complex and too broad to be quantified by any single set of indicators, but those in the table shed light on countries' "technological base"—the availability of skilled human resources, the number of scientific and technical articles published, the competitive edge countries enjoy in high-technology exports, sales and purchases of technology through royalties and licenses, the number of patent applications filed, and trademarks issued.

The United Nations Educational, Scientific, and Cultural Organization (UNESCO) collects data on scientific and technical workers and R&D expenditures from member states, mainly through questionnaires and special surveys as well as from official reports and publications, supplemented by information from other national and international sources. UNESCO reports either the stock of scientists, engineers, and technicians or the number of economically active persons qualified in those fields. UNESCO supplements these data with estimates of the number of qualified scientists and engineers by counting the number of people who have completed education at ISCED (International Standard Classification of Education) levels 6 and 7; qualified technicians are estimated using the number of people who have completed education at ISCED level 5. The data are normally calculated in terms of full-time-equivalent staff, the quality of whose training and education varies widely. Similarly, R&D expenditures are no guarantee of progress; governments need to pay close attention to the practices that make them effective.

The data on science and engineering students refer to those enrolled at the tertiary level, normally after their successful completion of education at the secondary level. These data are reported to UNESCO by national education authorities. (For further details on UNESCO education surveys see *About the data* for table 2.12.)

The methodology used for determining a country's high-technology exports was developed by the Organisation for Economic Co-operation and Development in collaboration with Eurostat. Termed the "product approach" to distinguish it from a "sectoral approach," the method is based on the calculation of R&D intensity (R&D expendi-

ture divided by total sales) for groups of products from six countries (Germany, Italy, Japan, the Netherlands, Sweden, and the United States). Because industrial sectors characterized by a few high-technology products may also produce many low-technology products, the product approach is more appropriate for analyzing international trade than is the sectoral approach. To construct a list of high-technology manufactured products (services are excluded), the R&D intensity was calculated for products classified at the three-digit level of the Standard International Trade Classification revision 3. The final list was determined at the four- and five-digit levels. At these levels, since no R&D data were available, final selection was based on patent data and expert opinion. This methodology takes only R&D intensity into account. Other characteristics of high technology are also important, such as know-how, scientific and technical personnel, and technology embodied in patents; considering these characteristics would result in a different list. (See Hatzichronoglou 1997 for further details.) Note that the R&D for high-technology exports may not have occurred in the reporting country.

The counts of scientific and technical journal articles include those published in a stable set of about 5,000 of the world's most influential scientific and technical journals, tracked since 1985 by the Institute of Scientific Information's Science Citation Index (SCI) and Social Science Citation Index (SSCI). (See *Definitions* for the fields covered.) The SCI and SSCI databases cover the core set of scientific journals but may exclude some of regional or local importance. They may also reflect some bias toward English-language journals.

Most countries have adopted systems that protect patentable inventions. Under most patent legislation, to be protected by law (patentable), an idea must be new in the sense that it has not already been published or publicly used; it must be nonobvious (involve an inventive step), in the sense that it would not have occurred to any specialist in the industrial field had such a specialist been asked to find a solution to the problem; and it must be capable of industrial application, in the sense that it can be industrially manufactured or used. Information on patent applications filed is shown separately for residents and non-residents of the country. The World Intellectual Property Organization estimates that at the end of 1998 about 4 million patents were in force in the world.

A trademark provides protection to owner by ensuring the exclusive right to use it to identify goods or services or to authorize another to use it in return for payment. The period of protection varies, but a trademark can be renewed indefinitely beyond the time limit on payment of additional fees. The system helps consumers identify and purchase a product or service because its nature and quality, indicated by its unique trademark, meets their needs.

Definitions

• **Scientists and engineers in R&D** are people trained at the tertiary level to work in any field of science who are engaged in professional R&D activity. • **Technicians in R&D** are people engaged in professional R&D activity who have received vocational or technical training in any branch of knowledge or technology. Most such jobs require three years beyond the first stage of secondary education. • **Science and engineering students** include students at the tertiary level in the following fields: engineering, natural science, mathematics and computers, and social and behavioral sciences. • **Scientific and technical journal articles** refer to scientific and engineering articles published in the following fields: physics, biology, chemistry, mathematics, clinical medicine, bio-medical research, engineering and technology, and earth and space sciences. • **Expenditures for R&D** are current and capital expenditures on creative, systematic activity that increases the stock of knowledge. Included are fundamental and applied research and experimental development work leading to new devices, products, or processes. • **High-technology exports** are products with high R&D intensity. They include high-technology products such as in aerospace, computers, pharmaceuticals, scientific instruments, and electrical machinery. • **Royalty and license fees** are payments and receipts between residents and nonresidents for the authorized use of intangible, non-produced, non-financial assets and proprietary rights (such as patents, copyrights, trademarks, industrial processes, and franchises) and for the use, through licensing agreements, of produced originals of prototypes (such as manuscripts and films). • **Patent applications filed** are applications filed with a national patent office for exclusive rights for an invention—a product or process that provides a new way of doing something or offers a new technical solution to a problem. A patent provides protection for the invention to the owner of the patent for a limited period, generally 20 years. • **Trademarks** are distinctive signs that identify certain goods or services as those produced or provided by a specific person or enterprise.

Data sources

The data on technical personnel, science and engineering students, and R&D expenditures are from UNESCO's *Statistical Yearbook*. The data on scientific and technical journal articles are from the National Science Foundation's *Science and Engineering Indicators 2000*. The information on high-technology exports is from the United Nations' Commodity Trade (COMTRADE) database. The data on royalty and license fees are from the International Monetary Fund's *Balance of Payments Statistics Yearbook,* and the data on patents and trademarks are from the World Intellectual Property Organization's *Industrial Property Statistics.*

GLOBAL LINKS

Globalization and growth

Global integration has helped countries with a combined population of 3 billion—but countries with a combined population of 2 billion have fallen behind.

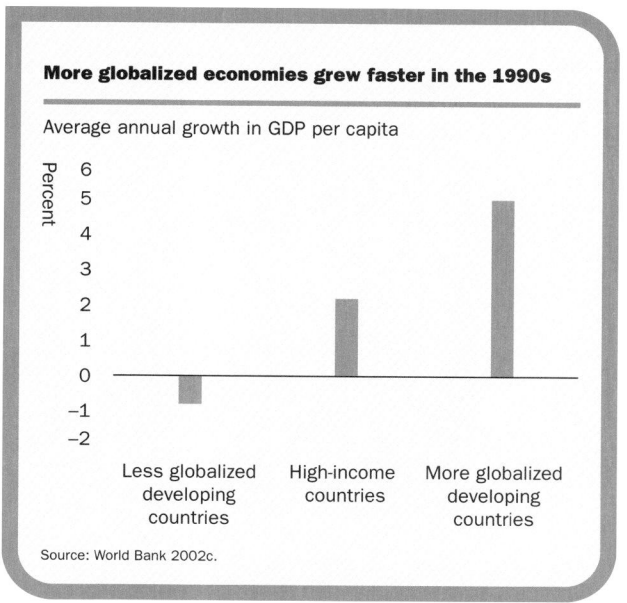

More globalized economies grew faster in the 1990s

Average annual growth in GDP per capita

Source: World Bank 2002c.

Building an inclusive world economy

What is globalization? In broad terms it reflects the growing links between people, communities, and economies around the world. These links are complex—the result of lower communications and transport costs and greater flows of ideas and capital between high- and low-income countries.

Integrating with the world economy can be a powerful spur to growth and poverty reduction. Low-income developing countries with about 3 billion people have switched from exporting primary commodities to exporting manufactures and services. Between the mid-1970s and 1998 manufactures increased from 25 percent of their exports to more than 80 percent. And per capita incomes in developing countries increased by about 5 percent a year in the 1990s, with the number of poor people declining by 125 million between 1990 and 1999.

But in developing countries with a combined population of about 2 billion, overall economic growth declined in the 1990s and poverty has been rising, in part because these countries trade less with the rest of the world and often suffer from conflicts, corruption, and poor governance. Their poverty goes beyond the loss of jobs and income—to limited voice and poor access to health and education, all needed for the climb out of poverty.

It is widely thought that economic integration will lead to cultural and institutional homogenization. But "globalizers" such as China, India, Malaysia, and Mexico have maintained rich cultural traditions. What is true is that global trade imposes standardization, making it important for trade and investment agreements to respect local customs, social policies, and labor and environmental standards.

Three waves of globalization

There have been three waves of globalization since 1870. Since the latest wave started in the 1980s many developing countries have evolved from exporting primary commodities to exporting manufactures and services.

The first wave of global integration, between 1870 and 1914, was led by improvements in transport technology (from sailing ships to steamships) and by lower tariff barriers. Exports nearly doubled to about 8 percent of world income.

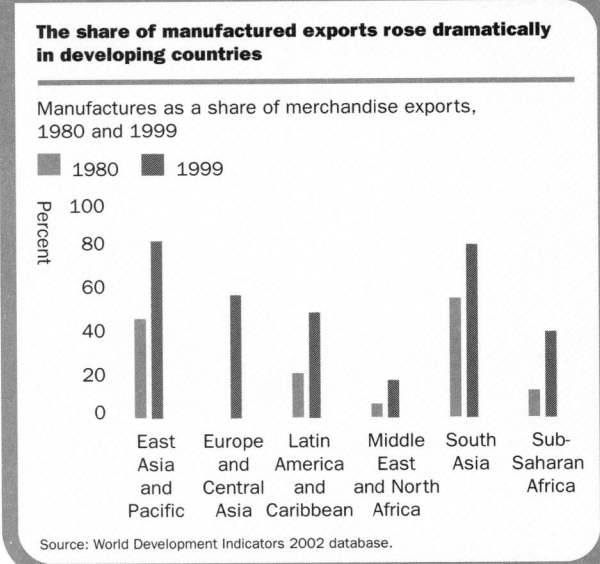

The share of manufactured exports rose dramatically in developing countries

Manufactures as a share of merchandise exports, 1980 and 1999

■ 1980 ■ 1999

Source: World Development Indicators 2002 database.

The second wave, from 1945 to 1980, was also characterized by lower trade barriers and transport costs. Sea freight charges fell by a third between 1950 and 1970. And trade regained the ground it lost during the Great Depression.

Spurring the third wave of integration has been further progress in transport (containerization and airfreight) and communications technology (falling telecommunications costs associated with satellites, fiber-optic cable, cell phones, and the Internet). And along with declining tariffs on manufactured goods in high-income countries, many developing countries lowered barriers to foreign investment and improved their investment climates.

Integration with the world economy has increased incomes and

Globalization and poverty

How has the third wave of globalization affected growth, poverty, and inequality? Growth for the new globalizers has accelerated, to rates even higher than those for rich countries, so they are catching up.

And growth is good for poor people. Studies show that their income rises one for one with overall growth (for every percentage point increase in overall per capita growth, poor people's incomes increase at the same rate). In developing economies the number of people in absolute poverty declined by 125 million between 1990 and 1999.

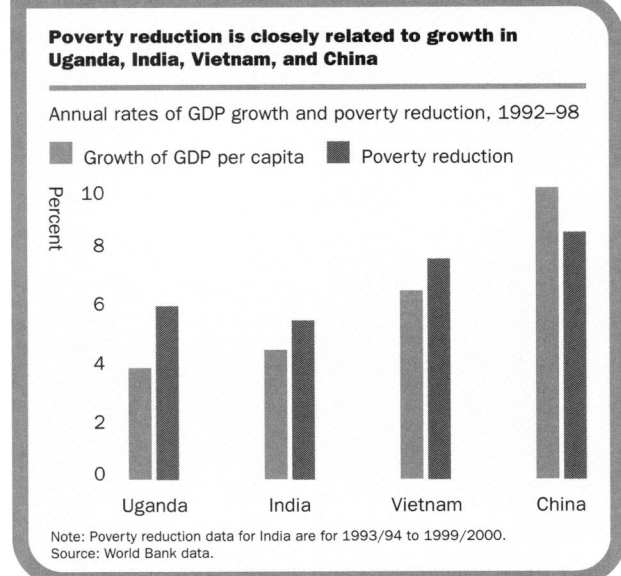

Poverty reduction is closely related to growth in Uganda, India, Vietnam, and China

Annual rates of GDP growth and poverty reduction, 1992–98

■ Growth of GDP per capita ■ Poverty reduction

Note: Poverty reduction data for India are for 1993/94 to 1999/2000.
Source: World Bank data.

In 1995 inequality between countries was less than half what it had been in 1960. And within economies people's incomes are generally more equally distributed in those that are more integrated. But while inequality has declined in some globalizing countries, overall for the globalizers inequality within countries has increased, mainly because of the rise in inequality in China—between rural and urban areas and between provinces with urban agglomerations and those without.

Although globalization leads to higher wages and employment in some sectors, some people still lose out, especially in the short run. So it is important to identify who has been left behind—and to offer support programs for the neediest.

Higher returns on education

Economic integration raises the return on education and highlights the importance of improvements in the delivery of social services.

Economic integration with global markets encourages people to invest in education. Why? Because as countries open to the global economy, new technologies and production processes are introduced, requiring a more skilled workforce. A "skill premium" (the extra pay that skilled workers get relative to unskilled workers) then raises the incomes of some of the

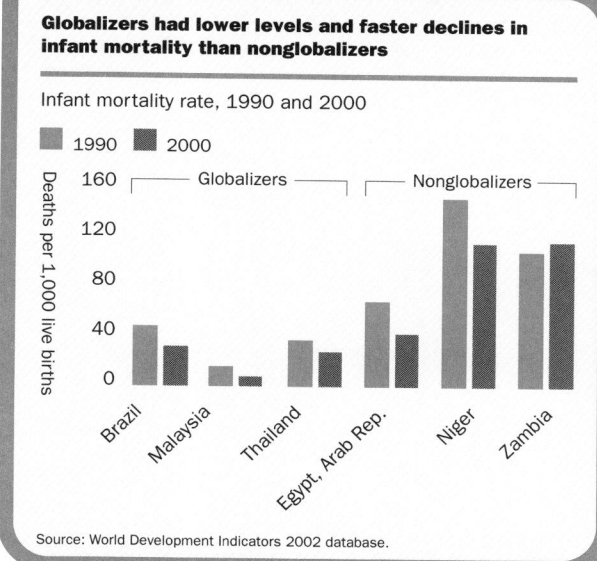

Globalizers had lower levels and faster declines in infant mortality than nonglobalizers

Infant mortality rate, 1990 and 2000

■ 1990 ▨ 2000

Deaths per 1,000 live births

Globalizers: Brazil, Malaysia, Thailand

Nonglobalizers: Egypt, Arab Rep., Niger, Zambia

Source: World Development Indicators 2002 database.

workers. But others who have not had good access to health and education services may fall behind. If this gap in incomes and access persists, globalization can lead to greater inequalities in society.

Affordable access to health and education services thus helps to ensure that the poor benefit from growth. Some of the more globalized developing countries reduced infant mortality by more than 30 percent during the 1990s, compared with an average decline of about 12 percent for all developing countries. Although infant mortality rates have also declined for some nonglobalizing countries, for others the rates are increasing to extremely high levels.

lowered poverty in some countries, but some have been left behind.

Culture and environment

These tangible effects on economic growth and living standards are not the only outcome. Globalization also affects culture and the environment. The greater economic power of the newly globalizing economies gives them more interest and influence in the international arena. Their rising incomes also reduce the risk of conflict, compared with

countries whose economies have stagnated or are in decline. In Africa, for example, where countries have become more dependent on primary commodity production and exports, there is a two-way relationship between conflict and economic performance. As economic performance worsens, the risk of conflict rises—and as performance improves, the risk of conflict diminishes.

And there are risks of cultural dilution. More diverse societies have broader sources of information and dynamic business networks that improve productivity, competition, and growth, especially under democratic governments that allow people to make choices and express preferences. But even in cultures that are very resilient, the traditions handed down from one generation to another can be weakened by the spread of ideas, goods, and advertising from abroad.

Economic integration may also pose threats to the environment. As production and consumption increase, both globalizers and non-globalizers face environmental challenges. But as incomes increase, countries can use the additional resources to tackle environmental issues. And environmental improvements can be made at low cost. For example, water quality can be upgraded by installing water filters, which can often remove close to half the pollutants.

Trade tariffs and the poor

Trade helps reduce poverty, but high tariffs reduce access to world markets.

Low-income developing countries often depend on agriculture and labor-intensive manufactures, which account for about 70 percent of the exports of least developed countries. Their agricultural exports help reduce rural poverty, and exports of textiles and clothing tend to reduce urban poverty.

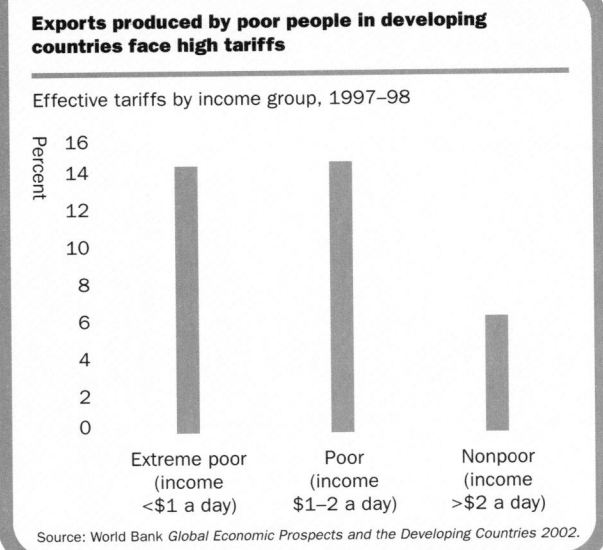

Exports produced by poor people in developing countries face high tariffs

Effective tariffs by income group, 1997–98

Source: World Bank *Global Economic Prospects and the Developing Countries 2002.*

Trade-related production is a major source of jobs and income for the poor, but the goods they produce face the highest tariffs in developed countries, reducing their access to world markets. The tariffs faced by the extreme poor (those living on less than $1 a day) and the poor (those living on $1–2 a day) are about twice as high as those faced by the nonpoor.

Integration with the world economy

Barriers to trade

Countries regulate imports by applying a combination of tariffs and other measures. Even when average tariffs are low, high or peak tariffs (rates exceeding 15 percent) may be placed on imports of "sensitive commodities," often the goods produced by the world's poorest people. In the European Union and Japan tariff peaks are common for agricultural products; in the United States, for labor-intensive textiles and clothing. For many developing countries tariff peaks cover a high proportion of imports, although the share is falling for such countries as Bangladesh, Brazil, and Zimbabwe.

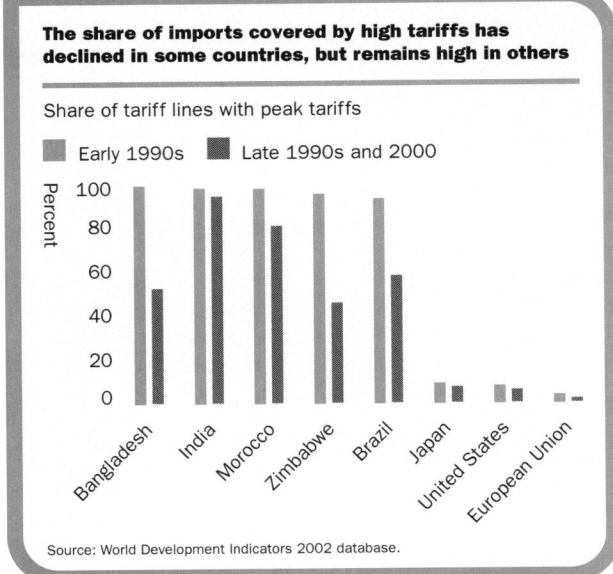

The share of imports covered by high tariffs has declined in some countries, but remains high in others

Share of tariff lines with peak tariffs

■ Early 1990s   ■ Late 1990s and 2000

Source: World Development Indicators 2002 database.

Nontariff barriers also limit imports of particular goods. They include quotas, prohibitions, licensing schemes, export restraint arrangements, and health and quarantine measures. And large subsidies to agricultural producers in high-income economies distort agricultural commodity trade by reducing their agricultural imports and the ability of developing country agricultural producers to export.

The European Union's new initiative, "Everything but Arms," phases in duty-free and quota-free access for all but 25 tariff lines related to arms trade. Policies such as this that grant "aid for trade" may help developing countries achieve greater development success.

Financial flows

Financial flows, used well, can contribute to growth and poverty reduction.

Private capital flows to developing countries—mainly foreign direct investment and portfolio investment—as measured by net long-term resource flows, increased dramatically in the 1990s, from $62 billion in 1991 to almost $226 billion in 2000, dropping to $160 billion in 2001.

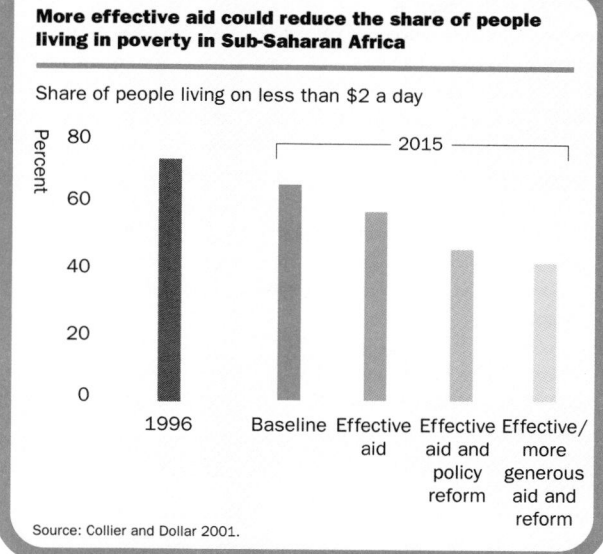

More effective aid could reduce the share of people living in poverty in Sub-Saharan Africa

Share of people living on less than $2 a day

Percent

Source: Collier and Dollar 2001.

But more capital does not automatically translate into higher growth. Also needed are better government policies and stronger institutions—especially if growth is to reduce poverty and inequality.

Take Sub-Saharan Africa. If current growth and policies remain through 2015, the share of the population living on less than $2 a day will decline from about 72 percent to 64 percent. That's based on average annual economic growth of a mere 0.1 percent. But policy reform and more effective aid could increase growth enough to reduce the poverty rate to about 42 percent by 2015.

through trade, finance, and migration

Migration

Of the 83 million people added to the world's population every year, 82 million are in developing economies, so the pressures for migration of unskilled workers will increase. Combining developed country capital and developing country labor could bring mutual economic benefits. But legal migration is very restricted, so illegal immigration is growing. Still, for most countries net migration rates are small relative to the total population. In 2000 Albania and Liberia had the highest rates of emigration, while Singapore had the highest immigration rate.

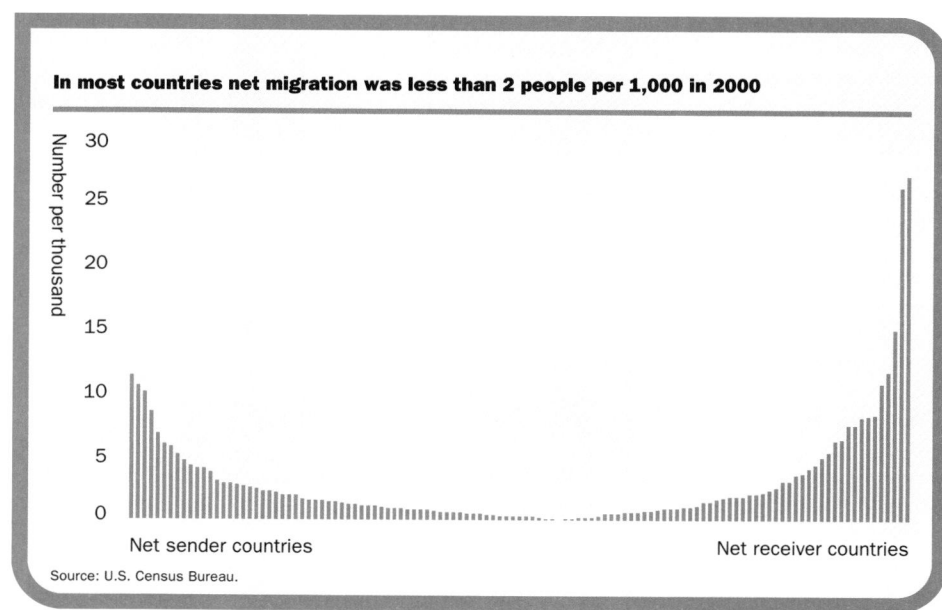

In most countries net migration was less than 2 people per 1,000 in 2000

Number per thousand

Net sender countries

Net receiver countries

Source: U.S. Census Bureau.

Seven actions—local and global

While many poor people may benefit from globalization, the challenge is to extend the improvements in income, health, education, and participation to those left behind. How? By taking actions in seven areas at local and global levels.

1 **Successfully complete the trade negotiations launched in Doha to reduce restrictions on global trade and improve developing countries' access to markets in both developing and high-income countries.**

• Curtail producer subsidies and other indirect support to agriculture in high-income countries, which amount to as much as $1 billion a day—several times all development assistance.

• Reduce tariffs in developing countries. Average tariffs on imported labor-intensive industrial products are highest in developing countries—about 35 percent in South Asia in 1997–99, while less than 5 percent in high-income countries.

• Take mutually reinforcing actions to support trade-led development. For high-income countries this means providing enhanced aid for trade (infrastructure, customs, education, and technical assistance to implement World Trade Organization accords). For developing countries it means undertaking pro-poor trade reforms. The resulting new growth could lift an additional 300 million people above the poverty line by 2015.

2 **Improve the investment climate—with good economic governance, control of corruption, well-functioning institutions, and sound infrastructure.**

• Good governance pays off: countries with good institutions and policies grew at about 3 percent a year (GDP per capita) in 1964–94; countries with poor institutional capability and policies, at only 0.4 percent.

• Surveys of firms in 10 Indian states show that value added per worker is 30 percent higher in states with good investment climates.

• Small and medium-size enterprises, important for generating new jobs, are a powerful force in poverty reduction. In Bosnia and Herzegovina small enterprises account for 61 percent of GDP and 75 percent of employment.

Agenda for action

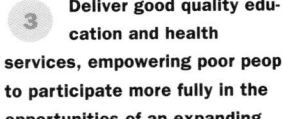

3 **Deliver good quality education and health services, empowering poor people to participate more fully in the opportunities of an expanding economy.**

• Good health and long life expectancy depend on access to health services, clean water and sanitation, and education, especially for women.

• The private sector can contribute here too. In Sub-Saharan Africa about a third of primary education is provided by the private sector. In India more than 80 percent of poor people seek treatment for acute respiratory illnesses in private health facilities.

4 **Provide social protection tailored to the labor market.** As people lose jobs, they may need temporary support.

• Some support programs for the unemployed, such as public works and job training, are designed to reach the poorest workers. Others, such as unemployment insurance or mandatory savings and severance pay, often do not.

• Argentina's *Trabajar* public works program provides temporary employment to improve infrastructure in poor communities. Since March 1996 it has created 730,000 jobs. About 80 percent of beneficiaries are from the poorest households.

• Bangladesh has addressed child labor with its Food-for-Education program, providing food to poor families that send their young children to school.

5 **Provide more and better managed aid for low-income countries that are undertaking reforms.** More money doesn't always result in better development outcomes, but it can make a difference in countries that have sound management.

• The quality of government spending can be more important than the quantity. In one study the 10 developing countries with the best child mortality rates spent less on health than the 10 with the worst rates.

• In Vietnam reform gave civil society more voice, and donors focused on policy advice and technical assistance during adjustment. As policies improved, aid increased from about 1 percent of GDP in the late 1980s to more than 3 percent by 1995.

• In Pakistan in the mid-1990s only 45 percent of young girls were in school, but an innovative program to support the startup of girls' schools in Baluchistan led to an immediate leap—to 70 percent—in girls' enrollment.

 **Offer debt relief to poor countries with unsustainable debt burdens.** Combined with sound economic management and an improved investment climate, debt relief can help countries with crushing debt burdens, especially in Africa.

• The Debt Initiative for Heavily Indebted Poor Countries (HIPCs) offers debt relief to poor countries adopting sound policies and poverty reduction strategies.

• In late 1998 the World Bank and the International Monetary Fund (IMF) joined nongovernmental organizations, churches, and civil society in a global consultative review, leading to an endorsement to cut external debt service by more than twice as much as under the earlier framework. The World Bank will reduce its debt claims by almost $11 billion, and the IMF by about $4 billion.

• In January 2002, 24 countries were receiving debt service relief under the enhanced HIPC initiative, relief that will total $36 billion over time.

7 **Tackle greenhouse gases and global warming—to avert environmental disasters that may result from global warming.**

• According to the Intergovernmental Panel on Climate Change, average global temperatures will rise between 1.4 and 5.8 degrees Celsius over the next 100 years, a rate of warming higher than in the past 10,000 years.

• Even small changes in temperature can be devastating for agricultural production and food security.

• Rising sea levels could displace millions of people in low-lying areas of the Ganges River and Nile Delta, and threaten the existence of small island states.

> We are convinced that globalization can and does contribute to development, but we cannot ignore those who are left out, nor can we fail to recognize how much better development progress could be.
>
> James D. Wolfensohn,
> President,
> World Bank

6.1 | Integration with the global economy

	Trade in goods				Changes in trade as shares of GDP	Growth in real trade less growth in real GDP	Gross private capital flows		Gross foreign direct investment	
	% of GDP		% of goods GDP		% change	percentage points	% of GDP		% of GDP	
	1990	2000	1990	2000	1980-1999	1990-2000	1990	2000	1990	2000
Afghanistan	..	..	..	..	..	..	..	..	..	..
Albania	29.0	35.7	34.5	46.2	..	7.8	18.0	6.5	0.0	3.8
Algeria	36.6	53.8	55.0	76.2	-24.6	-0.7	2.6	..	0.0	..
Angola	53.5	127.5	91.0	155.9	..	..	10.1	44.9	3.3	39.9
Argentina	11.6	18.1	27.0	49.8	154.9	7.0	8.2	10.9	1.3	4.5
Armenia	..	61.9	..	..	..	-12.7	..	17.8	..	6.6
Australia	26.4	34.7	71.3	89.5	72.9	3.8	9.3	17.4	3.7	5.3
Austria	55.9	70.1	140.5	168.0	72.5	3.3	9.8	49.7	1.5	6.5
Azerbaijan	..	59.6	..	102.0	..	13.2	..	3.0	..	2.5
Bangladesh	17.6	31.5	..	..	130.6	6.0	0.9	3.6	0.0	0.6
Belarus	..	53.0	..	93.0	..	-5.8	..	2.0	..	0.3
Belgium	120.3	138.1	316.6	412.8	44.5	2.5	18.5	120.5	6.7	26.6
Benin	30.0	45.1	60.8	86.0	-44.2	-2.1	10.7	13.4	3.7	2.8
Bolivia	33.1	35.9	..	..	46.3	1.0	3.1	14.2	0.7	8.9
Bosnia and Herzegovina	..	87.4	..	228.6	..	-1.0	..	..	..	..
Botswana	99.0	92.9	162.5	..	..	-3.4	9.1	6.9	4.4	1.4
Brazil	11.6	19.1	..	..	72.1	5.8	1.9	10.9	0.4	6.0
Bulgaria	48.9	93.1	70.8	190.3	..	3.3	39.2	20.7	0.0	8.4
Burkina Faso	24.9	35.3	44.4	67.3	-25.5	-3.8	1.1	..	0.0	..
Burundi	27.0	28.6	35.1	38.6	26.8	6.0	3.7	6.4	0.1	1.7
Cambodia	22.4	40.2	33.6	46.4	..	7.5	3.2	6.8	1.7	3.9
Cameroon	30.5	36.5	55.4	56.1	56.4	2.3	15.5	..	1.1	..
Canada	43.8	75.8	103.1	..	113.3	5.4	8.1	30.0	2.7	16.1
Central African Republic	18.4	29.1	26.4	37.9	..	..	2.2	..	0.5	..
Chad	27.2	33.6	54.9	61.6	-29.4	-4.3	5.6	..	0.0	..
Chile	52.9	51.4	100.1	110.7	65.5	3.3	15.0	24.1	2.2	12.0
China	32.5	43.9	47.4	65.8	..	-2.7	2.5	12.7	1.2	4.3
Hong Kong, China	223.5	256.2	784.5	1,142.7	209.7	4.4	..	188.8	..	89.2
Colombia	30.7	30.2	54.8	62.4	80.7	4.2	3.1	12.3	1.3	4.5
Congo, Dem. Rep.	20.2	14.7	34.6	..	38.2	-3.6	..	..	..	..
Congo, Rep.	57.2	105.4	107.0	138.5	10.9	6.0	6.6	..	0.0	..
Costa Rica	60.2	77.2	..	..	69.0	4.7	7.0	10.2	2.9	4.3
Côte d'Ivoire	47.9	75.9	86.0	147.1	38.8	1.0	3.5	6.5	0.4	2.5
Croatia	89.3	64.6	165.6	123.7	..	4.5	..	19.8	..	5.5
Cuba	..	..	..	..	..	..	..	..	..	..
Czech Republic	84.0	120.5	..	..	..	9.8	..	23.7	..	9.3
Denmark	52.6	57.9	144.1	160.1	55.3	2.1	15.1	54.9	2.0	38.1
Dominican Republic	73.2	78.8	163.2	174.2	51.5	-0.2	5.0	9.3	1.9	5.2
Ecuador	42.8	61.1	..	..	3.1	0.6	10.7	31.5	1.2	5.3
Egypt, Arab Rep.	27.4	18.9	54.2	35.3	-40.9	-1.3	6.8	6.7	1.7	1.3
El Salvador	38.4	59.2	88.5	146.7	48.7	7.5	2.0	9.3	0.8	1.5
Eritrea	..	..	..	..	..	0.0	..	..	..	..
Estonia	..	149.5	..	292.9	..	9.9	3.7	26.4	2.0	10.2
Ethiopia	20.2	..	31.3	..	..	2.7	2.0	3.4	0.0	..
Finland	39.2	65.5	86.5	150.1	57.6	5.4	17.4	88.6	3.6	34.4
France	37.1	46.6	101.6	136.3	63.1	4.2	20.6	36.1	3.9	16.4
Gabon	52.5	88.8	97.7	..	2.8	-1.7	18.0	24.5	8.4	14.5
Gambia, The	75.4	49.1	146.7	81.6	-34.7	-2.7	0.9	..	0.0	..
Georgia	..	34.8	..	..	..	24.7	..	4.9	..	4.3
Germany	46.0	56.3	106.2	156.6	40.6	3.4	9.8	40.8	1.8	13.3
Ghana	35.7	91.4	58.0	150.6	-1.3	6.9	2.7	4.5	0.3	2.1
Greece	33.2	32.5	83.5	79.1	103.1	3.9	3.9	16.1	1.2	2.9
Guatemala	36.8	39.1	..	..	-13.4	3.5	2.9	22.4	0.6	10.1
Guinea	26.3	40.2	45.5	64.1	..	-1.4	3.9	4.0	0.6	1.8
Guinea-Bissau	55.7	83.5	69.1	83.9	-27.9	2.6	23.0	1.3	0.0	..
Haiti	16.5	29.6	28.8	..	168.1	8.8	1.0	4.1	0.3	0.3
Honduras	57.9	70.9	106.4	131.6	-21.8	-0.2	7.2	9.5	1.4	4.8

	Trade in goods				Changes in trade as shares of GDP	Growth in real trade less growth in real GDP	Gross private capital flows		Gross foreign direct investment	
	% of GDP		% of goods GDP		% change	percentage points	% of GDP		% of GDP	
	1990	2000	1990	2000	1980-1999	1990-2000	1990	2000	1990	2000
Hungary	61.5	131.9	102.4	214.8	81.8	8.8	4.6	25.0	0.0	5.0
India	13.1	20.3	..	..	61.6	4.4	0.8	3.0	0.0	0.6
Indonesia	41.5	62.4	64.4	97.2	-16.5	1.3	4.1	8.5	1.0	4.2
Iran, Islamic Rep.	27.1	43.1	50.8	106.6	-63.3	-9.5	2.6	2.3	0.0	0.0
Iraq	41.2	..	..	..	..	..	..	..	..	..
Ireland	93.9	139.3	186.7	273.9	129.1	6.8	22.2	299.9	2.2	49.2
Israel	55.0	62.9	..	..	25.1	4.1	6.2	19.5	0.7	6.7
Italy	32.0	44.2	83.3	121.7	68.5	3.8	10.6	23.6	1.3	2.4
Jamaica	70.6	60.9	164.3	159.1	42.2	0.2	9.1	15.7	3.3	7.2
Japan	17.1	17.7	44.4	55.2	39.3	2.6	5.4	10.3	1.7	0.9
Jordan	91.1	77.2	205.2	208.4	-7.3	-3.2	6.3	5.9	1.7	2.0
Kazakhstan	..	77.8	..	142.2	..	-4.3	..	12.3	..	7.8
Kenya	37.0	46.7	66.4	97.9	-9.1	2.2	3.6	6.6	0.7	1.1
Korea, Dem. Rep.	..	..	..	..	..	..	..	..	..	..
Korea, Rep.	53.4	72.8	102.7	153.8	121.6	7.5	6.2	11.5	0.7	3.2
Kuwait	59.8	71.9	112.9	..	..	..	19.3	43.0	1.3	0.7
Kyrgyz Republic	..	81.3	..	119.4	..	-1.8	..	10.4	..	4.5
Lao PDR	32.3	52.7	42.5	..	..	..	3.7	8.7	0.7	5.4
Latvia	..	70.7	..	185.6	..	5.3	1.7	32.0	0.5	5.8
Lebanon	106.5	42.1	..	..	..	-3.1	..	..	..	..
Lesotho	118.8	100.1	185.0	155.9	0.9	-1.4	9.4	15.6	2.7	12.9
Liberia	..	..	..	..	..	..	..	..	..	..
Libya	..	..	..	..	..	..	..	..	..	..
Lithuania	..	81.9	..	179.9	..	10.0	..	14.3	..	3.4
Macedonia, FYR	103.8	100.3	168.9	186.8	..	7.2	..	17.4	..	4.9
Madagascar	28.9	24.8	43.6	..	-25.1	2.8	1.8	5.0	0.7	2.1
Malawi	53.1	55.4	71.0	86.4	-32.4	-2.8	3.2	..	0.0	..
Malaysia	133.3	201.3	232.1	356.5	124.8	4.2	10.3	16.8	5.3	2.0
Mali	40.4	54.0	64.5	83.2	125.5	1.2	2.0	..	0.2	..
Mauritania	84.1	68.5	134.0	119.4	-25.5	-2.5	48.8	40.6	0.7	0.0
Mauritius	106.4	81.6	200.3	180.0	32.6	0.3	7.2	26.2	1.6	6.4
Mexico	32.1	60.8	76.9	155.3	223.4	10.2	9.2	6.3	1.0	2.3
Moldova	..	96.8	..	177.9	..	12.7	..	34.6	..	9.9
Mongolia	..	93.4	..	180.2	..	..	..	10.1	..	3.4
Morocco	42.9	56.7	85.5	124.1	30.4	3.3	5.5	3.0	0.6	0.8
Mozambique	40.8	35.6	68.9	66.7	..	0.8	0.4	15.6	0.4	3.7
Myanmar	..	..	..	..	17.0	..	..	..	..	..
Namibia	88.9	85.2	174.4	165.8	..	1.4	17.0	11.4	4.7	3.6
Nepal	24.7	43.2	..	..	127.1	6.0	3.5	4.8	0.0	0.0
Netherlands	87.3	112.5	228.9	289.2	44.4	2.4	29.7	103.6	8.3	35.3
New Zealand	44.1	54.5	122.3	..	67.5	3.0	18.0	19.2	11.6	8.3
Nicaragua	95.9	100.9	183.0	183.8	65.2	6.2	9.0	22.1	0.0	10.6
Niger	27.0	40.3	49.9	68.6	-46.9	-2.5	2.8	..	1.6	..
Nigeria	67.8	80.3	91.2	105.3	-39.9	2.1	5.9	13.0	2.1	2.9
Norway	53.1	58.4	127.8	119.7	14.8	1.6	11.9	39.4	2.1	11.4
Oman	77.7	74.8	127.4	..	..	..	3.8	10.2	1.4	0.7
Pakistan	32.8	32.8	..	..	-13.3	-1.6	4.2	2.5	0.6	0.5
Panama	35.4	42.9	..	..	..	-1.5	106.6	49.2	2.6	7.1
Papua New Guinea	72.6	81.2	122.2	116.8	-7.5	-0.3	5.7	27.0	4.8	8.4
Paraguay	43.9	40.5	82.8	79.9	142.3	-0.7	5.4	8.9	1.5	1.7
Peru	25.5	29.5	..	..	45.9	4.2	3.2	5.1	0.2	1.3
Philippines	47.6	98.5	84.5	192.9	142.3	4.3	4.4	48.4	1.2	2.8
Poland	43.9	51.1	75.2	99.7	..	8.4	11.0	13.3	0.2	6.6
Portugal	58.8	58.6	141.0	151.9	118.5	3.9	11.5	53.4	3.9	15.9
Puerto Rico	..	..	..	..	..	..	..	..	..	..
Romania	32.8	63.8	45.2	116.7	..	7.9	2.9	7.7	0.0	2.8
Russian Federation	16.5	60.0	35.0	117.3	..	0.7	..	13.3	..	2.4

	Trade in goods				Changes in trade as shares of GDP	Growth in real trade less growth in real GDP	Gross private capital flows		Gross foreign direct investment	
	% of GDP		% of goods GDP		% change	percentage points	% of GDP		% of GDP	
	1990	2000	1990	2000	1980-1999	1990-2000	1990	2000	1990	2000
Rwanda	15.4	14.8	26.0	22.0	97.7	2.6	2.8	2.0	0.3	0.8
Saudi Arabia	65.4	66.0	106.7	..	..	..	9.8	10.8	1.8	1.1
Senegal	34.7	56.8	90.0	128.4	-21.0	-1.3	4.8	8.8	1.3	4.0
Sierra Leone	32.0	25.5	46.0	32.4	-62.6	-5.5	8.0	..	3.6	..
Singapore	309.9	295.3	892.4	858.0	..	..	54.6	48.5	20.7	11.6
Slovak Republic	110.8	128.5	192.1	290.2	..	9.3	..	30.6	..	12.2
Slovenia	102.4	103.9	196.5	209.6	..	0.5	3.4	12.5	0.9	1.3
Somalia	26.7	..	33.2	..	..	..	..	..	..	..
South Africa	37.5 a	47.4 a	75.2 a	101.3 a	23.2	4.2	2.2	13.1	0.2	1.2
Spain	27.9	47.8	70.1	128.5	154.6	7.2	11.3	47.9	3.4	16.5
Sri Lanka	58.1	73.3	..	..	40.1	2.7	13.1	7.6	0.5	1.1
Sudan	7.5	28.7	..	50.7	-32.2	..	0.3	4.6	0.0	3.4
Swaziland	144.7	131.2	224.2	..	38.1	0.0	11.2	17.3	5.2	5.4
Sweden	46.9	70.3	119.8	175.5	67.0	5.3	34.2	77.0	7.0	27.3
Switzerland	58.4	68.9	..	193.3	50.6	2.7	15.9	113.4	5.8	25.0
Syrian Arab Republic	53.7	47.8	102.4	88.1	-31.7	-0.9	18.0	17.8	0.0	1.6
Tajikistan	..	146.8	..	290.4	..	..	..	..	..	..
Tanzania	33.9	24.2	50.8	37.9	..	-1.8	0.2	3.3	0.0	2.1
Thailand	66.1	107.2	133.0	211.4	99.5	2.8	13.5	11.3	3.0	2.8
Togo	52.1	73.0	92.6	122.0	-22.3	-1.1	9.6	12.6	1.1	4.2
Trinidad and Tobago	65.9	107.4	130.7	243.4	43.7	1.6	11.4	13.6	3.1	11.9
Tunisia	73.8	74.0	162.1	180.1	9.3	-0.2	9.5	9.3	0.6	3.9
Turkey	23.4	40.0	44.5	77.1	..	7.5	4.3	9.3	0.5	0.9
Turkmenistan	..	93.1	..	76.6	..	2.4	..	..	..	..
Uganda	8.4	32.9	12.0	51.1	..	7.0	1.1	5.0	0.0	3.5
Ukraine	..	89.7	..	152.9	..	6.3	..	9.5	..	1.9
United Arab Emirates	93.5	119.9	146.6	..	..	..	..	..	..	..
United Kingdom	41.3	43.9	104.7	126.7	55.6	3.9	35.4	125.1	7.4	38.7
United States	15.8	20.7	..	..	99.1	5.0	5.7	16.9	2.8	5.1
Uruguay	32.7	29.2	85.0	103.6	90.9	4.4	12.7	14.7	0.0	1.5
Uzbekistan	..	75.9	..	120.0	..	0.5	..	..	..	..
Venezuela, RB	51.1	39.7	90.8	94.0	12.1	3.9	49.9	12.3	1.7	4.0
Vietnam	79.7	96.0	132.5	..	..	18.7	..	10.8	..	4.1
West Bank and Gaza	..	..	..	..	..	0.5	..	..	..	..
Yemen, Rep.	46.9	83.0	90.0	134.9	..	9.1	16.2	6.9	2.7	3.3
Yugoslavia, Fed. Rep.	..	64.2	..	..	..	..	..	..	..	..
Zambia	76.9	54.3	102.3	97.0	-45.1	2.9	64.7	..	6.2	..
Zimbabwe	40.7	44.9	74.5	89.5	139.6	6.1	1.7	..	0.1	..
World	32.4 w	40.0 w	96.2 w	118.9 w			10.3 w	29.1 w	2.7 w	8.8 w
Low income	26.7	41.3	..	..			3.0	4.8	0.5	1.6
Middle income	36.6	53.5	77.3	114.0			7.6	12.0	1.0	3.8
Lower middle income	38.8	52.5	67.1	90.9			5.4	12.8	1.1	3.5
Upper middle income	35.3	54.3	84.5	142.4			8.7	11.4	0.9	4.0
Low & middle income	34.6	51.6	76.3	113.1			6.7	10.9	0.9	3.5
East Asia & Pacific	48.8	65.6	84.9	112.6			5.3	13.3	1.5	3.9
Europe & Central Asia	28.7	65.6	53.1	110.3			..	13.6	..	3.8
Latin America & Carib.	23.2	37.7	68.8	115.2			7.9	10.5	0.9	4.5
Middle East & N. Africa	45.4	51.6	80.9	89.7			11.5	7.5	0.9	1.0
South Asia	16.5	24.3	..	..			1.4	3.1	0.1	0.6
Sub-Saharan Africa	41.2	56.8	76.1	96.4			5.1	11.0	1.0	1.8
High income	32.0	37.1	100.6	124.4			11.0	33.6	3.0	10.1
Europe EMU	44.9	56.3	112.6	141.9			14.1	49.3	2.9	14.8

a. Data refer to the South African Customs Union (Botswana, Lesotho, Namibia, South Africa, and Swaziland).

About the data

The growing integration of societies and economies has succeeded in reducing poverty in many countries. The number of poor people in developing economies declined by about 125 million between 1990 and 1999. Although global integration is a powerful force in poverty reduction, more needs to be done—2 billion people are in danger of becoming marginal to the world economy. All countries have a stake in helping developing countries integrate into the global economy and have better access to rich country markets and greater volumes of well-managed foreign aid can help countries as they improve their own policies and develop more effective institutions.

The growing importance of trade in the world economy is one indication of increasing global economic integration. Another is the increased size and importance of private capital flows to developing countries that have liberalized their financial markets. This table presents standardized measures of the size of trade and capital flows relative to GDP. The numerators are based on gross flows that capture the two-way flow of goods and capital. In conventional balance of payments accounting exports are recorded as a credit and imports as a debit. And in the financial account inward investment is a credit and outward investment a debit. Thus net flows, the sum of credits and debits, represent a balance in which many transactions are canceled out. Gross flows are a better measure of integration because they show the total value of financial transactions during a given period.

Trade in goods (exports and imports) is shown relative to total GDP and to "goods GDP" (GDP less services such as retail trade, restaurants and hotels, transport, storage and communications, business services) and community, social and personal services and public administration because as a result of the increasing share of services in GDP, trade as a share of total GDP appears to be declining for some economies. Measuring merchandise trade rela-tive to GDP after deducting value added in services thus provides a better measure of its relative size than does comparing it with total GDP, although this neglects the growing service component of most goods output.

Trade in services (such as transportation, travel, finance, communications, insurance, royalties, construction and cultural services), is an increasingly important element of global integration. The difference between the growth of real trade in goods and services and the growth of GDP helps to identify economies that have integrated into the global economy by undertaking trade liberalization, lowered barriers to foreign investment, and harnessed their abundant labor to gain a competitive advantage in labor-intensive manufactures and services.

The indicators covering capital flows—gross private capital flows and gross foreign direct investment—are calculated from detailed accounts since higher-level aggregates would result in smaller totals by netting out credits and debits. The comparability of these indicators between countries and over time is affected by the accuracy and completeness of balance of payments records and by their level of detail.

There are two changes in this table from previous editions. First, trade and capital flows are shown as a percentage of GDP in U.S. dollars, converted at the average official exchange rate reported by the International Monetary Fund for the year shown. An alternative conversion factor is applied if the official exchange rate is judged to diverge by an exceptionally large margin from the rate effectively applied to transactions in foreign currencies and traded products. Second, to give a better measure of the policy-induced component of trade, the *change in trade as a share of GDP* is presented. This measures the effect of trade on growth using the decade-over-decade change in a country's trade as a share of its GDP.

Definitions

- **Trade in goods as a share of GDP** is the sum of merchandise exports and imports measured in current U.S. dollars, divided by the value of GDP in U.S. dollars. • **Trade in goods as a share of goods GDP** is the sum of merchandise exports and imports divided by the value of GDP after subtracting value added in services, all in current U.S. dollars. • **Change in trade as a share of GDP** is the decade-over-decade change in trade as a share of GDP. • **Growth in real trade less growth in real GDP** is the difference between annual growth in trade of goods and services and annual growth in GDP. Growth rates are calculated using constant price series taken from national accounts and are expressed as a percentage. • **Gross private capital flows** are the sum of the absolute values of direct, portfolio, and other investment inflows and outflows recorded in the balance of payments financial account, excluding changes in the assets and liabilities of monetary authorities and general government. The indicator is calculated as a ratio to GDP in U.S. dollars. • **Gross foreign direct investment** is the sum of the absolute values of inflows and outflows of foreign direct investment recorded in the balance of payments financial account. It includes equity capital, reinvestment of earnings, other long-term capital, and short-term capital. This indicator differs from the standard measure of foreign direct investment, which captures only inward investment (see table 6.7). The indicator is calculated as a ratio to GDP in U.S. dollars.

Data sources

The data on merchandise trade are from the World Trade Organization. The data on GDP come from the World Bank, converted from national currencies to U.S. dollars using the official exchange rate, supplemented by an alternative conversion factor if the official exchange rate is judged to diverge by an exceptionally large margin from the rate effectively applied to transactions in foreign currencies and traded products. The data on real trade and GDP growth come from the World Bank's national accounts files. Gross private capital flows and foreign direct investment were calculated using the International Monetary Fund's Balance of Payments database.

Figure 6.1

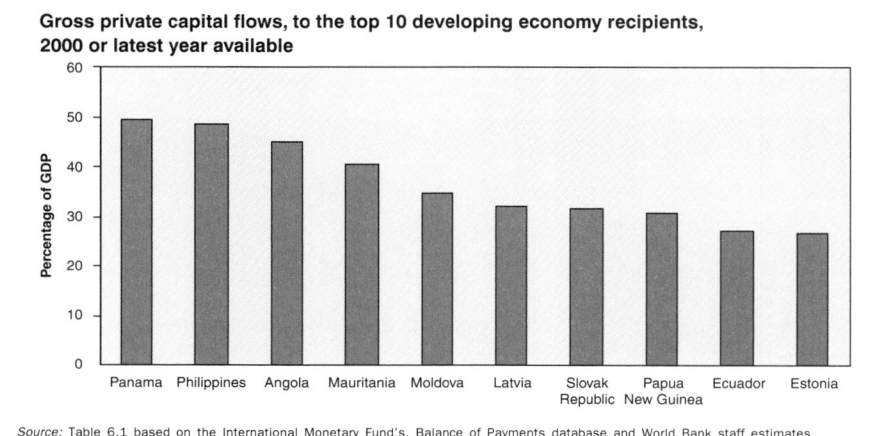

Gross private capital flows, to the top 10 developing economy recipients, 2000 or latest year available

Source: Table 6.1 based on the International Monetary Fund's, Balance of Payments database and World Bank staff estimates.

6.2 | Direction and growth of merchandise trade

High-income importers

Direction of trade % of world trade, 2000	European Union	Japan	United States	Other industrial	All industrial	Other high income	All high income
Source of exports							
High-income economies	29.4	3.1	11.7	6.0	50.1	5.6	55.8
Industrial economies	27.9	2.1	9.8	5.7	45.4	4.3	49.7
European Union	22.3	0.6	3.4	2.0	28.3	1.5	29.7
Japan	1.2		2.3	0.3	3.8	1.4	5.2
United States	2.6	1.0		3.1	6.7	1.1	7.9
Other industrial economies	1.8	0.4	4.1	0.2	6.6	0.3	6.9
Other high-income economies	1.5	1.0	2.0	0.3	4.8	1.3	6.1
Low- and middle-income economies	6.0	2.3	7.0	0.8	16.1	4.2	20.3
East Asia & Pacific	1.7	1.7	2.3	0.4	6.1	2.3	8.4
Europe & Central Asia	1.7	0.0	0.1	0.1	1.9	1.1	3.0
Latin America & Caribbean	0.7	0.1	3.4	0.2	4.3	0.2	4.5
Middle East & N. Africa	1.0	0.3	0.4	0.1	1.8	0.3	2.1
South Asia	0.5	0.1	0.5	0.1	1.2	0.3	1.5
Sub-Saharan Africa	0.4	0.0	0.3	0.0	0.8	0.1	0.9
World	35.3	5.4	18.8	6.8	66.3	9.8	76.1

Low- and middle-income importers

Direction of trade % of world trade, 2000	East Asia & Pacific	Europe & Central Asia	Latin America & Caribbean	Middle East & N. Africa	South Asia	Sub-Saharan Africa	All low- & middle- income	World
Source of exports								
High-income economies	8.0	3.0	1.9	1.4	0.7	0.8	15.7	72.9
Industrial economies	4.2	2.9	1.8	1.3	0.4	0.7	11.2	63.2
European Union	1.0	2.5	0.6	0.8	0.2	0.5	5.7	35.9
Japan	1.7	0.1	0.2	0.1	0.1	0.1	2.2	7.5
United States	1.1	0.2	0.9	0.2	0.1	0.1	2.6	12.1
Other industrial economies	0.4	0.1	0.1	0.1	0.0	0.0	0.8	7.7
Other high-income economies	3.8	0.1	0.1	0.1	0.2	0.1	4.5	9.6
Low- and middle-income economies	2.6	1.7	1.1	0.6	0.5	0.4	6.9	27.1
East Asia & Pacific	1.6	0.2	0.2	0.2	0.2	0.1	2.6	11.1
Europe & Central Asia	0.2	1.3	0.0	0.1	0.0	0.0	1.7	4.8
Latin America & Caribbean	0.1	0.0	0.8	0.1	0.0	0.0	1.1	5.8
Middle East & N. Africa	0.5	0.1	0.0	0.1	0.1	0.0	0.9	3.1
South Asia	0.1	0.0	0.0	0.0	0.0	0.0	0.3	1.0
Sub-Saharan Africa	0.1	0.0	0.0	0.0	0.0	0.2	0.4	1.3
World	10.6	4.7	3.1	1.9	1.1	1.2	22.6	100.0

High-income importers

Nominal growth of trade annual % growth 1990-2000	European Union	Japan	United States	Other industrial	All industrial	Other high income	All high income
Source of exports							
High-income economies	3.9	3.8	7.5	4.8	4.7	8.0	5.0
Industrial economies	3.7	2.5	7.4	4.7	4.5	7.6	4.7
European Union	3.7	2.9	7.4	2.4	4.0	8.2	4.2
Japan	2.9		4.7	0.7	3.7	7.5	4.6
United States	4.7	2.9		7.3	5.5	7.7	5.8
Other industrial economies	2.8	0.9	9.3	3.7	6.3	5.3	6.2
Other high-income economies	7.2	7.2	7.7	5.5	7.3	9.3	7.7
Low- and middle-income economies	8.7	7.6	13.2	10.6	10.3	13.5	10.9
East Asia & Pacific	12.9	9.4	13.5	13.2	12.0	10.3	11.5
Europe & Central Asia[a]	10.6	1.6	12.2	9.3	10.5	8.0	9.5
Latin America & Caribbean	3.2	1.1	16.0	11.0	11.8	11.2	11.8
Middle East & N. Africa	3.2	4.3	3.4	5.3	3.5	6.2	3.8
South Asia	7.6	2.6	14.0	9.2	9.4	12.7	9.9
Sub-Saharan Africa	4.7	10.0	6.6	4.6	5.6	21.3	6.2
World	4.4	5.1	9.2	5.3	5.7	9.0	6.0

Low- and middle-income importers

Nominal growth of trade annual % growth, 1990-2000	East Asia & Pacific	Europe & Central Asia	Latin America & Caribbean	Middle East & N. Africa	South Asia	Sub-Saharan Africa	All low- & middle- income	World
Source of exports								
High-income economies	9.4	8.0	7.5	1.3	4.7	1.5	7.2	5.6
Industrial economies	8.3	7.9	7.5	1.1	2.9	1.1	6.2	5.1
European Union	7.3	9.0	6.4	1.0	3.5	0.8	5.7	4.4
Japan	8.8	-1.6	6.5	-1.6	1.4	-1.2	6.7	5.2
United States	9.2	3.9	9.0	3.0	1.5	3.8	7.5	7.0
Other industrial economies	6.4	1.2	4.9	1.3	4.1	3.3	4.4	6.0
Other high-income economies	10.9	12.7	8.0	3.3	9.6	5.4	10.3	9.1
Low- and middle-income economies	19.5	13.6	11.9	5.6	12.0	11.4	13.7	11.4
East Asia & Pacific	20.2	9.4	19.4	9.9	13.6	12.4	16.7	12.2
Europe & Central Asia[a]	3.4	10.4	8.4	2.5	6.0	8.7	8.6	9.2
Latin America & Caribbean	8.5	2.1	11.7	2.1	11.8	5.2	9.7	11.3
Middle East & N. Africa	20.6	-3.7	-2.2	1.2	7.7	7.2	7.1	4.8
South Asia	16.4	-6.6	28.1	7.4	12.3	15.3	7.5	9.1
Sub-Saharan Africa	23.8	5.2	16.3	5.7	18.7	11.9	14.3	8.0
World	11.6	7.9	8.9	2.1	6.6	3.8	8.3	6.5

a. Refers to 1993-2000

6.2 | Direction and growth of merchandise trade

About the data

This table provides estimates of the flow of trade in goods between groups of economies. The source of these data is the International Monetary Fund's (IMF) *Direction of Trade Statistics Yearbook* (DOTSY), which covers 182 countries. Of these countries, about 100 report data on a timely basis, covering about 95 percent of trade for recent years. Trade by less timely reporters and by countries that do not report is estimated using reports of partner countries. Because the largest exporting and importing countries are reliable reporters, a large portion of the missing trade flows can be estimated from partner reports. Partner country data may introduce discrepancies due to overreporting of transit trade, different points of valuation and time of recording, different exchange rates, inclusion or exclusion of freight rates, confidentiality, and smuggling. In addition, estimates of intra-European Union trade have been significantly affected by changes in reporting methods following the creation of a customs union. Coverage by the new system for collecting data on trade between EU members, *Intrastat*, introduced in 1993, is less exhaustive than that by the previous customs-based system and has resulted in some asymmetry problems (estimated imports are about 5 percent below exports). Nevertheless, only a small portion of world trade is estimated to be omitted from the IMF's *Direction of Trade Statistics Yearbook*.

Most countries report their trade data in national currencies, which are converted using the IMF's published period average exchange rates (series rf or rh, monthly averages of the market or official rates) of the reporting country or, if those are not available, monthly average rates in New York. Because imports are reported at c.i.f. (cost, insurance, and freight) valuations, and exports at f.o.b. (free on board) valuations, the IMF adjusts country reports of import values by dividing those values by 1.10 to estimate equivalent export values. This approximation is more or less accurate, depending on the set of partners and the items traded. Other factors affecting the accuracy of trade data include lags in reporting, recording differences across countries, and whether the country reports trade according to the general or special system of trade. (For further discussion of the measurement of exports and imports see *About the data* for tables 4.5 and 4.6.)

The regional trade flows shown in this table were calculated from current price values. The growth rates presented are in nominal terms; that is, they include the effects of changes in both volumes and prices.

Figure 6.2

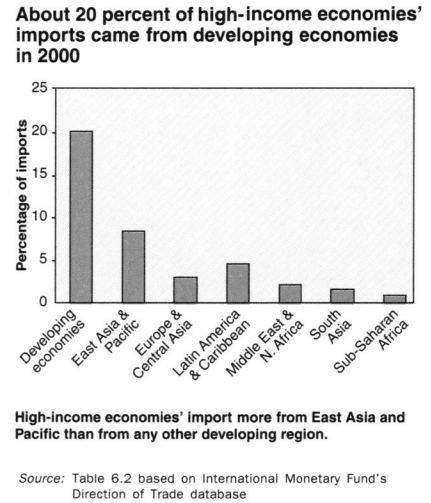

About 20 percent of high-income economies' imports came from developing economies in 2000

High-income economies' import more from East Asia and Pacific than from any other developing region.

Source: Table 6.2 based on International Monetary Fund's Direction of Trade database

Definitions

• **Merchandise trade** includes all trade in goods; trade in services is excluded. • **Low- and middle-income regional groupings** are based on World Bank classifications and may differ from those used by other organizations. • **High-income** includes those economies classified as high-income by the World Bank. • **Industrial countries** are those classified as such in the IMF's *Direction of Trade Statistics Yearbook* and include the countries of the European Union, Japan, the United States, and the other industrial economies listed below. • **European Union** comprises Austria, Belgium, Denmark, Finland, France, Germany, Greece, Ireland, Italy, Luxembourg, the Netherlands, Portugal, Spain, Sweden, and the United Kingdom. • **Other industrial economies** include Australia, Canada, Iceland, New Zealand, Norway, and Switzerland. • **Other high-income economies** include Cyprus, Hong Kong (China), Israel, Kuwait, Macao (China), Malta, Qatar, San Marino, Singapore, Taiwan (China), and the United Arab Emirates. Some small high-income economies such as Aruba, the Bahamas, and Bermuda have been included in the Latin America and Caribbean group.

Data sources

Intercountry trade flows are published in the IMF's *Direction of Trade Statistics Yearbook* and *Direction of Trade Statistics Quarterly;* the data in the table were calculated using the IMF's Direction of Trade database.

Exports to low- and middle-income economies	High-income OECD countries		European Union		Japan		United States	
	1990	2000	1990	2000	1990	2000	1990	2000
$ billions								
Food	34.1	53.1	15.8	22.9	0.4	0.6	11.6	20.2
Cereals	14.0	14.0	4.1	4.9	0.1	0.1	6.2	6.6
Agricultural raw materials	11.9	17.3	3.3	4.9	0.8	1.4	5.6	6.7
Ores and nonferrous metals	9.3	18.5	3.0	6.5	0.9	3.1	5.0	0.0
Fuels	8.5	18.4	2.5	6.5	0.8	0.8	3.3	6.8
Crude petroleum	0.3	2.3	0.0	0.6	0.0	0.0	0.0	0.1
Petroleum products	5.6	11.5	2.4	5.0	0.8	0.8	2.2	5.4
Manufactured goods	305.7	683.9	149.8	319.6	68.7	135.7	72.5	205.2
Chemical products	46.0	91.4	23.9	46.3	6.0	13.0	12.2	25.7
Machinery & transport equipment	175.7	411.3	80.6	180.0	43.9	89.9	44.5	130.3
Other	84.0	181.2	45.2	93.4	18.9	32.8	15.9	49.2
Miscellaneous goods	11.6	21.0	3.8	5.7	0.8	4.0	4.7	10.1
Total	**381.1**	**812.1**	**178.1**	**366.2**	**72.4**	**145.7**	**102.7**	**249.0**
% of total exports								
Food	8.9	6.5	8.9	6.2	0.5	0.4	11.3	8.1
Cereals	3.7	1.7	2.3	1.3	0.1	0.0	6.1	2.6
Agricultural raw materials	3.1	2.1	1.8	1.3	1.1	0.9	5.4	2.7
Ores and nonferrous metals	2.5	2.3	1.7	1.8	1.2	2.1	4.9	0.0
Fuels	2.2	2.3	1.4	1.8	1.1	0.6	3.2	2.7
Crude petroleum	0.1	0.3	0.0	0.2	0.0	0.0	0.0	0.0
Petroleum products	1.5	1.4	1.3	1.4	1.0	0.5	2.1	2.1
Manufactured goods	80.2	84.2	84.1	87.3	94.9	93.2	70.6	82.4
Chemical products	12.1	11.3	13.4	12.6	8.2	8.9	11.8	10.3
Machinery & transport equipment	46.1	50.6	45.3	49.2	60.6	61.7	43.3	52.3
Other	22.1	22.2	25.4	25.5	26.0	22.5	15.5	19.8
Miscellaneous goods	3.0	2.3	2.1	1.6	1.1	2.7	4.6	4.0
Total	**100.0**	**100.0**	**100.0**	**100.0**	**100.0**	**100.0**	**100.0**	**100.0**

Imports from low- and middle-income economies	High-income OECD countries		European Union		Japan		United States	
	1990	2000	1990	2000	1990	2000	1990	2000
$ billions								
Food	64.6	89.5	34.9	40.4	10.7	20.0	15.5	23.5
Cereals	1.3	2.3	0.5	0.9	0.5	0.5	0.2	0.6
Agricultural raw materials	17.7	23.0	9.9	13.0	5.0	4.5	2.3	4.4
Ores and nonferrous metals	30.2	52.1	15.0	22.8	9.1	12.6	5.1	12.0
Fuels	144.5	226.4	58.6	91.9	33.5	41.6	48.8	83.1
Crude petroleum	107.5	164.5	46.6	64.5	20.8	24.1	37.3	67.4
Petroleum products	23.6	34.1	6.2	12.8	5.9	5.9	10.8	14.4
Manufactured goods	210.7	781.8	85.3	270.3	24.6	94.1	85.5	366.4
Chemical products	14.5	36.9	8.0	16.7	2.3	5.2	3.0	11.8
Machinery & transport equipment	59.3	361.4	18.3	110.3	3.7	38.6	32.1	188.2
Other	136.9	383.5	59.0	143.2	18.6	50.2	50.4	166.5
Miscellaneous goods	5.6	15.6	2.1	1.6	0.5	2.1	2.6	11.8
Total	**473.3**	**1,188.5**	**205.7**	**440.1**	**83.5**	**174.9**	**159.8**	**501.2**
% of total imports								
Food	13.6	7.5	17.0	9.2	12.9	11.5	9.7	4.7
Cereals	0.3	0.2	0.2	0.2	0.6	0.3	0.1	0.1
Agricultural raw materials	3.7	1.9	4.8	3.0	6.0	2.6	1.5	0.9
Ores and nonferrous metals	6.4	4.4	7.3	5.2	10.9	7.2	3.2	2.4
Fuels	30.5	19.1	28.5	20.9	40.2	23.8	30.5	16.6
Crude petroleum	22.7	13.8	22.7	14.7	24.9	13.8	23.3	13.5
Petroleum products	5.0	2.9	3.0	2.9	7.0	3.3	6.8	2.9
Manufactured goods	44.5	65.8	41.4	61.4	29.5	53.8	53.5	73.1
Chemical products	3.1	3.1	3.9	3.8	2.8	3.0	1.9	2.4
Machinery & transport equipment	12.5	30.4	8.9	25.1	4.5	22.1	20.1	37.5
Other	28.9	32.3	28.7	32.5	22.2	28.7	31.5	33.2
Miscellaneous goods	1.2	1.3	1.0	0.4	0.7	1.2	1.6	2.4
Total	**100.0**	**100.0**	**100.0**	**100.0**	**100.0**	**100.0**	**100.0**	**100.0**

Note: For a listing of low- and middle-income economies, see front flap of book.

About the data

Developing countries in the trading system are becoming increasingly important. Since the early 1990s trade between OECD countries and low- and middle-income economies has grown faster than trade among OECD members. The increased trade benefits consumers and producers, but as the Doha World Trade Organization WTO ministerial conference in October 2001 illustrates, achieving more progress toward a pro-development outcome remains a major challenge, and will require strengthening international consultation. Negotiations after the Doha meetings will be launched (or continued) agriculture, services, manufactures, dispute settlement, WTO rules, disciplines on regional integration, environment, and intellectual property rights protection. These negotiations are scheduled to be concluded by 2005.

What would improved access to rich country markets mean for developing countries? They stand to gain $9 billion a year in textiles alone, and another $22.3 billion in other manufacturers. They would also reap large benefits from better access to one another's markets: opening their own markets would lead to gains of about $27.6 billion a year for manufacturers, and $31.4 billion for agricultural goods.

Trade flows between high-income members of the OECD and low- and middle-income economies reflect the changing mix of exports to and imports from developing economies. While food and primary commodities have continued to fall as a share of OECD imports, the share of manufactured goods supplied by developing countries has grown dramatically, from about 45 percent of total goods in 1990 to more than 65 percent in 2000. At the same time, developing countries have increased their imports of manufac-

tured goods from high-income countries—particularly capital-intensive goods, such as machinery and transport equipment. And trade between developing countries has grown substantially over the past decade as a result of a number of factors, such as the increasing share of developing country output in the world economy and the liberalization of developing country trade. With 40 percent of their exports going to other developing countries, the high trade barriers need to be reduced (more than 70 percent of the tariff burden faced by manufactured goods from developing countries is imposed by other developing countries). Despite the growth in trade between developing countries, high-income OECD countries remain the developing world's most important partners.

The aggregate flows in the table were compiled from intercountry flows recorded in the United Nations Statistics Division's Commodity Trade (COMTRADE) database. Partner country reports by high-income OECD countries were used for both exports and imports. Exports are recorded free on board (f.o.b.); imports include insurance and freight charges (c.i.f.). Revisions have been made to the time-series data as far back as 1990. Because of differences in sources of data, timing, and treatment of missing data, the data in this table may not be fully comparable with those used to calculate the direction of trade statistics in table 6.2 or the aggregate flows shown in tables 4.4–4.6. For further discussion of merchandise trade statistics see *About the data* for tables 4.4–4.6 and 6.2.

Definitions

The product groups in the table are defined in accordance with the Standard International Trade Classification (SITC) revision 1: food (0, 1, 22, and 4) and cereals (04); agricultural raw materials (2 excluding 22, 27, and 28); ores and nonferrous metals (27, 28, and 68); fuels (3), crude petroleum (331), and petroleum products (332); manufactured goods (5–8 excluding 68), chemical products (5), machinery and transport equipment (7), and other manufactured goods (6 and 8 excluding 68); and miscellaneous goods (9). • **Exports** are all merchandise exports by high-income OECD countries to low- and middle-income economies as recorded in the United Nations Statistics Division's COMTRADE database. • **Imports** are all merchandise imports by high-income OECD countries from low- and middle-income economies as recorded in the United Nations Statistics Division's COMTRADE database. • **High-income OECD countries** in 2000 were Australia, Austria, Belgium, Canada, Denmark, Finland, France, Germany, Greece, Iceland, Ireland, Italy, Japan, Luxembourg, the Netherlands, New Zealand, Norway, Portugal, Spain, Sweden, Switzerland, the United Kingdom, and the United States. • **European Union** comprises Austria, Belgium, Denmark, Finland, France, Germany, Greece, Ireland, Italy, Luxembourg, the Netherlands, Portugal, Spain, Sweden, and the United Kingdom.

Data sources

COMTRADE data are available in electronic form from the United Nations Statistics Division. Although not as comprehensive as the underlying COMTRADE records, detailed statistics on international trade are published annually in the United Nations Conference on Trade and Development's (UNCTAD) *Handbook of International Trade and Development Statistics* and the United Nations Statistics Division's *International Trade Statistics Yearbook*.

Figure 6.3

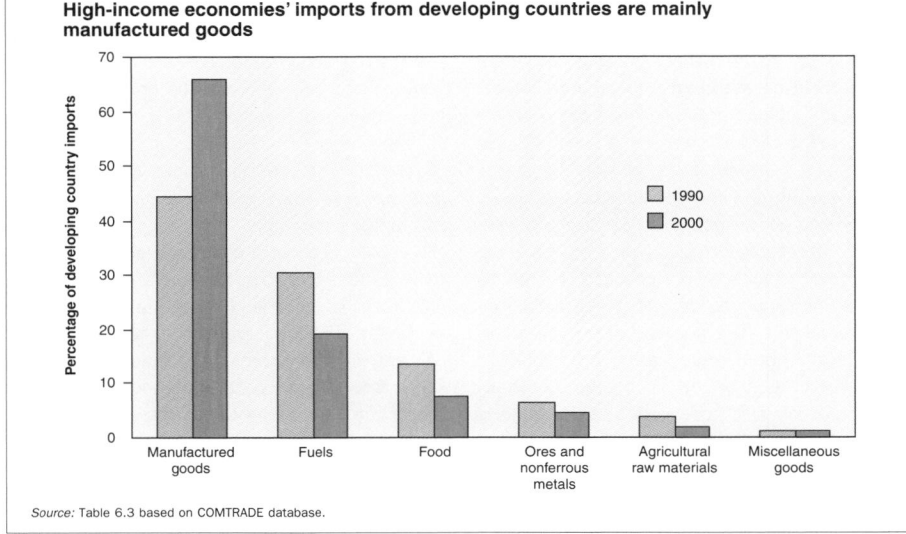

High-income economies' imports from developing countries are mainly manufactured goods

Source: Table 6.3 based on COMTRADE database.

6.4 | Primary commodity prices

	1970	1980	1990	1995	1996	1997	1998	1999	2000	2001
World Bank commodity price index (1990= 100)										
Non-energy commodities	156	159	100	104	103	114	99	88	89	82
Agriculture	163	175	100	112	113	124	108	93	90	83
Beverages	203	230	100	129	113	165	141	108	91	75
Food	166	177	100	100	111	112	105	88	87	89
Raw materials	130	133	100	116	114	110	88	89	94	80
Fertilizers	108	164	100	89	108	116	122	115	109	102
Metals and minerals	144	120	100	87	80	87	76	74	85	78
Petroleum	19	205	100	64	80	81	57	79	127	110
Steel products[a]	111	100	100	91	86	86	75	69	78	69
MUV G-5 index	28	79	100	117	111	104	100	100	97	97
Commodity prices (1990 prices)										
Agricultural raw materials										
Cotton (cents/kg)	225	260	182	182	159	169	145	118	134	109
Logs, Cameroon ($/cu. m)[a]	153	319	343	290	256	275	287	270	283	275
Logs, Malaysian ($/cu. m)	154	248	177	218	227	230	163	188	195	165
Rubber (cents/kg)	145	181	86	135	125	98	72	63	71	62
Sawnwood, Malaysian ($/cu. m)	625	503	533	632	666	641	486	604	612	497
Tobacco ($/mt)	3,836	2,889	3,392	2,259	2,746	3,411	3,347	3,055	3,055	3,125
Beverages (cents/kg)										
Cocoa	240	330	127	122	131	156	168	114	93	111
Coffee, robustas	330	412	118	237	162	168	183	150	94	63
Coffee, Arabica	409	440	197	285	242	403	299	230	197	142
Tea, avg., 3 auctions	298	211	206	127	149	199	205	185	192	165
Energy										
Coal, Australian ($/mt)	..	50.01	39.67	33.64	34.21	33.90	29.33	26.08	26.95	33.43
Coal, U.S. ($/mt)	..	54.71	41.67	33.47	33.44	35.15	34.50	33.32	33.94	46.41
Natural gas, Europe ($/mmbtu)	..	4.32	2.55	2.33	2.55	2.65	2.42	2.14	3.96	4.20
Natural gas, U.S. ($/mmbtu)	0.59	1.97	1.70	1.47	2.45	2.40	2.09	2.28	4.42	4.09
Petroleum ($/bbl)	4.31	46.80	22.88	14.68	18.35	18.52	13.11	18.15	28.98	25.19

About the data

During the 20th century, non-oil commodity prices fell about 1 percent a year relative to the prices of manufactures. Until the early 1970s oil prices had fallen even more rapidly. The decline in agricultural commodity prices was mainly due to productivity gains: rising yields, improved policies, and investment in infrastructure and irrigation. Metals and minerals commodity prices have declined relative to those of manufactures for similar reasons: better technology, policies, and management.

Agricultural commodity prices were down about 33 percent in 2000 compared with 1995. Although metals and minerals prices rose somewhat from the lows of 1999, by early 2001 they had dropped again due to weak demand. While oil prices rose sharply during 1999 and most of 2000, they weakened in late 2000 and into 2001.

Primary commodities are raw or partially processed materials that will be transformed into finished goods. They are often the most significant exports of developing countries, and revenues obtained from them have an important effect on living standards. Price data for primary commodities are collected from a variety of sources, including international study groups, trade journals, newspaper and wire service reports, government market surveys, and commodity exchange spot and near-term forward prices. This table is based on frequently updated price reports. When possible, the prices received by exporters are used; if export prices are unavailable, the prices paid by importers are used. Annual price series are generally simple averages based on higher frequency data. The constant price series in the table is deflated using the manufactures unit value (MUV) index for the G-5 countries (see below).

The commodity price indexes are calculated as Laspeyres index numbers, in which the fixed weights are the 1987–89 export values for low- and middle-income economies, rebased to 1990. Each index represents a fixed basket of primary commodity exports. The non-energy commodity price index contains 37 price series for 31 non-energy commodities. Separate indexes are compiled for petroleum and for steel products, which are not included in the non-energy commodity price index.

The MUV index is a composite index of prices for manufactured exports from the five major (G-5) industrial countries (France, Germany, Japan, the United Kingdom, and the United States) to low- and middle-income economies, valued in U.S. dollars. The index covers products in groups 5–8 of the Standard International Trade Classification (SITC) revision 1. To construct the MUV G-5 index, unit value indexes for each country are combined using weights determined by each country's export share.

	1970	1980	1990	1995	1996	1997	1998	1999	2000	2001
Fertilizers ($/mt)										
Phosphate rock	39	59	40	30	35	40	43	44	45	43
TSP	152	229	132	128	158	166	174	155	141	131
Food										
Fats and oils ($/mt)										
Coconut oil	1,417	855	336	573	675	634	660	740	462	329
Groundnut oil	1,350	1,090	964	847	806	976	912	791	733	704
Palm oil	927	741	290	537	477	527	673	438	318	296
Soybeans	417	376	247	221	274	285	244	203	217	203
Soybean meal	367	333	200	168	240	266	171	153	194	187
Soybean oil	1,021	759	447	534	496	545	628	429	347	366
Grains ($/mt)										
Grain sorghum	185	164	104	102	135	106	98	85	90	99
Maize	208	159	109	106	149	113	102	91	91	93
Rice	450	521	271	274	305	293	305	250	208	179
Wheat	196	219	136	151	187	154	127	113	117	131
Other food										
Bananas ($/mt)	590	481	541	380	422	499	491	375	435	603
Beef (cents/kg)	465	350	256	163	160	179	173	185	199	220
Oranges ($/mt)	599	496	531	454	442	443	444	433	373	630
Sugar, EU domestic (cents/kg)	40	62	58	59	61	61	60	59	57	55
Sugar, U.S. domestic (cents/kg)	59	84	51	43	44	47	49	47	44	49
Sugar, world (cents/kg)	29	80	28	25	24	24	20	14	19	20
Metals and minerals										
Aluminum ($/mt)	1,982	1,848	1,639	1,543	1,353	1,545	1,362	1,367	1,590	1,494
Copper ($/mt)	5,038	2,770	2,661	2,509	2,062	2,199	1,660	1,580	1,862	1,633
Iron ore (cents/dmtu)	35	36	32	24	27	29	31	28	30	31
Lead (cents/kg)	108	115	81	54	70	60	53	50	47	49
Nickel ($/mt)	10,148	8,274	8,864	7,031	6,741	6,691	4,645	6,038	8,868	6,150
Tin (cents/kg)	1,310	2,129	609	531	554	545	556	543	558	464
Zinc (cents/kg)	105	97	151	88	92	127	103	108	116	92

a. Series not included in the non-energy index.

Definitions

• **Non-energy commodity price index** covers the 31 non-energy primary commodities that make up the agriculture, fertilizer, and metals and minerals indexes. • **Agriculture**, in addition to beverages, food, and agricultural raw materials, includes sugar, bananas, beef, and oranges. • **Beverages** include cocoa, coffee, and tea. • **Food** includes rice, wheat, maize, sorghum, soybeans, soybean oil, soybean meal, palm oil, coconut oil, and groundnut oil. • **Agricultural raw materials** include timber (logs and sawnwood), cotton, natural rubber, and tobacco. • **Fertilizers** include phosphate rock and triple superphosphate (TSP). • **Metals and minerals** include aluminum, copper, iron ore, lead, nickel, tin, and zinc. • **Petroleum price index** refers to the average spot price of Brent, Dubai, and West Texas Intermediate crude oil, equally weighted. • **Steel products price index** is the composite price index for eight steel products based on quotations f.o.b. (free on board) Japan excluding shipments to China and the United States, weighted by product shares of apparent combined consumption (volume of deliveries) for Germany, Japan, and the United States. • **MUV G-5 index** is the manufactures unit value index for G-5 country exports to low- and middle-income economies. • **Commodity prices**—for definitions and sources see "Commodity Price Data" (also known as the "Pink Sheet") at the Global Prospects Web site (www.worldbank.org/prospects).

Data sources

Commodity price data and the G-5 MUV index are compiled by the World Bank's Development Prospects Group. Monthly updates of commodity prices are available on the Web at www.worldbank.org/prospects.

Merchandise exports within bloc
$ millions

	1970	1980	1985	1990	1995	1996	1997	1998	1999	2000
High-income and low- and middle-income economies										
APEC [a]	58,633	357,697	494,464	901,560	1,688,185	1,754,764	1,868,667	1,734,788	1,899,098	2,259,727
CEFTA	1,157	7,766	6,302	4,235	12,118	12,874	13,169	14,234	13,226	15,102
European Union	76,451	456,857	419,134	981,260	1,259,699	1,273,430	1,162,419	1,226,988	1,405,568	1,416,825
NAFTA	22,078	102,218	143,191	226,273	394,472	437,804	496,423	521,649	581,162	676,440
Latin America and the Caribbean										
ACS	758	4,892	4,123	5,401	10,449	10,847	11,985	12,547	11,582	13,780
Andean Group	97	1,161	768	1,312	4,812	4,762	5,524	5,408	3,921	5,177
CACM	287	1,174	544	671	1,595	1,723	1,973	2,038	2,154	2,477
CARICOM	52	576	414	448	307	900	968	1,020	1,134	1,078
Central American Group of Four	176	692	310	399	1,026	1,106	1,299	1,220	1,290	1,483
Group of Three	59	706	534	1,046	3,460	3,131	3,944	3,921	2,912	3,711
LAIA	1,263	10,981	7,139	12,331	35,299	38,373	44,809	42,864	34,747	42,665
MERCOSUR	451	3,424	1,953	4,127	14,199	17,075	20,772	20,352	15,313	17,925
OECS	..	8	10	29	39	33	34	36	36	38
Africa										
CEMAC	22	75	84	139	120	164	161	153	121	125
CEPGL	3	2	9	7	8	9	6	8	9	10
COMESA	412	616	466	963	1,386	1,610	1,545	1,501	1,348	1,534
Cross Border Initiative	209	447	294	613	1,002	1,191	1,144	1,156	964	1,091
ECCAS	162	89	131	163	163	212	211	198	167	181
ECOWAS	86	692	1,026	1,533	2,088	2,483	2,462	2,614	2,669	3,331
Indian Ocean Commission	5	10	4	24	64	69	75	95	91	116
MRU	1	7	4	0	1	4	7	8	8	10
SADC	483	617	843	1,630	3,373	3,963	4,471	3,865	4,224	4,419
UDEAC	22	75	84	139	120	163	160	152	120	124
UEMOA	52	460	397	614	555	665	707	753	841	847
Middle East and Asia										
Arab Common Market	102	661	504	911	1,368	1,149	1,146	978	936	1,238
ASEAN	1,456	13,350	14,343	28,648	81,911	86,925	88,773	72,218	81,020	100,818
Bangkok Agreement	132	1,464	1,953	4,476	12,070	13,128	13,647	13,175	15,272	17,218
EAEC	9,197	98,532	126,030	282,351	637,029	651,803	673,285	551,555	617,196	776,658
ECO	63	1,165	2,447	1,243	4,746	4,773	4,929	4,031	3,903	4,495
GCC	156	4,632	3,101	6,906	6,832	7,624	8,110	7,358	7,194	8,561
SAARC	99	613	601	863	2,024	2,144	2,004	2,834	2,615	2,798
UMA	59.5	109.1	274.1	958.4	1,109.5	1,115.3	924.2	881.1	918.5	1,081.4

Merchandise exports within bloc
% of total bloc exports

	1970	1980	1985	1990	1995	1996	1997	1998	1999	2000
High-income and low-										
and middle-income economies										
APEC [a]	57.8	57.9	67.7	68.3	71.9	72.1	71.8	69.7	71.9	73.2
CEFTA	12.9	14.8	13.8	9.9	14.6	14.4	13.4	13.0	12.1	12.1
European Union	59.5	60.8	59.2	65.9	62.4	61.4	55.5	57.0	63.3	62.1
NAFTA	36.0	33.6	43.9	41.4	46.2	47.6	49.1	51.7	54.6	55.7
Latin America and the Caribbean										
ACS	9.6	8.7	7.9	8.4	8.1	6.9	6.9	7.2	5.8	5.5
Andean Group	1.8	3.8	3.2	4.1	12.0	9.7	10.8	12.8	8.7	8.5
CACM	26.0	24.4	14.4	15.4	21.7	22.0	18.1	16.0	11.9	12.4
CARICOM	4.2	5.3	6.3	8.1	4.7	13.3	14.6	17.4	16.9	15.0
Central American Group of Four	20.1	18.1	10.9	13.7	22.0	22.0	19.9	17.0	12.0	12.1
Group of Three	1.1	1.8	1.3	2.0	3.2	2.4	2.7	2.6	1.7	1.7
LAIA	9.9	13.7	8.3	10.8	17.1	16.3	17.1	16.7	12.8	12.9
MERCOSUR	9.4	11.6	5.5	8.9	20.3	22.6	24.8	25.0	20.6	20.8
OECS	..	9.1	6.4	8.1	12.7	10.6	10.7	12.0	12.6	10.0
Africa										
CEMAC	4.8	1.6	1.9	2.3	2.2	2.3	2.1	2.3	1.6	1.2
CEPGL	0.4	0.1	0.8	0.5	0.5	0.5	0.4	0.6	0.7	0.8
COMESA	9.1	6.1	4.7	6.6	7.8	8.0	7.9	8.6	7.3	6.0
Cross Border Initiative	9.3	8.8	6.9	10.3	11.9	12.4	12.7	13.8	12.1	12.4
ECCAS	9.6	1.4	1.7	1.4	1.6	1.6	1.6	1.8	1.3	0.9
ECOWAS	2.9	10.1	5.2	7.8	9.8	9.3	9.6	11.6	12.0	10.8
Indian Ocean Commission	2.5	1.2	0.6	1.5	3.3	3.0	3.9	4.7	4.8	4.7
MRU	0.2	0.8	0.4	0.0	0.1	0.3	0.5	0.5	0.6	0.7
SADC	8.0	2.0	3.8	4.8	8.7	9.4	10.4	10.4	11.9	12.2
UDEAC	4.9	1.6	1.9	2.3	2.2	2.3	2.1	2.3	1.6	1.2
UEMOA	6.5	9.6	8.7	12.9	10.0	9.4	11.5	10.8	13.3	15.6
Middle East and Asia										
Arab Common Market	2.2	2.4	1.9	2.7	6.7	4.4	4.1	4.8	3.3	2.9
ASEAN	22.9	18.7	19.8	19.8	25.4	25.4	24.9	21.9	22.4	23.9
Bangkok Agreement	2.7	3.7	3.7	3.7	5.1	5.3	5.2	5.0	5.3	5.2
EAEC	28.9	35.6	34.3	39.9	48.3	49.3	48.3	42.2	44.1	47.0
ECO	1.5	5.4	9.9	3.2	7.9	7.1	7.5	6.9	5.7	5.5
GCC	2.9	3.0	4.9	8.0	6.8	6.4	6.5	8.1	6.7	5.2
SAARC	3.2	4.8	4.5	3.2	4.4	4.3	4.0	5.2	4.6	4.3
UMA	1.4	0.3	1.0	2.9	3.8	3.4	2.7	3.3	2.5	2.3

Total merchandise exports by bloc
% of world exports

	1970	1980	1985	1990	1995	1996	1997	1998	1999	2000
High-income and low-										
and middle-income economies										
APEC [a]	36.0	33.7	38.9	39.0	46.3	46.0	47.2	46.1	46.6	48.5
CEFTA	3.2	2.9	2.4	1.3	1.6	1.7	1.8	2.0	1.9	2.0
European Union	45.6	41.0	37.8	44.0	39.8	39.2	38.0	39.9	39.2	35.9
NAFTA	21.7	16.6	17.4	16.2	16.8	17.4	18.3	18.7	18.8	19.1
Latin America and the Caribbean										
ACS	2.8	3.1	2.8	1.9	2.5	3.0	3.1	3.2	3.5	3.9
Andean Group	1.9	1.7	1.3	0.9	0.8	0.9	0.9	0.8	0.8	1.0
CACM	0.4	0.3	0.2	0.1	0.1	0.1	0.2	0.2	0.3	0.3
CARICOM	0.4	0.6	0.3	0.2	0.1	0.1	0.1	0.1	0.1	0.1
Central American Group of Four	0.3	0.2	0.2	0.1	0.1	0.1	0.1	0.1	0.2	0.2
Group of Three	1.8	2.1	2.1	1.5	2.1	2.5	2.7	2.8	3.0	3.4
LAIA	4.5	4.4	4.6	3.4	4.1	4.5	4.8	4.8	4.8	5.2
MERCOSUR	1.7	1.6	1.9	1.4	1.4	1.4	1.5	1.5	1.3	1.4
OECS	..	0.0	0.0	0.0	0.0	0.0	0.0	0.0	0.0	0.0
Africa										
CEMAC	0.2	0.3	0.2	0.2	0.1	0.1	0.1	0.1	0.1	0.2
CEPGL	0.3	0.1	0.1	0.0	0.0	0.0	0.0	0.0	0.0	0.0
COMESA	1.6	0.6	0.5	0.4	0.4	0.4	0.4	0.3	0.3	0.4
Cross Border Initiative	0.8	0.3	0.2	0.2	0.2	0.2	0.2	0.2	0.1	0.1
ECCAS	0.6	0.3	0.4	0.3	0.2	0.3	0.2	0.2	0.2	0.3
ECOWAS	1.1	0.4	1.0	0.6	0.4	0.5	0.5	0.4	0.4	0.5
Indian Ocean Commission	0.1	0.0	0.0	0.0	0.0	0.0	0.0	0.0	0.0	0.0
MRU	0.1	0.0	0.1	0.1	0.0	0.0	0.0	0.0	0.0	0.0
SADC	2.2	1.6	1.2	1.0	0.8	0.8	0.8	0.7	0.6	0.6
UDEAC	0.2	0.3	0.2	0.2	0.1	0.1	0.1	0.1	0.1	0.2
UEMOA	0.3	0.3	0.2	0.1	0.1	0.1	0.1	0.1	0.1	0.1
Middle East and Asia										
Arab Common Market	1.6	1.5	1.4	1.0	0.4	0.5	0.5	0.4	0.5	0.7
ASEAN	2.3	3.9	3.9	4.3	6.4	6.5	6.5	6.1	6.4	6.6
Bangkok Agreement	1.8	2.2	2.8	3.6	4.7	4.7	4.7	4.9	5.1	5.2
EAEC	11.3	15.1	19.6	20.9	26.0	25.0	25.3	24.2	24.7	26.0
ECO	1.5	1.2	1.3	1.1	1.2	1.3	1.2	1.1	1.2	1.3
GCC	1.9	8.5	3.4	2.5	2.0	2.2	2.3	1.7	1.9	2.6
SAARC	1.1	0.7	0.7	0.8	0.9	0.9	0.9	1.0	1.0	1.0
UMA	1.5	2.3	1.5	1.0	0.6	0.6	0.6	0.5	0.6	0.8

Note: Regional bloc memberships are as follows: **Asia Pacific Economic Cooperation (APEC)**, Australia, Brunei Darussalam, Canada, Chile, China, Hong Kong (China), Indonesia, Japan, the Republic of Korea, Malaysia, Mexico, New Zealand, Papua New Guinea, Peru, the Philippines, the Russian Federation, Singapore, Taiwan (China), Thailand, the United States, and Vietnam; **Central European Free Trade Area (CEFTA)**, Bulgaria, the Czech Republic, Hungary, Poland, Romania, the Slovak Republic, and Slovenia; **European Union (EU; formerly European Economic Community and European Community)**, Austria, Belgium, Denmark, Finland, France, Germany, Greece, Ireland, Italy, Luxembourg, the Netherlands, Portugal, Spain, Sweden, and the United Kingdom; **North American Free Trade Area (NAFTA)**, Canada, Mexico, and the United States; **Association of Caribbean States (ACS)**, Antigua and Barbuda, the Bahamas, Barbados, Belize, Colombia, Costa Rica, Cuba, Dominica, the Dominican Republic, El Salvador, Grenada, Guatemala, Guyana, Haiti, Honduras, Jamaica, Mexico, Nicaragua, Panama, St. Kitts and Nevis, St. Lucia, St. Vincent and the Grenadines, Suriname, Trinidad and Tobago, and República Bolivariana de Venezuela; **Andean Group**, Bolivia, Colombia, Ecuador, Peru, and República Bolivariana de Venezuela; **Central American Common Market (CACM)**, Costa Rica, El Salvador, Guatemala, Honduras, and Nicaragua; **Caribbean Community and Common Market (CARICOM)**, Antigua and Barbuda, the Bahamas (part of the Caribbean Community but not of the Common Market), Barbados, Belize, Dominica, Grenada, Guyana, Jamaica, Montserrat, St. Kitts and Nevis, St. Lucia, St. Vincent and the Grenadines, Suriname, and Trinidad and Tobago; **Central American Group of Four**, El Salvador, Guatemala, Honduras, and Nicaragua; **Group of Three**, Colombia, Mexico, and República Bolivariana de Venezuela; **Latin American Integration Association (LAIA; formerly Latin American Free Trade Area)**, Argentina, Bolivia, Brazil, Chile, Colombia, Ecuador, Mexico, Paraguay, Peru, Uruguay, and República Bolivariana de Venezuela; **Southern Cone Common Market (MERCOSUR)**, Argentina, Brazil, Paraguay, and Uruguay; **Organization of Eastern Caribbean States (OECS)**, Antigua and Barbuda, Dominica, Grenada, Montserrat, St. Kitts and Nevis, St. Lucia, and St. Vincent and the Grenadines; **Economic and Monetary Community of Central Africa (CEMAC)**, Cameroon, the Central African Republic, Chad, the Republic of Congo, Equatorial Guinea, Gabon, and São Tomé and Principe; **Economic Community of the Countries of the Great Lakes (CEPGL)**, Burundi, the Democratic Republic of Congo, and Rwanda; **Common Market for Eastern and Southern Africa (COMESA)**, Angola, Burundi, Comoros, the Democratic Republic of the Congo, Djibouti, the Arab Republic of Egypt, Eritrea, Ethiopia, Kenya, Madagascar, Malawi, Mauritius, Namibia, Rwanda, Seychelles, Sudan, Swaziland, Uganda, Tanzania, Zambia, and Zimbabwe; **Cross-Border Initiative**, Burundi, Comoros, Kenya, Madagascar, Malawi, Mauritius, Namibia, Rwanda, Seychelles, Swaziland, Tanzania, Uganda, Zambia, and Zimbabwe; **Economic Community of Central African States (ECCAS)**, Angola, Burundi, Cameroon, the Central African Republic, Chad, the Democratic Republic of the Congo, the Republic of Congo, Equatorial Guinea, Gabon, Rwanda, and São Tomé and Principe; **Economic Community of West African States (ECOWAS)**, Benin, Burkina Faso, Cape Verde, Côte d'Ivoire, the Gambia, Ghana, Guinea, Guinea-Bissau, Liberia, Mali, Mauritania, Niger, Nigeria, Senegal, Sierra Leone, and Togo; **Indian Ocean Commission**, Comoros, Madagascar, Mauritius, Réunion, and Seychelles; **Mano River Union (MRU)**, Guinea, Liberia, and Sierra Leone; **Southern African Development Community (SADC; formerly Southern African Development Coordination Conference)**, Angola, Botswana, the Democratic Republic of the Congo, Lesotho, Malawi, Mauritius, Mozambique, Namibia, Seychelles, South Africa, Swaziland, Tanzania, Zambia, and Zimbabwe; **Central African Customs and Economic Union (UDEAC; formerly Union Douanière et Economique de l'Afrique Centrale)**, Cameroon, the Central African Republic, Chad, the Republic of Congo, Equatorial Guinea, and Gabon; **West African Economic and Monetary Union (UEMOA)**, Benin, Burkina Faso, Côte d'Ivoire, Guinea-Bissau, Mali, Niger, Senegal, and Togo; **Arab Common Market**, the Arab Republic of Egypt, Iraq, Jordan, Libya, Mauritania, the Syrian Arab Republic, and the Republic of Yemen; **Association of South-East Asian Nations (ASEAN)**, Brunei, Cambodia, Indonesia, the Lao People's Democratic Republic, Malaysia, Myanmar, the Philippines, Singapore, Thailand, and Vietnam; **Bangkok Agreement**, Bangladesh, India, the Republic of Korea, the Lao People's Democratic Republic, the Philippines, Sri Lanka, and Thailand; **East Asian Economic Caucus (EAEC)**, Brunei, China, Hong Kong (China), Indonesia, Japan, the Republic of Korea, Malaysia, the Philippines, Singapore, Taiwan (China), and Thailand; **Economic Cooperation Organization (ECO)**, Afghanistan, Azerbaijan, the Islamic Republic of Iran, Kazakhstan, the Kyrgyz Republic, Pakistan, Tajikistan, Turkey, Turkmenistan, and Uzbekistan; **Gulf Cooperation Council (GCC)**, Bahrain, Kuwait, Oman, Qatar, Saudi Arabia, and the United Arab Emirates; **South Asian Association for Regional Cooperation (SAARC)**, Bangladesh, Bhutan, India, Maldives, Nepal, Pakistan, and Sri Lanka; and **Arab Maghreb Union (UMA)**, Algeria, Libya, Mauritania, Morocco, and Tunisia.

a. No preferential trade agreement.

About the data

Trade blocs are groups of countries that have established special preferential arrangements governing trade between members. Although in some cases the preferences—such as lower tariff duties or exemptions from quantitative restrictions—may be no greater than those available to other trading partners, the general purpose of such arrangements is to encourage exports by bloc members to one another—sometimes called intratrade.

Most countries are members of a regional integration arrangement, and more than a third of the world's trade takes place within these arrangements. The structure of regional arrangements varies widely, but the main objective is the same: the reduction of trade barriers among member countries. But effective integration requires more than reducing tariffs and quotas. Economic gains from competition and scale may not be achieved unless other barriers that divide markets and impede the free flow of goods, services, and investments are lifted. For example, many regional trade blocs retain contingent protection or restrictions on intrabloc trade. These include antidumping, countervailing duties, and "emergency protection" to address balance of payments problems or to protect an industry from surges in imports. Other barriers include cumbersome and costly border formalities, differing product standards, and discrimination in public procurement.

Membership in a regional integration arrangement may reduce the frictional costs of trade, increase the credibility of reform initiatives, and strengthen security among partners. But making it work effectively is a challenge for any government. All sectors of an economy may be affected, and some sectors may expand while others contract, so it is important to weigh the potential costs and benefits that membership may bring.

Asia Pacific Economic Cooperation (APEC), which has no preferential arrangements, is included in the table because of the volume of trade between its members. The table shows the value of merchandise intratrade for important regional trade blocs (service exports are excluded) as well as the size of intratrade relative to each bloc's total exports of goods and the share of the bloc's total exports in world exports.

The data on country exports are drawn from the International Monetary Fund's (IMF) Direction of Trade database and should be broadly consistent with those from other sources, such as the United Nations Statistics Division's Commodity Trade (COMTRADE) database. However, trade flows between many developing countries, particularly in Africa, are not well recorded. Thus the value of intratrade for certain groups may be understated. Data on trade between developing and high-income countries are generally complete.

Membership in the trade blocs shown is based on the most recent information available, from the World Bank Policy Research Report *Trade Blocs* (2000a) and from consultation with the World Bank's international trade unit. Although bloc exports have been calculated back to 1970 on the basis of current membership, most of the blocs came into existence in later years and their membership may have changed over time. For this reason, and because systems of preferences also change over time, intratrade in earlier years may not have been affected by the same preferences as in recent years. In addition, some countries belong to more than one trade bloc, so shares of world exports exceed 100 percent. Exports of blocs include all commodity trade, which may include items not specified in trade bloc agreements. Differences from previously published estimates may be due to changes in bloc membership or to revisions in the underlying data.

Figure 6.5

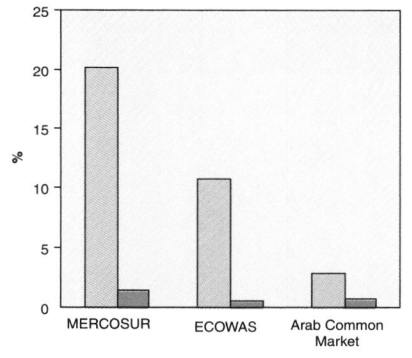

Exports within small regional blocs is often much higher their share of exports to the rest of the world . . .

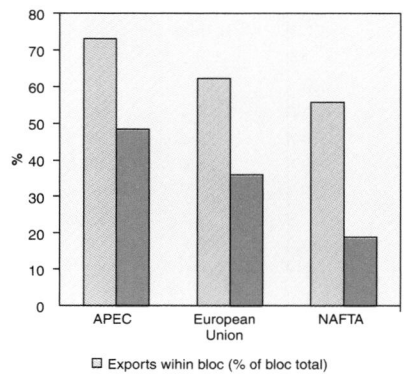

. . . but for some of the larger trade blocs, exports to the rest of the world are high as a share of world trade

☐ Exports wihin bloc (% of bloc total)
■ Exports by bloc (% of world's total)

Source: Table 6.5 based on the International Monetary Fund's Direction of Trade database.

Definitions

• **Exports within bloc** are the sum of exports by members of a trade bloc to other members of the bloc. They are shown both in U.S. dollars and as a percentage of total exports by the bloc. • **Total exports by bloc** as a share of world exports are the ratio of the bloc's total exports (within the bloc and to the rest of the world) to total exports by all economies in the world.

Data sources

Data on merchandise trade flows are published in the IMF's *Direction of Trade Statistics Yearbook* and *Direction of Trade Statistics Quarterly;* the data in the table were calculated using the IMF's Direction of Trade database. The United Nations Conference on Trade and Development (UNCTAD) publishes data on intratrade in its *Handbook of International Trade and Development Statistics*. The information on trade bloc membership is from the World Bank Policy Research Report *Trade Blocs* (2000a) and the World Bank's international trade unit.

		All products					Primary products		Manufactured products	
	Year	Simple mean tariff %	Standard deviation of tariff rates %	Weighted mean tariff %	Share of lines with international peaks %	Share of lines with specific tariffs %	Simple mean tariff %	Weighted mean tariff %	Simple mean tariff %	Weighted mean tariff %
Albania	1997	17.0	8.5	14.4	56.0	0.0	15.7	12.8	17.2	15.2
Algeria	1993	22.5	16.6	15.4	45.8	0.0	18.0	8.9	23.0	18.9
	1998	24.6	16.5	17.3	51.3	0.0	18.1	14.6	25.4	18.7
Argentina	1992	12.2	7.7	12.7	31.0	0.0	10.0	5.8	12.5	13.8
	2000	12.6	7.5	10.5	42.5	0.0	10.6	4.9	12.8	11.3
Australia	1991	13.1	14.3	9.1	30.3	1.4	3.2	1.6	14.3	10.3
	2000	5.8	6.5	4.0	6.2	1.0	1.7	0.8	6.2	4.5
Bangladesh	1989	106.6	79.3	88.4	98.2	1.3	79.9	53.5	110.5	112.2
	2000	21.3	13.6	21.0	51.8	0.0	24.1	18.6	21.0	21.7
Belarus	1996	12.2	8.7	8.8	30.9	0.0	9.6	6.4	13.0	10.5
	1997	13.0	8.3	9.5	31.9	0.0	10.4	7.0	13.8	11.2
Bhutan	1996	18.6	14.9	20.3	54.3	3.7	24.2	20.4	17.9	20.2
Bolivia	1993	9.7	1.1	9.4	0.0	0.0	10.0	10.0	9.7	9.3
	1999	9.5	1.6	9.1	0.0	0.0	10.0	10.0	9.4	8.9
Brazil	1989	42.2	17.2	31.9	92.2	0.5	37.9	18.8	42.5	37.9
	2000	14.4	7.0	12.7	57.4	0.0	11.3	6.3	14.7	15.0
Burkina Faso	1993	23.8	10.7	21.7	65.1	0.0	25.9	18.0	23.5	23.5
Cameroon	1994	19.2	10.4	13.9	53.6	0.0	22.6	14.3	18.7	13.8
	1995	18.5	9.5	14.5	51.3	0.3	21.1	17.0	18.0	13.5
Canada	1989	8.6	7.4	6.0	14.6	3.4	5.1	2.5	9.3	6.7
	2000	3.9	6.7	0.8	9.1	4.1	2.8	0.4	4.2	0.9
Central African Republic	1995	18.0	10.7	13.4	51.7	0.4	20.6	13.7	16.8	13.2
	1997	18.6	10.6	14.1	54.2	0.2	21.1	14.3	17.4	14.0
Chad	1995	15.7	10.8	14.6	43.4	0.0	15.9	16.1	15.6	13.5
	1997	15.7	10.8	14.6	43.4	0.0	15.9	16.1	15.6	13.5
Chile	1992	11.0	0.5	11.0	0.0	0.0	11.0	11.0	11.0	10.9
	2000	9.0	0.0	9.0	0.0	0.0	9.0	9.0	9.0	9.0
China†	1992	41.0	30.6	32.2	77.6	0.0	35.4	13.9	42.3	36.5
	2000	16.3	10.7	14.7	42.5	0.0	16.5	18.8	16.2	13.7
Hong Kong, China	1988	0.0	0.0	0.0	0.0	0.0	0.0	0.0	0.0	0.0
	1998	0.0	0.0	0.0	0.0	0.0	0.0	0.0	0.0	0.0
Colombia	1991	5.7	8.2	6.5	1.6	0.0	7.6	7.5	5.6	6.2
	2000	11.7	6.2	11.0	22.9	0.0	12.6	12.7	11.6	10.5
Congo, Rep.	1994	20.6	9.3	16.3	62.1	0.0	22.1	20.5	20.3	14.8
	1997	17.6	8.6	16.7	35.8	0.0	17.8	15.2	17.5	17.0
Costa Rica	1995	10.3	8.0	8.6	29.3	0.1	13.0	10.5	10.0	8.0
	2000	5.4	7.5	3.7	0.4	0.0	9.6	6.1	4.8	3.2
Côte d'Ivoire	1993	25.3	11.9	22.2	76.3	0.0	26.6	21.6	25.1	22.6
	1996	19.0	10.8	14.1	52.6	0.0	19.7	14.3	18.8	14.1
Cuba	1993	13.1	8.0	10.0	25.8	0.0	13.7	8.3	13.0	11.6
	1997	11.3	6.6	8.1	9.5	0.0	10.6	5.2	11.4	9.8
Czech Republic	1996	6.9	6.2	5.8	5.4	0.0	8.1	4.1	6.6	6.3
	1999	6.5	9.3	5.7	5.4	0.0	11.0	5.1	5.4	5.9
Dominican Republic	1997	14.9	9.1	15.8	33.3	0.0	16.5	10.4	14.7	17.8
Ecuador	1993	8.7	5.9	8.1	20.4	0.0	9.3	6.4	8.6	8.4
	1999	12.8	6.4	11.1	36.4	0.0	12.5	10.4	12.9	11.3
Egypt, Arab Rep.	1995	25.6	33.2	16.6	53.1	1.2	24.2	7.6	25.8	22.4
	1998	20.5	39.5	13.7	47.4	9.5	22.5	7.5	20.2	17.5
El Salvador	1995	10.3	7.8	9.1	27.4	0.0	12.6	10.2	9.9	8.8
	2000	7.4	8.6	6.5	9.8	0.0	10.4	8.2	6.8	5.5
Equatorial Guinea	1998	19.1	9.7	15.3	55.4	0.2	21.1	23.7	18.4	13.6
Estonia	1995	0.1	1.0	0.4	0.1	0.0	0.0	0.0	0.1	0.5
Ethiopia	1995	32.0	23.5	18.1	71.3	0.2	37.1	18.4	31.7	18.1
European Union	1989	4.1	5.9	3.8	3.9	18.2	8.7	2.7	2.7	4.4
	2000	2.4	4.4	1.8	1.8	7.2	4.6	1.3	1.8	1.9
Gabon	1995	20.4	9.6	16.1	60.6	0.0	23.4	20.0	19.7	15.1
	1998	20.4	9.8	16.0	61.1	0.3	23.4	20.2	19.7	14.7
Georgia	1999	9.9	3.2	10.1	0.0	1.0	11.9	12.0	9.5	8.3
†Data for Taiwan, China	1989	12.3	9.5	10.0	16.9	0.5	17.3	8.4	11.2	10.7
	2000	7.8	8.2	3.9	9.6	0.3	13.6	6.4	6.7	3.3

	Year	All products					Primary products		Manufactured products	
		Simple mean tariff %	Standard deviation of tariff rates %	Weighted mean tariff %	Share of lines with international peaks %	Share of lines with specific tariffs %	Simple mean tariff %	Weighted mean tariff %	Simple mean tariff %	Weighted mean tariff %
Ghana	1993	14.6	9.0	11.2	42.3	0.0	20.2	16.2	13.8	8.7
Guatemala	1995	10.0	7.4	8.7	25.3	0.0	12.6	10.2	9.6	8.1
	2000	7.2	7.8	5.8	9.6	0.0	9.3	7.5	6.9	5.2
Honduras	1995	9.8	7.5	9.0	25.1	0.0	13.3	12.9	9.3	7.6
	2000	7.9	7.5	8.3	25.9	0.0	11.6	12.3	7.3	6.7
Hungary	1991	12.7	10.9	10.1	18.9	0.0	14.7	5.5	12.4	11.8
	1997	8.2	14.7	4.5	10.4	0.0	25.9	6.8	4.6	3.9
Iceland	1993	3.6	7.6	3.4	5.5	0.0	3.8	5.2	3.6	2.8
	1996	5.7	13.1	3.6	4.2	0.7	9.5	5.9	4.9	2.9
India	1990	79.0	43.6	49.6	97.0	0.9	69.1	25.4	80.2	69.9
	1999	32.5	12.3	28.5	93.1	0.6	30.9	23.2	32.8	32.7
Indonesia	1989	21.9	19.7	13.0	50.3	0.3	19.9	5.8	22.3	15.6
	2000	8.4	10.8	5.2	11.2	0.0	6.3	2.8	8.9	6.7
Iran, Islamic Rep.	2000	4.9	4.2	3.1	0.6	0.0	2.9	0.9	5.1	3.8
Israel	1993	7.7	12.2	4.0	15.7	0.0	5.3	1.9	8.1	4.4
Jamaica	1996	20.8	9.0	17.8	44.0	41.2	21.2	14.2	20.7	20.9
	2000	10.6	11.3	9.6	33.3	0.0	15.5	9.0	9.4	10.0
Japan	1989	5.6	7.9	3.0	9.1	3.3	8.3	3.3	4.7	2.7
	2000	4.5	7.0	2.0	7.1	3.0	8.3	3.4	3.2	1.2
Jordan	2000	22.8	16.6	18.9	63.3	0.4	26.2	16.9	22.3	19.8
Kenya	1994	31.9	13.8	20.7	87.0	1.2	32.2	17.0	31.9	23.3
	2000	19.3	12.7	12.4	34.7	9.6	18.1	10.6	19.4	13.0
Korea, Rep.	1989	14.8	5.3	10.5	11.8	12.5	14.6	5.5	14.9	13.5
	1999	8.6	5.9	5.9	4.8	0.7	12.3	5.5	7.8	6.1
Kyrgyz Republic	1995	0.0	0.0	0.0	0.0	19.7	0.0	0.0	0.0	0.0
Lao PDR	2000	9.6	7.8	14.7	11.7	3.5	18.6	24.5	8.8	8.9
Latvia	1996	4.3	7.5	2.2	2.2	0.0	8.3	1.5	3.2	2.6
	1997	5.6	9.2	3.2	2.9	0.0	10.0	4.0	4.2	2.9
Lebanon	1999	12.6	9.9	12.2	23.9	0.1	13.0	11.8	12.5	12.4
	2000	17.9	14.2	19.1	37.1	1.7	23.9	24.3	16.9	16.0
Libya	1996	27.3	37.0	21.3	58.3	1.4	24.8	9.6	27.7	25.7
Lithuania	1995	3.8	8.5	2.6	6.9	0.0	8.3	3.7	2.6	1.8
	1997	3.8	7.9	2.3	6.4	0.0	7.5	3.3	2.8	1.8
Madagascar	1995	7.6	5.9	5.2	6.0	0.0	6.1	2.7	7.8	6.3
Malawi	1994	31.3	14.6	22.3	87.0	0.0	27.7	12.8	31.7	26.6
	1998	19.6	14.9	11.5	13.9	62.9	17.8	6.1	19.8	13.4
Malaysia	1988	17.0	15.1	9.4	46.1	7.2	15.2	4.6	17.4	10.5
	1997	9.3	33.3	6.0	24.7	0.4	7.0	10.0	10.3	5.4
Mali	1995	16.3	12.6	10.3	41.8	0.0	18.2	13.5	16.1	8.5
Mauritius	1995	36.2	28.5	23.5	64.7	0.0	26.2	25.7	37.5	22.7
	1998	31.0	27.8	23.8	28.9	50.0	23.8	15.2	32.0	26.9
Mexico	1991	13.2	4.3	11.9	18.9	0.0	12.2	8.2	13.3	13.1
	2000	16.2	9.2	15.4	50.7	0.5	18.3	20.2	16.1	14.8
Moldova	1996	6.3	9.2	1.6	19.9	1.2	10.3	0.8	4.8	2.7
	2000	4.6	5.5	2.3	0.1	0.7	9.3	1.7	4.0	2.8
Morocco	1993	66.5	29.5	45.4	96.8	0.1	55.1	30.2	68.1	55.8
	2000	33.6	22.0	25.8	79.9	0.0	42.4	27.1	32.3	25.3
Mozambique	1994	5.0	0.0	5.0	0.0	0.0	5.0	5.0	5.0	5.0
	1997	16.8	14.3	17.4	37.7	0.0	19.9	22.0	16.2	15.5
Nepal	1993	21.9	17.8	15.9	58.9	1.0	11.9	9.3	23.6	19.1
	2000	17.9	20.9	17.7	18.7	7.9	13.5	13.8	19.0	19.6
New Zealand	1992	10.4	11.0	8.5	36.0	2.8	5.9	3.7	11.2	9.6
	2000	3.3	4.4	2.3	0.0	5.8	1.6	0.5	3.6	2.9
Nicaragua	1995	7.5	7.9	5.6	20.4	0.0	8.7	7.1	7.4	4.6
	2000	3.2	4.7	2.9	0.2	0.0	5.1	3.8	2.9	2.3
Nigeria	1989	27.9	20.1	24.7	64.2	0.4	33.7	32.5	27.3	22.5
	1995	21.8	15.7	20.0	9.7	80.5	29.5	20.8	20.2	19.9
Norway	1988	1.9	5.2	0.7	5.1	8.0	0.9	0.2	2.1	0.9
	2000	2.9	15.6	1.1	4.4	8.6	8.7	2.5	2.1	0.8

		All products					Primary products		Manufactured products	
	Year	Simple mean tariff %	Standard deviation of tariff rates %	Weighted mean tariff %	Share of lines with international peaks %	Share of lines with specific tariffs %	Simple mean tariff %	Weighted mean tariff %	Simple mean tariff %	Weighted mean tariff %
Oman	1992	5.5	8.2	7.4	1.5	0.0	7.2	14.1	5.2	5.5
	1997	4.8	0.9	4.7	0.0	0.0	4.0	3.1	4.9	5.0
Pakistan	1995	50.9	21.5	46.4	91.4	4.4	45.7	23.0	51.5	51.0
	1998	46.6	21.2	41.7	86.3	4.2	43.6	30.1	46.9	44.1
Panama	1998	9.5	5.6	8.7	0.8	17.9	11.0	9.6	9.2	8.5
	2000	9.5	7.4	7.8	1.4	0.1	12.4	7.7	9.0	7.8
Papua New Guinea	1997	21.1	18.5	15.6	33.4	1.9	32.8	21.7	19.6	13.7
Paraguay	1991	15.6	11.5	11.9	41.8	0.0	13.8	3.6	15.8	14.5
	2000	10.9	6.7	10.5	33.6	0.0	11.9	8.6	10.8	11.4
Peru	1993	17.3	4.2	15.9	23.3	0.0	18.4	15.5	17.2	16.1
	1999	13.0	2.6	12.6	12.0	0.0	13.7	13.5	12.9	12.3
Philippines	1989	28.0	14.2	22.4	77.2	0.1	29.6	18.5	27.7	23.6
	2000	7.6	7.9	3.8	8.8	0.0	11.9	7.5	6.9	3.3
Poland	1991	12.2	9.0	10.5	24.6	0.0	11.8	8.2	12.2	11.3
	2000	10.0	9.8	7.4	14.3	5.0	17.6	6.2	8.4	7.8
Romania	1991	19.2	8.3	11.9	55.6	0.0	20.1	8.2	19.0	18.2
	1999	15.2	16.2	12.4	36.0	0.0	25.4	11.0	12.9	12.8
Russian Federation	1993	7.8	9.8	6.2	3.2	0.0	3.4	3.9	9.4	7.5
	1997	13.9	8.5	11.3	35.5	0.0	11.5	10.3	14.8	11.8
Rwanda	1993	28.3	26.8	25.5	59.6	1.7	37.8	36.7	27.5	21.7
Saudi Arabia	1994	12.5	3.3	10.7	10.3	0.1	12.2	9.1	12.6	11.0
	2000	12.3	3.1	10.3	8.2	4.1	11.9	7.9	12.4	10.9
Singapore	1989	0.6	3.0	1.1	0.3	1.6	0.7	2.5	0.6	0.6
	1995	0.0	0.0	0.0	0.0	0.2	0.0	0.0	0.0	0.0
Slovenia	1999	11.8	6.5	11.4	20.8	3.1	11.9	7.5	11.8	12.3
South Africa[a]	1988	12.7	11.8	12.0	32.3	18.8	6.3	4.3	12.9	12.4
	1999	8.5	10.2	4.4	21.9	20.6	8.0	1.8	8.6	5.1
Sri Lanka	1990	28.3	24.5	26.9	51.7	1.4	31.8	32.2	28.0	24.4
	2000	9.9	9.3	7.4	22.0	0.7	15.3	14.8	9.2	5.2
Sudan	1996	5.3	11.9	3.8	8.9	0.0	12.4	3.3	4.7	4.0
Switzerland	1990	0.0	0.0	0.0	0.0	53.3	0.0	0.0	0.0	0.0
	2000	0.0	0.1	0.0	0.0	31.2	0.0	0.0	0.0	0.0
Tanzania	1993	14.4	10.7	15.6	43.2	0.0	21.6	19.9	13.7	14.8
	2000	17.9	8.6	14.2	69.4	0.0	17.1	16.1	18.0	13.5
Thailand	1989	38.5	19.6	33.0	72.8	21.9	30.6	24.2	39.6	35.7
	2000	16.6	14.1	10.1	45.9	1.7	21.9	9.5	15.7	10.2
Trinidad and Tobago	1991	19.9	14.9	13.0	40.3	0.0	26.9	10.9	18.7	14.2
	1999	18.4	8.8	17.0	36.7	45.2	20.8	17.8	17.8	16.7
Tunisia	1990	28.3	10.1	25.9	97.1	0.0	24.4	17.4	28.7	28.6
	1998	30.0	13.1	28.8	90.4	0.0	28.7	21.2	30.2	30.2
Turkey	1993	7.4	5.0	6.1	5.9	0.0	6.0	7.9	7.6	5.4
	1997	8.1	12.8	5.7	8.2	0.3	22.2	5.2	5.9	5.8
Turkmenistan	1998	0.0	0.0	0.0	0.0	0.0	0.0	0.0	0.0	0.0
Uganda	1994	16.8	9.3	13.6	53.6	0.0	17.0	17.5	16.8	12.4
	2000	8.3	5.8	6.1	0.0	0.0	9.4	5.6	8.2	6.3
Ukraine	1995	9.0	9.4	9.5	14.5	0.0	13.1	15.6	7.6	6.4
	1997	10.4	11.0	5.2	23.7	0.0	16.8	3.4	8.2	7.2
United States	1989	5.6	6.8	3.8	8.0	12.7	3.7	2.0	6.0	4.1
	2000	4.0	10.7	1.8	5.8	8.0	4.3	1.4	4.0	1.9
Uruguay	1992	7.5	5.8	5.8	0.0	0.0	8.0	5.7	7.5	5.8
	2000	11.1	8.3	6.2	37.9	6.9	9.1	2.5	11.3	7.8
Venezuela, RB	1992	15.7	11.4	16.4	47.4	1.0	17.7	14.5	15.5	16.7
	2000	12.6	5.9	13.4	25.4	0.0	13.0	13.5	12.5	13.4
Vietnam	1994	12.8	17.9	20.2	32.6	1.0	21.4	46.4	12.0	13.0
	1999	15.2	17.8	18.7	37.3	0.5	22.5	34.9	14.3	14.8
Zambia	1993	25.2	11.0	17.9	90.9	0.0	29.5	12.4	24.5	20.0
	1997	14.7	8.8	13.1	32.2	0.0	17.1	13.9	14.4	12.9
Zimbabwe	1996	40.8	15.0	39.2	94.4	1.5	34.3	40.3	41.4	38.9
	1998	21.4	20.1	16.4	45.1	0.0	26.2	20.4	20.9	15.9

a. Data refer to the South African Customs Union (Botswana, Lesotho, Namibia, South Africa, and Swaziland).

About the data

Poor people in developing countries work primarily in agriculture and labor-intensive manufactures, the very sectors that confront the greatest trade barriers. Removing barriers to merchandise trade could increase growth by about 0.5 percent a year in developing countries. If trade in services (financial, business, telecommunications, and retailing services) were also liberalized, growth would be even higher. In general, tariffs in high-income countries on imports from developing countries, though low, are four times those collected from industrial countries. But protection is also an issue for developing countries, which also have high tariffs on agricultural commodities, labor-intensive manufactures, and other products and services. In some developing regions new trade policies could make the difference between achieving important Millennium Development Goals— such as poverty reduction, lowering maternal and child mortality, and improving educational attainment—falling short by a large margin.

Economies regulate their imports through a combination of tariff and nontariff measures. The most common form of tariff is an ad valorem duty, based on the value of the import, but tariffs may also be levied on a specific, or per unit, basis or may combine ad valorem and specific rates. Tariffs may be used to raise fiscal revenues or to protect domestic industries from foreign competition—or both. Nontariff barriers, which limit the quantity of imports of a particular good, take many forms. Some common ones are quotas, prohibitions, licensing schemes, export restraint arrangements, and health and quarantine measures.

Nontariff barriers are generally considered less desirable than tariffs because changes in an exporting country's efficiency and costs no longer result in changes in market share in the importing country. Further, the quotas or licenses that regulate trade become very valuable, and resources are frequently wasted in attempts to acquire these assets. A high percentage of products subject to nontariff barriers suggests a protectionist trade regime, but the frequency of nontariff barriers does not measure how much they restrict trade. Moreover, a wide range of domestic policies and regulations (such as health regulations) may act as nontariff barriers. Because of the difficulty of combining nontariff barriers into an aggregate indicator, they are not included in this table.

The table shows data on average tariffs, the dispersion of tariff rates, the proportion of tariff lines with duties exceeding 15 percent, and the proportion of lines subject to specific tariffs. The rates used in calculating the indicators are effectively applied rates, which reflect the rates actually applied to partners in preferential trade agreements such as the North American Free Trade Agreement. Countries typically maintain a hierarchy of trade preferences applicable to specific trading partners. In previous years the indicators were based on most-favored-nation rates, which are equal to or higher than effectively applied rates.

Two measures of average tariffs are shown: the simple and the weighted mean tariff. Weighted mean tariffs are weighted by the value of the country's trade with each of its trading partners. Simple averages are frequently a better indicator of tariff protection than weighted averages, which are biased downward because higher tariffs discourage trade and reduce the weights applied to these tariffs. Specific duties— duties not expressed as a proportion of the declared value—have not been included in this year's table, but work is under way to estimate ad valorem equivalents.

Some countries set fairly uniform tariff rates across all imports. Others are more selective, setting high tariffs to protect favored domestic industries. The standard deviation of tariffs is a measure of the dispersion of tariff rates around their mean value. Highly dispersed rates increase the costs of protection substantially. But these nominal tariff rates tell only part of the story. The effective rate of protection—the degree to which the value added in an industry is protected—may exceed the nominal rate if the tariff system systematically differentiates among imports of raw materials, intermediate products, and finished goods.

Two other measures of tariff coverage are shown: the share of tariff lines with international peaks (those for which ad valorem tariff rates exceed 15 percent) and the share of tariff lines with specific duties (those not covered by ad valorem rates). Some countries—for example, Switzerland—apply only specific duties.

The indicators in this table were calculated from data supplied by the United Nations Conference on Trade and Development (UNCTAD). Data are classified using the Harmonized System of trade at the six- or eight-digit level. Tariff line data were matched to Standard International Trade Classification (SITC) revision 2 codes to define the commodity groups and import weights. Import weights were calculated for 1995 using the United Nations Statistics Division's Commodity Trade (COMTRADE) database. Data are shown only for the first and last year for which complete data are available. To conserve space, countries for which only a single year is available and countries that are members of the European Union have not been included. Data for the whole of the European Union are shown.

Definitions

• **Primary products** are commodities classified in SITC revision 2 sections 0–4 plus division 68 (nonferrous metals). • **Manufactured products** are commodities classified in SITC revision 2 sections 5–9 excluding division 68. • **Simple mean tariff** is the unweighted average of the effectively applied rates for all products subject to tariffs. • **Standard deviation of tariff rates** measures the average dispersion of tariff rates around the simple mean. • **Weighted mean tariff** is the average of effectively applied rates weighted by the product import shares corresponding to each partner country. • **International peaks** are tariff rates that exceed 15 percent. • **Specific tariffs** are tariffs that are set on a per unit basis or that combine ad valorem and per unit rates.

Data sources

All indicators in this table were calculated by World Bank staff using the World Integrated Trade Solution (WITS) system. Tariff data were provided by UNCTAD. Data on global imports come from the United Nations Statistics Division's COMTRADE database.

6.7 | Global financial flows

	Net private capital flows $ millions		Foreign direct investment $ millions		Portfolio investment flows				Bank and trade-related lending $ millions	
					Bonds $ millions		Equity $ millions			
	1990	2000	1990	2000	1990	2000	1990	2000	1990	2000
Afghanistan	..	..	..	..	..	..	..	..	..	..
Albania	31	142	0	143	0	0	0	0	31	-1
Algeria	-424	-1,212	0	10	-16	0	0	4	-409	-1,226
Angola	235	1,206	-335	1,698	0	0	0	0	570	-492
Argentina	-203	16,620	1,836	11,665	-857	4,847	13	450	-1,195	-343
Armenia	..	159	..	140	..	0	..	0	..	19
Australia	..	..	8,111	11,527	..	..	..	..	..	..
Austria	..	..	653	9,066	..	..	..	..	..	..
Azerbaijan	..	175	..	130	..	0	..	0	..	45
Bangladesh	58	269	3	280	0	0	0	3	55	-14
Belarus	..	123	..	90	..	0	..	0	..	33
Belgiumª	..	..	5,987	17,902	..	..	..	..	..	..
Benin	1	30	1	30	0	0	0	0	0	0
Bolivia	3	923	27	733	0	0	0	0	-24	190
Bosnia and Herzegovina	..	4	..	0	..	0	..	0	..	4
Botswana	77	27	95	30	0	0	0	0	-19	-3
Brazil	563	45,672	989	32,779	129	164	0	5,016	-555	7,713
Bulgaria	-42	1,114	4	1,002	65	0	0	5	-111	107
Burkina Faso	-1	10	0	10	0	0	0	0	-1	0
Burundi	-5	12	1	12	0	0	0	0	-6	0
Cambodia	0	126	0	126	0	0	0	0	0	0
Cameroon	-125	-21	-113	31	0	0	0	0	-12	-52
Canada	..	..	7,581	62,758	..	..	..	..	..	..
Central African Republic	0	5	1	5	0	0	0	0	-1	0
Chad	-1	14	0	15	0	0	0	0	-1	-1
Chile	2,098	4,833	590	3,675	-7	672	320	18	1,194	469
China	8,107	58,295	3,487	38,399	-48	-2,451	0	22,198	4,668	148
Hong Kong, China	..	..	..	..	..	..	..	..	..	..
Colombia	345	3,130	500	2,376	-4	1,225	0	26	-151	-497
Congo, Dem. Rep.	-24	1	-12	1	0	0	0	0	-12	0
Congo, Rep.	-100	14	0	14	0	0	0	0	-100	0
Costa Rica	23	912	163	409	-42	220	0	0	-99	-20
Côte d'Ivoire	57	-47	48	106	-1	-46	0	6	10	-113
Croatia	..	2,451	..	926	..	833	..	0	..	692
Cuba	..	..	..	..	..	..	..	..	..	..
Czech Republic	876	3,299	207	4,583	0	-325	0	617	669	-1,576
Denmark	..	..	1,132	34,192	..	..	..	..	..	..
Dominican Republic	130	1,142	133	953	0	-4	0	74	-3	119
Ecuador	184	904	126	710	0	0	0	0	58	194
Egypt, Arab Rep.	668	1,967	734	1,235	-1	0	0	619	-65	114
El Salvador	8	338	2	185	0	132	0	0	6	22
Eritrea	..	35	..	35	..	0	..	0	..	0
Estonia	..	485	..	387	..	110	..	-29	..	16
Ethiopia	-45	42	12	50	0	0	0	0	-57	-8
Finland	..	..	812	9,125	..	..	..	..	..	..
France	..	..	13,183	43,173	..	..	..	..	..	..
Gabon	103	142	74	150	0	0	0	0	29	-8
Gambia, The	-8	14	0	14	0	0	0	0	-8	0
Georgia	..	155	..	131	..	0	..	0	..	24
Germany	..	..	2,532	189,178	..	..	..	..	..	..
Ghana	-5	71	15	110	0	0	0	17	-20	-57
Greece	..	..	1,005	1,083	..	..	..	..	..	..
Guatemala	44	178	48	230	-11	-31	0	0	7	-22
Guinea	-1	63	18	63	0	0	0	0	-19	0
Guinea-Bissau	2	0	2	0	0	0	0	0	0	0
Haiti	8	13	8	13	0	0	0	0	0	0
Honduras	76	301	44	282	0	0	0	0	32	19

	Net private capital flows		Foreign direct investment		Portfolio investment flows				Bank and trade-related lending	
					Bonds $ millions		Equity $ millions			
	$ millions		$ millions						$ millions	
	1990	2000	1990	2000	1990	2000	1990	2000	1990	2000
Hungary	-308	1,721	0	1,692	921	-1,218	150	0	-1,379	1,247
India	1,872	8,771	162	2,315	147	4,916	105	2,117	1,458	-576
Indonesia	3,235	-11,210	1,093	-4,550	26	-2,050	312	379	1,804	-4,988
Iran, Islamic Rep.	-392	-610	-362	39	0	0	0	0	-30	-649
Iraq	..	..	..	..	..	..	..	..	..	..
Ireland	..	..	627	22,778	..	..	..	..	..	..
Israel	..	..	151	4,392	..	..	..	..	..	..
Italy	..	..	6,411	13,175	..	..	..	..	..	..
Jamaica	92	898	138	456	0	485	0	0	-46	-43
Japan	..	..	1,777	8,227	..	..	..	..	..	..
Jordan	254	455	38	558	0	-95	0	12	216	-20
Kazakhstan	..	1,900	..	1,250	..	350	..	0	..	300
Kenya	122	53	57	111	0	0	0	4	65	-61
Korea, Dem. Rep.	..	..	..	..	..	..	..	..	..	..
Korea, Rep.	1,038	13,215	788	9,283	151	1,333	518	7,784	-418	-5,185
Kuwait	..	..	..	16	..	..	..	..	..	..
Kyrgyz Republic	..	-65	..	-2	..	0	..	0	..	-62
Lao PDR	6	72	6	72	0	0	0	0	0	0
Latvia	..	583	..	407	..	-30	..	0	..	206
Lebanon	12	2,028	6	298	0	1,040	0	4	6	687
Lesotho	17	111	17	118	0	0	0	0	0	-7
Liberia	0	12	0	12	0	0	0	0	0	0
Libya	..	..	..	..	..	..	..	..	..	..
Lithuania	..	799	..	379	..	312	..	151	..	-43
Macedonia, FYR	..	187	..	176	..	0	..	0	..	12
Madagascar	7	83	22	83	0	0	0	0	-15	0
Malawi	2	45	0	45	0	0	0	0	2	0
Malaysia	770	3,228	2,333	1,660	-1,239	477	293	542	-617	550
Mali	-8	76	-7	76	0	0	0	0	-1	0
Mauritania	6	3	7	5	0	0	0	0	-1	-2
Mauritius	86	-7	41	266	0	-150	0	0	45	-123
Mexico	8,253	11,537	2,634	13,286	661	-2,636	563	3,517	4,396	-2,631
Moldova	..	209	..	128	..	0	..	0	..	81
Mongolia	..	27	..	30	..	0	..	0	..	-3
Morocco	341	-293	165	10	0	-30	0	147	176	-419
Mozambique	35	138	9	139	0	0	0	0	26	-1
Myanmar	153	188	161	255	0	0	0	0	-8	-66
Namibia	..	..	..	..	..	..	..	..	..	..
Nepal	-8	-4	6	4	0	0	0	0	-14	-8
Netherlands	..	..	10,676	54,138	..	..	..	..	..	..
New Zealand	..	..	1,735	3,209	..	..	..	..	..	..
Nicaragua	20	395	0	254	0	0	0	0	20	141
Niger	9	13	-1	15	0	0	0	0	10	-2
Nigeria	467	908	588	1,082	0	0	0	2	-121	-177
Norway	..	..	1,003	5,882	..	..	..	..	..	..
Oman	-259	56	141	23	0	0	0	11	-400	23
Pakistan	181	-53	244	308	0	0	0	0	-63	-361
Panama	127	947	132	603	-2	249	0	0	-4	95
Papua New Guinea	204	128	155	130	0	0	0	48	49	-50
Paraguay	67	-16	76	82	0	0	0	0	-9	-98
Peru	59	1,553	41	680	0	0	0	205	18	668
Philippines	639	2,459	530	2,029	395	797	0	290	-286	-656
Poland	71	13,195	89	9,342	0	2,450	0	871	-18	532
Portugal	..	..	2,610	6,227	..	..	..	..	..	..
Puerto Rico	..	..	..	..	..	..	..	..	..	..
Romania	4	1,900	0	1,025	0	-75	0	0	4	950
Russian Federation	5,556	2,200	0	2,714	310	-1,018	0	1,075	5,246	-571

	Net private capital flows $ millions		Foreign direct investment $ millions		Portfolio investment flows				Bank and trade-related lending $ millions	
					Bonds $ millions		Equity $ millions			
	1990	2000	1990	2000	1990	2000	1990	2000	1990	2000
Rwanda	6	14	8	14	0	0	0	0	-2	0
Saudi Arabia	..	..	..	..	..	..	..	..	..	..
Senegal	42	106	57	107	0	0	0	0	-15	-2
Sierra Leone	36	1	32	1	0	0	0	0	4	0
Singapore	..	..	5,575	6,390	..	..	..	..	..	..
Slovak Republic	278	2,185	0	2,052	0	758	0	0	278	-625
Slovenia	..	..	..	176	..	..	..	..	..	..
Somalia	6	0	6	0	0	0	0	0	0	0
South Africa	..	2,736	..	961	..	1,193	..	864	..	-282
Spain	..	..	13,984	36,023	..	..	..	..	..	..
Sri Lanka	53	262	43	173	0	-50	0	6	10	133
Sudan	0	392	0	392	0	0	0	0	0	0
Swaziland	28	33	30	-44	0	0	0	0	-2	0
Sweden	..	..	1,982	22,125	..	..	..	..	..	..
Switzerland	..	..	5,987	17,902	..	..	..	..	..	..
Syrian Arab Republic	62	107	71	111	0	0	0	0	-9	-4
Tajikistan	..	64	..	24	..	0	..	0	..	40
Tanzania	5	182	0	193	0	0	0	0	5	-11
Thailand	4,380	-1,383	2,444	3,366	-87	-1,218	449	1,044	1,574	-4,575
Togo	0	30	0	30	0	0	0	0	0	0
Trinidad and Tobago	-69	673	109	650	-52	128	0	0	-126	-106
Tunisia	-121	966	76	752	-60	-371	0	0	-137	585
Turkey	1,782	11,416	684	982	597	6,484	35	2,701	466	1,250
Turkmenistan	..	..	..	..	..	0	..	0	..	..
Uganda	16	231	0	220	0	0	0	0	16	11
Ukraine	..	927	..	595	..	-33	..	0	..	365
United Arab Emirates	..	..	..	..	..	..	..	..	..	..
United Kingdom	..	..	33,504	133,974	..	..	..	..	..	..
United States	..	..	48,490	287,680	..	..	..	..	..	..
Uruguay	-192	574	0	298	-16	284	0	0	-176	-8
Uzbekistan	..	18	..	100	..	0	..	0	..	-82
Venezuela, RB	-126	5,454	451	4,464	345	-751	0	71	-922	1,670
Vietnam	16	581	16	1,298	0	0	0	0	0	-717
West Bank and Gaza	..	..	..	..	..	..	..	..	..	..
Yemen, Rep.	30	-201	-131	-201	0	0	0	0	161	0
Yugoslavia, Fed. Rep.	-837	0	67	0	0	0	0	0	-904	0
Zambia	194	191	203	200	0	0	0	0	-9	-9
Zimbabwe	85	29	-12	79	-30	0	0	1	127	-50

World	.. s	.. s	199,954 s	1,167,987 s	.. s	.. s	.. s	.. s	.. s	.. s
Low income	6,636	4,581	2,201	6,562	142	2,787	416	2,528	3,876	-7,296
Middle income	35,937	221,265	21,918	160,129	1,062	14,091	2,343	48,340	10,614	-1,295
Lower middle income	18,660	79,672	8,724	61,018	543	-2,071	449	25,902	8,944	-5,177
Upper middle income	17,045	141,329	13,194	99,087	519	16,162	1,894	22,438	1,438	3,642
Low & middle income	43,556	225,846	24,119	166,691	1,204	16,879	3,743	50,867	14,490	-8,591
East Asia & Pacific	19,402	65,693	11,135	52,130	-802	-3,113	2,290	32,285	6,779	-15,609
Europe & Central Asia	7,692	45,446	1,051	28,495	1,893	8,598	235	5,391	4,513	2,962
Latin America & Carib.	12,630	97,305	8,177	75,088	145	4,986	1,111	9,378	3,196	7,853
Middle East & N. Africa	384	1,074	2,458	1,209	-148	544	0	795	-1,926	-1,474
South Asia	2,162	9,254	464	3,093	147	4,866	105	2,126	1,446	-831
Sub-Saharan Africa	1,287	7,074	834	6,676	-31	997	2	893	482	-1,492
High income	..	..	175,835	1,001,296	..	..	..	..	..	..
Europe EMU	..	..	58,480	401,868	..	..	..	..	..	..

a. Includes Luxembourg

About the data

The most recent wave of global integration, starting around 1980 and continuing today, has seen improvements in the investment climate and an opening to foreign trade and investment in many developing economies. Private capital flows to developing economies have increased dramatically, from around $44 billion in 1990 to $257 billion in 2000, while official flows have decreased from $57 billion to $39 billion during the same period. Foreign direct investment has become the major form of international finance for developing countries, accounting for about 70 percent of the private capital flows in 2000. Mergers and acquisitions were the most important source of this increase in foreign direct investment, especially those resulting from the privatization of public companies.

The data on foreign direct investment are based on balance of payments data reported by the International Monetary Fund (IMF), supplemented by data on net foreign direct investment reported by the Organisation for Economic Co-operation and Development (OECD) and official national sources. The internationally accepted definition of foreign direct investment is that provided in the fifth edition of the IMF's *Balance of Payments Manual* (1993).

Under this definition foreign direct investment has three components: equity investment, reinvested earnings, and short- and long-term intercompany loans between parent firms and foreign affiliates. However, many countries fail to report reinvested earnings, and the definition of long-term loans differs among countries. Foreign direct investment, as distinguished from other kinds of international investment, is made to establish a lasting interest in or effective management control over an enterprise in another country. As a guideline, the IMF suggests that investments should account for at least 10 percent of voting stock to be counted as foreign direct investment. In practice, many countries set a higher threshold.

The OECD has also published a definition, in consultation with the IMF, Eurostat, and the United Nations. Because of the multiplicity of sources and differences in definitions and reporting methods, there may be more than one estimate of foreign direct investment for a country and data may not be comparable across countries.

Foreign direct investment data do not give a complete picture of international investment in an economy. Balance of payments data on foreign direct investment do not include capital raised locally, which has become an important source of financing for investment projects in some developing countries. In addition, foreign direct investment data capture only cross-border investment flows involving equity participation and thus omit nonequity cross-border transactions such as intrafirm flows of goods and services. For a detailed discussion of the data issues see the World Bank's *World Debt Tables 1993–94* (volume 1, chapter 3).

Portfolio flow data are compiled from several official and market sources, including Euromoney databases and publications, Micropal, Lipper Analytical Services, published reports of private investment houses, central banks, national securities and exchange commissions, national stock exchanges, and the World Bank's Debtor Reporting System.

Gross statistics on international bond and equity issues are produced by aggregating individual transactions reported by market sources. Transactions of public and publicly guaranteed bonds are reported through the Debtor Reporting System by World Bank member economies that have received either loans from the International Bank for Reconstruction and Development or credits from the International Development Association. Information on private nonguaranteed bonds is collected from market sources, because official national sources reporting to the Debtor Reporting System are not asked to report the breakdown between private nonguaranteed bonds and private nonguaranteed loans. Information on transactions by nonresidents in local equity markets is gathered from national authorities, investment positions of mutual funds, and market sources.

The volume of portfolio investment reported by the World Bank generally differs from that reported by other sources because of differences in the classification of economies, in the sources, and in the method used to adjust and disaggregate reported information. Differences in reporting arise particularly for foreign investments in local equity markets because clarity, adequate disaggregation, and comprehensive and periodic reporting are lacking in many developing economies. By contrast, capital flows through international debt and equity instruments are well recorded, and for these the differences in reporting lie primarily in the classification of economies, the exchange rates used, whether particular tranches of the transactions are included, and the treatment of certain offshore issuances.

Definitions

• **Net private capital flows** consist of private debt and nondebt flows. Private debt flows include commercial bank lending, bonds, and other private credits; nondebt private flows are foreign direct investment and portfolio equity investment. • **Foreign direct investment** is net inflows of investment to acquire a lasting management interest (10 percent or more of voting stock) in an enterprise operating in an economy other than that of the investor. It is the sum of equity capital, reinvestment of earnings, other long-term capital, and short-term capital, as shown in the balance of payments. • **Portfolio investment flows** are net and include non-debt-creating portfolio equity flows (the sum of country funds, depository receipts, and direct purchases of shares by foreign investors) and portfolio debt flows (bond issues purchased by foreign investors). • **Bank and trade-related lending** covers commercial bank lending and other private credits.

Data sources

The data in this table are compiled from a variety of public and private sources, including the World Bank's Debtor Reporting System, the IMF's International Financial Statistics and Balance of Payments databases, and other sources mentioned in *About the data*. These data are also published in the World Bank's *Global Development Finance 2002*.

6.8 | Net financial flows from Development Assistance Committee members

Net flows to part I countries

Net flows to part I countries	Net official development assistance				Other official flows	Private flows					Net grants by NGOs	Total net flows
	Total	Bilateral grants	Bilateral loans	Contributions to multilateral institutions		Total	Foreign direct investment	Bilateral portfolio investment	Multilateral portfolio investment	Private export credits		
$ millions, 2000												
Australia	987	758	..	229	573	-219	-726	507	..	..	150	1,491
Austria	423	260	-3	167	21	560	421	..	..	139	63	1,067
Belgium	820	477	..	343	-9	1,394	1,441	-494	..	447	75	2,281
Canada	1,744	1,184	-24	583	5	4,621	3,814	821	..	-14	113	6,483
Denmark	1,664	1,011	13	641	-3	482	482	..	..	..	32	2,176
Finland	371	219	-2	154	2	672	493	-494	..	673	5	1,050
France	4,105	3,116	-287	1,276	14	1,439	2,740	-1,301	..	..	..	5,557
Germany	5,030	2,696	-10	2,343	-456	7,000	4,571	2,635	-1,684	1,478	846	12,420
Greece	226	97	1	127	3	..	..	..	..	..	..	229
Ireland	235	155	..	80	..	416	..	416	..	..	90	741
Italy	1,376	525	-148	999	-103	9,537	1,414	7,292	..	832	37	10,846
Japan	13,508	5,678	4,090	3,740	-5,200	2,725	2,874	702	-52	-799	231	11,264
Luxembourg	127	93	..	33	..	..	..	..	..	..	7	133
Netherlands	3,135	2,334	-92	892	38	3,469	2,135	1,980	-646	..	306	6,947
New Zealand	113	85	..	28	..	17	17	..	..	..	12	142
Norway	1,264	925	9	330	..	-5	-36	..	..	31	179	1,437
Portugal	271	320	-141	92	78	4,273	4,011	..	..	262	..	4,622
Spain	1,195	603	117	475	3	22,272	22,286	..	..	-14	..	23,471
Sweden	1,799	1,222	19	557	..	2,127	871	..	..	1,256	26	3,952
Switzerland	890	608	20	263	8	997	1,134	..	-638	500	159	2,054
United Kingdom	4,501	2,563	146	1,792	-72	2,093	834	1,706	..	-447	536	7,058
United States	9,955	8,093	-688	2,550	562	10,666	18,456	-10,724	-365	3,299	4,069	25,252
Total	**53,737**	**33,022**	**3,021**	**17,694**	**-4,537**	**74,537**	**67,234**	**3,046**	**-3,385**	**7,642**	**6,935**	**130,673**

Net flows to part II countries

Net flows to part II countries	Net official aid				Other official flows	Private flows				Net grants by NGOs	Total net flows
	Total	Bilateral grants	Bilateral loans	Contributions to multilateral institutions		Total	Foreign direct investment	Bilateral portfolio investment	Private export credits		
$ millions, 2000											
Australia	8	2	..	6	3	-1,164	-646	..	..	..	-1,154
Austria	187	144	..	43	..	2,090	2,090	..	..	8	2,285
Belgium	74	5	..	69	12	-175	17	-188	-4	10	-78
Canada	165	165	..	..	1,652	1,199	1,139	78	-18	55	3,070
Denmark	189	104	15	71	67	284	284	..	..	13	554
Finland	58	33	0	25	0	1,009	882	123	3	..	1,066
France	1,657	1,001	83	573	-34	10,393	5,221	..	..	..	12,016
Germany	647	325	-102	424	499	20,123	11,156	9,187	-220	60	21,330
Greece	12	10	..	2	..	..	..	..	..	..	12
Ireland	..	..	..	..	..	..	..	..	..	..	..
Italy	406	16	197	193	196	2,821	144	1,382	1,296	..	3,424
Japan	-54	171	-263	39	492	3,504	3,332	-271	443	..	3,942
Luxembourg	2	2	..	..	..	..	..	..	..	..	2
Netherlands	306	228	-21	99	-10	599	2,341	-2,412	671	..	895
New Zealand	0	0	..	..	..	..	..	..	..	..	0
Norway	27	27	..	..	4	1,294	1,257	..	37	..	1,325
Portugal	27	0	..	26	..	1,067	1,060	..	7	..	1,093
Spain	12	12	0	..	..	1,747	1,747	..	..	..	1,759
Sweden	122	119	0	3	-1	1,734	1,902	0	-168	..	1,855
Switzerland	58	57	1	..	..	6,460	6,305	0	155	8	6,526
United Kingdom	439	88	0	350	4	-154	-2,045	3,026	-1,135	7	297
United States	2,506	2,435	27	45	825	17,015	16,101	503	411	2,362	22,708
Total	**6,848**	**4,944**	**-64**	**1,968**	**3,708**	**69,848**	**52,286**	**11,429**	**1,478**	**2,524**	**82,928**

Note: Totals may not sum due to gaps in reporting.

About the data

The high-income members of the Development Assistance Committee (DAC) of the Organisation for Economic Co-operation and Development (OECD) are the main source of official external finance for developing countries. Net disbursements of official development assistance (ODA) by some important donor countries that are not DAC members are shown in table 6.8a. The main table shows the flow of official and private financial resources from DAC members to official and private recipients in developing and transition economies. DAC exists to help its members coordinate their development assistance and to encourage the expansion and improve the effectiveness of the aggregate resources flowing to developing and transition economies. In this capacity, DAC monitors the flow of all financial resources, but its main concern is ODA. DAC has three criteria for ODA: it is undertaken by the official sector. It promotes the economic development and welfare of developing countries as a main objective. And it is provided on concessional terms, with a grant element of at least 25 percent on loans (calculated at a rate of discount of 10 percent).

This definition excludes military aid and nonconcessional flows from official creditors, which are considered other official flows. The definition includes capital projects, food aid, emergency relief, post-conflict peacekeeping efforts, and technical cooperation. Also included are contributions to multilateral institutions, such as the United Nations and its specialized agencies, and concessional funding to the multilateral development banks. In 1999, to avoid double counting extrabudgetary expenditures reported by DAC countries and flows reported by the United Nations, all United Nations agencies revised their data to include only regular budgetary expenditures since 1990 (except for the World Food Programme and the United Nations High Commissioner for Refugees, which revised their data from 1996 onward).

DAC maintains a list of developing countries and territories that are aid recipients. Part I of the list comprises those considered by DAC members to be eligible for ODA. Part II of the list, comprises countries in transition: more advanced Central and Eastern European countries and the new independent states of the former Soviet Union and more advanced developing countries. Flows to these recipients that meet the conditions of eligibility for inclusion in ODA are termed official aid.

The data in the table were compiled from replies by DAC member countries to questionnaires issued by the DAC Secretariat. Net flows of ODA, official aid, and other official resources are defined as gross disbursements of grants and loans minus repayments on earlier loans. Because the data are based on donor country reports, they do not provide a complete picture of the resources received by developing and transition economies, for three reasons. First, flows from DAC members are only part of the aggregate resource flows to these economies. Second, the data that record contributions to multilateral institutions measure the flow of resources made available to those institutions by DAC members, not the flow of resources from those institutions to developing and transition economies. Third, because some of the countries and territories on the DAC recipient list are normally classified as high income, the reported flows may overstate the resources available to low- and middle-income economies. High-income countries receive only a small fraction of all development assistance, however.

Definitions

- **Net official development assistance** comprises grants and loans (net of repayments) that meet the DAC definition of ODA and are made to developing countries and territories in part I of the DAC list of aid recipients. • **Net official aid** comprises grants and loans (net of repayments) that meet the conditions for inclusion in ODA, and are made to countries and territories in part II of the DAC list of aid recipients. • **Bilateral grants** are transfers of money or in kind for which no repayment is required.
- **Bilateral loans** are loans extended by governments or official agencies that have a grant element of at least 25 percent (calculated at a rate of discount of 10 percent) and for which repayment is required in convertible currencies or in kind. • **Contributions to multilateral institutions** are concessional funding received by multilateral institutions from DAC members in the form of grants or capital subscriptions.
- **Other official flows** are transactions by the official sector whose main objective is other than development or whose grant element is less than 25 percent. • **Private flows** consist of flows at market terms financed from private sector resources. They include changes in holdings of private long-term assets by residents of the reporting country. • **Foreign direct investment** is investment by residents of DAC member countries to acquire a lasting management interest (at least 10 percent of voting stock) in an enterprise operating in the recipient country. The data reflect changes in the net worth of subsidiaries in recipient countries whose parent company is in the DAC source country. • **Bilateral portfolio investment** covers bank lending and the purchase of bonds, shares, and real estate by residents of DAC member countries in recipient countries.
- **Multilateral portfolio investment** records the transactions of private banks and nonbanks in DAC member countries in the securities issued by multilateral institutions. • **Private export credits** are loans extended to recipient countries by the private sector in DAC member countries to promote trade; they may be supported by an official guarantee. • **Net grants by NGOs** are private grants by nongovernmental organizations, net of subsidies from the official sector. • **Total net flows** comprise ODA or official aid flows, other official flows, private flows, and net grants by NGOs.

Table 6.8a

Official development assistance from selected non-DAC donors

Net disbursements ($ millions)

	1996	1997	1998	1999	2000
OECD members (non-DAC)					
Czech Republic	..	..	16	15	16
Korea, Rep.	159	186	183	317	212
Poland	..	..	19	20	29
Slovak Republic	..	..	..	7	6
Turkey	88	77	69	120	82
Arab countries					
Kuwait	432	373	278	147	165
Saudi Arabia	327	251	288	185	295
United Arab Emirates	31	115	63	92	150
Other donors					
Estonia	..	..	0.2	0.4	0.5

Note: China also provides aid but does not disclose the amount.
Source: OECD data.

Data sources

The data on financial flows are compiled by DAC and published in its annual statistical report, *Geographical Distribution of Financial Flows to Aid Recipients,* and the DAC annual *Development Co-operation Report.* Data are available in electronic format to registered users on the Web site at www.oecd.org/dac/htm/online.htm and on the OECD's *International Development Statistics* CD-ROM.

6.9 | Aid flows from Development Assistance Committee members

Net flows to part I countries	$ millions		% of GNI		Net official development assistance — annual average % change in volume[b] 1994-95 to 1999-2000	Per capita of donor country[b] $	$	Aid appropriations — % of central government budget		Untied aid[a] — % of total ODA commitments	
	1995	2000	1995	2000		1995	2000	1995	2000	1995	2000
Australia	1,194	987	0.34	0.27	-0.7	60	56	1.2	1.0	..	77.4
Austria	767	423	0.33	0.23	-4.1	78	60	..	..	25.0	59.2
Belgium	1,034	820	0.38	0.36	2.0	83	91	..	0.0	..	85.7
Canada	2,067	1,744	0.38	0.25	-4.1	67	55	1.4	1.5	31.5	24.9
Denmark	1,623	1,664	0.96	1.06	4.3	274	348	2.5	3.2	61.3	80.5
Finland	388	371	0.32	0.31	6.1	63	80	1.0	1.1	75.8	89.5
France	8,443	4,105	0.55	0.32	-7.3	122	80	..	..	58.4	*68.0*
Germany	7,524	5,030	0.31	0.27	-1.9	75	71	..	..	60.3	93.2
Greece		226		0.20			25		..		23.5
Ireland	153	235	0.29	0.30	13.2	42	68	..	..	..	..
Italy	1,623	1,376	0.15	0.13	-5.5	29	27	..	..	59.8	38.2
Japan	14,489	13,508	0.27	0.28	3.9	94	102	1.1	..	96.3	86.4
Luxembourg	65	127	0.36	0.71	18.1	136	320	..	..	..	96.7
Netherlands	3,226	3,135	0.81	0.84	5.5	173	221	3.0	..	78.9	95.3
New Zealand	123	113	0.23	0.25	4.9	28	34	0.6	0.6	..	..
Norway	1,244	1,264	0.86	0.80	2.1	264	276	1.8	..	77.0	97.7
Portugal	258	271	0.25	0.26	0.9	24	30	0.8	0.1	98.1	98.2
Spain	1,348	1,195	0.24	0.22	1.5	31	34	1.0	0.0	0.0	47.2
Sweden	1,704	1,799	0.77	0.80	1.3	174	223	..	..	93.9	85.4
Switzerland	1,084	890	0.34	0.34	2.1	122	137	2.9	2.7	91.3	93.6
United Kingdom	3,202	4,501	0.29	0.32	1.5	63	79	1.1	..	86.2	91.5
United States	7,367	9,955	0.10	0.10	0.2	30	35	1.3	0.8	27.3	..
Total or average	**58,926**	**53,737**	**0.26**	**0.22**	**0.4**	**65**	**67**	**1.3**	**0.8**	**69.6**	**81.1**

Net flows to part II countries	Net official aid — $ millions		% of GNI		annual average % change in volume[b] 1994-95 to 1999-2000	Per capita of donor country[b] $	$
	1995	2000	1995	2000		1995	2000
Australia	4	8	0.00	0.00	7.7	0	0
Austria	313	187	0.14	0.10	-4.5	32	26
Belgium	89	74	0.03	0.03	1.4	7	8
Canada	250	165	0.05	0.02	0.9	8	5
Denmark	170	189	0.10	0.12	4.2	29	40
Finland	76	58	0.06	0.05	3.8	12	13
France	770	1,657	0.05	0.13	16.0	11	32
Germany	4,514	647	0.18	0.03	-24.5	45	9
Greece		12		0.01			1
Ireland	21	0	0.04	0.00	..	6	0
Italy	286	406	0.03	0.04	2.2	5	8
Japan	250	-54	0.00	0.00	-48.2	2	0
Luxembourg	9	2	0.05	0.01	-20.3	19	5
Netherlands	305	306	0.08	0.08	-0.1	16	22
New Zealand	1	0	0.00	0.00	-14.4	0	0
Norway	61	27	0.04	0.02	-17.3	13	6
Portugal	22	27	0.02	0.03	2.9	2	3
Spain	120	12	0.02	0.00	-37.1	3	0
Sweden	152	122	0.07	0.05	0.4	16	15
Switzerland	102	58	0.03	0.02	-6.9	11	9
United Kingdom	406	439	0.04	0.03	1.1	8	8
United States	1,280	2,506	0.02	0.03	8.3	5	9
Total or average	**9,202**	**6,848**	**0.04**	**0.03**	**-2.5**	**10**	**9**

a. Excluding administrative costs in 1995, and administrative costs and technical cooperation in 2000. b. At 1999 prices.

About the data

Developing and developed countries have a shared interest in reducing global poverty and improving the lives of people everywhere. Developing countries have an interest in becoming a part of the global economy and seeing a reduction in poverty and inequalities. Developed countries are vitally interested in making development work better for all in terms of markets, investment, and sustainable growth.

Effective aid supports institutional development and policy reforms that are at the heart of successful development. For aid to be effective,and to have a greater effect on global poverty reduction, there needs to be a partnership among recipient countries, aid agencies, and donor countries. Effective aid complements private investment and requires improvements in economic institutions and policies. And aid agencies need to find alternative approaches and windows of opportunities to nurture reform efforts where traditional methods have failed.

As part of its work, the Development Assistance Committee (DAC) of the Organisation for Economic Co-operation and Development (OECD) assesses the aid performance of member countries relative to the size of their economies. As measured here, aid comprises bilateral disbursements of concessional financing to recipient countries plus the provision by donor governments of concessional financing to multilateral institutions. Volume amounts, at constant prices and exchange rates, are used to measure the change in real resources provided over time. Aid flows to part I recipients—official development assistance (ODA)—are tabulated separately from those to part II recipients—official aid (see *About the data* for table 6.8 for more information on the distinction between the two types of aid flows).

Measures of aid flows from the perspective of donors differ from aid receipts by recipient countries. This is because the concessional funding received by multilateral institutions from donor countries is recorded as an aid disbursement by the donor when the funds are deposited with a multilateral institution and recorded as a resource receipt by the recipient country when that institution makes a disbursement.

Ratios of aid to gross national income (GNI), aid per capita, and aid appropriations as a percentage of donor government budgets are calculated by the OECD. The denominators used in calculating these ratios may differ from corresponding values elsewhere in this book because of differences in timing or definitions.

DAC members have progressively introduced the new System of National Accounts, which replaced GNP with GNI. Because GNI includes items not previously included in GNP, ODA-GNI ratios are slightly lower than previously reported ODA-GNP ratios.

The proportion of untied aid is reported here because tying arrangements require recipients to purchase goods and services from the donor country or from a specified group of countries. Tying arrangements may be justified on the grounds that they prevent a recipient from misappropriating or mismanaging aid receipts, but they may also be motivated by a desire to benefit suppliers in the donor country. The same volume of aid may have different purchasing power depending on the relative costs of suppliers in countries to which the aid is tied and the degree to which each recipient's aid basket is untied. Thus tying arrangements may prevent recipients from obtaining the best value for their money and so reduce the value of the aid received.

Definitions

• **Net official development assistance** and **net official aid** record the actual international transfer by the donor of financial resources or of goods or services valued at the cost to the donor, less any repayments of loan principal during the same period. Data are shown at current prices and dollar exchange rates. • **Aid as a percentage of GNI** shows the donor's contributions of ODA or official aid as a share of its gross national income. • **Average annual percentage change in volume** and **aid per capita of donor country** are calculated using 1999 exchange rates and prices. • **Aid appropriations** are the share of ODA or official aid appropriations in the donor's national budget. • **Untied aid** is the share of ODA that is not subject to restrictions by donors on procurement sources.

Data sources

The data on financial flows are compiled by DAC and published in its annual statistical report, *Geographical Distribution of Financial Flows to Aid Recipients*, and the DAC annual *Development Co-operation Report*. Data are available in electronic format to registered users from the Web site at www.oecd.org/dac/ htm/online.htm and on the OECD's *International Development Statistics* CD-ROM.

Figure 6.9

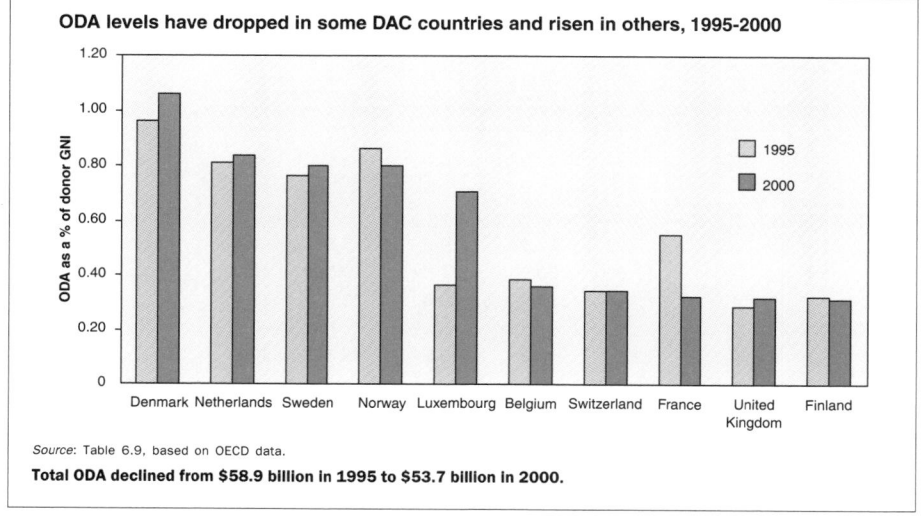

ODA levels have dropped in some DAC countries and risen in others, 1995-2000

Source: Table 6.9, based on OECD data.

Total ODA declined from $58.9 billion in 1995 to $53.7 billion in 2000.

| | Net official development assistance or official aid | | Aid per capita | | Aid dependency ratios | | | | | | | |
| | $ millions | | $ | | Aid as % of GNI | | Aid as % of gross capital formation | | Aid as % of imports of goods and services | | Aid as % of central government expenditure | |
	1995	2000	1995	2000	1995	2000	1995	2000	1995	2000	1995	2000
Afghanistan	214	141	10	5	..	..	..	..	..	..	..	..
Albania	182	319	56	93	7.3	8.3	41.7	45.6	21.1	21.1	24.2	28.6
Algeria	312	162	11	5	0.8	0.3	2.4	1.3	2.4	1.2	2.4	0.6
Angola	418	307	37	23	17.2	6.5	..	12.3	9.7	3.8	..	..
Argentina	144	76	4	2	0.1	0.0	0.3	0.2	0.4	0.2	0.4	0.2
Armenia	218	216	58	57	7.6	11.2	41.0	58.9	29.4	21.2	..	..
Australia												
Austria												
Azerbaijan	119	139	15	17	4.1	2.8	17.8	10.3	9.2	5.8	23.3	16.4
Bangladesh	1,292	1,171	11	9	3.4	2.5	17.8	10.8	19.1	12.5	..	21.4
Belarus	223	40	22	4	1.1	0.1	4.4	0.6	3.8	0.5	6.4	1.3
Belgium												
Benin	280	239	51	38	14.3	11.1	71.2	55.9	30.3	29.6	..	..
Bolivia	719	477	97	57	11.1	5.9	70.5	31.6	39.7	19.5	50.7	23.9
Bosnia and Herzegovina	932	737	273	185	57.4	16.0	250.0	82.0	..	..	..	..
Botswana	90	31	62	19	1.9	0.6	6.8	6.1	3.5	0.9	5.2	..
Brazil	273	322	2	2	0.0	0.1	0.2	0.3	0.4	0.3	..	0.2
Bulgaria	114	311	14	38	0.9	2.7	5.5	15.7	1.6	3.7	2.1	6.7
Burkina Faso	491	336	49	30	22.6	15.5	87.3	55.6	71.0	49.1	..	..
Burundi	288	93	47	14	29.1	13.8	300.1	150.2	102.1	55.9	94.1	39.8
Cambodia	556	398	52	33	19.1	12.6	86.8	83.5	38.6	21.5	..	..
Cameroon	444	380	33	26	6.0	4.6	38.4	26.0	20.3	12.7	42.2	31.1
Canada												
Central African Republic	169	76	50	20	15.3	8.0	111.3	73.4	52.1	47.2	..	..
Chad	236	131	35	17	16.8	9.4	159.4	54.9	43.6	26.7	..	..
Chile	157	49	11	3	0.3	0.1	0.9	0.3	0.7	0.2	1.2	0.3
China	3,531	1,735	3	1	0.5	0.2	1.2	0.4	2.3	0.6	6.1	2.2
Hong Kong, China	18	4	3	1	0.0	0.0	0.0	0.0	0.0	0.0	..	..
Colombia	171	187	4	4	0.2	0.2	0.7	1.9	0.9	1.0	1.4	1.9
Congo, Dem. Rep.	196	184	4	4	4.0	2.5	37.0	..	8.6	5.5	41.8	..
Congo, Rep.	125	33	48	11	8.1	1.5	16.2	4.2	6.6	1.5	18.1	4.0
Costa Rica	34	12	10	3	0.3	0.1	1.6	0.4	0.7	0.1	1.3	0.3
Côte d'Ivoire	1,213	352	87	22	13.5	4.1	89.7	30.4	25.4	8.4	45.8	18.0
Croatia	54	66	12	15	0.3	0.4	1.6	1.6	0.6	0.6	0.6	0.7
Cuba	64	44	6	4	..	..	..	..	..	..	..	..
Czech Republic	148	438	14	43	0.3	0.9	0.8	2.9	0.5	1.1	0.8	2.3
Denmark												
Dominican Republic	120	62	16	7	1.1	0.3	5.2	1.3	1.7	0.5	6.5	6.6
Ecuador	227	147	20	12	1.3	1.2	6.8	6.4	3.4	2.3	..	..
Egypt, Arab Rep.	2,015	1,328	35	21	3.3	1.3	19.5	5.6	11.0	5.6	9.9	..
El Salvador	297	180	52	29	3.2	1.4	15.4	8.0	7.9	3.0	..	8.1
Eritrea	149	176	42	43	21.6	25.3	134.9	76.2	33.3	35.0	..	..
Estonia	58	64	39	47	1.2	1.4	4.5	5.0	2.0	1.2	4.6	4.0
Ethiopia	883	693	16	11	15.4	10.9	93.0	76.6	65.1	34.0	..	..
Finland												
France												
Gabon	144	12	134	10	3.4	0.3	12.3	0.9	5.8	0.4	..	..
Gambia, The	47	49	42	38	12.4	11.8	60.5	67.3	19.3	14.8	..	..
Georgia	209	170	39	34	11.5	5.6	273.2	38.6	23.5	11.4	..	45.4
Germany												
Ghana	651	609	38	32	10.3	12.1	50.3	49.5	28.8	17.6	..	..
Greece												
Guatemala	210	264	21	23	1.4	1.4	9.5	8.3	5.3	4.4	..	..
Guinea	417	153	63	21	11.6	5.2	68.2	22.8	37.6	14.9	..	32.6
Guinea-Bissau	119	80	110	67	50.2	39.6	209.2	210.8	107.4	67.2	..	..
Haiti	726	208	101	26	27.7	5.1	316.7	48.1	87.2	20.7	..	54.2
Honduras	406	449	72	70	11.0	7.8	32.5	21.6	19.2	12.9	..	..

	Net official development assistance or official aid ($ millions)		Aid per capita ($)		Aid dependency ratios							
					Aid as % of GNI		Aid as % of gross capital formation		Aid as % of imports of goods and services		Aid as % of central government expenditure	
	1995	2000	1995	2000	1995	2000	1995	2000	1995	2000	1995	2000
Hungary	-244	252	-24	25	-0.6	0.6	-2.3	1.8	-1.1	0.7	-1.1	1.2
India	1,739	1,487	2	1	0.5	0.3	1.8	1.4	3.1	1.8	3.2	1.9
Indonesia	1,391	1,731	7	8	0.7	1.2	2.2	6.3	2.3	2.6	4.7	7.8
Iran, Islamic Rep.	191	130	3	2	0.2	0.1	1.1	0.6	1.2	0.7	0.8	0.2
Iraq	339	101	16	4	..	..	..	..	..	..	..	..
Ireland												
Israel	336	800	61	128	0.4	0.8	1.5	3.7	0.8	1.4	0.8	1.6
Italy												
Jamaica	108	10	43	4	2.4	0.1	7.5	0.5	2.6	0.2	7.5	0.3
Japan												
Jordan	540	552	129	113	8.3	6.6	24.3	32.7	10.2	8.8	25.7	21.0
Kazakhstan	66	189	4	13	0.3	1.1	1.4	7.4	1.0	1.9	..	7.2
Kenya	734	512	28	17	8.4	5.0	46.3	39.0	18.9	13.0	28.5	16.0
Korea, Dem. Rep.	14	75	1	3	..	..	..	..	..	..	..	..
Korea, Rep.	57	-198	1	-4	0.0	0.0	0.0	-0.2	0.0	-0.1	0.1	..
Kuwait	3	3	2	1	0.0	0.0	0.1	0.1	0.0	0.0	0.0	0.1
Kyrgyz Republic	285	215	63	44	8.8	17.6	46.7	102.9	37.2	28.8	68.8	87.2
Lao PDR	309	281	66	53	17.6	16.8	67.3	80.6	40.5	41.5	..	..
Latvia	63	91	25	38	1.3	1.3	7.4	4.7	2.8	2.2	4.4	4.0
Lebanon	187	197	47	45	1.6	1.1	4.7	6.6	2.5	..	4.8	3.3
Lesotho	114	41	61	20	8.6	3.6	20.2	11.4	9.4	5.0	24.6	15.0
Liberia	124	68	45	22	..	..	..	..	..	..	..	..
Libya	6	15	1	3	..	..	..	..	0.1	0.1	..	..
Lithuania	179	99	48	27	2.8	0.9	11.3	4.2	4.5	1.6	11.8	3.2
Macedonia, FYR	79	252	40	124	1.8	7.1	8.5	42.2	..	10.9	..	..
Madagascar	301	322	23	21	10.0	8.5	87.1	51.5	25.9	20.3	54.8	48.7
Malawi	435	445	47	43	31.5	26.8	179.0	200.5	49.0	43.3	..	..
Malaysia	109	45	5	2	0.1	0.1	0.3	0.2	0.1	0.0	0.6	..
Mali	541	360	56	33	22.4	15.9	95.9	69.3	52.0	32.5	..	..
Mauritania	230	212	101	80	22.7	23.3	111.9	75.3	41.2	46.0	..	..
Mauritius	23	20	21	17	0.6	0.5	2.3	1.8	0.9	0.7	2.6	2.0
Mexico	385	-54	4	-1	0.1	0.0	0.7	0.0	0.4	0.0	0.8	0.0
Moldova	66	123	15	29	2.2	9.0	8.6	42.8	6.4	11.3	12.8	32.2
Mongolia	211	217	93	91	22.7	22.8	80.3	74.7	38.3	27.7	96.8	76.5
Morocco	495	419	19	15	1.6	1.3	7.2	5.2	3.9	3.1	4.6	5.9
Mozambique	1,064	876	67	50	49.9	24.9	201.6	69.3	84.8	49.7	..	..
Myanmar	151	107	3	2	..	..	..	..	7.0	3.7	1.3	0.3
Namibia	192	152	121	86	5.2	4.4	25.2	18.3	8.2	6.9	15.4	12.2
Nepal	433	390	21	17	9.6	6.9	39.1	29.1	28.0	21.5	61.9	45.6
Netherlands												
New Zealand												
Nicaragua	653	562	148	111	44.2	26.6	142.6	68.1	44.1	25.3	104.3	56.5
Niger	274	211	30	19	15.0	11.7	199.4	108.8	53.8	46.8	..	..
Nigeria	212	185	2	1	0.8	0.5	4.6	2.0	1.3	1.0	..	..
Norway												
Oman	59	46	27	19	0.6	..	..	..	1.0	0.6	1.1	0.8
Pakistan	824	703	7	5	1.4	1.2	7.3	7.3	5.6	5.1	6.1	5.2
Panama	40	17	15	6	0.5	0.2	1.7	0.6	0.4	0.2	2.0	0.5
Papua New Guinea	371	275	82	54	8.3	7.5	36.5	33.8	15.4	12.2	27.6	22.6
Paraguay	140	82	29	15	1.5	1.1	6.5	4.9	2.6	2.3	..	..
Peru	373	401	16	16	0.7	0.8	2.8	3.7	3.0	3.3	3.6	3.9
Philippines	890	578	13	8	1.2	0.7	5.3	4.3	2.5	1.4	6.7	4.0
Poland	3,790	1,396	98	36	3.0	0.9	15.1	3.3	10.3	2.3	7.4	2.6
Portugal												
Puerto Rico												
Romania	299	432	13	19	0.8	1.2	3.5	6.1	2.6	2.9	2.7	3.1
Russian Federation	1,612	1,565	11	11	0.5	0.7	1.9	3.6	1.8	2.1	1.9	2.6

362

2002 World Development Indicators

| | Net official development assistance or official aid ($ millions) | | Aid per capita ($) | | Aid dependency ratios | | | | | | | |
| | | | | | Aid as % of GNI | | Aid as % of gross capital formation | | Aid as % of imports of goods and services | | Aid as % of central government expenditure | |
	1995	2000	1995	2000	1995	2000	1995	2000	1995	2000	1995	2000
Rwanda	702	322	110	38	54.4	18.1	364.0	118.1	179.4	75.0	..	..
Saudi Arabia	17	31	1	1	0.0	0.0	0.1	0.1	0.0	0.1	..	..
Senegal	666	423	80	44	15.4	9.9	89.0	48.9	32.8	22.0	..	..
Sierra Leone	206	182	46	36	23.6	29.6	..	358.5	73.4	68.6	145.2	52.5
Singapore	17	1	5	0	0.0	0.0	0.1	0.0	0.0	0.0	0.1	0.0
Slovak Republic	98	113	18	21	0.5	0.6	2.0	2.0	0.9	0.7	..	1.5
Slovenia	53	61	26	31	0.3	0.3	1.2	1.2	0.5	0.5	0.7	0.8
Somalia	189	104	26	12	..	..	..	..	..	..	..	..
South Africa	389	488	10	11	0.3	0.4	1.4	2.6	1.0	1.3	0.8	1.3
Spain												
Sri Lanka	555	276	31	14	4.3	1.7	16.6	6.1	8.8	3.2	14.5	6.6
Sudan	242	225	9	7	3.9	2.3	..	13.7	10.7	7.1	..	27.0
Swaziland	58	13	65	13	4.3	0.9	22.0	4.6	4.3	1.1	..	3.2
Sweden												
Switzerland												
Syrian Arab Republic	359	158	25	10	3.1	1.0	11.6	4.5	5.5	2.4	2.8	0.9
Tajikistan	65	142	11	23	2.9	15.2	9.6	72.1	7.3	15.9	..	144.6
Tanzania	877	1,045	30	31	17.1	11.6	84.4	65.3	38.5	48.6	..	..
Thailand	859	641	15	11	0.5	0.5	1.2	2.3	1.0	0.8	3.2	2.9
Togo	192	70	49	15	15.2	5.8	91.1	27.9	27.0	10.3	..	..
Trinidad and Tobago	25	-2	20	-1	0.5	0.0	2.3	-0.1	1.0	0.0	1.7	..
Tunisia	71	223	8	23	0.4	1.2	1.6	4.2	0.7	2.2	1.2	3.6
Turkey	307	325	5	5	0.2	0.2	0.7	0.7	0.7	0.5	0.8	0.4
Turkmenistan	28	32	6	6	0.5	0.7	..	1.8	1.3	1.2	..	..
Uganda	835	819	43	37	14.7	13.3	88.3	73.0	57.3	40.0	..	76.8
Ukraine	320	541	6	11	0.7	1.8	2.4	9.1	1.7	2.8	..	6.1
United Arab Emirates	5	4	2	1	0.0	0.0	..	..	..	..	0.1	0.1
United Kingdom												
United States												
Uruguay	68	17	21	5	0.4	0.1	2.4	0.6	1.6	0.3	1.2	0.3
Uzbekistan	84	186	4	8	0.8	2.5	3.0	21.9	2.2	5.8	..	..
Venezuela, RB	44	77	2	3	0.1	0.1	0.3	0.4	0.2	0.3	0.3	0.3
Vietnam	837	1,700	11	22	4.2	5.4	15.3	19.8	8.4	9.4	16.9	26.1
West Bank and Gaza	499	636	208	214	12.2	12.5	37.8	44.6	..	..	..	..
Yemen, Rep.	169	265	11	15	4.2	3.6	18.3	16.2	5.5	6.7	6.2	23.0
Yugoslavia, Fed. Rep. [a]	95	1,135	9	107	..	13.4	..	93.6	..	..	..	..
Zambia	2,034	795	226	79	63.0	28.5	367.5	149.5	103.7	48.7	..	..
Zimbabwe	492	178	43	14	7.2	2.5	35.1	19.1	14.9	7.9	19.4	..
World	68,287 s	58,369 s	.. w	.. w	.. w	.. w	.. w	.. w	.. w	.. w	.. w	.. w
Low income	27,748	22,894	12	9	3.0	2.3	11.4	10.3	10.7	7.2	..	..
Middle income	26,583	20,968	10	8	0.5	0.4	1.9	1.4	1.7	0.9	..	..
Lower middle income	19,165	15,919	10	8	1.0	0.7	3.0	2.3	2.9	1.8	..	..
Upper middle income	6,582	3,874	11	6	0.2	0.1	1.0	0.6	0.8	0.3	..	..
Low & middle income	66,802	56,482	14	11	0.9	0.7	3.3	2.6	3.1	1.8	..	..
East Asia & Pacific	10,026	8,464	6	5	0.6	0.4	..	..	1.6	1.0	..	..
Europe & Central Asia	11,602	10,867	25	23	1.0	1.0	4.0	4.6	2.6	1.9	..	..
Latin America & Carib.	6,344	4,987	13	10	0.3	0.2	1.6	1.0	1.6	0.7	..	..
Middle East & N. Africa	5,621	4,609	21	16	1.2	0.8	5.5	3.8	2.8	2.0	..	..
South Asia	5,187	4,241	4	3	1.1	0.7	4.2	3.0	5.8	3.5	..	..
Sub-Saharan Africa	18,880	13,453	33	20	5.8	4.0	30.3	21.4	15.3	9.5	..	..
High income	1,485	1,887	..	..	..	..	..	..	..	..	..	..
Europe EMU												

Note: Regional aggregates include data for economies not specified elsewhere. Income group totals include aid not allocated by country or region.

a. Aid to the states of the former Socialist Federal Republic of Yugoslavia that is not otherwise specified is included in regional and income group aggregates.

About the data

Although foreign aid is important in promoting development, it is most effective when coupled with sound policies and high-quality public institutions. Improvements in the quality of life—higher incomes, poverty reduction, improvements in education and health, and environmentally sustainable development—require a broad development strategy that puts in place growth-enhancing, market-oriented policies (a stable macroeconomic environment, effective law and order, trade liberalization) and the provision of basic public services not supplied by private markets.

Ratios of aid to gross national income (GNI), gross capital formation, imports, and public spending provide a measure of the recipient country's dependency on aid. But care must be taken in drawing policy conclusions. For foreign policy reasons some countries have traditionally received large amounts of aid. Thus aid dependency ratios may reveal as much about the donors' interests as they do about the recipients' needs. Ratios in Sub-Saharan Africa are generally much higher than those in other regions, and they increased in the 1980s. These high ratios are due only in part to aid flows. Many African countries saw severe erosion in their terms of trade in the 1980s, which, along with weak policies, contributed to falling incomes, imports, and investment. Thus the increase in aid dependency ratios reflects events affecting both the numerator and the denominator.

As defined here, aid includes official development assistance (ODA) and official aid. The data cover loans and grants from Development Assistance Committee (DAC) member countries, multilateral organizations, and non-DAC donors. They do not reflect aid given by recipient countries to other developing countries. As a result, some countries that are net donors (such as Saudi Arabia) are shown in the table as aid recipients (see table 6.8a).

The data in the table do not distinguish among different types of aid (program, project, or food aid; emergency assistance; post-conflict peace-keeping assistance; or technical cooperation), each of which may have a very different effect on the economy. Technical cooperation expenditures do not always directly benefit the economy to the extent that they defray costs incurred outside the country on the salaries and benefits of technical experts and the overhead costs of firms supplying technical services.

In 1999, to avoid double counting extrabudgetary expenditures reported by DAC countries and flows reported by the United Nations, all United Nations agencies revised their data to include only regular budgetary expenditures since 1990 (except for the World Food Programme and the United Nations High Commissioner for Refugees, which revised their data

from 1996 onward). These revisions have affected net official development assistance and official aid and, as a result, aid per capita and aid dependency ratios.

Because the table relies on information from donors, it is not consistent with information recorded by recipients in the balance of payments, which often excludes all or some technical assistance—particularly payments to expatriates made directly by the donor. Similarly, grant commodity aid may not always be recorded in trade data or in the balance of payments. Moreover, DAC statistics exclude purely military aid.

The nominal values used here tend to overstate the amount of resources transferred. Changes in international prices and in exchange rates can reduce the purchasing power of aid. The practice of tying aid, still prevalent though declining in importance, also tends to reduce its purchasing power (see *About the data* for table 6.9).

The values for population, GNI, gross capital formation, imports of goods and services, and central government expenditure used in computing the ratios are taken from World Bank and International Monetary Fund databases. The ratios shown may therefore differ somewhat from those computed and published by the Organisation for Economic Co-operation and Development (OECD). Aid not allocated by country or region—including administrative costs, research on development issues, and aid to nongovernmental organizations—is included in the world total. Thus regional and income group totals do not sum to the world total.

Definitions

• **Net official development assistance** consists of disbursements of loans made on concessional terms (net of repayments of principal) and grants by official agencies of the members of DAC, by multilateral institutions, and by non-DAC countries to promote economic development and welfare in developing countries on Part I of the DAC list of aid recipients. Loans with a grant element of at least 25 percent (calculated at a rate of discount of 10 percent) are included in ODA. • **Net official aid** refers to aid flows, net of repayments, from official donors to more advanced Central and Eastern European countries, to the new independent states of the former Soviet Union, and to certain advanced developing countries and territories on Part II of the DAC list of aid recipients. Official aid is provided under terms and conditions similar to those for ODA. • **Aid per capita** includes both ODA and official aid. • **Aid dependency ratios** are calculated using values in U.S. dollars converted at official exchange rates. For definitions of GNI, gross capital formation, imports of goods and services, and central government expenditure see *Definitions* for tables 1.1, 4.9, and 4.12.

Data sources

The data on financial flows are compiled by DAC and published in its annual statistical report, *Geographical Distribution of Financial Flows to Aid Recipients,* and in the DAC annual *Development Co-operation Report.* Data are available in electronic format to registered users on the Web site at www.oecd.org/ dac/ htm/online.htm and on the OECD's *International Development Statistics* CD-ROM. The data on population, GNI, gross capital formation, imports of goods and services, and central government expenditure are from World Bank and International Monetary Fund databases.

$ millions, 2000	Total	Ten major DAC donors										Other DAC donors
		Japan	United States	France	Germany	United Kingdom	Netherlands	Sweden	Canada	Denmark	Norway	
Afghanistan	87.5	0.2	2.4	0.7	10.6	12.7	10.2	11.5	6.7	0.3	12.6	19.7
Albania	141.4	7.1	44.7	1.8	19.5	9.6	3.8	0.4	1.3	3.4	3.6	46.3
Algeria	27.1	-4.9	..	57.3	5.8	..	0.1	0.2	1.6	0.0	1.1	-34.1
Angola	189.1	21.5	37.3	7.7	11.3	8.3	11.7	17.1	3.6	7.7	16.6	46.3
Argentina	43.5	37.3	-2.5	7.5	7.4	9.5	0.2	0.2	1.1	-0.6	0.0	-16.7
Armenia	139.3	9.1	103.1	2.5	8.9	2.8	4.7	0.7	0.4	0.1	2.1	4.9
Australia												
Austria												
Azerbaijan	70.7	36.4	18.9	0.8	9.2	0.8	0.8	0.1	0.3	..	2.2	1.2
Bangladesh	616.5	201.6	62.5	21.3	36.7	103.4	32.6	31.9	38.5	33.7	18.4	36.1
Belarus	14.9	0.2	4.4	1.2	4.5	0.2	..	2.7	0.1	1.1	0.1	0.5
Belgium												
Benin	190.5	6.2	29.7	74.3	21.7	0.1	4.4	0.2	3.3	19.5	..	31.1
Bolivia	336.1	43.7	97.4	8.3	45.3	12.6	33.3	18.8	5.7	20.9	2.8	47.4
Bosnia and Herzegovina	452.2	24.4	85.8	19.9	91.5	7.1	43.3	23.9	5.5	2.7	30.8	117.5
Botswana	23.5	6.1	1.0	0.6	6.7	3.7	0.1	0.7	0.3	1.2	2.7	0.6
Brazil	222.5	169.6	-57.9	23.7	49.5	9.8	2.0	1.6	3.2	0.0	2.3	18.6
Bulgaria	207.0	20.7	119.2	10.2	29.1	4.6	0.7	0.3	0.2	2.1	0.0	20.0
Burkina Faso	227.8	21.3	9.3	82.2	22.2	0.5	16.1	1.2	8.3	24.5	0.4	41.7
Burundi	40.9	0.2	1.0	4.8	3.0	1.7	4.4	4.3	1.3	..	5.3	14.9
Cambodia	248.0	99.2	21.5	21.5	19.4	13.0	7.4	16.8	2.6	2.0	6.2	38.5
Cameroon	213.5	15.8	2.5	86.2	47.0	8.1	4.3	0.1	6.3	1.0	0.7	41.5
Canada												
Central African Republic	53.1	22.8	1.1	18.7	7.2	0.0	..	0.3	0.1	..	0.3	2.6
Chad	53.3	0.2	4.1	24.7	14.9	0.4	..	0.2	0.2	..	0.1	8.5
Chile	41.0	21.4	-19.1	8.5	21.9	0.2	0.6	2.2	0.8	0.8	0.7	3.2
China	1,257.5	769.2	1.6	46.0	212.8	83.4	24.9	11.0	29.2	-1.7	9.9	71.2
Hong Kong, China	4.2	2.6	..	0.5	1.0	..	..	0.0	..	..	..	9.6
Colombia	178.5	8.1	105.1	8.9	13.1	3.4	9.0	4.4	2.4	0.1	5.8	18.2
Congo, Dem. Rep.	102.7	0.5	12.8	8.2	12.8	8.0	4.7	7.7	5.6	0.0	5.7	36.9
Congo, Rep.	22.2	0.1	3.5	9.8	2.3	0.0	..	1.6	0.7	-0.1	2.0	2.2
Costa Rica	17.2	-6.3	-30.6	2.7	1.4	15.2	7.4	1.7	11.2	0.7	0.6	13.2
Côte d'Ivoire	250.1	23.4	10.0	156.3	15.7	1.1	10.3	0.2	3.5	..	0.2	29.4
Croatia	42.5	1.7	11.9	1.7	5.2	1.6	4.2	2.9	0.6	..	5.0	7.6
Cuba	30.8	2.0	1.4	1.2	2.5	0.2	1.5	1.1	2.6	..	0.8	17.6
Czech Republic	25.3	1.8	..	6.7	9.8	0.9	0.3	0.2	0.8	1.4	0.0	3.5
Denmark												
Dominican Republic	44.6	29.6	-18.8	3.2	9.2	6.4	0.0	1.3	0.2	0.2	0.2	13.1
Ecuador	137.4	20.1	47.1	4.9	11.3	0.9	6.5	0.9	5.1	6.6	2.1	32.0
Egypt, Arab Rep.	1,138.9	85.9	634.8	241.7	65.2	4.1	17.5	2.6	9.2	42.4	1.1	34.5
El Salvador	172.3	66.9	36.6	1.0	14.5	5.0	2.8	7.9	1.7	2.4	1.2	32.2
Eritrea	111.9	0.4	39.5	3.3	3.6	1.1	15.8	5.5	1.8	11.0	6.4	23.5
Estonia	23.7	0.4	1.8	1.3	2.9	0.3	0.1	4.1	0.7	6.8	0.3	5.0
Ethiopia	379.5	34.0	129.8	9.4	38.6	11.4	25.7	20.7	10.9	2.6	23.6	72.7
Finland												
France												
Gabon	-11.7	-1.5	1.3	-14.5	1.0	..	0.0	0.1	1.3	..	..	2.0
Gambia, The	14.6	3.3	3.2	0.1	2.6	2.1	0.2	0.7	0.2	0.0	0.2	6.4
Georgia	120.3	11.4	74.6	0.8	19.1	1.7	2.2	1.8	0.3	..	2.1	13.4
Germany												
Ghana	385.0	102.9	63.3	3.3	32.0	79.9	27.6	5.9	16.2	37.2	3.2	0.0
Greece												
Guatemala	230.3	67.1	58.0	1.5	18.7	23.2	10.6	13.4	4.4	5.4	8.1	3.8
Guinea	92.8	19.1	25.7	19.7	17.4	0.4	0.0	0.1	6.7	..	..	19.5
Guinea-Bissau	41.6	..	0.6	6.7	0.7	0.2	11.1	2.5	0.2	0.3	0.0	0.0
Haiti	153.9	13.5	91.0	10.9	4.2	0.0	4.0	0.5	19.7	0.1	1.7	61.9
Honduras	310.6	50.1	110.3	7.7	17.3	1.0	8.7	41.7	7.0	3.0	2.0	0.1

$ millions, 2000	Total	Ten major DAC donors										Other DAC donors
		Japan	United States	France	Germany	United Kingdom	Netherlands	Sweden	Canada	Denmark	Norway	
Hungary	53.5	6.6	2.0	6.4	24.0	3.3	0.2	0.4	0.5	0.7	..	17.3
India	650.3	368.2	14.6	-11.6	15.6	204.2	-8.9	15.4	6.8	20.9	8.0	229.3
Indonesia	1,617.2	970.1	174.2	21.7	6.4	33.9	144.0	4.1	26.5	1.4	5.8	14.5
Iran, Islamic Rep.	112.8	44.9	..	7.9	37.2	2.9	0.1	0.1	..	0.1	5.2	10.9
Iraq	84.1	0.0	..	2.0	31.7	14.0	3.6	7.2	0.7	..	14.0	2.3
Ireland												
Israel	800.4	0.7	867.2	5.3	-75.1	..	..	..	0.1	..	..	-2.5
Italy												
Jamaica	-26.4	-12.2	-26.2	-0.8	1.3	4.7	3.2	0.2	5.5	..	0.4	9.9
Japan												
Jordan	385.3	104.7	187.8	17.1	44.3	7.4	1.1	0.9	1.9	6.9	3.4	2.4
Kazakhstan	159.3	83.3	58.3	1.4	10.3	1.4	0.3	0.2	0.7	0.1	1.0	19.6
Kenya	293.0	66.9	45.9	4.0	38.4	73.1	14.2	14.2	5.4	8.4	2.9	6.6
Korea, Dem. Rep.	26.9	..	1.6	1.7	1.5	1.3	0.2	3.5	2.4	..	3.3	0.1
Korea, Rep.	-196.6	-183.7	-44.4	13.9	17.4	..	0.0	0.0	..	..	..	0.3
Kuwait	2.0	0.1	..	1.0	0.6	..	..	..	..	..	..	8.1
Kyrgyz Republic	91.3	47.8	24.6	0.4	4.8	2.2	1.9	0.3	0.6	0.3	0.3	21.0
Lao PDR	194.3	114.9	2.7	12.8	13.3	2.1	2.0	14.6	0.4	2.1	8.5	3.5
Latvia	34.3	2.0	1.2	1.1	5.7	0.4	..	8.9	1.4	9.8	0.5	8.8
Lebanon	90.5	2.2	31.8	31.1	5.5	0.9	0.6	3.8	2.1	..	3.7	10.1
Lesotho	21.8	0.9	1.3	-0.5	3.2	4.5	0.3	0.1	0.1	1.7	0.2	1.1
Liberia	23.8	0.0	15.9	0.8	-1.3	3.3	2.0	1.4	0.2	0.1	0.3	9.3
Libya	11.9	0.2	..	1.0	1.4	..	..	..	..	..	..	0.3
Lithuania	46.1	2.0	2.0	1.5	4.0	0.3	1.3	14.7	0.8	17.5	1.7	0.0
Macedonia, FYR	110.9	7.9	37.3	8.2	6.7	8.5	20.9	0.4	0.7	1.3	1.0	0.6
Madagascar	138.7	26.3	31.6	46.5	14.2	2.1	1.3	0.2	0.2	0.2	4.5	4.0
Malawi	269.2	38.5	59.3	..	25.5	96.9	1.6	5.1	6.7	24.9	6.8	-0.1
Malaysia	43.3	23.9	0.2	-2.8	5.5	0.2	0.3	0.1	2.2	13.5	0.2	2.1
Mali	299.8	32.2	56.4	98.1	31.6	1.0	42.5	0.4	12.7	0.1	6.6	21.1
Mauritania	82.5	29.9	4.2	23.4	7.6	1.0	4.6	0.2	2.1	..	0.4	2.3
Mauritius	12.4	2.1	-0.6	9.5	-2.8	0.7	0.0	..	0.2	..	0.9	0.0
Mexico	-68.4	-92.6	23.8	-11.2	15.3	5.7	-2.0	0.2	1.6	-0.2	0.4	1.0
Moldova	61.5	2.6	35.0	1.0	1.9	1.1	13.5	2.4	0.1	..	0.7	4.3
Mongolia	150.8	104.5	12.6	1.5	18.8	0.8	3.8	1.8	0.3	1.0	1.4	0.0
Morocco	293.1	103.3	14.0	154.7	6.2	0.2	-0.1	0.8	5.2	-0.9	0.1	140.6
Mozambique	623.5	20.0	115.5	16.1	47.8	82.7	61.6	46.3	8.0	46.9	38.2	4.2
Myanmar	68.1	51.8	3.4	1.2	1.5	1.0	1.6	0.5	0.2	..	2.9	14.2
Namibia	96.8	5.4	9.5	3.1	24.4	4.8	3.2	21.1	0.3	3.7	7.2	1.7
Nepal	231.2	99.9	16.0	2.0	21.8	23.0	5.7	1.2	4.2	25.0	8.9	0.0
Netherlands												
New Zealand												
Nicaragua	325.9	76.5	72.8	3.4	26.9	1.7	15.6	33.3	2.8	27.2	13.3	21.4
Niger	105.8	15.0	5.3	41.3	11.6	1.6	1.6	0.1	2.6	4.9	0.5	4.3
Nigeria	84.3	2.6	32.5	4.1	11.3	22.9	0.3	0.8	1.8	3.2	0.5	2.9
Norway												
Oman	9.2	11.2	-3.0	0.7	0.2	..	..	..	..	..	..	20.1
Pakistan	475.1	280.4	88.5	19.6	2.4	23.7	19.1	1.7	13.1	-0.1	6.7	0.3
Panama	11.7	3.0	-8.8	0.3	2.5	0.4	0.2	..	1.0	0.1	..	205.9
Papua New Guinea	268.6	55.8	1.0	0.4	3.9	..	1.2	0.2	0.0	..	0.2	6.1
Paraguay	72.9	51.5	6.4	0.7	4.4	0.0	..	0.8	0.0	..	2.9	13.0
Peru	372.7	191.7	92.3	6.3	34.0	10.4	9.2	3.7	8.8	1.9	1.4	56.1
Philippines	502.3	304.5	75.5	5.9	23.3	3.2	10.0	2.7	9.9	6.9	4.6	127.7
Poland	552.5	-3.4	32.7	197.3	44.3	6.0	0.6	5.8	121.9	19.6	0.0	0.0
Portugal												
Puerto Rico												
Romania	157.7	19.5	61.4	17.0	24.7	5.2	0.6	1.0	1.7	8.2	0.1	218.4
Russian Federation	1,344.2	6.5	915.2	17.0	63.5	39.2	4.1	31.6	16.6	13.7	18.4	27.9

$ millions, 2000	Total	Ten major DAC donors										Other DAC donors
		Japan	United States	France	Germany	United Kingdom	Netherlands	Sweden	Canada	Denmark	Norway	
Rwanda	175.4	3.4	22.9	7.5	13.8	52.7	20.4	14.6	6.7	1.2	4.3	12.5
Saudi Arabia	18.0	13.9	..	2.6	1.1	..	0.4	..	..	..	..	32.1
Senegal	288.4	48.5	22.9	147.2	16.8	2.4	5.9	0.4	11.3	-0.6	1.7	0.1
Sierra Leone	115.6	0.0	8.0	0.7	3.5	68.3	2.7	3.7	3.8	0.0	8.8	0.3
Singapore	0.7	2.9	..	1.7	-4.5	0.3	..	..	0.1	..	..	4.8
Slovak Republic	25.3	3.0	2.0	3.6	5.7	1.6	..	0.1	0.9	3.5	0.1	1.3
Slovenia	0.6	0.6	..	0.9	-2.4	0.0	..	0.3	..	..	0.1	18.3
Somalia	56.4	..	9.9	0.6	3.1	1.1	6.2	4.5	0.5	3.2	20.1	26.4
South Africa	353.6	19.8	105.9	18.4	41.6	42.6	24.2	32.4	10.7	17.0	14.7	10.1
Spain												
Sri Lanka	240.2	163.7	-3.9	0.2	21.2	9.9	6.9	16.7	1.4	-0.6	14.6	0.0
Sudan	90.3	0.7	5.2	6.5	12.0	5.7	15.3	12.4	2.4	0.6	14.2	1.8
Swaziland	2.8	6.0	0.2	0.0	-0.9	-3.7	0.0	0.0	0.3	0.3	0.1	4.5
Sweden												
Switzerland												
Syrian Arab Republic	97.3	64.4	..	13.2	12.0	0.2	0.1	1.0	0.3	..	1.7	6.3
Tajikistan	38.1	2.1	22.6	0.0	3.5	0.1	0.2	1.8	0.4	0.1	1.1	57.4
Tanzania	778.7	217.1	24.5	15.8	34.8	152.7	97.3	63.5	11.6	68.8	35.2	-37.4
Thailand	625.2	635.3	12.6	-10.9	19.2	0.7	0.8	4.0	2.1	-1.5	0.4	155.8
Togo	51.9	8.5	1.9	28.8	8.7	0.4	0.0	0.6	0.2	..	0.1	3.4
Trinidad and Tobago	4.4	1.8	0.8	0.8	0.2	0.4	0.1	..	0.2	..	..	2.0
Tunisia	150.3	72.1	-19.7	92.9	1.9	0.2	-1.5	0.4	1.8	0.0	0.2	19.2
Turkey	97.5	144.5	-61.9	7.8	-21.0	0.5	0.6	2.6	5.1	-1.7	1.8	0.1
Turkmenistan	9.9	1.1	7.5	0.2	0.7	0.1	..	..	0.0	..	0.1	0.0
Uganda	578.2	22.4	57.9	7.6	18.3	216.6	43.3	22.7	1.6	59.8	21.0	13.1
Ukraine	352.1	2.7	244.8	5.1	38.3	13.9	3.1	4.0	19.2	5.6	2.4	0.0
United Arab Emirates	2.7	0.1	..	1.9	0.7	0.1	..	..	..	..	..	1.6
United Kingdom												
United States												
Uruguay	15.3	5.8	0.3	1.6	5.3	0.2	0.1	0.1	0.2	..	0.0	1.3
Uzbekistan	133.8	82.2	35.7	4.2	9.3	0.7	0.0	0.2	0.2	..	0.1	13.0
Venezuela, RB	61.3	4.6	6.8	3.5	5.5	1.4	0.2	1.3	0.5	0.6	0.3	105.1
Vietnam	1,247.6	923.7	6.8	52.9	33.3	7.9	18.8	37.3	14.6	41.0	6.2	0.0
West Bank and Gaza	305.2	61.2	60.1	14.2	17.3	14.7	16.2	32.4	0.4	8.0	27.9	13.2
Yemen, Rep.	159.6	21.0	56.6	6.5	31.8	4.6	34.4	0.9	0.1	0.1	0.1	45.0
Yugoslavia, Fed. Rep.	592.9	4.8	107.7	10.9	98.7	28.3	71.5	33.5	..	..	71.5	18.0
Zambia	486.2	31.9	46.1	13.0	112.2	111.4	51.2	19.1	8.4	23.1	24.8	14.0
Zimbabwe	192.6	62.4	13.1	3.2	12.5	20.2	11.3	14.8	9.0	22.5	9.8	10.4
World	40,904.9 s	9,654.2 s	9,866.1 s	3,914.7 s	2,912.4 s	2,796.4 s	2,449.5 s	1,361.0 s	1,325.1 s	1,142.1 s	960.6 s	4,522.8 s
Low income	14,689.6	4,459.0	2,149.3	1,175.5	1,021.2	1,516.8	839.9	483.2	325.4	541.4	385.2	1,792.7
Middle income	14,050.7	3,542.3	3,609.3	1,329.3	1,378.3	628.1	397.6	388.3	355.4	253.0	312.8	1,856.2
Lower middle income	11,364.0	3,408.0	2,969.8	884.6	1,038.8	368.1	348.2	319.3	156.8	164.8	253.1	1,452.6
Upper middle income	1,669.8	102.8	101.3	419.7	276.4	153.6	32.7	56.2	151.5	64.1	31.6	280.0
Low & middle income	39,134.2	9,646.7	8,976.6	3,150.6	2,988.1	2,794.7	2,273.8	1,360.6	1,324.9	1,142.1	960.2	4,515.9
East Asia & Pacific	6,755.7	4,001.1	449.4	232.1	380.9	167.9	216.2	104.5	93.7	66.5	53.0	990.5
Europe & Central Asia	5,724.7	531.3	2,222.1	361.7	524.6	246.6	198.9	190.1	216.5	146.8	154.1	932.0
Latin America & Carib.	3,867.5	799.6	1,343.3	109.5	348.9	229.7	142.8	164.9	111.8	76.7	59.4	480.9
Middle East & N. Africa	3,010.1	595.5	979.3	676.3	265.5	49.9	73.4	53.2	28.3	57.3	60.6	170.9
South Asia	2,347.8	1,129.2	180.0	32.2	109.6	377.3	69.6	78.6	71.3	89.1	70.6	140.6
Sub-Saharan Africa	8,651.6	955.7	1,477.2	1,240.0	790.0	1,128.1	584.9	394.6	199.7	404.0	335.8	1,141.6
High income	1,770.7	7.5	889.5	764.0	-75.6	1.7	175.7	0.3	0.2	0.0	0.4	6.9
Europe EMU												

Note: Regional aggregates include data for economies not specified elsewhere. World and income group totals include aid not allocated by country or region.

About the data

Private flows to developing countries have gone mainly to productive activities in agriculture and industry. So official development assistance (ODA) has become more concentrated in the social sectors, whose share increased from about 20 percent of bilateral aid in the late 1970s to about 30 percent in the late 1990s. Emergency aid also grew during this period, and debt relief increased substantially. The geographic distribution of aid has changed, because many of the large developing country recipients, such as India, Indonesia, and Brazil, have been able to tap private capital markets to fund infrastructure development. At the end of the 1960s India, Indonesia, and Brazil accounted for almost a quarter of bilateral aid from Development Assistance Committee (DAC) members, but by the late 1990s their share had fallen to about 7 percent.

The data in the table show net bilateral aid to low- and middle-income economies from DAC members of the Organisation for Economic Co-operation and Development (OECD). The DAC compilation includes aid to some countries and territories not shown in the table and small quantities of aid to unspecified economies that are recorded only at the regional or global level. Aid to countries and territories not shown in the table has been assigned to regional totals based on the World Bank's regional classification system. Aid to unspecified economies has been included in regional totals and, when possible, in income group totals. Aid not allocated by country or region—including administrative costs, research on development issues, and aid to nongovernmental organizations—is included in the world total; thus regional and income group totals do not sum to the world total.

In 1999 all United Nations agencies revised their data to include only regular budgetary expenditures since 1990 (except for the World Food Programme and the United Nations High Commissioner for Refugees, which revised their data from 1996 onward). They did so to avoid double counting extrabudgetary expenditures reported by DAC countries and flows reported by the United Nations.

Because the data in the table are based on donor country reports of bilateral programs, they cannot be reconciled with recipient country reports. Nor do they reflect the full extent of aid flows from the reporting donor countries or those to recipient countries. A full accounting would include donor country contributions to multilateral institutions and the flow of resources from multilateral institutions to recipient countries as well as flows from countries that are not members of DAC. In addition, the expenditure countries report as official development assistance have changed. For example, some DAC members providing aid to refugees during the first 12 months of their stay within the donor's borders have reported these expenditures as ODA.

Some of the aid recipients shown in the table are themselves significant donors. See table 6.8a for a summary of ODA from non-DAC countries.

Definitions

• **Net aid** comprises net bilateral official development assistance to part I recipients and net bilateral official aid to part II recipients (see *About the data* for table 6.8). • **Other DAC donors** are Australia, Austria, Belgium, Finland, Greece, Ireland, Italy, Luxembourg, New Zealand, Portugal, Spain, and Switzerland.

Data sources

Data on financial flows are compiled by DAC and published in its annual statistical report, *Geographical Distribution of Financial Flows to Aid Recipients,* and the DAC annual *Development Co-operation Report.* Data are available in electronic format to registered users from the Web site at www.oecd.org/dac/htm online.htm and on the OECD's *International Development Statistics* CD-ROM.

Figure 6.11

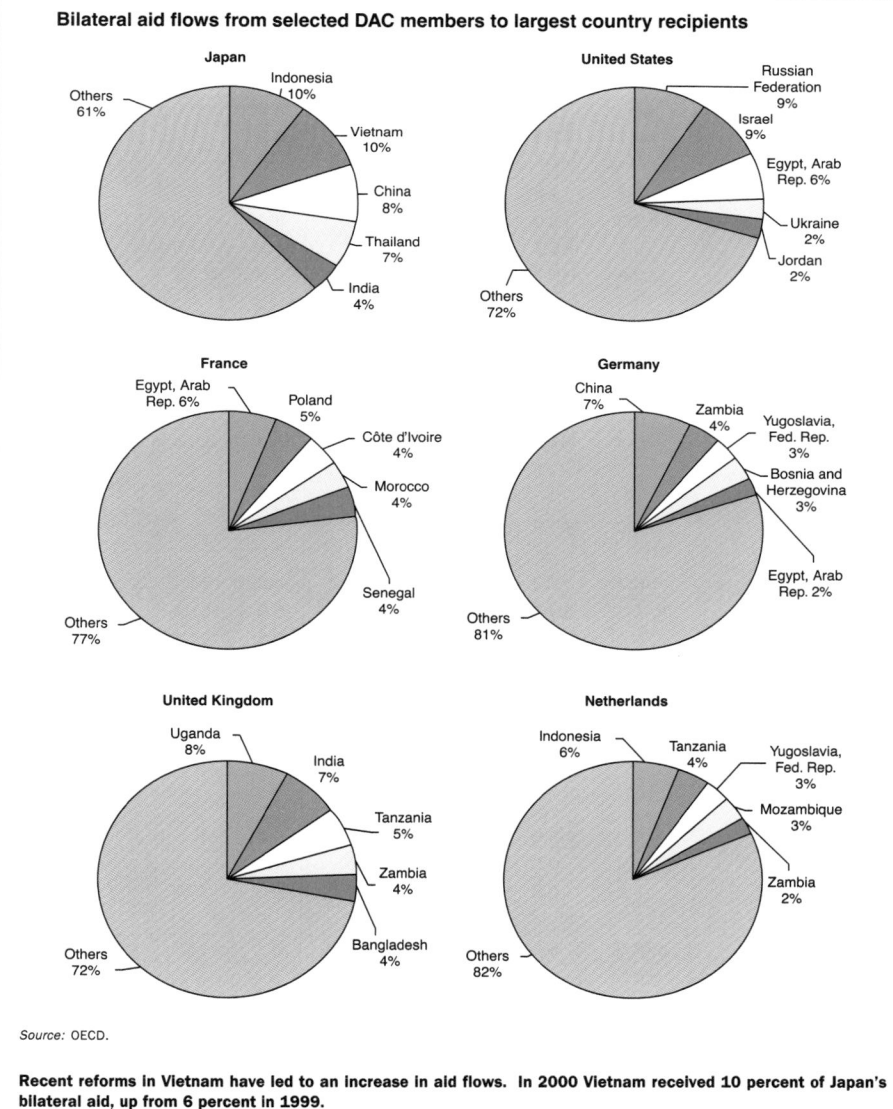

Bilateral aid flows from selected DAC members to largest country recipients

Source: OECD.

Recent reforms in Vietnam have led to an increase in aid flows. In 2000 Vietnam received 10 percent of Japan's bilateral aid, up from 6 percent in 1999.

	International financial institutions							United Nations					Total
	World Bank		IMF		Regional development banks								
$ millions, 2000	IDA	IBRD	Conces-sional	Non-concessional	Conces-sional	Non-concessional	Others	UNDP	UNFPA	UNICEF	WFP	Others	
Afghanistan	..	..	..	..	..	..	..	4.8	0.8	8.8	6.7	14.0	35.0
Albania	64.4	0.0	11.6	0.0	0.0	0.0	15.4	2.4	0.2	1.2	0.0	7.0	102.2
Algeria	0.0	-113.7	0.0	-92.6	0.3	38.3	60.8	0.7	0.4	0.7	2.4	5.4	-97.2
Angola	23.7	0.0	0.0	0.0	-1.5	-23.6	-2.4	2.0	1.3	4.4	38.4	9.5	51.8
Argentina	0.0	480.7	0.0	814.7	-0.9	618.4	0.0	-0.5	0.0	1.0	0.0	26.7	1,940.0
Armenia	54.4	-0.4	0.0	-15.8	0.0	-5.2	1.8	1.1	0.1	0.7	2.6	2.8	42.2
Australia													
Austria													
Azerbaijan	27.2	0.0	0.0	-51.4	0.0	9.6	10.7	2.1	0.6	1.0	2.4	4.8	6.9
Bangladesh	275.2	-5.3	0.0	-85.7	184.9	11.3	17.0	18.8	3.7	12.5	8.9	10.9	452.3
Belarus	0.0	-8.8	0.0	-55.6	0.0	-11.7	0.0	0.5	0.1	0.0	0.0	1.4	-74.1
Belgium													
Benin	30.3	0.0	0.0	-3.6	11.1	0.0	-1.0	3.0	0.7	2.0	1.9	2.8	47.1
Bolivia	50.6	-11.9	-14.8	0.0	62.5	-25.4	17.0	1.4	1.1	1.1	5.7	4.3	91.6
Bosnia and Herzegovina	44.1	0.0	0.0	15.8	0.0	15.0	-159.9	-2.3	0.1	0.9	0.0	24.6	-61.5
Botswana	-0.5	-7.4	0.0	0.0	0.2	-13.8	-3.0	0.9	0.4	0.7	0.0	2.7	-19.8
Brazil	0.0	805.4	0.0	-6,693.0	3.0	2,488.1	-3,136.7	-0.4	0.9	1.3	0.0	93.3	-6,438.1
Bulgaria	0.0	44.3	0.0	137.0	0.0	0.7	57.7	0.8	0.1	0.0	0.0	1.5	242.1
Burkina Faso	35.2	0.0	0.0	-2.5	10.0	-1.9	-2.4	4.2	1.1	3.3	1.1	3.9	52.1
Burundi	27.6	0.0	-4.5	0.0	-0.3	0.0	0.0	6.4	0.7	2.9	2.1	6.3	41.0
Cambodia	36.6	0.0	4.1	0.0	38.4	0.0	1.8	3.1	3.2	3.6	10.2	7.8	108.8
Cameroon	48.7	-53.3	0.0	49.9	3.2	-16.7	-2.6	1.0	1.5	2.1	0.4	3.1	37.4
Canada													
Central African Republic	7.2	0.0	-0.8	0.0	0.0	0.0	1.9	1.1	0.7	1.3	1.6	4.2	17.3
Chad	13.3	0.0	12.9	0.0	9.4	0.0	-0.5	4.3	1.0	1.9	3.5	4.2	49.9
Chile	-0.7	-66.7	0.0	0.0	-1.3	4.6	0.6	1.1	0.1	0.8	0.0	1.8	-59.7
China	313.6	949.7	0.0	0.0	0.0	417.2	8.8	12.7	3.5	18.1	7.5	11.4	1,742.6
Hong Kong, China	..	..	..	..	..	..	..	..	..	..	..	..	..
Colombia	-0.7	24.5	0.0	0.0	-12.3	63.2	-8.2	-0.2	0.3	1.2	3.2	4.8	75.9
Congo, Dem. Rep.	0.0	0.0	0.0	0.0	0.0	0.0	0.0	3.1	0.7	16.6	2.1	25.1	47.6
Congo, Rep.	-0.9	-2.4	0.0	13.9	-0.4	-1.7	0.1	1.0	0.2	1.4	0.1	6.5	17.9
Costa Rica	-0.2	-27.2	0.0	0.0	-11.1	16.0	21.8	0.3	0.2	0.5	0.0	2.4	2.7
Côte d'Ivoire	75.4	-57.5	-39.3	0.0	43.3	-35.4	-20.9	1.3	1.1	2.4	0.8	10.5	-18.3
Croatia	0.0	33.5	0.0	-28.8	0.0	-4.0	9.3	0.1	0.0	0.2	0.0	10.7	21.0
Cuba	..	..	..	..	..	..	..	0.8	0.3	0.8	2.0	2.0	6.0
Czech Republic	0.0	-42.9	0.0	0.0	0.0	0.0	51.0	0.2	0.0	0.0	0.0	1.1	9.4
Denmark													
Dominican Republic	-0.7	17.8	0.0	0.0	-4.2	24.1	8.7	1.0	0.6	0.9	1.0	7.9	57.0
Ecuador	-1.1	-20.6	0.0	149.5	-15.5	167.3	46.3	0.4	0.6	1.0	2.3	2.5	332.7
Egypt, Arab Rep.	26.3	-80.5	0.0	0.0	3.4	-83.1	16.6	2.0	1.9	3.2	9.1	5.3	-95.8
El Salvador	-0.8	17.0	0.0	0.0	-13.0	89.0	-25.9	1.3	0.6	0.8	0.9	1.4	71.2
Eritrea	31.6	0.0	0.0	0.0	0.7	0.0	6.4	2.2	0.6	1.5	1.7	5.5	50.3
Estonia	0.0	-9.4	0.0	-5.1	0.0	-2.7	-6.1	0.3	0.0	0.0	0.0	0.1	-22.9
Ethiopia	115.6	0.0	-13.0	0.0	22.7	-18.4	5.3	18.8	3.0	13.5	36.0	27.6	211.0
Finland													
France													
Gabon	0.0	-3.9	0.0	7.6	0.0	-30.1	0.1	0.1	0.2	0.5	0.0	3.3	-22.2
Gambia, The	5.4	0.0	7.5	0.0	1.6	-0.7	4.2	1.6	0.4	0.6	1.6	2.7	24.9
Georgia	18.1	0.0	0.0	-25.9	0.0	0.7	1.2	1.8	0.1	0.9	2.0	5.0	3.9
Germany													
Ghana	178.9	-8.1	0.0	-1.8	0.7	-13.5	1.6	4.9	1.8	2.9	1.5	4.0	173.0
Greece													
Guatemala	0.0	38.2	0.0	0.0	-5.4	20.6	33.7	1.8	0.3	0.9	2.7	1.6	94.3
Guinea	17.5	0.0	-8.0	0.0	0.6	-8.8	9.2	1.7	0.6	2.6	1.3	21.0	37.6
Guinea-Bissau	10.7	0.0	6.5	1.9	0.0	0.0	-0.3	0.9	0.2	1.1	0.2	2.1	23.3
Haiti	1.5	0.0	-3.0	0.0	35.1	0.0	-0.5	2.6	1.2	2.6	6.1	0.7	46.3
Honduras	35.9	-32.9	0.0	16.4	51.5	-15.1	165.1	2.7	0.8	0.4	0.9	1.8	227.4

$ millions, 2000	International financial institutions							United Nations					Total
	World Bank		IMF		Regional development banks								
	IDA	IBRD	Conces-sional	Non-concessional	Conces-sional	Non-concessional	Others	UNDP	UNFPA	UNICEF	WFP	Others	
Hungary	0.0	-56.7	0.0	0.0	0.0	3.3	-12.1	0.1	0.0	0.0	0.0	1.3	-64.1
India	655.2	-304.8	-251.0	0.0	0.0	159.8	41.5	21.2	9.0	31.9	27.0	33.7	423.5
Indonesia	33.2	290.1	0.0	1,122.7	17.9	203.9	-10.5	3.2	2.5	6.7	0.0	11.2	1,680.8
Iran, Islamic Rep.	0.0	44.4	0.0	0.0	0.0	0.0	-27.9	0.6	1.1	1.9	0.1	13.5	33.7
Iraq	..	..	..	..	..	..	..	0.9	0.3	2.8	0.1	5.4	9.5
Ireland													
Israel	..	..	..	..	..	..	..	0.0	0.0	0.0	0.0	0.4	0.4
Italy													
Jamaica	0.0	37.1	0.0	-19.1	-4.7	88.8	10.8	0.1	0.2	0.8	0.0	2.0	116.0
Japan													
Jordan	-2.6	-14.8	0.0	-11.3	0.0	0.0	-15.3	0.9	0.4	0.9	1.2	81.5	40.8
Kazakhstan	0.0	29.7	0.0	-442.1	3.6	18.0	13.0	0.8	0.8	0.8	0.0	1.8	-373.5
Kenya	141.5	-40.4	1.9	0.0	1.6	-15.2	-5.7	4.9	1.9	4.1	19.4	21.4	135.4
Korea, Dem. Rep.	..	..	..	..	..	..	..	1.2	0.4	0.7	0.6	4.1	6.9
Korea, Rep.	-3.5	-187.6	0.0	0.0	0.0	-39.7	0.0	0.3	0.0	0.0	0.0	1.8	-228.8
Kuwait	..	..	..	..	..	..	..	0.0	0.0	0.0	0.0	0.8	0.8
Kyrgyz Republic	51.7	0.0	0.0	7.4	37.7	0.0	7.6	1.7	0.4	0.9	0.0	1.5	108.9
Lao PDR	16.7	0.0	-7.7	0.0	39.2	0.0	13.1	2.8	1.4	2.2	1.0	2.8	71.5
Latvia	0.0	53.8	0.0	-10.1	0.0	14.1	-30.7	0.2	0.1	0.0	0.0	0.7	28.0
Lebanon	0.0	25.8	0.0	0.0	0.0	0.0	42.0	0.6	0.3	1.1	0.0	51.3	121.0
Lesotho	5.3	6.0	0.0	-5.2	1.0	-1.8	-2.4	0.7	0.2	0.7	1.2	1.4	7.2
Liberia	0.0	0.0	0.0	-0.6	0.0	0.0	0.0	2.0	0.7	1.7	12.7	14.5	31.0
Libya	..	..	..	..	..	..	..	-0.2	0.0	0.0	0.0	3.4	3.2
Lithuania	0.0	56.9	0.0	-27.3	0.0	1.2	-3.3	0.4	0.0	0.0	0.0	0.4	28.3
Macedonia, FYR	38.4	9.6	2.3	-17.8	0.0	0.6	10.5	1.1	0.0	0.5	0.0	9.2	54.3
Madagascar	76.9	0.0	45.1	0.0	19.6	-5.6	15.4	5.9	1.4	5.7	2.7	3.0	170.0
Malawi	81.2	-7.6	-0.6	0.0	15.6	-1.1	0.0	2.4	1.1	3.9	1.8	2.9	99.6
Malaysia	0.0	-85.9	0.0	0.0	0.0	9.4	-2.4	0.4	0.2	0.4	0.0	1.7	-76.3
Mali	40.7	0.0	0.0	-8.2	4.7	0.0	3.4	2.0	0.8	5.0	2.0	3.2	53.5
Mauritania	53.1	-1.9	-3.0	0.0	6.3	-5.8	10.8	1.9	0.7	1.3	2.2	3.2	68.8
Mauritius	-0.6	-14.4	0.0	0.0	-0.5	-2.8	12.9	0.5	0.1	0.6	0.0	1.0	-3.2
Mexico	0.0	418.0	-4,298.9	0.0	-1.1	300.6	0.0	0.7	1.2	1.1	0.0	8.3	-3,570.2
Moldova	30.1	0.8	12.2	-24.6	0.0	0.4	-4.2	0.7	0.1	0.7	0.0	1.2	17.4
Mongolia	14.1	0.0	1.5	0.0	19.8	0.0	0.3	1.4	1.5	1.2	0.0	1.9	41.7
Morocco	-1.4	-168.8	0.0	0.0	3.5	22.3	-4.4	1.3	1.3	1.2	2.2	2.7	-140.3
Mozambique	93.7	0.0	0.0	30.4	12.6	1.8	6.3	5.5	3.4	7.1	3.4	4.0	168.2
Myanmar	0.0	0.0	0.0	0.0	0.0	0.0	-1.2	14.9	0.8	6.3	0.0	12.9	33.7
Namibia	..	..	..	..	..	..	..	1.0	0.4	0.8	0.3	4.7	7.2
Nepal	34.4	0.0	0.0	-4.4	67.5	0.0	4.7	8.2	2.5	3.7	6.3	10.6	133.6
Netherlands													
New Zealand													
Nicaragua	85.5	-4.8	0.0	21.3	59.9	-9.1	0.9	2.8	1.2	0.8	8.4	1.5	168.4
Niger	59.8	0.0	9.4	0.0	-0.4	0.0	-3.7	5.5	1.0	5.9	3.0	5.3	85.7
Nigeria	51.0	-242.4	0.0	0.0	12.7	-70.2	-2.0	6.1	3.7	18.9	0.0	15.2	-207.0
Norway													
Oman	0.0	-2.9	0.0	0.0	0.0	0.0	1.5	0.0	0.0	0.8	0.0	1.6	0.9
Pakistan	76.8	-67.2	-14.5	-73.1	153.7	119.0	-31.4	4.0	0.7	11.6	2.7	26.6	208.8
Panama	0.0	-2.4	0.0	-51.8	-9.6	37.7	4.5	0.0	0.2	0.7	0.0	1.5	-19.2
Papua New Guinea	-2.7	14.5	0.0	18.7	-0.7	0.0	1.6	2.0	0.7	1.4	0.0	2.6	38.3
Paraguay	-1.5	27.9	0.0	0.0	-1.1	83.1	-2.6	0.2	0.6	0.8	0.0	1.2	108.5
Peru	0.0	172.9	0.0	-141.3	-6.6	5.3	137.2	-0.2	1.4	1.2	3.9	5.4	179.1
Philippines	7.2	-197.5	0.0	305.3	21.8	-77.2	-2.7	3.5	1.0	2.9	0.0	3.6	67.9
Poland	0.0	149.8	0.0	0.0	0.0	0.0	0.0	-0.2	0.1	0.0	0.0	2.2	151.9
Portugal													
Puerto Rico													
Romania	0.0	293.2	0.0	18.3	0.0	19.0	163.5	0.7	0.3	0.7	0.0	1.6	497.2
Russian Federation	0.0	273.6	0.0	-2,888.0	0.0	-9.4	-2.4	0.7	0.2	0.0	0.0	12.3	-2,613.0

| $ millions, 2000 | International financial institutions | | | | | | | United Nations | | | | | Total |
| | World Bank | | IMF | | Regional development banks | | | | | | | | |
	IDA	IBRD	Conces-sional	Non-concessional	Conces-sional	Non-concessional	Others	UNDP	UNFPA	UNICEF	WFP	Others	
Rwanda	30.9	0.0	0.0	14.0	-0.9	-0.1	-0.5	5.4	0.7	3.1	20.0	11.1	83.7
Saudi Arabia	..	..	..	..	..	..	..	0.0	0.0	0.1	0.0	10.9	11.0
Senegal	76.7	-2.8	-3.7	0.0	2.5	-12.0	-21.4	3.4	1.0	2.3	3.0	4.5	53.4
Sierra Leone	68.3	-0.3	-25.2	13.7	1.4	0.0	-2.5	0.9	0.2	2.2	0.0	4.7	63.5
Singapore	..	..	..	..	..	..	..	0.0	0.0	0.0	0.0	0.4	0.4
Slovak Republic	0.0	-22.2	0.0	-127.3	0.0	-33.7	27.8	0.4	0.0	0.0	0.0	1.1	-153.9
Slovenia	..	..	..	..	..	..	..	0.0	0.0	0.0	0.0	1.1	1.2
Somalia	0.0	0.0	0.0	0.0	0.0	0.0	0.0	5.2	0.4	4.9	0.7	12.6	23.8
South Africa	0.0	2.7	0.0	0.0	0.0	0.0	0.0	3.2	0.3	1.1	0.0	6.7	14.0
Spain													
Sri Lanka	28.3	-5.3	-85.6	0.0	44.6	0.0	2.8	5.0	0.6	0.7	2.5	8.4	1.9
Sudan	-2.2	-2.1	0.0	-54.2	0.0	0.0	-0.1	6.9	1.6	4.1	6.7	17.1	-22.2
Swaziland	-0.3	-0.1	0.0	0.0	1.2	8.1	-0.7	0.3	0.2	0.6	0.0	1.9	11.2
Sweden													
Switzerland													
Syrian Arab Republic	-1.5	-14.2	0.0	0.0	0.0	0.0	-42.0	1.1	0.9	1.0	4.6	27.1	-23.0
Tajikistan	22.8	0.0	25.5	-9.9	3.2	0.0	9.5	2.0	0.4	1.2	4.9	3.6	63.1
Tanzania	109.4	-4.4	0.0	27.4	27.2	-2.2	13.5	8.7	2.4	11.5	2.5	28.1	224.1
Thailand	-3.4	275.1	0.0	-197.9	-2.1	-269.8	-2.3	2.0	0.6	0.8	0.0	9.1	-187.9
Togo	9.9	0.0	-9.4	0.0	2.5	0.0	-0.1	2.8	0.5	1.2	0.0	1.9	9.3
Trinidad and Tobago	0.0	3.8	0.0	0.0	-0.1	-11.1	-0.8	0.1	0.0	0.0	0.0	0.9	-7.1
Tunisia	-2.1	-14.5	0.0	-40.1	0.0	-65.0	73.7	0.5	0.4	0.7	0.0	1.7	-44.8
Turkey	-5.9	805.8	0.0	3,372.0	0.0	0.0	-316.8	1.1	0.5	1.1	0.0	5.1	3,862.8
Turkmenistan	0.0	19.6	0.0	0.0	0.0	-2.7	-0.7	0.9	0.4	0.8	0.0	0.8	19.2
Uganda	175.6	0.0	0.0	-37.2	17.8	-0.8	17.3	4.1	2.6	6.5	8.6	16.4	211.0
Ukraine	0.0	88.2	0.0	-598.1	0.0	-29.4	0.0	1.7	0.1	0.0	0.0	3.2	-534.3
United Arab Emirates	..	..	..	..	..	..	..	0.3	0.0	0.0	0.0	1.0	1.3
United Kingdom													
United States													
Uruguay	0.0	76.3	0.0	0.0	-1.7	107.3	-4.3	0.3	0.1	0.6	0.0	0.6	179.1
Uzbekistan	0.0	26.8	0.0	-65.1	1.2	56.9	0.0	1.3	0.6	1.5	0.0	1.8	24.9
Venezuela, RB	0.0	-157.6	0.0	-507.1	0.0	159.5	77.8	0.4	0.3	0.9	0.2	3.2	-422.3
Vietnam	172.5	0.0	-15.9	-5.3	146.4	0.0	21.3	11.6	4.2	5.4	10.1	3.9	354.1
West Bank and Gaza	..	..	..	..	..	..	..	2.9	1.1	1.6	1.1	152.5	159.2
Yemen, Rep.	51.3	0.0	0.0	-71.4	0.0	0.0	-16.5	7.2	1.8	3.1	7.1	7.4	-10.0
Yugoslavia, Fed. Rep.	0.0	0.0	0.0	80.8	0.0	0.0	0.0	1.0	0.1	0.0	0.2	69.1	151.2
Zambia	205.8	-7.8	0.0	26.4	25.0	-14.9	-9.8	3.1	3.4	4.5	4.2	11.9	251.9
Zimbabwe	7.3	-27.4	-35.7	-34.8	3.7	-7.3	-25.0	1.8	0.5	1.7	0.0	5.4	-109.7
World	.. s	.. s	.. s	.. s	.. s	.. s	.. s	395.7 s	134.2 s	580.0 s	357.3 s	1,872.0 s	
Low income	3,545.6	-428.9	-309.4	153.0	1,062.0	261.8	52.4	254.5	81.3	264.1	290.9	500.7	5,727.9
Middle income	629.0	3,823.0	-4,385.5	-6,437.0	179.2	4,145.6	-2,743.6	78.6	34.3	75.8	66.4	811.9	-3,722.3
Lower middle income	616.4	1,705.1	-86.6	-3,218.3	201.2	539.2	502.5	66.8	28.7	61.8	62.8	526.0	1,005.7
Upper middle income	-10.2	2,117.9	-4,298.9	-3,218.7	-22.0	3,606.4	-3,258.8	9.5	5.0	13.5	0.2	247.5	-4,808.7
Low & middle income	4,174.6	3,394.1	-4,694.9	-6,284.1	1,241.2	4,407.4	-2,691.2	396.0	134.1	580.0	357.3	1,866.0	2,880.4
East Asia & Pacific	589.6	1,051.8	-18.1	1,243.6	290.7	244.4	23.0	69.2	23.8	54.7	36.6	142.1	3,751.4
Europe & Central Asia	345.2	1,745.4	51.5	-761.3	45.7	40.5	-156.9	21.5	5.4	15.9	12.2	196.3	3,083.9
Latin America & Carib.	174.3	1,795.0	-4,316.6	-6,426.1	174.4	4,215.8	-2,630.7	21.3	14.9	23.4	37.3	219.0	-6,698.1
Middle East & N. Africa	73.5	-339.2	0.0	-214.1	10.1	-87.5	40.5	14.4	9.1	17.0	21.8	399.8	-54.6
South Asia	1,076.1	-382.6	-351.1	-163.1	452.8	290.0	35.5	66.2	19.1	70.5	55.6	108.0	1,277.0
Sub-Saharan Africa	1,916.0	-476.2	-60.6	37.0	267.5	-295.9	-3.0	165.8	49.5	165.8	190.6	570.7	2,527.3
High income	..	..	..	..	..	..	..	-0.3	0.0	0.0	0.0	6.0	..
Europe EMU													

Note: The aggregates for the regional development banks, United Nations, and total net financial flows include amounts for economies not specified elsewhere.

About the data

The regional distribution of multilateral assistance differs from that of bilateral assistance. For example, while bilateral donors have increased the share of their aid to Sub-Sarharan Africa over the past 15 years to about a quarter, the share of multilateral assistance to the region has averaged more than 40 percent over the same period. The seven major (G-7) industrial countries—Canada, France, Germany, Italy, Japan, the United Kingdom, and the United States—have contributed about 77 percent of total multilateral assistance in the past 30 years.

This table shows concessional and nonconcessional financial flows from the major multilateral institutions—the World Bank, the International Monetary Fund (IMF), regional development banks, United Nations agencies, and regional groups such as the Commission of the European Communities. Much of these data come from the World Bank's Debtor Reporting System.

The multilateral development banks fund their nonconcessional lending operations primarily by selling low-interest, highly rated bonds (the World Bank, for example, has a AAA rating) backed by prudent lending and financial policies and the strong financial backing of their members. These funds are then on-lent at slightly higher interest rates, and with relatively long maturities (15–20 years), to developing countries. Lending terms vary with market conditions and the policies of the banks.

Concessional flows are defined by the Development Assistance Committee (DAC) as those containing a grant element of at least 25 percent. The grant element of loans is evaluated assuming a nominal market interest rate of 10 percent. The grant element of a loan carrying a 10 percent interest rate is nil, and for a grant, which requires no repayment, it is 100 percent.

Concessional, or soft, lending by the World Bank Group is carried out through the International Development Association (IDA), although some loans made by the International Bank for Reconstruction and Development (IBRD) are made on terms that may qualify as concessional under the DAC definition. Eligibility for IDA resources is based on gross national income (GNI) per capita; countries must also meet performance standards assessed by World Bank staff. Since 1 July 2001 the GNI per capita cutoff has been set at $885, measured in 2000 using the Atlas method (see *Users guide*). In exceptional circumstances IDA extends eligibility temporarily to countries that are above the cutoff and are undertaking major adjustment efforts but are not creditworthy for IBRD lending. An exception has also been made for small island economies. Lending by the International Finance Corporation is not included in this table.

The IMF makes concessional funds available through its Enhanced Structural Adjustment Facility (ESAF), the successor to the Structural Adjustment Facility, and through the IMF Trust Fund. Low-income countries facing protracted balance of payments problems are eligible for ESAF funds.

Regional development banks also maintain concessional windows for funds. In the *World Development Indicators* loans from the major regional development banks—the African Development Bank, Asian Development Bank, and Inter-American Development Bank—are recorded according to each institution's classification. In some cases nonconcessional loans by these institutions may be on terms that meet DAC's definition of concessional.

In 1999, all United Nations agencies revised their data to include only regular budgetary expenditures since 1990 (except for the World Food Programme and the United Nations High Commissioner for Refugees, which revised their data from 1996 onward). They did so to avoid double counting extrabudgetary expenditures reported by DAC countries and flows reported by the United Nations.

Definitions

• **Net financial flows** recorded in this table are disbursements of public or publicly guaranteed loans and credits, less repayments of principal. • **IDA** is the International Development Association, the soft loan window of the World Bank Group. • **IBRD** is the International Bank for Reconstruction and Development, the founding and largest member of the World Bank Group. • **IMF** is the International Monetary Fund. Its nonconcessional lending consists of the credit it provides to its members, principally to meet their balance of payments needs. It provides concessional assistance through the Enhanced Structural Adjustment Facility and the IMF Trust Fund. • **Regional development banks** include the African Development Bank, based in Abidjan, Côte d'Ivoire, which lends to all of Africa, including North Africa; the Asian Development Bank, based in Manila, Philippines, which serves countries in South Asia and East Asia and Pacific; the European Bank for Reconstruction and Development, based in London, England, which serves countries in Europe and Central Asia; the European Development Fund, based in Brussels, Belgium, which serves countries in Africa, the Caribbean, and the Pacific; and the Inter-American Development Bank, based in Washington, D.C., which is the principal development bank of the Americas. • **Others** is a residual category in the World Bank's Debtor Reporting System. It includes such institutions as the Caribbean Development Bank and the European Investment Bank. • **United Nations** includes the United Nations Development Programme (UNDP), United Nations Population Fund (UNFPA), United Nations Children's Fund (UNICEF), World Food Programme (WFP), and other United Nations agencies, such as the United Nations High Commissioner for Refugees, United Nations Relief and Works Agency for Palestine Refugees in the Near East, and United Nations Regular Program for Technical Assistance. • **Concessional financial flows** cover disbursements made through concessional lending facilities. • **Nonconcessional financial flows** cover all other disbursements.

371

2002 World Development Indicators

Data sources

The data on net financial flows from international financial institutions come from the World Bank's Debtor Reporting System. These data are published in the World Bank's *Global Development Finance 2002* and electronically as *GDF Online*. The data on aid from United Nations agencies come from the DAC annual *Development Co-operation Report*. Data are available in electronic format to registered users on the Web site at www.oecd.org/dac/htm/online.htm and on the OECD's *International Development Statistics* CD-ROM.

Selected OECD countries	Foreign population[a] (thousands)		Foreign population[a] (% of total population)		Foreign labor force[b] (% of total labor force)		Inflows of foreign population — Total thousands[c]		Inflows of foreign population — Asylum seekers thousands	
	1990	1999	1990	1999	1990	1999	1990	1999	1990	1999
Austria	456	748	5.9	9.2	7.4	10.0	..	..	23	20
Belgium	905	897	9.1	8.8	7.1	..	50	58	13	36
Denmark	161	259	3.1	4.9	2.4	4.4	15	21	5	6
Finland	26	88	0.5	1.7	..	1.5	6	8	3	3
France	3,597	3,263	6.3	5.6	6.2	5.8	102 [d]	104 [d]	55	31
Germany	5,343	7,344	8.4	8.9	..	8.8 [e]	842	674	193	95
Ireland	80	118	2.3	3.1	2.6	3.4	..	22 [d]	0	8
Italy	781	1,252	1.4	2.2	1.3	3.6	..	268 [d]	5	33
Japan	1,075	1,556	0.9	1.2	0.1	0.2	224	282	..	..
Luxembourg	113	159	29.4	36.0	45.2 [e]	57.3 [e]	9	12	0	3
Netherlands	692	652	4.6	4.1	3.1 [e]	3.4	81	78	21	43
Norway	143	179	3.4	4.0	2.3	3.0	16	32	4	10
Portugal	108	191	1.1	1.9	1.0	1.8	14 [d]	11 [d]	0	0
Spain	279	801	0.7	2.0	0.6	1.0	..	..	9	8
Sweden	484	487	5.6	5.5	5.4	5.1	53	35	29	11
Switzerland	1,100	1,369	16.3	19.2	18.9	18.1	101	86	36	46
United Kingdom	1,723	2,208	3.2	3.8	3.3	3.7	204 [d]	277 [d]	38	91

	Foreign-born population[a] (thousands)		Foreign-born population[a] (% of total population)		Foreign-born labor force[b] (% of total labor force)		Inflows of foreign population — Total thousands[c, d]		Inflows of foreign population — Asylum seekers thousands	
	1990	1999	1990	1999	1990	1999	1990	1999	1990	1999
Australia	3,886	4,482	22.8	23.6	25.7	24.6	121	84	4	8
Canada	4,343	4,971	16.0	17.4	18.5	..	214	190	37	29
United States	19,767 [f]	28,180 [g]	7.9 [f]	10.3 [g]	9.4	11.7	1,536	647	74	43

a. Data are from population registers or from registers of foreigners, except for France and the United States (censuses), Italy, Portugal, and Spain (residence permits), and Ireland and the United Kingdom (labor force surveys), and refer to the population on 31 December of the year indicated. b. Data include the unemployed, except in Italy, Luxembourg, the Netherlands, Norway, and the United Kingdom. Cross-border workers and seasonal workers are excluded unless otherwise noted. c. Inflow data are based on population registers and are not fully comparable because the criteria governing who gets registered differ from country to country. Counts for the Netherlands, Norway, and especially Germany include substantial numbers of asylum seekers. d. Data are based on residence permits or other sources. e. Includes cross-border workers. f. From the U.S. Census Bureau, *1990 Census of Population Listing*. g. From the U.S. Census Bureau, *Current Population Report* (March 2001).

About the data

The data in the table are based on national definitions and data collection practices and are not fully comparable across countries. Japan and the European members of the Organisation for Economic Co-operation and Development (OECD) have traditionally defined foreigners by nationality of descent. Australia, Canada, and the United States use place of birth, which is closer to the concept used in the United Nations' definition of the immigrant stock. Few countries, however, apply just one criterion in all circumstances. For this and other reasons, data based on the concept of foreign nationality and data based on the concept of foreign-born cannot be completely reconciled. See the notes to the table for other breaks in comparability between countries and over time.

Data on the size of the foreign labor force are also problematic. Countries use different permit systems to gather information on immigrants. Some countries issue a single permit for residence and work, while others issue separate residence and work permits. Differences in immigration laws across countries, particularly with respect to immigrants' access to the labor market, greatly affect the recording and measurement of migration and reduce the comparability of raw data at the international level. The data exclude temporary visitors and tourists (see table 6.14).

OECD countries are not the only ones that receive substantial migration flows. Migrant workers make up a significant share of the labor force in Gulf countries and in southern Africa, and people are displaced by wars and natural disasters throughout the world. Systematic recording of migration flows is difficult, however, especially in poor countries and those affected by civil disorder.

Figure 6.13

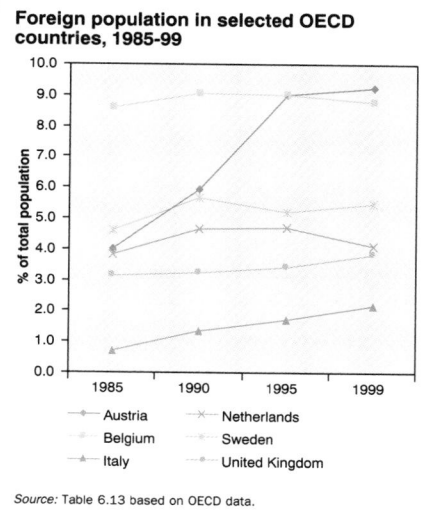

Foreign population in selected OECD countries, 1985-99

Source: Table 6.13 based on OECD data.

Definitions

• **Foreign (or foreign-born) population** is the number of foreign or foreign-born residents in a country. • **Foreign (or foreign-born) labor force, as a percentage of total labor force,** is the share of foreign or foreign-born workers in a country's workforce. • **Inflows of foreign population** are the gross arrivals of immigrants in the country shown. The total does not include asylum seekers, except as noted. • **Inflows of foreign workers** are the gross arrivals of foreign workers with legal employment status. The workers may be permanent or temporary. • **Asylum seekers** are those who apply for permission to remain in the country for humanitarian reasons.

Data sources

International migration data are collected by the OECD through information provided by national correspondents to the Continuous Reporting System on Migration (SOPEMI) network, which provides an annual overview of trends and policies. The data appear in the OECD's *Trends in International Migration 2001.*

6.14 | Travel and tourism

| | International tourism | | | | International tourism receipts | | | | International tourism expenditures | | | |
| | Inbound tourists thousands | | Outbound tourists thousands | | $ millions | | % of exports | | $ millions | | % of imports | |
	1990	2000	1990	2000	1990	2000	1990	2000	1990	2000	1990	2000
Afghanistan	8	4	..	..	1	1	..	..	1	..	..	..
Albania	30	39	..	18	4	211	1.1	38.8	4	12	0.8	1.1
Algeria	1,137	866	3,828	903	64	24	0.5	0.2	149	..	1.5	..
Angola	67	51	..	..	13	18	0.3	0.2	38	..	1.1	..
Argentina	1,930	2,991	2,398	4,786	1,131	2,903	7.6	9.4	1,505	4,107	22.0	12.6
Armenia	15	30	..	..	..	45	..	10.1	..	34	..	3.7
Australia	2,215	4,946	2,170	3,210	4,088	8,442	8.2	10.2	4,535	5,792	8.5	6.9
Austria	19,011	17,982	8,527	3,954	13,417	11,440	21.1	12.1	7,748	9,803	12.6	10.1
Azerbaijan	77	681	..	1,204	42	81	..	6.3	..	139	..	7.3
Bangladesh	115	200	388	1,103	11	59	0.6	0.9	78	212	1.9	2.5
Belarus	..	355	..	..	..	17	..	0.2	..	116	..	1.7
Belgium	5,147	6,457	3,835	7,773	3,721	7,039	2.7	3.5	5,477	10,057	4.1	5.3
Benin	110	152	418	..	28	33	7.7	5.9	12	7	2.6	0.9
Bolivia	254	342	242	196	91	160	9.3	11.0	130	165	12.0	8.3
Bosnia and Herzegovina	1	110	..	..	..	17	..	..	..	..	..	..
Botswana	543	843	192	..	117	234	5.8	7.7	56	143	2.8	5.7
Brazil	1,091	5,313	1,188	2,679	1,444	4,228	4.1	6.6	1,559	3,893	5.5	5.4
Bulgaria	1,586	2,785	2,395	2,592	320	1,074	4.6	15.3	189	524	2.4	8.0
Burkina Faso	74	218	..	16	11	42	3.2	10.5	32	..	4.2	..
Burundi	109	30	24	16	4	1	4.5	1.8	17	8	5.3	6.2
Cambodia	17	466	..	49	50	228	15.9	15.2	..	8	..	0.6
Cameroon	89	135	..	..	53	40	2.4	1.7	279	..	14.5	..
Canada	15,209	20,423	20,415	18,368	6,339	10,768	4.2	3.3	10,931	11,345	7.3	4.4
Central African Republic	6	10	..	..	3	6	1.4	3.9	51	..	12.4	..
Chad	9	44	24	..	8	10	3.0	2.7	70	..	14.4	..
Chile	943	1,742	768	1,567	540	827	5.3	3.7	426	806	4.6	4.5
China	10,484	31,229	2,134	10,473	2,218	16,231	3.9	5.8	470	10,864	1.0	5.7
Hong Kong, China	6,581	13,059	2,043	4,175	5,032	7,886	5.0	3.2	..	..	..	..
Colombia	813	530	781	1,098	406	1,028	4.7	6.6	454	1,078	6.6	8.0
Congo, Dem. Rep.	55	53	..	50	7	2	0.3	..	16	..	0.6	..
Congo, Rep.	33	26	..	..	8	11	0.5	0.4	113	60	8.8	4.5
Costa Rica	435	1,106	191	353	275	1,102	14.0	14.4	148	428	6.3	6.0
Côte d'Ivoire	196	301	2	..	51	108	1.5	2.1	169	237	4.9	5.4
Croatia	7,049	5,831	..	..	1,704	2,758	..	31.9	729	751	..	7.7
Cuba	327	1,700	12	56	243	1,756	..	..	..	..	..	..
Czech Republic	7,278	5,700	3,510	39,977	419	2,869	..	8.0	455	1,474	..	4.3
Denmark	1,838	2,088	3,929	4,841	3,322	4,025	6.8	5.7	3,676	5,084	8.9	8.7
Dominican Republic	1,305	2,977	137	364	900	2,918	49.1	32.6	144	282	6.4	3.0
Ecuador	362	615	181	386	188	402	5.8	6.7	175	271	6.9	6.5
Egypt, Arab Rep.	2,411	5,116	2,012	2,886	1,100	4,345	12.0	27.2	129	1,078	0.9	5.1
El Salvador	194	795	525	787	18	254	1.8	7.0	61	80	3.8	1.7
Eritrea	169	70	..	..	..	36	..	37.7	..	..	..	..
Estonia	372	1,100	..	1,780	27	505	4.1	10.5	19	217	2.7	5.1
Ethiopia	79	125	89	..	25	24	3.7	2.4	11	55	1.0	2.9
Finland	1,572	2,700	1,169	5,314	1,167	1,401	3.7	2.7	2,791	2,021	8.3	5.4
France	52,497	75,500	19,430	16,709	20,184	29,900	7.1	7.9	12,423	18,631	4.4	5.4
Gabon	109	155	161	..	3	7	0.1	0.2	137	183	7.6	10.3
Gambia, The	100	96	..	..	26	49	15.5	18.6	8	..	4.2	..
Georgia	..	384	..	373	..	400	..	54.1	..	270	..	21.2
Germany	17,045	18,983	56,261	73,400	14,288	17,812	3.0	2.8	33,771	48,495	8.0	7.9
Ghana	146	373	..	..	81	304	8.2	12.3	13	36	0.9	0.9
Greece	8,873	12,500	1,651	..	2,587	9,221	19.9	31.3	1,090	3,989	5.6	11.2
Guatemala	509	823	289	391	185	518	11.8	13.3	100	183	5.5	3.6
Guinea	..	33	..	..	30	12	3.6	1.4	30	31	3.1	3.3
Guinea-Bissau	..	..	..	..	..	..	..	..	..	..	..	..
Haiti	144	143	..	..	46	55	14.5	9.8	37	37	7.2	3.6
Honduras	290	408	196	235	29	240	2.8	9.6	38	60	3.4	2.0

	International tourism				International tourism receipts				International tourism expenditures			
	Inbound tourists thousands		Outbound tourists thousands		$ millions		% of exports		$ millions		% of imports	
	1990	2000	1990	2000	1990	2000	1990	2000	1990	2000	1990	2000
Hungary	20,510	15,571	13,596	10,622	824	3,424	6.8	10.8	477	1,191	4.3	4.2
India	1,707	2,641	2,281	3,811	1,513	3,296	6.6	5.2	393	2,010	1.2	3.0
Indonesia	2,178	5,064	688	..	2,105	5,749	7.2	8.1	836	2,353	3.0	5.6
Iran, Islamic Rep.	154	1,700	788	1,450	61	850	0.3	2.9	340	918	1.5	5.8
Iraq	748	78	239	..	55	13	..	..	..	..	..	..
Ireland	3,666	6,728	1,798	3,576	1,883	3,571	7.0	4.0	1,163	2,620	4.7	3.7
Israel	1,063	2,400	883	3,203	1,396	3,100	8.1	6.9	1,442	2,566	7.1	6.3
Italy	26,679	41,182	16,152	18,962	16,458	27,439	7.5	9.3	10,304	16,913	4.7	6.3
Jamaica	989	1,323	..	..	740	1,333	33.4	37.2	114	227	4.8	5.7
Japan	3,236	4,757	10,997	16,358	3,578	3,374	1.1	0.6	24,928	32,808	8.4	8.3
Jordan	572	1,427	1,143	1,560	512	722	20.4	20.4	336	355	9.0	7.1
Kazakhstan	..	..	..	..	..	363	..	5.2	..	394	..	5.8
Kenya	814	943	210	..	443	304	19.9	11.3	38	115	1.4	3.5
Korea, Dem. Rep.	115	130	..	..	..	..	..	..	..	..	..	..
Korea, Rep.	2,959	5,322	1,561	5,508	3,559	6,609	4.9	3.2	3,166	6,377	4.1	3.3
Kuwait	15	77	..	..	132	243	1.6	1.8	1,837	2,510	25.6	21.1
Kyrgyz Republic	..	69	..	32	2	8	..	1.3	..	3	..	0.3
Lao PDR	14	300	..	..	3	114	2.9	22.8	1	12	0.5	2.1
Latvia	..	490	..	2,256	7	131	0.6	4.0	13	268	1.3	7.4
Lebanon	210	742	..	1,650	..	742	..	34.7	..	..	..	..
Lesotho	171	186	..	..	17	19	17.0	8.8	12	12	1.6	1.4
Liberia	..	..	..	..	..	..	..	..	..	..	..	..
Libya	96	40	425	..	6	28	0.1	0.4	424	150	4.7	3.1
Lithuania	780	1,226	..	3,482	..	391	..	7.7	..	341	..	6.4
Macedonia, FYR	562	224	..	..	45	37	..	2.3	..	..	..	..
Madagascar	53	160	34	..	40	116	8.5	9.8	40	111	4.9	9.3
Malawi	130	228	..	..	16	27	3.6	5.5	16	..	2.9	..
Malaysia	7,446	10,222	14,920	26,067	1,667	4,563	5.1	4.1	1,450	1,973	4.6	2.6
Mali	44	91	..	..	47	50	11.2	7.1	62	29	7.5	3.0
Mauritania	..	24	..	..	9	28	1.9	7.7	23	55	4.4	13.3
Mauritius	292	656	89	154	244	585	14.2	22.2	94	187	4.9	6.6
Mexico	17,176	20,643	7,357	11,081	5,467	8,295	11.2	4.6	5,519	5,499	10.6	2.9
Moldova	226	17	49	37	4	4	..	0.6	..	58	..	7.5
Mongolia	147	158	..	..	5	28	1.0	5.3	1	41	0.1	6.2
Morocco	4,024	4,113	1,202	1,612	1,259	2,040	20.2	19.5	184	440	2.4	3.7
Mozambique	..	..	..	..	..	..	..	..	..	..	..	..
Myanmar	21	208	..	..	9	35	1.4	2.2	16	18	1.4	0.7
Namibia	213	614	..	..	85	288	7.0	17.9	63	88	4.0	4.6
Nepal	255	451	82	122	64	168	16.9	14.6	45	71	5.9	4.7
Netherlands	5,795	10,200	9,000	14,180	4,155	6,951	2.6	2.7	7,376	11,366	5.0	4.9
New Zealand	976	1,787	717	1,185	1,030	2,068	8.8	11.6	958	1,493	8.2	8.5
Nicaragua	106	486	173	452	12	116	3.1	12.2	15	74	2.2	3.6
Niger	21	50	18	10	17	24	3.2	7.5	44	26	6.0	5.7
Nigeria	190	813	56	..	25	142	0.2	1.4	576	620	8.3	5.1
Norway	1,955	4,481	2,667	..	1,570	2,229	3.3	3.7	3,679	4,751	9.5	9.4
Oman	149	502	..	..	69	104	1.2	1.4	47	47	1.4	0.8
Pakistan	424	543	..	..	156	86	2.5	0.9	440	180	4.7	1.5
Panama	214	479	151	221	172	576	3.9	7.5	99	184	2.4	2.3
Papua New Guinea	41	58	66	106	41	76	3.0	3.5	50	53	3.3	2.9
Paraguay	280	221	264	281	128	66	5.1	2.4	103	109	4.7	3.1
Peru	317	1,027	329	781	217	1,001	5.3	11.6	295	443	7.2	4.9
Philippines	1,025	2,171	1,137	1,755	1,306	2,534	11.4	6.5	111	1,308	0.8	3.6
Poland	3,400	17,400	22,131	55,097	358	6,100	1.9	13.2	423	3,600	2.8	6.9
Portugal	8,020	12,037	2,268	..	3,555	5,206	16.5	15.7	867	2,266	3.2	4.9
Puerto Rico	2,560	3,341	996	1,134	1,366	2,541	..	..	630	815	..	..
Romania	3,009	3,274	11,247	6,274	106	364	1.7	3.0	103	395	1.0	3.5
Russian Federation	3,009	21,169	4,150	18,371	752	7,510	1.4	8.9	..	7,434	..	14.0

	International tourism				International tourism receipts				International tourism expenditures			
	Inbound tourists thousands		Outbound tourists thousands		$ millions		% of exports		$ millions		% of imports	
	1990	2000	1990	2000	1990	2000	1990	2000	1990	2000	1990	2000
Rwanda	16	2	..	..	10	17	6.9	15.0	23	18	6.4	4.0
Saudi Arabia	2,209	3,700	..	..	1,884	1,462	4.0	3.4	..	..	..	..
Senegal	246	369	..	..	167	166	11.5	11.5	105	..	5.7	..
Sierra Leone	98	10	..	..	19	12	9.1	13.8	4	4	1.9	2.7
Singapore	4,842	6,258	1,237	3,971	4,937	6,370	7.3	3.8	1,893	2,749	2.9	2.2
Slovak Republic	822	1,053	188	343	70	432	..	3.1	181	295	..	2.0
Slovenia	650	1,090	..	..	721	957	8.5	8.9	282	539	4.1	4.7
Somalia	46	10	..	..	..	..	..	..	..	..	..	..
South Africa	1,029	6,001	616	3,363	992	2,526	3.6	7.5	1,117	1,806	5.3	6.0
Spain	34,085	48,201	10,698	4,794	18,593	31,000	22.2	18.4	4,254	5,523	4.2	3.2
Sri Lanka	298	400	297	524	132	253	5.8	4.0	74	219	2.5	3.2
Sudan	33	50	203	..	21	2	4.0	0.2	51	35	3.5	2.3
Swaziland	263	319	..	..	30	35	4.6	3.5	35	45	4.6	3.7
Sweden	1,900	2,746	6,232	10,500	2,906	4,107	4.1	3.8	6,286	7,557	8.9	8.0
Switzerland	13,200	11,400	9,627	12,009	7,411	7,303	7.6	6.0	5,873	6,842	6.1	6.4
Syrian Arab Republic	562	916	1,041	..	320	474	6.4	6.9	249	630	8.4	12.1
Tajikistan	..	511	..	..	..	..	..	..	..	..	..	..
Tanzania	153	459	301	..	65	739	12.1	57.7	23	550	1.6	25.8
Thailand	5,299	9,509	883	1,909	4,326	7,119	14.8	8.7	854	2,065	2.4	2.9
Togo	103	60	..	..	58	6	8.7	1.3	40	2	4.7	0.3
Trinidad and Tobago	195	336	254	..	95	210	4.2	6.2	122	67	8.6	2.1
Tunisia	3,204	5,057	1,727	1,480	948	1,496	18.2	17.4	179	239	3.0	2.6
Turkey	4,799	9,587	2,917	4,758	3,225	7,636	15.3	14.9	520	1,471	2.0	3.0
Turkmenistan	..	300	..	357	..	192	..	22.6	..	..	..	..
Uganda	69	151	..	..	10	149	4.1	20.5	8	141	1.2	7.7
Ukraine	..	4,232	..	7,399	..	2,124	..	12.5	..	1,774	..	11.6
United Arab Emirates	633	2,481	..	..	169	607	..	..	..	..	..	..
United Kingdom	18,013	25,191	31,150	53,881	13,762	19,544	5.8	4.9	17,560	35,631	6.6	8.7
United States	39,363	50,891	44,623	58,386	43,007	85,153	8.0	8.0	37,349	59,351	6.1	4.9
Uruguay	1,267	1,968	..	778	262	652	12.1	17.5	111	280	6.7	7.0
Uzbekistan	..	272	..	..	..	21	..	0.6	..	..	..	..
Venezuela, RB	525	469	309	891	496	656	2.6	3.0	1,023	1,646	10.8	9.7
Vietnam	250	2,140	..	168	85	86	4.4	0.7	..	..	..	..
West Bank and Gaza	..	330	..	..	..	155	..	..	..	..	..	..
Yemen, Rep.	52	73	..	..	20	76	1.3	1.8	64	83	2.9	2.8
Yugoslavia, Fed. Rep.	1,186	152	..	..	419	17	..	..	..	..	..	..
Zambia	141	574	..	..	41	91	3.0	9.7	54	..	2.8	..
Zimbabwe	605	1,868	200	331	60	202	3.0	8.6	66	131	3.3	4.8
World	463,576 t	701,855 t	508,753 t	644,804 t	265,062 t	475,817 t	6.1 w	6.2 w	268,266 t	417,084 t	6.3 w	6.0 w
Low income	12,955	25,684	..	..	7,825	14,275	4.9	7.6	..	10,938	3.8	5.0
Middle income	135,859	235,398	150,412	240,320	45,559	123,119	6.5	7.2	31,956	67,555	4.8	5.1
Lower middle income	47,704	108,139	44,071	61,463	17,820	58,528	7.8	8.2	..	31,582	2.5	6.3
Upper middle income	87,623	126,468	..	181,055	27,703	64,408	5.9	6.6	21,959	35,907	6.3	4.1
Low & middle income	149,346	263,586	..	299,419	53,380	139,533	6.3	7.1	38,313	78,539	4.7	5.0
East Asia & Pacific	30,463	67,978	23,210	49,961	15,682	44,091	6.5	5.4	7,146	22,989	2.9	4.1
Europe & Central Asia	59,843	97,311	..	176,460	9,737	38,042	7.4	10.9	..	21,927	2.6	7.7
Latin America & Carib.	33,010	51,058	17,576	28,727	15,157	33,109	8.0	7.1	13,002	19,251	9.1	5.0
Middle East & N. Africa	17,053	28,105	..	..	7,057	13,120	4.9	8.9	..	..	..	..
South Asia	3,004	4,714	3,503	6,255	1,968	4,230	5.8	4.7	1,048	2,744	2.1	2.9
Sub-Saharan Africa	7,075	17,455	..	..	3,079	6,597	3.8	8.4	3,683	5,202	5.5	5.9
High income	311,017	435,443	274,397	328,625	210,970	337,014	6.1	5.9	228,359	338,638	6.6	6.2
Europe EMU	184,112	255,007	..	..	100,879	152,168	6.6	7.1	87,712	132,360	6.0	6.2

About the data

The data in the table are from the World Tourism Organization. They are obtained primarily from questionnaires sent to government offices, supplemented with data published by official sources. Although the World Tourism Organization reports that progress has been made in harmonizing definitions and measurement units, differences in national practices still prevent full international comparability.

The data on international inbound and outbound tourists refer to the number of arrivals and departures of visitors within the reference period, not to the number of people traveling. Thus a person who makes several trips to a country during a given period is counted each time as a new arrival. International visitors include tourists (overnight visitors), same-day visitors, cruise passengers, and crew members.

Regional and income group aggregates are based on the World Bank's classification of countries and differ from those shown in the World Tourism Organization's *Yearbook of Tourism Statistics*. Countries not shown in the table but for which data are available, are included in the regional and income group totals. World totals are no longer calculated by the World Tourism Organization. The aggregates in the table are calculated using the World Bank's weighted aggregation methodology (see *Statistical methods*) and differ from aggregates provided by the World Tourism Organization and published in previous editions of the *World Development Indicators.*

Definitions

• **International inbound tourists** are the number of visitors who travel to a country other than that in which they have their usual residence for a period not exceeding 12 months and whose main purpose in visiting is other than an activity remunerated from within the country visited. • **International outbound tourists** are the number of departures that people make from their country of usual residence to any other country for any purpose other than a remunerated activity in the country visited. • **International tourism receipts** are expenditures by international inbound visitors, including payments to national carriers for international transport. These receipts include any other prepayment made for goods or services received in the destination country. They also may include receipts from same-day visitors, except in cases where these are important enough to justify a separate classification. Their share in exports is calculated as a ratio to exports of goods and services. • **International tourism expenditures** are expenditures of international outbound visitors in other countries, including payments to foreign carriers for international transport. These expenditures may include those by residents traveling abroad as same-day visitors, except in cases where these are so important as to justify a separate classification. Their share in imports is calculated as a ratio to imports of goods and services.

Data sources

The visitor and expenditure data are available in the World Tourism Organization's *Yearbook of Tourism Statistics* and *Compendium of Tourism Statistics, 2001*. The data in the table were updated from electronic files provided by the World Tourism Organization. The data on exports and imports are from the International Monetary Fund's *International Financial Statistics* and World Bank staff estimates.

Figure 6.14

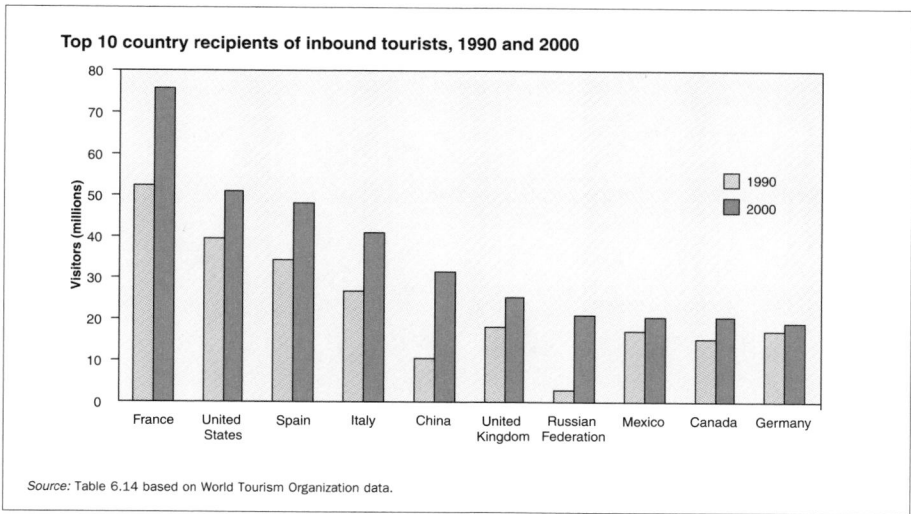

Top 10 country recipients of inbound tourists, 1990 and 2000

Source: Table 6.14 based on World Tourism Organization data.

This section describes some of the statistical procedures used in preparing the *World Development Indicators.* It covers the methods employed for calculating regional and income group aggregates and for calculating growth rates, and it describes the World Bank's Atlas method for deriving the conversion factor used to estimate gross national income (GNI) (formerly referred to as GNP) and GNI per capita in U.S. dollars. Other statistical procedures and calculations are described in the *About the data* sections that follow each table.

Aggregation rules

Aggregates based on the World Bank's regional and income classifications of economies appear at the end of most tables. These classifications are shown on the front and back cover flaps of the book. This year's edition of the *World Development Indicators,* like the two previous editions, includes aggregates for the member countries of the European Monetary Union (EMU). Members of the EMU on 1 January 2001 were Austria, Belgium, Finland, France, Germany, Ireland, Italy, Luxembourg, the Netherlands, Portugal, and Spain. Other classifications, such as the European Union and regional trade blocs, are documented in *About the data* for the tables in which they appear.

Because of missing data, aggregates for groups of economies should be treated as approximations of unknown totals or average values. Regional and income group aggregates are based on the largest available set of data, including values for the 148 economies shown in the main tables, other economies shown in table 1.6, and Taiwan, China. The aggregation rules are intended to yield estimates for a consistent set of economies from one period to the next and for all indicators. Small differences between sums of subgroup aggregates and overall totals and averages may occur because of the approximations used. In addition, compilation errors and data reporting practices may cause discrepancies in theoretically identical aggregates such as world exports and world imports.

Five methods of aggregation are used in the *World Development Indicators:*

- For group and world totals denoted in the tables by a *t,* missing data are imputed based on the relationship of the sum of available data to the total in the year of the previous estimate. The imputation process works forward and backward from 1995. Missing values in 1995 are imputed using one of several proxy variables for which complete data are available in that year. The imputed value is calculated so that it (or its proxy) bears the same relationship to the total of available data. Imputed values are usually not calculated if missing data account for more than a third of the total in the benchmark year. The variables used as proxies are GNI in U.S. dollars, total population, exports and imports of goods and services in U.S. dollars, and value added in agriculture, industry, manufacturing, and services in U.S. dollars.

- Aggregates marked by an *s* are sums of available data. Missing values are not imputed. Sums are not computed if more than a third of the observations in the series or a proxy for the series are missing in a given year.

- Aggregates of ratios are generally calculated as weighted averages of the ratios (indicated by *w*) using the value of the denominator or, in some cases, another indicator as a weight. The aggregate ratios are based on available data, including data for economies not shown in the main tables. Missing values are assumed to have the same average value as the available data. No aggregate is calculated if missing data account for more than a third of the value of weights in the benchmark year. In a few cases the aggregate ratio may be computed as the ratio of group totals after imputing values for missing data according to the above rules for computing totals.

- Aggregate growth rates are generally calculated as a weighted average of growth rates (and indicated by a *w*). In a few cases growth rates may be computed from time series of group totals. Growth rates are not calculated if more than half the observations in a period are missing. For further discussion of methods of computing growth rates see below.

- Aggregates denoted by an *m* are medians of the values shown in the table. No value is shown if more than half the observations for countries with a population of more than 1 million are missing.

Exceptions to the rules occur throughout the book. Depending on the judgment of World Bank analysts, the aggregates may be based on as little as 50 percent of the available data. In other cases, where missing or excluded values are judged to be small or irrelevant, aggregates are based only on the data shown in the tables.

Growth rates

Growth rates are calculated as annual averages and represented as percentages. Except where noted, growth rates of values are computed from constant price series. Three principal methods are used to calculate growth rates: least squares, exponential endpoint, and geometric endpoint. Rates of change from one period to the next are calculated as proportional changes from the earlier period.

Least-squares growth rate. Least-squares growth rates are used wherever there is a sufficiently long time series to permit a reliable calculation. No growth rate is calculated if more than half the observations in a period are missing.

The least-squares growth rate, *r,* is estimated by fitting a linear regression trend line to the logarithmic annual values of the variable in the relevant period. The regression equation takes the form

$$\ln X_t = a + bt,$$

which is equivalent to the logarithmic transformation of the compound growth equation,

$$X_t = X_o (1 + r)^t.$$

In this equation X is the variable, t is time, and $a = \ln X_o$ and $b = \ln(1 + r)$ are parameters to be estimated. If b^* is the least-squares estimate of b, the average annual growth rate, r, is obtained as $[\exp(b^*) - 1]$ and is multiplied by 100 for expression as a percentage.

The calculated growth rate is an average rate that is representative of the available observations over the entire period. It does not necessarily match the actual growth rate between any two periods.

Exponential growth rate. The growth rate between two points in time for certain demographic indicators, notably labor force and population, is calculated from the equation

$$r = \ln(p_n/p_1)/n,$$

where p_n and p_1 are the last and first observations in the period, n is the number of years in the period, and $\ln$ is the natural logarithm operator. This growth rate is based on a model of continuous, exponential growth between two points in time. It does not take into account the intermediate values of the series. Nor does it correspond to the annual rate of change measured at a one-year interval, which is given by $(p_n - p_{n-1})/p_{n-1}$.

Geometric growth rate. The geometric growth rate is applicable to compound growth over discrete periods, such as the payment and reinvestment of interest or dividends. Although continuous growth, as modeled by the exponential growth rate, may be more realistic, most economic phenomena are measured only at intervals, in which case the compound growth model is appropriate. The average growth rate over n periods is calculated as

$$r = \exp[\ln(p_n/p_1)/n] - 1.$$

Like the exponential growth rate, it does not take into account intermediate values of the series.

World Bank Atlas method
In calculating GNI and GNI per capita in U.S. dollars for certain operational purposes, the World Bank uses the Atlas conversion factor. The purpose of the Atlas conversion factor is to reduce the impact of exchange rate fluctuations in the cross-country comparison of national incomes.

The Atlas conversion factor for any year is the average of a country's exchange rate (or alternative conversion factor) for that year and its exchange rates for the two preceding years, adjusted for the difference between the rate of inflation in the country and that in the G-5 countries (France, Germany, Japan, the United Kingdom, and the United States). A country's inflation rate is measured by the change in its GDP deflator.

The inflation rate for G-5 countries, representing international inflation, is measured by the change in the SDR deflator. (Special drawing rights, or SDRs, are the IMF's unit of account.) The SDR deflator is calculated as a weighted average of the G-5 countries' GDP deflators in SDR terms, the weights being the amount of each country's currency in one SDR unit. Weights vary over time because both the composition of the SDR and the relative exchange rates for each currency change. The SDR deflator is calculated in SDR terms first and then converted to U.S. dollars using the SDR to dollar Atlas conversion factor. The Atlas conversion factor is then applied to a country's GNI. The resulting GNI in U.S. dollars is divided by the midyear population to derive GNI per capita.

When official exchange rates are deemed to be unreliable or unrepresentative of the effective exchange rate during a period, an alternative estimate of the exchange rate is used in the Atlas formula (see below).

The following formulas describe the calculation of the Atlas conversion factor for year t:

$$e_t^* = \frac{1}{3}\left[e_{t-2}\left(\frac{p_t}{p_{t-2}} \middle/ \frac{p_t^{S\$}}{p_{t-2}^{S\$}}\right) + e_{t-1}\left(\frac{p_t}{p_{t-1}} \middle/ \frac{p_t^{S\$}}{p_{t-1}^{S\$}}\right) + e_t\right]$$

and the calculation of GNI per capita in U.S. dollars for year t:

$$Y_t^\$ = (Y_t/N_t)/e_t^*,$$

where e_t^* is the Atlas conversion factor (national currency to the U.S. dollar) for year t, e_t is the average annual exchange rate (national currency to the U.S. dollar) for year t, p_t is the GDP deflator for year t, $p_t^{S\$}$ is the SDR deflator in U.S. dollar terms for year t, $Y_t^\$$ is the Atlas GNI per capita in U.S. dollars in year t, Y_t is current GNI (local currency) for year t, and N_t is the midyear population for year t.

Alternative conversion factors
The World Bank systematically assesses the appropriateness of official exchange rates as conversion factors. An alternative conversion factor is used when the official exchange rate is judged to diverge by an exceptionally large margin from the rate effectively applied to domestic transactions of foreign currencies and traded products. This applies to only a small number of countries, as shown in *Primary data documentation*. Alternative conversion factors are used in the Atlas methodology and elsewhere in the *World Development Indicators* as single-year conversion factors.

Primary data documentation

The World Bank is not a primary data collection agency for most areas other than living standards surveys and debt. As a major user of socio-economic data, however, the World Bank places particular emphasis on data documentation to inform users of data in economic analysis and policymaking. The tables in this section provide information on the sources, treatment, and currentness of the principal demographic, economic, and environmental indicators in the *World Development Indicators*.

Differences in the methods and conventions used by the primary data collectors—usually national statistical agencies, central banks, and customs services—may give rise to significant discrepancies over time both among and within countries. Delays in reporting data and the use of old surveys as the base for current estimates may severely compromise the quality of national data.

Although data quality is improving in some countries, many developing countries lack the resources to train and maintain the skilled staff and obtain the equipment needed to measure and report demographic, economic, and environmental trends in an accurate and timely way. The World Bank recognizes the need for reliable data to measure living standards, track and evaluate economic trends, and plan and monitor development projects. Thus, working with bilateral and other multilateral agencies, it continues to fund and participate in technical assistance projects to improve statistical organization and basic data methods, collection, and dissemination.

The World Bank is working at several levels to meet the challenge of improving the quality of the data that it collates and disseminates. At the country level the Bank is carrying out technical assistance, training, and survey activities—with a view to strengthening national capacity—in the following areas:

- Poverty assessments in most borrower member countries.
- Living standards measurement and other household and farm surveys with country partner statistical agencies.
- National accounts and inflation.
- Price and expenditure surveys for the International Comparison Programme.
- Projects to improve statistics in the countries of the former Soviet Union.
- External debt management.
- Environmental and economic accounting.

	National currency	Fiscal year end	National accounts					Balance of payments and trade			Government finance	IMF special data dissemi- nation
			Reporting period[a]	Base year	SNA price valuation	Alternative conversion factor	PPP survey year	Balance of Payments Manual in use	External debt	System of trade	Accounting concept	
Afghanistan	Afghan afghani	Dec. 31	CY	1975	VAB							
Albania	Albanian lek	Dec. 31	CY	1995 [b]	VAP		1996	BPM5	Actual	G	C	G
Algeria	Algerian dinar	Dec. 31	CY	1980	VAB			BPM5	Actual	S	B	
Angola	Angolan kwanza	Dec. 31	CY	1997	VAP	91-96		BPM4	Actual	S		
Argentina	Argentine peso	Dec. 31	CY	1993	VAB	1971-84	1996	BPM5	Preliminary	S	C	S*
Armenia	Armenian dram	Dec. 31	CY	1996 [b,c]	VAB	1993-95	1996	BPM5	Actual	S		G
Australia	Australian dollar	Jun. 30	FY	1995 [b,c]	VAB	1990-95	1996	BPM5		G	C	S*
Austria	Austrian schilling [d]	Dec. 31	CY	1995 [b]	VAB		1996	BPM5		S	C	S*
Azerbaijan	Azeri manat	Dec. 31	CY	2000 [b,c]	VAB	1987-95	1996	BPM5	Actual	G	C	G
Bangladesh	Bangladesh taka	Jun. 30	FY	1996 [b]	VAP	1971-2000	1993	BPM5	Actual	G	C	
Belarus	Belarussian rubel	Dec. 31	CY	1990 [b,c]	VAB	1987-2000	1996	BPM5	Actual	G	C	
Belgium	Belgian franc [d]	Dec. 31	CY	1995 [b]	VAB		1996	BPM5		S	C	S*
Benin	CFA franc	Dec. 31	CY	1985	VAP	1992	1993	BPM4	Actual	S		G
Bolivia	Boliviano	Dec. 31	CY	1990 [b]	VAP	1960-85	1996	BPM5	Preliminary	S	C	G
Bosnia and Herzegovina	Convertible mark	Dec. 31	CY	1996 [c]	VAB			BPM5	Preliminary			
Botswana	Botswana pula	Dec. 31	CY	1986	VAP	1999	1993	BPM5	Preliminary	G	B	
Brazil	Brazilian real	Dec. 31	CY	1995	VAB	1999	1996	BPM5	Preliminary	S	C	S*
Bulgaria	Bulgarian lev	Dec. 31	CY	1990 [b,c]	VAB	78-89, 91-92	1996	BPM5	Actual	G	C	G
Burkina Faso	CFA franc	Dec. 31	CY	1985	VAB	1992-93		BPM4	Actual	G	C	G
Burundi	Burundi franc	Dec. 31	CY	1980	VAB			BPM5	Estimate	S	C	
Cambodia	Cambodian riel	Dec. 31	CY	1989	VAP			BPM5	Preliminary	G		
Cameroon	CFA franc	Jun. 30	FY	1980	VAB	1970-99	1993	BPM5	Preliminary	S	C	G
Canada	Canadian dollar	Mar. 31	CY	1995 [b]	VAB		1996	BPM5		G	C	S*
Central African Republic	CFA franc	Dec. 31	CY	1987	VAB			BPM4	Estimate	S		
Chad	CFA franc	Dec. 31	CY	1995	VAB			BPM5	Preliminary	S	C	
Chile	Chilean peso	Dec. 31	CY	1986	VAB		1996	BPM5	Actual	S	C	S*
China	Chinese yuan	Dec. 31	CY	1990	VAP	1987-93		BPM5	Estimate	S	B	
Hong Kong, China	Hong Kong dollar	Dec. 31	CY	1990	VAB		1993	BPM5		G		S*
Colombia	Colombian peso	Dec. 31	CY	1994	VAB	1992-94	1993	BPM5	Actual	S	B	S*
Congo, Dem. Rep.	Congo Franc	Dec. 31	CY	1987	VAP	1993-99		BPM5	Actual	S	C	
Congo, Rep.	CFA Franc	Dec. 31	CY	1978	VAP	1993	1993	BPM4	Estimate	S	C	
Costa Rica	Costa Rican colon	Dec. 31	CY	1991 [b]	VAB			BPM5	Actual	S	C	S*
Côte d'Ivoire	CFA franc	Dec. 31	CY	1986	VAP		1993	BPM5	Estimate	S	C	G
Croatia	Croatian kuna	Dec. 31	CY	1997 [b]	VAB		1996	BPM5	Actual	G	C	S*
Cuba	Cuban peso	Dec. 31	CY	..	..					G		
Czech Republic	Czech koruna	Dec. 31	CY	1995 [b]	VAB		1996	BPM5	Preliminary	G	C	S*
Denmark	Danish krone	Dec. 31	CY	1995 [b]	VAB		1996	BPM5		G	C	S*
Dominican Republic	Dominican peso	Dec. 31	CY	1990	VAP			BPM5	Actual	G	C	
Ecuador	Ecuadorian sucre	Dec. 31	CY	1975	VAP	1999	1996	BPM5	Estimate	S	B	S*
Egypt, Arab Rep.	Egyptian pound	Jun. 30	FY	1992	VAB	1965-91	1993	BPM5	Actual	S	C	
El Salvador	Salvadoran colone	Dec. 31	CY	1990	VAP	1982-90		BPM5	Actual	S	B	S*
Eritrea	Eritrean Nakfa	Dec. 31	CY	1992	VAB			BPM4	Actual			
Estonia	Estonian kroon	Dec. 31	CY	1995 [b]	VAB	1990-95	1996	BPM5	Preliminary	G	C	S*
Ethiopia	Ethiopian birr	Jul. 7	FY	1981	VAB	1989-99		BPM5	Actual	G	B	
Finland	Finnish markka [d]	Dec. 31	CY	1995 [b]	VAB		1993	BPM5		G	C	
France	French franc [d]	Dec. 31	CY	1995 [b,c]	VAB		1996	BPM5		S	C	S*
Gabon	CFA franc	Dec. 31	CY	1991	VAP	1993	1993	BPM5	Actual	S	B	S*
Gambia, The	Gambian dalasi	Jun. 30	CY	1987	VAB			BPM5	Actual	G	B	
Georgia	Georgian lari	Dec. 31	CY	1994 [b,c]	VAB	1990-94	1996	BPM5	Actual	G	C	G
Germany	Deutsche mark [d]	Dec. 31	CY	1995 [b]	VAB		1996	BPM5		S	C	S*
Ghana	Ghanaian cedi	Dec. 31	CY	1975	VAP	1973-87		BPM5	Estimate	G	B	
Greece	Greek drachma [d]	Dec. 31	CY	1995 [b,c]	VAB	1993		BPM4	Estimate	S	C	
Guatemala	Guatemalan quetzal	Dec. 31	CY	1958	VAP	1985-86	1980	BPM5	Actual	S	B	
Guinea	Guinean franc	Dec. 31	CY	1994	VAB	1986	1993	BPM5	Estimate	S	C	
Guinea-Bissau	CFA franc	Dec. 31	CY	1986	VAB	1970-86		BPM5	Estimate	G		G
Haiti	Haitian gourde	Sep. 30	FY	1976	VAP	1991-97		BPM5	Preliminary	G		
Honduras	Honduran lempira	Dec. 31	CY	1978	VAB	1988-89		BPM5	Actual	S		

	Latest population census (incl. registration based censuses)	Latest demograhic, household, or health survey	Vital registration complete	Latest agricultural census	Latest industrial data	Latest water withdrawal data	Latest survey of scientists and engineers engaged in R&D	Latest survey of expenditure for R&D
Afghanistan						1997		
Albania	1989	MICS, 2000	Yes	1995	1990	1970		
Algeria	1998	MICS, 2000		1973	1996	1990		
Angola	1970			1964-65		1987		
Argentina	2001		Yes	1988	1996	1995	1999	1999
Armenia	1989	DHS, 2000	Yes		1991	1994	1999	2000
Australia	2001		Yes	1990	1997	1985	1998	1996
Austria	2000		Yes	1990	1998	1991	1993	1998
Azerbaijan	1999	MICS, 2000	Yes			1995	1996	
Bangladesh	1991	DHS, 1999-00		1976	1997	1990	1995	
Belarus, Rep.	1999		Yes	1994		1990	1996	1997
Belgium	2001		Yes	1990	1997	1980	1997	1991
Benin	1992	DHS, 1996		1992-93	1981	1994	1989	
Bolivia	2001	DHS, 1998			1998	1987	1996	
Bosnia and Herzegovina	1991	MICS, 2000	Yes		1991	1992		
Botswana	1991	MICS, 2000		1993	1994	1992		
Brazil	2000	DHS, 1996		1996	1996	1992	1995	1996
Bulgaria	1992	LSMS, 1995	Yes		1998	1988	1999	1999
Burkina Faso	1996	DHS, 1998-99		1993	1997	1992	1997	
Burundi	1990	MICS, 2000			1991	1987	1989	1989
Cambodia	1998	DHS, 2000				1987		
Cameroon	1987	DHS, 1998		1972-73	1998	1987		
Canada	2001		Yes	1991	1997	1991	1995	1998
Central African Republic	1988	DHS, 1994-95			1993	1987	1996	1996
Chad	1993	DHS, 1996-97				1987		
Chile	1992		Yes	1997	1997	1987	2000	2000
China	2000	Population, 1995		1996	1998	1993	1996	1994
Hong Kong, China	2001		Yes		1998	1995		
Colombia	1993	DHS, 2000		1988	1997	1996		
Congo, Dem. Rep.	1984			1990		1990		
Congo, Rep.	1996			1986	1988	1987	2000	
Costa Rica	2000	CDC, 1993	Yes	1973	1997	1997	1996	1996
Côte d'Ivoire	1998	DHS, 1999		1974-75	1997	1987		
Croatia	2001		Yes		1992		1996	1995
Cuba	1981		Yes		1989	1995	1995	
Czech Republic	1991	CDC, 1993	Yes	..	1998	1991	1999	1998
Denmark	2001		Yes	1989	1998	1990	1998	1998
Dominican Republic	1993	DHS, 1996			1971	1984	1994	
Ecuador	2001	CDC, 1999			1997	1998	1997	1997
Egypt, Arab Rep.	1996	DHS, 2000	Yes	1989-90	1997	1993	1991	2000
El Salvador	1992	CDC, 1994		1970-71	1998	1992	1992	1992
Eritrea	1984	DHS, 1995			1998			
Estonia	2000		Yes	1994		1995	1999	1999
Ethiopia	1994	DHS, 2000		1988-89	1998	1997	1987	
Finland	1990		Yes	1990	1998	1991		
France	1999		Yes	1988	1998	1990	1998	1997
Gabon	1993	DHS, 2000		1974-75	1982	1987		
Gambia, The	1993	MICS, 2000			1982	1982		
Georgia, Rep.	1989	CDC, 1999	Yes			1990		
Germany	–		Yes	1993		1991	1997	1998
Ghana	2000	DHS, 1998		1984	1995	1970		
Greece	2001		Yes	1993	1996	1980	1997	1997
Guatemala	1994	DHS, 1998-99	Yes	1979	1988	1992	1988	1988
Guinea	1996	DHS, 1999		1996		1987		
Guinea-Bissau	1991	MICS, 2000		1988		1991		
Haiti	1982	DHS, 2000		1971	1996	1991		
Honduras	1988	CDC, 1994		1993	1997	1992		

Primary data documentation

	National currency	Fiscal year end	Reporting period[a]	Base year	SNA price valuation	Alternative conversion factor	PPP survey year	Balance of Payments Manual in use	External debt	System of trade	Accounting concept	IMF special data dissemination
Hungary	Hungarian forint	Dec. 31	CY	1994 [b]	VAB	1996		BPM5	Actual	S	C	
India	Indian rupee	Mar. 31	FY	1993	VAB	1971-2000		BPM5	Preliminary	S	C	S*
Indonesia	Indonesian rupiah	Mar. 31	CY	1993	VAP	1993		BPM5	Preliminary	S	C	S*
Iran, Islamic Rep.	Iranian rial	Mar. 20	FY	1982	VAB	1980-90	1993	BPM5	Estimate	G	C	S*
Iraq	Iraqi dinar	Dec. 31	CY	1969	VAB					S		
Ireland	Irish pound[d]	Dec. 31	CY	1995 [b]	VAB		1996	BPM5		G	C	
Israel	Israeli new shekel	Dec. 31	CY	1995 [b]	VAP		1996	BPM5		S	C	S*
Italy	Italian lira[d]	Dec. 31	CY	1995 [b]	VAB		1996	BPM5		S	C	S*
Jamaica	Jamaica dollar	Dec. 31	CY	1986	VAP	1995-96, 99	1993	BPM5	Actual	G	C	S*
Japan	Japanese yen	Mar. 31	CY	1995	VAB		1996	BPM5		G	C	
Jordan	Jordan dinar	Dec. 31	CY	1994	VAB		1993	BPM5	Preliminary	G	B	S*
Kazakhstan	Kazakh tenge	Dec. 31	CY	1993 [b, c]	VAB	1987-95	1996	BPM5	Actual	G	C	G
Kenya	Kenya shilling	Jun. 30	CY	1982	VAB		1993	BPM5	Actual	G	B	G
Korea, Dem. Rep.	Dem. Rep. of Korea won	Dec. 31	CY	..	..			BPM5				
Korea, Rep.	Korean won	Dec. 31	CY	1995 [b]	VAB		1993	BPM5	Actual	S	C	
Kuwait	Kuwaiti dinar	Jun. 30	CY	1984	VAP			BPM5		S	C	S*
Kyrgyz Republic	Kyrgyz som	Dec. 31	CY	1995 [b, c]	VAB	1992-96	1996	BPM5	Actual	G	B	G
Lao PDR	Lao kip	Dec. 31	CY	1990	VAB	1960-89	1993	BPM5	Preliminary	G		
Latvia	Latvian lat	Dec. 31	CY	1995 [b]	VAB	1987-95	1996	BPM5	Actual	G	C	
Lebanon	Lebanese pound	Dec. 31	CY	1994	VAB			BPM4	Preliminary	G	V	S*
Lesotho	Lesotho loti	Mar. 31	CY	1995	VAB			BPM5	Preliminary	G	C	
Libya	Libyan dinar	Dec. 31	CY	1975	VAB	1986		BPM5		G		
Liberia	Liberian dollar	Dec. 31	CY	1971	VAB				Estimate			
Lithuania	Lithuanian litas	Dec. 31	CY	1995 [b]	VAB	1987-95	1996	BPM5	Actual	G	C	S*
Macedonia, FYR	Macedonian denar	Dec. 31	CY	1995 [b]	VAB		1996	BPM5	Actual	G		S*
Madagascar	Malagasy franc	Dec. 31	CY	1984	VAB		1993	BPM5	Preliminary	S	C	
Malawi	Malawi kwacha	Mar. 31	CY	1994	VAB		1993	BPM5	Estimate	G	B	
Malaysia	Malaysian ringgit	Dec. 31	CY	1987	VAP		1993	BPM5	Estimate	G	C	
Mali	CFA franc	Dec. 31	CY	1987	VAB		1993	BPM4	Preliminary	G		G
Mauritania	Mauritanian ouguiya	Dec. 31	CY	1985	VAB			BPM4	Actual	G		
Mauritius	Mauritian rupee	Jun. 30	CY	1992	VAB		1993	BPM5	Actual	G	C	
Mexico	Mexican new peso	Dec. 31	CY	1993 [b]	VAB		1996	BPM5	Actual	G	C	G
Moldova	Moldovan leu	Dec. 31	CY	1996	VAB	1987-95	1996	BPM5	Actual	G	C	S*
Mongolia	Mongolian tugrik	Dec. 31	CY	1998	VAP		1996	BPM5	Estimate	S	C	
Morocco	Moroccan dirham	Dec. 31	CY	1980	VAP		1983	BPM5	Actual	S	C	G
Mozambique	Mozambican metical	Dec. 31	CY	1995	VAB	1992-95		BPM5	Preliminary	S		
Myanmar	Myanmar kyat	Mar. 31	FY	1985	VAP	1980-82		BPM5	Estimate	G	C	
Namibia	Namibia dollar	Mar. 31	CY	1995	VAB			BPM5	Estimate		B	
Nepal	Nepalese rupee	Jul. 14	FY	1985	VAB	1973-2000	1993	BPM5	Actual	S	C	G
Netherlands	Netherlands guilder[d]	Dec. 31	CY	1995 [b, c]	VAB		1996	BPM5		S	C	
New Zealand	New Zealand dollar	Mar. 31	FY	1995	VAB		1996	BPM4		G	B	S*
Nicaragua	Nicaraguan gold cordoba	Dec. 31	CY	1980	VAP	1970-93		BPM5	Actual	S	C	
Niger	CFA franc	Dec. 31	CY	1987	VAP	1993		BPM5	Preliminary	S		G
Nigeria	Nigerian naira	Dec. 31	CY	1987	VAB	1971-98	1993	BPM5	Estimate	G		
Norway	Norwegian krone	Dec. 31	CY	1995 [b, c]	VAB		1996	BPM5		G	C	
Oman	Rial Omani	Dec. 31	CY	1978	VAP		1993	BPM5	Actual	G	B	S*
Pakistan	Pakistan rupee	Jun. 30	FY	1981	VAB	1972-2000	1993	BPM5	Preliminary	G	C	
Panama	Panamanian balboa	Dec. 31	CY	1982 [c]	VAP		1996	BPM5	Actual	S	C	
Papua New Guinea	Papua New Guinea kina	Dec. 31	CY	1983	VAP	1989		BPM5	Actual	G	B	G
Paraguay	Paraguayan guarani	Dec. 31	CY	1982	VAP	1982-88		BPM5	Actual	S	C	G
Peru	Peruvian new sol	Dec. 31	CY	1994	VAP	1985-91	1996	BPM5	Actual	S	C	
Philippines	Philippine peso	Dec. 31	CY	1985	VAP		1993	BPM5	Actual	G	B	S*
Poland	Polish zloty	Dec. 31	CY	1990 [b, c]	VAB		1996	BPM5	Actual	S	C	S*
Portugal	Portuguese escudo[d]	Dec. 31	CY	1995 [b]	VAB		1996	BPM5		S	C	S*
Puerto Rico	U.S. dollar	Dec. 31	CY	1954	VAP					G		S*
Romania	Romanian leu	Dec. 31	CY	1993 [c]	VAB	1987-89, 92	1996	BPM5	Actual	S	C	G
Russian Federation	Russian ruble	Dec. 31	CY	1997 [b, c]	VAB	1987-94	1996	BPM5	Estimate	G	C	

	Latest population census (incl. registration based censuses)	Latest demograhic, household, or health survey	Vital registration complete	Latest agricultural census	Latest industrial data	Latest water withdrawal data	Latest survey of scientists and engineers engaged in R&D	Latest survey of expenditure for R&D
Hungary	2001		Yes	1994	1997	1991	1999	1998
India	2001	National family health, 1998-99		1986	1997	1990	1996	1996
Indonesia	2000	Socioeconomic, 1998		1993	1998	1990		1994
Iran, Islamic Republic	1991	Demographic, 1995		1988	1996	1993	1994	1994
Iraq	1997	MICS, 2000		1981	1997	1990		
Ireland	1996		Yes	1991	1997	1980	1997	1997
Israel	1995		Yes	1983	1996	1986	1997	1999
Italy	2001		Yes	1990	1994	1990	1997	1996
Jamaica	2001	CDC, 1997	Yes	1979	1996	1993		
Japan	2000		Yes	1990	1998	1992	1997	1997
Jordan	1994	Annual Survey, 1999		1997	1997	1993		
Kazakhstan	1999	DHS, 1999	Yes			1993		1997
Kenya	1999	DHS, 1998		1981	1998	1990		
Korea, Dem. Rep.	1993					1987		
Korea, Rep.	1995			1991	1997	1994	1999	1997
Kuwait	1995	FHS, 1996	Yes	1970	1997	1994	1997	
Kyrgyz Republic	1999	DHS, 1997	Yes			1994	1997	1997
Lao PDR	1995			1999		1987		
Latvia, Rep.	2000		Yes	1994	1998	1994	1999	1999
Lebanon	1970	MICS, 2000		1999		1994		
Lesotho	1996	DHS, 1991		1989-90	1985	1987		
Libya	1995	PAPCHILD, 1995		1987	1997	1994	2000	1997
Liberia						1987		
Lithuania	2001		Yes	1994		1995	1996	
Macedonia, FYR	1994		Yes	1994	1996		1999	1999
Madagascar	1993	DHS, 1997		1984	1988	1984	1994	1995
Malawi	1998	DHS, 2000		1992-93	1998	1994		
Malaysia	2000		Yes		1996	1995	1998	1998
Mali	1998	DHS, 1995-96		1978	1997	1987		
Mauritania	2000	PAPCHILD, 1990		1985		1985		
Mauritius	2000	CDC, 1991	Yes		1997	1974	1992	1989
Mexico	2000	Population, 1995		1991	1995	1998	1995	1997
Moldova	1989	MICS, 2000	Yes			1992	1997	1997
Mongolia	2000	Repro. Health, 1998			1998	1993	1999	1999
Morocco	1994	DHS, 1995		1997	1998	1991		
Mozambique	1997	DHS, 1997				1992		
Myanmar	1983	DHS, 1996		1993	1998	1987		
Namibia	1991	DHS, 2000		1995	1994	1991		
Nepal	1991	DHS, 1996		1992	1996	1994	1980	1980
Netherlands	2001		Yes	1989	1998	1991	1998	1997
New Zealand	2001		Yes	1990	1997	1991	1997	1997
Nicaragua	1995	DHS, 1998		1963	1997	1998	1987	
Niger	1988	DHS, 1998		1980	1998	1988		
Nigeria	1991	DHS, 1999		1960	1994	1987	1987	1987
Norway	2001		Yes	1989	1998	1985	1999	1997
Oman	1993	FHS, 1995		1979	1998	1991		
Pakistan	1998	RHS, 2000-01		1990	1996	1991	1997	1997
Panama	2000			1990	1998	1990		
Papua New Guinea	2000	DHS, 1996				1987		
Paraguay	1992	DHS, 1990; CDC, 1998		1991	1997	1987		
Peru	1993	DHS, 2000		1994	1994	1992	1997	1989
Philippines	2000	DHS, 1998		1991	1997	1995	1992	1992
Poland	1988		Yes	1990	1997	1991	1999	1998
Portugal	2001		Yes	1989	1997	1990	1999	1997
Puerto Rico	1990		Yes	1987	1998			
Romania	1992	CDC, 1999	Yes		1997	1994	1994	1991
Russian Federation	1989	LSMS, 1992	Yes	1994-95	1998	1994	1999	1999

	National currency	Fiscal year end	National accounts					Balance of payments and trade			Government finance	IMF special data dissemi- nation
			Reporting period[a]	Base year	SNA price valuation	Alternative conversion factor	PPP survey year	Balance of Payments Manual in use	External debt	System of trade	Accounting concept	
Rwanda	Rwanda franc	Dec. 31	CY	1985	VAB			BPM5	Estimate	G	C	
Saudi Arabia	Saudi Arabian riyal	Hijri year	Hijri year	1970	VAP		1993	BPM4	Estimate	G		
Senegal	CFA franc	Dec. 31	CY	1987	VAP		1993	BPM5	Preliminary	S	B	G
Sierra Leone	Sierra Leonean leone	Jun. 30	CY	1990	VAB	71-79, 87	1993	BPM5	Actual	G	B	
Singapore	Singapore dollar	Mar. 31	CY	1990	VAP		1993	BPM5		G	C	
Slovak Republic	Slovak koruna	Dec. 31	CY	1995 [b]	VAP		1996	BPM5	Actual	G	C	S*
Slovenia	Slovenian tolar	Dec. 31	CY	1993 [b]	VAB		1996	BPM5	Actual	S	C	S*
Somalia	Somali shilling	Dec. 31	CY	1985	VAB							S*
South Africa	South African rand	Mar. 31	CY	1995	VAB			BPM5	Estimate	S	C	
Spain	Spanish peseta [d]	Dec. 31	CY	1995 [b]	VAB		1996	BPM5		S	C	S*
Sri Lanka	Sri Lankan rupee	Dec. 31	CY	1996	VAB		1993	BPM5	Actual	G	B	S*
Sudan	Dinar	Jun. 30	CY	1982	VAB	1980-91		BPM5	Estimate	G	B	G
Swaziland	Lilangeni	Dec. 31	CY	1985	VAB				Estimate		B	
Sweden	Swedish krona	Jun. 30	CY	1995 [b, c]	VAB		1996	BPM5		G	C	
Switzerland	Swiss franc	Dec. 31	CY	1995	VAB		1996	BPM5	Estimate	S	C	S*
Syrian Arab Republic	Syrian pound	Dec. 31	CY	1995	VAP	1970-00	1993	BPM5	Estimate	S	C	S*
Tajikistan	Tajik somoni	Dec. 31	CY	1985 [b]	VAB	1987-95	1996	BPM5	Actual	G	C	
Tanzania	Tanzania shilling	Dec. 31	CY	1992	VAB		1993	BPM5	Preliminary	S		G
Thailand	Thai baht	Sep. 30	CY	1988	VAP		1993	BPM5	Preliminary	G	C	
Togo	CFA franc	Dec. 31	CY	1978	VAP		1993	BPM5	Preliminary	S		G
Trinidad and Tobago	Trinidad and Tobago dollar	Dec. 31	CY	1985	VAP		1993	BPM5	Estimate	S	C	
Tunisia	Tunisian dinar	Dec. 31	CY	1990	VAP		1993	BPM5	Actual	G	C	S*
Turkey	Turkish lira	Dec. 31	CY	1994	VAB		1996	BPM5	Actual	S	C	
Turkmenistan	Turkmen manat	Dec. 31	CY	1987 [b]	VAB		1996	BPM5	Estimate	G		S*
Uganda	Uganda shilling	Jun. 30	FY	1991	VAB	1980-99		BPM5	Preliminary	G	B	
Ukraine	Ukrainian hryvnia	Dec. 31	CY	1990 [b, c]	VAB	1988-95	1996	BPM5	Actual	G	C	G
United Arab Emirates	U.A.E. dirham	Dec. 31	CY	1985	VAB		1993	BPM4		G	B	
United Kingdom	Pound sterling	Dec. 31	CY	1995 [b]	VAB		1996	BPM5		G	C	
United States	U.S. dollar	Sep. 30	CY	1995 [b, c]	VAB		1996	BPM5		G	C	S*
Uruguay	Uruguayan peso	Dec. 31	CY	1983	VAP	1993-99	1993	BPM5	Actual	S	C	S*
Uzbekistan	Uzbek sum	Dec. 31	CY	1997 [b, c]	VAB	91-94, 96-00	1996	BPM5	Actual	G		
Venezuela, R.B.	Venezuelan bolivar	Dec. 31	CY	1984	VAB		1993	BPM5	Preliminary	G	C	G
Vietnam	Vietnamese dong	Dec. 31	CY	1989	VAP	1991	1993	BPM4	Preliminary	G	B	
West Bank and Gaza	Israeli new shekel	Dec. 31	CY	1997	VAB		1993					
Yemen, Rep.	Yemen rial	Dec. 31	CY	1990	VAP	1991-96	1993	BPM5	Preliminary	G	B	G
Yugoslavia, Fed. Rep.	Yugoslav new dinar	Dec. 31	CY	2000	VAP				Estimate	S		
Zambia	Zambian kwacha	Dec. 31	CY	1994	VAB	1990-92	1993	BPM5	Preliminary	G	B	
Zimbabwe	Zimbabwe dollar	Jun. 30	CY	1990	VAB	1991, 1998	1993	BPM5	Preliminary	G	C	

Note: For explanation of the abbreviations used in the table see the notes.

a. Also applies to balance of payments reporting. b. Country uses the 1993 System of National Accounts methodology. c. Original chained constant price data are rescaled. d. European Monetary Union member sharing single currency Euro.

	Latest population census (incl. registration based censuses)	Latest demograhic, household, or health survey	Vital registration complete	Latest agricultural census	Latest industrial data	Latest water withdrawal data	Latest survey of scientists and engineers engaged in R&D	Latest survey of expenditure for R&D
Rwanda	1991	DHS, 2000		1984	1986	1993	1999	
Saudi Arabia	1992	Demographic, 1999		1983		1992		
Senegal	1988	DHS, 1999		1960	1997	1987	1996	
Sierra Leone	1985	MICS, 2000		1985	1986	1987		
Singapore	2000	General household, 1995	Yes		1998	1975	1995	1995
Slovak Republic	1991		Yes		1998	1991	1999	1995
Slovenia	1991		Yes	1991	1998		1998	1998
Somalia						1987		
South Africa	2001	DHS, 1998			1996	1990	1993	1993
Spain	2001		Yes	1989	1998	1991	1999	1998
Sri Lanka	2001	DHS, 1993	Yes	1982	1995	1990	1996	
Sudan	1993	DHS, 1989-90			1997	1995		
Swaziland						1980		
Sweden	1990		Yes	1981	1997	1991	1999	1997
Switzerland	2000		Yes	1990	1998	1991	1996	1992
Syrian Arab Republic	1994	PAPCHILD, 1995		1981	1998	1993	1997	
Tajikistan	2000	MICS, 2000	Yes	1994		1994	1993	
Tanzania	1988	DHS, 1999		1995	1997	1994		
Thailand	2000	DHS, 1987		1993	1996	1990	1996	1997
Togo	1981	DHS, 1998		1996	1997	1987	1994	1995
Trinidad and Tobago	1990	DHS, 1987	Yes	1982	1997	1997	1997	1997
Tunisia	1994	DHS, 1998		1961	1998	1990	1997	1997
Turkey	1997	DHS, 1998		1991	1997	1992	1997	1997
Turkmenistan	1995	DHS, 2000	Yes			1994		
Uganda	1991	DHS, 2000		1991	1997	1970	2000	1999
Ukraine	2001	CDC, 1999	Yes			1992	2000	2000
United Arab Emirates	1995			1998	1981	1995		
United Kingdom	2001		Yes	1993	1998	1991	1998	1997
United States	2000	Current population, 1997	Yes	1997	1997	1990	1997	1996
Uruguay	1996		Yes	1990	1997	1965		
Uzbekistan	1989	DHS, 1996	Yes			1994	1992	
Venezuela, R.B.	2001	LSMS, 1993	Yes	1997-98	1996	1970	2000	2000
Vietnam	1999	DHS, 1997		1994	1998	1990	1995	
West Bank and Gaza	1997	Demographic, 1995		1971				
Yemen, Rep.	1994	DHS, 1997		1982-85		1990		
Yugoslavia, Fed. Rep.	1991	MICS, 2000	Yes	1981	1998		1999	1998
Zambia	1990	DHS, 1996		1990	1997	1994		
Zimbabwe	1992	DHS, 1999		1960	1997	1987		

• **Fiscal year end** is the date of the end of the fiscal year for the central government. Fiscal years for other levels of government and the reporting years for statistical surveys may differ, but if a country is designated as a fiscal year reporter in the following column, the date shown is the end of its national accounts reporting period. • **Reporting period** for national accounts and balance of payments data is designated as either calendar year basis (CY) or fiscal year (FY). Most economies report their national accounts and balance of payments data using calendar years, but some use fiscal years, which straddle two calendar years. In the *World Development Indicators* fiscal year data are assigned to the calendar year that contains the larger share of the fiscal year. If a country's fiscal year ends before June 30, the data are shown in the first year of the fiscal period; if the fiscal year ends on or after June 30, the data are shown in the second year of the period. Saudi Arabia follows a lunar year whose starting and ending dates change with respect to the solar year. Because the International Monetary Fund (IMF) reports most balance of payments data on a calendar year basis, balance of payments data for fiscal year reporters in the *World Development Indicators* are based on fiscal year estimates provided by World Bank staff. These estimates may differ from IMF data but allow consistent comparisons between national accounts and balance of payments data. • **Base year** is the year used as the base period for constant price calculations in the country's national accounts. Price indexes derived from national accounts aggregates, such as the GDP deflator, express the price level relative to prices in the base year. Constant price data reported in the *World Development Indicators* are rescaled to a common 1995 reference year. See *About the data* for table 4.1 for further discussion. • **SNA price valuation** shows whether value added in the national accounts is reported at basic prices (VAB) or at producers' prices (VAP). Producers' prices include the value of taxes paid by producers and thus tend to overstate the actual value added in production. See *About the data* for tables 4.1 and 4.2 for further discussion of national accounts valuation. • **Alternative conversion factor** identifies the countries and years for which a World Bank-estimated conversion factor has been used in place of the official (IFS line rf) exchange rate. See *Statistical methods* for further discussion of the use of alternative conversion factors. • **PPP survey year** refers to the latest available survey year for the International Comparison Programme's estimates of purchasing power parities (PPPs). • **Balance of Payments Manual in use** refers to the classification system used for compiling and reporting data on balance of payments items in table 4.15. BPM4 refers to the fourth edition of the IMF's *Balance of Payments Manual* (1977), and BPM5 to the

fifth edition (1993). Since 1995 the IMF has adjusted all balance of payments data to BPM5 conventions, but some countries continue to report using the older system. • **External debt** shows debt reporting status for 2000 data. *Actual* indicates data are as reported, *preliminary* indicates data are preliminary and include an element of staff estimation, and *estimate* indicates data are staff estimates. • **System of trade** refers to the general trade system (G) or the special trade system (S). For imports under the general trade system, both goods entering directly for domestic consumption and goods entered into customs storage are recorded, at the time of their first arrival, as imports; under the special trade system goods are recorded as imports when declared for domestic consumption whether at time of entry or on withdrawal from customs storage. Exports under the general system comprise outward-moving goods: (a) national goods wholly or partly produced in the country; (b) foreign goods, neither transformed nor declared for domestic consumption in the country, that move outward from customs storage; and (c) nationalized goods that have been declared from domestic consumption and move outward without having been transformed. Under the special system of trade exports comprise categories (a) and (c). In some compilations categories (b) and (c) are classified as re-exports. Direct transit trade, consisting of goods entering or leaving for transport purposes only, is excluded from both import and export statistics. See *About the data* for tables 4.5 and 4.6 for further discussion. • **Government finance accounting concept** describes the accounting basis for reporting central government financial data. For most countries government finance data have been consolidated (C) into one set of accounts capturing all the central government's fiscal activities. Budgetary central government accounts (B) exclude central government units. See *About the data* for tables 4.11, 4.12 and 4.13 for further details. • **IMF special data dissemination** shows the countries that subscribe to the International Monetary Fund's (IMF) Special Data Dissemination Standard (SDDS) or the General Data Dissemination System (GDDS). *S* refers to countries that subscribe to the SDDS; *S** indicates subscribers that have posted data on the Dissemination Standards Bulletin Board web site; while *G* refers to countries that subscribe to the GDDS. (Posted data can be reached through the IMF Dissemination Standard Bulletin Board at dsbb.imf.org/.). The SDDS was established by the IMF to guide members that have or that might seek, access to international capital markets in the provision of their economic and financial data to the public. The GDDS helps guide member countries in the dissemination to the public of comprehensive, timely, accessible, and reliable economic, financial, and sociodemographic statistics. Member countries of the IMF

voluntarily elect to participate in either the SDDS or the GDDS. Both the GDDS and the SDDS are expected to enhance the availability of timely and comprehensive data and therefore contribute to the pursuit of sound macroeconomic policies; the SDDS is also expected to contribute to the improved functioning of financial markets. • **Latest population census** shows the most recent year in which a census was conducted and at least preliminary results have been released. • **Latest household or demographic survey** gives information on the surveys used in compiling household and demographic data presented in section 2. PAPCHILD is the Pan Arab Project for Child Development, DHS is Demographic and Health Survey, LSMS is Living Standards Measurement Study, SDA is Social Dimensions of Adjustment, CDC is Centers for Disease Control and Prevention, and SHEHEA is Survey of Household Expenditure and Household Economic Activities. • **Vital registration complete** identifies countries judged to have complete registries of vital (birth and death) statistics by the United Nations Department of Economic and Social Information and Policy Analysis, Statistical Division, and reported in *Population and Vital Statistics Reports*. Countries with complete vital statistics registries may have more accurate and more timely demographic indicators. • **Latest agricultural census** shows the most recent year in which an agricultural census was conducted and reported to the Food and Agriculture Organization. • **Latest industrial data** refer to the most recent year for which manufacturing value added data at the three-digit level of the International Standard Industrial Classification (revision 2 or revision 3) are available in the UNIDO database. • **Latest water withdrawal data** refer to the most recent year for which data have been compiled from a variety of sources. See *About the data* for table 3.5 for more information. • **Latest surveys of scientists and engineers engaged in R&D and expenditure for R&D** refer to the most recent year for which data are available from a data collection effort by UNESCO in science and technology and research and development (R&D). See *About the data* for table 5.11 for more information.

Acronymns and abbreviations

Technical terms

AIDS	acquired immunodeficiency syndrome
BOD	biochemical oxygen demand
CFC	chlorofluorocarbon
c.i.f.	cost, insurance, and freight
CO$_2$	carbon dioxide
COMTRADE	United Nations Statistics Division's Commodity Trade database
CPI	consumer price index
cu. m	cubic meter
DHS	Demographic and Health Survey
DMTU	dry metric ton unit
DOTS	directly observed treatment, short-course (strategy)
DPT	diphtheria, pertussis, and tetanus
DRS	World Bank's Debtor Reporting System
ESAF	Enhanced Structural Adjustment Facility
f.o.b.	free on board
GDP	gross domestic product
GEMS	Global Environment Monitoring System
GIS	geographic information system
GNI	gross national income (formerly referred to as GNP)
GNP	gross national product (now referred to as GNI)
ha	hectare
HIPC	heavily indebted poor country
HIV	human immunodeficiency virus
ICD	International Classification of Diseases
ICRG	International Country Risk Guide
ICSE	International Classification of Status in Employment
ICT	information and communications technology
IP	Internet Protocol
ISCED	International Standard Classification of Education
ISIC	International Standard Industrial Classification
ISP	Internet service provider
kg	kilogram
km	kilometer
kwh	kilowatt-hour
LIBOR	London interbank offered rate
M0	currency and coins (monetary base)
M1	narrow money (currency and demand deposits)
M2	money plus quasi money
M3	broad money or liquid liabilities
mmbtu	millions of British thermal units
mt	metric ton
MUV	manufactures unit value
NEAP	national environmental action plan
NGO	nongovernmental organization
NO$_2$	nitrogen dioxide
ODA	official development assistance
PC	personal computer
PPI	private participation in infrastructure
PPP	purchasing power parity
R&D	research and development
S&P/IFCG	Standard & Poor's/International Finance Corporation Global (index)
S&P/IFCI	Standard & Poor's/International Finance Corporation Investable (index)
SDR	special drawing right
SITC	Standard International Trade Classification
SNA	System of National Accounts
SO$_2$	sulfur dioxide
SOPEMI	Continuous Reporting System on Migration
sq. km	square kilometer
STD	sexually transmitted disease
TB	tuberculosis
TFP	total factor productivity
ton-km	metric ton-kilometers
TSP	total suspended particulates

Organizations

ADB	Asian Development Bank
AfDB	African Development Bank
APEC	Asia Pacific Economic Cooperation
CDC	Centers for Disease Control and Prevention
CDIAC	Carbon Dioxide Information Analysis Center
CEC	Commission of the European Community
DAC	Development Assistance Committee of the OECD
EBRD	European Bank for Reconstruction and Development
EDF	European Development Fund
EFTA	European Free Trade Area
EIB	European Investment Bank
EMU	European Monetary Union
EU	European Union
Eurostat	Statistical Office of the European Communities
FAO	Food and Agriculture Organization
FYR	former Yugoslav Republic
G-5	France, Germany, Japan, United Kingdom, and United States
G-7	G-5 plus Canada and Italy
G-8	G-7 plus Russian Federation
GEF	Global Environment Facility
IBRD	International Bank for Reconstruction and Development
ICAO	International Civil Aviation Organization
ICP	International Comparison Programme
ICSID	International Centre for Settlement of Investment Disputes
IDA	International Development Association
IDB	Inter-American Development Bank
IDC	International Data Corporation
IEA	International Energy Agency
IFC	International Finance Corporation
ILO	International Labour Organization
IMF	International Monetary Fund
IRF	International Road Federation
ITU	International Telecommunication Union
IUCN	World Conservation Union
MIGA	Multilateral Investment Guarantee Agency
NAFTA	North American Free Trade Agreement
NATO	North Atlantic Treaty Organization
NSF	National Science Foundation
OECD	Organisation for Economic Co-operation and Development
PAHO	Pan American Health Organization
PARIS21	Partnership in Statistics for Development in the 21st Century
S&P	Standard & Poor's
UIP	Urban Indicators Programme
UN	United Nations
UNAIDS	Joint United Nations Programme on HIV/AIDS
UNCED	United Nations Conference on Environment and Development
UNCHS	United Nations Centre for Human Settlements (Habitat)
UNCTAD	United Nations Conference on Trade and Development
UNDP	United Nations Development Programme
UNECE	United Nations Economic Commission for Europe
UNEP	United Nations Environment Programme
UNESCO	United Nations Educational, Scientific, and Cultural Organization
UNFPA	United Nations Population Fund
UNHCR	United Nations High Commissioner for Refugees
UNICEF	United Nations Children's Fund
UNIDO	United Nations Industrial Development Organization
UNRISD	United Nations Research Institute for Social Development
UNSD	United Nations Statistics Division
USAID	U.S. Agency for International Development
WCMC	World Conservation Monitoring Centre
WFP	World Food Programme
WHO	World Health Organization
WIPO	World Intellectual Property Organization
WITSA	World Information Technology and Services Alliance
WTO	World Trade Organization
WWF	World Wide Fund for Nature

Credits

This book has drawn on a wide range of World Bank reports and numerous external sources, listed in the bibliography following this section. Many people inside and outside the World Bank helped in writing and producing the *World Development Indicators*. The team would like to particularly acknowledge the help and encouragement of Nicholas Stern, Senior Vice-President and Chief Economist. It is also grateful to those who provided valuable comments on the entire book, especially Jean Baneth. This note identifies those who made specific contributions. Numerous others, too many to acknowledge here, helped in many ways for which the team is extremely grateful.

1. World view

was prepared by Eric Swanson and K. M. Vijayalakshmi. Eric Swanson wrote the introduction. David Cieslikowski, Mona Fetouh, Masako Hiraga and Sulekha Patel assisted in developing and preparing tables and figures. Valuable suggestions were received from members of the World Bank Human Development Network. Yonas Biru and William Prince provided substantial assistance with the data, preparing the estimates of gross national income in purchasing power parity terms. Azita Amjadi, Aki Kuwahara (UNCTAD), and Jerzy Rozanski helped in preparing the market access indicators.

2. People

were prepared by Masako Hiraga and Sulekha Patel in partnership with the World Bank's Human Development (HD) Network and the Development Research Group in the Development Economics Vice Presidency. The Institute of Statistics of the United Nations Educational, Scientific, and Cultural Organization (UNESCO) provided substantial help in preparing the education data for this section. Barbara Bruns and Nicholas Wilson from the Education anchor of the HD Network provided estimates of primary completion rates. Sulekha Patel wrote the introduction, based on an outline provided by Harold Alderman, Advisor, Nutrition Policy in the Bank's Environmentally and Socially Sustainable Development network and Milla McLaughlin, Senior Nutrition Advisor in the HD Network. Substantial input was also provided by Lynn Brown, Judith McGuire, and Claudia Rokx. Contributions to the section were provided by Eduard Bos and Mila McLaughlin (demography, health, and nutrition); Raquel Artecona and Martin Rama (labor force and employment); Shaohua Chen and Martin Ravallion (poverty and income distribution); Montserrat Pallares-Miralles and Robert Palacios (vulnerability and security); and Barbara Bruns, Saida Mamodova, Robert Prouty, Lianqin Wang, and Nicholas Wilson (education). Comments and suggestions at various stages of production also came from Jean Baneth, Eduard Bos, Vilay Soulatha and Eric Swanson. Vivienne Wang provided invaluable assistance in preparing data.

3. Environment

was prepared by M. H. Saeed Ordoubadi and Mona Fetouh in partnership with the World Bank's EESD network and in collaboration with the World Bank's Development Research Group and Transportation, Water, and Urban Development Department. Important contributions were made by Robin White and Christian Layke of the World Resources Institute, Orio Tampieri of the Food and Agriculture Organization, Laura Battlebury of the World Conservation Monitoring Centre, Gerhard Metchies of GTZ, and Christine Auclair, Moses Ayiemba, Bildad Kagai, Guenter Karl, Pauline Maingi, and Markanley Rai of the Urban Indicators Programme, United Nations Centre for Human Settlements. Mehdi Akhlaghi managed the databases for this section, and Mona Fetouh assisted with research and data preparation. The World Bank's Environment Department and Rural Development Department devoted substantial staff resources to the book, for which the team is very grateful. Drawing on a draft of the forthcoming World Bank's Rural Development strategy, M. H. Saeed Ordoubadi wrote the introduction to the section with valuable comments from John Dixon, Kirk Hamilton, Nwanze Okidegbe, Eric Swanson and Bruce Ross-Larson who edited the text. Other contributions were made by Susmita Dasgupta, Craig Meisner, and David Wheeler (water pollution); Juan Blazquez Ancin, Jan Bojö, Katja Erickson, Surhid Gautam, and Kirsten Oleson (government commitment); and Katie Bolt and Kirk Hamilton (adjusted savings). Valuable comments were also provided by Jean Baneth, Victor Gabor, Barbro Hexeberg, and Vilay Soulatha.

4. Economy

was prepared by K. M. Vijayalakshmi in close collaboration with the Macro-economic Data Team of the World Bank's Development Data Group, led by Soong Sup Lee. K. M. Vijayalakshmi and Michael Lewin wrote the introduction with substantial contributions from Punam Chuhan, Eric Swanson and Hans Timmer. Contributions to the section were provided by David Cieslikowski and Barbro Hexeberg (national accounts), Azita Amjadi (trade), and Punam Chuhan and Ibrahim Levent (external debt). The national accounts and balance of payments data for low- and middle-income economies were gathered from the World Bank's regional staff through the annual Unified Survey. Maja Bresslauer, Raquel Fok, Victor Gabor, Barbro Hexeberg, Soong Sup Lee and Naoko Watanabe worked on updating, estimating, and validating the databases for national accounts. The national accounts data for OECD countries were processed by Mehdi Akhlaghi. The team is grateful to Guy Karsenty, Andreas Maurer, Vudda Meach, and Wladimir Tislenkoff at the World Trade Organization, and Sanja Blazevic, Arunas Butkevicius and Aurelie von Wartensleben at the United Nations Conference on Trade and Development (UNCTAD) for providing data on trade in goods, to Tetsuo Yamada for help in obtaining the United Nations Industrial Development Organization (UNIDO) database, and to Jean Baneth and Michael Ward for helpful comments.

5. States and markets

was prepared by David Cieslikowski in partnership with the World Bank's Private Sector and Infrastructure Network, its Poverty Reduction and Economic Management Network, the International Finance Corporation, and external partners. Mona Fetouh gave invaluable assistance in preparing data. David Cieslikowski wrote the introduction to the section, with substantial inputs from staff in the Development Economics Vice Presidency, Mona Fetouh, and Eric Swanson. Other contributors include Ada Karina Izaguirre and Shokraneh Minovi (privatization and infrastructure projects); Alka Banerjee , Isilay Cabuk, Shannon Laughlin, and Sangmin Lee (Standard & Poor's emerging stock market indexes); Yonas Biru (purchasing power parity conversion factors); Mariusz Sumlinksi (private investment); Esperanza Magpantay and Michael Minges of the International Telecommunication Union (communications and information); Louis Thompson (transport); Maria-Helena Capelli-Miguel, S.K. Chu, and Diane Stukel of UNESCO's Institute for Statistics (culture, research and development, scientists and engineers data); Anders Halvorsen of the World Information Technology and Services Alliance (ICT data); Dan Gallik of the U.S. Department of State (military expenditures); and Lise McLeod of the World Intellectual Property Organization (patents data).

6. Global links

was prepared by David Cieslikowski who wrote the introduction, drawing in part on ideas developed in *Globalization Growth, and Poverty: Building an Inclusive World Economy,* written by Paul Collier and David Dollar under the supervision of Nicholas Stern. Mona Fetouh and Eric Swanson also contributed to the introduction. Mona Fetouh gave invaluable assistance in preparing data. Substantial help came from Azita Amjadi (trade); Betty Dow (commodity prices); Aki Kuwahara of UNCTAD and Jerzy Rozanski (tariffs); Shelly Fu, Ibrahim Levent, and Gloria Reyes (financial data); Cecile Thoreau of the OECD (migration); Yasmin Ahmad of the OECD (data on aid flows); and Antonio Massieu and Rosa Songel of the World Tourism Organization (tourism data).

Other parts

The maps on the inside covers were prepared by the World Bank's Map Design Unit. The *Users guide* was prepared by David Cieslikowski. *Statistical methods* was written by Eric Swanson. *Primary data documentation* was coordinated by K. M. Vijayalakshmi, who served as database administrator. Mehdi Akhlaghi was responsible for database updates and aggregation. *Acronyms and abbreviations* was prepared by Estela Zamora. The index was collated by Richard Fix.

Data management

Database management was coordinated by Mehdi Akhlaghi with cross-team participation of DECDG staff to create an integrated WDI database. This database was used to generate the WDI tables and other WDI-related products such as *WDI Online*, *The Little Data Book*, and the *WDI CD-ROM*.

Administrative assistance and office technology support

Estela Zamora provided administrative assistance, and assisted in updating the databases. Jean-Pierre Djomalieu, Nacer Megherbi, and Shahin Outadi provided office technology support.

Design, production, and editing

Richard Fix coordinated all aspects of production with the Graphic Visions Associates team, led by Roger Berwanger and Francis Knab. Roger Berwanger provided overall direction for design and planning. The team would also like to thank Mike James for the design. The section introductions were edited by Bruce Ross-Larson and designed by Communications Development Incorporated with input from Grundy and Northedge, London.

Client services

The Development Data Group's Client Services Team (Azita Amjadi, Elizabeth Crayford, Richard Fix, Anat Lewin, Gonca Okur, and William Prince) contributed to the design and planning of the *World Development Indicators* and the *Atlas* and helped coordinate work with the Office of the Publisher.

Publishing and dissemination

The Office of the Publisher, under the direction of Dirk Koehler, provided valuable assistance throughout the production process. Randi Park coordinated printing and Carlos Rossel supervised marketing and distribution. Lawrence MacDonald of Development Economics and Andrew Kircher of External Affairs managed the communications strategy, and the regional operations group headed by Paul Mitchell helped coordinate the overseas release.

The Atlas

Production was managed by Richard Fix. The preparation of data benefited from the work on corresponding sections in the *World Development Indicators*. William Prince assisted with systems support and production of tables and graphs. Jeffrey Lecksell and Greg G. Prakas from the World Bank's Map Design Unit coordinated map production.

World Development Indicators CD-ROM

Design, programming, and testing were carried out by Reza Farivari and his team: Azita Amjadi, Ying Chi, Elizabeth Crayford, Sathyanarayanan Govindaraju, and Nacer Megherbi. Yusri Harun prepared the text files. Masako Hiraga produced the social indicators tables. William Prince coordinated production and provided quality assurance.

WDI Online

Design, programming, and testing were carried out by Reza Farivari and his team: Mehdi Akhlaghi, Azita Amjadi, Elizabeth Crayford, Sathyanarayanan Govindaraju, and Nacer Megherbi. William Prince coordinated production and provided quality assurance. Cybèle Bourgougnon, Hafed Al-Ghwell and Stacey Leonard-Frank of the Office of the Publisher were responsible for the implementation of the *WDI Online* and the management of the subscription service.

Client feedback

The team is also grateful to the many people who took the trouble to provide comments on its publications. Their feedback and suggestions have helped improve this year's edition.

AbouZahr, Carla. 2000. "Maternal Mortality." *OECD Observer* (223): 29–30.

Ahmad, Sultan. 1992. "Regression Estimates of Per Capita GDP Based on Purchasing Power Parities." Policy Research Working Paper 956. World Bank, International Economics Department, Washington, D.C.

———. 1994. "Improving Inter-Spatial and Inter-Temporal Comparability of National Accounts." *Journal of Development Economics* 44: 53–75.

Alderman, Harold, Simon Appleton, Lawrence Haddad, Lina Song, and Yisehac Yohannes. 2001. "Reducing Child Malnutrition: How Far Does Income Growth Take Us?", World Bank. Washington, D.C.

American Automobile Manufacturers Association. 1998. *World Motor Vehicle Data*. Detroit, Mich.

Ball, Nicole. 1984. "Measuring Third World Security Expenditure: A Research Note." *World Development* 12(2): 157–64.

Barro, Robert J. 1991. "Economic Growth in a Cross-Section of Countries." *Quarterly Journal of Economics* 106(2): 407–44.

Barro, Robert J., and Jong-Wha Lee. 2000. "International Data on Educational Attainment Updates and Implications." NBER Working Paper 7911. National Bureau of Economic Research. Cambridge, Mass.

Beck, Thorsten and Ross Levine. 2001. "Stock Markets, Banks, and Growth: Correlation or Causality." Policy Research Working Paper 2670. World Bank, Washington, D.C.

Behrman, Jere R., and Mark R. Rosenzweig. 1994. "Caveat Emptor: Cross-Country Data on Education and the Labor Force." *Journal of Development Economics* 44: 147–71.

Bloom, David E., and Jeffrey G. Williamson. 1998. "Demographic Transitions and Economic Miracles in Emerging Asia." *World Bank Economic Review* 12(3): 419–55.

Brown, Lester R., and others. 1999. *Vital Signs 1999: The Environmental Trends That Are Shaping Our Future*. New York and London: W. W. Norton for Worldwatch Institute.

Brown, Lester R., Christopher Flavin, Hilary F. French, and others. 1998. *State of the World 1998*. Washington, D.C.: Worldwatch Institute.

Brown, Lester R., Michael Renner, Christopher Flavin, and others. 1998. *Vital Signs 1998*. Washington, D.C.: Worldwatch Institute.

Brunetti, Aymo, Gregory Kisunko, and Beatrice Weder, 1997. "Institutional Obstacles for Doing Business: Data Description and Methodology of a Worldwide Private Sector Survey." Background paper to World Development Report 1997. World Bank, Washington, D.C.

Bulatao, Rodolfo. 1998. *The Value of Family Planning Programs in Developing Countries*. Santa Monica, Calif.: Rand.

Caiola, Marcello. 1995. *A Manual for Country Economists*. Training Series 1, vol. 1. Washington, D.C.: International Monetary Fund.

Centro Latinoamericano de Demografía. Various years. *Boletín Demográfico*. Santiago.

CGAP (Consultative Group to Assist the Poorest.) 2000. *Report 2000*. Washington, D.C.: [www.cgap.org/assets/images/CGAPReport2000.pdf].

Chen, Shaohua, and Martin Ravallion. 2000. "How Did the World's Poorest Fare in the 1990s?" Policy Research Working Paper 2409. World Bank, Development Research Group, Washington, D.C.

Clarke, George R. G. 2001. "How the Quality of Institutions Affects Technological Deepening in Developing Countries." Policy Research Working Paper 2603. World Bank, Washington, D.C.

Collier, Paul, and David Dollar. 1999. "Aid Allocation and Poverty Reduction." Policy Research Working Paper 2041. World Bank, Development Research Group, Washington, D.C.

———. 2001. "Can the World Cut Poverty in Half? How Policy Reform and Effective Aid Can Meet the International Development Goals." Policy Research Working Paper 2403. World Bank, Washington, D.C.

Collins, Wanda W., Emile A. Frison, and Suzanne L. Sharrock. 1997. "Global Programs: A New Vision in Agricultural Research." *Issues in Agriculture* (World Bank, Consultative Group on International Agricultural Research, Washington, D.C.) 12: 1–28.

Corrao, Marlo Ann, G. Emmanuel Guindon, Namita Sharma, and Donna Fakhrabadi Shokoohi, eds. 2000. *Tobacco Control Country Profiles*. Atlanta: American Cancer Society.

Dahlman, Carl, and Jean-Eric Aubert . 2001. *China and the Knowledge Economy: Seizing the 21st Century*. World Bank Institute Studies. Washington, D.C.

Demirgüç-Kunt, Asli, and Enrica Detragiache. 1997. "The Determinants of Banking Crises: Evidence from Developed and Developing Countries." Working paper. World Bank and International Monetary Fund, Washington, D.C.

Demirgüç-Kunt, Asli, and Ross Levine. 1996a. "Stock Market Development and Financial Intermediaries: Stylized Facts." *World Bank Economic Review* 10(2): 291–321.

———. 1996b. "Stock Markets, Corporate Finance, and Economic Growth: An Overview." *World Bank Economic Review* 10(2): 223–39.

———. 1999. "Bank-Based and Market-Based Financial Systems: Cross-Country Comparisons." Policy Research Working Paper 2143. World Bank, Washington, D.C.

de Onis, Mercedes, and Monika Blossner. 2000. "Prevalence and Trends of Overweight among Pre-School Children in Developing Countries." *American Journal of Clinical Nutrition*. 72: 1032-39.

Devarajan, Shantayanan, David Dollar, and Torgny Holmgren, eds. 2001. *Aid and Reform in Africa: Lessons from Ten Case Studies*. World Bank: Washington, D.C.

Devereux, Stephen. 2001. "Food Security and Information Systems." In Stephen Devereux and Simon Maxwell, eds., *Food Security in Sub-Saharan Africa*. London: ITDG Publishing.

Dixon, John, and **Paul Sherman**. 1990. *Economics of Protected Areas: A New Look at Benefits and Costs*. Washington, D.C.: Island Press.

Djankov, Simeon, Rafael La Porta, Florencio Lopez de Silanes, and Andrei Shleifer. 2001. "The Regulation of Entry." Policy Research Working Paper 2661. World Bank, Washington, D.C.

DKT International. 1998. *1997 Contraceptive Social Marketing Statistics*. Washington, D.C.

Dollar, David, and Aart Kraay. 2001a. "Growth Is Good for the Poor." Policy Research Working Paper 2587. World Bank, Washington, D.C.

———. 2001b. *Trade, Growth, and Poverty*. A World Bank Working Paper 2615. Washington, D.C.

Doyle, John J., and Gabrielle J. Persley, eds. 1996. *Enabling the Safe Use of Biotechnology: Principles and Practice*. Environmentally Sustainable Development Studies and Monographs Series, no. 10. Washington, D.C.: World Bank.

Drucker, Peter F. 1994. "The Age of Social Transformation." *Atlantic Monthly* 274 (November).

Easterly, William. 2000. "Growth Implosions, Debt Explosions, and My Aunt Marilyn: Do Growth Slowdowns Cause Public Debt Crises?" Policy Research Working Paper 2531. World Bank, Development Research Group, Washington, D.C.

Economic Commission for Europe. 2000. Women and Men in Europe and North America. New York and Geneva.

Economist. 2001. "Globalisation and Its critics: A Survey of Globalisation." 29 September, pp. 1-30.

Euromoney. 2001. September. London.

Eurostat (Statistical Office of the European Communities). Various years. *Demographic Statistics*. Luxembourg.

———. Various years. *Statistical Yearbook*. Luxembourg.

Evenson, Robert E., and Carl E. Pray. 1994. "Measuring Food Production (with Reference to South Asia)." *Journal of Development Economics* 44: 173–97.

Faiz, Asif, Christopher S. Weaver, and Michael P. Walsh. 1996. *Air Pollution from Motor Vehicles: Standards and Technologies for Controlling Emissions*. Washington, D.C.: World Bank.

Fallon, Peter, and Zafiris Tzannatos. 1998. *Child Labor: Issues and Directions for the World Bank*. Washington, D.C.: World Bank.

Fankhauser, Samuel. 1995. *Valuing Climate Change: The Economics of the Greenhouse*. London: Earthscan.

FAO (Food and Agriculture Organization). 1986. "Inter-Country Comparisons of Agricultural Production Aggregates." Economic and Social Development Paper 61. Rome.

———. 1996. *Food Aid in Figures 1994*. Vol. 12. Rome.

———. 2001. *State of the World's Forests 2001*. Rome.

———. Various years. *Fertilizer Yearbook*. FAO Statistics Series. Rome.

———. Various years. *Production Yearbook*. FAO Statistics Series. Rome.

———. Various years. *The State of Food Insecurity in the World*. Rome.

———. Various years. *Trade Yearbook*. FAO Statistics Series. Rome.

Frankel, Jeffrey. 1993. "Quantifying International Capital Mobility in the 1990s." In Jeffrey Frankel, ed., *On Exchange Rates*. Cambridge, Mass.: MIT Press.

Frankhauser, Pierre. 1994. "Fractales, tissus urbains et reseaux de transport." *Revue d'economie politique* 104: 435–55.

Fredricksen, Birger. 1993. *Statistics of Education in Developing Countries: An Introduction to Their Collection and Analysis*. Paris: UNESCO.

French, Kenneth, and James M. Poterba. 1991. "Investor Diversification and International Equity Markets." *American Economic Review* 81: 222–26.

Gallup, John L., and Jeffrey D. Sachs. 1998. "The Economic Burden of Malaria." Harvard Institute for International Development, Cambridge, Mass.

Gannon, Colin, and Zmarak Shalizi. 1995. "The Use of Sectoral and Project Performance Indicators in Bank-Financed Transport Operations." TWU Discussion Paper 21. World Bank, Transportation, Water, and Urban Development Department, Washington, D.C.

Gardner, Robert. 1998. "Education." Demographic and Health Surveys, Comparative Study 29. Macro International, Calverton, Md.

Gardner-Outlaw, Tom, and Robert Engelman. 1997. "Sustaining Water, Easing Scarcity: A Second Update." Population Action International, Washington, D.C.

Goldfinger, Charles. 1994. *L'utile et le futile L'économie de l'immatériel*. Paris: Editions Odile Jacob.

Greaney, Vincent, and Thomas Kellaghan. 1996. *Monitoring the Learning Outcomes of Education Systems*. A Directions in Development book. Washington, D.C.: World Bank.

Grigorian, David A., and Albert Martinez,. 2000. "Industrial Growth and Quality of Institutions: What Do (Transition) Economies Have to Gain from the Rule of Law?" Policy Research Working Paper 2475. World Bank, Washington, D.C.

GTZ (German Agency for Technical Cooperation). 1999. *Fuel Prices and Taxation*. Eschborn, Germany.

Gupta, Sanjeev, Hamid Davoodi, and Erwin Tiongson. 2000. "Corruption and the Provision of Health Care and Education Services." IMF Working Paper 00/116, Washington, D.C.

Gupta, Sanjeev, Brian Hammond, and Eric Swanson. 2000. "Setting the Goals." *OECD Observer* (223): 15–17.

Haggarty, Luke, and Mary M. Shirley. 1997. "A New Database on State-Owned Enterprises." *World Bank Economic Review* 11(3): 491–513.

Hallward-Driemeier, Mary. 2001. "Openness, Firms, and Competition." Development Research Group Background paper. World Bank, Washington, D.C.

Hamilton, K., and M. Clemens. 1999. "Genuine Savings Rates in Developing Countries." *World Economic Review* 13 (2): 333–56.

Happe, Nancy, and John Wakeman-Linn. 1994. "Military Expenditures and Arms Trade: Alternative Data Sources." IMF Working Paper 94/69. International Monetary Fund, Policy Development and Review Department, Washington, D.C.

Harrison, Ann. 1995. "Factor Markets and Trade Policy Reform." World Bank, Washington, D.C.

Hatzichronoglou, Thomas. 1997. "Revision of the High-Technology Sector and Product Classification." STI Working Paper 1997/2. OECD Directorate for Science, Technology, and Industry, Paris.

Hazell, Peter. 2001. "Agriculture and Environment", in Environment and Development Economics, 6 (4). Beijer Institute of Ecological Economics and Royal Sweden Academy of Sciences.

Heck, W. W. 1989. "Assessment of Crop Losses from Air Pollutants in the U.S." In J. J. McKenzie and M. T. El Ashry, eds., *Air Pollution's Toll on Forests and Crops*. New Haven, Conn.: Yale University Press.

Heggie, Ian G. 1995. *Management and Financing of Roads: An Agenda for Reform*. World Bank Technical Paper 275. Washington, D.C.

Hellman, Joel S., Geraint Jones, Daniel Kaufmann, and Mark Schankerman. 2000. "Measuring Governance, Corruption, and State Capture: How Firms and Bureaucrats Shape the Business Environment in Transition Economies." Policy Research Working Paper 2312. World Bank, Washington, D.C.

Heston, Alan. 1994. "A Brief Review of Some Problems in Using National Accounts Data in Level of Output Comparisons and Growth Studies." *Journal of Development Economics* 44: 29–52.

Hettige, Hemamala, Muthukumara Mani, and David Wheeler. 1998. "Industrial Pollution in Economic Development: Kuznets Revisited." Policy Research Working Paper 1876. World Bank, Development Research Group, Washington, D.C.

Hill, Kenneth, Carla AbouZahr, and Tessa Wardlaw. 2001. "Estimates of Maternal Mortality for 1995." *Bulletin of the World Health Organization*. 79 (3): pp. 182-193.

IEA (International Energy Agency). Various years. *Energy Balances of OECD Countries*. Paris.

———. Various years. *Energy Statistics and Balances of Non-OECD Countries*. Paris.

———. Various years. *Energy Statistics of OECD Countries*. Paris.

IFC (International Finance Corporation). 2001a. *Trends in Private Investment in Developing Countries 2001*. Washington, D.C.

———. 2001b. *SME: World Bank Group Review of Small Business Activities*. Washington, D.C.

IFPRI (International Food Policy Research Institute). 1999. *Soil Degradation: A Threat to Developing-Country Food Security by 2020*. Washington, D.C.

ILO (International Labour Organization). 1990. *ILO Manual on Concepts and Methods*. Geneva: International Labour Office.

———. 2002. *Key Indicators of the Labour Market 2001–2002*. Geneva: International Labour Office.

———. Various years. *Sources and Methods: Labour Statistics* (formerly *Statistical Sources and Methods*). Geneva: International Labour Office.

———. Various years. *Yearbook of Labour Statistics*. Geneva: International Labour Office.

IMF (International Monetary Fund). 1977. *Balance of Payments Manual*. 4th ed. Washington, D.C.

———. 1993. *Balance of Payments Manual*. 5th ed. Washington, D.C.

———. 1995. *Balance of Payments Compilation Guide*. Washington, D.C.

———. 1996a. *Balance of Payments Textbook*. Washington, D.C.

———. 1996b. *Manual on Monetary and Financial Statistics*. Washington, D.C.

———. 2000. *Exchange Arrangements and Exchange Restrictions Annual Report, 2000*. Washington, D.C.

———. 2001. *A Manual on Government Finance Statistics*. Washington, D.C.

———. Various years. *Balance of Payments Statistics Yearbook*. Parts 1 and 2. Washington, D.C.

———. Various issues. *Direction of Trade Statistics*. Quarterly. Washington, D.C.

———. Various years. *Direction of Trade Statistics Yearbook*. Washington, D.C.

———. Various years. *Government Finance Statistics Yearbook*. Washington, D.C.

———. Various issues. *International Financial Statistics*. Monthly. Washington, D.C.

———. Various years. *International Financial Statistics Yearbook*. Washington, D.C.

IMF (International Monetary Fund), OECD (Organisation for Economic Co-operation and Development), United Nations, and World Bank. 2000. *A Better World for All: Progress towards the International Development Goals*. Washington, D.C.

Institutional Investor. 2001. September. New York.

International Association for the Evaluation of Educational Achievement. 2000. *Third International Mathematics and Science Study, 1999*. Boston College, Lynch School of Education, International Study Center.

International Civil Aviation Organization. 2001. *Civil Aviation Statistics of the World, 1998–99*. Montreal.

International Road Federation. 2001. *World Road Statistics 2001*. Geneva.

International Telecommunication Union. 2001. *World Telecommunication Development Report 2001*. Geneva.

International Working Group of External Debt Compilers (Bank for International Settlements, International Monetary Fund, Organisation for Economic Co-operation and Development, and World Bank). 1987. *External Debt Definitions*. Washington, D.C.

Inter-Secretariat Working Group on National Accounts (Commission of the European Communities, International Monetary Fund, Organisation for Economic Co-operation and

Development, United Nations, and World Bank). 1993. *System of National Accounts*. Brussels, Luxembourg, New York, and Washington, D.C.

IPCC (Intergovernmental Panel on Climate Change). 2001. *Climate Change 2001*. Cambridge: Cambridge University Press.

Irwin, Douglas A. 1996. "The United States in a New Global Economy? A Century's Perspective." Papers and Proceedings of the 108th Annual Meeting of the American Economic Association. *American Economic Review* (May).

Isard, Peter. 1995. *Exchange Rate Economics*. Cambridge: Cambridge University Press.

IUCN (World Conservation Union). 1998. *1997 IUCN Red List of Threatened Plants*. Gland, Switzerland.

———. 2000. *2000 IUCN Red List of Threatened Animals*. Gland, Switzerland.

Jamison, D. T. 1990. "Child Malnutrition and School Performance in China." *Journal of Development Economics* 20: pp. 299–310.

Journal of Development Economics. 1994. Special issue on Database for Development Analysis. Edited by T. N. Srinivasan. Vol. 44, no. 1.

Kaminsky, Graciela L., Saul Lizondo, and Carmen M. Reinhart. 1997. "Leading Indicators of Currency Crises." Policy Research Working Paper 1852. World Bank, Latin America and the Caribbean Region, Office of the Chief Economist, Washington, D.C.

Klein, Michael, Carl Aaron, and Bita Hadjiumichael. 2001. "Foreign Direct Investment and Poverty Reduction." Policy Research Working Paper 2613. World Bank, Washington, D.C.

Knetter, Michael. 1994. "Why Are Retail Prices in Japan So High? Evidence from German Export Prices." NBER Working Paper 4894. National Bureau of Economic Research, Cambridge, Mass.

Komives, K., D. Whittington, and X. Wu. 2000. "Infrastructure Coverage and the Poor: A Global Perspective." Paper presented at the Conference Infrastructure for Development: Private Solutions and the Poor. 31 May – 2 June. London.

Kunte, Arundhati, Kirk Hamilton, John Dixon, and Michael Clemens. 1998. "Estimating National Wealth: Methodology and Results." Environmental Economics Series, no. 57. World Bank, Environment Department, Washington, D.C.

Lanjouw, Jean O., and Peter Lanjouw. 2001. "The Rural Non-Farm Sector: Issues and Evidence from Developing Countries." *Agricultural Economics* 26: 1-23.

Lanjouw, Peter and Gershon Feder. 2001. "Rural Non-Farm Activities and Rural Development: From Experience Toward Strategy." Rural Strategy Discussion Paper 4. World Bank, Washington, D.C.

Leete, Richard. 2000. "Reproductive Health." *OECD Observer* (223): 31–32.

Lele, Uma, William Lesser, and Gesa Horstkotte-Wessler, eds. 2000. *Intellectual Property Rights in Agriculture: The World Bank's Role in Assisting Borrower and Member Countries*. Washington, D.C.: World Bank.

Lewis, Karen K. 1995. "Puzzles in International Financial Markets." In Gene Grossman and Kenneth Rogoff, eds., *Handbook of International Economics*. Vol. 3. Amsterdam: North Holland.

Lewis, Stephen R., Jr. 1989. "Primary Exporting Countries." In Hollis Chenery and T. N. Srinivasan, eds., *Handbook of Development Economics*. Vol. 2. Amsterdam: North Holland.

Lovei, Magdolna. 1997. "Toward Effective Pollution Management." *Environment Matters* (fall): 52–53.

Lucas, R. E. 1988. "On the Mechanics of Economic Development." *Journal of Monetary Economics* 22: 3–22.

Maddison, Angus. 1995. *Monitoring the World Economy 1820–1992*. Paris: OECD.

Mani, Muthukumara, and David Wheeler. 1997. "In Search of Pollution Havens? Dirty Industry in the World Economy, 1960–95." World Bank, Policy Research Department, Washington, D.C.

McCarthy, Desmond, and Holger Wolf. 2001. *Comparative Life Expectancy in Africa*. A World Bank Working Paper 2668. Washington, D.C.

McGuire, Judith S. 1996. *The Payoff from Improving Nutrition*. The World Bank. Washington, D.C. (processed).

Meashanm, Anthony R. 2001. "Assessing Malnutrition in the Africa Region: Why Bother?" Africa Region Health, Nutrition, and Population, World Bank, Washington, D.C.

Midgley, Peter. 1994. *Urban Transport in Asia: An Operational Agenda for the 1990s*. World Bank Technical Paper 224. Washington, D.C.

Moody's Investors Service. 2002. *Sovereign, Sub-national and Sovereign-Guaranteed Issuers*. January. New York.

Morgenstern, Oskar. 1963. *On the Accuracy of Economic Observations*. Princeton, N.J.: Princeton University Press.

Morisset, Jacques. 2000. "Foreign Direct Investment in Africa: Policies Also Matter." Policy Research Working Paper 2481. World Bank, Washington, D.C.

Moulton, Jeanne. 2001. "Improving Education in Rural Areas: Guidance for Rural Development Specialists." World Bank. Washington, D.C. (Processed).

Murray, Christopher J. L., and Alan D. Lopez. 1996. *The Global Burden of Disease*. Cambridge, Mass.: Harvard University Press.

———. eds. 1998. *Health Dimensions of Sex and Reproduction: The Global Burden of Sexually Transmitted Diseases, HIV, Maternal Conditions, Perinatal Disorders, and Congenital Anomalies*. Cambridge, Mass.: Harvard University Press.

National Science Foundation. 2000. *Science and Engineering Indicators 2000*. Arlington, Va.

Netcraft. 2001. *Netcraft Secure Server Survey*. [http://www.netcraft.com/]

Obstfeldt, Maurice. 1995. "International Capital Mobility in the 1990s." In P. B. Kenen, ed., *Understanding Interdependence: The Macroeconomics of the Open Economy*. Princeton, N.J.: Princeton University Press.

Obstfeldt, Maurice, and Kenneth Rogoff. 1996.

Foundations of International Macroeconomics. Cambridge, Mass.: MIT Press.

OECD (Organisation for Economic Co-operation and Development). 1985. *Measuring Health Care 1960–1983: Expenditure, Costs, Performance*. Paris.

———. 1996. *Trade, Employment, and Labour Standards: A Study of Core Workers' Rights and International Trade*. Paris.

———. 1997. *Employment Outlook*. Paris.

———. 1999. *OECD Environmental Data: Compendium 1999*. Paris.

———. 2000. *Enhancing the Competitiveness of SMEs through Innovation*. Workshop for Conference in Bologna, Italy. 14-15 June.

———. Various issues. *International Development Statistics*. CD-ROM. Paris.

———. Various years. *National Accounts*. Vol. 1, *Main Aggregates*. Paris.

———. Various years. *National Accounts*. Vol. 1, *Main Aggregates*. Paris.

———. Various years. *National Accounts*. Vol. 2, *Detailed Tables*. Paris.

———. Various years. *Trends in International Migration: Continuous Reporting System on Migration*. Paris.

OECD, Development Assistance Committee. Various years. *Development Co-operation*. Paris.

———. Various years. *Geographical Distribution of Financial Flows to Aid Recipients: Disbursements, Commitments, Country Indicators*. Paris.

O'Meara, Molly. 1999. "Reinventing Cities for People and the Planet." Worldwatch Paper 147. Worldwatch Institute, Washington, D.C.

Palacios, Robert, and Montserrat Pallares-Miralles. 2000. "International Patterns of Pension Provision." Social Protection Discussion Paper 0009. World Bank, Human Development Network, Washington, D.C.

Pearce, David, and Giles Atkinson. 1993. "Capital Theory and the Measurement of Sustainable Development: An Indicator of Weak Sustainability." *Ecological Economics* 8: 103–08.

Pfefferman, Guy P. 2000. "Paths Out of Poverty: The Role of Private Enterprise in Developing Countries." International Finance Corporation. Washington, D.C.

Pilling, David. 1999. "In Sickness and in Wealth." *Financial Times*, 22 October.

Plucknett, Donald L. 1991. "Saving Lives through Agricultural Research." *Issues in Agriculture* (World Bank, Consultative Group on International Agricultural Research, Washington, D.C.) 16.

PricewaterhouseCoopers. 2001a. *Corporate Taxes 2001–2002: Worldwide Summaries*. New York.

———. 2001b. *Individual Taxes 2001–2002: Worldwide Summaries*. New York.

PRS Group. 2001. *International Country Risk Guide*. CD-ROM. December. East Syracuse, N.Y.

Rama, Martin, and Raquel Artecona. 1999. "A Database of Labor Market Indicators across Countries." World Bank, Development Research Group, Washington, D.C.

Ravallion, Martin. 1996. "Poverty and Growth: Lessons from 40 Years of Data on India's Poor." DECNote 20. World Bank, Development Economics Vice Presidency, Washington, D.C.

———. 2001. "Growth, Inequality and Poverty: Looking Beyond Averages." Policy Research Working Paper 2558. World Bank, Washington, D.C.

Ravallion, Martin, and Shaohua Chen. 1996. "What Can New Survey Data Tell Us about the Recent Changes in Living Standards in Developing and Transitional Economies?" World Bank, Policy Research Department, Washington, D.C.

———. 1997. "Can High-Inequality Developing Countries Escape Absolute Poverty?" *Economic Letters* 56: 51–57.

Rodrik, Dani. 1996. "Labor Standards in International Trade: Do They Matter and What Do We Do about Them?" Overseas Development Council, Washington, D.C.

Romer, P. M. 1986. "Increasing Returns and Long-Run Growth." *Journal of Political Economy* 94: 1002–37.

Ruggles, Robert. 1994. "Issues Relating to the UN System of National Accounts and Developing Countries." *Journal of Development Economics* 44(1): 87–102.

Ryten, Jacob. 1998. "Fifty Years of ISIC: Historical Origins and Future Perspectives." ECA/STAT.AC. 63/22. United Nations Statistics Division, New York.

Sen, Amartya. 1988. "The Concept of Development." In Hollis Chenery and T. N. Srinivasan, eds., *Handbook of Development Economics*. Vol. 1. Amsterdam: North Holland.

Serageldin, Ismail. 1995. *Toward Sustainable Management of Water Resources*. A Directions in Development book. Washington, D.C.: World Bank.

Shiklovanov, Igor. 1993. "World Fresh Water Resources." In Peter H. Gleick, ed., *Water in Crisis: A Guide to Fresh Water Resources*. New York: Oxford University Press.

Smith, Lisa C. 1998. "Can FAO's Measure of Chronic Undernourishment be Strengthened?" *Food Policy* 23 (5) 425–445.

Smith, Lisa C., and Lawrence Haddad. 2000. *Overcoming Child Malnutrition in Developing Countries: Past Achievements and Future Choices*. International Food Policy Research Institute. Washington, D.C.

Soemantri, A. G., E. Pollitt, and I. Kim. 1985. "Iron Deficiency Anemia and Educational Achievement." *American Journal of Clinical Nutrition* 42: 1221–1228.

Srinivasan, T. N. 1994. "Database for Development Analysis: An Overview." *Journal of Development Economics* 44(1): 3–28.

Standard & Poor's. 2000. *The S&P Emerging Market Indices Methodology, Definitions, and Practices*. New York.

———. 2001. *Emerging Stock Markets Factbook 2001*. New York.

———. 2002. *Credit Week*. January. New York.

Stern, Nicholas. 2001a. "A Strategy for Development." Keynote Address, Annual World Bank Conference on Development Economics, Washington, D.C., May.

———. 2001b. "Building a Climate for Investment, Growth, and Poverty Reduction in India." Speech at the Export-Import Bank of India, Mumbai. 22 March.

Taylor, Alan M. 1996a. "International Capital Mobility in History: Purchasing Power Parity in the Long Run." NBER Working Paper 5742. National Bureau of Economic Research, Cambridge, Mass.

———. 1996b. "International Capital Mobility in History: The Saving-Investment Relationship." NBER Working Paper 5743. National Bureau of Economic Research, Cambridge, Mass.

Thomas, Duncan, and John Strauss. 1977. "Health and Wages: Evidence on Men and Women in Urban Brazil. *Journal of Econometrics*, 77 (1): 159–186.

UNACC/SCN (United Nations Administrative Committee on Co-ordination, Subcommittee on Nutrition). Various years. *Update on the Nutrition Situation*. Geneva.

———. 2000. *Fourth Report on the World Nutrition Situation*. Geneva.

UNAIDS (Joint United Nations Programme on HIV/AIDS) and WHO (World Health Organization). 2000. *AIDS Epidemic Update*. December.

UNCTAD (United Nations Conference on Trade and Development). Various years. *Handbook of International Trade and Development Statistics*. Geneva.

UNEP (United Nations Environment Programme). 1991. *Urban Air Pollution*. Nairobi.

UNEP (United Nations Environment Programme) and WHO (World Health Organization). 1992. *Urban Air Pollution in Megacities of the World*. Cambridge, Mass.: Blackwell.

———. 1995. *City Air Quality Trends*. Nairobi.

UNESCO (United Nations Educational, Scientific, and Cultural Organization). 1998. *World Education Report 1998*. Paris: UNESCO Publishing and Bernan Press.

———. Various years. *Statistical Yearbook*. Paris: UNESCO Publishing and Bernan Press.

UNICEF (United Nations Children's Fund). 2001. *Progress since the World Summit for Children. A Statistical Review*. UN, New York.

———. Various years. *The State of the World's Children*. New York: Oxford University Press.

UNIDO (United Nations Industrial Development Organization). Various years. *International Yearbook of Industrial Statistics*. Vienna.

United Nations. 1947. *Measurement of National Income and the Construction of Social Accounts*. New York.

———. 1968. *A System of National Accounts: Studies and Methods*. Series F, no. 2, rev. 3. New York.

———. 1990. *International Standard Industrial Classification of All Economic Activities, Third Revision*. Statistical Papers Series M, no. 4, rev. 3. New York.

———. 1992. *Handbook of the International Comparison Programme*. Studies in Methods, Series F, no. 62. New York.

———. 1993. *System of National Accounts*. New York.

———. 2000. *We the Peoples: The Role of the United Nations in the 21st Century*. New York.

United Nations Economic and Social Commission for Western Asia. 1997. *Purchasing Power Parities: Volume and Price Level Comparisons for the Middle East, 1993*. E/ESCWA/STAT/1997/2. Amman.

United Nations Population Division. 1996. *International Migration Policies 1995*. New York.

———. 1998. *World Population Prospects: The 1998 Revision*. New York.

———. 2000. *World Urbanization Prospects: The 1999 Revision*. New York.

———. Various years. *Levels and Trends of Contraceptive Use*. New York.

United Nations Statistics Division. 1985. *National Accounts Statistics: Compendium of Income Distribution Statistics*. New York.

———. 1993. *Integrated Environmental and Economic Accounting*. New York.

———. Various years. *Energy Statistics Yearbook*. New York.

———. Various years. *International Trade Statistics Yearbook*. New York.

———. Various issues. *Monthly Bulletin of Statistics*. New York.

———. Various years. *National Accounts Statistics: Main Aggregates and Detailed Tables*. Parts 1 and 2. New York.

———. Various years. *National Income Accounts*. New York.

———. Various years. *Population and Vital Statistics Report*. New York.

———. Various years. *Statistical Yearbook*. New York.

U.S. Census Bureau. 1990. *1990 Census of Population Listing*. Washington, D.C.

———. 2000. *Current Population Report*. March. Washington, D.C.

U.S. Department of Health and Human Services. 1997. *Social Security Systems throughout the World*. Washington, D.C.

U.S. Department of State, Bureau of Verification and Compliance. 2002. *World Military Expenditures and Arms Transfers 2000*. Washington, D.C.

U.S. Environmental Protection Agency. 1995. *National Air Quality and Emissions Trends Report 1995*. Washington, D.C.

Wagstaff, Adam, and Harold Alderman. 2001. "Life and Death on a Dollar a Day: Does It Matter Where You Live?" World Bank, Washington, D.C.

Walsh, Michael P. 1994. "Motor Vehicle Pollution Control: An Increasingly Critical Issue for Developing Countries." World Bank, Washington, D.C.

Watson, Robert, John A. Dixon, Steven P. Hamburg, Anthony C. Janetos, and Richard H. Moss. 1998. *Protecting Our Planet, Securing Our Future: Linkages among Global Environmental Issues and Human Needs*. A joint publication of the United Nations Environment Programme, U.S. National Aeronautics and Space Administration, and World Bank, Nairobi and Washington, D.C.

WCMC (World Conservation Monitoring Centre). 1992. *Global Biodiversity: Status of the Earth's Living Resources.* London: Chapman and Hall.

——. 1994. *Biodiversity Data Sourcebook.* Cambridge: World Conservation Press.

WHO (World Health Organization). 1995. *Trends and Challenges in World Health: Report by the Secretariat.* WHO Executive Board Document EB 105/4. Geneva.

——. 1977. *International Classification of Diseases.* 9th rev. Geneva.

——. 1997. *Coverage of Maternity Care.* Geneva.

——. 1999. *Global Tuberculosis Control Report 1999.* Geneva.

——. Various years. *World Health Report.* Geneva.

——. Various years. *World Health Statistics Annual.* Geneva.

WHO (World Health Organization) and UNICEF (United Nations Children's Fund). 1992. *Low Birth Weight: A Tabulation of Available Information.* Geneva.

——. 2000. *Global Water Supply and Sanitation Assessment 2000 Report.* Geneva.

WITSA (World Information Technology and Services Alliance). 2002. *Digital Planet 2002: The Global Information Economy.* Based on research by International Data Corporation. Vienna, Va.

Wolf, Holger C. 1997. "Patterns of Intra- and Inter-State Trade." NBER Working Paper 5939. National Bureau of Economic Research, Cambridge, Mass.

Wolfensohn, James D. 2001. "Responding to the Challenges of Globalization." Speech to the G-20 Finance Ministers and Central Governors, Ottawa, 17 November.

World Bank. 1990. *World Development Report 1990: Poverty.* New York: Oxford University Press.

——. 1991. *World Development Report 1991: The Challenge of Development.* New York: Oxford University Press.

——. 1992. *World Development Report 1992: Development and the Environment.* New York: Oxford University Press.

——. 1993a. *The Environmental Data Book: A Guide to Statistics on the Environment and Development.* Washington, D.C.

——. 1993b. *Purchasing Power Parities: Comparing National Incomes Using ICP Data.* Washington, D.C.

——. 1993c. *World Development Report 1993: Investing in Health.* New York: Oxford University Press.

——. 1996a. *Environment Matters* (summer). Environment Department, Washington, D.C.

——. 1996b. *Livable Cities for the 21st Century.* A Directions in Development book. Washington, D.C.

——. 1996c. *National Environmental Strategies: Learning from Experience.* Environment Department, Washington, D.C.

——. 1997a. *Can the Environment Wait? Priorities for East Asia.* Washington, D.C.

——. 1997b. *Expanding the Measure of Wealth: Indicators of Environmentally Sustainable Development.* Environmentally Sustainable Development Studies and Monographs Series, no. 17. Washington, D.C.

——. 1997c. *Private Capital Flows to Developing Countries: The Road to Financial Integration.* A World Bank Policy Research Report. New York: Oxford University Press.

——. 1997d. *Rural Development: From Vision to Action.* Environmentally Sustainable Development Studies and Monographs Series, no. 12. Washington, D.C.

——. 1997e. *Sector Strategy: Health, Nutrition, and Population.* Human Development Network, Washington, D.C.

——. 1997f. *World Development Report 1997: The State in a Changing World.* New York: Oxford University Press.

——. 1998. *1998 Catalog: Operational Documents as of July 31, 1998.* Washington, D.C.

——. 1999a. *Fuel for Thought: Environmental Strategy for the Energy Sector.* Environment Department, Energy, Mining, and Telecommunications Department, and International Finance Corporation, Washington, D.C.

——. 1999b. *Greening Industry: New Roles for Communities, Markets, and Governments.* A World Bank Policy Research Report. New York: Oxford University Press.

——. 1999c. *Health, Nutrition, and Population Indicators: A Statistical Handbook.* Human Development Network, Washington, D.C.

——. 1999d. *World Development Report 1999/ 2000—Entering the 21st Century: The Changing Development Landscape.* New York: Oxford University Press.

——. 1999e. *Towards a Virtuous Circle: A Nutrition Review of the Middle East and North Africa.* Middle East and North Africa Working Paper Series No. 17. Washington, D.C.

——. 2000a. *Trade Blocs.* A World Bank Policy Research Report. New York: Oxford University Press.

——. 2000b. *World Development Report 2000/2001: Attacking Poverty.* New York: Oxford University Press.

——. 2000c. *Reforming Public Institutions and Strengthening Governance: A World Bank Strategy.* Washington, D.C.

——. 2001. "Private Sector Development Strategy—Directions for the World Bank Group." Discussion draft. Washington, D.C.

——. 2002a. *World Development Report 2002: Building Institutions for Markets.* New York: Oxford University Press.

——. 2002b. *Global Economic Prospects and the Developing Countries: Making Trade Work for the World's Poor.* Washington, D.C.

——. 2002c. *Globalization, Growth, and Poverty: Building an Inclusive World Economy.* A World Bank Policy Research Report. New York: Oxford University Press.

——. 2002d. *Financial Impact of the HIPC Initiative: First 24 Country Cases.* [www.worldbank.org/hipc]

——. 2002e. *Social Protection in Latin America and the Caribbean.* Fact Sheet. Latin America and Caribbean Region, Human Development Network, Washington, D.C.

——. 2002f. *World Development Report 2003: Transforming Growth: Neighbor, Nature, Future.* Draft Report. Washington, D.C.

——. 2002g. "Achieving Education for All by 2015: Simulation Results for 47 Low-Income Countries". Africa Region and Education Department, Human Development Network. World Bank. (Processed).

——. Forthcoming. *Poverty Reduction and the World Bank: Operationalizing the WDR 2000–01.* Washington, D.C.

——. Various issues. *Global Commodity Markets.* Quarterly. Washington, D.C.

——. Various years. *Global Development Finance* (formerly *World Debt Tables*). Washington, D.C. (Also available on CD-ROM.)

——. Various years. *Global Economic Prospects and the Developing Countries.* Washington, D.C.

——. Various years. *World Development Indicators.* Washington, D.C.

World Bank and EBRD (European Bank for Reconstruction and Development) 2000. *Business Environment and Enterprise Performance Survey, 1999-2000.* Washington, D.C.

World Energy Council. 1995. *Global Energy Perspectives to 2050 and Beyond.* London.

World Intellectual Property Organization. 2001. *Industrial Property Statistics.* Publication A. Geneva.

World Resources Institute, International Institute for Environment and Development, and IUCN (World Conservation Union). Various years. *World Directory of Country Environmental Studies.* Washington, D.C.

World Resources Institute, UNEP (United Nations Environment Programme), and UNDP (United Nations Development Programme). 1994. *World Resources 1994–95: A Guide to the Global Environment.* New York: Oxford University Press.

World Resources Institute, UNEP (United Nations Environment Programme), UNDP (United Nations Development Programme), and World Bank. Various years. *World Resources: A Guide.386 to the Global Environment.* New York: Oxford University Press.

World Tourism Organization. 2001a. *Compendium of Tourism Statistics 2001.* Madrid.

——. 2001b. *Yearbook of Tourism Statistics.* Vols. 1 and 2. Madrid.

WTO (World Trade Organization). Various years. *Annual Report.* Geneva.

Young, Helen. 2001. "Nutrition and Intervention Strategies." In Stephen Devereux and Simon Maxwell, eds: ITDG Publishing. *Food Security in Sub-Saharan Africa.* London.

Yusuf, Shahid. 2001. "Globalization and the Challenge for Developing Countries." Policy Research Working Paper 2618. World Bank, Washington, D.C.

Zook, Matthew. 2000. "Internet Metrics: Using Host and Domain Counts to Map the Internet." *International Journal on Knowledge Infrastructure Development, Management and Regulation* (University of California at Berkeley) 24(6/7).